ENCYCLOPEDIA OF HUMAN RIGHTS

EDITORIAL BOARD

ENCYCLOPEDIA OF
HUMAN
RIGHTS

DAVID P. FORSYTHE

EDITOR IN CHIEF

VOLUME 1

Afghanistan–Democracy and Right to Participation

OXFORD
UNIVERSITY PRESS
2009

OXFORD
UNIVERSITY PRESS

Oxford University Press, Inc., publishes works that further
Oxford University's objective of excellence
in research, scholarship, and education.

Oxford New York
Auckland   Cape Town   Dar es Salaam   Hong Kong   Karachi
Kuala Lumpur   Madrid   Melbourne   Mexico City   Nairobi
New Delhi   Shanghai   Taipei   Toronto

With offices in
Argentina   Austria   Brazil   Chile   Czech Republic   France   Greece
Guatemala   Hungary   Italy   Japan Poland   Portugal   Singapore
South Korea   Switzerland   Thailand   Turkey   Ukraine   Vietnam

Copyright © 2009 by Oxford University Press

Published by Oxford University Press, Inc.
198 Madison Avenue, New York, NY 10016
www.oup.com

Oxford is a registered trademark of Oxford University Press

The Library of Congress Cataloging-in-Publication Data

Encyclopedia of human rights / David P. Forsythe, editor in chief.
p. cm.
Includes bibliographical references and index.
ISBN 978-0-19-533402-9 (alk. paper) – ISBN 978-0-19-533688-7
1. Human rights–Encyclopedias. 2. Civil rights–Encyclopedias. I. Forsythe, David P., 1941-
JC571.E673 2009
323.03–dc22
2009006268

3 5 7 9 8 6 4 2

Printed in the United States of America
on acid-free paper

EDITORIAL AND PRODUCTION STAFF

Acquiring Editor
Damon Zucca

Development Editor
Timothy H. Sachs

Editorial Assistants
Stephen Alsa   Holly Seabury

Production Editor
Peter Pickow

Copyeditors
John Barclay   Dorothy Bauhoff   Patricia B. Brecht   Nancy Clements   John Fitzpatrick
Gretchen Gordon   Archibald Hobson   Jean Fortune Kaplan   Robin Perlow
Mary Hawkins Sachs   Ben Sadock   Michael Sandlin   Lisa Vecchione   Heidi Yerkes

Proofreaders
Dorothy Bauhoff   Patricia B. Brecht

Index Prepared by
Katharyn Dunham, ParaGraphs

Compositor
SPi

Manufacturing Controller
Genieve Shaw

Interior and Cover Design
Joan Greenfield

Cartography
Mapping Specialists, Ltd.

Managing Editor
Mary Araneo

Executive Editor, Development
Stephen Wagley

Publisher
Casper Grathwohl

CONTENTS

ENCYCLOPEDIA OF

HUMAN RIGHTS

LIST OF ARTICLES

VOLUME 1

VOLUME 2

ix

VOLUME 3

FOREWORD

The story of human rights is one that belongs to everyone, unfolding in every language of every people the world over. And it is a story that is still being told, in international forums, national legislatures, movements for social justice, and in countless other places where collective and individual aspirations are being expressed.

The Encyclopedia of Human Rights makes a major contribution to our understanding of what we have endured together and achieved together as an international community, and it helps us to see what is still left to be done. Most important, it exists as a tool for all those who are interested in increasing their own capacity to advance the realization of human rights in their community, their nation, and our common world.

Although our collective interest in human dignity and well-being did not originate with the Universal Declaration of Human Rights, this document serves as an important gauge for assessing how far the world has progressed in achieving these goals. Using its own words, the Declaration provides "a common standard of achievement for all peoples and all nations." Far from being merely aspirational or utopian, human rights embody an international consensus on the minimum conditions for a life of dignity. They provide a foundation for action at home, as well as for international assistance and cooperation. They bring transparency and accountability to decision-making processes, and they provide a common forum for dialogue and for planning work together.

The types of social, political, and legal transformations chronicled in these five volumes demand political commitment, generated by people—individually and together—who work for their ideals, who hold politicians to account, and who defend principles wherever they are: in their homes, in the streets, or on the international stage. In addressing the development of collective capacity to advance the promotion and protection of human rights from a variety of perspectives, *The Encyclopedia of Human Rights* chronicles key developments in international law, in terms of both legal instruments and institutions, and it provides an overview of the political and social action that led to their birth. It gives insight into key debates, events, and personalities that are essential to understanding the realization of human rights in a range of settings, and it points to some of the key challenges that remain ahead. Producing a succinct and systematic work such as this one is a very ambitious undertaking. I congratulate the editor, Professor David Forsythe, and the many contributors to this work, for taking on this challenging project and seeing it to a successful completion.

The possibility for people to claim their human rights entitlements through legal and other processes is essential for human rights to have meaning for those most at the margins, a vindication of their equal worth and a profound expression of human agency. I am confident that this five-volume set will provide useful assistance to those who stand up for rights, their own and those of others.

Louise Arbour
United Nations High Commissioner
for Human Rights, 2004–2008

PREFACE

Over the past decade measurable progress, however fitful, has been made in efforts to create an international rules-based system to protect human rights. This progress, reflected in many of the entries in this encyclopedia, can be measured in several ways: ideas endorsed, operations created for implementation, and organizational structures in place.

Unresolved disputes do remain, of course, also often noted in the entries of this project. Some of these complex disputes involve, for example: (1) the unintended consequences of some of the organizational innovations such as the International Criminal Court, (2) whether there are effective ways in which to operationalize the enforcement of human rights, particularly in conflicts and failing states, and (3) the trade-offs between human rights legal norms and other values such as resolution of conflicts and humanitarian aid operations—which may be affected, sometimes in profound and ambiguous ways, by the application of these human rights norms. Some of these disputes will never be fully resolved, as they reflect the ambiguities of the real world, which are seldom easy to address with simple formulas.

The American and European notions of human rights share many things in common, but on some issues differences remain. The American concept, best described in the U.S. Declaration of Independence and Bill of Rights, takes a more narrow and individualistic view, influenced by classical liberalism, arguing that human rights should protect the individual *from* undue interference from the state or from other social structures, emphasizing the sovereignty of the individual. This view is memorialized in the first half of the UN Universal Declaration of Human Rights. While the European tradition, influenced by the social democratic tradition, certainly endorses this view of human rights, it extends the protections of what most Europeans term "human rights" to rights of individuals *to* certain public services such as housing and health care, to food, and to a clean environment, among other things. These rights *to* public services and goods are enshrined in the second half of the UN Universal Declaration of Human Rights (although the drafting of the Universal Declaration of Human Rights, including these rights to public services, was heavily influenced by an American—Eleanor Roosevelt). These rights extend the meaning of the term well beyond the narrower American definition, and imply an increase in the responsibility and power of the state, as some institution must ensure people are provided these services if they are to be taken seriously.

Entries in this project cover both the Canadian John P. Humphrey and the Frenchman René Cassin, both social democrats, who played leading roles in the development of the 1948 Universal Declaration of Human Rights, as well as Eleanor Roosevelt and her key mediating and lobbying role. Franklin D. Roosevelt and his views of human rights are covered as well.

The growing role of developing countries in the evolution of these notions of human rights leads to another difference in emphasis: the centrality of group, rather than individual, rights. The increase in the number and ferocity of intranational conflicts after the end of the cold war has led to increased interest in the notion of the rights of racial, religious, ethnic, and tribal groups. These domestic conflicts have been driven by the very vulnerability of groups to abuse by the state or by other more powerful factions. In many intranational conflicts individuals have been abused principally because they belong to a group, and thus perhaps the strong Western focus on individual rights, whether defined by Americans or Europeans, may not deal adequately with the danger certain groups face on the ground. There is an entry in this reference work on North-South views on human rights, and many intranational conflicts are covered—from Rwanda to Chechnya, from Tibet to Darfur.

At the same time that these various differences persist, there is evidence of some agreements. The position of these same developing countries on human rights has undergone profound changes since the end of the cold war. Early in the 1990s many developing countries viewed with great suspicion the creation of the UN Office of the Coordinator of Humanitarian Affairs, because it represented to them a dangerous, interventionist erosion of the principle of state sovereignty (particularly *their* sovereignty) by meddling Western democracies. These same countries nevertheless approved at UN meetings the new doctrine of the "responsibility to protect" in late 2005. This doctrine was a step forward in the evolution in human rights law, particularly to protect group rights during civil conflicts, and the rights of internally displaced people during conflict, who have traditionally been at a great disadvantage compared with refugees, who are protected by a much older and better developed body of law. The "responsibility norm" proclaims, in short, that sovereign states have the duty to protect human rights in their jurisdictions, and, if they do not, the international community has the responsibility to intervene to stop gross violations of human rights. These developments further eroded the notion of absolute state sovereignty. While this erosion has been happening gradually since the end of the Cold War, this UN resolution has formalized and accelerated this erosion.

Several essays that follow address the subject of humanitarian intervention from different angles. And there are entries on the rights of refugees and internally displaced persons.

A more cynical and perhaps troubling view, which may explain acceptance by some developing countries (particularly those that abuse their own people) of this expansion in human rights doctrine, is that the practical effects on the ground of the erosion of state sovereignty has been limited or even negligible. This raises the greatest conundrum facing human rights advocates the world over, namely, how enforceable in the real world are these doctrinal advances in human rights? How much difference do these international norms actually make to those who are threatened with abuse or even death? We have more than two dozen UN resolutions on Darfur (Sudan), and yet the war there continues as of the time of writing. Normative agreement is noteworthy, but does it really affect behavior and policy?

If a comprehensive survey were taken, most human rights practitioners would argue, I suspect, that there is a growing, rather than diminishing, gap between the promise of human rights and their application in an increasingly complicated world. Part of this is caused by the fact that doctrine and theory have evolved faster than organizational structure and operational systems. Thus attempts to implement human rights law have become a question of much greater focus for practitioners now than at any time in the past. The 1990s saw a rising tide of international treaties and doctrines signed by most countries, including some of the worst offenders, to deal with various human rights problems, the results of which have been disappointing in practice. It is unclear how much difference the conventions on the rights of the child, on the ban on antipersonal landmines, and on child soldiers have actually had on the ground. It may be substantial; we simply do not have rigorous evidence. Even if these conventions have led to progress in improving the human condition, it may be very difficult to show it other than through unsatisfying anecdotes. Many of the entries in this encyclopedia do try to address the "so what" question. Given the agreement on human rights norms, has this agreement changed behavior and public policy?

We do know from nearly two decades of practical experience some operational measures that can be taken to constrain abuse and protect civilians in conflict zones. The perpetrators of atrocities anywhere do not like outsiders to witness their barbarism, and so the very presence of international observes, aid workers, and UN peacekeeping troops appears to constrain this abuse, though not eliminate it. Once the international humanitarian aid infrastructure was in place at the end of 2004 in Darfur there was a precipitous drop in atrocities. Detailed and comprehensive reports by international human rights nongovernmental organizations (NGOs), the International Committee of the Red Cross, and UN rapporteurs that carefully document what is taking place in situations of risk appear to have a constraining affect on atrocities as well. Western governments have begun enforcing travel bans on people accused of mass atrocities; these "smart sanctions" have happened in the cases of Bosnia, Zimbabwe, and Sudan. We know that international media coverage of atrocities, particularly via electronic media, does appear to unnerve perpetrators, or why else would they go to such lengths to harass or even kill reporters, prevent them from interviewing victims, or control what they report? We know that electronic media can be used, as it was most notoriously in Rwanda through Radio Télévision Libre des Mille Collines (RTLM), as an active instrument of genocide, and it can also be used to constrain atrocities, as radio was successful in doing in Burundi during the same period.

Globalization of electronic news coverage is perhaps the most powerful new force now at work in the world to change the calculation of those abusing human rights. The instant and dramatic coverage of atrocities, genocide, and systemic abuse is being replayed across the globe for the first time in human history on television and radio in real time. Few places remain in the world for human rights abusers to hide from the light of public disclosure. We do not yet fully comprehend the consequences for human rights of this very recent phenomenon, but I suspect it is greater than we may understand. Entries in this encyclopedia dealing with both the media and with the internet probe this subject.

Alexis de Tocqueville's fascinating description of the role of civil society in the building of the American social order, written during his celebrated visit to America in the 1830s, contains lessons for other societies in our time experiencing the massive growth of a robust civil society composed of nongovernmental organizations (including indigenous human rights NGOs), religious institutions, independent trade unions, business and professional associations, women's groups, and fraternal orders, among others. One of the most encouraging signs of progress over the past decade on operationalizing human rights is this massive expansion in the number of these indigenous organizations in countries where the rule of law is weak and the freedom of the press constrained. These groups may have the greatest impact of all over the long term because they are rooted in the societies at risk and do not parachute in and then depart when violence starts, and they can build local constituencies and organizations to protect human rights over time, acting as watchdogs over state power and abuse. The relatively peaceful transition of Indonesia from dictatorship to a robust democracy in a few short years has been attributed to the rich civil society that had developed in the country prior to its democratization.

The institutionalization of human rights protection over the past decade has not been limited to these indigenous organizations, but has taken place in the international system as well. The International Criminal Court, the UN High Commissioner for Human Rights, and the Special Human Rights courts all reflect this relatively recent institutional development. Some of these institutional changes show mixed results. The long standing UN Commission on Human Rights was replaced in 2006 with the UN Human Rights Council, after criticism that the Commission had included some of the worst abusers of human rights. Unfortunately, in some respects the new Council quickly fell into the same pattern of action as the old Commission. Human rights organizations and democratic governments have criticized the new council because of its nearly exclusive focus on Israel, which was condemned fifteen times in two years. Myanmar was condemned once, and other states such as Zimbabwe, North Korea, and Cuba went unnoticed. The Council expressed "concern" over the situation in Darfur. At the same time, the new Council started the Universal Periodic Review of the human rights record of all UN member states. This was intended to reduce the political selectivity so evident in the old Commission.

The Office of the UN High Commissioner for Human Rights, established by General Assembly action in 1993, has gradually constructed an effective institutional structure and capacity; in 2006–2007 it had a budget of $85 million, with a staff of 850, including 240 human rights monitors serving with UN peace keeping missions around the world. It had offices in eleven countries and seven regional missions with three mandates: standard setting, monitoring, and implementation.

The International Criminal Court (ICC), established by an international convention now signed by 105 countries, went into operation in 2002. Luis Moreno-Ocampo, former Argentine public prosecutor, was elected by the ICC as Chief Prosecutor in 2003. Critics of the court who believe the court would politicize prosecutions in the fashion of the Human Rights Council, have thus far been proven wrong, while some supporters of the court have been uneasy with the slow pace of prosecutions and enforcement problems. Some critics, in unexpected places, argue that the law of unintended consequences may now be in operation in what they call the "ICC effect" as heads of state or leaders of rebel movement accused of abuse stubbornly remain in office because of fear that if they leave they will be prosecuted. Some have even called this the Charles Taylor effect (after the former Liberian president who is on trial at the ICC for war crimes), because it appears the Mugabe government in Zimbabwe refused to accept their apparent defeat in the 2008 elections out of fear of prosecution if they were to leave office. Other critics argue that the fear of prosecution has prolonged conflicts, such as between the Lord's Resistance Army and the government of Uganda, making conflict mediators' work more difficult.

I found while I was Special U.S. Envoy to Sudan that the Sudanese government's fear of ICC prosecution for the atrocities in Darfur was influencing, perhaps in a very negative way, their willingness to hold free and fair democratic elections, which are required under the North/South peace agreement. However, it is also the case that the decline in the number of civilian deaths in Darfur following the indictment of a single senior Sudanese official for war crimes may be partially attributable to ICC action. Supporters of the Court argue that war criminals and rights abusers should no longer get impunity, no matter what the diplomatic consequences, or the world will continue to witness Bosnias, Rwandas, and Darfurs. Regardless of which side of the argument one might be on, what cannot be denied is that the ICC is now operational, making its weight felt, and causing human rights abusers to recalculate their actions because of the fear of prosecution. Special Courts were created, before the ICC was operational, to confront the atrocities in Rwanda and Bosnia, as was the Truth Commission in South Africa.

Several entries in this project delve into the various complexities of the ICC, the situations in Uganda and Darfur, and the role of the ICC prosecutor Moreno Ocampo. There are also analyses of the UN Human Rights Commission and Human Rights Council.

Encouraging institutional innovations have taken place in protecting human rights through nongovernmental organizations. To take just one example, the first operational human rights nongovernmental organization to come out of the evangelical Christian tradition in the United States, the International Justice Mission, collects actionable criminal evidence on cases of systemic human rights abuses such as human trafficking, child labor, and abuse, and takes the cases to court to prosecute them in countries where such cases have never before been tried, but where the national laws prohibit the abuse. Many on their staff are retired FBI agents and criminal prosecutors: they have had some surprising successes.

This encyclopedia comes at a momentous time in the global movement to protect human rights, because it is now maturing into a force to be reckoned with. Only history will tell us whether the movement's full promise is realized.

Andrew S. Natsios
Walsh School of Foreign Service,
Georgetown University

INTRODUCTION

There have been remarkable developments in the evolution of human rights thinking, but that thinking is under serious challenge. More international human rights standards have been developed in the period since 1945 than ever before in world history, but their effectiveness has been seriously challenged by such developments as the rise of authoritarian China as a world power and the U.S. emphasis on a tough and extensive quest for national security after the terrorist attacks on the Pentagon outside of Washington, D. C., and the World Trade Center in New York City on 11 September 2001. So while there is much "rights talk" and "rights law," there are many rights violations. This encyclopedia is an attempt to put these twin and contradictory developments into perspective.

OVERVIEW OF RIGHTS DEVELOPMENTS

Human rights were mostly unknown in general international law until 1945. France and the United States had both proclaimed the existence of the "rights of man" in the last quarter of the eighteenth century, building on philosophical arguments from the Enlightenment. But no general treaties existed on the subject until the United Nations era. There had been some rights talk in diplomacy, and a few treaties on certain minority rights and rights of aliens (foreigners). But it was only after the carnage and atrocities of the 1930s and 1940s that Franklin D. Roosevelt and others pushed for mention of human rights in the UN Charter, the closest document we have to a global constitution. He believed that human rights were linked to international peace and security, and that some of the origins of World War II lay in the human rights violations of Nazi Germany and Imperial Japan. There had been no mention of human rights in the Covenant of the League of Nations, although in 1919 Japan had pushed for a statement on racial equality, and the United Kingdom and the United States had been initially interested in a statement on religious freedom.

With human rights mentioned but not specified in the UN Charter, and with member states obligated very generally to cooperate in their promotion, states begin to define them as an international matter in the 1948 Universal Declaration of Human Rights. This UN General Assembly resolution, which was not legally binding at the time of adoption, laid out thirty principles pertaining to civil, political, economic, social, and cultural rights. UN developments thus reflected a broad conception of human rights consistent with the philosophy of social democracy held by key personalities like Eleanor Roosevelt of the United States (first president of the UN Human Rights Commission and a U.S. representative), Rene Cassin of France (who as a French representative was central in the drafting process), and John P. Humphrey of Canada (the latter being a member of the UN secretariat and also an important player behind the scenes). Certain other actors, especially various social democratic governments in Latin American, but also including the representatives of India, Lebanon, and the Philippines, and various nongovernmental organizations (NGOs) were actively engaged in the process.

By 1966 states had (slowly) negotiated the International Covenant on Civil and Political Rights (ICCPR) and the companion International Covenant on Economic, Social, and Cultural Rights (ICESCR). These, combined with the 1948 Universal Declaration, constituted the composite "International Bill of Human Rights" and the core of the new norms on internationally recognized human rights. By 2008, 162 states had ratified, and thus formally consented to be bound by, the ICCPR, and 159 had similarly accepted the ICESCR. (UN membership was 192.) The International Bill of Rights was then followed by a deluge of human rights treaties at the UN on such subjects as racial discrimination, apartheid (legally enforced racial segregation), women's rights, the rights of the child, religious freedom, torture and mistreatment, secret detention (enforced disappearances), and more. Not only states but also NGOs and international civil servants played important roles in these legislative developments.

One of the reasons for this proliferation of rights standards particularly in the form of general treaty law was that the original enforcement mechanisms were weak. So if one had difficulty in enforcing the provisions, say, of the ICCPR, the practical solution was seen in drafting new treaties on torture or enforced disappearances, among other subjects, to continue to shine the international spotlight on persistent violations. The fact was that while most states were willing to ratify general human rights treaties, albeit sometimes with reservations to particular provisions, many were not willing to create a UN human rights court with strong enforcement authority. They were only willing to set up a diplomatic review or monitoring process through which international bodies, frequently composed of independent experts rather than governmental representatives, could raise question about, but not compel change in, governmental policies. So in general, international human rights standards proliferated at the UN, but enforcement measures remained very weak for several decades. The fundamental cause of this situation was not lack of intelligence and creativity by those interested in international human rights, but governmental unwillingness to see state sovereignty, and hence freedom of policy choice, significantly restricted in the name of human rights. They might have wanted to be associated with rights talk, but they also wanted to retain considerable freedom of policy making when dealing with economic, security, and other issues. International relations showed not only growing attention to universal human rights, but also the continuing strength of a narrow, provincial, or noncosmopolitan nationalism.

This general situation was partially remedied by human rights developments in certain regions, where strong regional treaties on human rights were negotiated accompanied by strong enforcement measures. This was clearly the case in Europe where one found the European Convention on Human Rights and Fundamental Freedoms enforced by the supranational European Court of Human Rights. Also in Europe one found the European Union and its supranational European Court of Justice. These latter bodies increasingly manifested a human rights dimension or component.

Also, in the Americas one found the Organization of American States, the American Declaration and Inter-American Convention on Human Rights, and the Inter-American Court of Human Rights. (There was also the Inter-American Commission on Human Rights.) The regional human rights institutions in the Western Hemisphere functioned in a way that was mostly inferior to those in Europe but superior to UN arrangements.

In Africa, as the African Union replaced the Organization of African states, one found the African Charter of Human and People's Rights, along with a Human Rights Commission and embryonic Human Rights Court. But African arrangements functioned less well than in Europe and the Americas. No other regional human rights courts existed, although various regional organizations were involved in human rights matters. Thus such bodies as the Arab League, the Organization of the Islamic Conference, the Association of Southeast Asian Nations, and other organizations all

found themselves dealing with human rights issues. But these latter organizations, while they might have manifested human rights diplomacy, did not manifest strong and authoritative enforcement procedures.

The persistent problem of weak enforcement of internationally recognized human rights standards was also partially remedied by certain institutional developments from the 1990s. After World War II the Nuremberg and Tokyo Trials held certain German and Japanese individuals accountable for war crimes, crimes against humanity, and aggression (crimes against peace). For about fifty years there were no other international criminal courts. In 1993 and 1994 the UN Security Council created international criminal courts for certain international crimes committed in the territory of the Former Yugoslavia from 1991 and in Rwanda during 1994. Hence the idea of international criminal courts was resurrected for the crimes of genocide, crimes against humanity, and war crimes, covering particular areas during particular times.

Building on these developments, in 1998 states, with many NGOs playing a strong supporting role, created the International Criminal Court. It become operational in 2002, the first ever permanent international criminal court with potentially global reach to try individuals for gross violations of human rights—namely, genocide, crimes against humanity, and war crimes. By 2008, one trial was scheduled (arising out of the Democratic Republic of the Congo), several investigations and indictments possibly leading to trials were underway (pertaining to Uganda, for example), and indictments had been issued charging certain high officials and seeking their arrest (in relation to events in Darfur, Sudan).

So the idea of international criminal courts trying individuals (or in some cases partially internationalized or mixed or hybrid criminal courts) helped to remedy the problem of weak enforcement of at least certain human rights norms. At the same time, on rare occasions the International Court of Justice (or World Court), which heard disputes between states, but only with the consent of states, also ruled on human rights matters in its binding and advisory proceedings—for example regarding genocide in the Balkans, or the Israeli security wall and the Fourth Geneva Convention of 1949 to protect individuals in occupied territory. (As a companion to international human rights law, one finds international humanitarian law, or the laws of war, much of which seeks to protect human dignity in war, legally known as armed conflict. International courts deal both with human rights law, such as prohibiting torture, and humanitarian law, such as prohibiting torture of those detained in relation to armed conflict.)

To be sure, criminal courts of various types were not the only responses chosen to deal with human rights violations. The notion of transitional justice became more prevalent. That is, in the transition from a situation of major rights violations to a situation of institutionalized rights protection, one might rely on not just criminal prosecution but also on other measures including truth commissions and reports, reparations, apologies, and certain nonjudicial punishments such as denial of holding public office (lustration). In general, the international community experimented with a wide variety of measures for enhancing human rights in general—and humanitarian law in times of armed conflict and occupation.

It cannot be stressed enough that both the negotiation of human rights standards and also their enforcement depends greatly on states and their foreign policies. Private individuals might play important roles, along with NGOs and officials of intergovernmental organizations, but it is states that approve the treaties, and states that either push for strong enforcement or not. They might work with or resist the other actors. Many nonstate actors are important in international relations—from corporations to terrorist groups to heads of UN agencies. Still, it was the territorial state, said to possess sovereign authority, that was of great importance to many human rights developments.

In retrospect one can see since 1945: (1) the development of an extensive international law of human rights and humanitarian affairs (or if one prefers, human rights norms in peace and war); (2) from about 1970 an increasing seriousness devoted to the subject through the hard law of court cases and the soft law of diplomacy, much of it occurring under pressure from a growing number of NGOs interested in human rights; and (3) a persistent concern by many states, including some liberal democracies, to be associated with rights talk but to try to preserve as much national or unilateral freedom of policy making as possible.

In fact, this last problem is as old as it is central. Franklin Roosevelt and Harry Truman, both supportive of certain developments on human rights in international relations, realized that if one constructed a strong international legal regime for human rights, it would reduce national freedom of policy making—and in the case of the United States spotlight difficulties, particularly on race relations in the south. These presidents might have been in favor of progressive change concerning American racial discrimination, but they were aware that certain treaty language on human rights would never be consented to by the U.S. Senate in that era, given the power of southern senators in that body. Hence, from the beginning of the UN era, there was a persistent and palpable tension between the goal of advancing human rights around the world and the necessity to accommodate strong oppositional forces at home. In quite a few countries during certain eras, those opposed to a strong international law on human rights (and on humanitarian affairs) controlled the executive branch and the conduct of foreign policy. They might have given lip service to internationally recognized human rights, but their nationalism caused them to place emphasis on state sovereignty. International relations remained a modified system of territorial states, said to possess sovereignty or ultimate legal authority, even as universal rights talk and international rights standards proliferated.

THIS ENCYCLOPEDIA

To deal with the rich and complex developments outlined above, the five volumes of *The Encyclopedia of Human Rights* might be said in simplified form to cover four major categories of entries: rights, organizations, persons, and situations. The focus is 1945 to the present, but with some attention to developments before the creation of the UN Charter. As suggested above, human rights as a positivistic and global matter are defined according to international law and diplomacy—those fundamental rights of the person that are internationally recognized. (Some believe that human rights are more fundamentally defined by moral argument, with human rights in international law and diplomacy more or less approximating the preceding list of rights in moral philosophy.)

Readers will thus find here expert and extended commentary on these four aspects of internationally recognized rights. It was sometimes said of certain earlier efforts at a human rights encyclopedia that while those projects offered definitions, short descriptions, and reproduction of documents, one had to look elsewhere for in-depth expert commentary. The present work emphasizes precisely that type of commentary.

Users of this work will certainly find the expected core coverage. For example, with regard to rights, there is an entry on freedom from genocide, and also an entry on freedom from torture. With regard to this first category of specific human rights, sometimes we focus on a key right, such as religious freedom or freedom from arbitrary arrest. Sometimes we focus on a legal concept, such as universal jurisdiction, or human rights in emergencies. Sometimes in this category of entries the focus is on a collection of related rights, such as rights of due process; or civil and political rights; or economic, social, and cultural rights. And sometimes the focus is on a process, such as democracy promotion or economic sanctions for violation of rights. The emphasis is on richness of analysis rather than simple definition of rights.

With regard to organizations, we cover a selection of public and private global, regional, and national human rights organizations. For example, one entry analyzes Human Rights Watch, while another summarizes the human rights dimension of the United Nations Security Council. Concerning these various organizations, in addition to noting the distinction between public (governmental or intergovernmental) and private organizations (usually called nongovernmental organizations when referring to human rights advocacy groups), we provide coverage of multinational corporations (also called transnational corporations) in the entry on business and human rights. And we cover various "hot" and "cold" sources of information in the entry on the media and human rights. Moreover we discuss the major religious traditions; so in this case, we define organization broadly. We also provide entries on many groups traditionally called development or relief groups, such as Oxfam, because they either increasingly adopt a human rights dimension, or their work overlaps with human rights concerns in significant ways. In some entries in the category of organizations we focus on a particular organization, such as Amnesty International, but in some entries we provide a collective coverage, such as Jewish nongovernmental organizations and Arab nongovernmental organizations. There are literally tens of thousands of private groups that get involved in human rights issues around the world, so some collective coverage is necessary given the limitations of space, and even with collective coverage we are limited to a representative and not exhaustive list of organizations. We try to cover most of the organizations with prominent roles on human rights issues at the United Nations.

The section on persons presents leading figures who made major contributions to the advancement of human rights, or tried to, and those who did major damage to human rights, including Hitler, Stalin, and Mao Zedong. One entry creates a portrait of Roméo Dallaire, the Canadian military official who did so much to try to stop the 1994 Genocide in Rwanda, while another presents an analysis of Augusto Pinochet, the Chilean dictator. There is also an entry on Mary Robinson, the outspoken second UN High Commissioner for Human Rights, and another on Tito, the longtime leader of communist Yugoslavia whose suppression of certain civil and political rights both maintained stability in that part of the Balkans for several decades and also eventually led to the bloody Balkan wars of the 1990s after his death. It is a difficult judgment call as to which

personality merits particular and singular attention (such as Nicolae Ceausescu in communist Romania, a particularly brutal and reactionary leader) and which should be treated as part of the analysis of a situation (such as Charles Taylor in Liberia). We made some systematic choices, covering all recent UN secretaries-general (but not the earlier ones, since human rights did not figure so prominently then), and we cover all Nobel laureates who had a pronounced link to human rights.

Concerning situations, one entry covers South Africa, while another goes back in history to analyze the human rights situation in the Belgian Congo. Situations may cover countries, regions, or incidents. The coverage of situations presented a number of difficult choices. There are 192 UN members, which is too large a number for particular in-depth coverage of all of them in this project. Moreover, the U.S. State Department annually presents its Country Reports on Human Rights Practices, covering in fairly brief form mostly but not entirely civil and political rights in 191 of them—exempting only itself. These are widely regarded as relatively objective, even if not always tightly linked to actual U.S. foreign policy toward a particular country. Still further, the private organization Freedom House, on which we have an entry, presents an annual statistical overview of each country in the world concerning civil and political rights. From 2006, the relatively new UN Human Rights Council, on which we have an entry, started a "Universal Periodic Review" of all UN members. Thus, because of these and still other published sources, there already exists systematic information, mostly reliable, on the human rights record of the countries of the world.

Given the facts above, we decided to present an in-depth analysis of selected countries, emphasizing broad analysis in historical perspective; but in some cases we also decided for regional or comparative analysis, such as human rights trends in North Africa, or past human rights problems in the Southern Cone of South America during the era of the "national security state," or contemporary human rights trends in the populist democracies of South America (Bolivia, Ecuador, Peru, Venezuela). This in-depth approach nicely supplements the other sources already available. We encouraged our authors to make in-depth analyses rather than present short and superficial description.

As already noted in passing, we also decided to reach back before 1945 in some entries, either because of the gravity of the human rights situation (such as the Irish famine, Armenians in the Ottoman Empire, the Holocaust, the Soviet gulag, Japanese atrocities in the 1930s and 1940s), or to ensure a proper understanding of colonialism (such as

Germany's colonial wars against the Herero and Nama in Namibia, the nature of King Leopold's rule in the Belgian Congo, now the Democratic Republic of the Congo, which has an entry, too), or to note important formative developments (such as the American and French revolutions). There is also a general entry on the historical evolution of human rights. To more fully understand human rights today, it is important to understand their absence or weakness in the past. According to a number of scholars, we have developed human rights standards today because of the obvious human wrongs of yesterday. Some human wrongs before 1945 are important in this regard, as well as some historical efforts to correct those wrongs. Yet the focus remains 1945 to the present, which is for some commentators the era of human rights.

By combining a focus on rights (discussed in various ways), organizations (of various types), persons (with both a positive and negative effect on human rights), and situations (presented so as to not to duplicate U.S., UN, and Freedom House reports), we are able to provide broad coverage on internationally recognized human rights, including humanitarian affairs. We include subject matter about rights being negotiated and/or projected for the future, such as international standards regarding sexual and gender diversity.

But there is much more here than the usual core coverage. In addition to entries on Rwanda and also on humanitarian intervention, one entry presents an analysis of foreign policy decision making with regard to the lack of humanitarian intervention in the face of atrocities, explaining the politics of the lack of decisive response. To give other examples of how we go beyond traditional core coverage, one entry presents an analysis of the Internet from a human rights perspective, and another presents a primer on quantitative studies of human rights. Still further beyond the usual legal focus on human rights as defined in law, one entry analyzes the concept of peacebuilding from a human rights perspective, while another dissects the notion of global justice and human rights. One entry covers forensic science and human rights, since forensic science is being increasingly used in international criminal justice. There is also an entry on art and images from a human rights view. One entry analyses individual human rights in comparison to an emphasis on community. Another focuses on film and human rights. These entries are indicative of our broad approach.

THE ENCYCLOPEDIA: ORIGINS, OTHER CONSIDERATIONS

The inspiration for embarking on this project was the single-volume *Encyclopedia of Human Rights*, edited by the late Edward Lawson, first published in 1991 and updated in 1996. Our five-volume encyclopedia of human rights builds on the commitment to human rights education established by Lawson, and we take a new, more in-depth, multifaceted approach to the topic that better serves the needs of today's students, scholars, and general readers. Unlike Lawson's personalized efforts, we reached out to a broad range of experts, and declined to reproduce human rights documents because they are so readily available on the Internet.

In fact, the rapid improvements in information dissemination provided by the explosive growth of Internet access and the increased availability of electronic resources in the years since Lawson's second edition has meant that our encyclopedia must be different. Ours is much more than a compilation of brief entries that describe the human rights–related activities of the United Nations, reproductions of key U.N. documents, and brief descriptions of countries and situations around the world. Thanks to the information age (though one must acknowledge that much of the world still does not have any, or uncensored, internet access) vast amounts of data and documents related to human rights are freely available online from mostly reliable sources such as the United Nations, other intergovernmental organizations, the U.S. State Department, and a variety of well-respected nongovernmental organizations.

We asked experts from different disciplines to write the analytical entries. Professors in philosophy and law had pioneered in the study of human rights. Political scientists had studied rights as part of political and diplomatic processes. Sociologists and economists had increasingly addressed the subject. Historians, journalists, and public policy specialists had added their unique perspectives as well. We made sure to include an interdisciplinary perspective across the five volumes. The team of authors, editors, and referees contained lawyers, political scientists, historians, sociologists, journalists, and independent scholars. If most entries were written by lawyers or political scientists, those from the other disciplines and professions left their mark as well.

Approximately one-third of the entries are written by women, and we made a concerted effort to include entries that pertain in one way or another to women, gender, or sexuality, such as entries on Louise Arbour, Aung San Suu Kyi, Simone de Beauvoir, Carla del Ponte, Shirin Ebadi, Female Genital Mutilation and Female Genital Cutting, Arvonne Fraser, Gender Violence, Human Trafficking, Japanese Sexual Slavery, Rigoberta Menchu, Mary Robinson, Eleanor Roosevelt, Sisterhood is Global, United Nantions

Commission on Status of Women, and Women's Rights Groups in the Middle East. Moreover many other entries, although having a more general focus, pay particular attention to gender and sexual issues, such as the entry on the UN High Commissioner for Refugees, since many refugees are women, and since gender and sexual persecution constitutes for UNHCR a well-founded fear of persecution, thus leading to refugee status. The entries on International Criminal Justice and Humanitarian Law cover the special attention paid to women in those domains. The entries on the International Criminal Tribunal for Former Yugoslavia (ICTY) and for Rwanda (ICTR) note some of the case law developed there regarding gender and sex, such as rape as a war crime, as a crime against humanity, and as an indication of genocide.

This project also made a considerable effort to enlist non-Western authors and to cover issues of particular interest to the non-Western world. Already mentioned is the coverage of some of the brutalities of Western colonialism inflicted on those under its control. The British historian Niall Ferguson has noted that while British colonialism helped spread such notions as the rule of law and democracy, it also had its brutal aspects. There is an entry on views toward human rights by the global South compared to the global North. There is an entry on the argument that East Asian values are superior to global human rights as presently defined. There is an entry on the violence that accompanied the independence of India and Pakistan. While the editorial team is composed of scholars in law and the social sciences from the North Atlantic area, all have traveled and lived in other parts of the world, and all interact with close colleagues who are non-Western—hence our recruitment of scholars from around the world. We believe that what counts is sensitivity to points of view and quest for balance and objectivity, not place of residence.

USING THE ENCYCLOPEDIA

We have recognized the necessity of some overlap of coverage across the entries, and the reader is well advised to make ample use of the index and the topical outline found in volume five in order to locate the multiple points where a subject might be covered. There are, for example, four entries primarily dealing with torture: "Torture and International Law," "Convention against Torture," "European Convention on Prevention of Torture," and "Torture Treatment Organizations." Other entries also touch upon the subject, such as the analysis of the United States and its "War against Terrorism." The key to the use of this five-volume work is the index and its multiple references to various subjects. If one is interested in the regional protection of human rights in, say, Europe, one needs to use the index to consult: the European Union, the European Social Charter, the European Bank for Reconstruction and Development, the European Union Charter of Fundamental Rights, the European Convention on Human Rights and Fundamental Freedoms (Council of Europe), the Helsinki Accord and CSCE/OSCE, and so on. The index is the essential access point.

All entries have been refereed, and a conscious effort has been made to present information in clear and understandable prose. We avoided legalistic or otherwise obtuse presentations. Some entries, it should be noted, are beautifully written, original and creative, and could stand alone as important contributions to scholarship. The merits of the encyclopedia rest primarily with the authors, who devoted their expertise and time, mainly because of an interest in human rights education and a commitment to professional service.

We endeavored to explain all legal terms so that this reference work would be of assistance to nonadvanced students and the general public. The emphasis on clear, jargon-free language, of course, does not preclude use by those more advanced in the subject matter. A selective bibliography at the end of each entry tells the reader where further basic information may be found. A few key references may be found within certain entries, but the intent was not to encumber the essays with extensive references, since the authors are in effect distilling the collective current state of knowledge about each topic, and each sentence could in theory include a reference.

Each entry contains cross-references to other relevant entries in our five volumes. The more than three hundred entries are arranged alphabetically, each starting on a new page. Note that entries that begin with "Right to" are alphabetized under the word that follows, so the "Right to Development" entry is found under "Development, Right to," following the entry on the Democratic Republic of Congo and preceding the entries on disability rights. Similarly, the entries on North Korea and South Korea appear in the letter K. The encyclopedia includes seven maps in the front matter of each volume. Volume five contains the topical outline, the index, and the directory of contributors.

ACKNOWLEDGMENTS

I would like to thank especially the editorial board of Peter R. Baehr, Michael Freeman, Mark Janis, Rhoda

Howard-Hassmann, Barbara Stark, and David Weiss-brodt. They all wrote and refereed entries, and they all helped locate expert authors—sometimes on short notice and sometimes with repeated efforts. Several referees selected by the publisher were helpful in structuring the project initially. I would also like to thank the sympathetic, efficient, and agreeable persons at Oxford University Press who rescued this project from some early difficulties not of our making, and who saw it through in timely fashion to completion—first Damon Zucca and then more closely over time Tim Sachs. Finally, I would like to thank profusely the authors of the project, many of whom wrote beautiful and even definitive essays, sometimes multiple essays, sometimes on short notice, and sometimes in accommodating demanding referees. In the last analysis the project reflects their willingness to contribute their expertise to advancing the understanding of human rights.

David P. Forsythe
April 2009

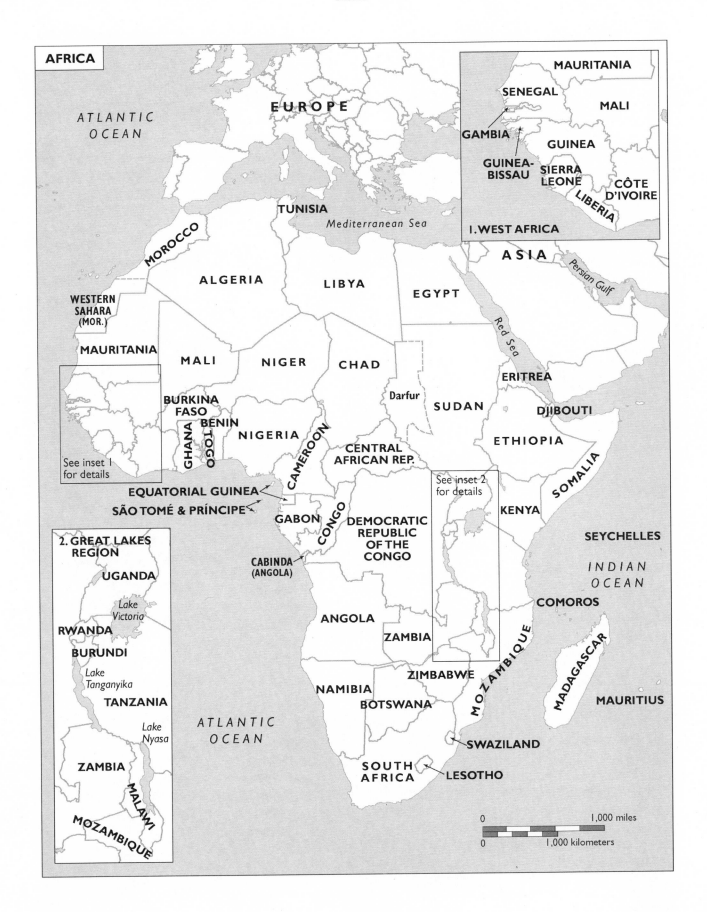

AFRICA

ATLANTIC OCEAN

EUROPE

ASIA

MAURITANIA

SENEGAL

GAMBIA

MALI

GUINEA-BISSAU

GUINEA

SIERRA LEONE

CÔTE D'IVOIRE

LIBERIA

1. WEST AFRICA

TUNISIA

Mediterranean Sea

Persian Gulf

MOROCCO

ALGERIA

LIBYA

EGYPT

WESTERN SAHARA (MOR.)

Red Sea

MAURITANIA

MALI

NIGER

CHAD

Darfur

SUDAN

ERITREA

DJIBOUTI

BURKINA FASO

BENIN

NIGERIA

GHANA

TOGO

CAMEROON

CENTRAL AFRICAN REP.

ETHIOPIA

See inset 1 for details

EQUATORIAL GUINEA

SÃO TOMÉ & PRÍNCIPE

GABON

CONGO

See inset 2 for details

KENYA

SOMALIA

SEYCHELLES

CABINDA (ANGOLA)

DEMOCRATIC REPUBLIC OF THE CONGO

INDIAN OCEAN

2. GREAT LAKES REGION

UGANDA

COMOROS

Lake Victoria

RWANDA

BURUNDI

ANGOLA

ZAMBIA

MOZAMBIQUE

MADAGASCAR

Lake Tanganyika

TANZANIA

Lake Nyasa

ZIMBABWE

MAURITIUS

ZAMBIA

NAMIBIA

BOTSWANA

MALAWI

ATLANTIC OCEAN

MOZAMBIQUE

SWAZILAND

SOUTH AFRICA

LESOTHO

0   1,000 miles

0   1,000 kilometers

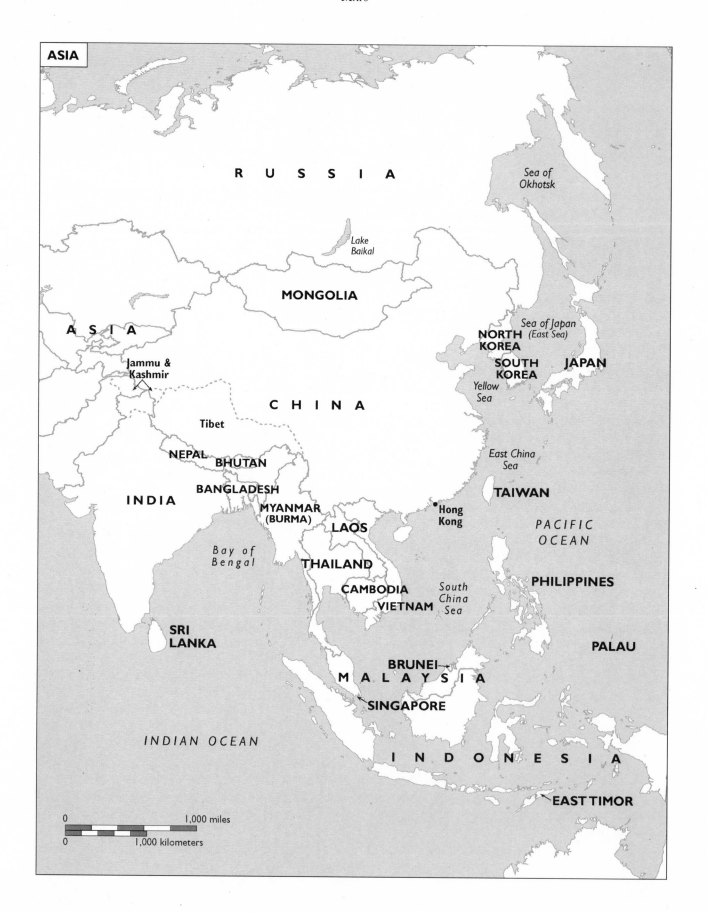

ASIA

RUSSIA

Sea of Okhotsk

Lake Baikal

MONGOLIA

ASIA

Jammu & Kashmir

CHINA

Tibet

NEPAL

BHUTAN

BANGLADESH

INDIA

MYANMAR (BURMA)

LAOS

Bay of Bengal

THAILAND

CAMBODIA

VIETNAM

SRI LANKA

NORTH KOREA

Sea of Japan (East Sea)

SOUTH KOREA

JAPAN

Yellow Sea

East China Sea

TAIWAN

Hong Kong

PACIFIC OCEAN

South China Sea

PHILIPPINES

PALAU

BRUNEI

MALAYSIA

SINGAPORE

INDIAN OCEAN

INDONESIA

EAST TIMOR

0   1,000 miles

0   1,000 kilometers

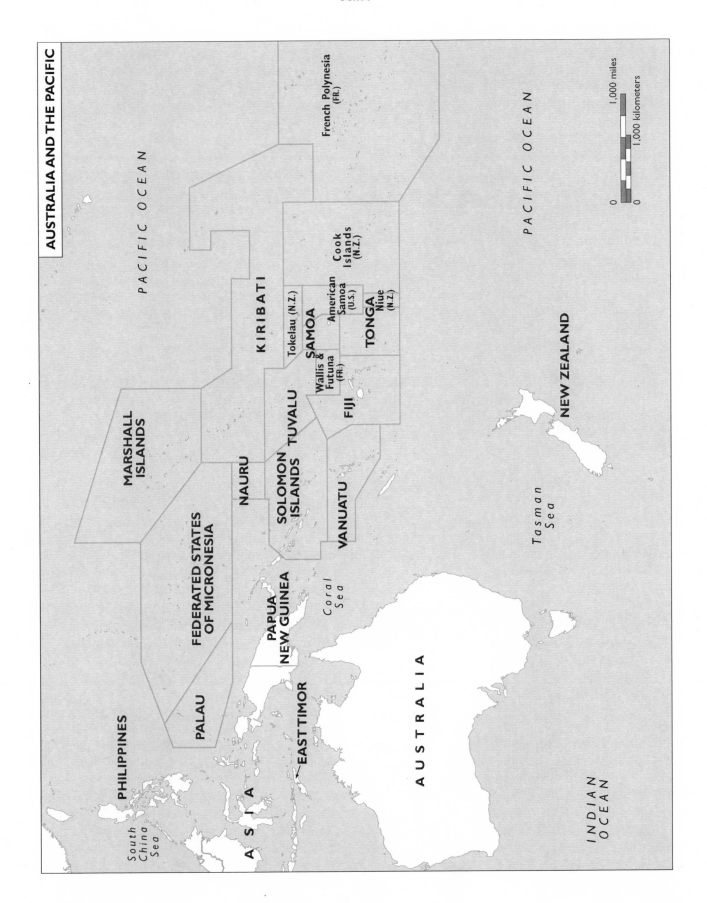

AUSTRALIA AND THE PACIFIC

PACIFIC OCEAN

PACIFIC OCEAN

French Polynesia
(FR.)

1,000 miles

1,000 kilometers

0

0

KIRIBATI

Cook
Islands
(N.Z.)

Tokelau (N.Z.)

American
Samoa
(U.S.)

SAMOA

Niue (N.Z.)

TONGA

Wallis &
Futuna
(FR.)

FIJI

MARSHALL
ISLANDS

TUVALU

NAURU

SOLOMON
ISLANDS

VANUATU

NEW ZEALAND

FEDERATED STATES
OF MICRONESIA

PAPUA
NEW GUINEA

Coral
Sea

Tasman
Sea

PALAU

PHILIPPINES

EAST TIMOR

A S I A

AUSTRALIA

South
China
Sea

INDIAN
OCEAN

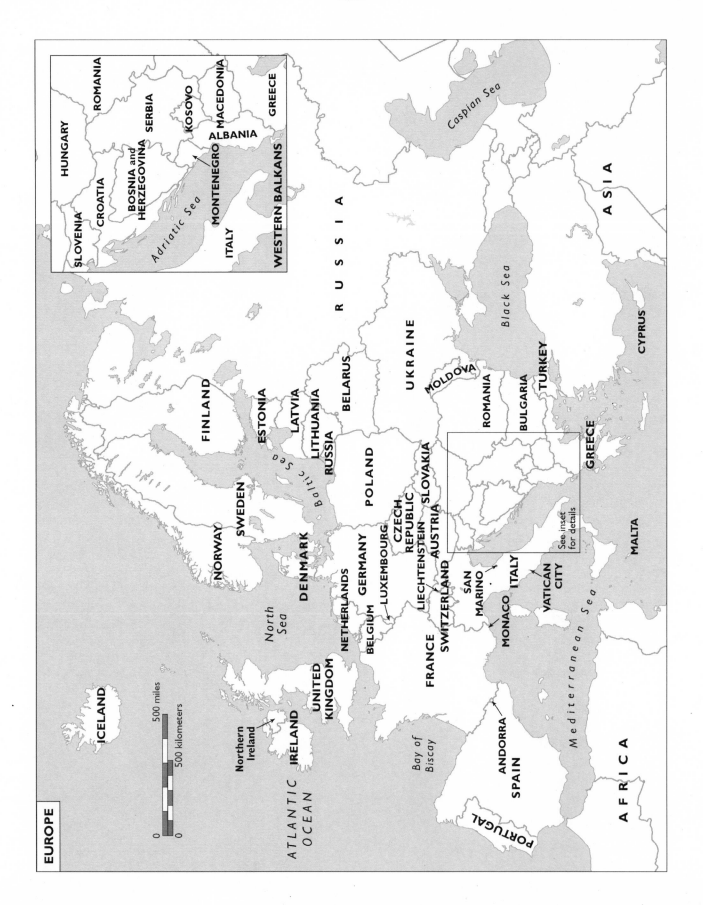

EUROPE

SLOVENIA
HUNGARY
CROATIA
ROMANIA
BOSNIA and HERZEGOVINA
SERBIA
KOSOVO
MACEDONIA
MONTENEGRO
ALBANIA
GREECE
ITALY
Adriatic Sea
WESTERN BALKANS

Caspian Sea

A S I A

R U S S I A

Black Sea

CYPRUS

UKRAINE

TURKEY
MOLDOVA
ROMANIA
BULGARIA
GREECE

FINLAND
ESTONIA
LATVIA
LITHUANIA
BELARUS
RUSSIA
POLAND
Baltic Sea

NORWAY
SWEDEN
DENMARK
CZECH REPUBLIC
SLOVAKIA
AUSTRIA
LIECHTENSTEIN

See inset for details

MALTA

North Sea

NETHERLANDS
GERMANY
BELGIUM
LUXEMBOURG
SWITZERLAND
FRANCE
SAN MARINO
MONACO
ITALY
VATICAN CITY

Mediterranean Sea

A F R I C A

ICELAND

500 miles
500 kilometers

Northern Ireland
IRELAND
UNITED KINGDOM

ATLANTIC OCEAN

Bay of Biscay

ANDORRA
SPAIN
PORTUGAL

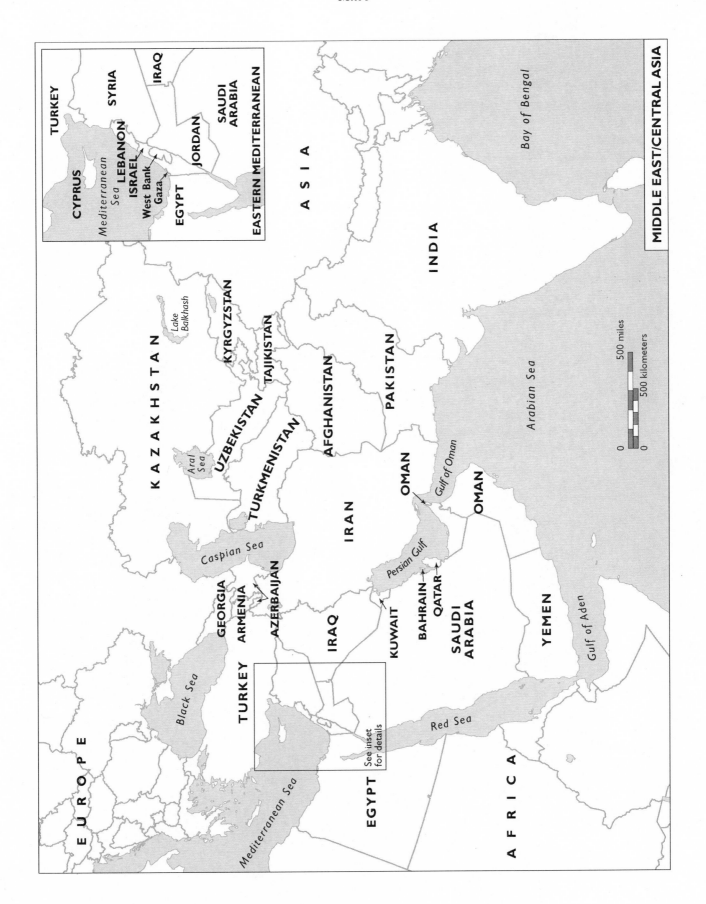

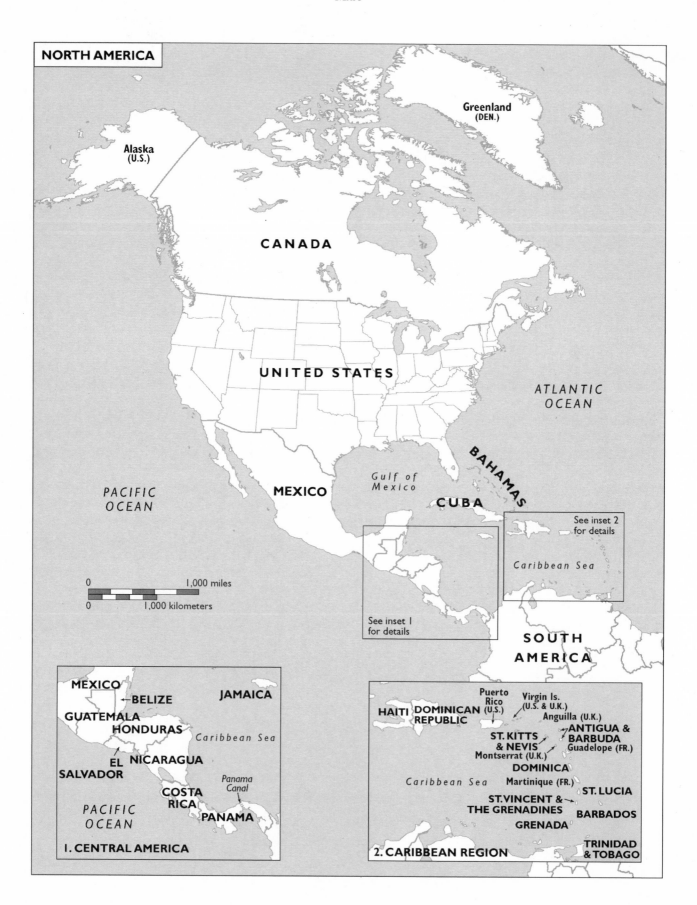

NORTH AMERICA

Greenland
(DEN.)

Alaska
(U.S.)

CANADA

UNITED STATES

ATLANTIC
OCEAN

PACIFIC
OCEAN

MEXICO

Gulf of
Mexico

BAHAMAS

CUBA

See inset 2
for details

Caribbean Sea

0   1,000 miles

0   1,000 kilometers

See inset 1
for details

SOUTH
AMERICA

MEXICO

BELIZE

JAMAICA

GUATEMALA

HONDURAS

Caribbean Sea

EL
SALVADOR

NICARAGUA

PACIFIC
OCEAN

COSTA
RICA

Panama
Canal

PANAMA

1. CENTRAL AMERICA

HAITI

DOMINICAN
REPUBLIC

Puerto
Rico
(U.S.)

Virgin Is.
(U.S. & U.K.)

Anguilla (U.K.)

ANTIGUA &
BARBUDA

ST. KITTS
& NEVIS

Guadelope (FR.)

Montserrat (U.K.)

DOMINICA

Caribbean Sea

Martinique (FR.)

ST. LUCIA

ST. VINCENT &
THE GRENADINES

BARBADOS

GRENADA

TRINIDAD
& TOBAGO

2. CARIBBEAN REGION

AFGHANISTAN

by Christa Meindersma

Since 1979 Afghanistan has been the scene of conflict involving foreign occupation and interference, resulting in more than a million people dead and millions of refugees in neighboring countries. Decades of war destroyed Afghanistan's political, social, and economic infrastructure and took a heavy toll on its civilian population.

Following the terrorist attack on the World Trade Center in New York on 11 September 2001 by Afghan-based Al Qaeda operatives, the United States attacked Afghanistan in retaliation. The U.S. invasion toppled the Taliban regime, which had given sanctuary to Al Qaeda, and initiated a process toward political transition, stabilization, and reconstructing a representative Afghan state that continues to date.

As of 2001, a UN-mandated, NATO-led military operation, International Security and Assistance Force (ISAF, established by UN Security Council Resolution 1386 in 2001), and a civilian United Nations mission, United Nations Assistance Mission in Afghanistan (UNAMA, established by Security Council Resolution 1401 in 2002) are assisting the Afghan government to extend its authority throughout Afghanistan and to establish a functioning state. Alongside the ISAF, the American Operation Enduring Freedom (OEF) continues to pursue terrorist operatives, such as members of Al Qaeda and the Taliban.

Human rights violations in Afghanistan now take place against the backdrop of a sustained history of conflict, ongoing insurgency by Taliban and Al Qaeda fighters, and over seven years of humanitarian and military intervention by the international community. Human rights violations are both a consequence and cause of the conflict in Afghanistan. The failure of the international community to meet the most basic needs of the Afghans has created the space for antigovernment forces to gain renewed strength.

BACKGROUND

Afghanistan is a mountainous landlocked country with a population of approximately 30 million people. It is strategically located at the crossroads of southern and European Asia and shares borders with Pakistan, Iran, China, Tajikistan, Turkmenistan, Uzbekistan, and that part of the disputed territory of Jammu and Kashmir that is controlled by Pakistan. Its population is a mix of Pashtun (42 percent), Tajik (27 percent), Hazara (9 percent), Uzbek (9 percent), Aimak, Turkmen, Baloch, and numerous smaller ethnic groups and tribes. Religiously, approximately 80 percent is Sunni and 20 percent Shia Muslim.

Afghanistan's history is marked by wars, conflict, and foreign invasions and interference. During the colonial period, Afghanistan was not subjugated but maintained as a buffer state in the "Great Game" between Russia and the British Empire. Its current borders were delineated in the late nineteenth century without much Afghan involvement. The contested Durand Line, the 1,610-mile border between Afghanistan and Pakistan that cuts through the Pashtun tribal belt and divides the Pashtun tribal people between Pakistan and Afghanistan, remains a source of tension between both countries. Afghanistan joined the United Nations in 1946 and enjoyed a period of relative calm until the 1970s, when the ousted prime minister, Mohammed Daoud, launched a coup against the ruling king, Mohammed Zahir.

In 1979 Soviet forces invaded Afghanistan, which became a playground for Cold War confrontations. The United States and the West supported and armed the mujahideen opposition against the Russian Communist regime in Afghanistan. Pakistan supported the anti-Communist effort by arming and strengthening Islamic Pashtun fighters against the Soviet occupation. During the ten-year war of attrition against the Soviets, 3 million refugees fled to Pakistan and 1.5 million to Iran, the economy was crippled, the school system destroyed, and more than half of the population was displaced. The Soviet occupation lasted until 1989.

Following Soviet withdrawal, war continued, first between the mujahideen and the pro-Soviet regime, and after the regime's collapse in 1992, between the various mujahideen factions. While the interest by the international community in Afghanistan waned, civil war between various factions and warlords intensified. By 1990 6.3 million Afghans had fled Afghanistan and lived in exile—3.3 million in Pakistan (mainly Pashtun) and 3 million in Iran (mainly Tajiks, Uzbeks, and Hazaras). Various peace accords among Afghan leaders did not stop the fighting.

In 1994 the Taliban was created, funded and inspired by Pakistan, in order to resolve the chaos in southern Afghanistan. Originally a movement of sons and orphans of mujahideen raised in religious schools in Pakistan (madrassas), the Taliban seized power in Kabul in 1996 and imposed strict Islamic rule. Full-scale war between the Taliban and a coalition of mujahideen, the Northern Alliance, ensued and continued unabated. By 2000 the Taliban controlled most of the territory of Afghanistan.

Under the Taliban regime, Afghanistan became a sanctuary and training ground for international terrorists, including Al Qaeda fighters. The Taliban regime was renowned for some of the worst human rights atrocities in the recent history of Afghanistan, particularly against women and girls, including the banning of girls' education and employment. By 2000 one-quarter of all children born in Afghanistan were dying of preventable diseases before the age of five. Afghan women were nearly five times more likely to die in childbirth than in other developing countries. Typhoid and cholera epidemics were rampant, and pneumonia and malaria had reemerged as public health threats. The condition of women had deteriorated markedly, and only one in twenty girls received any kind of education. By the late 1990s Afghanistan had also become the source of nearly 80 percent of the world's illicit opium. In the late 1990s Afghanistan was hit by a series of natural disasters—earthquakes, severe flooding, and drought.

Following the U.S. invasion and the toppling of the Taliban regime with the help of the Northern Alliance in 2001, the Northern Alliance took Kabul. Subsequently, several Afghan factions consolidated their control of the countryside, creating an unstable security situation. While military victory was quickly achieved over the Taliban and Al Qaeda, less planning was done to prepare for a political transition. A meeting of Afghan political leaders was hastily convened in Bonn under United Nations auspices in December 2001. The result was the formation of an Afghan Interim Authority and a roadmap for a political transition. The Bonn process has been criticized for not being representative. During a subsequent *loya jirga*, a grand council of tribal elders, held in 2002,

Hamid Karzai was elected interim president. Previously he had been politically close to the United Kingdom and United States. In 2004 a constitutional *loya jirga* drafted a new Afghan constitution. That same year, presidential elections were held that confirmed Karzai as president. In 2005 parliamentary elections followed.

More than six years after the U.S. invasion, the security situation in Afghanistan remained volatile. In much of Afghanistan, the rule of power rather than the rule of law reigned. By 2005 fighting between resurgent forces of the Taliban and ISAF and OEF forces had intensified, particularly in the south of Afghanistan. Active pursuit of Taliban fighters by international troops was stepped up. Reportedly, by 2008 the Taliban had a permanent presence in 54 percent of Afghanistan and ran parallel governments in a number of districts (Senlis Council, *Afghanistan*. By that time the Taliban had started to use such tactics as suicide bombings, hitherto largely unknown to Afghanistan and probably derived from experience in Iraq, resulting in growing numbers of civilian casualties. According to a survey into past human rights violations carried out by the Afghan Independent Human Rights Commission, 69 percent of Afghans consider themselves victims of war. In 2007 Afghanistan ranked 174 out of 178 on the UN Human Development Index (HDI).

UNITED NATIONS HUMAN RIGHTS INVOLVEMENT

In 1980 an attempt by the United Nations Security Council to condemn the Soviet invasion failed due to a Soviet veto. Consequently, the situation in Afghanistan was periodically reviewed by the UN General Assembly. In 1985 the assembly appointed a special rapporteur for the human rights situation in Afghanistan. In its first consideration of what was to become an annual review of the situation, the assembly expressed concern at widespread disregard for human rights and large-scale violations, as well as the severe consequences for the civilian population of indiscriminate bombardments and military operations aimed primarily at villages and agricultural structures.

In subsequent years the assembly issued fifteen more resolutions on the human rights situation in Afghanistan. Each year (except 1996) the assembly expressed deep concern about the human rights situation, in particular violations against Afghan women. In addition, rapporteurs reported regularly on the situation in Afghanistan since the 1980s, and the UN High Commissioner for

Human Rights issued reports after 1993. For instance, in 1993 the UN Committee against Torture expressed concern over the way Islamic law was incorporated into Afghan criminal law. The special rapporteur on violence against women, appointed in 1994, has critically reviewed the situation of Afghan women.

Except for the human rights mechanisms, Afghanistan was largely ignored by the international community after the Soviet withdrawal. A UN-brokered peace deal for a political transition collapsed. Between 1992 and 1996 the UN Security Council had only one debate on Afghanistan. In addition to monitoring and reporting on human rights, the United Nations, until the arrival of the ISAF, OEF, and UNAMA, predominantly engaged in humanitarian efforts, with some political initiatives aimed at establishing peace. An important part of the problem was that the U.S. government also lost interest in Afghanistan, being satisfied with the Soviet withdrawal. This neglect allowed a power vacuum to develop, filled by the Taliban and Al Qaeda.

In 1997 the UN secretary-general appointed Lakhdar Brahimi as special envoy for Afghanistan. In 1999 he convened a "six plus two" process, aimed at bringing together Afghanistan's neighbors, Russia, and the United States to negotiate peace. The process did not achieve its aim and Brahimi resigned shortly thereafter. Brahimi was reappointed to oversee the Bonn process following the U.S. invasion and toppling of the Taliban regime in 2001.

HUMAN RIGHTS VIOLATIONS UNDER THE TALIBAN REGIME (1996–2001)

In 1996 a group of young students managed to take over Kabul. These students, who called themselves Taliban (literally translated, "students of Islam"), were a mujahideen faction out to bring order and stability back to Afghanistan. In reality, the Taliban turned out to be a radical Islamist movement that enforced a strict interpretation of Sharia law on Afghan citizens.

Initially, Afghanistan's citizens welcomed the Taliban to rid the country of the corrupt mujahideen factions that had been terrorizing the population. The Taliban eventually exerted control over approximately 80 to 90 percent of the country, with power centered in the city of Kabul. During the Taliban's regime it had approximately ten to twenty-five thousand members, operating mainly in Pakistan and Afghanistan. Their members consisted primarily of Pashtuns, an ethnic group that forms almost half of Afghanistan's citizens, specifically from the Durrani and Ghilzai tribes in southern Afghanistan.

The Taliban regime was known for its brutal suppression of human rights, particularly of women, ethnic minorities, children, and homosexuals. It was officially recognized by only three countries: Pakistan, Saudi Arabia, and the United Arab Emirates. The Taliban's strict regulations were issued by the Ministry for the Propagation of Virtue and the Suppression of Vice, which was part of the Ministry of Religious Affairs. The ministry employed approximately thirty-five hundred Taliban members as religious police. It was their job to ensure that the Sharia laws were strictly adhered to. Afghanistan's citizens were constantly watched and interrogated by the religious police. Whenever any of the Taliban's regulations were not obeyed, immediate repercussions would follow.

Response of the international community.

The Taliban's maltreatment of Afghan citizens was widely known internationally. In 1993, a few years before the Taliban's arrival, the UN General Assembly established the United Nations Special Mission to Afghanistan (UNSMA) to help Afghanistan with reconstruction and state-building efforts. However, in retaliation for the U.S. decision to close the Taliban office in New York, the Taliban ordered the closure of the UNSMA office in 1998, making it harder to monitor the deteriorating human rights situation.

Special rapporteurs of the United Nations regularly requested visits to Afghanistan during the Taliban regime. Mostly they were denied permission to enter because of so-called urgent preoccupations. When a rapporteur was allowed to enter, he would usually be confined to the city of Kabul. During the Taliban regime it also became harder for Western nongovernmental organizations (NGOs) to continue operations in Afghanistan, due to restrictive visa regulations. The Taliban would try to use their influence over NGO workers. Afghan women were only allowed to work at NGOs if accompanied by a *mahram*, a blood relative. In 1998 the reciprocal frustrations became so bad that the Taliban eventually decided to close the operations of NGOs present in Afghanistan. They were not allowed or able to return until 2001, when the Taliban regime was removed.

In November 2000 the Taliban and the secretary-general of the United Nations agreed "to pursue a process of dialogue under the auspices of the Secretary-General from which neither side would unilaterally withdraw until all the items on its agenda were exhausted" (UN General Assembly, p. 4).

Women.

Among their most disreputable violations were the restrictions the Taliban put on women. The Taliban installed a system of gender apartheid, in which women were subservient to men. During the years of the Taliban regime, Afghanistan consistently ranked at the bottom of the UN Gender Disparity Index. In 1997 the Interagency Gender Mission to Afghanistan found that sixteen of the main articles of the Convention on the Elimination of All Forms of Discrimination against Women, to which Afghanistan was a party, were violated. While the Taliban claimed they imposed restrictions on women to protect them from harm, many women were beaten or executed if they were considered guilty of violating Taliban's rules. Constant fear of reprisals made Afghan women follow the Taliban's regulations.

The position of women deteriorated markedly under Taliban rule. Afghan women were prohibited from working outside the home, from entering schools and universities, and from leaving the house unattended by a male relative. Outside the house women had to wear a burka, covering their body from head to toe, with a small mesh through which they could breathe. Women were often beaten for showing their ankles, wearing the wrong shoes or burka, or simply for laughing too loud.

Afghan women were not allowed to visit a male doctor, nor were they allowed to become doctors themselves. The Taliban eventually allowed some international nongovernmental organizations to enter the country to provide health care to women. However, restricted access to health care claimed the lives of many Afghan women. Women were also not allowed any leisure time at their homes, since music, the Internet, and other leisure activities were forbidden. This resulted in high numbers of Afghan women becoming depressed.

Women were punished for adultery or fornication. Punishment was often meted out on the spot. In addition, every Friday "adulterous" women were brought to a stadium in which they were publicly humiliated. It was difficult for a woman to prove that she was raped, since she needed four men to attest to the rape. If the victim failed to prove this, she might end up being accused of adultery, her complaint constituting proof of extramarital sexual intercourse. The women that were sexually abused often had trouble seeking professional help. A feeling of shame or stigma caused many women to stay quiet about these incidents.

Children and education.

Many of Afghanistan's children died at a young age under the Taliban. Some died before they reached the age of eight, often due to lack of health care. Many children became ill because of the poor living conditions or died from diseases that could not be cured in time. Eventually, Afghanistan's child mortality rate became the highest in the world.

The majority of children witnessed violence and murder during the war years. More than half had seen family members being killed or beaten. Many children suffered from posttraumatic stress, living in constant fear. In addition, a great number of children suffered from malnutrition. Owing to the bad economic situation, many families could not afford to buy sufficiently nutritious food, leading to a great number of children not being able to fully develop physically or intellectually.

Reforming the educational system into purely religious schooling was one of the Taliban's priorities. Secular education was no longer allowed, and only boys were permitted to receive education. They were taught the Arab language and the teachings of the Qur'an. Children had to learn parts of the Qur'an by heart and recite prayers and rituals in addition to studying Islamic morals and values.

Girls were not allowed to receive an education from age eight, since they had to prepare themselves for their lives at home. In 1998 all girls' schools were closed. Women were not allowed to receive a secondary or tertiary education, and those who already had received some kind of education were no longer allowed to work. Although the ban on girls attending schools was most strictly enforced in the cities, the regime also made it harder for girls to enter schools outside of the cities, where 80 to 90 percent of the population lived. Communities did establish their own schools without Taliban intervention, and a number of girls were able to attend these. However, overall it was made extremely hard for girls to receive any formal education.

In addition to violating women's rights, the Taliban also imposed restrictions on men. For instance, men were obliged to grow their beards and attend prayers at mosques. The religious police were also checking on them. Men of ethnic minorities especially had a lot to endure under the Taliban regime.

Ethnic minorities.

Hazaras, an ethnic minority living primarily in north-central Afghanistan, were another target of the

Taliban regime. Hazaras make up approximately 9 percent of the Afghan population and had faced persecution for several decades. Reportedly, the Taliban's aim was to "exterminate all Hazaras" because of their Shia beliefs. During persecutions citizens were obliged to cite Sunni rituals, to make sure that they were indeed Shia. This religious persecution took place during the five years the Taliban regime was effective, leading to many deaths.

In August 1998 a massacre took place in Mazar-i-Sharif, a city in northern Afghanistan inhabited mainly by Hazaras, when the Taliban opened fire indiscriminately on people in Hazara neighborhoods. Subsequently, Taliban members searched people's homes for male family members and their weapons. Some men were summarily executed, others were imprisoned in overcrowded jails. Although most of the prisoners were Hazaras, some Tajiks and Uzbeks were also imprisoned. The Mazar-i-Sharif massacre was only one of several during the Taliban regime. In 2001 another major massacre took place in Yakawalang when men were taken from their houses and executed by a firing squad. Reportedly, victims were tortured prior to the execution.

The Taliban regime triggered a new flow of refugees into neighboring countries, especially from the minority groups they targeted. Others became internally displaced in Afghanistan. Occasionally, Taliban members entered refugee camps and attacked the people inside. Some women were raped, and men were beaten or forced to stay inside of their tents.

HUMAN RIGHTS ISSUES FROM 2001

In addition to the devastating consequences of almost three decades of war, the violence and insecurity associated with the conflict following the 2001 invasion—which after 2005 —pose serious challenges to the achievement of the basic human rights of Afghans. According to the report of the UN High Commissioner for Human Rights, summarizing the human rights situation in Afghanistan in 2008:

> The escalation of the armed conflict in Afghanistan has had a significant impact on civilians in conflict-affected areas, in particular on those who are already vulnerable. The intensifying conflict has also resulted in a disturbing rise in civilian casualties and has contracted the space for humanitarian action. Long-standing discrimination against women and minority groups is manifest in their lack of access to justice and other basic services. Important gains made recently by women in the public sphere are in danger of receding.

> Mounting attacks on the freedom to express views that challenge existing power structures as well as social and religious norms that usually marginalize women cast doubts on the Government's ability to ensure a free and democratic space where human rights are fully respected. This is especially vital in an elections period. While important initiatives to reform the justice sector and improve the administration of justice were launched in 2008, the judicial system remains weak, corrupt and dysfunctional, and at times does not comply with international human rights obligations. Compounded by a surge in criminal violence and decline of public law enforcement authorities, control over parts of the country, a culture of impunity prevails as demonstrated by the failure to prosecute perpetrators for past and contemporary human rights violations and abuses. (p. 1)

The most pressing human rights challenges are the rights of women, access to and quality of education, and violence against civilians associated with the ongoing conflict.

Rights of women.

Despite some positive developments for women since the fall of the Taliban, such as participation of women in parliament, inclusion of equal rights for men and women in the Afghan constitution, the establishment of a Ministry for Women, and improved access to education and health care, the human rights situation of women in Afghanistan remains frail.

Maternal mortality is among the highest in the world, with 1,600 deaths per 100,000 live births in the period 2000–2006, while according to a 2009 report by the United Nations Children's Fund (UNICEF), infant mortality rated 165 per 1,000 life births. One in four Afghan children die before their fifth birthday. Afghanistan is the only country in the world where life expectancy is lower for women than men (forty-four years for women and forty-five for men in 2006). Despite war casualties, men still outnumber women by an average of 104 to 100 for all age groups. The level of malnutrition is estimated at 45 to 55 percent, with women and children mostly at risk. Forty percent of the rural population are unable to satisfy their most basic needs, and as few as 23 percent of Afghans have access to clean drinking water. Despite progress in recent years, primary school enrollment is among the lowest in the world, with half as many girls enrolled in primary education as boys. In southern Afghanistan, according to a 2006 report filed by the special rapporteur on violence against women, girls constitute only 15 percent of the pupils in primary schools.

Violence against women continues to be an all-pervasive phenomenon, tolerated and perpetuated by a traditional patriarchal society and culture. Perpetrators are often male family members, who enjoy immunity as informal systems of dispute settlement are biased against women and formal justice systems absent or dysfunctional in cases affecting women. The preponderance of domestic violence, rape, and trafficking is also fueled by the war and the postconflict situation of lawlessness and insecurity. Kidnapping and rape of women by militia and warlords continue to be widespread, including execution by local dispute-settlement councils. The United Nations special rapporteur on violence against women identified four factors underlying women's vulnerability and the perpetuation of violence: the traditional patriarchal gender order, the erosion of protective social mechanisms, lack of the rule of law, and poverty and insecurity.

Afghan women and girls are at risk of violence inside and outside of the home. Marital rape, sexual assault, and other forms of violence against women at home are common. In most cases, women do not report these crimes or, if they do, are returned to male family members by the police. Safe houses for women do exist but are generally not accepted by Afghan society, which considers these places for women of ill repute.

Child and forced marriages are considered to be at the root of most violence against women and girls in Afghanistan. Though the legal age for marriage is fifteen (eighteen for boys) and child marriage is prohibited by law, many girls are married at the age of ten or even younger. The Afghan Independent Human Rights Commission estimates that 60 to 80 percent of all marriages in Afghanistan are forced marriages and that 57 percent of girls are married before the age of sixteen. Consequently, girls may become pregnant before their bodies are fully developed, negatively affecting their health. Enforcing existing laws on child and forced marriages is complicated by the fact that only 5 percent of marriages are registered, though registration is required by law.

Legal provisions protecting women from violence, forced and early marriage, and discrimination do exist in civil and criminal law but are rarely applied in practice. For instance, marriage without the consent of a girl is punishable by—albeit short—imprisonment, and when this is done as compensation (baad), the term of imprisonment goes up to years.

Notwithstanding the existence of formal laws, in rural areas lives are governed by tribal practices and social codes. In traditional areas of Afghanistan, women are subordinated to men, excluded from public life, and at the mercy of male family members. In Pashtun-inhabited areas of Afghanistan, for instance, the practice of baad is widespread, according to which girls are given away to settle a dispute upon the orders of a local council in order to prevent a blood feud. Thus girls are reduced to property, an economic asset to be transferred at the behest of male family members and local elders. Another illustration of the treatment of girls as property is the fact that widows can be forced to marry a brother-in-law or be given to a stranger by her in-laws. Given the prevalence of child marriages, young women may face this situation.

In addition, there are few effective mechanisms of redress for women who have been subjected to violence or discrimination. Women are hesitant to report crimes. There are few women police, and the chief of police is often the local militia commander. Police are known to return women victims of violence to their families. Judges in the formal judicial system lack legal training and may be at the same time members of traditional councils that adjudicate disputes. Typically, cases of violence against women and girls tend to be settled out of court through mediation by traditional councils rather than law enforcement. These councils, traditionally composed of men, are perceived as discriminatory toward women.

In reality, women who have been violated may be accused of sexual offenses and face imprisonment while the perpetrator goes free. For instance, sexual intercourse outside marriage is punishable by whipping or stoning. However, women who have been raped or have become the victim of incest may have difficulty proving the rape—requiring four male witnesses—and be convicted for adultery instead, their complaint of rape being the proof of sexual intercourse outside marriage. Most women in Afghan prisons are incarcerated for sexual offenses related to adultery, prostitution, or illicit sexual intercourse. Some of these women were arrested when they remarried after divorce and were then accused by their former husbands of having an illicit relationship. Some women are held in prison on charges of "running away from home," which is not a crime, either in criminal law or under the Islamic Sharia code.

To escape violence, and in the absence of formal mechanisms of redress, some girls and women try to set themselves on fire (self-immolation). The Afghan Independent Human Rights Commission documented 380 cases between September 2003 and April 2004, the majority of which resulted in death. The same organization recorded 1,545 cases of violence against women in

2006, including self-immolation, exchange of girls, forced marriage, and sexual violence; in 2007 the number of cases rose to 2,374. The hospital in Herat registered 100 cases between 2002 and 2005 and almost 200 in Herat province alone in 2006.

Efforts to improve the situation of women.

Afghanistan's strategy to curb violence against women and improve the position of women consists of economic development, improving access to education and health care, and lifting women's societal position. A Ministry of Women was created in 2002 with four priority areas: health, education, legal protection, and empowerment. Other ministries have prioritized women's concerns such as maternal mortality and women's access to microcredit and participation in small-scale development.

In 2005 the Afghan government created an Inter-Ministerial Task Force to Eliminate Violence against Women. The task force produced a work plan that identified ten objectives, activities, and entities responsible for implementation. A law on family violence has been drafted and submitted to parliament for approval. Also in 2005, family response units were established in a number of cities, including Kabul, Herat, and Mazar-i-Sharif.

Education.

One of the biggest challenges to Afghanistan's reconstruction and development is the lack of education of a large part of the Afghan population. Following the fall of the Taliban, some tangible progress in education was made. Girls' education was no longer prohibited, and in 2001 three-quarters of a million children returned to school. In 2008 this number had risen to 6 million children, including an estimated 1.9 million girls.

Under the Afghan constitution, education up to grade nine is compulsory and free. Yet Afghanistan faces a 72 percent illiteracy rate. The country has the lowest female literacy rate in the world (18 percent), and only 40 percent of girls between the ages of seven and twelve attend school (UNICEF, 2009). Many children in rural areas have no access to schools at all. At the secondary level, between 2000–2007 only 6 percent of all girls were attending as compared to 18 percent of all boys. At the primary level, this was 66 versus 40 percent. Of an estimated 2 million children not attending school, approximately 1.3 million are girls (Human Rights Watch, *Lessons in Terror*).

The worsening security situation in general has had a negative impact on education. The Taliban have increasingly attacked soft targets such as schools, teachers, and girls attending schools, as well as NGOs working in schools, to instill terror in the population. Attacks on educational facilities and personnel, throughout the country, increased by 24 percent from 236 incidents in 2007 to 293 in 2008. According to Human Rights Watch, anti-government forces target schools "either because of ideological opposition to secular education generally or to girls' education specifically, or because teachers and schools represent symbols of the government or the work of foreigners" (*The Human Cost*, p. 75). Insurgent tactics ranged from night letters (letters posted on doors at night warning girls or students not to attend school) and verbal threats to arson, grenade, or rock attacks and the killing of teachers and students. According to UNICEF, in 2008, 92 people were killed and 169 injured as a result of such attacks. In 2008 more than 640 schools remain closed due to insecurity, depriving 230,000 students of their education. In some of the southern provinces, 80 percent of the schools are closed (this according to security statistics released by the Afghan Ministry of Education September 2008).

Recent, insurgent attacks have especially targeted girls attending school or girls' schools. In general, in a society where girls' movements are more restricted than those of boys and given parents' concern about sexual harassment and violence against girls, parents are more inclined to pull girls out of school when the security situation deteriorates.

The reasons for the Taliban's efforts to disrupt the education of a new generation are clear: in rural areas, schools and teachers are often the first—and sometimes the only—point of interaction between the government and ordinary Afghans. Education is also a major contributor and prerequisite to modernizing and developing Afghan society and emancipating its women. Some NGOs have therefore suggested that access to education should be a key benchmark for measuring progress on the security front.

Although more children are in school as of 2008 than at any other period in Afghanistan's history, girls are not catching up, even at the primary level, partly because of societal attitudes demanding strict separation of girls and boys' education. There are also cases where designated girls' schools have been used for other purposes.

Education is crucial to the development of Afghanistan. The continuing denial of education to the majority of Afghan girls is an impediment to the development of Afghanistan and the participation of women in economic, social, and political life. Yet neither the Afghan government nor the international community has developed a strategy to end attacks on schools and teachers and to make education truly accessible to all.

HUMAN RIGHTS AND THE ONGOING CONFLICT

Human rights cannot be viewed in isolation from the ongoing armed conflict between the Taliban, Al Qaeda, and other insurgent groups, on the one hand, and international and Afghan forces, on the other. Attacks by insurgent groups and counterinsurgency campaigns by coalition forces have created a renewed sense of insecurity, caused fresh civilian casualties, and resulted in new displacement. Violence linked to the ongoing conflict was the deadliest in 2008 since the fall of the Taliban. In 2008 UNAMA recorded the highest civilian death toll of any year since 2001: a total of 2,118 civilian casualties, an increase of almost 40 percent on the 1,523 civilian deaths recorded in 2007. Of these, 55 percent were attributed to the Taliban and other armed opposition groups and 39 percent to coalition forces (UNAMA, 2009).

Violations by the Taliban and other armed groups.

Since early 2006 antigovernment armed groups, including the Taliban and Hezb-e Islami, have carried out an increasing number of attacks either directed against civilians or causing a disproportionate number of innocent civilian casualties. Attacks have targeted persons associated with the Afghan government, including teachers, doctors, tribal elders, and health workers, Afghan security forces—in particular Afghan police—Afghans associated with international forces and organizations, humanitarian workers, and private contractors. Targeted assassinations against district and provincial government employees have been a particularly worrying trend, discouraging Afghans from participating in the institutions of governance.

In 2008 the armed opposition was responsible for 1,160 civilian deaths, an increase of 65 percent over 2007. Eighty-five percent died as a result of suicide and improvised explosive devises (IEDs). Recent years saw a distinct pattern of Taliban attacks carried out in crowded residential areas and with apparent disregard for the extensive damage they cause to civilians. There have also been reports of Taliban using civilians as human shields and deliberately basing themselves in civilian areas.

In 2005 the average number of insurgent attacks was 130 per month. By late 2006 and into 2007 insurgent attacks had soared to 600 a month, with over 1,000 in June 2007. Human Rights Watch documented 350 cases in 2006 in which insurgent attacks such as bombings, shootings, kidnapping, and executions caused a total of at least 669 civilian deaths and more injuries. These numbers exclude civilians killed in fighting between insurgent and international or government forces.

The Taliban employ additional tactics to instill fear in the population, such as the "night letters" mentioned above, which are also posted on mosques and individual houses, threatening violence if a community cooperates with international organizations or forces. In some districts, Taliban members have enforced justice.

A new phenomenon in Afghanistan is suicide attacks, which have come to be an integral part of the Taliban's strategy. Afghanistan's first suicide attack occurred on 9 September 2001, but such attacks remained rare until 2005. From 2005 onward they started to happen with some regularity. In 2006 more than 800 Afghans were killed or injured in 123 suicide attacks. In 2007 160 attacks were recorded, in addition to 68 thwarted attempts. In 2008 in addition to 146 suicide attacks and 1,297 detonated IEDs killing 725 people, 93 suicide attacks and 843 IEDs were discovered before they could be detonated. While suicide attacks have targeted mostly national and international security forces, the large majority—80 percent—of victims has been civilian (UNAMA, 2009).

As far as is known, the perpetrators of suicide attacks are often uneducated youth drawn from the madrassas or from poor families in Pakistan. The impact of suicide attacks goes much beyond their immediate effects in terms of people killed or injured. Suicide attacks target and impact societies as a whole. They instill fear into the population, intimidate and traumatize people and communities, undermine the legitimacy of state institutions and their ability to protect the population, hamper reconstruction efforts and business activities, and thus have repercussions far beyond the immediate results of the attack itself.

Insurgent groups have also executed or mutilated persons who have allegedly collaborated with the Afghan government or with international forces, particularly civilian staff such as truck drivers or construction workers. In Helmand, persons accused of collaboration have been hanged or beheaded. Civilian vehicles have been ambushed and their passengers killed or mutilated on the spot. Insurgents have also resorted to the taking of hostages and kidnapping journalists, aid workers, and medical personnel. Hostages have been exchanged for Taliban fighters or executed when demands have not been met. For instance, on 17 March 2007 passengers of a civilian convoy contracted to deliver food to the UN International Security Assistance Force (ISAF) in Nuristan province were mutilated for their collaboration with foreigners.

Military operations by international troops.

In Afghanistan two sets of international forces are active. Alongside the approximately twenty-five thousand troops in the American-led antiterrorist Operation Enduring Freedom (OEF) as of April 2008, the UN Security Council has mandated the ISAF to support the Afghan government to establish its authority throughout Afghanistan. In August 2008 the ISAF consisted of about forty-five thousand troops from thirty-seven NATO and non-NATO countries, under a single NATO Strategic Command.

Military operations by international troops against Taliban fighters, which intensified between 2006 and 2008, have caused increasing numbers of civilian casualties. Air strikes are responsible for the largest number of deaths, as well as excessive use of force in search operations and civilians being killed after failing to follow instructions from international troops. Human rights NGOs and the United Nations have expressed concern that aerial bombardments carried out by international forces have failed to discriminate between civilians and military targets and have resulted in the excessive killing of innocent civilians and destruction of civilian property. For instance, in August 2008 an American attack in the western Afghan village of Azizabad struck a suspected Taliban compound, killing more than ninety people, including seventy-five women and children.

The issue of civilian casualties is complicated by potential disagreements between international military forces and Afghans about what constitutes a civilian. For instance, during a *shura* (meeting of traditional elders) following the fighting in Chora in south Afghanistan in 2007, locals demanded an explanation as to why so many civilians had been killed. According to NATO, these had been Taliban fighters who carried arms and had fought the international troops. The elders explained that as these young men had been coerced by the Taliban to fight, they were not Taliban but should be considered civilian. Perception matters. Killing by international troops of what are perceived as civilians by Afghans may inspire revenge killings.

Both President Karzai and the head of the United Nations Assistance Mission in Afghanistan (UNAMA) have condemned civilian deaths caused by the ISAF and insurgents and cautioned both NATO and the Taliban to avoid civilian casualties at all costs. At the end of 2006,

NATO issued a statement that civilian casualties were its single biggest failure. Civilian deaths, displacement following military operations, heavy-handed searches of private properties, and renewed hardship have decreased support for the international forces and the Afghan government. Causing civilian casualties also risks driving people into the hands of the Taliban and other armed groups that oppose the government.

There have also been complaints about international and Afghan security forces using abusive treatment and excessive force during raids and searches of private homes, resulting in the destruction of property and the killing and beating of civilians. However, even inappropriate or culturally insensitive conduct that does not reach this level of severity may negatively impact relations with Afghans and undermine the efforts of the international community. Human rights groups have also expressed concern about the detention procedures used by the ISAF, which may result in the torture or mistreatment of Afghan nationals who are handed over to Afghan security forces.

REFUGEES

Years of protracted conflict in Afghanistan caused millions of Afghans to flee abroad. Each stage of the conflict caused fresh waves of refugees, resulting in what the United Nations Human Rights Commission has described as "one of the most protracted, complex and tragic humanitarian dilemmas in contemporary history" (*Searching for Solutions*, p. 3). Throughout these years, Pakistan hosted the largest continuing refugee caseload in the world. The first wave of refugees arrived in Pakistan well before the Soviet takeover. By 1981, 2.4 million refugees had sought refuge in Pakistan, peaking at 3.3 million in 1990. The influx of so many Afghans had a dramatic impact on cities such as Peshawar and Quetta. The rise of the Taliban in the 1990s caused renewed waves of refugees and internally displaced persons.

Since 2002 more than 2.4 million refugees have returned to Afghanistan from Pakistan. As of 2008, some 3 million Afghan refugees continued to live in Pakistan, 1 million of whom lived in camps. Most of the Afghans still living in Pakistan arrived there after the Soviet invasion and were reluctant to go home for economic rather than security reasons. Meanwhile, tens of thousands of people cross the border between Afghanistan and Pakistan every day.

Over the years, approximately 3 million Afghan refugees fled to Iran. About 1 million remain in Iran, reluctant to return due to the lack of security in Afghanistan. In March 2008 Iran announced that it planned to resume deportation of most of the million remaining "illegal" Afghans, after suspending deportation in January 2008 due to cold weather.

ASSESSMENT

Seven years after the toppling of the Taliban regime, Afghanistan was at a tipping point. The failure of the Afghan government and the international community to meet the most basic human needs and rights of the Afghan people hampered the stabilization and reconstruction of the country. The lack of a tangible peace dividend for many ordinary Afghans created the space for the Taliban to reemerge and operate. The increasing insecurity in Afghanistan showed the inability of the Afghan authorities and the international coalition forces to provide basic security and negatively impacted every aspect of Afghan life.

The insecurity caused by prolonged and resurgent conflict cannot be overcome by military means alone. To stabilize the situation and counter the growing insurgency, an integrated approach firmly rooted in human rights and including serious political efforts is required. Ordinary Afghans need to experience a tangible improvement in their daily lives in order to gain confidence in the dividend of peace. Human rights are a precondition for peace and stability; continued insecurity and widespread human rights violations feed the insurgency.

Though improvement in women's rights and girls' education are often cited as signs of progress in Afghanistan since the toppling of the Taliban, a large percentage of Afghan children, particularly girls, remain without access to education. Another lost generation will greatly hamper Afghanistan's reconstruction, development, and modernization. Societal mores and traditional practices continue to work against an appreciation of women and girls as human beings worthy of equal respect and dignity. This, no doubt, is the greatest human rights challenge in Afghanistan and a barometer of the success of its human rights performance.

[*See also* Osama bin Laden and Al Qaeda; Pakistan; Terrorism; *and* United States: War on Terrorism.]

BIBLIOGRAPHY

Afghan Independent Human Rights Commission. *A Call for Justice: A National Consultation on Past Human Rights Violations in Afghanistan.* January 25, 2005. http://www.ictj.org.

Amnesty International. *Women in Afghanistan: Pawns in Men's Power Struggles.* ASA 11/011/1999.

Erturk, Yakin. *Integration of the Human Rights of Women and a Gender Perspective: Violence against Women. Report of the Special Rapporteur on Violence against Women, Its Causes and Consequences.* UN Doc. E/CN.4/2006/61/Add.5, February 15, 2006.

Human Rights Watch. *Afghanistan: The Massacre in Mazar-i-Sharif.* New York: Human Rights Watch, 1998. http://www.hrw.org/reports/1998/afghan/.

Human Rights Watch. *The Human Cost: The Consequences of Insurgent Attacks in Afghanistan.* New York: Human Rights Watch, 2007. http://www.hrw.org/reports/2007/afghanistan0407/.

Human Rights Watch. *Humanity Denied: Systematic Violations of Women's Rights in Afghanistan.* New York: Human Rights Watch, 2001. http://www.hrw.org/reports/2001/afghan3/.

Human Rights Watch. *Lessons in Terror: Attacks on Education in Afghanistan.* New York: Human Rights Watch, 2006. http://www.hrw.org/reports/2006/afghanistan0706/.

Human Rights Watch. *Massacres of Hazaras in Afghanistan.* New York: Human Rights Watch, 2001. http://www.hrw.org/reports/2001/afghanistan/.

Karlsson, Pia, and Amir Mansory. *Afghan Dilemma: Education, Gender, and Globalisation in an Islamic Context.* Stockholm, Sweden: Institute of International Education, Stockholm University, 2007.

Physicians for Human Rights. *The Taliban's War on Women: A Health and Human Rights Crisis in Afghanistan.* Cambridge, Mass.: Physicians for Human Rights, 1998.

Save the Children. *Afghanistan: Children in Crisis.* http://www.savethechildren.org/publications/afghanistan_children.pdf.

Senlis Council. *Afghanistan: Decision Point 2008.* http://www.senliscouncil.net.

Senlis Council. *Stumbling into Chaos: Afghanistan on the Brink.* http://www.senliscouncil.net.

Sheridan, Michael. "How the Taliban Slaughtered Thousands of People." *Sunday Times,* November 1, 1998.

Their, J. Alexander. "Afghanistan." In *Twenty-First-Century Peace Operations,* edited by W. J. Durch, pp. 467–572. Washington, D.C.: United Institute of Peace, 2006.

United Nations Assistance Mission in Afghanistan. *Suicide Attacks in Afghanistan 2001–2007.* September 2007. http://www.unama-afg.org/docs/_UN-Docs/unama-suicide-attacks-study.pdf.

United Nations Assistance Mission in Afghanistan. Human Rights Unit. Afghanistan: 2008. *Annual Report on Protection of Civilians in Armed Conflict.* January 2009.

United Nations Children's Fund (UNICEF). *State of the World's children 2009: Statistics on Afghanisthan.* http://www.unicef.org/infobycountry/afghanistan_statistics.html.

United Nations General Assembly. *Interim Report of the Special Rapporteur of the Commission on Human Rights on the Situation of Human Rights in Afghanistan.* UN Doc. A/56/409.

United Nations High Commissioner for Human Rights. *Report of the High Commissioner for Human Rights on the Situation of Human Rights in Afghanistan and on the Achievements of Technical Assistance in the Field of Human Rights.* A/HRC/4/98, March 5, 2007.

United Nations High Commissioner for Human Rights. *Report of the High Commissioner for Human Rights on the Situation of Human Rights in Afghanistan and on the Achievements of Technical Assistance in the Field of Human Rights.* A/HRC/7/27, February 21, 2008.

United Nations High Commissioner for Human Rights. *Report of the Special Rapporteur on Violence aganist Women, Its Causes and Consequences, Mission to Afghanistan.* E/CN.4/2006/61/Add 5, 2006.

United Nations Human Rights Commission. *Searching for Solutions: Twenty-five Years of UNHCR-Pakistan Cooperation on Afghan Refugees.* June 2005. http://www.un.org.pk/unhcr/.

Ward, Jeanne, Christopher Horwood, Claire McEvoy, Pamela Shipman, and Lauren Rumble. *The Shame of War: Sexual Violence against Women and Girls in Conflict.* Nairobi, Kenya: United Nations Office for the Coordination of Humanitarian Affairs, 2007. http://www.crin.org/.

World Bank. *GenderStats: Database of Gender Statistics.* http://www.genderstats.worldbank.org.

AFRICAN UNION
BANJUL CHARTER

by Rachel Murray

The African Charter on Human and Peoples' Rights, also known as the Banjul Charter, was adopted in Banjul, The Gambia, in 1981 and came into force in 1986. It is unique among both regional and international human rights treaties in that it contains not only civil and political rights (including the rights to life, freedom from torture, fair trial, and free expression) but also economic, social, and cultural rights (such as the rights to work, education, and the best attainable state of health), peoples' rights (such as the rights to self determination, development, and a satisfactory environment), and a list of duties for the individual. As a result, it challenges many traditionally held views of what human rights are. In the early years of the African Charter's existence, observers had concerns that the treaty was unworkable, that the way some of the rights were termed gave far too much discretion to states, and that the inclusion of provisions on individual duties would be another opportunity for rights to be watered down. In practice these fears have not been borne out. While for many years the focus of its implementing body, the African Commission on Human and Peoples' Rights, was interpreting mostly civil and political rights generated by cases submitted to it by nongovernmental organizations (NGOs), since 2000 it began to look more closely at the more unusual provisions of the charter, and it is in these areas that it has made a particularly significant contribution to the development of international human rights law.

CIVIL AND POLITICAL RIGHTS

Infringements on rights on the basis of the ethnicity of an individual are a violation of Article 2, which concerns nondiscrimination. Thus, where Burundian nationals and members of the Tutsi ethnic group were subject to attacks, harassment, extrajudicial executions, and other violations, the commission found a violation of this provision. Article 3 of the African Charter provides for rights to equal protection under the law. Consequently, when an individual was subjected to numerous arrests and was detained because of his political beliefs, causing him to go into hiding, the commission found a violation of this right under Article 3(2). When Zambia amended its constitution to require that those who wished to contest the office of president must have parents who were Zambian by birth or descent, the African Commission found violations of Articles 2 and 3(1).

Many cases of extrajudicial executions have been found to be in violation of the right to life under Article 4 of the charter. If the state "purposefully" lets a person die in custody, for example, through denial of medication, it is a violation of Article 4.

In a significant number of cases the African Commission has found torture or inhuman or degrading treatment or punishment, contrary to Article 5 of the African Charter. So where individuals were subject to treatment in detention that included "solitary confinement, shackling within a cell, extremely poor quality food and denial of access to adequate medical care," a violation of Article 5 was found (African Commission on Human and Peoples' Rights, Communications 64/92, 68/92, 78/92, *Krischna Achutan [on Behalf of Aleke Banda], Amnesty International on Behalf of Orton and Vera Chirwa, Amnesty International on Behalf of Orton and Vera Chirwa v. Malawi*, 1995).

When some students were subjected to lashings in public on their convictions for offenses of immoral conduct in Sudan, the African Commission was asked to consider whether the punishment amounted to a violation of Article 5. Reiterating that this provision should be "interpreted as widely as possible to encompass the widest possible array of physical and mental abuses," the African Commission held that there was a violation of this provision and called on the government to abolish this penalty and compensate the victims (African Commission on Human and Peoples' Rights, Communication 236/2000, *Curtis Francis Doebbler v. Sudan*, 2003).

The African Commission's creation of a special rapporteur on prisons and conditions of detention in Africa in 1996 also enabled it to focus on the applicability of Articles 5 and 6 in certain states. The reports adopted by the special rapporteur on prisons have set out concerns and recommendations that the state should address. States have been willing to accept suggestions by the special rapporteur, and on some occasions there have been changes as the result of a visit, in particular where, as was the case with Mozambique, the special rapporteur made a follow-up visit.

Similarly, the Robben Island Guidelines (Resolution on Guidelines and Measures for the Prohibition and Prevention of Torture, Cruel, Inhuman, or Degrading Treatment or Punishment in Africa), adopted in 2002 by the African Commission, clarify the content of Article 5 in more detail. They set out obligations for states with respect to prohibition of torture and promotion of international mechanisms. There are also provisions on criminalization of torture, making it an extraditable offense; non-refoulement; and combating impunity. The guidelines provide for measures to be taken by states to prevent torture, including protection for those deprived of their liberty, education, and awareness. The implementation of these guidelines is overseen by the Follow-Up Committee, composed of members of both the commission and the NGO community.

In a large number of cases the African Commission has found arbitrary detention and violations of the right to a fair trial, contrary to Articles 6 and 7 of the African Charter. Many of these cases have been against Nigeria, submitted by an active NGO population trying to achieve some resolution to the situation in that county. Detaining individuals without charge and on account of their political beliefs violates Article 6 of the charter. Furthermore, any organ that makes a decision on detention must be impartial under Article 6.

Using military tribunals, where the tribunals are composed of the armed forces and police, to try civilians is in violation of Article 7. Where the state has attempted to oust the jurisdiction of the courts in respect to particular legislation, the African Commission has found that not only will domestic remedies "be prolonged . . . and certain to yield no results" but that this amounts to a violation of Article 7 of the charter (African Commission on Human and Peoples' Rights, Communication 129/94, *Civil Liberties Organisation v. Nigeria*, 1996).

In a series of important cases against Sudan, one of the issues the African Commission was asked to consider was the application of Sharia law to non-Muslims and the alleged persecution of non-Muslims in the country. The African Commission held with respect to Article 8 of the African Charter: "Trials must always accord with international fair-trial standards. Also, it is fundamentally unjust that religious laws should be applied against non-adherents of the religion. Tribunals that apply only Shari'a are thus not competent to judge non-Muslims, and everyone should have the right to be tried by a secular court if they wish" (African Commission on Human and Peoples' Rights, Communications 48/90, 50/91, 52/91, 89/93, *Amnesty International, Comité Loosli Bachelard, Lawyers' Committee for Human Rights, Association of Members of the Episcopal Conference of East Africa v. Sudan*, 2000). Harassment and persecution of Christians and others on the basis of their religion were also found to violate Article 8.

The African Commission adopted the Resolution on the Adoption of the Declaration of Principles on Freedom of Expression in Africa in 2002. This important document sets out further standards for the protection of Article 9 of the African Charter, including that authorities take positive measures to promote diversity and elaborating on the right to freedom of information and the need to encourage an independent private broadcast media. There are further provisions on regulating the media, dealing with complaints, and protecting reputations, among others. The appointment of a special rapporteur on freedom of expression has also kept the attention of the African Commission focused on this issue, although in contrast to the work of some of the special rapporteurs and working groups of the commission, concrete outputs are less apparent.

The African Commission has held that proscription of newspapers violates Article 9 of the African Charter, as does requiring the payment of excessively high registration fees by newspapers. The commission has stressed the "close relationship" among Articles 9(2), 10(1), and 11, and where there were allegations, not contradicted by the government, that a trial and resultant death sentences were passed because of the views expressed by the individuals, the commission found a violation of Articles 10(1) and 11.

The African Commission has held that Article 12 of the African Charter "should read as a general protection of all those who are subject to persecution that they may seek refuge in another state" and that arbitrary expulsion, on the basis of their nationality, of individuals from the country of asylum is in violation of this provision (African Commission on Human and Peoples' Rights, Communications 27/89, 46/91, 49/91, 99/93, *Organisation*

Mondiale Contre la Torture and Association Internationale des Juristes Democrates, Commission Internationale des Juristes [CIJ], Union Interafricaine des Droits de l'Homme v. Rwanda, 1997). Similarly, mass expulsion "of any category of persons" was a "special violation of human rights" that impacted on numerous other rights in the charter (African Commission on Human and Peoples' Rights, Communication 159/96, *Union Interafricaine des Droits de l'Homme, Federation Internationale des Ligues des Droits de l'Homme, Rencontre Africaine des Droits de l'Homme, Organisation Mondiale des Droits de l'Homme au Sénégal, and Association Malienne des Droits de l'Homme v. Angola*, 1998).

The African Commission has also addressed the positions of refugees and internally displaced persons in general through not only the appointment of a special rapporteur on the issue but also by working with the United Nations High Commissioner for Refugees. It thus adopted a memorandum of understanding in 2003 in which the two institutions promised to cooperate in their promotion and protective capacities, including undertaking joint research and supporting each others' procedures and work.

Article 13, the right to participate freely in government, has been held to encompass the "right to vote for a representative of one's choice" (African Commission on Human and Peoples' Rights, Communication 102/93, *Constitutional Rights Project and Civil Liberties Organisation v. Nigeria*, 1999). Annulling the results of a free and fair election was held to be a violation of this provision. In one important case relating to the treatment of mental health patients in The Gambia, the African Commission found that Article 13 of the charter encompassed a right to vote and that "there are no objective bases within the legal system of the Respondent State to exclude mentally disabled persons from political participation" (African Commission on Human and Peoples' Rights, Communication 241/2001, *Purohit and Moore v. The Gambia*, 2003).

In its 1996 Resolution on Electoral Process and Participatory Governance, the African Commission asserted that "elections are the only means by which the people can elect democratically the government of their choice in conformity to the African Charter on Human and Peoples' Right" (African Commission on Human and Peoples' Rights). It called on governments to guarantee the credibility of the electoral process and emphasized the importance of allowing observation of elections.

ECONOMIC, SOCIAL, AND CULTURAL RIGHTS

The manner in which the African Charter has been interpreted indicates that economic, social, and cultural rights can be the subject of cases before an international body. It is in relation to these rights that the African Commission has made some of its most important contributions to the development of international human rights law.

In its Pretoria Declaration on Economic, Social, and Cultural Rights, adopted in 2004, the African Commission refers to the rights in Articles 14–18 of the African Charter. States have to ensure "at the very least, the minimum essential levels" of these rights, which requires them in general to tackle issues of good governance, corruption, equitable distribution of income from natural resources, refugees and internally displaced persons, and privatization and discrimination, among other things (African Commission on Human and Peoples' Rights). It then sets out obligations for states, such as the need to ratify African and international instruments and adopt certain measures at the national level. This declaration in addition provides some interpretations of the various rights in the African Charter.

The Pretoria Declaration refers to the right to property in Article 14 of the African Charter as encompassing the rights to not be deprived of property arbitrarily; equitable access to property; adequate compensation where publicly acquired; equitable distribution of land, in particular to deal with historical or gender injustices; protection of lands for indigenous communities; and equal access to housing and acceptable living conditions. In a case against Nigeria, the African Commission said that this encompasses "a right to have access to property of one's own and the right not for one's property to be removed" and that sealing up the premises of newspaper houses violated this provision (African Commission on Human and Peoples' Rights, Communications 105/93, 128/94, 130/94, 152/96, *Media Rights Agenda, Constitutional Rights Project, Media Rights Agenda and Constitutional Rights Project v. Nigeria*, 1999). Furthermore, in a series of cases against Mauritania the African Commission held that "confiscation and looting of the property of black Mauritanians and the expropriation or destruction of their land and houses before forcing them to go abroad" violated Article 14 (African Commission on Human and Peoples' Rights, Communications 54/91, 61/91, 98/93, 164/97–196/97, 210/98, *Malawi African Association, Amnesty International, Ms Sarr Diop, Union Interafricaine des Droits de l'Homme and RADDHO, Collectif des Veuves et Ayants-Droit, Association Mauritanienne des Droits de l'Homme v. Mauritania,* 2000).

In a case where an individual accused of public order issues was dismissed from his post as magistrate and then not given back his job, unlike others also accused, the commission found a violation of the individual's right to work and called on the government to reinstate him in his position under Article 15 of the African Charter, concerning the right to work. Denying an individual who is held in custody access to doctors and medical assistance while his or her health is worsening violates Article 16. The African Commission on other occasions also implied that unlawful deportations of individuals out of a country impact on other rights, including those to work, education, and property. The Pretoria Declaration also underlines rights to equal opportunities in relation to access to work and remuneration, satisfactory conditions of work, equality for women, freedom of association, and rest and leisure.

It is also worth spending some time outlining the African Commission's findings in one of its most well-known cases. This case (Communication 155/96, *The Social and Economic Rights Action Center and the Center for Economic and Social Rights v. Nigeria,* 2002) alleged that the Nigerian government's involvement in oil exploration with the multinational company Shell in the Ogoni-land region of the country violated the rights of the people who lived there. In a decision that included both individual (civil and political and economic, social, and cultural) and group rights, the African Commission found a series of violations of the African Charter and set out a number of recommendations for the government to remedy the situation. It found that oil exploration in the area had led to environmental damage and pollution, which not only violated the right of the Ogoni as a people to a satisfactory environment but also their rights as individuals to the best attainable level of health. The African Commission also found a violation of Article 21, peoples' right to dispose of their natural resources and wealth, through the lack of benefits that oil exploration brought to the local population. Although it is not expressly mentioned in the African Charter, the African Commission also interpreted the express provisions to include a right to housing and shelter and a right to food, both of which it found the Nigerian government had violated.

Some other references to economic, social, and cultural rights are littered throughout cases the African Commission has decided. For example, the commission found violations of a number of rights of mental health patients detained in hospitals in Gambia, including their right to health. In addition, in an earlier case against what was then Zaire, the African Commission found that the failure of the government to provide basic services, including safe drinking water, electricity, and sufficient medicines, and the closure of universities and secondary schools violated the rights to health and education under Articles 16 and 17, respectively. Furthermore, the Pretoria Declaration contains greater elaborations of both these rights, including references to availability and accessibility of affordable health facilities; access to minimum food, shelter, reproductive services, education on HIV/AIDS, free compulsory basic education, and affordable secondary and higher education; and the liberty of parents to choose their childrens' schools.

Article 17 has not received a large amount of attention from the African Commission, but interpretations of this provision are interesting. In the cases against Mauritania, the African Commission held that language was an integral part of culture and that to deprive an individual of its usage would be to deprive him or her of his or her identity. In the Pretoria Declaration the commission reiterated that this provision includes "positive African values consistent with international human rights realities and standards" and the need for participation in determining cultural policies (African Commission on Human and Peoples' Rights). The African Commission has also stated on numerous occasions that "harmful traditional practices," particularly those against women and girls, should be eradicated (African Commission on Human and Peoples' Rights).

Article 18 has received considerable attention in relation to the rights of women. This will be dealt with below.

PEOPLES' RIGHTS

Given that few international treaties contain rights for peoples or groups, the inclusion in the African Charter of rights for peoples offered an important opportunity for some law to be developed in these areas. Although it took the African Commission some years to start to examine these provisions, the contribution it has made to international human rights law should be welcomed. Prompted by the submission of some innovative cases by NGOs and others, the African Commission has been willing to interpret dynamically the provisions in Articles 19–24 of the African Charter, thereby enhancing protection for rights in general. Besides the important Communication 155/96 relating to the Ogoni people, as outlined above, a few other significant examples are worth detailing.

The right to self-determination is not exclusive to the African Charter and is found in other international treaties, including the two United Nations (UN) human rights covenants. However, unlike those instruments, where it has not been possible to bring a case before the relevant UN body alleging a violation of these rights by a representative of a people, the African Commission, in its Communication 75/92, *Katangese Peoples' Congress v. Zaire*, 1995, permitted the Katangese Peoples' Congress to submit a case calling for recognition of the congress as a liberation movement entitled to support for independence from Zaire, recognizing the independence of Katanga, and securing Zaire's evacuation from the area. Although the commission did not find in the congress's favor, it did establish the principle that cases could be submitted by not only individuals and NGOs but also peoples. In addition, the commission made some statements that add to the jurisprudence on self-determination. Thus, it held that "self determination may be exercised in any of the following—independence, self-government, local government, federalism, confederalism, unitarism or any other form of relations that accords with the wishes of the people but fully cognizant of other recognised principles such as sovereignty and territorial integrity." However, "in the absence of concrete evidence of violations of human rights to the point that the territorial integrity of Zaire should be called into question" and in the absence of proof that the people of Katanga could not participate in government, the sovereignty of Zaire was affirmed (African Commission on Human and Peoples' Rights, Communication 75/92, *Katangese Peoples' Congress v. Zaire*, 1995).

A less radical interpretation of the notion of self-determination examines the manner in which the existing state is governed. Article 20 has been linked expressly with the right of individuals in Article 13 of the African Charter, Article 20 being "the counterpart of the right enjoyed by individuals under Article 13" (African Commission on Human and Peoples' Rights, Communication 102/93, *Constitutional Rights Project and Civil Liberties Organisation v. Nigeria*, 1999). Where ethnic black Mauritanians were subject to discrimination on the basis of their ethnicity, resulting in attacks on their villages, the African Commission not only found violations of their rights as individuals but also referred to Article 19, the right of a people to equality, and Article 23, the right of a people to peace and security, in its decision.

It is perhaps, however, the African Commission's work on indigenous peoples that has been the most surprising contribution to human rights law. When the term "indigenous peoples" was first introduced as an item for discussion at its sessions, many on the African Commission and within civil society found it difficult to deal with, noting the term's derogatory use in the colonial context and stressing the belief that all Africans were indigenous. Gradually, however, significant strides were taken in highlighting the concerns of groups such as the Maasai, Tuareg, Batwa, San, and others on the continent to the extent that the African Commission's work in some respects stretched far beyond what was undertaken by even the UN bodies. Through the establishment of a Working Group on Indigenous Populations/Communities, composed of commissioners, NGOs, and representatives from particular indigenous groups, the African Commission maintained the concerns of indigenous peoples as an item on its agenda, adopted an important report outlining the violations that such groups are subject to, and attempted to define the characteristics of these groups.

INDIVIDUAL DUTIES

The inclusion of a section for duties of individuals within the African Charter sparked many writing on the charter in its early years to express concern that these provisions would be used to water down the rights provided for. The inclusion of duties, although not unique, is certainly unusual and challenges traditional notions that human rights are rights of the individual owed by the state. Although the African Commission has made little reference to these provisions in its work, in one important decision it put to rest the fears many had about their negative impact on rights. Communication 105/93, 128/94, 130/94, 152/96, *Media Rights Agenda, Constitutional Rights Project, Media Rights Agenda and Constitutional Rights Project v. Nigeria*, 1999, addresses the issue that the government of Nigeria had imposed a number of restrictions on freedom of expression. The African Commission held that

> the only legitimate reasons for limitations to the rights and freedoms of the African Charter are to be found in Article 27 (2). . . . The reasons for possible limitations must be founded in a legitimate state interest and the evils of the limitations must be strictly proportionate with and absolutely necessary for the advantages which are to be obtained. Even more important, a limitation may never have as a consequence that the right itself becomes illusory. (African Commission on Human and Peoples' Rights, Communication 105/93, 128/94, 130/94, 152/96, *Media Rights Agenda, Constitutional Rights Project, Media Rights Agenda and Constitutional Rights Project v. Nigeria*, 1999)

The government did not give any evidence that its restrictions on the rights were compatible with this interpretation of Article 27(2), and the commission therefore found a violation of the right to freedom of expression.

UNUSUAL ASPECTS OF THE AFRICAN CHARTER

Unlike other regional or international human rights treaties, the African Charter does not contain a derogation clause, that is, a general provision that enables states to disregard certain rights during times of war or other public emergency. Such provisions commonly permit derogation of the rights to life and freedom from torture but not the right not to be arbitrarily detained. One might expect, given the many civil wars and conflicts on the African continent, that the African Commission would have taken a similar line and allowed states to derogate during these times. However, in a case against Chad and subsequently in other cases, the African Commission said that "unlike other human rights instruments, [the African Charter] does not allow for states parties to derogate from their treaty obligations during emergency situations. Thus, even a civil war in Chad cannot be used as an excuse by the state violating or permitting violations of rights in the African Charter" (African Commission on Human and Peoples' Rights, Communication 74/92, *Commission Nationale des Droits de l'Homme et des Libertés v. Chad*, 1996). Many may view this as unrealistic, but it can be seen as a pragmatic response to a continent where many states fluctuate between situations of conflict and relative peace.

Finally, it is also necessary to highlight the attention that has been paid to the African Charter in terms of women's rights. Prompted by NGO lobbying and concerns that the African Charter made scant explicit reference to the rights of women, the African Commission established a working group and a special rapporteur on the rights of women in Africa. Their proposals suggested creating the Protocol to the African Charter on Human and Peoples' Rights on the Rights of Women in Africa. It was hoped that this would give particular attention to the situation of women and provide more concrete legal obligations. After several drafts, lobbying, and discussion by governments and legal experts, the protocol was adopted in 2003. It required fifteen states to agree to be bound to it in order for it to become operational, and sufficient states did so by December 2005.

This protocol sets out many rights and in some respects goes further than other international instruments. It refers to the elimination of harmful traditional practices, ensures that men and women are regarded as equal partners in marriage as well as in divorce and separation, and sets out rights for the protection of women during armed conflict, including requiring that rape and other sexual offenses be considered war crimes, genocide, and crimes against humanity. There is also protection in terms of health, food security, and education as well as specific provisions for widows, those with disabilities, and older women. Although it draws upon the provisions of the African Charter and interprets them for women, it does not include all of the African Charter rights, and it also takes its cue from the United Nations Convention on the Elimination of All Forms of Discrimination against Women and other international documents. It is to be enforced by states reporting on what they have done to implement it and through reports submitted under Article 62 of the African Charter. Given that in writing their reports, states already mention the position of women in practice, it is difficult to see what this will add to the implementation measures in the charter. However, it has been hailed by many as an inspirational document, an indication of the importance states attach to the rights of women, and a potentially useful lobbying tool in ensuring they comply with their obligations under the African Charter.

ASSESSMENT

Despite some initial concerns that the African Charter was unworkable in the rights that it provided, the African Commission has been dynamic in its interpretation of the provisions and, as a result, has made an important contribution to the development of international human rights law. It is more difficult to measure whether this has had an impact on governmental behavior and the extent of compliance with the African Commission's decisions. The African Commission does not have a formal follow-up mechanism by which it can track implementation of its decisions by states. It has, however, questioned states about decisions when examining their reports submitted under Article 62 of the charter. The responses are not often made public, however, and may not reveal the situation on the ground. The little research in this area displays mixed results. In many cases it is difficult to obtain information on the government response to commission decisions (for example, Communication 205/97), and in some instances by the time the African Commission released its decision, the situation in the country had changed dramatically (for example, Communication 27/89).

Although there is some indication of laws being repealed and individuals being released after a decision by the African Commission, this may be attributed to other political factors. For example, a change to the constitution in Sudan repealed many of the laws that were found to be in violation of the African Charter by the commission in its communications against the country (for example, Communications 48/90). In addition, although the government of Nigeria made an attempt to address some of the issues raised in the communication relating to the impact of oil exploration on the Ogoni (Communication 155/96), the response was limited, and the extent to which it was the result of the African Commission's decision is not clear. However, some of the earlier cases against Nigeria (for example, Communication 87/93) suggest that decisions by the African Commission imposed significant pressure on the government to act.

Beyond these few instances and without dismissing the importance of the African system in contributing to the development of international human rights law standards, the extent to which the African Charter and the work of its commission are known in African countries is reflected in the relatively few cases the African Commission has received. Although there may be increasing awareness of human rights standards and commitments of governments across the continent, the knowledge of how individuals, NGOs, and others can use the African mechanism is poor. Every anniversary of the African Charter on Human and Peoples' Rights brings hope for an opportunity to increase the visibility of the work of these African human rights institutions.

[*See also* African Union: Commission and Court of Human Rights; Humanitarian Law; *and* Nongovernmental Organizations: Overview.]

BIBLIOGRAPHY

African Commission on Human and Peoples' Rights. http://www.achpr.org.

African Commission on Human and Peoples' Rights. *Pretoria Declaration on Economic, Social and Cultural Rights, Resolution on Economic, Social and Cultural Rights*, ACHPR/Res.73(XXXVI)04, 2004.

African Commission on Human and Peoples' Rights. *Resolution on Electoral Process and Participatory Governance*, ACHPR/Res.23(XIX)96, 1996.

Banda, F. *Women, Law and Human Rights: An African Perspective*. Oxford: Hart Publishing, 2005.

Evans, Malcolm D., and Rachel Murray, eds. *The African Charter on Human and Peoples' Rights: The System in Practice, 1986–2006*. 2d ed. New York: Cambridge University Press, 2008.

Murray, R. "Decisions by the African Commission on Human and Peoples' Rights on Individual Communications Under the African Charter on Human and Peoples' Rights." *International and Comparative Law Quarterly* 46 (1997): 412–434.

Viljoen, F. *International Human Rights Law in Africa*. Oxford: Oxford University Press, 2007.

COMMISSION AND COURT ON HUMAN RIGHTS

by Rachel Murray

The African Charter on Human and Peoples' Rights was adopted in 1981 by the Organization of African Unity (OAU). The OAU was the regional political organization for the continent, and human rights had not been a particular focus of its work since its inception in 1963. But both the European and American continents had established regional human rights treaties by this time, and against the background of a number of notable atrocities in Africa, the charter was adopted. It came into force in 1986 and was eventually ratified by all African states. The African Charter provides for an eleven-member independent African Commission on Human and Peoples' Rights, which was established in 1987 and whose secretariat is based in Banjul, Gambia. In 1998 the OAU adopted an additional protocol to the African Charter, establishing an African Court on Human and Peoples' Rights. This came into force in January 2004, although it did not begin to operate immediately.

THE ORGANIZATION OF AFRICAN UNITY AND THE AFRICAN UNION

Although the focus of this section will be on the African Charter and its commission and court, it is worth outlining the context in which the African Charter has to operate and the role of its parent institution, the OAU, now the African Union (AU). The OAU, whose headquarters were in Addis Ababa, Ethiopia, was geographically removed from its human rights institution, the African Commission on Human and Peoples' Rights, on the other side of the continent. While one of the reasons for this separation initially was to ensure the independence of the African Commission, its practical outcome was isolation of the work of the commission from the rest of the OAU. This had an impact on the extent to which the African Commission's recommendations and decisions were known and taken seriously by the political

bodies and individuals who determined its funding and debated its reports.

There was some hope, however, that this would change. In 2001 the OAU transformed itself into the African Union, reflecting a desire not only to revitalize the organization, which was initially established to assist newly independent states and to help others gain independence, but also to make some necessary institutional reforms. The founding document of the AU, the Constitutive Act, unlike the Charter of the OAU, makes significant reference to human rights among the principles and objectives of the union. Although many of the organs that existed under the OAU are replicated in the AU structures, a few important innovations are worth mentioning. These include the Peace and Security Council, which is to prevent, manage, and resolve conflicts in Africa; the Pan-African Parliament, which is composed of over two hundred legislators from over forty African states; the Economic, Social, and Cultural Council, which is an advisory organ composed of a large number of civil society organizations; and the African Court of Justice.

The AU is supported by a commission, the Commission of the Union, its administrative arm, that facilitates the operations of the organs of the union and is composed of eight commissioners with specific portfolios. Among these are the commissioner on political affairs, whose responsibilities include human rights, good governance, and humanitarian and refugee issues; the commissioner on peace and security; and the commissioner on social affairs. These positions offer a greater opportunity for human rights to remain on the AU agenda than was the case in the past. The knowledge of the African Commission among those working at the AU, however, is still limited. Discussions on reform of the working practices of the African Commission led to various attempts to remedy this situation through greater involvement of the African Commission in the decision-making processes of the AU.

The New Partnership for Africa's Development (NEPAD), whose focus is on socioeconomic development, has operated outside the auspices of the union but is being subsumed under the AU umbrella. The standards applied to states under NEPAD encompass a broad range of issues but include human rights requirements. NEPAD is implemented by states voluntarily agreeing to be subject to the African Peer Review Mechanism, permitting a team under an expert panel to visit the country and assess compliance with NEPAD standards. At first only a few states were visited, but by February 2006 twenty-three states had acceded to the peer review. The detailed list of benchmarks and indicators in the review process includes provisions on democracy and political governance, outlining, among other matters, protection of civil and political as well as economic, social, and cultural rights; separation of powers; fighting corruption; and protection of the rights of women and other vulnerable groups.

The African Court of Justice is intended to be the principal judicial organ of the AU. A separate protocol to establish the court was adopted by the AU, and a certain number of states had to agree to this protocol before it could come into being. A decision adopted in July 2004 by the Assembly of Heads of State and Government of the AU approved that the African Court of Justice and the African Court on Human and Peoples' Rights should be "integrated into one Court" (African Union, Decision on the Seats of the African Union, Assembly/AU/Dec.45[III]). The reasons behind this are not entirely clear but stem in part from concerns about the financial implications in establishing two judicial bodies rather than one. This decision caused considerable confusion and delay over what should happen to the African Court on Human and Peoples' Rights, whose protocol had by that stage received acceptance and legally come into force.

Eventually, the AU decided that any decision on the merged court should not delay the operations of the African Court on Human and Peoples' Rights and proceeded, at its summit in January 2006, to appoint judges to this eleven-member court. Those appointed were from Algeria, Burundi, Burkina Faso, Ghana, Lesotho, Libya, Mali, Rwanda, Senegal, South Africa, and Uganda. They included only two women despite the requirement in the protocol that in the election of judges the assembly should ensure adequate gender representation. Many of those appointed came from a judicial background, and they had varying degrees of human rights experience. In the meantime a draft protocol for the merged African Court

of Justice and African Court on Human and Peoples' Rights was being considered, and this protocol on an African Court of Justice and Human Rights was finally adopted by the AU in July 2008. The new protocol requires fifteen ratifications for it to come into force, and this merged African Court of Justice and Human Rights will replace the African Court on Human and Peoples' Rights.

As a result, many questions remained unanswered, including the exact nature of the relationships among the existing Human and Peoples' Rights Court, the future merged court, the African Commission on Human and Peoples' Rights, and other AU organs.

THE AFRICAN COMMISSION ON HUMAN AND PEOPLES' RIGHTS

The African Commission is an eleven-member independent body elected by the AU Assembly from nominations by states parties. Despite the African Charter's directive that the commissioners serve in their personal capacities, some of those appointed to the commission have simultaneously held government positions. These have included ambassadors, government officials, and even at one stage the attorney general of Zimbabwe himself. Prompted by increasing concern that this jeopardized the reputation of the African Commission, the AU in April 2005 issued a note verbale highlighting that a number of positions on the African Commission were due to expire and reminding states of positions that were incompatible with that of commissioner, including member of government, diplomatic representative, minister, or legal adviser. This approach appeared to have been successful, particularly in the July 2005 round of appointments. The AU was also successful in ensuring gender representation on the African Commission to the extent that in July 2008 five out of the eleven members were women, far exceeding the records of other similar regional and many international bodies.

Commissioners meet twice a year in sessions lasting about two weeks held either in the country of its headquarters, The Gambia, or in other African locations. The benefit of holding sessions across the continent is the increased publicity for the work of the African Commission and the charter. With sessions in several African countries, local nongovernmental organizations (NGOs) have been prompted to attend and subsequently apply for observer status with the African Commission and submit cases against their governments. In turn, governments hosting the sessions have sometimes felt obliged to submit their

Article 62 reports for examination and have nominated individuals to sit on the commission in subsequent elections.

The African Commission is serviced by a secretariat based in Banjul, The Gambia. It is headed by a secretary who is supported by staff. The commission and staff are supposed to be funded by the AU primarily; however, given that financial support has been limited, external donors have also funded the staff to the commission, sometimes on a temporary basis. As a result, the secretariat of the commission has not been as adequately resourced or stable as one might hope for in an institution of this nature, and the total number of staff members at the commission at any one time is usually not in excess of twenty. This inevitably has an impact on the ability of the secretariat to function effectively. The AU in 2008 significantly increased the budget of the African Commission and thus raised hopes that this situation will be remedied to some extent.

The African Commission is mandated under Article 45 of the African Charter with a broad assignment, including both promotion and protective functions. Its promotional work has included holding seminars with NGOs, the latter usually being required to provide the funding to do so, and disseminating information about the African Charter across the continent and farther afield. The African Commission has also adopted a worthwhile practice of allocating each of its members certain countries for which they are responsible in promotional terms. Commissioners visit these states and their governments and civil society and, in doing so, have enhanced the awareness of the commission and the charter. The African Commission produces a number of reports, including its final communiqués for each of its sessions and its Annual Activity Reports. These documents are usually available, although not necessarily immediately, on its Web site. The African Commission is also served by an documentalist. The individuals who have held this position have proven to be invaluable sources of information for those outside the commission.

States are required under Article 62 of the African Charter to provide reports every two years on the legislative and other measures they have taken to implement the charter. The report is submitted to the African Commission, which sends questions to the state in advance of the meeting, often drawing upon information from other sources, such as NGOs. The state is then invited to the next session of the African Commission to present its report in public and to answer a series of questions posed by commissioners. The African Commission has on some

occasions, but not all, adopted concluding observations on the reports. As with other international obligations of this type, states have been notoriously behind in submitting their reports, and as of 2008, over a third had yet to submit even one. The African Commission adopted a policy of accepting one report as fulfilling all overdue reports but still requires states to attend a commission session before obligations are fulfilled. In only one case, that of the Seychelles, which submitted a report in 1995 but by 2006 had still yet to attend a session of the commission to present it, has the Commission gone ahead to examine the report without the presence of state representatives.

While states submitted increasingly weighty reports and sent senior high-level delegations, often composed of at least one minister from government, the process of examining the report did not necessarily facilitate the constructive dialogue it was meant to achieve. Because there are usually only a few hours available to examine each report, states submit the reports infrequently, questions are posed together and then answered together by the delegate, and the commission is inconsistent in providing concluding observations to the report, the process is inefficient. However, the state reporting mechanism has been successful in getting states to attend the sessions of the African Commission and in starting to engage with it over a period of time.

The African Commission also receives communications or cases alleging violations of the rights in the African Charter. It can receive cases from states (Articles 47–54) and others (Articles 55–59). As of July 2008, one registered case had been submitted by a state against other states (Communication 227/99, *Democratic Republic of Congo v. Burundi, Rwanda, and Uganda*), and the decision was published by the Commission in 2006. It is possible that this was due to the submission of a case before the International Court of Justice on the same facts. All of the other cases the African Commission dealt with were submitted by individuals and NGOs, with NGOs submitting the majority of them. The African Commission has not interpreted the charter as restricting access to only victims or those acting on their behalf and has received complaints from NGOs alleging violations on behalf of others and allegations that particular legislation violates the charter (for example, Communication 129/94, *Civil Liberties Organisation v. Nigeria*, 1996). In addition, contrary to other international bodies, because the African Charter contains a list of rights for peoples, the African Commission has been willing to accept complaints from those representing a people (for example, Communication 75/92, *Katangese Peoples' Congress v. Zaire*, 1995) and those alleging violations against peoples (for example, Communication 155/96, *The Social and Economic Rights Action Center and the Center for Economic and Social Rights v. Nigeria*, 2002).

Those submitting cases, as with other international communications procedures, have to satisfy admissibility requirements as set out in Article 56 of the charter. These reflect similar requirements in other human rights treaties, for example, that the communication cannot be anonymous and that it must not have been settled by another international body. The African Commission has interpreted the requirement that applicants exhaust domestic remedies as requiring that only those remedies that are "of a judicial nature, are effective and are not subordinate to the discretionary power of the public authorities" need be exhausted (African Commission on Human and Peoples' Rights, Communications 48/90, 50/91, 52/91, 89/93, *Amnesty International, Comité Loosli Bachelard, Lawyers' Committee for Human Rights, Association of Members of the Episcopal Conference of East Africa v. Sudan*, 2000). In addition, where there is prima facie evidence of serious or massive violations, for example, where there is a large number of victims or a broad range of violations, the African Commission will presume that the state already has notice of these violations and therefore had an opportunity to remedy them. The case will therefore be admissible (for example, Communications 25/89, 47/90, 56/91, 100/93, *Free Legal Assistance Group, Lawyers' Committee for Human Rights, Union Interafricaine des Droits de l'Homme, Les Temoins de Jehovah v. Zaire*, 1996). In a number of cases in which the Nigerian government attempted to oust the jurisdiction of the courts from examining particular pieces of legislation, the African Commission also found that remedies were not only prolonged but would not yield any results (for example, Communication 129/94, *Civil Liberties Organisation v. Nigeria*, 1996). One more unusual admissibility requirement in the African Charter is that the communication must not be written in "disparaging or insulting language directed against the state concerned and its institutions or to the Organisation of African Unity" (Article 56[3]) (African Union, African [Banjul] Charter on Human and Peoples' Rights). In Communication 65/92, *Ligue Camerounaise des Droits de l'Homme v. Cameroon*, 1997, the African Commission agreed with the government that statements such as "Paul Biya must respond to crimes against humanity," "thirty years of

the criminal neo-colonial regime incarnated by the duo Ahidjo/Biya," "regime of torturers," and "government barbarisms" amounted to insulting language. The case was declared inadmissible on this and other grounds. Similarly, in Communication 322/2006, *Tsikata v. Ghana*, with respect to claims made by the complainant that the judiciary was not independent and that the government was determined to have him found guilty, the Commission held that this was not disparaging or insulting language as "they are only facts of the allegations" and the complainant was expressing his "fears" (Twenty-first Activity Report of the African Commission, 2006, para. 32).

Once the African Commission has examined the admissibility requirements in the communication, it then considers the merits of the case, namely, whether any violations of particular rights in the charter can be found. Although most of the procedure is carried out through written documentation, the African Commission does permit complainants and states to attend its session and present their cases in an oral hearing.

The decision of the African Commission is published in its annual activity report, and the parties are informed. Although there is no formal follow-up mechanism, the African Commission has used the state reporting procedure to question states about the extent to which they have complied with its decisions, and commissioners have raised these issues in their promotional visits to states. In one case against Nigeria, the complainants, among other alleged violations, drew the African Commission's attention to the failure of the government to comply with a previous decision of the commission (Communication 87/93, *Constitutional Rights Project [in respect of Zamani Lakwot and Six Others] v. Nigeria*, 1995). The African Commission held that "in ignoring this decision, Nigeria has violated Article 1 of the African Charter" (Communications 137/94, 139/94, 154/96, 161/97, *International Pen, Constitutional Rights Project, Interights on Behalf of Ken Saro-Wiwa Jr. and Civil Liberties Organisation v. Nigeria*, 1999).

In connection with some communications and in addition to them, the African Commission has undertaken a number of protective missions to states parties. These differ from the regular promotional missions that individual commissioners take to their assigned countries. The protective or on-site missions have proved more controversial and problematic. It is not entirely clear whether all of these have been prompted by communications pending before the commission and therefore whether they are intended to find further evidence relating to those alleged violations or not. The African Commission has taken missions to a number of countries, including Nigeria (March 1997), Zimbabwe (June 2002), and Sudan (December 1996 and July 2004). In some of its fact-finding missions, but not all, it has produced a report of its findings, the conclusions of which have been in some instances damning. However, the reports have rarely been released immediately after the missions, and on some occasions it has taken years for them to appear. While the visibility of their contents is limited and the aim of the African Commission in undertaking these missions not clear, states do appear to take them seriously, and it is possible that some influence is brought to bear on the states behind closed doors as a result of the missions.

After 1994 the African Commission adopted a practice of appointing special rapporteurs and working groups on particular thematic issues. All special rapporteurs have been commissioners, a fact questioned by many who argue that individuals external to the African Commission might be more expert in the area and more able to commit time to the post. In the early twenty-first century, however, the African Commission still preferred to keep the positions in-house. The decision to appoint a special rapporteur on a particular subject has been primarily the result of NGO pressure. Consequently, the African Commission has looked first to NGOs to fund the work of the special rapporteurs, which on some occasions has proved successful but not on others. The first special rapporteur, that on summary, arbitrary, and extrajudicial executions, was appointed in April 1994 during the session that took place at the same time as the genocide in Rwanda. This was followed in October 1996 with the appointment of a special rapporteur on prisons and conditions of detention in Africa and in April 1998 with the appointment of a special rapporteur on the rights of women in Africa.

There was then a suspension in further appointments given concerns, particularly around the special rapporteur on summary, arbitrary, and extrajudicial executions, that the special rapporteurs produced few visible results. While reconsidering the missions and functions of these posts, the African Commission in the meantime appointed "focal points" on particular issues and looked at the creation of working groups (see below). Once there was some agreement over the role of special rapporteurs, the African Commission changed these focal points into special rapporteurs. As of July 2008, there were five special rapporteurs: on the rights of women in Africa; on prisons and conditions of detention in Africa; on refugees, asylum seekers, migrants, and internally displaced persons; on the

human rights defenders in Africa; and on freedom of expression in Africa. When Commissioner Ben Salem resigned from the post of special rapporteur on summary, arbitrary, and extrajudicial executions in 2000, he was not replaced. The special rapporteurs have carried out important work, some more visible than others. The special rapporteur on prisons and conditions of detention has in the past been particularly successful due in part to the support provided by the NGO Penal Reform International and the commitment of the Commissioners Victor Dankwa and Vera Chirwa, who held this post. There have been examples of states accepting their recommendations and making improvements to some of the places of detention the special rapporteur visited.

In conjunction with creating the special rapporteurs, the African Commission has also established a number of working groups. Again prompted by NGO lobbying, the African Commission has established groups on indigenous populations/communities; on economic, social, and cultural rights; on the death penalty; and on specific issues relating to the work of the African Commission and created a follow-up committee on the Robben Island Guidelines relating to torture. These have been composed of two or three commissioners, one of whom chairs the group, and representatives of NGOs, experts, or other representatives. They have been particularly important in drafting guidelines and setting standards on provisions in the charter, often following seminars and conferences on these issues. Thus the Working Group on Indigenous Populations/Communities adopted an extensive report outlining violations suffered by indigenous groups in Africa and provisions in the African Charter for both individual and peoples' rights that could be used for their protection. This report was well received by the international community, including the relevant offices in the United Nations.

The African Commission also adopts resolutions on issues. These have included resolutions on ending impunity and protection of human rights and the rule of law while countering terrorism in addition to resolutions on particular countries (for example, in 2005 on Zimbabwe, the Democratic Republic of the Congo, Sudan, Uganda, Eritrea, Ethiopia, and Togo). These country-specific resolutions were prompted by concerns raised at the commission's sessions about the situations in particular states. In these resolutions the African Commission highlighted abuses and called on the relevant authorities to comply with their international human rights obligations under the African Charter.

RELATIONSHIP WITH OTHER ACTORS

Mention of the work of the African Commission would not be complete with reference to the significant role played by NGOs within the African system. Both African-based and international NGOs can apply for observer status before the African Commission. They must submit a number of documents, including statutes; proof of legal existence; lists of members, constituent organs, and sources of funding; the last financial statement; and a statement on activities. Their applications are, under the responsibility of a particular commissioner, discussed in a public forum, and a decision is taken on whether status should be granted. Of the few applications that fail to gain status, most are due to lack of information or relevant documentation. As at July 2008, over 370 NGOs had observer status, which entitled them to participate in the sessions of the commission, have access to relevant public documents, disseminate their own material, and make statements on agenda items. Many of those NGOs with observer status, however, do not attend every session of the commission, although a significant number attend the NGO forum held in the two or three days preceding the session. At this forum NGOs have a chance to network and to adopt resolutions that are forwarded to the African Commission and that are influential in some situations in what the commission chooses to do.

National human rights institutions (NHRIs), namely, those usually established by legislation or constitutions within particular states, are entitled to apply for affiliated status before the African Commission. By July 2008 twenty-one had done so. Affiliated status permits the NHRI to attend the sessions of the commission and make statements on agenda items. To gain this status, an NHRI must submit relevant documentation indicating that it is established by law, constitution, or decree; that it is an institution of a state that is party to the African Charter; and that the NHRI conforms with the Paris Principles, the United Nations General Assembly guidelines relating to such institutions. Few of the affiliated NHRIs attend the sessions of the African Commission and participate in the discussions.

The sessions of the African Commission permit oral participation not only by commissioners and states but also by NGOs and NHRIs. Those with observer and affiliated status are permitted to comment on all the agenda items discussed in the public forum, and the sessions offer a valuable opportunity for networking with states and commissioners outside of the formal sittings.

ASSESSMENT

Despite concerns that the African Charter did not provide for an effective institution by only establishing an African Commission, the way this commission interpreted its mandate and the increasing seriousness with which states take its deliberations suggest differently. The future role of the African Commission, in light of the relatively new organs of the AU and the establishment of the African Court on Human and Peoples' Rights, became open to debate. It is hoped that the experience the African Commission has gained and the respect it has acquired from states will continue and be built upon. However, the African Commission must consider carefully its role not only in relation to the new court but also within the AU as a whole. A working group composed of commissioners and NGOs reviewed the African Commission's Rules of Procedure and in the process examined the commission's effectiveness across its whole mission as well as how it can establish its place in the AU. The anniversaries of the adoption of the African Charter and its coming into force provide valuable opportunities for the African Commission and the AU to take stock and evaluate successes and obstacles to ensure an effective regional human rights system for the future.

[*See also* African Union: Banjul Charter; Inter-African Commission on Traditional Practices; *and* Nongovernmental Organizations: Overview.]

BIBLIOGRAPHY

African Commission on Human and Peoples' Rights. http://www.achpr.org.

African Union. http://www.africa-union.org/root/au/index/index.htm.

African Union. African [Banjul] Charter on Human and Peoples' Rights. http://www.africa-union.org/official_documents/Treaties_%20Conventions_%20Protocols/Banjul%20Charter.pdf.

African Union. *Decision on the Seats of the African Union.* Assembly/AU/Dec.45(III). http://www.asil.org/rio/african union.html.

Ankumah, Evelyn A. *The African Commission on Human and Peoples' Rights: Practices and Procedures.* The Hague: Martinus Nijhoff, 1996.

Coalition for an Effective African Court on Human and Peoples Rights. http://www.africancourtcoalition.org.

Evans, Malcolm D., and Rachel Murray, eds. *The African Charter on Human and Peoples' Rights: The System in Practice,*

1986-2006. 2d ed. New York: Cambridge University Press, 2008.

Magliveras, K. D., and Gino J. Naldi. "The African Union: A New Dawn for Africa?" *International and Comparative Law Quarterly* 51, no. 2 (2002): 415–425.

Manby, Bronwen. "The African Union, NEPAD, and Human Rights: The Missing Agenda." *Human Rights Quarterly* 26 (2004): 983–1027.

Murray, Rachel. *The African Commission on Human and Peoples' Rights and International Law.* Oxford: Hart, 2000.

Murray, Rachel. *Human Rights in Africa: From the OAU to the African Union.* Cambridge, U.K.: Cambridge University Press, 2004.

Naldi, Gino J. *The Organization of African Unity: An Analysis of Its Role.* 2d ed. London: Mansell, 1999.

Odinkalu, Chidi Anselm, and Camilla Christensen. "The African Commission on Human and Peoples' Rights: The Development of Its Non-State Communication Procedures." *Human Rights Quarterly* 20, no. 2 (1998): 235–280.

Ouguergouz, Fatsah. *The African Charter on Human and People's Rights: A Comprehensive Agenda for Human Dignity and Sustainable Democracy in Africa.* The Hague: Martinus Nijhoff, 2003.

Ouguergouz, Fatsah. *The African Charter on Human and Peoples' Rights: A Comprehensive Agenda for Human Rights.* The Hague: Kluwer Law International, 2003.

Udombana, Nsongurua J. "An African Human Rights Court and an African Union Court: A Needful Duality or a Needless Duplication?" *Brooklyn Journal of International Law* 28 (2003): 811–866.

Viljoen, Frans, and Evarist Baimu. "Courts for Africa: Considering the Co-Existence of the African Court on Human and Peoples' Rights and the African Court of Justice." *Netherlands Quarterly of Human Rights* 22, no. 2 (2004): 241–267.

AIDS/HIV

by Amy S. Patterson

According to the Joint United Nations Programme on HIV/AIDS (UNAIDS), in 2005 an estimated 38.6 million people worldwide were infected with the human immunodeficiency virus (HIV) that causes the acquired immune deficiency syndrome (AIDS). Approximately 2.8 million people died of AIDS in 2005. Of the world's HIV-positive individuals, more than 90 percent (35 million) lived in developing countries, and of those, 24.5 million inhabited sub-Saharan Africa. Lesotho, Zimbabwe, Swaziland, and Botswana each had more than 20 percent of their populations infected with HIV. In spite of the fact that fewer than 1 percent of people in India were HIV positive, that country had the most individuals with HIV in the world (5.7 million in 2005). Although the first AIDS cases appeared in the United States, AIDS has become a disease that disproportionately affects people in poor countries.

HIV is spread through heterosexual and homosexual contact, intravenous drug use with contaminated needles, transfusions with contaminated blood or blood products, and mother-to-child transmission. In the latter, HIV-positive HIV-pregnant women may pass the virus to the infant in the womb or during childbirth; mothers also may transmit the virus during breastfeeding. In sub-Saharan Africa, HIV has spread primarily through heterosexual contact and mother-to-child transmission. In Latin America, the majority of AIDS cases have been among intravenous drug users (IDUs) and men who have sex with men, although Argentina reported in 2004 that 50 percent of its people living with HIV/AIDS (PLWHAs) had been infected through heterosexual contact. Most AIDS cases in Asia are among IDUs and sex workers. In China, roughly 10 percent of PLWHAs are former plasma donors (primarily in Henan province) who contracted HIV through contaminated blood given to donors.

Since the first AIDS cases appeared in 1981, HIV prevalence rates have increased globally. HIV prevalence measures the percentage of people living with HIV in a given population, usually individuals between fifteen to forty-nine years old. Instead of gathering AIDS case data in poor countries, UNAIDS often relies on HIV tests of women attending prenatal clinics to discern larger population rates. Because not all pregnant women attend clinics and HIV suppresses fertility, these estimates may be somewhat inaccurate. In 2005 UNAIDS began providing "plausibility ranges" for estimates, and in 2006 it readjusted some of its prevalence rates downward.

AIDS in the developing world is closely linked to human rights. AIDS stigma and discrimination violate tenets of the Universal Declaration of Human Rights (UDHR, adopted 1948) that prohibit unequal treatment of individuals. In poor countries, most politicians and legal institutions have inadequately addressed such human rights violations. Despite the fact that the vast majority of developing countries have ratified the Convention on the Rights of the Child (CRC, adopted 1989) and the Convention for the Elimination of All Forms of Discrimination against Women (CEDAW, adopted 1979), social, political, and economic exclusion have increased women and children's vulnerability to HIV and the negative impact of AIDS on them. AIDS has called attention to unequal access to health care despite the human right of the world's citizens to health and well-being. Violations of political and civil rights prevent AIDS organizations from educating citizens about HIV and lobbying for AIDS policies.

AIDS AND HUMAN RIGHTS: A NEW WAY TO VIEW PUBLIC HEALTH

The late Jonathan Mann, director of the Global AIDS Program at the World Health Organization (WHO) from 1986 until 1990, argued that AIDS and human rights went hand in hand. Mann's approach was novel, because the conventional wisdom was that disease eradication was divorced from the political, economic, social, and cultural situation of individuals. Mann brought three understandings to the AIDS–human rights nexus, and each remained crucial for fighting AIDS in the early twenty-first century.

First, Mann challenged widespread calls for the quarantine and exclusion of PLWHAs. By 1987 more than eighty countries had laws to control PLWHAs or people thought to be at risk of infection, such as homosexuals and sex workers. Discrimination in housing, travel, health care, and employment was common. Mann called for compassion for PLWHAs and comprehensive education to prevent HIV infection. He noted that discriminatory practices were counterproductive, as they stigmatized PLWHAs, discouraged people from being tested for HIV, and caused them to hide their HIV status from family and partners. In 1988 the WHO officially acknowledged the destructive impact of discrimination on fighting AIDS.

Second, Mann asserted that people excluded in society—those whose human rights often were not realized because of their race, gender, sexual orientation, education level, nationality, and/or income—were most vulnerable to HIV infection. The political and social processes that violate human rights and contribute to disease include political repression, unemployment, migration, cultural practices that devalue women, and inadequate educational opportunities. For example, economic underdevelopment has forced men (and some women) to migrate to urban areas and across borders, leaving behind their families for long periods. Studies of male migrants in South Africa indicate that they suffer loneliness, depression, health problems, and high rates of alcohol use. These factors have made migrants more likely to engage in casual sex with multiple partners, increasing their risk of HIV infection.

Third, Mann argued that PLWHAs were not passive victims but essential voices in AIDS policy making. During the initial years of the epidemic in the United States, Gay Men's Health Crisis (GMHC) and AIDS Coalition to Unleash Power (ACT UP) educated members about HIV prevention, demanded media attention to AIDS, and lobbied for government policies. Mann urged the WHO, bilateral donors, and governments to partner with civil society organizations. This approach empowered PLWHAs, particularly in Brazil and South Africa, where activists lobbied their governments to develop AIDS programs. In Uganda, the AIDS Support Organization (TASO) became the largest voice of HIV-positive people in that country, providing testing, counseling, and support to people with the disease. Civil society's role in the AIDS fight was explicitly recognized in the Declaration of Commitment on HIV/AIDS unanimously approved at the 2001 UN General Assembly Special Session on HIV/AIDS.

STIGMA, DISCRIMINATION, AND AT-RISK POPULATIONS

Stigma is the process of devaluing an individual. AIDS stigma reinforces the negative connotations linking the disease to marginalized behaviors such as drug use, promiscuity, sex work, and male homosexual relations. Often rooted in lack of knowledge about AIDS, stigma reinforces fears of "outsiders," such as migrants or prisoners. Studies indicate stigma prevents people from being tested for HIV and from disclosing their HIV status. Stigma has caused husbands to leave their HIV-positive wives and villagers to force AIDS orphans from communities. It has led religious organizations to shun their HIV-positive members and, at times, to condemn them for sinful behavior. Stigma also has caused political leaders to ignore AIDS or to support incomplete solutions to the disease. For example, former Kenyan president Daniel arap Moi denied media reports of AIDS cases in his country in the 1980s, claiming foreign journalists were out to destroy Kenya.

Stigma may be manifested in discrimination, or the unequal treatment of people without justification because of their suspected or confirmed HIV status. The UN Commission on Human Rights has determined that discrimination based on health status including HIV/AIDS violates human rights law. As of 2005, only half of sub-Saharan African countries (and only one-third of countries globally) had laws to protect HIV-positive individuals from discrimination. In poor countries with such laws, judges may not enforce them and attorneys may be unwilling to take on discrimination cases. The AIDS Law Project in South Africa is somewhat exceptional, because it has successfully sued the government over unequal treatment of HIV prisoners, job discrimination of HIV-positive workers, and rape victims' access to HIV prophylaxis. More common is the situation that Human Rights Watch (HRW) outlined in Kenya, where hundreds of AIDS orphans have lost property they legally should inherit because they had no advocates and traditional leaders did not protect their legal rights.

Soldiers also may suffer discriminatory treatment. Because HIV prevalence is thought to be higher in the military than in the general population (although HIV-prevalence rates in militaries are difficult to obtain), many countries have made HIV testing mandatory for recruits. Ghana has required that any soldier who participates in a UN peacekeeping mission be HIV-negative. Because such missions are prestigious and higher-paying than regular military service, Ghana hopes the policy will encourage soldiers to protect themselves from HIV. Eritrea and Sudan will not accept HIV-positive soldiers in peacekeeping missions. Although the rationale for these policies is that military preparedness necessitates healthy soldiers and that HIV-positive soldiers may put local populations at risk, the increased use of AIDS treatment for HIV-positive soldiers and AIDS-prevention efforts among soldiers may diminish such concerns.

HIV testing raises human rights issues related to personal autonomy and nondiscrimination. Testing is crucial to the AIDS fight, because 90 percent of HIV-positive people worldwide do not know their status, cannot protect their partners from infection, and cannot access AIDS treatment programs. From the epidemic's beginning, testing in the developing world was modeled on Western voluntary counseling and testing (VCT) services. VCT requires patients to ask for the test, to voluntarily consent to it, and to receive counseling before and after the test. Providers pledge that test results will be confidential. Although VCT was intended to guarantee that people who tested positive would not suffer recrimination and that they were psychologically prepared for the implications of a positive result, the lengthy process and focus on the individual in isolation from the community often prevented patients from being tested.

By 2004 these problems led Botswana, a country with a 24 percent HIV-prevalence rate in 2005, to develop a new model of routine testing. After 2001 Botswana provided HIV-positive citizens with AIDS treatment, but few people enrolled in the programs because they did not know their HIV status. In routine testing, all patients receive the HIV test as part of a medical visit unless they explicitly refuse it. Confidentiality, informed consent, and post-test counseling for those who test positive are supposed to remain part of routine testing. By 2006 Botswana's testing program had greatly increased the number of people in AIDS treatment programs, and most citizens viewed the policy positively. Many public-health officials argued that the policy removed the "exceptional" status of AIDS and protected patients' right to health care, because access to AIDS treatment is impossible without the HIV test. Botswana's policy became the model for countries such as Lesotho (23.2 percent prevalence), which called for the village-to-village testing of all its citizens by 2007. Although human rights organizations agree that testing is essential, some caution that routine testing, particularly as incorporated in Lesotho, could be potentially coercive. Community-wide testing would be less likely to be confidential, a factor that could put those who test positive

(particularly women or men who have sex with men) at risk for violent recriminations.

Although the human rights implications of routine testing are uncertain, the impact of Cuba's AIDS policies on human rights is more evident. Some AIDS activists and human rights advocates assert that Cuba has egregiously violated the rights of HIV-positive people. Between 1986 and 1993 the country forcibly quarantined in sanatoriums anyone who tested HIV-positive. During the program's initial years, patients could not leave the facilities, family visits were limited, and inhabitants lived in wards and wore similar clothing. In time, some of these rules were relaxed. In 1993 mandatory quarantine ended, although to live outside sanatoriums, HIV-positive citizens in Cuba must disclose their sexual partners (who are traced and tested) and assure health authorities that they are sexually responsible. Sanatorium residents are entitled to 100 percent of their former salary; those living outside receive 50 percent. In 2003 roughly half of Cuba's four thousand HIV-positive people chose to live in the sanatoriums. Patients report that while they receive excellent medical treatment in the sanatoriums, they also suffer isolation. For those who want to leave, convincing health authorities they are sexually responsible can be difficult. Although the Cuban government asserts the country's low prevalence rate (0.1 percent in 2005) is a direct result of its policy, AIDS activists claim these policies discourage sexually active adults from getting tested and they fuel homophobia because most people with HIV are gay men.

Though not as systematic as Cuba's policies, discriminatory behaviors and laws can hamper the AIDS fight among sex workers, men who have sex with men, and IDUs. In India, Vietnam, China, and several Caribbean and West African countries, sex workers are a large component of the HIV-positive population. For example, an estimated 20 percent of China's HIV-positive people are sex workers. In Ghana and Senegal, both countries with low HIV prevalence rates (roughly 3 and 0.9 percent, respectively), an estimated 30 to 40 percent of urban sex workers have HIV. Because sex work is illegal in most countries, sex workers are less likely to receive access to health care and HIV prevention information. Only one-third of sex workers in southern Africa knew they were at risk of contracting HIV if they had unprotected sex. Similarly low levels of knowledge are evident in India, a country with between 2 and 8 million female sex workers.

Many developing world governments and donor aid agencies have either ignored or tended to scapegoat sex workers. In India, thousands of prostitutes have had their homes bulldozed or been imprisoned. China prohibits the selling and purchasing of sexual services, although punishment is unequal for sex workers and customers. Sex workers often are sent to prison or reform-through-education programs, whereas customers usually get a fine. Such unequal legal treatment further stigmatizes sex work and discourages sex workers from seeking out or attending AIDS education programs. Starting in 2005, the U.S. government required any organization that receives U.S. funds for AIDS to promise that it does not promote or support prostitution. Although the so-called antiprostitution pledge is intended to curb sex trafficking, many public-health officials and AIDS activists have argued that the policy increases the AIDS stigma and limits outreach among individuals who can spread HIV to the general population. In contrast, Senegal and Thailand have recognized that educating sex workers about condom use and regularly testing them for sexually transmitted diseases like HIV are crucial in the AIDS fight. Senegal's legalized prostitution facilitates such practices. Public discussions initiated by Thailand's health minister and Thailand's 100 percent condom-use policy for brothels also have helped to fight AIDS.

The group labeled men who have sex with men includes not only self-identified gay and bisexual men but also men who engage in male–male sex but identify themselves as heterosexuals. HIV prevalence among this population in some communities can be high. For example, in Bogotá, Colombia, and Montevideo, Uruguay, an estimated 20 percent of such men are HIV-positive, in contrast to fewer than 5 percent of sex workers. Many countries have criminalized sex between men. In Malawi, for example, such relations can be punished with a fourteen-year prison sentence. Criminal penalties push these individuals from accessing health services, with only 5 percent of these men receiving HIV prevention information. (Most men exposed to AIDS education live in the United States, Western Europe, Brazil, Chile, and Argentina.) Health officials in several developing countries have complained that AIDS programs have no component to serve this at-risk population.

One-third of new HIV infections outside of sub-Saharan Africa occur among IDUs. This population accounts for almost half of HIV infections in China, Vietnam, and South America, and roughly 80 percent of infections in Eastern and Central Europe. Drug use and sex work often overlap, with a high percentage of those working in the sex trade also using drugs. In some Chinese provinces, for example, half of sex workers are also IDUs. Sex workers who use drugs tend to have more customers and to be less likely to use condoms. Because of their legal and social status, 95 percent of IDUs worldwide lack access to HIV prevention efforts such as needle-exchange and drug-substitution programs. In China, where heroin use is a significant problem, IDUs must first endure two rounds at prisonlike drug rehabilitation centers before they can access government methadone treatment centers. Forced rehabilitation and periodic police sweeps at methadone centers dissuade addicts from enrolling in the program. U.S. foreign assistance policies also negatively impact HIV prevention among IDUs, because the U.S. Congress has consistently prohibited funding for needle-exchange programs. Even though the vast majority of public health experts agree on the benefits of needle exchange for HIV prevention, many governments in developing countries have ignored IDUs in their AIDS efforts or refused needle exchange for fear it will escalate drug use. For AIDS activists, these approaches encroach on IDUs' human right to health and, ultimately, life.

WOMEN AND AIDS

AIDS and women's human rights are closely related. Globally, more than 50 percent of HIV-positive people are women; in sub-Saharan Africa, the number is 57 percent. The gender disparity in infection rates is most apparent among Africans who are fifteen to twenty-four years old, with three HIV-positive women in this age group for every one HIV-positive man. (In Kenya, the ratio is almost 7 to 1.) Biology contributes to this discrepancy, because the virus easily passes through vaginal membranes, especially the immature membranes of young women. Women are seven times more likely to be infected during sexual intercourse with an infected partner than men are. But biology is not the only reason for the disproportionate impact of AIDS on women: women's human rights situation also affects their vulnerability to HIV and shapes their responses to the disease.

Because many developing world societies emphasize marriage and large family size, women tend to marry and have their first sexual relations at a young age. In Kenya, for example, one-fourth of girls marry by the age of eighteen. Women often marry men who are older than they are and who may have more sexual experiences prior to marriage. Despite their support for CEDAW, which includes women's right to choose a spouse, determine the number of children they have, and be free from domestic violence, most governments in the developing world have been slow to challenge traditional marriage patterns and patriarchal norms. Few African countries have laws against domestic violence, a practice that limits women's ability to resist sex and insist on their spouse's fidelity or condom use. In South Africa, one in six women is thought to be in a violent relationship, and gang rape and coercion often accompany a woman's first sexual encounter. Sexual violence increases women's risk of HIV infection, because the virus can pass through torn cervical membranes. The payment of "bride wealth," while intending to solidify marriage arrangements and to compensate the bride's family for her lost labor, can increase pressure on women to stay in such abusive relationships. Fear of violence also prevents women from freely obtaining an HIV test.

Because of the link between AIDS and stigmatized populations, married women often believe they are not at risk for HIV infection. However, because married women are less likely to use condoms even if they believe their husbands are unfaithful or HIV-positive, HIV infection rates are roughly 10 percent higher for married women than unmarried women in Kenya and Zambia. In Uganda, 88 percent of women with HIV are married. In India, husbands who spend months away from home as truck drivers and traders often engage in sex with sex workers or with other men; when they return home, they may infect their wives with HIV. A 2006 study determined that almost 40 percent of India's HIV-positive people are women, with a large number of them monogamous wives of husbands with multiple sex partners.

Because few HIV prevention programs target married women, their level of knowledge on HIV/AIDS is often lower than men's. Roughly half of women in India knew about AIDS prevention methods in comparison to 63 percent of men. AIDS education programs that focus on abstinence until marriage and monogamy in marriage may ignore women's lack of economic and social power to refuse sex with husbands who have been unfaithful. More broadly, AIDS activists, human rights organizations, and public-health officials have criticized the HIV prevention programs of Uganda and the United States that teach young people to abstain from premarital sex and to be sexually monogamous, but provide limited information on condoms, negotiating sex with a condom, and women's empowerment. In a 2005 report, Human Rights Watch argued that access to complete health information is essential to realizing the human right to the highest attainable standard of health. In response, both the Ugandan and U.S. governments have maintained that condom distribution, particularly for at-risk populations, remains part of their AIDS prevention strategies.

Customary practices that may be rooted in beliefs about women's inferiority and that reflect women's lack of choice in marriage can facilitate the spread of HIV/AIDS. Because it adds partners into a sexual circle, polygamy may increase the risk of HIV infection, particularly in countries with high HIV prevalence rates. Marriage of girls younger than eighteen years old, a practice prevalent in Southeast Asia, sub-Saharan Africa, and the Middle East, cuts short their schooling, increases the period of years during which they regularly engage in sexual relations, and adds to their childbearing years. These outcomes can limit women's economic choices and make them economically dependent on their husbands. This dependence makes it difficult for women to refuse sex with unfaithful or HIV-positive spouses. Because they have not been exposed to HIV/AIDS education programs in school, these young women often have low levels of knowledge about the disease. In 2003 UNAIDS found that only 16 percent of rural, married women in Lesotho, 7 percent in Cameroon, and 10 percent in Indonesia had comprehensive knowledge about AIDS.

Widow inheritance and ritual sexual cleansing, cultural practices in parts of sub-Saharan Africa, challenge women's human rights and increase their vulnerability to HIV. In traditional African society, a male relative of a dead husband often marries the widow, so her children remain in the family lineage and receive care. Although some women consent to such a marriage, others may be coerced in order to keep their property and children, an act that violates women's right to choice in marriage. If the widow is HIV-positive (because her husband died of AIDS), this practices introduces AIDS into yet another sexual circle. In sexual cleansing, the dead husband's family pays a social outcast to have sex with the widow to cleanse the dead husband's evil spirits from her. The practice may be coerced, the man rarely uses a condom, and he may have had multiple partners. In communities with many AIDS deaths, this practice increases vulnerability to AIDS.

Economic dependence on men also makes women more likely to engage in sexual encounters that put them at risk for HIV infection. In 2003 the literacy rate for adult women in the world's poorest countries (primarily those in sub-Saharan Africa and South Asia) was 70 percent of adult men's rate. Women's lower educational levels prevent them from finding employment; even with formal sector jobs, women are paid less and work more hours than men doing comparable work. Given these economic challenges, women may exchange sexual favors for food, housing, or money to pay for children's school or health care. In southern Africa, economies based on male migration have sometimes forced wives left behind to engage in such survival sex. Such women rarely consider themselves to be prostitutes. Young girls may have sexual relations with older men ("sugar daddies") in order to pay for school fees. Although a violation of women's human rights, male government officials may demand sexual services from female merchants in return for positive business inspection reports or low customs duties. Male teachers may insist on sex from girls for passing grades. Such practices prey on power inequalities between genders and make women more vulnerable to HIV infection, because these men may have had multiple sexual partners. For HIV-positive women, their limited economic resources make it more difficult for them to afford AIDS treatment. Even if treatment is free, the cost of diagnostic tests and transportation to hospitals may be too high. Some studies show that when male and female family members are HIV-positive, men are more likely to receive treatment than women.

Although the lack of protection of women's human rights in marriage, education, and employment makes them vulnerable to HIV infection, it also means that women bare the burden of AIDS in poor countries. Customs and the legal system may not protect a woman's access to her husband's property when he dies. Instead, property may return to the husband's family. This property grabbing discriminates against women, and may plunge their children and them into dire poverty. But women's lack of access to resources also occurs before male household members die. Because of increased costs for medicines and foods, and lost income from sick breadwinners, AIDS-infected households must ration resources. To save money, parents may remove girls from school, and women and female children may receive less food to eat. Because of social expectations about women's role in the household, women and girls provide most of the care for the ill, at the cost of their education, economic and social advancement, and autonomy.

Given the gender bias of AIDS in poor countries, governments, traditional leaders, and donors have sought to design programs to prevent the spread of AIDS among women. Some programs have tried to decrease women's economic dependence on men, by giving women employable skills or making education, textbooks, and school uniforms free. Some of these solutions, however, have reinforced women's unequal status in society. For example, in the mid-1990s, there was a resurgence of virginity testing among women in southern Africa. In the practice, women testers inspect a young girl's vaginal canal for evidence of the hymen to determine if the girl is sexually chaste; testers may grade girls using unscientific criteria and these grades may be shared with the community. Initiated by older women, the practice can be viewed as an attempt to regain control over younger women's sexuality. The UN Commission on Human Rights, on the other hand, has said the practice violates women's right to privacy and bodily integrity. Moreover, because the practice puts the onus of HIV prevention (and sexual purity) on women, not men, it is discriminatory. It ignores the larger social pressures on young people to have premarital sex. Finally, many donor programs have yet to fully incorporate the promotion of women's human rights into AIDS prevention. Human rights advocates argue that women's right to comprehensive information about HIV prevention must be coupled with increased educational and employment opportunities for women. Discriminatory social and economic barriers to health care must also not hinder women's access to HIV testing and AIDS treatment.

CHILDREN AND AIDS

In 2005 a spokesperson for the United Nations Children's Fund (UNICEF) said that children are the missing face of AIDS. In that year, UNAIDS estimated that 2.3 million children under fifteen years old had HIV worldwide; of these, 2 million lived in sub-Saharan Africa. Roughly 570,000 children died of AIDS in 2005. In addition, there were an estimated 15.2 million AIDS orphans globally, of which 12 million lived in sub-Saharan Africa. (UNAIDS defines an AIDS orphan as any child under seventeen years old who has lost one or both parents to AIDS.) Because it makes millions of adults too ill to teach, parent, or care for young people, AIDS affects large numbers of children. The situation of HIV-positive children, AIDS orphans (only some of whom may be HIV-positive), and AIDS-affected children raises particular concerns about the rights of children to survival, education, family support and care, and protection from sexual and economic exploitation.

Most HIV-positive children contract the virus through mother-to-child transmission. In the West, widespread HIV testing of pregnant women and the use of antiretroviral drugs (ARVs) for prevention of mother-to-child transmission (PMTCT) meant only 700 HIV-positive children were born in the Untied States and Western Europe in 2005. In contrast, because of the lack of prenatal care and drugs for PMTCT, roughly 540,000 HIV-positive infants—470,000 in sub-Saharan Africa—were born in poor countries that same year. In 2005 less than 5 percent of HIV-positive women in Angola, Ethiopia, Ghana, Mali, Namibia, Somalia, Cambodia, Honduras, and Paraguay received drugs for PMTCT.

Diagnosis of HIV infection in children is difficult, because clinical symptoms may not be apparent or they may be confused with other childhood illnesses. The use of HIV antibody tests in infants is complicated by the fact that an infant acquires maternal antibodies, which may remain in the child's blood for up to eighteen months. Sophisticated laboratory equipment is needed to determine if the HIV antibodies are the child's or the mother's. For these reasons, HIV in poor children is often not detected until they are quite ill.

In 2006 only about 5 percent of HIV-positive children globally had access to ARVs. As a result, most children with HIV/AIDS will die before they are five years old. Usually prescribed in combinations of three drugs, ARV therapy destroys the protein that HIV uses to reproduce itself. ARV therapy has made AIDS a chronic medical condition for many people living with HIV and AIDS (PLWHAs) and has greatly decreased AIDS deaths in the West. Treating a child with AIDS is up to four times more costly than treating an adult because of the lack of generic pediatric ARVs and because drugs commonly have to be administered as syrups or powers mixed with water. More expensive than tablets or capsules, these drug forms often require refrigeration, accurate measurement by caregivers, and clean water. UNICEF and the WHO only developed standardized treatment guidelines for children in 2006. While increasing, the number of children in ARV programs remains small. For example, in U.S.-funded treatment programs, the number of children increased from roughly 4,000 in 2003 to 17,500 in 2005. Despite this fact, adults remain the focus of government and donor ARV programs. Such gradual responses contradict Article 6 of the Convention on the Rights of the Child (CRC), which calls on states to "ensure to the maximum extent possible the survival and development of the child."

The CRC also outlines the rights of children to an adequate standard of living for their physical, mental, spiritual, moral, and social development (Article 27). Nevertheless, many AIDS orphans worldwide do not have access to family support, education, sufficient food, or medical care. AIDS orphans and AIDS-affected children are more likely to leave school, less likely to attend at an age-appropriate grade, and less likely to have family resources to spend on education than children AIDS does not affect. Even before the death of a parent from AIDS,

children may be forced to leave school to work or do household chores. Although extended family members care for most AIDS orphans, the growing number of such children increases the burden on adults. Surveys of AIDS orphans also show that they are less likely to have access to AIDS prevention messages, because schools are the primary arena in which they learn about AIDS. AIDS orphans are more likely than nonorphans to suffer depression, to use drugs, to engage in unprotected sex, and to begin sexual activities at a younger age. Without parents to provide love and support, they are vulnerable to powerful adults, who may economically and/or sexually exploit children's need for food, money, and acceptance. Communities may also stigmatize AIDS-affected children, by refusing to let them attend schools or live in certain neighborhoods. The lack of child advocates, police trained to work with children, and judges attuned to their needs means these children have been subject to property grabbing, discrimination in health care, and social ostracism.

Because children are relatively powerless and because adult policy makers have often ignored their plight, few programs exist for orphans and AIDS-affected children in poor countries. Although community organizations and faith-based groups are desperately trying to provide for these children, these efforts often lack resources. In 2005 only about 10 percent of Kenyan and Zambian households with orphans received outside assistance such as educational fees, food resources, and/or medicine. Uganda and Kenya have sought to ensure that these children attend schools by abolishing school fees, but some local administrators have refused to enroll children who lack birth certificates or who cannot pay for books and uniforms. Not only does the lack of attention to children violate their human rights, it may also have high costs for AIDS-affected societies, if children without education, care, and support turn to antisocial behavior.

THE HUMAN RIGHT TO MEDICINE: ACCESS TO AIDS TREATMENT

In 2006 the UN secretary-general reported that 1.3 million people in the developing world had access to ARVs, representing an increase from 400,000 in 2003. In Africa, the percentage of PLWHAs who receive needed ARVs ranges from 1 percent in Somalia to 50 percent in Uganda; in Asia, from 7 percent in India to 60 percent in Thailand; in Latin America, from 16 percent in Honduras to 97 percent in Panama. Compared regionally, only 17 percent of Africans needing ARVs received them, whereas

66 percent of similar Latin Americans did. Although low, these numbers have increased since 2001. Before then, officials at bilateral and multilateral donor agencies argued that AIDS treatment was not sustainable in developing countries. They maintained that without a health-care infrastructure and doctors trained to administer ARVs, widespread treatment efforts in poor countries would fail. They doubted that poor, uneducated individuals could adhere to complex treatment regimens, and they argued that limited financial resources could be better used for HIV prevention efforts.

In response, a global movement emerged in the late 1990s to demand access to ARVs in poor countries. At the 2000 International Conference on AIDS in Durban, South Africa, an ad hoc coalition led by Health Global Access Project (Health GAP) staged protests that gained widespread media attention. Formed in 1998, its members included ACT UP, Search for a Cure, Health Action International, Doctors without Borders (Médecins sans frontières), Partners in Health, the South Africa-based Treatment Action Campaign (TAC), the AIDS Treatment Data Network, and Ralph Nader's Consumer Project on Technology. In time, additional human rights advocates, faith-based groups, and development organizations joined the effort. The coalition coupled protests with studies demonstrating the feasibility of ARV use in poor countries. In South Africa, Doctors without Borders set up pilot ARV treatment programs in several black townships, where patients were poor, uneducated, and unemployed. Partners in Health demonstrated in Haiti and Peru that people with AIDS and/or tuberculosis could adhere to difficult drug regimens. Both organizations trained community members to monitor patients, a move that also built local support for AIDS prevention and care programs. Health GAP argued that the most effective advocates for prevention were HIV-positive people; lengthening their lives could help societies fight AIDS. These arguments persuaded UN member states to assert in the 2001 Declaration of Commitment on HIV/AIDS that access to medication in the context of pandemics is essential for the "full realization of the right of everyone to enjoyment of the highest attainable standard of physical and mental health." In 2003 the WHO initiated a program to put 3 million HIV-positive people on ARVs by 2005. Although the WHO did not reach its goal, the effort reinforced the right to health and medicines for PLWHAs.

The right to AIDS treatment clashed with tenets of the neoliberal global economy. When countries formed the World Trade Organization (WTO) in 1995, they supported the Trade-Related Intellectual Property Rights (TRIPS) Agreement. Because TRIPS protects the intellectual property of companies through patents, it effectively gave pharmaceutical companies monopoly power to set prices. In 2001 the lack of market competition meant that ARVs cost between $10,000 and 15,000 per patient per year, a sum few PLWHAs in poor countries could afford. Producers argued they needed patent protection to recoup their investments in drug research and to encourage the development of new drugs. Critics asserted that patents were never intended to take precedence over public health and that companies used patent protection to gain huge profits.

Pressured by AIDS activists and pushed by the right to health outlined in their countries' constitutions, South Africa and Brazil passed policies that challenged TRIPS. In 1996 Brazil announced that it would provide ARVs to all citizens who needed them. To do so, it would produce generic versions of some drugs by requiring the patent holder to license its product to a domestic manufacturer (a process called compulsory licensing), and it would negotiate discounts with pharmaceutical companies for imported drugs. Coupled with an aggressive prevention effort, the treatment plan decreased AIDS deaths by 50 percent and saved the government $1.2 billion in hospital costs between 1996 and 2002. Brazil's efforts also demonstrated to other poor countries that treatment is feasible. In South Africa, the legislature passed the 1997 Medicines Act, which cited AIDS as a health emergency and allowed the government to issue compulsory licenses to produce AIDS drugs. In response, forty Western pharmaceutical companies, with the support of Western governments, sued South Africa for violations of TRIPS. AIDS activists in South Africa and the West used mass protests to call attention to the lawsuit, and to publicly chastise Western politicians such as then U.S. presidential candidate Al Gore for supporting the companies. The resulting negative publicity led the companies to drop the suit in 2001.

Because of changing opinions on ARV access, WTO negotiators agreed in 2001 to the Doha Declaration on the TRIPS Agreement and Public Health, which asserts that countries have the right to issue compulsory licenses in "public health crises, including those relating to HIV/AIDS, tuberculosis, malaria and other epidemics." In 2003 the Doha Declaration was clarified to allow companies that produce generics, primarily in India, to export those products to eligible countries. In response, the William J. Clinton Foundation began to negotiate with generic producers to buy ARVs at a bulk rate and provide them to nongovernmental organizations (NGOs) and African governments. In 2003 the United States passed the $15 billion, five-year President's Emergency Plan for AIDS Relief (PEPFAR) that focuses on fifteen AIDS-affected countries (Zambia, Namibia, South Africa, Botswana, Uganda, Rwanda, Ethiopia, Nigeria, Côte d'Ivoire, Kenya, Mozambique, Tanzania, Haiti, Guyana, and Vietnam). PEPFAR allocates 55 percent of its funding for AIDS treatment, and since 2005, it has used some generic ARVs. Generic competition caused the price of the most common ARV combination therapy to drop to less than $200 per patient per year in 2006.

The global treatment movement coincided with activist demands in South Africa for government ARV programs. Even though the country passed the Medicines Act and it counted more than 5 million HIV-positive citizens in 2003, President Thabo Mbeki (elected in 1999) refused to provide free ARVs at government hospitals. Mbeki argued that a universal AIDS treatment program was unsustainable and too expensive. His critics countered that South Africa has a gross domestic product per capita ten times that of most other African countries and South African pharmaceutical companies have the capacity to produce ARVs. The president's hesitancy also reflected his concern about ARV toxicity and his public questioning of the link between HIV and AIDS. A TAC-led coalition used mass protests and lawsuits to advocate for the ARV program. Setting an important precedent, the South African Constitutional High Court ruled in 2002 that the constitutional right to health required the government to provide ARVs to all HIV-positive mothers for PMTCT. TAC pressure and divisions within the ruling party pushed the government in late 2003 to announce it would provide universal access to ARVs. Despite the promise, government inefficiencies have hampered the ARV rollout; only 20 percent of PLWHAs who needed ARVs in 2005 received them.

The treatment-access movement has rooted its arguments in the language of human rights. TAC, Health GAP, Doctors without Borders, and Partners in Health (among others) assert that because of their mere humanity, HIV-positive citizens in poor countries have the same right as Western PLWHAs to access the benefits of medical technology and pharmaceutical research. Economic status, nationality, educational level, or gender should not prevent the realization of the human right to health. These organizations also argue that access to medicine for PLWHAs facilitates their autonomy, enables them to make important life choices, teaches society that living in dignity with AIDS is possible, and empowers those with the disease to contribute to their communities. ARVs enable PLWHAs

to work, HIV-positive parents to care for their children, and teachers with AIDS to educate millions of students. In doing so, HIV-positive individuals help to foster the realization of the human right to education, health, development, and child survival for all people.

POLITICAL RIGHTS AND THE STRUGGLE AGAINST AIDS

Several human rights documents, most notably the Universal Declaration of Human Rights and the International Covenant on Civil and Political Rights (ICCPR, adopted 1966), explicitly call on states to protect citizens' rights to free political participation, free expression of thought, free assembly, ownership of property, and equal protection before the law. The lack of recognition of civil and political rights in some countries, however, has hampered the fight against AIDS and prevented PLWHAs from accessing the information, medical treatment, and care they need. Zimbabwe and China provide two examples.

Although Zimbabwe's HIV prevalence rate declined from roughly 25 percent in 2000 to 21 percent in 2005, the country's political and economic situation has undermined its AIDS efforts. After the 2005 parliamentary elections, which President Robert Mugabe's party won, the government evicted residents in poor urban neighborhoods and razed their homes and businesses; an estimated 1 million people were displaced. Many Zimbabwe observers speculated that the government was punishing urban residents, who had disproportionately supported the opposition party. The actions disrupted the treatment and health-care programs of hundreds of PLWHAs and forced them to live in poor, crowded housing that increased their vulnerability to opportunistic infections such as tuberculosis. As part of the evictions, police destroyed two thousand outlets for distributing condoms and intimidated or closed several AIDS education organizations. Moreover, because most destroyed businesses were in the informal sector, an economic arena in which women disproportionately work, many women lost their economic livelihoods. To support themselves, some turned to high-risk behaviors such as unprotected sex with male benefactors or sex work. More broadly, the regime's harassment and tight legal control over civil society organizations have prevented AIDS organizations, which UNAIDS credits with helping to decrease Zimbabwe's HIV rate, from advocating for the rights of PLWHAs and from providing needed AIDS prevention, care, support, and treatment programs.

Although the Chinese government has become more open about AIDS, particularly after the 2003 outbreak of severe acute respiratory syndrome (SARS), the country has periodically shown how limited political freedoms can harm its AIDS efforts. In 2002 AIDS activist Wan Yanhai published on his Web site a report claiming that between 70,000 and 250,000 plasma donors in Henan province were HIV-positive. This action led to his incarceration, possibly because Yanhai's report suggested some of the plasma centers had continued to use unsafe collection procedures even after the government knew about the high HIV infection rates. Since then the government has continued to harass and arbitrarily detain AIDS activists who have protested the government's AIDS policies. In early 2006 activist Hu Jia was detained for forty-one days without explanation, and in March 2006 AIDS activists in Henan province were placed under house arrest to prevent them from bringing their petitions for economic redress to the National People's Congress. National laws also hamper the registration of AIDS organizations that represent PLWHAs, provide AIDS education programs, and fight continued AIDS stigma and discrimination.

AIDS AND LESSONS ABOUT THE HUMAN RIGHT TO HEALTH

AIDS in the developing world highlights crucial elements of the global human rights regime. The 2001 Declaration of Commitment on HIV/AIDS states that realizing all people's human rights and fundamental freedoms is essential to reduce vulnerability to HIV/AIDS and that respecting the human rights of PLWHAs is crucial for an effective response to the pandemic. At-risk groups such as IDUs, men who have sex with men, and sex workers have been particularly marginalized in the AIDS fight because of their legal and social status. AIDS in the developing world demonstrates the high cost of ignoring the economic and social rights of women. Legal, social, and political obstacles to women's access to education, health care, marriage choices, and control of their bodies have contributed to the growing gender bias in the pandemic. Because of their lack of power and the inability or unwillingness of states to protect their right to health, education, and survival, AIDS has had a large impact on children. AIDS has called attention to global inequality in access to medicine, and activists worldwide have used the language of human rights to demand ARVs for all the world's PLWHAs. In doing so, they have sought to reframe our understanding of public health in a neoliberal economy. In addition, the pandemic has demonstrated the link between good governance and health, with countries that ignore citizens' political rights negatively affecting the AIDS fight.

AIDS has changed the way that public-health officials view disease. The economic, political, and social structures of society that hamper the realization of individuals' rights to education, autonomy, marriage choice, and employment also limit their rights to health. Civil-society organizations have been crucial in linking health and human rights. This new paradigm has helped to contribute to increases in global spending on AIDS from $300 million in 1996 to $8.3 billion in 2005. This new view also has helped bring more attention to other diseases such as malaria and tuberculosis, and led to the development of public and private funding institutions such as the Clinton Foundation, the Bill & Melinda Gates Foundation, and the Global Fund to Fight AIDS, Tuberculosis and Malaria. Whether the commitment to a human rights approach to AIDS (and more broadly, health) can be sustained with increasing HIV infections, more people on ARVs, and an estimated $22 billion needed annually to fight AIDS in 2008 remains to be seen.

[*See also* Children's Convention (Convention on the Rights of the Child); Doctors without Borders; Right to Health and Health Care; Human Rights Watch; Intellectual Property; Sexual and Gender Diversity; Women: Convention on the Elimination of Discrimination against Women; Women: Women's Rights; World Health Organization; *and* Zimbabwe.]

BIBLIOGRAPHY

Barnett, Tony, and Alan Whiteside. *AIDS in the Twenty-First Century: Disease and Globalisation.* 2d ed. New York: Palgrave MacMillan, 2006.

Behrman, Greg. *The Invisible People: How the U.S. Has Slept Through the Global AIDS Pandemic, the Greatest Humanitarian Catastrophe of Our Time.* New York: Free Press, 2004.

Booth, Karen. *Local Women, Global Science: Fighting AIDS in Kenya.* Bloomington: Indiana University Press, 2004.

Cameron, Edwin. *Witness to AIDS.* New York: I. B. Tauris, 2005.

Campbell, Catherine. *"Letting Them Die": Why HIV/AIDS Prevention Programmes Fail.* Bloomington: Indiana University Press, 2003.

D'Adesky, Anne-Christine. *Moving Mountains: The Race to Treat Global AIDS.* New York: Verso, 2004.

Farmer, Paul. *Pathologies of Power: Health, Human Rights and the New War on the Poor.* Berkeley: University of California Press, 2005.

Harris, Paul, and Patricia Siplon, eds. *The Global Politics of AIDS: Suffering, Power, and the International Struggle for Public Health.* Boulder, Colo.: Lynne Rienner, 2007.

Human Rights Watch. "China: House Arrests Stifle HIV/AIDS Petitions." Press release, March 11, 2006. http://www.hrw.org/english/docs/2006/03/11/china12874.htm.

Human Rights Watch. *A Dose of Reality: Women's Rights in the Fight against HIV/AIDS.* Report for Human Rights Watch, March 21, 2005. http://www.hrw.org/english/docs/2005/03/21/africa10357_txt.htm.

Human Rights Watch. *The Less They Know, the Better: Abstinence-Only HIV/AIDS Programs in Uganda.* Report for Human Rights Watch, March 30, 2005. http://www.hrw.org/reports/2005/uganda0305.

Human Rights Watch. *Letting Them Fail: Government Neglect and the Right to Education for Children Affected by AIDS.* Report for Human Rights Watch, August 11, 2005. http://www.hrw.org/reports/2005/africa1005.

Human Rights Watch. *No Bright Future: Government Failures, Human Rights Abuses and Squandered Progress in the Fight Against AIDS in Zimbabwe.* Report for Human Rights Watch, July 28, 2006. http://www.hrw.org/reports/2006/zimbabwe0706.

Human Rights Watch. *Preventing the Further Spread of HIV/AIDS: The Essential Role of Human Rights.* Report for Human Rights Watch, January 12, 2006. http://www.hrw.org/wr2k6/hivaids/3.htm.

Human Rights Watch. *In the Shadow of Death: HIV/AIDS and Children's Rights in Kenya.* Report for Human Rights Watch, June 1, 2001. http://www.hrw.org/reports/2001/kenya.

Joint United Nations Programme on HIV/AIDS. *HIV-Related Stigma, Discrimination and Human Rights Violations: Case Studies of Successful Programmes.* Report for UNAIDS, 2005. http://www.data.unaids.org/publications/irc_pub06/JC999-HumRightsViol_en.pdf.

Joint United Nations Programme on HIV/AIDS. *Report on the Global AIDS Epidemic 2006.* http://www.unaids.org/en/HIV-data/2006GlobalReport/default.asp.

Patterson, Amy S. *The Politics of AIDS in Africa.* Boulder, Colo.: Lynne Rienner, 2006.

Patterson, Amy S., ed. *The African State and the AIDS Crisis.* Aldershot, U.K.: Ashgate Publishers, 2005.

Poku, Nana, and Alan Whiteside, eds. *The Political Economy of AIDS in Africa.* Aldershot, U.K.: Ashgate Publishers, 2004.

Stillwaggon, Eileen. *AIDS and the Ecology of Poverty.* New York: Oxford University Press, 2006.

United Nations General Assembly. *Declaration of Commitment on HIV/AIDS.* http://www.un.org/ga/aids/coverage/FinalDeclarationHIVAIDS.html.

United Nations Secretary-General. *Declaration of Commitment on HIV/AIDS: Five Years Later.* Report from the Secretary-General, March 24, 2006. http://data.unaids.org/pub/Report/2006/20060321_SGReport_GA_A60736_en.pdf.

United States Government Accountability Office. *Spending Requirement Presents Challenge for Allocating Prevention Funding under the President's Emergency Plan for AIDS Relief.* Report to Congressional Committees, April 2006. http://www.gao.gov/new.items/d06395.pdf.

Walker, Liz, Graeme Reid, and Morna Cornell. *Waiting to Happen: HIV/AIDS in South Africa.* Boulder, Colo.: Lynne Rienner, 2004.

Weiser, Sheri D., Michele Heisler, Karen Leiter, Fiona Percy-de Korte, Sheila Tlou, Sonya DeMonner, Nthabiseng Phaladze, David R. Bangsberg, and Vincent Iacopino. "Routine HIV Testing in Botswana: A Population-Based Study on Attitudes, Practices, and Human Rights Concerns." *PLOS Medicine* 3, no. 7 (2006): 1013–1022.

ALGERIAN WAR

by Rita Maran

The Algerian War was a major event in international relations and in human rights, and its lessons continue to be debated today. This entry first reviews some relevant history, and then addresses the general nature and course of the war. Special attention is paid to torture and terror, for the war saw major violations of human rights on both sides. The arrival of General Charles de Gaulle on the political scene and the ambiguity of his statements in favor of and against Algerian independence, ending in his decision in favor of an independent Algeria, are also discussed. This revolutionary war was fought with arms, unconventionally, on urban streets in Algeria, as well as without arms, unconventionally, in international diplomatic circles, including at the United Nations. Definitive figures for military and civilian casualties suffered by both sides, not only during the war but also in the related killings afterward, were not reliably recorded or maintained. Alistair Horne estimates one million Algerians and twenty thousand French were casualties of the war. The conclusion addresses the significance of the war for human rights.

BACKGROUND

Out of the French Revolution had come the Declaration of the Rights of Man and of the Citizen of 1789. The Declaration is the foundation of what is referred to in the French language as "les droits de l'homme" (the rights of man) and what in other languages is called "human rights." The Declaration narrowed the power of governments and strengthened the rights of individuals. Every French constitution since 1789 has reaffirmed the Declaration, and France thereafter prided itself on being one of the first nations to give legal standing to human rights.

The Declaration had been in existence almost forty-one years when on 14 June 1830 a French expeditionary corps led by Louis-Auguste-Victor de Bourmont landed in Sidi Ferruch, on the north coast of Algeria, and began bombardment of the nearby capital, Algiers. By 5 July the ruler of Algiers, the dey, had surrendered control to the French. A royal ordinance issued by King Louis-Philippe on 22 July 1834 defined Algeria as a French possession and ordered it to be under the rule of a governor-general, who would derive his power from the French minister of state for war. Civil and military duties in Algeria were assigned to a single commanding officer.

Four times larger than France, with uninhabited desert covering nine-tenths of its land, Algeria at the time of the French invasion had a population of at least 1.5 million Arabs who lived clustered in the hospitable land of the north. Over the following years, Thomas-Robert Bugeaud commanded French forces occupying Algeria, ending with the surrender of the ruler, the emir Abdelkader, in 1847. Bugeaud, referred to familiarly in French schoolbooks as "Père Bugeaud," proceeded with the "pacification" of Algeria by establishing an education system, roads, markets, hospitals, and other social and economic projects. The system of justice was administered by French and indigenous Muslim authorities, with one exception: Muslim tribunals were not granted the authority to pronounce the death penalty, for which the final authority remained in Paris.

France is divided into *départements* (departments). After Algeria's status in law was established in 1848, it was officially designated as three departments of France: Algiers, Constantine, and Oran. The Sahara Desert was designated separately. The Mediterranean Sea on the north coast linked France's departments in Europe and North Africa. French laws and decrees of 14 July 1865 and 26 June 1889 granted French nationality to indigenous Muslims. In the late nineteenth and early twentieth centuries, driven by economic and agricultural failures in Europe, tens of thousands of Europeans from France, Malta, Corsica, Spain, and Italy migrated to Algeria.

In 1936 the Blum-Violette Bill requested the French National Assembly to grant Muslim Algerians the political rights of French citizens, allowing them to vote in French national elections, while not modifying their civil rights. The bill and its assimilationist approach failed, making peaceful coexistence between *colons* (European settlers) and indigenous Algerians more problematic. Subsequently, the Statute of Algeria of 1947 affirmed French citizenship for all Algerians. Algerian-born Muslims were legally entitled to the same rights as those of French citizens in mainland France, but in practice Algerian-born Muslims' rights were more similar to those of people in French colonies than to those of French citizens in mainland France.

Muslim discontent with French rule precipitated a crisis in 1945 in Sétif, a market town in the Kabyle Mountains of northeast Algeria that was considered one of the main centers of radical nationalist activities. Ten years before the outbreak of the Algerian War, large-scale exchanges of gunfire between local Muslims and French gendarmes had been occurring in the region, raising the French government's concern about the possibility of a general uprising.

On 8 May 1945, V-E Day (Victory in Europe Day) celebrations of the end of World War II, arranged by Muslim Algerians and authorized by the French authorities, were held at a monument to Muslim war dead in Sétif. When the gathering turned into a rally for Algerian independence, which the authorities had not authorized, violence broke out between the Muslim crowd and the police. After Muslims went on to kill over a hundred European civilians, French troops were called in, killing thousands of Muslims in reprisals. The French government's estimate of the number of Muslim dead was 1,005, while historians such as Alistair Horne and George Armstrong Kelly estimated the number starting at six thousand and rising as high as fifty thousand. The Sétif killings added a strong dimension of militancy to the burgeoning Algerian nationalism.

ALGERIAN NATIONALIST LEADERSHIP

From the late 1920s on, Muslim Algerian nationalists, less and less willing to be ruled from Paris, organized revolutionary movements to seek Algeria's independence. During World War II Algerian nationalism had been stimulated by patriotic radio messages emanating from Washington, London, and Moscow reporting on Allied troops fighting for liberty and equality. Ninety percent of young Algerian soldiers who joined the fighting in that war were Muslim, deployed mainly in frontline positions. The other 10 percent, mostly of European descent, were employed in behind-the-lines support duties.

The views of the younger generation of Muslim Algerians diverged from those of the older generation.

While both generations had been raised in Algeria, the older generation had little experience of the world outside Algeria and was more at ease within the dominant French culture that surrounded them.

Intellectual and political leaders.

The ideology underlying France's invasions of Africa in the nineteenth century was the *mission civilisatrice* (civilizing mission). Although the civilizing mission defied formal definition, it nonetheless encompassed what France assumed as a responsibility—namely, to contribute what France identified as the benefits of its civilization to peoples whose lands it had invaded and occupied. Those benefits included not only new roads, hospitals, and schools but also the French language and social, cultural, ethnic, and political mores.

These French influences shaped the development of Algerian revolutionaries such as Ferhat Abbas, who was born in Algeria in 1899 to French-acculturated landowners and was educated in the French system. Abbas was broadly representative of Muslim Algerians who identified strongly with French culture and used the French language. Few Algerian nationalists of that generation were accustomed to the use of Arabic. Abbas sought at first to achieve nonviolently an assimilated Algeria having greater autonomy within a French community. In 1936 he wrote, "Had I discovered the Algerian nation, I would be a nationalist. . . . However, I will not die for the Algerian nation, because it does not exist" (Horne, p. 40).

After the massacre at Sétif, Abbas's political views altered, becoming increasingly sympathetic to the idea of an Algerian state. His initiatives for organizing intellectuals began to reflect his view that colonialism, being born of violence, must be met with violence. He disavowed his early advocacy of nonviolence and reappraised ways to combat what he defined as the structural violence inherent in colonialism. Abbas continued working for better conditions for Algerians and organized the Algerian Muslim Students Association and the Union Démocratique du Manifeste Algérien (Democratic Union of the Algerian Manifesto). He is the author of *Guerre et révolution d'Algérie* (The Algerian War and Revolution, 1962).

Influenced by the U.S. president Franklin D. Roosevelt's speeches on rights and freedom, Abbas brought together influential Algerian professionals, who signed *Le manifeste du peuple algérien* (The Manifesto of the Algerian People) in 1943. The manifesto, organized by Abbas and Ahmed Messali Hadj, called for equal participation of Muslims in government; the abolition of colonization; the granting of Algeria's own constitution guaranteeing all rights and freedoms; the restoration of the sovereign, democratic, and social Algerian state within the framework of Islamic principles; and the preservation of all fundamental freedoms without distinction as to race or religion.

Abbas's fellow organizer Messali Hadj was born in 1898 and raised in Paris among Marxists. As a young leader of the Parti du Peuple Algérien (Algerian People's Party; PPA), Mouvement National Algérien (National Algerian Movement; MNA), Union Nationale des Musulmans Nord-Africaine (National Union of North African Muslims), and later of the Mouvement pour le Triomphe des Libertés Démocratiques (Movement for the Victory of Democratic Freedoms; MTLD), Hadj organized support among poor, less-educated Muslim Algerians.

Ahmed Ben Bella, born in 1918, was among the next generation of Algerian nationalists whose education was shaped by the theories of Abbas and Hadj. One of the founders of the FLN, he later became the first president of the Algerian nation. In reaction to Sétif, Ben Bella expressed impatience with manifestos and demonstrated an eagerness for action, saying "the horrors [at Sétif] . . . succeeded in persuading me of the only path, Algeria for the Algerians" (Horne, p. 28).

Saadi Yacef, another of the younger generation of Algerian nationalists, born in 1928, fought in Europe and returned to Algeria ready to fight again, if necessary, to bring about an independent Algerian state. Yacef played a character based on himself in the Gillo Pontecorvo film *Battle of Algiers* (1966), which was inspired by his book, written in French, *Souvenirs de la bataille d'Alger, decembre 1956–septembre 1957* (Memories of the Battle of Algiers, December 1956–September 1957, 1962).

Frantz Fanon, a psychiatrist born in Martinique in 1925, wrote *Les damnés de la terre* (The Wretched of the Earth, 1961), which chronicled the repressed anger and violence of colonized peoples. Although not an Algerian, Fanon helped give identity to the nascent Algerian nationalism he perceived around him, as exemplified in his *L'an cinq de la révolution Algérienne* (1959; English translation, *A Dying Colonialism*, 1965). He expressed concern that France's benign social and economic improvements might weaken Algerians' drive for independence. Further, he argued that colonized peoples fighting to win a war of liberation must "do so cleanly, without 'barbarity,'" and leave it to the world to judge that "the European nation that practices torture is a blighted nation" (*A Dying Colonialism*, p. 24).

Organizations.

The Comité Révolutionnaire pour l'Unité et l'Action (Revolutionary Committee for Unity and Action; CRUA) was founded in March 1954, several months before the outbreak of the war. The CRUA's goal was to unite the various nationalist movements in an armed insurrection and to internationalize the conflict. Led by a collective of nine dedicated revolutionaries—Hocine Aït Ahme, Ahmed Ben Bella, Mostefa Ben Boulaid, Larbi Ben M'hidi, Rabah Bitat, Mohamed Boudiaf, Mourad Didouche, Mohamed Khider, and Belkacem Krim—the CRUA subdivided the northern region of Algeria into six autonomous sectors, or *wilayas*, each with its local leader and troops. On 10 October 1954 the CRUA dissolved and became part of the Front de Libération Nationale (National Liberation Front; FLN). As other nationalist parties began to dissolve, most pledged support to the FLN. The Parti Communiste Algérien (Algerian Communist Party; PCA), founded in 1924, was an exception; its commitment was to the international Communist movement, and it did not join the FLN.

The FLN assumed responsibility for mobilizing the population and exercising strict control over activities it prohibited Muslim Algerians from engaging in, such as working for Europeans, smoking, attending the cinema, appearing before French justice systems, and having their children attend French educational institutions. Failure of Muslim Algerians to comply with those restrictions often resulted in their physical mutilation by FLN soldiers.

THE WAR

At the outbreak of the revolution there were 9 million Algerians: 8 million Muslim Algerians and 1 million European Algerians, mainly of French, Spanish, and Italian origin. The majority of settlers owned their own businesses or worked as civil servants for the French. A small but influential number of *colons* spearheaded effective lobbying in the French National Assembly. Their strategies to obtain financial and political benefits were generally successful, influencing France's policy in Algeria.

1954–1955.

On All Saints' Day, 1 November 1954, a coordinated series of attacks by the FLN marked the beginning of an armed insurrection against the French. FLN policy prioritized opposition to colonialism and the creation of a sovereign, democratic Algerian state. The FLN issued a proclamation launching what it called "the true revolutionary struggle." It called on all Algerians to rally to the cause of Algerian independence through "restoration of the Algerian state, sovereign, democratic, and social, within the framework of the principles of Islam." In an unusual action for a liberation group, but one that foreshadowed its future strategy, it listed as an objective the assertion, "through the framework of the United Nations Charter, of our active sympathy towards all nations that may support our liberating action" (Horne, p. 95).

An unspecified number of soldiers, estimated to be between seven hundred and three thousand, were in service in the Armée de Libération Nationale (National Liberation Army; ALN), the military arm of the FLN, in 1954. Only a few hundred were trained, armed, and ready to fight. After the All Saints' Day attacks, young Muslim Algerians, now eager to achieve an independent Algeria, readily joined the ALN.

The Algerian jurist Mohammed Bedjaoui characterized the ALN as "a regular, national and belligerent army in law" (p. 53), in accordance with international legal standards. Bedjaoui, who in later years served as president of the International Court of Justice in The Hague, further stated, "When an insurrectional movement has the goal of liberation from colonialism, it can be nothing other than legitimate both politically and juridically." The FLN thus began a process of establishing legal legitimacy for a revolutionary war through identification of the war's foundations in international law.

By the beginning of 1955, the military objectives of the French army in Algeria were twofold. First, the program of pacification was to be expanded, establishing contact with the indigenous populations to regain their confidence and obtain political and military information about the revolutionaries. The second objective was to achieve a military victory over the FLN after finding and destroying its core personnel, property, and support elements.

While around fifty-four thousand French forces were in Algeria in November 1954, not more than thirty-five hundred were considered by the commander in chief, General Paul Cherrière, to be combat-ready. As a result, reservists who had been released from duty in Indochina were recalled, and thousands of new conscripts were drafted. By mid-1956 reinforcements brought the total number of French soldiers and auxiliaries in Algeria to nearly half a million.

In August 1955 the FLN unleashed a planned, savage attack on the French civilian population near Philippeville, an easterly Algerian coastal town. The immediate retaliation by the French army and local *pieds noirs* (literally "black feet," a term commonly used to describe European émigrés in Algeria) was no less barbarous, with government sources claiming that 71 Europeans and 1,273 Muslim Algerians had died. The FLN cited names and addresses of 12,000 Muslims who they claimed had died.

Jacques Soustelle, appointed governor-general of Algeria in 1955 by Prime Minister Pierre Mendès-France and serving until early 1956, reflected a growing despair in France about the possibility of achieving peace if, as it appeared, victory was unattainable. Soustelle had forbidden the application by French authorities of collective responsibility, under which entire groups could be indiscriminately subjected to reprisals whether or not everyone in the group had participated in the wrongdoing in question. He further ordered that "police operations . . . interrogations, etc., must be conducted without brutality" (Horne, p. 113). Soustelle's policy called for finding and punishing only the specific individuals responsible for identified criminal acts. However, in direct contradiction of Soustelle's order, his subordinate, General Cherrière, ordered troops around Philippeville to apply collective responsibility vigorously. After the FLN attacks of August 1955 the French soldiers followed Cherrière's orders, and the reprisal was immediate and severe; almost every Muslim found in the region was summarily executed, and several villages were eradicated.

Germaine Tillion, a French anthropologist and social worker, had been authorized by Soustelle to set up structural reforms in the Algerian countryside, to include improved sanitation, education, and living conditions. As atrocities by both sides increased during 1955 and 1956, Tillion spoke out publicly about the "deadly sequence: terrorism, reprisals, executions, torture" rife in those years. In *France and Algeria: Complementary Enemies* (1961), Tillion described her frank discussion with the FLN leader Saadi Yacef in 1957 about torture and terrorism being carried out by both the French and the Algerians. To Tillion's sad but firm statement to Yacef, "You are murderers," he replied "Yes, Madame Tillion, we are murderers" (p. 35).

The armed buildup on both sides intensified. Muslim Algerians who were not actively supportive of the FLN were maimed and killed by FLN terrorists. FLN terrorist acts against the French were met by the French army's increasingly brutal acts in return.

1956–1962.

In June 1956 the French government executed two members of the FLN, resulting in immediate reprisals by that organization. A number of European Algerians were randomly shot dead on the streets of Algiers. In response, hard-liner French Algerians planted a bomb in the Casbah of Algiers in August 1956, killing over seventy Muslims. The FLN retaliated in September with bombings during a busy hour at the Milk-Bar and La Cafétéria, two cafés popular with young *pieds noirs*. Three people died and more than fifty were injured. Governor-General Robert Lacoste called in military reinforcements. The Battle of Algiers was underway.

General Jacques Massu was assigned on 7 January 1957 to serve as both military commander in chief and governor-general of Algiers. He ordered the Tenth Parachute Division under his command to comb the mosques systematically, clear out suspected terrorists, and, if deemed necessary in order to obtain information, to torture suspects. Massu was credited with having captured or killed most of the FLN leaders by October 1957, bringing the conflict to a close. In his two books, *La vraie bataille d'Alger* (The Real Battle of Algiers, 1971) and *Le torrent et la digue* (The Flood and the Dike, 1972), Massu gave an unabashed description of ordering torture in good conscience, in the course of fulfilling his duties.

By October 1957, through widespread use of torture of Muslim Algerians, meant to frighten the population into submission and sometimes resulting in information about the rebels, Massu's forces had captured or killed most of the leaders of the FLN. The Battle of Algiers came to a close with the disbanding of Algerian revolutionary groups. The revolutionary uprising appeared at that juncture to have ended in a victory for France. Had France lost the Battle of Algiers, its loss of all of Algeria would have seemed inevitable. In fact, the apparent victory of Massu's paratroops was reversed by the FLN's ongoing policy of politicization at the international level of the struggle for independence.

Despite their loss in the Battle of Algiers, the FLN continued to fight. The ALN grew to a total strength of about 30,000, with another 30,000 irregulars operating in the interior. Of those 60,000, the French claimed to have killed or captured over 25,000 in the first half of 1958. The FLN launched a political "second front," founding the Gouvernement Provisoire de la République Algérienne (Provisional Government of the Algerian Republic; GPRA) on 19 September 1958. The GPRA acted as a government-in-exile for an Algerian state that the FLN was dedicated, through both military and diplomatic means, to bringing into existence.

In January 1960 a German newspaper published an interview with General Massu in which he criticized President de Gaulle's policy of self-determination for Algeria and said that many of his officers would not unconditionally execute de Gaulle's orders. Massu was summarily dismissed by de Gaulle, which led to a protest of the dismissal by the settlers. The "journées des barricades" (days of the barricades) took place along Algiers's main thoroughfares from 24 to 31 January 1960. For the first time French troops were operating under competing loyalties to different commanders, and French were firing upon French. The French military command invoked a state of siege.

In April 1961 dissatisfied French army field commanders—Generals Maurice Challe, Edmond Jouhaud, André Zeller, and Raoul Salan—created the Organisation de l'Armée Secrète (Secret Army Organization; OAS) in order to mount military opposition to any weakening of Algeria's status as part of France. They launched a coup attempt to overthrow de Gaulle, which failed, although the OAS continued to operate in Algeria. *Colons* strongly supported the OAS's pursuit of a military victory, which they agreed was necessary in order to keep Algeria French. However, on 3 July 1962 de Gaulle recognized Algeria as an independent state. Algeria was admitted to the United Nations on 9 October 1962. According to the French government, during the Algerian War more than 300,000 Muslim Algerians and more than 25,000 French were killed.

RESPONSES TO TORTURE AND TERRORISM

Torture had been abolished in France in 1789; it carried the penalty of death for anyone found guilty of committing it. In the 1940s and 1950s reports of torture were noted on police records, in government documents, and by the counterespionage sections of the police, the Direction de la Sécurité du Térritoire (Homeland Security Administration). During a National Assembly session in 1947, newly elected Muslim members recounted their personal experience of torture.

In July 1954 the nine-year-long Indochina war, in which the French army had been defeated, concluded with the signing of the Geneva Peace Agreements. Four months later, the revolutionary war in Algeria broke out. At that moment in time, the French nation, both military and civilian, having just expended great resources of personnel and matériel, was slow in producing the effort required for waging another war. As a result, the incipient Algerian revolution received less than full attention and was referred to somewhat dismissively in France as "les évènements" (the events). Under the cover of this relative neglect, the extremes of brutality and torture practiced by the French army in Indochina were transferred to the French army's practices in Algeria.

Reports and criticisms.

Between 1954 and January 1957 the phenomenon of torture was acknowledged in reports in the official French parliamentary record, the *Journal officiel* (Official Journal). Jacques Fonlupt-Espéraber, a member of the Conseil d'État (the highest administrative court), stated in the National Assembly in 1955, "In 1950 (I have documents to prove this), eighty complaints of acts of torture were laid before the public prosecutor. I have no evidence that these complaints produced the smallest result" (p. 4517). Prime Minister Guy Mollet reminded the National Assembly in March 1957 that France was "the nation of the rights of man," even as he downplayed the accuracy of accusations of torture against the government and the army (*Journal officiel,* 27 March 1957, p. 1911).

François Mitterrand, the minister of the interior from 1954 to early 1955, facing growing numbers of authenticated reports of torture, ordered an internal governmental report on breaches of the law and appointed Inspector-General Roger Wuillaume to carry out the investigation. The Wuillaume report, delivered on 2 March 1955, confirmed that previous reports of torture were indeed true, that torture had been in regular usage for a very long time, that its necessity and usefulness in gathering information had long since been proven, and that it was too late to prohibit "all but legal procedures." Wuillaume therefore recommended authorizing extralegal procedures. In addition, he recommended letters of congratulation be sent to those who had performed illegal acts, to relieve any sense of wrongdoing they might have.

Maître Paul Teitgen, a lawyer and respected Catholic intellectual and the prefecture secretary-general in Algiers, was a major force behind a different report in 1957. In April of that year Teitgen helped establish the Commission de Sauvegarde des Droits et des Libertés Individuels (Committee for the Safeguard of Individual Rights and Liberties) to investigate complaints of torture and other abuses prohibited under Article 5 of the Universal Declaration of Human Rights of 1948, the First Convention of the four Geneva Conventions of 1949, and Article 186 of the French Penal Code. The committee's final report, published in full in the newspaper *Le Monde* on 14 December 1957, confirmed the acts of torture. Teitgen

resigned in September 1957 because he refused to remain silent about the torture taking place within his jurisdiction.

Books by the military.

In France's internal military affairs, growing unrest concerning torture was exemplified by the actions of an officer under General Massu's command. General Jacques Pâris de Bollardière, an illustrious career officer in the French army, received orders from General Massu in 1957 for the torture of prisoners. Bollardière refused to carry out the order, asked to be relieved of his command, and returned the prestigious Medal of the Legion of Honor to the French government, explaining that moral and religious principles forbade him from committing torture or causing it to be committed. Bollardière wrote an autobiography, *Bataille d'Alger, bataille de l'homme* (Battle of Algiers, Battle of Man, 1972), and went on to become a leading figure in Le Mouvement Altérnatif Nonviolent (Nonviolent Alternative Movement; MAN), a grassroots nonviolent organization active throughout France.

A body of literature about the war was produced by others who also served in the military in Algeria. Jean-Jacques Servan-Schreiber, editor of *L'Express,* who served with honor in World War II and again in the Algerian War, wrote *Lieutenant en Algérie* (Lieutenant in Algeria, 1957), an insider's view of French soldiers' rationalizations for the necessity of torture. Jules Roy, a French Algerian playwright and former colonel in the French Air Force, wrote in *The War in Algeria* (1961), "The [French Intelligence Agency] seizes men and tortures them. The FLN does the same thing." Colonel Roger Trinquier's *Modern Warfare* (1964) described the need for torture in fighting terrorists, and Bernard Fall's introduction to that book cites Trinquier's belief that "torture is the particular bane of the terrorist." Pierre Leulliette, in *St. Michael and the Dragon* (1961), wrote about the impossible goals laid out for French soldiers, who were ordered to achieve both a military victory and pacification, and in addition to use methods including torture.

Among French soldiers serving in Algeria, a number voiced concern about obeying orders for torture that they feared might conflict with religious and moral precepts, as well as with the Nuremberg principles developed after World War II. As cited by General de Bollardière, some said, "If one day there is a new Nuremberg Tribunal, we shall all be condemned" (Bollardière, p. 139; translation by the author).

French intellectuals.

Left-wing intellectuals criticized the government for failing to publicly condemn and end the policy and practice of torture and for failing to bring those responsible to justice. Right-wing intellectuals criticized the left-wing critics, declaring their criticism detrimental to the morale of the French army and the nation. French Catholics on both the right and the left faced a dilemma: on the one hand, they considered themselves bound by religious and moral precepts to criticize the practice of torture by their government; on the other hand, they felt the pressure of their duty as good citizens to refrain from criticizing the government, even when the situation involved the extreme of torture.

The Catholic press had published reports of torture by the French army during the war in Indochina in 1949 in *Témoignage chrétien* (Christian Testimony). It did so again in the Algerian War, in 1957, in a special edition, *Müller dossier* (Müller File). The Catholic Comité de Résistance Spirituelle (Committee of Spiritual Resistance) published *Des rappelés témoignent* (Reservists Offer Testimony, 1957), a collection of letters and statements by soldiers critical of the French army's conduct of the war. The published testimony expressed soldiers' profound distress about the torture they had committed or had seen others commit.

Jean-Paul Sartre, troubled by the institutionalization of colonialism and the racism he perceived in the Algerian War, wrote the play *The Condemned of Altona* (1959). It expressed Sartre's moral outrage at the oppression of Muslim Algerians and the torture committed by the French military. In sympathy with Algerian nationalists, Sartre wrote a preface to Henri Alleg's *La question* and to Frantz Fanon's *Les damnés de la terre*. Along with Simone de Beauvoir and other prominent intellectuals, he signed the "Manifesto of the 121," subtitled "Declaration on the Right of Insubordination in the Algerian War." With other writers, artists, scientists, and left-wing political parties, he supported the right of conscripts to refuse to serve in the Algerian war.

Pierre-Henri Simon, an influential Catholic scholar, condemned torture on moral and religious grounds. In his book *Contre la torture* (Against torture, 1957), Simon considered that public criticism of the torture carried out under the cloak of the French government should in fact be held up as a positive achievement. It proved, said Simon, France's ethical adherence to the highest principles of a civilized society, which would not countenance gross violations of human rights. Georges Bidault, a right-leaning

deputy of the National Assembly and former prime minister, who opposed torture and yet believed in the legitimacy, if not the necessity, of France's continued presence in Algeria, was moved by Simon's moral argument.

At the time of the Battle of Algiers in 1957, the French newspapers *Le Monde, Esprit, L'Express,* and *Le Figaro* published firsthand reports from victims of torture, as well as intellectuals' writings on the battle and the torture. The philosopher Paul Ricoeur, who wrote frequently for *Esprit*, opposed the war but believed that encouraging draft avoidance and desertion from the army was a serious danger to the preservation of the state. The Nobel laureate François Mauriac wrote "Bloc-notes" for *L'Express* in 1955 and 1956, proposing that the government institute practical remedies through structural reforms in Algeria to address unemployment, that public education be improved, and that the French army and police be prevented from torturing.

In *La raison d'état* (Reasons of State, 1962) and *La torture dans la République* (1963; English translation, *Torture: Cancer of Democracy—France and Algeria, 1954–1962*), the esteemed historian Pierre Vidal-Naquet chronicled and documented the incremental institutionalization of torture in state policy and state practice and raised critical moral and legal questions surrounding torture involving officers of the state. Alec Mellor's *La torture: son histoire, son abolition, sa réapparition au xxe siècle* (Torture: Its History, Abolition, and Reappearance in the Twentieth Century, 1949) noted with regret the need to enact additional prohibitions against torture, since despite Article 5 of the Universal Declaration of Human Rights, the use of torture continued.

Literature by and about torture survivors.

Djamila Boupacha (1962), a book coauthored by Simone de Beauvoir and Maître Gisèle Halimi, a member of the Paris Bar, chronicles the story of the young Algerian Muslim woman, Djamila Boupacha, who was accused of being an FLN agent and was forced to confess under torture. Boupacha brought a case against the French government and was represented in court by Halimi. One of the best-known books dealing with torture during the Algerian War, *Djamila Boupacha* drew governmental and public attention to torture as an institutionalized phenomenon.

Henri Alleg, born in 1921, a *pied noir* and member of the Algerian Communist Party, was the editor of the daily Algerian newspaper *Alger républicain* from 1950 until 1955, when it was banned by the government. Alleg was arrested in June 1957 and charged with endangering the safety of the state. His memoir, *La question* (The Question, 1958), seized by the French government in March 1958, graphically describes the tortures to which he was subjected, including having electrodes attached to his body and water forcibly pumped into his stomach. The account shocked the public and marked a turning point for many in France who had remained ignorant, willfully or not, of torture being committed by their government.

Maurice Audin, born in 1932, another Algerian of French ancestry, was a professor at the University of Algiers, a member of the Algerian Communist Party, and a sympathizer with the FLN program of decolonization via revolution. His death while in French custody in June 1957 was widely believed to have resulted from torture. The Comité Maurice Audin (Maurice Audin Committee), founded in his memory in 1960, reprinted testimony, entitled *Sans commentaire* (No Comment, 1961), taken from actual court cases involving torture.

Djamal Amrani, born in 1935 into a Muslim Algerian family that identified itself as loyal to France, wrote in *Le témoin* (The Witness, 1960) of the painful aftereffects of torture that he suffered. Nevertheless, he expressed gratitude to the members of the French left who had rallied around him.

PRESIDENT DE GAULLE AND THE SHIFT IN FRENCH POLICY

France's Fourth Republic (1946–1958) governed under the seventh constitution in force since 1830. In the four years from 1954 to 1958 France had six prime ministers, whose short terms of office made for an unstable situation. After the collapse of the Fourth Republic, the National Assembly recalled Charles de Gaulle to power as president on 1 June 1958, in the expectation that his return would provide much-needed stability to the French government.

Later that month, de Gaulle traveled to Algiers to calm and reinspire the population. He declared that in Algeria everyone was French, with all the rights and obligations of the French, and ended with the now classic phrase "Je vous ai compris" (I have understood you). This ambiguous statement seemed to convince different populations with diametrically opposed views that he sided with their wishes. De Gaulle spoke often of keeping Algeria French, as desired by the *colons* and the army; he also spoke often of granting limited autonomy to Algeria within a federal community, a talking point designed to placate the nationalists seeking independence. In a constitutional referendum on the Fifth Republic in September 1958, in which the relationship between the metropole and its outlying territories was redefined, Algeria continued to be formally included as part of France. However, in a speech a few months later, de Gaulle declared Algeria's right to self-determination.

Speaking to the nation on television on 29 January 1960, de Gaulle called for pledges of loyalty from the troops, from the *colons*, and from all French people. To that end, he undertook a "tournée des popotes" (tour of army officers' messes) in Algeria in March 1960, with the purpose of raising French soldiers' morale and loyalty, assuring the continuing support of the *colons*, and raising additional support for a successful end to the war.

Facing criticism from other countries, including Great Britain and the United States, about France's colonialist policies, de Gaulle again repositioned himself so as not to be a victim of Algeria's looming independence. On 14 June 1960 he indicated his willingness to negotiate with the FLN, indirectly intimating that Algeria would in the near future be governed by Algerians. In Algeria a growing exodus of *colons* began, many moving to Europe. In November 1960 de Gaulle made the first mention of "l'Algérie Algérienne" (Algerian Algeria).

In a referendum on 8 January 1961 the French public overwhelmingly endorsed de Gaulle's call for Algerian self-determination, for which he claimed to have been progressively preparing them. The French government immediately began collaborating with the Provisional Government of the Algerian Republic (GPRA). On 19 March 1962 negotiations at Evian between the French government and the GPRA concluded with agreements that called for a vote by the Algerian population on Algerian independence. The agreements also covered four main objectives: a cease-fire, Algeria's independence, guarantees for the minority of European origin, and French-Algerian cooperation. The cease-fire was declared at Evian the next day. On 1 July 1962, in keeping with the Evian agreements, a referendum was put before the Algerian population, which favored independence by a vote of 5,993,754 to 16,478, with 10 percent of the population (mainly *pieds noirs*) abstaining.

The new Algerian government made provisions for the security of the French minority as well as for others who wished to go on living in Algeria. Thousands of Muslim Algerians who had worked as civilians or soldiers for the French before and during the war, and who either chose to remain in Algeria or could not find a way to leave, were left to face a problematic future in nationalist Algeria.

INTERNATIONAL DEVELOPMENTS

The inaugural conference of the Non-Aligned Movement, initially comprising twenty-nine newly decolonized Asian and African governments, was held in Bandung, Indonesia, in 1955. The GPRA participated in that and subsequent Non-Aligned Movement conferences as an unofficial delegate with observer status. Although an Algerian government had not come into existence, the conference participants unanimously adopted Algeria's motion declaring its right to independence, citing Articles 1, 55, and 73 of the UN Charter. Algerian independence became a rallying point for the Non-Aligned Movement, this being the first time a subject people who did not control any of the territory they claimed had declared independence and had proceeded to win international recognition that led to independence.

In 1955, at the request of thirteen Asian and African countries, the UN secretary-general Dag Hammarskjöld included a new item, "The Question of Algeria," on the agenda at the General Assembly's tenth session. The French government protested the agenda item, saying the rebellion going on at that moment was a domestic matter, and it called for compliance with Article 2(7) of the UN Charter, which asserts that "nothing . . . shall authorize the United Nations to intervene in matters which are essentially within the domestic jurisdiction of any state." The French government further stated that since Algerians were formally part of the French state, every French person was already entitled to the full exercise of rights. The French government's final point was that Algeria was not a non-self-governing territory and therefore was not subject to regulation under Chapter 11 of the charter, the Declaration Regarding Non-Self-Governing Territories.

When, on 8 February 1958, the French military bombarded Sakiet Sidi Youssef, a Tunisian border village being used by the Algerian dissidents as a base for operations against the French, the incident was internationalized by the GPRA, who brought it forward for attention at the United Nations. The fourth annual discussion on Algeria in the General Assembly in December 1958 ended with a resolution calling for negotiations between the "two parties." The French government considered the phrase "two parties" to imply equal and legitimate standing for the GPRA, and it therefore did not find the negotiations acceptable. After "The Question of Algeria" had appeared as an item on the agenda of the General Assembly for five years, the General Assembly formally recognized the right of the Algerian people to self-determination and independence.

At the United Nations as well as at international conferences, Mohammed Bedjaoui, who served as legal counselor to the GPRA, promulgated innovative international norms defining the revolution's legal standing. Bedjaoui referred to the right of peoples to self-determination as recognized in Article 1 and Article 55 of the UN Charter, and declared that the charter "confirmed the legal character of decolonization by the very fact that it has laid down the various stages of the process" (p. 11). In the anticolonialist atmosphere prevalent in the General Assembly in that period, national delegations sympathetic to Algerian independence referred to the same UN Charter articles, which constituted the basis of their support for Algeria's independence.

The GPRA named Ferhat Abbas as its first prime minister in 1958 and sent a note to all foreign chancelleries defining the GPRA as the sole representative of Algeria. It requested recognition of the Algerian state and government under the principle that these "were not new legal entities. It was less a question of recognizing a new State than of confirming the legal resurrection of a preexisting State" (Bedjaoui, p. 15). The GPRA's efficiency in lobbying at the United Nations, and in the use of UN mechanisms and procedures in making the case for Algeria's right to self-determination, resulted in recognition of the Algerian state and government by twenty-five countries in 1961, nineteen of them de jure and six de facto.

LEGACY

After the war, the film *The Battle of Algiers* (1966), directed by the Italian filmmaker Gillo Pontecorvo and based on a screenplay by Saadi Yacef, graphically presented to audiences around the world the nature and ferocity of contemporary revolutionary warfare, fought not on a conventional battlefield but in an indigenous people's alleyways and homes. The film shocked the conscience of international audiences with its vivid reenactments of French paratroops' use of torture and of the FLN's terrorist attacks.

The Algerian War had a profound impact on international relations as well as on French, Algerian, and other societies' intellectual opinion. The war was an important part of the larger and longer decolonization process, from which Algeria differed by making its case for self-determination based on the authority of legal norms rather than resorting mainly to military force. Initiatives to that end took place in diplomatic as well as military settings.

In addition to Algeria's independence and France's defeat in spite of its early victory in the Battle of Algiers, one outcome of the war was the recognition of a people's right to national self-determination, laid out in Article 1 of the International Covenant on Economic, Social, and Cultural Rights of 1966 and again in Article 1 of the International Covenant on Civil and Political Rights of 1966.

The Algerian War also led to a continuing debate about the efficacy and necessity of torture and about ways for governments to deal with terrorists who by definition are nonstate actors operating outside the ambit of state-based international law. The FLN employed much terror, in particular in attacks on civilians, and the French side used much torture, authorized at times at high government levels. One school of thought maintains that the Battle of Algiers shows the effectiveness of torture and inhuman or degrading interrogation, leading a number of French authors to defend the practice. Another school of thought finds that the French won the Battle of Algiers not so much through use of torture but more through the ability to "pacify" an area and use information it obtained from the public. The debate continues in the face of growing international agreement about the absolute nature of the prohibition of torture and, conversely, in the face of frequent international disregard for actual implementation of the prohibition.

There is no doubt that the Algerian War tested severely the application of standards of both international human rights law and international humanitarian law (laws of war). Among scholars and policy makers of Algeria and France, and indeed of other past or presently troubled countries, the applicability of the war and its brutal history to later events continues to produce a rich and disturbing legacy.

[*See also* Colonialism; French Revolution; North Africa; Terrorism; *and* Torture: International Law.]

BIBLIOGRAPHY

Abbas, Ferhat. *Guerre et révolution d'Algérie*. Paris: R. Juilliard, 1962.

Alleg, Henri. *The Question*. Translated by John Calder. Lincoln: University of Nebraska Press, 2006.

Beauvoir, Simone de, and Gisèle Halimi. *Djamila Boupacha*. Translated by Peter Green. New York: Macmillan, 1962.

Bedjaoui, Mohammed. *La révolution algérienne et le droit*. Brussels, Belgium: International Association of Democratic Lawyers, 1961.

Bollardière, Jacques Pâris de. *Bataille d'Alger, bataille de l'homme*. Paris: Desclée de Brouwer, 1972.

Connelly, Matthew James. *A Diplomatic Revolution: Algeria's Fight for Independence and the Origins of the Post–Cold War Era*. Oxford and New York: Oxford University Press, 2002.

Fanon, Frantz. *A Dying Colonialism*. Translated by Haakon Chevalier. New York: Grove, 1965.

Greenberg, Eldon Van Cleef. "Law and the Conduct of the Algerian Revolution." *Harvard International Law Journal* 11 (Winter 1970): 37–72.

Horne, Alistair. *A Savage War of Peace: Algeria, 1954–1962*. New York: New York Review of Books, 2006.

Journal officiel de la république Française: Assemblée nationale. 2d session, March 27, 1957.

Journal officiel de la république Française: Assemblée nationale. 3d session, July 29, 1955.

Kelly, George Armstrong. *Lost Soldiers: The French Army and Empire in Crisis, 1847–1962*. Cambridge, Mass.: M.I.T. Press, 1965.

Lacouture, Jean. *De Gaulle*. Translated by Patrick O'Brian and Alan Sheridan. 2 vols. New York: W.W. Norton, 1990.

Massu, Jacques. *La vraie bataille d'Algers*. Paris: Plon, 1971.

Milgram, Stanley. *Obedience to Authority: An Experimental View*. New York: Harper and Row, 1974.

Newman, Frank, and David Weissbrodt. *International Human Rights: Law, Policy, and Process*. 2d ed. Cincinnati, Ohio: Anderson, 1996.

O'Balance, Edgar. *The Algerian Insurrection, 1954–62*. London: Faber and Faber, 1967.

Rejali, Darius. *Torture and Democracy*. Princeton, N.J.: Princeton University Press, 2007.

Saadi, Yacef. *Souvenirs de la bataille d'Alger, décembre 1956–septembre 1957*. Paris: R. Juilliard, 1962.

Tillion, Germaine. *France and Algeria: Complementary Enemies*. Translated by Richard Howard. New York: Alfred A. Knopf, 1961.

Trinquier, Roger. *Modern Warfare: A French View of Counterinsurgency*. Translated by Daniel Lee. New York: Praeger, 1964.

Vidal-Naquet, Pierre. *Torture: Cancer of Democracy, France and Algeria, 1954–1962*. Translated by Barry Richard. Baltimore: Penguin, 1963.

AMERICAN CIVIL LIBERTIES UNION (ACLU)

by William J. Aceves

Although the American Civil Liberties Union (ACLU) was founded in 1920, its roots extend back to at least 1917, with the formation of the Civil Liberties Bureau by Roger Baldwin and Crystal Eastman. During this era, fears of war and the threat of communism fueled a growing climate of hostility toward civil liberties in the United States. The notorious Palmer Raids of 1919–1921, authorized by U.S. Attorney General Alexander Mitchell Palmer, resulted in numerous civil rights violations, including arrests without probable cause, denial of right to counsel, and lack of judicial review. Individuals were detained in crowded cells and subjected to physical and mental abuse. Many immigrants detained in these raids were subsequently deported, with no opportunity to challenge their detention or deportation.

Against this backdrop of civil liberties violations, Roger Baldwin established the American Civil Liberties Union on 19 January 1920. Although several civil rights organizations already existed in the United States, including the National Association for the Advancement of Colored People (NAACP) and the Anti-Defamation League, the ACLU offered a broader vision of civil liberties and a commitment to defend this vision through litigation, public education, lobbying, and civic engagement.

The ACLU consists of a national administrative structure and a set of affiliate offices located throughout the country. The ACLU national headquarters is located in New York and works closely with a legislative office in Washington, D.C., and several program-specific offices, including the Immigrants' Rights Project; Capital Punishment Project; Lesbian, Gay, Bisexual, and Transgender Project; and the Women's Rights Project. ACLU policy is established by the National Board of Directors in consultation with staff. The ACLU affiliates play an integral role in implementing ACLU policy at the local level. Although the affiliates work closely with the national administrative structure, they maintain significant autonomy and can implement their own policies. Case selection

occurs at both the national and local levels. Financially, the ACLU receives funding from several sources, including member contributions and private foundations. In 2008 the ACLU had an annual budget of approximately $106 million. Most funding, which includes support of the program-specific offices as well as affiliate offices, is allocated to ACLU legal programs.

International human rights norms, and especially civil and political rights, have always played a role in the ACLU's work and can be found in the treaties and customary practices of the international community. These norms took on greater significance for the ACLU in the late twentieth century and became an integral feature of ACLU work following the 9/11 terrorist attacks.

LITIGATING CIVIL LIBERTIES

The ACLU has litigated many cases in defense of civil liberties and has supported many more through activism and educational outreach. The ACLU's docket encompasses a wide variety of civil liberties issues, including racial equality; voting rights; reproductive freedom; women's rights; and freedom of speech, religion, and association. Other prominent issues are protecting immigrant rights; defending the rights of lesbian, gay, bisexual, and transgendered people; working on behalf of prisoners' rights; protecting privacy; and working to abolish the death penalty.

One of the first ACLU cases is also one of the most significant in American history. The Scopes Monkey Trial examined the legality of a Tennessee law that prohibited the teaching of evolution theory in public schools. Adopted in 1925, the Tennessee law was the first in the country to criminalize the teaching of evolution. Because of the law's implications for academic freedom and separation of church and state, the ACLU announced its interest in defending any teacher who was prosecuted for violating the law. The Tennessee school teacher

John Scopes, who taught science in Dayton, Tennessee, agreed to challenge the law. Seeking to publicize the case, Dayton officials hired the noted lawyer and former presidential candidate William Jennings Bryan to prosecute the case. Clarence Darrow, a respected litigator and national figure, agreed to represent Scopes on behalf of the ACLU. The trial received extensive media attention and brought significant publicity to the ACLU. Scopes pleaded not guilty, asserting that the Tennessee law was unconstitutional, although he readily admitted violating the law. From the outset, the proceedings did not go well for Scopes. Despite objections, the trial judge started each day of the trial with a prayer. Darrow's efforts to submit testimony on science and religion were rejected by the judge. Students testified at trial that Scopes had taught evolution in class, and Darrow never introduced testimony to deny this. Seeking to bolster his case, Darrow then convinced Bryan to testify as an expert witness about creationism and evolution. Even though Darrow managed to undermine Bryan's credibility, the jury ultimately convicted Scopes, who was fined a hundred dollars. Scopes responded that he would continue "to oppose this law in any way. . . . Any other action would be in violation of my ideal of academic freedom—that is, to teach the truth as guaranteed in our constitution, of personal and religious freedom" (*The World's Most Famous Court Trial*, p. 313). On appeal, the Tennessee Supreme Court reversed the conviction, yet it upheld the legality of the statute. The ACLU, however, continued to challenge the constitutionality of anti-evolution statutes. The Tennessee statute remained in effect until it was repealed in 1967. The U.S. Supreme Court ultimately rejected the legality of anti-evolution statutes the following year in *Epperson v. Arkansas*. According to the Supreme Court, "The law's effort was confined to an attempt to blot out a particular theory because of its supposed conflict with the Biblical account, literally read. Plainly, the law is contrary to the mandate of the First, and in violation of the Fourteenth Amendment to the Constitution."

Another prominent set of ACLU cases took place during World War II. Following the Japanese attack on Pearl Harbor, President Franklin Delano Roosevelt, on 19 February 1942, signed Executive Order 9066, which authorized the establishment of military areas in the United States and the exclusion of any individuals from these areas. The order was then used as the basis for imposing restrictions on Japanese Americans in the United States, including their evacuation and exclusion from most of the West Coast and their eventual internment. These restrictions were imposed for discriminatory reasons, as no credible evidence existed that Japanese Americans posed any security threat to the United States. Eventually, 120,000 Japanese Americans were evacuated from their homes on the West Coast and forced to relocate in internment camps scattered throughout the United States. When the restrictions were first announced, a great debate ensued within the ACLU as to how to respond. Although some ACLU members argued for an emphatic rejection of these discriminatory policies, other groups within the organization were reluctant to challenge the U.S. government in a time of war.

Eventually, the ACLU decided to challenge the discriminatory practices. The organization agreed to represent Fred Korematsu, a Japanese American citizen who refused to comply with an internment order and was subsequently arrested and convicted in San Leandro, California. The ACLU also represented Gordon Hirabayashi, who was arrested for violating a curfew and relocation order in Seattle, Washington. Both cases ultimately reached the U.S. Supreme Court. In June 1943 the Court unanimously upheld Hirabayashi's conviction. In December 1944 the Court also upheld Korematsu's conviction, although this decision was not unanimous and resulted in vigorous dissents by three justices.

The Japanese internment cases represent a failure of each branch of government to protect civil liberties in time of war, from the president's decision to authorize the evacuation, exclusion, and internment of Japanese Americans; to Congress's acceptance of the policies; to the courts' unwillingness to condemn them. The U.S. government later rejected the legacy of the Japanese internment cases: in 1984 a federal court overturned Korematsu's criminal conviction, finding that the United States had withheld relevant information during the criminal proceedings and provided misleading information to the courts. Although this judgment did not reverse the legal status of the Supreme Court's decision, it effectively removed its last vestiges of legitimacy. According to the court, "Korematsu remains on the pages of our legal and political history. As a legal precedent it is now recognized as having very limited application. As historical precedent it stands as a constant caution that in times of war or declared military necessity our institutions must be vigilant in protecting constitutional guarantees." In 1988 Congress adopted the Civil Liberties Act, which acknowledged "the fundamental injustice of the evacuation, relocation, and internment of United States citizens and permanent resident aliens of Japanese ancestry during

World War II" and apologized "on behalf of the people of the United States for the evacuation, relocation, and internment of such citizens and permanent resident aliens." The Act authorized the payment of $20,000 to each survivor as reparation for this treatment.

One of the ACLU's most controversial cases involved the right of Nazi sympathizers to march in a predominantly Jewish community in Skokie, Illinois. In April 1977 the National Socialist Party of America (NSPA) announced that it would hold a thirty-minute demonstration in front of the Skokie Village Hall. Skokie was home to one of the largest groups of Holocaust survivors in the country, and several hundred survivors lived in Skokie and the surrounding communities. In response to public outcry, Skokie village leaders sought and received a court injunction barring the demonstration. The NSPA then contacted the ACLU and requested legal representation to challenge the injunction. When the ACLU agreed to represent the NSPA, it received significant criticism, both within the organization and throughout the country. The ACLU argued that the injunction impermissibly infringed on free speech principles protected by the First Amendment. Restricting demonstrations because of community fears would create a "heckler's veto," thereby preventing any unpopular speech. Critics charged, however, that the ACLU's support of the NSPA encouraged racism and was an affront to democratic principles. The Cook County Circuit Court rejected the First Amendment challenge, upheld the injunction, and enjoined the demonstration. Seeking to prevent future demonstrations, Skokie village leaders also adopted three ordinances that imposed extensive requirements for holding demonstrations. After protracted litigation, the federal district court held that the three ordinances were unconstitutional because they lacked content neutrality for political expression. According to the court, "The First Amendment means that government has no power to restrict expression because of its message, its ideas, its subject matter, or its content." The ruling was affirmed by the Seventh Circuit Court of Appeals and the U.S. Supreme Court. Despite the NSPA's legal victories, it never conducted its demonstration in Skokie.

The Skokie case was a seminal moment in ACLU history. The ACLU lost thousands of members, who criticized the organization for representing the NSPA at Skokie. But it gained even more members after the case, many of whom respected the ACLU's position on the First Amendment and the principles underlying the freedom of speech. As Roger Baldwin noted, "Tolerance of what we hate is a daring doctrine and a hard lesson to learn. Our natural instincts may tell us to suppress such dangerous threats to freedom as Nazis. However, the problem has always been, who decides?"

The ACLU has litigated countless cases in support of civil liberties, both as direct counsel on behalf of litigants and in an amicus capacity. (In an amicus capacity, the ACLU can submit a legal brief to the court even though it is not a direct party in the case.) In *Escobedo v. Illinois* (1964), for example, the ACLU argued that a criminal defendant has a right to counsel when in police custody. In a 5 to 4 decision the Supreme Court agreed. In *Tinker v. Des Moines* (1967), the ACLU represented a young student who was suspended from school for wearing a black armband to protest the Vietnam War. In a 7 to 2 decision the Supreme Court held that the armband was akin to pure speech and was protected by the First Amendment. In *Doe v. Bolton* (1973), the companion case to *Roe v. Wade*, the ACLU successfully argued that the constitutional right to privacy encompasses reproductive choice, including a woman's right to continue or terminate her pregnancy. In *ACLU v. Reno* (1997), the ACLU successfully challenged the 1996 Communications Decency Act, which prohibited the online dissemination of patently offensive displays. In a 7 to 2 decision the Supreme Court held that these provisions abridged the freedom of speech protected by the First Amendment. In *Sosa v. Alvarez-Machain* (2004), the ACLU served as counsel in a case seeking civil remedies for the abduction and detention of a Mexican doctor under the Alien Tort Statute. By a 6 to 3 margin, the Supreme Court found that federal courts had jurisdiction to hear the case, although no remedy was available for the underlying claims. In addition to this litigation, the ACLU filed amicus briefs in other prominent cases, including *Brown v. Board of Education* (1954), *New York Times v. Sullivan* (1964), *Miranda v. Arizona* (1966), *New York Times Co. v. United States* (1971), *United States v. Nixon* (1974), *Atkins v. Virginia* (2001), *Grutter v. Bollinger* (2003), *Lawrence v. Texas* (2003), and *Rasul v. Bush* (2004).

ACLU AND INTERNATIONAL HUMAN RIGHTS

Although the ACLU has always relied on the U.S. Constitution to guide its work, it has also recognized the role of international human rights law in promoting civil liberties in the United States. Indeed, Roger Baldwin long championed the importance of international law and regularly sought to infuse international human rights norms into the ACLU's civil liberties work. Following World War II, greater U.S. involvement overseas also increased calls within the ACLU to address human rights standards in U.S. foreign policy. There was, however, some reluctance within the organization to address civil liberties matters outside the United States, particularly when they did not directly involve the United States.

In 1973 the ACLU National Board adopted Policy 401, which formally recognized the role of international human rights in the ACLU's work. The National Board revised Policy 401 in 1983 and 1992. According to the 1992 version, "International human rights are significant to the ACLU . . . because active and expressed support for human rights by the United States government, international organizations and other bodies further legitimizes and otherwise strengthens the values of civil liberties and civil rights in the United States as well as in the rest of the world."

Policy 401 affirms ACLU support for several international human rights instruments that protect civil liberties, including the Genocide Convention, the Convention on the Elimination of All Forms of Discrimination against Women, the Convention on the Elimination of All Forms of Racial Discrimination, the Forced Labor Convention, and the International Covenant on Civil and Political Rights. It then calls on the United States to ratify these treaties. It notes, however, that the ACLU opposes any international agreements that discriminate against U.S. citizens.

In addition, Policy 401 urges greater reliance by the ACLU on international law and institutions. It recognizes that international law can strengthen arguments in support of civil liberties. Thus, "Lawyers arguing in American courts should more frequently invoke international legal standards. The citing of international legal principles can help the effort to fully incorporate these standards into our legal codes." Furthermore, the policy states, ACLU lawyers should also consider using international institutions such as the United Nations to pursue civil liberties claims. "The United Nations . . . has developed a number of procedures for the protection of the rights of individuals and groups that need to be used. The Union can further this use of United Nations procedures by distributing a manual or manuals, prepared by groups with expertise in the field, on procedures in United Nations tribunals affecting human rights." The 1992 revisions to Policy 401 coincided with increased use of international human rights law by the ACLU. Consistent with the

policy, ACLU litigation began to reference international human rights norms in support of civil liberties. The ACLU also highlighted these international norms in other ways, including public education campaigns and lobbying efforts.

In 2004 the ACLU established its Human Rights Program "to ensure that the U.S. government complies with universal human rights principles in addition to the U.S. Constitution. The Program uses human rights strategies to complement existing ACLU advocacy on national security, immigrants' rights, women's rights and racial justice." The program relies on both national and international institutions to address U.S. compliance with human rights standards. It works closely with other ACLU offices, including the National Security Program and the Immigrants' Rights Project. The adoption of Policy 401 and the establishment of the Human Rights Program increased the role of international human rights norms in the ACLU's work. The effects were twofold. First, the ACLU increasingly cited human rights law in support of its civil liberties work in U.S. courts. Second, the ACLU looked to international tribunals and organizations to challenge violations of civil liberties in the United States.

THE ACLU'S RESPONSE TO 11 SEPTEMBER 2001

The ACLU's human rights work became even more significant following the 9/11 terrorist attacks. The U.S. government's response to the attacks threatened civil liberties in numerous ways: surveillance programs monitored the activities of U.S. citizens and foreign nationals without probable cause or court order; immigration policies resulted in thousands of arrests, many motivated solely on ethnic, national, or religious grounds; detention policies authorized extended incarceration without access to counsel or judicial review; the writ of habeas corpus was significantly curtailed; abusive treatment of detainees was justified on national security grounds. The ACLU denounced each of these policies by campaigning for legislative reform and promoting public awareness. Many were challenged through litigation.

To promote transparency of U.S. government policy, the ACLU sought the release of U.S. government documents relating to the war on terror through the Freedom of Information Act. The ACLU was forced to litigate for the documents' release when the United States refused to make them public. Through this litigation, thousands of documents were released. They offered details about detainee abuse at U.S. military installations in Iraq, Afghanistan, and Guantánamo; they also revealed the expansive nature of U.S. government policy toward surveillance, torture, and detention. In addition, the ACLU monitored military commission proceedings at Guantánamo. (The military commissions were established by the Bush administration to prosecute alleged terrorists for war crimes.) The ACLU's regular reports from Guantánamo raised concerns about the treatment of detainees and the legitimacy of the proceedings.

To promote accountability, the ACLU sought to hold human rights abusers responsible for their actions. In *El-Masri v. Tenet*, for example, the ACLU represented Khaled El-Masri, who was abducted and transferred to Afghanistan by the United States under its extraordinary rendition program. El-Masri was then detained at a CIA detention center in Afghanistan for several months. Upon his release, El-Masri sued the former director of the CIA and three aviation corporations for their involvement in his kidnapping, transfer, and detention. The federal courts eventually dismissed the lawsuit, asserting that allowing the case to proceed would be harmful to U.S. national security. In *Ali v. Rumsfeld*, the ACLU filed a lawsuit against senior government officials for their role in implementing policies that resulted in the torture and abusive treatment of detainees in Iraq and Afghanistan. The federal courts dismissed this case as well, holding that U.S. government officials were exempt from liability.

Along with domestic litigation, the ACLU used international institutions to challenge U.S. violations of civil liberties. In 2004, for example, the ACLU filed a complaint against the United States with the UN Working Group on Arbitrary Detention, concerning the detention of immigrants in the United States. The Working Group subsequently found that U.S. detention policies violated international law. The ACLU also filed reports with several other UN bodies, including the Human Rights Committee, the Committee against Torture, and the Committee on the Elimination of All Forms of Racial Discrimination. In addition to these international bodies, the ACLU pursued human rights claims before the Inter-American Commission on Human Rights.

ASSESSMENT

Since its formation in 1920, the ACLU has defended civil liberties in the United States through litigation, public education, lobbying, and civic engagement. As a nonpartisan organization, the ACLU has consistently denounced federal, state, and local policies that threaten civil liberties, regardless of the political implications. Although international human rights norms always played a role in ACLU work, these norms became integral to its work in the late twentieth century.

[*See also* Conflict among Human Rights Norms; History of Human Rights; Franklin Delano Roosevelt; *and* United States: War on Terrorism.]

BIBLIOGRAPHY

Klein, Woody. *Liberties Lost: The Endangered Legacy of the ACLU.* Westport, Conn.: Praeger, 2006.

Kutulas, Judy. *The American Civil Liberties Union and the Making of Modern Liberalism*, 1930–1960. Chapel Hill: University of North Carolina Press, 2006.

Larson, Edward J. *Summer of the Gods: The Scopes Trial and America's Continuing Debate over Science and Religion.* New York: Basic Books, 1997.

Markmann, Charles Lam. *The Noblest Cry: A History of the American Civil Liberties Union.* New York: St. Martin's Press, 1965.

Neier, Aryeh. *Defending My Enemy: American Nazis, the Skokie Case, and the Risks of Freedom.* New York: Dutton, 1979.

Robinson, Greg. *By Order of the President: FDR and the Internment of Japanese Americans.* Cambridge, Mass.: Harvard University Press, 2001.

Romero, Anthony. *In Defense of Our America: The Fight for Civil Liberties in the Age of Terror.* New York: William Morrow, 2007.

Strum, Philippa. *When the Nazis Came to Skokie: Freedom for Speech We Hate.* Lawrence: University Press of Kansas, 1999.

Walker, Samuel. *In Defense of American Liberties: A History of the ACLU.* New York: Oxford University Press, 1990.

The World's Most Famous Court Trial: State of Tennessee v. John Thomas Scopes. New York: Da Capo Press, 1971.

Yamamoto, Eric K., Margaret Chon, Carol L. Izumi, Jerry Kang, and Frank H. Wu. *Race, Rights, and Reparation: Law and the Japanese American Internment.* Gaithersburg, Md.: Aspen Law and Business, 2001.

AMERICAN REVOLUTION

by Ari Kohen and Sara W. Lunsford

When thinking about the American Revolution, one is soon confronted by the puzzle of precisely which revolution is up for discussion. As many scholars of American political thought have noted, one can make a strong case for two revolutionary moments in the founding days of the American republic: the declared separation from Britain in 1776 and the 1789 constitutional revolution. While both of these distinctive moments profoundly influenced the way people think about rights, this essay will focus on the initial revolutionary statement, the American Declaration of Independence. Doing so will enable us to examine closely both the immediate and the lasting impact of the American colonists' decision to break away from the British Empire—a move prompted by the perceived infringement on their basic rights.

The first section of the entry looks closely at the philosophical roots of the American declaration and the rights that it put forward, while the second section considers the declaration from a comparative perspective. The first part looks at the relationship between Jefferson's ideas and those of political philosopher John Locke, while the second part considers the relationship between the American declaration, the English Bill of Rights that preceded it, and the French declaration which came after it. Next, an argument is made about universality and particularity with regard to basic rights, especially noting the language employed by the American founders. Finally, and closely related to the universality debate, the argument is put forth that—while the American Revolution represented a great leap forward with regard to the idea of basic human rights—the founders also left much work to be done, particularly in terms of applying those rights to an ever-expanding circle of individuals and groups.

THE REVOLUTION'S PHILOSOPHICAL FOUNDATION

The American founders owe an intellectual debt to many who came before them. Although the experiment they undertook in the late eighteenth century was unique, the ideas upon which it was founded were already in the air, having been written about and debated by some of the greatest minds in Europe. While there are a great many political theorists whose ideas laid the foundation upon which Hamilton, Jefferson, Madison, and others built, the foremost of those is John Locke. His Second Treatise (the second part of his famous *Two Treatises of Government*, 1690) undoubtedly influenced Jefferson's thinking, as the ideas and even some of the language can be seen in the American declaration. The most obvious example of this influence can be seen in a comparison of the descriptions of human beings in their natural state. According to Locke (p. 271), "The state of nature has a law of nature to govern it, which obliges every one: and reason, which is that law, teaches all mankind, who will but consult it, that being all equal and independent, no one ought to harm another in his life, health, liberty, or possessions." Echoing this sentiment, Jefferson writes that "all men are created equal; that they are endowed by their Creator with certain unalienable rights; that among these are life, liberty and the pursuit of happiness." The similarities of language are clear, as is the emphasis that both authors place on the idea of natural rights, but more important are two other foundational ideas upon which Jefferson relies. These are Locke's arguments that legitimate governments must be founded upon the consent of the governed and that subjects have a right to change their government to avoid being tyrannized.

On these two related points, Locke's Second Treatise is explicit. After detailing what men are like in their natural state, quite dissimilar from Thomas Hobbes's unhappy picture of the "warre of every man against every man" in *Leviathan*, Locke makes an argument for the origins of government. For Locke, the biggest problem with the state of nature is that independent judgment, legislative clarity, and executive enforcement are lacking; for this reason only, men contract together to form a commonwealth. In doing so, they give up a measure of the power that is theirs by nature and invest it in those who will create and enforce laws. Because men have consented in this way to be ruled, Locke argues that they might withdraw their consent if their chosen rulers do not discharge their duties properly. Toward the end of the Second Treatise, then, Locke articulates two ways by which a government can be dissolved. The first is when the legislative power is altered in any way not agreed upon by the people, while the second is when the executive neglects or abandons his charge by failing to properly enforce the laws that have been enacted. In those instances, the people have the right to discontinue their obedience to the laws and create a new legislative or executive power.

Jefferson, of course, directly addresses both of these ideas in the American declaration, noting that "to secure these rights, governments are instituted among men, deriving their just powers from the consent of the governed" and that "whenever any form of government becomes destructive of these ends, it is the right of the people to alter or to abolish it, and to institute a new government." Furthermore, he dedicates the majority of the declaration to listing the myriad ways in which George III had broken faith with the American colonists and ruled them tyrannically. This list is very much in keeping with Locke's understanding of appropriate revolutionary moments. After all, Locke is not a proponent of revolution in all cases; rather, he argues that rebellion ought to be undertaken only in rare, necessary cases when it is clear that further delaying a revolution will result in enslavement to a tyrant.

THE DECLARATION OF INDEPENDENCE FROM A COMPARATIVE PERSPECTIVE

The American Declaration of Independence belongs to a larger tradition of rights-asserting documents that also includes the English Bill of Rights of 1689 and the French Declaration of the Rights of Man and of the Citizen of 1789. All three are responses to monarchs' abuses of power, and they contain many ideas in common, yet they differ significantly, each a product of the circumstances of its creation. The American declaration is a bridge between the other two documents: inspired by the English Bill of Rights, elements of the Declaration of Independence were later incorporated into the Declaration of the Rights of Man.

In 1689, eighty-seven years before the signing of the Declaration of Independence, members of the British Parliament passed the Bill of Rights. They wrote it during the reign of William III of England (also known as William of Orange). A Protestant, William began his rule

following the 1688 Glorious Revolution that ousted his uncle and father-in-law, James II, a Catholic. The Bill of Rights was a response to the tyranny of James II.

The influence of the English Bill of Rights is evident in the Declaration of Independence; it set a precedent for the American colonists by declaring to their king that they had rights, the king had violated those rights, and they would not tolerate any such violations in the future. Both documents declare that the authors and their constituents possess certain rights, although their justification and the particular rights claimed differ. They also both include lists of grievances; some that they share in common are the king acting as if he were superior to the laws, the maintenance of standing armies in peacetime, and the forced quartering of troops in private homes.

Although the influence of the English Bill of Rights on the American declaration is clear, significant differences exist between the two documents. The American founders did not simply copy the ideas found in the English Bill of Rights; they modified and expanded upon those ideas in a way that reflects the political and philosophical environment of eighteenth-century colonial America. The most striking difference between the documents is the authors' opinion of the sovereignty of the British monarchy. The Bill of Rights explicitly affirms the right of the king to rule Britain—though it requires that he be a Protestant—whereas the Declaration of Independence cuts ties with the British government entirely, asserting America's status as a separate and independent political entity. Another difference is the source from which the authors derive the rights that they claim. The Bill of Rights understands rights in a particularistic sense, resulting from the British civil tradition, but the American declaration assumes the universality of its rights by referring to "all men." Finally, although the Bill of Rights confines itself to only the specific rights set forth in the document, the Declaration of Independence takes the broader stance that all men possess the rights to "life, liberty and the pursuit of happiness," which imply other, more specific rights that are necessary for the attainment of the three that are stated. For example, the right to liberty suggests the right to due process of law in the case of imprisonment. The broader scope of the Declaration of Independence updates the ideas set forth in the English Bill of Rights in a way that is more readily accessible to oppressed people throughout the world, not just in areas controlled by Great Britain.

The French embraced the American revolutionary example. Between 1776 and 1783, there were nine different translations of the Declaration of Independence into French. Undoubtedly, these played a role in the creation of the Declaration of the Rights of Man and of the Citizen, which was approved by the National Assembly of France on 26 August 1789. As the delegates met to write the French declaration, opposition to the monarchy increased among the populace, leading to an attack on the Bastille, a French state prison and a symbol of royal power, on 14 July 1789. The Declaration of the Rights of Man and of the Citizen was so radical that the king refused to endorse it. Following the events of August 1789, popular revolutionary sentiment continued to increase, leading to the eventual overthrow of the monarchy.

The Marquis de Lafayette was the primary author of the Declaration of the Rights of Man. He received advice from Thomas Jefferson, which helps to explain some of the similarities between the French document and the American Declaration of Independence. Both embrace universal language, emphasizing that rights derive from nature, not from some sort of agreement between the king and his subjects. Additionally, the French declaration's assertion of the rights to "liberty, property, security, and resistance to oppression" sounds nearly as similar to the American rights to "life, liberty and the pursuit of happiness" as those words sound to Locke's rights to "life, health, liberty, or possessions."

Despite the striking similarities between the Declaration of Independence and the Declaration of the Rights of Man, some differences do exist between the two documents. Unlike the American colonists, the deputies to the French National Assembly were not ready to deny explicitly the sovereignty of the king, and so do not mention the king at all in the declaration. However, the intentions of the two groups of signers were perhaps more similar than is immediately obvious, since the French declaration *did* declare the nation to be sovereign and, as Lynn Avery Hunt asks, "If the nation was sovereign, what was the role of the king, and who best represented the nation?" (p. 133). Another divergence from the Declaration of Independence is that the French declaration lists particular rights belonging to citizens. In this manner, it is comparable to the English Bill of Rights and to the forthcoming Bill of Rights in the U.S. Constitution (1791), claiming rights such as representative government (Article 6) and due process (Article 8).

The English Bill of Rights, the American Declaration of Independence, and the French Declaration of the Rights of Man and of the Citizen represent different points in the process of asserting the rights of the people against an overreaching monarch. The differences between the three reflect the times and places of the documents' creations. Oliver Cromwell's brutal dictatorship as lord protector after the English Civil War (1642–1651) was still too fresh in British collective memory in 1689 to support another overthrow of the monarchical system. In America, by 1776, the environment was quite different. After King George III repeatedly ignored the colonists' petitions to treat them more fairly, American revolutionaries were ready to apply the philosophy of John Locke and others and declare their independence. Finally, in France of 1789, the many political and economic failures of the aristocratic ancien régime resulted in overwhelming anger among the impoverished peasants, propelling forward the ideals of liberty, equality, and fraternity upon which the revolution stood. The documents that resulted from the revolutionary movements in Britain, America, and France helped to advance and diffuse ideas about human rights.

UNIVERSALS AND PARTICULARS IN THE AMERICAN FOUNDING

At the beginning of the revolutionary period, few colonists—even those who would go on to become the framers of the American Constitution—saw themselves as anything other than British subjects living abroad. By 1776, however, that sentiment had dwindled significantly. To be sure, there remained quite a few loyalists—many of whom fled to Canada or to England during the Revolutionary War—but the founders began to perceive of themselves as American instead of British. Even Franklin, the oldest of the Founding Fathers and thus presumably the least likely to become a revolutionary, rejected the possibility that the impasse could be resolved without a split between subjects and sovereign.

Indeed, the specificity of language in the American declaration can be attributed to the unusual circumstances surrounding its drafting, for it needed to describe the feelings of British subjects seeking a separation from the British Empire because of their treatment as British subjects. Thus, the list of complaints against George III is one compiled by subjects who believe that they are being treated unfairly as subjects. For Edmund Burke, who was not a great supporter of revolutionary movements, this distinction is critical because it accords with his sentiment that all rights are particular. Thus, in supporting the American revolutionary sentiment from his position in the British Parliament, Burke points out that these are

British subjects asserting the rights that all British subjects possess as a result of their particular history. But this, of course, contrasts markedly with the language employed in the preliminary clauses of the declaration, which is universalistic in tone and which invokes the rights of all men rather the particular rights of British subjects.

Finally, from a theoretical perspective, one of the more interesting questions arising from the drafting of the American declaration involves the language the founders chose to describe natural rights and how closely that language is in accordance with their intentions. Clearly, the language is universal, referring to the natural rights of *all* men. This word choice certainly calls to mind a debate about whether Jefferson understood women to possess these rights; it also seems clear from Jefferson's other writings, notably his *Notes on the State of Virginia*, that a great many people were either not considered men by many of the founders or simply were not believed to possess these rights.

LAYING THE FOUNDATIONS

The American Revolution was a key event in the progression of human rights in what is now the United States. Most important, the colonists broke away from the British monarchy, established a republic, and—through the Declaration of Independence—centered American political rhetoric on freedom and equality. Despite these advances, the American Revolution nonetheless left a great deal of work to be done in the field of human rights.

Only by situating the American Revolution in its philosophical and historical context can its outcomes be properly evaluated. The English Bill of Rights set a practical example of a people (albeit the elites of a people) asserting their rights as subjects. Enlightenment philosophy, particularly through the writings of John Locke, also helped to pave the way for declaring independence from Britain by providing an ideological justification.

By declaring independence, the Americans took the first step toward establishing a republic. From a human rights perspective, the major advantages of a republic are that, unlike a monarchy, it does not presume that some people are more worthy than others simply because of parentage, and that, in theory at least, citizens can use the vote to prevent tyrannical behavior by those in power. The Revolution put a stop to certain illiberal practices that had occurred under British rule. For example, after the war the Church of England lost its status as the official religion. In addition to these direct advances, the revolutionary focus on freedom and equality helped to put these values at the center of America's collective consciousness, thereby laying the foundation for later human rights advances in the United States.

Although the American Revolution played an undeniably important role in advancing human rights, many in the new republic did not gain access to either freedom or equality. The government denied some or all rights to people without property, women, slaves, free blacks, and Native Americans. Economically, as well, the early United States was quite unequal, prompting Thomas Jefferson to remark, "The property of this country is absolutely concentrated in a very few hands" (Ishay, *History of Human Rights*, p. 108). Furthermore, although there was no longer an established religion, several state constitutions allowed the allocation of taxes to churches in order to preserve Christianity, and some states had religious requirements for public office. Finally, under the Articles of Confederation that served as the first postrevolutionary form of government, Americans lacked a sufficiently strong national government to protect the rights that the Revolution secured.

The failures of the weak national government finally led Americans to take the next step and draft the Constitution. Although observers today can quite rightly criticize the founders as having too limited a conception of who possessed human rights, their ideas were progressive for their time and served as a foundation on which later generations built expanded notions of rights. The process of the expansion of rights that started with the Revolution continued through the Civil War, the granting of the vote to African Americans and women, and the civil rights movement. In the early twenty-first century, the same values of liberty and equality that prompted the Revolution remain key components of the way Americans think about their government and themselves.

[*See also* French Revolution.]

BIBLIOGRAPHY

Adams, Willi Paul. *The First American Constitutions: Republican Ideology and the Making of State Constitutions in the Revolutionary Era.* Lanham, Md.: Rowman & Littlefield, 2001.

Bailyn, Bernard. *The Ideological Origins of the American Revolution.* Cambridge, Mass., and London: Belknap Press, 1992.

Burke, Edmund. *Reflections on the Revolution in France* (1790). Edited and with an introduction by L. G. Mitchell. Oxford: Oxford University Press, 1993.

Hobbes, Thomas. *Leviathan* (1651). Edited by Richard Tuck. Cambridge, U.K., and New York: Cambridge University Press, 1996.

Hunt, Lynn Avery. *Inventing Human Rights: A History*. New York: W. W. Norton, 2007.

Isaacson, Walter. *Benjamin Franklin: An American Life*. New York: Simon & Schuster, 2003.

Ishay, Micheline R. *The History of Human Rights: From Ancient Times to the Globalization Era*. Berkeley: University of California Press, 2004.

Ishay, Micheline R., ed. *The Human Rights Reader: Major Political Essays, Speeches, and Documents from the Bible to the Present*. 2d ed. New York: Routledge, 2007.

Locke, John. *Two Treatises of Government* (1690). Edited and with an introduction by Peter Laslett. Cambridge, U.K., and New York: Cambridge University Press, 1988.

Lubert, Howard L. "Thomas Hutchinson and James Otis on Sovereignty, Obedience, and Rebellion." In *History of American Political Thought*, edited by Bryan-Paul Frost and Jeff Sikkenga. Lanham, Md.: Lexington Books, 2003.

Rakove, Jack N. *Original Meanings: Politics and Ideas in the Making of the Constitution*. New York: Vintage Books, 1997.

Wood, Gordon S. *The American Revolution: A History*. New York: Modern Library, 2002.

Wood, Gordon S. *The Radicalism of the American Revolution*. New York: Vintage Books, 1993.

Zuckert, Michael P. *The Natural Rights Republic: Studies in the Foundation of the American Political Tradition*. South Bend, Ind.: University of Notre Dame Press, 1999.

IDI AMIN DADA OUMEE

by Susan Dicklitch

Idi Amin Dada Oumee ruled Uganda from 1971 to 1979. He was notorious for a reign of terror that plunged Uganda into the darkest period of its history and resulted in the murder of an estimated 350,000 Ugandans. His eight-year rule nearly destroyed Uganda, once considered the "Pearl of Africa" by Sir Winston Churchill.

EARLY LIFE AND RISE TO POWER

Amin was born in the small rural village of Koboko, Uganda, near Arua in the West Nile Province of northern Uganda. Although no official record of his birth exists, it has been estimated that he was born around 1925. Amin died in exile in Jidda, Saudi Arabia, of apparent multiple organ failure on 16 August 2003. Amin had two siblings, a brother and a sister. His father was a Muslim of the Kakwa tribe and his mother, a Christian of the Lugbara tribe. Amin's parents separated very early in his childhood, and he went to live with his mother in Buganda, in southern Uganda. Amin received very little education, so he was considered only functionally literate.

Although Amin was not known for his intellect, he did distinguish himself in athletics. He was not only a champion swimmer but also the heavyweight boxing champion of Uganda from 1951 to 1960. Weighing in at 280 pounds, and 6 feet 4 inches tall, he stood head and shoulders above his countrymen. Amin converted to Islam and practiced polygamy. He had at least five wives and an estimated fifty children.

Amin worked his way up through the military. At age eighteen, he enlisted in the British Army in the King's African Rifles. He fought for the British in Kenya during the Mau Mau revolt (1952–1956). Distinguishing himself in the field, he rose to the rank of lieutenant in 1961, becoming one of only two Ugandans to be commissioned during British rule. In 1962 Amin was sent to repress cattle stealing by Kenyan Turkani tribesmen in northern Uganda. The troops, under Amin's control, were accused of committing the Turkana Massacre, in which victims were tortured, beaten to death, and even buried alive. Instead of court-martialing Amin for the torture, Milton Obote, the new prime minister of an independent Uganda, subsequently promoted him. In 1963, just one year after independence, Amin was promoted to colonel and in 1964 to commander of the army and air force. By 1968 then President Obote promoted Amin to major general.

The honeymoon between Amin and Obote was short-lived, however. In November 1970 President Obote removed Amin from his command position and demoted him to an administrative role. Amin soon discovered that Obote intended to arrest him on charges of misappropriation of millions of dollars of military funds. Instead, on 25 January 1971, while Obote was attending a commonwealth summit in Singapore, Amin staged what seemed at the time a relatively bloodless coup d'état.

Obote subsequently fled into exile in Tanzania. Although Amin's military takeover was initially welcomed with great euphoria, especially by the Buganda ethnic group that witnessed the exile of their beloved *kabaka* (king), Edward Mutesa II, under Obote, the country's honeymoon with Amin was soon to end as well. Amin presented himself as the great peacemaker—a leader who would reconcile all ethnic groups and religions. Amin promised many things to Ugandans, including elections within months and a return to civilian rule within five years. Instead, he declared himself president and general and, a year after taking power, promoted himself to field marshal. Amin dissolved the National Assembly and instead ruled by decree.

Amin did disband the hated Obote secret police—the General Service Unit—and release many political prisoners, but, in turn, he created the equally brutal State Research Bureau (SRB) and Public Safety Unit (PSU), which were responsible for thousands of murders. Ugandans were soon to learn that Amin was anything but a peacemaker.

REIGN OF TERROR: 1971 TO 1979

Amin's reign of terror began with mass killings of former Obote security operatives hailing from the defunct General Service Unit, the special forces, and the police. Prisons were turned into slaughterhouses, and bodies were dumped in forests, along roadways, and in rivers and lakes. These bodies were frequently mutilated beyond recognition, with eyes gouged out, lips cut off, and body parts severed and stuffed into victims' mouths. Amin's brutal terror tactics earned him the title of "Butcher of Africa." Many from the Lango and Acholi ethnic groups that had made up a large portion of Obote's security forces and military were especially targeted by Amin's killing machine, but nobody was safe: Amin's brutality was indiscriminate, fearless, and merciless. Amin was even suspected of cannibalism and practicing traditional Kakwa blood rituals on his slain enemies.

Amin had politicians, archbishops, soldiers, and foreigners as well as journalists and other innocent civilians killed without hesitation. For example, Amin's agents murdered Chief Justice Ben Kiwanuka, a former prime minister and Democratic Party leader, brazenly abducting him from Uganda's High Court on 21 September 1972. Kiwanuka's crime? He had angered Amin for releasing—for lack of evidence—a British citizen arrested by Amin's men. Janan Luwum, the Anglican archbishop of Uganda, Rwanda, Burundi, and Zaire, was later killed by Amin's forces in 1977 because of a letter written by the House of Bishops concerning the Amin regime's human rights abuses. The archbishop and two cabinet ministers, Erunayo Oryema and Charles Oboth-Ofumbi, were killed in a car accident, but contradictions in official reports suggest that Amin's government was complicit in their deaths.

Several Americans and British citizens were also killed by Amin's forces, including Dora Bloch, a British hostage on the ill-fated Air France jet that was hijacked by the Palestine Liberation Organization (PLO) in Athens in 1976 and flown to Entebbe Airport in Uganda. The killings continued under Amin's capricious rule and increased with every failed military coup d'état. Amin purged the army of Acholi and Lango officers in 1972 after Obote attempted a coup d'état from Tanzania (the Acholi and Lango had been Obote's chief supporters during his prior rule of Uganda).

AMIN'S ECONOMIC WAR

In 1972, just one year after assuming power, Amin declared that in a dream God had ordered him to expel Indo-Pakistani Asians from the country. Thus began Amin's economic war against Asians and his "Africanization" of the Ugandan economy. In 1972 he gave all Asians, an estimated fifty thousand to seventy thousand people who lived in Uganda, ninety days to leave, taking with them only what they could carry. Some of the Asians had been born in Uganda and were Ugandan citizens, whereas many others held foreign passports. For Amin, this did not matter—they were foreigners and spies in his country and needed to be expelled. The Asians held many civil service jobs and essentially formed the middle class. With their expulsion, Amin established the foundation for the destruction of the Ugandan economy. He seized the pillaged Asian assets and properties for himself and his cronies. Some estimates suggest that this amounted to more than five thousand firms, factories, ranches, and agricultural estates and about $400 million in personal possessions.

In January 1973 Amin decided to nationalize all British-owned businesses in Uganda—without compensation. This naturally strained ties between Great Britain and Uganda, and the situation came to a head when Amin embraced Libya and the former Soviet Union over Britain and Israel, Uganda's traditional allies. The United States closed its embassy in Uganda in 1973, and Britain followed suit, shuttering the doors of its high commission in 1976. Amin also expelled Israelis from Uganda, instead allying his government with the Arab world and, in particular, the PLO and Libya.

Amin's economic war was initially met with jubilation from many Ugandans, who believed that Asians were foreigners who had profited off the backs of Ugandans. Little did they know at the time that Amin's pillaging would not stop with the Asians' property and assets.

The impact of Amin's economic war on the Ugandan economy was not felt immediately, because the nation's main export, coffee, continued to do well on the international market. But by 1977 the Ugandan economy was in shambles, with inflation averaging 1,000 percent. The Ugandan infrastructure was also in bad shape, with an inept civil service. Soon the economy collapsed. Peasants refused to grow coffee, as often they were not paid for months, if at all.

BUFFOON, RUTHLESS KILLER, OR JUST PARANOID?

By 1975 Amin had declared himself Ugandan president for life. He insisted on being referred to as "His Excellency, Field Marshal, Al-Haji, Dr. Idi Amin Dada, Life

President of Uganda, Conqueror of the British Empire, Distinguished Service Order of the Military Cross, Victoria Cross, and Professor of Geography" in any public appearances. Amin's being named chairman of the Organization of African Unity (OAU) in 1975 did not curb his insatiable lust for power and respect.

Perhaps it was the multiple failed coups d'état, in April 1973 and March 1974, led by Kakwa officers, his fellow tribesmen, that increased Amin's paranoia. After the failed coup attempts, Amin purportedly lived in constant fear that Obote would successfully overthrow him. He also believed that there was an international conspiracy to overthrow him. Consequently, Amin banned all "imperialist" newspapers from Uganda, for allegedly being against him and the Ugandan government.

Amin's coup de grâce began in 1976 with his backing of the PLO hijacking of Air France Flight 139 during a stopover in Athens. The hijackers used Uganda's Entebbe Airport as their base to hold 256 hostages, mostly Jews, in return for the release of fifty-four PLO prisoners. Amin and his military gave the hijackers their support. Israel forces stormed Entebbe in a daring ninety-minute operation, rescuing almost all the hostages. It was a grand embarrassment for Amin and his military, who became the laughing stock of Uganda. Amin retaliated with more repression and coveted additional support from the former Soviet Union and the Arab world, especially Libya.

In October 1978 Amin decided to divert attention away from the disintegrating economy and infighting within the military by invading Tanzania. He claimed that the territory north of the Kagera River, known as the Kagera Salient, was Ugandan, and he planned to annex it. By now Tanzania's President Julius Nyerere had had about enough of Amin. With a ragtag force of some six thousand exiled Ugandan rebels and the fifty thousand–plus Tanzanian army, the Tanzanian People's Defence Force (TPDF) launched a counteroffensive against Amin's army of seventy thousand troops in December 1978. Libya and the PLO sent troops to help Amin, but by then Amin's troops were demoralized. On 11 April 1979 the Ugandan rebels, the Uganda National Liberation Army (UNLA), with the help of Tanzanian soldiers, captured Kampala, the capital of Uganda, and forced Amin into exile. Yoweri Kaguta Museveni, a future president of Uganda, was the leader of the Front for National Salvation (FRONASA), one of the Ugandan rebel forces in the UNLA.

Yusuf Lule, the former Makerere University vice-chancellor and chairman of the UNLA's political wing, formed an interim government. Amin's reign of terror was finally over. Amin first fled to Libya and lived there for ten years (1979 to 1989), but after an alleged falling out with Colonel Muammar al-Qaddafi, the leader of Libya, he relocated to Saudi Arabia, where he died in 2003.

Idi Amin Dada Oumee will be remembered as the "Butcher of Africa"—dragging Ugandans into one of the darkest periods of their history. Some considered him a buffoon; others saw him as a rational, calculated murderer who was obsessed with retaining power. Although never tried for his crimes against humanity, Amin earned nearly universal condemnation for the murder of hundreds of thousands of his compatriots. He was surely one of the more noteworthy abusers of human rights in the twentieth century.

[See also Uganda.]

BIBLIOGRAPHY

Hansen, Holger Bernt, and Michael Twaddle, eds. *Uganda Now: Between Decay and Development.* Athens, Ohio: Ohio University Press, 1988.

Jørgensen, Jan Jelmert. *Uganda: A Modern History.* London: Croom Helm, 1981.

Karugire, Samwiri Rubaraza *A Political History of Uganda.* Nairobi, Kenya: Heinemann Educational Books, 1980.

Kasfir, Nelson. "State, 'Magendo,' and Class Formation in Uganda." *The Journal of Commonwealth and Comparative Politics* 21, no. 3 (November 1983): 84–103.

Kasozi, A. B. K. *The Social Origins of Violence in Uganda: 1964–1985.* With the assistance and collaboration of Nakanyike Musisi and James Mukooza Sejjengo. Buffalo, N.Y.: McGill-Queen's University Press, 1994.

Mutibwa, Phares. *Uganda since Independence: A Story of Unfulfilled Hopes.* London: Hurst, 1992.

Ofcansky, Thomas P. *Uganda: Tarnished Pearl of Africa.* Boulder, Colo.: Westview Press, 1996.

Saul, John. "The Unsteady State: Uganda, Obote, and General Amin." *Review of African Political Economy* 3, no. 5 (January–April 1976): 12–38.

AMNESTY INTERNATIONAL

by Peter R. Baehr

As of 2008, Amnesty International (AI) is the largest international nongovernmental organization (NGO) in the field of human rights in the world. It has more than 2.2 million members, subscribers, and regular donors in over 150 countries and territories and over 6,000 volunteer groups in more than 74 countries. There are 50 nationally organized sections, 22 of them in Latin America, Africa, Asia, and the Middle East, and 23 offices in other countries of the global south and eastern and central Europe, where a formal section has not yet been recognized. The International Secretariat in London has more than 320 staff from over 50 countries. AI's consolidated global budget for 2004 and 2005 was approximately £100 million (almost $200 million).

The organization started in 1961 when an article by a London lawyer, Peter Benenson, appeared in *The Observer*. Published as an "Appeal for Amnesty," it urged governments to release prisoners who were being held in jail because their political or religious views differed from those of their government. In the article, the notion of "prisoners of conscience" was introduced and defined as "any person who is physically restrained (by imprisonment or otherwise) from expressing (in any form of words or symbols) any opinion which he honestly holds and which does not advocate or condone personal violence" (p. 1). The listed aims of the appeal were the following:

1. To work impartially for the release of those imprisoned for their opinions
2. To seek for them a fair and public trial
3. To enlarge the right of asylum and help political refugees to find work
4. To urge effective international machinery to guarantee freedom of opinion

The appeal elicited many reactions in the United Kingdom and other parts of the world and eventually led to the founding of Amnesty International.

OBJECTIVE AND METHODS

The objective of the organization is to contribute to the observance throughout the world of human rights as outlined in the Universal Declaration of Human Rights and other international human rights standards. Amnesty's work is based not on arbitrary values held by certain individuals, many of whom reside in Western countries, but on a set of universally accepted values—the "common standard of achievement for all peoples and all nations" to which the preamble of the Universal Declaration refers.

From its founding in 1961 until the early 1990s AI focused its work on the human rights of prisoners. Amnesty moved from this prisoner orientation to expand considerably its scope of work, so as to include the prevention and ending of grave abuses of the rights to physical and mental integrity, freedom of conscience and expression, and freedom from discrimination, within the context of its work to promote all human rights. What was formerly regarded as the mandate of the organization, which originally strongly emphasized the freeing of prisoners of conscience, was broadened in subsequent years to include the fight against torture or other cruel, inhuman, and degrading treatment or punishment, the death penalty, extrajudicial executions, and involuntary "disappearances." The organization assists asylum-seekers who are at risk of being returned to a country where they will be subject to violations of basic and fundamental human rights. Over the course of the years, its activities have been further expanded gradually to also cover economic, social, and cultural rights, in addition to the classical civil and political rights. Examples of subjects of recent work on economic, social, and cultural rights include:

- The right to food (in North Korea and Zimbabwe)
- The right to mental health (in Bulgaria and Romania)

- Housing rights (in Angola, Israel, the Occupied Territories, and Swaziland)
- The right to health (in Rwanda, Argentina, and the Democratic Republic of Congo)

The basic premise has always been of a highly practical nature: to be effective within a clearly defined area and thus to contribute to the struggle for the maintenance of all human rights.

The vision and mission of the organization and its core values are contained in Amnesty International's International Statute. The statute may be amended by the International Council, which represents the international membership and meets once every two years, by a majority of two-thirds of the votes cast. The council can also, by ordinary majority, adopt resolutions to further specify or interpret the statute. The International Statute calls for the development of an Integrated Strategic Plan that is determined for a period of six years by the International Council.

The methods of the organization are based on the accurate disclosure of human rights abuses, both of individual cases and patterns of such abuses. Its findings are published, and public pressure is then exercised on governments and others to stop these abuses. Among its methods are well-known Amnesty techniques, such as reporting, letter-writing campaigns, membership drives, approaches to governments and intergovernmental organizations, trial observation, and research missions. Accuracy in its reporting is considered of prime importance. Over the years, Amnesty has built a reputation of reliability, which lies at the basis of its success and which the organization goes to great lengths to maintain. Draft reports are checked and double-checked before being released. This may be to the detriment of a speedy response to abuses.

A government that is the target of systematic reporting may do its best to discredit the organization by questioning its motives (for instance, attempting to dismiss them as political) or financial resources. For many years, the Soviet Union accused Amnesty of being CIA-supported, whereas military dictatorships in Latin America and elsewhere called it a "Communist umbrella organization." In order to safeguard its impartiality, as well as preserve an impartial image in the eyes of the outside world, Amnesty does not accept any government financial or other support for its human rights activities. In the early years of its existence, the organization was strongly tied to, and received financial support from, the United Kingdom, threatening its impartiality (Berenson). That practice led

to a crisis in the organization and as a result a full and principled rejection of such aid from any government.

The issues Amnesty faces often call for a fine-tuning of its activities, sometimes in the form of difficult interpretations of existing rules, sometimes by having to create new rules. The organization has had to face many relevant questions over the years. Should Amnesty's policy on the imprisonment of political opponents of a regime include administrative detention? If so, what type? Should its opposition to the death penalty include various forms of extralegal or extrajudicial execution, and how should such executions be distinguished from criminal assassination? Should excessive force used by security forces resulting in the death of peaceful demonstrators be considered extrajudicial executions, or only if the killings were the result of targeted shooting? If governments are criticized for their human rights violations, what about similar acts by nongovernmental entities, and how should these entities be distinguished from criminal groups such as the Mafia? Should hostage taking by terrorist groups be included in the mandate? In order to avoid difficult discussions about terminology denoting the same group of people as terrorists, rebels, or freedom fighters, Amnesty usually refers to such groups as "armed political groups."

Final policy decisions are made by the International Council. In the period between two councils, formal authority rests with Amnesty's International Executive Committee, whereas the International Secretariat, headed by a secretary-general, is responsible for the organization's day-to-day activities.

Deciding what Amnesty's core business should be, when new issues come up, is often very difficult. The average Amnesty member usually lacks firsthand experience with and knowledge of decisions made in the past that may have created precedents. Only a handful of members and certain individuals in the International Secretariat have the necessary command of the intricacies of human rights issues to knowledgeably identify Amnesty's core business and develop options that are sufficiently clear for the membership to act on. Records are kept on earlier decisions, but many of these cases raise complicated legal issues not easily interpreted by those not directly involved in the cases. Thus, the departure of experienced staff from the secretariat may complicate matters from the point of view of organizational memory—much of which in the instance of Amnesty is preserved in the minds of a limited number of individuals.

The International Statute applies to the entire membership of Amnesty International. Members are supposed to adhere to every aspect of it and, in principle, be ready to promote the statute in its entirety. Certain issues covered in the statute may be more popular among some segments of the membership than others, but it is not a menu from which one can pick and choose. For instance, Amnesty's opposition to the death penalty receives more wholehearted support in western Europe and North America than among its African members who may find it hard to apply in their society. The same is true for Amnesty's work for the release of individuals detained for their homosexuality—an issue that only after extensive debates among the membership was acted on by the organization.

As Amnesty International is a membership organization, some of its members' involvement is limited to paying their annual dues, whereas others are actively involved in decision making and helping to craft the overall policy of the organization. Other members take an active part in implementing Amnesty's objectives, for instance, participating in letter-writing and the movement's various other campaigns.

It is hard to say what the precise impact of the organization is. Governments rarely admit to changes of policies as the result of pressure by Amnesty International or other human rights organizations. The organization itself is reluctant to claim successes, although it does tend to emphasize "good news stories," for instance, the release of prisoners of conscience on whose behalf it had made appeals. Little doubt also exists that some of AI's world campaigns, such as those conducted against torture, disappearances, and other forms of human rights abuses, have played an important role. The organization helped to establish the function of UN High Commissioner for Human Rights in 1993 and was strongly involved in the creation of an International Criminal Court in 1998. In the early twenty-first century it is heavily engaged in putting an end to the violation of the rights of women, including trafficking and sexual abuse. The organization often succeeds in placing human rights matters that might otherwise have remained ignored on the international political agenda. That is one important way in which Amnesty International—together with its fellow NGOs—can make an impact.

CRITERIA

Amnesty International's program of action needs to be sufficiently flexible to develop with changing circumstances in the world. Thus, it was because of the changing nature of human rights violations throughout the years that opposition to extrajudicial executions as well as the fight against disappearances was added to the organization's program. At the same time, in order to obtain the necessary consensus among the membership, such changes could not be too radical. Only after long discussions was it decided that Amnesty would work on "all" human rights and deal more specifically with aspects of economic, social, and cultural rights, as had been suggested by critics, who accused Amnesty of maintaining a Western bias. This impression of such a bias is reinforced by the fact that the bulk of AI's membership resides in Western nations. Amnesty for its part has always tried to combat this impression by stressing its commitment to the standards set forth in the Universal Declaration of Human Rights, by trying—without much success—to expand its membership in non-Western countries, by appointing qualified staff members from such countries, including since 1992 a secretary-general from Senegal (Pierre Sané, 1992–2001) and Bangladesh (Irene Khan, 2001 to the present).

The notion of political impartiality is stressed in the sense that the nature of the political or economic system under which violations of human rights occur is of no concern to the organization. This approach has had important consequences for Amnesty's method of work. The International Statute formerly mentioned the need for the organization to maintain an "overall balance between its activities in relation to countries adhering to different world political ideologies and groupings." Therefore, for many years, Amnesty groups working for the release of prisoners of conscience were expected to do so simultaneously for three detainees: one from a Western country, one from a Communist country, and one from a nonaligned nation. This practice has been gradually abolished for lack of sufficient cases from all three systems, and in 1991 the text of the International Statute was revised, with the word "balance" replaced by "impartiality," focusing once more on the fate of the victims of human rights violations, regardless of political systems.

Political impartiality is seen as contributing to Amnesty's credibility and thus its effectiveness. The need to maintain political impartiality, as well as the wish to avoid even the appearance of bias, was the main reason why Amnesty did not condemn the best known legally based system of human rights violations in the world: apartheid in South Africa. Amnesty also avoided taking up all kinds of discriminatory legislation in other parts of the world, limiting itself to "condemning and opposing those laws and practices of Apartheid which permit the imprisonment of people on grounds of conscience or race; the denial of fair trial to political prisoners; torture; or the death penalty." This compromise text was arrived at with considerable difficulty. It was challenged at regular intervals at meetings of the membership. African members of the organization, in particular, found it difficult to accept the fact that Amnesty did not openly condemn the South African government's policy of apartheid. An equally divisive issue was AI's decision to not adopt the long-time-imprisoned Nelson Mandela as a prisoner of conscience, as he had not ruled out the use of violence in the struggle against apartheid.

The nonviolence clause in the International Statute was based on Amnesty's wish to uphold its impartiality. The organization sought to avoid involvement in situations where it would have to state whether or not a particular circumstance justified the use of violence. As with political impartiality, consistency is also seen as contributing to the credibility of the organization. Consistency means that similar cases are dealt with in a similar fashion. However, the problem Amnesty faces in this regard is that cases tend to be similar only up to a point, and deciding what sort of action the principle of consistency requires in a given case is often difficult. Should all killings by the agents of a government, if they are not carried out to satisfy a judicial death sentence, be considered extrajudicial executions? No, obviously not, as Amnesty does not deal with killings in a combat situation, although it may call on the parties to a conflict to adhere to the rules of international humanitarian law. This raises the problem of those complicated and ambiguous gray areas, which represent neither war nor peace, but something in between, and where Amnesty's course of action may not always be clear. This issue has been especially significant when the organization has had to address human rights abuses by nongovernmental entities (see below).

INVOLVED ACTORS

The development of Amnesty's Integrated Strategic Plan depends a great deal on who takes an interest in it. There are at least three types of parties interested in the plan:

Staff of the International Secretariat and other "insiders"
Overall membership of Amnesty International
Outside world, including governments, other NGOs, the
    press, and the public

Amnesty's staff is, of course, vitally interested in the development of the Strategic Plan. They use it to decide on which cases to act. It may also serve to increase their opportunity for action, while at the same time directly confronting the limits of personnel and financial resources. Although the membership may be inclined to expand the activities of the organization, it is the task of the secretary-general and permanent staff to determine the resource implications of such expansion. An inherent structural tension exists between members wanting the organization to take on continuously more types of human rights violations and staff pointing to limited resources. This difference in perspective does not have much to do with so-called radicalism or conservatism; it is rather the result of the role each party plays. Such tension is not necessarily a bad phenomenon, provided the leaders of the organization, that is, the International Executive Committee and secretary-general, jointly ensure that it does not get out of hand. It should also be added that at times the opposite dynamic exists: with individual staff members seeking the expansion of activities and members urging restraint.

Members of Amnesty International continuously confront new instances of human rights violations in the world—as does the staff—and may chafe at the limitations of the organization. Should a journalist imprisoned for not divulging his sources be adopted as a prisoner of conscience? Should restrictions on freedom of movement be acted on? What assistance ought to be provided to individuals denied the right to leave their country? Should house demolition as a means of repression be acted on, or is this circumstance limited to one particular geographic location (the Occupied Territories)? What should Amnesty's position on forcible resettlement be? Should prisoners carrying the immunodeficiency virus (HIV) or suffering from AIDS who are subject to human rights violations be given special attention? These are only some of the many issues that have been raised at International Council meetings. Their discussion was brought about by rightful indignation over reprehensible practices by governments in violation of international human rights standards. Some of these issues were eventually incorporated in the Strategic Plan, whereas others will not or may become the subject of further study. In reaching a decision on such matters, consistency as well as resource implications are taken into account.

Such issues may lead to heated, passionate debates among Amnesty's membership. Peter Benenson referred in his 1961 *Observer* article to Voltaire's well-known pronouncement: "I detest your views, but am prepared to die for your right to express them." The example of Salman Rushdie is a case in point. There are clearly limits to the principle of free speech. One of these limits is, for example, the advocacy of national, racial, or religious hatred that constitutes incitement of discrimination, hostility, or violence. Does this mean that the advocacy of such hatred should be allowed and defended? Should an author be imprisoned for writing a book claiming that the Holocaust never took place? The mere mention of the Rushdie example in an internal document led to strong reactions within the AI organization. Should Amnesty International take on the cause of such an author, the suppression of his views, or should his "attack on historical truth" (as one Amnesty faction claimed) not be acted on?

Certain governments are seldom or never mentioned in Amnesty International's reports. They may enter into discussions with Amnesty about the implications of its Strategic Plan and make informal suggestions for its further development. Other governments seek ways to avoid Amnesty's attention. Although the most effective way of accomplishing this would be to put an end to human rights abuses, this is not necessarily what happens. Such governments will instead search for ways to discredit the organization, for instance, by pointing out alleged factual errors in its reports or by suggesting that a discrepancy exists between AI's emphasis on human rights violations by some governments and lack of interest in similar abuses by nongovernmental entities (see below). A continued professional approach, factual correctness, and political impartiality are crucial to the effectiveness of Amnesty's work.

The press and public opinion are also crucial to Amnesty's effectiveness. The press is important because if Amnesty's reports are not widely circulated and reported on, offending governments can more easily ignore them. The media may call attention to alleged inconsistencies or factual errors in the reports. The media are less interested in the intricacies of a program, unless these happen to have political repercussions. Thus, the debate on AI's adoption of imprisoned homosexuals as prisoners of conscience received relatively wide coverage in the Western press, partly encouraged by an active campaign on the part of interested gay rights organizations. The same is generally true of interested public opinion that will, on occasion, critically review Amnesty's claim of political impartiality. Public opinion is in the final analysis Amnesty's strongest ally, and the organization deploys it in its campaigns of "mobilization of shame" against offending governments.

NONGOVERNMENTAL ENTITIES

According to classical doctrine, governments are accountable under international law for violations of human rights. They must see to it that international standards are applied. As far as these standards have been codified in international treaties, states are parties to such treaties and must meet their related obligations. This classical doctrine is the approach that Amnesty normally takes in confronting governments once it becomes aware of human rights violations in their territory. However, it is a well-known fact that some governments are barely able to exert their authority in their own capital city, let alone the remainder of the territory they are supposed to govern. Examples that come to mind are the governments of Colombia, the Democratic Republic of Congo, Nepal, Sri Lanka, and Sudan. In the case of Somalia, a government in the formal sense hardly exists. In these nations, circumstances may differ, but they usually include one or more of the following characteristics:

Civil war: two or more groups fighting each other, claiming central or partial political control

Threat of break-up: that is, the chance of the country dissolving, while the allocation of governmental authority remains at least temporarily unresolved (as has happened in the Soviet Union and the former Yugoslavia)

Certain degree of control by the armed opposition: it may control part of the territory and the population, either on a permanent or temporary basis

This state of affairs gives rise to a number of questions. Should nongovernmental entities be expected to honor the same commitments in the field of human rights as the formal government of their country? Should they be asked to give their prisoners fair and prompt trials? Apart from the technical difficulty of identifying a central authority in many of these cases, how realistic is it to treat such groups as if they were governments? And to what extent would the making of such demands imply some sort of recognition? Governments regard such armed opposition groups as rebels or terrorists, if not outright criminals. These governments usually adopt a somewhat ambivalent attitude with regard to the question of upholding human rights standards. Although they want the armed opposition to be judged by the same human rights criteria as they are, they also do not want to publicly offer the opposition this kind of recognition.

Amnesty—like other human rights organizations—has struggled with the dilemma of confronting nongovernmental entities whose abuses are as bad as or even worse than the violations committed by governments, finding it difficult to decide how to approach such entities. For a long time, Amnesty took the position that it would condemn the torture or killing of prisoners by opposition groups, but not directly confront such groups. According to some critics, directly addressing such groups would signify that the organization was moving into the area of crime fighting, because when an individual or opposition group commits a killing, perpetrates torture, or takes a hostage, this should be regarded as a crime rather than as an abuse of human rights. International human rights instruments are binding only for states parties, that is, governments. On the other hand, however, some governments accused Amnesty of being less forceful in pursuing its aims with regard to nongovernmental entities than governments. As a consequence, the organization began to deal with abuses by nongovernmental entities, but refused to deal with them on the same level as with governments.

For a number of years, Amnesty distinguished a separate category of nongovernmental entities, what it chose to call "quasi-governmental entities," having a number of characteristics that made them look very much like governments. These characteristics were the following:

Having effective authority over territory and peoples such that individuals may be subject to abuses, whereas the formal government is excluded as a source of protection
Being political organizations in the sense of acting in pursuit of a political program

In practice, however, Amnesty has found it difficult to maintain the distinction between nongovernmental entities in general and quasi-governmental entities. The authority exerted by the quasi-governmental entity is often rather transient in nature. It may control parts of the population for a while, then lose that control or take over the government according to the fortunes of war. Some entities may gain control of part of a territory at night, only to have to relinquish it during daytime. In some cases, deciding the following can also be rather arbitrary: if an entity is or is not in pursuit of a political program, thus distinguishing it from groups that are purely criminal such as the Mafia or dealers in narcotic drugs. Political groups may engage in criminal activities to support their cause, whereas criminals may opt for some kind of semipolitical control. Amnesty does address abuses by political nongovernmental entities, whether or not the entity has the attributes of a government, in effect abolishing the distinction between nongovernmental and quasi-governmental entities.

A continuum of political nongovernmental organizations may exist, ranging from those that are very similar to governments to those organizations having little in common with governments. The organization decided that as a priority Amnesty would concentrate its resources on those entities having greater control over people, territory, and the use of force and develop criteria by which political nongovernmental entities might be distinguished from groups falling outside the scope of Amnesty's work, including common criminal organizations.

The question of how to approach nongovernmental entities received special emphasis in relation to the issue of hostages taken by nongovernmental entities. Originally, Amnesty did not condemn the taking of hostages, but only the torture or killing of such hostages, or the threat to do so. However, sometimes hostages are taken for political reasons. And the issue became whether Amnesty should call for the release of these hostages. Moreover, the question arose whether it was logical to condemn hostage-taking, but not killings in the street by those same nongovernmental entities. Amnesty decided to do both: to bring the taking of hostages by nongovernmental entities into the scope of its activities as well as other deliberate and arbitrary killings, for example, the killings of people under the nongovernmental entity's immediate control and killings carried out solely by reason of the victim's ethnic origin, sex, color of skin, language, religion, or political views or other beliefs.

It may be expected that in the remaining decades of the twenty-first century the activities of nongovernmental entities will receive greater attention from human rights organizations such as Amnesty International. The dilution of state power seems to be on the increase. With the dilution of state power and the demise of governments comes an upsurge of new, "nongovernment" groups who seem to have little in common except an abundant supply of weapons and a striving for power. Together with that come killings of civilians, torture, extrajudicial executions, and other abuses of international human rights standards. The existence and contents of those standards are usually little known to the perpetrators. This will only further complicate the already daunting tasks of organizations such as Amnesty International.

ASSESSMENT

On issues such as prisoners of conscience, fair trials, torture, the death penalty, extrajudicial executions, and "disappearances," Amnesty International has developed an expertise that is second to none. Governments seek its advice when having to take a position on difficult issues and Amnesty willingly provides the requested information. Problems have ensued, though, in the delineation of its program, those gray areas, where Amnesty continuously has to review its position. Issues that have been debated include killings in armed conflicts, refugee guidelines, forcible exile and relocation, administrative detention, racial discrimination, unfair trials, and other grave measures against freedom of conscience and expression such as the demolition of homes, extrajudicial executions, harsh prison conditions, and ill-treatment in psychiatric settings.

Amnesty's activities are still true to the principal ideas originally envisaged in 1961. The world has changed since then, however, and so has the nature of some of the major human rights violations. The main internal issue in the coming years is whether Amnesty will be able to hold together various culturally based views within the organization. As the great majority of its members are from Western countries, the organization may be seen as a purely Western organization—a characterization it wants to avoid. "Multicultural perspectives" were reflected in Amnesty's homosexuality debate and in the debate on the demolition of houses in the Occupied Territories. In relation to the latter, specific reference was made in the debate to the fact that it was important in the context of significant mandates such as that on homosexuality to look at wider issues and to ensure that changes in the organization's activities are multiculturally balanced. The issue of female genital mutilation arouses similar culturally determined differences of view. That is of tremendous importance because in the long run Amnesty's effectiveness may depend to a considerable degree on whether it will be able to relate effectively to human rights concerns in countries worldwide, including Africa and Asia.

[*See also* Peter Benenson *and* Nongovernmental Organizations: Overview.]

BIBLIOGRAPHY

Amnesty International Web site. http://www.amnesty.org.

Baehr, Peter R. "Amnesty International and Its Self-Imposed Limited Mandate." *Netherlands Quarterly of Human Rights* 12, no. 1 (1994): 5–21.

Benenson, Peter. "The Forgotten Prisoners." *The Observer* (London), May 28, 1961.

Clark, Ann Marie. *Diplomacy of Conscience: Amnesty International and Changing Human Rights Norms*. Princeton, N.J.: Princeton University Press, 2001.

Cook, Helena. "Amnesty International at the United Nations." In *The Conscience of the World: The Influence of Non-Governmental Organizations in the UN System*, edited by Peter Willets, pp. 181–213. London: C. Hurst, 1996.

Hopgood, Stephen. *Keepers of the Flame*. Ithaca, N.Y.: Cornell University Press, 2006.

Kaufman, Edy. "Prisoners of Conscience: The Shaping of a New Human Rights Concept." *Human Rights Quarterly* 13, no. 3 (1991): 339–367.

Larsen, Egon. *A Flame in Barbed Wire: The Story of Amnesty International*. London: Frederick Muller, 1978.

Martens, Kerstin. "An Appraisal of Amnesty International's Work at the United Nations: Established Areas of Activities and Shifting Priorities since the 1990s." *Human Rights Quarterly* 26, no. 4 (2004): 1050–1070.

Poe, Steven C., Sabina C. Carey, and Tanya C. Vazquez. "How Are These Pictures Different? A Quantitative Comparison of the U.S. State Department and Amnesty International Human Rights Reports 1976–1995." *Human Rights Quarterly* 23, no. 3 (2001): 650–677.

Power, Jonathan P. *Like Water on Stone: Forty Years Amnesty International*. Harmondsworth, U.K.: Penguin Books, 2001.

Winston, Morton. "Assessing the Effectiveness of International Human Rights: Amnesty International." In *NGOs and Human Rights: Promise and Performance*, edited by Claude Welch, pp. 25–54. Philadelphia: University of Pennsylvania Press, 2001.

ANGOLA

by Ana Leao

Angola, considered the seventh largest country in Africa, overlooks the West African coast. Under Portuguese colonial administration from the late fifteenth century until 1975, its territory includes 990 miles (1,600 kilometers) of South Atlantic coast and borders with the Republic of the Congo, the Democratic Republic of the Congo (DRC), Zambia, and Namibia. It also includes a small but oil-rich enclave to the north—Cabinda—surrounded by both Congos. Angola is a scarcely populated country with demographic levels on the narrow coastal plain substantially higher than those in the central plateau. Although endowed with natural resources and possessing both industrial and agricultural potential, Angola ranked 160 (out of 175 countries) in the 2005 Human Development Index (HDI). Decades of war and conflict, the main contributing factor to the appalling human indicators in Angola, ended with the signing of the Luena Memorandum of Understanding (also known as the Luena Accords) in April 2002 and renewed hopes of lasting peace and stability that would enable the country to fulfill its economic potential.

FROM COLONIALISM TO INDEPENDENCE

Colonialism came to Angola with the added repression of the fascist dictatorship in mainland Portugal; the advent of a dictatorship in Portugal in 1926 almost coincided with the consolidation of colonial administration in Angola. Even though Portugal claimed a presence in the territory starting in the late fifteenth century, colonial administration had hardly penetrated beyond a handful of coastal cities and inland trading posts until the Conference of Berlin in 1885 when the Portuguese claimed possession of the territories and sought to extend their administration to them. However, it was only after 1910 that colonial authority began, in earnest, to assert itself in the African colonies.

Until the late 1850s Angola's economy was dominated by the slave trade to such a degree that its impact on African peoples and their cultures is incalculable. Adding to the demographic depletion, the procurement of slaves from African traders led to the development of some local kingdoms through the subjugation of others, thus creating social tensions that still remain ill-understood today. When in 1858 the slave trade was abolished in Angola, the colonial authorities embarked on expansionist campaigns based on military strategies financed by higher hut taxes levied on the local population. Resentment toward this and other unpopular policies led Angolans to evade areas under Portuguese control and to sporadic rebellions repressed with renewed brutality in a cyclic pattern of violence that persisted until the liberation struggles of the 1960s.

Angolan resentment of taxation was compounded by employment policies based on racial discrimination that greatly limited the economic base for the local population. Under the colonial regime, the population was divided into *indígenas*, the great mass of black Africans mostly ignored by the authorities; *assimilados*, black Africans, and mestizos, those of mixed race, who could speak Portuguese, were literate, acted in a "civilized" manner, and maintained jobs in the secondary sector; and white settlers with rights to full citizenship even though many of them were illiterate and had as little or less marketable skills than the *assimilados*.

As the number of white settlers increased, the privileges previously enjoyed by Africans decreased: white settlers all but replaced the mestizos and *assimilados*, while *indígenas* became subject to the payment of a head tax with either currency or six months of unsalaried labor. As most Portuguese settlers were poor and without access to capital, they relied on cheap labor for profitable rural or industrial undertakings. Although the imposition of a hut tax pushed Angolans into the labor market, this was not enough to satisfy the labor needs of the settlers. Forced labor policies started with legislation in 1899, but it was after 1928 that abusive labor practices were institutionalized. In spite of much international criticism, these laws remained in effect until 1961 when they were officially (if not de facto) abolished. Concurrently with labor demands, the *indígenas* also had to meet quotas in certain crops, most commonly cotton for the mills in Portugal. These crops competed with food crops, and famines evolved with the concomitant deaths of thousands of Angolans.

António de Oliveira Salazar, the Portuguese dictator and mentor of the Estado Novo (New State), came to power in 1928 and ruled with an iron fist until suffering a stroke in 1968; Estado Novo lasted until 1974 when it was overthrown by a military coup. At a time when most colonial powers were taking the first steps toward granting total independence to their colonies, Portugal tightened the grip on what were considered its overseas provinces. The rise of national consciousness in Angola thus coincided with escalating political and military repression. But no amount of repression could contain the emergence of a local political class (even when forced into exile) or the resentment of the African population toward colonial policies, which provided a fertile ground for nationalist recruitment.

The three Angolan liberation movements that soon resulted embodied the social contradictions of Portuguese colonialism, as John Marcum (1969) illustrates in Volume 1 of *The Angolan Revolution* (1959–1962). The Popular Movement for the Liberation of Angola (MPLA) founded in 1956 in Luanda—the capital of Angola—represented the mestizo and Mbundu urban elites along the coast; the National Front for the Liberation of Angola (FNLA) was established in 1957 with the full support of the northeastern Bakongo people and the southern Ovimbundu. In 1964 Jonas Savimbi, an Ovimbundu leader, split from the FNLA to found the National Union for the Total Independence of Angola (UNITA). In spite of the many diplomatic moves to unite the three movements under a single umbrella, personal and ideological differences set their leaders apart and they fought each other as much as the colonial army. The tensions among the three groups would be fully played out at the time of independence and during the three decades thereafter; they would lead to a full-scale civilian war.

Fernando Andresen Guimarães's *The Origins of the Angolan Civil War: Foreign Intervention and Domestic Political Conflict* (1998) provides an exhaustive account of the development of the Angolan liberation movements and their alliances with foreign actors in a world divided by the Cold War scenario. In short, the MPLA made alliances with the Soviet bloc countries and Cuba through the Portuguese Communist Party, whereas the FNLA developed ties with Mobutu Sese Seko's Zaire and the United States. UNITA was open to support from any source: from Communist China to apartheid South Africa and the United States. In spite of the ethnic bias of each movement at the inception of the liberation struggle, as the conflict evolved, so too did popular support for the different groups change, and analysis of the conflict based on ethnicity cannot explain more recent political events, such as the outcome of the 1992 elections. The 1992 elections were held between the MPLA and UNITA and awarded a clear victory to the ruling party, the MPLA. Had the vote been divided along ethnic lines, such a victory would not have been possible, as estimates put the Ovimbundu peoples, which UNITA claimed to represent, at 37 percent of the total population.

Militarily, none of the liberation movements represented a real threat to colonial authority, and the repression of civilians did not abate, nor were there significant investments in social expenditure. Using special police forces, colonial authorities exerted violence against their perceived political opponents: indiscriminate imprisonments, interrogations under torture, denied legal representation, exile, and summary executions were but a few human rights abuses on the long list perpetrated by colonial authorities in Angola. These were compounded by massacres meted out to communities allegedly loyal to the rebels; forced labor and labor abuses; lack of access to health, education, and the most basic needs; and racial discrimination.

The April 1974 coup in Portugal resulted from pressures placed by both the independence movements in the colonies and Portuguese antifascist resistance. Essentially military in nature, the coup of 25 April failed to articulate a political agenda beyond the end of the colonial war, its main aim. Whereas in Portugal different political forces debated models of decolonization, security in the colonies deteriorated by the day, with the independence movements clamoring for an immediate transfer of power and independence and the white settlers fleeing en masse. It was within this political instability that decolonization took place. On 15 January 1975 the three Angolan liberation movements signed the first of many peace agreements—the Alvor Accords—establishing Angola's independence on 11 November 1975 and laying out guidelines for the political handover. Mistrust among the warring parties, misgivings about the neutrality of the mediator (Portugal), and the Cold War geography of the era created an environment of uncertainty conducive to political and military maneuvering rather than peaceful consolidation.

CIVIL WAR(S)

It was chaotic decolonization that created the opportunity for open military intervention in Angola, but foreign involvement turned war into an option, by arming and training reluctant parties for a political solution. Civil war in Angola started before formal independence, the perception being that whoever controlled the capital, Luanda, would control the country. As the date of independence approached, so grew the tension among the three movements and foreign support for each of them. The two superpowers of the Cold War closely monitored the situation in Angola and competed for the provision of war equipment and training to their Angolan allies, thus bringing war to a new level where human life and human rights considerations played no part.

The United States supported covertly the FNLA through Mobutu's Zaire and later, after the FNLA's military defeat, UNITA; the Soviet bloc and Cuba openly supported the MPLA. South African intervention in Angola involved regional and domestic considerations: to prevent logistical support to Namibian freedom fighters (South West Africa People's Organization or SWAPO) and the African National Congress (ANC), and the establishment of a Soviet-backed government in a neighboring country. U.S. intervention was limited to the provision of war equipment; its operations would switch from covert to open, depending on the domestic situation. In *In Search of Enemies: A CIA Story* (1978), John Stockwell suggests that the goal of U.S. support was neither to end the civil war nor bring about a change in the regime; the goal was to not allow a Soviet-backed government rule no matter what, regardless of the cost in human lives. Soviet and Cuban aid to Angola had a strong component of military support, complemented by assistance to development programs that were hard to pursue given the prevailing insecurity.

Although the Soviet bloc was openly pouring weapons and military advisors into Angola, with Cuba supplying troops, the supply of weapons from the United States to the FNLA occurred via Zaire and, according to David Birmingham (1992), to UNITA via Zambia in order to enhance military leverage vis-à-vis the Russian-backed MPLA. In October 1975 the South African Defence Force (SADF) invaded Angola in support of UNITA, aiming to increase pressure on the MPLA that was then being attacked from the north by FNLA and Zairian troops. The attack on Luanda, however, proved to be the wrong move; the FNLA and Zairian troops were disbanded by Cuban and MPLA troops (People's Armed Forces for the Liberation of Angola or FAPLA) and retreated to Zaire. FNLA never recovered from this setback and the movement and its leader, Holden Roberto, would only return to Luanda in 1991 as a political party. Apartheid support to UNITA discredited the movement and had the immediate effect of the MPLA government's official recognition by the Organization of African Unity (OAU) and subsequently the rest of the world, except for the United States.

However, the military defeat of the MPLA's opponents did not translate into continued peace. On the contrary, the newly inaugurated government had to not only respond to constant border clashes in the east and south, but also to secure the Cabinda oil fields, the main source of state revenue and patronage. Hence, the need for additional Cuban troops developed; they were paid with the royalties the Angolan government received from the United States to secure the oilfields explored by American companies. Cabinda was by now the stage for a secessionist struggle based on questionable historical evidence. As Cabinda was the main oil-producing province, the government of Angola was not willing to part with it, and government troops had to contend with not only the separatists but also UNITA (and Zairian) attacks. Initially represented by one movement that later split in three, the Cabinda separatists started their struggle in 1963 against the Portuguese government first and after 1975 against any government in mainland Angola.

Until 1991, the year the Peace Accords for Angola (otherwise known as the Bicesse Accords) were signed, the civil war exhibited a cyclic pattern of violence and witnessed many full-scale conventional battles, the most famous being Cuíto Cuanavale. During this battle in October 1987, the FAPLA backed by Cuban troops inflicted an embarrassing defeat on UNITA forces and South African troops. UNITA's survival from 1979 until the Bicesse Accords was based on its alliance with the United States via apartheid South Africa. In 1984 U.S. President Ronald Reagan was able to convince Congress to repeal the Clark Amendment (which prohibited CIA covert assistance to the Angolan rebels without explicit congressional approval) and thus openly support UNITA, leading to a new escalation of the conflict that spread to the highlands and ultimately the entire country. It was during this cycle of war that the population was heavily plundered for supplies and manpower by both parties, resulting in the inevitable human rights abuses characteristic of such scenarios. Torture and summary executions of prisoners were equally common practices.

Already in 1975, according to Jan Breytenbach in *The Buffalo Soldiers: The Story of South Africa's 32 Battalion, 1975–1993* (1992), UNITA was torturing and summarily executing war prisoners. Stockwell also refers to the summary execution of sixteen Cuban prisoners of war during the first phase of the civil war. There is no reason to believe the government would operate differently except for white prisoners of war, deemed too valuable to be executed and better presented to the international media as proof of foreign interference. The repression and violence that the government of Angola unleashed on the supporters of Nito Alves in 1977, leaving 28,000 dead and over 3,000 "disappeared," perfectly illustrate the government's contempt for human rights considerations. Alves belonged to the central committee of the MPLA and was well known for his opposition to the group's then leader—Agostinho Neto. In May 1977 Alves and Zé Van-Dunen were accused of fomenting rebellion; they were tortured and summarily executed, with their perceived supporters suffering a similar fate or imprisonment.

The massive destruction of Angola's infrastructure did not allow for development and the violence perpetrated on the population disrupted communities, displacing them to safer urban areas or refugee camps in neighboring countries. International support to both sides ruled out a clear military victory, but by the late 1980s the international backdrop was beginning to change: Mikhail Gorbachev's glasnost policies were in place and the worldwide oil crisis was over (for the time being). In South Africa, social unrest was spiraling out of control and the government felt the need to concentrate on the domestic situation rather than regional strategies. It was in this context that another peace agreement for Angola was negotiated.

Angola, South Africa, and Cuba signed the Tripartite Agreement in December 1988 in New York. It mandated the withdrawal of foreign troops from Angolan territory, granting concurrently independence to Namibia. The implementation of this agreement was overseen by the United Nations (UN), through the UN Angola Verification Mission I (UNAVEM I), and it was believed that the lack of international interference would help bring about a political resolution of the conflict. Although diplomatic pressure brought the warring parties to the negotiating table and influenced them to sign the Bicesse Accords in May 1991, whose implementation the UN Angola Verification Mission II (UNAVEM II) undertook, the process was almost as flawed as that for the Alvor Accords and had a similar outcome.

The Bicesse peace agreement was intended to mark the transition from conflict to political cohabitation. With the process mediated by Portugal, the former Soviet Union and the United States were observers to it (these three countries constituted what became known as the troika). Among the agreement's clauses calling for a cease-fire and the disarmament of both warring parties (the government of Angola and UNITA) was a clause known as the "triple zero" clause that prevented either party from procuring new weapons. Although not explicitly worded, the Bicesse Accords contained provisions relating to human rights—namely the free circulation of people and goods, the release of civilian and military prisoners, and an end to acts of violence against civilians. The monitoring and supervision of compliance were the joint responsibility of a commission that included representatives from Portugal, the United States, Russia, and the UN. There were no provisions relating to human rights abuses committed during the civil war.

As it turned out, none of the parties lived up to their commitments and the process was marred by numerous violations, with both sides restricting the free circulation of people and goods and delaying the release of prisoners. UNITA obviously did not disarm and the government established partisan paramilitary forces given the complacency of the international community. The government mobilized the nation's entire administration and state-owned media for propaganda and electoral purposes, while UNITA relied on threats of renewed war to harness support for a political victory. The 1992 electoral process went on unhindered by these violations and resulted in a turnout of 91 percent of all registered voters, with 54 percent voting for the MPLA and 34 percent for UNITA. In the presidential elections, 49.6 percent of the populace voted for José Eduardo dos Santos (the leader of the MPLA) and 40.7 percent for Jonas Savimbi. The Bicesse peace process ended when UNITA, alleging electoral fraud, refused to accept the poll results. Under the pretext of a suspected coup, government supporters unleashed unprecedented violence against UNITA, expelling its followers from the nation's primary urban areas. Meanwhile, Savimbi began to rebuild its war machine throughout the country. However, the elections conferred on the government an international legitimacy it had never enjoyed, while UNITA lost its main ally—the United States—when the administration of Bill Clinton finally recognized the government of Angola in mid-1993. Later that same year the UN Security Council, invoking systematic violations, imposed an international arms embargo on UNITA.

Rising oil prices brought unexpected revenue to the Angolan government; UNITA for its part controlled the diamond-producing areas of the northeast—the Lunda provinces. Ignoring the Bicesse Accords' triple zero clause, both sides could once again afford to further procure armaments, hence leading to another escalation of the conflict. In seeking arms, UNITA violated not only the triple zero clause but also the UN-imposed sanctions as of September 1993, but it found allies other than former Western supporters willing to assist. The support of African allies, such as Zaire and Togo, enabled UNITA to resist the Angolan Armed Forces (FAA) offensive and by 1994 the civil war had reached another stalemate. This so-called third war killed, according to Human Rights Watch (HRW), an estimated 300,000 Angolans—almost 3 percent of the population. This period of war was characterized by gross violations of the laws of war by both sides, including the indiscriminate bombing and shelling of cities under siege for extended periods; the massive destruction of property; abduction and forced conscription, including the use of young men and children as soldiers, and girls as sex slaves; the use of mercenaries; and accusations of massacres perpetrated on civilians by both sides. It was in this context that the MPLA and a very reluctant UNITA signed the Lusaka Protocol in 1994.

As reluctantly as the parties reached a peace agreement, in one regard their efforts did not falter: both received a general pardon for atrocities committed during the war, even though mass graves and accounts of massacres were well known and documented by, among others, Amnesty International (AI). The Lusaka Protocol contained provisions for a cease-fire; defined the role of the new UN mission (UNAVEM III) to supervise the implementation of the protocol; stipulated the release of prisoners and division of political power. Nevertheless, the protocol's implementation was marred by UNITA's resistance to handing over areas to government control and its refusal to join parliament and the Government of National Unity and Reconciliation (Governo de Unidade Nacional or GURN) in Luanda. UNITA's constant violations of the protocol caused the UN Security Council to impose further sanctions on it in October 1997, including travel bans and the freezing of foreign bank accounts. In May 1998 UN sanctions were broadened to ban UNITA's diamond exports and to prevent transportation to geographic areas under its control. In 1999 the government launched offensives against UNITA strongholds and called for an end to the UN Observer Mission in Angola (MONUA), which had replaced UNAVEM III in June 1997, and to the Lusaka peace process. The escalation of the conflict was inevitable and violence against civilians,

including UN staff and equipment, erupted as never before. Internal displacement affected some 1 million people, with refugees flowing into neighboring countries.

According to AI, the Lusaka Protocol expanded some of the human rights provisions included in the 1991 Bicesse Accords, in spite of the general amnesty for crimes of war. Specifically, the Lusaka Protocol called for the respect of human rights and basic freedoms; an end to acts of violence against civilians; freedom of movement, speech, and association; the release of prisoners; and the neutrality of the police. UNAVEM III's mandate included provisions for specifically monitoring human rights in Angola, but the mission was unable to prevent abuses.

Although violence abated after the protocol was signed, both sides engaged in cease-fire violations, aimed at controlling food aid and movements of people, leading to the death of hundreds of civilians. Forced conscription and kidnapping did not stop and the movements of troops and equipment intensified, particularly in the diamond-producing provinces—Lunda North and Lunda South. The laying of landmines continued in clear violation of the protocol; freedom of speech, association, and movement were systematically denied; journalists were arrested, threatened, and even killed; prisoners of war were slow to be released; and there were no investigations into the thousands of "disappeared." Government security and partisan forces harassed and murdered political opponents; UNITA did not stop its kidnappings and abductions or violence against defenseless civilians, particularly government officials and traditional chiefs. Mutilation, sexual abuse, and enslavement are but some of the accusations against UNITA. HRW mentions frequent reports of forced labor and forced recruitment in areas under UNITA control, as well as pillage, indiscriminate shelling, and the forced habitation of people in areas where food was scarce. The government responded with arbitrary killings, indiscriminate arrests and the general harassment of UNITA supporters, forced recruitment, indiscriminate bombing of towns under UNITA control, mistreatment of prisoners, pillage and looting of aid agencies, and manipulation and harassment of the media. In addition, the government opposed the opening of humanitarian corridors until almost the end of 1999.

In the following years the conditions under which UNITA fought and operated further worsened: UN sanctions could still be violated but transactions were more difficult and expensive. The forced displacement of people from rural to urban areas under government control decreased markedly the amount of food available to

UNITA as well as logistical support, although HRW suggests that collusion may have existed between UNITA and government officials in sidestepping UN sanctions on water and fuel supplies. Hunger and deteriorating living conditions led to mass desertions from UNITA ranks; once under government control, these men were organized into special units that hunted down any remaining UNITA fighters. In February 2002 UNITA's leader, Jonas Savimbi, died in combat with government troops in the eastern province of Moxico. In April of that same year the military leaders of both warring factions met in Luena to sign a memorandum mandating the demobilization and disarmament of UNITA fighters and re-enforcing the commitments subscribed to under the Lusaka Protocol.

Having brought an end to the war with UNITA, the government could now concentrate on controlling the separatist movements in Cabinda by deploying over thirty thousand troops to the territory and systematically targeting and killing civilians. HRW's report *Angola: Between War and Peace in Cabinda* (1996) provides an accurate description of the situation at the time.

ASSESSMENT

In the early twenty-first century Angola is experiencing what is perhaps the longest period of peace in its history. However, Angola has a long tradition of impunity with regard to human rights violations, and in spite of lasting military peace, human rights abuses seem embedded in daily life: corruption, embezzlement of the state's property, police brutality, forced displacements, evictions, violations of freedom of speech and religion, persecution of journalists, mistreatment of migrants, and abuse of power prevail. Most Angolans are still denied basic rights, including health, education, and housing, by a corrupt political elite bent on keeping its unwarranted privileges.

[*See also* African Union: Commission and Court on Human Rights; Cuba under Castro; *and* Demise of Soviet Communism.]

BIBLIOGRAPHY

Agualusa, José. *Catálogo de sombras.* Lisbon, Portugal: Dom Quixote Publicaçoes, 2003.

Amnesty International. *Angola, the Lusaka Protocol: What Prospect for Human Rights.* http://www.web.amnesty.org/library/index/ENGAFR120021996.

Anstee, Margaret J. *Orphan of the Cold War. The Inside Story of the Collapse of the Angolan Peace Process, 1992–93.* New York: St. Martin's Press, 1996.

Bender, Gerald J. *Angola under the Portuguese: The Myth and the Reality.* Trenton, N.J.: Africa World Press, 2004.

Birmingham, David. *Frontline Nationalism in Angola & Mozambique.* Trenton, N.J.: Africa World Press, 1992.

Breytenbach, Jan. *The Buffalo Soldiers: The Story of South Africa's 32 Battalion, 1975–1993.* Alberton, South Africa: Galago, 2002.

Bridgland, Fred. *Jonas Savimbi. A Key to Africa.* Edinburgh, Scotland: Mainstream, 1986.

Brittain, Victoria. *The Death of Dignity: Angola's Civil War.* London: Pluto Press, 1998.

Chabal, Patrick, ed. *A History of Postcolonial Lusophone Africa.* Bloomington: Indiana University Press, 2002.

Clarence-Smith, W. G. *Slaves, Peasants, and Capitalists in Southern Angola 1840–1926.* Cambridge, U.K.: Cambridge University Press, 1979.

Cofré, Margrit, and Fergus Power, eds. *Stories for Trees.* Luanda, Angola: Development Workshop, 2002.

Comerford, Michael G. *The Peaceful Face of Angola: Biography of a Peace Process (1991–2002).* Luanda, Angola: M.G. Comerford, 2005.

Davidson, Basil. *In the Eye of the Storm: Angola's People.* London: Longman, 1972.

Edward, George. *The Cuban Intervention in Angola, 1965–1991: From Che Guevera to Cuito Cuanavale.* New York: Frank Crass, 2005.

Guimarães, Fernando Andresen. *The Origins of the Angolan Civil War: Foreign Intervention and Domestic Political Conflict.* New York: St. Martin's Press, 1998.

Hodges, Tony. *Angola: From Afro-Stalinism to Petro-Diamond Capitalism.* Bloomington: Indiana University Press, 2001.

Human Rights Watch. *Angola Arms Trade Violations of the Laws of War since the 1992 Elections.* New York: HRW, 1994.

Human Rights Watch. *Angola. Between War and Peace: Arms Trade and Human Rights Abuses since the Lusaka Protocol.* New York: HRW, 1996.

Human Rights Watch. *Angola. Some Transparency No Accountability: The Use of Oil Revenue in Angola and Its Impact on Human Rights.* New York: HRW, 2004.

Human Rights Watch. *Angola Unravels: The Rise and Fall of the Lusaka Peace Process.* New York: HRW, 1999.

Human Rights Watch. *Struggling Through Peace: Return and Resettlement in Angola.* New York: HRW, 2003.

Kapućiński, Ryszard. *Another Day of Life.* Translated from Polish by William R. Brand and Katarzyna Mroczkowska-Brand. San Diego, Calif.: Harcourt Brace Jovanovich, 1987.

Luanda Antena Comercial (LAC). *UNITA que futuro?* Luanda, Angola: Editorial Nzila, 2002.

Maier, Karl. *Angola: Promises and Lies.* London: Serif, 2007.

Marcum, John A. *The Angolan Revolution. Volume 1: The Anatomy of an Explosion (1959–1962).* Cambridge, Mass.: MIT Press, 1969.

Meijer, Guus, ed. *From Military Peace to Social Justice? The Angolan Peace Process.* London: Conciliation Resources, 2004.

Mendes, Pedro Rosa. *Bay of Tigers: A Journey through War-Torn Angola.* London: Granta Books, 2004.

Messiant, Christine. *Why Did Bicesse and Lusaka Fail? A Critical Analysis.* http://www.sarpn.org.za/documents/d0001958/Bicesse_Lusaka_2005.pdf.

Newitt, Malyn. *Portugal in Africa: The Last Hundred Years.* London: C. Hurst & Co., 1981.

Schneidman, Witney W. *Engaging Africa: Washington and the Fall of Portugal's Colonial Empire.* Lanham, Md.: University Press of America, 2004.

Stockwell, John. *In Search of Enemies: A CIA Story.* New York: W.W. Norton, 1978.

Winden, Bob van der, ed. *A Family of the Musseque: Survival and Development in Postwar Angola.* Oxford: WorldView Publishing, 1996.

KOFI ANNAN

by Courtney B. Smith

Kofi Atta Annan served as the seventh secretary-general of the United Nations (UN) from 1 January 1997 to 31 December 2006. He was appointed to this position after working for nearly thirty-five years in the UN bureaucracy, making him the first secretary-general to rise from the ranks of the organization. His tenure began at a time when the UN faced myriad global problems that demanded its attention, and the focus of much of this activity was centered on the secretary-general. Unfortunately, these expanding demands were not accompanied by a corresponding increase in the resources or authority enjoyed by the organization or Annan's office. Despite these challenges, his actions and achievements led him to be widely considered among the most effective of the secretaries-general. Annan faced his share of disappointments and frustrations, in particular after the beginning of the Iraq War, in 2003, but these developments should not overshadow his deep concern for human dignity and his significant contributions to the promotion of human rights.

PERSONAL BACKGROUND

Annan and his twin sister were born in Kumasi, Ghana, on 8 April 1938. He was baptized Anthony, but his parents preferred to use traditional names; hence, he was called Kofi (born on Friday) and Atta (twin). Annan had at least two older sisters and one younger brother. His parents were both of noble lineage in the Fante tribe, although his father was also partially of Ashanti descent. The most significant influence on Annan as a child was his father, who worked as an executive for the United Africa Company, a subsidiary of Unilever. His father also held a number of tribal and governmental positions during and after his business career, which made him a man whose counsel on issues was valued by others. Stories of Annan's childhood recount several lessons learned from his father, including the importance of self-confidence and honesty.

As a teenager, Annan enrolled in Mfantsipim, Ghana's oldest and most prestigious boarding school, where he began to hone the skills of negotiation and persuasion that later served him as secretary-general. He developed a knack for talking his way out of trouble with upperclassmen and teachers, and he successfully led a hunger strike to protest the quality of food. After Mfantsipim, Annan studied at the then new Kumasi Institute of Science and Technology, where he was elected vice president of the Ghana Student Union. Annan then applied for and received a Ford Foundation scholarship to attend Macalester College in Saint Paul, Minnesota. Given Macalester's international interests, Annan fit in well and became engaged in many activities, including debate, soccer, and track, in which he set the school's record in the sixty-yard dash. Important influences on him were his athletic career, which taught him how to lose gracefully, and the cold weather, which taught him to respect the wisdom of the local population.

After his graduation, Annan moved to Geneva, Switzerland, studying economics at the Graduate Institute of International Studies. Although Annan never finished this degree, he did earn a Master of Science degree one decade later, at MIT's Sloan School of Management. While in Geneva, Annan met a Nigerian woman, Titilola Alakija, who became his first wife in 1965. During the next fifteen years they had a daughter, Ama, and a son, Kojo, but they also moved for Annan's career nearly ten times, which certainly contributed to the end of their marriage. In 1980 Annan returned with his son to Geneva, where he met Nane Lagergren, the niece of the heroic Swedish diplomat Raoul Wallenberg. The two shared important similarities: both worked for the Office of the UN High Commissioner for Refugees, and both were single parents, with Nane raising a daughter, Nina. When Annan was reassigned to New York in 1983, Nane followed, and the couple married there in 1984.

ANNAN'S RISE TO SECRETARY-GENERAL

When Annan assumed his first position in the UN system in 1962, as an administrative and budget officer at the World Health Organization, he did not intend to remain an international civil servant for his entire career; he planned instead to return home to Ghana. After assignments with the Economic Commission for Africa in Addis Ababa and the Second UN Emergency Force in Ismailia, he did leave the UN for two years, in 1974. During this time he worked as managing director of the Ghana Tourist Board in Accra, but military rule in his native country made the job nearly impossible. As a result, he returned to the UN and stayed there for the remainder of his career, moving through increasingly senior posts in New York and Geneva, dealing primarily with human resources, finance, and budgeting.

Annan's career at the UN unfolded in support roles until 1990, when he was sent to Baghdad to secure the release of the UN's international staff in advance of the first Gulf War. His success led Boutros Boutros-Ghali, his predecessor as secretary-general, to appoint him as the second-ranking officer in the newly formed Department of Peacekeeping Operations in 1992. In this position, Annan developed a particularly positive relationship with the United States, which subsequently pushed to have him take over the department as undersecretary-general in 1993. Annan was seen as being more flexible toward U.S. interests, a view that was confirmed in 1995, when Annan authorized North Atlantic Treaty Organization (NATO) bombing in the former Yugoslavia while the secretary-general was out of contact with UN headquarters. Soon thereafter, Boutros-Ghali sent Annan to be his special representative in the region, which some observers viewed as an attempt to sideline a popular potential rival. There is likely some merit to this view, as the United States clearly preferred Annan as the candidate to replace Boutros-Ghali, who was denied a second term. Although France initially opposed Annan's nomination, nearly all member states liked and respected him, and the French soon acquiesced.

Annan's background and the manner of his rise to secretary-general created divergent expectations of his performance in office. The United States supported him because he promised to be more secretary than general, a person who would focus his energies and talents on managing the institution. Some from the developing world saw him as "the first American secretary-general," but they nonetheless also viewed him as one of their own, someone they hoped would be a general, vocally advocating for their positions and priorities. In his work on human rights, Annan excited and disappointed both views.

ANNAN'S COMMITMENT TO HUMAN DIGNITY

Annan's early work at the UN involved little interaction with the organization's human rights activities. However, once he became secretary-general, his deep concern for human dignity made human rights one of the hallmarks of his tenure. His most dramatic and controversial statement on human dignity came during his annual address to the UN General Assembly on 20 September 1999. In advocating what some later called the Kofi doctrine, Annan argued that the international community must place the need to protect individuals from those who abuse them above the desire to respect state sovereignty. He was criticized by myriad diplomats, policy makers, academics, and journalists who feared that his doctrine might set a precedent for unending humanitarian wars, but he was also praised by an equally diverse group who felt that Annan was finally placing human rights and the responsibility to protect civilians on the proper stage.

During his tenure, Annan viewed the UN's wide-ranging efforts to promote human rights as an essential means to enhance human dignity. This was a critical contribution to the international human rights discourse, and it is not surprising that Annan's focus on these issues was deeply rooted in his own personal experiences. One of the reasons he cared so deeply about human dignity lay in the failures of the UN and its member states during the mid-1990s in Rwanda, Bosnia, and Somalia. Annan was head of UN peacekeeping at the time, and he acknowledged his own sense of responsibility for the inability of the international community to mobilize the political will to respond as required. In the case of Rwanda, for example, Annan (and others) placed traditional UN principles of impartiality and neutrality above the need to intervene, a decision for which he later expressed organizational and personnel regret. Although Annan's reputation survived, at least in the eyes of most observers, these events influenced him and what he hoped to accomplish as secretary-general. The early roots of his concern for human dignity, however, were present long before those events, especially in regard to his experiences dealing with race, equality, and civil rights while in college. Annan learned important lessons about being in the minority, and it is telling that his most vivid memory of these events was the embarrassment of those who had treated him so poorly.

These experiences cultivated in Annan a great compassion for the well-being of others, especially the most vulnerable victims of human tragedy. He considered it his responsibility as secretary-general to call attention to the needs of groups and individuals who lacked voices of their own. This commitment anchored Annan's address when he accepted the Nobel Prize for Peace on 10 December 2001, in which he asserted that improving the lives of individual people was the true measure of everything the UN does.

SCOPE OF ANNAN'S HUMAN RIGHTS WORK

Annan's second major contribution was his expansive definition of the scope of human rights. He chose to address some of the most difficult traditional human rights issues, including genocide, oppression, political freedoms, and the promotion of democracy, even over the opposition of important member states. Annan's work to shine an international spotlight on Darfur and to press this issue behind the scenes as necessary is a prime example of his desire not to let the international community repeat the mistakes of the past, regardless of the political sensitivities involved. But he also brought a human rights dimension to the UN's activities in a range of other issues, such as HIV/AIDS and terrorism, both of which were cited by the Norwegian Nobel Committee when it selected him for the award. Furthermore, Annan strongly advocated for improvement in the institutional structures through which the UN addresses human rights, proposing that the ineffectual Commission on Human Rights be replaced by a more robust Human Rights Council. A deep moral commitment to human rights guided these efforts, but he also understood that political trade-offs would be required in order to make essential progress.

Annan's expansive view of human rights was reflected in many of his most important initiatives. For example, his report *In Larger Freedom* (2005) examines the interconnections among human rights, security, and development, the UN's three most essential activities. In addition, the eight components of the Millennium Development Goals all relate to issues of human rights and human dignity: poverty, hunger, education, gender equality, health, and environmental sustainability. Even in reaching out to new partners, such as the private sector, through his Global Compact, Annan conceptualized human rights on a broad scale, through links to labor, the environment, and corruption.

ANNAN'S LEGACY

A common debate in the study of leadership is the extent to which the leader makes the office or the office makes the leader. In the case of Annan and human rights, it is clear that his deep commitment to human dignity made the office more effective than it had previously been. This was possible in part because of Annan's personal attributes, which were almost perfectly suited to the tasks he faced: his personal sense of dignity, his persuasive ability and negotiating skill, his patience and modesty, his calm and reserved demeanor, and his astute interpersonal skills. However, these formidable talents were not sufficient to keep him out of controversy, especially in regard to the secretary-general's only real source of influence: moral authority. Annan's moral authority was compromised from the beginning in the eyes of some observers because of his role in the UN's failures of the 1990s. When the Oil-for-Food scandal emerged late in his second term, additional criticisms were raised concerning the actions of Annan's son and apparent lapses in Annan's management style. As these issues were combined with the ongoing difficulties of addressing the situation in Iraq, Annan spent part of his final years as secretary-general disappointed and depressed.

Fortunately for Annan, these negative evaluations of his moral authority and his overall performance as secretary-general remain a minority view. Although definitive assessments of his tenure await the passage of time, most early-twenty-first-century UN scholars believe that Annan will be considered one of the most effective secretaries-general and that his important human rights work was an essential component of his success.

[*See also* Boutros Boutros-Ghali; Darfur; Peacebuilding; Rwanda; *and* United Nations Human Rights Council.]

BIBLIOGRAPHY

Barnett, Michael. *Eyewitness to a Genocide: The United Nations and Rwanda.* Ithaca, N.Y.: Cornell University Press, 2002. A deeply moving evaluation of the UN and the international community in regard to the events in Rwanda, written by a scholar on fellowship at the time at the U.S. Mission to the UN.

Chesterman, Simon, ed. *Secretary or General? The UN Secretary-General in World Politics.* Cambridge, U.K.: Cambridge University Press, 2007. A collaborative study of the role and responsibilities of the UN secretary-general that includes contributions from well-known scholars and distinguished practitioners.

Gourevitch, Philip. "The Optimist: Kofi Annan's U.N. Has Never Been More Important and More Imperiled." *The New Yorker,* March 3 2003, 50–73. A detailed and generally well-balanced examination of Annan's strengths and weaknesses as secretary-general, completed as the Iraq crisis was unfolding.

In Larger Freedom: Towards Development, Security, and Human Rights for All. UN Doc. A/59/2005, March 21, 2005. One of Annan's most important reports as secretary-general, prepared in advance of the World Summit held to celebrate the UN's sixtieth anniversary.

Kille, Kent J. *From Manager to Visionary: The Secretary-General of the United Nations.* New York: Palgrave Macmillan, 2006. A comparative analysis of the leadership qualities of three UN secretaries-general; includes a detailed evaluation of Annan's strategic style.

Meisler, Stanley. *Kofi Annan: A Man of Peace in a World of War.* Hoboken, N.J.: John Wiley & Sons, 2007. The first book-length biography of Annan, completed with the secretary-general's cooperation near the end of his second term.

Rivlin, Benjamin, and Leon Gordenker, eds. *The Challenging Role of the UN Secretary-General: Making "The Most Impossible Job in the World" Possible.* Westport, Conn.: Praeger, 1993. A classic scholarly study of the office of UN secretary-general, completed before Annan's tenure; includes a chapter by the future secretary-general on the responsibilities of the office in regard to the UN budget.

Shawcross, William. *Deliver Us from Evil: Peacekeepers, Warlords, and a World of Endless Conflict.* New York: Simon & Schuster, 2000. Although not focused on the secretary-general, this book includes a number of significant insights about Annan, based on personal interviews.

Smith, Courtney B. "Politics and Values at the United Nations: Kofi Annan's Balancing Act." In *The UN Secretary-General and Moral Authority: Ethics and Religion in International Leadership,* edited by Kent J. Kille, pp. 299–336. Washington, D.C.: Georgetown University Press, 2007. Written as part of a comparative analysis of the first seven secretaries-general, this chapter focuses on how Annan's ethical and religious values influenced his behavior in office.

Traub, James. *The Best Intentions: Kofi Annan and the UN in the Era of American World Power.* New York: Farrar, Straus and Giroux, 2006. Although often described as a biography of Annan, and written with his cooperation, this text is better understood as an analysis of the UN and the secretary-general's role in it in the era of American power that began with the end of the Cold War.

ANTI-SLAVERY INTERNATIONAL

by Claude E. Welch Jr.

Anti-Slavery International (often simply referred to as Anti-Slavery) justly claims to be the world's oldest continuous human rights organization. Founded in 1839, when many hopes of abolitionists had fallen short of accomplishment, it has continued to press for the total elimination of slavery in all its forms. The phenomenon of slavery has changed dramatically in the many decades since the establishment of Anti-Slavery. Hence, the organization has adapted new approaches and strategies while maintaining its steady focus on slavery. The more than 170 years since its founding have seen slavery transformed from a relatively widely accepted practice to one condemned by public opinion and contrary to both customary and conventional international law. However, reaching formal, legally enforceable definitions on the global level has remained difficult. States have been reluctant to commit themselves to restrictions on their sovereignty; individuals and groups caught in slavery-like conditions lack the resources to organize; world public opinion has not fully recognized the nature and scope of the issues involved; and, despite efforts by Anti-Slavery International and similar groups, relatively little popular mobilization has been undertaken.

No human rights abuse has resulted in more formal international treaties than slavery. More than six hundred agreements in the nineteenth century sought to eliminate trade in slaves and chattel practices. Its reduction and abolition motivated the establishment of the first international human rights nongovernmental organization (NGO). Anti-Slavery International, founded under the name of the Anti-Slavery Society in 1839, remains a significant protagonist in such efforts. It encourages the adoption of global agreements. In spite of them, however, slavery-like practices and servitude remain widespread phenomena. A definition crafted in 1926 (drawn from a broadly worded international agreement of 1890) continues to be contested and imperfectly implemented in the early twenty-first century.

The 1926 treaty, negotiated under the League of Nations, defined slavery as the "status and/or condition of a person over whom any or all of the powers attaching to the right of ownership are exercised" and mentioned a range of slavery-like practices. The 1956 supplementary convention, adopted by the United Nations (UN), went into considerably greater detail about contemporary forms of slavery. Like its predecessor, however, it provided no international enforcement mechanisms. A 1949 agreement on trafficking in persons (updated by the 2000 optional protocol on trafficking) covered related ground. Several of the more than 180 conventions adopted by the International Labour Organization (ILO) deal with child labor, forced labor, or debt bondage. All involve slavery-like conditions from which individuals cannot escape. The UN dubbed 2004 the International Year to Commemorate the Struggle against Slavery and Its Abolition. The fifty-seven-page 2006 annual report of the ILO was entitled *The End of Child Labour: Within Reach.* Clearly, there has been plenty of talk about prohibiting slavery, leading to global treaties. Much remains to be done in terms of enforcement, however. This has proven to be the Achilles heel, as in many other areas where human rights agreements exist on paper but are not effectively implemented.

Not only legal agreements—formal human rights conventions and bilateral treaties among states—bar slavery, moreover. The buying and selling of persons are contrary to customary international law. All governments are obligated, under an *erga omnes* responsibility (obligations owed to all), to stamp out this practice through direct action. Slavery, whether in the form of chattel ownership or more modern guises, is a crime against humanity; it falls under the purview of the recently established International Criminal Court (ICC).

A PERSISTENT PROBLEM

Slavery and slavery-like practices affecting millions of people persist in the third millennium. New forms of

78

bondage have emerged and constitute the "frontier," in a sense, of current human rights concern. The chattel slavery familiar to nineteenth-century abolitionists (although still extant in a few countries) provides a misleading model. Early-twenty-first-century manifestations of slavery are far more subtle than those of captured, racially differentiated slaves imported into a society to fill specific labor needs, the form most familiar to Westerners. Slavery in the twenty-first century is a deep-rooted feature in many societies, justified by existing norms, in which selected groups in the populace are particularly liable to slavery-like practices, often on the basis of descent—that is, because of their race, ethnic group, or status in society, such as the Dalits (untouchables) of South Asia.

A curious institutional gap confronts antislavery activists. Although slavery is universally recognized as a gross abuse of human rights, neither it nor related slavery-like practices fall under a specific monitoring UN treaty body. Most major UN human rights treaties provide for their own monitoring mechanism, usually a supervisory committee that utilizes diplomatic means to ensure that ratifying states honor their legal obligations under the particular agreements. Neither the 1926 Convention (the League of Nations' Slavery, Servitude, Forced Labour, and Similar Institutions and Practices Convention; the so-called Slavery Convention) nor the 1956 Supplementary Convention (the UN's Supplementary Convention on the Abolition of Slavery, the Slave Trade, and Institutions and Practices Similar to Slavery) provided means of enforcement or set meaningful obligations for submitting information for analysis. Similar gaps exist in the 1949 Convention for the Suppression of the Traffic in Persons and the Exploitation of the Prostitution of Others, the 2000 Protocol against the Smuggling of Migrants by Land, Sea, and Air, and the 2000 Protocol to Prevent, Suppress, and Punish Trafficking in Persons, Especially Women and Children.

No organization has played a lengthier and more important role in the effort to widen awareness of contemporary forms of servitude than the venerable NGO Anti-Slavery. Founded in 1839 as the Anti-Slavery Society, it has gone through a series of changes, most notably in the 1990s. The organization modernized its program of action, changing its name to Anti-Slavery International, to cope with new types of slavery-like practices and professionalized its operations. What had been a small, narrowly based group of British supporters, working almost completely on a volunteer basis, moved closer to becoming an international NGO led by a core of relatively low-paid professionals, few in number, with the majority of its members located in the United Kingdom. Anti-Slavery's major attention is focused on public opinion, governments (especially that in Great Britain), the ILO, and various UN bodies.

HISTORIC ROLES OF ANTI-SLAVERY

Anti-Slavery was founded by a small, largely Quaker group of British subjects. They drew on their wealth and strong social concerns, stressing the sinfulness of slavery as a means of building support and moral legitimacy for their political activism. The history of Anti-Slavery illustrates different types of networks. For most of the organization's life, they were personal in nature, centered in a London-based group of politically influential and often economically successful individuals.

Pre-1919: Establishment, stagnation, and indirect pressure.

Anti-Slavery was an organization born of disappointed expectations. The triumph of 1833, when the House of Commons, besieged by petitions, abolished the ownership of slaves in the British Empire, in fact made only a limited dent on a large, profitable traffic. Freed slaves had been consigned to debt servitude as "apprentices" in the West Indies. Exports of humans (particularly to Brazil and Cuba) continued unabated in the late 1830s, despite British efforts to suppress it, with upwards of 300,000 people exported from West Africa during the decade. Almost as many persons were shipped from East Africa to the Gulf region. Moreover, the British East India Company did not outlaw slavery, but simply declared that it had no legal standing within British India. Not until 1860 did it become an offense to own slaves in India.

Anti-Slavery operated for the first 150 years of its existence essentially as a face-to-face, London-based group. Membership was measured in the hundreds: 236 in 1840, 461 in 1841, 850 by 1847. A number of local affiliates sprang up, largely as a result of organized petition campaigns. Business was conducted through a general committee that met approximately every two months in London. Although there was a secretary and one or two assistants, the staff played a restricted role—as late as 1990, the general committee approved expenses above £50 (approximately $100 in 2008), and the minutes of its meetings were not made available to staff. The relatively small number of activists, drawn from the same social milieu, could readily agree on strategy, in terms of both networks and direct representations to government.

The strategy of nineteenth-century British antislavery activists was appropriate to the times and circumstances, nonetheless. A natural stratagem for human rights NGOs is to concentrate on the politically well placed, to leverage and thereby increase their organizations' influence. Anti-Slavery tried to affect what the British government could accomplish through its diplomatic pressure, economic clout, and imperial spread. Success resulted far more from personal links than from organizational size.

From 1890 to 1926: at the edges of (largely imperial) diplomacy.

A late-nineteenth-century landmark in the global struggle against slavery for which Anti-Slavery could claim some credit was the so-called Brussels Act, the General Act for the Suppression of the African Slave Trade. Signed by or on behalf of the governments or sovereigns of nineteen countries on 2 July 1890, the Brussels Act was based on the belief that better, expanded, and hence effective colonial administration would provide the best protection against slavery in Africa. It helped create a principle of international responsibility for "native welfare" and internationalized slavery as a human rights issue.

For Anti-Slavery, this 1890 document ushered in a gradual change from almost exclusively British condemnation toward multinational pressure against slavery and the slave trade. This shift was gradual, however, and had limited effect on how Anti-Slavery operated within Great Britain. The organization continued primarily to rely on well-connected British activists influencing diplomats and politicians of powerful Western countries, almost always the United Kingdom. Anti-Slavery's objectives were to achieve universal recognition of slavery and similar institutions and practices as gross abuses of human rights, and to establish effective mechanisms to stamp out these abuses. The means were primarily documentation, publicity, and leverage. The instruments included influencing public opinion in Great Britain, involving British political and social elites in legislative and diplomatic steps, building international pressure for broad, clear definitions of slavery and similar practices, and (most important) enforcing the elimination of what had been agreed on.

In 1909 the organization merged with the Aborigines' Protection Society. Its major focus remained sub-Saharan Africa. The new organization counted a somewhat larger number of members and a wider mandate. It could afford to employ a full-time head, recruiting John Harris, an antislavery activist deeply moved by practices in the Belgian Congo, as its secretary. During his lengthy period of service (1910–1940), he, more than any other person, drew international attention to institutions and practices similar to slavery.

At the end of World War I, when international treaties were realigned, major colonial powers believed that the slave trade was no longer a live issue. Anti-Slavery sharply disagreed. When the Brussels Act lapsed, the group turned to new forms of pressure through the new League of Nations. Far broader in its composition than the handful of (largely) European states that had ratified the Brussels Act, the League could claim a moral prestige and global spread advantageous in combating an international phenomenon. Harris bombarded both the League and the British government with reports, memoranda, and the like. He also used personal connections, persuading the New Zealand delegate to the League—concurrently a British member of parliament—to introduce a resolution in the League's assembly calling for the global investigation of slavery and reports from all members about slavery in their territories.

As a result of these pressures, the League of Nations established a Temporary Slavery Commission (TSC) in 1924. It could take evidence from individuals and NGOs, but only after approval from the governments concerned. The commission met in private, twenty-one times over a ten-day period. Its reports could only be published with League concurrence, and after the colonial administrations had reviewed them. The TSC had no bite and very little bark. Publicity was restricted in advance. Nonetheless, the TSC brought numerous social and economic questions into the international arena. It condemned not just slavery but also serfdom, the sale of children for domestic service, concubinage, and slave dealing under the guise of adoption or marriage. Harris, Sir Frederick Lugard (a distinguished British colonial administrator and member of the TSC), and other highly motivated individuals thus sowed the seeds for the expanded definition of slavery that appeared in the landmark 1926 Convention.

The Temporary Slavery Commission recommended that a new international agreement against the slave trade be negotiated under the auspices of the League of Nations. Lugard's draft was adopted by the commission in a narrow 4 to 3 vote. However, these ideas were too radical for the times. After significant watering down, the 1926 Convention was approved by the League of Nations Assembly and subsequently ratified by states. Nonetheless, many significant advances were made. The convention sought to bring about "progressively and as soon as possible the complete abolition of slavery *in all its forms*" (italics added). It lacked details about these forms, however. It defined slavery and the slave trade, but provided only weak injunctions against forced or compulsory labor, lest they degenerate into slavery. As a result, the agreement was replete with insufficient sanctions against some behaviors. It also omitted many items (such as debt bondage or childhood betrothal of girls in order to exploit their labor) desired by antislavery activists. The treaty said essentially nothing about how and by whom instances of banned practices would be reviewed. Nor did it speak to enforcement at an international level, if League member states refused to take action.

Practical application: the 1926 Convention.

The absence of a monitoring committee weakened the 1926 agreement significantly. Nonetheless, the International Labour Organization started to work on an agreement against forced labor, with urging from NGOs and the League of Nations; colonial administrations had to review their laws; and NGOs continued to hammer away at abuses. Under pressure from Harris and Anti-Slavery, the British government in 1929 called on the assembly of the League to create a small, permanent group of experts that could collect and publish information on slavery and conduct investigations. The resulting Committee of Experts on Slavery (CES) was both temporary and toothless, however. It could meet, in private, only for one year, consider just slavery (not forced labor) under the 1926 Convention, and look only at reports submitted by or through governments. Direct input from NGOs was excluded. Were a report to contain allegations unfavorable to a particular country, that government would have the opportunity to receive and comment on such information before the CES could take note of it. All seven members were drawn from European colonial powers; moreover, many were directly or indirectly linked to individual governments. However, the seeds of change were germinating. The committee recommended that it be succeeded by a permanent body. After lengthy debate, the colonial powers agreed to the establishment of the Advisory Committee of Experts on Slavery (ACES)—to that date, the closest approximation to an international mechanism to end this abuse.

The 1926 Convention defined slavery as the "status and/or condition of a person over whom any or all of the powers attaching to the right of ownership are exercised." However, the League never defined these words and moved cautiously in naming experts who could interpret and apply them. Not until 1934, when the League was afflicted by the Depression and reeling under the threat of an impending major war, was the ACES appointed. Its level of activity was dictated primarily by the national interests of representatives' countries and severely restricted by the financial constraints of the League. Little effective action could be undertaken.

Although never formally dissolved, the Advisory Committee of Experts died of attrition before World War II. The birth of the United Nations resulted in renewed steps for global abolition. The initiative passed to a substantial extent from London-based Anti-Slavery and the Geneva, Switzerland-based League of Nations to newer NGOs and the New York–based United Nations. Anti-Slavery had assisted in the creation of the Advisory Committee of Experts on Slavery but, beyond that, its concerns and efforts during the Depression and World War II were overshadowed by more pressing issues.

Efforts at the United Nations, 1945 to 1956.

In recognition of its seriousness, freedom from slavery stands near the start of the Universal Declaration of Human Rights (UDHR, adopted 1948) and successor documents such as the International Covenant on Civil and Political Rights (ICCPR, adopted 1966). Article 4 of the UDHR succinctly states, "No one shall be held in slavery or servitude; slavery and the slave trade shall be prohibited in all their forms." The Universal Declaration helped to lay the foundation for the next major advance, the 1956 Supplementary Convention. Discussion about this new agreement ran afoul of new fault lines within the United Nations, notably the Cold War and rapid decolonization in Africa and Asia, however. These changed the political orientation of the General Assembly and, as a result, the effectiveness of human rights bodies reporting to it.

Nonetheless, Anti-Slavery helped stimulate international action among NGOs and sympathetic states. It noted with concern that the 1926 Slavery Convention was not included when the League of Nations was dissolved and its treaty-maintaining functions were transferred to the United Nations. The only significant action came in 1951, when the UN appointed a five-member ad hoc committee, including the secretary of Anti-Slavery. He was burning with enthusiasm and single-handedly produced a lengthy, integrative minority report on the nature and extent of slavery-like practices, thereby laying important groundwork for the Supplementary Convention. The impact of Anti-Slavery was, in essence, the impact of one dedicated person, namely John Harris.

The ad hoc committee made three significant recommendations. First, the United Nations should take responsibility for the 1926 Convention, which would require a "protocol" to it. Second, the practices prohibited under the 1926 agreement should be extended through a supplementary convention. Both these objectives were attained in the 1956 Supplementary Convention. The ad hoc committee believed that the creation of international supervisory machinery for the abolition of slavery and other forms of servitude was urgent and should be undertaken immediately. It further recommended that serfdom be defined and prohibited, that ratifying states provide annual reports, that slave trading on the high seas be declared an international crime with universal jurisdiction, that female genital mutilation and "inchoate forms of enslavement" be prohibited, that a minimum age of consent to marriage be set at fourteen, and that the registration of marriages be encouraged.

In the context of the times, these were striking proposals. The 1956 Supplementary Convention achieved many, but not all, of the goals of Anti-Slavery. The organization was disappointed that defense of traditional state sovereignty, unwillingness to risk potentially divisive social change, and extraneous international rivalries scuttled a provision allowing the search and seizure of a ship of a ratifying state reasonably suspected of conveying slaves in international waters. It was more chagrined by the unwillingness of governments to incorporate even a weak system of reporting. On the other hand, the 1956 agreement officially extended international supervision over many practices not mentioned in the 1926 Convention. "Institutions and practices similar to slavery" now fall under international jurisdiction, thanks largely to the advocacy of Anti-Slavery.

"OLD" AND "NEW" FORMS OF SLAVERY: SOCIETAL REALITIES, TREATY DEFINITIONS

Kevin Bales has contrasted the familiar form of chattel possession—the "old slavery" against which Anti-Slavery fought in the nineteenth century—with the "new slavery" characteristic of the early twenty-first century. According to him in *Disposable People: New Slavery in the Global Economy* (1998), the three key causes of the new slavery include the population explosion, economic globalization, and the chaos of greed, violence, and corruption created by these in developing countries. Millions of victims exist, Bales argues, with very few identifiable perpetrators. This makes eradication difficult. In short, the "causal chain" cannot be readily discerned between those who suffer and those responsible. Defining what slavery is thus remains problematic. Only by analyzing specific contexts closely can one determine whether practices similar to slavery exist in particular cases.

The 1956 Supplementary Convention added four institutions and practices of "servile status":

- Debt bondage, in which the value of reasonably assessed personal services of a debtor is not applied to liquidating his or her debt, or the length and nature of these services are not limited and defined;
- Serfdom, in which a tenant is bound by law, custom, or agreement to live and labor on another's land and is not free to change his or her status;
- Certain marriage practices, notably (1) when a woman is given or promised in marriage, without the right to refuse, for payment in money or kind, (2) when a woman may be transferred by her husband, his family, or his clan to another for value received, or (3) widow inheritance; and
- Exploitation of children, in which a child or young person under eighteen is delivered by a parent or guardian to another "with a view to the exploitation of the child or young person or of his labour."

The Supplementary Convention stresses how debt bondage results in servile status. The obligations of the Supplementary Convention have had varying and usually minimal impact, however. Several states where offenses are the worst have not ratified the relevant agreements. Many factors have mitigated the impact of ILO and NGO efforts. Nonwage agricultural and domestic labor falls outside the ILO's purview. International pacts on corporate codes of conduct have also fallen short. Other slavery-like practices defined in the 1956 Supplementary Convention cut counter to social norms in numerous states, reducing the likelihood of effective government action.

RESEARCH AND LOBBYING EFFORTS BY ANTI-SLAVERY

Documenting and publicizing the exploitation of children have become a major objective of Anti-Slavery. The organization has launched campaigns focused on child camel jockeys in the Persian Gulf area. Other campaigns by Anti-Slavery include forced labor in North Korea; trafficking for forced labor in the United Kingdom; fair and ethical trade; child begging and street children; child soldiers; and the responsibilities of transnational corporations.

Forced marriage and the sale of wives constitute still other institutions and practices similar to slavery. Both may be deeply embedded in cultural norms, although they also constitute responses to difficult economic circumstances. Both have also been long recognized as abuses. Accordingly, abolition will be difficult and protracted—and the potential work for Anti-Slavery to be measured in decades.

UPDATING ANTI-SLAVERY AS AN ORGANIZATION

Although it remains based in London, Anti-Slavery has pursued some of its activities in Geneva, through the UN and ILO. It has professionalized its staff and approaches. Even though relatively small, the organization increased in size, moving from one full-time professional employee in 1990 to twenty in 2002. Strategic planning has become a watchword. Anti-Slavery expanded its work on debt bondage and exploitative child labor. At the same time, it reduced its involvement with indigenous peoples. Asia supplanted Africa as its primary geographic focus. Although the organization's concern with chattel slavery remains, its attention to slavery-like institutions and practices has increased. The lack of an international monitoring mechanism for the 1956 Supplementary Convention continues to occupy much of Anti-Slavery's attention. It identifies six forms of twenty-first-century slavery: bonded labor; forced labor; forced marriage; worst forms of child labor; human trafficking; and slavery by descent.

Anti-Slavery has long desired to create effective international mechanisms to oversee and evaluate governments' efforts to abolish institutions and practices similar to slavery. This concern surfaced in 1966, when the UN Economic and Social Council (ECOSOC) debated a recommendation from a specially appointed expert that a small committee of experts on slavery be established. Opposition stemmed from almost every side. The British government wanted a high commissioner for human rights, whereas Anti-Slavery requested both a high commissioner and a committee focused on slavery. The Communist bloc and the United States opposed the creation of the proposed committee. Countries recently freed from colonial rule spoke out sharply as well, focusing on the continued existence of apartheid and colonialism. Accordingly, no committee of experts was established by ECOSOC in 1966. Antislavery advocates found other avenues to publicize slavery and slavery-like practices in various international forums. The UN Commission on Human Rights (UNCHR) debated slavery for the first time in March 1967.

Anti-Slavery during this period followed an outmoded operational model. Power in the organization rested within its general committee, with membership fixed between twenty-one and forty, that convened regularly to run the group's business. The atmosphere at Anti-Slavery's meetings was decidedly patrician, with most of its members elderly. They did recognize, however, the need to update their image. They published a twenty-four-page pamphlet, *Its Task Today*, to set forth Anti-Slavery's broadened goals.

This brochure reiterated the organization's three major aims at the time: eradication of slavery "in all its forms"; abolition of labor systems "resembling slavery"; and "protection and advancement of aboriginal and primitive peoples." It advocated close work with governments, "the only authorities able to realize the Society's aims." The British government served as the chief focus, for "it was relatively easy to influence an administration having an image of Christian foundations to maintain and which at least shared the Society's basic assumptions." However, "Her Majesty's Government is no longer available as a central agency subject to such pressure." This last sentence signaled an important shift. Anti-Slavery saw HMG as a target of criticism, not only a focus of hope for pressure at the international level. At the same time, new agreements had strengthened Geneva-based foundations for human rights. Hence, *Its Task Today* identified Anti-Slavery's immediate aim as "to bring about the establishment of permanent machinery responsible for informing and advising the United Nations on slavery and for supervising the implementation of the slavery conventions." However, the pamphlet concluded, "there is no likelihood of slavery being eliminated in the foreseeable future." For the next several years, Anti-Slavery's pressure at the global level focused on potential "permanent machinery" and on providing detailed information to the UN and ILO.

Another effort at institutional reorientation came in 1987. Twelve activists on the general committee exchanged views on the present state of the society and its future direction. Serious institutional transformation started at this brainstorming session. Implementation took most of a decade. The most important decision, in

TABLE 1. Income and Expenses, Anti-Slavery International, 1990–2006 (in £ sterling)

	1990	1991	1992	1993	1994	1995	1996	1997	1998	1999	2000	2001	2002	2003	2004	2005	2006
Income	285,552	158,712	163,145	232,417	212,588	247,178	402,701	363,321	554,141	669,078	445,167	720,067	932,639	985,579	1,136,697	1,326,081	1,700,725
Direct costs	79,757	80,144	108,599	132,678	180,463	229,445	270,293	293,860	409,494	478,413	453,999	568,545	698,541	828,295	869,194	922,875	
Fund-raising	36,477	17,144	17,816	18,879	26,689	31,678	35,163	28,327	35,794	22,435	44,437	54,505	63,539	66,038	134,823	131,696	
Administrative costs	46,416	62,056	63,985	67,623	39,463	42,355	41,678	43,785	40,368	45,596	46,535	52,078	62,900	59,805	68,654	51,140	

Data prior to 2000 derive from annual reports; since 2000 from personal communication with Jeff Howarth, 30 April 2007.
The income for 1990 includes £148,813 received as a result of Anti-Slavery's 150th anniversary appeal.

retrospect, was to move away from the unwieldy, self-perpetuating committee in which the organization's chief responsibilities had been vested, toward a larger permanent staff of professionals working with a trimmer executive committee. The reforms included a significant increase in the organization's funding, and greater staff and campaign activity. A new director, Michael Dottridge, was hired from Amnesty International. The organization started to receive enough funds to upgrade its publications and to support a growing cadre of researchers and activists, as shown in Table 1.

One of the chief avenues for Anti-Slavery's face-to-face contacts has been the Geneva-based UNCHR Working Group on Contemporary Forms of Slavery, formed in 1975. Despite concerns about the benefits relative to costs, leaders of Anti-Slavery often visit Geneva. At the heart of this working group are five of the twenty-six experts of the UN Sub-Commission on the Promotion and Protection of Human Rights. Anti-Slavery has furnished the overwhelming bulk of the working group's documentation—reports totaling a quarter of a million words in the first three years, for example—and is regarded as the most significant, best-informed organization in the group.

Overall, the working group has enjoyed little clout, prestige, or influence. However, near total disregard when it was formed and almost total rejection of its recommendations for minimal power throughout most of its history have changed somewhat. An increasing number of governments send observers. Greater attention to women's and children's rights has also made a difference. The working group devotes increasing time to the knotty problems of prostitution, child labor, and the sale of organs for transplants. NGO attendance has grown, albeit modestly, although the numbers remain far below those recorded for sessions of the Sub-Commission on the Promotion and Protection of Human Rights, the Human Rights Council (HRC), or the council's predecessor, the Commission on Human Rights

Creating an active, informed monitoring mechanism has been the most consistent objective of Anti-Slavery, but the least successful. However, the working group is not the ultimate target. It is an entry point into the hierarchical UN human rights system and global public opinion. The strongest official action an NGO can obtain from the Working Group on Contemporary Forms of Slavery is a recommendation to the Sub-Commission on the Promotion and Protection of Human Rights that it adopt a specific resolution. And, since NGOs such as Anti-Slavery (working collegially with certain sub-commission members)

propose many of the draft resolutions, they exert influence that, over time, may be translated into the power of changing public opinion. Anti-Slavery remains active both vis-à-vis the council itself and its advisory body—as well as with various special procedures.

Neither the 1926 Convention nor the 1956 Supplementary Convention would have been initiated at the times they were without pressure from Anti-Slavery. However, many governments' follow-up to both treaties continues to be unimpressive. The modest means of enforcement reflect the tremendous imbalance in power between states and NGOs, in addition to the vague terminology of treaties. And given the close links between culture and several institutions and practices similar to slavery, the debate over what abuses can be effectively measured and combated will remain vigorous.

Yet another international mechanism should be mentioned: the special rapporteur on contemporary forms of slavery, one of the "special procedures" tasked to the UNCHR and HRC. The first, David Weissbrodt, was appointed by the commission in 2002. He and Michael Dottridge, the director of Anti-Slavery, coauthored an extensive report in 2000 on the legal foundations of international steps against slavery. The relationship between Anti-Slavery and the special rapporteur remains symbiotic and highly professional.

Although the relative importance of chattel slavery has diminished, the significance of institutions and practices similar to slavery has increased dramatically. While outright ownership of slaves exists in only a small handful of countries, alternate forms of lifelong subordination to others continue to endure. Major issues of the early twentieth century (including bonded labor, child labor, and the exploitation of indigenous peoples) remain major problems of the early twenty-first century. Pressure on governments—from below in terms of mobilized public opinion, from within in terms of influence exerted as a result of expertise and of personal contacts between NGO leaders and policy makers, and from above in terms of intergovernmental discussions—is a constant objective for Anti-Slavery. And, finally, it is working increasingly in concert with NGOs in developing countries and others in the affluent north.

THE CHANGING DYNAMICS OF ANTI-SLAVERY

Without question, the early-nineteenth-century antislavery movement in Great Britain represented one of the earliest mobilizations of mass support for a human rights objective. However, this phase of widely supported popular pressure proved temporary. Anti-Slavery's survival as an organization throughout the rest of the Victorian era and into the twentieth century may have been a historical accident. The society's survival and the successes it achieved resulted from its geographic location and the dedication of a few key members. Its merger with the Aborigines' Protection Society in 1909 and appointment of John Harris as secretary rescued the group from the political sidelines and possible extinction at that time. Anti-Slavery worked closely with and through the British government. It claimed success if HMG pressured other governments explicitly on slavery-related issues, or if Great Britain changed its own practices and policies when its "national interest" dictated otherwise. This close cooperation remained reasonably constant until the early 1950s. The group's attempts to revise and expand its image to metamorphose into more of an international NGO only became particularly marked during the 1990s.

Being physically located in London, Anti-Slavery enjoyed one distinct advantage. With some of its leading members serving concurrently in Parliament, British abolitionists worked within the social and political parameters of one system, in order to change social and political parameters elsewhere. Anti-Slavery remains reformist and in favor of an incremental approach rather than being revolutionary and an organization of the masses. It was and is primarily nationally based, but internationally oriented.

Anti-Slavery faces a different political dynamic in Geneva than in London. With respect to intergovernmental organizations (IGOs), coalitions with many like-minded governments usually prove more effective than strong ties with one. Affinity can be established with several states, rather than with a single patron, and with numerous NGOs, rather than going it alone. Ant-Slavery's close ties with other NGOs, particularly through the Working Group on Contemporary Forms of Slavery, should profit from further development. Its yeoman efforts must be complemented by studies and political mobilization by others for future success, however. Effective global efforts to end contemporary forms of slavery, in particular, will require support from larger numbers of NGOs from developing countries. Only as activists from disadvantaged groups speak up, organize, put pressures on their governments, and work for social change will there be an effective global movement against contemporary forms of slavery.

[*See also* Belgian Congo; Colonialism; International Labour Organization; United Nations Commission on Human Rights; United Nations Sub-Commission on Human Rights; *and* Universal Declaration of Human Rights.]

BIBLIOGRAPHY

Amnesty International. *Mauritania: A Future Free from Slavery?* London: Amnesty International, 2002. AFR 38/003/2002.

Amnesty International and Anti-Slavery International. *Enhancing the Protection of the Human Rights of Trafficked Persons: Amnesty International and Anti-Slavery International's Recommendations to Strengthen Provisions of the July 2004 Draft European Convention against Trafficking in Human Beings.* London: Amnesty International, 2004. IOR 61/016/2004.

Anti-Slavery International. *Its Task Today.* London: ASI, 1967. http://www.adam-matthew-publications.co.uk.

Anti-Slavery Reporter. http://www.antislavery.org. Anti-Slavery's quarterly journal.

Bales, Kevin. *Disposable People: New Slavery in the Global Economy.* Berkeley: University of California Press, 1998.

Bales, Kevin. *Ending Slavery: How We Free Today's Slaves.* Berkeley: University of California Press, 2007.

Bales, Kevin, and Peter T. Robbins. "No One Shall Be Held in Slavery or Servitude: A Critical Analysis of the International Slavery Agreements and Concepts of Slavery." *Human Rights Review* 2, no. 2 (2001): 18–45.

Coupland, Reginald. *The British Anti-Slavery Movement.* London: Frank Cass, 1964.

Dottridge, Michael, and David Weissbrodt. "Review of the Implementation of and Follow-up to the Convention on Slavery." In *German Yearbook of International Law*, pp. 242–292. Berlin: Duncker & Humblot, 2000.

Grant, Kevin. *Civilised Slavery: Britain and the New Slaveries in Africa, 1884–1926.* New York: Routledge, 2005.

Greenidge, C. W. W. *Slavery.* London: George Allen and Unwin, 1958.

Harris, John. *A Century of Emancipation.* London: J.M. Dent & Sons, 1933.

Human Rights Watch. *Contemporary Forms of Slavery in Pakistan.* New York: Human Rights Watch, 1995.

Human Rights Watch (Children's Rights Project and Human Rights Watch/Asia). *The Small Hands of Slavery: Bonded Child Labor in India.* New York: Human Rights Watch, 1996.

Miers, Suzanne. *Slavery in the Twentieth Century.* Walnut Creek, Calif.: Altamira, 2003.

Quirk, Joel Forbes. "The Anti-Slavery Project: Linking the Historical and Contemporary." *Human Rights Quarterly* 28, no. 4 (2006): 565–598.

Rassam, A. Yasmine. "Contemporary Forms of Slavery and the Evolution of the Prohibition of Slavery and the Slave Trade under Customary International Law." *Virginia Journal of International Law* 39, no. 2 (1999): 303–352.

Skinner, E. Benjamin. *A Crime So Monstrous: Face-to-Face with Modern-Day Slavery.* New York: Free Press, 2008.

Temperley, Howard. *British Antislavery 1833–1870.* London: Longman, 1972.

LOUISE ARBOUR

by William A. Schabas

Canadian jurist and the fourth United Nations (UN) High Commissioner for Human Rights from 2004 to 2007, Arbour was also the third prosecutor of the International Criminal Tribunal for the Former Yugoslavia (ICTY) and the second prosecutor for the International Criminal Tribunal for Rwanda (ICTR), holding office from 1996 to 1999. Arbour made important contributions to the development of all three institutions, where she was a dynamic, effective, and popular leader with her staff. Some states, however, did not always agree with her criticisms of their policies.

BACKGROUND

Louise Arbour was born in Montreal, Canada, on 10 February 1947. Her father Bernard managed hotels in rural Quebec. Following the breakup of her parents' marriage, she lived with her mother Rose, who supported the family with income from a women's clothing boutique in Montreal. From the age of ten, Louise Arbour attended a convent school, Collège Regina Assumpta, from which she graduated in 1967. Arbour obtained a law degree at the Law Faculty of the University of Montreal, graduating in 1970. A distinguished student, she obtained a prestigious clerkship with Justice Louis-Philippe Pigeon at the Supreme Court of Canada. While working for Justice Pigeon, she also undertook postgraduate studies at the Law Faculty of the University of Ottawa. She was called to the Quebec Bar in 1971, and she later joined its Ontario equivalent, the Law Society of Upper Canada.

During 1972 and 1973 Arbour worked as a research officer for the Law Reform Commission of Canada. In 1974 she began a legal academic career at Osgoode Hall Law School of York University in Toronto, where she specialized in criminal law. In 1987 Arbour left the academy for an appointment as justice of the Ontario Supreme Court. Three years later, she was promoted to the Ontario Court of Appeals. As a senior Canadian judge, she participated in important rulings applying Canada's new constitutional charter, a document that was largely based on

texts drawn from international human rights instruments. For example, she voted that prisoners had the right to participate in democratic elections and that the state had an obligation to organize this in an effective manner. Arbour also joined a majority of the court in upholding the acquittal of a Hungarian émigré charged with Nazi war crimes and crimes against humanity—it was one of Canada's first prosecutions based on universal jurisdiction. The ruling was controversial in some circles and was subsequently confirmed by the Supreme Court of Canada.

As vice president of the Canadian Civil Liberties Association, Arbour took strong and often controversial positions that reflected her deep attachment to the rights of the accused. For example, she criticized so-called rape-shield provisions that prevent defendants in sexual assault cases from cross-examining complainants about previous relations. In 1994 and 1995 Arbour served as the single member of a commission of inquiry into certain events at the Prison for Women in Kingston, Ontario; she made scathing criticisms of the prevailing conditions and put forward forceful recommendations for change.

INTERNATIONAL DIMENSION

Arbour's international career began in 1995 when Richard Goldstone, who was then prosecutor of the UN International Criminal Tribunals for the Former Yugoslavia and Rwanda, proposed her as his successor to Secretary-General Boutros Boutros-Ghali. Goldstone had first met Arbour some years earlier, when she had attended a conference at Witwatersrand University. Her candidacy provoked some initial hesitations from skeptical human rights nongovernmental organizations (NGOs), based on concerns about some of her views, such as the opposition to rape-shield legislation.

Arbour obtained leave from the Ontario Court of Appeals, taking up the position as international prosecutor in September 1996. There, she directed the first trials at the Yugoslavia and Rwanda tribunals, steering them through difficult formative years as the two institutions struggled to obtain custody of important suspects and to ensure prompt proceedings of those taken into custody. At the Yugoslavia tribunal, UN peacekeeping forces initially resisted her appeals for them to arrest alleged offenders, but they gradually became more cooperative as a result of Arbour's persistent complaints coupled with intense lobbying campaigns at the UN and with powerful states. Nothing in Arbour's background, either as a law professor and judge, had prepared her for what were essentially political functions at a high international level, but she quickly excelled in that environment.

Many of the cases she directed raised innovative arguments and broke new ground in international criminal law. Arbour undertook the first international prosecution of the crime of genocide since adoption of the Convention on the Prevention and Punishment of the Crime of Genocide in 1948. The *Akeyesu* judgment, and several others that followed during her tenure as prosecutor of the International Criminal Tribunal for Rwanda, helped clarify many legal issues, such as the quantitative dimension of the crime and the scope of protected groups. The definition of genocide requires that there be the intent to destroy a "national, ethnical, racial or religious group, in whole or in part." However, these concepts had received little judicial interpretation prior to *Akayesu*. In the same case, she successfully managed to get rape and sexual violence characterized as crimes against humanity, which was another important innovation. The prosecutor's office was somewhat careless with regard to the procedural rights of certain Rwandan detainees—something for which it was scolded in a 1999 Appeals Chamber.

While Arbour acted as prosecutor of the two tribunals, the negotiations leading to adoption of the Rome Statute of the International Criminal Court (ICC) took place. Arbour contributed to the debates, offering informed opinions on the relationship between international tribunals and national governments and justice systems that built on her own experience. One of the most significant developments at the Rome Conference was the delegates' acceptance of an independent prosecutor, with authority to initiate prosecutions even in the absence of a particular mandate from either the UN Security Council or a member state. Arbour herself served as a reassuring model, and she was held up as an example of a determined, competent, independent, and fair prosecutor in answer to those who were concerned that a reckless, irresponsible individual might assume such a position.

Arbour remained sceptical about the underlying premise of prosecutions at the International Criminal Court, which were based on deference to national justice systems. Under the principle of "complementarity," the court could not take up a case unless the prosecutor could prove that domestic courts were either unwilling or unable to proceed. Her own experience with regimes in the former Yugoslavia had made her extremely wary of the obstructive and uncooperative role they might play when confronted with possible action by international judicial institutions.

Under Arbour's stewardship at the international criminal tribunals, prosecutorial strategies evolved toward a focus on individuals in leadership positions. In May 1999, during NATO bombing of the former Yugoslavia (in response to the persecution of ethnic minorities in Kosovo), Arbour obtained an indictment of the country's sitting president, Slobodan Milošević, for war crimes and crimes against humanity; she also obtained an order freezing his assets around the world. This was the first time that an acting head of state had ever been charged by an international tribunal. The indictment probably contributed to shortening the conflict by putting additional pressure on the Serbian leader, and ultimately helped bring about his political downfall and subsequent transfer to The Hague for trial.

RETURN TO CANADA

Shortly after charging Milošević, Louise Arbour announced that she was leaving the tribunals to take up an appointment as justice of the nine-member Supreme Court of Canada, where she replaced Peter Cory as one of three judges traditionally appointed from the Province of Ontario. In *Burns and Rafay v. United States*, she joined the other members of the court in denying an extradition request for two accused murderers: on the grounds that exposure to capital punishment in the United States would violate fundamental rights. The judgment drew on international human rights law authorities and expressed concerns about the danger of a wrongful conviction by American courts. Another decision was more troublesome from a human rights standpoint. In *Suresh v. Canada*, a Supreme Court of Canada decision reached during the politically volatile post-9/11 context, she concurred with a ruling that deportation of a terrorist suspect—despite concerns he might be subject to torture—could be permitted in exceptional circumstances. It was a judgment premised on a balance between fundamental human rights and the prerogatives of counterterrorism and national security.

Arbour was in the minority of the court in a case dealing with the corporal punishment of children.

She voted to strike down a section of the Canadian Criminal Code that provides parents and teachers with a defense when they use physical force for disciplinary purposes (*Canadian Foundation for Children, Youth and the Law v. Canada*), saying it "violates the constitutional rights of children to safety and security." Arbour's dissenting judgment noted the importance of evolving standards of international human rights law on this issue, explaining that "Canada's international obligations with respect to the rights of the child must also inform the degree of protection that children are entitled to." In support of her opinion, she cited recent Concluding Observations of the UN Committee on the Rights of the Child, calling for Canada to repeal its legislation authorizing corporal punishment of children.

Arbour also dissented in a case concerning the role of economic and social rights in constitutional litigation. She considered that regulations denying social welfare benefits to young adults were discriminatory and contrary to fundamental principles of justice. Arbour argued that the Canadian constitutional protection of the right to "life, liberty and security of the person" included "a positive dimension" that was enforceable by the courts, and that extended to cover certain necessities of life such as food, housing, and medical care.

RETURN TO INTERNATIONAL LIFE

When the Rome Statute of the International Criminal Court entered into force in July 2002, Arbour's name circulated as an ideal candidate for the institution's first prosecutor, but she soon confirmed that she was not interested in the job. Then, in 2003, following the murder of High Commissioner for Human Rights Sergio Vieira de Mello in Iraq, Secretary-General Kofi Annan approached Louise Arbour to take up the premier human rights position in the UN. She initially turned down the offer, but after later reconsidering it, she resigned from the Supreme Court of Canada and was appointed to the four-year term of High Commissioner for Human Rights, effective 1 July 2004.

During the course of her mandate as high commissioner, Arbour presided over an enormous expansion of the office. As a consequence of important reforms in 2005 and 2006, the budget was dramatically increased, and Arbour used the new resources to develop an extensive network of field offices throughout the world. In 2005 she expressed disappointment with the politicization of the Commission on Human Rights (UNCHR), contributing to a process that brought about the abolition of that body

and its replacement by the Human Rights Council. Arbour navigated the Office of the High Commissioner (OHCHR) through a difficult period of change and adjustment to the UN human rights machinery. Her approach to the new Council was supportive but also cautious, and she jealously protected the independence of the OHCHR. She was unsuccessful in efforts to reform the "treaty bodies," the expert committees such as the Human Rights Committee, the Committee for the Elimination of Racial Discrimination, and the Committee against Torture whose activities have proliferated with the adoption of new conventions and the growth in numbers of ratifying states.

Arbour was less confrontational than her celebrated predecessor, Mary Robinson. Nevertheless, she could be forthright and outspoken when this seemed necessary. In July 2006, as war raged in Lebanon, she warned that "those in positions of command and control" were subject to "personal criminal responsibility," angering some who viewed these remarks as directed principally against Israeli officials. She also publicly criticized U.S. detention and interrogation policies after 9/11, saying she had no hesitancy in characterizing "water boarding" as torture.

Arbour encouraged an autonomous role for the OHCHR in the development of human rights norms. Her career as judge and academic ideally suited her for this. She issued authoritative opinions on legal issues such as the illegitimacy of so-called diplomatic assurances by which states promise that individuals transferred to their jurisdiction will not be tortured. Arbour insisted that if such assurances were necessary, the practice of torture in the receiving state was already too serious. She promoted an orientation within the OHCHR directed at economic and social rights, insisting that extreme poverty constituted one of the greatest threats to the respect of human dignity. In this way, she built on previous similar steps by Mary Robinson.

The Darfur crisis was one of the major human rights issues during her term as high commissioner. Arbour was very forceful about the violations, substantially increasing the number of field officers and producing several extensive reports on human rights violations, including sexual violence. In late 2004 the OHCHR organized a fact-finding mission to Darfur at the request of the UN Security Council. Its report, issued in January 2005, concluded there was strong evidence that war crimes and crimes against humanity had been committed, recommending referral of the situation in Darfur to the Security Council. Two months later, the Security Council gave the International Criminal Court the necessary authorization to open an investigation: this was the first time it had ever done so at the request of the Council, a measure that was necessary to establish jurisdiction given that Sudan was not a party to the Rome Statute.

As high commissioner, Arbour signed amicus curiae briefs that were submitted to national and international tribunals, including the U.S. Supreme Court and the International Criminal Court. When judges at the International Criminal Court expressed concern about the pace of the Darfur investigation, she disputed the prosecutor's contention that it was not possible to conduct investigations within the affected region. Before the Iraqi Special Tribunal, she argued that former president Saddam Hussein should not be executed following his conviction for genocide, crimes against humanity, and war crimes.

As her four-year term came to a close, Arbour announced that she would not seek a second mandate. She cited personal reasons for the decision, although there was speculation that a renewal might have been opposed by some large states that were annoyed by positions she had taken—notably with respect to human rights violations by Israel. She left the UN at the age of sixty-one; she was in good health and at the height of her powers but was without any apparent projects for the future. In 2008 she was appointed a Companion of the Order of Canada, the country's highest civilian honor, "for her contributions to the Canadian justice system and for her dedication to the advancement of human rights throughout the world." She has been awarded more than thirty honorary doctorates. Arbour has three children—Emilie, Patrick, and Catherine Taman—and one grandchild.

ASSESSMENT

Louise Arbour has made important contribution to human rights at both the institutional and substantive levels.

As a senior officer of the two ad hoc international criminal tribunals, and then as the head of the OHCHR, she steered all of these organizations through difficult periods of growth and expansion. They were all stronger, better established, and more credible after her tenure. She seemed to have a natural aptitude for the combination of administrative and political skills that were required. As a leader, she was greatly appreciated by those who worked within the institutions, exercising her authority with confidence, modesty, and generosity of spirit. She also ably managed the tightrope act of speaking out in defense of human rights while trying to maintain the multigovernmental support on which international authority depends.

[*See also* Darfur; International Criminal Tribunal for Rwanda (ICTR); International Criminal Tribunal for the Former Yugoslavia (ICTY); *and* United Nations High Commissioner for Human Rights.]

BIBLIOGRAPHY

Arbour, Louise. "Crimes against Women Under International Law." *Berkeley Journal of International Law* 21 (2003): 196.

Arbour, Louise. "The Crucial Years." *Journal of International Criminal Justice* 2 (2004): 396.

Arbour, Louise. "History and Future of the International Criminal Tribunals for the Former Yugoslavia and Rwanda." *American University International Law Review* 13 (1998): 1498.

Arbour, Louise. "The Prosecution of International Crimes: Prospects and Pitfalls." *Washington University Journal of Law and Policy* 13 (1999): 1.

Off, Carol. *The Lion, the Fox and the Eagle: A Story of Generals and Justice in Rwanda and Yugoslavia.* Toronto: Random House Canada, 2000.

ARMENIANS IN THE OTTOMAN EMPIRE

by Peter Balakian

The Armenians emerged as a distinct culture in the sixth century BCE and inhabited an area that in the early twenty-first century included the Republic of Armenia, most of eastern Turkey, and border areas of Azerbaijan, Georgia, and Iran. At its height in 70 CE, it stretched from the Mediterranean to the Caspian Sea. Today the Republic of Armenia, founded after the fall of the Soviet Union, is in the southwest Caucasus and is one-tenth of its historic size. In 301 CE Armenia declared Christianity its national religion, becoming the first Christian nation.

For centuries Armenians were ruled by Persia, the Byzantines, and the Arabs, until, from the eleventh century on, they lived under the rule of Seljuk and Ottoman Turkic tribes that had come from the regions of the Gobi Desert to colonize Anatolia and Asia Minor.

INFIDEL STATUS IN THE OTTOMAN EMPIRE

The Ottomans conquered Constantinople in 1453 and controlled Anatolia. Under the Ottoman system, Muslims were separated from *dhimmi* (non-Muslims such as Armenians, Assyrians, Greeks, and Jews), who lived in self-governing communities called *millets*. Armenians were allowed to run their communities' internal affairs under government protection and rule.

In this system, however, *dhimmi* had few legal rights, and none in Islamic courts; thus Armenians—with no protection from theft and extortion and the rape and abduction of women—were in perpetual jeopardy. They were not allowed to own weapons or join the military or civil service, which excluded them from the power structure and made them prey, subjected to a corrupt tax-farming system wherein they were forced to pay redundant rounds of taxes to extorting local officials. They were required to wear distinctive dress and defer to Muslims in public.

THE ARMENIAN QUESTION

What came to be known as the "Armenian question" grew out of two Tanzimat (restructuring) reform programs (1839, 1856), in which the empire's minorities were promised reforms and equality under the law. When the reforms failed to materialize, Armenians sought protection from the increasing abuses of a military autocracy and a decaying feudal system.

Pressure for Armenian reforms overlapped with four Russo-Turkish wars between 1806 and 1877, fought over control and domination of strategic areas in the Balkans and the Crimea and Russia's concern for the plight of Christians under Ottoman rule. The Greeks broke free by 1828, and in the 1870s other Balkan states were pressing for autonomy, eliciting violent Ottoman reprisals, such as the massacres of the Bulgarians.

In their final war, the Russians defeated the Turks and occupied the heavily populated Armenian territories of eastern Anatolia. The peace treaty of San Stefano (1878) stated that Russian troops would evacuate the Armenian provinces once Turkey agreed to implement the reforms and guarantee the Armenians protection. The Turks hated Russian and European intervention in their internal affairs and appealed to the British to intervene. As Russian gains were a threat to British interests, Britain was sympathetic to the sultan's request and demanded that Russo-Turkish issues be settled by the European powers. The Treaty of Berlin (1878) that followed returned to Turkey many of its losses, including two Armenian provinces, thus putting the very sultan who had been abusing the Armenians in charge of protecting them from himself.

An angry Sultan Abdülhamid II now referred to European concern for the improvement of life for the Armenians as "the everlasting persecutions and hostilities of the Christian world" (Alder and Dalby, p. 360). Consequently, social and political conditions for the Armenians grew worse. The sultan now sent masses of Muslim refugees (*muhajirs*), whom the Russo-Turkish wars had driven from the Balkans and the Caucasus, into eastern Anatolia to claim Armenian land, and violence was sanctioned. By 1890 he had created the Hamidiye (belonging to Hamid), his private army of Kurds, which allowed the sultan to deal directly with the Armenian problem.

As Armenian frustration grew, protests and activism emerged. Progressive ideas about equality and human rights had come to Armenians in Turkey from Armenian intellectuals in Russia, and the European Enlightenment had reached them through education, trade, and travel and through the American Protestant missionary schools in Turkey.

The formation of political parties (Hunchaks and Dashnaks) now gave voice to Armenian aspirations. In 1890, in Erzerum, about two hundred Armenians met publicly with a petition to protest Armenian conditions. In Constantinople, Armenians demonstrated outside their cathedral. In both cases, police broke up the protests; some protesters who resisted were killed, and hundreds of Armenians were wounded. The British ambassador Sir William White called it "the first occasion since the conquest of Constantinople by the Turks on which Christians have dared resist soldiers in Stamboul" (Walker, p. 132). In 1893 Armenian activists were placing placards on the public walls in towns in western and central Turkey, calling for Muslims to stand up to the despotic sultan. In their peaceful protests, Armenians asked a fundamental question: can a Christian be the equal of a Muslim in the Ottoman Empire?

THE HAMIDIAN ERA MASSACRES

In 1891 and 1892 Armenian reformers went to Sasun to help the Armenian agrarian community organize resistance to tax extortion. The resistance led to a confrontation in which a few Kurds and Armenians were killed. Shortly thereafter, the sultan ordered nomadic Kurds to invade Sasun and the Armenian villages of the region.

When, in the spring of 1894, the Sasun Armenians were confronted with tax extortion, they resisted and were accused of rebellion. By the middle of September, the sultan had sent in his Hamidiye. Within weeks, more than three thousand Hamidiye burned villages and massacred, without regard to age or sex, three thousand Armenians. The massacre at Sasun, unprecedented in modern history, caused terror in the Armenian provinces, sent shock waves through the empire, and became a dramatic human rights issue in the West. A European investigative commission found that the Armenians were not guilty of anything but self-defense and demanded that the sultan implement the promised reforms.

Frustration and fear grew, and on 1 October 1895 the Hunchak Party staged a rally in Constantinople; two thousand Armenians marched to the Sublime Porte to deliver a "protest-demand." It protested the Sasun massacre, the condition of the Armenians, and the inaction of the central government. An extraordinary statement about civil rights, given its time and place, it demanded fair taxation; guarantees of freedom of conscience; the right of public meeting; equality before the law; protection of life, property, and honor ("honor" meant protection of women from rape and abduction); and the cessation of political arrests and torture. As Vahakn Dadrian has noted, it was "the first time in Ottoman history that a non-Muslim, subject minority had dared to confront the central authorities in the very capital of the empire" (*History of the Armenian Genocide*, p. 120).

Although the rally was peaceful, the sultan's cavalry and police attacked the protestors: twenty were killed, hundreds wounded, and a massacre, assisted by the *softas* (Islamic theological students), began in the capital and continued for more than a week, even as foreign diplomats sent a collective message to the Porte asking for an end to the killings. The killing in the capital finally stopped, but it set off a new wave of violence against Armenians.

In the autumn of 1895, the map of Armenia in Turkey went up in flames. From Constantinople to Van to Diyarbekir and across central and eastern Turkey—the heartland of historic Armenia—the killing and plunder unfolded, from October into the early months of 1896.

On 26 August 1896 twenty-five Dashnaks stormed Constantinople's Ottoman Bank with a letter informing the European powers that they had two days to convince the sultan to meet their demands or they would destroy the bank. Their petition demanded justice, anticipating modern civil rights ideas. Fighting broke out between police and Armenians in the bank, and soon Armenians all over the city were being massacred by police and mobs. Two days later, when the killing stopped, at least six thousand Armenians were dead, none of whom were associated with the Ottoman Bank takeover. European newspapers condemned Abdülhamid, and some applauded the Armenian activists for their pursuit of justice. Three weeks later the sultan massacred two thousand Armenians in Egin, the home city of Papken Siuni, one of the bank takeover's slain leaders.

When the main period of the Hamidian massacres ended in 1896, the death toll of innocent civilians exceeded anything the modern era had known. A German Foreign Ministry operative estimated it at 200,000; the French historian Pierre Renouvin put it at 250,000. Johannes Lepsius, a German pastor who traveled to the killing fields, estimated 100,000 dead from the killing and another 100,000 from famine and disease (Dadrian, *History of the Armenian Genocide*; Lepsius, *Armenia and Europe.*

HUMAN RIGHTS RESPONSES

The massacres provoked outrage in Europe and the United States and began a process of international humanitarian relief. Abdülhamid was called "the bloody sultan," "the great assassin," and "le sultan rouge." Newspapers and magazines in the United States and Europe covered the massacres widely, often in bold images that brought human rights atrocities to popular culture in new ways (Balakian, *The Burning Tigris*).

The British prime minister William Gladstone spoke and wrote continually about the mistreatment of the Christian subjects in the Ottoman Empire. Five major British organizations were devoted to raising funds for Armenian relief, and influential British figures such as Gladstone and the Oxford historian (and later foreign minister) James Bryce rallied public support for the Armenian cause.

In the United States, numerous organizations and prominent Americans such as Julia Ward Howe and Alice Stone Blackwell worked hard to relieve and publicize the Armenian crisis. A broad range of literary figures spoke out passionately about the massacres, as did many industrialists and clergy. Clara Barton took the Red Cross, for the first time, out of America to the Armenian provinces of Turkey, in January 1896. In rescuing Armenians from famine and disease and helping them rebuild their economy, the mission set the stage for a modern era of international human rights intervention in the United States (Balakian, *The Burning Tigris.*

Although Abdülhamid was rebuked by Western leaders and condemned in the Western press, no international body existed to impose sanctions on Turkey. The massacres went unpunished, and the Armenians were now more vulnerable than ever.

THE RISE OF THE YOUNG TURK MOVEMENT

As financial debt mounted and its colonized peoples grew desirous of autonomy, the Ottoman Empire was sinking into an increasingly corrupt feudal system, and Turkish intellectuals too began to clamor for the constitutional reforms promised by Tanzimat. They formed secret societies, the best known of which was the Young Ottomans, later called the Young Turks, which evolved into the Committee of Union and Progress (CUP).

After 1902 the Young Turk movement, which many *dhimmi* supported, took hold, mostly at military schools and army centers, and mutinies began to break out across the empire. In June 1908 several officers, including Enver Bey, who was twenty-seven, led an insurrection outside of Salonika; it led to a coup that the sultan was unable to put down. On 24 July 1908 he assented to the Young Turks' demand that he step down as political leader and that the constitution be restored.

The revolution was greeted with great enthusiasm; with the promise of constitutional reform, a triumphant Enver Bey declared that all nationalities and religious minorities of the empire were now brothers. Many Armenians believed that equality between Christians and Muslims would finally be achieved.

As this euphoric moment faded, however, religious and political antagonisms reemerged. By April 1909 anti-government protests instigated by counterrevolutionaries who hoped to bring back the sultan were taking place throughout the country. The losses of Bosnia and Herzegovina to Austria, Crete to Greece, and then Bulgaria's independence, continued the erosion of Ottoman territories and fueled nationalist sentiment.

MASSACRES AT ADANA, 1909

After the Young Turks' coup, the *dhimmi* had gained some rights and were hopeful about others, but given the counterrevolutionary mood, Armenian optimism was an affront to the poorer Muslims—particularly in the Mediterranean region of Adana, where some Armenians constituted a prosperous merchant and small-business class. It was a familiar story of a disliked minority (like the Chinese in Southeast Asia or the Jews in Europe) being perceived as too aggressive or pushy.

On 13 April 1909, the day the counterrevolution was declared in Constantinople, in Adana, Turkish gangs began killing Armenians and the town "was full of a howling mob looting the shops" (FO 420/219, p. 80). The British vice-consul of Mersin, Charles Doughty-Wylie, was enraged when the local governor refused to intervene, and he and his men tried to control the mob violence. In two days, it left two thousand Armenians massacred and the Armenian quarter destroyed.

After the Young Turks put down the counterrevolution in Constantinople, they sent regiments to Adana to restore order, but on the pretext of being provoked by Armenians—trying to protect women and children from rape and murder—the new CUP army began to massacre them in "one of the most gruesome and savage blood-baths ever recorded in human history" (Dadrian, *History of the Armenian Genocide*, p. 183). In the end, Doughty-Wylie estimated the deaths at fifteen to twenty-five thousand; other estimates put the toll at thirty thousand (FO 420/219).

In Adana in 1909, the issue of equal citizenship for Christians and Muslims in the Ottoman Empire had been tested again, and again it had failed. This chain of Armenian massacre that began in 1894–1896 and continued in 1909 created what Irvin Staub in *The Roots of Evil* calls a "continuum of destruction" —a historical and cultural orientation that can lead to conditions for genocide. The "long history of devaluation and mistreatment of the Armenians" included "large-scale mass killings" planned by government bureaucracy, which encouraged ordinary people to participate. Scapegoating and devaluing a minority group are often the result of the majority group seeking to raise its self-esteem in a time of crisis: here, the Turks felt their empire threatened by European intervention on behalf of the Christian minorities in Anatolia and the Balkans.

Those responsible for the Hamidian and Adana massacres went unpunished. Massacre committed with impunity sanctioned the Ottoman government's tactic of solving its "Armenian question" with state-sponsored violence and further devaluing a marginalized group.

A NEW TURKISH NATIONALISM

The Ottoman Empire's road to World War I and to its final solution for the Armenians was accelerated by the Balkan Wars (1912–1913). While the Christian nations and cultures of the Balkans were fighting to end centuries of what the Bulgarian premier Ivan Geshov called "unbearable Turkish tyranny" (Dadrian, *History of the Armenian Genocide*), the Turks saw their empire in Europe dissolving, their imperial hegemony greatly diminished, and their leadership under attack.

Like the Anatolian Armenian provinces, the Balkan states were historically Christian, and from the fifteenth century to 1913, they were called Turkey in Europe. In the last quarter of the nineteenth century they had continually petitioned for reform. By 1912, as new Balkan alliances were formed in opposition to Ottoman rule,

violence broke out. From October 1912 until the spring of 1913, during two sets of Balkan wars, Turkey lost 70 percent of its European population and 85 percent of its European territory.

The death toll of Turks in the Balkans and their expulsion were a shock that renewed hatred of Christian minorities and provoked a new nationalism. The enormous influx of Muslim refugees on the streets of Constantinople created chaos and was a symbol of Turkey's defeat. In this moment of insecurity and humiliation, the nationalist faction of the CUP staged a coup d'état. Mehmet Talât and Enver and their followers marched into the Sublime Porte and assassinated the minister of war and, later, the grand vizier. Talât, Enver, and Ahmed Jemal emerged as the ruling triumvirate of the CUP party, devoted to a militant Turkish nationalism.

The chief CUP propagandist, Zia Gökalp, despised constitutional reform and asserted that Turkey could reclaim its glory only if it rid itself of its non-Muslim elements. Turkey for the Turks was his theme "as Muslims had to use 'the weapon of nationalism'" (Akçam, p. 88); this included proto-Nazi race hygiene, as Armenians were likened to "dangerous microbes" infecting the state (Dadrian, "The Role of Turkish Physicians in the World War I Genocide of Ottoman Armenians," p. 175), and "Greeks, Armenians, and Jews" were "a foreign body in the national Turkish state" (Heyd, p. 132). To reclaim its golden age of Turkic warriors (Genghis Khan and Tamerlane), a homogenous empire would be forged by unifying all Turkic peoples from the Caucasus to Central Asia.

At this moment of Turkish vulnerability and rising nationalism, Armenians persuaded the European powers to push the Turks on some of the reforms for which they had been clamoring. In February 1914 the Armenian reforms agreement was initiated by the Europeans, and included European inspectors to oversee them. The Turks saw the reforms as one more humiliating European intervention and feared that they might turn into an eastern version of the recent Balkan humiliation (Akçam, *A Shameful Act*).

European intervention for human rights issues inside Turkey was also pursued through the Capitulations, which began in the sixteenth century as privileges the Ottoman government granted to non-Ottoman subjects who were traveling or living on Ottoman soil. Through them, Europeans could sidestep Ottoman laws and exert some financial and diplomatic influence. For the

Armenians, the Capitulations had meant the possibility of assistance from the European powers, adding to Turkey's resentment of this system.

THE GERMAN-TURKISH ALLIANCE AND WORLD WAR I

Turkey's relatively new alliance with Germany accelerated the Ottoman militarization program. By 1914 the Germans were entrenched in the empire, and high-ranking German officers held commanding positions in the Ottoman army and navy. In entering World War I on the side of Germany, the CUP saw a unique opportunity to solve problems that had plagued it for decades. The Turks believed the Germans would help them defeat Russia and enable Turkey to unite all the Turkic peoples, many of whom were living under Russian rule. The Armenians of the Caucasus, who were a roadblock to that dream, would have to be eliminated (Akçam, *A Shameful Act*). They hoped the Germans would free them of all foreign interventions, especially the hated Capitulations and the nineteenth-century treaties with Europe.

In November 1914, just after the Ottomans entered the war, the Sheikh-ul-Islam in Constantinople made a formal declaration of jihad against the Christians of Europe in an attempt to get the Muslims of the Ottoman Empire to join the war effort with zeal. Although the effort failed, the jihad, as Henry Morgenthau observed, "started passions that afterward spent themselves in the massacres of the Armenians and other subject people" (p. 170).

With Germany's help, Turkey was freed of the hated Capitulations and nineteenth-century treaties—and the detested Armenian Reform Agreement. James Bryce and Arnold Toynbee noted a pattern here, in which Armenian requests for reform were followed by sanctioned government violence: "At the close of 1914, the Armenians found themselves in the same position they were in 1883; the measures designed for their security had fallen through, and left nothing behind but the resentment of the Government that still held them at its mercy" (pp. 635–636).

Jay Winter noted that World War I created for the Turks a condition of total war: an armed and mobilized society, a paranoia about national security, a deepened xenophobia, and the chaos that accompanies war. In the Armenian case "total war created the military, political, and cultural space in which [genocide] could occur, and occur again," opening up a new phase in the history of warfare by providing an environment for the CUP to wage a campaign of race annihilation against the Armenians by deeming them "the internal enemy" (Winter, p. 39).

Enver Pasha's humiliating defeat by the Russians at Sarikamish in January 1915, for which he blamed the Armenians, claiming they were helping their brethren in the Russian army, and the landing of European and Australian troops at Gallipoli in April propelled Turkey further into a siege mentality and an obsession with "internal enemies"—especially the Armenians, whom Turkey feared could regain, with Russian help, some of their historic lands on the Russian border.

GOVERNMENT-PLANNED GENOCIDE

In the spring of 1915, the final solution for the Armenians was put into motion by the CUP leadership in a plan conducted by the bureaucracy of the central government. In every city, town, and village across Turkey, Armenians were rounded up, arrested, and either shot outright or put on deportation marches. Most often, the able-bodied men were arrested in groups, taken out of the town or city, and shot en masse. The women, children, infirm, and elderly were given short notice that they could gather some possessions and would be deported to what they were told was "the interior." The Turks often told the Armenians, as the Nazis would later tell the Jews, that they could return after the war.

The deportations and massacres spanned the length and width of Turkey, from Constantinople to Ankara to the Armenian *vilayets* in the east, where the majority of the Armenian population had lived on their historic lands for nearly three thousand years. Along the Black Sea region in the north, and from Adana and other historic Cilician Armenian cities in the south, the massacre network led to the northern Syrian desert: east of Aleppo, in the region of Deir el-Zor, more Armenians died than perhaps anywhere else, and some were stuffed into caves and asphyxiated by brush fires—primitive gas chambers.

Richard Rubenstein described the Turkish extermination of the Armenians as the "first full-fledged attempt by a modern state to practice disciplined, methodically organized genocide" (pp. 11–12). Like the Nazis, the CUP understood that bureaucracy could create a totally vulnerable, "expendable" people. The extermination plan proceeded from a series of roughly sequential planned events:

- *The onset of World War I*. Armenian men were conscripted into army labor battalions (*amele taburlari*) and put to work on roads and railways or carrying supplies on foot. After Enver Pasha's defeat at Sarikamish, Enver had them disarmed and then massacred.

- *Winter 1915*. The CUP's Special Organization organized killing squads for the purpose of exterminating the Armenians (Dadrian, "Special Organisation").

- *Early spring 1915*. The government ordered all civilian Armenians who were suspected of possessing arms to surrender them. This resulted in what Bryce and Toynbee called a "reign of terror." (p. 638). Local officials broke into homes, demanding weapons when often there were none, sometimes planting them, and arresting and executing innocent civilians arbitrarily.

- *8 April*. The first deportation was ordered in the mountain town of Zeitun, where Armenians had resisted massacre in 1895–1896; a trial run, it was done on foot and for the first time by railway (Bryce and Toynbee, Treatment of *Armenians in Ottoman Empire*).

- *17 April*. The Armenians in the city of Van refused a demand of the *vali* (governor), Jevdet Bey, who had terrorized the region with mass arrests and executions all winter, for four thousand Armenian men for the army's labor battalions. The Armenians knew the men would be murdered en masse. Their refusal led to a Turkish attack on Van, and Armenians resisted, which became another pretext for the CUP to claim the Armenians were disloyal during wartime (Walker, *Armenia*). Because the events at Van have been so important to Turkish claims that Armenians were disloyal, it must be noted that a stateless, Christian minority population, without any military organization, that is also under siege, cannot engage in civil war. As the German ambassador Count Paul Wolff-Metternich explained, the local uprisings at Van and in several other towns in the spring of 1915 were "defensive acts" to avert being massacred (Dadrian, *The Determinants of the Armenian Genocide*).

- *24 April*. The CUP arrested some 250 Armenian intellectuals and cultural leaders in Constantinople, an unprecedented event that began the process of liquidating Armenian intellectuals and cultural leaders throughout the country.

- *Spring through fall 1915*. Deportations, which were death marches, and massacres were carried out throughout Turkey in a deliberate and systematic way.

The CUP's plan harnessed the bureaucracy to organize and implement the deportations—to form killing squads, create legislation, and utilize technology and communications. The final solution for the Armenians was directed by the minister of the interior, Talât, who told the U.S. ambassador, Henry Morgenthau, "the deportations were the result of long and careful deliberation" (Morgenthau, p. 333). The bureau in charge of the Armenian plan was a covert group called the Special Organization (SO or Teshkilat-i Mashusa). High-ranking party officials (Mehmed Nazim, Gökalp, Behaeddin Shakir) were instrumental in the planning. The SO recruited, organized, released, and deployed thirty to thirty-four thousand convicts from prisons for the purpose of mass killing (Dadrian, "Special Organisation"). The organization of the ex-convict killer-bands (*chetes*) bore resemblance to the Nazis' mobile killing units (Einsatzgruppen), but the *chetes* were augmented by the military police and by provincial police known as gendarmes or police-soldiers.

The extermination plan was overseen by a hierarchical administration within the SO that worked closely with the local CUP clubs. The German ambassador Wolff-Metternick wrote, "The Committee demands the extirpation of the last remnants of the Armenians" (Dadrian, *The Determinants of the Armenian Genocide*, p. 13).

To accelerate the plan and give it further legitimacy, Talât pushed through two acts of emergency legislation. The Temporary Law of Deportation (May 1915) gave the military and local commandants authorization to deport any groups of the population that were considered suspicious or threats to the state. The Temporary Law of Expropriation and Confiscation (September 1915) authorized the expropriation of Armenian wealth and property. The U.S. consul in Aleppo, Jesse Jackson, called it "a gigantic plundering scheme as well as the final blow to extinguish the [Armenian] race" (United States National Archives, RG59, 867.4016/219, p. 867).

The Turks implemented a groundbreaking use of technology for mass killing. Talât and others used the telegraph (a new technology) to relay orders for deportation and massacre across hundreds of miles to CUP offices in the provinces. In addition, the railway, crucial for the Nazis, was likewise important for the Turks. As Hilmar Kaiser notes, "the Ottoman government introduced into modern history . . . railway transport of civilian populations" as part of the plan of "extermination" (p. 75). Armenians were crammed into the cattle cars of the Anatolian and the Baghdad Railway, and sent south and east, many dying on the way.

Diplomats and journalists at the time estimated that between 800,000 and 1.2 million Armenians died in 1915 alone (Bryce and Toynbee, Treatment of *Armenians in Ottaman Empire*). In the summer of 1916 another 200,000 were massacred in the Syrian desert around Deir el-Zor. In addition, tens of thousands of women were abducted into harems or Muslim families, and as many children were taken into families and forced to convert to Islam. After the war, further massacres took place, in Marash in 1920 and Smyrna in 1922. In the end, from one-half to two-thirds of the more than 2 million Armenians living in their historic homeland in the Ottoman Empire were annihilated. In his autobiography, *Totally Unofficial Man*, Raphael Lemkin, the legal scholar who invented the concept of genocide as an international crime, put the figure at 1.2 million. The International Association of Genocide Scholars conservatively assesses that more than 1 million Armenians were killed, probably 1.2 to 1.3 million. Some historians put the figure at about 1.5 million. The survivors were dispersed across the world, mostly in North America, Russia, the Middle East, and Europe, in what was a major twentieth-century diaspora.

HUMANITARIAN RESPONSES

Foreign diplomats and missionaries stationed across Turkey were primary witnesses to the massacres and played pivotal roles in rescue and relief. Diplomatic reports and dispatches corroborated the extermination plan and process.

The U.S. consuls Leslie A. Davis (Harput), Jesse B. Jackson (Aleppo), Oscar Heizer (Trabzon), William Peter (Samsun), Edward Nathan (Adana/Mersin), and George Horton (Smyrna) communicated with Ambassador Henry Morgenthau in Constantinople via reports that Morgenthau shared with the Committee on Armenian Atrocities, formed in New York City in 1915. The organization then, and later as Near East Relief, raised over $100 million for Armenians and other refugees in the former Ottoman Empire.

The U.S. National Archives has more than forty thousand pages of consular accounts of the Armenian genocide, perhaps the first record of diplomatic witness to modern genocide. Consul Jackson wrote Morgenthau in September 1915 that the survival rate of the deportation marches was about 15 percent, which put the toll of vanished Armenians at about 1 million. "You cannot make it too black. The sides of the roads are strewn with bones or decaying bodies" (United States National Archives, RG59, 867.4016/298). An extensive archive of diplomatic reports from German, Austrian, British, and French foreign offices also documents the genocide.

In the United States, relief efforts for the "starving Armenians" continued into the early 1920s. The American Board of Commissioners for Foreign Missions played a key role. The press covered the Armenian genocide thoroughly: *The New York Times* in 1915 alone published 147 articles on the massacres. American writers and political figures continued to speak out about the atrocities, including the former president Theodore Roosevelt, who called the Armenian massacres "the greatest crime of the war" (Balakian, *The Burning Tigris*, p. 308).

POSTWAR CONDITIONS

In 1917, with the collapse of the czar's empire and the retreat of the Russian army, the Turks recaptured the Armenian provinces the Russians occupied, and Russian Armenia (now part of a short-lived Transcaucasian Federation) was caught between the chaos of a defunct Russian empire and a hostile Turkey. In 1918 the Ottoman army invaded Transcaucasian Armenia, massacring civilians. Reciprocally, some Armenian irregulars, having survived the genocide, attacked Turkish civilian populations to avenge the atrocities of 1915. (The Turkish government today, in its efforts to deny the Armenian genocide, has dated these 1918 wartime killings to 1915 in support of their claims that Armenians were seditious in 1915.)

By May 1918 the Turks reached Sardarabad, in Armenia's heartland, where the Armenians made a desperate last stand. An army of genocide survivors, outnumbered two-to-one by the Turks, drove them back and kept Armenia from being expunged. With no help coming from Russia or any Allied country, on 28 May 1918 Armenia was forced to declare its independence. It was a small landlocked area of 11,000 square miles (29,000 square kilometers) with a population of 600,000, 300,000 of whom were starving refugees. But for the first time since 1375, Armenia was self-ruled.

ARMENIA AND THE RISE OF MUSTAFA KEMAL'S NATIONALISM

The emergence of Mustaf Kemal, a hero of the Ottoman victory at Gallipoli, as a charismatic political leader gave the Turks a new nationalist force to negotiate the

Paris Conference's plans for a defeated Turkey. With permission from the Allies, Greek troops landed at Smyrna in May 1919 and engulfed Greece and Turkey in a war that helped Kemal's nationalism attract thousands of followers, who joined to fight the Greeks.

At the Paris Conference, on 10 August 1919, the Ottoman government, under Damad Ferid, signed the Treaty of Sèvres, of which Section 6, Articles 88–93, stipulated that Turkey was to recognize Armenia as a free and independent state; that the U.S. president would determine the boundary between Armenia and Turkey, which would entail the provinces of Erzerum, Trabzon, Van, and Bitlis and include an outlet for Armenia on the Black Sea; and that Turkey would renounce any claim to the ceded land.

In the United States, President Woodrow Wilson was advocating that America become the mandatory protector of the new democratic Republic of Armenia. Two U.S. commissions, the King-Crane Commission and the Harbord Commission, went to Turkey to evaluate the fate of the Armenians. They corroborated the voluminous accounts: the Armenians had been wiped out by a systematic campaign implemented by the central government, and the death toll was 1 million or more.

The Kemalists were determined to nullify the Treaty of Sèvres, and demanded all of Turkish Armenia plus Kars and Ardahan, then part of the Armenian republic. In the fall of 1920 Kemal launched an offensive against the Armenian republic, ordering General Kâzim Karabekir to "politically and physically eliminate Armenia" (Dadrian, *The History of the Armenian Genocide,* pp. 357–358). Within weeks, Karabekir took several towns, including Sarikamish, and finally, the stronghold of Kars (Hovannisian, *Armenia on the Road to Independence*).

After much delay, in November 1920 President Wilson finally announced the official award to Armenia. In accordance with the Treaty of Sèvres, it awarded Armenia 42,000 square kilometers (16,380 square miles) in areas of Turkish Armenia and Russian Armenia, including 400 kilometers (156 square miles) of coastline on the Black Sea. Despite the Wilson award, the Turks continued into the Armenian heartland, massacring Armenians until the Soviets intervened, working quickly to bring Armenia into the Soviet Union. The boundaries of the Armenian Soviet Socialist Republic were shaped by the Treaty of Moscow (16 March 1921) and the Treaty of Kars (13 October 1921), and Armenia was forced to cede to Turkey Kars and the surrounding areas the Turks had invaded and to declare the Treaty of Sèvres null and void. When Kemal

demanded that the Europeans redo the postwar treaty for Turkey, the Lausanne Conference was convened in Switzerland in 1922: in the new Treaty of Lausanne, the word "Armenia" did not appear.

OTTOMAN COURT MARTIAL TRIALS, 1919–1920

After the war, the British government, occupying Constantinople, called on Turkey (the former CUP leadership had fled the country) to hold a military tribunal to try those responsible for the Armenian massacres and crimes against war prisoners. The British foreign secretary, Lord Curzon, declared that the Young Turk leaders "had murdered hundreds of thousands of their own subjects . . . and deserved any fate which was inflicted upon them" (Bass, p. 113). The Ottoman grand vizier, Damad Ferid, admitted the need to bring to justice "the truly responsible authors of these terrible crimes" (Lloyd George, p. 651).

The Ottoman foreign minister, Ahmed Reshid, told Britain's high commissioner in Constantinople that "with regard to the Armenian massacres, it was not merely the intention but the firm decision of the Government to punish the guilty" (Bass, p. 120). Those arrested included Said Halim Pasha (grand vizier, 1913–1917), numerous government ministers and provincial administrators, and some former provincial governors. According to Gary Bass, atleast 107 important CUP leaders were held in jail.

The tribunal prepared more than two hundred files to indict those in the military, the CUP, and at the top level of government; four major trials were set up on the basis of municipal law and the Ottoman penal code, legitimizing the trials in a national legal context. The key indictment was premeditated (*ta'ammtiden*) mass murder organized by the Central Committee of the CUP and the SO. The records of all of these trials can be found in *Takvim-i Vekayi*, the official gazette of the Ottoman parliament.

At the Yozgat trials (February–April 1919), dozens of authenticated ciphers were introduced that repeatedly disclosed that the word "deport" in fact meant "massacre." A secret telegram of 17/18 July 1915, from the gendarmerie chief of Boghazlyan in the Yozgat district, informed his superiors that the Armenians of the region were to be "deported, that is, destroyed [*sevkiyat, yani mahv manasina*]" (Dadrian, "A Texual Analysis of the Key Indictment of the Turkish Military Tribunal Investigation of the Armenian Genocide," p. 9).

The main verdict of the Trabzon trials (22 May 1919) corroborated the findings of the Yozgat trials. Again, "deportation" meant "massacre." The verdict read,

> The men were separated from the women in the convoy of the Armenians, who were deprived of the means of protection. The brigands, deployed . . . first robbed [the deportees] of their goods and possessions and then [proceeded to] kill and destroy [the men]. . . . Under the pretext of transporting them by the sea route to another place, the male and female infants [*zukur ve inas cocuklari*], taken in split groups on board of barges and caiques to the high seas, and hidden from sight [*gözden nihan olduktan sonar*], were thrown overboard to be drowned and destroyed [*bahra ilka etmekle bogdurup mahv edildikleri*]. (Dadrian, "The Armenian Genocide in Official Turkish Records," p. 45)

The tribunal concluded that all of the midlevel bureaucrats of the CUP, especially the Responsible Secretaries, were "accessories to the criminal decision-making of the Central Committee of the party," and they "ventured to commit particularly such crimes as those which were connected with deportations and massacres, including appropriating the riches and plundering the properties" (Dadrian, "The Armenian Genocide in Official Turkish Records," p. 75).

The evidence against top CUP members was delivered in the key indictment, with forty-two incriminating documents appended. These documents—telegrams, decoded telegrams, memos, statements, and depositions—highlighted the role of the Central Committee and confirmed that the campaign to exterminate the Armenians was premeditated and deliberate. Furthermore, they revealed that the SO engineered the killing squads, the majority of whom were "criminals released from prisons." The key indictment also stated that "the Special Organization was set up by the leaders of the CUP" and that the chief organizer of the operation was the SO chief, Dr. Behaeddin Shakir. Third Army Commander General Mehmed Vehib testified,

> In summary, here are my convictions. The Armenian deportations were carried out in a manner entirely unbecoming to [the ideals of] humanity, civilization, and government. The massacre and annihilation of the Armenians, and the looting and plunder of their properties were the result of the decision of the Central Committee of Ittihad and Terakki. The butchers of human beings, who operated in the command zone of the Third Army, were procured and engaged by Dr. Behaeddin Shakir. The high ranking governmental officials did submit to

his directives and orders. . . . He stopped by at all major centers where he orally transmitted his instructions to the party's local bodies and to the governmental authorities. (Dadrian, "The Armenian Genocide in Official Turkish Records," pp. 59–60)

By the end of 1919, faced with the Kemalist takeover of Turkey, Grand Vizier Damad Ferid resigned, and with the new nationalism in Turkey and British postwar fatigue, Britain's commitment to the trials waned. To appease the Kemalists, Britain's War Office, in 1921, led by the new secretary of war, Winston Churchill, decided to free its Turkish prisoners held at Malta in exchange for the British prisoners the Turks held, and the trials were abandoned. It was a pragmatic deal that, as one member of the Foreign Office noted, destroyed Part VII (Penalties) of the Treaty of Sèvres and was "tantamount to a complete capitulation to Turkish blackmail" (Bass, p. 142).

In August 1921 the British released forty-three Turkish prisoners accused of perpetrating the Armenian massacres. Although there were three hangings and many prison convictions, none of the convicted served out their prison sentences, and after the British-Turkish prisoner exchange, the majority of the perpetrators escaped punishment.

Britain's deal came at great cost to international justice. Nevertheless, the trials produced critical evidence about the organized plan to exterminate the Armenians, evidence that came from Turkish officials who were participants in the killing and from a wealth of official government documents. Gary Bass called the trials a milestone in the history of war crimes tribunals and an antecedent to the Nuremberg Trials.

After the war, some Armenians pursued the chief architects of the Armenian genocide who had fled Turkey. Armenian avengers killed Said Halim, former grand vizier, in Rome in 1921 and Behaeddin Shakir in Berlin in 1922. Jemal Pasha was killed by Armenians in Tiflis in July 1922. Enver Pasha died at Bukhara in August 1922 during a battle led by an Armenian Bolshevik officer. The young Armenian Soghoman Tillerian assassinated Talât Pasha in Berlin in 1921, which led to a celebrated trial; when Talât's role in the Armenian massacres was revealed, Tillerian was acquitted.

THE AFTERMATH AND TURKISH DENIAL

Every episode of genocide is followed by forms of denial, often by the perpetrator and sometimes by those who identify with the perpetrator. Denialist literature has followed the Holocaust and other genocides, but the denialist texts on the Armenian genocide are unusually extreme, in part because they have been aggressively promoted by the Turkish government from the very time of the crime.

Sultan Abdülhamid and then the CUP denied any culpability for the Armenians' deaths. Yet in a candid moment, Talât said to Ambassador Morgenthau, "We will not have the Armenians anywhere in Anatolia" (Morgenthau, p. 338), and Enver bragged to the ambassador, "I have no desire to shift the blame on our underlings. . . . The Cabinet itself has ordered the deportations" (Morgenthau, p. 352).

Talât established the template for the Turkish government's denial by asserting that the Armenians were to blame for what happened to them because, first, the Russians used them to invade eastern Turkey; second, "Armenian bandits . . . killed more than 800,000 Mohammedans"; and third, the government did not order any massacres—rather, it was the fault of local authorities: "I am innocent of ordering any massacres," he wrote (pp. 294–295).

Talât's early example of denying the Armenian genocide created a counterfeit version of history that would be used by successive Turkish regimes. While the outside world was shocked by such statements, inside Turkey they took hold. After World War I, the policy of erasing Armenia from Turkish history would become part of the Turkish republic's founding mythology. The Turkish historian Taner Akçam notes in *From Empire to Republic* that the Kemalists created an extreme nationalism built on several myths and taboos, including the following: Turkey is a society without class distinctions; Turkey is a society without ethnic minority groups or cultures; and there was never an Armenian genocide.

In 1934 Turkey stepped up its denialist campaign by demanding that the U.S. State Department stop MGM from continuing its film production of Franz Werfel's best-selling novel, *The Forty Days of Musa Dagh*, about Armenians who had heroically resisted Turkish massacre in 1915. Turkey said the film would damage relations between the two countries. The State Department yielded and got MGM to drop the project. Four years later, Hitler invoked the erosion of memory when he said, eight days before invading Poland in August 1939, "Who today, after all, speaks of the annihilation of the Armenians?" (Lochner, p. 2).

After Armenians began worldwide annual commemorations of the genocide, on 24 April 1965, Turkey's official policy of denial intensified. Turkey began to pressure the press not to use the word "genocide." The Turks began referring to "the alleged Armenian genocide" and calling it a "civil war." Even though, during the period of the trials, Turkish officials had admitted that close to 1 million Armenians had been killed, the number dropped to 600,000 and has fallen to the 300,000 espoused as of 2007. Richard Falk, emeritus professor of international law at Princeton University, has called the Turkish campaign of denial "sinister" and "a major, proactive, deliberate government effort to use every possible instrument of persuasion at its disposal to keep the truth about the Armenian genocide from general acknowledgment" (Dadrian, "The Armenian Genocide in Official Turkish Records," p. i).

A small number of scholars have accommodated Turkey's denial and produced statements and books attempting to give academic legitimacy to Turkey's claims. In their efforts to sanitize the history and negate the genocidal nature of the event, Bernard Lewis, Stanford Shaw, Justin McCarthy, and Gunther Lewy, most notably, have ignored the evidence and conclusions of the massive record of documents and decades of scholarship as well as the 1948 UN Genocide Convention's definition of genocide (Power, *A Problem from Hell*). Denialist scholars have engaged in what is called unethical practice: "Where scholars deny genocide in the face of decisive evidence . . . they contribute to false consciousness that can have the most dire reverberations, and lend their considerable authority to the acceptance of this ultimate crime" (Smith, Markusen, and Lifton, p. 16.)

In 1980, 1985, 1989, 2000, and 2007, the Turkish government used its military alliance with the United States to pressure the State Department to block passage of various nonbinding congressional resolutions affirming the Armenian genocide and paid lobbyists millions of dollars annually to work against them. Turkey has lobbied to stop Jewish American organizations from acknowledging the genocide and pressed them to work against the resolutions. Most dramatically, in 2007, after the Anti-Defamation League, a major Jewish American organization, acknowledged the events of 1915 as genocide, Turkey demanded that Israel intercede and force the ADL to retract its statement, lest the well-being of Jews in Turkey be affected.

WORLD OPINION AND REJECTION OF DENIAL

In the face of Turkish denial, scholars, organizations, and nations, motivated by an ethical sense and the value of historical honesty, have made statements of acknowledgment and affirmation of the Armenian genocide. The International Association of Genocide Scholars has issued several open letters which underscore that the historical record on the Armenian genocide is overwhelming and unambiguous, noting Raphael Lemkin's first use of the term "genocide" to describe the Armenian case and the applicability of the 1948 United Nations Convention on the Prevention and Punishment of the Crime of Genocide. Twenty countries as well as the Vatican and the European Parliament have passed resolutions acknowledging the events of 1915 as genocide.

The Nobel laureate Elie Wiesel has called Turkish denial a "double killing" that strives to kill the memory of the event. Deborah Lipstadt has written, "Denial of genocide whether that of the Turks against the Armenians, or the Nazis against the Jews is not an act of historical reinterpretation. . . . The deniers aim at convincing innocent third parties that there is 'another side of the story' . . . when there is no credible 'other side.' . . . Denial of genocide strives to reshape history in order to demonize the victims and rehabilitate the perpetrators . . . [and] is the final stage of genocide" (p. 138). While Turkish denial has been discredited by the mainstream scholarly community, students of the Armenian genocide should be alert to the nature of denialist literature and its connection to Turkish nationalism.

[*See also* Crimes against Humanity *and* Genocide.]

BIBLIOGRAPHY

Akçam, Taner. *From Empire to Republic: Turkish Nationalism and the Armenian Genocide.* London and New York: Zed, 2004.

Akçam, Taner. *A Shameful Act: The Armenian Genocide and the Question of Turkish Responsibility.* New York: Metropolitan, 2006. The first book by a Turkish scholar on the subject, making new use of Turkish sources.

Alder, Lory, and Richard Dalby. *The Dervish of Windsor Castle: The Life of Arminius Vambery.* London: Bachman and Turner, 1979.

Balakian, Grigoris. *Armenian Golgotha: A Memoir of the Armenian Genocide.* New York: Alfred A. Knopf, 2009. The most comprehensive and detailed personal account of the Armenian genocide.

Balakian, Peter. *The Burning Tigris: The Armenian Genocide and America's Response.* New York: HarperCollins, 2003. This study brings together a history of the Armenian genocide and a history of how and why the Armenian cause became a groundbreaking human rights movement in the United States.

Bass, Gary Jonathan. *Stay the Hand of Vengeance: The Politics of War Crime Tribunals.* Princeton, N.J.: Princeton University Press, 2000.

Bloxham, Donald. *The Great Game of Genocide: Imperialism, Nationalism, and the Destruction of the Ottoman Armenians.* Oxford and New York: Oxford University Press, 2005.

Bryce, James, and Arnold Toynbee. *The Treatment of the Armenians in the Ottoman Empire, 1915–1916: Documents Presented to Viscount Grey of Falloden by Viscount Bryce.* Edited and introduced by Ara Sarafian. 2d ed. London: The Gomidas Institute, 2005. A major collection of witness accounts of the Armenian genocide from 1915 through the summer of 1916 by American and European observers in Turkey.

Chalk, Frank, and Kurt Johassohn, eds. *The History and Sociology of Genocide.* New Haven, Conn.: Yale University Press, 1990. A view of the history of genocide from ancient times through the Cambodian genocide.

Dadrian, Vahakn. "The Armenian Genocide in Official Turkish Records." Foreword by Richard Falk, introduction by Roger Smith. *Journal of Political and Military Sociology* 22, no. 1 (Summer 1994): 1–208. Reprinted with corrections, spring 1995. The most extensive collection of the Ottoman government's official gazette (*Takvimi Vekayi*), whose supplements served as a judicial journal, recording the proceedings of the Turkish military tribunal that tried the perpetrators of the Armenian genocide in Constantinople, 1919–1920.

Dadrian, Vahakn. *The Determinants of the Armenian Genocide.* New Haven, Conn.: Yale Center for International and Area Studies, 1998. Paper presented at the Genocide Studies program seminar, Yale University.

Dadrian, Vahakn. *The History of the Armenian Genocide.* 4th rev. ed. New York and Oxford: Berghahn, 2003.

Dadrian, Vahakn. "The Role of the Special Organisation in the Armenian Genocide during the First World War." In *Minorities in Wartime*, edited by Panikos Panayi, pp. 5–82. Oxford and Providence, R.I.: Berg, 1993.

Dadrian, Vahakn. "The Role of Turkish Physicians in the World War I Genocide of Ottoman Armenians." *Holocaust and Genocide Studies* 1, no. 2 (1986): 169–192.

Dadrian, Vahakn. "A Texual Analysis of the Key Indictment of the Turkish Military Tribunal Investigation of the Armenian Genocide." *Armenian Review* 44, no. 173 (Spring 1991).

Fromkin, David. *A Peace to End All Peace: The Fall of the Ottoman Empire and the Creation of the Modern Middle East.* New York: Henry Holt, 2001.

Great Britain, Foreign Office. Archives, referenced in text as FO.

Great Britain, Foreign Office. *Turkey*, no. 1 and no. 2. London: Harrison and Sons, 1896.

Gust, Wolfgang. *The Genocide of the Armenians 1915/16. Documents from the Political Archives of the German Foreign Office.* [In German.] Hamburg, Germany: Carl Hanser, 2005. http://www.armenocide.de/armenocide/armgende.nsf.

Heyd, Uriel. *Foundations of Turkish Nationalism (1950)*. Westport, Conn.: Hyperion Press, 1979.

Hovannisian, Richard G. *Armenia on the Road to Independence, 1918*. Berkeley, Calif.: University of California Press, 1967.

Hovannisian, Richard G., ed. *Remembrance and Denial: The Case of the Armenian Genocide*. Detroit: Wayne State University Press, 1998.

International Association of Genocide Scholars. *Open Letter to Turkish Prime Minister Recep Tayyip Erdogan*. May 2006. http: www.genocidescholars.org/home.html.

Kaiser, Hilmar. "The Baghdad Railway and the Armenian Genocide, 1915–1916: A Case Study in German Resistance and Complicity." In *Remembrance and Denial: The Case of the Armenian Genocide*, edited by Richard G. Hovannisian, pp. 67–112. Detroit: Wayne State University Press, 1998.

Kloian, Richard D. *The Armenian Genocide: News Accounts from the American Press, 1915–22*. 3d ed. Berkeley, Calif.: Anto Printing, 1987.

Landau, Jacob M. *Pan-Turkism: From Irredentism to Cooperation*. 2d rev. ed. Bloomington: Indiana University Press, 1995.

Lepsius, Johannes. *Armenia and Europe*. London: Hodder and Stoughton, 1897.

Lewis, Bernard. *The Emergence of Modern Turkey*. 3d ed. New York: Oxford University Press, 2002.

Lipstadt, Deborah. House Committee on International Relations, Hearing on H. Res. 398, The United States Training on and Commemoration of the Armenian Genocide Resolution, 106th Congress, 2nd session, September 14, 2000.

Lloyd George, David. *Memoirs of the Peace Conference*. New Haven, Conn.: Yale University Press, 1939.

Lochner, Louis P. *What about Germany?* New York: Dodd, Mead & Company, 1942. Lochner records the occasion of Hitler's famous remark about the extermination of the Armenians.

Melson, Robert. *Revolution and Genocide: On the Origins of the Armenian Genocide and the Holocaust*. Chicago: University of Chicago Press, 1992. Quoted in Melson: United Kingdom House of Commons, Correspondence Relating to Asiatic Provinces of Turkey, "Events at Sassoun and Commission of Inquiry at Moush."

Morgenthau, Henry. *Ambassador Morgenthau's Story*. Preface by Robert Jay Lifton, introduction by Roger Smith, afterword by Henry Morgenthau III. Edited by Peter Balakian. Detroit: Wayne State University Press, 2003. The first major narrative of the Armenian genocide in English, originally published in 1918.

Power, Samantha. *A Problem from Hell: America and the Age of Genocide*. New York: Basic Books, 2002. Power uses the Armenian genocide to contextualize the pioneering work of Raphael Lemkin and his creation of the concept of genocide; Lemkin first used the term "genocide" to describe the Armenian atrocities on a CBS News broadcast in 1949, footage of which can be found in Andrew Goldberg's PBS documentary *The Armenian Genocide* (2005).

Ramsaur, Ernest Edmondson. *The Young Turks: Prelude to the Revolution of 1908*. Princeton, N.J.: Princeton University Press, 1957.

Rubenstein, Richard. *The Cunning of History: The Holocaust and the American Future*. New York: Harper & Row, 1975.

Sarafian, Ara, ed. *United States Official Documents on the Armenian Genocide*. Vol. 1, *The Lower Euphrates*. Watertown, Mass.: Armenian Review, 1993.

Smith, Roger W., Eric Markusen, and Robert Jay Lifton. "Professional Ethics and the Denial of the Armenian Genocide." In *Remembrance and Denial: The Case of the Armenian Genocide*, edited by Richard G. Hovannisian, pp. 271–296. Detroit: Wayne State University Press, 1998.

Staub, Ervin. *The Roots of Evil: The Origins of Genocide and Other Group Violence*: Cambridge, U.K., and New York: Cambridge University Press, 1989. A social-psychological view of how perpetrators marginalize and harm minority groups.

Talât, Memhet. "The Posthumous Memoirs of Talaat Pasha." In *Current History*, pp. 287–295. New York: New York Times, 1921.

Toynbee, Arnold J. *Armenian Atrocities: The Murder of a Nation*. London and New York: Hodder & Stoughton, 1915.

United States National Archives. Record Group 59, Records of the Department of State, 867 Series, Internal Affairs of Turkey 1910–1929, File 867.4016 Race Problems. Available at http://www.armenian-genocide.org/sampledocs.html.

Walker, Christopher J. *Armenia: The Survival of a Nation*. 2d ed. New York St. Martin's Press, 1990.

Wiesel, Elie. Quoted in "Statement by Concerned Poets and Scholars Commemorating the Armenian Genocide." *New York Times*, April 24, 1998.

Winter, Jay, ed. *America and the Armenian Genocide of 1915*. Cambridge, U.K., and New York: Cambridge University Press, 2004. Includes Jay Winter's "Under the Cover of War: Genocide in the Context of Total War."

Zurcher, Erik J. *Turkey: A Modern History*. 3d ed. London and New York: I.B. Tauris, 2004.

ART AND IMAGES

by Caroline Turner

The European Court of Human Rights has declared that "those who create, perform, distribute or exhibit works of art contribute to the exchange of ideas and opinions which is essential for a democratic society" (Chinkin, p. 14). Artists may create beauty, celebrate life, and help us see our world and humanity in different ways. But artists and their images are also intimately and profoundly linked to issues of human rights and the visualization of human wrongs. Art can be a testament and a memorial to human suffering. The work of creative artists explores ideas critical to the definition of humanity: happiness, fear, love, hate, justice, injustice, and ambivalent issues for which there are no stark clarities of right and wrong.

Art alone cannot change the world. However, as many artists throughout the history of humankind have shown, it can protest greed, environmental degradation, cultural loss, exploitation, injustice, war, racism, oppression, and crimes against humanity, such as genocide. There is an ancient Chinese saying that the true artist is one who turns his or her back on the world, but artists through the centuries have had the courage to connect with their world and to oppose injustice, sometimes at the cost of their own lives. The role that artists can play in cultural and social transformation by engaging at the community level with issues of violence, social justice, and reconciliation has been shown to be a critical one. Art can help communities and individuals survive present injustice, overcome trauma, communicate with one another, begin a process of healing, and construct new futures. Appreciation of the artistic creations of other cultures can build bridges to understanding and tolerance. The immense importance of art for human rights lies in the fact that it can speak in ways universally understood, often where no other form of speech is possible.

This entry concentrates on visual art, though literature, film, music, and the performing arts are equally important in relation to human rights. Visual artists have over the centuries explored themes of human emotion: great sculptural decorations from ancient civilizations that document victory and defeat in war, slaves in procession, and triumphs of the conquerors serve as reminders of the vicissitudes of fear, exaltation, and despair in human existence. Artists also celebrate life through their art by creating images of beauty and illustrating stories of universal significance. The often exquisite creations of religious art have been made for not only rulers but also ordinary people, providing solace in all cultures and at all times. Creating beauty is a fundamental human aspiration; ordinary people create their own art forms, such as embroidery or carving, to decorate their homes, commemorate loved ones, and amuse their children. Many artists have sought refuge from pain in creating art for private spaces. Creative activity itself can be seen to be a human right. Art related to human rights does not have to be realistic or representational. Nor does it have to be an art about atrocities. It can equally be a celebration of life in speaking to and for our common humanity.

Images are a powerful means of expressing ideas. And writers often evoke images for us through words. George Orwell, for example, provided a frightening metaphor of violence in his novel *1984*: "If you want a picture of the future, imagine a boot stamping on a human face—for ever."

Images are a source of knowledge about the world and of ideas. Early humans painted on the walls of caves to pass on such knowledge to their tribes. Important images as well as written texts were copied through the centuries. After a means of mechanical production of images was introduced, the circulation of images greatly increased. Artists like Albrecht Dürer in the sixteenth century responded to social change and religious ferment by creating art in print media, such as woodblock prints and engravings. Artists traveled with voyages of exploration and recorded new places and peoples, and these images were published in books, atlases, and newspapers. Cartoons and caricatures in journals and newspapers, an important form of political expression since the eighteenth century, have contributed to political debates and have often been the subject of censorship. In the twentieth and twenty-first centuries, images created by new visual processes, such as photography and film, and broadcast through new media, such as television and the Internet, have become a dominant means of communication—often replacing the written word. People of the modern era have witnessed and been moved by photographic and televised images of torture, violence, concentration camps, civilian victims, napalmed children, and refugees. Sadly, images are often also the medium of communication for messages of hatred and violence and are capable of shaping opinion through mass dissemination. In addition, it is possible to deliberately manipulate images to distort reality and thus serve the purposes of propaganda. Images therefore have power to work both for and against human rights.

HUMAN RIGHTS LEGISLATION

Since the Universal Declaration of Human Rights was adopted by the United Nations in 1948, legislation in both national and international law has created a major shift in world culture toward acceptance of a concept of human rights that applies to all human beings. But human rights have not always been respected by nations or individuals. Some of the worst abuses of human rights have indeed occurred since the Universal Declaration of Human Rights was adopted.

The distinguished international human rights lawyer Christine Chinkin observes that the provisions of the declaration "offer a vision of human dignity and choice through the affirmation of a broad range of civil and political, economic, social and cultural rights" (p. 13). Among these rights are freedom of religion, an adequate standard of living, equality before the law, and a number that she argues are especially pertinent to artists, including "freedom of expression and communication" and the rights of individuals "freely to participate in the cultural life of the community; to enjoy the arts." There are also moral rights for artists through copyright and professional associations protected by legislation. People in every nation, including creative artists, have become more aware, since the declaration, of the concept of "universal" rights and of the international fora to which they can appeal. Chinkin and others have referred to the need to further develop a rights culture to advance the promotion and implementation of human rights. Art offers ways to extend this culture through education; for example, the United Nations has presented exhibitions that help translate ideas important to understanding human rights into local settings.

Another distinguished international lawyer, Hilary Charlesworth, in a 2003 speech at the Humanities Research Centre at the Australian National University in Canberra, pointed to the "silences" in human rights legal frameworks. She has drawn attention to the fact that there are marginalized groups, including women, children, and indigenous peoples, who through their lack of power within their own societies are often excluded from human rights discourse and practice. In this area as well, art connects with human rights, and artists can work to extend an understanding of rights to include marginalized groups.

The South African poet and writer Mbulelo Mzamane argues that the connection between art and human rights extends to issues such as cultural survival or health—life and death issues for those in poorer countries. Hunger, starvation, poverty, and illnesses such as AIDS are among the issues that many artists in the third world confront in their work. In a 2003 speech at the Humanities Research Centre at the Australian National University in Canberra, Mzamane suggested that artists, through creative practice, storytelling, and the creation of images, are working toward a better society and are actively contributing to human rights.

Art can thus help people know their rights. Art can also help individuals reach their full potential as human beings and can help in the preservation of identities and cultures. Art can help in the fight for free expression in a political context. It can be an important tool for communication between peoples and in promoting tolerance. There are three significant areas in which art plays a key role in the defense of human rights within the world culture that has grown in the aftermath of the Universal Declaration of Human Rights in 1948: witnessing, resistance and restorative justice, and cultural survival and affirmation.

WITNESSING

Witnessing is one of the most profound ways art connects and has always connected to human rights. Witnessing might be described as art that evokes a sense of the tragedy of injustice, without indicating a specific course of action to be adopted in response or a specific perpetrator to be condemned. It does not overtly assign blame or call for retribution. An example is the Indonesian artist Dadang Christanto's invocations of "the unspeakable horror" of the Indonesian massacres of hundreds of thousands of people in 1965–1966. In Christanto's sculptural installations—such as *They Give Evidence*, in which the figures of human beings, both male and female, hold in their out-stretched arms bundles that resemble bodies—there are no specific victims identified, no perpetrators revealed. These figures are silent witnesses to injustice throughout history and in every time and place. The emotional impact of Christanto's art has resonated perhaps most widely with audiences who are unaware of the circumstances in Indonesia that inspired the works; the works convey a sense of human tragedy in universal terms.

Pablo Picasso's *Guernica* (1937) might similarly be said to inspire a reaction of horror and almost unbearable grief without any overt indication of when and why or by whom the horror was committed. Francisco Goya's *Los desastres de la guerra* (*Disasters of War*, 1810–1814) does indeed identify the perpetrators as either French invaders or the Spanish resistance, but its theme manifestly relates to the universal human condition, in which people of all races and beliefs do appalling things to one another. Depictions of the sufferings inflicted by war have a long history in art, from ancient times to the present day. Examples would be Jacques Callot's *The Miseries of War* in the seventeenth century, Eugène Delacroix's *Massacre at Chios* in the nineteenth century, or the French artist Georges Rouault's *Miserere et guerre* in the twentieth century. Responses to World War I include, from Germany, the former soldier Otto Dix's shocking depictions of the effect on soldiers and Käthe Kollwitz's powerful statements about war from the perspective of a mother whose son had been killed. These themes of pain and disillusion were echoed thirty years later by the Japanese artist Chimei Hamada, a conscript in World War II, who depicted a young conscript killing himself because he could no longer endure the fighting. The German Anselm Kiefer's ominous and evocative postwar artworks, addressing the Nazi era and German mythology, are some of the most powerful works produced in response to war and its aftermath. There have also been many artists through the centuries whose work promotes the necessity of peace, including art depicting the horrors of the effects of the dropping of the atomic bombs on Hiroshima and Nagasaki.

Social tragedies have also inspired artists. Examples include the works of nineteenth-century British artists depicting the Highland Clearances, the Irish Famine, and the miseries of the working class. Gustave Courbet's *Stone Breakers* (1849) is an appalling vision of the degradation of sections of the working class in France, though it contains no hint of what might be or ought to be done to alleviate their conditions and Courbet himself was without question subjectively revolutionary in his views.

The Impressionist painter Camille Pissarro was a committed political anarchist, and his vision of the life of peasants is deeply sympathetic to them as individuals but not overtly ideological. The work of Mexican artists such as Diego Rivera, José Clemente Orozco, and David Alfaro Siqueiros in the twentieth century gave witness to the lives of the poor in Mexico and gave hope of a better life, while Frida Kahlo's psychological explorations of a female self became an inspiration to women and to later feminists.

Art witnessing to wrongs was produced by the victims of the Nazi concentration camps in Europe, even in the extermination camps Auschwitz and Buchenwald. Such artistic expression was of course forbidden. But the artists wished to record the terrible events and violations of human rights they were enduring or simply to respond to the human impulse to create some small expression of beauty in the midst of horror. The images that have survived are deeply moving and have been termed "spiritual resistance."

An oft-cited statement about art and creative practice since World War II and its horrors is that of Theodor Adorno, who suggested in 1949 that to write poetry after Auschwitz would be barbaric. Yet, many artists in the second half of the twentieth century have found it more important than ever to write poetry and produce art in response to terrible wrongs, including genocide. And what of "cultural genocide," the deliberate destruction of a people's cultural heritage? Raphael Lemkin, out of the chaos of the 1930s and 1940s in Europe, defined genocide as a term that could be used to seek restorative justice; in the words of Kofi Annan, Lemkin almost single-handedly drafted an international multilateral treaty declaring genocide an international crime, and he hoped to have cultural genocide included in the same legislative framework.

If the Universal Declaration of Human Rights of 1948 was a product of the idealism born after World War II, a war that had torn Europe apart and produced the Holocaust, then the loss of such idealism in the early twenty-first century is perhaps equally evident. Christian Boltanski was born in 1944 in France to a Catholic mother and a Jewish father who spent much of the war in hiding from the Nazis. His art is deeply informed by his own experiences growing up in the 1950s in the immediate aftermath of the war, in a France still marked by anti-Semitism. Boltanski's art, which evokes a sense of loss and catastrophe and mourning despite the lack of allusion to specific events, suggests that horror, death, and loss are not confined to any groups of individuals. He thus implies that human beings are all potentially capable of great crimes and can only make a difference in small local ways. He said: "Art is always a witness, sometimes a witness to events before they actually occur . . . but I don't think art has real power. . . . I think what's more important for all of us is to be witnesses of what has happened" (Boltanski, p. 37).

The Belgian Luc Tuymans also reflects this renewed spirit of existential despair, which for an artist can nonetheless be an incentive to positive action. Tuymans's paintings are, at first sight, of ordinary people and objects, but they refer to the hidden problems of Western society, such as child abuse. He was extremely sensitive to the historical circumstances of his own time and to his own Belgian historical past, compromised inevitably by the record of Belgian colonialism and collaboration with the Nazis, and he was immensely concerned about the rise of neo-Fascism in Europe. He said: "Every art has failed. How we fail is another matter" (Riemschneider, Grosenick, and Larsen, p. 514). There is no ambiguity about the nature of the fears expressed in Tuymans's work other than the ambiguity inherent in an art that achieves its effect through what is left unseen rather than what is seen.

The African American artist Jacob Lawrence provides another striking example of the power of art to bear witness to injustice while eschewing any element of propaganda. Lawrence's works have explored the history of African Americans, including slavery in the United States. His delicate and restrained evocations of natural and unnatural tragedies derive their impact precisely from what is left out: a study of a lynching, for example, depicts only a branch, an empty noose, and the form of a mourning woman, leaving to the imagination of the observer any image of a dangling tortured body and a jeering mob of spectators.

Many artists open up questions in their art rather than providing answers. The Chinese artist Xu Bing's *A Book from the Sky* was shown in the 1989 China Avant-Garde exhibition in Beijing, held just before the protests at Tiananmen Square. Xu Bing took three years to carve wooden blocks to print massive and elegant books with what look like ancient Chinese characters but are in fact meaningless script. This work was officially denounced in China as a challenge to authority. The artist, like so many of his talented generation, left China shortly after Tiananmen. The Taiwanese artist Wu Mali has explored the complex histories of her Taiwanese homeland but also looks for ways to connect people though collective art projects and metaphors, such as the sea. In Australia the Chinese-born artist Guan Wei has produced monumental

artworks about ethical, social, and environmental questions. The installations and video works of the Malaysian Wong Hoy Cheong brilliantly reverse the colonial gaze to remind us that anybody can be colonized and anybody can be a colonizer and to confront the issue of racial stereotyping. Yinka Shonibare, a Nigerian British artist, has produced evocative and humorous sculptural installations, often using textiles from Asia and Africa, that explore serious issues of race, colonialism, and crosscultural engagement. The Iranian-born artist Shirin Neshat, who lived in New York, created poetic works in photography and film about Islam and particularly about women in the Muslim world. Her photographic series *Women of Allah*, showing a Muslim woman wearing a chador holding guns and also containing poems in Farsi, explores issues of cultural difference, violence, belief, and even martyrdom, undermining Western stereotypes of Islamic women. The Chinese-born artist Chen Zhen explored the near impossibility of communication between different cultures. For the fiftieth anniversary of the United Nations in 1995, he completed his *Round Table* installation in Geneva, with a round table (such as for a Chinese meal) and chairs symbolizing the nations of the world. However, the chairs could not be used, pointing to the difficulties of cross-cultural understanding.

Witnessing has been a critical aspect of art in our times outside Europe and North America. In India, Vivan Sundaram has worked in his art to combat religious fundamentalism. In Pakistan, Salima Hashmi has produced quiet and beautiful works, such as her semiabstract painting *People Wept at Dawn*, which acts as a memorial to suffering for those who protest human rights abuses. Artists in Pakistan, India, Bangladesh, and Sri Lanka have produced much powerful work confronting the legacies of colonialism, partition between India and Pakistan, and civil and religious violence in the Indian subcontinent. This art protests against violence and intolerance, witnesses to the destructive effects of religious and partisan hatreds, and pleads for tolerance, especially religious tolerance. Jagath Weerasinghe in Sri Lanka confronted the civil war in his country through the concept of nonviolence. Rummana Hussain, an Indian artist, developed the concept of a space for healing to confront intolerance, inspired in part by the mobs who demolished the Babri Mosque in Ayodhya in 1992.

The history of art since 1948 contains many examples of artists who have connected their art to political, social, and economic issues. Sometimes this art is created in opposition to their own governments. There are many examples of such artworks from Eastern Europe and many artists who resisted the conformity of art imposed in the former Soviet Union. The Jane Voorhees Zimmerli Art Museum at Rutgers University, for example, holds seventeen thousand items of Soviet "dissident" art.

Artists in the postwar era confronted the rise of dictatorships in many Latin American countries and abuses of human rights, including the use of torture and death squads, by witnessing to those events by allusion rather than specific denunciation. Latin American art in this era has produced some of the most powerful art of the late twentieth century. The Colombian artist Doris Salcedo's quiet and poetic installations evoke terrible underlying currents of fear. Her works include human bones in beautifully crafted furniture or rows of empty discarded women's shoes, inevitably invoking the possibility that their wearers were among "the disappeared"—those taken away by police and soldiers and never heard of again. The Chilean-born artist Juan Davila evoked the shock for his countrymen when their country fell under a military dictatorship; the faces in his painting of the Australian Chilean community, "a diaspora of mourning," reflect the tragic realization that their country, after 140 years of constitutional government, had in 1973 become subject to a military dictatorship that murdered or tortured some eighty thousand people. Among those tortured was the artist Guillermo Núñez, director of the Museo de Arte Contemporáneo at the time of the 1973 coup d'état. Artists in the many countries with military dictators found ways of witnessing to violence, repression, militarization, censorship, and the struggles of marginalized groups through art that is psychologically alienated; sometimes, as with the Brazilians Hélio Oiticica, Cildo Meireles, and Ivens Machado, creating their art was a form of liberty.

Many women artists have identified with and shown the sufferings of women and children as well as social and religious injustice to women in times of violence and war and in situations in which perpetrators believe they can commit violent acts with impunity. For example, in India, Navjot Altaf and Vasudha Thozhur have treated the rapes and attacks on women in the 2002 Guyarat religious riots, and Nilima Sheikh explored the deliberate murder, by burning, of brides in India by their in-laws for their dowries. In Pakistan, Saira Wasim represented the so-called honor killings of women by their relatives.

Many artists, as the cultural theorist Jennifer Webb has pointed out, see their art as a "beacon against forgetting" (p. 36). Art can point to what has been termed collective amnesia, the history that societies do not want to remember. Katsushige Nakahashi, a Japanese artist, has produced deeply disturbing works about World War II, for example, his replica of a crashed fighter plane made from thousands of photographs of a toy plane. This work is a statement about defeat and loss in war. A work of mourning, it is also a controversial work in Japan, where many do not wish to remember that defeat. The Japanese female artist Yoshiko Shimada has produced work documenting the suffering of the so-called comfort women from other parts of Asia who were imprisoned and subjected to sexual violence by the Japanese Imperial Army during the war. Some of the former "comfort women" have also produced their own art as a means of overcoming trauma.

An example of art as a "beacon against forgetting" is the work of William Kentridge, the son of the eminent South African human rights lawyer Sydney Kentridge. William Kentridge reminds us through his art not only that some artists stood against apartheid but also of the need to keep remembering what such a regime does to a society. But Kentridge does not see himself as a "political artist" of apartheid. He said: "I have never tried to make illustrations of apartheid, but the drawings and films are certainly spawned by and feed off the brutalized society left in its wake. I am interested in a political art, that is to say an art of ambiguity, contradiction, uncompleted gestures, and certain endings; an art (and a politics) in which optimism is kept in check and nihilism at bay."

RESISTANCE AND RESTORATIVE JUSTICE

Chinkin has referred to the "power of artists to confront their governments with unwelcome messages" (p. 15). This function might be termed resistance. Artists over the centuries have had work censored and even suffered imprisonment not just for political views but for diverging from the accepted norms and introducing new ideas or refusing to depict images of propaganda and hate. The distinction between resistance and witnessing is of course nuanced. The art of the victims of the Nazi concentration camps was equally an art of witnessing and resistance. Many artists play both roles. For example, the Mozambique artist Malangatana Ngwenya's paintings about violence and social injustice were an inspiration to the Mozambique independence movement, and he was imprisoned. In the late twentieth and early twenty-first centuries, as an international goodwill ambassador for the United Nations Educational, Scientific, and Cultural Organization (UNESCO), he has used his art to combat violence and social injustice throughout the world. The Colombian Fernando Botero, best known for his studies of the human figure, has also produced horrific portrayals of discrimination and injustice in his native Latin America and of the effects on prisoners of the events at Abu Ghraib prison in Iraq. Vasan Sitthiket of Thailand is an example of a resistance artist. A devout Buddhist, Vasan depicted the figure of the Buddha to condemn political and religious corruption in Thailand. The Burmese artist Htein Lin created works related to his Buddhist faith while a political prisoner of the military regime in Burma.

The Indonesian artist Heri Dono relied on depicting and satirizing the symbols of oppression and injustice rather than identifying guilty individuals specifically, although no one with any knowledge of Indonesian affairs could be in any doubt as to the identity of those being satirized. The U.S. artist Leon Golub, who painted in a figurative style, similarly depicted generalized types of agents of oppression, such as mercenaries and torture and death squads, but the titles of some of his works, for example, *Napalm and Vietnam*, leave no doubt as to the sources of his outrage. In the nineteenth century the caricaturist, painter, and sculptor Honoré Daumier was a satirist of his society in France. Théodore Géricault in the same century depicted the horrors of the slave trade. Delacroix's *Liberty Leading the People*, depicting the Paris uprising of 1830, is an icon of popular resistance and an invocation of revolutionary idealism, a celebration of the victory of the people against absolute monarchy. Many artists have used satire to critique their societies, such as the German artists of the 1920s and 1930s who depicted with devastating precision the effects of war and the Depression. Others evoked the tragedy of the times. Kollwitz's works about the effects of war and its aftermath on ordinary people are one of the great statements of resistance in art from the perspective of the oppressed. Max Beckmann, whose career spanned disillusion and social criticism after World War I, was condemned by the Nazis as an exponent of "degenerate" art. He saw his works confiscated and destroyed, and he fled Germany.

There is a complex link between art and power, which needs to be confronted in any discussion of the art of resistance. An art of protest can mean different things in different times. In some nations it is also much easier to produce such art. In the 1960s to the 1980s many Latin American artists responded to the suffering of their fellow citizens under dictators with allusions to skeletons and torture instruments rather than specific denunciation.

In the early twenty-first century there were many artists whose work dealt with oppressive regimes and who were both witnessing and resisting injustice.

Indonesia provides a case study of art that moves between witnessing and resistance. Modern Indonesian art was deeply informed by the struggle for independence against the Dutch. The artists Sindutomo Sudjojono, Affandi, and Hendra Gunawan shaped Indonesian art through their emphasis on the lives of ordinary Indonesian people. Hendra was imprisoned under the Suharto regime because he was seen as too closely linked to the group Lekra, identified with support for Communism, which was outlawed in 1966 after the fall of Sukarno. Hendra spent thirteen years in prison but was able to continue painting and continued to focus on the often hard lives of ordinary people. In the 1980s and 1990s a new generation of Indonesian artists produced an art concerned with documenting human rights abuses under the Suharto government. They sided with ordinary people in opposing the taking of their land for economic development and in their sufferings, such as economic exploitation and worse. For example, Moelyono lives and works as an art teacher in remote villages in Java affected by economic loss, such as land taken for dams, and he has helped that community through communal art projects. His artwork about Marsinah, a woman trade union leader brutally raped and murdered by soldiers in the 1990s, helped bring soldiers to trial in Java. FX Harsono, Heri Dono, and Dadang Christanto, among others, produced work shown in international exhibitions outside Indonesia, especially in the 1990s. Other artists were prominent through street theater and other activities, such as making banners, in the revolution leading to the overthrow of Suharto.

In the last half of the twentieth century confronting the legacies of Western colonialism as well as the injustices of some regimes of the independence era and about social justice was characteristic of art outside the West—in Africa, Asia, the Pacific, and Latin America—though artists in developed nations also addressed these issues. The Niuean-born Pacific Islander artist John Pule, who lived in New Zealand, passionately denounced the arrogance of power in his *American Series*. The Australian artist Pat Hoffie has dealt movingly with issues of injustice and reconciliation related to Aboriginal people in Australia and injustices suffered by interned refugees in Australia as well as the continuing exploitation of the developing world by industrialized nations. Jayce Salloum in Canada has used photography and film for decades to explore questions such as divisions in the Middle East.

Artists in many parts of the world in the early twenty-first century confronted the issues of economic survival and the immediacy of the trauma of war—for example, the war in Lebanon in the work of Walid Raad and the Atlas Group. An example of resistance against wrongs committed throughout the world is the work of the Indian artist Nalini Malani. Through drawing, painting, animation, and film, she reflects on Western as well as local histories of violence. She is particularly concerned with the vulnerability of women in a broader consideration of oppression. The *Mutants* series, for example, expressed her reaction to U.S. hydrogen bomb tests at Bikini Atoll in 1954 and the deformed babies subsequently born to Micronesian mothers. The Chilean-born artist Alferedo Jaar, who lived in the United States, is concerned with racially motivated violence, poverty, exploitation, war, and genocide. His work *Gold in the Morning* was about the drudgery of miners in the northeastern Amazon rain forest. In his *Rwanda Project* of site-specific "interventions," he chose in the photo-based work *The Eyes of Gutete Emerita* to show only the eyes of one woman who had seen her family massacred in 1994 and must live with that memory.

Linking art and politics is controversial among scholars, and many art textbooks approach art from the perspective of movements and styles rather than in relation to protest or social involvement. Many argue that the link to politics distorts art and can diminish its aesthetic focus, reducing it to the level of propaganda. This is particularly the case with the art of resistance. Art that connects to the streets or to the emotions of the moment may indeed not always be great art. But it can be great art, and it can reflect passionately felt emotions that can encapsulate human aspirations and even change history. Issues are not always clear-cut, and many artists remind us through their work that it is often dangerous to see such issues only in terms of "good" and "evil." Artists can also be partisan. Throughout the centuries artists have referred to their contemporary societies in their work, and art historians have shown that art as diverse as ancient Chinese scroll paintings and European portraits contain coded messages that link to social and political ideas of the time. Many artists in fact would contend that all art is political and that even to do nothing is to espouse a position.

Protest art has a long history in the United States, from art in support of political freedoms in the eighteenth century to the Guerrilla Girls activism of the feminist movement in the twentieth century. The Vietnam War inspired much protest art in the United States; Nancy

Spero, for example, devoted five years of her art to protesting the Vietnam War. Hans Haacke is another example of an artist activist whose work explores how the control of ideas can rest with those with financial or corporate power.

The Nigerian-born curator Okwui Enwezor opened up a vital aspect of these issues when he asked "How to bear witness and ensure democratic representation?" in a conference in New Delhi in 2001 designed to examine "the central arguments that form the judicial and social methods of the 'Truth Commissions' as they pertain to state crime and violence" and also to reflect on other complex conflicts (ethnic, racial, religious, and sectarian) (Enwezor, p. 17). This choice of subject for the art exhibition Documenta XI in 2002 in Germany seems prophetic in light of the political uncertainties so vividly exposed since 11 September 2001. Transnational survey exhibitions like Documenta and the other biennials and triennials around the world devoted to contemporary art can also serve as venues for more radical art expressions. Important exhibitions in the 1990s included the biennials of Venice, Lyon, Johannesburg, Gwangju (Korea), Shanghai, Guangzhou, São Paulo, Sydney, Yokohama, Istanbul, Havana, and Singapore as well as the Indian and Bangladesh triennials, the Asia-Pacific triennial exhibitions (Brisbane), the Fukuoka Asian Art Shows and Fukuoka triennials, and the European exhibitions Manifesta, Documenta (Kassel), and Cities on the Move (Vienna). Art exhibitions can be an important source of exchange for art and ideas, an example being inIVA in the United Kingdom, which focuses on artists from marginalized backgrounds.

Artists have espoused the cause of nonviolence in their works, as in the Indian artist Amar Kanwar's art film *A Season Outside* (1997–1998) in which the narrator, using the words of Mohandas "Mahatma" Gandhi, explains that one cannot respond to violence by inflicting pain on others. There are many organizations of artists specifically committed to activism for peace and artists who work with nongovernmental organizations. Exhibitions have included a 1998 "arms into art" campaign by the Christian Council in Mozambique calling for weapons to be handed in and featured in made into tools, featuring artworks made from AK-47 machine guns, land mines, and other weapons; the Aar-Paar project, where artists in Mumbai, India, and Karachi, Pakistan, exchanged works that were inserted into public spaces to promote better understanding of each others' culture; and In the Time of Shaking: Irish Artists for Amnesty International in 2004, featuring works by one hundred Irish artists. There have been exhibitions in Bosnia and Serbia to promote understanding between former foes. Artists have produced many projects for peace, for example, the many exhibitions in Hiroshima related to the dropping of the atomic bombs. The artist Yoko Ono even inaugurated her own peace prize, giving the first awards to Israeli and Palestinian artists.

Many artists in the early twenty-first century, especially women artists, dealt with the psychological affects of violence, fear, and unease. Mona Hatoum, a Beirut-born artist of Palestinian heritage who lived in Britain, explored ideas of identity and difference in allusive ways. Hatoum explored themes of separation, migration, and violence through her performances, videos, and installations. The work of some artists is deliberately confrontational. The Cuban-born artist Coco Fusco uses performance, writing, and video to treat themes of migration, race, and ethnic divides particularly relating to women and the exploitation of women. Artists in the former Soviet Union, such as the Russian female performance artist Elena Kovylina, founder of the charitable organization Red Shelter in Saint Petersburg, have attempted to question the role of art in addressing problems of society while redefining identity and confronting significant social and political transition. The women artists Tania Bruguera from Cuba and Lida Abdul from Afghanistan have defined complex issues related to power, authority, and repression. Artists often choose to pose questions for which there are no easy answers and to work in ambiguous ways in creating artworks exploring new possibilities. Emily Jacir from Ramallah and New York created extremely beautiful work about memory and displacement as well as works that can involve many others collectively, such as her *Memorial to 418 Palestinian Villages Destroyed, Depopulated, and Occupied by Israel in 1948*. The African American writer bell hooks in her book *Black Looks: Race and Representation* suggests that artists and others can transform images, especially racially defined stereotypes: "It is also about transforming the image, creating alternatives, asking ourselves questions about what type of images subvert, pose critical alternatives, and transform our world views" (p. 4).

CULTURAL SURVIVAL AND AFFIRMATION

Is art for self or community? Sometimes the rights of individuals can be in conflict with the rights of communities. Nevertheless, many artists devote their work to community projects and to helping communities or disadvantaged groups within communities through volunteer action, and many define their work as being about cultural human rights.

Chinkin has defined another role of art in the context of human rights as that of being "an essential element in the preservation of the identities of people and their cultures" (p. 14). The most astonishing demonstration of this function of art is the explosion on the international art scene of Australian Aboriginal (Indigenous) art, the essence of which is indeed to represent pictorially the stories and traditions of the Aboriginal people, particularly in terms of their relationship with the land on which they have lived for some forty thousand years. Much of their work in effect consists of "spiritual maps," using traditional images from sand drawings and body painting to create new work. Elders in the Central Desert made a decision in the 1970s to share their stories and culture with the world outside, thereby also preserving their culture and at the same time developing new modes of expression through the use of media, such as acrylic paints on canvas. The images of contemporary Australian Aboriginal art are both overwhelmingly beautiful and at the same time powerful statements of cultural survival and affirmation. The works of these artists have not only had a great impact internationally but have also been used to establish legal claims to traditional lands as well as providing economically for the physical and spiritual survival of their communities. Art by Australian indigenous artists has also dealt with fundamental issues of human rights, such as the large number of suicides of Aboriginal people in prisons. At the same time art skills learned in prisons have provided a way for many Aboriginal people to rediscover their heritage and to break a terrible cycle of poverty.

The twenty- and early-twenty-first-century art of the Pacific region reveals much about the role that art can play in social transformation by engaging with issues of cultural survival. Such art demonstrates the continuing relevance of religion, spirituality, and tradition, especially for indigenous peoples. The Papua New Guinean artist Michael Mel has pointed out that in his culture there is no distinction between art and life. He was nominated in 2006 as a laureate by the Prince Claus Foundation in the Netherlands because of his outstanding work in cultural survival through art for Pacific communities.

To use traditional design motifs, stories, dances, and songs in a contemporary way is the force behind the work of Michel Tuffery, an artist of Samoan, Tahitian, and Palagi (European) descent who lived and worked in

New Zealand. His *Povi Tau Vaga* is about the challenge to cultures under threat. It is also about the interaction between Pacific First Nation peoples as well as their shared history of colonization. It is in no way a symbol of defeat but rather a dynamic affirmation of a living and evolving culture and a further proof that for indigenous people their past is their future. Many artists have assisted marginalized groups in society to reclaim culture through projects to revive traditions and provide cultural rights, such as several projects in the slums in Brazil. Connecting to contemporary culture is also a vital form of cultural affirmation. In the new South Africa, artists have produced art that expresses life in the urban townships. Willie Bester, a black artist whose work documents the apartheid regime, has used found objects in the townships to create assemblages and sculptures, and David Koloane helped set up initiatives for black artists. Two artists from Kyrgyzstan, Gulnara Kasmalieva and Muratbek Djumaliev, began working in the early 1990s to find a new mode of art in their country in the post-Soviet era through both myth and legend and by confronting the reality of social and economic problems in the present.

UNESCO, in its task of preserving culture, has developed a new category, "intangible heritage," which recognizes the people whose knowledge and culture produce the physical objects of tangible heritage. Many cultures thought lost or on the verge of extinction have been revived through art and culture. For example, the Ainu people in northern Japan have used their ancient arts to gain recognition through major museums, and Taiwan aborigines have revived lost tribal communities through the creative revival of cultural practice.

Women's art and cultural practice have a special place in all this for, as is known, women are in many cases the transmitters of culture and of life itself in nurturing future generations. The revival of Palestinian women's embroidery in refugee camps in Palestine has been an important social and cultural means of confronting loss and trauma. The United Nations World Conference on Human Rights held in Vienna in 1993 urged the United Nations and individual governments to make a priority the full and equal participation of women in political, civil, economic, social, and cultural life at the national, regional, and international levels and the eradication of all forms of discrimination on grounds of sex. Women's rights, including those relating to cultural development, have been stressed as a critical challenge by Mary Robinson, former United Nations High Commissioner for Human Rights.

Many women are denied access to education and the chance to become artists. Nevertheless, women, while underrepresented in the international art world, often create traditional art forms and "crafts." For example, Sonabai, a tribal Indian artist, is famous for her revival of a village craft tradition of decorating homes with clay animals. Sometimes women's creative work helps their families economically. Women in the former Indonesian colony of East Timor have used traditional weaving for cultural and economic development, and Aboriginal women in central Australia have created fabric designs and batik art as well as paintings that are sold for the benefit of their families and their communities. Many aid agencies use the sale of traditional art objects and craftwork by men and women as a way out of destitution and poverty, and some UNESCO projects, such as at Ha Long Bay in Vietnam, have the revival of local arts and crafts at the core of redevelopment projects.

UNDERSTANDING AND EDUCATION

Art can also provide a means of education about human rights. For example, art competitions sponsored by the United Nations create a greater awareness of human rights. Art has also been used for adults and children as a way of overcoming trauma from displacement or war.

Many artists engage in helping communities survive the present and build new futures. Art offers, through communication, interaction, and collaboration, an important means of educating by being able to communicate in ways that are commonly understood by ordinary people. AIDS campaign posters in Papua New Guinea use cartoon characters to convey health messages. The Congolese artist Chéri Samba employs a comic style of social commentary that is highly accessible. He believes that artists must appeal to people's consciences. Artists in many countries have formed artist groups to help the poor and disadvantaged others, sometimes producing artworks that involve whole communities. Artists in Indonesia associated with Cemeti Art House in Yogyakarta, run by Mella Jaarsma and Nindityo Adipurnomo, have developed communal projects in the face of the postrevolution issues and the 2004 tsunami. The Open Circle Arts Trust in India works with communities in that country. In the Philippines many artists have undertaken communal art projects to help counter the destructive and continuing effects of colonialism, poverty, and exploitation. In the words of the Philippine artist Santiago Bose: "The artist cannot but be affected by his society. It is hard to ignore the pressing needs of the nation while making art that serves the nation's elite. . . . The artist takes a stand through the practice of creating art."

[*See also* Culture and Human Rights; Film; Index on Censorship; Intellectual Property; Internet; Media; United Nations Educational, Scientific, and Cultural Organization (UNESCO); *and* Universal Declaration of Human Rights.]

BIBLIOGRAPHY

Adorno, Theodor. "Cultural Criticism and Society." In *Prisms*, translated by Samuel and Sherry Weber, pp. 17–34. Cambridge, Mass.: MIT Press, 1997.

Beke, László, et al. *Global Conceptualism: Points of Origin, 1950s–1980s.* New York: Queens Museum of Art, 1999.

Blazwick, Iwona, ed. *Century City: Art and Culture in the Modern Metropolis.* London: Tate Gallery Publishing, 2001.

Boltanski, Christian. "Conversation with Tamar Garb." In *Christian Boltanski*, edited by Didier Semin, Tamar Garb, and Donald Kuspit. London and New York: Phaidon, 2001.

Bose, Santiago. "A Savage Look at Indigenous Art: Notes in Transit." *In the Bag* 1, no. 3 (1999). http://www.members.tripod.com/~in_the_bag/savagenotes.htm.

Chinkin, Christine. "The Language of Human Rights Law." In *Witnessing to Silence: Art and Human Rights*, edited by Caroline Turner and Nancy Sever, pp. 13–15. Canberra: Humanities Research Centre and Drill Hall Gallery, Australian National University, 2003.

Douzinas, Costas, and Lynda Nead, eds. *Law and the Image: The Authority of Art and the Aesthetics of Law.* Chicago and London: University of Chicago Press, 1999.

Enwezor, Okwui. "Introduction." In *Experiments with Truth: Transitional Justice and the Processes of Truth and Reconciliation; Documenta 11, Platform 2*, edited by Okwui Enwezor et al., p. 17. Ostfildern-Ruit, Germany: Hatje Cantz, 2002.

hooks, bell. *Black Looks: Race and Representation.* Boston: South End, 1992.

Kentridge, William. "In Conversation with Christov-Bakargiev." *Revuenoire*, 1999.

Kleinert, Sylvia, and Margo Neale, eds. *The Oxford Companion to Aboriginal Art and Culture.* Melbourne, Australia: Oxford University Press, 2000.

Mary and Leigh Block Museum of Art. *The Last Expression: Art and Auschwitz.* http://www.lastexpression.northwestern.edu/.

Pejic, Bojana, and David Elliott, eds. *After the Wall: Art and Culture in Post-Communist Europe.* Stockholm, Sweden: Moderna Museet, 1999.

Ramírez, Mari Carmen, and Héctor Olea. *Inverted Utopias: Avant-Garde Art in Latin America.* New Haven, Conn., and London: Yale University Press, 2004.

Riemschneider, Burkhard, Uta Grosenick, and Lars Bang Larsen, eds. *Art at the Turn of the Millennium.* Cologne, Germany: Taschen, 1999.

Soares, Paulo. "Art on the Move." In *Art from the Frontline: Contemporary Art from Southern Africa.* London: Frontline States and Karia, 1990.

Tawadros, Gilane, ed. *Changing States: Art and Ideas in an Era of Globalisation.* London: Institute of International Visual Arts, 2004.

Turner, Caroline, ed. *Art and Social Change: Contemporary Art in Asia and the Pacific.* Canberra, Australia: Pandanus Books, 2005.

United Nations Educational, Scientific, and Cultural Organization. *UNESCO Artists for Peace.* http://www.portal.unesco.org/en/ev.php-URL_ID=8843&URL_DO=DO_TOPIC&URL_SECTION=201.html.

Vanderlinden, Barbara, and Elena Filipovic, eds. *The Manifesta Decade: Debates on Contemporary Art Exhibitions and Biennials in Post-Wall Europe.* Cambridge, Mass.: MIT Press, 2005.

Van der Plas, Els, Maul Halasa, Marlous Willemsen, eds. *Creating Spaces of Freedom.* London: Saqi Books; The Hague: Prince Claus Fund Library, 2002.

Webb, Jen. "William Kentridge: "A Beacon against Forgetting." In *Witnessing to Silence: Art and Human Rights*, edited by Caroline Turner and Nancy Sever, pp. 36–39. Canberra: Humanities Research Centre and Drill Hall Gallery, Australian National University, 2003.

ARTICLE 19

by Peter Noorlander

Article 19 (spelled here as Article 19) is an international human rights organization that defends and promotes freedom of expression and freedom of information all over the world. It takes its name from Article 19 of the Universal Declaration of Human Rights (UDHR), which states:

> Everyone has the right to freedom of opinion and expression; this right includes freedom to hold opinions without interference and to seek, receive, and impart information and ideas through any media and regardless of frontiers.

Article 19 believes that freedom of expression and access to information are not a luxury but a fundamental human right, the full enjoyment of which is crucial to preempt repression, conflict, and war as well as to achieve individual freedoms and develop democracy. It works on themes such as the conflict between free expression and defamation laws, broadcast regulation, and access to information, and emphasizes the value of free expression to democracy and other rights. Article 19 has a particular expertise in legal and policy issues and has developed numerous sets of principles on freedom of expression that have been widely endorsed, including by United Nations (UN) bodies. These include its Johannesburg principles on freedom of expression and national security, its "Defining Defamation" principles on freedom of expression and the protection of reputation, and its "Right to Know" principles on freedom of information. The organization does not believe in an "absolute" right to free expression; it sees freedom of expression as one—albeit an important one—of the rights guaranteed in the Universal Declaration of Human Rights and believes in all peoples' harmonious enjoyment of them.

Article 19 has its headquarters in London. It does not have a membership; it is a charitable organization overseen by an international advisory board and a smaller board of trustees. It has various regional offices in North America, South America, Africa, and the Middle East. It maintains a core staff of approximately twenty in London,

while each of its offices abroad employs a smaller number of staff members. Article 19's working method is based on a strong belief in the value of partnership: in all its work, the organization partners with other, often local, organizations that bring added value to its work.

HISTORY AND ORGANIZATION

Article 19 started in the mid-1980s as the brainchild of J. Roderick MacArthur, an American businessman and philanthropist, whose dying wish was "that there be a world without censorship" (*Article 19 Bulletin*, 1997, p. 1). MacArthur had long had an interest in journalism and human rights and, in particular, the protection of alternative voices. During World War II he reported for Associated Press (AP) from Mexico, and in the 1980s he was instrumental in ensuring the survival of *Harper's Magazine* in the United States. Shortly after MacArthur's death in 1984, a small group of people, including his children Greg, Rick, and Solange MacArthur, and human rights activists Martin Ennals, Frederieke Knabe, and Douwe Korff, set to work on a blueprint for the organization. After discussing and rejecting several options—one early suggestion having been to supply printing presses to Eastern Europe—the newly founded Article 19: International Centre against Censorship was formally established in 1986 and started operations in 1987. In 2000 it changed its name to Article 19: Global Campaign for Free Expression, as it was felt that its work was far broader than merely fighting censorship.

Article 19's founding trustees included the civil rights campaigner Aryeh Neier, broadcaster William Shawcross, and activist Ben Hooberman; the trustees as of 2008 are chaired by Heather Rogers, a respected media lawyer in the United Kingdom, and include broadcaster George Alagaiah and Richard Sambrook, the BBC's director of global news. Its international advisory board includes renowned human rights attorneys and journalists such as Dato' Param Cumaraswamy, a former UN special rapporteur on the independence of judges and lawyers, and Goenawan Mohamad, the founding editor of *Tempo*, the leading weekly news magazine in Indonesia.

Article 19's staff is led by its executive director, who oversees a team of forty based mainly in London. In 2006 the organization decided to strengthen its global presence and located offices and staff in Mexico City, Nairobi, Beirut, São Paolo, Buenos Aires, and Dakar, among other places. The executive director in 2008 was Agnès Callamard; previous directors were Andrew Puddephatt, Frances D'Souza, and Kevin Boyle.

OBJECTIVES AND WORKING METHODS

Article 19's statutes state the organization's objectives simply and plainly: "to promote and protect throughout the world Article 19 of the Universal Declaration of Human Rights." Article 19 is not a defender of an absolute right to freedom of expression. And although it recognizes the intrinsic value of freedom of expression, in its campaigning and advocacy work, the organization does tend to emphasize the value of free expression as a gateway to democracy and as a "leverage right" for the enjoyment of all other human rights. William Shawcross, the first chair of Article 19's board, wrote in the preface to the organization's 1988 world report:

> The essential point which Roderick MacArthur grasped, and for which he founded Article 19, is that the abuse of power which is embodied in censorship can lead to all the other abuses of power. Censorship is essential to tyranny. Not all tyrants torture but all tyrants censor. Freedom of speech is the essential right if all others are to be sought. It is the fundamental defence of the individual against government. Perhaps it cannot always be an adequate defence, but it is vital nonetheless. (Boyle, p. vii)

Nor does Article 19 see freedom of expression as primarily a media issue. Although much of the group's work has focused on defending the freedom of the media, it has also done significant work on the expression and information rights of vulnerable groups, such as refugees. In 2003 it published a report that criticized segments of the UK media that provided grossly distorted coverage of refugee issues and denied refugee groups "their voice." Similarly, in its work on broadcasting, Article 19's emphasis is often the right of the public to a free and pluralistic media rather than the rights of broadcasters per se. The organization is also a strong believer in the importance of public service broadcasting.

Article 19's organizational policy is guided by international human rights law. Its mandate requires it to promote Article 19 of the UDHR, and the interpretation of that instrument—as supplemented by other human rights instruments such as the International Covenant on Civil and Political Rights (ICCPR) as well as the jurisprudence of bodies such as the UN Human Rights Committee and the European and Inter-American Human Rights Courts—is seen as its guiding line. This lends Article 19's policy recommendations considerable strength: in its dealings with governments, the organization often makes the strong point that what it advocates is not an esoteric ideal, but a settled point of international human rights law that governments are required to respect and implement. The notable instances when the organization does deviate from settled points of law are when it attempts to push the envelope. For example, it would like the European Court of Human Rights (ECtHR) to recognize and state that the concept of criminal libel is outdated, or that the right to freedom of expression includes a right of access to government-held information. Both issues are examples of policy areas where Article 19 believes that the ECtHR has not moved far enough in the protection of freedom of expression.

Article 19 undertakes virtually all its work in partnership with others. When it works in a particular country, Article 19 typically partners with domestic journalists or a human rights organization, whereas its regional work often occurs in partnership with other international organizations. But its work increasingly transcends the "narrow" arena of free expression, and so Article 19 in the early twenty-first century frequently partnered with organizations that have other thematic specializations. For example, it has worked on access to reproductive and sexual health information in partnership with women's rights organizations. Article 19 is also a founding member of the International Freedom of Expression Exchange (IFEX), a global network of organizations working to defend and promote the right to free expression. Article 19's partners additionally include intergovernmental organizations (IGOs) such as United Nations Educational, Scientific, and Cultural Organization (UNESCO) and the Organization for Security and Cooperation in Europe (OSCE).

Article 19 is also among the few human rights nongovernmental organizations (NGOs) that have publicly adhered to a policy of total transparency. Under its own April 2007 "freedom of information" policy, Article 19 committed to publishing online all its reports and financial data, a list of staff including short bios, and a list of all its partners. Furthermore, it committed to disclosing on request any information it holds, subject to a few exemptions: it will not disclose personal information; legally privileged or otherwise confidential information; or information that would undermine its ability to operate, unless the overall public interest in disclosure outweighs the interest in maintaining confidentiality.

ARTICLE 19'S WORK

Article 19's early work focused on reporting abuses of freedom of expression. It published two significant world reports, in 1988 and 1991, that reviewed the state of freedom of expression in seventy-seven countries around the world. This work was much valued: a reviewer of the 1991 world report, writing in the *Human Rights Quarterly*, described the organization as "one of the most exciting and creative non-governmental organizations created since the explosion of interest in international human rights began" (Drinan, p. 573). During this period the organization made numerous protests about freedom of expression abuses in countries around the world, including the United States. For example, it joined forty-three other organizations in a petition before the U.S. Supreme Court arguing that the Flag Protection Act violated the international guarantee of freedom of expression. During this same period it also published many country-specific reports, detailing the bureaucratic and legal machinery of censorship in countries such as Syria and Myanmar (the former Burma).

Although Article 19 continued to expose and detail censorship throughout the 1990s, it published no further world reports beyond the first two. An important part of its work in the early 1990s instead became the defense of author Salman Rushdie, against whom a fatwa had been issued in 1989. Article 19 spearheaded the International Committee for the Defence of Salman Rushdie and His Publishers.

Throughout the 1990s Article 19 also published a series of books and reports emphasizing the link between free expression and other rights. The first of these, entitled *Starving in Silence* (1990), made explicit the link between the free flow of information and famine. Other such thematic publications included a pamphlet on the need to abolish the crime of blasphemy (*The Crime of Blasphemy*, 1989), a book on access to reproductive health information (*The Right to Know*, 1995; published jointly with the University of Pennsylvania Press), and a book on "hate speech" (*Striking a Balance*, 1992; copublished with

the International Centre Against Censorship, Human Rights Centre, and the University of Essex). Article 19 also published exposés on the role of the media in the Balkan wars of the 1990s (*Forging War*, 1999; published jointly with the University of Luton in Bedfordshire) and the Rwandan genocide (*Broadcasting Genocide*, 1996). These publications are generally regarded as highly valuable and have been helpful in establishing the content and boundaries of the right to freedom of expression.

From the mid-1990s onward Article 19 increasingly emphasized the need for a proper legal and regulatory framework for the realization of the right to free expression. This work started in 1993 with the publication of *Press Law and Practice*, an overview of media law in various countries, and continued with the steady expansion of its legal team. Since 2003 the legal team has every year assessed some fifty draft laws from various countries on compliance with international free expression standards, and its legal analyses have become extremely important to its domestic partners as well as the field offices of such international organizations as UNESCO and the OSCE.

In the 1990s Article 19 also increasingly focused on standard setting. Its 1993 *Freedom of Expression Handbook* took stock of the state of international and comparative freedom of expression law. From that point on, Article 19 increasingly campaigned to both elaborate and strengthen international standards on the right to freedom of expression. It used several strategies to achieve this end. First, it utilized its observer status with IGOs. Throughout the 1990s Article 19 lobbied the United Nations Commission on Human Rights (replaced by the Human Rights Council in 2006) to adopt country-specific resolutions as well as thematic resolutions on issues of concern. From 2000 onward it chose instead to focus its energies on regional human rights bodies, where it decided more might be achieved. As of 2008, Article 19 had observer status with various expert and steering groups at the Council of Europe (CoE) and contributed to the drafting of numerous CoE standard-setting instruments, including one on the protection of journalists' sources. It has also worked intensively with the African Commission on Human and Peoples' Rights, resulting in that body's adoption of a Declaration of Principles on Freedom of Expression in Africa, in October 2002.

The organization has also tried to influence the development of the content of the right to freedom of expression by organizing conferences and sponsoring publications discussing specific aspects of this right. The first of these conferences and publications focused on the interplay between freedom of expression and national security concerns. Following a meeting of experts in Johannesburg, South Africa, in 1995, Article 19 published *The Johannesburg Principles on National Security, Freedom of Expression and Access to Information* in 1996 and began to lobby for their international endorsement. It was very successful: the Johannesburg principles, as they came to be known, have since been endorsed by numerous individuals and organizations, including the UN special rapporteur on freedom of expression. In quick succession, the organization then published three further sets of principles: *Defining Defamation*, on the interplay between free expression and the protection of defamation; *The Public's Right to Know*, on freedom of information; and *Access to the Airwaves*, on broadcast regulation. Each of these has gained considerable international recognition. The organization has also published "model laws" on access to information and public service broadcast regulation. In 2006, following a period of standard-setting inactivity, Article 19 was instrumental in the drafting of the *Transparency Charter for International Financial Institutions*, which was originally published by the Global Transparency Initiative.

Another way by which Article 19 attempts to contribute to the development of international standards is through organizing annual meetings of the four intergovernmental mandates for the protection of the right to freedom of expression and helping draft their annual resolutions. Each year it brings together the UN special rapporteur on freedom of opinion and expression, the OSCE representative on freedom of the media, the OAS special rapporteur on freedom of expression, and the African Commission on Human and Peoples' Rights special rapporteur on freedom of expression to discuss specific topics. These meetings have taken place since 1999, and the joint declarations adopted at them have indicated the rapporteurs' stance on issues such as media regulation, antiterror laws, and defamation law, to name but a few.

Finally, Article 19 engages in strategic litigation at international human rights courts and tribunals. It intervenes in key cases, such as *Reyes v. Chile* in 2006 in which the Inter-American Court of Human Rights held that Article 13 of the American Convention on Human Rights requires states to enact freedom of information laws. In a select number of cases, it has also acted on behalf of victims before the UN Human Rights Committee and the African Commission on Human and Peoples' Rights.

IN CONCLUSION

Measuring the extent of Article 19's impact is not easy. However, it is clear that since the organization was established in 1986, standards in the field of freedom of expression have been developed and become internationally accepted, and the organization has played a vital role in this. For example, Article 19 was an early proponent of the right to freedom of information, with its work predating by a decade the wave of "access to information laws" enacted around the world. Article 19 is also a firm supporter of the intergovernmental rapporteurs on freedom of expression: at the OSCE, UN, OAS, and African Commission on Human and Peoples' Rights. It is unlikely that the latter's mandate would have been established if it were not for Article 19's continued lobbying of the African Commission.

At the national level, governments are not in the habit of admitting that they have introduced change at the behest of an NGO. But it is striking that many of Article 19's recommendations to governments for legal change go on to be implemented. This may result, in part, because those recommendations are grounded in international law, but it also may be the case because Article 19 increasingly works in coalition with national NGOs and IGOs. These alliances—sometimes overt, sometimes behind the scenes—can be very fruitful.

Another important outcome of Article 19's work has been the building and nurturing of civil society organizations in the countries where it works. Because of its belief in active partnerships, a significant exchange of knowledge and expertise has occurred between it and its partner organizations. This is an important outcome of Article 19's work in countries such as Bulgaria or in the Balkans, where strong domestic free expression organizations have sprung up, and remains a key element of its work in other nations.

In the remaining years of the early twenty-first century Article 19 will face many challenges. Although international standards in the field of free expression have certainly advanced since the mid-1980s, they are still often honored in the breach rather than in the observance, and the organization will need to further maximize its campaign and advocacy work to retain its relevance. In addition, Article 19 will need to find a credible voice in the debate concerning free speech on the Internet, from which it has been largely absent as of 2008.

[*See also* Martin Ennals; Salman Rushdie; Rights to Thought, Speech, and Assembly; United Nations Commission on Human Rights; United Nations Human

Rights Council; *and* Universal Declaration of Human Rights.]

BIBLIOGRAPHY

Article 19. *Broadcasting Genocide: Censorship, Propaganda, and State-Sponsored Violence in Rwanda, 1990–1994.* London: 1996.

Article 19. *Defining Defamation: Principles on Freedom of Expression and Protection of Reputation.* http://www.article19.org/pdfs/standards/definingdefamation.pdf.

Article 19. *International Freedom and Censorship: World Report 1991.* London: Library Association, 1991.

Article 19. *The Johannesburg Principles on National Security, Freedom of Expression and Access to Information.* http://www.article19.org/pdfs/standards/joburgprinciples.pdf.

Article 19. *The Public's Right to Know: Principles on Freedom of Information Legislation.* http://www.article19.org/pdfs/standards/righttoknow.pdf.

Article 19. *Starving in Silence: A Report on Famine and Censorship.* London: 1990.

Article 19. *Transparency Charter for International Financial Institutions: Claiming Our Right to Know.* http://www.article19.org/pdfs/standards/transparency-charter-english.pdf.

Article 19 Bulletin, Issue 24 (1997).

Boyle, Kevin, ed. *Article 19 World Report 1988: Information, Freedom, and Censorship.* New York: Times Books, 1988.

Coliver, Sandra. *Article 19 Freedom of Expression Handbook: International and Comparative Law, Standards and Procedures.* London: Article 19, 1993. http://www.article19.org/pdfs/publications/1993-handbook.pdf.

Coliver, Sandra, ed. *Press Law and Practice: A Comparative Study of Press Freedom in European and Other Democracies.* London: Article 19 for UNESCO, 1993.

Coliver, Sandra, ed. *The Right to Know: Human Rights and Access to Reproductive Health Information.* London: Article 19 and Philadelphia: University of Pennsylvania Press, 1995.

Coliver, Sandra, ed. *Striking a Balance: Hate Speech, Freedom of Expression, and Non-discrimination.* London: Article 19, International Centre Against Censorship, Human Rights Centre, and University of Essex, 1992.

Drinan, Robert. "Book Review." *Human Rights Quarterly* 14 (1992): 573–576.

International Committee for the Defence of Salman Rushdie and His Publishers. *The Crime of Blasphemy: Why It Should Be Abolished.* London: Article 19, 1989.

Thompson, Mark. *Forging War: The Media in Serbia, Croatia, Bosnia, and Hercegovina.* Revised ed. London: Article 19, and Bedfordshire, U.K.: University of Luton, 1999.

ASSOCIATION OF SOUTHEAST ASIAN NATIONS (ASEAN)

by Kenneth Christie

The Association of Southeast Asian Nations (ASEAN) is a regional organization based in Southeast Asia. This article begins with an overview of ASEAN and the problems of human rights in the region. The huge differences in the perceptions of human rights among the ASEAN states have increased in the light of the global "war on terrorism" initiated after the attacks of 11 September 2001. The article provides specific information on the state of human rights in selected countries in the ASEAN region, particularly on some pressing early-twenty-first-century problems. The article then summarizes the prospects and challenges for human rights throughout the ASEAN region. Rather than a uniform version of human rights, the region and ASEAN contain multifaceted versions of what human rights constitute, how they are implemented, and their practice, due in part to individual ASEAN states' retention of sovereignty over domestic affairs.

THE REGIONAL CONTEXT

In the early twenty-first century ASEAN included Brunei, Myanmar (the former Burma), Cambodia, Indonesia, Laos, Malaysia, the Philippines, Singapore, Thailand, and Vietnam. The organization was formed in 1967 by Indonesia, Malaysia, the Philippines, Singapore, and Thailand to increase economic growth among its members, promote social progress and cultural development, and provide stability and peace in a region where countries are widely seen as disparate. In the association's early days it was also concerned with nation building, as many of these countries had recently gained independence from the colonial powers. In the organizational structure of ASEAN, sovereignty is retained at the national level, and various principles were established to ensure this, such as noninterference, avoidance of force, and nonconfrontation. The founders agreed to an implicit

bargain about nonintervention in each member's affairs. As a result, the institutionalization and legalization of regional cooperation have proven difficult, and more often than not the management of ASEAN has taken place through consultation and a search for consensus among member governments. Consequently, ASEAN experienced fairly severe political difficulties after the Asian economic crisis of 1997.

The development of ASEAN took place in two phases: first, in the 1960s, when it was viewed essentially as a "club" for dictators, and, second, in the post–Cold War period, when political change allowed it to become more expressive in regional economic ambitions and in developing a security dialogue. Its major achievement in the early 1990s was its contribution to solving the Cambodian conflict through mediation among the various parties. Nevertheless, much of its potential failed to materialize, and after the financial upheavals of 1997 ASEAN was in tremendous organizational disarray. Internal developments and external problems led to strategic incoherence and an apparent lack of will to make decisions. The organization experienced a lack of leadership over issues such as the continual haze problem from forest fires in Indonesia that affected Singapore and Malaysia. Indonesia, the largest and most powerful member of ASEAN, has done little to take the initiative in problem solving, and this lack of leadership has extended to human rights issues.

There was also little agreement on foreign policy issues. ASEAN's policy of "constructive engagement," aiming to appease dictatorships like that in Myanmar, failed, and the more democratic governments in the region, like the Philippines and Thailand, advocated abandoning the policy and moving toward "flexible engagement." The more illiberal members of the organization rejected the proposal, however. ASEAN member states focused on antiterrorism policies in their regional meetings while paying little attention to the consequences of these policies for the condition of human rights within member states. More specifically, due to its weakness ASEAN failed at a regional level to protect and promote human rights.

The enlargement of ASEAN to incorporate members whose human rights records were less than exemplary affected its international standing. Its reputation on rights, in short, degraded over time. The members that joined in stages after 1995, including Vietnam and Myanmar, brought different issues to the ASEAN table. In the early twenty-first century civil society in any real sense existed in only a few members, such as Thailand, the Philippines, and Indonesia, where people contributed to the political process without major restraints. Myanmar clearly did not have civil society by any stretch of the imagination. In turn, many ASEAN members returned to an illiberal tendency, reflected in the individual behaviors of some of its members. ASEAN proved a bit more successful in the area of free trade liberalization and various cultural activities, but organizationally it remained politically underdeveloped.

Interestingly, ASEAN successfully made collective decisions on the international stage through various well-established dialogue mechanisms. This process started in 1972 with a dialogue between ASEAN and the European Union (EU) and continued through a network of regional and global meetings that included such major players as the United States, China, and Japan. In 1993 ASEAN also developed the ASEAN Regional Forum (ARF), which introduced a framework for developments concerning security. In 1997 an informal meeting established the ASEAN Plus Three (APT), through which the organization developed closer relations with China, Japan, and South Korea.

A DIVERGENCE OF VIEWS

It might be argued that Asia has no history of human rights as understood in Western, liberal terms. Human rights in this conception, to which Asians have been obliged to react, not only apply to all groups of people in all societies, regardless of socioeconomic status, but are also conceived of as basic entitlements that trump all other considerations that may arise from an individual's relationship to social networks or the state. Southeast Asia, however, has no tradition of such entitlements. Rather, the political culture stresses basic duties, not rights. These duties arise from a person's status or group affiliation, which is extremely important in society. For many Asian governments, to the extent that they are interested in

human rights, the priority of second-generation (economic and social) rights has always been featured more than individual, liberal political rights.

The subject of human rights in Southeast Asia became more prominent with the Asian values debate in part because of the region's dynamic economic expansion and its subsequent crisis in 1997. Some have argued that the region is resistant to the ideas and practice of democracy and human rights agendas. Although the paths of democratization may appear universal in the West, something different took place in this region. The Asian values debate of the 1990s was used to justify authoritarian rule and was sponsored by illiberal regimes protecting themselves from opposition. The idea that Asian values were inherently superior to Western values was for the most part discarded extraordinarily quickly as it seemed the Asia-Pacific century might not materialize after all. The whole point of the Asian values movement was to maintain high rates of economic growth without developing the social pathologies that followed affluence in the West; that is, to enjoy the positive aspects of modernization without the negatives. This debate largely ceased with the devastating effects of the financial crisis as the less appealing aspects of modernization, such as unemployment, crime, and decline in social welfare, came to the region. This caused illiberal Southeast Asian states to lower their voices, because they had largely lost the moral high ground in the values debate.

THE WAR ON TERRORISM

Of the far-reaching changes affecting human rights agendas, problems, and prospects in the region, the aftermath of the terrorist attacks in the United States on 11 September 2001 was most significant. The war on terrorism generated a crisis for rights in many parts of the ASEAN region, as authoritarian regimes reinvigorated suppression of domestic oppositions. The notion of a new, very serious threat enabled states that previously were improving their human rights records to suppress dissent by prioritizing national security issues. That is, in view of terrorism and its operatives around the world, issues of domestic security acquired new import, and the restriction and even abolition of civil liberties became the agenda of many Asian governments. As terrorism provided a new enemy for the United States in the absence of Communism, states in the region fell in line. In particular, the governments of Singapore and Malaysia seized 9/11 as a justification for increased suppression of internal dissent and a means to bolster their legitimacy. Brad Adams, executive director of the Asia Division of Human Rights Watch (HRW), warned that "ASEAN is right to focus on the threat of terrorism, but should commit to building in protections for due process and human rights. The campaign against terror must not be a green light for indefinite detention without trial or torture" (Human Rights Watch).

Following 9/11, in varying degrees, individual ASEAN governments expressed sympathy and solidarity with the victims and with the United States. ASEAN governments made statements condemning terrorism and calling for international cooperation in the wake of the attacks. Most Southeast Asian states endorsed United Nations (UN) Security Council Resolution 1368, passed one day after 9/11, which condemned the attacks and recognized the basic rights of individual and collective self-defense. However, state responses in other ways varied from strong support (the Philippines) to criticism of U.S. policy regarding Muslim states (Malaysia) and criticism of the handling of the "war." ASEAN members did sign a joint declaration with the United States for cooperation in combating international terrorism. Adopted on 1 August 2002, the declaration provided for intelligence sharing and capacity building. Unfortunately, this also made Myanmar a signatory to a joint declaration with the United States. The declaration did several things. It boosted law enforcement and intelligence gathering in Southeast Asia and allowed illiberal leaders to reassert themselves. It also committed the United States to participating in development in the region, whereas previously it had distanced itself from the region.

On a thematic level, critics contend that the United States has had a negative impact on Southeast Asian politics. According to Jim Glassman, a professor of geography, U.S. efforts are simply an attempt to regain the hegemony forfeited at the end of the Vietnam War. In the region the relationships with the United States vary according to states' strategic interests. For instance, Singapore, the Philippines, and Thailand are generally supportive of the United States and the war on terrorism, but others have argued for a reduced U.S. role.

After 9/11 the global war on terrorism produced a more difficult and complex world. There is little doubt that human rights as an issue became increasingly marginalized. The counterterrorist measures of the United States and its allies proved counterproductive, as governments often used these measures to perpetuate widespread abuse against people with legitimate grievances.

OTHER PROBLEMS

Southeast Asia confronted several other issues. The majority of ASEAN countries argued for a UN solution to the Iraq problem, with the exceptions of the Philippines (the strongest U.S. supporter in the area) and Singapore. Myanmar, Laos, and Vietnam opposed interventionist policies, and Malaysia criticized the actions of the United States and the West in Iraq. However, no ASEAN state enjoyed great bilateral relations with the others. For instance, there are no extradition treaties between members. ASEAN was also weakened by an overemphasis on consultation and consensus; it avoided ownership of controversial issues, concentrating instead on those in which it could develop consensus. In short, there was little if any leadership on issues that might affect its political standing.

The region was also severely affected by the Indian Ocean tsunami on 26 December 2004 that left as many as 290,000 people dead. The Aceh area in Indonesia, where 230,000 people were killed, was hit the hardest. Although natural disasters of this magnitude cannot be equated with violations of human rights, they do highlight the nature of some of the societies. For instance, the crisis illustrated how closed the Indonesian government was to allowing freedom of movement and access in areas like Aceh, the site of a long-standing insurgency.

Although the size and diversity of the region induce caution in making generalizations, authoritarian states there have tended to view human rights as a threat to national security. Some cases illustrate the general points.

The Philippines.

According to a member of the Philippine Alliance of Human Rights Advocates, "The painful scenario of the human rights situation in the Philippines today only proves that the 'war against terrorism' being waged by Arroyo's strong republic is an all out war against the Filipino people." According to the Canada-based British Columbia Committee for Human Rights in the Philippines, in the early twenty-first century there were nineteen cases of human rights violations every week in which at least two people were killed. The majority of these cases (almost 70 percent) were perpetrated by the army and special forces. From January 2001 to October 2002, 9,206 civilians were victims of bombings and indiscriminate firing by military, paramilitary, and police forces. In 2003 there were 167 political prisoners in the Philippines. Rodolf Stavenhagen, the UN envoy for the rights of indigenous people, noted reports of native people being prosecuted for terrorist activity because of their involvement in legitimate protest or in the defense of their rights. This shows an extenuation of the counterterrorism policies adopted by the Philippine government. According to critics, perhaps like the United States in some ways, the Philippines was headed toward a militarized society.

The war on terrorism had a disproportionate effect on civilians in the Philippines. According to Luis H. Francia, ordinary Filipinos' lives worsened as a result: "The war itself can be regarded as terroristic, particularly in Mindanao, where the army has aggressively engaged the MILF and where the number of internal refugees at its peak rose as high as half a million." In particular, the Philippine government demonstrated strong support for the global war on terrorism. This may have damaging effects for human rights policies in a society that prides itself on being one of the most democratic countries in ASEAN.

Indonesia.

Indonesia is the world's largest Muslim nation and a country of strategic and political importance to the West. Only in the early twenty-first century did it begin progress toward democracy and respect for human rights. The country held national elections for parliament and president in April, July, and September 2004, an illustration of democratization. Indonesia was regarded as crucial in the global war on terrorism. Between 2002 and 2007 more than two hundred civilians were killed in bomb attacks that mainly targeted Western institutions, including the Australian Embassy, the Marriott Hotel in Jakarta, and a nightclub in Bali. Victims included Indonesian citizens and Australian tourists, among others. In response to Western pressure, the Indonesian government passed new antiterrorist laws that restricted human rights and used them to justify repression and crackdowns in Aceh and Papua. The repercussions in these provinces, which were campaigning for independence, were serious, and the Indonesian government enacted harsh security measures and repressed separatism, easily categorized as part of its war on terrorism.

In Timor-Leste (formerly East Timor), the long-standing issue within Indonesia's human rights record reflected an overall failure to bring to justice those responsible for human rights abuses despite efforts by the Indonesian government to appoint more judges and prosecutors. The question of justice for the atrocities perpetrated under Indonesian rule continued to dominate much of the Timorese political scene in the early twenty-first

century. Moreover, mainland human rights commissions, such as the Indonesian National Human Rights Commission (Komisi Nasional Hak Asasi Manusia or Komnas HAM), became more and more ineffective and marginalized from human rights activities, a pattern reflected in the treatment of human rights advocates across the region.

In Aceh, the conflict between the Indonesian military and the Free Aceh Movement (Gerakan Aceh Merdeka or GAM) intensified. In 2002 an estimated 1,230 people were killed in Aceh. By mid-2003 at least 25,000 military personnel operated there, despite the provision of a new special autonomy law issued on 1 January 2002. The Indonesian government declared a state of military emergency in Aceh and a state of martial law in May 2003, after the failure of peace talks, and launched full-scale military operations in the province. Nearly 40,000 troops were sent to deal with an estimated 5,000 members of the GAM. The situation became uncertain and extremely worrying for human rights in the province, including concerns that humanitarian aid workers were prevented from accessing areas.

In West Papua (formerly Irian Jaya), the security situation also deteriorated. Civilians and human rights advocates bore the brunt of the problems despite the approval of a special autonomy law for Papua in October 2001. U.S. proposals to spend millions of dollars to equip a domestic peacekeeping force were criticized by human rights advocates as another way of repressing human rights. More than 100,000 West Papuans were killed between 1963, when Indonesia took control of the province from the Dutch, and the early twenty-first century.

As of 2008, both peripheries continued to be subject to widespread violence, random killings, and human rights abuses. Furthermore, senior Indonesian officials used the term "terrorism" in their rhetoric when referring to domestic groups that were seen as a threat to the overall unity of Indonesia. Because of Indonesia's large Islamic population, the country was regarded as one of the most important states in the war on terrorism. The government's actions do not augur well for the positive development of human rights.

Vietnam.

Human rights conditions in Vietnam, which could be described as "poor at best" in the early twenty-first century, included severe restrictions on freedom of speech, but the greatest violations were in the area of religious freedom. The human rights problems in Vietnam emanated from the authorities' treatment of ethnic minorities.

Documents show that the Montagnards were one of the main minorities subjected to such violations. The abuses committed against them included assaults on church leaders by police and other officials, destruction of churches, banning of night-time gatherings and travel outside villages, and large-scale appropriation of farmland by the authorities. Montagnard Christians were the principal targets of the attacks and persecution, and many fled. Cambodia refused asylum, forcing Montagnard Christians to go into hiding in Vietnam. In early 2003, for example, more than one hundred Montagnards were forcibly returned to Vietnam from Cambodia. In April 2004 a peaceful demonstration by this group during Easter turned violent when security forces ambushed the demonstrators, killing at least ten and injuring dozens more. In the early twenty-first century more than 124 Montagnards were imprisoned for involvement in church activities and demonstrations. The status of ethnic minorities and refugees is a human rights concern because the situation corresponds to renewed state repression following the attacks of 9/11. Ethnic or minority groups are treated as terrorist threats to national security.

Singapore, Malaysia, and Thailand.

The major issues in Singapore and Malaysia relate to the lack of freedom of expression. Despite their developed status (Singapore more so than Malaysia), these countries continued to restrict freedom of speech and effectively curbed and weakened opposition activists by either imprisoning them (as in the case of Malaysia) or issuing defamation suits against opponents (as in the case of Singapore).

After more than two decades as prime minister of Malaysia, Mohamed Mahathir retired in 2003, and Abdullah Badawi was elected to the post. In September 2004 Anwar Ibrahim, the former deputy prime minister who was imprisoned during Mahathir's tenure, was released from prison. Badawi achieved some openness; however, restrictions remained. Scores of Islamists and suspected terrorists were arrested in the wake of 9/11, and few if any were brought to trial.

The harsh treatment of asylum seekers and refugees in Malaysia reflected the global trend. In 2001 Malaysia enacted strict laws against illegal immigrants, which prompted an exodus of at least 300,000 workers to Indonesia. Another 400,000 workers remained in Malaysia with no financial support. The government at the time agreed to a one-month extension of the departure deadline, but those who remained still faced huge fines, prison sentences in some cases, and even caning by the authorities. In May 2003 thousands of Indonesians fled from the brutal conflict in Aceh to Malaysia but did not receive the status or treatment normally given to refugees as a result of conflict and persecution. Those who managed to avoid deportation were subjected to harsh conditions and poverty.

In the early twenty-first century Malaysia avoided terrorist attacks on its soil, and the government attributed this to its Internal Security Act (ISA), which allows authorities to detain suspects for ninety days. By 2005 some ninety terror suspects had been held in this way. In April 2005 Amnesty International (AI) accused Malaysian police of human rights abuses, including a "pattern of torture and ill-treatment" of detainees in custody. The Malaysian government asserted that only thirty-nine suspects died in police custody between 2000 and 2003.

In 2002 members of religious groups in Singapore, such as Jehovah's Witnesses, were imprisoned for conscientious objection to the country's compulsory military service. Similarly, members of Falun Gong were arrested for holding a vigil in memory of group members who had died in custody in China.

In 2003 the government of Thailand waged a war on drugs that resulted in many extrajudicial killings. More than twenty-five hundred people died in these killings, and more than fifty thousand were arrested. In conjunction the Thai government resumed executions by lethal injection. Southern Thailand, where much of the country's Muslim population is concentrated, experienced widespread violence. There several Muslim lawyers and human rights defenders were intimidated and harassed by security forces. In 2005 bombings, shootings, and arms theft became commonplace in Thailand's Muslim south. The Thai government attributed the situation to Al Qaeda networks, which also operated in Malaysia, Indonesia, and the Philippines. In Thailand nearly 6 million of the nation's 63 million population were Muslim, and tensions escalated gradually. In October 2004 eighty-six protestors were killed by security forces in the Muslim south. At the end of March 2005 fifteen people were injured in bomb attacks and shoot-outs in the southern region. Thailand moved from a positive standard of human rights in the region to become a country of high concern. Much of the steady progress Thailand made in the last decade of the twentieth century in human rights was rolled back under Thaksin Shinawatra's government.

PROSPECTS FOR HUMAN RIGHTS

The prospects for establishing a human rights culture in the ASEAN region following the September 2001 attacks in the United States appear problematic. The U.S. response to the events of 9/11 led to the establishment of a much more unilateral, hard-line stance on terrorism, with dramatic implications for local populations in parts of Southeast Asia. Soft authoritarian states such as Singapore, Malaysia, Indonesia, and others now justified internal repression with reference to the threat of terrorism within their societies. The Philippines, with a convenient home-grown Islamist movement, Abu Sayyaf, on its doorstep to justify repressive measures, suppressed internal dissent with the aid of the U.S. military. Then U.S. president George W. Bush, for instance, provided an unqualified endorsement to Manila's counterterrorism actions against Muslim insurgents, while some American officials warned that the southern Philippines could become the next Afghanistan. Clearly, the stakes were raised with greater military aid made available, and the United States declared that it wanted to play an active role in hunting terrorists in Southeast Asia. In other words, for the United States and the West the war on terrorism was a higher priority than human rights. Indeed, this encouraged many developing states with less than adequate human rights records to enhance and securitize their reactions to internal dissent.

GLOBALIZATION

In some ways, it is difficult to discuss the development of human rights in Asia without reference to globalization, which not only played its part in the region's dramatic economic growth but was also a factor in its rapid downfall with the economic crisis in mid-1997. Questions of illegal (and legal) migration, labor standards, prostitution, child labor, and discrimination against ethnic minorities, to name just a few, impact human rights in the ASEAN countries. Groups that have been marginalized by globalization are vulnerable and susceptible and therefore are often the victims of human rights abuse. Legitimate ethnic grievances suffered as a result of the war on terrorism have been disregarded in states that ignore rights and the rule of law. This has become a global phenomenon.

The rise of a radical form of Islam also had significant implications for Southeast Asia. In the early twenty-first century Al Qaeda continued strong operations in the region, which will continue to be a theater for its operations for some time to come. The globalization of security concerns about terrorism following 9/11 meant that human rights suffered around the world, and states in Southeast Asia reinvigorated their internal security mechanisms and increased their military power. The nation-state was further strengthened because ASEAN was weak and incoherent in its response to terrorism. In turn, the United States became reengaged in the region, as seen in its support for the Philippines and Indonesia. But most importantly for human rights, the war on terrorism allowed states in Southeast Asia to justify repression, and in consequence they faced little criticism from the United States. The global war on terrorism gave these a countries a new opportunity to exploit the security nexus of the state in violating human rights. In the early twenty-first century this trend appeared set to continue, and ASEAN had done little to protect the citizens of the individual societies its organization represents.

[*See also* Human Security; Islam; *and* United States: War on Terrorism.]

BIBLIOGRAPHY

Abuza, Zachary. *Militant Islam in Southeast Asia: Crucible of Terror.* Boulder, Colo.: Lynne Reinner, 2003.

Acharya, Amitav. *Constructing a Security Community in Southeast Asia: ASEAN and the Problem of Regional Order.* London: Routledge, 2001.

Acharya, Amitav. *The Quest for Identity: International Relations of Southeast Asia.* Oxford: Oxford University Press, 2000.

Acharya, Amitav. "Realism, Institutionalism, and the Asian Economic Crisis." *Contemporary Southeast Asia* 21 (1999): 1–29.

Asia Watch. *Human Rights in the APEC Region.* New York: Asia Watch, 1993.

Bauer, Joanne R., and Daniel A. Bell, eds. *The East Asian Challenge for Human Rights.* Cambridge, U.K.: Cambridge University Press, 1999.

Capie, David. "Between a Hegemon and a Hard Place: The 'War on Terror' and Southeast Asian–US Relations." *Pacific Review* 17, no. 2 (2004): 223–248.

Christie, Kenneth. "Regime Security and Human Rights in Southeast Asia." *Political Studies* 43 (1995): 204–218.

Christie, Kenneth, and Denny Roy. *The Politics of Human Rights in East Asia.* London: Pluto, 2001.

Connors, Michael K., Rémy Davidson, and Jörn Dosch. *The New Global Politics of the Asia-Pacific.* London: RoutledgeCurzon 2004.

Cotton, James. "Southeast Asia after September 11." *Terrorism and Political Violence* 15, no. 1 (Spring 2003).

Eldridge, Philip J. *The Politics of Human Rights in Southeast Asia.* London: Routledge, 2002.

Francia, Luis H. "Meanwhile in Manila . . . : Bush's War Has Internationalized Internal Conflicts on the Archipelago." *The Nation*, October 27, 2003. http://www.thenation.com/directory/bios/luis_h_francia.

Gershman, John. "Is Southeast Asia the Second Front?" *Foreign Affairs* (July–August 2002): 60–65. http://www.foreignaffairs.org/20021001faupdate10329/john-gershman.

Glassman, Jim. "The War on Terrorism Comes to Southeast Asia." *Journal of Contemporary Asia* 35, no. 1 (February 2005): 3–28.

Haacke, Jürgen. *ASEAN's Diplomatic and Security Culture: Origins, Developments, and Prospects*. London: RoutledgeCurzon, 2003.

Human Rights Watch. "Asian Security Talks Risk Giving Green Light to Repression." *Human Rights News*, June 16, 2003. http://www.hrw.org/press/2003/06/asean061603.htm.

Narine, Shaun. "ASEAN in the 21st Century: Problems and Prospects." *Pacific Review* 12, no. 3 (1999): 357–380.

Ravenhill John. "A Three Bloc World? The New East Asian Regionalism." *International Relations of the Asia-Pacific* 2, no. 2 (2002): 167–195.

AUNG SAN SUU KYI

by Monique Skidmore

Throughout Myanmar (known as Burma prior to its 1989 government-mandated name change) Aung San Suu Kyi is referred to as "The Lady" and the "Iron Butterfly," and her significance as an abiding beacon of hope and symbol of resistance to military rule for the vast majority of Burmese people cannot be overstated. In the worldwide media she is often referred to as the "Nelson Mandela of Asia," testimony to her international renown, but in Myanmar she is a revered person along with her father Aung San. Since forming a political party, the National League for Democracy (NLD), in 1989, Aung San Suu Kyi has become the most prominent human rights advocate in not only Myanmar but also all of Southeast Asia.

Suu Kyi has spoken often of the formidable influence of her father's political beliefs and personal values, and of the importance of Theravada Buddhist practices (such as *vissipana*, insight meditation) and values including forgiveness, kindness, and compassion in forging her political philosophy. She has also acknowledged the teachings and practices of Mohandas ("Mahatma") Gandhi as important to the development of a political consciousness based in spirituality, humanism, and nonviolence. Many of these ideas permeate her collected writings, the most well-known of her books being *Freedom from Fear and Other Writings* (1995).

BACKGROUND

Aung San Suu Kyi was born on 19 June 1945, into an affluent family in the then capital of Rangoon (now known as Yangon). Her father Aung San is one of Myanmar's most important historical figures, having founded the Burma Independence Army and mediated the agreement for independence with the British. He was assassinated in 1947, and Suu Kyi and her two brothers, Aung San Lin (who died in an accident when he was eight years old) and Aung San Oo (who now resides in America), were raised by their mother, Khin Kyi. In 1960 Suu Kyi left Yangon for New Delhi, where her mother began

service as the Burmese ambassador to India. Suu Kyi graduated from Lady Shri Ram College in New Delhi in 1964.

Suu Kyi then attended St. Hugh's College, Oxford, and in 1967 received a BA in philosophy, politics, and economics. It was in England that Aung San Suu Kyi met her future husband, Michael Aris, then a student of Tibetan civilization who was to become an internationally renowned scholar on Tibet.

In 1969 Suu Kyi moved to the United States for graduate study, but postponed her studies to join the United Nations (UN) Secretariat in New York. Burma's U Thant was secretary-general at that time and Suu Kyi was appointed assistant secretary of the Advisory Committee on Administrative and Budgetary Questions.

On 1 January 1972 Aung San Suu Kyi married Aris at the home of Sir Paul Gore-Booth, a former British ambassador to Burma, in a Buddhist ceremony. During this period, Aris was a tutor to the royal family of Bhutan, a small kingdom in the Himalayas; he was also working as both head of Bhutan's Translation Department and as a researcher on Bhutan's official history. Suu Kyi moved to Bhutan to be with her husband, and there she was appointed a research officer in the Royal Ministry of Foreign Affairs.

In 1973 the married couple returned to England for the birth of their first son, Alexander. Their second son, Kim, was born there in 1977. While in England, Aris commenced postgraduate studies at the School of Oriental and African Studies at the University of London, and in 1976 was appointed a university faculty member at Oxford. While raising her children, Suu Kyi worked in the Bodleian Library's Oriental Department and began to write and research a biography of her father, published as *Aung San* in 1984. The following year she published *Let's Visit Burma* for young readers, as well as several books on Nepal and Bhutan.

In 1985 Suu Kyi was a visiting scholar at the Center of Southeast Asian Studies at Kyoto University, Japan; in 1987 she received a fellowship at the Indian Institute for

Advanced Studies in Simla, India. She and her family then returned to Oxford, and Suu Kyi began to pursue a postgraduate degree at the School of Oriental and African Studies at the University of London.

The year 1988 proved to be a decisive one. In March, upon learning that her mother had suffered a stroke, Aung San Suu Kyi returned to Yangon to care for Khin Kyi. Aris has written this of that phone call: "Our sons were in bed, and we were reading when the telephone rang . . . She put down the phone at once and started to pack. I had a premonition that our lives would change forever" (Aris quoted in Hoge, 1999, p. C27). Suu Kyi's flight to her mother's bedside was the beginning of her unwitting transformation into what Aris described as "an icon of popular hope and longing" for the Burmese people.

METAMORPHOSIS

General Ne Win, leader of the Burma Socialist Programme Party (BSPP) and military dictator of Burma since 1962, resigned in July 1988. Still, popular demonstrations of protest against military rule and demanding free elections continued, peaking in mass uprisings across the country on 8 August 1988. Known as the 8-8-88 or the "Four Eights," the pro-democracy movement was violently suppressed by the military, and estimates of its death toll during this period range around the ten thousand mark. In her first political action on 15 August, Aung San Suu Kyi sent an open letter to the government in which she asked for the formation of an independent committee to lay the groundwork for multiparty elections. Four days later the man known as the "Butcher of Burma," Sein Lwin, resigned and Maung Maung Kha became the leader of the nation.

In her first public speech before several hundred thousand people at the Shewdagon Pagoda in Yangon one week later, Suu Kyi called for a democratic Burmese government. On 18 September, however, a cartel of military officers seized power, calling themselves the State Law and Order Restoration Council, best known by its Orwellian-like acronym, SLORC. The new military government pledged to hold multiparty elections while simultaneously implementing a series of laws that repressed civil society and political and social freedoms.

Undeterred, nine days later, the NLD formed, with U Tin Oo as its chairman and Suu Kyi the general secretary, a post she continues to hold. In defiance of a SLORC order banning the public political gatherings of more than four people, for the rest of the year Aung San Suu Kyi and U Tin Oo delivered speeches throughout the country to ever-growing audiences.

At her mother's funeral in January 1989, Suu Kyi pledged to continue serving the cause of the Burmese people. Despite harassment and threats from the military, she continued her campaign. On 17 February 17 SLORC announced that Aung San Suu Kyi would be unable to run as a candidate in the national general election and placed her under house arrest on 20 July. The following year, on 27 May 1990, despite the fact that its leaders had been unable to run for election, the NLD won 392 out of 485 seats contested in the general election. However, SLORC refused to hand over power, and in the early twenty-first century Suu Kyi remained under house arrest. The candidate who most likely would have played a major leadership role, perhaps as Myanmar's first democratically elected female prime minister or president, was thus, like her father before her, denied that opportunity by violent means. International condemnation of the military regime was fierce, and a number of international peace and human rights prizes were awarded to Aung San Suu Kyi in 1990 and 1991. In 1990, for example, Suu Kyi was awarded the Professor Thorolf Rafto Memorial Prize; in 1991 she received the Sakharov Prize for Freedom of Thought and the Nobel Prize for Peace. In December 1991 her *Freedom from Fear and Other Writings* was published, and because she was unable to leave Myanmar with any hope of return, her sons accepted the Peace Prize in Oslo on her behalf. SLORC offered Aung San Suu Kyi her freedom in return for exile and a withdrawal from politics, but she refused. In 1992 she announced the creation of a trust fund to be used for health and education projects in Myanmar financed by her Nobel Prize for Peace monies (U.S. $1.3 million).

Aung San Suu Kyi was released briefly from house arrest in July 1995, although her movements were still restricted, and a vehement and abusive propaganda campaign was waged against her in the state-controlled media. While she was at first able to speak to large gatherings of people, leaning over the front fence of her home, the junta stopped this in 1996. On 15 November 1997 SLORC transformed itself into a successor military council known as the State Peace and Development Committee (SPDC). The policy toward Suu Kyi did not change as SLORC's senior leadership also remained in place. From 1996 until 1998 Suu Kyi was again placed under house arrest. During the period 1998–2000 the conditions of her imprisonment ameliorated: she remained under severe restrictions but was able to travel around Yangon and could attend NLD meetings, and social and ceremonial events. Nevertheless, she was not able to make any public speeches during this period.

In addition, Aung San Suu Kyi's ability to see her family has been severely restricted by the military regime since December 1995. In 1997 Aris, then living in London, was diagnosed with prostate cancer; he died two years later, without having been allowed to see his wife. During this time the military regime attempted to prevent all forms of communication between Suu Kyi and her family, in the continued hope that she would choose exile over house arrest. On several occasions her sons visited her in Yangon when military authorities relented.

In October 2000 Aung San Suu Kyi was again placed under house arrest. She was released in May 2002, after secret negotiations instigated by the UN. All restrictions on her were subsequently lifted, and she took the opportunity to travel around the country, reopening NLD branch offices and giving public speeches. A tacit agreement existed between the NLD and the military regime that neither would criticize the other in their propaganda, and Suu Kyi further agreed that she would not undertake so-called treasonous activities, such as calling for the overthrow of the military regime.

In the twelve months that followed, a spontaneous groundswell of popular support for the NLD and Aung San Suu Kyi became apparent during her travels throughout the country. Alarmed by this visible sign of resurgent support for the NLD, the SPDC organized a competing social welfare organization, the Union Solidarity and Development Association (USDA). In what has become known as the Depayin Massacre, on 30 May 2003 a large group of people led by the USDA attacked the convoy in which Suu Kyi and U Tin Oo were traveling. Many of Suu Kyi's supporters were killed or wounded during this incident, and she was briefly imprisoned at Insein Prison in Yangon. Later that year she was again placed under house arrest, where she has remained in strict detention, unable to meet with anyone but her private doctor.

CONTRIBUTIONS AND CONTROVERSIES

Critics of Aung San Suu Kyi include former confidants, expatriate activists, and some Western commentators and academics. She has been accused of inflexibility regarding her stance on the illegitimacy of Myanmar's military government and of causing the ruling generals to lose face, thus hardening their attitudes toward her and the NLD, and undermining the cause of democracy and human rights. A few Burmese activists have suggested that the hard-line stance of NLD leadership since its founding in 1989 is impeding movement toward a compromise solution. In particular, such critics point to the withdrawal of the NLD from the National Convention constitutional drafting process. It refused to participate in 2004 because Suu Kyi and U Thin Oo remained in detention, although the NLD had attended an earlier National Convention in 1995–1996, a period when Suu Kyi also was held in detention.

On those few occasions when Aung San Suu Kyi has made conciliatory gestures and suggested compromises, even proposing that she rejoin the National Convention in 2004, the military government has spurned the offers. She possesses a unique power in contemporary Myanmar, and the military regime continues to try and suppress it. The movement of the Burmese capital from Rangoon to Pyinmana in March 2006 and the regular renewal of Suu Kyi's period of house arrest signal the regime's resolve to isolate her from all political processes and decisions.

The military regime reviles Aung San Suu Kyi, as evidenced by a series of articles published in the state media and then as a collected volume, *Who Is Aung San Suu Kyi? Whither Goest She?* (1997). In these articles she is portrayed as a foreigner who has renounced her Burmese heritage, as a prostitute, a lesbian, a puppet of Western forces, a person of status lower than that of Indian traders in Myanmar, an ogress, not to mention other degrading, racist, sexist, and anti-Buddhist representations. This propaganda aims to convince Burmese people that Suu Kyi is not Burmese "enough," an analysis advanced by Monique Skidmore (2004). It is failing, but it has had the effect of heightening gender stereotypes and reducing women's ability to take action in a public sphere, especially the political one in contemporary Myanmar.

ASSESSMENT

The 1991 Nobel Peace Prize laureate Aung San Suu Kyi has spent most of the years since 1989 under house arrest in Yangon. In the eyes of the great majority of the Burmese population, this has only increased the significance of her fight for human rights, democracy, and the rule of law in Myanmar. As secretary of Myanmar's main opposition party, she is a visible and constant symbol of defiance against military rule, repression, and human rights violations in her homeland. Her father is regarded as the architect of Burmese independence, and together Aung San and Aung San Suu Kyi are the two most important figures in Myanmar's political history since the fall of the Burmese monarchy in 1885. Other figures also have been significant, such as former prime minister U Nu and military dictator Ne Win, but no other figure commands both the respect and love of the Burmese people as much as Aung San Suu Kyi. She is a figure of international repute for the human rights movement, the women's movement, and the Burmese diaspora.

[*See also* Burma (Myanmar) *and* History of Human Rights.]

BIBLIOGRAPHY

Abrams, Irwin, ed. "Aung San Suu Kyi—Biography." In *Les Prix Nobel/ Nobel Lectures, Peace 1991–1995*. Singapore: World Scientific, 1999. http://www.nobelprize.org/peace/laureates/1991/kyi-bio.html.

Aung San Suu Kyi, ed. *Freedom from Fear and Other Writings*. Introduction by Michael Aris. 2d ed., revised. London: Penguin, 1995.

Hoge, Warren. "Michael V. Aris, 53, Dies: Scholarly Husband of Laureate." *The New York Times*, March 30, 1999, obituary.

Houtman, Gustaaf. *Mental Culture in Burmese Crisis Politics: Aung San Suu Kyi and the National League for Democracy*. Tokyo: Tokyo University of Foreign Studies, Institute for the Study of Languages and Cultures of Asia and Africa, 1999.

Pe Kan Kaung. *What Is Aung San Suu Kyi? Whither Goest She?* Yangon: Myanmar News and Periodicals Enterprise, 1997.

Skidmore, Monique. *Karaoke Fascism: Burma and the Politics of Fear*. Philadelphia: University of Pennsylvania Press, 2004.

Skidmore, Monique, and Patricia Lawrence, eds. *Women and the Contested State: Religion, Violence and Agency in South and Southeast Asia*. South Bend, Ind.: University of Notre Dame Press, 2007.

JOSÉ AYALA LASSO

by Alfred de Zayas

José Ayala Lasso was the first United Nations High Commissioner for Human Rights (1994–1997). Born in Quito, Ecuador, on 29 January 1932, he became a career officer in the diplomatic service of Ecuador, serving as foreign minister on three occasions and as ambassador to Belgium, France, Luxembourg, Peru, the Vatican, and the European Economic Community. He was Ecuador's permanent representative to the United Nations (UN) (1989–1994) and Ecuador's representative on the UN Security Council (1991–1992), serving as its president in August 1991 and again in September 1992.

Paragraph 18 of part 2 of the Vienna Declaration and Programme of Action of 25 June 1993 recommended to the General Assembly that it establish the office of a High Commissioner for Human Rights. Ayala Lasso chaired the UN General Assembly working group that considered the Vienna Declaration and drafted Resolution 48/141, adopted by consensus on 20 December 1993, establishing the post and defining its mandate. Secretary-General Boutros Boutros-Ghali nominated Ayala Lasso, and the General Assembly confirmed the appointment. Ayala Lasso started his four-year mandate on 5 April 1994.

WORK AS HIGH COMMISSIONER

The priorities of the office had yet to be determined. When, how, and where should the high commissioner act? Ayala Lasso's first task was to establish the authority and credibility of the office vis-à-vis the member states and the different UN organs. He set the following goals: crisis management and urgent action; preventive strategies; universal ratification of human rights conventions; development of a follow-up capacity to ensure that states implemented the decisions of the treaty bodies; assistance to states in transition to democracy; expansion of national human rights infrastructures; and promotion of "enabling rights," such as the right to peace, the right to development, and the right to one's homeland.

Ayala Lasso's first challenge was the human rights crisis resulting from the genocide in Rwanda. He traveled repeatedly to the troubled country and personally interceded on behalf of thousands of Tutsi trapped in Kigali. Although he did not receive credit for it, he successfully rescued thousands, similar to Raoul Wallenberg's rescue of thousands of Jews from Hungary in 1944. Ayala Lasso's personal appeal to the chief of staff of the interim government resulted in the evacuation of some fifteen hundred Tutsi trapped at the Hôtel des Mille Collines and other sites. Ayala's report of 19 May 1994 described the killings in Rwanda as "a human rights tragedy of unprecedented dimensions," and he insisted that those in command of the killings must be held individually responsible for their violations of international law (*Report of the UN High Commissioner for Human Rights on His Mission to Rwanda*, p. 2).

Ayala also addressed the grave human rights violations in the former Yugoslavia and conferred with many politicians and negotiators, including Cyrus Vance of the United States, in an effort to devise a peaceful solution. After the signing of the Dayton Peace Accords in December 1995, Ayala offered the assistance of his office for the postconflict institutional reconstruction of Bosnia and Herzegovina. He was a strong advocate of the International Criminal Tribunal for the Former Yugoslavia and the International Criminal Tribunal for Rwanda. He stated, "We must rid this planet of the obscenity that a person stands a better chance of being tried and judged for killing one human being than for killing 100,000" (*Report of the President of the International Criminal Tribunal for the Former Yugoslavia to the Security Council*, p. 11). Ayala Lasso's years as high commissioner were marked by a continuous effort to give greater visibility to the UN human rights program. He opened and expanded field offices in all regions of the world, including Colombia, Burundi, Cambodia, Rwanda, and Bosnia and Herzegovina. As a seasoned diplomat, he excelled in quiet diplomacy and traveled extensively to confer with leaders worldwide, including a trip in November 1994 to Cuba, where he met not only with Fidel Castro and his ministers but also with political dissidents. Ayala Lasso spoke out frequently against capital punishment; interceded on behalf of persons under sentence of death; and, in November 1995, made an urgent appeal to the president of Nigeria on behalf of the Ogoni leader Ken Saro-Wiwa and his eight co-defendants. When they were executed, Ayala Lasso strongly condemned the action.

Ayala Lasso's vision was to transform the former Centre for Human Rights from a passive conference services secretariat into a proactive center of excellence with an expert secretariat and an expanded mandate to conduct projects throughout the world. Under his leadership the Office of the High Commissioner for Human Rights began to develop an operational capacity similar to that of the Office of the High Commissioner for Refugees. He emphasized that he was appointed to serve all humanity and to defend all victims in all parts of the world, regardless of privilege and without discrimination. He rejected opportunism and emphasized the overarching principle of equality, including the equality in human dignity of all victims, speaking against the fiction of "politically correct," or "consensus," victims and those unfortunates who could be safely ignored. He demonstrated courage in giving enhanced attention to the "unsung victims," among them the indigenous peoples of the world, particularly in his own Latin America. On 28 May 1995 he also gave the forgotten survivors among the 15 million Germans expelled from East Prussia, Pomerania, Silesia, East Brandenburg, Bohemia, Moravia, and other parts of central and eastern Europe at the end of World War II eloquent and unexpected recognition:

> The right not to be expelled from one's homeland is a fundamental right. . . . I submit that if in the years following the Second World War the States had reflected more on the implications of the enforced flight and the expulsion of the Germans, today's demographic catastrophes, particularly those referred to as "ethnic cleansing," would, perhaps, not have occurred to the same extent. (de Zayas, "The Right to One's Homeland," p. 257)

In this context, Ayala Lasso gave effective support to the Sub-Commission on Prevention of Discrimination and Protection of Minorities special rapporteur on the human rights dimensions of population transfer, Awn Shawkat Al-Khasawneh (who subsequently became a judge at the International Court of Justice). Al-Khasawneh produced a seminal study, *Human Rights and Population Transfer*, which includes a Draft Declaration on Population Transfer and the Implantation of Settlers.

As high commissioner, Ayala Lasso observed the priorities established by the General Assembly, including the Third Decade to Combat Racism and Racial Discrimination (1993–2003), the International Decade of the World's Indigenous People (1995–2004), the UN Decade for Human Rights Education (1995–2004), and the UN International Year for Tolerance (1995). In September 1995 the Fourth World Conference on Women was held in Beijing, resulting in the Beijing Platform for Action. Back in Geneva, Ayala Lasso proved to be a strong supporter of gender mainstreaming.

As an administrator, Ayala Lasso was remembered fondly by most of his staff because of his openness and kindness. Less successful were his efforts at restructuring, primarily because of the failure of the General Assembly to approve an adequate budget for the office. Indeed, when Ayala Lasso took office, he contended with a secretariat of only two hundred staff members and less than US $40 million per annum, which was reduced by $2.6 million in financial crisis. Economy has always been a high a priority of the UN. But as Ayala Lasso observed, it is hard on the staff members to have to explain to people deprived of their rights that one cannot help them because the necessary material means are insufficient. Of course, no high commissioner can be expected to solve the enormous problems of human rights in their towering extent and complexity. Rather, the main task should be to develop step-by-step a human rights culture to assist all people to become aware of their rights and to learn how to claim them.

AFTER HIGH COMMISSIONER SERVICE

Ayala Lasso resigned on 31 March 1997 to return to Ecuador to broker the peace negotiations between Ecuador and Peru that led to the treaty of 1998 settling the border dispute. After his retirement from public service, he continued his public advocacy for human rights. At a major event in Berlin on 6 August 2005, with German chancellor Angela Merkel, he delivered a speech in which he reasserted his faith in human dignity and the rights of indigenous peoples:

> I am convinced that the United Nations and, in particular, the Office of the High Commissioner for Human Rights . . . will persevere in its patient task of building a universal culture of human rights. . . . Among the collective human rights, the right to self-determination is, of course, of particular relevance to all of us. The United Nations played an

important role in the process of decolonization in Asia and Africa, and in the abolition of Apartheid. Other collective rights, including the rights of minorities, and the right to one's homeland have not been fully realized. Of course, the right to one's homeland is not merely a collective right, but it is also an individual right and a precondition for the exercise of many civil, political, economic, social and cultural rights. (de Zayas, *Die Nemesis von Potsdam*)

ASSESSMENT

As high commissioner, Ayala Lasso proved to be an honest broker, a discreet man who did not blow his own horn. His contribution to human rights is considerably greater than he has been given credit for. Some critics in the nongovernmental organization (NGO) community have pointed out that he did not take on the big powers, but it might be noted that his mandate did not allow him to do many things he would have wanted to do, even if his office had been properly funded, which alas it was not. He understood his function as establishing the credibility of the new office without overstepping his mandate and thus gradually building confidence with governments and NGOs alike. His supporters believe he proceeded wisely in establishing the new office on a firm footing, although some of his critics believe he might have been more dynamic in confronting some of the major rights problems of his time.

Ayala Lasso earned degrees in law and economics, international law, and political and social sciences from Pontificia Universidad Católica del Ecuador, Universidad Central del Ecuador, and Université Catholique de Louvain in Belgium. He taught at Instituto de Derecho Internacional of the Universidad Central del Ecuador.

[*See also* Indigenous Peoples; United Nations Commission on Human Rights; *and* United Nations Human Rights Council.]

BIBLIOGRAPHY

Ayala Lasso, José. "Contemporary International Law Issues: Conflicts and Convergence." 1995 Joint Conference, the American Society of International Law. The Hague, the Netherlands: Nederlandse Vereniging voor International Recht, 1996.

Ayala Lasso, José. "Defining the Mandate: New UN Efforts to Protect Human Rights." *Harvard International Review* (Winter 1994–1995): 38–78.

Ayala Lasso, José. "Foreword." In *The United Nations High Commissioner for Human Rights*, edited by Bertrand G. Ramcharan. The Hague: Martinus Nijhoff, 2002.

Ayala Lasso, José. "Grusswort." In *Dokumentation der Gedenkstunde in der Paulskirche zu Frankfurt am 28 Mai 1955: 50 Jahre Flucht, Deportation Vertreibung, Bonn, 1995*, edited by Dieter Blumenwitz, pp. 4–5. The original English version is reproduced in de Zayas, Alfred. *Nemesis at Potsdam*. Rockland, ME: Picton Press, 2003.

Ayala Lasso, José. "Making Human Rights a Reality in the Twenty-First Century." *Emory International Law Review* 10 (1996): 497–508.

Ayala Lasso, José. *Report of the UN High Commissioner for Human Rights, Mr. José Ayala Lasso, on His Mission to Rwanda 11–12 May 1994*. UN Doc. E/CN.4/S-3/3.

Ayala Lasso, José. *Report of José Ayala Lasso, High Commissioner for Human Rights, to the 1995 Session of the Commission on Human Rights*. UN Doc. E/CN.4/1995/98.

Ayala Lasso, José. *Report of the High Commissioner for Human Rights to the 1994 Session of the General Assembly*. UN Doc. A/49/36.

Ayala Lasso, José. *Report of José Ayala-Lasso, High Commissioner for Human Rights, to the 1996 Session of the Commission on Human Rights*. UN Doc. E/CN.4/1996/103.

Ayala Lasso, José. *Statement by the High Commissioner for Human Rights to a Joint Meeting of the Commission's Rapporteurs, Representatives, Experts, and Working Groups*. UN Doc. E/CN.4/1995/5/Add.1.

de Zayas, Alfred. *Die Nemesis von Potsdam*. 14th rev. ed. Munich: Herbig, 2005.

de Zayas, Alfred. "Human Rights, United Nations High Commissioner." In *A Concise Encyclopedia of the United Nations*, edited by Helmut Volger, pp. 216–223. The Hague and New York: Kluwer Law International, 2002.

de Zayas, Alfred. "The Right to One's Homeland, Ethnic Cleansing, and the International Criminal Tribunal for the Former Yugoslavia." *Criminal Law Forum* 6 (1995): 257–314.

de Zayas, Alfred. "United Nations High Commissioner for Human Rights." In *Encyclopedia of Public International Law*, edited by Rudolf Bernhardt, vol. 4. Amsterdam and New York: North-Holland, 2000.

Report of the President of the International Criminal Tribunal for the Former Yugoslavia to the Security Council. UN Doc. A/51/292, S/1996/665, 16 August 1996.

BAHÁ'Í FAITH

by Brian D. Lepard

The Bahá'í Faith is an independent world religion. Founded in 1844 in Persia (modern-day Iran), it had, in the first decade of the twenty-first century, more than 5 million followers who resided in virtually every country and came from a wide variety of racial, ethnic, and cultural groups. Members of the Bahá'í Faith (Bahá'ís) follow two prophets: Siyyid 'Ali-Muhammad, known as the Báb (the Gate), and Mirza Husayn-'Alí, known as Bahá'u'lláh (the Glory of God). Bahá'u'lláh proclaimed that he was the promised one of all religions. He taught as cardinal principles the oneness of the human family, the unity of the major world religions, and respect for the fundamental rights of all human beings.

Followers of the Báb and Bahá'u'lláh have suffered persecution since the earliest days of the religion. This persecution has been particularly systematic and intense in Iran, based on the view of many Muslims that Bahá'ís are apostates of Islam. New waves of persecution were unleashed in the last two decades of the twentieth century and the opening decade of the twenty-first century.

HISTORY OF THE BAHÁ'Í FAITH AND ITS TWO PROPHETS

The Báb was born in Shiraz, in southwest Persia, on 20 October 1819. During his lifetime many followers of the "Twelver" school of the Shia branch of Islam—the predominant branch in Persia—anticipated the return of the twelfth, or "hidden," Imam, a messianic figure. In 1844 Mulla Husayn-i-Bushru'i, a follower of the teachings of Siyyid Kazim-i-Rashti, a Twelver Shiite, went to Shiraz, where he believed the twelfth Imam would appear. There, he met the Báb, with whom he had a long conversation at the Báb's home on 22 May 1844. During that conversation the Báb declared to Mulla Husayn-i-Bushrú'i that he was the promised twelfth Imam, the Báb, the Gate of God.

The Báb appointed Mulla Husayn-i-Bushrú'i his first disciple and eventually appointed seventeen others, known as Letters of the Living. Followers of the Báb were referred to as Bábis. One of the Letters of the Living was a woman known as Tahirih (the Pure One). At a conference of Bábis in 1848, she removed her veil as a symbol of the equality of women with men, a new teaching of the Báb. This and other teachings of the Báb posed a challenge to the religious leaders in Persia at the time. The shah (a general term for the ruler of Persia) and other government officials set out to suppress the new religion through a relentless campaign of torture and intimidation. Between 1844 and 1852 several thousand Bábis were killed, including Tahirih.

The Báb was imprisoned for the remainder of his life. In the fortress of Mah-Kú, he wrote his most significant work, the *Persian Bayán*, in which he foretold the coming of a greater prophet. He urged his followers to turn to the new prophet when he appeared. Eventually, the government and religious authorities decided that the Báb himself had to be killed to eliminate the religion. He was executed on 9 July 1850.

Bahá'u'lláh was born in Tehran on 12 November 1817. His father was a high-ranking government minister. Bahá'u'lláh came to be known for his generosity to the less fortunate. He became a follower of the Báb, and his stature in the Bábi community quickly ascended. In 1852 two Bábis attempted to murder the shah of Persia. Their attempt failed. Although Bahá'u'lláh was not involved in the plot, the government imprisoned him in a foul prison in Tehran, a former underground sewer, known as the Siyah-Chal (Black Pit). Bahá'u'lláh spent four months in the dungeon, restrained in heavy chains. In this prison, around October 1852, Bahá'u'lláh had a vision in which he fully recognized that he was the prophet promised by the Báb.

To thwart Bahá'u'lláh's expanding influence, the government authorities exiled him and his family to Baghdad, Iraq, in early 1853. Bahá'u'lláh lived in Baghdad for ten years, from 1853 to 1863, during which time he revealed two of his best-known works—*The Hidden Words*, a series of meditations, and the *Kitab-i-Iqan* (Book of Certitude), which affirms the unity of all the prophets of God.

The Ottoman authorities decided to send Bahá'u'lláh farther away from Persia, to Constantinople (modern-day Istanbul). Before his departure, in April 1863, Bahá'u'lláh announced his prophetic station publicly in a garden on the outskirts of Baghdad known as the Garden of Ridván (Garden of Paradise). Following his announcement, the vast majority of Bábis turned to Bahá'u'lláh and recognized him as the prophet promised by the Báb. They became known as Bahá'ís, meaning "followers of Bahá."

Bahá'u'lláh and his family lived under house arrest in Constantinople for four months. They were then sent to Adrianople (now Edirne), where they spent five years. In a final effort to squelch Bahá'u'lláh's growing influence, in 1868 the Ottoman government decided to send him and his family to one of the worst prisons in the Ottoman Empire, 'Akka (Acre), a fortified prison-city in Palestine. For two years Bahá'u'lláh was confined to a bare prison cell. The Ottoman authorities tried to prejudice the local population against Bahá'u'lláh and the Bahá'ís. However, according to reports, the kindness of the Bahá'ís gradually won over the population. Bahá'u'lláh and his family were then allowed to live in various dwellings within 'Akka while still under house arrest. Bahá'u'lláh revealed the *Kitab-i-Aqdas*, his book of laws, in one of these houses. During his stay in 'Akka, he also wrote many letters to world leaders, including Queen Victoria of England, Czar Alexander II of Russia, and Napoleon III of France. He urged these leaders to reduce their armaments, to create a system of collective security for the maintenance of peace, to promote representative government, to abolish tyranny, and to uphold justice for their people.

Eventually, Bahá'u'lláh was allowed to take up residence in an abandoned house known as Bahjí outside the city walls of 'Akka. There, he spent the remaining years of his life. He continued to write copiously. He decreed that the remains of the Báb, which had been secretly safeguarded, should be buried on Mount Carmel, in Haifa, Israel, not far from 'Akka, in a tomb subsequently known as the Shrine of the Báb. Bahá'u'lláh also ordainedthat Mount Carmel should be the world center of his religion. Bahá'u'lláh died on 29 May 1892. His remains are buried in a small building at Bahjí, known as the Shrine of Bahá'u'lláh, which for Bahá'ís is a place of pilgrimage.

In his will, Bahá'u'lláh appointed his eldest son, 'Abdu'l-Bahá (Servant of the Glory), as his successor and as the authorized interpreter of his teachings. 'Abdu'l-Bahá traveled to the West, including to Europe and North America, to proclaim his father's message. The number of Bahá'ís grew rapidly. 'Abdu'l-Bahá was knighted by the British government in recognition of his humanitarian services to the population of the Holy Land during World War I. He died in 1921. In his will he appointed his eldest grandson, Shoghi Effendi, to the position of Guardian of the Bahá'í Faith.

In accordance with principles established by Bahá'u'lláh and 'Abdu'l-Bahá, the Bahá'í Faith is administered by elected assemblies or councils at the local, regional, national, and international levels. The international governing body of the Bahá'í Faith, the Universal House of Justice, has nine members and carries out its work on Mount Carmel. In July 2008 the United Nations Educational, Scientific, and Cultural Organization declared the Shrine of the Báb on Mount Carmel and the Shrine of Bahá'u'lláh at Bahjí as World Heritage sites.

BAHÁ'Í TEACHINGS ON HUMAN RIGHTS

The writings of the Báb, Bahá'u'lláh, and 'Abdu'l-Bahá (known as the Bahá'í writings) uphold principles of human rights. They prohibit religious hatred and fanaticism. They declare that all the prophets of God—including Abraham, Krishna, Moses, Zoroaster, Buddha, Jesus, Muhammad, the Báb, and Bahá'u'lláh—have taught the same eternal spiritual truths but have also brought particular social laws adapted to the needs of the age in which the prophet appeared.

Some of the social laws taught by Bahá'u'lláh, which Bahá'ís believe are appropriate for this epoch in humanity's development, are the unity and equality of people of all races, ethnicities, cultures, and religions; the elimination of all forms of prejudice; universal recognition and observance of human rights; the abolition of slavery; the full equality of women and men; the right of everyone to universal education, including women and girls; the right of everyone to investigate the truth for him- or herself; full freedom of religion and belief; the eradication of extremes of wealth and poverty; the harmony of science and religion; and the implementation of a global collective security system to prevent war and human rights atrocities. Bahá'u'lláh also enjoined Bahá'ís not to become involved in partisan politics, to show loyalty to their governments, and to eschew violence.

The worldwide Bahá'í community supported the adoption of the Universal Declaration of Human Rights in 1948 because it promoted many of these principles and because Bahá'u'lláh and 'Abdu'l-Bahá taught that a global standard of human rights should be recognized and adopted. Bahá'í communities and individual Bahá'ís around the world have been active in promoting human rights for all and in undertaking social and economic development projects. The Bahá'í International Community United Nations Office, which represents the worldwide Bahá'í community at the United Nations (UN), enjoys consultative status with the UN Economic and Social Council and collaborates with many human rights nongovernmental organizations (NGOs) on a wide variety of human rights issues. It also shares a Bahá'í perspective on these issues with UN bodies, governments, and NGOs and makes proposals for improving the UN human rights system and advancing international human rights law.

PERSECUTION OF BAHÁ'ÍS

Bahá'ís have been subject to various forms of persecution in Iran since the birth of the Bahá'í Faith in that land. In the first decade of the twenty-first century, there were some three hundred thousand Bahá'ís in Iran, constituting the country's largest religious minority. Many Muslims, owing to their understanding of the title of "Muhammad" as the "Seal of the Prophets," consider Bahá'ís apostates—Muslims who have renounced the true faith of Islam—even though the Bahá'í Faith is an independent world religion. Moreover, these Muslims believe that Bahá'ís have committed a particularly egregious religious transgression by accepting prophets after Muhammad, whom these Muslims regard as the final prophet. Some Muslim religious leaders have also resented Bahá'ís because Bahá'u'lláh abolished the institution of clergy, thus threatening their power, and taught the equality of women and men.

Thousands of Bábis, and later numerous Bahá'ís, perished in Iran in brutal pogroms during the nineteenth century. The persecution of Bahá'ís continued into the twentieth century. Bahá'ís were oppressed under the regime of Reza Shah Pahlavi, who founded the Pahlavi dynasty and assumed the title of shah in 1925. Beginning in the 1930s, a ban was imposed on the distribution of Bahá'í literature and the recognition of Bahá'í marriages, and all Bahá'í schools throughout Iran were closed. A wave of anti-Bahá'í violence followed in 1955, during the regime of Reza Shah Pahlavi's son and successor, Muhammad Reza Shah Pahlavi. Bahá'ís were targeted and harassed by the shah's secret police, SAVAK.

Persecution of Bahá'ís escalated dramatically after the installation in 1979 of the Islamic Republic of Iran, which replaced the Pahlavi dynasty. The new constitution recognized the rights of Christian, Jewish, and Zoroastrian minority religious communities only, deliberately excluding the Bahá'í community. This gave the government a legal basis for denying Bahá'ís all human rights. The government rounded up Bahá'ís, imprisoned them, tortured them in an effort to force them to recant their faith, and executed many when they refused to do so. More than two hundred Bahá'ís were killed between 1978 and 1998. In 1980 all nine members of the elected national governing body of the Bahá'ís of Iran were kidnapped and "disappeared". It is presumed that they were executed. A new governing council was elected, but eight of its members were abducted the following year and were executed. In 1983 ten Bahá'í women, the youngest aged seventeen, were hanged for the crime of teaching moral education classes for Bahá'í children. All had been tortured and given the opportunity to spare their lives by disavowing their faith, but all refused.

From 1979 to 2005 nearly one thousand Bahá'ís were arrested and imprisoned. Many have been tortured in order to persuade them to renounce their religion. Bahá'ís have been dismissed from their employment, and their financial assets, including their pensions, have been confiscated. Under a decree issued in 1981, the government refused to allow Bahá'í youth to enroll in colleges and universities and prohibited employment of Bahá'í professors. During the 1980s Bahá'í children were also refused admission to primary and secondary schools. In 1983 the government ordered all Bahá'í administrative institutions disbanded. After 1979 the government seized all properties and assets held by the Bahá'í community. Bahá'í cemeteries were desecrated. Some of the most revered Bahá'í holy places, including the house of the Báb, in Shiraz, were razed.

The Iranian government confirmed and formalized its calculated and systematic attempt to eradicate the Bahá'í community in a secret memorandum prepared in 1991. Titled "The Bahá'í Question," it was drafted by the Iranian Supreme Revolutionary Cultural Council and was signed by Iran's supreme leader, Ali Khamenei. This document affirmed that the "progress and development" of the Bahá'í community "shall be blocked." (Bahá'í International Community, *The Bahá'í Question*, p. 20). It was made public in 1993 by the UN special representative on Iran, Reynaldo Galindo Pohl, who had been appointed by the UN Commission on Human Rights.

Beginning in 1980, UN human rights organs adopted resolutions condemning the persecution of Bahá'ís in

Iran. These organs included the Commission on Human Rights and its subcommission. In 1985 the UN General Assembly adopted a resolution expressing its deep concern over allegations of violations of human rights in Iran, including the right of religious minorities such as the Bahá'ís to practice their own religions. Subsequently, the General Assembly adopted numerous resolutions on the human rights situation in Iran that call on Iran to cease its oppression of Bahá'ís.

From 1984 to 2002 the UN Commission on Human Rights appointed special representatives to report on human rights in Iran, including the situation of the Bahá'ís. These special representatives, including Pohl, investigated and documented the human rights violations committed by the Iranian government against Bahá'ís. UN special rapporteurs on freedom of religion or belief, including Asma Jahangir, also verified and publicized these violations.

The Council of Europe and the European Parliament, among other intergovernmental organizations, adopted resolutions on the oppression of Bahá'ís in Iran. Numerous national legislatures passed resolutions, and heads of state and other government officials made statements deploring Iran's treatment of the Bahá'í community. NGOs such as Amnesty International, Human Rights Watch, and the Minority Rights Group International prepared reports on the persecution of Bahá'ís. These reports confirmed that Bahá'ís are peaceful, law-abiding citizens of Iran who have been targeted solely because of their religion.

International attention to the atrocities committed against Bahá'ís appeared to have a deterrent effect on the Iranian government. In the mid-1980s the number of killings of Bahá'ís dropped dramatically. Bahá'í leaders believe that the international outcry against the persecution of Bahá'ís prevented far worse atrocities against the Bahá'í community in Iran. At the same time, the Iranian government persisted in less visible systematic efforts to strangle the Bahá'í community culturally and socially.

Acts of intimidation against the Bahá'í community began to escalate again in the early twenty-first century. In 2004 government authorities destroyed the home of Bahá'u'lláh's father. Between 2004 and 2008 the government ostensibly began admitting Bahá'ís to universities for the first time since 1981 but then ordered their expulsion. In 2007 more than two-thirds of Bahá'í university students were dismissed because of their religion. During the same period frequent attacks were launched against Bahá'ís in government-sponsored media. Bahá'ís

were placed under surveillance and were summarily arrested and imprisoned without charge. Their homes were searched by government officials, and many personal items, and sometimes the homes themselves, were confiscated. Bahá'í children in primary and secondary school were harassed by their teachers. In the spring of 2008, all seven national Bahá'í leaders were arrested in an attempt to intimidate the entire Iranian Bahá'í community. This action was ominously reminiscent of the abduction of the national leaders of the Bahá'í community in 1980 and 1981.

Bahá'ís have also suffered oppression in other countries. In Egypt the Bahá'í Faith was officially banned in 1960. The Bahá'í community has been under constant police surveillance, and Bahá'ís have been arrested. In the early twenty-first century the Bahá'ís of Egypt faced a new form of oppression. They were denied government-mandated identification cards and other essential documents. According to a new government policy, the only way for Bahá'ís to obtain these documents would be to lie and declare themselves Muslims, Christians, or Jews on their applications, which they refused to do and would in any event be illegal as a false statement. Because most civil rights in Egypt are ultimately dependent on possession of these documents, this policy had the effect of depriving Egyptian Bahá'ís of their basic rights. A December 2006 judgment of the highest administrative court in Egypt validated the government policy, but some lower courts ruled in favor of the Bahá'ís both before and after that judgment. In mid-2008 the legal rights of Egyptian Bahá'ís remained in jeopardy.

[See also Iran from 1979; Islam; Minority Rights: Overview; and Religious Freedom.]

BIBLIOGRAPHY

Bahá'í Faith. http://www.bahai.org. The official international Web site of the Bahá'í Faith, containing information about its history and beliefs and about the persecution of Bahá'ís.

Bahá'í International Community. The Bahá'í Question: Cultural Cleansing in Iran. New York: Bahá'í International Community, 2005. http://www.question.bahai.org. A comprehensive account of the persecution of the Bahá'ís in Iran, prepared by the Bahá'í International Community, which represents the Bahá'í community at the United Nations.

Bahá'í International Community. Closed Doors: Iran's Campaign to Deny Higher Education to Bahá'ís. New York: Bahá'í International Community, 2005. http://www.denial.bahai.org. A detailed report on Iran's denial of the right to a university education to Bahá'í youth.

Bigelow, Katherine R. "A Campaign to Deter Genocide: The Bahá'í Experience." *In Genocide Watch*, edited by Helen Fein, pp. 189–196. New Haven, Conn.: Yale University Press, 1992. A survey of international efforts to protest the persecution of the Bahá'ís in Iran, written by a high-level Bahá'í official involved in those efforts.

Cooper, Roger. *The Bahá'ís of Iran*. Rev. ed. Minority Rights Group report no. 51. London: Minority Rights Group, 1985. An independent report by the NGO Minority Rights Group on the persecution of Bahá'ís.

Ghanea, Nazila. *Human Rights, the UN, and the Bahá'ís in Iran*. Oxford; George Ronald: The Hague, the Netherlands; New York: Kluwer Law International, 2002. An exhaustive scholarly account of the persecution of Bahá'ís in Iran and the UN's response.

Hatcher, William S., and J. Douglas Martin. *The Bahá'í Faith: The Emerging Global Religion*. Wilmette, Ill.: Bahá'í Publishing, 2002 A general reference work on the Bahá'í Faith.

Human Rights Watch, Egyptian Initiative for Personal Rights. *Egypt: Prohibited Identities: State Interference with Religious Freedom*. New York: Human Rights Watch, Egyptian Initiative for Personal Rights, 2007. A thorough report prepared by independent human rights organizations on Egypt's identification card policy, including its discrimination against Bahá'ís.

Iran Human Rights Documentation Center. *A Faith Denied: The Persecution of the Bahá'ís of Iran*. New Haven, Conn.: Iran Human Rights Documentation Center, 2006. http://www.iranhrdc.org/httpdocs/English/pdfs/Reports/A-Faith-Denied_Dec06.pdf. An extensive and well-documented report on the persecution of Bahá'ís in Iran, prepared by an independent and nonpartisan NGO.

Kazemzadeh, Firuz. "The Bahá'ís in Iran: Twenty Years of Repression." *Social Research* 67 (Summer 2000): 537–558.

BALKAN WARS

by Božo Repe

Following the death of Josip Broz Tito in 1980, Yugoslavia, a Communist country with open borders and a specific system of so-called self-management socialism, or "Titoism," entered a period of crisis. Tito ruled with an iron fist and did not allow any nationalism other than Yugoslav nationalism. Individuals expressing unauthorized nationalist or chauvinistic nationalist ideas were dealt with by the police and in the courts. Tito took it upon himself to remove non-Yugoslav nationalist-oriented politicians and whole leaderships of republics if necessary (as with the Croatian leadership in the period of the so-called mass movement in the early 1970s). In 1968, when nationalist unrest broke out in the predominantly Albanian Kosovo, he used the army to intervene and suppress Albanian sentiment. Crimes committed by the Croatian nationalist Ustashas, the Serbian nationalist Chetniks, and others during World War II were discussed, but politicians were careful not to let those discussions escalate into new outbursts of hatred against ethnic or nationalist communities. On an individual level, however, memories and national hatred were passed down quietly from generation to generation.

THE END OF "BROTHERHOOD AND UNITY" AND THE RISE OF NATIONALISM

After Tito's death, censorship gradually decreased and there were voices demanding increased democracy and the abolition of Communism. In addition, literary, film, theater, television, and journalistic works were produced discussing topics that until then had been taboo, relating to the period during and after World War II. The Yugoslav League of Communists tried in vain to fight these phenomena with various administrative measures and by organizing ideological conferences. The media focused on the issues relating solely to their own republics. In addition, the leaders of some republics in the second half of the 1980s began appealing to nationalist sympathies, and all of this created a very explosive nationalist basis for war. Each ethnic group in Yugoslavia

felt ethnically threatened and exploited. Yugoslav nationalism, while generally weak, was strongest in Sarajevo and other communities in Bosnia and Herzegovina where there were many mixed marriages that crossed ethnic and religious lines.

The conflict between Serbs and Albanians and between Serbs and Croats from the period before and during World War II was revived. In Serbia, Slobodan Milošević was gaining power and established close ties with nationalist intellectuals. In the spring of 1985 these intellectuals, who were also members of the Serb Academy of Arts and Sciences, secretly started to write a memorandum that became public in September 1986. The memorandum claimed that the Serbs in Yugoslavia were in an inferior position, presenting them as victims of the Slovene-Croatian coalition. The key demand of the memorandum was the unification of all Serbs in one state in accordance with the old assertions that the borders of Greater Serbia lay along the Karlobag-Karlovac-Virovitica line.

Though human rights violations occurring in the 1980s in Yugoslavia had different backgrounds, the country mostly witnessed violations of national minority and universal democratic rights, with both types resulting from the nature of the Communist regime itself and from Yugoslav legislation. Violations of national minority rights were related either to violence against Serbs in Kosovo committed by Albanians out of hostility and the desire to recover lost territory (which led to mass emigration of Serbs from the region) or to violence against Albanians in Kosovo committed by the state. In 1981 the Yugoslav federal authorities declared a state of emergency in order to suppress mass Albanian demonstrations. In the late 1980s also the right to self-determination guaranteed by Yugoslav federal and republic constitutions became disputable.

With Yugoslav legislation allowing trial for the so-called verbal delict (criticism of the authorities, the system, individual politicians, or the Yugoslav army), several intellectuals found themselves in the dock in certain Yugoslav republics (Bosnia and Herzegovina, Serbia, Croatia). With conscientious objection also not recognized under Yugoslav law, men of various religious beliefs who did not want to be armed or serve in the army were sentenced to several years in prison. In addition, several forms of media control existed. In general, the extent of human rights violations largely depended on the state of affairs, the influence of the general public, and informal opposition in individual republics.

By the spring of 1989 Milošević mobilized mass rallies of his supporters, dispatching them from Kosovo and Serbia to other parts of Yugoslavia (referring to the planned activities of this mob as an "anti-bureaucratic revolution"), and deposed the leaderships of the autonomous province of Vojvodina and of the republic of Montenegro. Serbia gained supremacy over Kosovo by amending the Serbian constitution, revoking Kosovo's autonomy, and essentially negating the Yugoslav constitution's definition of Kosovo and Vojvodina as autonomous provinces. The Kosovo Albanians organized demonstrations against the changes; a group of miners from Trepča even went on a hunger strike in February 1989. The federal presidency reimposed a state of emergency, which led to judicial proceedings, uncontrolled homicides, and various forms of "isolation" (imprisonment in prisons or special camps, torture, and abuse). A few months later, on 28 June 1989, the six hundredth anniversary of the original Battle of Kosovo, Milošević threatened with war those who did not want to accept his idea of a centralized Yugoslavia.

Like the Serb leadership, the Yugoslav People's Army (YPA) considered itself a guardian of Communist Yugoslavia. Army leadership pointed to the last Yugoslav constitution, created in 1974, as the cause of Yugoslav disintegration because it granted the six Yugoslav republics the status of states (with the exception of foreign policy, defense, and a uniform market and currency). After 1987 military leaders prepared several scenarios for military coups against Slovenia based on the Kosovo model. On 25 March 1988 the Military Council, a consultative body of the Federal Secretariat for National Defense, accepted an assessment stating that a war and counterrevolution, with the support of the Slovene authorities, were raging in Slovenia. This assessment served as a basis for the army to prepare measures against Slovenia.

In the spring of 1990, when Slovenia held the first multiparty elections in Yugoslavia, the vote brought the right-wing coalition Democratic Opposition of Slovenia (DEMOS) to power. DEMOS advocated confederate status for Yugoslavia, but in reality it was working toward Slovenia's independence. After the DEMOS victory, tension between the army and Slovenia intensified considerably. On 7 March 1991 the Slovene Assembly passed a law freeing Slovenes from obligatory service in the YPA. Slovene authorities in individual municipalities hid the lists of conscripts so that the army would have no access to them. A few days later, on 12 March, half of the members of the presidency of SFRY rejected the demand for the introduction of a state of emergency in Yugoslavia. A secret mission on the part of the Yugoslav defense minister Veljko Kadijević for support from the Soviet defense minister Dmitry Jazov brought no results. In April the public learned about a secret army document outlining steps to intervene in Slovenia. In May several provocations occurred as a preparatory stage for military intervention. The green light for open intervention after the declaration of Slovene independence on 25 June 1991 was given by the last federal prime minister, Ante Marković, who had tried to reform Yugoslavia with help from the West but had lacked political support. On 26 June the federal government passed a decree to secure all borders on the territory of the Republic of Slovenia.

THE WAR IN SLOVENIA

The war in Slovenia, defined as a limited intervention, was started by the army on 27 June (26 June in the Primorska region). The army units left from both Croatian territory and individual army barracks in Slovenia. Initially, they had no difficulty securing Slovene border crossings and the airports. Then came the response from the Slovene Territorial Defense and the police. The army was still ethnically mixed. Soldiers of all Yugoslav ethnicities, including Slovenes, were confused and a great number of them deserted. Of twenty-five thousand soldiers in Slovenia, eight thousand deserted. Slovene authorities fed them, bought them tickets, and sent them home. Yugoslav officers who had lived in Slovenia with their families for decades found themselves in a dilemma. Many soldiers on the Slovene side were also facing a psychological crisis as they confronted their (until then) fellow countrymen, with no previous experience of having to kill the "enemy." On 28 and 29 June the European Community intervened diplomatically, and in Zagreb the so-called threesome including the Yugoslav government, Slovenia, and Croatia agreed on a cease-fire and a three-month moratorium on independence. The Yugoslav Army withdrew from Slovenia by October 1991. Before that some high-ranking army officers tried to retaliate against Slovenia with another attack by special units, but it was already too late for it to be effective. Milošević realized that Slovenia was lost, which meant the end of the concept of a centralized Yugoslavia under Serb control. The Yugoslav Army, which was fast being transformed into a Serb army (by the first half of 1992 Milošević forced 135 out of 200 generals in the Yugoslav Army into retirement), retreated to the planned borders of Greater Serbia, which included parts of Croatia and of Bosnia and Herzegovina.

Following an unsuccessful conference on Yugoslavia at the end of the year, the European Union, mostly under pressure from Germany, decided to grant recognition to the Yugoslav republics who requested it. Slovenia and Croatia thus gained international recognition at the beginning of 1991. On 6 April 1992, a day after war started, the European Union also recognized Bosnia and Herzegovina, and the three states were accepted into the United Nations in May 1992. Macedonia declared its independence in November 1991, gained international recognition a few months later, and became a member of the United Nations in April 1993. The rest of Yugoslavia consisted of Serbia and Montenegro and was known as the Federal Republic of Yugoslavia.

During the war of independence, Slovenia lost five members of the Territorial Defense forces and six members of the police. Eleven members of the Territorial Defense died of other causes. Two Slovenes were killed as members of the Yugoslav People's Army. There were six dead among the citizens of the Republic of Slovenia, ten foreign citizens, mostly truck drivers who found themselves trapped in roadblocks, and forty-three members of the YPA (eighty-three casualties altogether). A number of factors explain why the number of victims was relatively low, especially in comparison with the wars that followed: the short duration of the fighting, the limited nature of the armed conflicts (the desire to "discipline" Slovenia so that it would remain in Yugoslavia), the successful combination of Slovene military and diplomatic measures and rapid diplomatic intervention by the European Union (responding to the first armed conflict on European soil after World War II), and, above all, the fact that Slovenia was not part of the plans for Greater Serbia. Psychological factors played an important role as well since the Yugoslav Army leaders, believing that Slovenes were poor soldiers and would surrender in twenty-four hours, did not supply the army units with enough ammunition or even with enough food and water for more than a day.

The Yugoslav Army accused Slovenes of maltreating prisoners and published a propaganda report about it. An investigation confirmed that officers were placed in ordinary prisons and treated as prisoners at first, only being given the status of prisoners of war after a few hours. There were also allegations that three army soldiers who tried to surrender were shot and killed at Holmec, the border crossing with Austria, but a later investigation proved these allegations wrong. (Three soldiers were indeed killed during the fighting, but at different times, and they were not the same ones that tried to surrender, as claimed. All three of them—two of whom were Slovenes—were still living.) In general, there were no major violations of human rights during the time of the conflict in Slovenia, which can be attributed to the short duration of the war.

In the period after independence, many former officers of the YPA found themselves in a difficult position. They were subjected to checks by military and secret police units without proper legal cause, and some were denied entrance to Slovenia or asked to leave Slovenia even though they had families and permanent residence there. They were thus unable to deal with issues such as their retirement. The biggest problem from the human rights viewpoint was the so-called erased. The deadline for citizens of other former Yugoslav republics to apply for Slovene citizenship was 1991. Those who did not do so became legally foreign citizens, and state officials removed their names from the register of permanent residents. Their total number was 18,305; by 2008 it stood at 4,000. They lost the right to permanent residence, to work, and to social and health insurance, and the organs of the Interior Ministry began to destroy their documents. In 1999 the Constitutional Court determined that the erasing of permanent residents in 1992 was illegal. The problem remained unsolved, however, as the Slovene parliament, because of lack of consensus, did not pass an appropriate law, and right-wing parties even forced a referendum on the issue in 2004. The referendum drew only 31 percent of voters, who with a 94 percent majority voted against the law that would settle the rights of the erased.

THE WAR IN CROATIA

The first multiparty elections in Croatia in April and May of 1990 brought to power the Croatian Democratic Union (Hrvatska Demokratska Zajednica [HDZ]), under the leadership of Franjo Tudjman, a general under Tito, who had been imprisoned twice because of Croatian nationalist statements. The new regime was justifiably accused of nostalgia for the Ustashas' Independent State of Croatia, a Fascist state that cooperated with the Nazis during World War II. The government tried to change the ratio of power between political and ethnic groups in the republic, 15 percent (580,000) of whom were Serbs. Serbs held many important positions in the Yugoslav Army and administration because of their role during the national resistance movement in World War II—they founded the resistance movement in Croatia—and because of their loyalty to the League of Communists. Their fear that the pre–World War II situation would return, when the Ustashas authorities tried to implement measures to exile one-third of the Serbs from Croatia, kill the second third, and forcibly convert the remaining third from Orthodox to Catholicism, triggered a Serb rebellion. The rebellion was largely instigated from Belgrade, which also provided arms and fighters. The Serbs were primarily against the intention of the new nationalist Croatian government to secede from Yugoslavia. Tudjman tried to stifle their protests through a series of police actions that should have given him control over Serb territory but instead escalated into a war that lasted from 1991 to 1995 (it is difficult to determine the exact date it began because of the many minor incidents that took place). After the Croatian declaration of independence on 25 June 1991, the YPA openly intervened. It had done so even before that date, following orders from the federal presidency, presumably to prevent conflicts and to protect the civilian population, but its "neutrality" was only a camouflage; in reality the army was firmly on the Serb side, which it also helped to arm.

On 25 July 1990 approximately 100,000 Croatian Serbs had gathered in the center of Lapac municipality (Lika) and adopted a declaration on the sovereignty and autonomy of the Serb ethnic group within the borders of Croatia. Two days later the assembly of the Knin municipality declared the establishment of the Joint Municipality of Northern Dalmatia and Lika. By August most other municipalities with a majority Serb population joined the new formation. On the occasion of the celebration of Vidov Dan on 2 July 1990, they published a draft declaration of a Serb autonomous province and the name of the would-be president: Dr. Milan Babić (first leader was Jovan Rasković, but he died). On 25 July all thirteen Serb municipalities rejected the initiatives for amending the Croatian constitution. They adopted the declaration of the sovereignty and autonomy of the Serb nation, giving the Serbs in Croatia the right to secede. They also rendered void all legal documents that either diminished their autonomous rights or denied their right to self-determination.

On August 8 the first armed Croatian unit was established, formally as a police unit, with eighteen hundred members. Other police units followed, as well as the formation of the National Guard Corps (Zbor Narodne Garde), out of which grew the Croatian army. Serbs began to build roadblocks around Knin. In the press this resistance was referred to as the "log" (balvan) revolution, after the logs used to block the roads. Because of the distribution of Serb settlements, Croatia was practically split into two parts. In the fall of 1990 the rebellious Serbs attacked the police stations in Glina, Petrinja, Kostanjica, and Dvor na Uni; they laid mines to stop the water supply in and around Zadar and also mined some railroad lines, some of which actually exploded. On 21 December 1990, the day before the announcement of the new Croatian Constitution, the Joint Municipality of Northern Dalmatia and Lika became the Serb Autonomous Region (SAO) Krajina, with headquarters in Knin. On 28 February 1991 the SAO Krajina seceded from Croatia. The YPA directly intervened at the beginning of March 1991. Police officers of Serb ethnicity disarmed their colleagues in the town of Pakrac on 1 March, and the next day a special unit of Croatian police again took over the police station. The YPA artillery units arrived in town to protect the Serb population. This was followed by a mass rally in Belgrade, where protesters demanded a showdown with Croats. Milan Martić, a local police chief and one of the Croatian Serb leaders, founded his own militia and on 29 March 1991 occupied the Plitvice Lakes (in 2007 Martić was sentenced by the Hague Tribunal to thirty-five years of imprisonment for ethnic cleansing and other war crimes). On 31 March 1991 a new armed skirmish between Croatian police and the SAO Krajina militia broke out in Plitvice, killing two police officers, one Serb and one Croat.

Paramilitary groups began to arrive en masse in Croatian territory (the first ones were spotted building roadblocks in August 1990 near Benkovac), especially in Slavonia. Various "guards" (the Chetniks and others), such as the Beli Orli (White Eagles) and Tigri (Tigers), under the command of Željko Ražnjatović, were organized by Serbian parties, who recruited their members from the lower rungs of the social ladder, especially criminals. After Milošević's victory in the election of December 1990, these groups received illegal or semi-legal aid in arms and equipment from the Serb state. One group, known as Crvene Baretke (Red Berets) and later renamed the Special Operations Unit, was a direct product of Serb state authorities in the Interior Ministry. Serbs from Croatia joined the Krajina militia and the territorial defense organized by the Krajina authorities. After Serb Chetniks killed twelve Croatian police officers in Borovo Selo, Slavonia, on 2 May 1991, the YPA arrived with tank units that gradually positioned themselves all over Slavonia. Because of the Pakrac police station incident, the Yugoslav presidency ordered the YPA to deploy its forces in all Croatian territories with a Serb majority to prevent ethnic conflicts; the army used that as an excuse to provoke conflicts with Croatian armed forces. At the same time, paramilitary units repeatedly invaded Croatian territory, burning property, killing, raping, and implementing the plan of ethnic cleansing on territories that were to be included in Greater Serbia. At first they did that on their own, but when the war escalated, they accompanied or followed YPA units and carried out their activities after military operations were over.

Even though the Croatian Assembly declared Croatian sovereignty on the same day as Slovenia, Croatia was far less prepared for independence than the ethnically homogenous Slovenia. Slovenia and Croatia were allies brought together by the circumstances, and in January 1991 their ministers signed an agreement on joint defense that could, in the short term, help Slovenia should the YPA attack it but could at the same time drag it into a much worse war between the Serbs and Croats. The agreement was thus couched in very diplomatic language. At the time of YPA aggression toward Slovenia, Croatia heeded Tudjman's direct order and did not react. It did nothing to prevent the army's march from Croatia to Slovenia, even though some top army officials were in favor of stopping it. Tudjman counted on finding a common language with Milošević and the YPA and reaching an agreement with them. Later, he labeled the Slovene war as the "operetta" war and accused Slovenia of making a deal with Serbia in order to be allowed to leave Yugoslavia at Croatia's expense. In view of his policies and his government's attitude toward the Serbs, Tudjman's idea that Croatia could avoid war proved to be totally unfounded.

The war for Croatian independence (referred to as the war for the homeland by the Croats) was much longer and much bloodier than the Slovene one, and the fighting raged throughout ethnically mixed territories (Slavonia, Banija, Kordun, Lika, Dalmatia), as well as in those territories where the majority population was Croatian but the Serbs still considered as their own. Only the central and northwestern parts of Croatia were spared. There life

went on as usual, even in luxury—a frequent reproach from other parts of the country that suffered in the war. It is true, however, that Zagreb also came under rocket attack once. Initially the YPA was winning, but again massive defections undercut its successes. Croatia badly lacked arms and made a number of strategic mistakes, mostly because of Tudjman's unpredictability and his attempts to make a deal with Milošević (including the partition of Bosnia and Herzegovina). Despite its nationalist policy, its treatment of Croatian Serbs, and its open appetite for Bosnian territories, Croatia won the sympathy of the international community, largely owing to the Serb siege and occupation of Vukovar and the siege of Dubrovnik.

Vukovar, the port town on the Danube in eastern Slavonia along the border with Serbia, fell after three months of heavy fighting, on 18 November 1991. In August 1991, after Serbian paramilitary units had ethnically cleansed the surrounding areas, the YPA had attacked Vukovar, which was defended by eight hundred members of the Croatian National Guard Corps and approximately one thousand volunteers. The town was surrounded, which made it very difficult to gain access and provide assistance. The Croatian military and political leadership, especially Tudjman, were accused of having surrendered Vukovar to the Serbs. The invaders perpetrated a massacre. Approximately 260 civilians, captured Croatian soldiers, and some medical personnel were taken to nearby Ovčara Mountain (where there was also a concentration camp), and as many as two hundred were killed. Some of those responsible for the massacre were brought to trial by the International Criminal Tribunal for the Former Yugoslavia in The Hague in 2007. Mile Mrkšić was sentenced to twenty years of imprisonment, Veselin Šljivančan to five years (but was released because he had already served his sentence for a different crime), and Miroslav Radić was acquitted. The sentences triggered sharp protests in Croatia. An indictment was also brought against Vojislav Šešelj, the president of the Serb Radical Party and a Chetnik leader, who was accused of sending his troops to Vukovar and to other battlefields.

Dubrovnik, a world-famous historical city, came under attack by units from Herzegovina and Montenegro. The city's location close to both the Bosnian-Herzegovinian and Montenegrin borders made it vulnerable. The surrounding areas were occupied by the YPA in October 1991 and consequently looted by both the YPA and the various paramilitary units (the so-called weekend fighters) from Montenegro and Serbia. Even the highest officials of the YPA are known to have looted yachts, works of art, cars, and the like. The besieged city was exposed to shelling for several months before January 1992, when a cease-fire agreement calmed down the situation somewhat. Owing to the war in Bosnia, however, the city's fate remained uncertain for a long time there after.

Members of the Croatian National Guard Corps had begun to build defenses and minefields around Dubrovnik in the summer of 1991. A number of skirmishes broke out, and in Montenegro volunteers were recruited for the military. In line with Montenegrin military tradition, the mobilization initially met with a massive response. In September 1991 most YPA units left Montenegro and moved to eastern Herzegovina (in the republic of Bosnia and Herzegovina), while some participated in the attacks on Dubrovnik. The Montenegrin leadership (Milo Djukanović, Momir Bulatović) managed to avoid taking responsibility for aggression against Dubrovnik, but Bulatović especially, as a fervent Milošević supporter, lived in fear of receiving a subpoena from the Hague Tribunal for many years.

Since the outbreak of larger armed conflicts in Croatia in June 1991, there had been a special European Community Monitoring Mission (ECMM) on the ground. It was unable to stop the fighting, but on 2 January 1992 the international community pressured the YPA and the Croatian army into signing a cease-fire in Sarajevo. This was a prerequisite for the implementation of the UN peace operation in accordance with the so-called Vance Plan (after Cyrus Vance, the special envoy of the secretary-general of the United Nations), which was accepted by the Croatian government, the Yugoslav (Serb) government, the YPA, and the representatives of the Croatian Serbs (who were the most reluctant to do so). Four UN Protected Areas (UNPA) were created in those parts of Croatia where the majority of the population was Serbian (the exception was eastern Slavonia, where part of the territory was under Croatian control). The YPA withdrew from Croatia but used that as an excuse for strengthening Serb forces in Bosnia. Military units within the protected areas were supposed to be disarmed, an order enforced by the UN Protection Force (UNPROFOR). The status of UN Protected Areas was to remain the same until an adequate all-Yugoslav solution was found. The UNPROFOR units were deployed in the spring of 1992, at a time when the war in Bosnia and Herzegovina was already underway.

The arrival of UNPROFOR brought a halt to major fighting but not the shelling of cities and the destruction of transport infrastructure. Southern Dalmatia in particular was cut off. The ethnic cleansing of the Croatian population in Serb territories continued, while their property and historical and religious monuments were destroyed. UNPROFOR tried to prevent this, but in most cases it was helpless. The Croatian side continued with individual military operations and gradually liberated parts of its territory. In 1992 it liberated southern Dalmatia around Dubrovnik, while the controversial Prevlaka peninsula on the border between Croatia and Montenegro came under the control of the UN monitors. In January 1993 the area around Zadar was liberated and the key road across the Maslenica Bridge was no longer subjected to constant shelling.

Between 9 and 17 September 1993 the Croatian forces expelled the Serbs from the villages near Gospić. Two years earlier in October 1991, the area had been the scene of war crimes committed by both sides. The Croatian Army had killed between fifty and one hundred civilians, mostly Serbs, a few days after the Serbs had killed approximately forty civilians, mostly Croats, but also five Serbs who did not want to join the Serb paramilitary units and participate in the killings. Croatian military personnel in the 1993 operation were also involved in war crimes against the Serb population. Three individuals were accused of war crimes by the Hague Tribunal: General Rahim Ademi, Mirko Norac, and General Janko Bobetko, the commander of Croatian army headquarters. Bobetko died in his home in Zagreb in 2003 before being handed over to The Hague. Ademi and Norac were transferred back to a Croatian court, and in 2007 Norac received a seven-year sentence, while Ademi was acquitted.

On 1 May 1995 the Croatian army launched Operation Bljesak (Flash) and freed Slavonia. Between 4 and 7 August 1995 the army liberated Knin in Operation Oluja (Storm), with the help of American private consultants and the army of Bosnia and Herzegovina. Approximately 150,000 soldiers participated on the Croatian side. The operation resulted in the mass exodus of Serbs (approximately 200,000), the burning of villages (over 20,000 houses were razed, even according to Croatian data), looting, and killings (according to Croatian sources, a few hundred cases; according to Serbs, 2,500). Because of the negative international reaction to such activities, the Croatian army stopped short of liberating the Serb-occupied territory in Baranja and eastern Slavonia. Instead, these territories were quietly reintegrated into Croatia after the Dayton Peace Accords, between 1996 and 1998, with the help of the UN Transitional Administration in Eastern Slavonia (UNTAES).

The so-called homeland war claimed 13,233 lives on the Croatian side; 1,149 were declared missing and 33,043 wounded. As of 2008, there were no confirmed data on the number of Serb casualties.

War produced brutal ethnic cleansing and numerous war crimes on both sides. Several hundred thousand people were forced to flee their homes. The flow of Croatian refugees reached its peak at the end of 1991, the Serbian one after final operations in 1995. Croatia found it hard to face up to the traumas of war. Both handing war criminals over to the Hague Tribunal and putting them on trial at home have been traumatic and would probably have been even more so if Franjo Tudjman had been tried in The Hague. Such a (likely) scenario was precluded by his death.

THE WAR IN BOSNIA AND HERZEGOVINA

The war in Croatia was a prelude to the anticipated but far crueler war in Bosnia and Herzegovina. That republic was the most ethnically mixed in the former Yugoslavia. According to the 1991 census data, 44 percent of the population was Muslim, 31 percent Serb, 17 percent Croat, and 8 percent other. They were dispersed like stripes on a tiger, and no clear delimitation lines between individual ethnicities could be drawn.

The burden of history was hard to bear. During the Nazi occupation and the civil war between the Communist Partisans, the Serbian nationalist Chetniks, and the Croatian nationalist Ustashas in World War II, 164,000 Serbs, 75,000 Muslims, and 64,000 Croats were killed. The Ustashas also killed around 14,000 Jews. Ethnicity did not decide allegiance: Serbs were both Partisans and Chetniks, Muslims and Croats both Ustashas and Partisans. As in other parts of Yugoslavia, memories of that history were still very much alive in Bosnia and Herzegovina and only intensified with the discovery of mass graves after 1990. The first multiparty elections took place in December 1990 and, in accordance with the ethnic structure of the population, three ethnic parties won: the Democratic Action Party, led by the Muslim Alija Izetbegović; the Serb Democratic Party, led by Radovan Karadžić; and the Croatian Democratic Union (HDZ) of Bosnia and Herzegovina (a sister party to the Croatian HDZ), led by Stjepan Kljuić. (Karadžić was arrested and turned over to the Hague Tribunal in July 2008; Izetbegović was probably saved from the tribunal by death; Kljuić, a fervent advocate of independent and multiethnic society, barely escaped death by poisoning at the hands of the HDZ

because of his views. He later established a new party.) The three parties received 71 percent of votes altogether and formed a parliamentary coalition. The presidency was held by Alija Izetbegović. After Slovene and Croatian independence in 1991, Bosnia and Herzegovina accepted the proposal of the European Community (based on the decision of the so-called Badinter Commission) that the Yugoslav republics should decide whether or not they wished to become independent and try to meet the requirements for international recognition. The parties were split in this respect: Serbs wanted to remain within Yugoslavia (or become part of the Greater Serbia), Croats in Herzegovina wanted to join Croatia or, in the interim phase, establish their own state, and Muslims were in favor of independence because they believed that their numbers and demographic trends would guarantee them a dominant position. After the European Community tried unsuccessfully to use ethnicity criteria to divide the state into separate cantons, a referendum was held on 29 February 1992, in which Muslims and Croats voted for an independent state (67 percent of the population voted, and 98 percent were for independence), while Serbs boycotted the referendum for the most part. On 3 March 1992 an independent state was declared, with strong support from the United States, who had hoped that in this way a war in Bosnia could be avoided.

Ethnic tensions mounted soon after the elections. Serbs began to form autonomous governments on the model of Croatian Serbs. They enjoyed the support of Belgrade and had enough equipment and weapons brought by the YPA from Slovenia, western Croatia, and Macedonia to last for a few years of fighting. In August the Serb Democratic Party began to boycott the meetings of the presidency, and on 24 October it recalled its delegates from the Bosnian assembly and established the Serb National Assembly, with headquarters in Banja Luka. In November 1991 the Bosnian Serbs held their own referendum and voted to remain within a common state together with Serbia and Montenegro. In January 1992 they declared the Republic of the Serb People of Bosnia and Herzegovina. On 28 February 1992 they adopted a constitution that declared the Serb Republic of Bosnia and Herzegovina (a slightly changed name) to be a part of the Yugoslav federal state. The government of Bosnia and Herzegovina declared all these actions to be unconstitutional and invalid. In response the Bosnian Serbs declared independence on 7 March, and in August they dropped the name of Bosnia and Herzegovina, becoming simply the Republic of Srpska. Following the Serb example, on

18 November 1992 the Croats declared the Croatian Community of Herceg-Bosna, which had its seat in the Croatian section of Mostar and was headed by Mate Boban (who died in 1997, while most of his colleagues were tried in The Hague). This community declared itself the Croatian Republic of Herzeg-Bosna on 28 August 1993 and lasted until March 1994. It had its own military units, the Croatian Council of Defense (Hrvaško Vijeće Obrane [HVO]), which were formed on 8 April 1992 in Grude and were helped and supplied mostly by Croatia. Some Bosniaks (Bosnian Muslims) also joined them in the beginning. The HVO fought against the Serbs and, between April 1993 and March 1994, also against Bosniaks. Both Serb and Croatian entities engaged in ethnic cleansing, destroying each other's cultural and religious monuments.

The policy of Serbs and Croats in Bosnia stemmed from the agreement reached between Tudjman and Milošević on 25 March 1991. The meeting was called after a series of many unsuccessful meetings of the presidents of the Yugoslav republics. Tudjman and Milošević made a deal about splitting Bosnia and Herzegovina among themselves, accompanied by the removal of Ante Marković from the position of Yugoslav prime minister. It was not clear, however, how the division should be implemented (Milošević demanded 66 percent of the territory), so it was left up to the situation on the ground—to war and the ratio of forces. In May 1992 Boban and Radovan Karadžić, in the same spirit, agreed to cooperate in joint military operations against the Bosniaks.

On 7 April 1992, the day the United States recognized Bosnia and Herzegovina, Serb paramilitary units began intensive artillery shelling of Sarajevo from the surrounding hills. The YPA marched on Zvornik, Foča, Višegrad, and other towns. At the beginning of military operations, on 12 May 1992, the YPA units became the Army of the Republic of Srpska. It had eighty thousand soldiers, its commander became Ratko Mladić, and it continued to be funded by Yugoslavia (Serbia). The Serb plan was relatively simple: to occupy the Drina valley and the Posavje region, establish a unified territory with the Republic of Srpska Krajina in Croatia, occupy as much of the Herzegovinian territory as possible, and encircle Sarajevo, thus breaking Muslim resistance. As the territories were ethnically mixed, this implied massive ethnic cleansing, killing civilians, placing men in concentration camps, and raping women. The ethnic cleansing plan was implemented in its entirety. In six weeks Serbs gained control of two-thirds of the Bosnian territory. At the peak of their power in 1994, the percentage of Serb-controlled territory increased to 70 percent. Croats and Bosniaks offered weak resistance, and in Bosnia "a war of everybody against everybody else" broke out. Thus there were conflicts between Bosniaks in 1993, and in 1994 between the Army of Bosnia and Herzegovina and Izetbegović's political opponent Fikret Abdić in the Cazin region. Bosniaks and Croats were also fighting each other because the latter had become the allies of the Serbs and jointly attacked the Bosniaks.

The UN weapons embargo for the former Yugoslav republics inflicted damage primarily on Bosniaks and Croats. The divided views of different countries (France and Great Britain were more in favor of Serbia, while Germany and the United States continued to support the Croats and Muslims), coupled with the ineffectiveness of the European Union, only added to Bosnian agony. Such circumstances resulted in smuggling, crime, and secret weapons purchases. The United Nations limited its activities to humanitarian aid and refused to get involved in the war. Only later did the United States agree to create the so-called safe areas. Among the many unsuccessful diplomatic initiatives to end the war and solve the crisis was the so-called Vance-Owen Plan at the January 1993 peace conference, which proposed dividing Bosnia into ten autonomous provinces, with Sarajevo as a demilitarized zone. The prerequisite for that, however, was a cease-fire. Each ethnic group was supposed to have a majority in three of the ten provinces, while Sarajevo was to remain ethically mixed. The plan was rejected by Serbs and largely criticized by the international community.

In March 1994, under pressure from the United States, the Croats and Bosniaks signed the Washington Agreement establishing an alliance and a federation. The Bosniak and Croatian Army was trained by American "consultants," and the United States quietly ignored the supply of arms from Muslim countries. The first consequences of the changed American policy in Croatia could be seen in the operations Flash and Storm.

THE GENOCIDE IN SREBRENICA; THE CONSEQUENCES OF THE BALKAN WARS (1992–1995)

The Srebrenica genocide in July 1995, the largest massacre in Europe after World War II, has to be seen within the context of American policy. The genocide, in which eight thousand Bosniaks were first stripped naked, robbed of personal belongings, and then shot dead, was carried out by the Republic of Srpska Army led by Ratko Mladić and by paramilitary units from Serbia (known as the Scorpions). The armed forces invaded the so-called protected area under the control of four hundred poorly equipped and restrictively mandated Dutch soldiers, who had a peacekeeping (not an enforcement) mandate and thus did nothing to prevent the deportation of Bosniaks, even though they knew the fate that awaited them (later the families concerned filed suit against the Dutch government).

Many women and children were also killed during the massacre, so that the final number of casualties rose to 8,373. The International Criminal Tribunal for the Former Yugoslavia labeled it as genocide. When, only a month later, the Serbs shelled Sarajevo from the surrounding hills (Sarajevo was under constant Serb fire for over a thousand days) and committed a new massacre, the international community finally ran out of patience and stopped pretending not to see what was happening. The American diplomat Richard Holbrooke undertook an effective international initiative, which also entailed many compromises and negative side effects (among other things, it seems, the commitment not to bring to the Hague Tribunal Radovan Karadžić and Ratko Mladić, the main culprits for the military and ethnic cleansing and genocide in Bosnia and Herzegovina). Holbrooke in his book *To End a War* said his job was to negotiate peace, not pursue criminal justice, although the latter was generally mentioned in the Dayton Peace Accords.

A broad international coalition was formed against the Serbs, who found themselves isolated. NATO planes began to bomb their positions on the ground, and Croatian and Muslim units launched a broad offensive and reclaimed a large amount of territory. After a month of fighting, even Milošević was forced to renounce his support to Bosnian Serbs because of unfavorable external circumstances.

On 1 November 1995 negotiations between all parties involved began at the Wright-Patterson Air Force Base near Dayton, Ohio, and ended on 21 November. Bosnia and Herzegovina remained an independent state, made up of the Bosnian-Croatian Federation (51 percent of the territory) and of the Republic of Srpska (49 percent). The United Nations and NATO were to guarantee its existence. On 14 December an agreement to this effect was signed in Paris, and approximately sixty thousand members of international forces were deployed to Bosnia and Herzegovina. The war claimed over 200,000 dead, according to some sources, over 2.2 million refugees (almost half of the population), approximately 50,000 tortured, and 20,000 women raped. There were 715 concentration camps in the country. In response to the crimes committed by all three sides (but more by far by the Serbs), the UN Security Council set up the International Criminal Tribunal for the Former Yugoslavia (ICTY).

After the Balkan Wars of 1912–1913 and World War I and II, the Yugoslav wars, which also included Kosovo and limited conflicts in Macedonia between Macedonians and Albanians, were the fourth conflict in the Balkans in the twentieth century. They left behind several hundred thousand dead, millions of refugees, and dozens of ruined cities and villages. They were a combination of cultural, religious, and ethnic conflicts deeply rooted in history. Ethnic states that were formed on the territory of the former Yugoslavia more or less successfully "cleansed" their territories. Their positions differ from each other: some have managed to stabilize and become members of the European Union (Slovenia), some are approaching that goal (Croatia), while the situation in the others remains uncertain. This is true particularly of the initiator of the wars, Serbia. (In February 2007 the International Court of Justice, in a much criticized judgment, declared that Serbia was not directly responsible for the genocide in Bosnia, while holding that Serbia should have done more to prevent what did occur. But historically it is a fact that it was Serb nationalism that tore Yugoslavia apart and triggered the wars.) The cost and the consequences of the wars will continue to be paid for generations to come. In their wake the region as a whole continues to be a "powder keg," just as it was labeled at the beginning of the twentieth century.

[*See also* Ethnic Cleansing; Humanitarian Intervention: Policy Making; International Criminal Tribunal for the Former Yugoslavia (ICTY); Internationally Administered Territories; Slobodan Milošević; *and* Tito.]

BIBLIOGRAPHY

Bianchini, Stefano, and Marco Dogo, eds. *The Balkans: National Identities in a Historical Perspective*. Ravenna, Italy: Longo Editore, 1998.

Bennet, Christopher. *Yugoslavia's Bloody Collapse: Causes, Course, and Consequences*. London: Hurst, 1995.

Bethlehem, Daniel, and Marc Weller, eds. *The Yugoslav Crisis in International Law: General Issues*. Cambridge, U.K., and New York: Cambridge University Press, 1997.

Bildt, Carl. *Peace Journey: The Struggle for Peace in Bosnia*. London: Weidenfeld & Nicholson, 1998.

Calic, Marie-Janine. *Krieg und Frieden in Bosnien-Herzegovina.* Frankfurt, Germany: Suhrkamp, 1996.

Castellan, Georges. *Le monde des Balkans: Poudrière ou zone de paix?* Paris: Vuibert, 1994.

Daalder, Ivo H. *Getting to Dayton: The Making of America's Bosnia Policy.* Washington, D.C.: Brookings Institution Press, 2000.

Glenny, Misha. *The Fall of Yugoslavia: The Third Balkan War.* 3d ed. New York: Penguin, 1996.

Gow, James. *Triumph of the Lack of Will: International Diplomacy and the Yugoslav War.* New York: Columbia University Press, 1997.

Guskova, Jelena. *Istorija Jugoslavskogo krizisa.* Moscow: Izdatel' A. Solov'ev, 2001.

Hartmann, Florence. *Paix et châtiment.* Paris: Flammarion, 2007.

Holbrooke, Richard C. *To End a War.* Rev. ed. New York: Modern Library, 1999.

Owen, David. *Balkan Odyssey.* New York: Harcourt Brace, 1995.

Pirjevec, Jože. *Le guerre Jugoslave, 1991–1999.* Ljubljana, Slovenia: Cankarjeva založba, 2003.

Ramet, Sabrina P. *Balkan Babel.* Boulder, Colo.: Westview, 2002.

Ramet, Sabrina P., and Ljubiša Adamovich, eds. *Beyond Yugoslavia: Politics, Economics, and Culture in a Shattered Community.* Boulder, Colo.: Westview, 1995.

Repe, Božo. *Jutri je nov dan: Slovenci in razpad Jugoslavije.* Ljubljana, Slovenia: Modrijan, 2002.

Rizman, Rudolf Martin. *Uncertain Path: Democratic Transition and Consolidation in Slovenia.* College Station: Texas A&M University Press, 2006.

Šarinić, Hrvoje. *Svi moji tajni prezgovori sa Slobodanom Miloševićem: Izmedju rata i diplomacije 1993–1995 (1998).* Zagreb, Croatia: Globus International, 1999.

Silber, Laura, and Allan Little. *Yugoslavia: Death of a Nation.* Rev. ed. New York: Penguin, 1997.

Unfinished Peace: Report of the International Commission on the Balkans. Washington, D.C.: Carnegie Endowment for International Peace, 1996.

Woodward, Susan. L. *Balkan Tragedy: Chaos and Dissolution after the Cold War.* Washington, D.C.: Brookings Institution Press, 1995.

Žabkar, Anton. *Analyses of the Conflict in Former Yugoslavia.* Vienna: National Defence Academy, 1994.

Zimmermann, Warren. *Origins of a Catastrophe: Yugoslavia and Its Destroyers.* New York: Random House, 1999.

SIMONE DE BEAUVOIR

by Sonia Kruks

Simone de Beauvoir (b. 9 January 1908; d. 14 April 1986) is best known as the author of *The Second Sex*, a book often described as the bible of the late-twentieth-century feminist movement. She was also a major figure within French existentialism after World War II and was the author of important essays on ethics and politics that engage with questions about freedom and responsibility in human existence. Her ideas have strong affinities with those of her lifelong companion Jean-Paul Sartre but are not the same as his. Her thinking was also shaped by the work of others in the European tradition of existential philosophy, including Søren Kierkegaard, Martin Heidegger, and Maurice Merleau-Ponty, and by the German phenomenologist Edmund Husserl. As an existentialist, Beauvoir argues that the capacity for freedom, in the sense of being free to choose how one acts in the world, is the most significant quality of a human life. Freedom is, in this sense, ontological; that is, it is intrinsic to our being human. However, without an effective field for action in the world we cannot adequately exercise our ontological freedom; thus freedom is also a practical social and political matter.

The Second Sex (*Le deuxième sexe*) was published in 1949 and was translated into English in 1952. Millions of copies were later sold in the Anglophone world as the women's liberation movement, or Second Wave feminism, developed during and after the 1970s. The ideal of universal human rights was very much in the air when Beauvoir published her book, as the United Nations had promulgated the Universal Declaration of Human Rights shortly before, in December 1948. Beauvoir notes in her introduction that the United Nations had declared that inequality between the sexes was now at an end (*The Second Sex*, p. xxxiii). However, although the rights of women is a topic that Beauvoir treats in *The Second Sex*, it is not her central concern. She insists that guaranteeing rights to women does not necessarily ensure their capacity to exercise their freedom effectively. Rights are often too abstract, and the concrete practices that shape women's daily lives may be more significant in supporting, or negating, their effective freedom. Furthermore, as she argues more fully in some of her other works, too much faith in rights as the fundamental means for augmenting human freedom may actually be dangerous—it may function as a pretext for avoiding careful examination of the specifics of situations of oppression. Thus Beauvoir's work greatly complicates the assumptions of First Wave European feminism, in the late nineteenth and early twentieth centuries, that the granting of equal rights to women would automatically result in their equality.

WOMEN'S RIGHTS IN *THE SECOND SEX*

The Second Sex is divided into two volumes. The first, "Facts and Myths," describes the ways women have been constructed as men's subordinates both historically and in the contemporary world. The second volume, "Lived Experience," describes "from within," through the use of memoirs and other more subjective sources, how women experience their lives as members of a subordinate or oppressed group. It also describes the ways they may still make their lives meaningful or resist their oppression. Although freedom in its ontological sense is possible even within highly constrained situations, Beauvoir argues that we have an obligation to struggle for greater effective or practical freedom for others. Equality of all kinds—social, economic, political—is necessary for the fullest exercise of an individual's ontological freedom. Thus struggle for the extension of rights may be one important element within a wider struggle to enhance the effective freedom of all.

Beauvoir's discussions of rights for women range from a historical treatment of the rights of women in ancient Greece and Rome to the significance of the vote for women in modern democracies—a right granted in France only in 1945. She also addresses, long before the term was actually coined, the issue of "reproductive rights" for women: the right freely to choose—or refuse—maternity through access to birth control and abortion.

Throughout the book Beauvoir acknowledges that the presence or absence of rights is important to women while also insisting that they are not necessarily the most fundamental element of women's freedom. In comparing ancient Greece and Rome, for example, Beauvoir notes that, although the rights of women were extremely limited in both states, the situation of many women in Rome was one of greater freedom than in Greece. Paradoxically this was so even though they were legally "more enslaved" than in Greece. For, she observes, "abstract rights are not enough to define the actual concrete situation of woman; this depends in large part on her economic role; and frequently abstract liberty and concrete powers vary in inverse ratio" (Beauvoir, *The Second Sex*, p. 93).

This insight, that women's formal rights and their "concrete powers," or effective freedom, do not necessarily advance in a smooth parallel, informs Beauvoir's analysis of women's situation in the West up to the present. Examining the situation in France since the French Revolution, she argues that women's entry into wage work—followed by the gradual development of legislation that reduced their exploitation at work—was of equal, or perhaps greater, importance than political rights in women's progress toward greater freedom. While in her own era—and arguably still in the early twenty-first century—she notes that, although Western women have won most of the same formal rights as men, they still do not have the same degree of effective freedom. Contrary to the optimistic expectations of First Wave feminists, who campaigned for women to have equal rights to enter into contracts and own property, to receive education and enter the professions, to sue for divorce, and to have full political participation, including the vote, the actual attainment of such rights has not in practice produced equality between the sexes.

Beauvoir identifies several aspects of women's situation that interact and contribute to the perpetuation of their lack of effective freedom: their unequal participation in economic life, which makes them dependent on men for their livelihood and so coerces them into marriage; their lack of control over their fertility, which forces motherhood upon them; and the general cultural attitudes and moral values that make man "the Absolute" and woman his "Other" (*The Second Sex*, p. xxii). These last—attitudes and values—are perhaps the most difficult to address. For she notes that even in the Soviet Union, where women did enter the paid workforce in vast numbers and legalized abortion gave them a degree of control over their fertility (at least prior to the Stalinist period), they still remained

the "second sex" and did not attain equal effective freedom with men. None of this is to dismiss rights as irrelevant to improving women's situation. However, Beauvoir warns against a politics that fixates on women's formal rights as a panacea and does not acknowledge the many other changes necessary for their liberation. She is also aware that differences among women, such as social class, or religion, or age (in the early twenty-first century ethnicity or race often would be added), will differentially shape the impact that rights may have upon various groups.

Beauvoir also distinguishes herself from the earlier generation of feminists by her explicit concern with what have since come to be called "reproductive rights." In the chapter of *The Second Sex* entitled "The Mother," she forges a radically new analysis of women's subordination as she develops a critique of what she calls "enforced maternity" (p. 485). It is only when women can voluntarily choose maternity that it may begin to become a site for free and meaningful action, she argues, and until then it is a source of oppression. But such a free choice is precluded not only by cultural norms and pressures but also by legal prohibitions on women's control of their own fertility. Thus it is at the level of the physical body itself, and in what has previously been deemed an exclusively "private" sphere, that new rights must be demanded: the rights to avoid or to plan pregnancies through contraception (broadly illegal in France until 1967) and legal and safe abortion. Until these are granted women will be forced to have children they do not want, or whom they cannot afford to care for, or else to undergo the dire physical, emotional, and social risks associated with illegal abortion.

However, even as she makes this argument, Beauvoir is aware that the absence or presence of reproductive rights will not affect all women in a similar way and that their presence will not benefit all equally. Wealthier women are already able to obtain "therapeutic" abortions and have better knowledge of (still illicit) contraceptive techniques. Thus the lack of reproductive rights bears more heavily on some women than on others. She notes that abortion is correctly referred to as a "class crime" because it is predominantly poor women who must resort to it. Many of the women who have abortions already have children but cannot afford to have more, so ironically "the repulsive aborted woman is also the splendid mother cradling two blond angels in her arms: one and the same person" (Beauvoir, *The Second Sex*, p. 487). Thus while the achievement of reproductive rights will be important for all women, their liberating effect will be greater for some than for others. Moreover, the benefit of such formal rights will also be enhanced or limited by other aspects of a woman's situation, such as cultural and religious attitudes to maternity, or by her level of economic dependence on a man. Reproductive rights (along with the rights to property ownership, the right to vote, and so forth) will constitute only one significant aspect, among many others, in the totality of a woman's situation.

THE AMBIGUITY OF RIGHTS

Beauvoir's limited optimism about the role that formal rights may play in extending women's freedom is consistent with her broader distrust of indubitable faith in any set of political ideals. For when ideals, such as a belief in the sanctity of human rights, are enthroned as incontestable articles of faith, they become no more than mindless dogmas; they become a dangerous substitute for making our own judgments. In *The Ethics of Ambiguity*, written shortly before *The Second Sex*, as well as in numerous other works Beauvoir argues that our ontological freedom requires that we must always choose for ourselves the values we affirm and that we must take responsibility for our actions and the consequences—including the negative consequences—that may flow from them. To refuse to acknowledge our responsibility for consequences, to claim that because we followed a lofty ideal or principle, we should not be blamed for any harmful consequences that may ensue, is to attempt to evade our freedom in what Beauvoir calls "bad faith" or "seriousness."

Our ontological freedom is what makes us human, but it is also acutely painful. This freedom is a source of intense anxiety because it means that we must act without a preordained purpose in life and without fixed moral rules. Instead, we must acknowledge the ambiguity of all values and all actions. To attempt to rid oneself of one's freedom by claiming that one's will is subordinate to predetermined ends is in "bad faith." One must not, for example, mask one's freedom "under the shield of rights" (*The Ethics of Ambiguity*, p. 48). The person in "bad faith" is not only self-deluded but is also dangerous to others. For example, by claiming that the state or the church should decide what is "right," and thus dishonestly claiming to be constrained in one's decisions by "objectively existing" duties and values, such a person may unleash carnage on others while claiming to have a clear conscience and "clean hands." Thus the Fascist justifies mass extermination in the name of the "race" or "nation" with a clear

conscience. Or, to give an early twenty-first-century example, those who murder workers at abortion clinics easily justify their actions in the name of the "rights of the unborn child." Thus also, in the name of "rights" or "democracy," are military invasions and occupations often justified.

However, this is not to say that actions that may result in injustice to others, suffering, oppression, or even death for others, may never be justified. Beauvoir is not a pacifist. Rather, her claim is that we can never justify our actions a priori in the name of our ideals. For the world of politics is ambiguous: it is not a domain of clear-cut outcomes and uncomplicated moral relationships. Rather, it is a world of unpredictability and of conflicting goods, a world in which even responsible actions may have dire effects on others. Thus, as Beauvoir puts it in the title of another essay, we need responsibly to navigate between "Moral Idealism and Political Realism" (1945). It may, for example, be necessary to violate the rights of some individuals in the course of the struggle to obtain rights for others—as she noted in her support for the violent actions sometimes carried out by the independence movement in French-ruled Algeria. Or rights may be, in some situations, less important in enabling effective freedom than other goods. There are no definitive rules to follow here. Instead, we must evaluate each concrete situation in its particularities in order to arrive at the best judgment possible, even though we also know that our judgment is fallible. In *The Ethics of Ambiguity*, Beauvoir affirms that political judgment is "at the same time a wager and a decision" (p. 148). To say it is a "wager" is not, however, to say that we must proceed wholly blindly, for we certainly should be guided by an ethical commitment to enlarging the field of effective freedom of others. However, we must be aware that this commitment provides no assurances as to what the best path to follow is in practice—and sometimes no path is the best. Thus Beauvoir profoundly complicates claims that the pursuit of universal human rights is an unerring source of good in politics.

In this Beauvoir anticipates criticisms of rights-driven politics made by some early-twenty-first-century feminist and postcolonial theorists. Some argue that notions of human rights developed within a Western, liberal framework may be deleterious when introduced (and especially when forcefully introduced) into non-Western contexts. For, they point out, practices that are deemed oppressive from a rights perspective may also be important to the well-being of a community and highly meaningful to its members, including women. However, Beauvoir does not go as far as some of these critics do in defending all culturally specific practices against criticisms made in the name of women's human rights. For example, she asserts in a late interview that the refusal of some Western feminists to criticize practices of clitoridectomy in Africa because they are not themselves African expresses a lack of care about young girls in Africa that is itself "a kind of racism" (Wenzel, pp. 15–16). She also points out that some African women usefully assert the claims of universal women's rights in resisting the practice. On this particular issue, then, human rights are far from irrelevant. However, Beauvoir's more general position is that, although human rights are important in specific instances, they are far from being a panacea whose enactment will bring about freedom for all.

[*See also* Female Genital Mutilation and Female Genital Cutting; Universal Declaration of Human Rights; *and* Women: Women's Rights.]

BIBLIOGRAPHY

Beauvoir, Simone de. *The Ethics of Ambiguity*. Translated by Bernard Frechtman. New York: Citadel, 1967. English translation of *Pour une morale de l'ambiguïté*, first published in 1947. Beauvoir's most extended philosophical work on ethics and politics.

Beauvoir, Simone de. "Moral Idealism and Political Realism." In *Philosophical Writings, Simone de Beauvoir*, edited by Margaret A. Simons with Marybeth Timmermann and Mary Beth Mader, pp. 175–193. Urbana: University of Illinois Press, 2004. English translation of "Idéalisme moral et réalisme politique," first published in 1945. An accessible short introduction to Beauvoir's ideas on ethics and politics.

Beauvoir, Simone de. *The Second Sex*. Translated by H. M. Parshley, preface by Deirdre Bair. New York: Vintage Books, 1989. English translation of *Le deuxième sexe*, first published in 1949. Beauvoir's pathbreaking treatise on women.

Wenzel, Hélène. "Interview with Simone de Beauvoir." *Yale French Studies* 72 (1986): 5–32. Interview conducted in 1984; translated by Wenzel.

BELGIAN CONGO

by Adam Hochschild

The territory that eventually became known as the Belgian Congo—although it has borne other names before and since—largely consists of the great swath of central Africa drained by the Congo River. The river is the world's second biggest; only the Amazon carries more water. It descends over more than two hundred miles (more than 320 kilometers) of intermittent, enormous rapids shortly before pouring into the Atlantic Ocean, and, until late in the nineteenth century, these rapids blocked the efforts of European explorers to get their boats onto the upper reaches of the river and the tributaries they presumed must flow into it.

The rapids did not, however, prevent exploitation of the region's people by outsiders. Portuguese mariners first landed near the great river's mouth in 1482, missionaries, soldiers and adventurers soon followed, and by several decades later thousands of Africans were being shipped every year as slaves from this area to the New World. The land that surrounded the river's mouth and extended some distance inland and to the south, the kingdom of Kongo, was controlled by a ruler known as the Manikongo. In 1506 a Manikongo named Nzinga Mbemba assumed the throne. He learned Portuguese and took on the name of Affonso. During the nearly forty years of his rule, he saw his kingdom decimated by the slave trade. An eloquent set of letters from Affonso to successive kings of Portugal are the first known documents written by a black African in a European language. "Each day," Affonso wrote in desperation to King João III of Portugal in 1526, "the traders are kidnapping our people—children of this country, sons of our nobles and vassals, even people of our own family. . . . Our land is entirely depopulated."

Affonso's pleas were in vain. For several centuries the Atlantic slave trade continued to victimize both the people of this kingdom and Africans living for hundreds of miles into the interior. All told, several million Africans were taken from the region around the river's mouth and its hinterland, chiefly to work on the plantations of Brazil.

Similarly, over an even longer period of time, Arab and Afro-Arab slave traders had been ravaging the east coast of Africa, buying slaves as far inland as the eastern side of the Congo River basin, and shipping them to the Arab and Islamic world. Slave ship captains and traders could buy slaves so easily on both coasts because most people in Africa south of the Sahara Desert lived in slave societies. The ethnic groups of the Congo River basin were no exception; Affonso himself, for example, owned slaves. In some ways, indigenous African slavery was less brutal than slavery in the Americas: slaves were more status objects than a source of labor; they could often intermarry with free people and frequently earned their freedom after several generations. But in other ways, African slavery was harsh: slaves were sometimes killed in human sacrifice rituals—many might be slain when an important chief died, for example, to give his soul company on its journey to the next world. When a treaty was made between two rival tribes or groups, a male slave might have his bones broken and be left to die painfully in a remote spot, as a symbol of what might happen to anyone who broke the treaty. People could become slaves in Africa as a punishment for a crime, as payment for a family debt, or, most commonly, by being captured as prisoners of war. The widespread heritage of indigenous slavery would eventually mean that when the Congo became notorious as the site of a forced labor system run by King Leopold II of Belgium and his successors, there were local chiefs willing to collaborate in supplying these laborers.

Soon after the Atlantic slave trade finally came to an end in the middle of the nineteenth century, the major part of Europe's conquest and colonization of Africa began. The Scramble for Africa, as it is often called, was one of the greatest land grabs in history—and one of the swiftest. In 1870 roughly four-fifths of sub-Saharan Africa was governed by local chiefs, kings, or other indigenous rulers. A mere forty years later, in 1910, nearly all this vast expanse of territory had become colonies or protectorates controlled by European countries or, as in South Africa (where Europeans had arrived much earlier), by white settlers. The bloodiest single phase of Africa's colonization was centered on the territory known, from the river that flowed through it, as the Congo.

Besides the river's huge rapids, heat and tropical diseases had long kept the Congo's interior a mystery to Europeans. The big step forward for them—although arguably a step backward for Africans—came between 1874 and 1877, when the British explorer-journalist Henry Morton Stanley (1841–1904) made an epic journey across Africa from east to west. Stanley's travels made him a great celebrity. He was also a brutal taskmaster, quick to flog his porters or to lay waste to any African villages that threatened to impede his progress, and, at all times, to shoot first and ask questions later. These traits were visible in the best-selling books he wrote about his journeys, but biographers and historians did not begin to focus on them until some three-quarters of a century after his death, in a world that had left outright colonialism behind.

Despite the dead bodies left in his wake, Stanley's crossing of Africa was a rare and difficult feat for a European at the time. He also became the first white man to map most of the course of the Congo River. For much of his journey he floated down it, noting with great awe that its many tributaries potentially constituted, in the age of steamboats, a built-in transportation network of thousands of miles for whoever could take control of the region.

KING LEOPOLD II

Stanley hoped that the Congo's colonial master would be Great Britain, but the British were coping with various rebellions and crises elsewhere in their empire and had little interest in adding to it the Congo, with its troublesome rapids, heat, malaria, and sleeping sickness. Someone who did lust after this territory, however, was King Leopold II of Belgium. Leopold (1835–1909) had taken his country's throne in 1865. An imposing, bearded, august man of great charm, ruthlessness, and greed, he was openly frustrated at heading such a small country, and, moreover, at doing so at a time in history when western European monarchs were rapidly losing power to elected parliaments. He had long wanted a colony where he could rule supreme, and in Stanley he saw someone who could help secure it for him. The Belgian government at the time did not want colonies, which seemed an extravagance for a small nation with no navy

and no merchant fleet. To Leopold, the Belgian cabinet's lack of desire for colonies posed no problem; if they were not interested, he would acquire one of his own.

Leopold courted and flattered Stanley, and before long he persuaded the explorer to return to the Congo as the king's agent. Although Stanley is conventionally remembered as the man who had years earlier found the missing explorer David Livingstone, by far his greatest impact on history derived from the five years he spent staking out the Congo for Leopold. From 1879 to 1884 he set up riverbank outposts, built a road around the rapids, and, using small steamboats that exhausted African porters had carried up the road in pieces, traveled up and down the river network. Alternately passing out gifts and displaying the power of his men's repeating rifles, Stanley forced or bamboozled hundreds of African chiefs into signing away their land to King Leopold II. Virtually all were illiterate and had little or no idea of what they were agreeing to.

Stanley returned to Europe with these treaties in 1884. Meanwhile, Leopold had already begun an ultimately successful campaign to persuade first the United States, and then the nations of Europe, to recognize his claim. With a great mastery of public relations, he presented himself as a philanthropist earnestly striving to abolish the Arab slave trade that still flourished in east Africa. Making a profit, he implied, was the farthest thing from his mind. Leopold made further progress toward his goal at a diplomatic conference in Berlin in 1884 and 1885, at which the European powers began the process of dividing the spoils in Africa. By the spring of 1885 most major nations had recognized his claim to the Congo. He then proclaimed its existence as the greatly misnamed État Indépendant du Congo, or, as it was known in English, the Congo Free State. He took the title of king-sovereign, sometimes in future years referring to himself as the Congo's "proprietor." His was the world's only major colony owned by one man.

Over the following two decades, Leopold asserted his control of the vast territory. Its inhabitants were armed only with spears or antiquated muskets left over from slave-trading days, while the king put together a 19,000-man private army. With black soldiers under European officers, the army was equipped with repeating rifles, machine guns, Krupp cannons, and steamboats for fast transport on the river network. Army posts sprang up along the riverbanks.

The royal conquest met frequent resistance. In the far south, for example, a chief named Mulume Niama led warriors of the Sanga people in a rebellion that killed one of the king's officers. Congo state troops pursued them, trapping Mulume Niama and his soldiers in a large cave. They refused to surrender, and when Leopold's troops finally entered the cave three months later, they found 178 bodies. Nzansu, a chief in the region near the great Congo River rapids, led rebels who killed a hated colonial official and pillaged several state posts, although they carefully spared the homes of nearby Swedish missionaries with whom they had good relations. Nzansu's men fought on sporadically for five years more, and no record of his fate exists.

The regime also faced resistance from within its own army, whose resentful African conscripts sometimes joined forces with the rebel groups they were supposed to be suppressing. The largest mutiny involved three thousand troops and an equal number of auxiliaries and porters, and continued for three years. "The rebels displayed a courage worthy of a better cause," acknowledged the army's official history—which, remarkably, devoted fully one-quarter of its pages to the various campaigns against mutineers from the army's own ranks.

In the early years, what Leopold and the agents he sent to Africa sought most avariciously was ivory. Because it was durable and could be carved into a variety of shapes, ivory served some of the uses of plastic today, but with the added cachet of its exotic origin. It was used to make jewelry, piano keys, small statuary, and even, in a faint echo of its original use to the elephant, false teeth. Like illegal drugs in a later era, ivory had high value and low bulk: thousands of false teeth could be made from a single tusk.

As a young steamboat officer, the writer Joseph Conrad spent six months working in the Congo in 1890, and he gives a searing description of the search for ivory in his great novel based on that experience, *Heart of Darkness*. "The word 'ivory' rang in the air, was whispered, was sighed," says Conrad's hero and alter-ego, Marlow. "You would think they were praying to it." Marlow gives a crisp summary of the colonial economy: "a stream of rubbishy cottons, beads, and brass-wire set into the depths of darkness and in return came a precious trickle of ivory." The most memorable figure in the book is its villain, Mr. Kurtz, the brutal ivory-crazed state agent far in the interior, with a collection of severed African heads set on fence posts outside his house. The fictional Kurtz is an amalgam of several men of this era (including the similarly ruthless Henry Morton Stanley), but in giving Kurtz the habit of collecting severed African heads, Conrad was

not inventing anything. At least four white men who worked in the Congo during this period boasted openly of collecting the heads of African rebels they killed; two of them Conrad is likely to have met, and two more were people he almost certainly heard about.

From the very beginning of Leopold's colony, the foundation of its economy, as in most of colonial Africa, was forced labor. The black soldiers of the king's private army were conscripts, often sent to posts hundreds of miles away from their villages so that they could not easily desert and go home. The porters who transported the ivory tusks out of the interior and carried back everything from ammunition to bottles of wine for the European ivory agents were forced laborers. So were the workers who built a railway around the impassable river rapids. *Heart of Darkness* gives a vivid picture, closely based on what Conrad observed, of some of the latter being worked to death. "I could see every rib, the joints of their limbs were like knots in a rope, each had an iron collar on his neck and all were connected together with a chain whose bights swung between them, rhythmically clinking." The woodcutters who traveled with each steamboat to gather fuel for its boilers—up to several dozen men for a larger boat—were forced laborers. Convoys of sullen men in chains, force-marched from remote villages to wherever colonial officials needed them, were part of business as usual in central Africa. "The conquest of the earth," Marlow says in *Heart of Darkness*, "which mostly means the taking it away from those who have a different complexion or slightly flatter noses than ourselves, is not a pretty thing when you look into it too much."

In Europe and North America few did much looking. Most people continued to think of Leopold as the philanthropic king who was fighting evil Arab slave traders. Very little information on the true nature of the Congo Free State, especially the way it was founded on forced labor, reached the outside world. The first person to fully expose the regime was a remarkable American visitor, George Washington Williams. Williams, like Conrad, spent some six months in the Congo in 1890, and in early August of that year, their steamboats probably crossed paths in Stanley Pool, a bulge in the Congo River at what was then the small post of Leopoldville.

Williams was an American Civil War veteran, a historian and journalist, a Baptist minister, a lawyer, and the first black member of the Ohio state legislature. As a journalist, he had interviewed King Leopold II in Brussels and, like almost everyone, was charmed by the apparently modest and altruistic monarch. But when, on a trip around Africa, Williams reached the Congo, he was appalled to find what he called "the Siberia of the African Continent." He took extensive notes and was virtually the only early visitor to interview Africans about their white colonizers. From Stanley Falls, a thousand miles up the river, Williams wrote one of the great documents of human rights reporting, "An Open Letter to His Serene Majesty Leopold II, King of the Belgians and Sovereign of the Independent State of Congo." It was the first comprehensive eyewitness indictment of the regime and its forced labor system. Published in many American and European newspapers, it caused Leopold considerable embarrassment. The uproar would doubtless have been prolonged had Williams lived to write the book on the Congo he was planning, but, sadly, he died of tuberculosis on his way home from Africa, at the age of forty-one. This first brave critic of the Congo regime also fired off several other letters from Africa, and in one of them, to the American secretary of state, he used a phrase not commonly heard again until the Nuremberg Trials more than half a century later. Leopold, Williams declared, was guilty of "crimes against humanity."

THE RUBBER ERA

Ivory remained valuable, but in the early 1890s a much larger source of Congo wealth suddenly loomed. A few years before, the industrialized world had seen the invention of the inflatable bicycle tire, followed by that of the automobile. In addition, the network of telephone and telegraph wires starting to span the globe needed rubber insulation, and thousands of types of industrial machinery required rubber belts or other rubberized parts. An international rubber boom thus began. In tropical territory everywhere, planters rushed to set up rubber plantations. But new rubber trees can require as much as fifteen years to reach the point at which they may be tapped. This created a time window during which vast amounts of money could be made by whoever owned the land where rubber grew wild. No one possessed more such land than King Leopold II, for the equatorial African rain forest, rich in wild rubber vines, covered roughly half of his Congo state.

These spongy vines were hundreds of feet long; one might twine upward around a palm or other tree to a hundred feet or more above the ground, where it could get some sunlight, then wind and branch its way through the limbs of half a dozen more trees. The vines were scattered quite widely and sparsely through the forest. Even with a forced labor system in place, how could villagers be compelled to disperse for miles to gather the sap that these vines produced? Leopold's officials quickly devised a harshly effective system. The army would send a detachment of soldiers into a village and seize the women as hostages. To secure their wives' release, the men of each village would then have to go into the forest to begin the painstaking job of tapping the wild rubber vines and collecting the slow, milky drip of sap. They were given a monthly quota to fulfill, and, as rubber prices soared in Europe, the quotas rose as well. All the rubber vines near each village were soon drained dry, which meant that men had to sometimes walk for days to reach fresh vines. Eventually, men could be gone as long as several weeks out of each month, in the urgent scramble to reach their quota and get their wives briefly released.

Discipline was pitiless: villagers who failed to gather enough rubber, like reluctant military conscripts or disobedient porters before them, fell victim to the notorious *chicotte,* a whip made of sun-dried hippopotamus hide with razor-sharp edges. A hundred lashes of the *chicotte*— a common punishment—could be fatal. Colonial officials earned bonuses that were based on how much rubber was collected in the area each controlled, a system that rewarded ruthless, devastating plunder.

The forced labor system for gathering rubber was at the core of a tremendous death toll in the Congo during and immediately after Leopold's rule. Many of the male forced laborers were, in effect, worked to death. Large numbers of women hostages—frequently raped by the regime's soldiers during their captivity—starved. And, with the women chained up in compounds and much of the male population off the in the forest desperately trying to meet their monthly rubber quota, the birthrate plummeted. Few able-bodied adults were left in the villages to harvest food, hunt, or fish. Famine spread. Local uprisings against the regime erupted more frequently. They continued to do so over some two decades and occasionally recurred later as well; tens of thousands more people died as the army suppressed them. A large but unknown number of additional men, women, and children fled the forced labor regime, but they had nowhere to go except to more remote parts of the rain forest, where there was little food or shelter. Years later, travelers would come upon their bones.

The greatest toll of all came as soldiers, caravans of porters, and refugees from the rubber terror, all moved back and forth across the country, bringing new diseases to people with no resistance to them. Many illnesses, particularly sleeping sickness, became far more lethal for people weakened by trauma and hunger. As the experience of those in Nazi and Soviet concentration camps would show decades later, in a regime of terror, firing squads or crematoria are not always required to cause the death of millions.

THE PROTEST MOVEMENT

Unlike many other human rights catastrophes in history, what happened in Leopold's Congo was seen by outside witnesses—some of them with cameras. These were the missionaries.

Belgium was heavily Catholic, and Catholic missionaries in the Congo basically acted like agents of the regime, running schools, for example, that trained boys to become soldiers. But to curry diplomatic favor, Leopold had allowed several hundred Protestant missionaries into the territory: British, American, and Swedish. Most made no protest, but some were outraged at the forced labor system. In articles in church magazines and in speeches in the United States and Europe on visits home, they described what they had seen: Africans whipped to death, rivers full of corpses, and—a detail that quickly seared itself into the world's imagination—piles of severed hands. For the white officers of Leopold's army often demanded of their black conscripts a dead rebel's hand in return for each bullet issued to the soldier, as proof that it had been used as ordered and not wasted in hunting, or worse yet, saved for use in a mutiny. If a soldier had fired at someone and missed, he sometimes would cut off the hand of a living person, so as not to have to brave his officer's wrath. Missionaries photographed a number of people without hands, some of them children. One American missionary saw a soldier slice off someone's hand "while the poor heart beat strongly enough to shoot the blood from the cut arteries."

E. V. Sjöblom of Sweden was one of the first and most outspoken Congo missionaries. Alice Harris, a British Baptist, took photographs of the atrocities she witnessed. William Morrison, a white man, and William Sheppard, the first black missionary in the Congo, were Virginia Presbyterians whose writing and speaking so infuriated Congo colonial authorities that they finally put the men on trial for libel.

Around 1900 Leopold's most formidable enemy surfaced in Europe, and suddenly the concerned missionaries had someone who could carry their stories to a far wider audience. A British shipping company had the monopoly on all cargo traffic between the Congo and Belgium, and every few weeks it sent to the Belgian port of Antwerp a burly, mustachioed junior official, Edmund Dene Morel. There he would supervise the unloading of a ship arriving from Africa and its loading for the voyage back. Morel, in his mid-twenties at the time, noticed that when his company's ships steamed in from the Congo, they were filled to the hatch covers with enormously valuable cargoes of rubber and ivory. But when the ships turned around and headed to Africa, they carried no merchandise in exchange. Nothing was being sent to the Congo to pay for the goods flowing to Europe. Instead, the ships carried soldiers and large quantities of firearms and ammunition. Standing on the dock at Antwerp, Morel realized that before his shocked eyes lay irrefutable proof that a forced labor system was in operation some four thousand miles (6500 kilometers) away. "I was giddy and appalled at the cumulative significance of my discoveries," he wrote later. "It must be bad enough to stumble upon a murder. I had stumbled upon a secret society of murderers with a King for a croniman" (Morel, 1968, pp. 41–42). This young shipping clerk's stunning moment of realization gave rise to the first great international human rights movement of the twentieth century.

Morel went to the head of the steamship company to protest. The man tried to promote him to another job in another country. When that did not work, his boss tried to pay Morel some money to stay quiet. That did not work either. Morel soon quit his job and in short order turned himself into the greatest British investigative journalist of his time. He was filled, he wrote, with "determination to do my best to expose and destroy what I then knew to be a legalized infamy . . . accompanied by unimaginable barbarities and responsible for a vast destruction of human life" (Morel, 1968, p. 5). *For* a dozen years, from 1901 to 1913, working sometimes fourteen to sixteen hours a day, he devoted his formidable energy and eloquence to putting the story of forced labor in King Leopold's Congo on the world's front pages. In Britain, where returned missionaries had already begun to find large audiences for their slide shows of Congo atrocities, Morel founded the Congo Reform Association. Affiliated groups quickly sprang up in the United States and other countries.

Morel wrote three books on the Congo, several dozen pamphlets, and hundreds of newspaper articles, making much use of eyewitness testimony from the missionaries. He traveled throughout Britain speaking to large audiences and was adept at recruiting bishops, peers, and other luminaries to join him on the lecture platform. More than one thousand mass meetings to protest forced labor in the Congo were held, mostly in Britain and the United States, but also in continental Europe and as far away as Australia and New Zealand. The devout sang hymns about suffering in the Congo, and Morel enlisted prominent authors in his cause: Mark Twain wrote a satirical pamphlet on the subject, *King Leopold's Soliloquy: A Defense of His Congo Rule* (1905), and Sir Arthur Conan Doyle—who shared many speaking platforms with Morel—a book, *The Crime of the Congo* (1909). In a decade, the campaign inspired more than four thousand newspaper articles about the Congo atrocities.

After Morel orchestrated a protest resolution by the House of Commons in 1903, the British government, in response, asked its representative in the Congo to investigate his charges. The British consul, a black-bearded Irishman named Roger Casement, who later in life was to die on the gallows as an Irish patriot, took the assignment seriously. Renting a missionary steamboat, he spent more than three months traveling in the interior. He produced an excoriating, detailed report, complete with sworn testimony, which was in many ways a model for the reports that began to be produced more than fifty years later by Amnesty International and other human rights organizations. In the first decade of the twentieth century, the efforts of Morel, Casement, key missionaries, and their supporters succeeded in making the forced labor system of King Leopold's Congo the most widely publicized human rights scandal of its time. The king was condemned in the press, poets thundered against him, and cartoonists throughout Europe portrayed him surrounded by human skulls and severed hands.

Leopold himself never went to the Congo. Something of a hypochondriac, he always worried about germs. And perhaps he had good reason to do so, for Europeans had not yet found ways of combating all the major tropical diseases. Leopold knew—and kept secret—statistics showing that before 1900 about one-third of all white men who went to the Congo ended up succumbing to disease and dying there. The king chose to stay in Europe, where he spent his Congo profits on grand buildings and public monuments in Belgium, a huge array of clothes for his teenage mistress, and an expanding array of properties on the French Riviera.

As a result of the international agitation over the atrocities, Leopold was finally pressured into relinquishing his private ownership of the Congo, reluctantly transferring it to the Belgian state in 1908—while making

Belgium pay him for so doing. He died the following year, having made a profit from the territory conservatively estimated as equal to more than $1.1 billion in the American dollars of a century later.

Although the human rights violations in Leopold's Congo were egregious and the avaricious king an easy villain to target, in a sense, the protest movement's focus on that territory alone was unfair. For the king's system of exploitation became a model for surrounding colonies which also had rain forests rich in wild rubber: Portuguese-controlled Angola, the Cameroons under the Germans, and the French Congo, part of French Equatorial Africa, across the river from Leopold's Congo. Seeing what profits Leopold was reaping from forced labor, officials in the other colonies soon adopted exactly the same system—including women hostages, male forced labor, and the *chicotte*—with equally high death rates. Forced labor of one kind or another was widely used in most parts of the continent until several decades into the twentieth century, although seldom with such fatal consequences as during the rubber boom in central Africa.

After 1908, in the newly christened Belgian Congo, men were forced to continue gathering rubber, for its price remained high. Eventually, just before World War I, the price fell as rubber plantations elsewhere in the world began producing. The Congo's wild rubber vines were also largely tapped out. But the war brought new hardships: large numbers of Africans were conscripted as porters, carrying supplies for Belgian military campaigns against Germany's African colonies. In 1916, according to statistics kept by Belgian officials, one district of the eastern Congo with a population of 83,518 adult men supplied more than 3 million man-days of porterage. Exactly 1,359 of these porters were worked to death or died of disease.

THE DEATH TOLL

Starting in the early 1920s, however, the system became considerably less draconian, mainly because colonial officials realized that otherwise they would soon have no labor force left. "We run the risk of someday seeing our native population collapse and disappear," declared the permanent committee of the National Colonial Congress of Belgium in 1924, "so that we will find ourselves confronted with a kind of desert." Between 1880, when Leopold started to assume control of the Congo, and the 1920s, when the forced labor system became less severe, what happened could not, by strict definition, be called genocide, for there was no deliberate attempt to wipe out all members of one particular ethnic group. But the slashing of the territory's population—through the combination of forced labor and the consequent disease, famine, and diminished birthrate, plus the suppression of rebellions—indisputably occurred on a genocidal scale.

In estimating population losses without the benefit of complete census data, demographers are more confident speaking of percentages than absolute numbers. Using a wide variety of local and church sources, Jan Vansina, the leading ethnographer of Congo basin peoples, calculates that the Congo's population dropped by some 50 percent during this period, an estimate with which a number of other modern scholars concur. Interestingly, a long-time high colonial official, Major Charles C. Liebrechts, made the same estimate in 1920. Shocked by local census statistics that showed less than one child per woman, the official Commission Instituée pour la Protection des Indigènes (Commission for the Protection of the Natives) made a similar reckoning in 1919. Its report that year to the Belgian king warned that the situation had reached "the point of threatening even the existence of certain Congolese peoples" and could completely depopulate the entire region. R. P. Van Wing, a Belgian Jesuit missionary who had long worked in the region, estimated that one subgroup of the Bakongo people had seen 80 percent of its population disappear.

More precise statistics do not exist, for census data before 1920 are scanty and only local. Furthermore, just before the Congo state was transferred out of his hands in 1908, King Leopold II ordered its archives burned. But numerous surviving records from the rubber-bearing land in the adjoining French Congo, which closely followed the model of the Leopoldian forced labor system, suggest a population loss there of also approximately 50 percent. If the estimates from varied sources of a 50 percent toll in King Leopold's Congo are correct, how many people perished? In the early 1920s the first territory-wide census, when adjusted for undercounting, placed the number of the colony's inhabitants at around 10 million. If that figure is accurate and it represents 50 percent of what the population had been in 1880, this would suggest a loss of some 10 million people.

Some writers, almost entirely in Belgium, where the government and conservative academics have long tried to deny the size of the death toll, claim that such estimates are exaggerated. But other scholars use even higher numbers. Although neither figure is well documented, Hannah Arendt's seminal *The Origins of Totalitarianism* cited an estimated minimum population loss of 11.5 million, and a Congolese historian writing in 1998, Isidore Ndaywel è Nziem, estimated the loss at roughly 13 million. We will never know even the approximate toll with any certainty, but beyond doubt what happened in the Congo during and just after the years of Leopold's control was one of the great human rights catastrophes of modern times.

A NEW PHASE OF COLONIALISM

In the 1920s, in what was now the Belgian Congo, colonial officials began constructing the rudiments of a public health system and what eventually became one of the continent's best networks of primary schools. Colonialism's defenders often point to these, plus the wide network of roads and railways, as examples of the great positive benefits white rule brought to Africa. The clinics and schools were indeed built in the Congo, as elsewhere, but because Belgian industrialists and mine owners wanted a healthy work force with enough education to be trained. And the roads and railways were built almost entirely to carry ore, rubber, palm oil, and other products to the ports where it could be shipped to Europe.

Although the death toll began dropping dramatically in the 1920s, Congolese had few legal rights, no vote, and, when it came to politics, little free speech. Along with the forced labor system, these were violations of human rights common throughout colonial Africa. In 1921, for example, Congo authorities became deeply alarmed at the large following attracted by a religious prophet, Simon Kimbangu, who was said to heal the sick and make the blind see. His preaching was not overtly political, but thousands of workers left their jobs to follow him. He was swiftly arrested and kept in prison until his death, thirty years later.

Sporadic uprisings continued. In 1931 white officials set out to conscript palm oil workers by seizing some women of the Pende ethnic group as hostages. The officials raped some of the women, and the Pende rose in revolt. Hundreds of troops were called out. By the time it was over, 344 Pende had been killed, 45 wounded, and 1,356 arrested. Of the latter, 2 were sentenced to death, 47 to be whipped, and 39 to lengthy prison terms—during which 9 of them died.

Although it gradually took on a less murderous form, forced labor remained a crucial part of the Belgian Congo's economy. The enforcement mechanism of taking women or chiefs as hostages gradually was replaced by that of taxes—and the threat of severe punishment for Congolese who did not pay them. Throughout sub-Saharan Africa, European colonists and settlers used head taxes or hut taxes to force people away from subsistence agriculture and into mines, factories, and other parts of the colonial economy that required labor.

The decades immediately after World War I saw the growth of Belgian Congo production of copper, gold, tin, and palm oil. The *chicotte* remained a key tool of control, now often in the hands of private corporations. At the gold mines of Moto, on the Uele River, records show that 26,579 lashes were administered to miners in the first half of 1920 alone. When the key railway line around the great Congo River rapids was widened and rebuilt between 1923 and 1932, the regime mobilized 68,000 forced laborers and members of their families, of whom 7,700 died. (This was colonial business as usual: a competing railway built at the same time in French Equatorial Africa cost 20,000 lives.) To Africans throughout the Congo conscripted to work on these and other works of the white men's corporations, the business bankruptcies and slow-downs caused by the Great Depression brought, paradoxically, lifesaving relief.

The coming of World War II, in which the Congo's treasure house of natural resources was a key source of supply for the Allies, saw the legal maximum for forced labor increased to 120 days per man per year. The penalty for evasion was six months in prison. Workers labored at everything from the railways to the heavily guarded uranium mine of Shinkolobwe, which produced more than 80 percent of the uranium used in the atomic bombs dropped on Hiroshima and Nagasaki. The Allied armies also wanted ever more rubber for the tires of hundreds of thousands of military trucks and warplanes. Some of it now came from the Congo's new plantations of cultivated rubber trees. But in the forest villages Africans were forced to go into the rain forest, sometimes for weeks at a time, to search for wild rubber vines once again.

INDEPENDENCE AND AFTER

The Belgian Congo developed economically much more rapidly after 1945, and the health and education levels of its population rose. But Belgium was taken by surprise by the demand for self-government that swept across the African continent in the 1950s, igniting mass demonstrations in the Congo's capital, Leopoldville, in 1959 that were brutally suppressed by the colonial army. When pressure grew still stronger and Belgium hastily granted independence in 1960, there were, in the entire territory,

fewer than thirty African university graduates. No Congolese had been trained as engineers, agronomists, doctors, or army officers. Of some five thousand management-level positions in the civil service, only three were filled by Africans.

Like the other colonial powers, Belgium gave in to the demands for independence in its colonies because it was convinced it could retain ownership of mines and industries and keep profits flowing back to Europe. To a large extent, this assumption proved correct. To make sure, however, the Belgians and Americans decided to depose the newly independent Congo's coalition-government prime minister, Patrice Lumumba, who had taken power in 1960 as a result of the first democratic election the territory had ever experienced. It would be, for well over four decades, the last.

The fiery, mercurial Lumumba was a charismatic speaker who believed that political independence was not enough for Africa; the continent must cease to be an economic colony of Europe as well. His presence in office immediately set off alarm bells in Western capitals, because American, Belgian, and other European corporations by now had vast investments in the Congo, particularly in mining. Less than two months after Lumumba took office, a U.S. National Security Council subcommittee on covert operations, which included CIA chief Allen Dulles, authorized his assassination. President Dwight D. Eisenhower agreed.

Although CIA officials made strenuous efforts to arrange Lumumba's death, getting close to him was difficult, and in the end both the CIA and Belgians still working in the Congo's army and police supported anti-Lumumba factions in the government, confident they would carry out the job. And they did. After being arrested and repeatedly beaten, the prime minister was secretly shot in early 1961. Covertly urged on by their own government, a Belgian pilot flew the plane that took Lumumba to the city where he was executed, Elizabethville, and a Belgian officer commanded the firing squad. Two Belgians then cut up his body and dissolved it in acid, to leave no martyr's grave. We cannot know whether, had he survived, Lumumba would have stayed true to the radical hopes he embodied for so many people in Africa, but the United States and Belgium saw to it that he had no chance to try.

A rising figure at the time of Lumumba's death was army chief of staff Joseph Désiré Mobutu. Early on the Western powers identified Mobutu as someone who would look out for their interests, and President John F. Kennedy received him at the White House in 1963. With

U.S. encouragement, Mobutu assumed power in a coup in 1965 and remained the country's dictator for the next thirty-two years. In 1971 he changed his name to Mobutu Sese Seko and his country's name to Zaire. During his decades in office, the United States gave him well over a billion dollars in civilian and military aid; European powers, especially France and Belgium, contributed more. In return the United States. and its allies got a regime that protected their investments, was reliably anti-Communist, and could serve as a secure staging area for CIA and French military operations. Mobutu was received several times at the White House by President Ronald Reagan, who praised him as "a voice of good sense and good will." President George H. W. Bush, who welcomed him as well, called him "one of our most valued friends."

During his three decades in power, Mobutu became perhaps the most spectacular example of a type of ruler all too common in postcolonial Africa, the authoritarian kleptocrat. His political enemies he killed, imprisoned, tortured, exiled, or co-opted. Government services gradually ceased to function as state revenues flowed into the hands of Mobutu and an entourage of several thousand, largely from his own ethnic group. When he ran out of money, he printed new currency. Garbage piled up in heaps, uncollected. Government support of schools, universities, and hospitals dwindled to almost nothing. Some of the country's mines continued producing, but the profits flowed almost entirely to foreign corporations, with kickbacks into the pockets of Mobutu and the people around him. Mobutu became one of the world's wealthiest men, amassing a fortune estimated at $4 billion.

In a striking number of ways, he resembled King Leopold II. Both men saw African lakes renamed after themselves. Both treated the territory as a private preserve whose main purpose was to enrich them. Both lived much of the time on yachts: Mobutu on the Congo River, Leopold in the Mediterranean. Both invested their profits in European real estate. Mobutu's luxurious Villa del Mare, a colonnaded château on the French Riviera, lay a mere dozen miles down the coast from Leopold's equally palatial estate.

Despite the uncanny manner in which Mobutu almost seems to have modeled himself on Leopold (reportedly, he boasted of this to his advisors), it would be a mistake to blame all the Congo's postindependence problems entirely on colonialism. Colonial rule did indeed establish government as an organized system for plunder, and the forced labor system did cause millions of deaths. Yet from Ireland to South Korea, countries that were once ruthlessly colonized have nonetheless, on these unpromising foundations, managed to build reasonably just, prosperous, and democratic societies.

The reasons most of Africa has not done so go far beyond the colonial heritage. One major factor is the abysmal position of women, and all the violence, repression, and prejudices that go with that. Another is the deep-seated popular tolerance and even hero worship of leaders such as Mobutu, for whom politics is solely a matter of enriching themselves and their extended clan or ethnic group. Finally, perhaps above all, is the way the long history of indigenous slavery is still deeply and disastrously woven into the African social fabric.

These same handicaps exist elsewhere. Education and full rights for women are closely linked to social justice and economic development in all countries. Many societies, from the Balkans to Afghanistan, have had trouble building nation-states when power-hungry demagogues enrich their own ethnic group and ignore others. And Africa is not alone in its heritage of slavery: the writer Anton Chekhov, knowing the weight of his own country's history of serfdom, spoke of how Russians must squeeze the slave out of themselves, drop by drop. Russia's continuing troubles show how long and hard a task this is.

These then are some of the burdens of its past that the Congo labors under, in addition to all that was suffered during its unusually painful experience of colonialism. In 1997 Mobutu was overthrown; he died from cancer the same year. The country then became the Democratic Republic of Congo. Under that heading, its story, sadly again one involving gross abuses of human rights and mass deaths, is continued elsewhere in this volume.

[*See also* Colonialism; Democratic Republic of Congo; *and* Slavery and the Slave Trade.]

BIBLIOGRAPHY

Anstey, Roger. *King Leopold's Legacy: The Congo Under Belgian Rule, 1908–1960* . London: Oxford University Press, 1966.

Ascherson, Neal. *The King Incorporated: Leopold II in the Age of Trusts*. London: Allen & Unwin, 1963.

Benedetto, Robert, ed. *Presbyterian Reformers in Central Africa: A Documentary Account of the American Presbyterian Congo Mission and the Human Rights Struggle in the Congo, 1890–1918*. Leiden, Netherlands: E.J. Brill, 1996.

Bierman, John. *Dark Safari: The Life behind the Legend of Henry Morton Stanley*. New York: Alfred A. Knopf, 1990.

Cline, Catherine Ann. *E. D. Morel 1873–1924: The Strategies of Protest*. Dundonald, Belfast: Blackstaff Press, 1980.

Conrad, Joseph. *Heart of Darkness: An Authoritative Text, Backgrounds and Sources, Criticism.* 3d ed., edited by Robert Kimbrough, Norton Critical Series. New York: W.W. Norton, 1988.

Cookey, Sylvanus John Sodieyne. *Britain and the Congo Question: 1885–1913.* New York: Humanities Press, 1968.

De Witte, Ludo. *The Assassination of Lumumba.* London: Verso, 2001.

Forbath, Peter. *The River Congo: The Discovery, Exploration, and Exploitation of the World's Most Dramatic River.* New York: Harper & Row, 1977.

Franklin, John Hope. *George Washington Williams: A Biography.* Chicago: University of Chicago Press, 1985.

Harms, Robert. *River of Wealth, River of Sorrow: The Central Zaire Basin in the Era of the Slave and Ivory Trade, 1500–1891.* New Haven, Conn.: Yale University Press, 1981.

Hochschild, Adam. "In the Heart of Darkness." *The New York Review of Books* 52, no. 15 (October 6, 2005): 39–42.

Hochschild, Adam. *King Leopold's Ghost: A Story of Greed, Terror and Heroism in Colonial Africa.* Boston: Houghton Mifflin, 1998.

Inglis, Brian. *Roger Casement.* London: Hodder and Stoughton, 1973.

Kelly, Sean. *America's Tyrant: The CIA and Mobutu of Zaire: How the United States Put Mobutu in Power, Protected Him from His Enemies, Helped Him Become One of the Richest Men in the World, and Lived to Regret It.* Lanham, Md.: American University Press, 1993.

Lagergren, David. *Mission and State in the Congo. A Study of the Relations between Protestant Missions and the Congo Independent State Authorities with Special Reference to the Equator District, 1885–1903.* Lund, Sweden: Gleerup, 1970.

Lindqvist, Sven. *Exterminate All the Brutes: One Man's Odyssey into the Heart of Darkness and the Origins of European Genocide.* Translated from Swedish by Joan Tate. New York: New Press, 1996.

Marchal, Jules. *E. D. Morel contre Léopold II. L'histoire du Congo, 1900–1910* [E. D. Morel vs. Leopold II: The History of the Congo 1900–1910]. 2 vols. Paris: Éditions L'Harmattan, 1996.

Marchal, Jules. *L'état libre du Congo: Paradis perdu. L'histoire du Congo, 1876–1900* [The Congo Free State: Paradise Lost. The History of the Congo, 1876-1900]. 2 vols. Borgloon, Belgium: Éditions Paula Bellings, 1999.

Marchal, Jules. *Forced Labor in the Gold and Copper Mines: A History of Congo under Belgian Rule, 1910–1945.* Volume 1, translated from French by Ayi Kwei Armah. Popenguine, Senegal: Per Ankh, 2003.

McLynn, Frank. *Stanley: The Making of an African Explorer.* London: Constable, 1989.

McLynn, Frank. *Stanley: Sorcerer's Apprentice.* London: Constable, 1991.

Morel, E. D. *E. D. Morel's History of the Congo Reform Movement.* Edited by William Roger Louis and Jean Stengers. Oxford, U.K.: Clarendon Press, 1968.

Morel, E. D. *King Leopold's Rule in Africa.* London: Heinemann, 1904.

Morel, E. D. *Red Rubber: The Story of the Rubber Slave Trade Which Flourished on the Congo for Twenty Years, 1890–1910.* Revised ed. Manchester, U.K.: National Labour Press, 1919.

Nelson, Samuel H. *Colonialism in the Congo Basin, 1880–1940.* Athens, Ohio: Ohio University Center for International Studies, 1994.

Northrup, David. *Beyond the Bend in the River: African Labor in Eastern Zaire, 1865–1940.* Athens, Ohio: Ohio University Center for International Studies, 1988.

O Síocháin, Séamas, and Michael O'Sullivan, eds. *The Eyes of Another Race: Roger Casement's Congo Report and 1903 Diary.* Dublin: University College Dublin Press, 2003.

Phipps, William. *William Sheppard: The Congo's African American Livingstone.* Louisville, Ky.: Geneva Press, 2002.

Samarin, William J. *The Black Man's Burden: African Colonial Labor on the Congo and Ubangi Rivers, 1880–1900.* Boulder, Colo.: Westview Press, 1989.

Shaloff, Stanley. *Reform in Leopold's Congo.* Richmond, Va.: John Knox Press, 1970.

Sheppard, William H. *Presbyterian Pioneers in Congo.* Richmond, Va.: Presbyterian Committee of Publication, 1916.

Slade, Ruth. *English-Speaking Missions in the Congo Independent State (1878–1908).* Brussels, Belgium: Académie Royale des Sciences Coloniales, 1959.

Vangroenweghe, Daniel. *Du sang sur les lianes.* Brussels, Belgium: Didier Hatier, 1986.

Vansina, Jan. *Paths in the Rainforest.* Madison: University of Wisconsin Press, 1990.

Wrong, Michela. *In the Footsteps of Mr. Kurtz: Living on the Brink of Disaster in Mobutu's Congo.* New York: HarperCollins, 2001.

PETER BENENSON

by Kirsten Sellars

Peter Benenson was a champion of "prisoners of conscience" and founding member of Amnesty International. During his six years at its helm, he developed an approach to campaigning that provided a blueprint for the human rights movement. He was ambitious, innovative, and occasionally reckless, sparking controversies that would cast a shadow over the organization he had founded.

Peter James Henry Solomon Benenson was born in London on 31 July 1921. His mother was of Russian Jewish extraction; his father, a British Army officer, died when Peter was young. He enjoyed a privileged upbringing: after being tutored by W. H. Auden, he was educated at Eton College (where he raised funds to rescue young Jews from Germany) and then at Balliol College, Oxford. During the war, he worked in military intelligence at the Bletchley Park code-breaking center; after it, he was called to the English Bar and unsuccessfully stood for Parliament as a Labour Party candidate. In 1954 he traveled to Spain on behalf of the Society of Labour Lawyers to observe the trial of Basque trade unionists. Two years later he visited the British colony of Cyprus to advise lawyers representing those who had fallen foul of the authorities. During this period, he founded Justice, the British section of the International Commission of Jurists, and converted to Catholicism—thereafter a strong influence on his life.

THE FOUNDING OF AMNESTY

In 1960 Benenson read that two students had been jailed in Portugal for the "crime" of toasting freedom, and decided to campaign on behalf of those imprisoned for their beliefs. Assisted by influential friends such as fellow lawyer Louis Blom-Cooper, Quaker Eric Baker, and editor David Astor, he launched Amnesty in *The Observer* newspaper on 28 May 1961 ("The Forgotten Prisoners," p. 21). The campaign proclaimed that the organization would work impartially on behalf of so-called prisoners of conscience, rising above the Cold War fray by taking on cases equally from the East, the West, and the third

world. As Benenson explained in his *Persecution 1961*: "If [Amnesty] were ever to fall under the control of one country, ideology or creed, it will have failed in its purpose" (p. 152).

The campaign soon gathered momentum. In 1962, already thinking along international lines, Benenson traveled to Paris and New York to drum up support for new sections. Meanwhile, other senior figures in Amnesty traveled abroad to plead the case of prisoners: Seán MacBride to Czechoslovakia, Louis Blom-Cooper to Ghana, Neville Vincent to Portugal, and Prem Khera to East Germany. At the same time, fledgling groups of activists mounted letter-writing campaigns on behalf of prisoners from each of the world's power blocs. The following year, Amnesty embarked on an investigation in southern Africa, paid £90 (U.S.$252 at 1963 rates) a month to prisoners' families in apartheid South Africa, and sent several parcels of clothes to Spain.

Despite his pledge of organizational independence, and unbeknownst to its membership, Peter Benenson also began to offer advice to and gain support from a partisan entity—the British government. During the 1960s the United Kingdom was still in the process of withdrawing from its colonies, and government departments such as the Colonial Office and Foreign Office welcomed information from those familiar with human rights issues. The relationship between Amnesty and Whitehall was placed on a more solid footing in 1963, when the Foreign Office wrote to overseas missions urging "discreet support" for Amnesty: discreet, because its public endorsement would have seriously undermined the campaign's credibility. It also explained that Amnesty would remain "independent," in the sense that officialdom would not be responsible for its activities, "some of which might from time to time embarrass us" (UK National Archives Kew, LCO 2/8097, Intel: "Amnesty International," 9 May 1967, which recaps the 1963 decision).

Benenson thrived as a go-between. In 1963 he wrote to Lord Lansdowne, the Colonial Office minister, about an

Amnesty proposal to install a "refugee counselor" in the British protectorate of Bechuanaland (present-day Botswana). The aim was to assist people fleeing across the border from neighboring South Africa, but not those actively engaged in the struggle against apartheid. "I would like to reiterate our view that these [British] territories should not be used for offensive political action by the opponents of the South African Government," he wrote. "Communist influence should not be allowed to spread in this part of Africa, and in the present delicate situation, Amnesty International would wish to support HMG [Her Majesty's Government] in any such policy" (UK National Archives, Kew: CO 1048/570, Benenson to Lansdowne, 26 September 1963). The following year the organization dropped antiapartheid activist Nelson Mandela as a prisoner of conscience because he had been convicted for an act of violence—namely, sabotage.

TRIP TO HAITI

In 1964 Benenson asked the Foreign Office to assist him to obtain a visa to Haiti, the impoverished Caribbean nation ruled by President François ("Papa Doc") Duvalier, so that he might conduct an investigation of human rights abuses there. The Foreign Office obliged and cabled its Port-au-Prince representative Alan Elgar to say that "we support the aims of Amnesty International" (UK National Archives, Kew: FO 371/174252, FO to Port-au-Prince, 18 December 1964). Benenson was to travel under his own name but with a false identity as a painter, enabling him to meet the regime's opponents without attracting the attention of Duvalier's security force, the Tontons Macoutes. This ploy would also disguise the fact that the investigation was being carried out with the official blessing of Whitehall. As Minister of State Walter Padley reminded him before he left: "We shall have to be a little careful not to give the Haitians the impression that your visit is actually sponsored by Her Majesty's Government" (UK National Archives, Kew: FO 371/174252, Padley to Benenson, 18 December 1964).

Benenson arrived in Port-au-Prince in January 1965 and began his investigation. Elgar introduced him to prominent expatriates such as the American ambassador, the Canadian chargé d'affaires, and "reliable people" in the business community. (Benenson noted that of these individuals, the ambassador was the only apologist for Duvalier.) His mission in Haiti remained a secret while he was there, but on the way home he called a press

conference in Paris. Assuming it to be an off-the-record briefing, he revealed his cover as a "painter," with unpredicted consequences. *The Times* named him as the Amnesty representative who had traveled to Haiti, and the *New York Times* revealed how he had "obtained his entry visa as an 'artist' and circumvented restrictions on internal travel by a ruse."

Foreign Office officials were displeased: Elgar, for example, declared himself to be "shocked by Benenson's antics." Benenson apologized to Padley but blamed the newspapers. "I really do not know why the *New York Times*, which is generally a responsible newspaper, should be doing this sort of thing over Haiti," he wrote. "I can only suppose that some of the editorial staff are rather indignant about the present regime on the island and are using every opportunity to shake the US administration into action" (UK National Archives, Kew: FO 371/179555, Benenson to Elgar [Haiti], 24 January 1965).

REPORT ON ADEN

More drama followed. In July 1966 Dr. Selahuddin Rastgeldi of Amnesty's Swedish section traveled to the British colony of Aden to investigate allegations of torture at the Ras Morbut interrogation center. Hans Goran Franck, chairman of the Swedish section, then contacted Prime Minister Harold Wilson. "Dr. Rastgeldi has gathered reliable information on the practice of torture in the British interrogation centres in Aden," he wrote. This included: "Undressing the detainee and letting him stand naked during interrogation . . . forcing the prisoner to sit on a pole entering his anus . . . hitting and twisting his genital organs . . . extinguishing cigarettes on his skin . . . keeping him in filthy toilets with the floor covered with faeces and urine" (UK National Archives, Kew: PREM 13/1294, Franck to Wilson, 18 October 1966).

Amnesty released the Franck letter in October 1966, but not Rastgeldi's report. There were conflicting explanations for the delay. Peter Benenson claimed that the Amnesty general secretary Robert Swann had suppressed it in deference to the Foreign Office. But according to cofounder Eric Baker, both Benenson and Swann had met Foreign Secretary George Brown in September and told him that they were willing to hold up publication if the Foreign Office "made concessions about procedure which would ensure that no such incidents could recur" (Amnesty International circular: "Aden", October 1966). A memo by Lord Chancellor Gerald Gardiner to

Wilson in November states that "Amnesty held the Swedish complaint as long as they could simply because Peter Benenson did not want to do anything to hurt a Labour government" (UK National Archives, Kew: PREM 13/1294, Lord Chancellor to Prime Minster, 4 November 1966).

That same month Benenson traveled to Aden and was shocked by what he found there. "During many years spent in the personal investigation of repression. . . I never came upon an uglier picture than that which met my eyes in Aden," he wrote to Gardiner, adding that he was sickened by "the deliberate cruelty and affronts to the human dignity of the Arab population." Regarding Rastgeldi's report, he admitted that "there is to say the least a strong possibility that some if not all the rather horrifying allegations are correct" (UK National Archives, Kew: LCO 2/8097, Benenson to Gardiner, 6 January 1967). (Brown later denounced the report's "wild allegations" in the House of Commons [*Hansard*, Commons, Vol. 738, 19 December 1966, Col. 1007].)

THE "HARRY" LETTERS

Further controversy followed in the spring of 1967, with the revelation that the International Commission of Jurists had been founded and covertly funded by the CIA through an American affiliate, the American Fund for Free Jurists. Its secretary-general, Seán MacBride (who was also head of Amnesty's International Secretariat), denied knowledge of this covert support. Then, shortly thereafter, a similar scandal hit Amnesty.

Polly Toynbee, then a twenty-year-old volunteer and later a prominent British journalist, contacted the press with evidence suggesting that Amnesty was being covertly funded by the British government. In 1966 she had traveled first to Nigeria and then to the Southern Rhodesia (now Zimbabwe) with the organization. During her six weeks in Salisbury (now Harare), she and other volunteers dispensed funds to detainees' families and tried to arrange legal aid for prisoners. Money seemed to be no object— "I could go to the bank and pull out £200 [U.S.$560] at a time, there was no one to check up"—and rumors circulated about the source of it (Duff Hart-Davis). When Benenson paid a visit to Salisbury, he had apparently admitted to her that the money had come from the British government.

When Toynbee and others were expelled from Rhodesia in March 1966, she brought with her correspondence that she claimed to have found abandoned in a safe; it included letters from Benenson's address to Amnesty's general secretary Swann and others working in Rhodesia. These appeared to indicate that Amnesty had asked "Harry" (Harold Wilson's Labour government) for money to pursue its work in Rhodesia, and that "Harry" had paid up in late January 1966.

When the press published excerpts from the "Harry" letters in March 1967, Amnesty formally denied knowledge of the payments. Benenson, however, conceded that the government *had* provided secret funds, but claimed they were a direct gift to prisoners and their families in Rhodesia, and not funds for the organization itself. A private letter written by Benenson to Gardiner two months before Toynbee's revelations revealed that the British government had asked a third party, Charles Forte, the owner of a catering and hotel chain, to donate £10,000 (U.S.$28,000 at 1966 rates) to the Rhodesian work. Benenson suggested that in return for the donation, "it was not altogether unlikely that the name of such a well-known caterer would appear on a future honours list" (UK National Archives, Kew: LCO 2/8097, Benenson to Gardiner, 6 January 1967).

Whatever the truth of the matter, Benenson decided to return the money. He wrote to Gardiner that "rather than jeopardise the political reputation of those members of the Government involved in these secret payments, I had decided to sell sufficient of my own securities to repay the secret donor." His motive, he explained, was "to clear the record so that it could be said that the money sent for succour to HM [Her Majesty's] loyal subjects in Rhodesia came from a . . . private person with a known interest in the cause." Benenson was also keen to divest himself of unspent Foreign Office funding for two other human rights organizations with which he was involved: Justice and the Human Rights Advisory Service, which he had set up in January 1966 and which was also active in Rhodesia. "In my view," he wrote, "under present circumstances it would be better if the money went back whence it came" (UK National Archives, Kew: LCO 2/8097, Benenson to Gardiner, 6 January 1967).

In addition to his nervousness about a possible scandal over the covert funds, Benenson also expressed his bitter disappointment over the British government's handling of human rights issues. "I believed on the evidence of my friends' record and their public declarations that they would set an example to the world in the matter of human rights," he wrote to Gardiner. "Alas, such an example has been set, but it is not a good example" (UK National Archives, Kew: LCO 2/8097, Benenson to Gardiner, 6 January 1967).

BENENSON'S DEPARTURE FROM AMNESTY

At the height of the controversy over the "Harry" letters, Amnesty staffer Stephanie Grant wrote to G. C. Grant in Salisbury: "Peter Benenson has been levelling accusations . . . which can only have the result of discrediting the organisation which he has founded and to which he dedicated himself." She continued: "All this began after soon after he came back from Aden, and it seems likely that the nervous shock which he felt at the brutality shown by some elements of the British army there had some unbalancing effect on his judgment" (UK National Archives, Kew: FCO 36/100, S. Grant to G. C. Grant, 7 March 1967). Benenson resigned as Amnesty's president on the grounds that its London office was bugged and infiltrated by the secret services, and announced that he could no longer live in a country where such activities were tolerated.

In March 1967 Amnesty delegations from Europe and America gathered for a conference in Elsinore, Denmark. Chairman Seán MacBride submitted a written report that referred pointedly to Benenson's "erratic actions" and "unilateral initiatives" (Power, p. 17). Benenson did not attend but submitted a resolution demanding MacBride's resignation on the grounds that a section of the International Commission of Jurists had been funded by the CIA. After the conference, Amnesty's leadership passed to a caretaker, Eric Baker.

The relationship between Amnesty and the British government was suspended. Amnesty vowed that in future, it "must not only be independent and impartial but must not be put into a position where anything else could even be alleged" (Peter Burns, "Elsinor: Mandate for Change," *Air* [Amnesty International Review], 19 May 1967). In May 1967 the Foreign Office reversed its 1963 instructions about the organization and cautioned that "for the time being our attitude to Amnesty International must be one of reserve" (UK National Archives, Kew: LCO 2/8097, Intel: "Amnesty International," 9 May 1967).

Peter Benenson withdrew from the scene but reemerged in the 1980s as the champion of new causes. He chaired the Association of Christians Against Torture, founded organizations to aid fellow sufferers of celiac disease and manic depression, organized aid for Romanian orphans, and spoke out for Mordachai Vanunu (the technician imprisoned for revealing some of Israel's nuclear secrets). In the meantime he mended fences with Amnesty International, which grew into one of the world's leading human rights groups, with sections in sixty-four countries. When he died in Oxford on 25 February 2005, the organization paid fulsome tribute. "Peter Benenson's life was a courageous testament to his visionary commitment to fight injustice around the world," said general secretary Irene Khan. "He brought light into the darkness of prisons."

[*See also* Amnesty International; Colonialism; Haiti; International Commission of Jurists; Seán MacBride; Refugees; Religious Freedom; South Africa; Torture: International Law; *and* Zimbabwe.]

BIBLIOGRAPHY

Benenson, Peter. *Gangrene.* Introduction. London: Calderbooks, 1959.

Benenson, Peter. *Persecution 1961.* Harmondsworth, U.K.: Penguin, 1961.

Hart-Davis, Duff. "Strange Secrets of the Amnesty Row." *Sunday Telegraph*, March 5, 1967.

Kamm, Henry. "Reign of Terror Reported in Haiti." *New York Times*, January 22, 1965.

Larsen, Egon. *A Flame in Barbed Wire: The Story of Amnesty International.* New York: W.W. Norton, 1979.

The Observer. "The Forgotten Prisoners," May 28, 1961.

Power, Jonathan. *Amnesty International: The Human Rights Story.* New York: McGraw-Hill, 1981.

Rabben, Linda. *Fierce Legion of Friends: A History of Human Rights Campaigns and Campaigners.* Hyattsville, Md.: Quixote Center, 2002.

Sellars, Kirsten. *The Rise and Rise of Human Rights.* Stroud, Gloucestershire, U.K.: Sutton, 2002

Winner, David. *Peter Benenson: Taking a Stand Against Injustice.* Milwaukee, Wis.: Gareth Stevens, 1991.

STEVE BIKO

by Mark Sanders

Bantu Stephen Biko, a leader of the Black Consciousness movement in South Africa, became a subject for human rights posthumously, for it was at the hearings in connection with his death that human rights came to be invoked. The first of these hearings took place in 1977. At a coroner's inquest held to determine the cause of his death in police custody on 12 September 1977, the security policemen responsible produced a version of events convincingly impeached by the lawyers for the Biko family. The complicity of the chief medical examiner with the police in particular brought the question of human rights to the fore. Instead of upholding accepted medical ethics, the medical examiner, Benjamin Tucker, and his deputy, Ivor Lang, bowed to the exigencies of the security police and failed to undertake the appropriate care of their patient. Despite examinations diagnosing the likelihood of brain damage from his assault by the police, Biko was never treated, continued to be detained, and eventually died after being transported unconscious in a police vehicle over seven hundred miles from Port Elizabeth to Pretoria.

THE TRUTH AND RECONCILIATION COMMISSION

Although the United Nations had declared apartheid a crime against humanity, the invocation of human rights did not become well established inside the country as a strategy of political mobilization against apartheid or in the legal representation of the political accused or plaintiffs until after Biko's death and the ensuing international outcry over the systemic detention and torture of South African political activists. The 1977 Biko inquest and the medical hearings that followed in 1980 and 1985 led to efforts in South Africa to make doctors answerable to the Universal Declaration of Human Rights. A product of these efforts was the founding of the National Medical and Dental Association in 1982 as an alternative body to the official South African Medical and Dental Council,

which was widely perceived to have covered up the complicity of the doctors involved in Biko's death.

When twenty years later, in 1997, the policemen who assaulted Biko appeared before the Truth and Reconciliation Commission, human rights had been firmly established in South Africa as the dominant discourse in framing legal treatment of political cases. With a bill of rights entrenched in the interim constitution of 1993 and then in the final constitution of 1996, there was the sense that South Africa had brought itself into step politically and juridically with the best that international constitutional law could offer. Part of the reason for a relative lack of human rights legal activism in apartheid South Africa was the absence of a bill of rights and the operation of the principle of parliamentary sovereignty. Human rights, embodied in a series of international agreements, was by the 1990s rapidly providing the overarching framework for transnational juridico-legal action. When the Truth and Reconciliation Commission was established at the end of 1995, it was natural for it to be given a mandate to "investigat[e] and . . . establish . . . as complete a picture as possible of the nature, causes and extent of gross violations of human rights" (South Africa, p. 55) committed in the political conflicts of 1960–1994 at the height of the apartheid era and in its immediate aftermath. It should be noted that the commission's interpretation of its mandate has been criticized for individualizing rights violations to almost archetypal identities of "victim" and "perpetrator" and for not attending to the structural violence of apartheid, which affected people insofar as they were members of groups. One of the most controversial measures adopted by the Truth Commission was a conditional amnesty for perpetrators of gross human rights violations on condition that full disclosure be made and that the acts committed were carried out in the pursuit of a political goal and proportional to it.

This was how the policemen responsible for the death of Biko came to testify before the Truth and Reconciliation Commission. Ruben Marx, Gideon Nieuwoudt,

Daniel Petrus Siebert, and Harold Snyman applied for amnesty. After several days of hearings in which they endeavored to alter certain details of the account that they had given in 1977, they convinced few people that they were telling the truth. And because they did not admit that they had killed Biko, an act for which amnesty would have been applicable, their application was refused. One of the ironies of this series of events was that Biko's widow, Ntsiki Biko, had been one of the principal opponents of the commission's amnesty provisions, joining other plaintiffs in taking the case in 1996 to the Constitutional Court, which decided for the commission. She and the others were in effect opponents of a juridical process that, by massively actualizing a growing tradition in human rights activism in unprecedented ways, drew its energy in significant part from a response to Biko's death.

BIKO'S LIFE AND POLITICS

Biko's life and politics were more complicated than this dimension of his legacy. Born on 18 December 1946 in Tarkastad in the Eastern Cape, he grew up in humble circumstances. Remembered as the leading figure in the Black Consciousness movement, he came from a Christian family and received his high school education at Lovedale and at Saint Francis College in Mariannhill, run near Durban by the Catholic Church. Biko continued a dialogue throughout his career with Christian groups. He had close friendships with the Anglican priests David Russell and Aelred Stubbs, with whom he debated the role of religion in his life—for instance, his love relationship, as a married man, with Mamphela Ramphele—and in the struggle of blacks against apartheid. Realizing that no mass mobilization of Africans could take place in South Africa without acknowledging the central role of Christianity (a large majority of South Africans are Christians), he nevertheless criticized the various churches for allowing the political status quo to remain unchallenged. Like the liberation theologians in South Africa, he advocated an interpretation of the Bible that would make moral sense of life under apartheid and suggest ways of changing those conditions.

Biko is rightly best known for his role as a leader of the South African Students' Organisation (SASO). Influenced by Frantz Fanon and black-nationalist and civil-rights leaders of the United States, such as Malcolm X, Martin Luther King Jr., and James Cone, Biko and fellow medical students at the University of Natal Non-European Section, including N. Barney Pityana and Ramphele, developed in the late 1960s a thinking that was novel in the South African context. Instead of viewing racial oppression simply as something imposed from the outside through apartheid policies and institutions, Biko and his contemporaries developed a theory of how these policies were reinforced by the profound acceptance by black African people of their own inferiority through a process of mental "internalization." In 1970 Biko defined "Black Consciousness" as an "inward-looking process" designed "to infuse [the black man] with pride and dignity, to remind him of his complicity in the crime of allowing himself to be misused and therefore letting evil reign supreme in the country of his birth" (Biko, *I Write What I Like*, p. 29). Biko's solution therefore was to raise consciousness of this complicity and, through a process of fostering autonomy, to develop the mental and political self-reliance necessary to mobilize against the system.

The effects of Black Consciousness thinking were far-reaching. One sees, for example, the development, in dialogue with Jean-Paul Sartre's *Black Orpheus* (1948) and Maurice Merleau-Ponty's *Phenomenology of Perception* (1945), of a Black Consciousness existential psychology in N. Chabani Manganyi's *Being-Black-in-the-World* (1973). The immediate political consequence of Black Consciousness, however, was a breaking away of SASO, a black student organization, from the umbrella student political body, the National Union of South African Students (NUSAS), in 1969. It had become clear to members of SASO that, while black student interests were being represented by white student leaders, black articulations would not come to maturity. For Biko, the integration achieved by NUSAS was "a one-way course, with the whites doing all the talking and the blacks the listening" (Biko, *I Write What I Like*, p. 20). Although traumatic for NUSAS, the break transformed the political landscape of South Africa.

Believing that a separatist black student organization might help it promote apartheid "separate development" and dilute the African National Congress (ANC) tradition of nonracialism (the ANC kept a studied distance), the government allowed Black Consciousness to organize, with comparatively little harassment, on black university campuses. As Black Consciousness became more popular, however, especially among township high school students, the government cracked down. The most public facet of this crackdown was the trial of the leaders of SASO on charges of terrorism that took place from August 1975 to December 1976. This trial, rather than blunting the force of Black Consciousness, publicized it and gave Biko, who had by then left his medical studies for law, the opportunity to expound its ideas. Testifying at length, Biko was conciliatory and, for example, astutely linked the protest of Soweto students against classroom instruction in Afrikaans with the struggle of Afrikaner nationalists for the parity of Afrikaans with the English in the 1920s. He also revealed himself to have been Frank Talk, the pseudonymous author of the influential column in the *SASO Newsletter* titled "I Write What I Like." Collected under that title, these columns are some of the key writings in South African political history.

The ideology of Black Consciousness was, in certain superficial respects, alien to human rights. In the fashion of the Négritude writers, it stood for an African communitarianism in which the individual is subordinate to the community. Its assertion of black pride and self-confidence, through the Black is Beautiful campaign and through cultural activities, however, led it to a redefinition of freedom as liberation not only from political oppression and economic exploitation but from the internalized racism dominating one's life. It was thus an intensification of the liberalism that, in public at least, was its main antagonist—as is vividly depicted in *Cry Freedom*, Richard Attenborough's 1987 film about Biko's friendship with the newspaper editor Donald Woods. It is also important to note that an explicit use of the discourse of rights might also have associated Black Consciousness with the ANC and its Freedom Charter (1955), which declared that "all shall enjoy human rights" (Suttner and Cronin, p. 264). Yet Black Consciousness was an eclectic mix of ideas, and the language of rights did come into play from time to time even before emerging with the force that it did at the hearings investigating Biko's death.

By the time of the SASO trial, Black Consciousness had moved out from the university campuses. Famous for its community outreach work through Black Community Programmes led by Bennie Khoapa in health care (its leaders were medical students), the movement also evolved in 1972 into the Black People's Convention, a national body for uniting Black Consciousness organizations. The Soweto uprising of 1976 against Afrikaans as a medium of instruction in black schools, which is generally considered the beginning of the end of the apartheid state, will perhaps always be remembered as the most graphic moment in the influence of Biko. After the state reacted to the uprising with killings, mass arrests, and torture, large numbers of high school students crossed the borders of South Africa into exile. Many joined the ANC, bringing with them the aggressive Black Consciousness thinking that in turn galvanized the nationwide resistance to apartheid in the townships and on shop floors in the 1980s and eventually forced the state to the negotiating table. Instrumental in this mobilization, the influence of Black Consciousness was strong also in cultural politics, as its self-assertion was translated into a rejection of aesthetic standards associated with white domination. "We will have to *donder* [smash] conventional literature," Mothobi Mutloatse declared in 1980. "We are going to pee, spit and shit on literary convention before we are through; we are going to kick and pull and push and drag literature into the form that we prefer. We are going to experiment and probe and not give a damn about what the critics have to say. Because we are in search of our true selves—undergoing self-discovery as a people" (p. 5). The writings of Njabulo S. Ndebele, collected in *South African Literature and Culture: Rediscovery of the Ordinary* (1994), are perhaps the most intensive critical elaboration, in dialogue with Marxism, of these ideas.

LEGACY

Members of the Black Consciousness movement remained prominent in the early twenty-first century, especially in the fields of education, development, and human rights. Ramphele became vice chancellor of the University of Cape Town in 1996 before moving to the World Bank as managing director responsible for human development in 2000. She was succeeded as vice chancellor by Ndebele. Ramphele subsequently became chair of Circle Capital Ventures, a black empowerment company based in Cape Town. Pityana, for a time also an academic at the University of Cape Town, became chair of the Human Rights Commission in 1995, leading its controversial investigation and public hearings into racism in the South African media in 2000. Among those who served political apprenticeship in Black Consciousness structures were Thenjiwe Mtintso, commander in Umkhonto we Sizwe during the struggle against apartheid, formerly chair of the Commission on Gender Equality, and in the early twenty-first century deputy secretary-general of the ANC. The ideas of Biko and Black Consciousness also influenced radical whites. When they tried to raise consciousness of internalized racism among whites, Rick Turner, Breyten Breytenbach, and Nadine Gordimer all took their cue from Biko. Biko's legacy is marked by an annual Steve Biko Memorial Lecture at the University of Cape Town, instituted in 2000. Speakers have included Ndebele, Ramphele, Ngugi wa Thiong'o, and Nelson Mandela.

[*See also* Right to Health and Health Care; South Africa; *and* Torture: International Law.]

BIBLIOGRAPHY

Biko, Steve. *I Write What I Like*. Edited by Aelred Stubbs. London: Bowerdean, 1978.

Biko, Steve. *Steve Biko: Black Consciousness in South Africa*. Edited by Millard W. Arnold. New York: Random House, 1978.

Gerhart, Gail M. *Black Power in South Africa: The Evolution of an Ideology*. Berkeley: University of California Press, 1978.

Mutloatse, Mothobi. "Introduction." In *Forced Landing: Africa South, Contemporary Writings*, edited by Mothobi Mutloatse, pp. 1–7. Johannesburg, South Africa: Ravan, 1980.

Ndebele, Njabulo S. *The First Steve Biko Memorial Lecture: Iph' Indlela*. Braamfontein, South Africa: Skotaville, 2000.

Ndebele, Njabulo S. *South African Literature and Culture: Rediscovery of the Ordinary*. Manchester, U.K.: Manchester University Press, 1994.

Pityana, N. Barney. "Medical Ethics and South Africa's Security Laws: A Sequel to the Death of Steve Biko." In *Bounds of Possibility: The Legacy of Steve Biko and Black Consciousness*, edited by N. Barney Pityana, Mamphela Ramphele, Malusi Mpumlwana, and Lindy Wilson, pp. 78–98. Atlantic Highlands, N.J.: Zed Books, 1992.

Pityana, N. Barney, Mamphela Ramphele, Malusi Mpumlwana, and Lindy Wilson, eds. *Bounds of Possibility: The Legacy of Steve Biko and Black Consciousness*. Atlantic Highlands, N.J.: Zed Books, 1992.

Sanders, Mark. *Complicities: The Intellectual and Apartheid*. Durham, N.C.: Duke University Press, 2002.

South Africa, Truth and Reconciliation Commission. *Truth and Reconciliation Commission of South Africa Report*. 7 vols. Cape Town, South Africa: Truth and Reconciliation Commission, 1998–2003.

Suttner, Raymond, and Jeremy Cronin. *30 Years of the Freedom Charter*. Johannesburg, South Africa: Ravan, 1986.

Wilson, Lindy. "Bantu Stephen Biko: A Life." In *Bounds of Possibility: The Legacy of Steve Biko and Black Consciousness*, edited by N. Barney Pityana, Mamphela Ramphele, Malusi Mpumlwana, and Lindy Wilson, pp. 15–77. Atlantic Highlands, N.J.: Zed Books, 1992.

Woods, Donald. *Biko*. New York: Paddington, 1978.

OSAMA BIN LADEN AND AL QAEDA

by Mahmood Monshipouri

Osama bin Muhammad bin Laden was born in Riyadh, Saudi Arabia, on 30 July 1957, the seventeenth son of fifty-four children (twenty-four boys and thirty girls) of Muhammad bin Laden, who was Saudi Arabia's wealthiest construction magnate. Little is known of Osama's mother, Hamida, the daughter of a Syrian family with whom Muhammad had business connections. Osama was raised in Medina and the Hejaz and attended King Abdulaziz University in Jiddah, where he acquired a degree in civil engineering. While at university in Jiddah, Osama was taught Islamic studies by Muhammad Qutb, the brother of Sayyid Qutb, the ideologue of the Muslim Brotherhood, and Abdullah Azzam, both of whom would heavily influence his thinking in years to come.

BIN LADEN AND THE JIHAD

After the Soviet invasion of Afghanistan on 26 December 1979, bin Laden left Saudi Arabia to join the Afghan resistance and freedom fighters known as mujahideen. With the support of the U.S. Central Intelligence Agency (CIA) and Pakistan's security apparatus, the Inter-Services Intelligence (ISI), some thirty-five thousand Muslim radicals from forty Muslim countries joined the Afghan jihad against the Soviet Union. The mujahideen guerrillas promoted the production of heroin in their campaign against the Soviets. This so-called narco-jihadism received a wink and a nod from the CIA, which had, for all practical intents and purposes, given up the drug war to fight its Cold War enemy.

Saudi Arabia provided funding for the Afghan resistance movement. From the Pakistani border, bin Laden also raised funds and provided the mujahideen with logistical and humanitarian aid. At the same time, bin Laden participated in several battles as a guerrilla commander, including the fierce battle of Jalalabad, which resulted in a conventional military victory of the sort that drove the Soviets from Afghanistan in 1989.

In 1988 bin Laden established Al Qaeda (the base), a transnational terrorist organization of former mujahideen and other supporters, with the mission of channeling fighters and funds to the Afghan resistance. After the Soviet withdrawal from Afghanistan in 1989, bin Laden returned to Saudi Arabia. In the aftermath of the Iraqi invasion of Kuwait (1990), the United States and Saudi Arabia forged an alliance to dislodge Iraqi troops from Kuwait. Bin Laden objected to the presence of half a million American troops on Saudi soil. He joined the ranks of Saudi dissidents, voicing his opposition to the stationing of U.S. forces on the Saudi peninsula. Osama left Saudi Arabia for Pakistan in April 1991, where he conducted a campaign against the Saudi royal family. His messages, either as pamphlets or cassettes, began to circulate in homes, private businesses, and mosques.

Meanwhile, the National Islamic Front (NIF), led by Hassan al-Turabi, the Sudanese spiritual leader, which came to power in Sudan in 1989, sent a delegation to Peshawar in northwestern Pakistan to meet with bin Laden. The Sudanese fledgling Islamic state welcomed bin Laden; its leaders hoped that bin Laden would bring funding and investment. In 1994 the Saudi government confiscated his passport after accusing him of subversion. Bin Laden's inheritance and massive fortune (estimated to be $300 million) placed him in a unique position to shore up his activities and organizational operations even beyond Afghanistan. Bin Laden agreed to train NIF members in guerrilla warfare in their war against the largely Christian Sudan People's Liberation Army (SPLA) fighting for independence in the southern part of the country, and he decided to relocate Al Qaeda's infrastructure to Sudan. He went to Khartoum, Sudan, by 1992, establishing several commercial firms while supporting Islamist groups with funds, training, and weapons.

After Al Qaeda's failed attempt to assassinate Egyptian president Hosni Mubarak, the pressure on Sudan to expel Osama increased. The United States mounted a campaign to pressure Sudan by giving military assistance to its hostile neighbors Uganda, Eritrea, and Ethiopia. While still in Sudan, bin Laden directed the bombing of the World Trade Center in New York on 26 February 1993.

Saudi Arabia had tolerated bin Laden as long as he operated outside Saudi Arabia. On 9 April 1994 the Saudi government revoked bin Laden's citizenship and froze his assets in Saudi Arabia. In March 1995 Ramzi Yousef, who had masterminded the 1993 World Trade Center bombing, was captured in Pakistan and extradited to the United States. The U.S. investigators believed that he was linked financially to bin Laden. Under pressure by the U.S. and Saudi governments, in May 1996 Sudan's leaders expelled bin Laden. He moved back to Afghanistan, where a new force called the Taliban (seekers of knowledge), with the assistance of Pakistan's ISI, had seized control of two-thirds of the country.

In the aftermath of the Soviet Union's dissolution in the early 1990s, the Afghan state collapsed, and the country devolved into heavily armed networks of power. Seeking a political settlement, the Saudi and Pakistani governments agreed to promote orthodox Islamic factions and institutions throughout Afghanistan. With the end of the Cold War, Afghanistan had become a country without foreign aid. The armed forces, the sole remaining institution, dissolved and were absorbed into the country's regional-ethnic power networks.

The collapse of the state administration and community leadership in many places in the early to mid-1990s increased the importance of the mosques, the mullahs, and the Taliban who staffed them. The network of madrasas (Islamic schools), which created ties among potential new elites while other institutions were being destroyed, penetrated society as never before. The Taliban movement presented an Islamic solution to the problems of a failed state. Meanwhile, the devastation of Afghanistan enabled Osama bin Laden and others to create a base for global terror.

Taliban membership was drawn largely from Afghan youths who witnessed the Afghan war against Soviet troops and some mujahideen leaders living in Pakistan. A staunch supporter of bin Laden, Maulana Fazlu Rehman, the Jamiat Ulema Islam leader, controlled a complex of madrasas in Pakistan that actually provided recruits for the Taliban. Pakistan's ISI trained and provided the military wing of the Taliban with munitions, supplies, and advisers. Bin Laden later moved to Kandahar at the request of Mullah Omar, the Taliban's leader, to be placed under his regime's protection, which at the time controlled nearly 90 percent of Afghan territory. India and Iran supported the Northern Alliance to offset the Taliban's power. The Afghan Northern Alliance was made up of diverse ethnic and religious groups of rebel movements united in their goal of toppling the ruling Taliban. Made up of mainly non-Pashtun ethnic groups, it relied on some fifteen thousand Tajik and Uzbek troops defending the northern stronghold, Badakhshan, eastern Takhar province, the Panjshir Valley, and part of the Shomadi plain north of Kabul. The alliance was led by General Ahmed Shah Masood, who until his assassination received support from Iran, Russia, and Tajikistan.

On 7 August 1998 two simultaneous explosions at U.S. embassies in Nairobi, Kenya, and Dar es Salaam, Tanzania, bore a clear Al Qaeda imprint, as they were centrally directed by what the U.S. intelligence agencies called "Al Qaeda Central." The bomb in Nairobi killed 213 people, including twelve U.S. nationals. The bomb in Dar es Salaam killed eleven persons, but no Americans. To retaliate against these bombings, U.S. cruise missiles attacked suspected terrorist training camps in Afghanistan and also bombed Al Shifa, a pharmaceutical plant in Khartoum, which was believed to be linked to chemical weapons production. The Sudanese government vehemently denied these charges. Further evidence later discredited this claim by U.S. intelligence sources.

Following the previously mentioned U.S. futile assassination attempts, Osama was turned into a leading jihadist among Islamist groups and organizations throughout the Muslim world. On 16 January 1999 the U.S. Attorney's office filed an indictment against Osama bin Laden and eleven other suspected members of his terrorist organization. The grand jury charged the men with conspiring to kill American nationals in the embassy bombings.

11 SEPTEMBER 2001

On 11 September 2001 nineteen terrorists attacked American icons of military and economic power by hijacking four airplanes and flying two of them into the World Trade Center in New York City and one into the Pentagon in suburban Washington, D.C. These attacks were coordinated by Al Qaeda, whose intention was to demonstrate that the United States was fallible and vulnerable. Approximately two thousand people lost their lives in New York, as two of the world's tallest buildings crumbled, while more than a hundred died at the Pentagon. The fourth hijacked plane was brought down in Pennsylvania while headed, apparently, for the White House or Capital in Washington, D.C.

Bin Laden's first reaction following the attacks was published on 28 September 2001, in the Pakistani periodical *Umma*. There, he denied any responsibility for the hijackings, just as he had previously denied any involvement in the 1998 embassy bombings and the bombing of the U.S.S

Cole in Aden, Yemen, in November 2000. Instead, he placed the blame on America, "which has no friends," and on Israel's intelligence service, Mossad. On 7 October 2001 Al Jazeera broadcast a videotape in which bin Laden praised the courage of "the blessed Muslim vanguard" who had sacrificed their lives for the greater cause of jihad. In a tape aired on 17 April 2002, bin Laden finally admitted Al Qaeda's role in the destruction of the Twin Towers. He also acknowledged Al Qaeda's responsibility for subsequent bombings in Bali, Istanbul, and Madrid.

In retaliation for these terrorist attacks, on 7 October 2001, the United States launched its military operation in Afghanistan, which toppled the Taliban regime and dismantled part of the Al Qaeda infrastructure. While bin Laden went underground, many of his associates were captured. The worldwide outrage against the Taliban and Al Qaeda, along with the effectiveness of U.S. airpower and the cooperation of such neighboring countries as Iran and Pakistan to bring down the Taliban regime, showed that bin Laden had grossly miscalculated his support in the region.

Bin Laden operated from the assumption that U.S. interventions in Vietnam, Lebanon, and Somalia had proved unsustainable. This view was widely shared in the case of Iraq, as the prolongation of the U.S. occupation stirred up local turmoil. Bin Laden's reading of the situation in Afghanistan, however, proved to be fundamentally flawed. First, he underestimated the extent to which the Afghani people were disenchanted with the Taliban regime, as well as the fact that the Pashtun tribesmen, who supported the Taliban, were unwilling to lose their lives and property for a vague universal cause—that is, jihad against the mighty United States. Second, he overestimated the popular reaction on Arab streets. What motivates the Arabs and leads to their political mobilization is almost always linked to Arab—not Islamic—issues, such as the conflicts in Palestine and Iraq. In short, bin Laden's transnational agenda—or more accurately his theory of global jihad—conspicuously lacked a wider appeal in Afghanistan. It is important to bear in mind that the notion that an Islamic state should be created through jihad no longer resonates deeply among most in the Muslim world.

From the U.S. standpoint, 9/11 conveyed the dangers of abandoning a poor country such as Afghanistan in the post–Cold War period. The nagging question is whether U.S. military presence and UN operations in the aftermath of routing the Taliban and destroying the Al Qaeda terrorist networks would bring about a political settlement. Moreover, there is widespread anger among the Muslims at perceived U.S. failure to resolve the continuing conflict between Israel and the Palestinians. Public resentment not only helped bin Laden's jihad against the West flourish, it also turned him into a symbol of resistance to U.S. military interventions in Afghanistan and Iraq.

Although some Islamic groups were blamed for the terrorist assaults of 9/11, other Islamic organizations were mobilized by the United States to fight against the Serbs in the Balkans and Soviet troops in Afghanistan. Some analysts have asserted that U.S. foreign policy created violent political Islam inadvertently as part of its Cold War strategy. Before the Afghan jihad, right-wing political Islam was an ideological tendency with little organizational infrastructure or power on the ground. The war against the Soviet invasion of Afghanistan gave it a much-needed organizational, ideological, and strategic potency. In the words of one observer, "America created an infrastructure of terror but heralded it as an infrastructure of liberation" (Mamdani, 2005).

THE AL QAEDA NETWORK

Al Qaeda has never really existed as a centralized organization with a clear hierarchy of command and control. Rather, it is a virtual network that is distinctly religious. Its modern networks and use of sophisticated global communications systems defy any conventional definition of a terrorist organization. Unlike the terrorists of the 1970s and 1980s, Al Qaeda is not guided by territorial jurisdiction. Its system of operations and support is global; instead of resisting globalization, its forces use global means and targets worldwide for their ends. Its puritanical ideology notwithstanding, Al Qaeda is a modern network bent on exploiting modern technology, relying on satellite phones, using laptops and Web sites.

One expert noted that "the very intangibility of the Al Qaeda network precluded a traditional military conquest" (Kepel, p. 114). Bin Laden's mentor, the Palestinian–Jordanian ideologue Abdullah Azzam, had conceptualized Al Qaeda in 1987, laying down the guidelines for training the "pious group and the pioneering vanguard" in early 1988 (Gunaratna, p. 4). After Azzam's death, bin Laden was largely guided and influenced by the Egyptian Ayman Muhammad Rabi' al-Zawahiri, a physician by training. Many insiders have argued that Osama was transformed from a guerrilla into a terrorist by al-Zawahiri. Both of these men are archetypes of a new generation of terrorists who come from educated and well-to-do families, as did the 9/11 hijackers. Both are followers of the Salafi strand of Islam, which is associated with Wahhabism.

As the first multinational terrorist network of the twenty-first century, Al Qaeda has gone beyond using terrorism as a technique of protest and resistance by turning it into a global vehicle to compete with and challenge Western power and influence throughout the Muslim world. This terrorist network is financed by several companies in sectors ranging from shipping to agriculture to investment banking, which support Al Qaeda's movement of soldiers and procurement of weapons. These companies are linked to terror operations in Saudi Arabia, Pakistan, Yemen, Egypt, Algeria, Lebanon, Mauritania, and Palestine. Many of the people involved in Al Qaeda's linked terror operations were originally affiliated with a specific national organization, such as Egypt's Islamic Jihad or Algeria's Armed Islamic Group, but their allegiance has shifted to bin Laden and they now fight for his causes.

Al Qaeda merged—and continues to work—with several other extremist groups. Thus, it draws on almost three decades of terrorist expertise. Moreover, it has inherited a full-fledged training and operational infrastructure that was funded by the CIA, European countries, Saudi Arabia, the United Arab Emirates, and other governments for use in the anti-Soviet resistance. The merging of Al Qaeda with the Egyptian Islamic Jihad in 1988 greatly bolstered bin Laden's global reach and capacity. Following this expansion, the focus of Islamic jihad shifted from overthrowing the current Egyptian government to attacking U.S. interests.

A new phase of violence perpetrated by groups linked to Al Qaeda erupted following the U.S. invasion and occupation of Iraq in mid-March 2003. The subsequent bombings in Riyadh, Casablanca, and Istanbul, which targeted a residential complex, a synagogue, a Jewish center, and a British bank, demonstrated that the U.S. invasion of Iraq had failed to stem the terrorist attacks. Furthermore, the March 2004 bombing of trains in Madrid and the July 2005 bombing in London pointed to the ability of Al Qaeda to strike European targets. These attacks were apparently a reaction to the British and Spanish governments' support of U.S. occupation of Iraq.

Al Qaeda members have routinely shifted money around the world to bail prisoners out of jail in countries such as Algeria and Canada and to finance applications for political asylum to enable the planting of terrorist cells in western Europe. Evidence of Al Qaeda cells emerged in more than forty countries after the 9/11 attacks, as the United States investigated the extent of Al Qaeda's financial support structure. U.S. officials have pointed to evidence that bin Laden used a series of shops that sell honey to generate revenue, as well as to clandestinely move weapons, drugs, and agents throughout his terrorist network. U.S. officials in the past have underestimated the amount of income that Al Qaeda has generated by its involvement in the trade of diamonds, gold, uranium, and tanzanite. In Sudan in 1991 bin Laden launched several companies. One of these, the Al Shamal Isla Bank, had a complete Web site with a list of correspondent banking relationships, including institutions in New York, Geneva, Paris, and London. Bin Laden also established agricultural and construction companies.

Al Qaeda has fully exploited the tolerance and freedom of association enshrined in Western liberal democracies. Beyond its ideological penetration of Muslim communities by recruiting imams and other religious officials, Al Qaeda has created a huge network by establishing, infiltrating, and even trying to gain control of many Islamic nongovernmental organizations (NGOs). One-fifth of all Islamic NGOs worldwide, according to the CIA, have been infiltrated by Al Qaeda and other terrorist support groups. Al Qaeda and its associates as such have sought to mobilize the Islamic diaspora.

As for the dismantling of the Taliban regime, it cannot be said with confidence that Al Qaeda's infrastructure in Afghanistan has been fully destroyed and that a viable government has been established. Although Hamid Karzai, the country's president, enjoys the financial and political backing of the United States and the international community, he has yet to effectively extend his authority beyond Kabul. Many parts of the country are still ruled by tribal warlords, as was the case in the early 1990s before the Taliban took over. Moreover, Al Qaeda's chief financier (bin Laden) and key ideologue (Zawahiri) have thus far eluded capture. Instead of moving rapidly to eliminate the international network controlled by bin Laden, U.S. policy makers shifted their focus to Iraq, a country with no direct links to the tragic events of 9/11.

[See also Afghanistan; Saudi Arabia; and Terrorism.]

BIBLIOGRAPHY

Chossudovsky, Michel. *Who Is Osama Bin Laden?* Center for Research on Globalization, Montreal, September 12, 2001. http://www.globalresearch.ca/articles/CHO109C.html.

Coll, Steve. *Ghost Wars: The Secret History of the CIA, Afghanistan, and Bin Laden from the Soviet Invasion to September 10, 2001.* New York: Penguin Books, 2004.

Combs, Cindy C. *Terrorism in the Twenty-First Century.* 3d ed. Upper Saddle River, N.J.: Prentice Hall, 2003.

Feldman, Noah. *After Jihad: America and the Struggle for Islamic Democracy.* New York: Farrar, Straus and Giroux, 2003.

Gunaratna, Rohan. *Inside Al Qaeda: Global Network of Terror.* New York: Columbia University Press, 2002.

Kepel, Gilles. *The War for Muslim Minds: Islam and the West.* Cambridge, Mass.: Belknap Press of Harvard University Press, 2004.

Mamdani, Mahmood. "Inventing Political Islam," *Global Agenda* 3 (January 2005): 46–48. http://www.vicisu.com/wp-content/mamdani.pdf.

Rashid, Ahmed. "The Taliban: Exporting Extremism." *Foreign Affairs* 78 (1999): 22–35.

Robinson, Adam. *Bin Laden: Behind the Mask of the Terrorist.* New York: Arcade Publishing, 2001.

Roy, Olivier. *Globalized Islam: The Search for a New Ummah.* New York: Columbia University Press, 2004.

Rubin, Barnett R. *The Fragmentation of Afghanistan: State Formation and Collapse in the International System.* 2d ed. New Haven, Conn.: Yale University Press, 2002.

BOTSWANA AND LESOTHO

by Robert K. Hitchcock

Botswana and Lesotho in southern Africa are representative of developing nations dealing with significant human rights, health, minority, and poverty alleviation issues. Both countries were protectorates of the British from 1895 to the 1960s. Botswana was known as the Bechuanaland Protectorate and Lesotho as Basutoland. Along with Swaziland, they were termed high commission territories, and their histories are somewhat different from other countries in Africa. The two were "frontline states," in the forefront of the struggle against the apartheid ("apartness" or separate development) policies of their neighbor South Africa prior to the democratic elections and majority rule there in April 1994.

There are major cultural similarities between Botswana and Lesotho as the majorities of the populations in both countries share cultural traditions, belief systems, and language. Both Botswana and Lesotho had traditional authorities (chiefs, headmen, and headwomen) who played significant roles in dealing with societal issues ranging from enforcing customary law to overseeing land allocation. Their societies were organized along class lines, with chiefs or kings, nobles, and commoners. Botswana also had hereditary servants (*bolata*) who worked for other people for little or no pay.

The population of Botswana is ethnically diverse, with some thirty languages spoken by its residents. Its population in July 2008 was 1,842,323. Population density is relatively low in the Kalahari Desert, which makes up three-quarters of the country's land area, with most of the people found in the eastern hardveld portion of the country and around the Okavango Delta. Lesotho had a higher population than Botswana in July 2008 at 2,128,180. It is less ethnically diverse than Botswana, with five existing languages in the early twenty-first century. The majority of the population in Lesotho speaks Sesotho, a language related to Setswana, which is spoken by many Batswana (people of Botswana).

Botswana is a landlocked country in the center of southern Africa. With a total area of approximately 581,730 square kilometers (approximately 220,000 square miles), it is approximately the size of France, Kenya, or Texas. Botswana is considered by many to be a model of "development success" as measured by public participation in decision making, economic growth, income levels, and average standards of living. It is Africa's oldest parliamentary democracy, having been through half a dozen multiparty elections since its founding on 30 September 1966. According to Human Rights Watch (HRW) and the U.S. State Department's Country Reports on Human Rights, Botswana had no political prisoners and one of the best human rights records of any country on the African continent in the early twenty-first century.

Lesotho is a much smaller country, 30,355 square kilometers (about 11,720 square miles), and is also landlocked. Surrounded by South Africa, Lesotho has had to contend with the economic and political significance of its neighbor. Since the early 1900s Lesotho has been heavily dependent on the South African mining economy, with as many as 110,000 Basotho (people of Lesotho) going to work in the mines and sending remittances home to their families. As of 2007, Lesotho had a high rate of poverty, with 36.4 percent of its people living on less than $1 per day, according to the United Nations (UN) Human Development Report published that year. Development agencies and donors have invested heavily in Lesotho, trying to enhance incomes and agricultural production and reduce poverty. In general, the Lesotho government respects the rights of its citizens, although there have been cases of violations of the right to life, security, or integrity at the hands of the security forces and the police.

The populations of Botswana and Lesotho were heavily dependent on agriculture in the past, and cattle and other livestock were significant sources of subsistence, income, and to some extent social status. Drought and occasional floods are significant environmental challenges in both Botswana and Lesotho, as are outbreaks of livestock diseases, such as foot-and-mouth disease and in 1896–1897 rinderpest.

Minerals, especially diamonds, contribute to the economies of both countries. Botswana has what can be described as a mineral-led economy and in the early twenty-first century was the world's largest producer of gem diamonds. Lesotho is fortunate to have significant water resources in the Senqu and other rivers that rise in the Maluti Mountains, which dominate much of the landscape in the country. Both countries attract tourists, Botswana because of its wildlife and unique habitats, including the Okavango Delta and the Makgadikgadi Pans. Lesotho is known for its magnificent mountains, rivers, waterfalls, and picturesque villages.

Lesotho is one of the smallest countries in Africa. A significant portion of the country, some 61 percent, is mountainous, the so-called highlands, averaging between 2,100 and 3,000 meters (between 1.3 and 1.9 miles) in elevation, with some peaks in the Maluti Mountains as high as 3,482 meters (about 2.2 miles). The lowlands make up about a fifth of the country (20 percent) and are primarily on the western and northern boundary. The foothills make up 15 percent of the land area. The fourth major ecological zone, the Senqu River valley, makes up 4 percent. Of the total area of the country, 2 percent is residential.

In 1986 the governments of Lesotho and South Africa agreed to establish the Lesotho Highlands Water Project (LHWP), a large-scale physical infrastructure project that transfers water to South Africa and provides hydroelectric power to Lesotho. This project was one of the largest and most expensive of its kind undertaken in Africa in the late twentieth and early twenty-first centuries. One purpose of the LHWP is to transfer water from the headwaters of the Gariep River (the Senqu River in Lesotho) to the Vaal River catchment in South Africa and on to the commercial and industrial heartland in Gauteng. In exchange, the government of South Africa provides royalty payments to the government of Lesotho. The other purpose of the LHWP is to provide hydroelectric power to Maseru, the capital, and other towns in Lesotho.

In addition, the LHWP provided for compensation to the people affected by the works, resettlement of those households directly affected by the roads, reservoirs, and other infrastructure, and a wide variety of development programs aimed at restoring livelihoods. Some of the social, economic, and environmental impacts of the LHWP are seen as negative.

The Lesotho Highlands Development Authority and nongovernmental organizations (NGOs) working in the project area also undertook environmental rehabilitation, tree planting, and conservation programs. Efforts were made to conserve endangered species, such as the Maloti minnow (*Pseudobarbus quathlambae*), the bearded vulture (lammergeier, *Gypaetus barbarus*), and the spiral aloe (*Aloe polyphylla*). Some protected areas were established, including a new national park, Ts'ehlenyane, and an important new cultural park at Liphofung, an archaeologically significant rock shelter containing rock paintings that are likely the work of Bushmen (San) who resided in the mountains for thousands of years.

Botswana and Lesotho both have grazing resources, and livestock development has been a focus of governmental strategies in both countries. Botswana initiated a series of livestock development projects supported by the World Bank and the European Union (EU) in the 1970s through the 1990s. Lesotho's Range and Livestock Management Project, supported by the U.S. Agency for International Development (USAID), focused on communal grazing management through the establishment of local-level livestock cooperatives known as range management associations (RMAs). Lesotho embarked on large-scale integrated rural development projects that have had mixed success. Unemployment rates in the two countries differ, 39.3 percent in Lesotho and 23.8 percent in Botswana in 2007. Both countries see poverty alleviation, raising living standards, and access to development assistance as key national objectives.

MINORITY RIGHTS IN BOTSWANA

One of the most contentious human rights issues facing Botswana relates to the treatment of minority groups, particularly the Basarwa, also known as the San or Bushmen. Basarwa, who number approximately fifty thousand in the country, are historically disadvantaged.

The majority of Basarwa live in rural areas, although some reside in the towns and cities of Botswana. Many Basarwa are poor, living on less than $1 per day. Some Basarwa lack access to land, and unemployment levels among them are high. They are sometimes arrested and detained for hunting illegally in Botswana, and in several cases the detainees have been allegedly mistreated by police, game scouts, or members of the Botswana Defence Force (BDF). Basarwa in many ways are on the lowest rung of a several-tiered socioeconomic system in Botswana.

Basarwa see themselves as indigenous peoples, and as such, they believe that they should have the same rights as other indigenous peoples around the world. The Botswana government, on the other hand, takes the position that all citizens of the country are indigenous. The Botswana government is not a signatory to the Indigenous and

Tribal Peoples Convention, No. 169, of the International Labour Organization (ILO), but it did sign the UN Declaration on the Rights of Indigenous Peoples on 13 September 2007.

The government of Botswana announced in 1986 that people residing in the Central Kalahari Game Reserve, the largest protected area in the country, would be encouraged to leave the reserve and take up residence in government-sponsored settlements, where they would be provided with water and development assistance. The residents of the Central Kalahari brought legal action against the government of Botswana in the High Court in 2002, but the case was dismissed. The dismissal was appealed, and a new trial began in 2004. On 13 December 2006 the High Court ruled in favor of the Basarwa and Bakgalagadi residents of the reserve, asserting that they had the right to return to the Central Kalahari and that their rights to subsistence hunting should be recognized.

Botswana has one of the most successful formal education systems in Africa, claiming universal basic education of up to ten years. It has also invested a great deal of resources in providing children in remote areas with the opportunity to attend government schools to at least the fourth (or standard) grade. However, there are indications that minority children do not reap the same benefits as do other children in the country. Minority students have a lower rate of attendance and drop out much more often than students from other groups. There are particular problems in schools with boarding facilities, the so-called remote area dweller (RAD) hostels, where Basarwa children are sometimes exposed to corporal punishment and other forms of mistreatment. Basarwa parents have also raised the question of how useful education is in terms of long-term employment. In some ways, they argue, education may create a desire for more jobs that the state and the private sector cannot provide, thus increasing relative poverty and dissatisfaction.

A serious educational obstacle for Basarwa and other linguistic minority students is the Botswana government's language policy. An important part of Botswana's state-building strategy after its independence in 1966 rested on the identification of all of its citizens with the Batswana ethnic identity. The building of this national identity relied heavily on the promotion of Setswana as the primary language of its citizens. Accordingly, the first years of school are taught in Setswana before switching to English as the medium of instruction. No provision exists for mother tongue primary education for minority-language children. They must begin primary school in a foreign language (Setswana) and then transition to another (English) before they have even mastered the first one. As a result, some minority children face difficulties in school. For this reason, Basarwa and other minority groups would like to see the Botswana government change its educational and language policies.

HEALTH AND HUMAN RIGHTS IN BOTSWANA AND LESOTHO

The governments and civil societies in both Botswana and Lesotho face significant social, economic, and health issues, including HIV/AIDS. HIV (human immunodeficiency virus) is the cause of AIDS (acquired immunodeficiency syndrome). In Botswana and Lesotho, the transmission of HIV occurs primarily through heterosexual sex, although cases have been reported in which individuals became infected through the use of infected needles. The treatment of HIV/AIDS involves the application of highly active antiretroviral therapies that help suppress the virus and therefore enable affected people to live longer, healthier lives. The drugs used to treat HIV tend to work more effectively when they are combined in "cocktails," which in essence are mixtures of these drugs. Antiretroviral drugs (ARVs) have reduced HIV-related morbidity (illness) and mortality in Botswana and Lesotho dramatically. There is a danger, however, that the use of these drugs could lead to the evolution of drug-resistant strains of HIV.

In the early twenty-first century the two countries were stretched to the limit in attempting to cope with the HIV/AIDS epidemic. The disease affected people at highly productive ages (roughly eighteen to forty-four) and caused large numbers of deaths. In 2006 Botswana had an estimated 350,000 people who were HIV-positive, and Lesotho had 320,000. Life expectancy in Botswana declined considerably, from sixty-five years to forty-seven.

Both countries put in place AIDS prevention and treatment programs in the early 2000s, and they made considerable investments in the health sector to curb the spread of HIV. In the past, mortality rates were considerable, but the availability of ARVs and food distribution programs in the two countries have brought down the death rates.

The social impacts of the HIV/AIDS crisis in Botswana and Lesotho are staggering. Cemeteries are filled to overflowing, and the time allotted to funerals in some places is fifteen minutes, compared with the previous several-day period. As some Batswana and Basotho have pointed out, more funds are invested in the dead and dying than in the living, in part because of the stigma attached to AIDS. People do not want to admit that they have a relative, a father, a mother, a son, a daughter with the virus because it is seen as a death warrant. The fortunes of entire families have been drained both because of their attempts to pay for those who are ill and because of their efforts to cope with the expenses of funerals and burials for relatives.

An estimated ten thousand traditional medical practitioners (traditional healers) play a role in meeting the needs of the populations in both urban and rural areas in Botswana and Lesotho. Traditional healers provide more than 50 percent of the countries' medical consultations. These healers help people in a number of ways, not least through the provision of counseling. They offer herbal and other kinds of medicines, although none of these traditional medicines have been found to cure AIDS, in spite of the claims of some healers. Training of traditional healers on HIV/AIDS prevention and care is provided by NGOs in both countries.

Botswana and Lesotho struggled to get a handle on the scale of the AIDS epidemic and to make ARV treatment available to those most in need. These two countries, like Brazil, offer universal access to ARV treatment. The escalating cost of drugs, however, poses an enormous challenge, especially for the poor.

Both the Botswana and the Lesotho governments are fully aware of the need to address the deadly combination of poverty and HIV/AIDS. If Botswana and Lesotho are to sustain themselves and their populations in the face of the HIV/AIDS crisis, they will not only have to deal with the disease itself but also address issues of food insecurity and equitable access to clean water. In the absence of a large-scale expansion of prevention, treatment, and care efforts, the AIDS death toll will rise.

COPING WITH THE HIV/AIDS CRISIS IN BOTSWANA

Princess Marina Hospital in Gaborone, the capital of Botswana, is the largest care provider for people with HIV/AIDS. It is a study in contrasts. One the one hand, the AIDS wards were filled to overflowing in the early twenty-first century. On the other hand, its gleaming new laboratories were filled with recently purchased equipment for testing samples and the development of drugs.

As of 2006, Botswana had one of the highest HIV/AIDS prevalence rates in the world, second only to Swaziland. There were an estimated 120,000 AIDS orphans in

the country that same year, according to the United Nations Children's Fund.

A visible sign of the AIDS epidemic in Botswana is the large number of women dressed in mourning for their late husbands. Another sign is the significant expansion of programs aimed at helping AIDS orphans and people suffering from HIV/AIDS. Government officials said that there were over ninety NGOs in Botswana working on HIV/AIDS-related issues in 2008, compared with about thirty in Lesotho.

HIV/AIDS has exacerbated social and economic problems in Botswana, and as a result, enormous expenditures of resources have been devoted to prevention, treatment, and care. A National AIDS Orphans Program was established in 1999 with funds made available in the form of a "food basket" for orphans along with funds to pay for school fees, transportation, and school uniforms. Unlike most other African countries, the number of orphans in school in Botswana is approximately the same as that of other children.

Botswana was the first African country to pledge the provision of ARVs to all its citizens in need of them. The constraints faced in achieving this goal, however, are considerable. A sizable proportion of Botswana's population resides in rural areas, some quite remote. Over half of the country's population (51.2 percent) lives on less than $2 per day. In the past relatively few people could afford much in the way of medical assistance. Although the rollout of ARVs in Botswana has been impressive, in the early twenty-first century there remained areas where people lacked access to the drugs and segments of society with lower ARV coverage than others.

The first AIDS case in Botswana was diagnosed in 1985. The government responded relatively quickly. Botswana passed an official AIDS policy in 1993 and in 1999 established the National AIDS Coordinating Agency (NACA), which works under the National AIDS Council chaired by the president of Botswana. The government has developed a multisectoral set of responses to HIV/AIDS.

Botswana has received considerable support from donors to assist the country in coping with HIV/AIDS. As of 2008, the country was involved in the African Comprehensive HIV/AIDS Partnerships (ACHAP), which also includes the Bill and Melinda Gates Foundation and the Merck Company Foundation. The Centers for Disease Control and Prevention (CDC) of the United States and the Botswana government collaborated on a research and development program called the BOTUSA Project that became part of the U.S.-funded President's Emergency

Plan for AIDS Relief (PEPFAR). This program was funded at $15 billion and slated for expansion to $50 billion. In the early twenty-first century some 1.5 million people in Africa, the Caribbean, and Vietnam received ARVs and other assistance under PEPFAR.

One of the human rights issues relating to PEPFAR is its emphasis on the use of mainstream (and expensive) ARVs as opposed to much cheaper generic drugs. A second issue is the program's stipulation that drugs must be disseminated by licensed pharmacists, only a few of whom may be found in rural areas in Botswana and Lesotho.

Another human rights issue relates to equity in access to health assistance, including access to medicines and health care. In Botswana some segments of society, especially those minority populations residing in remote areas, have lower access to high-quality medical care than do better-off people in urban areas. Even in those settlements where health facilities are provided, such as the remote area dweller settlements in the Ghanzi, North west, Kweneng, Southern, Central, and Kgalagadi districts, doctors and nurses are rare, and medicines are often unavailable to patients.

It is interesting to note that the Basarwa of Botswana appear to have much lower HIV/AIDS prevalence rates than do other populations in the country. Part of the reason is the fact that they reside in remote areas and have had less exposure to HIV/AIDS. Another reason, according to some of the NGOs working with Basarwa, is that they have had the opportunity to take part in AIDS awareness programs.

In some remote area communities, notably New Xade in the Ghanzi district and Kaudwane in the Kweneng district, HIV/AIDS rates are increasing rapidly. Basarwa complain that they do not have sufficient access to ARVs and health services. They have also asserted that women and girls must cope with sexual exploitation by teachers and government workers in schools within the settlements, which has contributed to high dropout rates among girls. Girls have also dropped out of school because of pregnancy. In addition, according to remote area settlement residents and NGO spokespersons, AIDS education programs are limited, with more emphasis placed on abstinence programs as opposed to the use of condoms and behavior modification as preventive measures.

Although women's rights have been officially recognized in Botswana, there were still significant challenges to overcome in the early twenty-first century. Greater numbers of women than men were infected with HIV, similar to the situations in Lesotho and other countries in southern Africa. Women in Botswana continued to face constraints on access to employment, credit, and education. Women whose husbands had died sometimes ended up in poverty because they did not have the same inheritance rights as their male children. Some poverty-stricken women had to exchange sex for survival, exposing them to HIV. Women in some cases believed that they lacked the right to say no to sex and to insist that their husbands or partners use condoms. In 2006 and 2007 discrimination, prejudice, and violence were realities for women and people with HIV not just in Botswana but throughout sub-Saharan Africa.

Health is a human right, according to Botswana AIDS activists and to the Botswana Centre for Human Rights. Without equitable access to HIV/AIDS education, treatment, and care, women, children, minorities, and the poor in Botswana will continue to be denied a core human right that is crucial to their survival.

COPING WITH THE HIV/AIDS CRISIS IN LESOTHO

Lesotho's history is different from that of Botswana in part because it is ruled by a king and considered a constitutional parliamentary monarchy. The country has had periods of autocratic rule, including military rule occurring as a result of a military coup in 1986 and lasting until 1993. It has also experienced military interventions by other countries, notably South Africa and Botswana, which entered Lesotho in October 1998 to stop the rioting that occurred after a contested election.

Lesotho is poorer than Botswana, with high levels of poverty particularly evident in remote mountain areas and in households on the peripheries of towns in the early twenty-first century. The majority of the population is agropastoral, living on a combination of agricultural and livestock production along with wage labor. Because of recent changes in the South African economy, the numbers of migrant miners recruited from countries outside of South Africa, including Lesotho, decreased substantially, lowering the cash flows through remittances to households in Lesotho.

In 2006 there were ninety-seven thousand AIDS orphans in Lesotho. Concerned about the situations facing orphans and children with no visible means of support, the government of Lesotho developed an orphaned and vulnerable children's policy. Lesotho's Labor Code Amendment Act of 2006 provided for the implementation of HIV/AIDS policies in the workplace, and private companies developed AIDS policies.

In 2006 Lesotho's life expectancy was lower than that of Botswana and its population growth was -0.046 percent. The government established the National AIDS Commission in August 2005, and on 1 December 2005, World AIDS Day, King Letsie launched a Know Your Status campaign, an ambitious voluntary testing campaign. People who have HIV or AIDS suffer considerable stigma, and there thus is a reluctance to make one's status known publicly. Knowing one's status, however, can enable individuals to modify their behavior to protect other people, including sexual partners.

Like Botswana, Lesotho developed a National HIV and AIDS Strategic Plan and a national AIDS policy. The government of Lesotho and NGOs working in the country pioneered innovative approaches to HIV/AIDS, such as the effort to focus HIV/AIDS awareness programs in high transmission areas, including places along borders where truckers, traders, taxi and bus drivers, police, military personnel, migrant laborers, and transient sex workers tend to congregate. Efforts were also made to implement HIV/AIDS prevention and awareness programs in such places as the Lesotho highlands, where the LHWP was ongoing, and in textile factories that employ a considerable number of Basotho, many of them women.

It is important to note that the implementation of the LHWP may have contributed to the increase in HIV/AIDS prevalence in the highlands. Whereas the HIV prevalence rate in the highlands was about 0.5 percent in 1988, it was estimated to be 23.9 percent in 2007, according to the Human Sciences Research Council. It is possible that the substantial increase in HIV prevalence resulted, in part, from the huge influx of construction workers from outside the highlands, some of whom had sexual contact with local people.

Lesotho has not had as much success as Botswana in the distribution of ARVs, with a coverage rate of only 14 percent in 2005. The Lesotho government, the United Nations, NGOs, and the private sector have ramped up their activities aimed at making ARVs more widely available. Lesotho has also endeavored to ensure the availability of food, vitamins, and nutritional supplements for people with HIV/AIDS.

Poverty affects the success of HIV/AIDS programs. Lesotho is one of the poorest countries in Africa, and it is characterized by extreme inequality in income distribution. As in other parts of the world, wealthier people, many of them in urban areas, tend to have greater access to HIV/AIDS prevention, treatment, care, and support programs than do the poor. Some NGOs and faith-based organizations in Lesotho continue to pressure the government to increase the availability of AIDS prevention and treatment programs. If Lesotho is to cope with the HIV/AIDS epidemic, it must address not only health issues but also socioeconomic inequality.

ASSESSMENT

In 2008 there were an estimated 224,000 AIDS orphans in Botswana and Lesotho, many of whom lacked relatives and friends to help them. Sometimes termed "orphans of the storm," AIDS orphans face difficult circumstances. Many roam the streets of cities like Maseru, Lesotho, and Gaborone and Francistown, Botswana. They try to eke out a living but face victimization, including sexual exploitation, by adults and occasionally by law enforcement personnel. These children are among the least likely individuals to have access to information on HIV prevention, sex education, and AIDS drugs formulated specifically for the needs of children. Women, children, and the poor tend to fall between the cracks and are not always in a position to get HIV/AIDS information and treatment.

At a high-level UN meeting on HIV/AIDS in 2006, government leaders stated, "The full realization of all human rights and fundamental freedoms for all is an essential element in the global response to the HIV/AIDS epidemic" (International Consultation on HIV/AIDS and Human Rights). The Office of the High Commissioner for Human Rights and the Joint United Nations Programme on HIV/AIDS (UNAIDS) issued the International Guidelines on HIV/AIDS and Human Rights in 1998, with a revision and additional guidelines in 2002. The first guideline proclaims, "States should establish an effective national framework for their response to HIV which ensures a coordinated, participatory, transparent and accountable approach, integrating HIV policy and programme responsibilities across all branches of government." Guideline 6 asserts, "States should enact legislation to provide for the regulation of HIV-related goods, services and information, so as to ensure widespread availability of quality prevention measures and services, adequate HIV prevention and care information, and safe and effective medication at an affordable price" (International Consultation on HIV/AIDS and Human Rights).

In the early twenty-first century plans developed to boost HIV/AIDS prevention and treatment programs in Botswana and Lesotho, but there were still many obstacles to overcome, according to AIDS activists, human rights organizations, and scientists. More funding and greater efforts to improve the health and delivery systems are required as well as more effective measurements of the number of people infected with HIV. Although the methods to estimate HIV prevalence have improved substantially over time, population-wide surveys indicate that prenatal clinics, which in the past were the major source of information on HIV prevalence rates, may overestimate HIV infection rates by about 20 percent. Greater efforts have to be made to provide more accurate estimates of the HIV/AIDS situation.

HIV/AIDS counseling and testing are a human rights issue throughout Africa. In 2004 Botswana initiated a policy in which everyone who visited a clinic or health post would be offered an HIV test. Individuals had the right to opt out of the test if they so chose. As M. J. Heywood points out, "Although the offer of an HIV test does not in and of itself violate the established principles of informed consent, it does shift the onus of requesting the test from the patient to the provider" (p. 13). This approach raises some fundamental questions about informed consent, access to counseling and HIV/AIDS information, and the rights of individuals to make decisions on their own. As Heywood puts it, the arguments about HIV testing "artificially pits a person's right to autonomy against his or her right to health and well-being—as if the two can be separated" (p. 16). There are also fears that HIV and other diseases such as malaria are interacting to exacerbate the AIDS crisis and are fueling the spread of both HIV and malaria.

HIV/AIDS and other human rights issues in Botswana and Lesotho can be addressed adequately if as much money, energy, and technical knowledge are invested in efforts to cope with health and economic problems as in the global arms race. By law health care is available broadly to the populations of the two countries, but there are constraints on delivery and, in Lesotho, financial resources and government ministry capacity. In Botswana, with a good record on political rights in particular, serious human rights issues remain, especially in regard to HIV/AIDS. According to human rights organizations and AIDS activists in Botswana and Lesotho, it is time to turn the tide. As one young AIDS orphan in Botswana said, "This can happen only if our governments and societies have the political will to do so."

[*See also* AIDS/HIV *and* Right to Health and Health Care.]

BIBLIOGRAPHY

Abu-Raddad, Laith J., Padjama Patnaik, and James G. Kublin. "Dual Infection with HIV and Malaria Fuels the Spread of Both Diseases in Sub-Saharan Africa." *Science* 314 (2006): 1603–1606.

Barnett, Tony, and Alan Whiteside. *AIDS in the Twenty-first Century: Disease and Globalization.* New York: Palgrave Macmillan, 2002.

Botswana Rural Development Coordination Division. *Study of Poverty and Poverty Alleviation in Botswana (Phase One).* Vol. 1: *Overall Poverty Assessment.* Gaborone, Botswana: Rural Development Coordination Division, 1997.

Chakela, Q. K., ed. *State of the Environment in Lesotho 1997.* Maseru, Lesotho: National Environment Secretariat, Ministry of Environment, Gender, and Youth Affairs, 1997.

Ditshwanelo. *Conference on HIV/AIDS, the Law, and Human Rights: 7th December, 1999.* Gaborone, Botswana: Ditshwanelo, 2000.

Ellenberger, D. Fred, and J. C. Macgregor. *History of the Basuto, Ancient and Modern.* London: Caxton, 1912.

Ferguson, James. *The Anti-Politics Machine: "Development," Depoliticization, and Bureaucratic Power in Lesotho.* Minneapolis: University of Minnesota Press, 1994.

Gay, John, and David Hall. *Poverty and Livelihoods in Lesotho, 2000: More Than a Mapping Exercise.* Maseru, Lesotho: Sechaba Consultants, 2000.

Hamnett, Ian. *Chieftainship and Legitimacy: An Anthropological Study of Executive Law in Lesotho.* London: Routledge and Kegan Paul, 1975.

Heywood, M. J. "The Routine Offer of HIV Counseling and Testing: A Human Right." *Health and Human Rights* 8, no. 2 (2005): 13–19.

Hitchcock, Robert K. *Field notes,* Mogapelwa, Botswana, July 16, 2005.

Holm, John D., and Patrick Molutsi, eds. *Democracy in Botswana.* Gaborone: Botswana Society and Athens: Ohio University Press, 1989.

Horta, Korinna. "The Mountain Kingdom's White Oil: The Lesotho Highlands Water Project." *Ecologist* 25, no. 6 (1995): 227–231.

Human Sciences Research Council. *Main Report: Findings from the 2005/2006 Monitoring and Evaluation Survey Conducted in the Phase 1A and 1B Project Areas of the LHWP: Mohale, Katse, 'Muela, and Matsoku.* Pretoria, South Africa: Human Sciences Research Council; Maseru: Lesotho Highlands Development Authority, 2007.

Iliffe, John. *The African AIDS Epidemic.* Athens: Ohio University Press, 2006.

International Consultation on HIV/AIDS and Human Rights. *International Guidelines on HIV/AIDS and Human Rights.* Geneva, Switzerland: UNAIDS, 2006. http://www2.ohchr.org/english/issues/hiv/guidelines.htm.

Joint United Nations Programme on HIV/AIDS (UNAIDS). *Botswana: Country Situation Analysis.* Geneva, Switzerland: UNAIDS, 2006.

Joint United Nations Programme on HIV/AIDS. *Lesotho: Country Situation Analysis.* Geneva, Switzerland: UNAIDS, 2006.

Joint United Nations Programme on HIV/AIDS. *Report on the Global AIDS Epidemic.* Geneva, Switzerland: UNAIDS, 2006.

Joint United Nations Programme on HIV/AIDS. *Report on the Global AIDS Epidemic.* Geneva, Switzerland: UNAIDS, 2007.

Klaits, Frederick. "The Widow in Blue: Blood and the Morality of Remembering in Botswana's Time of AIDS." *Africa* 75, no. 1 (2005): 46–62.

Lee, Richard B., and Ida Susser. "Confounding Conventional Wisdom: The Ju'hoansi and HIV/AIDS." In *Updating the San: Image and Reality of an African People in the 21st Century,* edited by Robert K. Hitchcock, Kazunobu Ikeya, Megan Biesele, and Richard B. Lee, pp. 45–60. Senri Ethnological Studies no. 70. Osaka, Japan: National Museum of Ethnology, 2006.

Leith, J. Clark. *Why Botswana Prospered.* Montreal: McGill-Queens University Press, 2005.

Lye, William F., and Colin Murray. *Transformations on the Highveld: The Tswana and the Southern Sotho.* Cape Town, South Africa, and London: David Philip, 1980.

Measure Evaluation Project, Tulane University, and Sechaba Consultants. *Priorities for Local AIDS Control Efforts (PLACE) for Use in Border Areas of Lesotho and South Africa.* Maseru, Lesotho, and Tshwane, South Africa: U.S. Agency for International Development Regional AIDS Project for Southern Africa, 2005.

Mogwe, Alice. *Who Was (T)here First? An Assessment of the Human Rights Situation of Basarwa in Selected Communities in the Gantsi District, Botswana.* Gaborone: Botswana Christian Council, 1992.

Murray, Colin. *Families Divided: The Impact of Migrant Labour in Lesotho.* Johannesburg, South Africa: Ravan and Cambridge, U.K.: Cambridge University Press, 1981.

Physicians for Human Rights. *Epidemic of Inequality: Women's Rights and HIV/AIDS in Botswana and Swaziland.* Cambridge, Mass.: Physicians for Human Rights, 2007.

Schapera, Isaac. *A Handbook of Tswana Law and Custom.* London: Frank Cass, 1938.

Schapera, Isaac. *Tribal Innovators: Tswana Chiefs and Social Change 1795–1940.* London: Athlone, 1970.

Schapera, Isaac. *The Tswana.* London: International African Institute, 1953.

Sheddick, Vernon George John. *The Southern Sotho.* London: International African Institute, 1953.

Tarantola, Daniel. "HIV Testing: Breaking the Deadly Cycle." *Health and Human Rights* 8, no. 2 (2005): 37–42.

Thamae, Mabusetsa Lenka, and Lori Pottinger, eds. *On the Wrong Side of Development: Lessons Learned from the Lesotho Highlands Water Project.* Maseru, Lesotho: Transformation Resource Centre, 2006.

United Nations Children's Fund. *State of the World's Children 2008: Child Survival.* New York: United Nations Children's Fund, 2008.

United Nations Development Programme (UNDP). *Human Development Report 2007/2008.* New York: UNDP, 2007.

Urdang, Stephanie. "The Care Economy: Gender and the Silent AIDS Crisis in Southern Africa." *Journal of Southern African Studies* 32, no. 1 (2006): 165–177.

World Bank. *Lesotho Poverty Assessment.* Report no. 13171 LS. Washington, D.C.: Population and Human Resources Division, Southern Africa Department, Africa Regional Office, World Bank, 1994.

Wright, John B. *Bushman Raiders of the Drakensberg, 1840–1870.* Pietermaritzburg, South Africa: University of Natal Press, 1971.

Wright, John B., and Aron Mazel. *Tracks in a Mountain Range: Exploring the History of the Ukhahlamba-Drakensberg.* Johannesburg, South Africa: Witwatersrand University Press, 2007.

Zungu-Dirwayi, Nompumelelo, Olive Shisana, Eric Odjo, Thaang Mosala, and John Seager. *An Audit of HIV/AIDS Policies in Botswana, Lesotho, Mozambique, South Africa, Swaziland, and Zimbabwe.* Cape Town, South Africa: Human Sciences Research Council Publications, 2004.

BOUTROS BOUTROS-GHALI

Anthony F. Lang Jr.

Boutros Boutros-Ghali, best known for serving as secretary-general of the United Nations from 1992 through 1996, played an important role in the way the United Nations addressed human rights in the immediate post–Cold War period. As an international legal scholar, he came to the office with already developed ideas about human rights and the role of the state and international organizations in promoting those rights. His intellectual and personal background also played a key role in his efforts to promote development and democracy as human rights issues.

PERSONAL BACKGROUND

Boutros Boutros-Ghali was born on 14 November 1922 in Cairo, Egypt. He was raised in a wealthy Coptic Christian family that had a distinguished reputation in Egyptian politics; his grandfather was the first Christian prime minister of Egypt, and one of his uncles served as a foreign minister. He received his Ph.D. in international law from the Sorbonne in 1949 and was then appointed a professor of international law at Cairo University, a position he held until 1977. In that year, he was asked by the Egyptian president Anwar Sadat to serve in his cabinet, eventually accompanying Sadat to Jerusalem and playing a key role in the negotiations that led to peace between Egypt and Israel. He served in the Egyptian Foreign Ministry in different contexts, although never as foreign minister; according to Boutros-Ghali in *Egypt's Road to Jerusalem*, this was because the majority Muslim political establishment would not accept a Christian in such a key post.

After Sadat was assassinated in 1981, Boutros-Ghali continued to serve as an adviser to the new president, Hosni Mubarak, on foreign affairs. He focused his attention on defending Egyptian interests in Arab and African diplomatic circles, particularly in response to claims that Egypt had sold out the Arab world in its peace treaty with Israel. A number of African leaders suggested that he place himself forward as a candidate for the position of secretary-general of the United Nations in 1991. After receiving the approval of Mubarak, Boutros-Ghali actively canvassed for the position, relying primarily on the French to support him, while also courting the other permanent members of the Security Council. He was elected in 1991 and took office on 1 January 1992. Unlike every other secretary-general, Boutros-Ghali served only one term, ending his tenure in 1996. He wished to continue in office, but believed (and most would agree) that he was forced from office by his disagreements with the American administration of Bill Clinton.

Once he left office, Boutros-Ghali took on the position of secretary-general of La Francophonie, the international organization sponsored by the French government that seeks to promote the French language and culture throughout the world. Serving in that position from 1997 through 2002, Boutros-Ghali sought to invigorate the association through engaging more directly in political affairs. He then served for three years (2003–2006) as chairman of the South Centre, an NGO devoted to the advancement of the development and rights of states traditionally considered a part of the developing world. He was also appointed chairman of the National Council of Human Rights in Egypt in 2003, a position he still occupied in 2008. This organization has come under criticism for being an attempt by the Egyptian government to mollify critics without making any substantive changes in its politics. As of 2008, he was active in both Egyptian political affairs and international legal circles.

HUMAN RIGHTS IN THE UNITED NATIONS, 1992–1996

As secretary-general in the immediate post–Cold War period, Boutros-Ghali played an important role in the way the United Nations conceptualized and promoted human rights through its institutional structure. In 1993 the World Conference on Human Rights was held in Vienna. It had been planned before Boutros-Ghali came to office, which meant his role in the conference was somewhat limited. His most important contribution was delivering an opening address that captured the centrality of human rights for the new world order. In that speech, he presented a more scholarly analysis of human rights, arguing that they bring us "face to face with the most challenging dialectical conflict ever: between 'identity' and 'otherness.'" This idea, more commonly found in philosophical pieces, suggests that human rights forces us to consider how our identities as members of particular groups—cultures, states, religious traditions—must be placed alongside our identities as members of the human race with certain shared qualities that demand protection. In other words, the universality of human rights does not always sit easily with particularistic locations in specific contexts. But while this dialectic is admittedly a challenge, Boutros-Ghali believed that human rights are fundamental to the international system. As he stated quite clearly, "Human rights are, by definition, the ultimate norm of all politics" (*Papers*, vol. 1, pp. 673–674).

The conference produced a plan of action that included the creation of a new position—office of high commissioner for human rights. According to Boutros-Ghali, the idea for such a position was first proposed to him by representatives of the Carter Center in Atlanta prior to the conference. At that meeting, Boutros-Ghali argued against creating such a position. As he wrote in his memoirs,

> This might simply create one more big bureaucracy, I said. I was having a hard enough time dealing with the United Nations' new human rights center in Geneva. Moreover, the effort to "coordinate" would be regarded as an attempt to consolidate pressure against countries of the third world, and that would only strengthen their resistance to progress in human rights. The very title "high commissioner" was a vestige of British colonialism and should be abandoned.
>
> (*Unvanquished*, p. 167)

Despite these concerns, the General Assembly did approve the recommendations of the conference, including the creation of a new position of high commissioner for human rights. Boutros-Ghali appointed José Ayala Lasso, an Ecuadorian diplomat, to the position in 1994, who established the office through his active campaigning around the world.

Boutros-Ghali's skepticism about this office reflected his concerns about the clash between quiet diplomacy and vocal advocacy for human rights. He relates in his memoirs the story of the Chinese dissident Shen Tong, who had been invited to address the United Nations Correspondents Association. When the Chinese delegation discovered this, they protested vigorously, and Boutros-Ghali refused to allow Shen Tong to speak there. He argued that it was more important to retain the integrity of the United Nations Secretariat, its impartiality, than to offend one of the member states. His decision was roundly condemned by advocates and politicians who saw it as a violation of free speech and human rights more broadly.

THE AGENDA DOCUMENTS

As a scholar, Boutros-Ghali came to office with ideas about human rights and politics more generally. Some of these ideas appeared in the three agenda documents he wrote while in office. None of them addressed human rights specifically, but they all touched on it in important ways.

When he first took office, the new secretary-general was asked by the Security Council to develop new thinking on peacekeeping. This he did in his seminal document *An Agenda for Peace*. This paper became influential for a fundamental rethinking of humanitarian intervention, but it was not focused directly on human rights. Boutros-Ghali revisited the ideas in this paper in his *Supplement to an Agenda for Peace*, which was issued in January 1995. In that follow-up document, he noted that the breakdown of political order in states subject to intervention demands that the United Nations play a greater role in protecting human rights through the coordination of police and criminal justice procedures.

His next two agenda documents, however, addressed human rights more directly. In *An Agenda for Development*, he boldly stated, "Development is a fundamental human right" (*Amicorum*, vol. 2, p. 1528). While the agenda document does not explore this assertion in any depth, it seems to be more than simply boilerplate rhetoric. Boutros-Ghali, drawing on his experience as a minister from a developing country, had understood development to be something central to the rights of individuals. For him, development was more than simply economic wealth, although the agenda document is devoted to the centrality of economic welfare for the betterment of the human condition. He begins by emphasizing the role of peace in development, turns to economics, but then explores the centrality of sustainability for the success of any development scheme. Finally, he concludes the text by emphasizing the centrality of democracy for development, a point that leads him naturally to the final agenda document.

His final agenda document, *An Agenda for Democratisation*, did not arise from the same set of requests that produced the other two agendas. In 1994 the General Assembly requested from the secretary-general a document on how to support emerging democracies. Drawing on a recent speech he had given, Boutros-Ghali presented a third agenda document, one that some of his colleagues believed went beyond the mandate of the General Assembly request. While he emphasized that the report was about democratization and not about democracy per se, he made a strong case that democracy was essential to the realization of human rights.

THE STATE AND HUMAN RIGHTS

Boutros-Ghali's background as an international lawyer fundamentally shaped his approach to human rights issues. Although he remained a strong advocate of rights throughout his tenure and after leaving the United Nations, Boutros-Ghali believed that rights could only truly be obtained within the state. This put him at odds with those who believed in a more global or cosmopolitan approach to the human rights agenda. Some of his early writing in international law demonstrates a concern with protecting sovereignty as the means to keep the state system egalitarian, as when he argues that the international legal system is premised on protecting the de jure equality of states, especially through their participation in international organizations. For Boutros-Ghali, the importance of the state was even a moral principle. In meeting Pope John Paul II, he noted that the pope supported his view that "the rights of nations, which like human rights, are derived from a universal moral law" (*Unvanquished*, p. 253).

In dealing with the conflict in the Balkans, he made clear that the state was the best institution for protecting the rights of individuals. In his opening statement to the London Conference in 1992, at which the European Union and United Nations sought to develop an approach to the problem, he argued that human rights in this context could best be protected through nation-state structures. While recognizing that Yugoslavia no longer existed, he maintained that the new states must "possess all the rights and duties held by their fellow-states in the international community." He argued that each ethnic group within Bosnia-Herzegovina should not be allowed to create its own nation-state, for this would result in

endless fragmentation. Instead, returning to an issue that he learned from his experience as a minority in Egypt, he argued for the importance of protection of minority rights:

> One requirement for solutions to these problems lies in commitment to human rights with a special sensitivity to those of minorities, whether ethnic, religious, social, or linguistic. The General Assembly will soon have before it a declaration on the rights of minorities. That instrument, together with the increasingly effective machinery of the United Nations dealing with human rights, should enhance the situation of minorities as well as the stability of States. One approach to the solution of this crisis should include a special appeal to the leaders of all religious denominations. In them is enshrined the moral and spiritual responsibility to defend and uphold the dignity and life of each human life regardless of creed. (*Papers*, vol. 1, p. 231)

Boutros-Ghali's attempt to orient the conference toward a regime that would focus on the protection of minorities was, ultimately, not the course of action pursued by the international community. Instead, Bosnia was eventually broken into "entities" that have not been able to resolve their differences to this day.

Clearly, Boutros-Ghali did not object to the United Nations playing a key role in the promotion of and protection of human rights; David Forsythe notes that he was more aggressive in pursuing this agenda in the United Nations than some of his predecessors (*Human Rights*, pp. 67–68). At the same time, his foundation in an international legal tradition that privileged the state over international organizations led him to emphasize the centrality of the state for the protection of human rights.

PEACE AND HUMAN RIGHTS

Boutros-Ghali stressed in both his written work and his activities in the United Nations that his primary goal was peace. This goal, at times, created conflict with the protection of human rights. This tension is not unique to Boutros-Ghali, but has long been a struggle for activists from the conflict resolution and human rights communities; the former believes that bringing opposing sides to a reconciliation should be the primary emphasis, while the latter believes that the protection of human rights is central.

For Boutros-Ghali, reconciliation and peace came first. In reflecting upon his contribution to various attempts at postconflict reconciliation—a focus of much of his tenure as secretary-general—Boutros-Ghali stated that "forgiveness is often more important than justice" (Lang, p. 269). He cited South Africa and El Salvador as places where truth commissions demonstrated that reconciliation was more important than "punishing criminals." As he noted, "the pursuit of justice can create new conflicts," leading him to conclude that reconciliation must be part of any peacemaking process (Lang, p. 270). He also emphasized, however, that each community will engage in the process of reconciliation in different ways. Citing his involvement in El Salvador, Boutros-Ghali noted that every community needs to find the proper balance between reconciliation, peace, and justice.

Boutros-Ghali's record at the United Nations most certainly had its flaws; the genocide in Rwanda and the chaos over peacekeeping in the Balkans will always be seen as black marks on his record. His attitude toward human rights, which emphasized the state and peace, might give the impression that he was less concerned with rights than others, particularly advocates who sought to push the United Nations toward greater activism. At the same time, his ideas as expressed in the agenda documents sought to locate human rights more widely through the political system. Whether or not the United Nations and the secretary-general can actively promote and protect human rights remains a challenge beyond the work of this one individual.

[See also Balkan Wars; La Francophonie; Rwanda; and United Nations High Commissioner for Human Rights.]

BIBLIOGRAPHY

Boutros-Ghali, Boutros. Amicorum Discipulorumque Liber: Peace, Development, Democracy. 2 vols. Brussels: Bruylant, 1998.

Boutros-Ghali, Boutros. Egypt's Road to Jerusalem: A Diplomat's Story of the Struggle for Peace in the Middle East. New York: Random House, 1997.

Boutros-Ghali, Boutros. En attendant la prochaine lune: Carnets 1997–2002. Paris: Fayard, 2004.

Boutros-Ghali, Boutros. Le principe d'égalité des états et les organisations internationales. Paris: Leydes, 1960.

Boutros-Ghali, Boutros. The Papers of United Nations Secretary-General Boutros Boutros-Ghali. Edited by Charles Hill. 3 vols. New Haven, Conn.: Yale University Press, 2003.

Boutros-Ghali, Boutros. Unvanquished: A U.S.-U.N. Saga. New York: Random House, 1999.

Forsythe, David P. Human Rights in International Relations. 2d ed. Cambridge, U.K., and New York: Cambridge University Press, 2006.

Lang, Anthony F., Jr. "A Realist in the Utopian City: Boutros Boutros-Ghali's Ethical Framework and Its Impact." In The UN Secretary-General and Moral Authority, edited by Kent J. Kille, pp. 265–297. Washington, D.C.: Georgetown University Press, 2007.

Lombardo, Caroline. "The Making of an Agenda for Democratization: A Speechwriter's View." Chicago Journal of International Law 2, no. 1 (Spring 2001): 253–266.

Report of the World Conference on Human Rights: Report of the Secretary-General United Nations General Assembly Document A/Conf.157/24, October 13, 1993. http://www.unhchr.ch/huridocda/huridoca.nsf/(Symbol)/A.CONF.157.24+(PART+I).En?OpenDocument.

BRAZIL

by Anthony W. Pereira

Brazil's history includes two processes that involved some of the most egregious human rights violations in history: the Iberian conquest of the New World and the transatlantic slave trade. In the twentieth century the country endured two relatively long-lived dictatorships (1930–1945 and 1964–1985) in which political repression, including torture and killings committed by agents of the state, was common. After briefly reviewing the country's early history, this analysis focuses on the second of these dictatorships as the period in Brazil's history in which a consciousness of human rights in the modern sense first developed. The dictatorship engaged in new and widespread forms of state violence, but opposition groups adapted their resistance tactics in response to that repression. By linking up with each other and with transnational human rights networks, these groups expressed moral disapproval of the authoritarian regime and became part of the broad coalition that supported the transition to civilian rule. This article argues that the resistance to authoritarianism generated an emerging civil society in which the norm of human rights for all citizens was articulated. This civil society expanded after the demise of military rule, and it was during this postauthoritarian period in the late 1980s and the 1990s that Brazil belatedly joined the post–World War II "rights revolution" (Forsythe, 2006).

This article discusses some of the obstacles to a fuller realization of human rights in Brazil. The country gained notoriety for its extreme income inequality; for police massacres of street children, the landless, the urban poor, and other vulnerable groups; and for the violence of its cities, in which large slums (*favelas*) often lie in close proximity to middle- and upper-class neighborhoods. The fourth section of the article discusses the struggle to curb police violence and make the police more accountable to citizens. The fifth section analyzes two constraints on the promotion of human rights: increasing violence and crime and the so-called war on terrorism. The final section argues that despite these obstacles the decades since the mid-1970s have seen significant achievement

in terms of the Brazilian state's formal recognition of human rights.

HISTORICAL ANTECEDENTS

Brazil was a Portuguese colony from the sixteenth century until the early nineteenth century. Seeking mineral wealth and agricultural commodities for their expanding commercial empire, the Portuguese began producing sugar along the Brazilian coast soon after laying claim to the territory. Portuguese descriptions of what is now Brazil tended toward the lyrical in the sixteenth century, but the encounter between the Europeans and the indigenous people was usually violent, as it was in Spanish America. Portuguese attempts to enslave indigenous people were generally unsuccessful, so as early as 1538 the Portuguese imported African slaves to Brazil. Over the course of the next three centuries an estimated 3 to 4 million African slaves were transported to Brazil (Burns, 1980; Eakin, 1999; Fausto, 1998). At the beginning of the nineteenth century Brazil had the largest slave population in the world—roughly 50 percent of its population of 3 million (Eakin, 1999). Despite the claim of an earlier generation of historians that Brazilian slavery was more benign than its counterpart in the United States, the consensus among early-twenty-first-century historians was that it was not.

In 1826 the Brazilian government, under pressure from Great Britain, formally abolished the slave trade while in practice permitting it to continue. The formal prohibition was said to be "para o ingles ver" (for the English to see"). In other words, formal commitments were not to interfere with actual practice. This is an example of the unusually ambiguous nature of Brazilian legality, which sets it apart from other countries in Latin America, such as Chile and Uruguay, which have more legalistic traditions. Brazilians celebrate their resort to the *jeito*, the trick or maneuver, and drawing on personal favors and exceptions to deal with laws that are abundant, changeable, complex, and often unequally and arbitrarily applied.

After 1850 the slave trade was suppressed in Brazil. After a long and gradual struggle, slavery itself was also abolished in 1888. Brazil was the last country in the Americas to eliminate the institution. However, the centuries of slavery marked Brazil, creating a hierarchical society in which the distribution of effective rights was profoundly unequal. Brazil was also the only country in the Americas to inherit a monarchy after independence, becoming an empire in 1822 and preserving the monarchy until 1889. The state greatly reflected the interests of the slave-owning, plantation-owning ruling class, serving as an intermediary between the latter's commercial interests and the financial sectors of Britain and later the United States. In Steven Topik's words, "The Brazilian state always had one eye on the interior and one on the City of London" (p. 130).

Under the first republic (1889–1930), an oligarchic political system prevailed. The interests of coffee planters and other plantation owners in the largest states were dominant; elections took place, but the franchise was small. The enforcement of the human rights of workers and peasants was minimal; the power of landowners over their dependents went virtually unchecked by the state, and the middle class was weak. This system came to an end in 1930, when economic depression in the United States and Europe reduced demand for Brazil's exports and plunged the economy and political system into crisis.

Out of the crisis emerged Getúlio Dornelles Vargas, who was to lead Brazil for the next fifteen years (1930–1945). Vargas became a dictator, but under his regime some rights of Brazil's working class were formally recognized by the state for the first time. A Ministry of Labor was created, and labor unions were accorded legal status. As industrialization proceeded, the working class grew. Brazil was still an agrarian society, but its cities developed, its economy became more complex, and republican ideas of equality of citizenship were promulgated. The middle class expanded, and a civil service run on meritocratic lines was created within the state apparatus.

Vargas was deposed in 1945, ushering in a second republic with elections and an expanded franchise that endured until 1964. During this period Brazil's participation in the first few decades of the post–World War II human rights "revolution," marked by the approval of the Universal Declaration of Human Rights at the United Nations in 1948, was minimal (Forsythe, 2006). According to the politician and human rights activist Nilmário Miranda (2006), one of the few instances of human rights being debated in the public arena during this period was a 1956 bill in the Brazilian Congress to create a Council for the Defense of the Rights of the Human Person (Conselho de Defesa dos Direitos da Pessoa Humana or CDDPH). The bill languished in Congress until March 1964, when it was finally approved. Unhappily for the cause of human rights in Brazil, the bill was signed into law fifteen days before a military coup.

THE MILITARY DICTATORSHIP

The coup toppled the elected government of João Goulart and initiated what became a twenty-one-year military dictatorship from 1964 to 1985. It had repercussions throughout South America and was followed by military seizures of power in Argentina in 1966 and in Chile and Uruguay in 1973. The takeover was supported by the United States, which lent logistical and diplomatic assistance to the coup makers (Parker, 1979) and supported the military regime for most of its history (Huggins, 1998). Under the dictatorship, torture came to be practiced on a large scale and affected as many as twenty thousand victims, placing the country beyond the pale of prevailing international human rights norms and treaties. As many as fifty thousand people were imprisoned for political reasons during military rule (Pereira, 2005). Paradoxically, it was during the military regime, when human rights abuses were part of state policy, that human rights norms were eventually strengthened in the country. This also occurred in other countries in the region, such as Chile. The strengthening of human rights norms in Brazil took place, as it did in Chile, as a result of both internal dynamics and international human rights pressure, as this section will show.

In the first few months after the 1964 coup, tens of thousands of people were detained, many for just a short time. As part of the military's Operation Clean-Up, purges of suspected Communists were carried out in Congress, the civil service, universities, trade unions, state-owned firms, and the armed forces (Alves, 1988). During the early years of the military regime, it appeared that the dictatorship might only endure for a few years. The first military president, General Humberto Castelo Branco, at first seemed to want to administer a caretaker government until elections for a civilian president could be held in 1965. However, Castelo Branco's successor as president was a more hard-line military officer, and the regime began to move in a more dictatorial direction after 1967. In the cultural realm, dismay at the regime's increasing authoritarianism was voiced by musical artists, such as Caetano Veloso and Chico Buarque, who along with many other artists and intellectuals participated in the Passeata dos Cem Mil (March of the One Hundred Thousand), a largely middle-class protest against the regime's policies organized in Rio de Janeiro in June 1968. At this time small pockets of armed resistance to military rule also began to emerge.

In December 1968 the regime decreed its notorious Institutional Act 5 (AI-5), which ushered in a new period of repression. AI-5 imposed censorship on the media, strengthened the powers of the executive in relation to other branches and levels of government, and forbade writs of habeas corpus in cases involving violations of national security (which was broadly defined). The latter provision enabled the security forces to detain suspected "subversives" for long periods, subjecting them to electric shocks, beatings, and other forms of torture.

AI-5 polarized public opinion in Brazil. Conservative commentators, such as the celebrated Brazilian scholar Gilberto Freyre, welcomed it. Freyre wrote in 1970 that "drastic changes in the political system of the country have reduced some liberal electoral aspects in favor of more pragmatic authoritarian procedures without abolishing what has always been an essentially democratic tendency toward social and political flexibility" and that Brazil was "simply trying to develop a style of political democracy suited to its own needs" (*Order and Progress*, p. xxiii). However, many skeptics and opponents of military rule denounced AI-5, calling it a "coup within the coup," and added their voices to what became a wave of criticism of Brazil's military rule.

Despite its lack of commitment to human rights, the dictatorship created the CDDPH in 1968. The bill creating the council had been passed into law in 1964 but not enacted until 1968. The council was mainly a public relations operation designed to deflect international criticisms of the military regime. At the same time the security forces stepped up their clandestine war against small, scattered guerrilla groups. From 1969 to 1974 torture was widely practiced, and during that period most of the more than three hundred or so political killings and disappearances committed by the regime took place. The worst example of this was the systematic disappearance of members of the Maoist Communist Party of Brazil (Partido Comunista do Brasil), a guerrilla group operating in the Araguaia region of Pará in the eastern Amazon. About sixty members of this group were killed and their bodies buried or destroyed in a secret operation by the army in 1973 and 1974, with the news only coming to light in the late 1970s.

Criticisms of the military regime grew in the 1970s, and the international dimension was crucial in mounting and sustaining the human rights movement. In this decade what Margaret Keck and Kathryn Sikkink (1988) call "transnational advocacy networks" in the area of human rights had an important impact on, and gained impetus from, developments in Brazil. International nongovernmental organizations (NGOs), such as Amnesty International (AI) and Human Rights Watch, protested the treatment of political prisoners in Brazil, documenting and disseminating information about human rights abuses there. Groups of Brazilian exiles in Europe and North America were vital to these efforts. The number of Brazilian political exiles between 1964 and 1979 has been estimated at ten thousand. Many of these exiles were well-educated, middle-class opponents of the regime, and some were able to form alliances with sympathizers in countries such as France, Britain, Italy, and the United States.

In the United States, for example, exiles teamed with church leaders and academics to publicize and criticize human rights abuses in Brazil in the 1960s and 1970s (Green, 2009). In 1970 the Inter-American Commission on Human Rights (IACHR) responded to a complaint and asked the Brazilian government for more information about human rights abuses. The exchange continued for several years until the IACHR mildly rebuked the Brazilian government in 1974 and moved on to other issues. In 1971 a committee in the U.S. Congress presided over by Senator Frank Church issued a report critical of the U.S. Office of Public Safety (OPS) police program in Brazil, under which the United States had supplied training and technology to police involved in human rights abuses. In 1972 OPS ended its operations in Brazil. In the United Kingdom and the United States in 1976, AI waged a campaign on behalf of 240 "prisoners of conscience" languishing in Brazilian prisons for political reasons. AI also took information about the abuse of human rights in Brazil to the United Nations Commission on Human Rights in February 1976. None of these developments were decisive in changing the dictatorship's practices, but together they helped create a climate of opinion unfavorable to the military regime and supportive of the opposition.

Within Brazil itself during the first part of the 1970s nonviolent opposition to the regime gathered strength while the scattered guerrilla groups were being crushed. The bar association (Organização dos Advogados do Brasil) and the press association (Associação Brasiliera de Imprensa) were noteworthy critics of the regime. The Catholic Church played a particularly important role in the opposition to human rights abuses. For example, the National Bishops' Conference (Conferência Nacional dos Bispos do Brasil) denounced the repressive practices of the military regime, as did the Brazilian Commission for Amnesty (Comissão Brasileira de Anistia).

The Peace and Justice Commission (Comissão Justiça e Paz or CJP) in São Paulo, supported by Cardinal Paulo Evaristo Arns of the Catholic Church, was another significant voice in support of more humane treatment of political prisoners (Serbin, 2000). Because of its protection by the church, the CJP was one of the few organizations in Brazil at the time with the ability to challenge the regime about particular cases of human rights abuses. Run by well-known members of the liberal professions, the CJP also included activists from the student and labor movements. Many of these members went on to play important roles in the debates over state violence in the 1980s and 1990s.

In 1974 the military regime announced its intention to engage in a gradual liberalization, and for the next eleven years opposition groups waged a protracted struggle to reestablish democracy in the country. An important event was the ecumenical mass held in 1975 in the São Paulo cathedral to honor the prominent journalist Vladimir Herzog, who had been tortured to death by the security forces. Although he had been warned by the military authorities not to conduct the mass, Arns went ahead with the event, which was attended by several thousand people. The mass showed the resolve of opposition groups to continue protesting against the military regime's abuse of human rights.

The inauguration of President Jimmy Carter in the United States in 1977 further increased the pressure on the Brazilian military regime. U.S.-Brazilian relations reached a low point under the Carter administration (1977–1980), in part because of criticisms of Brazilian human rights violations by the administration. Opposition to the military regime continued to grow, with many business groups supporting liberalization at this point and trade unions launching major strikes in greater São Paulo in 1978 and 1979. These strikes spread well beyond São Paulo in 1979, including rural as well as urban trade unions, and received support from intellectuals, progressive activists in the Catholic Church, members of allied social movements, and opposition politicians. In addition, a landless movement began to emerge in the late 1970s and early 1980s, helped in part by church activists. The last few years of the military regime were thus marked by the political mobilization of previously excluded social sectors and new claims for long-repressed rights. These

various mobilizations grew to eventually include neighborhood organizers, environmentalists, women, indigenous people, sexual minorities, and other groups.

In 1979 the military regime abolished AI-5 and issued a law (Law 6,683 of 28 August 1979) that granted amnesty to participants in the political conflict under military rule—both political prisoners and members of the security forces. The amnesty led to the acquiescence of most of the military to political liberalization and allowed the return of thousands of political exiles to Brazil. But the law set severe constraints on subsequent efforts to bring the regime's torturers and murderers to justice. Despite the amnesty, a network of groups consisting of relatives of the killed and disappeared, such as Torture Never Again (Tortura Nunca Mais) and the Commissions of the Relatives of the Dead and Disappeared (Comissões de Familiares dos Mortos e Desaparecidos), continued to press for information about the remains of their loved ones. Supported by international NGOs, such as Americas Watch and AI, these groups remained active into the early 2000s.

In the late 1970s Arns and a Protestant minister, Jaime Wright, initiated a secret project to photocopy the transcripts of trials of political prisoners in Brazil's military courts to document human rights abuses. The project lasted five years. When it was completed, a microfilm of the entire collection of documents was sent to the headquarters of the World Council of Churches in Switzerland and then a book, *Brasil: Nunca Mais* (Brazil: Never Again), was published in 1985. This book used the records of the military regime to show how torture had been routinely employed by the security forces, destroying the credibility of apologists for the military regime who had denied the reality of such occurrences. The *Brasil: Nunca Mais* project epitomizes the domestic and international pressures, exerted through transnational networks, that wore down the dictatorship. The book topped the best seller list in Brazil for twenty-five weeks after its publication, just as the military regime was finally being replaced by a new government with an indirectly elected civilian president.

AFTER THE MILITARY REGIME

Civilian rule formally began in 1985, with the first direct election for president since 1960 occurring in 1989. The military had returned to the barracks, but the personnel of the various security agencies—intelligence agencies, police forces, parts of the armed forces—were still largely the same. The regime transition was a conservative one that involved little immediate reform of the police, who changed their focus from political repression to the repression of common crime, with few alterations of methods. Transitional justice or "the processes of trials, purges, and reparations that take place after the transition from one political regime to another" was also largely absent in Brazil (Elster, p. 1). Unlike its Argentine and Chilean counterparts, the Brazil government did not initiate any trials of those accused of human rights abuses during military rule. Similarly, the government did not establish an official truth commission immediately after the regime transition, as was done in Argentina, Chile, El Salvador, and South Africa. The official history of the authoritarian period was contested but largely outside of the government itself, where the gradual and conservative transition resulted in a large degree of continuity of personnel, institutions, and policies from one regime to the next.

However, beginning in the second half of the 1980s, the Brazilian government began to sign and ratify the myriad treaties that constitute the scaffolding of the international human rights system. In addition, 1988 saw the ratification of a new constitution by the Brazilian Congress. The constitution was the outcome of considerable popular mobilization and incorporated a series of popular amendments proposed by various social movements. It formally committed the country to the recognition and enforcement of a variety of rights. These include civil rights (to liberty, privacy, freedom of expression, and property); political rights (to vote, be voted for, and participate in political life); and social rights (to education, social assistance, health, and work). The 1988 constitution also decentralized the political system to a considerable extent, transferring some tax revenues to municipal governments and putting public health care and education under a greater degree of local government control (Roberts, 2005). To some extent, this "localized" the struggle for social, economic, and cultural rights.

Formal commitments to human rights were further strengthened in the 1990s. In 1992 the Brazilian Congress finally ratified the International Covenant on Civil and Political Rights and the International Covenant on Economic, Social, and Cultural Rights, treaties that were negotiated in 1966 and that had gained a sufficient number of signatories to acquire legal force internationally in 1976 (Forsythe, 2006). Another step forward occurred after the 1993 United Nations Conference on Human Rights in Vienna. After participating in the conference, the Brazilian delegation returned to the capital Brasília to meet with representatives of human rights organizations and develop a national human rights plan. That plan was approved in 1996. Earlier the lower house of Congress had created a Human Rights Committee at the beginning of 1995, at the start of the government of President Fernando Henrique Cardoso (1995–2003). At the same time the Cardoso government created the Special Secretariat for Human Rights within the Ministry of Justice, a secretariat that has ministerial status. Furthermore, in 1997 Brazil recognized the jurisdiction of the Inter-American Court of Human Rights. During this time it also began to receive United Nations representatives. These representatives periodically visited the country to report on the enforcement of United Nations treaties and agreements that Brazil signed. Thus during the late 1990s, the formal defense of human rights was consolidated as a state policy in Brazil.

Under the Cardoso administration, there were other significant developments in human rights at the official level. An annual national prize for human rights was created. The National Council for Handicapped People (Conselho Nacional da Pessoa Portadora de Deficiência) was established in 1999 to coordinate public policy for the handicapped. In addition, some 41 million hectares of indigenous lands were demarcated by the government from 1995 to 2001 (Presidency of the Republic of Brazil, 2002). Protecting these reserves from encroachment is difficult, but demarcation is a first, important step toward the preservation of the territory and culture of indigenous people. Another policy initiated at this time was affirmative action—quotas for Afro-Brazilians were put in place in some government ministries, a practice that was subsequently initiated in the admissions policies of some state and federal universities. In addition, limited governmental support for communities of descendants of runaway slaves (quilombos) started to become available (Presidency of the Republic of Brazil, 2002).

In the realm of transitional justice, some recognition of the crimes of the dictatorship occurred in Brazil in the late 1990s. Although the number of people killed by the military regime was small in comparison to the number killed by authoritarian regimes in neighboring countries, such as Argentina and Chile, many human rights activists believe that allowing complete impunity for past crimes is not a strong foundation for a new democracy. They thus keep up pressure on the government to better account for what happened under the dictatorship, and new information sporadically leaks out of the Brazilian government. In 1995 a Special Commission on the Politically Killed and Disappeared (Comissão Especial dos Mortos e Desaparecidos Políticos) was established to investigate the killed and disappeared under military rule, to compensate family members of those who died while in state custody, and to find the remains of the disappeared. This commission made considerable progress in achieving the first two objectives but not the third. It examined hundreds of cases, paying compensation to the families in many instances and replacing official lies with more accurate accounts of the deaths of dissidents and opposition activists during military rule (Pereira, 2000).

Another development in transitional justice took place under President Luís Ignácio Lula da Silva (2003–). In 2007 the Secretariat of Human Rights published *Direito à Memória e à Verdade* (The Right to Memory and Truth), a book based on the eleven years of work of the Special Commission on the Politically Killed and Disappeared. The book suggested that the remains of the disappeared—and in particular the guerrillas of Araguaia—might still be found if the archives of the armed forces were opened. But the book was published so quietly—an exclusive print run of five thousand copies was not made available for sale to the public but distributed to select individuals—suggests that the Lula government was reluctant to disturb the sensibilities of supporters of the military regime.

Transitional justice is likely to periodically reemerge in Brazilian politics for some time. Some of the state governments, for example, responded to pressure from human rights groups by initiating their own programs of compensation for victims of the authoritarian repression and by opening the archives of the now extinct political police (Departamento de Ordem Política e Social). Brazilian groups that applauded such initiatives are likely to push for further measures in the future, aided by international NGOs, such as the International Center for Transitional Justice, and activist judges, such as Spain's Baltasar Garzón, who was reported in 2008 to be investigating Brazilian military officers involved in Operation Condor, a network of repression that linked the military regimes of Argentina, Brazil, Chile, Paraguay, and Uruguay in the 1970s (as reported in the *Folha de São Paulo*, 11 January 2008).

In summary, the consciousness of and demand for human rights developed within civil society under the military regime, facilitated by transnational issue networks. The nascent human rights movement focused first on the torture of political prisoners, demanding amnesty for the latter, and then broadened its approach to the issue of the treatment of ordinary criminal suspects by the police, courts, and prisons (Caldeira, 2006). After the end of military rule in the mid-1980s, the state formally recognized its responsibility for a broad array of human

rights, and new institutions dedicated to rights enforcement were created. Legal prohibitions of torture and other types of human rights abuses abound in Brazil, and a plethora of enforcement institutions, such as ombudsmen and secretariats of human rights, exist. In the early twenty-first century the problem remined enforcement—the effective realization of rights in practice.

CURBING POLICE VIOLENCE

Of particular concern is the existence of police forces with poor reputations for engaging in corruption, torture, and killing. In the words of one specialist, "Brazil's police are among the world's most violent and corrupt, and human rights, particularly those of socially marginalized groups, are violated with impunity on a massive scale" (Hagopian, pp. 128–129).

The bulk of Brazilian police work is carried out by the uniformed, patrolling military police (*polícia militar*) and the plainclothes, investigative civil police (*polícia civil*), both controlled by state governments. In the late twentieth century and early twenty-first century, as Brazilian civil society became more active, the pressure to reform the police and make them more accountable, efficient, and respectful of human rights came from various organizations with a variety of ideological leanings. In response to this pressure, a number of important changes in policing occurred in Brazil. These changes include the creation of new mechanisms of accountability external to the police forces and internal organizational and managerial reforms. The reforms have been enacted at different times and in different ways in the patchwork quilt of Brazil's twenty-six states and federal districts.

One of the most important changes is the creation of police ombudsmen's offices. These offices are state-level agencies where members of the public (and police) can make complaints—anonymously if they like—about police misconduct. These complaints are then supposed to be investigated by the internal affairs units of the civil and military police forces (*corregedorias*). As of 2008, fourteen of Brazil's states had police ombudsmen. Observers argue that the ombudsmen provide an important feedback function, making police misbehavior more transparent and establishing the right of the public to oversee and control the state's use of force. From 2004 to 2007 the European Union (EU) donated financial support and technical assistance to Brazil's Secretariat of Human Rights to promote the work of the police ombudsmen (Secretariat of Human Rights).

However, substantial institutional variation exists among the police ombudsmen's offices across the Brazilian states. For example, some police ombudsmen are appointed to fixed mandates and have considerable autonomy and capacity, whereas others serve at the discretion of the state governor and lack genuine independence, visibility, capacity, and influence. Similarly, some offices were created by a decree law issued by the governor, meaning that they could be revoked immediately by decree law as well, whereas others were created by ordinary legislation and are thus more firmly entrenched. In addition, because the final outcome of complaints made about the police are rarely made public by the ombudsman's office and because the ombudsman's influence is often hard to perceive, citizens have little ability to gauge the effectiveness of this particular accountability mechanism.

Other reforms have attempted to improve the efficiency of the police in the areas of both crime prevention and investigation. The federal Secretariat of Public Security (Secretaria Nacional de Segurança Pública or SENASP) promoted the integration of the military and civil police in terms of planning (called *gestão integrada* or integrated management); human rights courses for the police; and the development of better relations between the police and communities. Civil society organizations became active participants in the police reform movement as well. Foundations such as the São Paulo Institute against Violence (Instituto São Paulo contra Violência) and Viva Rio, funded by donations from businesses, established partnerships with state agencies aimed at improving policing. In universities a new generation of academic centers arose that combined traditional preoccupations with human rights with a focus on policing and ways to improve it. These include the Center for Studies of Criminality and Public Security (Centro de Estudos de Criminalidade e Segurança Pública) at the Federal University of Minas Gerais in Belo Horizonte; the Center for Studies of Security and Citizenship (Centro de Estudos de Segurança e Cidadania) at the Candido Mendes University in Rio de Janeiro; and the Center for the Study of Violence (Núcleo de Estudos da Violência) at the University of São Paulo.

A fundamental question about Brazil's various police reforms is whether or not they reinforce the cause of human rights. Diane Davis (2006) argues that in Mexico police reforms have hurt human rights because they reflect a hard-line mentality that demands security at all costs. She writes that public security–minded NGOs have been eclipsing human rights–oriented associations in Mexico City and that these NGOs, heavily supported by business, care more about curbing criminality and insecurity than human rights. In Davis's words, "The emphasis has shifted . . . to criminalization, with human rights shunted to the sidelines" (p. 78). Some observers argue that this approach has long been adopted in many of Brazil's large cities, such as Rio de Janeiro, where an anti-insurgency approach is the dominant police strategy in many of that city's slums (Amnesty International, 2007; Arias, 2006).

This tension, however, is not necessarily inevitable. For example, spokespersons for public security–minded NGOs, such as the city of Recife's Antônio Carlos Escobar Institute (Instituto Antônio Carlos Escobar), insist that more efficient police must also respect the law. The police reformer and former Brazilian congressman Marcus Rolim, who studied police methods in Canada, the United States, and Europe, argues that the wave of reform can end "the political-cultural cycle in which public security and human rights were seen as opposed values and constituting inexorably contradictory issues" (p. 14). Another police reformer, Luiz Eduardo Soares, who briefly headed SENASP in 2003, also insists on the lack of contradiction between human rights and police reform (2002).

In summary, although important improvements have been initiated, curbing police violence remains a major challenge in Brazil. The violation of civil rights by the police affects the ability of citizens to fulfill many other human rights as well. Some observers argue that support for the cause of human rights became more difficult in the early twenty-first century because of various trends, and it is to two of those developments that this article now turns.

CONSTRAINTS ON THE STRUGGLE FOR HUMAN RIGHTS

The first, the rise of violent crime, is influenced by international forces but is primarily national and has been occurring gradually for several decades. The second, the war on terrorism, is global and more recent.

Violent crime has increased in Brazil since 1980. The homicide rate, for example, almost tripled by 2008. Although in many countries economic growth is associated with increases in property crime but decreases in crimes against life, Brazil's economic development has been accompanied by increases in the rates of both kinds of reported crime. This has led to increasing pressure on elected officials to respond to the perceived insecurity of Brazil's cities and has made the struggle for human rights more difficult than it otherwise would be.

For example, after the criminal group the First Command of the Capital (Primeiro Comando da Capital or PCC) staged coordinated attacks on buses, police officers, and prison guards in São Paulo in May 2006, many public officials expressed their support for hard-line police tactics in response. In the wake of the attacks, the São Paulo police killed dozens of suspected members of the PCC, some of them apparently in summary executions (Cavallaro and Dodge, 2007). In such an atmosphere of polarization and fear, police, prosecutors, judges, and other officials committed to the defense of human rights do not necessarily form majorities within their organizations and may be afraid to condemn such heavy-handed actions for fear of ostracism and retaliation.

State violation of the rights of criminal suspects is nurtured by a counter–human rights ideology that asserts rights should only be afforded to "good" people (*homens de bem*) and not "bandits" (*bandidos*). As one saying has it, "direitos humanos são para os humanos direitos" (human rights are for good humans). Aggressively propagated by radio talk show hosts, the presenters of television crime programs, some public security officials, and elected representatives, this view feeds on popular discontent with the criminal justice system, which is seen as biased and inefficient. It champions police death squads, vigilantism, and militias as a solution to problems of crime and insecurity (Rose,). Its language is mirrored by the statements of organized criminal groups such as the PCC, which also justifies the summary execution of its enemies (Caldeira, 2006).

Evidence suggests that such hard-line, anti-human rights perspectives are popular with at least some segments of the Brazilian population. Teresa P. R.Caldeira quotes an eighteen-year-old resident of a poor neighborhood on the outskirts of São Paulo as saying: "I wish the Esquadrão da Morte (Death Squad) still existed. The Esquadrão da Morte is the police who only kill; the Esquadrão da Morte is justice done by one's own hands" (p. 110). Survey research reveals such preferences as well. One study conducted as part of the Brazilian Social Research project (Pesquisa Social Brasileira) and published in 2007 revealed that a high percentage of respondents believed it was correct for the police to execute suspected thieves and muggers. This view varied somewhat across the five major regions of the country but averaged 31 percent.

In this climate human rights campaigners in Brazil face an uphill battle in spreading their message. In many instances they are simplistically said to be defending "criminals," and their ties with international NGOs can also be used, through nationalist discourse, to further tarnish their legitimacy. To what extent the human rights community has been able to associate its cause with the interests of all Brazilians, and to make formal commitments to human rights a practical reality, is a contested issue.

The second obstacle for human rights is the U.S. war on terrorism. The aggressive claims of executive privilege by the latter country since the terrorist attack of 11 September 2001 have worsened the prospects for human rights worldwide. These U.S. actions include the indefinite detention of alleged "unlawful combatants" in a prison at Guantánamo Bay, the practice of "rendition" of prisoners to countries that routinely practice torture, the notorious White House memo of 1 August 2002 justifying torture, and the prolonged detention of citizen enemy combatants, such as José Padilla. Such actions and declarations constitute one part of the United States' "mixed signals" about human rights and represent a significant retreat from the "moral high ground" by the U.S. government. The United States has projected a vision of human rights in international affairs since the 1970s and made major contributions to the creation of the global framework of human rights protection. In Brazil in the late twentieth and early twenty-first centuries, this included support for campaigns against child labor and trafficking in women. However, when its own security was threatened by the 9/11 attack, the U.S. executive branch seemed to retreat to a posture of "do as I say, not as I do." This posture stands in stark contrast to the official positions of the EU countries, some of which (such as Spain) have also suffered terrorist attacks but maintained a firmer commitment to human rights standards nonetheless.

It is unclear how the war on terrorism has affected Brazilian policies, both domestically and internationally, since 2001. Brazil takes an independent position on human rights in world affairs. However, it is influenced by U.S. actions, both indirectly in having to cope with an international environment marked by increasing tension, conflict, and militarism and directly through U.S. pressure to adhere to various antiterrorism initiatives. It is difficult to avoid reaching the conclusion that these developments have been largely negative for human rights in Brazil as has been the case elsewhere.

HUMAN RIGHTS IN BRAZIL: PROGRESS, STAGNATION, OR RETROCESSION?

Many people question whether or not Brazil is stagnating or even backsliding in its struggle to promote human rights. The authors of the third national report on human rights in Brazil, a state-by-state account of developments in the field, gloomily conclude that human rights are regressing in Brazil (Mesquita Neto and Affonso, 2007). However, before accepting such a conclusion, it should be acknowledged that there are at least three different conceptions of human rights competing for supremacy within the country.

The first is an ample vision of human rights that includes social and economic rights. The National Movement for the Defense of Human Rights (Movimento Nacional de Defesa dos Direitos Humanos), an umbrella organization for a variety of grassroots groups, holds this view. The second is a narrower conception that sees human rights as essentially civil and political rights. The third is an even narrower perspective that does not exist within the human rights movement itself but is adhered to by people who have a skeptical or hostile view of human rights as a universal principle. This is the dualistic perspective that human rights should only be available to "good people," as discussed earlier.

Diplomatically, the Brazilian Foreign Ministry and Ministry of Justice's Special Secretariat for Human Rights have tended to support the first, ample view of rights. This was evident at the 1993 United Nations conference in Vienna, where a broad view of rights was approved with the support of the Brazilian government. In this respect the official Brazilian position on human rights is closer to the social democratic vision prevalent in the EU than the classical liberal, U.S. view that human rights should only include political and civil rights. (This position exists despite the fact that social democracy is far from being achieved in Brazil.) The Brazilian government adheres to an ample view of rights, independent from the U.S. position, in other areas as well. For example, it supported the creation of the International Criminal Court in spite of U.S. opposition to this measure. And it became a member of the United Nations Human Rights Council in 2008 in spite of the U.S. refusal to participate. An independent, broad approach to rights that combines civil and political with economic, social, and cultural rights is also symbolized by the activities within the United Nations of Brazilians such as Paulo Sergio Pinheiro, an independent expert for the United Nations secretary-general's study on violence against children from 2003 to 2006, and Sergio Vieira de Mello. The latter, who started his career at the United Nations High Commission for Refugees and became the secretary-general's special representative on Iraq, was tragically killed by a bomb in Baghdad in 2003.

A major question is whether, despite increasing crime and violence domestically and the war on terrorism internationally, Brazil is pushing forward in the area of human rights. Nilmário Miranda, who served as the minister of human rights from 2003 to 2005 in the first government of President Lula, believes that progress has been and will continue to be made. He believes that Brazil has created institutions at the federal level that reflect the global human rights initiatives of the last several decades and that these institutions have the capacity to improve human rights enforcement on the ground. On the other hand, some scholars argue that the neoliberal economic order relegates human rights to a secondary plane in international affairs and that the existence of a formally democratic regime does not necessarily guarantee the enforcement of human rights. In "low-intensity" democracies such as Brazil's, authorities are often more concerned with formal commitments to rights and the creation of institutions than they are to the realization of rights in daily life.

How can one interpret this disagreement and the evident gap between formal institutions and official commitment to human rights, on the one hand, and a lack of effective human rights guarantees in Brazil, on the other? One interpretation is that the formal institutions and official commitments are the first step on a path and that with time actual practice will fall into line, as citizens become more aware of their rights and more confident in the institutions entrusted with investigating rights violations and disciplining and prosecuting those responsible for them. Another interpretation sees no inevitable convergence between the ideal and the actual or the formal, elite-level politics of human rights and the grassroots experience of rights on the streets and public spaces of Brazil. Brazil's history of creating institutions "para o inglês ver" is cited to reinforce this second position.

Interpretations clearly vary depending on what aspect of human rights is being discussed, but taking a historical view and noting the series of changes enacted, it is hard to resist the logic of the more optimistic view of human rights presented above, despite the global reality of neoliberal economics, big power politics, and violent crime. As a middle-income country experiencing steady if slow economic growth, Brazil is becoming a society with a much better-fed, better-educated population with more access to information than in the past. The international dimension, especially transnational human rights networks, is crucial to sustaining this progress. Although that dimension will probably always be more influential in small countries, such as Chile and those in Central America, it has also played and will continue to exercise an important role in Brazil. The flow of influence will also be two-way, as Brazil continues to make contributions to the movement for human rights worldwide.

Improvements strengthen the predisposition and capacity of the Brazilian people to claim the rights they believe they are entitled to under law, and the creation of new institutions charged with monitoring human rights violations makes it easier to press those claims. In the early twenty-first century the challenge is to use these institutions to enforce human rights on the ground and to fulfill the promise of citizenship inherent in democracy. Hope exists that Brazilians can continue to make progress toward effective human rights enforcement in the future.

[*See also* Belgian Congo *and* Chile in the Pinochet Era.]

BIBLIOGRAPHY

Almeida, Alberto Carlos. *A cabeça do Brasileiro* [The Head of the Brazilian]. Rio de Janeiro, Brazil: Editora Record, 2007.

Alves, Maria Helena Moreira. *State and Opposition in Military Brazil.* Austin: University of Texas Press, 1988.

Amnesty International. *From Burning Buses to Caveirões: The Search for Human Security.* May 8, 2007. http://www.web.amnesty.org/library/Index/ENGAMR190112007?open&of=ENG-BRA.

Arias, Enrique Desmond. *Drugs and Democracy in Rio de Janeiro: Trafficking, Social Networks, and Public Security.* Chapel Hill: University of North Carolina Press, 2006.

Avritzer, Leonardo. *Democracy and the Public Space in Latin America.* Princeton, N.J.: Princeton University Press, 2002.

Barahona de Brito, Alexandra, and Francisco Panizza. "The Politics of Human Rights in Democratic Brazil: *A lei não pega.*" *Democratization* 5, no. 4 (Winter 1998): 20–51.

Brinks, Daniel. *The Judicial Response to Police Killings in Latin America: Inequality and the Rule of Law.* Cambridge, U.K.: Cambridge University Press, 2007.

Burns, E. Bradford. *A History of Brazil.* 2d ed. New York: Columbia University Press, 1980.

Caldeira, Teresa P. R. "'I Came to Sabotage Your Reasoning!': Violence and Resignification of Justice in Brazil." *In Law and Disorder in the Postcolony,* edited by Jean Comaroff and John Comaroff, pp. 102–149. Chicago: University of Chicago Press, 2006.

Cavallaro, James Louis, and Raquel Ferreira Dodge. "Understanding the São Paulo Attacks." *ReVista: Harvard Review of Latin America* 6, no. 3 (Spring 2007): 53–55.

Dassin, Joan. *Torture in Brazil: A Report by the Archdiocese of São Paulo.* Translated by Jaime Wright. New York: Vintage, 1986.

Davis, Diane. "Undermining the Rule of Law: Democratization and the Dark Side of Police Reform in Mexico." *Latin American Politics and Society* 48, no. 1 (2006): 55–86.

Dunn, Christopher. *Brutality Garden: Tropicália and the Emergence of a Brazilian Counterculture.* Chapel Hill: University of North Carolina Press, 2001.

Eakin, Marshall. *Brazil: The Once and Future Country.* New York: St. Martin's Griffin, 1998.

Elster, Jon. *Closing the Books: Transitional Justice in Historical Perspective.* Cambridge, U.K.: Cambridge University Press, 2004.

Evans, Tony. *The Politics of Human Rights: A Global Perspective.* London: Pluto, 2005.

Fausto, Boris. *A Concise History of Brazil.* Cambridge, U.K.: Cambridge University Press, 1999.

Forsythe, David P. *Human Rights in International Relations.* 2d ed. Cambridge, U.K.: Cambridge University Press, 2006.

Freyre, Gilberto. *The Masters and the Slave: A Study in the Development of Brazilian Civilization.* Translated by Samuel Putnam. New York: Alfred A. Knopf, 1978.

Freyre, Gilberto. *Order and Progress: Brazil from Monarchy to Republic.* Translated by Rod W. Horton. Berkeley: University of California Press, 1986.

Green, James. *"We Cannot Remain Silent": Opposition to the Brazilian Military Dictatorship in the United States, 1964–85.* Durham, N.C.: Duke University Press, 2009.

Hagopian, Frances. "Brazil and Chile." *In Assessing the Quality of Democracy,* edited by Larry Diamond and Leonardo Morlino, pp. 123–162. Baltimore: Johns Hopkins University Press, 2005.

Hinton, Mercedes. *The State on the Streets: Police and Politics in Argentina and Brazil.* Boulder, Colo.: Lynne Rienner, 2006.

Huggins, Martha. *Political Policing: The United States and Latin America.* Durham, N.C.: Duke University Press, 1998.

Keck, Margaret, and Kathryn Sikkink. *Activists beyond Borders: Advocacy Networks in International Politics.* Ithaca, N.Y.: Cornell University Press, 1998.

Levinson, Sanford. "Preserving Constitutional Norms in Times of Permanent Emergencies." *Constellations* 13, no. 1 (2006): 59–73.

Macaulay, Fiona. "Knowledge Production, Framing, and Criminal Justice Reform in Latin America." *Journal of Latin American Studies* 39, no. 1 (2007): 627–651.

Macaulay, Fiona. "Problems of Police Oversight in Brazil." Working Paper 33-02. Centre for Brazilian Studies, Oxford University, 2002.

Maxwell, Kenneth. *Naked Tropics: Essays on Empire and Other Rogues.* New York: Routledge, 2003.

Mesquita Neto, Paulo. "Public-Private Partnership for Police Reform in Brazil." *In Public Security and Police Reform in the Americas,* edited by John Bailey and Lucía Dammert, pp. 44–57. Pittsburgh, Pa.: University of Pittsburgh Press, 2006.

Mesquita Neto, Paulo, and B. S. A. Affonso. *Terceiro relatório nacional sobre os direitos humanos no Brasil* [Third National Report on Human Rights in Brazil]. São Paulo, Brazil: Centre for the Study of Violence at the University of São Paulo and the Teotônio Vilela Commission for Human Rights, 2007.

Miranda, Nilmário. *Por que direitos humanos* [Why Human Rights]. Belo Horizonte, Brazil: Autêntica Editora, 2006.

Page, Joseph. *The Brazilians.* Reading, Mass.: Perseus, 1995.

Parker, Phyllis. *Brazil and the Quiet Intervention, 1964.* Austin: University of Texas Press, 1979.

Pereira, Anthony. *Political (In)justice: Authoritarianism and the Rule of Law in Brazil, Chile, and Argentina.* Pittsburgh, Pa.: University of Pittsburgh Press, 2005.

Pereira, Anthony. "An Ugly Democracy? State Violence and the Rule of Law in Postauthoritarian Brazil." *In Democratic Brazil: Actors, Institutions, and Processes,* edited by Peter Kingstone and Timothy Power, pp. 217–235. Pittsburgh, Pa.: University of Pittsburgh Press, 2000.

Pope, Clara. "Human Rights and the Catholic Church in Brazil, 1970–1983." *Journal of Church and State* 27, no. 3 (2006): 429–452.

Power, Samantha. *Chasing the Flame: Sergio Vieira de Mello and the Fight to Save the World.* New York: Penguin, 2008.

Presidency of the Republic of Brazil. *Brazil 1994–2002: The Era of the Real.* Brasília, Brazil: State Secretariat for Government Communication, 2002.

Roberts, Bryan R. "Citizenship, Rights, and Social Policy." *In Rethinking Development in Latin America*, edited by Charles H. Wood and Bryan R. Roberts, pp. 137–158. University Park: Pennsylvania State University Press, 2005.

Rolim, Marcos. *A síndrome da rainha vermelha: Policiamento e segurança pública no século XXI* [The Red Queen Syndrome: Policing and Public Security in the Twenty-first Century]. Oxford and Rio de Janeiro: Centre for Brazilian Studies, University of Oxford, and Jorge Zahar Editora, 2006.

Rose, R. S. *The Unpast: Elite Violence and Social Control in Brazil, 1954–2000.* Athens, Ohio: Center for International Studies, Ohio University, 2005.

Scheuerman, William. "Carl Schmitt and the Road to Abu Ghraib." *Constellations* 13, no. 1 (2006): 100–124.

Secretariat of Human Rights. *Direito à memória e à verdade* [The Right to Memory and Truth]. Brasília, Brazil: Special Commission on the Killed and Disappeared, Ministry of Justice, 2007.

Serbin, Kenneth. *Secret Dialogues: Church-State Relations, Torture, and Social Justice in Authoritarian Brazil.* Pittsburgh, Pa.: University of Pittsburgh Press, 2000.

Sikkink, Kathryn. *Mixed Signals: U.S. Human Rights Policy and Latin America.* Ithaca, N.Y.: Cornell University Press, 2004.

Skidmore, Thomas. *The Politics of Military Rule in Brazil, 1964–85.* Oxford: Oxford University Press, 1988.

Soares, Luiz Eduardo. "Prefácio" [Preface]. In *Direitos humanos: Os desafios do século XXI* [Human Rights: The Challenges of the Twenty-first Century]. Brasília, Brazil: Brasília Juridica, 2002.

Topik, Steven. "The Hollow State: The Effect of the World Market on State-Building in Brazil in the Nineteenth Century." In *Studies in the Formation of the Nation State in Latin America,* edited by James Dunkerley, pp. 112–132. London: Institute of Latin American Studies, University of London, 2002.

Weschler, Lawrence. *A Miracle, a Universe: Settling Accounts with Torturers.* Chicago: University of Chicago Press, 1998.

B'TSELEM

by Jasmin Habib

B'Tselem: The Israeli Information Centre for Human Rights in the Occupied Territories champions human rights and humanitarian law as the foundation for transforming the conflict between Israel and the Palestinians. The scope of B'Tselem's efforts and postcolonial aspirations for coexistence between Israeli Jews and Palestinians has extended beyond Israel, due in no small part to the global interest in human rights activism.

ESTABLISHMENT, FUNDING, AND PARTNERS

Established in 1989 by Israeli academics, lawyers, members of Knesset, activists, and journalists, B'Tselem is dedicated to educating Israelis and the international community about the effects of military occupation and administration in the Occupied Territories of the West Bank and the Gaza Strip. Its guiding principle is the protection of the human rights of Palestinians and Israelis. B'Tselem gathers, analyzes, and distributes evidence of human rights violations, lobbies for change at the juridical and political levels, and organizes public meetings to engage the Israeli public in these issues.

While describing itself as "an Israeli organization" whose efforts are "directed at violations committed by our government on behalf of all of us," B'Tselem has also criticized the Palestinian Authority's abuses of power, for example, calling for an end to its policy of executing collaborators.

According to B'Tselem's own documents, the name of the organization means "in the image of," which is a reference to Genesis 1:27: "And God created humans in his image. In the image of God did He create him." In the context of the Israel-Palestine conflict, B'Tselem calls upon Israelis to reflect on the image that they project to other Israelis, to the Palestinians, and to the world. In the context of its advocacy on behalf of those who are the victims of human rights abuses, B'Tselem wishes to reflect a more humane and humanitarian image.

B'Tselem is independently funded by individual donors from Israel and worldwide and several government and nongovernmental organizations including, but not limited to (in 2006), the British Foreign and Commonwealth Office, Commission of the European Communities, Federal Department of Foreign Affairs of Switzerland, the Norwegian Foreign Ministry, the New Israel Fund (Israel), the Ford Foundation (United States), the Development Corporation Ireland (DCI), Evangelischer Entwicklungsdienst (EED, Germany), Foundation for Middle East Peace, and the International Commission of Jurists—Swedish Section.

B'Tselem has forged close ties to several Israeli and Palestinian human rights NGOs, including the Association for Civil Rights in Israel; Bimkom—Planners for Planning Rights; HaMoked: Center for the Defence of the Individual; Physicians for Human Rights—Israel; the Public Committee against Torture in Israel (PCATI); as well as LAW—The Palestinian Society for the Protection of Human Rights and the Environment and the Palestinian Human Rights Monitoring Group.

B'TSELEM'S ACTIVITIES

B'Tselem's executive director oversees its research, data coordination, fieldwork, communications, and administration departments. Field researchers staff each of the Palestinian districts. Academics, lawyers, journalists, civil rights leaders, and activists compose its board of directors. Its multilingual Web site (English, Hebrew, Arabic, and Russian) allows access to all of its publications, including its comprehensive reports, press releases, and information bulletins, which outline developments on current matters of concern. Press reports are disseminated to legislators, jurists, activists, other human rights and nongovernmental organizations, and journalists, as well as to the wider public, using Web banners on popular Israeli sites as well as newspaper inserts and, most recently, a music video.

B'Tselem presents its political, juridical, and social history of the conflict from a human rights perspective. Data and evidence of abuse, which include eyewitness accounts of everyday life under occupation, are collected by Israeli and Palestinian fieldworkers. Illustrating the effects of the occupation by drawing upon the testimony of those most affected by rights violations, B'Tselem conveys the immediacy and urgency of the situation while privileging the perspective of the victimized over the victimizer, although the Centre makes every effort to provide the official perspective when it has been made available.

As of spring 2006, B'Tselem had published more than seventy reports, all available and accessible in several formats on the Internet. Among them are the following titles: *Neither Law nor Justice* (1995), *Demolishing Peace* (1997), *Routine Torture* (1998), *Illusions of Restraint* (2000), *Excessive Force* (2001), *Human Shields* (2002), *Trigger Happy* (2002), *Through No Fault of Their Own* (2004), *Forbidden Roads* (2004), *Forbidden Families* (2004), *Under the Guise of Security* (2005), and *Take No Prisoners* (2005). The titles are provocative, but what is notable is their comprehensive and collaborative nature; many are coauthored with other Israeli and Palestinian organizations.

Designed to reach multiple audiences, B'Tselem's compilations appear to be broadly conceived as legal dossiers, often providing a brief history; a statement outlining the nature of the violations and allegations of the nature of the abuses suffered (often appearing in the title of the report); a description of the violator (often the Israel Defense Force [IDF]); a section on the methods used for the collection of data (often testimonials gathered by fieldworkers); the applicability of various legal regimes that have been violated (such as the Fourth Geneva Convention or the Convention on the Rights of the Child); a condemnation of these practices; and an immediate call to action that may include an official inquiry, compensation to the victims, or a call to conform to international law and to remedy the situation.

Since 2003 B'Tselem has also provided free access to its digital photo and video archives, which include footage of house demolitions, testimonials by those who allege to have been victimized, as well as interviews with IDF soldiers. B'Tselem's maps of the Occupied Territories feature the location of Jewish settlements (both those recognized and unrecognized by the Israeli Ministry of the Interior), the proposed and already built route of the Separation Barrier (also known as the Wall, the Security Fence, and the Anti-Terrorist Fence), as well as the location of military checkpoints and roadblocks. Also available are pertinent statistics ranging from the number of Palestinian minors in IDF detention to data on Palestinian and Israeli fatalities, including individual names and the circumstances of death.

In an effort to communicate human rights concerns to Israeli soldiers, B'Tselem publishes and distributes full-color "pocket guides"—pamphlets designed to educate them about their responsibilities to those living in the occupation zones.

POLICY AND POSITIONS

In accordance with United Nations rulings and with the position taken by the majority of the world's governments, B'Tselem identifies the West Bank and Gaza as militarily occupied territories whose population must be governed in conformity with humanitarian law. At the broader political level, B'Tselem's position is that all Israeli settlements in the territories are illegal and that they must be evacuated. Moreover, the Centre claims that the courts have been manipulated by policy makers who, though claiming that land expropriations are necessary for the security of the state, actually aim to change the demographic character of these areas in order to thwart any serious efforts for Palestinian self-determination and to make territorial annexation to the state of Israel more viable.

At a number of levels (historical, juridical, and political), the government of Israel and its High Court of Justice have been consistent in refusing this "occupying power" designation, arguing instead that, save for the annexation of Jerusalem, the status of these territories, while an integral part of the state, is disputed. Furthermore, Israel argues that its settlement practices are entirely legal and that its security procedures are measured and taken only within the context of a state facing emergency or exceptional circumstances.

In the main, B'Tselem argues that human rights abuses are part and parcel of Israel's intention to destroy the economic and social fabric of Palestinian society in the West Bank and Gaza. In all of its publications, including Web site information bulletins, press releases, and reports, B'Tselem alerts Israelis and the world to the structural and direct violence of the occupation that Palestinians are forced to endure.

REPORTS AND STATEMENTS

Since its occupation of the territories in 1967, and especially throughout the 1980s and 1990s, Israel remapped the Occupied Territories, establishing and expanding settlements, as well as building new roads to provide exclusive Israeli access to these areas.

B'Tselem consistently describes Israel's practices in the territories as a "separation cum discrimination regime, in which it maintains two systems of laws, and a person's rights are based on his or her national origin." In the period since 1967, legislation enacted by Israel allows for "extra-territorial status for Israeli civilians." Settlers who live in the Territories are accorded the same rights as Israeli citizens living within the Green Line—the 1949 Armistice line—while Palestinians are denied these legal and social guarantees. According to B'Tselem, the principle of equality before the law is violated when an individual's nationality determines the legal system that applies. Moreover, B'Tselem asserts that "it is doubtful that any comparable system has existed since the end of apartheid in South Africa," though it argues that because there is no official document which sets out these restrictions, a "lack of transparency" persists that makes it "difficult to criticize such a policy and challenge its legality."

B'Tselem claims that since the beginning of the Palestinian uprising against military occupation in 2000 known as the Al-Aqsa intifada, "restrictions on movement . . . significantly affected the daily lives of Palestinians in commerce, in access to medical treatment and educational institutions, and in conducting social activities." These restrictions include the use of checkpoints, roadblocks, and curfews as well as the construction of the Separation Barrier. Not convinced that Israel's restrictions have anything to do with protecting Israel, B'Tselem argues that the settlement policy only exacerbates the conditions under which Palestinians are forced to live.

With respect to curfews, B'Tselem accuses the military of disproportionate harm to the civilian population, charging that the IDF does not properly notify the local population of curfews and that its enforcement practices, which include using live fire on a civilian population, testify "to a shameful disregard for human life and a 'trigger happy' attitude." On the Emergency Powers (Detentions) Law that allows for the administrative detention of hundreds of Palestinians, often without charge or proper representation, B'Tselem contends that neither "security of the area" nor "public security" are defined and that consequently "their interpretation [is] being left to the military commanders."

Furthermore, it states: "If the restrictions were intended to prevent attacks inside Israel, and not in the settlements, the policy would still be illegal because it is sweeping and disproportionate, giving it a semblance of collective punishment which is forbidden." In this position, B'Tselem follows what Iain Scobbie has interpreted

as the International Court of Justice's position in the Advisory on the Wall. He writes: "It would be odd to conclude that Israel may rely on self-defense to justify its response to acts that denote a breakdown of the order for which it ultimately bears responsibility under international law" (p. 83).

On the Separation Barrier, B'Tselem supports the International Court's Advisory Ruling in 2004, which found that the Fourth Geneva Convention applied to the occupied Palestinian territory and that the barrier was not in accordance with international law. While B'Tselem contends that Israel has a right to self-defense, it claims that the barrier is "the most extreme solution that causes the greatest harm to the local population." Moreover, the Centre charges that Israel chose the route through the West Bank in order "to avoid the political price to be paid if the Green Line were set as Israel's border." B'Tselem recommends that any fence should be "built along the Green Line or on Israeli territory."

On the highly charged matter of Jerusalem, B'Tselem declares that "East Jerusalem is occupied territory" and that "the annexation of East Jerusalem breaches international law." Moreover, the group's documentary analysis reveals that Jerusalem-born Palestinians are not accorded citizenship but rather "permanent resident" (in effect "new immigrant") status. Most significantly, this has implications for their movement in and out of the city as well as their access to social services.

As further evidence of the dual system of law, B'Tselem charges that Israeli "enforcement agencies" all but ignore "routine" settler violence against Palestinians and their property, noting that "these actions are intended to force Palestinians to leave their homes and farmland, and thereby enable the settlers to gain control of them."

Consistent with the position that laws governing civilians in the Occupied Territories should apply to all who reside there, B'Tselem is critical of any and all attacks on Israeli settlers, which, the Centre writes, "undermine all rules of morality and law. Whatever the circumstances, such acts are unjustifiable." Furthermore, it notes:

The illegality of the settlements has no effect at all on the status of their civilian residents. The settlers constitute a distinctly civilian population, which is entitled to all the protections granted civilians by international law. The Israeli security forces' use of land in the settlements or the membership of some settlers in the Israeli security forces does not affect the status of the other residents living among them, and certainly does not make them proper targets of attack.

RESPONSE AND IMPACT

B'Tselem's reports appear to be held in high regard by Israeli officials, as evidenced, for example, by the almost immediate, albeit critical, response by the Israel Ministry of Foreign Affairs, "Human Rights Issues for the Palestinian Population." B'Tselem's invitations to speak before Knesset committees and the success of several of its petitions before the High Court demonstrate the Centre's efficacy.

According to the activity reports, nearly every press release and comprehensive report received national and international media attention. Among their many claims, they celebrate those campaigns that led to changes in policy and practice, including pressure that led the Israeli Knesset to establish a committee to oversee IDF activities at checkpoints and roadblocks; pressure that led the IDF to form a special committee to evaluate and then to reconsider its housing demolition policy's efficacy; and engagements with the courts that led to the rare conviction of border police for abuse, court rulings on the legality and use of torture, as well as prohibitions against the use of Palestinian civilians in military missions, what the Israeli army called "prior use warning procedure" or the "neighbor procedure."

B'Tselem, along with Al Haq (Law in the Service of Man), West Bank, in 1989 received the Carter-Menil Award for Human Rights awarded to organizations for "their outstanding commitment, at the risk of their lives, to opposing human rights violations."

B'TSELEM'S CRITICS

Alongside academic and juridical scholars who accept Israel's position with respect to the Occupied Territories and the need for extraordinary measures to provide security for the state (Byman, 2006; Gavison, 2005), a number of interrelated Internet-based nongovernmental watchdog groups (Committee for Accuracy in Middle East Reporting in America [CAMERA], Independent Media Review and Analysis [IMRA], and NGO Monitor) that are highly critical of virtually all human rights organizations have been particularly critical of B'Tselem's methodology, repeatedly arguing that its fatality statistics are "unreliable" because they do not distinguish among those who were militarily engaged with the IDF and those who were not. It should be noted, however, that B'Tselem does include a disclaimer taking up this very issue, stating as follows:

> The listing of a person as a civilian, or having not participated in the fighting, or the inclusion of any other details

regarding the cause of death, does not indicate that the person or entity that killed the individual violated the law, or that the deceased was innocent, or that any other legal or moral conclusion can be drawn from the facts. The lists of fatalities relate to persons killed during incidents related to the al-Aqsa intifada, and are to be viewed solely in that light.

While a Factiva data service search in 2006 revealed extensive worldwide coverage of B'Tselem's press releases, there is no independent study citing the Centre's direct impact on Israeli, Palestinian, or worldwide attitudes. Despite its overall congratulatory tone, B'Tselem's activity reports are also self-reflexive. For example, in 2004 the organization noted: "The grave human rights violations that once captured headlines have now become part of the routine to which Israelis are accustomed, and the public and media have become increasingly apathetic to such incidents."

ASSESSMENT

The homepage on B'Tselem's Web site notes: "Readers of B'Tselem publications may decide to do nothing, but they cannot say, 'We didn't know.'" Read as a whole or in part, B'Tselem documents provide an invaluable resource for those interested in learning which human rights issues have engaged scholars, activists, jurists, and legislators in the Israel-Palestine conflict. They also highlight the challenges faced by human rights activists working on behalf of those living in the region.

Ronit Avni, who worked with PCATI, a key organization in the fight to end Israel's use of torture, writes: "In the end, it was a web of GSS [General Security Service, the Israeli internal security service] deceptions that the HCJ [High Court of Justice, the Israeli supreme court] could no longer tacitly permit, rather than any successful mobilization of popular opinion turned squarely against the practice." Nonetheless, she acknowledges that "without the vigilance and hard work of human rights groups such as B'Tselem, Physicians for Human Rights, and the Palestinian Human Rights Monitoring Group, abuses would continue, and the perpetrators would be able to casually deny, deflect, or discredit allegations made against them" (p. 206).

Reading B'Tselem's publications reveals the value as well as the limitations of human rights law and humanitarian law. With little enforcement capabilities, such groups take every opportunity to educate, communicating in order to agitate for change at every possible level. The weakness seems to lie less in their goals and practices than in the capacity for compassion between and among those caught in protracted militarized conflicts.

[*See also* Humanitarian Law; Israel; *and* West Bank and Gaza.]

BIBLIOGRAPHY

Avni, Ronit. "Mobilizing Hope: Beyond the Shame-Based Model in the Israeli-Palestinian Conflict." *American Anthropologist* 108, no. 1 (March 2006): 205–214.

Ben-Naftali, Orna, and Keren R. Michaeli. "Justice-Ability: A Critique of the Alleged Non-justiciability of Israel's Policy of Targeted Killings." *Journal of International Criminal Justice* 1 (2003): 368–405.

B'Tselem: The Israeli Information Centre for Human Rights in the Occupied Territories. http://www.btselem.org.

Byman, Daniel. "Do Targeted Killings Work?" *Foreign Affairs* 85, no. 2 (March/April 2006): 95–112.

CAMERA: Committee for Accuracy in Middle East Reporting in America. http://www.camera.org/.

Cohen, Stanley. "Government Responses to Human Rights Reports: Claims, Denials, and Counterclaims." *Human Rights Quarterly* 18, no. 3 (1996): 517–543.

Gavison, Ruth. "War and the Rule of (International) Law in the 21st Century—Lessons from Israel." *Democracy and Security* 1, no. 2 (March 2005): 119–126.

IMRA: Independent Media Review Analysis. http://www.imra.org.il/.

NGO Monitor. http://www.ngo-monitor.org/.

Scobbie, Iain. "Words My Mother Never Taught Me: 'In Defense of the International Court.'" *American Journal of International Law* 99, no. 1 (January 2005): 76–88.

Watson, Geoffrey R. "The 'Wall' Decisions in Legal and Political Context." *American Journal of International Law* 99, no. 1 (January 2005): 6–26.

BURMA (MYANMAR)

by Monique Skidmore and Trevor Wilson

This entry describes the human rights abuses perpetrated in Burma (Myanmar) in the modern era. It begins with a short historical background explaining the turbulent events of the nineteenth and twentieth centuries that brought the military to power in 1962. The discussion of human rights abuses in Burma under authoritarian rule is divided into three periods of military governance. These are the Burma Socialist Programme Party (BSPP), which ruled the country under General Ne Win (1962–1988); the State Law and Order Restoration Council (SLORC) period (encompassing the years 1988–1997); and the State Peace and Development Council (SPDC), a period of military rule that began in 1997 and was still operating as of 2008. The entry then describes the characteristics of human rights abuses during the SLORC and SPDC eras and international responses to these abuses. The process of charting Burma's human rights abuses is then examined, as well as the main human rights indicators that attempt to quantify the severity and scope of these abuses. In the summation attention is given to the limitations of the disaster relief provided to survivors of Cyclone Nargis.

HISTORICAL BACKGROUND

The history of the country known as Burma or Myanmar is a turbulent one. The twentieth century, in particular, saw the country move through forms of governance as diverse as colonialism, fascism, democracy, Buddhist socialism, and military dictatorship. There is much academic debate about Burmese prehistory and the existence of a unified Burman Kingdom in the central riverland plains and valleys of Burma. It is clear that many kingdoms rose and fell in central Burma, and in other areas of Burma as well. These included the Mon Kingdom of the ninth–eleventh, thirteenth–sixteenth, and eighteenth centuries, as well as the kingdoms established by the Burmans of Pagan (Bagan) (849–1287), Toungoo (1486–1752), and Konbaung dynasties (1758–1885). The geographic periphery of Burma is home to over a hundred minority groups, and Burma's current borders reflect colonial and postcolonial boundaries that often bear little resemblance to the long-established boundaries of traditional social groups. These older boundaries were created largely by topographical barriers such as mountain ranges and rivers. As a result, ethnic groups in Southeast and South Asia are often separated by nation-state boundaries, which has led to ineffectual state control in peripheral areas of the modern territorial states.

Burma is the junction of South and Southeast Asia and many of its minority groups straddle the country's international borders. This continues to be the source of much conflict in Burma, conflict that often spills over into Thailand and India. British colonization began with the annexation of Lower Burma in 1824 and resulted in the fall of the Burmese monarchy in 1886. Civil war against the British was waged in many parts of the country until the Japanese invaded during World War II (1942). The British returned following the war (in 1946), but a growing and increasingly united nationalist movement resulted in an agreement for independence for 1947. In that same year, the architect of the agreement, General Aung San, and most of his parliamentary cabinet were assassinated by an armed group (reputed to be hired by a rival politician, U Saw) before he could take office.

In January 1948 Burma was granted independence from Britain under the leadership of U Nu. Successive insurgencies plagued the new government for the next decade, including by the Burma Communist Party, members of the Karen minority group in eastern Burma, and former supporters of the assassinated Aung San. The coming to power in China of the Communist Party in 1949 resulted in remnants of the Chinese nationalist army, the Kuomintang under Chiang Kai-shek, entering northern Burma. The defection of Karen forces and Communists within the armed forces (in 1948) created civil war within the country once again. The new government found itself controlling only the immediate countryside around Rangoon. The turbulent times provided the crucible in which a reorganized and purposeful armed forces was reborn.

The army was not the only unifying force during these times, as the Socialist Party was also unifying the populace. The army outsted the remaining Karen commanders (1949) and a new leader emerged, General Ne Win, supreme commander of the armed forces. The economy revived somewhat during this period but continued political instability led the prime minister, U Nu, in 1958 to ask General Ne Win to temporarily step in to stabilize the country in preparation for nationwide elections. Ne Win handed power back to U Nu when the latter won the 1960 elections with a large majority.

HUMAN RIGHTS ABUSES IN BURMA UNDER AUTHORITARIAN RULE

The years 1960–1962 saw the reinstatement of democratic governance in Burma and attempts to rescue the flailing economy. Burmese politics and everyday life experienced a watershed year in 1962 with the staging of a military coup in March of that year. The postcolonial democratic government of Prime Minister U Nu was usurped by the chief of the armed forces, General Ne Win, permanently ending democratic governance in Burma.

The Burma Socialist Programme Party (BSPP).

From 1962 to 1988 Ne Win presided over the Burma Socialist Programme Party (BSPP) and ruled the country as military dictator. The BSPP was led by a seventeen-member Revolutionary Council, whose ideological platform was the "Burmese Road to Socialism." This involved the nationalization of most of the country's enterprises, resulting in everyday living essentials becoming available only on the black market. This nationalization went hand in hand with the demonetization of large bank notes and the removal of most of the Indian-Chinese mercantile class from the country.

Under General Ne Win, Burma was hardly a bastion of liberty. Arbitrary arrest and detention of political prisoners were the norm, severe restrictions were imposed on freedom of expression, and lip service was paid to the rule of law. But these shortcomings were not the subject of much international criticism as long as other formalities, such as parliamentary processes and elections, were followed. While Burma rhetorically adhered to the neutralist principles of the 1954 Bandung Conference and participated nominally in the United Nations, its actual acceptance of the norms of multilateral human rights instruments was very limited. Before 1988 it had not adhered to any international human rights conventions

and the only UN human rights organization Burma joined was the International Labour Organization. Burmese law was equally slim in the human rights protections it offered the people; many of the draconian internal security provisions of the British colonial period continue to the present day, including the repressive Penal Code and the forced labor provisions of the notorious Towns and Villages Acts.

Dissension, activism, and acts of resistance occurred throughout the BSPP period. This was a time of hardship, repression, and economic mismanagement. The BSPP period was also characterized by the strategic use of political violence to engender and perpetuate fear among the Burmese populace in the cities and towns. The imposition of political might was considered by Burmese citizens to be arbitrary and excessive and the use of military intelligence and propaganda was seen as blunter and less sophisticated than the experience that the population has had with successive military regimes. In the nation's geographic peripheries, minority groups fought military campaigns against the Burmese armed forces in a civil war that continues in parts of the country.

While remaining as chair of the BSPP, Ne Win resigned from his position of president of the Republic of Burma, but his hand-picked successors in the army continued to rule the country.

State Law and Order Restoration Council (SLORC).

The nation once known as the rice bowl of Asia was declared by the United Nations a Least Developed Country (LDC) in 1987. Ne Win resigned in July 1988, but not before overseeing another episode of massive demonetization of large currency notes. These events were forerunners for a nationwide uprising on 8 August 1988, known as the "Four Eights," the day that marked the end of the Burmese Way to Socialism under the BSPP (whose name had been changed to the National Unity Party). This transformed forever the relationship between the Burmese of the cities and towns and the army, the Tatmadaw. The demonstrations for democracy that were held throughout the country led to a breakdown of law and order, which came to an abrupt halt when the Tatmadaw received orders to fire upon the demonstrators. The reported numbers of people killed vary widely, from 3,000 in Yangon (the former Rangoon) to 10,000 nationwide. A very small amount of video footage exists of the army firing into unarmed crowds in Yangon.

On 19 August 1988 General Sein Lwin resigned as president of Burma and chair of the BSPP. Known widely in Yangon and later abroad as the "Butcher of Burma," he is credited with giving the order to the Tatmadaw to fire upon the demonstrators. He was replaced by Dr. Maung Maung Kha, an eminent lawyer and academic. A civilian was not destined to last long in the role of president, however, and the following month, on 18 September, a military coup was staged and a group of military officers announced that the country was being run by a State Law and Order Restoration Council (SLORC). One of the first moves of the SLORC was to announce its intention to hold multiparty National Assembly elections in May 1989 and to return the country to a democratically elected government. General Saw Maung, commander in chief of the armed forces, became the country's new leader.

A week after the military coup that enshrined the SLORC, the National League for Democracy (NLD) was founded with Tin Oo, a former general, becoming chair of the coalition party and Aung San Suu Kyi taking on the role of general secretary. The party committed itself to the pursuit of democracy, human rights, and the well-being of the population. Other political parties arose to contest the elections, and U Nu declared a parallel government. The charisma and popular appeal of Aung San Suu Kyi, Tin Oo, and Kyi Maung in particular were quickly evident throughout the country, as the NLD launched a furious campaign against the SLORC. On 20 July 1989 the SLORC placed Aung San Suu Kyi and Tin Oo under house arrest and disqualified them from running in the Parliamentary General Election, which was held on 27 May 1990. The National League for Democracy won 392 of the 485 seats contested in the elections.

Contrary to its stated commitment to hand the nation back to democratic rule, the SLORC refused to accept the results of the election. Two months later, on 27 July, Secretary Number One Khin Nyunt signed into existence Declaration No. 1/90. This Declaration nullified the 1945 Constitution and instituted martial law. Under martial law, it proclaimed that only the SLORC had the right to exercise legislative, executive, and judicial power.

During the next few years, the format for succession of the various graduating officer classes became routinized. The tripartite leadership strategy proved particularly successful. The SLORC was headed by Senior General Than Shwe, who relied on two senior generals to carry out his commands. The first was General Khin Nyunt, who headed the Office of the Chief of Military Intelligence. Khin Nyunt became the most feared and visible member of the SLORC and ruled the cities through fear, propaganda, and a network of informers and intelligence

officers. It was he who engineered the continuing repression of the NLD and the student movement. He ran the legion of surveillance operators and informers, torture chambers, and listening posts. He outlawed faxes, computers, satellite technology, mobile phones, and communication with foreigners. The other senior position was that of chief of the Armed Forces, held by General Maung Aye, who oversaw the division of the country into the domains of Armed Forces commanders. These commanders waged war in minority areas and were ultimately responsible for the most terrible human rights violations that have occurred during the civil war. In return for their services, they would later be moved back to the relative luxury of Yangon, and made members of the SLORC. At that time, the most corrupt of the SLORC members were "permitted to retire." The Armed Forces have found this to be an eminently satisfactory form of career progression, and the tension between Military Intelligence and the Armed Forces allowed Senior General Than Shwe to remain in power during the 1990s and the early twenty-first century.

One of the most pressing issues for the SLORC was the ongoing civil war and the desperate need for hard currency. When a mutiny inside the Communist Party of Burma broke out in 1989, Khin Nyunt realized that this was an opportunity for the SLORC to negotiate cease-fire agreements with most of the ethnic minority groups, (apart from the Karen National Union), and to secure an end to their opposition to the government in Yangon. The peace deals forged between former armed groups were largely remnants of the Communist Party of Burma, and they kept their autonomy and their economic networks and gave the SLORC a portion of the profits and agreed to stop fighting them. This has allowed former armed groups to have revenue from resource extraction and, often, production of heroin and methamphetamine. Typically, Kokang drug lords began appearing with SLORC leaders and were billed as economic entrepreneurs from ethnic minority areas. Later, this general situation led to the creation of cities in the middle of jungles and forests on Burma's outskirts, full of casinos, brothels, illegal wildlife markets, and people smuggling, where half the world's heroin and most of its methamphetamines trade hands. This is the hard currency that allowed the regime to limp along through the 1990s.

The other pressing issue for the SLORC was the resistance that was put up by the Sangha, or order of monks. In 1990, 133 monasteries were raided in Mandalay and significant amounts of weapons were confiscated. Many monks were derobed and a process began of suborning the Sangha. This took the form of the military government spending millions of dollars toward the building and running of new monasteries, pagodas, missionary training schools, and novitiate training. Monks were sent on lavish trips abroad and were given expensive imported goods such as televisions. Not only did the military regime pursue this system of "incentives" for senior monks to comply with the regime, the alternative strategy was also pursued, with the posting of soldiers outside major monasteries. Pro-democracy sentiment within monastic institutions was rooted out with ruthless efficiency, with monks being derobed and tortured in prison. Monks from Mon and Rakhine State have fared the worst in this regard.

On 10 July 1995 Aung San Suu Kyi was released from house arrest. She immediately began to campaign for democracy, and within a year, crowds of up to 10,000 people were gathering on University Avenue to hear her speak to them over her front fence. The SLORC was dismayed by the growing crowds and forbade her to speak in public. A virulent propaganda campaign was launched against her in the state media. Students, in particular, were frustrated by the renewed censorship of the National League for Democracy. In December 1996 and through January 1997, this frustration erupted into a series of student hit-and-run demonstrations in major cities and towns, but especially in Yangon. By 1996 the population had had a chance to rebuild its opposition after the 1988 uprising. The universities had been reopened and were the scene of increasing collective resistance to military rule. For about six weeks students held demonstrations in Yangon, Mandalay, and Bago (formerly Pegu). Troops were rushed to the scene of each demonstration. Taxis and cars took their license plates off, drove up to the students, and dropped great wads of cash at their feet. In Hledan Junction in Yangon, the students staged a peaceful sit-in. When the regime finally stormed the students, the residents of urban Hledan Township opened their doors and sat with the students, hardly daring to breathe, all night, until they could escape the next morning. From this moment on, in late 1996, it became clear that the regime's unceasing propaganda and nation-building endeavors had only hardened the population's hatred for the SLORC. The universities were shut down but eventually a small number of rural technical institutions reopened in their stead. These institutions were placed away from areas where students and democracy activists congregate to protest against the regime. Aung San Suu Kyi was kept under house arrest for a further five years until the regime judged that the threat posed by student activism had been quieted.

This mini-uprising hastened the reshuffle that resulted in the formation of the State Peace and Development Council (SPDC) and eventually to the downfall of Military Intelligence as the regime's enforcers in the cities.

State Peace and Development Council (SPDC).
Feeling very satisfied with its new vision of the future, in late 1997 the SLORC renamed itself the SPDC, the State Peace and Development Council. No longer concerned solely with the emergency provision of law and order in a time of social anarchy and crisis, it saw itself now as instituting a permanent state of peace and development. Again it moved up loyal commanders, promoted junior officers, and "permitted the older members of the ruling council to retire." This is a phrase often found in the state media.

A counterinsurgency war is still being waged against dissenting populations in eastern Burma, intensified with an unprecedented number of battalions engaging in military campaigns and the application of a "Four Cuts" policy. This is a policy designed to deny insurgents access to intelligence, finances, food, or recruits, provided by the population at large throughout the year. This intensification can be gauged through the increasing number of refugees fleeing the violence in neighboring Thailand; through the large number of villages, crops, and livestock destroyed by the Tatmadaw; and in the dire health situation of those populations on the run from the Burma Army.

Rape is used as a systematic tool of ethnic cleansing against Shan and Karen populations in the eastern states. The gang rape, torture, mutilation, and murder of Shan and Karen infants and girls as young as five by officers of the Burmese army has been continually documented by human rights groups. As long as the geopolitical situation remains, with China willing to protect Burma, these abuses of power by the SPDC will continue, as the human rights abuses are central to the government's effort to retain power.

DEALING WITH BURMA'S ENTRENCHED HUMAN RIGHTS ABUSES

After the military assumed power by force in 1988, widespread abuse of human rights by the Burmese military/authorities almost immediately came to notice. Initially this was through the tens of thousands of (mainly young) protesters and students who either fled the cities to take up their fight in the jungle or crossed the border into Thailand. Thailand would thereafter become "home" to these students as well as to many members of Burma's eastern border groups resisting the military takeover of power. Later human rights abuses came to attention through the spillover of displaced ethnic populations who were the victims of the SLORC/SPDC's intensified anti-insurgency campaigns and attempts to expand the territory under government control.

Characteristics of human rights abuses under SLORC and SPDC.

The initial refugees from Burma brought with them accounts of colleagues "disappearing" while in the custody of the security authorities, of systematic intimidation and ruthless repression of dissenters, the daily use of torture in interrogations, and of the harsh treatment of political prisoners, whose numbers have climbed to over 2,100 even as some political prisoners were released or (rarely) granted amnesty.

Along with the denial of democratic rights, civil human rights violations became the main grounds for international criticism of the SLORC/SPDC and were increasingly the justification for international sanctions against the regime (by the United States and the EU in the 1990s, and the majority of developed countries after 2003 and 2007). Human rights abuses by the SLORC/SPDC also became one of the main rationales for the long-running and relatively well-funded political campaigns by the expatriate Burmese opposition groups against the legitimacy of the SLORC/SPDC. It became increasingly clear that human rights abuses were a key instrument in the SLORC/SPDC's efforts to stay in power. The main perpetrators of human rights abuses were the Burmese Army, especially Military Intelligence and troops engaged in counterinsurgency actions along the eastern border of Burma, as well as officers from the Special Bureau, the Burmese Police Force, and prisons and correction establishments. Many of the techniques for torture or repression had in fact been practiced in Burma for a long time, including by the Ne Win regime, which was accorded considerable respect and help by the international community of the day. Forced labor, which had a historical background in Burma, grew more widespread as the SLORC/SPDC soon found itself short of funds and the army was forced to continually draw on local communities for its supply of labor for logistic support.

International responses to the SLORC/SPDC's human rights abuses.

The United Nations and its agencies soon began exposing the human rights abuses of the SLORC/SPDC and used a variety of means to mount pressure against the regime to change its behavior, although it was not until 2005 that the UN Security Council formally considered the situation in Burma. From 1991 the General Assembly Third Committee, which handles human rights issues, debated Burma every year, each year passing a (nonbinding) resolution citing a wide range of human rights abuses (from arbitrary detention without due process to extrajudicial killings, torture, forced relocation, lack of political freedoms, forced labor, etc.). A key issue, and obstacle, in achieving progress on human rights would be the question of access to victims (whether they were political prisoners or victims of forced labor or rape), since direct access to the country was not possible for virtually all international human rights organizations.

The main venue for examining Burma's human rights abuses was the UN Commission on Human Rights (CHR) in Geneva, which considered Burma's human rights situation at its annual sessions. As early as 1990 the CHR appointed Sadako Ogata of Japan, who was later to become the United Nations High Commissioner for Refugees, as a special envoy to report on the human rights situation in Burma. From 1992 a CHR resolution contained a mandate for the appointment of a special rapporteur on human rights in Burma. Although special rapporteurs were sometimes denied access to the country, their detailed reports became the most authoritative sources of information about human rights abuses in Burma, even though independent verification of human rights abuses was often made difficult by the lack of access to the country and to eye witnesses. Special rapporteurs were Yozo Yokota (Japan, 1992–1996), Rajsoomer Lallah (Mauritius, 1996–2000), and Paulo Sergio Pinheiro (Brazil, 2000–2008). Thomás Ojea Quintana (Argentina) was appointed to the position in March 2008 by the UN Human Rights Council, which replaced the Commission. Special rapporteurs, who did have access to prisons during their visits to Burma, reported in great detail and authoritatively on human rights abuses in Burma not only to the CHR in Geneva, but also to the Third Committee of the UN General Assembly in New York, where nonbinding resolutions critical of the SLORC/SPDC were passed annually. Understandably, these resolutions (passed by consensus and often without the support of Burma's Asian neighbors) were not very effective in changing the behavior of the SLORC/SPDC, although they suceeded in getting the regime's attention.

Although the UN Security Council, because of disagreements among member states, would not be able to take action on Burma until the end of 2005, the UN secretary-general used the mandate in a General Assembly resolution to appoint a special envoy on Burma from 1997. The special envoy's mission was to perform a "good offices" role by engaging in dialogue with the SLORC/SPDC and opposition representatives about the restoration of democracy, but the envoy also sought to make progress on the human rights situation. (The UN secretary-general appoints special envoys to only twenty-five other individual countries around the world.) Although the SLORC/SPDC denied the allegations of human rights abuses, it cooperated only partially with the special envoys, who were permitted to visit occasionally but sometimes denied access to the country altogether. Special envoys included Alvaro de Soto (Peru, 1997–1999; he also visited Burma 1995–1997) and Razali Ismail (Malaysia, 2000–2006). For a period after the latter's resignation, there was no special envoy because the SPDC refused to agree to the appointment of a successor, but in June 2006 Ibrahim Gambari, a former foreign minister of Nigeria and senior UN official, was appointed to the position. Gambari visited Burma in October 2006, November 2007, and March and August 2008. Special envoys have generally been permitted to meet NLD Leader Aung San Suu Kyi even when she has been under house arrest, as part of their attempts to assist the process of national political reconciliation. The August 2008 visit by Gambari is significant in that Aung San Suu Kyi refused to meet with him, signaling her frustration with the lack of progress the UN is making on political reform in Burma.

From 1991 the International Labour Organization (ILO) also increased its surveillance of Burma's breaches of various international labor conventions to which it was party by virtue of its membership in the ILO. Some of these breaches, including the use of forced labor, in particular, by the Burmese army and the denial of the right of workers to organize, had been the subject of ILO criticism for more than thirty years. In 1998, in response to a complaint by workers' representatives acting out of solidarity with Burmese workers and Burmese opposition parties, the ILO organized a Commission of Inquiry into forced labor, which reported in detail on the practice, although the Commission was not permitted to visit Burma to carry out its investigations. Thereafter, various ILO bodies passed resolutions criticizing Burma regularly and imposing limited sanctions on the SPDC. Unlike some multilateral agencies, the ILO was able to send official missions to the country for discussions with the SLORC/SPDC; in 2000, under threat of UN sanctions, these measures led

significantly to the formal rescinding of long-established Burmese laws permitting forced labor. While subsequent ILO reports confirmed some reduction in the incidence of forced labor, this was insufficient, as the overall pattern of forced labor persisted.

Cooperation by the SLORC/SPDC with the ILO was at times severely contested and at times relatively amicable, but it was always marked by uncertainty and challenge. It was not until 2001, for example, that the ILO was allowed to open an office in Burma, through which it initially insisted on the freedom to visit areas prone to forced labor. In a deliberate effort to move into areas of practical cooperation, the ILO also began discussing ways to eliminate forced labor gradually. One first step was a complaints mechanism, through the ILO Office in Yangon, which the SPDC permitted but only in a very circumscribed and unsatisfactory manner, which exacerbated poor relations with the ILO and prompted the SPDC to threaten to withdraw from the ILO (a threat it has not carried out). The ILO also commenced discussion of a technical assistance program for the eventual elimination of forced labor. As of mid-2008 this program had not been agreed to by the SPDC, after several years of negotiation. On many occasions, the SPDC chose to take its differences with the ILO right to the brink, illustrating how sensitive issues such as forced labor are for the military establishment.

A policy of "durable resettlement" is being practiced by the United Nations High Commissioner for Refugees (UNHCR). This means that in the Thai border refugee camps, medics, teachers, and other refugees are leaving to begin lives in third countries. The ramifications of this new policy and of the Royal Thai government allowing refugee camp members to gain work permits and employment in Thailand are as yet unknown. Other UN agencies operating humanitarian and assistance programs in Burma such as UNICEF have reported on the incidence of child soldiers. Further, UNHCR has reported on the mistreatment of minority groups seeking refuge from the SLORC/SPDC, such as the Muslim Rohingya refugees who came under pressure to leave Rakhine State and move to Bangladesh after 1992. The World Health Organization (WHO), and later the Joint United Nations Programme on HIV/AIDS (UNAIDS), monitored discrimination against HIV/AIDS sufferers and their families.

Over the years, the SLORC/SPDC's record of cooperation with the United Nations over human rights has been mixed. The standard SLORC/SPDC response to allegations of human rights abuses was to deny that they were occurring, to defend its practices on the grounds of threats to national security, and to accuse other countries of interfering in its internal affairs. It regarded UNCHR resolutions (such as that in 2000) as "factually incorrect, politically motivated and aimed at tarnishing the image of the country, and is used as a political instrument to exert pressure on the Government." It objected to UN Security Council action on Burma on the grounds that Burma is "not a threat to either international or regional peace and security" and that they were "matters that, under the Charter of the United Nations, lie within the domestic domain of [Burma]." It either completely blocked or significantly restricted the visits of most UN representatives to Burma.

Eventually, the human rights situation in Burma became a formal agenda item for the United Nations Security Council; the possible consequences of Security Council investigations and resolutions are not yet clear. Mass rallies have been held across Burma and Burmese people have been forced to participate at these rallies in the denouncement of the Security Council's deliberations. Clearly, Burma's military junta is uneasy about the increased international focus upon its human rights abuses, but the message it is relaying to the world via the state media and its co-opted citizens is one of ongoing defiance.

Documenting human rights abuses in Burma.

Charting of human rights abuses in Burma has since 1988 been increasingly undertaken by private nongovernmental organizations (NGOs). Establishment of a wide range of human rights reporting organizations on the Thai side of the Burmese border, with the generous support of such international philanthropic organizations as the Open Society Institute of George Soros, has enabled more systematic reporting of human rights abuses. Prodemocracy groups and their supporters were effective in generating publicity for the SLORC/SPDC's human rights abuses and thereby in mobilizing support for their campaigns for sanctions against the military regime. Many new groups were established with specific human rights mandates such as the Assistance Association of Political Prisoners, the Karen Human Rights Group, and the Shan Human Rights Foundation, and their documentation of human rights abuses gradually became more sophisticated and more valuable to UN agencies and others. At the global level, bodies like the International Committee of the Red Cross (ICRC), Amnesty International, Human Rights Watch, and later Reporters sans frontières (Reporters without Borders) began to focus on collecting data about

human rights abuses and providing these data to relevant UN agencies such as the Commission on Human Rights, the ILO, and the UNHCR.

The only organization among these NGOs that was able to maintain a presence inside the country was the ICRC, which maintained an office in Yangon from 1990 to 1995 and again beginning in 1999, as well as offices in some regional centers. The ICRC offices monitor human rights conditions, especially in relation to political prisoners, to whom it generally had access, although this stopped in late 2005. Despite closing its office in Yangon between 1995 and 1999, the ICRC was able to consolidate its presence with offices in regional centers. But after 2004 its relations with the SPDC deteriorated again, and by June 2007 it decided to depart from its normal practice to denounce publicly "major and repeated violations of international humanitarian law" in Burma. With the exception of the ICRC, these international human rights bodies were mostly denied access to Burma for the purposes of their work, apart from Amnesty International, which, unusually, was permitted to visit Burma twice in 2003 and allowed access to some human rights victims. However, the quality of international NGO reporting of human rights abuses was still extremely high and left no doubt about the nature and extent of abuses by the military regime. Amnesty International, for example, has produced numerous reports on aspects of human rights abuses in Burma in addition to its annual reports on the country, often based on a pattern of testimony from refugees fleeing in-country fighting or repression. More recently, the advent of "citizen journalism" in Burma, using mobile phone technology and Internet blogging, has meant that a larger volume of information is available from in-country sources, and this information is received much more quickly, as these new technologies escape much of the net of information suppression practiced by the military regime.

Efforts by UN agencies to persuade the SLORC/SPDC to change its behavior, to engage with relevant agencies to bring Burma into greater conformity with international human rights standards, and to even subscribe formally to additional international human rights instruments have achieved some progress, but the progress has been slow and the process frustrating. So far the only human rights conventions that Burma has signed are the Convention on the Rights of the Child (in 1991) and the Convention on the Discrimination against Women in 1997. Burma also provides regular reports on its observance of the provisions of both conventions. However, the regime is still acknowledged to be in breach of many of these instruments and fails to report adequately on measures it has taken to comply with the provisions of these instruments. Burma has not signed the International Covenant on Economic, Social, and Cultural Rights, although this was reported to be under consideration in the early 2000s. Not surprisingly, the SPDC has not signed the International Covenant on Civil and Political Rights. Burma is a party to the 1949 Geneva Conventions, which mandate humanitarian standards in internal as well as international war.

Yet, although concrete improvements in human rights are hard to identify, it is also evident that the SPDC on occasion listens to criticism of its human rights performance. After the appearance of the "Licence to Rape" report in 2002 by the Shan Human Rights Foundation (SHRF) and the Shan Women's Action Network (SWAN), the SPDC invited the special rapporteur to investigate the situation for himself. In 2000 the SPDC agreed to an Australian proposal to provide human rights capacity-building training to officials and others and began attending the Asian Forum for Human Rights and Development as an observer. The SPDC also established a Human Rights Committee, chaired by the minister for Home Affairs, as a precursor (it claimed) to establishing an independent Human Rights Commission. Although the Human Rights Committee functioned in a formal fashion for a few years, its activities ceased after the October 2004 purge of Prime Minister General Khin Nyunt and his Military Intelligence organization. In 2004 the SPDC enacted anti–people-trafficking legislation in response to criticisms of widespread prevalence of trafficking of women and children, and it has been cooperating with UN agencies and governments such as Australia to eliminate people trafficking.

Since enacting the legislation, the SPDC has prosecuted some offenders under its new people trafficking legislation, and a small number of soldiers have been charged with rape and forced labor, usually without publicity. But generally, members of the army are not held to account for any offenses they may have committed under civilian law, and any disciplinary action taken under the military code is not made public. There are no accounts of members of the army being charged with recruiting child soldiers, yet Burma is still believed to have the largest number of child soldiers in the world. (The numbers are not known, but figures as high as 80,000 are sometimes mentioned.) The rule of law is almost never applied to members of the army who may have carried out misdeeds against the general population, so human rights abuses

by the army, although they would appear to be common occurrences and are widely reported, mostly go unpunished.

In some areas, especially political freedoms, repressive measures by the SPDC that result in legally sanctioned human rights abuses remain as pervasive as ever. For example, party political activity is again severely restricted. The NLD is still the only political party allowed to have an identifiable office; it was allowed to re-open many of its offices across the country in 2002–2003, but all of these except the office in Yangon were subsequently closed again. Any expression of dissent whatsoever with the government is essentially treated as a subversive act, no matter its nature or the issue. This was most evident in the mass demonstrations in 2007 that started as protests against fuel price increases. Public gatherings of more than five people are still not allowed, and people are often detained for such "offenses," sometimes for long periods and often with no charges of any kind being made.

BURMA AND HUMAN RIGHTS INDICATORS

Various organizations now publish rankings of countries for performance in matters such as human rights. Burma is consistently ranked very low in these listings. For example:

- Freedom House deems Burma "not free" and gives it very poor scores for Political Rights (Score: 7) and Civil Liberties (Score: 7). (The highest score is 1, the worst is 7.)
- Press Freedom Index (Reporters without Borders): Burma ranks 164 out of 169 countries.
- In 2008 Transparency International's perceptions of the degree of corruption as seen by businesspeople and country analysts rank Burma 178 out of 180 countries, with a score of only 1.3 out of a possible 10.
- The United Nations Development Programme's Human Development Index 2007/2008 ranks Burma 132 in the world, out of 177 countries.
- Maximiliano Herrera's Human Rights Site nominates Burma as one of the most repressive nations in the world in 2007, along with and ahead of North Korea and Iraq.
- The World Audit of Democracy ranks Burma last out of 150 countries in its overall index of democracy in 2007.

The regime forcibly secured adoption of its constitution through a referendum in 2008 and proposes to hold national and local level elections in 2010, allowing the head of the junta, Senior General Than Shwe, to effectively retire and his hand-picked successors to have their role in the parliament enshrined through the constitution. Aung San Suu Kyi is now in her sixties and still under house arrest, while the student movement has been almost completely silenced through the 2007 arrest of the "88 Generation Students" leaders and the long prison sentences handed down to them. In addition, many monks who participated in the 2007 failed "Saffron Revolution" have been imprisoned or have fled the country.

ASSESSMENT

The human rights violations that are occurring in Burma cannot be fully captured by the standard reporting tools of human rights organizations, as they span a spectrum from the most egregious forms of extrajudicial killing and torture to the enforced poverty, denial of basic medicines, and inculcation of a permanent state of fear and vulnerability among the populace. Propaganda, self-censorship, anomie, and despair are common in Burma. The strategic use of political violence, rape, extortion, and threats creates an atmosphere where individual human rights violations are difficult to sort into discrete categories.

Across the country the number of political prisoners, deaths in custody, war casualties, and deaths due to violence occurring in forcibly relocated populations subject to unemployment and forced labor are generally decreasing as the SPDC "pacifies" more of the country. Although there may be an overall decrease in numbers in the late twentieth and early twenty-first centuries, war continues to be waged against groups that refuse to submit to the SPDC; forced relocation will continue to occur, especially in areas where large infrastructure is planned; rape, torture, and extrajudicial killings are still routinely reported in areas where the Tatmadaw (armed forces) is waging war; political opponents continue to be arrested, tortured, and die in prison under suspicious circumstances.

The 2006 move to a new, less accessible administrative capital, Naypyidaw, for example, was conducted during an increased period of arrest and incarceration of democracy advocates, most notably the student leaders of the 1988 prodemocracy uprising. The human rights of Burmese people will continue to be held hostage to the geopolitical realities of this part of Southeast Asia. Burma has become a heavily penetrated Chinese satellite nation and the United Nations Security Council is not able to pressure the Burmese military regime because of Burma's powerful backers, especially China.

The blockading and delaying of disaster relief for the survivors of Cyclone Nargis in the Irrawaddy Delta in May 2008 raised the specter of armed intervention in Burma under the "Mandate to Protect." This issue, however, was not taken up in the United Nations. Instead, the UN secretary-general maintained pressure on the military regime, which eventually accepted most of the offers of assistance.

[*See also* Aung San Suu Kyi.]

BIBLIOGRAPHY

Amnesty International. *Myanmar: Justice on Trial.* London: Amnesty International, 2003.

Amnesty International. *Myanmar: Travesties of Justice: Continued Misuse of the Legal System.* London: Amnesty International, 2005.

Assistance Association for Political Prisoners "The Darkness We See: Torture in Burma's Interrogation Centers and Prisons." Mae Sot, Tak, Thailand: Assistance Association for Political Prisoners, 2005.

Callahan, Mary P. *Making Enemies: War and State Building in Burma.* Ithaca, N.Y.: Cornell University Press, 2003.

Department of State, Bureau of East Asian and Pacific Affairs. "Conditions in Burma and U.S. Policy toward Burma for the Period September 28, 2005–March 27, 2006." Released to Congress April 17, 2006.

Department of State. *International Religious Freedom Report 2007. Bureau of Democracy, Human Rights, and Labor.* http://www.state.gov/g/drl/rls/irf/2007/90131.htm.

Freedom House. *The Worst of the Worst.* New York: Freedom House, May 2007.

Human Rights Watch. *Crackdown: Repression of the 2007 Popular Protests in Burma.* New York: Human Rights Watch, 2007.

Human Rights Watch. *Sold to Be Soldiers: The Recruitment and Use of Child Soldiers in Burma.* New York: Human Rights Watch, 2007.

International Committee of the Red Cross (ICRC). *ICRC Annual Report 2006: Myanmar.* Geneva, Switzerland: ICRC, 2007.

International Labour Organization. *Report of the Commission of Inquiry on Forced Labor in Myanmar.* Geneva, Switzerland: ILO, 1998.

Kinley, David, and Trevor Wilson. "Engaging a Pariah: Human Rights Training in Burma/Myanmar." *Human Rights Quarterly* 29, no. 2 (2007): 368–402.

Lintner, Bertil. *Outrage: Burma's Struggle for Democracy.* London: White Lotus; Cincinnati: Distributed in the United States by Seven Hill Books, 1990.

Myanmar Ministry of Foreign Affairs. *Annual International Religious Freedom Report 2005 Does Not Reflect True*

Situation in Myanmar. Yangon, Burma, 2005. http://www.myanmar-information.net/infosheet/2005/051043.htm.

Pilger, John, and David Munro. *Inside Burma: Land of Fear.* Oley, Pa.: Bullfrog Films, 1996.

Reporters without Borders. *Burma:—Annual Report 2008.* Paris, 2008.

Selth, Andrew. *Burma's Armed Forces: Power without Glory.* Norwalk, Conn.: EastBridge, 2002.

Shan Human Rights Foundation and Shan Women's Action Network. *Licence to Rape: The Burmese Military Regime's Use of Sexual Violence in the Ongoing War in Shan State.* Bangok, 2002.

Skidmore, Monique. *Karaoke Fascism: Burma and the Politics of Fear.* Philadelphia: University of Pennsylvania Press, 2004.

Smith, Martin. *Burma: Insurgency and the Politics of Ethnicity.* London; Atlantic Highlands, N.J.: Zed Books, 1991.

Smith, Martin. *Fatal Silence? Freedom of Expression and the Right to Health in Burma.* London: Article 19, 1996.

United Nations High Commissioner for Refugees (UNHCR). *The State of the World's Refugees: Human Displacement in the New Millennium.* New York: Oxford University Press, 2006.

BURUNDI

by René Lemarchand

In the spring and summer of 1972 the tiny central African republic of Burundi suffered a bloodletting of genocidal proportions. Over a period of five months, anywhere from 200,000 to 300,000 people were sent to their graves in the wake of an abortive insurrection led by a handful of opponents to the regime. In the early twenty-first century a number of questions remained unanswered, ranging from the exact number of victims to the identity of the insurgent leadership and the role of external actors.

On a number of points, however, there is widespread agreement among observers. While the uprising was directed against members of the ruling Tutsi minority, the victims of the repression were overwhelmingly Hutu, the majority group representing some 85 percent of a total population numbering roughly 5 million. Although the rebellion was highly localized, centering on the Nyanza and Rumonge provinces in the south, the retribution was countrywide, extending its avenging arm to every province and town. If the killings were largely the work of the Tutsi-dominated army, it received considerable assistance from the Tutsi-led Jeunesses Révolutionnaires Rwagasore (JRR), the youth wing of the ruling Union pour le Progrès National (Uprona) party. And the carnage began in early May, systematically targeting educated Hutu elements, and lasted well into August. By then virtually every Hutu politician, civil servant, and army officer and a vast number of university students down to secondary and primary schoolchildren were either dead or in exile. From this drastic surgery emerged a polity entirely dominated by members of the Tutsi minority. Finally in 1988 a series of reforms profoundly reshaped Burundi's mono-ethnic state.

Perhaps the most striking aspect of what must be described as independent Africa's first genocide is how little attention it received from the outside world. While Rwanda has become a household word, evocative of one of the worst genocides of the twentieth century, how many in the early twenty-first century, outside a small circle of Africanists, remember the Burundi tragedy?

A FORGOTTEN GENOCIDE

The silence of the international community surrounding the events of 1972 in Burundi is all the more surprising when one considers the highly emotional reaction of the White House at the time. President Richard Nixon's anger over the State Department's efforts to downplay the Burundi tragedy is vividly conveyed in a document made public in the early twenty-first century by a Canadian scholar, Christian Desroches. "This is one of the most cynical, callous reactions of a great government to a terrible tragedy I have seen," wrote Nixon in the margins of a memo from his national security adviser Henry Kissinger.

> When the Paks try to put down a rebellion in East Pakistan, the world screams. When Indians kill a few thousand Paks, no one cares; Biafra stirs us because of Catholics; the Israeli Olympics because of Jews; the north Vietnam bombings because of Communist leanings in our establishment. But when 100,000, one third of the population of a black country, are murdered, we say and do nothing, because we must not make blacks look bad, except of course when Catholic blacks are killed. I do not buy this double standard. (Desroches, pp. 3–4)

Nixon's emotional reaction never went beyond the confines of the Oval Office. The attitude of the State Department is appropriately captured in the title of the 1973 report of the Carnegie Endowment for International Peace, *Passing By: The United States and Genocide in Burundi, 1972.* It is hardly an exaggeration to say that the overall public reaction in the United States and abroad was one of almost total indifference.

In contrast to the extensive media coverage of the Rwanda bloodbath, the Burundi killings received only minimal attention in the American press. International organizations, including the Organization of African Unity (OAU)—now known as the African Union (AU)—and the United Nations (UN) either ignored the tragedy or felt obligated to convey pro forma expressions of sympathy to the Burundi authorities in charge of orchestrating mass murder. The most astonishing response came from the OAU secretary-general Diallo Telli following his visit to Bujumbura, the Burundi capital, on 22 May 1972. "The OAU," Telli opined, "being essentially an organization based on solidarity, my presence here in Bujumbura signifies the total solidarity of the Secretariat with the President of Burundi" (quoted in Hoyt). Hardly more edifying were the pious hopes expressed by the UN secretary-general Kurt Waldheim on the heels of a special visit of the UN mission to Burundi in June. Waldheim voiced his "fervent hopes that peace, harmony and stability can be brought about successfully and speedily, that Burundi will thereby achieve the goals of social progress, better standards of living and other ideals and principles set forth in the UN Charter" (Teltsch, p. 1).

For this extraordinary lack of public concern in the face of such appalling human rights violations there are several explanations. One is that in the early 1970s human rights issues had yet to dominate the conscience and policy agenda of the West to the extent that they do in the early twenty-first century. Another has to do with the severe restrictions placed on journalists seeking to investigate the circumstances and extent of the killings. The standard scenario awaiting reporters was one in which the government presented its own version of the facts—with the emphasis placed on the only "genocide" worth reporting about, that committed by the insurgents—and then only allowed interviews with members of the ruling oligarchy. In the months following the killings, a sustained effort was made by the government to give a hearing to its own "truth": at no time can the army be accused of committing genocide; its intervention can best be described as a heroic enterprise destined to prevent the Tutsi minority from being annihilated by Hutu insurgents. This version of events remained a central ingredient of the official truth manufactured by the Burundi authorities long after the killings stopped.

But perhaps the key explanation for the silence of the media in general and the international community in particular lies in the abyssal ignorance surrounding the most basic facts of the country's past and recent history. In the early twenty-first century Burundi conjures an image of Byzantine complexity that defies comprehension.

TOWARD ETHNIC POLARIZATION

Seen through the lens of precolonial history, this image seems entirely justified. Burundi and Rwanda are sometimes described as "false twins." Of roughly equal size, approximately 10,100 square miles, both were traditional kingdoms—"ancient" or "archaic" kingdoms, as sometimes characterized by anthropologists—and shared the same ethnic map, with the Hutu representing some 85 percent of the population, the Tutsi 14 percent, and the pygmoid Twa 1 percent. A closer look at Burundi, however, reveals a far more complicated picture. On a number of counts it differed from its neighbor to the north. The monarchy was not nearly as centralized as that in Rwanda, and the real holders of power were a group of traditional chiefly figures collectively known as *ganwa*. Relations between Hutu and Tutsi moreover were not as rigidly structured as in Rwanda, where the "premise of inequality," to use the title of Jacques Maquet's classic treatment of traditional Rwanda, found ample justification in social distance between the ruling Tutsi minority and the Hutu masses (Maquet, 1961). In Burundi, by contrast, if ethnic relations were more flexible, this was in part because the ethnic map was more complicated. For one thing the *ganwa* stood as a distinct ethnic category even though most were of Tutsi origins. Furthermore, there were major cultural differences between the Tutsi-Hima and the Tutsi-Banyaruguru, the former largely concentrated in the southern provinces and traditionally held in contempt by the Banyaruguru, who held a higher rank in the traditional pecking order. Finally, family ties were at least as important as ethnic identities in determining one's station in life. Thus a Hutu from a good family ranked higher than a Tutsi of lowly origins.

All of this helps explain why, in contrast with Rwanda, in Burundi it took a far longer period of time for the Hutu-Tutsi cleavage to become polarized. At the time they became independent in 1962, Rwanda was a republic under Hutu rule, while Burundi was still a monarchy, seemingly immune to ethnic tension. The central conflict was not between Hutu and Tutsi but between different *ganwa* factions—the Bezi versus the Batare, the first identified with the Union pour le Progrès National (Uprona; Union for National Progress), the other with the Parti Démocrate Chrétien (PDC; Christian Democratic Party). As 1962 drew to a close, the only party that stood for the rights of the Hutu was the Parti du Peuple (PP; Party of the People), whose membership was marginal compared to that of the main contenders. In the next few years the PP gained a substantial following among urban-based Hutu, while the Uprona became increasingly identified with Tutsi supremacy.

Behind the rise of a Hutu political consciousness lies first and foremost the growing attractiveness of the

Rwandan republic as an alternative model to the monarchy. For many Hutu in Burundi, Rwanda's dominant party, Parti de l'Émancipation du Peuple Hutu (Parmehutu; People's Emancipation Party), was exactly what its name said it was—the vehicle of Hutu emancipation. For the Tutsi minority, by contrast, Rwanda stood as the symbol of what had to be avoided at all costs, a violent revolution paving the way for the emergence of Hutu hegemony and the flight into exile of tens of thousands of Tutsi refugees. The message of what could happen to Burundi came through clear and loud in the countless stories of atrocities told by the thousands of Tutsi who poured into the country during and after the Rwandan Revolution (1959–1962). Thus what some viewed as a model to be emulated others saw as a nightmarish vision of what the future held in store unless Hutu threats were properly dealt with.

And dealt with they were, ruthlessly. A turning point in the rise of Hutu-Tutsi tensions was the assassination on 18 January 1965 of Pierre Ngendadumwe, Burundi's first Hutu prime minister, by a Tutsi refugee employed by the U.S. embassy. Shortly thereafter Hutu candidates scored a major victory in the legislative elections of May 1965, with twenty-three seats out of a total of thirty-three in parliament, but were soon robbed of their victory when the king, yielding to Tutsi pressures, appointed a *ganwa* as prime minister. This led to the next fatal step. At dawn on 19 October a group of Hutu gendarmerie officers attacked the royal palace but failed in their attempt to seize power. While the king, Mwambutsa, quickly left the country never to return, two days later thirty-eight Hutu officers were arrested and shot. On 28 October ten leading Hutu politicians were summarily tried and executed. In the following weeks eighty-six death sentences were handed down by improvised military tribunals. The next major purge occurred in September 1969, when rumors of an impending Hutu-engineered coup led to the arrests and executions of scores of influential Hutu personalities, many in the government and the army. By then the Hutu leadership had been virtually decapitated.

Thus even though its traditional system was unlike Rwanda in many respects, Burundi society by the early 1970s looked like the mirror image of its neighbor to the north—rent asunder by a split between Hutu and Tutsi. And just as in Rwanda, many resident Tutsi felt they had no other option than to seek asylum abroad, so also many Hutu in Burundi, including those later involved in the 1972 insurrection, decided to leave the country. Denied

every opportunity to gain a meaningful share of power, many were those who felt that there was no alternative to the use of force to press their claims.

THE DYNAMICS OF MASS MURDER

The timing of the Hutu insurgency draws attention to the emergence of bitter intra-ethnic rivalries among Tutsi. Beginning in 1971 a deep split emerged within the ruling oligarchy between Tutsi-Hima, the real holders of power, and the Tutsi-Banyaruguru. For months the country seemed to be tottering on the brink of anarchy. Rumors of plots and counterplots led to the arrests and bogus trials of scores of Banyaruguru politicians. President Michel Micombero, a Hima from Bururi, and his ruling clique saw their legitimacy plummet. The insurgents immediately grasped the strategic advantage that could be drawn from intra-Tutsi dissentions; on the other hand, nothing could have done more to restore unity to the Tutsi minority than the looming threat of a violent Hutu uprising.

Like a bolt out of the blue, the insurgency struck on 29 April, sending tremors through the lakeside towns of Rumonge and Nyanza-Lac in the south. In a matter of hours widespread violence was unleashed by Hutu upon Tutsi. Countless atrocities were reported by eyewitnesses. In the provincial capital of Bururi, the bastion of Hima elites, all military and civilian authorities were reported killed. After seizing the armories in Rumonge and Nyanza-Lac, they proceeded to kill every Tutsi in sight as well as a number of Hutu who refused to rally to their cause. At one point a group of rebels retreated to Vyanda, near Bururi, and proclaimed a mysterious People's Republic of Martyazo, an experiment quickly brought to an end by government troops sent to crush the rebellion. Although the uprising only lasted a few days, its cost in human lives went far beyond the hundreds or thousands of Tutsi killed by the insurgents.

How many Tutsi lost their lives at the hands of Hutu rebels is impossible to tell. Estimates vary widely from two thousand to five thousand, but the lower figure seems closer to the mark. Just as hard to assess is the number of insurgents. A French pilot who flew helicopter missions on behalf of the Burundi army came up with the number of one thousand, "including the majority of committed or conscripted Hutu, Mulelistes (a reference to the Congolese rebellion of 1964–1965, said to have been instigated by Pierre Mulele) and the organizers at the top" (quoted in Hoyt). Despite persistent reports of the presence of followers of Mulele, questions remain as to their numbers and motives. Although the core leadership was Hutu—involving, among others, three students from the University of Bujumbura, Albert Butoyi, Damien Ndabiruye, and Celius Mpasha, and a former parliamentarian, Ezechias Biyoero, all said to belong to the militantly pro-Hutu Burundi People's Party (BPP)—the rank and file of the rebellion included a substantial number of Congolese from the western shores of Lake Tanganyika. A fair number of these so-called Mulelistes were probably involved in the 1964–1965 rebellion in eastern Congo: as has been noted time and again, they displayed many of the ritual characteristics of the *simba* (lions) rebels of the 1960s, including a recourse to magic and drugs.

The racist underpinnings of the rebellion are revealed in the inflammatory tracts disseminated among the rural populations: "Arm yourselves and kill all the Tutsi!" "Let us unite in order to kill the Tutsi, army men and politicians!" "No trial for the Tutsi, only the grave!" (Chrétien and Dupaquier, p. 113). Though it is easy to detect the hand of the BPP in these incitements to racial hatred, ideology alone is not enough to explain why violence spread so swiftly through the lakeside provinces. Nor is it of much help in accounting for the number of Hutu killed by the rebels. Equally important is the social landscape of the region.

The area most directly affected by the insurgency consisted of an elongated strip of flatlands stretching southward along Lake Tanganyika known as the Imbo Plain. The area has always been considered different from the rest of the country. Though thickly populated with Hutu, it is also notable for the presence of a large number of Swahili-speaking migrants from the Congo. It remained administered by Hutu chiefs for many years after the advent of colonial rule, and when these were finally removed and replaced by Tutsi chiefs, anti-Tutsi sentiment became widespread. And furthermore, the ravages of famine and sleeping sickness left a legacy of extreme poverty. While all of this made the Imbo highly vulnerable to social unrest, there can be little doubt that Congolese migrants, including former *simbas*, played a key role in spreading violence through the region. And while many Hutu who refused to join the rebellion were killed by other Hutu, some also fell victim of the Mulelistes' indifference to ethnic distinctions once under the influence of drugs.

Of the seriousness of the threat posed by the uprising there can be no doubt. What followed, however, was not so much a repression as a ghastly slaughter of Hutu civilians. The carnage went on unabated for months.

By the end of August at least 200,000 had been killed. Boniface Fidel Kiraranganya, a distinguished civil servant of *ganwa* origins who witnessed firsthand, day after day, the scores of schoolchildren, students, professional people, and civil servants rounded up and sent to their graves, estimates the number of victims was "at least 300,000." He describes the carnage as "the paroxysm of madness, the most perfect example of what human beings are capable of doing when… freed of all obligation to control his destructive instincts" (Kiraranganya, p. 76).

The slaughter went through two distinctive phases. First came the wholesale eradication of Hutu rebels, lasting until 5 May, which involved a thorough cleansing of Hutu populations throughout the areas affected by the rebellion. Then came the genocidal killings, extending to virtually every province. Beginning with those few holding an officer's rank, most notably the highly popular and talented Martin Ndayahoze, Hutu elements within the army, numbering approximately 750, were the first to be executed by their Tutsi commanders. The same fate befell an estimated three hundred Hutu gendarmes, thus leaving the security forces entirely in Tutsi hands. Next in line were Hutu students and teachers. Some of the most gruesome scenes took place on the premises of the university in Bujumbura and in secondary and technical schools. In a scenario that was repeated again and again, groups of soldiers suddenly showed up in classrooms, called Hutu students by name, and took them away. Few ever returned. By June approximately 45 percent of primary schoolteachers and the near totality of secondary schoolteachers were reported killed. Nor was the church spared. Reporting from Bujumbura in early June, the *New York Times* correspondent Marvine Howe noted, "Twelve Hutu priests are said to have been killed, and thousands of Protestant pastors, school directors and teachers" (p. 4). What emerges from this bloodbath is a deliberate, systematic elimination of all Hutu elites. Even a glimmer of education was a death warrant. Irrespective of his or her level of education, a Hutu's wealth was enough to mark him or her. The appropriation of the victims' property by their executioners—ranging from bank accounts and houses to bicycles and cows—was standard practice, suggesting that ethnicity alone was not the only motive for turning against Hutu. At any rate, in a matter of months the whole of the Hutu middle classes, with the exception of those who found refuge in neighboring states, had been annihilated.

One of the most striking features of the genocide was the victims' total absence of resistance, as if struck by utter disbelief in the contemplation of their fate. It has been said, with reason, that Burundi's traditional culture of dependency tended to inhibit outward protest and thwart the will to resist among the Hutu masses. How far one can generalize from this thesis is open to debate. It is hard to detect anything like a dependency syndrome among the men who took the initiative in igniting the insurrection, but the fact remains that those tens of thousands who were rounded up and killed went to their graves with the docility of sheep taken to the slaughter house. To resist seemed both useless and contrary to their cultural dispositions.

The most notorious victim of the carnage, one might add, was neither Hutu, Tutsi, or *ganwa* but Mwambutsa's successor to the throne, young King Ntare, whose identity defied conventional categories. He was killed in the northern town of Gitega on 1 May shortly after his return from Uganda. Since his deposition by the army in 1966, Ntare no longer had legitimate claims to the throne; nonetheless, he was widely suspected by the Micombero government of plotting a restoration of the monarchy. His death thus ruled out the fearsome scenario of a Ntare-instigated revolt of the Hutu masses with the support of Banyaruguru elites.

The key institutional actors behind the carnage were the army and the JRR, the youth wing of the Uprona. Among the key organizers of the repression were Micombero, holding the rank of colonel, and his chief of staff Albert Shibura, who later became minister of the interior and justice. But the man who played the decisive role in expanding the killings was Artémon Simbananiye, who served as minister of foreign affairs in 1971 and subsequently as ambassador extraordinary and plenipotentiary during the killings. Described by Kiraranganya as "an extraordinarily cruel but stupid individual" (p. 89), Simbananiye was the chief planner and orchestrator of the killings. His influence reached far and wide among Tutsi networks, including the JRR, which played a major auxiliary role in identifying and rounding up Hutu suspects. At the height of the carnage he reportedly said, "At least now we'll have peace for the next thirty years." Apocryphal or not, the statement conveys the central rationale behind the genocide. From a youth organization the JRR quickly transformed itself into a central cog in the killing machine, with tentacles reaching out to every province and town.

What held these people together in their genocidal enterprise was first and foremost their ethnoregional identities. All were Tutsi-Hima from Bururi Province and, as such, represented the top echelons of what came to be known as the "Bururi lobby." Many were actively involved in the cabal against the Tutsi-Banyaruguru, the latter being seen as ardent supporters of King Ntare looking forward to the day when the monarchy would be restored and the Hima evicted from the seats of power. Most importantly, they sensed that the institutions of the state had been dangerously weakened by the continuing tug-of-war between the two groups.

Only in this context can one fully grasp the strategic goals of the organizers of the killings. Though the immediate aim was to crush the Hutu insurrection, a great deal more was at stake. The underlying objectives of the ruling oligarchy were (1) to ensure the long-term stability of the state through the wholesale elimination of all educated Hutu elites and potential elites; (2) to transform the instruments of force—army, police, gendarmerie—into a Tutsi-Hima monopoly and exclude all Hutu elements from future recruitment; (3) to rule out once and for all a return to the monarchy—hence the assassination of King Ntare only days after Micombero had sworn that nothing would happen to him; and (4) to create a new basis of legitimacy for the Hima-dominated state by projecting an image of the government as the protector of all Burundi against domestic and external foes. On each count Micombero's "prophylactic" repression met with resounding success, making Simbananiye's prediction sound like a prophecy. For the next thirty years—with the exception of the 1988 Hutu riots in the communes of Ntega and Marangara near the Rwandan border—Burundi experienced unprecedented peace. The country was by then virtually bereft of educated Hutu elites. The ever-present threat of another bloodbath was enough to deter all forms of protest. From a fragile edifice threatened from within and without, the state had become the all-powerful, unchallenged instrument of Tutsi hegemony under Hima rule.

THE REGIONAL AFTERMATH

A retrospective look at the regional spillover of the crisis brings into focus its wider implications. It brings to light the historical pattern of reciprocal influences between Rwanda and Burundi. Episodes of Hutu-Tutsi confrontation in Rwanda consistently impacted in Burundi in one form or another and vice versa. Just as the Hutu revolution in Rwanda (1959–1962) was the single most important factor behind the hardening of Hutu-Tutsi relations in Burundi, so also did the 1972 bloodbath significantly influence the course of events in Rwanda.

The backlash of the killings took the form of violent Tutsi riots in secondary schools and at the University of Rwanda in Butare, leaving scores of victims and causing a flight of dozens of Tutsi families to the Congo and Uganda. Most importantly, the growing unrest and incitements to violence by Hutu politicians were the pretext for the seizure of power by a group of officers from the north under the leadership of Juvenal Habyalimana. The events of 1972 thus played a major role in bringing about the Second Republic (1973–1994). The power shift had important regional dimensions in that it signaled the coming to power of northerners, the so-called Kiga—an ethnoregional label that distinguishes them sharply from the inhabitants of the Nduga region covering south and central Rwanda. While it is widely recognized that the Kiga were notoriously more distrustful of the Tutsi than the Hutu from the central and southern regions, owing to their relatively brief experience with the integrative bonds of Tutsi rule, this is hardly enough to suggest a causal relationship between the Burundi genocide and its 1994 counterpart in Rwanda. Once this is said, there is little question that the memories of the Burundi hecatomb contributed to the radicalization of anti-Tutsi sentiment in Rwanda.

The parallel with postrevolutionary Rwanda is striking. Just as the tens of thousands of Tutsi refugees who poured across the border into Burundi helped crystallize anti-Hutu feelings among the Tutsi of Burundi, the same phenomenon happened in Rwanda after tens of thousands of Hutu ran for their lives, streaming into Rwanda. The stories they told of the atrocities committed by the army and the JRR found a receptive audience in the hills and in the bars of the capital Kigali. The fresh outflow of Hutu refugees into Rwanda in the wake of the Ntega and Marangara "incidents" in 1988 underscored once again the sheer brutality of the Burundi army and gave additional weight to the tales of horror told by their predecessors. Among the refugees of 1972 were many Hutu elites who later surfaced in Bujumbura after President Pierre Buyoya, yielding to intense outside pressures, including that of the United States, decided in 1989 to open the way to multiparty democracy. One of those Hutu was Melchior Ndadaye, who, shortly after his election to the presidency in 1993, was assassinated by a group of army officers acting hand in hand with the more extremist elements in the government.

Given the thirty-one-year interval between the genocide and the killing of Ndadaye, it is easy to see why many among the Tutsi establishment bristled at the idea of surrendering their power to a Hutu president. Few anticipated the devastating consequences of their crime.

As the news of Ndadaye's death reached the hillside communities, gangs of Hutu youth suddenly seemed to materialize out of nowhere, slaughtering innocent Tutsi civilians. Again the number of victims is impossible to determine, but a conservative estimate of Tutsi killed by Hutu and Hutu killed by Tutsi during the subsequent repression suggests some thirty thousand deaths in each community. Whatever the case may be, the subtext of the 1972 mass murder came out clear and loud from the words of a Hutu clergyman: "When we told them (the Hutu gangs) not to spill Tutsi blood, they said 'look, since 1972 it is our blood that's being spilled! Now we hear President Ndadaye has been killed. If they did that it means we are next'" (Lemarchand, p. xiv). Memories of 1972 surfaced with an emotional charge made more potent still by intimations of yet another impending massacre of Hutu populations.

While all genocides are alike in the scale of violence and atrocities they conjure, each stands as a singular event, rooted in the particularities of specific historical situations. Although the parallel with Rwanda is reasonably clear, despite its more limited scale, the Burundi genocide cannot be seen as a carbon copy of the 1994 bloodbath where the roles of victims and killers were reversed. That they are nonetheless connected through a number of historical threads is undeniable. This is one of the many lessons to be learned from one of the least known of the many mass murders experienced in other parts of the continent.

[See also African Union: Commission and Court on Human Rights; Crimes against Humanity; Democratic Republic of Congo; Genocide; Minority Rights: Overview; Rwanda; and United Nations Commission on Human Rights.]

BIBLIOGRAPHY

Chrétien, Jean-Pierre, and Jean-François Dupaquier. *Burundi 1972: Au bord des génocides* [Burundi 1972: On the Edge of Genocides]. Paris: Karthala, 2007. Written thirty-five years after the event, this joint effort by a noted historian of Burundi and a journalist constitutes the richest body of sources on the 1972 bloodbath available to date. The wealth of interviews with survivors and witnesses is not the least of its virtues.

Desroches, Christian. "Burundi 1972 and Rwanda 1994: 45 Government Responses to Genocide in Central Africa." Unpublished manuscript, 2003. The author is indebted to his former graduate student at Concordia, Christian Desroches, for sharing this gem.

Howe, Marvine. "Slaughter in Burundi." *New York Times*, June 11, 1972.

Hoyt, Michael. "US Embassy Cables from Bujumbura to the State Department," April 29–August 29, 1972. Unpublished materials, available from the author's collection at the University of Florida, Gainesville, http://www.uflib.ufl.edu/cm/africana/fulltext.htm.

Kiraranganya, Boniface Fidel. *La vérité sur le Burundi*. Sherbrooke, Quebec: Éditions Naaman, 1985. A dispassionate, moving, and highly instructive account of the genocide by a close observer who also served Burundi in several official capacities prior to 1972.

Kissinger, Henry. "Memorandum for the President, September 20, 1972." In *Burundi*, Vol. I, Box 735, Country Files: Africa, NSC Files, NPMP, NARA II.

Lemarchand, René. *Burundi: Ethnic Conflict and Genocide*. Washington, D.C.: Woodrow Wilson Center Press; Cambridge and New York: Cambridge University Press, 1996. A broad analysis of the country's tumultuous evolution since independence in 1962, including a full chapter devoted to the roots and consequences of the genocide ten years later.

Lemarchand, René. "The Burundi Genocide." In *Century of Genocide: Eyewitness Accounts and Critical Views*, edited by Samuel Totten, William S. Parsons, and Israel W. Charny, pp. 317–333. New York: Garland, 1997. Examines the proximate causes and impacts of the genocide. Includes a set of personal accounts by survivors and eyewitnesses.

Lemarchand, René. "Le génocide de 1972 au Burundi: Les silences de l'histoire" [The 1972 Genocide in Burundi: The Silence of History]. *Cahiers d'Études Africaines* 167, no. 3 (2002): 551–567. An attempt to come to grips with the problem of oblivion and denial in the wake of the 1972 bloodletting, with emphasis on how memory, through distortion and selectivity, obscures political realities.

Malkki, Liisa H. *Purity and Exile: Violence, Memory, and National Cosmology among Hutu Refugees in Tanzania*. Chicago: University of Chicago Press, 1995. A fascinating exploration of the narratives of Hutu refugees in Tanzania that shows the impact of violence on the birth of "mythical histories." A major source on how the trauma of atrocities witnessed by refugees shapes their perceptions of the perpetrators.

Maquet, Jacques. *The Premise of Inequality in Rwanda*. London: Oxford University Press, 1961.

Reyntjens, Filip. *L'Afrique des Grands Lacs en crise: Rwanda, Burundi, 1988–1994* [The Great Lakes Region of Africa in Crisis: Rwanda and Burundi, 1988–1994]. Paris: Karthala, 1994. An excellent analysis of the reciprocal interactions between Rwanda and Burundi seen through the lens of their histories.

Teltsch, Kathleen. "Killings Go On in Burundi." *New York Times*, July 20, 1972.

Weissman, Stephen. "Living with Genocide." *Tikkun*, July–August 1997, pp. 53–57. A powerful critique of Western donors' responses to the genocide and subsequent crises.

BUSINESS AND HUMAN RIGHTS

by Scott Pegg

At first glance, the question of business and human rights can seem both simple and irrelevant. The question can appear irrelevant because sovereign states have traditionally been the duty-bearers (those with obligations under international law to respect and protect human rights) against whom human rights can be claimed and through whom they are enforced. Although international human rights laws and covenants create universal rights held by all, the obligations they create are solely for sovereign states. If states are the legal duty-bearers of human rights, then focusing on business and human rights is irrelevant because transnational corporations (TNCs) are not charged with ensuring respect for human rights. Alternatively, the question can seem simple because the Universal Declaration of Human Rights directs itself toward "every individual and every organ of society," certainly a broad enough formulation to include transnational corporations. As "organs of society," transnational corporations are subject to the strictures of the Universal Declaration of Human Rights and there is nothing particularly difficult or unique about their situation.

In reality, though, there are a series of debates involving business and human rights that are neither irrelevant nor easy to answer. Although concerns about business and ethics date back thousands of years, a series of high-profile cases in the 1990s sparked interest in the impact that business operations can have on human rights. A number of shoe and textile firms were accused of physically abusing workers and forcing them to labor under "sweatshop" conditions, while various resource extraction firms allegedly provided transportation, paid field allowances (monthly, weekly, or per diem monetary payments), or turned a blind eye to state security force abuses in their operating areas in such countries as Myanmar (the former Burma), Colombia, Indonesia, Nigeria, and Sudan. The term "conflict diamonds" entered the lexicon in the late 1990s over concerns that civil wars in Angola and Sierra Leone were largely being funded by transnational corporation purchases of diamonds from rebel groups.

The idea that transnational corporations can affect the human rights of their workers, local host communities, and host countries has thus gained acceptance. What this signifies and how business can best be brought into a human rights framework, however, remains hotly contested. Perhaps the most important question driving this debate is whether business practice in human rights can best be advanced through voluntary or legally binding initiatives. Incorporated into this larger debate are also such technical questions as whether or not parent corporations can be held liable for the actions of their subsidiaries, whether or not corporations as entities can be held responsible for human rights outside the actions of their individual employees, and what kinds of corporations should be held responsible for which kinds of human rights.

Recognizing the complexities and difficulties of applying a human rights framework to the business operations of transnational corporations does not, however, obviate the need for a rights-based approach. Indeed, there are a number of positive reasons to adopt a rights-based approach. First, as human rights standards have already been delineated in various widely accepted documents like the Universal Declaration of Human Rights, there is no need to start from scratch. Second, a human rights framework sets a minimal baseline standard that applies globally and can be pursued uniformly across different sovereign jurisdictions. This provides a welcome degree of coherence for large transnational corporations that might operate in dozens of different states around the world. Third, there is nothing about a rights-based approach that prevents companies from raising standards even higher should they want to do so. A rights-based approach sets a floor for corporate performance but does not impose a ceiling. Finally, businesses themselves are now starting to acknowledge the validity of a rights-based approach.

Dozens of corporations, for example, now formally incorporate support for the Universal Declaration of Human Rights into their general business practices.

This article will begin with some historical background to the contemporary emergence of what has come to be known as "corporate social responsibility" (CSR). It will then consider the fundamental question of whether corporate accountability for human rights standards can best be promoted through voluntary or legally binding initiatives. Voluntary initiatives at the company, industry, and global levels are then highlighted. It will conclude with national, regional, and global attempts at legal regulation.

HISTORICAL BACKGROUND

Although the specific form that concerns about business and human rights take has only emerged since the 1990s, debates over business ethics have a long historical pedigree. The Indian philosopher Kautilya in the fourth century BCE and the Roman statesman Cicero in the first century BCE both addressed the morality of specific business practices. Islam and the medieval Christian church censured usury. More recent antecedents of contemporary debates over business and human rights include the abolitionist boycott of sugar produced by slave labor and the international campaign against brutal working conditions in the rubber plantations of the Belgian Congo. The role of business in facilitating repression was formally addressed at the Nuremberg Trials after World War II, most famously resulting in the board of directors of the German company I. G. Farben being convicted for their individual involvement in gross human rights violations. In the United States, the Lockheed bribery scandal in the mid-1970s resulted in dramatic growth in the use of written corporate ethics policies. Contemporary debates about corporate social responsibility are thus modern versions of earlier conversations about the proper role of business in society.

A number of interrelated reasons account for the growth of interest in corporate social responsibility. Part of the explanation relates to changing social attitudes. The rise of conservative political ideology in the 1980s and the related deregulation, liberalization, and privatization of many economies contributed to a sense that along with the increased freedoms business enjoyed should come increased responsibilities to the societies in which they operate. Increasing globalization led more transnational corporations to source, produce, market, and service their products around the world. Along with this, labor unions and environmental groups increasingly "followed" transnational corporations as they established new facilities in overseas locations. Rapid growth in the nongovernmental organization (NGO) sector also contributed to an increased focus on the human rights performance of major business enterprises. The small but growing "ethical investment" sector offered incentives for corporations to think more carefully about issues such as diversity and environmental performance. Perhaps most important, the Internet and dramatically better and cheaper communications technologies greatly facilitated the monitoring of corporate performance around the world by NGOs, academics, consultants, and social movements. A series of highly publicized campaigns against such famous corporations as De Beers, Nike, and Royal Dutch/Shell in the 1990s made issues of corporate human rights behavior front-page news.

CORPORATE SOCIAL RESPONSIBILITY AND ITS CRITICS

Although corporate social responsibility is a broad umbrella term that encompasses a wide variety of meanings, it starts from the basic idea that corporations have larger social responsibilities that extend beyond simply maximizing profits for their shareholders. Socially responsible companies do not ignore profit considerations but instead embed them in a wider decision-making framework that also encompasses such things as their environmental performance, their social impact, and their respect for human rights. CSR is frequently measured in terms of the so-called triple bottom line, which maintains that companies should no longer be evaluated only by their financial results but should also be held accountable for their financial, environmental, and social performances. Importantly, though, CSR is conceived in solely voluntary terms. Corporations decide for themselves what responsibilities they have, how far their responsibilities extend, and to which groups. They voluntarily undertake CSR commitments but do not see themselves as legally bound to do so.

The rise of corporate social responsibility during the first decade of the twenty-first century has been stunning. The concept has gone from the margins of business thinking to being enthusiastically embraced by most of the world's leading corporations. CSR has literally become a growth industry, with business schools teaching it, consultants advising companies on how to implement it, accounting firms and NGOs trying to audit and monitor performance, and public relations firms trying to brand CSR initiatives and corporate identities.

Yet the concept is not without its critics. In broad terms, two principle schools of criticism can be identified, which Michael Blowfield and Jedrzej George Frynas (p. 505) term the "CSR is bad capitalism" school and the "weak CSR is bad development" school. The first of these schools, which comes primarily from liberal political economists, builds on Milton Friedman's famous argument that the only responsibility business firms have in a capitalist economy is to maximize profits for their shareholders. According to Friedman, "Few trends could so thoroughly undermine the very foundations of our free society as the acceptance by corporate officials of a social responsibility other than to make as much money for their stockholders as possible" (p. 133). In this view, asking company managers to assume other responsibilities outside of maximizing shareholder profits fundamentally misunderstands the nature of a free economy. A variant of this argument opposes CSR on the grounds that corporations are highly specialized entities and asking them to take on missions outside their narrow focus is unlikely to result in successful outcomes. In other words, we should expect mining companies to succeed in finding and producing minerals; we should not expect them to succeed at securing human rights for their host communities.

The second main line of critique, which principally comes from NGOs and activists, argues that corporate social responsibility is a poor voluntary substitute approach when what is truly needed is better legal regulation and enforcement of human rights, labor, and environmental standards. CSR, which relies on a company's goodwill or its own interpretation of what its social responsibilities are, cannot bring about substantive improvements in performance. In short, these critics argue that voluntary self-regulation is an inadequate and unsatisfactory mechanism for ensuring good corporate behavior. Some versions of this argument see CSR as destructive because it is designed solely to obviate the need for better legal regulation of corporate behavior.

THE VOLUNTARY VERSUS LEGAL CONTROVERSY

Perhaps the most important debate about business and human rights concerns the question of whether we can better improve corporate human rights performance through voluntary or legally binding initiatives. We will consider each of these arguments in turn.

The main proponents of a voluntary approach to business and human rights are transnational corporations themselves, along with pro-business politicians and liberal economists. Proponents of a voluntary approach start from a generally benign view of both globalization and the role of transnational corporations within it. Foreign direct investment is seen as a major driving force behind economic growth. In addition to creating jobs and generating export earnings, transnational corporations also transfer technology, managerial skills, and valuable training to their host countries. Transnational corporations typically pay higher wages than their domestic counterparts and offer their workers better working conditions than they previously enjoyed. There is little to no evidence of a "race to the bottom" whereby transnational corporations seek out the lowest wages and lowest environmental standards. Instead, transnational corporations are more likely to elevate standards in poor countries than lower them.

Advocates of a voluntary approach believe that there are certain inherent limits to the legal process that highlight the need for voluntary CSR initiatives. Legal approaches are by nature slow and reactive; voluntary initiatives are faster and more flexible. Beyond this, legal approaches are far better at prescribing minimum standards of conduct than they are at securing the best possible performance. Societal expectations of corporate behavior today already far exceed transnational corporations' legal obligations, and that gap is likely to grow unless voluntary CSR initiatives are allowed to flourish.

Voluntary approach supporters also believe it is unrealistic to attempt to start with universally binding legal codes. Most international treaties take decades to negotiate, if they ever come into effect at all. It is futile to expect international treaty agreements on business standards for human rights anytime soon. Focusing on the prospect of remotely possible legal treaties risks diverting time and attention away from more immediately fruitful voluntary approaches.

Furthermore, proponents of a voluntary approach also believe that using existing national legal systems to sue corporations for their human rights performance abroad is highly problematic. Attempting to apply one country's laws to events that occur in another country smacks of legal imperialism, violates fundamental principles of sovereignty, and constitutes an unwarranted intervention in the internal affairs of another country. Such actions can also threaten home-country political interests; the U.S. State Department, for example, argued that a legal suit against ExxonMobil for alleged human rights violations in Indonesia potentially threatened U.S. national interests in the war on terrorism.

Finally, and perhaps most importantly, supporters of a voluntary approach believe that voluntary initiatives work and can develop in the future. Voluntary codes of conduct that commit transnational corporations to monitor the labor practices of their suppliers create a financial incentive for them to do so. The very act of signing a nonbinding document like the UN Global Compact (a UN plan to get corporations to agree to a voluntary code of conduct) forces corporations to think about the issues they involve and creates an expectation that performance will be raised in these areas. Once corporations with reputations to protect commit themselves to voluntary initiatives, self-interest will ensure that they meet their commitments. Over time, voluntary initiatives gain added weight and legitimacy as new members sign on to them and better ways of monitoring and benchmarking performance are initiated. Voluntary commitments may not be enforceable, but that does not mean they are insignificant.

The main proponents of a legal approach tend to be social activists, NGOs, international lawyers, and some academics. They start from a more skeptical view of both globalization and the role of transnational corporations within it. They tend to subscribe to the view that globalization has led to a "race to the bottom" where governments are forced to lower labor and environmental standards to attract foreign investment and corporations seek out the lowest cost labor wherever they can find it. Transnational corporations have shown themselves to be quite comfortable investing in countries like China with poor human rights records, and their investments have propped up repressive regimes and military dictatorships. Transnational corporations have committed human rights violations themselves or been complicit in abuses committed by host country governments. They cannot be trusted to adhere to voluntary commitments, and if profits and human rights come into conflict, it is only logical to expect them to choose profits.

Advocates of a legal approach argue that much of the corporate interest in voluntary CSR commitments is solely being driven by public relations concerns. CSR is seen by many critics as "little more than a cosmetic treatment" that "does not go very deep" (Crook, p. 4). Only a relative handful of companies will enact meaningful reforms without being legally compelled to do so. Voluntary measures and self-regulation presume both high levels of trust and companies that sincerely care about regulating their social

and environmental impacts on their host communities. Yet, as Peter Newell points out,

> This assumption disregards the reasons why many companies choose to operate in locations where labor is cheap and natural resources abundant; where social and environmental impacts are inevitably large, but importantly are less regulated than in their home countries. (p. 553)

Critics of voluntary approaches believe there is a huge gap between corporate rhetoric about corporate social responsibility and the reality in poor countries. This illustrates the hypocrisy of many voluntary initiatives. De Beers, for example, maintained in its 1997 annual report that "the Company's Code of Business Conduct and Ethics requires employees to maintain the highest ethical standards in ensuring that business practices are conducted in a manner which . . . is above reproach." Yet, the human rights organization Global Witness has estimated that the Angolan rebel movement UNITA generated $3.7 billion in revenue throughout the 1990s from diamond sales to De Beers. Critics of voluntary approaches believe there is ample empirical evidence that voluntary self-regulation is inadequate and that corporate self-policing does not work. NGOs can monitor the performance of some corporations, but they depend on access to the corporate media to do this effectively. Such access is not always forthcoming, and NGOs have far fewer resources available to them than transnational corporations.

Proponents of a legal approach also believe that there are a number of distinct advantages to legal regulation, some of which should appeal to business leaders. Companies that are law-abiding and maintain high standards have nothing to fear from legal regulations. International legal codes can establish coherent universal standards that are unlikely to emerge from a competing array of voluntary initiatives. Coherent universal standards contribute to clarity and consistency and help establish a level playing field for all companies. Legal codes also do not prevent corporations that wish to do so from establishing higher standards.

Legal-approach supporters also feel that functioning national court systems that consider extraterritorial cases are essential to providing justice to the millions of people who live in countries without properly functioning judiciaries. The Alien Tort Claims Act (ATCA) is now being used to sue individuals and corporations in U.S. courts for crimes committed overseas. Contrary to the fears of some business groups, U.S. judges have not applied ATCA widely or indiscriminately. They have dismissed more than half of the ATCA cases filed without trial and they have narrowly focused on severe violations of universally recognized civil and political rights. ATCA cases and similar developments in other countries are vital avenues to justice for victims of human rights abuses and serve as an effective deterrent to future corporate complicity in such violations.

EXISTING VOLUNTARY INITIATIVES

Voluntary initiatives that address business and human rights issues have proliferated at four different levels: individual companies, industry associations, NGO codes of conduct and certification initiatives, and global codes. These levels are by no means exclusive. A transnational corporation could have its own code of conduct and also subscribe to an industry-wide agreement and to one or more global initiatives. These four levels should also be seen as ideal types, with some codes like the Kimberley Process Certification Scheme or the Voluntary Principles on Security and Human Rights having been developed by governments, NGOs, and various companies within the respective industries concerned. It is possible that some of these voluntary codes of conduct may also have legal implications, as when, for example, adherence to the company's code of conduct is included as a binding condition in a legal contract with a supplier or subcontractor. Voluntary codes at the industry-association level may also be mandatory in the sense that membership in the association is conditional upon adherence to the association's code of conduct.

At the level of the individual company, codes of conduct can vary from short mission statements to detailed documents with specific provisions and commitments. The content of individual codes varies widely. Some corporate codes of conduct address environmental, human rights, labor, and social issues, while others only address some of these components; this also varies by industry. Labor rights issues, for example, tend to show up most frequently in the textile, garment, footwear, sporting goods, and toy industries, while environmental provisions are more likely to appear in the chemicals and extractive industries.

In terms of business and human rights, companies such as ABN Amro, British Airways, Cadbury Schweppes, Chevron, and Nokia all make specific references to human rights in their respective codes of conduct. Another group of companies including The Body Shop, BP,

Diageo, GlaxoSmithKline, Ikea, Norsk Hydro, Reebok, and Royal Dutch/Shell explicitly declare their support for the Universal Declaration of Human Rights in their codes of conduct. In terms of labor rights, companies such as Federated Department Stores, JC Penney, Lands' End, and Nike all require their suppliers or subcontractors to comply with applicable child labor laws in their host country. Dress Barn, Fruit of the Loom, Liz Claiborne, and Wal-Mart specifically mandate a minimum age of fifteen for workers in any factories that make products for them.

Industry-wide codes of conduct are designed to address the "free rider" problem whereby one company adopting higher standards on its own could potentially suffer a loss of competitive advantage to other companies in the industry that did not adopt similarly high standards. Although the extent of this free rider problem is probably exaggerated, industry association codes have proliferated in recent years.

Perhaps the most sophisticated and well-developed industry association code in terms of environmental, health, and safety issues is the international chemical industry's Responsible Care initiative. The motivating idea behind Responsible Care is to continuously improve the chemical industry's safety, health, and environmental performance. Responsible Care is now in varying stages of implementation in fifty-two countries on six continents, accounting for nearly 90 percent of global chemicals production.

The Apparel Industry Partnership (AIP) was organized by the White House in response to a sweatshop scandal involving the American celebrity actress Kathie Lee Gifford, which attracted widespread publicity in the mid-1990s. The AIP was formed in 1996 and reached agreement on a workplace code of conduct and a system for monitoring adherence with these standards in 1997. The AIP commits its member firms not to employ workers younger than fifteen (or fourteen where legal under host country laws) or younger than the age for completing compulsory education in the host country if that is higher than fifteen. Member firms also pledge under the AIP's agreement to "recognize and respect the right of employees to freedom of association and collective bargaining."

The Kimberley Process Certification Scheme (KPCS) is an international certification scheme for rough diamonds that is designed to stop the trade in "conflict" or "blood" diamonds, which has been used in the past to fund civil wars in Angola, the Democratic Republic of the Congo, and Sierra Leone. The membership of the KPCS consists of forty-seven sovereign states and the European Union, representing all major rough diamond producing, importing, and exporting countries. The diamond industry participates via the World Diamond Council, and civil society is represented by the NGOs Global Witness and Partnership Africa Canada. All shipments of rough diamonds must be accompanied by a Kimberley Process certificate, and participants can only trade with other participants who have met the minimum requirements of the KPCS.

The industry-wide code that is perhaps most directly focused on issues of business and human rights is the Voluntary Principles on Security and Human Rights, which was negotiated by the U.S. and U.K. governments, extractive industry companies, and human rights NGOs. The Voluntary Principles specifically acknowledge the Universal Declaration of Human Rights and specific law enforcement documents such as the UN Basic Principles on the Use of Force and Firearms by Law Enforcement Officials. While acknowledging that "governments have the primary role of maintaining law and order, security and respect for human rights," the Voluntary Principles also state that "companies have an interest in ensuring that actions taken by governments, particularly the actions of public security providers, are consistent with the protection and promotion of human rights." Signatory companies should "encourage host governments to permit making security arrangements transparent and accessible to the public." If providing equipment to public security services, companies should "take all appropriate and lawful measures to mitigate any foreseeable negative consequences, including human rights abuses."

A third general form of voluntary codes of conduct consists of attempts by NGOs to set consistent and measurable standards that corporations agree to meet. The Coalition for Environmentally Responsible Economies (CERES) published a set of ten voluntary principles for corporate environmental performance in 1989. Adoption of the CERES principles is voluntary, but companies who make this commitment are required to fill out a standardized CERES report every year, with each signatory addressing the same set of questions.

Social Accountability 8000 (SA 8000) is an auditable certification standard managed by the NGO Social Accountability International. It is designed to encourage corporate adherence to a certifiable set of labor and human rights standards on such fronts as health and safety standards, the use of child labor, working hours, freedom of association, and the right to collective bargaining. SA 8000 standards are drawn from International Labour Organization (ILO) Conventions, the Universal Declaration of Human Rights, and the UN Convention on the Rights of the Child. Compliance with SA 8000 standards is audited by independent third parties certified by Social Accountability International.

The Forest Stewardship Council (FSC) similarly accredits third parties who certify that forests are managed according to FSC standards, which are set out in ten principles and fifty-seven criteria that address legal issues, indigenous rights, labor rights, and environmental impacts surrounding forest management. As one example of these standards, under FSC principle number three on indigenous peoples' rights, FSC members commit themselves to recognize and respect the "legal and customary rights of indigenous peoples to own, use and manage their lands, territories and resources."

Finally, voluntary initiatives on business and human rights have also taken place at the global level. Two of these initiatives emerged in the 1970s—the Organisation for Economic Cooperation and Development's 1976 Guidelines for Multinational Enterprises (revised in 2000) and the ILO's 1977 Tripartite Declaration on Principles Concerning Multinational Enterprises and Social Policy. Although both documents were developed under the auspices of intergovernmental organizations, they are voluntary and nonbinding.

Two other initiatives emerged in the 1990s during the period of rapidly rising popularity for the CSR concept. The Global Sullivan Principles were designed by the Rev. Dr. Leon H. Sullivan, the architect of a similar set of principles for doing business with apartheid-era South Africa. The Global Sullivan Principles describe themselves as "aspirational not apologetic" and "celebratory not punitive." They are designed to "apply to all workers, in all industries, in all countries." The principle with the most direct connection to human rights is that signatories will express their "support for universal human rights and, particularly, those of our employees, the communities within which we operate and parties with whom we do business" (Global Sullivan Principles Web site). Charter endorsers of the Global Sullivan Principles include American Airlines, Coca-Cola, Fannie Mae, General Motors, Kentucky Fried Chicken, Occidental Petroleum, Pepsico, Rio Tinto, Statoil, and the Tata Group.

Announced by then UN Secretary-General Kofi Annan in January 1999, the UN Global Compact comprises ten principles drawn from four existing documents. The first two principles on human rights are drawn from the

Universal Declaration of Human Rights. Principles 3–6 on labor rights come from the ILO's Declaration on Fundamental Principles and Rights at Work. Principles 7–9 on the environment derive from the Rio Declaration of the 1992 UN Conference on Environment and Development. The tenth principle, which proscribes corruption, is drawn from the UN Convention against Corruption. The Global Compact is a purely voluntary initiative and "is not a regulatory instrument—it does not 'police,' enforce or measure the behavior or actions of companies" (UN Global Compact Web site). As of 2008, there were more than fifty-six hundred participants, including over forty-three hundred businesses.

EXISTING LEGAL INITIATIVES

Attempts to hold transnational corporations legally accountable for their human rights performance can potentially occur at the national, regional, or global levels. At the national level, there are at least two distinct ways this can happen. First, home country governments can pass legislation that extraterritorially regulates the behavior of transnational corporations headquartered in their jurisdictions. One famous example of this is the passage of the U.S. Foreign Corrupt Practices Act (FCPA) in 1977. The FCPA makes it illegal under U.S. law for U.S. business executives to pay bribes to foreign government officials in order to secure or retain business. Although not directly focused on human rights per se, the FCPA clearly establishes the precedent that a home country government can regulate the activities of its transnational corporations extraterritorially. There is also some evidence that such extraterritorial regulation by the home country government can actually work. In a comprehensive study of extraterritorial sanctions applied by the U.S. government, Kenneth Rodman (in *Sanctions beyond Borders*) found that transnational corporate compliance with them frequently went beyond the letter of the law in order to avoid jeopardizing their relationship with the U.S. government.

There are, however, two fundamental problems that limit the utility of home country government regulation as a means of securing better transnational corporation human rights performance. First, given the power of business lobbying groups, many observers question whether or not any home country government will pass significant legislation that is perceived to be hostile to business interests. Given the clearly stated preference of transnational corporations for voluntary initiatives, any attempt to extend extraterritorial regulations in the area

of human rights would face fierce resistance. Second, there is a sharp distinction between passing legislation and actually enforcing it. In the first twenty-five years of the FCPA's history, the U.S. Justice Department only prosecuted about thirty cases. Although there is some evidence that extraterritorial regulation of transnational corporations can work, there does not appear to be sufficient political will to bring about such regulation.

The second main way that transnational corporations can be held accountable for their human rights impact at the national level is through legal cases filed against them in their home countries. The main approach here, in Ronen Shamir's phrasing, is that "activists try to mobilize the 'developed' legal systems of rich countries in order to police and sanction corporate practices in places where it is impractical or impossible to invoke local law" (p. 637). Such lawsuits have been filed in a number of countries. In 1994 *Rex Dagi v. Broken Hill Proprietary Company Limited*, a lawsuit representing thirty thousand indigenous persons from Papua New Guinea as plaintiffs, was filed in Melbourne, Australia, against BHP over environmental damages caused by the Ok Tedi mine. In England, there have been a number of cases where British transnational corporations were sued in British courts by foreigners for the actions of their subsidiaries abroad. In one such case, Rio Tinto was sued over health hazards relating to a uranium mine in Namibia, while in another case Thor Chemicals Holding Ltd. was sued over alleged mercury poisoning at a factory in South Africa.

This strategy, though, has arguably been pursued the furthest in the United States, where claims against transnational corporations have been filed under the Alien Tort Claims Act, an eighteenth-century U.S. law originally designed to allow victims of offshore piracy to sue onshore. ATCA cases have now been filed against Shell (*Wiwa v. Royal Dutch Petroleum Co. and Shell Transport and Trading Company PLC*) and Chevron (*Bowoto v. Chevron*) for alleged complicity in human rights violations in Nigeria; against Coca-Cola over allegations of harassment, torture, and murder of trade union leaders in Colombia (*Sinaltrainal v. Coca-Cola*); against Del Monte for torture, unlawful detention, and violation of fundamental labor rights in Guatemala (*Villeda v. Del Monte*); and against Unocal over allegations of forced labor in the construction of the Yadana gas pipeline in Myanmar (*Doe v. Unocal*).

In all of these cases, as Ronen Shamir points out, the "facts" of the case—that is, whether corporations actively committed or benefited from complicity in human rights violations—are usually not the center of the legal debate. Rather, "The concrete 'factual' dispute is often about chains of causality in general and about the responsibility of the corporation to the actions of state agents in particular" (p. 650). Within the context of the legal system, corporations have basically sought to respond to these cases primarily in two ways. First, they have filed *forum non conveniens* (literally, an inconvenient or inappropriate forum) motions that dispute the right of the U.S. (or Australian or U.K.) court to hear the case in the first place. In other words, the proper forum for these cases is the host country (Myanmar, Colombia, Nigeria, and so forth) where the alleged violations actually took place. As Richard Meeran explains in the context of England, "The plain truth of the matter is that claimants want to sue in England because they cannot get justice overseas and transnational corporations want to stay the claims for precisely the same reason" (p. 170). Second, transnational corporations attempt to distance themselves from the actual human rights violations by asserting that the parent corporation cannot be held accountable for the actions of legally distinct subsidiary corporations or for the governments with which those subsidiaries have entered into joint ventures. Thus, Chevron Nigeria Ltd. is claimed to be a completely separate entity from the parent Chevron corporation headquartered in California, and Coca-Cola emphasizes that it neither owned nor controlled Panamco, the Colombian bottling firm that exclusively bottles Coke products. Similarly, a company like Unocal (now part of Chevron) argues that it should not be held liable for human rights violations if those violations were actually committed not by Unocal itself, but by the Burmese military.

Corporations arguably have had mixed success with both approaches. In terms of *forum non conveniens* motions, *Doe v. Unocal* was the precedent-setting case that established transnational corporations could be tried in American courts under ATCA and potentially held liable for human rights abuses committed overseas if they knew or should have known that their business partner (in this case, the Burmese government) was committing human rights violations on behalf of the joint venture. Thus, transnational corporations could be tried in U.S. courts for their complicity in serious human rights abuses committed in foreign countries. Subsequently, a U.S. Court of Appeals ruling in *Wiwa v. Royal Dutch Petroleum Co. and Shell Transport and Trading Company PLC* held that the U.S. interest in pursuing claims for torture under both ATCA and the Torture Victim Prevention Act was a significant factor that should be addressed in responding to *forum non conveniens* motions. A U.S. District Court ruling in *Bowoto v. Chevron* also held that courts should look skeptically at *forum non conveniens* motions filed in ATCA cases. Corporations have succeeded in getting a number of ATCA cases thrown out and in having the ATCA statute interpreted narrowly, but they have not been able to prevent a number of these cases from moving forward.

In terms of the second strategy of distancing themselves from their subsidiaries, the corporate record is again mixed. Although the principle of separation of legal identity between different limited companies is firmly established in U.K. law, the CSR movement has arguably undercut this principle in two significant ways. First, the idea that transnational corporations can actively pursue CSR strategies in countries like Myanmar or Nigeria implies a degree of control over their operations that is at odds with their designation as totally separate legal subsidiaries—the approach adopted in their legal filings. The irony, as Ronen Shamir highlights, is that ATCA cases force transnational corporations "into a strategy of downplaying their ability to have a substantial impact upon their immediate social and physical environment, thereby implying a sort of diminished capacity to act responsibly in a proactive way" (p. 650). Second, in their voluntary commitments, transnational corporations have demonstrated that they have no problem being linked to their subsidiaries. The UN Global Compact, for example, lists only the name of the parent company on its participant list, "assuming that all subsidiaries participate as well." The Global Sullivan Principles are even more emphatic on this point: "All subsidiaries, local branches and plant/factory operations ARE accountable to their parent company that endorses the Global Sullivan Principles" (Global Sullivan Principles Web site). It is becoming increasingly difficult for transnational corporations to make such commitments on behalf of their subsidiaries and to claim that their active adherence to corporate social responsibility alone obviates the need for legal regulation while insisting that they have no control over or connections to their legal subsidiaries.

In April 2005 a potentially significant milestone was reached in ATCA cases when Unocal agreed to settle with the plaintiffs in the *Doe v. Unocal* case. Although the terms of the settlement remain confidential, the settlement is seen as a significant victory for the plaintiffs, one that will likely reverberate across other corporate boardrooms. Although transnational corporations will continue and intensify their lobbying campaign against ATCA, the settlement in the *Doe* case and the fact that other cases like *Bowoto* and *Wiwa* have now cleared numerous challenges to their legitimacy indicate that this is one potential route for holding transnational corporations legally accountable for their complicity in egregious human rights abuses.

Turning to the regional level, there are at least nascent or potential means of regulating transnational corporations in both North America and Western Europe. The treaties that established the North American Free Trade Agreement (NAFTA) also established the North American Agreement on Labor Cooperation (NAALC) and the North American Agreement on Environmental Cooperation (NAAEC). Neither of these bodies creates new labor standards or environmental regulations; rather, they are designed to ensure compliance with the preexisting standards of each member state. Citizens and NGOs can file complaints directly with each body. Although NAFTA has been sharply criticized for various weaknesses in terms of enforcing labor and environmental standards, it has, as Bill Meyer puts it, "institutionalized an international process for enforcing second and third generation human rights" (p. 45).

In Europe, the European Court of Justice (ECJ) has found that provisions of the European Union's (EU) founding document, the Treaty of Rome, that prohibit states from discriminating on the basis of nationality and require equal pay for equal work apply directly to private entities. In the view of Steven Ratner, the ECJ has thus "directly imposed on companies not only legal duties, but also human rights duties regarding nondiscrimination" (p. 484). Although by no means being designed specifically for transnational corporations and human rights, the EU's practice, Ratner emphasizes, demonstrates "that states can conclude treaties providing for direct corporate responsibility and implement those treaties effectively" (p. 485). Another potentially significant development within the EU was the passage by the European Parliament of a nonbinding resolution on a code of conduct for European enterprises operating in developing countries. That resolution requests that the European Commission and Council of Ministers put forward proposals "to develop the right legal basis for establishing a European multilateral framework governing companies' operations worldwide." As with the North American examples discussed above, while the actual legal regulation of transnational corporations' human rights performance is in its infancy, one can see potential avenues for future regulation at the regional level.

Finally, at the global level, one could perhaps see voluntary initiatives like the Organisation for Economic Cooperation and Development (OECD) Guidelines or the ILO Tripartite Declaration as being weak legal instruments. There are at least two more precedents of note as well at the global level since the 1990s. First, in 1997 the UN Human Rights Committee found in the case *Hopu and Bessert v. France* that a French tourism project in Tahiti developed by a private firm in conjunction with a government-owned company violated Articles 17 and 23 of the International Covenant on Civil and Political Rights.

Second, and perhaps far more significant, on 13 August 2003 the UN Sub-Commission on the Promotion and Protection of Human Rights passed the UN "Draft Norms on the Responsibilities of Transnational Corporations and Other Business Enterprises with Regard to Human Rights." According to David Weissbrodt and Maria Kruger, "The Norms are the first nonvoluntary initiative accepted at the international level" (p. 903). In their view, the UN Norms "as adopted are not a voluntary initiative of corporate social responsibility. The many implementation provisions show that they amount to more than aspirational statements of desired conduct" (p. 913). In this regard, the nonvoluntary nature of the Norms goes beyond the voluntary initiatives found in the OECD Guidelines, the ILO Tripartite Declaration, or the UN Global Compact.

The UN Norms essentially seek to reaffirm existing international human rights documents and apply their standards to the specific human rights responsibilities of business enterprises. They do not, however, have the status of treaty law yet. Like other UN Declarations, the Norms are what is sometimes referred to as "soft law." They have not yet been adopted by the Commission on Human Rights, the Economic and Social Council, or the General Assembly. Subsequent adoptions by these bodies with large majorities would certainly advance the limited standing of the existing Norms. In the words of Weissbrodt and Kruger, "The legal authority of the Norms now derives principally from their sources in international law as a restatement of legal principles applicable to companies, but they have room to become more binding in the future" (p. 915).

REMAINING ISSUES, FUTURE PROSPECTS

Compared even to the early days of the post–Cold War period, the extent of academic, civil society, corporate, government, and international-organization interest in the various debates surrounding business and human rights has exploded. Yet, amid this explosion of interest, two fundamental questions remain unanswered.

First, despite the rapid rise of corporate social responsibility, we simply do not have much firm data on the efficacy of CSR initiatives. Companies highlight select examples in their annual reports to paint a glowing picture of the shining new world of corporate social responsibility, while critics highlight other select examples where the gap between CSR rhetoric and CSR reality is huge. At this point, all we know, to quote Peter Newell, is that "CSR can work, for *some* people, in *some* places, on *some* issues, *some* of the time" (p. 556). The lack of empirical data and the obviously self-interested nature of many of the participants in the debate fundamentally limit any conclusions that can be drawn about the promise or peril of CSR.

Second, there has not been nearly enough discussion of what a human rights framework for business would ideally look like. There have been some attempts to outline the kinds of principles that might underlie such a framework but important questions—whether corporations as entities can be held accountable outside of the actions of individual employees, which kinds of human rights violations should corporations be held accountable for, or what degree of direct involvement or indirect complicity incurs liability for human rights violations—remain undertheorized. Specific answers are, indeed, emerging in certain cases. The Draft UN Norms and the Global Sullivan Principles, for example, answer the question of parent-company liability for subsidiaries in the affirmative that parent companies are in fact responsible for ensuring compliance from their subsidiaries. We still remain, however, in the very early days of what is likely to be a long debate on what kind of human rights framework should be designed for business firms.

The future prospects for voluntary initiatives relating to business and human rights are undoubtedly bright. CSR has been enthusiastically embraced by the vast majority of business firms. Many voluntary initiatives have reporting requirements that will ensure sustained corporate attention to environmental, human rights, and labor issues. Corporations that initiate annual reporting of their environmental and social performance are unlikely to stop doing so. The participants in the ever-growing CSR industry of consultants, monitors, academics, and auditors will also encourage the development of further voluntary initiatives. Presumably, at some point, the logic of competition might lead to certain voluntary schemes winning out over others and establishing themselves as the benchmark initiatives that all corporations want to be affiliated with. Such a process might reduce the existing plethora of voluntary schemes a bit, but it is unlikely to lead to any reduction in the corporate embrace of voluntarism as its preferred method for engaging with human rights issues.

The future prospects for legal initiatives relating to business and human rights are much more open to question. Concerted lobbying efforts are already under way to overturn ATCA in the United States, and corporations can be expected to resist any attempts to hold them legally accountable for their human rights performance. Companies that have enthusiastically embraced CSR and formally incorporated support for the Universal Declaration of Human Rights into their general business principles like Royal Dutch/Shell have actively supported the International Chamber of Commerce's lobbying efforts against the UN Norms on the Responsibilities of Transnational Corporations and Other Business Enterprises with Regard to Human Rights. The UN Norms as of 2008 have just made it out of one subcommittee and have not yet been endorsed by the Human Rights Council, let alone the General Assembly. Although there are significant debates yet to be resolved about how corporations could be incorporated into the existing human rights framework as duty-bearers, the fundamental problem is a lack of political will, not technically challenging legal questions. The movement to hold corporations legally accountable for their human rights impact has by no means been stopped or defeated. Its ultimate success, however, is far from assured.

Finally, the increased interest in business and human rights should not obscure the fundamental role that sovereign states will continue to play in the promotion, protection, and enforcement of human rights far into the foreseeable future. Although corporations have, in certain instances, adversely affected fundamental human rights, the fact remains that most corporations most of the time do not violate human rights. Sovereign states remain the fundamental duty-bearers of human rights obligations and any significant improvements in human rights will likely be driven by them and not by transnational corporations.

[*See also* Globalization; History of Human Rights; International Labour Organization; Labor Rights; Nongovernmental Organizations Overview; United Nations General Assembly; United Nations Human Rights Council; United

Nations Sub-Commission on Human Rights; *and* Universal Declaration of Human Rights.]

BIBLIOGRAPHY

Addo, Michael K. "Human Rights and Transnational Corporations—An Introduction." In *Human Rights Standards and the Responsibility of Transnational Corporations*, edited by Michael K. Addo, pp. 3–37. The Hague, The Netherlands: Kluwer Law International, 1999.

Bhagwati, Jagdish. *In Defense of Globalization*. Oxford: Oxford University Press, 2004.

Blowfield, Michael, and Jedrzej George Frynas. "Setting New Agendas: Critical Perspectives on Corporate Social Responsibility in the Developing World." *International Affairs* 81, no. 3 (May 2005): 499–513.

Christian Aid. *Behind the Mask: The Real Face of Corporate Social Responsibility*. London: Christian Aid, 2004.

Ciulla, Joanne B. "Why Is Business Talking about Ethics?: Reflections on Foreign Conversations." *California Management Review* 34, no. 1 (Fall 1991): 67–86.

Crook, Clive. "The Good Company: A Survey of Corporate Social Responsibility." *Economist*, January 22, 2005, 3–20.

Donnelly, Jack. "The Social Construction of International Human Rights." In *Human Rights in Global Politics*, edited by Tim Dunne and Nicholas J. Wheeler, pp. 71–102. Cambridge, U.K.: Cambridge University Press, 1999.

Elkington, John. *Cannibals with Forks: The Triple Bottom Line of 21st Century Business*. Oxford: Capstone Publishing, 1997.

Fabig, Heike, and Richard Boele. "The Changing Nature of NGO Activity in a Globalising World: Pushing the Corporate Responsibility Agenda." *IDS Bulletin* 30, no. 3 (July 1999): 58–67.

Friedman, Milton. *Capitalism and Freedom*. Chicago: University of Chicago Press, 1962.

Global Sullivan Principles. http://www.thesullivanfoundation.org/gsp/principles/faq/default.asp.

Global Witness. *A Rough Trade: The Role of Companies and Governments in the Angolan Conflict*. London: Global Witness, 1998.

Henderson, David. *Misguided Virtue: False Notions of Corporate Social Responsibility*. London: Institute of Economic Affairs, 2001.

International Council on Human Rights Policy. *Beyond Voluntarism: Human Rights and the Developing International Legal Obligations of Companies—Summary*. Versoix, Switzerland: International Council on Human Rights Policy, 2002.

Jenkins, Rhys. *Corporate Codes of Conduct: Self-Regulation in a Global Economy*. Geneva, Switzerland: United Nations Research Institute for Social Development, 2001.

Jungk, Margaret. "A Practical Guide to Addressing Human Rights Concerns for Companies Operating Abroad." In *Human Rights Standards and the Responsibility of Transnational Corporations*, edited by Michael K. Addo, pp. 171–186. The Hague, The Netherlands: Kluwer Law International, 1999.

Kirsch, Stuart. "Mining and Environmental Human Rights in Papua New Guinea." In *Transnational Corporations and Human Rights*, edited by Jedrzej George Frynas and Scott Pegg, pp. 115–136. New York: Palgrave Macmillan, 2003.

Kurlantzick, Joshua. "Taking Multinationals to Court: How the Alien Tort Act Promotes Human Rights." *World Policy Journal* 21, no. 1 (Spring 2004): 60–67.

Litvin, Daniel. *Empires of Profit: Commerce, Conquest, and Corporate Responsibility*. New York: Texere, 2003.

Maresca, John J. "A New Concept of Business." *Washington Quarterly* 23, no. 2 (Spring 2000): 155–163.

Mazur, Jay. "Labor's New Internationalism." *Foreign Affairs* 79, no. 1 (January–February 2000): 79–93.

Meeran, Richard. "The Unveiling of Transnational Corporations: A Direct Approach." In *Human Rights Standards and the Responsibility of Transnational Corporations*, edited by Michael K. Addo, pp. 161–170. The Hague, The Netherlands: Kluwer Law International, 1999.

Meyer, William H. "Activism and Research on TNCs and Human Rights: Building a New International Normative Regime." In *Transnational Corporations and Human Rights*, edited by Jedrzej George Frynas and Scott Pegg, pp. 33–52. New York: Palgrave Macmillan, 2003.

Monshipouri, Mahmood, Claude E. Welch Jr., and Evan T. Kennedy. "Multinational Corporations and the Ethics of Global Responsibility: Problems and Possibilities." *Human Rights Quarterly* 25, no. 4 (November 2003): 965–989.

Muchlinski, Peter T. "Human Rights and Multinationals: Is There a Problem?" *International Affairs* 77, no. 1 (January 2001): 31–47.

Nattrass, Nicoli. "The Truth and Reconciliation Commission on Business and Apartheid: A Critical Evaluation." *African Affairs* 98, no. 392 (July 1999): 373–391.

Newell, Peter. "Citizenship, Accountability, and Community: The Limits of the CSR Agenda." *International Affairs* 81, no.3 (May 2005): 541–557.

Ottaway, Marina. "Reluctant Missionaries." *Foreign Policy*, July–August 2001, 44–54.

Parkinson, John. "The Socially Responsible Company." In *Human Rights Standards and the Responsibility of Transnational Corporations*, edited by Michael K. Addo, pp. 49–62. The Hague: Kluwer Law International, 1999.

Pegg, Scott. "An Emerging Market for the New Millennium: Transnational Corporations and Human Rights." In *Transnational Corporations and Human Rights*, edited by Jedrzej George Frynas and Scott Pegg, pp. 1–32. New York: Palgrave Macmillan, 2003.

Ratner, Steven R. "Corporations and Human Rights: A Theory of Legal Responsibility." *Yale Law Journal* 111, no. 3 (December 2001): 443–545.

Rodman, Kenneth A. *Sanctions beyond Borders: Multinational Corporations and U.S. Economic Statecraft*. Lanham, Md.: Rowman & Littlefield, 2001.

Russell, James M. "The Ambivalence about the Globalization of Telecommunications: The Story of Amnesty International, Shell Oil Company, and Nigeria." *Journal of Human Rights* 1, no. 3 (September 2002): 405–416.

Shamir, Ronen. "Between Self-Regulation and the Alien Tort Claims Act: On the Contested Concept of Corporate Social Responsibility." *Law and Society Review* 38, no. 4 (December 2004): 635–664.

Spar, Debora L. "The Spotlight and the Bottom Line: How Multinationals Export Human Rights." *Foreign Affairs* 77, no. 2 (March–April 1998): 7–12.

Spar, Debora, and David Yoffie. "Multinational Enterprises and the Prospects for Justice." *Journal of International Affairs* 52, no. 2 (Spring 1999): 557–581.

UN Global Compact Web site. http://www.unglobalcompact. org/AboutTheGC/index.html.

UN Observer. "Shell Leads International Business Campaign against UN Human Rights Norms." March 15, 2004.

Wawryk, Alex. "Regulating Transnational Corporations through Corporate Codes of Conduct." In *Transnational Corporations and Human Rights*, edited by Jedrzej George Frynas and Scott Pegg, pp. 53–78. New York: Palgrave Macmillan, 2003.

Weissbrodt, David, and Maria Kruger. "Norms on the Responsibilities of Transnational Corporations and Other Business Enterprises with Regard to Human Rights." *American Journal of International Law* 97, no. 4 (October 2003): 901–922.

Woodroffe, Jessica. "Regulating Multinational Corporations in a World of Nation States." In *Human Rights Standards and the Responsibility of Transnational Corporations*, edited by Michael K. Addo, pp. 131–142. The Hague: Kluwer Law International, 1999.

CAMBODIA

by Lilian A. Barria

On 17 April 1975 the forces of the Communist Party of Kampuchea (CPK), more commonly know as the Khmer Rouge, entered Phnom Penh after a four-year civil war in Cambodia. The goal of the Khmer Rouge, or Red Khmers, was to create a utopian society in which social classes, money, education, and religion would no longer exist. In attempting to create such a society, it is estimated that the policies pursued by the Khmer Rouge led to the deaths of almost 2 million people between 1975 and 1979, the period during which the regime was in power. It took almost thirty years for the international community, through the United Nations (UN), and the succeeding Cambodian government to come to an agreement on how justice for the victims should be pursued. The establishment of the Extraordinary Chambers in the Courts of Cambodia (ECCC) in 2004 gave Cambodians hope that their suffering would not go unpunished.

This entry is divided into five sections. The first section will focus on the origins of Communism in Cambodia in order to understand the roots of the Khmer Rouge. The second will provide an overview of the Khmer Rouge regime of 1975–1979 and the policies that led to the atrocities committed against the Cambodian population. The third section addresses the efforts of the international community and the Cambodian government to bring the Khmer Rouge to justice between 1979 and 2004. The fourth section highlights the main features of the ECCC, the mixed tribunal agreed to by the UN and the government of Cambodia in 2004. Finally, the status of accountability efforts in the early twenty-first century is provided, as the ECCC is set to begin finally the trials against the accused.

THE ORIGINS OF COMMUNISM IN CAMBODIA

In 1930 Ho Chi Minh, the leader of the revolutionary struggle in Vietnam, established the Indochinese Communist Party (ICP), with members from Vietnam, Cambodia, and Laos, to fight against French colonialism.

It is important to note that the Cambodian ICP members were primarily ethnic Vietnamese and Chinese. This early core of the Communist movement was later rejected, persecuted, and eliminated by the Khmer Rouge, the ethnic Khmer Communists in Cambodia.

In 1951 the ICP disbanded, and separate Communist parties were created in Vietnam, Cambodia, and Laos. In Cambodia this new party was called the Khmer People's Revolutionary Party (KPRP). The KPRP continues to exist in the early twenty-first century under different guises, with ideological changes and a new name, the Cambodian People's Party (CPP), after 1989. The relationship between these newly created Communist parties became strained by the 1954 Geneva Conference on Indochina, which ended French colonialism. The KPRP was not allowed representation at the conference, and the Vietnamese Communists agreed to end their active support of the Communist struggle in Cambodia. Eventually, some members of the KPRP went into exile in Hanoi, Vietnam; others remained in Cambodia to continue the armed struggle; and still others formed the Krom Pracheachon, or People's Party, to participate openly in Cambodian politics.

Also by the early 1950s a number of ethnic Khmers who would eventually be known to the world as the leaders of the Khmer Rouge received scholarships to study in France. Khieu Samphan Hu Nim, and Hou Yuon received Ph.D.s in Paris. Ieng Sary and Saloth Sar (also known as Pol Pot) studied in Paris as well. Pot returned to a teaching position in Phnom Penh before joining the armed struggle. Son Sen became the director of studies of the National Teaching Institute at Phnom Penh after his return from France. Pol Pot's first wife, Khieu Ponnary (whose sister, Khieu Thirith, was married to Ieng Sary), was the first Cambodian woman to earn a baccalaureate degree. During their time in Paris, some of the group joined the Communist Party of France (the largest party in that country), which adhered to the Stalinist line. In addition, the Khmer students were exposed to the Maoist view that peasants constitute the revolutionary class.

As the members of the Paris group (as they would be known) returned to Cambodia, there were initially two lines of thought: Khieu Samphan, Hu Nim, and Hou Yuon saw benefit in supporting the government in order to fight U.S. imperialism, whereas Saloth Sar, Ieng Sary, and Son Sen (the Pol Pot group) argued for armed struggle against the government. The former group initially opted to participate openly in the political process and held several positions in the government. The Pol Pot group rose to prominence in the 1960 KPRP Second Party Congress; they created the Khmer Rouge as a party distinct from the KPRP and claimed the 1960 conference as its founding meeting, although it was not openly acknowledged as a party until 1967.

By 1963 the Pol Pot group and other prominent Communists had disappeared into the provinces as the government began to crack down on the Krom Pracheachon (Citizens Association) and those perceived to be on the Left. Also during this time, Pol Pot started to resent the manner in which the Vietnamese Communists, who were waging their struggle in Vietnam against U.S. forces, treated their "inferior" comrades in Cambodia. The 1967 Samlaut uprising, a rural peasant rebellion against a tax increase on rice in northwestern Cambodia, led to purges of Leftist elements within the government and the civil service. Khieu Samphan and Hou Yuon were accused of complicity in the uprising. It was time for the moderates also to join the armed struggle. Guerrilla warfare began in 1968 with the creation of the Revolutionary Army of Kampuchea (RAK), the military arm of the Khmer Rouge. The RAK instigated a series of armed operations against the government, initiating what soon escalated into a civil war. Both China and the Soviet Union provided military supplies to the government between 1968 and 1970. This convinced the Khmer Rouge leadership of the need for Cambodia to become self-reliant.

THE 1970 COUP AND PRINCE SIHANOUK

By 1968 the Khmer Rouge had begun its armed struggle within Cambodia; however, the event that gave impetus to the 1975 Khmer Rouge revolution occurred in 1970, when the government of Prince Norodom Sihanouk was deposed through a coup d'état. Sihanouk had been the leader of Cambodia since 1941, first under French colonial rule and later after independence in 1953. During Sihanouk's postcolonial leadership of Cambodia (1953–1970), the Left had a role in the government through the Krom Pracheachon, and Sihanouk tacitly allowed Vietnamese troops on Cambodian soil as part of the expanding theater of the Vietnam War. When he finally had to choose sides in the conflict in 1965, Sihanouk broke diplomatic relations and refused foreign aid from the United States, a move that was not well received by many in his government or by the military establishment.

In March 1970 Lon Nol, Cambodia's prime minister and the head of the army, and Sirik Matak, Sihanouk's cousin and the first vice president, seized power and quickly formed an alliance with the United States, which had instigated the coup and was happy to back the anti-Communist stance of the new Cambodian government. Sihanouk fled to Beijing, where, under Chinese insistence, he formed an alliance with the Khmer Rouge and other Leftist groups. The National United Front of Kampuchea was seen as the vehicle to fight Lon Nol and allow Sihanouk to regain power. The organization was composed of six different factions: the Khmer Rouge, KPRP members who had gone to Hanoi after 1954, KPRP members who had stayed in Cambodia after 1954 to continue the armed struggle, the Krom Pracheachonists, diverse Maoists allied with the Chinese Communist Party, and the followers of Sihanouk. Between 1970 and 1975 Cambodia was in a civil war.

In his alliance with the Khmer Rouge, Sihanouk became the head of state in exile of the Royal Government of Khmer National Unification. The RAK, which was controlled by the Khmer Rouge and which outnumbered the other factions, became the People's National Liberation Armed Forces of Kampuchea (PFLANK), under the command of Khieu Samphan, who was also named vice prime minister and minister of national defense in the exiled royal government. Hu Nim became minister of information and propaganda, and Hou Yuon was given the position of minister of the interior, communal reforms, and cooperatives. The PFLANK command authority was divided into six geographical military regions.

The National United Front of Kampuchea joined with Laotian and Vietnamese Communists under the banner of the United Front of the Three Indochinese Peoples to fight "U.S. imperialism." As Sirik Matak, now the prime minister of Cambodia, declared war on the North Vietnamese, the North Vietnamese Army became the main force fighting against the Cambodian government until 1972. In January 1973 the PFLANK launched its first full-scale offensive without assistance. Even though the Cambodian and Vietnamese Communists worked together in the early years of the civil war, the rift between them intensified as the PFLANK gained more strength, leading to a collapse of the United Front of the

Three Indochinese Peoples. By 1973 the Khmer Rouge had begun a policy of eliminating the other Communists in the National United Front of Kampuchea as well as ethnic Thai and other minority group members in the alliance. Many of them were sent to their deaths in battles against the government in order to eliminate any future challenge to the Khmer Rouge.

Sihanouk played an important role in calling for the mobilization of the peasants and their ultimate support for the Khmer Rouge, even though his relevance within the Royal Government of Khmer National Unification was continually reduced by the Khmer Rouge leadership. As the Khmer Rouge began to control more territory within Cambodia, it introduced the policy of collectivization. Although the peasantry did not wholeheartedly support the policy, the Khmer Rouge imposed it through force when necessary. This foreshadowed the events to come once the Khmer Rouge gained power.

In April 1975 the Khmer Rouge forces reached Phnom Penh, leading Lon Nol to resign and leave the country. Sirik Matak decided to stay and met his death at the hands of the Khmer Rouge. Sihanouk briefly assumed the position of head of state of the new Democratic Kampuchea regime. However, by April 1976 the Khmer Rouge forced Sihanouk to retire and appointed Khieu Samphan as his replacement. Sihanouk spent the rest of the period as a prisoner in the royal palace. It is important to note that even though many of Sihanouk's relatives perished under the Khmer Rouge, he continued his alliance with Pol Pot after the downfall of Democratic Kampuchea in 1979.

Of the Paris group, Hou Yuon was assassinated in August 1975, most likely under orders from Pol Pot. Hou Yuon had been opposed to the mass evacuation of the cities. Hu Nim continued in the position of minister of information and propaganda, which he had held under the Royal Government of Khmer National Unification until 1977, when he too was assassinated. Pol Pot became the prime minister of Democratic Kampuchea. Ieng Sary assumed the position of a deputy prime minister and minister of foreign affairs. Son Sen also became a deputy prime minister as well as the minister of defense. Khieu Thirith (or Ieng Thirith) was made minister of social affairs and head of Democratic Kampuchea's Red Cross Society, and her sister, Khieu Ponnary, was named the president of the Democratic Kampuchea Women's Association. Other individuals who rose to prominence in Democratic Kampuchea included Nuon Chea, or "Brother Number 2," who became the president of the Assembly of People's Representatives and minister of the interior.

Ta Mok was named the military commander of the Southwest regional army, and Kaing Khek Iev, or "Duch," headed the secret police and became the director of Security Prison 21 (S-21).

THE KHMER ROUGE IN POWER

Beginning on 17 April 1975, the Khmer Rouge began to empty all the major cities. More than 2 million people were relocated in the span of a week. None of the residents or refugees who had fled the countryside during the civil war were prepared for the forced migration that took place. Initially, the evacuation was presented as a temporary move to protect the population from a possible U.S. attack. Eventually, however, everyone was ordered to return to his or her home village, with no exceptions tolerated. Many hospital patients, the very young, and the very old died in the evacuation. Those who tried to defy the orders were shot as a warning to others. Official Democratic Kampuchea sources claim that up to three thousand people died during the evacuation; however, many observers consider these estimates to be low.

There were two interrelated reasons for the evacuations. First was the relative weakness of the Khmer Rouge forces, which had barely defeated the Lon Nol army. Second was the fear that the city dwellers would embark on a counterrevolution. The cities were seen as the centers of capitalist life, harboring the enemies of the regime. City dwellers were the "class enemy" responsible for the suffering of the peasantry and in collusion with U.S. imperialists. The urban population, or "new people," joined the peasantry, or "old people," in collective farms, an experiment that the Khmer Rouge had begun as early as 1973. Much of the forced migration took place from the Southwest to the more fertile Northwest, in order to grow rice.

The regime saw collectivization as the vehicle to achieve a Communist society while increasing the standard of living of the population. Collectivization would help the regime achieve self-sufficiency, and the surpluses in production would be sold on the international market to secure revenues to speed up development in the industrial and defense sectors. At the same time, collectivization would allow the Khmer Rouge to exercise more effective control over a population that might be hostile toward the regime, in order to fight both internal and external enemies.

Most of those who were taken to the countryside from the cities were not equipped to deal with the harsh working conditions, particularly given the inadequate food rations. Although agricultural production fed the army and gained export revenue, the populace was not given enough to eat. By early 1976 food became scarce, and the country faced famines in 1977 and 1978. Production quotas proved unrealistic, and the failure to achieve expected goals was perceived to be the work of internal and external enemies, thus increasing the level of repression. Chronic malnutrition coupled with overwork and medical neglect led to hundreds of thousands of deaths.

THE ENEMIES OF THE REGIME

According to the U.S. Central Intelligence Agency (CIA), before the Khmer Rouge entered Phnom Penh in 1975, the population of Cambodia stood at more than 7 million people. It is widely estimated that between April 1975 and January 1979, up to 2 million people died as a direct result of Khmer Rouge policies. The difficulty with making a precise estimate of the deaths during the Democratic Kampuchea era stems from the displacement and war-related deaths during the civil war of 1970–1975, when more than half a million people might have died. In addition, more than 2 million refugees had flooded into the major cities to escape the conflict in the countryside. Some fifty thousand people are also estimated to have fled to Thailand.

The Khmer Rouge targeted all those who were perceived to be opposed to the revolution, including domestic and foreign enemies. Within Cambodia the Khmer Rouge executed members of the Lon Nol regime, intellectuals and professional employees, skilled manual workers, and Khmer returning from overseas to help in the reconstruction of the country. The regime also targeted ethnic and national groups, such as the Vietnamese and the Chams. It is estimated that the Cham population dropped by 36 percent during the Democratic Kampuchea era. The Vietnamese minority was deported across the eastern border.

Suspicion also arose within the Khmer Rouge. By September 1976 a Khmer Rouge split precipitated a series of purges within the party. Hu Nim, the minister of information and propaganda, confessed to being a CIA agent in 1977, after being tortured. He subsequently was eliminated. Approximately twenty-five thousand high-ranking party members, military commanders, and officials became targets. Most were sent to the interrogation center at Tuol Sleng, or S-21, the site of a former high school in Phnom Penh, before being killed. Their bodies were dumped at Choeung Ek, or the "killing fields," 17 kilometers (10.6 miles) outside of the capital.

The policies of the Khmer Rouge had an international dimension, as the Khmer Rouge distrusted and loathed the Vietnamese. Part of Pol Pot's obsession with the Vietnamese "threat" stemmed from an extreme sense of Khmer nationalism as well as the perceived betrayal by the Vietnamese at the 1954 Geneva Conference. Although Pol Pot had relied on the Vietnamese Communist Party for support during the early part of the civil war, he resented his subservient position and what he considered the patronizing attitude of the Vietnamese, who insisted that Cambodia should subordinate its Communist struggle to that of Vietnam. In addition, the Khmer Rouge was interested in the possibility of creating a "greater Cambodia" that would include Cambodian ethnic minorities in the southern region of Vietnam. To counterbalance Vietnam as a client of the Soviet Union, China formed an alliance with the Pol Pot regime. China encouraged the belligerence of Democratic Kampuchea against the Vietnamese as relations between the two deteriorated after the Khmer Rouge victory in 1975. Democratic Kampuchea also served as a counterweight to the perceived Vietnamese expansionist designs in Indochina and Southeast Asia.

In 1976 Democratic Kampuchea began to mount direct attacks on Vietnam. The raids displaced almost half a million people on the Vietnamese side of the border. In December 1977 the Vietnamese launched a counteroffensive. While they retreated, a large number of Khmer followed these forces back to Vietnam as Pol Pot's military purges began to spiral out of control. Among those who fled in 1977 and 1978 were Heng Samrin and Hun Sen. Heng Samrin headed the Vietnamese-sponsored Kampuchean United Front for National Salvation, which eventually participated in the invasion of Cambodia at the end of 1978. Hun Sen became prime minister after the defeat of the Khmer Rouge.

By April 1978 more than 100,000 Vietnamese troops were amassed near the Cambodian border. In December 1978 the Vietnamese announced the creation of the Kampuchean United Front for National Salvation, which called for the overthrow of the Khmer Rouge regime. On Christmas Day 1978 Vietnamese forces invaded Cambodia, receiving the support of fifteen thousand Khmer resistance fighters. Phnom Penh fell on 7 January 1979. Cambodians who had gone into exile in Vietnam during the Khmer Rouge regime took power with Vietnamese support, renaming the country the People's Republic of Kampuchea. The new leaders also appropriated the name of the original Communist party in Cambodia, the Khmer People's Revolutionary Party (KPRP).

Pol Pot fled Phnom Penh in a helicopter with Ieng Sary and Nuon Chea, while other leaders took the train to Battambang. Khmer Rouge forces headed to the border with Thailand, where they constituted themselves into a guerrilla force. They took with them thousands of refugees at gunpoint. The Khmer Rouge treated the inhabitants of these refugee camps the same way they had treated the populace in Cambodia.

The 1978 Vietnamese invasion pushed China to call for the international isolation of Cambodia. The People's Republic of Kampuchea was widely viewed as a puppet regime of the Vietnamese, and the invasion was considered by many a breach of international law and the principle of sovereignty. China's position won support from the United States and the non-Communist Association of Southeast Asian Nations (ASEAN), which viewed the Vietnamese invasion with suspicion. This fear fit well in the era of the domino theory. The United States and China supported the Khmer Rouge in exile even as information about the atrocities committed became known to the world. The Khmer Rouge was seen as a preferable alternative to the Vietnamese-sponsored People's Republic of Kampuchea government.

THE ROAD TO ACCOUNTABILITY

After four years of the Khmer Rouge regime, Cambodia had almost no infrastructure, no currency or banks, no markets, and no public transport, and roads and railways had been badly damaged. There were no postal, telephone, or telegraph systems; clean water supplies; sanitation services; schools; or hospitals, and there was hardly any electricity. There were virtually no professionals or skilled workers. Old family and social networks had been destroyed. Cambodia was on the brink of famine when Vietnam invaded in 1978; however, the People's Republic of Kampuchea received almost no economic or humanitarian aid, because the regime was not recognized by the international community. Only the United Nations Children's Fund (UNICEF) and the International Red Cross assisted the country. Between 325,000 and 625,000 people died during 1979–1980, many from starvation.

The 1978 invasion by Vietnam also created a larger number of refugees and internally displaced people. At least half a million Cambodians fled to Thailand or to the Thai-Cambodian border. Thailand provided sanctuary to the retreating forces of the Khmer Rouge after 1979 with the encouragement of China. China, the ally of the Khmer Rouge, pledged to decrease its support to Communist insurgents in Thailand, to guarantee Thai security in the event of a Vietnamese attack, and to sell oil to Thailand at subsidized prices. In addition, the Thai government allowed China to supply weapons to the Khmer Rouge through its territory. Thailand's role as a military sanctuary also extended to the political realm, allowing for the creation of a "government in exile" on Thai territory.

The United States also supported the Khmer Rouge after 1979, leading Western nations to recognize Khieu Samphan as the legitimate representative of the Cambodian people at the UN. The United States pressured UN humanitarian organizations to provide assistance to the Khmer Rouge in the camps in Thailand. The World Food Program delivered aid that was destined to the Khmer Rouge through Thai military facilities. Moreover, the United States provided funds to the Khmer Rouge to finance their weapons purchases, although the U.S. government denied this. During the 1980s the Khmer Rouge controlled large parts of western and northwestern Cambodia, using bases on the Thai side of the border to continue to fight the People's Republic of Kampuchea.

The Vietnamese first attempted to have members of the Khmer Rouge regime tried for genocide. In August 1979 a special court, the People's Revolutionary Tribunal, was created to try Pol Pot and Deputy Prime Minister Ieng Sary, but the prosecution was conducted in absentia and amounted to nothing more than a show trial.

In June 1982 China brokered an anti-Vietnamese alliance that resembled the old alliance during the 1970–1975 civil war. The Khmer Rouge joined forces with Sihanouk's newly created United National Front for an Independent, Peaceful, and Cooperative Cambodia (FUNCINPEC) and Son Sann's Khmer People's National Liberation Front, a non-Communist resistance movement created in October 1979. The Coalition Government of Democratic Kampuchea had Sihanouk as president, Khieu Samphan from the Khmer Rouge as vice president, and Son Sann as prime minister. Although FUNCINPEC and the Khmer People's National Liberation Front had misgivings about joining in an alliance with the Khmer Rouge, especially after the extent of the death and violence during the 1975–1979 regime became clear, the coalition gained international support as the Cambodian "government in exile." The Coalition Government of Democratic Kampuchea was recognized by China, the United States, and ASEAN. The military forces of the Khmer Rouge, around thirty-five thousand strong, dominated the alliance and received the backing of members of the international community.

Any effort to de-escalate the conflict and bring stability to Cambodia in the early 1980s was rejected by several parties, both domestic and international. In 1980 Vietnam proposed to create a demilitarized zone on the border, which was rejected by Thailand. In 1981 the Soviet Union boycotted both a UN-sponsored international conference on Cambodia and a proposal by ASEAN to have the UN disarm all parties, assist in the withdrawal of the Vietnamese troops, and sponsor an election. In 1983 China rejected a proposal at the nonaligned summit for all parties to come to a conference. Sihanouk proposed direct talks with the People's Republic of Kampuchea as early as August 1984, just to be rebuffed by Chinese opposition. In 1985 the People's Republic of Kampuchea announced its willingness to talk to the Coalition Government of Democratic Kampuchea; however, it wanted the Khmer Rouge excluded. In 1986 a proposal by Austria to chair talks between all the parties was opposed by China.

However, the support of the Khmer Rouge by the United States, China, and ASEAN began to appear untenable by the mid-1980s. Vietnamese troops started withdrawing from Cambodia in 1982. The Heng Samrin–Hun Sen regime began to develop its own policies separate from Vietnamese pressures. In 1986 the Australian foreign minister Bill Hayden voiced the opinion that an international tribunal needed to be created to try the leaders of the Khmer Rouge. By the late 1980s ASEAN countries had changed their views on Vietnamese expansionism and on the People's Republic of Kampuchea as a puppet regime.

Beginning in 1987, there were several attempts to bring the different factions together. Indonesia backed an initiative that resulted in the beginning of regular meetings between Hun Sen and Sihanouk. The Sino-Soviet rapprochement and improving East-West relations increased the flexibility of the patrons, who began to exert pressure on the clients to reach a negotiated settlement. Vietnam's announcement that it would begin withdrawing troops from Cambodia because of declining aid from the Soviet Union led Hun Sen to approach Thailand and other countries in the region. In 1989 the People's Republic of Kampuchea changed its name to the State of Cambodia and renounced its socialist goals and ideology. The regime's political party, the KPRP, was renamed the CPP.

In 1989 members of the UN Security Council and other interested states convened the Paris Conference on Cambodia. The Khmer Rouge was one of four factions represented; the other three were FUNCINPEC, the Khmer People's National Liberation Front, and the State

of Cambodia. In September 1990 the four factions reached an agreement to create the Supreme National Council, composed of six members of the State of Cambodia, two members of each of the other three factions, and Sihanouk as the chairman and its thirteenth member. This arrangement paved the way for the signing of the Agreement on a Comprehensive Political Settlement of the Cambodian Conflict, commonly known as the Paris Agreement, on 23 October 1991. The Paris Agreement called for the creation of the United Nations Transitional Authority in Cambodia (UNTAC), to organize elections with full Khmer Rouge participation. The agreement also included a cease-fire; the verified permanent withdrawal of foreign forces; the end of foreign military assistance; the voluntary repatriation of refugees and displaced peoples; guarantees of Cambodia's neutrality, sovereignty, and territorial integrity; and rehabilitation and reconstruction support from the international community. In addition, Sihanouk stepped down as the leader of FUNCINPEC and assumed the ceremonial position of king of Cambodia.

Seeing a role for the Khmer Rouge in the Paris Agreement, the Chinese agreed to stop supplying them with weapons. The Chinese and Thai encouraged the Khmer Rouge to cooperate and be a party to the Paris Agreement. However, the Khmer Rouge continued to pursue policies aimed at driving ethnic Vietnamese out of the country, overthrowing the State of Cambodia, and regaining power. By June 1992 the Khmer Rouge refused to continue to abide by the Paris Agreement and ended its cooperation with UNTAC, which had begun operations in Cambodia in March 1992. By the end of 1992, there was an upsurge in violence, leading FUNCINPEC, the Khmer People's National Liberation Front, and the State of Cambodia to refuse to disarm fully and to demobilize. UNTAC even returned weapons to those three organizations for self-defense against the Khmer Rouge. However, the State of Cambodia seemed to have also used the situation to encourage violence against FUNCINPEC and the Khmer People's National Liberation Front.

Even though all parties had agreed to participate in and abide by the results of the elections scheduled for May 1993 under the supervision of UNTAC, the Khmer Rouge ultimately withdrew from the electoral contest when it perceived that it could not win. As the election date approached, the violence by both the Khmer Rouge and the State of Cambodia increased. The Khmer Rouge launched military attacks on State of Cambodia forces and threatened to kill people who voted. Voter turnout was more than 90 percent, even under the threat of attacks by the Khmer Rouge, but the constitutional requirement that a party win two-thirds of the seats in parliament to govern was not met, leading to an unstable alliance between two prime ministers—Hun Sen, representing the CPP, and Norodom Ranariddh (the son of Sihanouk and now the party leader), representing FUNCINPEC.

The United States formally changed its position on the Khmer Rouge in April 1994, when Congress passed the Cambodian Genocide Justice Act, which committed the United States to support efforts to bring members of the Khmer Rouge to justice. In July 1994 the Cambodian parliament passed a law outlawing the Khmer Rouge. While the new Cambodian government engaged in military campaigns against the Khmer Rouge, it also offered amnesty to those who agreed to defect from the organization. Khmer Rouge fighters began to defect and join the ranks of the military in January 1995, the deadline of one such amnesty. In August 1996 Ieng Sary negotiated another amnesty and defected alongside two military divisions. He denied responsibility for the atrocities committed under the Khmer Rouge and received a royal pardon. However, the government later clarified the amnesty deal, stating that Ieng Sary's amnesty only applied to his conviction at absentia in the 1979 People's Revolutionary Tribunal.

Ieng Sary's amnesty deal created another split within the Khmer Rouge in 1997 that further focused international attention on accountability for its atrocities. Son Sen and his family were executed, presumably under orders from Pol Pot. Ta Mok also became a target of Pol Pot. Although Ta Mok received assistance from some troops initially, they later mutinied against him. In 1998 Pol Pot died after a trial held by the remaining Khmer Rouge forces, for ordering the execution of Son Sen. The international community became increasingly concerned about the prosecution of Khmer Rouge leaders after Pol Pot's death.

The negotiations surrounding what was eventually called the Extraordinary Chambers in the Courts of Cambodia (ECCC) began eighteen years after the defeat of the Khmer Rouge regime by the Vietnamese forces in 1979. The UN secretary-general's special representative for human rights in Cambodia began the process that led to the negotiations between the UN and the Cambodian government. In July 1997 Hun Sen and Ranariddh were persuaded by the special representative to request assistance from the UN to establish an international tribunal to try members of the Khmer Rouge. The special representative ushered through the UN General Assembly Resolution 52/135, condemning the Khmer Rouge genocide and requesting that the secretary-general provide assistance to Cambodia. The UN Security Council was not involved in this effort, as there was concern over China's potential use of the veto.

However, as this process was moving forward, the CPP, in 1997, staged a coup ousting FUNCINPEC from the coalition government. The coup was the outcome of fears on both sides that an alliance with the Khmer Rouge forces was forthcoming. Former Khmer Rouge cadres were being integrated into government military structures that had allegiances to either the CPP or FUNCINPEC. Ranariddh was forced into exile under allegations that he was allying himself with the Khmer Rouge at the expense of the CPP. FUNCINPEC had been an ally of the Khmer Rouge under the Coalition Government of Democratic Kampuchea. After the coup, international pressure mounted on Hun Sen to schedule elections. The UN reacted by leaving vacant Cambodia's UN seat, as it was contested by both the CPP and FUNCINPEC representatives, and ASEAN delayed Cambodia's membership ascension for a year. Under these conditions, Hun Sen scheduled elections in 1998, at which time, although again not receiving two-thirds of the seats in parliament, the CPP became the dominant party and Hun Sen, the sole prime minister. Ranariddh returned to be president of the senate, and FUNCINPEC became a junior partner in the government coalition.

In December 1998 Hun Sen accepted a request by Khieu Samphan and Nuon Chea to return to Cambodia as ordinary citizens; however, Hun Sen later claimed that he did not offer them amnesty. Even as these events were unfolding in Cambodia, the UN secretary-general convened a group of experts to examine the available evidence regarding the atrocities committed by the Khmer Rouge; in March 1999 the experts' report found that members of the Khmer Rouge had committed not only war crimes and crimes against humanity but also genocide and other violations of the 1948 Genocide Convention. The report also recommended the creation of an international tribunal modeled on the International Criminal Tribunal for the Former Yugoslavia and the International Criminal Tribunal for Rwanda, owing to concerns regarding the levels of independence and transparency of the judicial system in Cambodia.

In March 1999 Ta Mok was captured and placed under military detention. He was soon followed by Duch, who was captured in May 1999. In the meantime, the Cambodian government rejected the recommendation for a purely international tribunal, arguing that it had the obligation to prosecute violations of human rights under Article 6 of the Genocide Convention and would do so within its domestic court system. By September 1999, however, Hun Sen presented two alternatives for UN involvement in a Cambodian tribunal: the UN could provide a legal team that would participate in the tribunal (established within the existing Cambodian court system), or the UN could provide a legal team that would only serve in an advisory capacity. Otherwise, Hun Sen suggested that the UN withdraw completely from the tribunal process, which was not the preferred option for the UN.

The Cambodian government created a task force to negotiate with the UN over its role and the structure of the court. The negotiations focused on creating a mixed tribunal, including both international and domestic judges. The Cambodian government drafted the tribunal statute, and in July 2000 the UN and the Cambodian government finalized details in a memorandum of understanding on the court structure. In January 2001 Cambodia's parliament enacted the Law on the Establishment of Extraordinary Chambers in the Courts of Cambodia for the Prosecution of Crimes Committed during the Period of Democratic Kampuchea.

The UN expressed concerns that the legislation approved by the parliament did not abide by the agreement in the memorandum of understanding with the UN, and in February 2002 the UN Office of Legal Affairs decided to end negotiations with the Cambodian government. The UN argued that the Cambodian government wanted UN assistance but under Cambodia's terms, without considering any recommendations. However, member states of the UN did not support this decision. In December 2002 the General Assembly passed Resolution 57/228A and Resolution 57/228B, calling for further negotiations between UN representatives and the Hun Sen government. On 6 January 2003, almost a year after the negotiations had collapsed, they resumed, and on 17 March the Cambodian government and UN officials agreed to a draft framework for a tribunal to prosecute the surviving leaders of the Khmer Rouge. This draft resolution was approved by the Cambodian government and the UN General Assembly by June 2003. However, the ratification of the agreement in the Cambodian parliament was delayed by the July 2003 election, in which again no political party received the two-thirds majority required by the constitution to govern. Talks on forming a coalition

bogged down over the insistence by opposition parties that Hun Sen step down as prime minister. The CPP rejected that demand and ruled as a caretaker government for more than a year, until, in June 2004, negotiations were brokered between the CPP and FUNCINPEC. Again FUNCINPEC assumed the position of junior partner in the government. In October 2004 the parliament finally debated and unanimously approved the UN agreement.

THE EXTRAORDINARY CHAMBERS IN THE COURTS OF CAMBODIA

The Agreement between the United Nations and the Royal Government of Cambodia concerning the Prosecution under Cambodian Law of Crimes Committed during the Period of Democratic Kampuchea established a "mixed" court with both international and domestic components. This is a departure from the International Criminal Tribunal for the Former Yugoslavia and the International Criminal Tribunal for Rwanda, which are purely international courts. As part of sharing responsibilities for the court, the Cambodian government agreed to cover the costs of the premises for the ECCC as well as those associated with Cambodian personnel, while the UN, through voluntary contributions from member states, would finance the international personnel, witness and defense expenses, safety and security, and other areas agreed to with the Cambodian government. The initial cost estimate was $56 million over three years. The Cambodian government would provide $13 million; UN voluntary contributions would cover the remaining $43 million.

Article 1 of the agreement states that the UN and the Cambodian government will cooperate in bringing to trial senior leaders of Democratic Kampuchea and those who were most responsible for the crimes and serious violations of Cambodian penal law, international humanitarian law and custom, and international conventions recognized by Cambodia. The temporal jurisdiction of the tribunal would cover the period between 17 April 1975 and 6 January 1979. This decision was controversial, as some in Cambodia believed that the period between 1970 and 1975 should be included, as there were many violations of human rights during the civil war. Others asserted that international supporters of the Khmer Rouge should also bear close scrutiny as well as the Vietnamese invaders. In addition, there was dissatisfaction in Cambodia with the limitation of trying only senior officials of the Khmer Rouge, and many wondered how to determine those "most responsible."

The court is composed of two chambers: the Trial Chamber and the Supreme Court Chamber. The chambers are composed of both international and Cambodian judges. According to the agreement, the secretary-general of the UN nominates no fewer than seven international judges, at least five of whom are appointed to the chambers by the Cambodian Supreme Council of the Magistracy, a body created in the 1993 constitution to guarantee the independence of the judiciary. The Trial Chamber is composed of three Cambodian judges and two international judges; the Supreme Court Chamber has four Cambodian judges and three international judges. The composition of the chambers gives a majority of the seats to Cambodian judges; however, decisions require a supermajority. In the case of the Trial Chamber, four judges need to agree with the decision; in the case of the Supreme Court Chamber, five judges have to agree. Judges are expected to be of high moral character and independent of any influence, including their governments. They are appointed to serve for the duration of the proceedings.

In addition to trial judges, the ECCC also has two investigating judges, one Cambodian and one international. The conduct of the prosecution is entrusted to co-prosecutors, one Cambodian and one international. The international investigating judge and the international prosecutor are selected by the Cambodian Supreme Council of the Magistracy from a list of two candidates for each position submitted by the UN secretary-general. To address possible disagreements between the investigating judges about whether to proceed with an investigation and what direction to take or between the prosecutors over how to proceed with the prosecution, a pretrial ruling by a chamber of five judges determines how to proceed. In this case, a supermajority of four is needed. However, if there is not a supermajority decision, the investigation or prosecution has to proceed.

Article 9 of the agreement establishes that the subject matter jurisdiction of the chambers includes (1) the crime of genocide as defined by the 1948 Convention on the Prevention and Punishment of the Crime of Genocide, (2) crimes against humanity as defined by the 1998 Rome Statute of the International Criminal Court, (3) grave breaches of the 1949 Geneva Conventions, and (4) other crimes defined in the Law on the Establishment of Extraordinary Chambers in the Courts of Cambodia, passed by Cambodia in 2001. The last includes crimes specified in the 1956 Penal Code of Cambodia, destruction of cultural property during armed conflict pursuant to the 1954 Hague Convention for the Protection of Cultural Property in the Event of Armed Conflict, and crimes against internationally protected persons pursuant to the 1961 Vienna Convention on Diplomatic Relations.

The procedures within the chambers are based on Cambodian law, but international standards are used in instances in which there are inconsistencies or the Cambodian law is silent. The 1966 International Covenant on Civil and Political Rights serves as a basis for establishing standards of justice, fairness, due process of law, and the rights of the accused. The maximum penalty for a conviction, in accordance with Cambodian law, is life imprisonment.

DEVELOPMENTS IN THE ECCC

One of the major issues facing the ECCC was funding. In December 2004 the UN secretary-general stated that the tribunal would begin its work once funding was secured for the three years of operation, with the first year's funding deposited in a trust fund. Donations were solicited, and pledging conferences took place in 2005 and 2006. Japan provided the largest contribution, some $21 million. Several countries also agreed to assist the Cambodian government with its $13 million share of the budget. However, neither China nor the United States made contributions. China did not support the idea of a court, and the United States expressed concerns over judicial independence and the application of internationally recognized standards of justice. The procedures within the chambers are based on Cambodian law, and the concern is that the penal code of Cambodia dates back to 1956. The application of Cambodian law still had many gray areas, and numerous domestic court decisions were destroyed during the Khmer Rouge regime, preventing the use of precedent to make decisions on the intent of the law and potential rulings.

Personnel became the next major issue. In June 2005 the UN requested that all states submit candidates for the international judge and prosecutor positions in the ECCC. By November 2005 a list a candidates was compiled, and in May 2006 the Supreme Council of Magistracy appointed seventeen Cambodian and thirteen international judges to serve. Two of those selected would act as prosecutors and fourteen as judges, with the rest in reserve. At that time, a tribunal spokesperson announced that trial proceedings would begin in 2007. However, work slowed because of disagreements over the internal rules of the court. A draft proposal was made public in November 2006, but international and national judges disagreed over several issues, including how to integrate

Cambodian law and international standards in navigating the Cambodian court system and what role the Defense Support Unit should have as it tried to include international defenders. Negotiations over these and other issues dragged on until June 2007.

In July 2007 the ECCC prosecutors presented the first introductory submission of their investigation to the investigating judges. The prosecutors identified five suspects who committed, aided, abetted, or bore superior responsibility for the alleged crimes. Duch was handed over to the ECCC and charged with crimes against humanity. In September 2007 Nuon Chea, the most senior surviving member of the Khmer Rouge, was arrested and charged with crimes against humanity. In November 2007 Ieng Sary, his wife Ieng Thirith, and Khieu Samphan were taken into custody. Ieng Sary and Khieu Samphan were charged with crimes against humanity and war crimes; Ieng Thirith was charged with crimes against humanity. The main issue in everyone's mind became whether the tribunal would work fast enough to bring to justice these surviving members of the Khmer Rouge. Khieu Ponnary, Pol Pot's first wife, died in July 2003, and Ta Mok died in July 2006. Most of the defendants are in their late seventies and eighties, which means they could avoid justice through death.

However, even though many questions remained unanswered regarding the ECCC's operations and the setbacks it could confront as it prepares to bring the accused to trial, great efforts have been made by the international community since the end of World War II, particularly in the 1990s, to bring to justice those responsible for gross violations of human rights across the world. Even at the thirtieth anniversary of the end of the Pol Pot regime, its actions were not forgotten. The UN and states around the world continue to work to promote the respect for, and enforcement of, international human rights.

[See also Association of Southeast Asian Nations (ASEAN); Civil and Political Rights: International Covenant on Civil and Political Rights; Crimes against Humanity; Genocide; Pol Pot; and Vietnam.]

BIBLIOGRAPHY

Chandler, David P. *A History of Cambodia.* 2d ed. Boulder, Colo.: Westview Press, 1992.

Chandler, David P. *The Tragedy of Cambodian History: Politics, War, and Revolution since 1945.* New Haven, Conn.: Yale University Press, 1991.

Clymer, Kenton. *Troubled Relations: The United States and Cambodia since 1870.* DeKalb: Northern Illinois University Press, 2007.

De Nike, Howard J., John Quigley, and Kenneth J. Robinson, eds. *Genocide in Cambodia: Documents from the Trial of Pol Pot and Ieng Sary.* Philadelphia: University of Pennsylvania Press, 2000.

Etcheson, Craig. *After the Killing Fields: Lessons from the Cambodian Genocide.* Westport, Conn.: Praeger, 2005.

Etcheson, Craig. *The Rise and Demise of Democratic Kampuchea.* Boulder, Colo.: Westview Press, 1984.

Fawthrop, Tom, and Helen Jarvis. *Getting Away with Genocide: Cambodia's Long Struggle against the Khmer Rouge.* London: Pluto Press, 2004.

Heder, Stephen R., with Brian D. Tittemore. *Seven Candidates for Prosecution: Accountability for the Crimes of the Khmer Rouge.* Washington, D.C.: War Crimes Research Office, American University, 2001.

Heder, Steve, and Judy Ledgerwood, eds. *Propaganda, Politics, and Violence in Cambodia: Democratic Transition under United Nations Peace-Keeping.* Armonk, N.Y.: M.E. Sharpe, 1996.

Kamm, Henry. *Cambodia: Report from a Stricken Land.* New York: Arcade, 1998.

Kiernan, Ben. *The Pol Pot Regime: Race, Power, and Genocide in Cambodia under the Khmer Rouge, 1975–79.* New Haven, Conn.: Yale University Press, 1996.

Kiernan, Ben, ed. *Conflict and Change in Cambodia.* London: Routledge, 2007.

Mason, Linda, and Roger Brown. *Rice, Rivalry, and Politics: Managing Cambodian Relief.* South Bend Ind.: University of Notre Dame Press, 1983.

Mayall, James, ed. *The New Interventionism, 1991–1994: United Nations Experience in Cambodia, Former Yugoslavia, and Somalia.* New York: Cambridge University Press, 1996.

Ramji, Jaya, and Beth van Schaack, eds. *Bringing the Khmer Rouge to Justice: Prosecuting Mass Violence before the Cambodian Courts.* Lewiston, N.Y.: Edwin Mellen Press, 2005.

Tully, John. *A Short History of Cambodia.* Crows Nest, New South Wales, Australia: Allen and Unwin, 2005.

Widyono, Benny. *Dancing in Shadows: Sihanouk, the Khmer Rouge, and the United Nations in Cambodia.* Lanham, Md.: Rowman & Littlefield, 2008.

CARE INTERNATIONAL

by Allison Burden

CARE International is an international confederation of independent humanitarian and development organizations that are committed to helping communities in the developing world achieve lasting victories over poverty. Since the organization's founding in 1945 as the Cooperative for American Remittances to Europe, the scope of its mission has changed considerably. CARE began as a group of twenty-two U.S. organizations sending food packages to war-torn Europe; as of 2008, it was a global confederation of organizations with more than twelve thousand employees working in seventy countries worldwide, with an average annual budget exceeding $600 million.

In 1999 CARE adopted a rights-based approach to development, which was reflected in a new organization-wide vision that commits the organization to fight for human dignity and social justice. The subsequent Strategic Plan (2001–2006) identified the adoption of a rights-based approach as one of its strategic directions, closely linked to efforts to address the underlying causes of poverty and social injustice.

HISTORY OF CARE

In 1945, as World War II ended, twenty-two U.S. charities combined their efforts to deliver food packages to Europe. The CARE package was born. As early as 1947, the scope of the package's contents began to change, with the inclusion of nonfood items such as tools, cloth, medicine, and other goods; in 1948, as the Soviet blockade of Berlin was lifted, CARE trucks were the first vehicles to enter the beleaguered town. By 1955 the last postwar packages were delivered and CARE had broadened its geographic reach.

CARE's expansion started in Asia, spreading in the early 1950s to Latin America and, by the 1960s, to Africa. CARE distributed medical services and supplies during wartime, sending relief workers to the affected areas. In 1953, in recognition of the broadening scope of its work, CARE changed its name to Cooperative Assistance for Relief Everywhere.

Through the 1960s onward, although CARE's work continued in response to human-made and natural disasters and focused on the provision of supplementary feeding programs (using surplus U.S. agricultural commodities), the contexts increasingly called for a broadening of the response to longer-term interventions for recovery, rehabilitation, and the renewal of resources.

In the 1970s and 1980s further changes took place. CARE developed its capacity in the agricultural, natural resources, primary health-care, and small-enterprise sectors. The board moved from consisting primarily of organizational representatives to a more diverse mix, with the inclusion of individual public members. The organization also began a careful transition to multinationalism. Germany, one of the first recipients of CARE packages in the 1940s, became the first country in Europe to raise funds for CARE programs in the developing world. In the early twenty-first century there were twelve members: the founder, CARE USA; Germany; Australia; Austria; Canada; Denmark; France; Japan; the Netherlands; Norway; Thailand; and the United Kingdom. Four of these are operational in the seventy countries where CARE works: CARE US, CARE Australia, CARE Canada, and CARE Thailand. All CARE members raise funds for development and humanitarian work worldwide, and the operational units (country offices, regional management units) can also raise funds for their work locally.

CARE International has a board, a secretary-general, a secretariat, and emergency personnel based in Geneva; it convenes a variety of committees from among its members to make strategic decisions, including the development of Strategic Plans. The most recent Strategic Plan (2007) recognizes concerns that the roles and accountabilities of each of the various CARE International and member decision-making bodies are blurred and that, as a result, decision-making modalities on organizational issues are perceived to be slow, especially on issues that affect CARE International's ability to speak independently or advocate collectively, or both. As a result, CARE International reviewed its internal governance structures, and members have provided resources to employ a full-time advocacy coordinator in the secretariat.

Having been founded as a charitable organization, CARE, throughout much of its history, has worked within (and not against) the systems and structures of power that dominate the world. For example, CARE's provision of food aid is a direct result of overproduction subsidies in the north that benefit U.S. producers and shipping companies but weaken developing-country producers. CARE also traditionally received most of its funding from the U.S. government, which carried its own restrictions and conditionality, often related to U.S. foreign policy interests.

Under a new president, Peter Bell, the mid-1990s saw CARE making efforts to ensure sustainable and appropriate development. The organization introduced a sustainable livelihoods framework (Household Livelihood Security) that led not only to a more strategic understanding and approach to the dynamics of poverty at the community level but also to a focus on gender equity and diversity that probed power relations within households and social structures more broadly. By the late 1990s CARE adopted a rights-based approach to development in a way that reflects this evolution of its learning. It defines a rights-based approach as follows:

A rights-based approach deliberately and explicitly focuses on people achieving the minimum conditions for living with dignity. It does so by exposing the roots of vulnerability and marginalization and expanding the range of responses. It empowers people to claim and exercise their rights and fulfill their responsibilities. A rights-based approach recognizes poor, displaced, and war-affected people as having inherent rights essential to livelihood security—rights that are validated by international law.

In 2001 CARE further defined the approach through a set of guiding principles (the CARE International Programming Principles) for enacting the rights-based approach: promoting empowerment, nonviolent resolution of conflict, and responsibility; working with partners; addressing discrimination; ensuring accountability; and seeking sustainable results.

For CARE, rights were a way of challenging its own history and incorporating its experience. The new approach recognized an understanding of poverty that was grounded in unequal power relations. The novelty of the rights framework lay in its ability to support the process of defining both the rights holders and those responsible for ensuring the enjoyment of rights. It broadened CARE's understanding of itself as an actor among others who could work for increasing inclusion and accountability and who would need to do so in new forms of partnership. The rights-based approach provided a coherent, comprehensive, and practical framework for the exploration of the root causes of vulnerability and exclusion in a given context and in all the sector work that CARE carries out.

CARE believes that the programming principles also provide it with the words and practices to make the programmatic and attitudinal shift to the rights-based approach. The programming principles were first defined as "the enacting behaviors of a rights-based approach" and subsequently edited and adopted by all CARE International confederation members as overarching principles.

CARE AND THE RIGHTS-BASED APPROACH

A rights-based view of development affirms people's right to participate in decisions that affect their lives. This view requires CARE to identify and address the root causes of poverty and social injustice; it also requires a focus on human dignity and an intolerance of discrimination. The rights-based approach is inherently moral and political. It calls for the transformation of power relations that govern the world.

At a conceptual level, CARE had, in the mid-1990s, developed a framework, Household Livelihood Security (HLS), which provided the organization with an understanding of the multidimensional dynamics of poverty. HLS also emphasized the importance of working in partnership and at multiple causal levels of change. The rights-based approach was incorporated into HLS, enabling CARE to expand its view of development beyond human needs to address relationships, rights, and responsibilities. This shift was predicated on the assumption that in addressing human rights, CARE would achieve a greater and more sustainable impact. It heralded the recognition that people are poor not only because they lack assets and skills but also because they suffer from social exclusion, marginalization, and discrimination.

To capture and promote the conceptual shift, CARE developed a Unifying Framework for Poverty Eradication and Social Justice (UF). The UF was not designed to replace HLS and other approaches; instead, the UF was developed to help clarify the connections and linkages and to demonstrate how the various frameworks and approaches complemented one another.

Through the UF, CARE expands on the concept of linking unmet needs to denied rights, addressing the social, political, and cultural structures that exacerbate poverty and discrimination. The UF focuses our attention on three broad outcome domains. The first seeks improvement in people's human condition. By human conditions, CARE means supporting people in their struggles to attain their rights to a minimum standard of overall agency and well-being. The second outcome area, social positions, requires CARE to focus on addressing the unequal power relations—embodied in social and cultural norms and practices at personal and institutional levels—that exacerbate poverty and discrimination. This means working with men and women, encouraging them to participate equally in negotiations to manage conflict, change attitudes and beliefs, address discrimination—and thus shift power relations or social positions. The third critical outcome area of the framework focuses on the enabling environment. The enabling environment refers to political, public, and civic institutions that together enable and foster an environment for just and equitable societies. Addressing the enabling environment is about promoting efforts to ensure that government recognizes and respects human rights, is open to political participation, promotes and regulates fair economic growth and trade, provides necessary social protection, mitigates conflict, and provides a sound legal and regulatory framework. Working to promote policies and practices that are sympathetic to the poor in the enabling environment will also increase the sustainability of poverty eradication and social justice efforts.

In terms of the shift in practice, questions and uncertainty still exist as to whether CARE's various approaches (HLS, rights-based approach, gender equity and diversity, civil society strengthening, and so on) complement or contradict each other. The incorporation of rights means challenging staff and program participants' well-rooted attitudes and beliefs, notions that have perpetuated a charitable mentality and fuzzy standards of impact in prior work. This is most evident in the unending cycle of project-based funding and activity—a perpetual-drip system that is adequate to sustain the aid system but does not constitute a program that aims to deliver at the level of systems change.

CHALLENGES AND DILEMMAS

Challenges relating to the adoption of a rights framework are numerous. First, the members of the CARE confederation did not all agree on the adoption of the rights-based approach. This has created practical obstacles,

for example, in the adoption of frameworks and principles, and has led to dilution of some of the rights language within them. This has also meant that CARE International has not drawn on the potential strength of the confederation to influence global change, provoking questions relating to the accountability of the organization in the implementation of strategies that will achieve its vision.

CARE is also a very large and decentralized organization, and its seventy country offices work relatively independently. As a result, the understanding and practical adoption of the concepts and frameworks differ across the spectrum of CARE's work. Furthermore, CARE depends primarily on institutional funding from governments; it does not raise large amounts of its own unrestricted money from individual donors. This can result in two different distorting impacts on its work. First, development practice has historically depended on the official aid system's quest for "efficient" technical fixes and tools that can be used in a given context and replicated elsewhere. The human rights framework requires a much more nuanced and adaptive response to a given context, requiring skills in power and risk analysis, facilitation and negotiation, advocacy and alliance building. Many of these skills have not traditionally been attracted to or rewarded within CARE. Second, a reliance on government funding can limit the organization's ability to take independent action, particularly when it relates to governmental policy, because challenging policy may result in the withdrawal of funding. This challenge has been highlighted in recent years in relation to the increasing militarization of humanitarianism (for example, in Iraq), the U.S. government's stance on food aid, and its restriction that organizations must have a policy explicitly opposing prostitution in order to be eligible for HIV and AIDS funding.

However, CARE has taken some stands in recent years, committing to abandoning the monetization of food by 2009 and to developing carefully negotiated policies on its work with sex workers, particularly in Asia. CARE also addressed the U.S. House Committee on Foreign Affairs as part of the U.S. Emergency Plan for AIDS relief (PEPFAR) reauthorization process in late 2007. Dr. Helene Gayle, the president of CARE USA, in her statement before the committee, pointed out the limitations of PEPFAR funding as experienced by CARE, stating,

PEPFAR's tendency to fund short-term interventions often neglects the social processes vital for real local ownership; . . . its emphasis on quick results produces incentives to "demonstrate big numbers"; and . . . its narrow focus and compartmentalized approach to prevention, treatment and care inhibit integrated, comprehensive programming. These are features of PEPFAR that must change, if lasting impact and real sustainability are to be realized.

Of interest in these examples is not that they are ideal results of the adoption of the rights-based approach, because they were both pragmatic solutions. The approach did not provide ideal answers for CARE; rather, it influenced CARE's negotiation of these decisions in a way that reflected the commitment to rights. Prior to the adoption of a rights-based approach, such discussions might not have taken place. More fundamentally, in order to diversify its funding, in 2003 CARE launched a new marketing campaign, "I am Powerful," that focuses on attracting funding and support from women in the United States. While CARE continues to raise funds from the national governments of members as well as from local sources in countries where CARE operates, the campaign has been successful in attracting diverse and less restricted sources of funding and in raising the awareness and understanding of poverty among women in America. The diversification of funding remains a primary goal of the 2007 Strategic Plan; in the early twenty-first century funding from the U.S. government fell, for the first time, below 50 percent of CARE's total spending.

There are real dilemmas as well within CARE's country office operations. The large majority of CARE's twelve-thousand-member staff is made up of nationals working in their own countries. Challenging state and culture carries risk; in some cases the risk is life-threatening. For example, in Darfur, where massive abuses of human rights led the former U.S. secretary of state, Colin Powell, to declare the situation genocidal, CARE's largely Sudanese ground team has had to take great care in its own positioning and statements and has often preferred behind-the-scenes advocacy. The risk of CARE's operations being closed in Sudan and its staff living with the consequences of public advocacy statements in terms of political and social marginalization is real. This situation is replicated across the world and particularly in contexts of conflict, or "fragile states." CARE, therefore, still needs to define its own position and role within human rights development practice to balance the challenging of power with its own ability to continue operating.

A further challenge relates to the measurement of impact. The adoption of the rights-based approach was, in considerable measure, based on the assumption that this method would have a positive impact on poverty. CARE adopted the Millennium Development Goals (MDGs) as indicators of its success in its Strategic Plan of 2001. Although the Millennium Development Declaration is couched in the language of rights, the goals themselves are not, and it therefore should not be assumed that efforts toward the achievement of the MDGs will contribute to the enjoyment of social and economic rights. CARE's attempts to go beyond MDG counts in measuring the impact of its rights-related work include a Strategic Impact Inquiry (SII) on women's empowerment. The inquiry shows that CARE has made valuable contributions to women's struggles to overcome the material and social roots of their poverty. CARE programs are expanding women's assets, skills, and attitudes, while fostering new modes of social and political relations between women and men in households, communities, and social organizations of the state and civil society. The study also makes clear, however, the need for a more strategic approach to mechanisms like women's groups, in order to support women's solidarity groups pursuing an empowerment agenda. The findings also show that CARE might not be aware of or taking action to minimize the potential harm to women that results from programs, for example, in the area of gender-based violence. Overall, the inquiry finds that despite exciting innovations in many projects, CARE has missed opportunities to work programmatically toward deeper, faster, and more sustainable positive changes in poverty and social injustice. The SII findings point directly back to the underlying structure and intent of the international aid system and call on the organization to seek its reform.

A mapping study of the level to which rights-based approaches and the programming principles had been adopted by CARE reinforce the SII findings. The mapping study concludes that, overall, there is increased understanding of the rights-based approach; it has made CARE think differently about its role, programs, and resources—and particularly the relationship CARE has with the people it seeks to serve. Through reflection, discussion, and debate, CARE's role in different contexts is increasingly shifting from that of direct implementer to that of facilitator, mediator, coordinator, and advocate. This means that some of CARE's programs are addressing long-term complex changes as well as short-term outcomes through service delivery. Although CARE has made significant commitments to deepening the theoretical understanding of rights-based approaches (and can point to some notable innovations), there is a need to work programmatically to scale up success and put rights-based approaches into more general practice across the portfolio. There is also a need to build accountability mechanisms, including solid impact measurement systems that ground the rights-based innovations in a learning framework. This framework will be one that shares important lessons on making change happen and can ensure that the same lessons are ploughed back into CARE's ongoing work for greater impact on the underlying causes of poverty and social injustice.

[*See also* Nongovernmental Organizations (NGOs): Overview.]

BIBLIOGRAPHY

Barrett, Christopher B., and Daniel G. Maxwell. *Food Aid after Fifty Years: Recasting Its Role.* New York: Routledge, 2005.

Jones, Andrew. *Incorporation of a Rights-Based Approach into CARE's Program Cycle, a Discussion Paper for CARE's Program Staff.* July 2001. http://www.pqdl.care.org.

Martinez, Eliza. *The Courage to Change: Confronting the Limits and Unleashing the Potential of CARE's Programming for Women. Synthesis Report: Phase 2.* CARE International Strategic Impact Inquiry on Women's Empowerment. February 2006. http://www.csps.emory.edu/SII%20Phase%202%20Synthesis%20Report%20Final.pdf.

McCaston, M. Catherine. *Moving CARE's Programming Forward, Unifying Framework for Poverty Eradiation and Social Justice and Underlying Causes of Poverty.* January 2005. http://www.pqdl.care.org.

Slim, Hugo. *Military Intervention to Protect Human Rights: The Humanitarian Agency Perspective.* Background Paper for the International Council on Human Rights' Meeting on Humanitarian Intervention: Responses and Dilemmas for Human Rights Organisations, Geneva, Switzerland, March 31–April 1, 2001. The Program Quality Digital Library. http://www.pqdl.care.org.

Slim, Hugo. "A Response to Peter Uvin, Making Moral Low Ground: Rights as the Struggle for Justice and the Abolition of Development." *PRAXIS: The Fletcher Journal of Development Studies* 17 (2002): 1–5.

United States House. Committee on Foreign Affairs. *Statement of Helene Gayle, MD, MPH President and Chief Executive Officer, CARE USA, before the U.S. House Committee on Foreign Affairs. Full Committee Hearing on "PEPFAR Reauthorization: From Emergency to Sustainability."* September 2007. http://www.foreignaffairs.house.gov/110/gay092507.pdf.

Uvin, Peter. "On High Moral Ground: The Incorporation of Human Rights by the Development Enterprise." *PRAXIS: The Fletcher Journal of Development Studies* 17 (2002): 1–11.

JIMMY CARTER

by Kirsten Sellars

Jimmy Carter's election as president of the United States in 1976 heralded a new era after the ordeals of Vietnam and Watergate. His emphasis on human rights was intended to signal a return to traditional American values, although the tension between his attempt to capture the public imagination and the need to maintain a flexible foreign policy resulted inevitably in compromise. His human rights policy has nevertheless endured, and its influence can be seen in the words and actions of all of his successors.

James Earl Carter Jr. was born on 1 October 1924 in Plains, Georgia, the son of James Earl Carter Sr., a farmer and businessman, and Lillian Gordy Carter, a nurse. Both parents were staunch Southern Baptists, and the church was a strong influence on Carter, as was his mother's commitment to racial integration. He was educated at Plains High School, Georgia Southwestern College, and the Georgia Institute of Technology. He married Rosalynn Smith in 1946; that same year, he also graduated from the U.S. Naval Academy at Annapolis and became a submariner, rising to the rank of lieutenant. After his father's death in 1953, Carter returned to Plains with his wife to run the family farming and warehousing business. His political career in Georgia began on boards and committees in Sumner County, and he later served as a Democrat in the state senate. In 1970 Carter was elected governor of Georgia, holding that office until 1974.

ROAD TO THE WHITE HOUSE

For a man whose presidency is synonymous with human rights, Carter was slow to embrace the issue. Some Democratic congressmen, led by Donald Fraser of Minnesota, had been agitating since 1973 for bans on U.S. aid to repressive regimes, but the future president took several years longer to take up the baton. Arthur M. Schlesinger Jr. noted, for example, that the phrase "human rights" did not appear in the foreign policy chapter of Carter's 1975 memoir *Why Not the Best?* If anything, Schlesinger noted, Carter "seemed to be moving in the opposite direction" by criticizing the Helsinki Agreement and the philosophy of foreign intervention (p. 513). At meetings to decide the Democratic Party's platform in the upcoming 1976 presidential election, Carter's team remained peripheral to the discussion of the issue. One participant, Patrick Moynihan, recalled that while the backers of George McGovern and Henry "Scoop" Jackson had strong views, Carter's were "at best neutral, giving the impression of not having heard very much of the matter" (p. 19).

By 1976 Carter was beginning to make up lost ground on the issue, having noted how his factional rivals were using human rights issues to attack the perceived amorality of the Republican administration. As one of his advisers noted, the incumbents lacked a "moral underpinning," and this created "a vacuum, and an environment where this issue would be very important" (Drew, p. 36). Carter expressed concern about covert American actions in Cambodia, Chile, and Angola and proposed a different ethical approach to that set out by then President Gerald Ford and Secretary of State Henry Kissinger. In this respect Carter was far from unique, as almost every presidential hopeful from Morris "Mo" Udall to Ronald Reagan proposed some kind of moral foreign policy. Indeed, it was precisely this new cross-party consensus that gave human rights concerns such a boost.

Carter thus raised the issue during his acceptance of the Democratic presidential nomination in July and returned to the theme at a B'nai B'rith convention two months later. (He was drawn to it, the speechwriter Patrick Anderson argued, "because it put him on high moral ground and . . . promised to win him friends among Jewish leaders," even though at that stage he did not have "deep emotional concern" for the plight of Russian Jews and political prisoners [p. 102].) During a preelection television debate with President Ford, Carter accused the Republicans of ignoring human rights, although the point was overlooked by journalists, who were more interested in Ford's curious claim that "there is no Soviet domination of Eastern Europe, and there never will be under a Ford Administration" (*Time*, p. 19).

THE HONEYMOON PERIOD

Carter won the presidential election with the promise of a new beginning, and now he had to deliver. There was a pressing need for positive policies, and in the months that followed the Democratic Party's inner circle looked increasingly to human rights. The party pollster Patrick Caddell reported that the issue pushed the right buttons with the electorate, because it appealed to both liberals, who saw it as a harbinger of progressive change, and conservatives, who embraced it as a return to core values. It also had the benefit of uniting factions within the Democratic Party and morally outflanking the Republicans. With Cold War anti-Communism on the wane during the détente years, it was an alternative "big idea" that seemed to offer a morally satisfying antidote to the mid-1970s American malaise.

"Our commitment to human rights must be absolute," declared Carter in his 20 January 1977 inauguration speech. A few days later he was presented with a perfect opportunity to display this commitment when Andrei Sakharov complained to him about Moscow's persecution of Soviet dissidents. Carter wrote back that the United States would "promote respect for human rights not only in our country but also abroad"—a bland statement that nonetheless provoked anger in Moscow (Boyd, p. 196). The State Department also pushed the new policy. During the first month of Carter's administration, it censured the Czech government for harassing dissidents, Idi Amin Dada Oumee for his rule of terror in Uganda, and Ian Smith's white minority government in Rhodesia. It also announced sanctions against Argentina, Uruguay, and Ethiopia on human rights grounds.

Carter described such actions as being in line with the "basic concepts on which our country was founded 200 years ago," and reactions from both the public and fellow politicians were positive. George McGovern and Barry Goldwater both congratulated the president on his stand, as did Henry Kissinger, who wrote that after "the traumas of Vietnam and Watergate," Carter had given Americans "a renewed sense of the basic decency of this country" (p. 60). Pundits also embraced the new credo. As Ronald Steel wrote in June 1977:

> The good grey liberals on the *New York Times* love it; so do the Friedmanites on the *Wall Street Journal*. Senator Henry Jackson thinks it's made in heaven, and the hitherto-ignored members of Amnesty International hope that at last it may

be coming down to earth. The hawkish neo-conservatives at *Commentary* and the dovish leftists at the *New York Review* have found one issue on which they can agree on—almost. Who can bad mouth human rights? It is beyond partisanship and beyond attack. (p. 14)

Carter had stumbled on the issue of human rights during the election campaign, and, as he acknowledged in his 1982 memoir *Keeping Faith*, "I did not fully grasp all the ramifications of our new policy" (p. 148). Nevertheless, the new government took full advantage of opportunities that presented themselves. One official admitted that there was no strategy, but "fate intervened—happenchance things, letters—that blew the issue up unexpectedly" (Drew, p. 41). As Carter's chief of staff Hamilton Jordan noted, one great benefit was that, alone among the administration's foreign policy initiatives, it was not considered to be "liberal" and thus provided "broad-based, non-ideological support for our foreign policy" (Dumbrell, p. 118). In the process it helped restore the credibility and resolve of the elite and improved America's self-image. As Carter publicly declared in 1977, "It re-establishes our country, I think, as kind of a beacon light for a principle that's right and decent and compassionate."

As well as these domestic benefits, human rights also provided the United States with a medium through which to renegotiate its relations with the developing world. In previous decades Washington had been preoccupied with the threat of radical insurgencies and had given priority to relationships with autocratic anti-Communist regimes. The thaw in the Cold War meant that Carter was able to pursue a more nuanced approach by maintaining relationships with dictatorial allies and encouraging them to implement domestic reforms. To this end, he strengthened the State Department's human rights bureau, headed by Patricia Derian, which agitated for improvements abroad.

POLICY SHIFTS

The first signs of trouble with the human rights policy came in March 1977, just two months after Carter's inauguration. When Congress raised a bill calling on the United States to use its "voice and vote" against loans to dictatorships by international financial institutions, Carter opposed it on the grounds that it would tie the administration's hands. Such restrictions, he argued, would remove his ability "to bargain with a foreign leader whom we think might be willing to ease off on the deprivation of human rights." It was a hard case to make after the grandiloquent statements that had preceded it, and it laid him open to accusations of bad faith.

This was not the administration's only problem. In addition to a restless Congress at home, it faced an obdurate Soviet leadership abroad. Not wishing to jeopardize the strategic arms limitation talks that were in progress, the administration decided to change tack. From the summer of 1977 on it eased off on criticisms of the Soviet bloc's human rights record, largely confining them to the "Helsinki" negotiations at Belgrade, Yugoslavia. At the same time, it shifted the human rights focus onto selected Latin American countries, which were more susceptible to U.S. pressure. This move was not universally popular. As one disappointed American human rights advocate noted, the government risked "dividing the world into two categories: countries unimportant enough to be hectored about human rights and countries important enough to get away with murder" (R. Cohen, p. 244).

The administration initially claimed that it would improve the human rights situation in Latin America and elsewhere by the judicious manipulation of aid. But sanctions did not produce the required result: the amount of aid cut was small, and the diplomatic costs were high. Not only that but the affronted governments of Argentina, Brazil, El Salvador, Guatemala, and Uruguay soon found alternative supplies of arms, development funds, and credit. This failure to bring about change prompted another shift in direction. Thereafter U.S. officials spoke less about halting specific abuses and more about improving America's image by distancing it from dictatorships. As Carter announced in September 1978, "We are no longer the best friend of every scurrilous, totalitarian government on Earth."

The inconsistencies of Carter's policy soon provided ammunition for critics. Some accused the administration of attacking the Soviet Union (or Rhodesia, Cuba, Chile, China, and others) too much, others too little. Some alleged that it was more willing to denounce the powerless than the powerful. They also fixed on the president's willingness to parley with the leaders of friendly but brutal regimes, such as the Shah of Iran, President Ferdinand Marcos of the Philippines, or President Mobutu Sese Seko of Zaire (Democratic Republic of the Congo). (Carter's 1977 toast to the Shah for creating "an island of stability" in Iran was soon to acquire a deeply ironic ring.) Whatever the political orientation of the critics, their argument

was the same: that the government was deploying human rights selectively and for its own purposes.

Some also noted that the administration paid lip service, but little more, to human rights laws that had been recently enacted by Congress. Jo Marie Greisgraber of the nongovernmental Washington Office on Latin America was not alone in arguing that it had "acted against the intent of the human rights legislation . . . by stretching loopholes beyond any common sense definition" (House Subcommittee on Human Rights and International Organizations, p. 155). In 1982, a former official Stephen B. Cohen confirmed the truth of this claim. Citing the example of Section 502B of the Foreign Assistance Act, which banned security assistance to repressive governments, he wrote that the administration had in some cases "adopted a highly strained reading of the statute, which . . . produced a result contrary to Congressional intent," while in others "the language was simply disregarded, so that decisions violated even the letter of the law" (p. 264).

THE POLITICAL PRICE

Carter effectively discarded his human rights campaign once the costs became too great. His noisier diplomatic forays abroad had alienated both enemies and friends, including, as he admitted, "the People's Republic of China, the Soviet Union, South Korea, Argentina, Chile, Brazil, the Philippines . . . and other countries." He was also hemorrhaging support on Capitol Hill, where some argued that the policy was undermining trade and others that it was jeopardizing security. As Carter said in 1979, "There are always delegations who come to me . . . and say, 'This particular dictator has been a valuable ally of ours, and when the United States makes a critical remark about political prisoners . . . it tends to shake our relationship with that country.'" In fact, Carter had sacrificed neither trade nor security to human rights, but that was not the way it seemed to opponents and eventually to the electorate at large—and this was what ultimately counted.

By the time the Iranians took the American hostages in November 1979 and the Soviets invaded Afghanistan in December, the president had more or less abandoned the issue of human rights except as a stick with which to beat Teheran or Moscow. Furthermore, his administration pursued policies that actually contributed to repression in several countries, including Cambodia, where it backed the Khmer Rouge against the Vietnamese-backed government after 1979, and South Korea, where it released

Korean troops under U.S. command to put down the Kwangju uprising in 1980.

Carter's commitment to human rights was not purely rhetorical, however. His government halted military aid to Argentina, Bolivia, El Salvador, Guatemala, Haiti, Nicaragua, Paraguay, and Uruguay and reduced economic assistance to Thailand, Afghanistan, and Morocco. Yet while the administration repeatedly polled Americans about the policy, it remained silent about its effects on the supposed beneficiaries abroad. The president himself was notably vague, stating that the United States could not take credit for specific improvements. This failure to capitalize frustrated Carter's colleagues. The influential House Democrat Dante Fascell, for example, complained that "regular, periodic *assessment of results* . . . was lacking in the Carter administration, and made the [human rights] policy unnecessarily vulnerable to criticism" (House Subcommittee on Human Rights and International Organizations, p. 48).

It fell to others to conduct a postmortem on Carter's actions overseas. A 1981 Congressional Research Service report by Stanley Heginbotham observed that, despite some marginal improvements in a few countries, the record abroad in the late 1970s was "hardly encouraging." A 1989 study by David Forsythe suggested that, while sanctions may have ameliorated abuses over time, they usually provoked a demonstrable "negative reaction" when first imposed (p. 181). And in 1987, David Carleton and Michael Stohl concluded that during the period 1976–1983 there was at best "no statistical relationship" between U.S. aid and human rights and at worst "a significant negative relationship; that is, the more abusive a regime, the more aid received" (pp. 1002–1003).

CARTER'S LEGACY

Carter's elevation of human rights to prominence within U.S. foreign policy endured well beyond his presidency. An early indication of its influence occurred in the first six months of Ronald Reagan's administration. The new Republican president attempted to distance himself from Carter by provocatively nominating Ernest Lefever—an academic who believed the United States had no business exporting rights—as the head of the State Department's human rights bureau. But the nominee was decisively voted down by the Republican-dominated Senate Foreign Relations Committee, thus proving that the appeal of human rights crossed party lines. The conservative academic Joshua Muravchik later conceded that in this

respect at least, "President Carter had wrought a lasting change" (p. xviii).

Since leaving the White House in 1981, Carter has continued to be a prominent advocate for human rights. The Carter Center, which he headed until 2005, runs programs devoted to upholding rights, mediating conflict, and eradicating disease. Over the years Carter has drawn attention to abuses in many places, including Chechnya, Colombia, Indonesia, Kenya, Nigeria, and Uzbekistan. Although many of his initiatives operate with the tacit support of the State Department, he is not averse to criticizing aspects of American policy, such as when he called for the closure of the Guantánamo Bay prison facility. He was awarded the Nobel Peace Prize in 2002.

[*See also* Afghanistan; Idi Amin Dada Oumee; Cambodia; Carter Center; Foreign Policy; Donald Fraser; Helsinki Accord and CSCE/OSCE; Iran from 1979; Palestine; Andrei Sakharov; *and* South American Southern Cone: National Security State, 1970s–1980s.]

BIBLIOGRAPHY

The American Presidency Project. Public Papers of the Presidents. *Jimmy Carter: Inaugural Address. January 20, 1977.* http://www.presidency.ucsb.edu/ws/index.php?pid=6575&st.

Anderson, Patrick. *Electing Jimmy Carter: The Campaign of 1976.* Baton Rouge: Louisiana State University Press, 1994.

Boyd, John A., ed. *Digest of United States Practice in International Law, 1977.* Department of State Publication No. 8960. Washington, D.C.: U.S. Government Printing Office, 1979.

Brinkley, Douglas. *The Unfinished Presidency: Jimmy Carter's Journey beyond the White House.* New York: Viking, 1998.

Carleton, David, and Michael Stohl. "The Role of Human Rights in U.S. Foreign Assistance Policy: A Critique and Reappraisal." *American Journal of Political Science* 31, no. 4 (November 1987): 1002–1018.

Carter Center. http://www.cartercenter.org/homepage.html.

Carter, Jimmy. *Keeping Faith: Memoirs of a President.* Fayetteville: University of Arkansas Press, 1995.

Cohen, Roberta. "Human Rights Decision-Making in the Executive Branch: Some Proposals for a Coordinated Strategy." In *Human Rights and American Foreign Policy,* edited by Donald P. Kommers and Gilburt D. Loescher, pp. 216–246. Notre Dame, Ind.: University of Notre Dame Press, 1979.

Cohen, Stephen B. "Conditioning U.S. Security Assistance on Human Rights Practices." *American Journal of International Law* 76, no. 2 (April 1982): 246–279.

Drew, Elizabeth. "Human Rights." *The New Yorker,* July 18, 1977, 32–62.

Dumbrell, John. *The Carter Presidency: A Re-evaluation.* Manchester, U.K.: Manchester University Press, 1993.

Forsythe, David P. *Human Rights and U.S. Foreign Policy: Congress Reconsidered.* Gainesville: University Presses of Florida, 1988.

Forsythe, David P. "U.S. Economic Assistance and Human Rights: Why the Emperor Has (Almost) No Clothes." In *Human Rights and Development: International Views*, edited by David P. Forsythe, pp. 171–231. Basingstoke, U.K.: Macmillan, 1989.

Fraser, Donald M. "Freedom and Foreign Policy." *Foreign Policy* 26 (Spring 1977): 140–156.

House Subcommittee on International Organizations. *Human Rights and U.S. Foreign Policy.* June 21, 1979.

House Subcommittee on Human Rights and International Organizations. *Implementation of Congressionally Mandated Human Rights Provisions*, Vol. 1. July 30, 1981.

Jimmy Carter: Interview with the President. Question-and-Answer Session with a Group of Publishers, Editors, and Broadcasters, June 24, 1977. http://www.presidency.ucsb.edu/ws/index.php?pid=7726&st.

Jimmy Carter: Interview with the President. Remarks and a Question-and-Answer Session with Editors and News directors, April 6, 1979. http://www.presidency.ucsb.edu/ws/index.php?pid=32170&st.

Jimmy Carter: International Human Rights Award. Remarks on an Accepting an Award from the Synagogue Council of America, October 24, 1979. http://www.presidency.ucsb.edu/ws/index.php?pid=31580&st.

Jimmy Carter: Remarks at a State Democratic Party Reception, Columbus, Ohio, September 23, 1978. http://www.presidency.ucsb.edu/ws/index.php?pid=29849&st.

Jimmy Carter: Remarks and a Question-and-Answer Session with Members of the Council. June 22, 1977. http://www.presidency.ucsb.edu/ws/index.php?pid=7713&st.

Jimmy Carter: The President's News Conference, April 15, 1977. http://www.presidency.ucsb.edu/ws/index.php?pid=7357&st.

Jimmy Carter: Toasts made by the President and the Shah at a State Dinner, Theran, Iran, December 31, 1977. http://www.presidency.ucsb.edu/ws/index.php?pid=7080&st.

Kissinger, Henry A. "Morality and Power." In *Morality and Foreign Policy: A Symposium on President Carter's Stance*, edited by Ernest W. Lefever, pp. 59–66. Washington, D.C.: Ethics and Public Policy Center, Georgetown University, 1977.

Moynihan, Daniel P. "The Politics of Human Rights." *Commentary*, August 1977, 19–26.

Muravchik, Joshua. *The Uncertain Crusade: Jimmy Carter and the Dilemmas of Human Rights Policy.* Lanham, Md.: Hamilton, 1986.

Neuringer, Sheldon. *The Carter Administration, Human Rights, and the Agony of Cambodia.* Lewiston, N.Y.: Edwin Mellen, 1993.

Schlesinger, Arthur M., Jr. "Human Rights and the American Tradition." *Foreign Affairs, America in the World, 1978* 57, no. 3 (1979): 503–526.

Schoultz, Lars. *Human Rights and United States Policy toward Latin America.* Princeton, N.J.: Princeton University Press, 1981.

Sellars, Kirsten. *The Rise and Rise of Human Rights.* Stroud, U.K.: Sutton, 2002.

Senate Committee on Foreign Relations. *Fiscal Year 1980 International Security Assistance Authorization.* February 28, 1979.

Shorrock, Tim. "Debacle in Kwangju." *The Nation*, December 9, 1996, 19–22.

Spencer, Donald S. *The Carter Implosion: Jimmy Carter and the Amateur Style of Diplomacy.* New York: Praeger, 1988.

Steel, Ronald. "Motherhood, Apple Pie, and Human Rights." *The New Republic*, June 4, 1977, 14–15.

Time. "The Blooper Heard round the World." October 18, 1976, 19–20.

Vogelgesang, Sandy. *American Dream, Global Nightmare: The Dilemma of U.S. Human Rights Policy.* New York: W.W. Norton, 1980.

CARTER CENTER

by Steven H. Hochman

The Carter Center is an international nongovernmental organization (NGO) founded in 1982 in Atlanta, Georgia, by the former U.S. president Jimmy Carter in partnership with Emory University. Its mission is comprehensive: "[The Center is] guided by a fundamental commitment to human rights and the alleviation of human suffering; it seeks to prevent and resolve conflicts, enhance freedom and democracy, and improve health."

With an Atlanta staff of about 160 and a budget of about $160 million in 2008, the center has carried out projects in more than seventy nations. Its headquarters is in the Carter Presidential Center, adjoining the Jimmy Carter Library and Museum. Programs are organized under two broad categories: peace and health. Although the human rights program is administered as one of the peace programs, an adherence to human rights also shapes the health programs.

The center has played an important role in the international human rights movement, particularly through its human rights program. It is one of the twelve member organizations of the Human Rights Leadership Coalition and has contributed to the development of international human rights structures through the United Nations. It has placed a special emphasis on supporting local human rights defenders around the world. When Carter was awarded the Nobel Peace Prize in 2002, his work through the Carter Center and, notably, its commitment to human rights were emphasized in the citation.

EARLY YEARS

When Carter left the U.S. presidency on 20 January 1981, he decided to create an institute to continue his work on the public issues most important to him. As president, he had successfully brokered the Camp David Accords and the subsequent peace treaty between Israel and Egypt. He also had raised human rights to a new level of prominence in U.S. foreign policy. Accordingly, in his early discussions about the proposed center, he indicated that peace and human rights were subjects he wished to emphasize.

In September 1982 the Carter Center quietly began operation at the same time as Carter began his appointment as Emory University Distinguished Professor. His inaugural public lecture, "Human Rights: Dilemmas and Directions," marked the beginning of a yearlong series of events at Emory devoted to human rights. This was a campuswide effort, with support from Carter and the small Carter Center staff. Planning for the center's own agenda focused on a variety of themes. The resolution of conflicts and disputes was projected as the major future area of concentration. Three initial projects, called consultations, were planned and launched. The first was to promote peace in the Middle East. The second addressed international security and arms control. The third, building on Emory's health resources, including the presence of the U.S. Centers for Disease Control in Atlanta, explored how to close the gap between what people knew about health and what was actually achieved for Americans. This was followed by "Risks Old and New: A Global Consultation on Health."

To Carter, a concern for human rights was implicit in all these activities. A more explicit focus on human rights began in 1986. In January, Thomas Buergenthal, a distinguished human rights jurist and member of the Emory Law School faculty, became the Center Fellow for Human Rights and International Law. He was also charged with creating and directing a human rights program. Later in the year came the announcement of the creation of the Carter-Menil Foundation, which would present a human rights prize every year on 10 December—the anniversary of the adoption of the UN Universal Declaration of Human Rights by the UN General Assembly—and would support the human rights program of the center. The financial backing for this came from the Houston philanthropist Dominique de Menil.

This all was part of a major expansion of the center. William Foege, a physician, became the new executive director and the Center Fellow for Health. He was the former director of the U.S. Centers for Disease Control, and he had directed the Carter Center's two initial health projects. On 1 October 1986 the new Carter Presidential Center facilities were dedicated. Housed there were nine fellows who were to develop programs in a variety of international public policy fields. Also included was the Task Force for Child Survival and the new Global 2000 field programs in agriculture and health. The Nobel Peace Prize winner Norman Borlaug led the agriculture initiative. Its goal was to bring the "green revolution" to sub-Saharan Africa. The health initiative, led by Foege, began with an effort to eradicate Guinea worm disease, then prevalent in sub-Saharan Africa, South Asia, and the Middle East.

Carter and the administrators of Emory established principles for the center that have continued into the twenty-first century. First, the work is strictly nonpartisan. The former U.S. president Gerald Ford and other prominent Republicans have co-chaired many initiatives with Carter. Second, the center does not duplicate work already being done by other institutions. It looks for vacuums to fill. Third, the center seeks projects that lead to action and implementation. It does not take on projects strictly for research purposes. Fourth, the center brings together institutions to foster cooperation rather than competition in addressing issues of public policy, and the center itself collaborates with other organizations to increase its own leverage.

THE CARTER-MENIL PRIZE AND THE DEVELOPMENT OF A HUMAN RIGHTS PROGRAM

On 10 December 1986 the first Carter-Menil Human Rights Prize of $100,000 was awarded jointly to Yuri Orlov, cofounder of the Moscow Helsinki Group, the Russian human rights organization, and to the Group for Mutual Support (GAM), an association of families of disappeared persons in Guatemala. The annual prize ceremonies continued through 1992; after the first year, Carter's remarks were presented as a "State of Human Rights" address. These ceremonies took place twice at the Rothko Chapel in Houston, once at New York University, once at a Senate office building in Washington, D.C., and three times at the Carter Center. On 14 May 1994 the final special prize was awarded in Oslo, Norway, to the Institute of Applied Social Science (FAFO) for facilitating the Oslo Agreement between Israel and the Palestine Liberation Organization. Following is the list of prize winners:

1986: Yuri Orlov, Soviet Union. Grupo de Apoyo Mutuo, Guatemala.

1987: La Vicaría de la Solidaridad, Chile.

1988: The Sisulu Family, South Africa.

1989: Al-Haq/Law in the Service of Man, West Bank. B'Tselem/The Israeli Information Center for Human Rights in the Occupied Territories, Jerusalem, Israel.

1990: The Consejo de Comunidades Etnicas Runujel Junam, Guatemala. The Civil Rights Movement (CRM) of Sri Lanka.

1991: The University of Central America in San Salvador, in honor of six Jesuit priests who were murdered.

1992: The Haitian Refugee Center, Miami, Florida. The Native American Rights Fund, Boulder, Colorado.

1994: Special Prize to the Institute of Applied Social Science (FAFO), Norway.

The decision to honor publicly those Carter called "human rights heroes," those who undertook great risks and often endured persecution for their cause, complemented Carter's strategy to use his influence privately to seek the release of prisoners of conscience and the end to specific human rights abuses. Carter worked confidentially with leaders of nations where abuses occurred; he believed this would be a more effective strategy than publicly condemning these leaders. In some cases, the center's humanitarian programs in health and agriculture worked in countries with questionable human rights policies. The level of trust he created through humanitarian programs helped Carter effectively address human rights issues in these countries. Carter asked the major human rights watch organizations to send to the human rights program staff their requests for him to help with difficult cases. The historian Douglas Brinkley, who has studied this topic, estimates that from 1981 to 1997, "Carter was directly responsible for the release of approximately 50,000 political prisoners whose human rights had been violated" (p. 212).

In his annual State of Human Rights address, Carter always would draw attention to the specific achievements of Carter-Menil Prize winners. He did not provide a comprehensive list of abuses during the year; instead, he focused on major issues. A consistent theme was the need to provide more support for the UN Charter, the Universal Declaration of Human Rights, and the UN covenants that legitimized the international human rights debate. He was critical of the United States for not ratifying international human rights instruments and of the international community for not establishing enforcement mechanisms. He called for strengthening the United Nations and for the establishment of an office of the UN high Commissioner for human rights. He also called for international human rights organizations to work together more effectively.

Carter moved beyond a focus on civil and political rights. He asserted that economic, social, and cultural rights must be promoted as well. He also called for the expansion of democracy. The need for peace was always a theme. In 1989 he bluntly declared that he would talk about "the greatest human rights crime of all, and that is war." These themes of his speeches reflected the direction in which he was taking the Carter Center. The center was addressing hunger and disease by developing agriculture and health programs in many of the poorest countries in Africa, Asia, and the Americas. It advocated and practiced conflict resolution in many of the same countries and in Europe. Promoting democracy and the peaceful resolution of conflicts, it observed and mediated elections, first in the Americas and later in Africa and Asia.

In the late 1980s the Carter Center played a role in the improving human rights dialogue between the East and West. Rosalynn Carter, the former first lady; Buergenthal; and the center staff engaged in meetings and a process begun in the Netherlands that developed into the DeBurght Conference. Also, in 1988, the center's human rights program and the Inter-American Institute of Human Rights co-sponsored a conference to build support in the English-speaking Caribbean for the American Convention on Human Rights. When Buergenthal left Emory and the Carter Center in the spring of 1989, Leah Leatherbee, a member of the center's staff, was promoted to director. In 1992 Jamal Benomar, who had been a prisoner of conscience in Morocco, succeeded her.

In July 1992 the center convened a major conference of human rights advocates and scholars to address the question of the role of human rights and human rights organizations in transitions of authoritarian to democratic governments. With the end of the Cold War, numerous nations with a history of human rights abuse were moving toward democracy. The themes of retribution vs. reconciliation and amnesty vs. justice were discussed at length. Carter described his admiration for organizations that expose human rights abuses. However, he called for a new proactive commitment to move from reaction to prevention of abuse. He believed this was an ideal time to work with emerging democracies. He sought the creation of a new human rights task force or council that would bring together human rights organizations. The participants supported this and created the International Human Rights Council, made up of leaders of organizations and of independent advocates. Kenneth Roth of Human Rights Watch and others, however, emphasized that they could not abandon their work of defending victims, even at the expense of the "political good." Roth pointed out that transitions in Haiti and the Philippines had demonstrated that a human rights watch remained necessary.

BALANCING THE GOALS OF THE CARTER CENTER

In the late 1980s and early 1990s, how to pursue simultaneously the goals of peace, democracy, health, and human rights was a notable challenge for the Carter Center. In June 1989 the violent repression of peaceful protests in Tiananmen Square in Beijing, China, presented the center with a difficult dilemma. The center was operating a program in China to train teachers of children and adults with disabilities and to assist with building a factory to manufacture modern prostheses. Historically, China's disabled citizens suffered terrible discrimination, and this program could help change this. The Carter Center could not simply continue with business as usual, but to abandon these people did not seem just. The decision was to suspend briefly, but not withdraw, the program. Carter would quietly support the victims of Tiananmen. This approach received little public attention until April 1991, when he traveled to China to mark the completion of the program. He used the visit with the Chinese leaders to raise the issues of imprisoned dissidents, asking for a universal amnesty for all those involved, and he gave a public address on human rights at the College of Foreign Affairs. When he returned to the United States, he authored an op-ed in the *New York Times* in which he discussed what had happened in China, calling on the Chinese to take innovative and generous action to address the Tiananmen tragedy; but he also called for reconciliation between the United States and China and for Congress to renew China's most-favored-nation status. This drew criticism from some human rights activists, and Carter was called an apologist for China.

Carter received additional support for the effort to pursue both human rights and conflict resolution when, in 1994, Harry G. Barnes became the director of both the conflict resolution and the human rights programs of the center. Barnes had served as a U.S. ambassador in three difficult and important posts—Romania, India, and Chile. His last post won him the respect of the human rights movement when he managed to help persuade the dictator General Augusto Pinochet to accept a presidential plebiscite that ultimately removed him from office and allowed a peaceful transition to democracy.

The period when Barnes was at the center proved to be one especially active in conflict resolution. Barnes, Carter, and other Carter Center staff engaged in high-profile mediations in North Korea, Haiti, Bosnia, and Sudan. In June 1994 a crisis over whether North Korea was developing nuclear weapons threatened to lead to a major international war. Carter led a Carter Center delegation to Pyongyang; and in meetings with North Korea's president, Kim Il-Sung, he was able to achieve a breakthrough that ended the crisis. In Haiti, Carter's delegation brought about a peaceful transition of government, rescuing the country from regime change via a forceful military invasion. In Bosnia and in Sudan, temporary cease-fires were negotiated. All of these conflicts were similar in that they involved controversial leaders who were viewed by many as abusers of human rights (or even as war criminals). Carter and the Carter Center received praise for their successful efforts on behalf of peace, but they also received condemnation for negotiating with tyrants.

Some of the criticism emanated from human rights activists who worked with the center. Along with Carter, Barnes decided to bring together leading practitioners of conflict resolution and leading advocates of human rights. They held a frank discussion about how to balance the search for justice with the search for peace. The Carter Center position, as voiced by Carter, was that "war is the greatest violation of human rights that one people can inflict upon another." Modern war, he argued, was especially vicious, bringing death and extreme suffering to ordinary men, women, and children. In order to stop or prevent war, it was necessary for enemies to communicate. Often, enemies demonized each other; but in order to reach peace, they needed to listen to each other. Justice, as well as peace, should be a goal of the negotiating process. The human rights advocates did not argue against holding negotiations with people who were identified as human rights abusers, but they argued against granting amnesty in order to get peace. Carter agreed that peace without justice was unacceptable, but he emphasized that justice was not the same as revenge. This conversation is one that has continued both within the Carter Center and outside it. How to reconcile conflict resolution and human rights,

as well as democracy and human rights, is a challenge both in theory and in practice.

CONTINUING DEVELOPMENTS

The Carter Center continued its efforts to strengthen the capability of the United Nations and the international system in the field of human rights. As an NGO, it encouraged the United Nations to take advantage of both its ability and that of other human rights NGOs to contribute to its work. After the United Nations established the office of UN High Commissioner for Human Rights (OHCHR) in December 1993, the center began to focus on the creation of the International Criminal Court (ICC). Activities included not only the sponsorship of a major conference in November 1997 on the U.S. role but also the sending of representatives to the ICC negotiations in Rome: these activities resulted in the statute creating the institution in July 1998. The Carter Center fellow and Emory law professor Johan van der Vyver, along with the Carter Center staff member Karin Ryan, focused on these activities.

The Carter Center reorganized in the middle and late 1990s. John Hardman, a physician, became executive director; a new board of trustees was established; and strategic planning took place. The center changed its institutional arrangement for human rights. Instead of basing the work in a separate program, human rights were considered integral to all of the center's work. Human rights staff members were assigned to work with all of the peace and health programs and also directly with Carter. After Barnes retired in 1999, the human rights attorney Ashley Barr was brought in to play a leading role.

In November 2003 the center, in partnership with the OHCHR, launched its first conference of "Human Rights Defenders on the Frontlines of Freedom." Activists from forty-one countries came to Atlanta to discuss the challenges of protecting human rights in the context of the war on terror. Many of the participants reported that counterterrorism efforts around the world had been used to suppress peaceful efforts on behalf of human rights. In June 2005 a second gathering of human rights defenders took place, again with the support of the OHCHR. This became an annual meeting, with sessions in 2006, 2007, and 2008. The international attention given to the defenders helped protect them from retaliation by government officials in their home countries.

The center continued its efforts to strengthen the United Nations. In December 2005 the center sponsored a seventeen-nation dialogue on a proposed new UN Human Rights Council. Carter gathered support from fellow Nobel Peace Prize laureates on behalf of the council. In March 2006 the General Assembly created the new council.

After a new round of strategic planning, the Carter Center reestablished a separate human rights program in September 2006. Ryan was appointed director; she had worked with the center in a variety of roles since 1988. In 2008 she was leading initiatives on human rights in the Congo and in the Palestinian Occupied Territories.

In the early twenty-first century the Carter Center remains committed to continuing a human rights emphasis throughout its programs. Providing access to health care and health resources inspires the efforts of the health programs to address neglected diseases in the developing world. The mental health program advocates full human rights for the mentally ill. Another human rights effort is that of the Access to Information initiative, led by the attorney Laura Neuman. This began in 1999 as part of the Americas program, and it expanded to other parts of the world as well. In February 2008 an international conference was hosted by the center; this produced the Atlanta Declaration and Plan of Action for the Advancement of the Right of Access to Information. This document is based firmly on the provisions of the Universal Declaration of Human Rights, the International Covenant on Civil and Political Rights, and regional conventions and charters. Access to information is seen as essential for good governance.

Another significant initiative is the development of democratic elections standards, led by David Carroll, the director of the center's democracy program. The center, a pioneer in international election observation, saw the need to develop standards as more organizations began to participate in the process. Meeting at the United Nations in October 2005, twenty-two intergovernmental and nongovernmental organizations endorsed a Declaration of Principles for International Election Observation. As the next step, the center has led an effort to determine what is necessary to fulfill the democratic rights described in the UN human rights documents. The goal is to establish basic standards for determining whether an election is free and fair.

THE VISION OF JIMMY CARTER

Throughout the existence of the Carter Center, Carter has been the chief spokesman for the center in the field of human rights. He has spoken and written widely on the subject and has served as the chair or co-chair of every significant conference. He continues to address many individual cases of alleged human rights abuse quietly through letters and telephone calls to heads of state. At times, he and Rosalynn Carter go public, particularly when the person of interest is facing the death penalty in the United States. Speaking out critically on certain issues, such as the American embargo on Cuba, or the conduct of the Israelis in their occupation of Palestinian territories, has generated considerable controversy. Although Carter often speaks independently of the Carter Center, it is difficult for the public to separate the two. Generally, the public does seem to understand that an organization addressing peace, democracy, and human rights will not always please everyone. Appreciation for the work of the center is demonstrated by the generous support received from individual donors, corporations, foundations, and governments around the world. In describing his vision of the future, Carter has said that the Carter Center must stay in the forefront of efforts to implement the commitments of the Universal Declaration of Human Rights.

[*See also* Jimmy Carter; Chile in the Pinochet Era; China: Tiananmen Massacre; Cuba under Castro; Electoral Supervision; Haiti; Human Rights Watch; International Criminal Court; Israel; Nongovernmental Organizations: Overview; Palestine; Terrorism; United Nations High Commissioner for Human Rights; United States: War on Terrorism; *and* Universal Declaration of Human Rights.]

BIBLIOGRAPHY

Brinkley, Douglas. *The Unfinished Presidency: Jimmy Carter's Journey beyond the White House.* New York: Viking, 1998.

Carter, Jimmy. *Beyond the White House: Waging Peace, Fighting Disease, Building Hope.* New York: Simon & Schuster, 2007.

Carter, Jimmy. *Talking Peace: A Vision for the Next Generation.* New York: Dutton, 1995.

RENÉ CASSIN

by Mark Weston Janis

René Samuel Cassin's most noteworthy accomplishment was his role, along with John Humphrey and Eleanor Roosevelt, in drafting the 1948 Universal Declaration of Human Rights, the first important formal expression of international human rights law. Cassin was a vibrant and enthusiastic proponent of human rights and was active in many walks of life. He was, at times, a soldier during World War I, a law professor, a member of Charles de Gaulle's Free French government in exile in London during World War II, a French government official, a French delegate both to the League of Nations and to the United Nations, a judge on the Permanent Court of Arbitration in the Hague and on the European Court of Human Rights in Strasbourg, and president of several nongovernmental organizations promoting peace and human rights. Cassin is probably the best-known twentieth-century French human rights activist.

PERSONAL BACKGROUND

Cassin was born in Bayonne in 1887, the son of Henri Cassin and Gabrielle Dreyfus Cassin. Raised in France, he was of Jewish descent and, as a young man, was deeply affected by the injustice done to Captain Alfred Dreyfus, the victim of a conviction for treason in a politicized, anti-Semitic process in 1894. After graduating with distinction from the lycée (high school) in Nice, Cassin attended the University of Aix-en-Provence, where he graduated in 1908 with outstanding degrees in both law and the humanities. Cassin then worked as a lawyer in Paris, from 1909 to 1914. He was awarded a doctorate in law, economics, and politics in 1914.

Cassin entered the French infantry in 1914, at the outset of World War I. Wounded and near death in 1916, Cassin later said that it was his experiences in World War I that left an indelible stamp on him. It was then that he decided it was essential to return to first principles and to promote respect for those who had sacrificed their lives. Discharged from of the army, Cassin married Simone Yzombard. Cassin became a professor of law at Aix-en-Provence in 1916. After World War I, Cassin helped organize military veterans to promote the pacifist cause. In 1920 Cassin took a professorship at the University of Lille. In 1924 he was chosen as a French delegate to the League of Nations. At the league from 1924 to 1938, he was particularly active in promoting disarmament. In 1929 Cassin joined the law faculty at the University of Paris, where he served until his retirement in 1960. He died in 1976.

DE GAULLE AND THE FREE FRENCH

After the fall of France to Nazi Germany in 1940, Cassin fled to London with General de Gaulle. Cassin was one of the earliest recruits to de Gaulle's London-based Free French resistance. In August 1940 Cassin led de Gaulle's team in its negotiations with the British government to draft what became the Charter of the Free French government in exile. De Gaulle paid homage to Cassin in his memoirs, remarking on his value in creating from nothing the internal and external structure of the government. In London between 1940 and 1944, Cassin played many roles. He acted as a member of de Gaulle's Council for the Defence of the Empire, commissioner for justice and public education, and vice president of the Juridical Committee. Returning to liberated France, Cassin was appointed president of the Council of the National School of Administration in 1945.

THE UNIVERSAL DECLARATION OF HUMAN RIGHTS

After World War II, Cassin, representing France, was one of the eighteen members of the United Nations Human Rights Commission. In 1947 and 1948 Cassin sat with the other delegates under the leadership of Eleanor Roosevelt, the widow of American president Franklin D. Roosevelt, as they debated and crafted what became the 1948 Universal Declaration of Human Rights.

The Universal Declaration owed a heavy intellectual debt to famous proclamations of rights in domestic settings: the English Magna Carta of 1215 and Bill of Rights of 1689, the American Declaration of Independence of 1776 and Bill of Rights of 1789, and the French Declaration of the Rights of Man and of the Citizen of 1789. However, the Universal Declaration of Human Rights was the first principal documentary venture into what became international human rights law. The Universal Declaration of Human Rights was, at that time and in the early twenty-first century, a bold invasion of state sovereignty. It was an important assertion that international human rights norms could trump domestic legal orders. The Universal Declaration became one of the foundations for modern international human rights law.

It is generally acknowledged that the principal draftsperson of the Universal Declaration was not Cassin but the Canadian international lawyer John Humphrey, who, as an international civil servant, was tasked by the United Nations to assist the Human Rights Commission. Leading a team of experts, Humphrey compiled a comparative survey of existing human rights instruments and prepared a first draft of what became the declaration itself, a document that Cassin termed, in his 1968 lecture accepting the Nobel Prize for Peace, "a historical event of the first magnitude. It is the first document of an ethical sort that organized humanity has ever adopted." However, it is Cassin's claim to fame that he was the one who transformed the Universal Declaration of Human Rights into such an eloquent, systematic, and plausible justification and explication of human rights.

Cassin set the ancient doctrine of human rights in a modern political context. It was Cassin who made plain that human rights were the heritage and expectation of all humanity. As Cassin explained in his Nobel lecture, an important "characteristic of the Declaration is its universality: it applies to all human beings without any discrimination whatever; it also applies to all territories whatever their economic or political regime."

FRENCH PUBLIC LEADER AND HUMAN RIGHTS ACTIVIST

Cassin continued to take an active part in French law and politics. He served as vice president of the French Council of State (Conseil d'État) from 1944 to 1960. In 1960 he became a member of the Constitutional Council, where he served until 1970. Five times (in 1946, 1948, 1950, 1951, and 1968) he represented France at the United Nations General Assembly. Cassin also served as president of the Hague Permanent Court of Arbitration between 1950 and 1960.

However, Cassin's principal passion remained the cause of human rights. In 1959 he was elected as one of the first judges on the European Court of Human Rights. He became president of that Strasbourg institution in 1965, a position he held until leaving the court in 1968.

Cassin also continued on serve on the United Nations Commission on Human Rights, where he had played such a significant role in helping to draft the Universal Declaration of Human Rights. He was a member of the commission throughout the 1950s, serving as chairperson from 1955 to 1957 and then as vice chairperson in 1959.

Cassin was an active promoter of two 1966 important United Nations treaties—the Covenant on Civil and Political Rights and the Covenant on Economic, Social, and Cultural Rights. The two put into legal form the moral aspirations of the 1948 Human Rights Declaration. Many feel that the Universal Declaration itself has passed into customary international law.

LEGACY

Central to all of Cassin's work was his belief in the universality of human rights and of humanity. At the close of his 1968 Nobel lecture, Cassin quoted the French poet Sully Prudhomme to express his guiding light: "My country imbues me with a love that overflows its borders, and the more French I am, the more I feel a part of mankind."

It is just this belief that human rights respect no national boundaries that is Cassin's principal contribution to human rights. Both as a drafter of the Universal Declaration of Human Rights and as a human rights activist, Cassin helped create the powerful discipline of international human rights law. Cassin, as much as any other figure in the twentieth century, moved human rights from its philosophical and national traditions into becoming an international legal field and endeavor.

[See also John Humphrey; Eleanor Roosevelt; and Universal Declaration of Human Rights.]

BIBLIOGRAPHY

Agi, Marc. *René Cassin: Fantassin des Droits de l'Homme.* Paris: Plon, 1979.

Cassin, René. *Nobel Lecture, December 11, 1968.* http://www.nobelprize.org/nobel_prizes/peace/laureates/1968/cassin-lecture.html.

De Gaulle, Charles. *The Complete War Memoirs of Charles de Gaulle*. New York: Simon & Schuster, 1964.

Glendon, Mary Ann. *A World Made New: Eleanor Roosevelt and the Universal Declaration of Human Rights*. New York: Random House, 2001.

Hobbins, A. J. "René Cassin and the Daughter of Time: The First Draft of the Universal Declaration of Human Rights." *Fontanus* 2 (1989): 7–26.

René Cassin: The Nobel Peace Prize 1968. http://www.nobelprize.org/nobel_prizes/peace/laureates/1968/cassin-bio.html.

CATHOLICISM

by William J. Wagner

atholicism possesses a rich and complex relevance to the topic of human rights. Its relevance to the topic has at least five distinct facets. First, the Catholic Church played an ascertainable role—as did Catholic statesmen and thinkers—in the historical origins of the international-law regime of human rights that today informs oversight by the international community regarding the respect that national legal systems accord to the freedom, dignity, and welfare of the human person.

Second, the Catholic Church, in the teachings of recent popes and the Second Vatican Council, has put forward its own contemporary statement of human rights. It has made this statement a leading component of the body of doctrine known as Catholic social doctrine. The Church proposes this statement of rights to guide the formation of desired attitudes among its own members, but also, critically, within the international "civic" realm occupied by nongovernmental organizations, to reinforce and to supplement the international-law human rights regime.

Third, by way of its associated tradition of intellectual and moral reflection, Catholicism enjoys a relationship of reciprocal intellectual influence with the human rights tradition. Catholicism, in this sense, is arguably a source of insight accounting, at least in part, for the historic emergence of the concept of human rights, or, at any rate, is amenable to being productively employed, if only after the fact, to ground human rights. In this aspect, the Catholic intellectual tradition offers a more particular direction and specific limits to the meaning of human rights. More recent Catholic thinkers have modified their discourse to conform to a human rights tradition ultimately finding its center outside the Catholic tradition. Admittedly, these Catholic thinkers reject any unqualified endorsement of the rights model.

Fourth, the Catholic Church, as an institution, has had a discernible role in the political dialectic within Western history, over time leading to constitutional and other legal protections for human rights. Early in its history and again in the Middle Ages, the Catholic Church arguably played a decisive role in, in some sense, initiating this historical process. Over time, its role has been ambiguous, however, and it has variously been in the vanguard, the rear guard, and the indifferent middle of human rights advocacy. Knowledge of the shifting place of the Catholic Church in this historical process is useful for following the historical evolution of human rights protections in Western law and social practice.

Fifth, as an institution possessing significant aggregate power and influence, the Catholic Church today is rightly the subject of evaluation of its contemporary human rights record. Catholics, perhaps more than non-Catholics, find cause in a demonstration that the Catholic Church has failed to respect human rights adequately to seek the reform of the Church. Such reform is assisted by awareness of where the Church's failures are the result not merely of insufficient dedication, but also of latent weaknesses in the Church's own conceptualization of human rights.

HUMAN RIGHTS AS NORMS IN AN INTERNATIONAL-LAW REGIME

The central case of what is meant by human rights is surely the usage reflected in the United Nations Universal Declaration of Human Rights (1948) and related United Nations documents, most notably the International Covenant on Economic, Social, and Cultural Rights (1966). Regional parallels include the European Convention on Human Rights (1950) and the American Human Rights Convention (1948). The meaning embodied in this usage derives, in turn, from the tradition of the revolutionary manifesto as in the American Declaration of Independence (1776) and the French Revolution's Declaration of the Rights of Man and of the Citizen (1789). The manifesto of rights finds its meaning, on the level of rhetoric, as an aspiration of a revolutionary order to be realized. After World War II, human rights concepts, previously conveying their meaning only on the level of the manifesto, received juridical status under conventions whose implementation was to be overseen by new international organizations, whether the United Nations, the European Economic Community, or the Organization of American States.

As an actor in international affairs, the Catholic Church helped set the stage for the adoption of what must remain, for now, the paradigm concept of human rights: the international-law human rights regime. During the totalitarian domination of Europe in the years before and during World War II, the Catholic Church, as is evident from the wartime Christmas addresses of Pope Pius XII, came to a policy judgment that postwar reconstruction should be based on some system of supranational oversight in defense of the human values trampled by totalitarian states. After the war, the Church publicly endorsed the Nuremberg Trials. It voiced its support for establishment of the United Nations. Individual Catholic statesmen like Robert Schumann, Konrad Adenauer, Alcide de Gaspari, and Jacques Maritain set about to contribute to the reconstruction of the international order on a model of common respect for supranational norms safeguarding respect for the freedom, dignity, and welfare of the human person. Drawing on his own prior philosophical work setting forth and justifying a comprehensive exposition of a human rights framework grounded in Catholic principles, Catholic philosopher Jacques Maritain had a leading role in inspiring, drafting, and promoting the United Nations Universal Declaration of Human Rights.

In the encyclical *Pacem in terris* (Peace on Earth, 1963), Pope John XXIII expressly endorsed both the creation of the United Nations and the promulgation of its Universal Declaration of Human Rights as major moral milestones for the human race. Subsequent popes—Paul VI, John Paul II, and Benedict XVI—have voiced, in addresses before the United Nations General Assembly and elsewhere, their fundamental affirmation both of the United Nations and the international framework of human rights centering on the Universal Declaration. These popes also publicly expressed their respect for regional rights arrangements such as the European Convention on Human Rights. Since 1964 the Vatican, as a sovereign state, has permanent observer status at the United Nations, where it maintains a mission. In this role, the Vatican participates in United Nations committees on human rights issues and in the United Nations international conferences on related questions. In its diplomacy, the Vatican exercises influence on behalf of the human rights regime expressed in the United Nations framework.

In keeping with its philosophical and theological commitments, the Vatican promotes a vision of human rights, including within their scope respect for the human being in all stages of its development, from conception to a natural death. The Vatican at times strongly disagrees with United Nations population policy and with some sexual and reproductive rights initiatives arising at the United Nations, and it conducts its diplomacy at the United Nations accordingly. While this disagreement is the source of some tension, the Vatican has not been led by it to qualify in any way its endorsement either of the United Nations or the international-law regime of rights centering on the United Nations Universal Declaration.

A human rights framework forms a leading component in the body of doctrine promulgated by popes and the Second Vatican Council known as Catholic social doctrine. The Catholic Church offers this rights framework as a model for desired attitudes among its members, but it also proposes it, within the international "civic" realm occupied by nongovernmental organizations, as public reinforcement of international-law human rights norms.

This framework dates to Pope Leo XIII's seminal encyclical, *Rerum novarum* (Rights and Duties of Capital and Labor, 1891). In less than a century after the setbacks it suffered through its too rigid alignment with monarchical rule during the period of the French Revolution, and after an interim of early-nineteenth-century alignment with the forces of reaction, the papacy had come to grasp that a just social order was not a natural given, but a constructive ideal. The methodology of *Rerum novarum* is remarkably similar to that of the social sciences just then coming into being. Leo built his encyclical on the social program of Wilhelm von Ketteler, Archbishop of Mainz, in a response to social unrest in mid-nineteenth-century Germany.

Pope Leo's rhetorical purpose was to set forth rights to galvanize constructive societal responses in the midst of a clash of ideas wherein undercurrents of Marxism threw into doubt traditional criteria of a just social order and Manchester-School Liberalism absolutized narrowly circumscribed individualism. Counter to Marx, Leo affirmed private property. But, counter to classical liberalism, and drawing on the thought of Thomas Aquinas, he also affirmed the universal destination of all created things as subject to appropriation by all. This doctrine implied a duty to yield surplus to those in need as well as the authority of the state to redistribute wealth. Leo identified the right to a living wage and the right to organize in unions. He affirmed a single social framework in which owner and worker alike were equal members. He assumed that rights are not conferred, but rather are possessed by virtue of the character of the person. He asserted that the realization of these rights depended upon the formation of society around individual initiative, the role of intermediate associations, and state intervention.

Pope Pius XI, in *Quadragesimo anno* (The Reconstruction of the Social Order, 1931), continued this line of teaching. Over and against contemporary Fascist regimes, Pius introduced the idea of subsidiarity, later to be incorporated into the basic structure of the European Union, which asserted a right to social cohesion at the most local level. In *Mit brennender Sorge* (With Burning Concern, 1937), Pope Pius XII similarly declared against the totalitarianism that society, as a matter of "man's nature . . . balances personal rights and social obligations . . . for the benefit of . . . the full development of individual possibilities . . . which by a give and take process, every one can claim for his own sake and that of others." Particular rights that he emphasized include the "absolute right" of free profession of religion and the education by parents of their children. He also denounced the ideology of race.

The issuance of Pope John XXIII's encyclical *Pacem in terris* in 1963 marks the zenith of the Catholic Church's endorsement of the human rights model and the closest parallel the Church offers to a rights charter. It encompasses moral and cultural rights, including freedom of academic inquiry, speech, and press, and also education; free exercise of religion, marriage, and family, with gender equality; economic rights including choice of job, healthy working conditions, a living wage, private property, and economic opportunity; freedom of association including of group association; freedom of travel; freedom of political participation, and a right to the constitutional protection of rights.

Two documents of the Second Vatican Council may be read as companions to *Pacem in terris*: *Dignitatis humanae* (Declaration on Religious Liberty, 1965) and *Gaudium et spes* (The Church in the Modern World, 1965). In *Dignitatis humanae* the Catholic Church, for the first time, endorsed the right of the free exercise of religion, premised on the respect merited by the human mind's capacity to know and to choose religious truth. The respect the mind is owed includes, therefore, respect even for conscientious adherence to error and thus respect for religious pluralism. In keeping with an emphasis on the social nature of the human person, the approval of religious free exercise, even on these terms, was not absolute. With a presumption favoring freedom, the state may nonetheless restrict religious freedom for the sake of "genuine public peace" or "public order," a "basic component of the

common welfare." Elements of such order included: "good order," "true justice," and "public morality." In *Gaudium et spes*, the Church articulated a Christian anthropology, justifying respect for freedom and pluralism, and called for a political-juridical framework of rights.

Thirty years later, Pope John Paul II returned to the themes of *Pacem in terris* to make explicit an assumption only implicit in 1963. In *Evangelium vitae* (On the Value and Inviolability of Human Life, 1995), he responded to subsequent rights discourse that voiced rights in term of reproductive and sexual autonomy, in order to place a gloss on *Pacem in terris*, stating that its charter depended upon "essential and innate human and moral values which flow from the very truth of the human being and express and safeguard the dignity of the person" such that inviolable respect is owed the human individual at all stages of its development, and that human sexuality has an intrinsically procreative significance.

In *Mater et magistra* (Mother and Teacher, 1961), Pope John launched what, in counterpoint to *Pacem in terris* with its rights charter, is a distinct line of Catholic social doctrine. Reaffirming *Rerum novarum* on economic and property rights, *Mater et magistra* shifts its emphasis to the role of the state in ensuring economic opportunity. It calls for the redistribution of wealth and for governmental economic intervention on a global scale. The Second Vatican Council's *Gaudium et spes* picks up these themes.

Except for *Evangelium vitae*, mentioned above, Catholic social encyclicals since that time are in this second tradition. These documents include Pope Paul VI's *Populorum progressio* (On the Development of Peoples, 1967) and *Octogesima adveniens* (A Call to Action, 1971), which both propose a plan of international development that has had less fully successful results, and also Pope John Paul II's *Laborem exercens* (On Human Work, 1981), *Sollicitudo rei socialis* (On Concern for the Social Order, 1987), and *Centesimus annus* (The Hundredth Year, 1991), all of which, by contrast, are of substantive and perhaps seminal importance. Beginning with *Mater et magistra*, these documents take a framework of named rights for granted. Where they employ rights language, it is not, moreover, in the sense of formal freedoms, but of substantive participation in various dimensions of well-being. John Paul II, for instance, emphasizes the right to work, specifically the right to a fully human working environment. Moreover, the later documents of Pope John Paul II move away from reliance on the rights model of discourse. In a parallel way, he draws back, as does Pope Benedict XVI following him, from any suggestion that the Catholic Church possesses any particular competency in economic theory as such.

Instead, John Paul emphasizes that the voice of the Church is one of evangelization. As centerpiece, he offers a vision of the teleology of the human person in terms of Christian personalism. He presents this vision, not so much as a basis for the statement of rights but of social policy and just social arrangements. Writing in a post–Cold War era, John Paul cautions against the danger of personal alienation. Likewise, he warns against the dangers of the consumer society, both to the natural environment and to human dignity and fulfillment ultimately grounded in "being" and not in "having."

When considered as a whole, the body of Catholic social doctrine affirms a comprehensive statement of human rights. It grounds such rights in a human dignity reflecting the human being's relationship with God, *imago dei*; insists that rights be correlated with duties; and insists that all rights, whether positive or negative, be related to a vision of substantive human fulfillment recognizing a hierarchy of basic values. The context within which human rights can be realized, in this view, is the open-ended quest for fulfillment in social solidarity and yielding a decisive role to the state. In recent social encyclicals, one receives the impression that the popes consider the formative moment of Catholic magisterial pronouncements on rights to be essentially over. The articulation of rights and their quasi-juridical definition will be left to international political organizations. The Church meanwhile has entrusted the cumulative wisdom of its own pronouncements in codified form as the *Compendium of the Social Doctrine of the Church* (2004).

HUMAN RIGHTS IN ROMAN CATHOLIC INTELLECTUAL TRADITION AND DISCOURSE

On the level of theory, the concept of human rights also enjoys a demonstrable relationship with Catholicism, viewed as a tradition of intellectual and moral reflection. Beginning with the apostolic and early Christian eras, the Church's witness was, in an essential way, one of adherence to the inviolable dignity of the human individual. The Church's self-understanding of its rupture from first-century Judaism, was, in the words of the evangelist, an objection to what the disciples of Christ perceived as one innocent man's being sacrificed for pragmatic reasons for the material security of the group (John 18:14). Admission to the Church was premised, in principle, on individual consent to baptism. Christians considered individuals morally entitled to refuse compliance with state obligations. The Church championed the rescue of abandoned infants, prostitutes, and slaves. Catholic clergy officiated at marriages between slaves and free individuals in violation of state prohibition. The conversion of Rome to Christianity occurred in part through public revulsion at imperial Roman torture and execution of individual believers and so implied a conversion to respect for the dignity (and ultimately rights) of the individual person.

As the Catholic Church gained the requisites of a fuller institutional identity and cultural influence, this original orientation was reflected in two distinct, intersecting emerging frameworks. One of these is juridically oriented canonical discourse and results from the integration of Roman law into the Church's structures and life. The other is philosophical and theological and results from the Church's integration of the intellectual discourse of antiquity, most fully in the writings of St. Augustine. Both developments reflect an integrative impulse characteristic of Catholicism, tending to relate faith to reason, and ecclesiology to rational principles of political order.

Canon law and juristic discourse.

By the fourth century, if not earlier, the Church had begun to formulate the theological implications of its creed and the requirements of Christian practice in authoritative norms known as canons and in other forms such as papal decretals, and to gather these in collections directing Church governance. The decisive moment in this process coincided with the great councils, especially Nicaea and Chalcedon, resolving key issues in Christology. The Church developed its own courts and cultivated its own juridical discourse. This discourse gave rise to insights relating to procedural rationality and fairness. Central commitments also included access to the sacraments and participation in marriage and family. Somewhat later, respect for the seal of confession and the clerical adjudication of a penitent's guilt in the rite of penance were undoubtedly a source of consciousness of individual rights. Also of key importance, over time, were guarantees belonging to corporate bodies upholding as separate their identities within the Church. An important culmination of this tradition is Gratian's twelfth-century *Decretum* or *Concordia discordantium canonum* (Concordance of Discordant Canons).

Under the Constantine settlement, this canonical tradition also influenced the formation of civil or secular law.

The insistence on juridical definitions at the great councils adequate to ensuring unity in faith had in fact originated with the emperor, as the state of the Church was critical to the unity of the empire. Thereafter, until the disestablishment of the Christian churches in the modern era, there existed a reciprocal openness of civil law structures in Europe to influence from the Church's canon law. Such influence occurred at the time of Emperor Justinian's law reform in the sixth century, and again in the high Middle Ages, especially through the *ius commune*, a body of supranational legal norms applied in civil courts throughout Christendom. In areas of the Church's primary jurisdiction, as in marriage and inheritance, this influence was even more direct. Particularly important for human rights jurisprudence is the medieval marriage law in which canonists fashioned a model of marriage based on equal consent. A parallel line of influence occurred through ecclesiastical politics in favor of what theologians and canonists referred to as "the freedom of the Church," above all in the context of internal Church appointments, but also in various jurisdictional issues. The effect of the Church's efforts was to influence the state in ways that tended to reform the assumptions and mores of the cultures in which the Church found itself.

Historical studies have shown that this tradition of canonical and juristic discourse lends itself to study in quest of deeper understanding of how law in changing circumstances can serve as an instrument of fairness. This research has drawn meaning from canonical reasoning applied, in a relatively decentralized pattern of authority, to local fact patterns according to a rule of reason. The centralizing effect of the Council of Trent and that of successive codifications of canon law in 1917 and 1983 are thought by some to have reduced the value of more recent discourse in canon law for reflection of this kind.

A Catholic tradition of theological and philosophical inquiry.

The same Constantinian juncture that gave rise to the tradition of canon law represents the stimulus for the initiation of a tradition of serious philosophical and theological reflection within Catholicism, beginning above all with St. Augustine. The starting point for this second kind of development is found, in particular, in the Christological and trinitarian definitions of the Councils of Nicaea and Chalcedon, according to which the human personality of Jesus retains its integrity even as his divine nature unites him with the Godhead in keeping with the doctrine of the Incarnation. These and related doctrinal formulations account for the introduction of the word "person" (from the Greek *prosopon*, which had previously borne a different and more limited meaning) into Western languages. It is this doctrinal definition that orients the Christian respect for the human person, *imago dei*. It lies in a direct line with the language of the Fourteenth Amendment of the United States Bill of Rights and of the United Nations Universal Declaration of Human Rights.

St. Augustine. In *City of God* (413–427), St. Augustine defended the Constantinian synthesis against the learned despisers of the Christian religion who blamed it for the precipitous decline of Roman world hegemony. For the sake of this defense, he enunciates a philosophy of history. In a radical departure from Plato and Aristotle, whose notions of fulfillment subordinate the identity of the human being to the structure of the social order, Augustine made the freedom, integrity, and dignity of the individual the key to the meaning of history. He took as his example the inviolate moral dignity of a Roman woman who has suffered, but not been morally compromised by, sexual assault by invaders. Augustine speaks to her personal experience of her dignity and her capacity for integration and personal wholeness as revelatory of the touchstone of providence and indeed of the totality of human history. Similarly, he offers the exposition of rule within a Christian household grounded in an ideal of the universal service of persons contrast to the "splendid vice" of Aristotle's and Plato's celebration of dominion in the subordination of the individual. In his dialogue *On the Free Choice of the Will* (388–395), Augustine traces moral equity likewise to radical freedom of the individual. Anticipating the social contract, Augustine relativizes the potential claims of the state over the individual person by limiting the purpose of the state to the attainment only of a "tranquility of temporal order," rather than any perfectionist scheme.

St. Thomas Aquinas. As the other path-breaking intellect of the Catholic tradition, St. Thomas Aquinas in his *Summa theologiae* (1267–1273) relied on newly uncovered sources in Aristotle to fashion a major alternative within the Catholic tradition to Augustinian political theory. The coalescence of a European Christian civilization led Thomas to abandon Augustinian minimalism in favor of a more activist vision of the polity based on a more optimistic moral epistemology. Rather than championing, as did Augustine, the individual person's worth as breaking beyond merely temporal bounds, Thomas presented the individual person as a constitutive element of a political order that is inherently both interpersonal and oriented to essential human fulfillment. For Thomas, law is a rule of reason that only has intelligible significance because it is rationally received by the individual person as subject. Thomas presented a right of self-preservation and rights of marriage and family as more fundamental than the state, and so particularly immune from state interference. Furthermore, he presents the social dimension of human choices as the outer bound of the law's reach, so that individuality enjoys what is, in effect, a privacy right.

School of Salamanca. The one remaining significant theoretical contribution of Catholicism to historical human rights discourse occurred in the early modern period among the Spanish scholastics associated with Salamanca. Francisco Suarez, SJ (1548–1617), a leading figure, advanced the cause of international law by his insight into the positive character of international-law norms. He also argued for the natural rights of life, liberty, and property, contested the divine right of kings, and declared that the framework of international law required respect for the sovereignty of indigenous peoples. Francisco de Vitoria, OP (1486–1546), another key representative, defended the rights of indigenous people to property, self-rule, and free consent in the choice of religion. Bartolome de las Casas, OP (1474–1566), a derivative figure, advocated before the Spanish Crown in favor of the indigenous peoples of the Caribbean on the terms articulated by de Vitoria, ultimately losing to the advocate of Aristotelian natural slavery, Juan de Sepulveda.

Modern trends. After an arid period of early modern rationalism and ecclesiastical dogmatism, a revival in the Catholic intellectual tradition relating to the grounding of human rights occurred following Pope Leo XIII's encyclical *Aeterni patris* (On the Restoration of Christian Philosophy, 1879), which had called for a return to reliance within Catholicism on original philosophical reasoning, especially as modeled by Aquinas. One outgrowth was the emergence in the early and mid-twentieth century of a school of thought recasting traditional law theory in natural-rights categories. Outstanding thinkers in this school included Jacques Maritain (1882–1973), who most fully expounded his rights theory in his work *The Rights of Man and Natural Law* (1943), and John Courtney Murray, SJ (1904–1967), who applied a popularizing version of Maritain's argument against the background of American constitutionalism, most notably in his work *We Hold These Truths* (1960). Neither Maritain nor Murray adopted a merely nominalist, pragmatic, or liberal construal of rights. Both grounded rights in interpretations

of Aquinas, centered on human dignity, and always correlated with responsibilities and affirming the inherently social nature of the human person. Subsequent Catholics have focused on relating the rights model within broader or traditional frameworks of Catholic reasoning about moral obligation and justice. For example, Brian Tierney has documented the continuity of medieval theory and practice and the natural rights model of early modernity. John Finnis, from a perspective influenced by British analytical and linguistic philosophy, construes the rights model as a "language" communicating requirements of justice more adequately understood within a general theory of natural law. More recent Catholic political philosophers have, to varying degrees, disputed the value and adequacy of the rights model. Skeptical of the Enlightenment and liberal tradition, they dispute that a universal moral language makes sense outside of a commitment to a particular tradition. Alasdair MacIntyre, for example, challenges the idea that natural rights now have anything other than fictitious meaning. Charles Taylor argues against liberal readings of rights, questioning whether communities and traditions can enter into dialogue based on abstract catalogues of rights without recourse to comparison of deeper cultural templates of moral knowledge. The liberation theology of thinkers like Juan Luis Segundo, Jon Sobrino, and Gustavo Gutierez sought, for its part, to reformulate Catholic social doctrine in terms alien to the rights model borrowed from Marxism. This line of thought has been discounted both by the demonstrable failure of Marxism in the Soviet experiment and by magisterial interventions (see, for example, the Sacred Congregation of the Doctrine of the Faith, *Instruction on Certain Aspects of "Theology of Liberation,"* 1984).

HISTORICAL ROLE OF THE CATHOLIC CHURCH IN THE PROCESS OF THE RECOGNITION OF RIGHTS

As distinct from its influence within the history of ideas, the Catholic Church, in its long institutional history, has also been an undeniable force in the historical dialectic by which human rights came, over time, to be acknowledged. Its role, in this latter respect, is ambiguous. At points in its history, the Church has contributed to the advancement of what we would now call human rights. At other times, it aligned itself with resistance to the emergence of such institutions. At times, it remained merely indifferent to what would today be considered human rights issues.

Catholicism as a force for human rights.

Certainly when viewed against the backdrop of the alternatives of the time, the Church's original witness in favor of the dignity of the person, its adoption of norms of reason and legality as fundamental to its identity, its relativizing view of the state, and an at least intermittently humanizing tendency in many of its administrative policies must be considered elements helping to explain subsequent progress with respect to human rights under Western institutions. The influence of these elements over time has been largely indirect and often even unconscious, but nonetheless real. To cite just one example, even when the Church departed from the human rights ideal, as in its eventual endorsement of the use of torture in the heresy trials of the medieval Inquisition, it moderated its procedures in relation to more general contemporary practice.

Such Catholic influence is traceable, more concretely, over time, to an ongoing political dynamic arising from the Church's perennial insistence, beginning at least with Pope Gelasius I (492–496), that the state recognize its separate and independent jurisdiction, thereby carving out a vantage for moral critique of the state. Harold Berman, in his *Law and Revolution* (1983), argues that the Catholic Church's insistence, under Pope Gregory VII (1073–1085), on its freedom to pursue its spiritual purposes over and against the state during the investiture controversy set the stage for the emergence of Western constitutionalism. In today's setting, the Catholic Church carries on this tradition, as the sole nongovernmental organization with international diplomatic privileges, on the whole, exerting diplomatic influence over a variety of secular states in favor of greater respect for human rights.

Catholicism as a force retarding respect for human rights.

On the other side of the ledger, key events reflect Catholicism's role as a force antagonistic to emergent values associated with the human rights model. Attending to several traits constitutive of Catholic identity may help explain this resistance. Finally, the meaning of this history for human rights theory and for contemporary Catholicism merits consideration.

The Catholic Church's past hostility to values associated with human rights appeared most notoriously in two interrelated phases. It appeared in antiquity and the Middle Ages in a reliance on state coercion to enforce orthodox religious belief among groups but also by individuals. It also appeared in the early and later modern era in a resort to coercion to suppress free scientific inquiry and the free formation of political opinion.

Reliance on state coercion to enforce orthodox belief. Beginning with Constantine's campaign against the Donatists of North Africa (317–321), the Church collaborated with the state in campaigns to eradicate groups considered heterodox. Further examples include the Crusade against the Albigensians (1209–1229) and the Papal persecution of the Waldensians (1188–Reformation). Such reliance appears in the Roman Inquisition (established by Pope Gregory IX in 1233 and reestablished by Pope Paul III in 1542) and the Spanish Inquisition (established by the Spanish Crown and approved by Pope Sixtus IV in 1478). This history is long and continuous, with the first execution for heresy occurring in 385 (Priscillian, at Treves). It included the burning of Czech reformer Jan Hus at the Council of Constance (1415) upon a betrayal of a promise of safe conduct, and it concluded with the last *autos da fé* (public executions by humiliation and burning at the stake) in Spain and Portugal continuing up to the early 1830s (such as the schoolmaster Cayetano Ripoll in Spain in 1826).

The Catholic Church similarly collaborated in state-sponsored coercion against non-Christians and other Christians of orthodox creedal faiths in campaigns of religio-cultural chauvinism aimed, in part, at securing Roman Catholic jurisdictional ambitions. Upon resisting Christian missionaries, the Saxons were converted by the sword in Charlemagne's military campaign of 772 to 805. The Fourth Lateran Council (1215) compelled the Jews to enter the ghetto, leading to their serial expulsion from various European nations. The Fourth Crusade, launched by Pope Innocent III, sacked and conquered the Byzantine Christian city of Constantinople (1202–1204). The Teutonic Knights, commissioned by Pope Celestine III (1191–1198) to undertake the Baltic Crusade, undertook a military assault on Slavic Orthodox Christians in an effort to force them to submit to Rome (the defeat of the Teutonic Knights in the Battle of the Ice in 1242 is to this day an emblem of Slavic cultural identity). The Catholic Hapsburgs employed the Inquisition to advance bloody repression of the Reformation in the Low Countries during the sixteenth century. The Spanish conquistadores systematically subjugated and enslaved native peoples, relying on the legalistic justification that they had defied the authority of the pope by failing to assent to the *Requiremento* when read, often at night in the jungle outside indigenous villages in a foreign language unintelligible to the people being addressed. The Spanish instituted this practice pursuant to an interpretation of the papal bull *Inter caetera* (Among Other Works, 1493), a practice repudiated by a papal bull issued in 1570.

The suppression of free scientific inquiry and free political opinion. With the rise of modernity, the Catholic Church entered a new and distinct phase in its opposition to rights-related values as it sought to respond to a social milieu proposing standards of truth independent of the Catholic Church's authoritative adjudications. Newly differentiated notions of truth accorded value to the free formation of political opinion and, in keeping with the scientific method, foresaw a free publication of hypotheses in a proffer for possible validation. These developments brought with them support for what would become the Enlightenment notion of the rights of man as a rational being capable of autonomy.

The movement to create constitutional and legal protections for individual rights elicited only resistance from the Church based on its entrenched support for the old or feudal order. Even in the Middle Ages, Pope Innocent III intervened characteristically to denounce England's Magna Carta in a bull entitled *Etsi carissimus* (Even If Most Cherished, 1215). Once human rights notions gained more general currency in modernity, the Catholic Church entered its strenuous overall objection, calling for what was essentially the restoration of the feudal order. The Church's rejection of the modern rights model received its most definitive statement in Pope Gregory XVI's encyclical *Mirari vos* (On Liberalism and Religious Indifferentism, 1832) and Pius IX's encyclical *Quanta cura* (Condemning Current Errors) and its accompanying *Syllabus errorum* (Syllabus of Errors, 1864).

The Church responded to the scientific revolution of early modernity by seeking, by coercive force, to subordinate scientific inquiry to the Church's comprehensive adjudication of truth, notwithstanding its lack of any corresponding competency. An often cited example is that of Giordano Bruno (1548–1600), who, though not a scientist himself, published Copernican ideas, challenged the divine origin of biblical miracles, and propounded what appeared to be a form of pantheism. Bruno was incarcerated by the Roman authorities for seven years without trial and, when eventually tried, was condemned to death and burned at the stake. Another example appears in the case of Galileo Galilei (1564–1642). St. Cardinal Robert Bellarmine, SJ, personally presided at Galileo's trial, at which implements of torture were displayed to remind the accused of his accountability to the Church.

Galileo was forced to recant and was sentenced to life imprisonment, a sentence commuted to lifelong imprisonment in his home.

While the Church justified its actions as being required to ensure the orthodoxy of Christian faith, in retrospect both men were punished essentially for the pursuit of open-minded scientific inquiry. The *Index librorum prohibitorum* (Index of Forbidden Books), first published by Pope Paul IV in 1557 to combat the Reformation, was put to use in attempting to further restrict and control the flow of scientific and other ideas. Inclusion on the list was erratic, and its impact was largely *in terrorem*. Galileo's scientific works, however, were placed on the *Index* and remained there until 1835.

Once the Church had lost this external battle with the new scientific establishment, it turned its attention inward, seeking closure within the Church against the influence of a now pluralistic social world. By the turn of the twentieth century, the Church had begun a campaign to eradicate "modernism" from its universities and seminaries. Pope Pius X initiated this program in his encyclicals *Pascendi dominici gregis* (On the Doctrine of the Modernists, 1907) and *Lamentabili sane* (With Truly Lamentable Results, 1907). In 1910 he added a mandatory *Oath against Modernism*. The *Index*, only abolished in 1966, was also enlisted as a tool in this struggle. Even since the relaxation of the Second Vatican Council, the Vatican has at times been thought to feature a bureaucracy that has a culture insufficiently sensitive to individual rights. One case entering the imagination of the educated public occurred in 1969, when *Time Magazine* reported that Ivan Illich, the founder of the Center for Intercultural Documentation in Cuernavaca, Mexico, upon reporting to Rome in response to a Vatican invitation to come for a conversation about his work, found himself led unceremoniously into a Vatican sub-basement, where, upon introducing himself with the words, "I am Illich," to the anonymous clerical figure seated there, he heard in response only, "I am your judge."

Sources of the problem potentially traceable to the characteristics of Catholicism.

The cumulative weight of these historical associations of the Catholic Church with antagonism to respect for human rights—perhaps best captured for the popular imagination by Fyodor Dostoyevsky's image of the grand inquisitor in the *Brothers Karamazov* or by Edgar Allen Poe in *The Pit and the Pendulum*—points to the need for critique and evaluation. The Catholic Church itself acknowledges its failures—both historic and contemporary—in the area of human rights and welcomes consideration of them. On 12 March 2000 Pope John Paul II, for example, marked the turn of the Christian millennium by publicly confessing and calling for repentance by Catholics for the sins of the Catholic Church against human rights, specifically against "the service of truth," "members of other Christian denominations," "the people of Israel," "the peoples of other cultures and religions," "the dignity of women," and "the fundamental rights of the person."

Such a critique must itself be tempered by awareness of the polemical influence on popular impressions of counter religious, political, and intellectual movements, which are themselves no less fair game for moral critique. Theologian Hans Urs von Balthasar moreover points to the unparalleled "weight of history" that rests upon the Catholic Church with its unequaled continuity, ensuring that it alone among contemporary institutions must account for practices that were once contemporaneous with institutions that vanished a millennium ago. Nonetheless, an understanding of several traits constitutive of Catholic identity can help to isolate several potential sources of Catholicism's historical resistance to human rights. Catholicism has a vertical and monarchical concept of its internal authority; it derives a distinctive language of adjudication from the unique form of confidence that it possesses in its capacity for discerning the meaning of empirical events in relation to nonverifiable spiritual realities; and it is devoted to the objective of *utilitas ecclesiae* (utility of the Church) as a fundamental reference in formulating many of its rules of decision.

An inherently vertical concept of authority. The Catholic Church derives its authority by divine delegation via apostolic succession. Both by virtue of the office of the papacy and the office of the episcopacy, the Church is monarchical. (At times, it may be considered an aristocracy, with certain extraordinary decisions being made by the pope together with the college of bishops.) Its leaders do not derive their authority from the consent of the Church's members or from their capacity to advance its members' welfare, but solely by divine and historic delegation. With the limited exception by a kind of analogy of the authority of religious orders as separate from that of the episcopacy, the principle of the separation of powers is essentially foreign to the ecclesiology and canonical structure of the Catholic Church. In the Church, a single authority, in ordinary instances, makes law, administers it, and applies it in concrete cases. In the Church's own courts, reflecting continental assumptions, there is no adversarial system. The relation of the legal subject to lawgiver is, moreover, inherently not so much one of a dialogue of reason, as St. Thomas describes that of civil governance, but rather, in the model of Christ's obedience to God the Father, fundamentally one of obedience.

A habit of adjudication based on definition of empirical events in relation to nonverifiable spiritual realities. The Catholic Church's concept of its authority is summarized in the concept of the "power of the keys." This concept derives from the words of Christ to Peter: "I will give you the keys of the kingdom of heaven, and whatever you bind on earth will be bound in heaven, and whatever you loose on earth will be loosed in heaven" (Matt. 16:19). This power has its central application in the administration of the sacrament of reconciliation and the conferral of indulgences. By its absolution, the Church considers itself able to eradicate sin and forestall divine punishment, neither of which is empirically verifiable. As custodian over a "trove of merits" won by the martyrs, the Church traditionally held itself to possess a fund to distribute to substitutes in the guise of sinners seeking relief.

Through its other empirical sacramental signs, the Church holds, in diverse additional ways, that it can make participation in grace possible, and even effectuate ineradicable metaphysical marks in human souls, again quantifying the nonverifiable. Moreover, the Church understands itself by its "power of the keys" capable of dogmatic pronouncements regarding the *Credendum* mediating the mind's access to saving truths of faith. With this power, it has established the dogmatic depository of what must, for the sake of salvation, be accepted by Catholics, with "religious assent of intellect and will."

This mode of thinking—which can be considered an aspect of what David Tracy calls the Catholic "analogical imagination"—despite all of its virtues, as viewed by Catholic theology, may incline the mind to disregard respect for human rights more readily, in certain settings at least. It may incline the mind to objectify and override human personality and dignity, as well as dimensions of reality beyond its competency, by purporting to assign them equivalencies within its universal rubric for measuring meaning, namely the meaning of the thing not in itself but "for the sake of our salvation," which, after all, purports to be fully sufficient "to all things human." Its orientation to sacramental signs making intangible realities present may inherently incline it to slide into inappropriate reliance on legal fictions. Infant baptism once thus was deemed by the Church constructively to establish the "consent" to the Church's jurisdiction that was a predicate for burning someone at the stake as a heretic. Similarly, the same orientation may incline it more readily to unwarranted reification of intangible qualities. Thus, Thomas Aquinas considered a heretic's ideas to be analogous to false coinage, so that a heretic was like a counterfeiter appropriately subject to capital punishment and to being burned alive.

The awkward fit of principle where benefits are relative to supererogatory goals. In understanding its relation to the state's calculus of just allocation, the Church begins from the notion of "the freedom of the Church." It holds that its divine commission to evangelize places it, in a certain sense, outside the jurisdiction of the state. The Church considers its own activities to ride above the ordinary set of comprehensive judgments that the state makes regarding the demands of the common good, which ordinarily establish the balance of just allocations within a society.

From the point of view of its internal governance, the Church, unlike the State, seeks to maintain not an order of persons within a universal framework of justice, as Kant means to describe with his ideal of the order of justice as a "Kingdom of Ends," that is, as an order of mutual respect among rational beings considered as Ends-in-Themeselves. Rather, the Church pursues an order of contingent purpose, namely the program of salvation entrusted to it in the economy of time by God's election. It asserts, then, its right or "freedom" to make all calculations necessary to this cause. As Thomas More wrote while imprisoned, he judged all goods "right naught" in comparison with salvation in Christ. From such a vantage, the instrumental advancement of the salvation of souls arguably trumps all other goods. Losses to some individuals can be written off for the sake of gain in the form of the salvation of others. The Church within its sacramental regime tallies and sums injustices against the backdrop of the eschaton and God's ultimate just judgment. The priest grants the individual absolution, while sitting as a judge, without ever hearing from the victims of confessed wrongs or adjudicating their rights. Maintenance of appearance to avoid disturbing the faithful and diverting them from the path of salvation becomes an overriding concern. The harm to the salvation of many through the scandal of negative truths may appear to outweigh the vindication of the truth for those it directly affects.

At all times, the Church, since it knows itself to be an authoritative sign of divine revelation, holds its own continuing self-constitution, never naturally a given, always its own nonnegotiable first objective, transcending all concrete good of its members and of society. In contrast to a particular state, no balance of considerations would ever lead it to liquidate itself or yield to another entity, regardless of the costs in the balance. Its second essential nonnegotiable objective becomes the upholding of a comprehensive order—in lieu of justice for persons—of offices and the administration of sacraments to ensure that it remains effective in fulfilling its commission.

As Pope Benedict XVI emphasizes in his encyclical *Deus caritas est* (God Is Love, 1995), the common good forming the object of ecclesial action is found on the supererogatory level of charity, rather than that of comprehensive concern for justice. The analogy is to the traditional notion of charitable immunity under civil law. To encourage charitable works, even civil courts until recently dispensed with the enforcement of norms of justice where negligence by charitable workers caused social harms. Niceties of justice are set aside to encourage welfare by relieving the Church from burdens for the sake of its altruistic giving.

Conclusions regarding the meaning of the record. Given these several characteristics of Catholicism, even when the Catholic Church is functioning in full harmony with its integrity, it may be doubtful that its character permits it to ever fully acknowledge individuals as bearers of rights in any strict sense. This even appears true when the contemporary Church seeks, in good faith, to absorb the language of rights into its framework of law, as it attempted to do in the 1983 revision of the Code of Canon Law. When it has departed from the norm of its integrity, these same traits have undoubtedly contributed to the Church having, at various points in history, resorted to techniques of coercion and control both in violation of human rights and incompatible with the spiritual and intangible values that it means to advance. The history of human rights abuses that have marred the Church's record shows, moreover, the fundamental unforeseen negative consequence of the Catholic Church's original Constantinian settlement, with the access that it ultimately gave the Church to resort to the coercive power of the state, a danger underscored, in fact, by the American theologian Roger Williams, namely that a church that seeks to put the state to its purposes will be twisted to the purposes of the state.

The solution to these problems has arisen not, in the first instance, in the Church itself, but within the political community that has recognized and put in place a separation of church and state. The Church, for its part, has learned from its historical experience and has accepted the separation of church and state, and has shown itself somewhat willing to relinquish responsibility for issues of law and justice for which by its nature it is ill-equipped. The Catholic Church now acknowledges its role, not as participant along with the state in some kind of universal dual juridical order, but as one intermediate social organization among others, devoted to charity and voluntary giving. The Church has also learned from its clash with science and, disavowing fundamentalism, now espouses a dialogic association of faith and reason (see John Paul II's *Fides et ratio* (Faith and Reason), 1998).

THE CATHOLIC CHURCH'S CONTEMPORARY HUMAN RIGHTS RECORD

Finally, separate from historical influence, the Catholic Church, as an institution functioning today in possession of significant power and scope, rightly is the subject of evaluation for its contemporary human rights record. Such current criticisms generally concern complicity in corrupt regimes, gender bias in the nonordination of women and the regulation of reproductive freedom, unjust treatment of its own employs and members, and, perhaps most critically, the exploitation of dependent and unemancipated persons among those receiving its services.

With respect to the question of complicity in regimes violating human rights, the Vatican, as mentioned, a sovereign state, maintains diplomatic relations with all states. It forms concordats or treaties regulating church-state collaboration in the conduct of schools and the conferral of state recognition on religious marriages. In this role, the Vatican, in cooperation with the Catholic episcopacies of various countries, exerts influence on behalf of human rights. For example, in the 1970s, with the support of the Vatican, the bishops of Chile opposed the Pinochet regime's reliance on torture. To cite another example, the Vatican seeks to exert influence against the United States' practice of the death penalty, which the Vatican understands as involving human rights violations. How well the Vatican strikes this balance over and against pragmatic accommodations in the interest of the Church, and whether these accommodations morally implicate Catholicism in violations of human rights must, as in the case of any other institution, be left to empirical investigation and whatever ethical critique of its diplomatic policies observers may wish to advance.

With regard to criticism based on women's and reproductive rights, one can more summarily deal with the first aspect concerned with reproductive rights. The Catholic Church proposes principled arguments in favor of a vision of rights based on the inviolable dignity of the individual and supported by substantive philosophical and theological arguments that are universally accessible; the Church stands by these arguments, however unpopular, with conviction. The difference with critics is generally one of principle. With regard to issues of gender equality that are implicated in the Church's denial of ordination to women, the Church relies on an argument from divine revelation, and this argument is not universally accessible. On this second point, the Church is in a more difficult posture in aligning its position with the general practice and discourse on human rights. Apart from the issue specifically of ordination, the Church espouses a position of equal rights for women, including equality of participation in politics, public life, and the market, while yet insisting that gender is the source of objective meaning for the intrinsic possibilities of human fulfillment (see John Paul II's encyclical *Mulieris dignitatem* (On the Dignity of Women), 1988).

Concerning the criticism of the unjust treatment of its employees and members, one can begin with the Catholic Church's policies in pursuing its rights under contracts and in litigation in civil courts. Here the Catholic Church, by the measure of its teaching on such issues as the living wage and the formation of labor unions, invites their application to itself, expressly doing so in the statement of the 1971 Synod of Bishops. Not infrequently, those affected are unconvinced that the Church's practices match such norms, almost invariably alleging that they depart from them in the direction of institutional self-interest. How often this is so is again open to empirical investigation and to the various ethical arguments observers wish to make. A key question for such argument is whether a charitable organization should in fact be held to a different standard than a for-profit entity.

Where the criticism concerns the Church's treatment of its own members, it again seems fair, by the measure of its teaching on such issues as a right to a juridically formulated and enforced order of respect for rights, and especially the normative role of the subsidiarity principle. The Church has specifically acknowledged that this is the case to a certain degree in the statement of the 1971 Synod of Bishops and in a concept of rights in the 1983 Code of Canon Law. However, those affected may find that the Church's own practices may depart from such norms and do so invariably, in this case, in the direction of its own administrative convenience. Again, the matter is open to empirical inquiry and to diverse ethical argument. Critical again is determining how exactly the relevant norms apply to an organization precisely like a church.

Finally, and perhaps most critically, there is the charge that the Church has a record of violating the rights of dependent and unemancipated persons receiving its services. A public scandal underway since about 2001 focuses on the sexual exploitation of children by Catholic priests. Changing societal norms regulating sexual harassment in the workplace, spousal abuse within marriage, and requisite consent under laws against rape led indirectly also to more extensive litigation of claims against the Catholic Church for exploitative sexual conduct, especially with minors and others to whom priests stand in a fiduciary relationship. This litigation has resulted in substantial financial liability being assessed by courts against the Church and in accompanying negative attention by the press. The Catholic Church has responded by acknowledging a pattern of pervasive rights abuse. More specifically, the pattern was one of disregard for the requirement of interpersonal consent as a moral principle governing sexual conduct, the abuse of power in violation of fiduciary duty, and violations of the order of justice by institutional units of the Church shown to have facilitated and covered up criminal conduct.

Various other patterns of abuse have also been alleged and proved in the setting of Roman Catholic philanthropic institutions such as schools, orphanages, and hospitals. Parallel charges have been raised and shown regarding patterns among Catholic and other Christian missionaries throughout the colonial era. An adequate assessment of this record requires careful attention to statistics establishing the frequency of such rights abuses in other institutions. However, all of these patterns, whether in the Catholic Church or elsewhere, can best be analyzed under the rubric of self-complacency characteristic of paternalism.

Exceptional characteristics of the Catholic Church ensure that its relationship to the topic of human rights is, in some respects, unique. The influence of its basic theological message and of its legal forms and policies over time arguably help account for the emergence of respect for human rights as a feature of Western legal institutions. Philosophers and theologians belonging to the intellectual tradition associated with it have provided concepts and theories useful in grounding and explaining human rights. In the twentieth century, the Catholic Church and Catholic statesmen contributed to the emergence and shape of supranational and international human rights conventions. The Church itself has promulgated its own parallel statements of rights within the documents of Catholic social doctrine; it attempts to exercise its own international diplomacy in favor of respect for human rights; and it acknowledges and seeks to meet the application of human rights to an evaluation of its own contemporary practices.

At the same time, historically, many hard-won insights of the human rights tradition at times emerged in the experience of negative aspects of the Catholic Church's practices and at times over its express objections. Its contemporary practices, when reviewed according to the norms of human rights, are sometimes found to be lacking. The Church, as an institution, thus provides many useful human rights lessons as teacher but also as example, both of success and failure. The richness and complexity of Catholicism's role in this regard reflects its unusually long and continuous history as an institution with an inescapably central role in the development of Western culture.

[See also Colonialism; Protestantism; and Religious Freedom.]

BIBLIOGRAPHY

Aquinas, Thomas. *Summa Theologiae.* II.II QQ. 57–79; I.II. QQ. 90–114. London: Benziger Brothers, 1947.

Augustine. *City of God.* New York: Penguin Classics, 1984.

Balthasar, Hans Urs von. "Die 'Seligkeiten' und die Menschenrechte." *IKZ/Communio* 10 (1981): 526–537.

Berman, Harold J. *Law and Revolution: The Formation of the Western Legal Tradition.* Cambridge, Mass.: Harvard University Press, 1985.

Coleman, John A., SJ. "Catholic Human Rights Theory: Four Challenges to an Intellectual Tradtion." *Journal of Law and Religion* 2 (1984): 343.

Finnis, John. *Natural Law and Natural Rights.* Oxford: Oxford University Press, 1980.

Glendon, Mary Ann. *Rights Talk: The Impoverishment of Political Discourse.* New York: Free Press, 1993.

Hamilton, Bernice. *Political Thought in 16th Century Spain: A Study of the Political Ideas of Vitoria, De Soto, Suárez, and Molina.* Oxford: Clarendon Press, 1963.

Hennelly, Alfred, and John Langan, eds. *Human Rights in the Americas.* Washington, D.C.: Georgetown University Press, 1982.

Hollenbach, David, SJ. *Claims in Conflict: Retrieving and Renewing the Catholic Human Rights Tradtions.* New York: Paulist Press, 1979.

Kaspar, Walter. "Theologische Bestimmung der Menschenrechte im neuzeitlichen Bewusstsein von Freiheit und Geschichte." In *Modernes Freiheitsethos und christlicher*

Glaube: Beiträge zur juristischen, philosophischen und theologischen Bestimmung der Menschenrechte, edited by Johannes Schwartländer, pp. 285–302. Munich: Matthias-Grünewald, 1981.

MacIntyre, Alasdair C. *Whose Justice? Which Rationality?* South Bend, Ind.: University of Notre Dame Press, 1989.

Maritain, Jacques. *The Rights of Man and Natural Law*. New York: Scribners, 1940.

Massaro, Thomas, and Shannon Thomas. *Vatican Council II: Constitutions, Decrees, Declarations*. New York: Costello Publishing, 1996.

Miller, J. Michael, ed. *The Encyclicals of John Paul II*. Huntington, Ind.: Our Sunday Visitor, 2001.

Murray, John Courtney, SJ. *We Hold These Truths: Catholic Reflections on the American Proposition*. New York: Sheed and Ward, 1960.

O'Brien, David J., and Thomas A. Shannon, eds. *Catholic Social Thought: The Documentary Heritage*. Maryknoll, N.Y.: Orbis Books, 1992.

O'Connell, Marvin R. *Critics on Trial: An Introduction to the Catholic Modernist Crisis*. Washington, D.C.: The Catholic University of America Press, 1994.

Peters, Edward M. *Inquisition*. Berkeley: University of California Press, 1989.

Pontifical Council for Justice and Peace. *Compendium of the Social Doctrine of the Church*. Washington, D.C.: United States Conference of Catholic Bishops, 2005.

Sigmund, Paul E. "The Catholic Tradition and Modern Democracy." *Review of Politics* 49 (1987): 530.

Taylor, Charles. *Sources of the Self: The Making of the Modern Identity*. Cambridge, U.K.: Cambridge University Press, 1989.

Tierney, Brian. *The Idea of Natural Rights: Studies on Natural Rights, Natural Law, and Church Law, 1150–1625*. Atlanta: Scholars Press, 1997.

Witte, John, and Frank S. Alexander. *The Teaching of Modern Roman Catholicism: On Law, Politics and Human Nature*. New York: Columbia University Press, 2007.

NICOLAE CEAUŞESCU

by Patrice C. McMahon

In 1965 Nicolae Ceauşescu (b. 26 January 1918; d. 25 December 1989) became the head of state of Communist Romania. By this time, this Eastern European country had already distinguished itself as unique among Warsaw Pact nations in distancing itself from the Soviet Union. On the face of it, the country's independence might have been positive in every respect, but for Ceauşescu's Romania, autonomy only served to foster the most repressive Communist regime in Eastern Europe. And while other East European countries gradually became more open and tolerant in the 1980s, experimenting with economic reform and allowing certain measures of political and social dissent, Romania remained a nepotistic dictatorship governed by the Ceauşescu family. After more than two decades of brutality and oppression, Romanians responded in kind, taking to the streets in December 1989 to remove Ceauşescu from power. On Christmas Day, Ceauşescu and his wife Elena were put on "trial" for their crimes against the nation and executed by a military tribunal.

This article looks at Ceauşescu's rise to power, the regime's unique and tenuous relationship to the Soviet Union, and its repressive policies toward its own population. Ceauşescu's popularity in Romania was due, in large part, to his ability to distance himself from the Soviet Union and ensure Romanian sovereignty. At least initially, his brash and independent foreign policy attracted loyal supporters as well as the support of the West. By the end of his rule, however, Romania was perhaps the most Stalinist country in the region. Ceauşescu was not only an embarrassment to the Western countries that once supported his leadership, but he was feared and detested by his own people.

THE RISE TO POWER

Nicolae Ceauşescu was born in a small village, like most Romanians of his time, and was from a large peasant family. Although many myths were propagated about Ceauşescu and his early life, it is known that he was largely a self-made man. That is to say, his active involvement in the Communist Party, starting when he was a teenager fighting against fascism, allowed him to overcome both poverty and a poor education. Ceauşescu's formal education ended with elementary school. Ceauşescu became a member of the Communist Party in the mid-1930s, spending many years in prison as a result. In 1944, shortly before the Soviets occupied Romania, Ceauşescu escaped from prison.

After World War II Ceauşescu rose rapidly through the ranks of the Romanian Communist Party hierarchy because of his ability to tap into and exploit Romanian nationalism and the country's need to modernize and develop economically. Though a committed Marxist, Ceauşescu recognized the power in appealing to tradition and nationalism to ensure domestic legitimacy.

Ceauşescu's rise to the top of the Communist Party was aided significantly by Gheorghe Gheorghiu-Dej, Romania's party leader and head of state from 1952 to 1965. From his mentor, Ceauşescu learned a great deal; in particular, Gheorghiu-Dej demonstrated the benefits that come from abolishing party organs and consistently reorganizing government institutions. During Ceauşescu's reign, he consciously reorganized institutions and regularly reshuffled party posts to weaken his rivals and solidify his personal rule over the country. Although Ceauşescu stayed out of the limelight during the early part of Gheorghiu-Dej's reign, he clearly understood the source of his predecessor's success: maintaining an independent foreign policy and emphasizing Romanian traditions and nationalism.

THE GOLDEN ERA OF CEAUŞESCU

In the first years following Gheorghiu-Dej's death, Ceauşescu worked behind the scenes to become the party leader and surround himself with loyal subordinates. Ceauşescu developed a number of mechanisms to legitimize what would become a unique form of Communist rule in the region. On the domestic front, Ceauşescu initially adopted a liberal approach to freedom of speech and was open to, if not supportive of, the right to discuss and debate the future of Communism in Romania. Among his domestic priorities, Ceauşescu focused on education, primarily in technical areas, though he emphasized the importance of the humanities and social sciences for the country's modernization. Ceauşescu even told foreign reporters that the Romanian Communist Party encouraged questioning and intellectual diversity. While Ceauşescu made vague promises to intellectuals, he simultaneously worked to improve the standard of living and the supply of consumer goods for the general population. Trade unions also benefited from his early liberalism, and in 1965 measures were adopted to improve working conditions and protect workers.

Yet even while Ceauşescu's Communist Party adopted a more liberal position on certain social issues, it simultaneously maintained a harsh and unequivocal policy on policies like abortion, divorce, and even smoking. In 1966, for example, in an effort to increase the country's low birthrate, the government made abortions and divorces almost impossible. It also carried out a series of campaigns against smoking, long hair, and miniskirts because of their association with Western decadence. The message emerging from the Ceauşescu-dominated party was clear: Romania's development would be assured only through hard work and sacrifice. His popularity in the 1960s was nonetheless genuine because of his promise to allow participatory politics, a higher standard of living, and greater social and cultural diversity.

By 1967 Ceauşescu had initiated major organizational and personnel changes, allowing him to consolidate his personal rule over Romanian politics. His power was also strengthened by international events, namely political challenges to Soviet rule coming from Czechoslovakia in 1968. By the time of the Prague Spring—Czechoslovakia's defiance of Soviet rule—Ceauşescu was already an outspoken critic of the Soviet Union. He had purged Romania's Ministry of Internal Affairs of pro-Soviet officers and created a new Department of State Security (the Securitate)—a secret police apparatus—to ensure his personal control over the Romanian population. His opposition to Soviet hegemony in the region and the Soviet Union's attempt to dominate Communist governments in Eastern Europe went a long way toward developing and sustaining Romanian nationalism. In a major speech on party history, Ceauşescu even blamed the interwar weakness of the Romanian Communist Party on the Soviet Union, claiming that foreigners did not understand Romania's unique history and situation. Tellingly, Ceauşescu singled out the Soviet Union's attempts to persuade Romanian leaders to characterize the country as a multinational state.

In August 1968 the Romanian Communist Party supported Czechoslovakia's right to determine policy within its party and state. After visiting with the leaders of France and Yugoslavia, Ceauşescu decided not to participate in the Warsaw Pact's military intervention of Czechoslovakia, asserting that he himself would rather fight than submit to foreign occupation. Regardless of the motivation behind it, this decision made Ceauşescu a national hero as well as an international leader of some stature; at the same time, it allowed him to further consolidate his power over Romania. Almost immediately following this international event, Ceauşescu launched a series of conservative, repressive policies. These policies ultimately characterized the Ceauşescu regime and its terrifying grip on Romanian society throughout the 1970s and 1980s.

THE DEMISE OF THE CEAUŞESCU REGIME

Ceauşescu became an absolute ruler and the object of a leadership cult that surpassed even that of Joseph Stalin. He came to hold a number of party and state positions, and was heralded as the "Genius of the Carpathians" and the "guarantor of the nation's progress and independence" (Fischer). Increasingly, Ceauşescu had to resort to coercion to maintain this fiction, relying primarily on the army and the Securitate. As Eastern Europe's largest secret police organization (in proportion to the total population), the Securitate was charged with guarding the internal security of the Ceauşescu regime and suppressing any unrest and disturbance. Yet Ceauşescu was not only intent on responding to unrest; he systematically worked to neutralize, if not obliterate, any challenges to his rule or attempts at autonomy from the Communist Party.

The intolerance of the government and its total disregard for human rights were particularly evident in the government's interaction with specific groups in society. Although workers actively supported Ceauşescu's rule in the 1960s, by the early 1970s the country's economy was at a breaking point. In spite of his promises to develop the country, his economic policies and priorities, emphasizing heavy industry financed largely by internal resources while neglecting consumer goods and services, impoverished the country. Instead of modernization and prosperity, Romanians suffered from food and energy shortages—electricity was frequently only available for a couple of hours a day—a toxic environment, and high infant mortality rates. In the 1980s, for example, critics of the Romanian government maintained that thousands of people died every year of starvation in Romania.

Starting in 1972 and continuing throughout the 1980s, workers registered their dissatisfaction with Ceauşescu's economic policies. Workers' strikes and protests were met with force and vindictiveness. After some thirty-five thousand miners went on strike in 1977, for example, the two leaders of the strike later "disappeared," while some four thousand strikers were dismissed from their jobs and others were transferred to distant areas. In 1979, when workers announced their plans to establish a Free Trade Union of Romanian Workers, the government responded by sentencing some organizers to imprisonment and confining others to psychiatric intuitions, and one of the founders disappeared for a long period of time. Accidents, dismissals, and disappearances were not uncommon in Ceauşescu's Romania, nor was the razing of villages to accommodate massive, but usually ill-conceived, industrialization projects.

At least compared to other Communist countries, Romania had adopted a relatively liberal policy toward the country's ethnic Hungarian minority (estimated to be about 10 percent of the country's population). The Romanian constitution, as well as a battery of other laws, made provisions for minority facilities and for the protection and promotion of minority rights. In practice, these protections and rights had little meaning, especially as Ceauşescu tightened his grip on the country. Starting in 1959, the Romanian government worked to curtail and then eliminate any minority privileges provided to the Hungarian minority after the war. In the 1970s, ostensibly as part of a massive modernization program, Ceauşescu completely disregarded the needs and interests of the Hungarian population; allegedly to improve the standard of living of the Hungarian minority, the government forcibly relocated Hungarians through job layoffs and reassignments to predominantly Romanian areas. Romanians, meanwhile, were relocated to places that were once dominated by minorities, thereby diluting the Hungarian population. At the same time, this Romanization program worked to assimilate minorities by shrinking the number of educational institutions providing instruction in minority languages and through the emphasis on Romanian as the one language whose mastery was essential both for the country's economic progress

and for the minorities' social mobilization. By the end of the 1970s, the Hungarian government even started to protest Ceauşescu's treatment of the Hungarian minority, and ethnic Hungarians who were members of the Romanian Communist Party resigned (risking severe penalty, if not death) because of the government's discriminatory policies against the country's ethnic minorities.

Ceauşescu's support for and encouragement of intellectual diversity was also short-lived. Instead of talking about pluralism and divergent views, the Ceauşescu government emphasized conformity, claiming that this was necessary to strengthen Communism and ensure economic development in Romania. Writers suspected of having independent minds (and were thus critical of Ceauşescu and the Communist Party) were either tempted into silence by being given positions of power within the party, as well as substantial material rewards, or were killed, severely punished, or merely banned. Yet, dissent in Romania was not significant because Romanians lived under a Romanian, rather than a foreign, occupation, which was ultimately more painful and more efficient than a foreign one.

Although Ceauşescu was brought up in a religious home, he did not look favorably on religious groups either. Communist Romania had always made clear the state's complete control over churches and religious organizations. Even the Romanian Orthodox church, which at one time had about three-quarters of the population as supporters, was treated as an extension of the party and a tool of the Romanian government. If anything, Ceauşescu treated members of religious organizations much the way he treated other groups, regularly intimidating and coercing groups into maintaining and advancing party goals. For instance, after a neo-Protestant group requested freedom of worship and an end to state interference in church affairs in 1978, leading members of the church were arrested or persuaded to emigrate.

Romania had actively participated in and signed the 1975 Helsinki Accords, which linked economic credits and trade to the observance of human rights, raising hopes in Romania that the government would ease its restrictions on communication and visits to the West, raise living standards, and allow for more intellectual freedom. These hopes were dashed again and again by the Romanian government in the 1980s, which continued to silence its critics with as much violence as was necessary. In 1982, despite U.S. support for Romania's neutrality in the East-West struggle, Ceauşescu's popularity among some Western countries started to wane because of the country's human rights record, which had become the worst in Eastern Europe. And as liberalization and democratization started to spread through the Communist bloc, the Romanian leader fell out of favor with countries in both the East and the West.

As Communist regimes in Eastern Europe started to crumble in 1989, Ceauşescu maintained, if not intensified, his grip on the country, renouncing its Most Favored Nation (MFN) status, refusing to sign international agreements on human rights, and even placing Romania's national representative to the UN Commission on Human Rights under house arrest for having released a devastating report on abuses in Romania. At the same time, the standard of living in Romania continued to deteriorate, though Ceauşescu and his extended family, which had come to occupy the most powerful positions in the country, lived lavishly and ostentatiously.

Years of repression and brutality provoked a strong reaction from the population once the international environment began to change. In December 1989 in the western city of Timişoara, protesters marching on the Communist Party headquarters were fired on by the security forces; approximately four thousand died in the following days. Within a week, antigovernment protests spread to Bucharest, the nation's capital, with over a hundred thousand demonstrators shouting "Down with the murders" and "Down with the dictatorship." Ultimately, the Romanian people forced Ceauşescu and his wife to flee Bucharest. On 25 December 1989 the one-time "savior" and "only hope for the world" was captured and executed for mass murder and other crimes against the Romanian nation.

[*See also* Helsinki Accord and CSCE/OSCE; Demise of Soviet Communism; *and* Joseph Stalin.]

BIBLIOGRAPHY

Campeanu, Pavel. *Ceauşescu: The Countdown.* Translated from the Romanian by Sorana Corneanu. Boulder, Colo.: East European Monographs; New York: Distributed by Columbia University Press, 2003.

Hale, Julian Anthony Stuart. *Ceauşescu's Romania. A Political Documentary.* London: George G. Harrap, 1971.

Fischer, Mary Ellen. *Nicolae Ceausescu: A Study in Political Leadership.* Boulder, Colo.: Lynne Rienner, 1989.

Nelson, Daniel N. *Romanian Politics in the Ceauşescu Era.* New York: Gordon and Breach Science Publishers, 1988.

Rothschild, Joseph. *Return to Diversity: A Political History of East Central Europe since World War II.* New York: Oxford University Press, 1993.

Shafir, Michael. *Romania, Politics, Economics, and Society.* London: F. Pinter, 1985.

CENTER FOR JUSTICE & ACCOUNTABILITY

by Beth Van Schaack

The Center for Justice & Accountability (CJA) is a nonprofit human rights law firm based in San Francisco, California. CJA uses litigation in the United States and Spain to hold perpetrators individually accountable for human rights abuses, to develop human rights law, and to advance the rule of law in countries transitioning from situations of armed conflict or governmental repression. CJA brings most of its cases under the principle of universal jurisdiction. Universal jurisdiction is a doctrine of international law which holds that certain crimes are so egregious that the perpetrators may be held accountable wherever they are found, regardless of the nationality of the perpetrator or victim, or the place of commission. Crimes subject to universal jurisdiction include genocide, crimes against humanity, war crimes, and torture. In the last three decades, survivors of human rights abuses have increasingly sought to enforce human rights norms through litigation in national courts, in part because of the lack of effective and accessible enforcement regimes at the international level.

The Center for Justice & Accountability was formed in 1998 by Gerald Gray, a psychotherapist and clinical social worker who specializes in providing psychological treatment to victims of human rights abuses. In 1998 one of Gray's clients became significantly retraumatized when he learned his torturer was living in the United States. Concerned about the impact of such encounters on his clients, and determined to ensure that human rights abusers would no longer enjoy safe haven in the United States, Gray worked with a number of prominent human rights lawyers and law professors to form CJA to track human rights abusers located in the United States and bring them to justice. Early funding came from Amnesty International, the UN Voluntary Fund for Victims of Torture, and several private individuals. Over time, CJA has received support from the U.S. government's Office of Refugee Resettlement, JEHT Foundation, Open Society Institute, and Oak Foundation.

Operating on a million-dollar annual budget, CJA has a small permanent staff of lawyers, interns, and administrative personnel, and it leverages its resources by partnering with the private bar, investigators, therapists, expert witnesses, and others working pro bono. CJA is governed by a board of directors that sets overall policy for the organization. The board consists of leading experts in universal jurisdiction litigation and human rights, members of the business community, and torture treatment practitioners. The Center for Justice & Accountability is run by an executive director who also serves as president of the board. The executive director works with a legal director and the staff attorneys to identify and pursue cases consistent with case selection criteria approved by the board. CJA also has a legal advisory council consisting of other human rights academics and practitioners that it relies on for advice on specific legal and policy questions.

The Center for Justice & Accountability is the only human rights organization in the United States devoted exclusively to providing free legal services to survivors of human rights abuses. For its work, CJA received the Thomas J. Dodd Prize in International Justice and Human Rights in 2007. The University of Connecticut awards the Dodd Prize biennially to an individual or group that has made a significant effort to advance the cause of international justice and global human rights. Previous honorees include Louise Arbour, former UN High Commissioner for Human Rights; the South African justice Richard J. Goldstone; Bertie Ahern, former prime minister of Ireland; and Tony Blair, former prime minister of Great Britian.

In the United States, CJA uses two federal statutes to hold perpetrators of international human rights abuses accountable: the Alien Tort Statute (ATS) and the Torture Victim Protection Act (TVPA). The ATS grants federal jurisdiction for "any civil action by an alien for a tort only, committed in violation of the law of nations or a treaty of the United States." The statute was first invoked in the human rights context in *Filártiga v. Peña-Irala*, in which a federal court found a Paraguayan national liable for acts of torture. In 1991 the United States enacted the TVPA following the United States' ratification of the UN

Convention against Torture and Other Cruel, Inhuman, or Degrading Treatment or Punishment. Whereas other human rights organizations have utilized these statutes to sue corporations and U.S. government officials, CJA limits its targets to individual perpetrators from abroad. As of 2008, CJA had initiated cases on behalf of victims from ten countries (Bosnia, Chile, China, El Salvador, Guatemala, Haiti, Honduras, Indonesia, Peru, and Somalia) and had been successful in all of its cases that went to trial. While CJA has won more than $285 million on behalf of its clients, it has recovered only $1.2 million, although enforcement efforts continue.

In 2006 CJA's board of directors decided to expand the organization's work to include litigation in Spain, where the law allows victims to pursue criminal actions by filing criminal complaints. In these private prosecutions (*acusaciones particulares*), *the victim becomes* a party to the case during the investigation and trial phases. Spanish law also allows those not directly connected to the crime to take part in certain criminal cases as popular prosecutors (*acusadores populares*). CJA is currently lead counsel in the Guatemala genocide case pending before the Spanish national court and initiated in 1999 by the Nobel laureate Rigoberta Menchú Tum. In all its work, CJA adopts a client-centered approach and ensures that its clients receive the necessary psychological support services before, during, and after litigation. Many of CJA's clients have gone on to become public spokespersons in the human rights and torture treatment movements.

Proponents of using domestic courts to enforce international human rights contend that such suits contribute to the rehabilitation of victims, the deterrence of future abuses, and the enunciation of human rights norms. Such cases also contribute to the fulfillment of states' obligations under international law to provide victims of human rights violations with redress and reparations. Despite efforts to create mechanisms of accountability for human rights abuses on the international level, few of these institutions are directly accessible to individual victims. Furthermore, many are quasi-judicial bodies that cannot hold individuals accountable or issue enforceable damage awards. CJA's mandate presumes that domestic courts have important roles to play in a decentralized system of international justice.

Critics of universal jurisdiction in both its civil and criminal manifestations argue that it is a form of plaintiffs' diplomacy that can complicate the host nation's foreign policy objectives. Although earlier administrations supported such suits, the former administration of George W. Bush had increasingly intervened in ongoing litigation in favor of dismissal on political questions and other grounds. With respect to civil suits, critics contend that a money judgment does not carry the moral impact of a criminal conviction, and any award of money damages will be incommensurate to the harm the individual victim suffers. In addition, the enforcement of judgments presents a perennial challenge to such litigation, given that defendants may not hold assets in the United States or may secrete their assets overseas pending litigation. With a civil suit, defendants can simply leave the country once suits are filed, especially those defendants who do not have permanent connections to the United States and are served with process while here temporarily. Or, the U.S. government has occasionally deported defendants at the outset of the suit. As a result, there is no guarantee that civil proceedings will be adversarial in nature, thereby denying the plaintiff the opportunity to face his or her adversary and to receive a clear articulation of the relevant law. Some criticize the historical justice cases as mere theater, where the abuses took place decades earlier and cases must proceed on the basis of a more scant evidentiary record.

[*See also* Amnesty International; Central America in the 1980s; Guatemala; Rigoberta Menchú; *and* Torture: Convention against Torture.]

BIBLIOGRAPHY

deLisle, Jacques. "Human Rights, Civil Wrongs, and International Politics: A 'Sinical' Look at the Use of U.S. Litigation to Address Abuses Abroad." *DePaul Law Review* 52 (2003): 473–561.

Eisenbrandt, Matt. "The Center for Justice and Accountability: Holding Human Rights Abusers Responsible in the United States and Abroad." In *Human Rights in Crisis*, edited by Alice Bullard, pp. 87–110. Burlington, Vt.: Ashgate, 2008.

Sikkink, Kathryn, and Ellen Lutz. "The Justice Cascade: The Evolution and Impact of Foreign Human Rights Trials in Latin America." *Chicago Journal of International Law* 2, no. 1 (Spring 2001): 1–33.

Stephens, Beth. "Translating *Filártiga*: A Comparative and International Law Analysis of Domestic Remedies for International Human Rights Violations." *Yale Journal of International Law* 27 (2002): 1, 6–9.

Stephens, Beth, and Michael Ratner. *International Human Rights Litigation in U.S. Courts*. Irvington, N.Y.: Transnational Publishers, 1996.

Van Schaack, Beth. "With All Deliberate Speed: Civil Human Rights Litigation as a Tool for Social Change." *Vanderbilt Law Review* 57 (2005): 2305–2348.

CENTRAL AMERICA IN THE 1980s

by Chandra Lehka Sriram

This study examines the causes and dynamics of conflict in the 1980s and the human rights violations that resulted in four Central American countries—El Salvador, Honduras, Guatemala, and Nicaragua. It discusses the enduring problems of democratic consolidation and peacebuilding in the 1990s that led to endemic violence and human rights violations in countries that had officially ended their internal armed conflicts or authoritarian rule. The study suggests that, while peace has formally been reached, causes of violent conflict and human rights violations in the subregion from the late 1970s through the early 1990s (beginning far earlier in Guatemala) endure, albeit at a lower level.

The societies of the region have an extremely uneven distribution of wealth, and land tenure in particular has been a key grievance underpinning several conflicts. Many leaders, specifically in Guatemala, El Salvador, and Nicaragua, have historically, in the face of strong opposition movements, turned to the military and created state apparatuses with tight control over society in order to ensure maintenance of power. Weak civilian control over the military and the security sector more generally enabled these forces to enjoy de jure or de facto control over political life. This in turn meant that the military became involved in internal political disputes. As a result, in the name of public security, civilians were often the targets of excesses by state forces, whether military or police, as well as (though generally less frequently) by rebel forces. While civilian control has been formally established and reform of the security sector, including human rights training, has been undertaken, this was an ongoing and incomplete process in the early twenty-first century.

Regional and international forces were also central to the conflicts and occasionally contributed to peace making. The Cold War meant that aid, military and otherwise, from the United States and Communist bloc countries propped up various regimes and their adversaries; U.S. support and training in particular fostered the *doctrina de seguridad nacional* (doctrine of national security) in the region. Spillover of conflicts across borders was inevitable

as rebels used neighboring countries as bases or refuges. At the same time, external political shifts helped form the basis for peace processes. The end of the Cold War reduced the superpowers' interest and prompted a shift in U.S. policy in particular. Regional peace processes helped end conflicts in the early 1990s.

Peacebuilding processes fostered by the United Nations (UN), the international financial institutions (IFIs), bilateral donors, and a host of others sought to address many of the causes and consequences of the conflicts that raged throughout the 1980s. However, democratic consolidation and peacebuilding remained incomplete in the early twenty-first century. Despite widespread reforms of military, police, and judicial institutions and measures addressing the claims of indigenous persons and disputes over land, continued corruption in institutions and ongoing impunity undermined attempts to build peace and embed respect for human rights. These incomplete transitions should disturb those concerned with protection of human rights and combating corruption, impunity, and systemic inequalities. Institutional and other reforms frequently included in peace agreements may not suffice.

This study examines only four Central American countries, rather than all seven countries in the subregion. These four countries, while having different political and social histories, have much in common, including serious violent conflicts, which were partly linked, that generated severe human rights violations and left patterns of impunity and abuses that endure. Honduras, the only country examined that did not experience a war per se, did experience serious violent conflict, both internally generated and as a result of conflicts in neighboring countries, and has struggled to address the legacy of past abuses. The study does not examine Costa Rica, which abolished its military in the mid–twentieth century, has not experienced serious internal violent conflict since that time, and has in fact served as the instigator and host for several regional peace processes. It also does not examine Belize, which did not experience such conflict, or Panama, which experienced strongman dictatorships propped up by the United States but no serious violent conflicts of a domestic nature. This is not, however, meant to discount the violence that each of these societies experienced and the risks that they continued to face in the early twenty-first century, or to ignore the positive roles they played in supporting national or regional initiatives for peace. In order to understand the conflicts and patterns of abuses in the four countries examined, it is important to understand state formation and the relationships among governments, militaries, and societies in these countries.

POLITICS OF STATE MAKING AND DECOLONIZATION

Numerous theories have been offered to explain trends until the early 1990s in Central America and much of Latin America generally, such as the dominance of politics by the military and a tendency toward oligarchic or authoritarian rule. A common explanation for this phenomenon is the legacy of Spanish colonialism. It can be argued that there was something peculiar about the militarization of rule in Spain that was transferred to its colonies. Alternatively, it can be argued that the departure of colonial control lent itself to state collapse and opened the space for military coups and military rule. Both theories can and have been ably critiqued. Claims that weak and underdeveloped states and social structures lend themselves to or even require strongmen should also be viewed critically. The ultimate cause of military penetration in political life and oligarchic or authoritarian rule matters less than the fact of its existence. It is worth recognizing further that military control itself changed in character over time. Nonprofessional militaries gave way to professionalized ones, but the military continued to dominate civilians in political life.

This phenomenon of the continued control of the state by a small group, often military, ostensibly for the good of the nation following transition, has been termed "protected democracy." Despite the presence of regular elections, liberalized institutions, and formal control of the security sector by civilians, democracy in many Latin American countries, not just in Central America, has thus been characterized as incomplete. While such control may have waned, the tradition of protected democracy engendered weak democracy and institutions vulnerable to impunity and corruption. These weak institutions, coupled with resurgent political violence and endemic crime, meant that human rights abuses continued on a regular, if reduced, basis in the early twenty-first century.

Weak democracy and military dominance over politics were further fostered by the U.S. bolstering of a number of Central American militaries. U.S. fear of Communism drove American funding and training of the military institutions of several states, most famously through the School of the Americas, which emphasized the *doctrina de seguridad nacional*. This doctrine emphasized the central role of the military as the protector of the nation and encouraged the treatment of opposition as necessarily a threat to national security. While the United States insisted that the school and the U.S. military were teaching democracy, the laws of war, and civilian control of the military, the simultaneous emphasis on the doctrine had an adverse effect, facilitating serious repression of normal political dissent and severe human rights abuses in many instances.

Finally, socioeconomic disparities were rife in all of the countries in the subregion examined here. Tensions between the peasantry and the oligarchy, the landed and the landless, and in some instances indigenous persons and those of Spanish descent manifested themselves in slightly different ways in each state. In three of the four states, however, these tensions gave rise to opposition and guerrilla movements and serious civil strife. Conflicts over scarce land and land tenure only escalated with the increase in export-oriented agriculture, which progressively limited the land available to the masses for sustenance farming. Expropriation of land by the government contributed to the growing scarcity of available land. The specific experiences of the four states are examined in greater detail in the following country histories. However, the authoritarian regimes, conflict, and rights abuses did not emerge in a vacuum, nor did the conflicts terminate in one. International and regional dynamics contributed to these phenomena.

STATE DEVELOPMENT, CONFLICT, AND HUMAN RIGHTS VIOLATIONS

Although regime type has varied over time and across the region, oligarchic states controlled by political elites or military rulers have predominated. Strong control at the top was compounded by economic stratification and divided states. The United States and its interests also affected the development of these states. This section discusses the development of regimes in the region, the emergence of conflict, and human rights violations in each country. It then considers briefly the peace-making processes and the enduring problems of political violence and human rights violations in each country.

Guatemala.

Guatemala, like other Central American nations, was susceptible to outside influences in the twentieth century. The United States was particularly involved because there were numerous U.S.-based agricultural enterprises in the country. The United States was also concerned about the spread of leftism or Communism in the hemisphere.

In 1954 the United States facilitated a coup and provided support to subsequent military regimes, and in future years its continuing support to repressive military governments was justified by the presence of strong left-wing guerrilla groups. The multiple left-wing groups eventually formed a united front, the Unidad Revolucionaria Nacional Guatemalteca (URNG), in 1982. Right-wing guerrilla groups also emerged, engaging in the torture and murder of suspected leftists. Military rule was carried out in Guatemala not through one-party control but through a multiparty system in which the army selected its preferred candidate and ensured the candidate's election through intimidation. Civil strife escalated into civil war and a series of conflicts and military-led regimes. In 1982 army officers staged a coup that brought General Efraín Ríos Montt to power, setting off new violence. Even though he was deposed in 1983, he remained powerful in politics. Civilian rule was installed in 1984–1985, but this did not halt the violence, which ultimately endured for thirty-six years and claimed some 200,000 lives.

Economic disparities were wide in Guatemala, and the lack of economic rights for many was a source of conflict. Land tenure was contentious, as development programs entailed seizure of land for the projects themselves and for roads. Many of those dispossessed in the 1960s and 1970s were poor farmers, a large number of whom were *indios*, or indigenous persons. These *indios* protested and became the subjects of violent crackdowns, as did activists who sought to unionize laborers. As the Guatemalan Commission for Historical Clarification and the Archbishop's Office for Human Rights reports found, the government was responsible for the vast majority of human rights violations, largely against unarmed civilians. Further, the conflict had a strong ethnic dimension—most of those killed were not just civilians but indigenous people.

As elsewhere in Latin America, rising civil and social conflict gave the armed forces the justification they needed to crack down, labeling opposition parties and leaders as guerrillas or terrorists. They also found a willing patron in the United States, which offered significant military aid to its protégé states and training that solidified the military's professionalism and also its self-concept as savior of the nation. Conflict that had been simmering for decades came to the fore, and violence rose in the late 1970s and early 1980s.

Civilian rule continued, with serious irregularities, after the overthrow of Ríos Montt, though the military continued to have significant control over the government. It was not until 1993–1994 that a peace process made serious strides, culminating in UN-brokered agreements first on human rights and later on other contentious issues, such as historical reporting on atrocities, in 1994. The final accords were signed in 1996. The national, regional, and international peace processes are discussed further below.

Broad institutional reforms were initiated with the conclusion and implementation of the peace accords in civil-military relations, the judiciary, and the police in particular. Some cases involving serious human rights violations went forward in national courts. Under pressure from the Inter-American Court of Human Rights, the government recognized its responsibility for a 1982 massacre at Dos Erres and settled with some victims' survivors in this and a number of other cases, though allegations persist that several officials responsible for the massacre remained in government service. However, some key provisions of the accords had not been implemented by the early twenty-first century, in particular the disbanding of the Presidential High Command and the appointment of a civilian as minister of defense. Civil Defense Patrols, which supported the armed forces during the civil war, demanded payment, generating widespread controversy, and continued to operate despite provision for their dissolution in the accords. The army has been called in repeatedly to support the police in dealing with violent crime, raising the risk of more permanent involvement by the army in internal security in violation of the accords. Serious abuses of human rights by the security forces have increased, as have reports of the growth of clandestine armed groups. These groups are allegedly linked to government officials, including individuals in the office of the prosecutor, in the police, and in the judiciary.

Attacks against human rights advocates and those seeking to implement key facets of the peace accords rose yet further in 2002. Attorney General Carlos David De León Argueta was the target of a gunshot attack, apparently linked to his investigations of several high-profile human rights cases and alleged official involvement in organized crime. Human rights advocates viewed this attack as part of a pattern that also included attacks against three sisters who had brought a case to the Inter-American Court of Human Rights, which in 2000 held the Guatemalan government responsible for the detention, torture, and extrajudicial execution of their brother. The human rights ombudsperson proposed the establishment of a new international investigative commission to address the widespread threats against the human rights community; the UN special rapporteur on human rights defenders also condemned the worsening security of human rights advocates.

Impunity for many past abuses continued as prosecutions were hampered by intimidation of those involved in the procedures. Concerns about corruption extend beyond the issue of impunity to the judicial system broadly due to corruption, lack of resources, and threats. The spread of small arms, allegedly imported by criminal groups linked to the police and the military, contributed to rising crime rates and general insecurity. At the same time, there was significant violence against union workers and reports that lynchings—with official support or complicity—and mob violence were on the rise. Deep divisions in the populace were revealed in May 1999, when a referendum on constitutional reforms dealing with, inter alia, national and social rights and the judiciary was rejected. Plans for a tax scheme to benefit former members of paramilitaries, many of whom had engaged in serious human rights abuses, were further cause for concern and possibly increased tensions.

Finally, the former dictator Ríos Montt, the leader of the ruling party, continued in his quest to recapture the presidency in the early twenty-first century. Courts twice denied him the right to run, citing a 1990 law barring coup leaders from office, but two courts considered his petition to run again. There are credible allegations that he was behind mob violence in late July 2003 that was meant to intimidate the judges considering his case, and the Constitutional Court ultimately granted him the right to run. He was not elected. Domestic murder charges were filed against him and subsequently dropped, and in 2006 Spain issued an international arrest warrant for him for genocide charges brought under Spain's universal jurisdiction legislation.

Human rights protections continued to be weak in Guatemala in the early twenty-first century. Of particular concern were lynchings; clandestine security structures; threats to judicial officials, witnesses, and human rights advocates; and the impunity of officials for past human rights abuses. Indigenous peoples faced discrimination and suffered economically and socially. Some progress was made institutionally with the creation of a new code of criminal procedure, the establishment of a commission to strengthen the judiciary, and the deployment of civilian police and advances in their professional training. Unfortunately, there remained significant problems with abuse and corruption in the security and judicial sectors.

El Salvador.

Like Guatemala, El Salvador has a history of socio-economic stratification, military interference in politics, and U.S. military support and intervention in politics. The result was a protracted social conflict, governmental repression, and the rise of guerrilla groups throughout the 1970s. This erupted in the early 1980s into a full-scale civil conflict, which resulted in some seventy-five thousand deaths and widespread human rights abuses.

The country's economics and politics were tightly controlled by a small elite that often exercised military control. Military involvement in politics, though not new, was consolidated with the rise in power of the "Tandona" (big class), the largest graduating class of military officers, in 1966. As tensions began to rise in the late 1970s, civilian leaders remained formally in power, but the military and security forces gained increasingly wide powers to maintain public order. The result was oligarchic rule with sporadic violence, particularly over the issue of land tenure.

Numerous left-wing groups emerged as violence escalated, and the military staged a coup in October 1979. The guerrilla groups joined to form the Frente Farabundo Martí para la Liberación Nacional (FMLN) in 1980, and the rising violence soon became a full-scale conflict that endured for some twelve years. According to the country's post-transition truth commission report, some 60 percent of the abuses complained of were extrajudicial executions, 25 percent were disappearances, and 20 percent were torture. Government forces, death squads, and allied paramilitaries were accused of responsibility for all but 5 percent of the complaints.

Dialogue and peace negotiations began with the inauguration of Alfredo Cristiani in 1989. The process was supported first by other Central American nations, but the UN joined the process at the request of the Central American presidents in 1990 and mediated talks that ultimately resulted in the peace accords completed in January 1992.

Great strides have been made in the implementation of the peace accords in El Salvador, and it is widely hailed as one of the UN's success stories. A new civilian police force, with a new doctrine and a new academy, was established and included vetted members of the old police force and of the FMLN. The civilian police were formally separated from the military, and a new military doctrine emphasized the military's role in external defense. Several of the more abusive security forces, such as the treasury police, were abolished, and the military was cut in half. Institutional purges also removed officers accused of human rights abuses and corruption. The FMLN was converted into a legitimate political party, winning municipalities and legislative seats.

Despite these advances, in the early twenty-first century serious difficulties remained in peacebuilding, particularly in the area of public security and protection of human rights. Rising crime rates challenged the capacity of the police. While the violence largely transitioned from explicitly political violence to common criminality, it remained a challenge to the weak state, according to a study by the government's human rights ombudsperson's office. The same study observed that, while accurate statistics were difficult to come by, El Salvador was second only to Guatemala in the subregion in experiencing serious violent crime per capita.

Further, the police were implicated and arrested in several high-profile crimes, and purification of the force was undertaken in late 2000. Police were involved in kidnapping of citizens for profit, and a presidential commission named twelve officers involved. Police also engaged in serious human rights violations, including killings and attempted killings. Investigation by the presidential commission resulted in the dismissal of some seventy-two officers. There were also some prosecutions for these abuses, but sentences were relatively light. However, there were no documented cases of politically motivated disappearances, and threats against human rights campaigners declined.

Despite the formal separation of the military and the police in the accords and institutionally, in 1995 the military began to offer support to the police in some areas where armed criminal bands were active. The military, however, remained under civilian control. Judicial reform was undertaken following the recommendations of the Truth Commission report. The entire supreme court was replaced in 1994. Replacement of lower-level magistrates and judges, however, proceeded less quickly. Constitutional reforms to improve the judiciary arising out of the peace agreements were completed in 1996, and the criminal procedure code was revised. Corruption and inefficiency continued in the judiciary and in the attorney general's office, ensuring that accused persons with political, economic, or institutional leverage could avoid penalty in many cases. Legislation was adopted in 2000 to combat this problem. The supreme court sanctioned and dismissed a number of judicial officers, albeit proportionately few in comparison to the numbers investigated.

On the salient issue of impunity, the Inter-American Commission of Human Rights found that the state violated rights to life, justice, and judicial protection, a decision the state disregarded, as it was nonbinding. In October 2000 the supreme court upheld 1993 amnesty legislation as constitutional, largely undermining the possibility of redress for past abuses, though the decision did leave judicial discretion to pursue cases occurring between 1989 and 1994. The status of children who disappeared during the war was contentious; the government refused to create a commission to investigate their fates. There were also complaints that the office of the human rights ombudsperson was ineffective in part due to politicization of the selection for the post.

Nicaragua.

Nicaragua, like its neighbors, had an uneven distribution of wealth and rule by a small elite. The Somoza family, which came to power in 1936, concentrated control until the leftist Frente Sandinista de Liberación Nacional (Sandinistas or FSLN) seized power in 1979. Under Anastacio Somoza Debayle, who controlled the state between 1952 and 1979, and his relatives, military and political authority were concentrated in the hands of a small group. Despite constitutional restrictions on reelection, Somoza remained in office, systematically repressing the Sandinistas and other opposition and guerrilla groups.

The Sandinistas engaged in low-intensity guerrilla warfare against the Somoza dynasty from the early 1960s onward. Violent conflict escalated throughout the 1970s, with the Sandinistas garnering support from more of the populace as government repression increased. In 1979 a Sandinista junta claimed control, and Somoza fled. Sandinista rule led the United States, fearing the spread of Communism, to support (and arguably create) the contras, a rebel group based largely on Honduran soil that sought to overthrow the Nicaraguan government throughout the 1980s. Casualty estimates of the protracted conflict vary, ranging from forty thousand to fifty thousand people dead.

The Sandinistas sought to rebuild the country, but efforts were hampered by a weak economy, the ongoing impact of the conflict, and a continuing debt crisis. Increasingly, aid from the United States and from the IFIs was cut or limited. However, land reform programs were successful as large tracts of land were seized and cooperatives created. Public control of a host of industries was also instituted.

Human rights abuses were committed both by government forces and by the contras, and there is dispute about the gravity and extent of abuses committed by each. Government forces held political prisoners and engaged in summary executions of persons suspected of being contra members or supporters. Contras abused prisoners and killed noncombatants and were accused more generally of launching indiscriminate attacks on civilians.

Pressure from home and abroad, combined with the end of the Cold War and a decline in external support for the Nicaraguan regime and from the United States for the contras, weakened the two primary actors in the conflict and paved the way for negotiations. The regime engaged in negotiations with the contras and agreed to elections in 1990. The electoral victor was Violeta Barrios de Chamorro, who engaged in a series of reforms to, inter alia, stabilize the economy, professionalize the army and the police, and privatize state-owned businesses.

Following the end of the Cold War and the election of Chamorro, a series of reforms sought to consolidate democracy, demobilize soldiers, and reform the security sector. The first civilian defense ministry was introduced in 1997; the president is chief of the defense and the security forces. However, electoral reforms introduced in 2000 were criticized by some as imposing difficult conditions for the creation of new political parties and the registration of candidates.

While the human rights record of the government generally improved, abuses by the police continued, and members of the security forces were responsible for torture and extrajudicial killings. The office of the inspector general sanctioned numerous officers accused of abuses; some were also dismissed. Budgetary limits and personnel shortages continued to plague the police despite support for training by international donors and nongovernmental organizations. Voluntary police were also implicated in numerous cases. They cannot be sanctioned, only dismissed, and continued to be used in light of poor resources and staffing though their numbers were cut. Allegations of death threats against human rights advocates pressing for investigation of abuses continued. Demobilization of soldiers was accomplished, but some observers argue that they were not properly reintegrated and suggest that some rearmed and engaged in criminal activity.

Though the judiciary remained weak and overburdened, a series of constitutional reforms in 1995 strengthened the independence of the supreme court, and in 2000 the number of supreme court justices was increased. The weakness of the judiciary impeded prosecution of human rights cases, though some proceeded but resulted in light sentences. In addition, the judiciary has been at times corrupt and susceptible to political influence, though the supreme court has sought to reduce incompetence and corruption by sanctioning and removing some judicial employees.

Respect for indigenous rights, while enshrined in legislation, has been limited. In 2000 the Inter-American Commission on Human Rights found that the government had violated the rights of an indigenous group in a case involving logging licenses.

Honduras.

Honduras has experienced numerous rebellions and civil conflicts with military domination of politics. The country was ruled by military officers from 1963, when the armed forces staged a coup, until the formal transition to democracy in 1982. This transition to democracy was itself carefully managed by the armed forces, which continued to maintain heavy involvement in politics even after ceding formal control. Even though formal armed conflict did not occur, political violence endured throughout the 1980s, including significant human rights violations and the disappearances of at least 184 people. Spillover effects from the other conflicts in the region, including refugee flows and the presence of the contras in Honduran territory, further destabilized the nation.

Honduras, like its neighbors, is very poor. It has relied heavily on banana and other exports, and this has brought with it extensive involvement of external firms in Honduras and its politics. However, while there is a concentration of land, wealth, and power in a relatively small elite, the concentration is not as great as in El Salvador and Guatemala. There have nonetheless been widespread protests by peasants seeking more land.

The military domination that continued through the period of civilianization was compounded by the unification of the police and the military under a single command as well as by the adoption by the military of the *doctrina de seguridad nacional*. The branding of the opposition as subversive enabled the security forces to justify disappearances and other human rights abuses; the U.S.-supported Battalion 3-16 largely carried out these disappearances. It is important to note that the disappearances, while tragic, were relatively few in number—under two hundred by most counts. Unlike its neighbors, Honduras did not experience open civil conflict, and consequently the degree of repression was not as significant as in El Salvador, Guatemala, and Nicaragua.

Nonetheless, effective military control over the state limited prospects for true democracy and resulted in serious human rights abuses. This was bolstered in part by U.S. support for the government, because the United States needed Honduras as a base of operations for the Nicaraguan contras that the United States supported. The U.S. Agency for International Development provided the Honduran government with substantial aid. U.S. bases on Honduran soil in turn provided support for the contras, trained Honduran troops, and trained Salvadoran troops to enable them to fight their leftist opposition. The contra camps on the border with Nicaragua prompted frequent incursions into Honduran territory by Sandinistas pursuing the rebels. This resulted in a number of clashes between the neighboring countries' militaries.

Civilian rule continued, though with heavy military influence over political life. With the election of President Carlos Roberto Reina in 1993, there was a push to address the abuses of the past. Shortly before his election a human rights commission was set up, which in 1993 issued a seminal report, "The Facts Speak for Themselves," on the disappearances and past human rights abuses. Efforts to address past abuses included the removal of some officers and the prosecution of others. Action was also taken to reform the security sector, although the process remains somewhat incomplete in part due to amnesties issued in 1987 and 1991.

The inauguration of President Reina following on the heels of the creation of a human rights commission was part of a shift toward greater respect for human rights and the strengthening of civilian control over the security sector. The country held its sixth consecutive democratic election in November 2001. Progress was made on ending the practice of forced recruitment into the armed forces, prosecution of those responsible for past abuses, separation of the military and the police, and release of information through the human rights commission, including requests for declassification of documents held by the U.S. government. However, progress came at a cost, with the security forces occasionally reacting strongly to steps impinging upon their autonomy. Thus while progress was made in curbing military autonomy, democratization remained arguably incomplete in Honduras in the early twenty-first century. The public prosecutor filed seminal cases against military officers in 1995 for kidnapping and torture. However, these were undermined by military intransigence, including alleged burning of documents.

Further, in response to public requests for information from the U.S. government by the human rights commissioner, the military sent tanks into the streets of the capital. The human rights commissioner and the judge hearing the case also received death threats. Nonetheless, indictments continued against other officers of the security forces. Several indicted officers went into hiding, protected by members of the security forces and in some instances continuing to draw salaries. The supreme court, in a key decision in 2000, ruled that illegal detention and execution by military officials were not covered by the 1987 amnesty legislation, potentially enabling further prosecutions.

Progress was made in the formal separation of the police and the military through constitutional reform. The formal transfer of the police to civilian control took place in 1997, and the body created to enable purification of the police offered a list of corrupt officials. Police reform legislation also created a civilian oversight body. While the budget of the security forces actually rose in 1995–1996, this was ostensibly for equipment and salaries and to combat rising crime; civilian control over budgetary matters was reestablished in 1996. In 1999 the first civilian was named as commander of the armed forces, and by 2000 the military was actually below its authorized strength. Rising crime, however, meant that the army was allowed to join the police in law enforcement. There were persistent accusations of criminal activities by the police, including drug trafficking. There were also reports of human rights abuses by the police; the attorney general's office initiated proceedings in these cases. In many of the numerous cases of alleged extrajudicial killings by the security forces, however, the office was unable to identify suspects. A purge was carried out in 2000. The government removed or demoted over two hundred military and police officers and judges. Between 2002 and 2007 extrajudicial killings of street children totaled some fifteen hundred, many of which can be attributed to the security forces according to the UN special rapporteur on extrajudicial, summary, or arbitrary executions. In March 2003 the government established a commission to investigate these deaths.

Nonetheless, impunity for a variety of abuses continues due in part to a weak and often corrupt judiciary with poor resources. The rise in crime led to the growth not only of unregulated private security services but also of neighborhood patrols that have been accused of engaging in vigilante justice. Human rights defenders have been increasingly attacked, not directly by the police but by organized crime networks and wealthy landowners.

Disputes over land reform, land tenure, and squatting have also led to violence. There have been allegations that, while the police may not be directly involved in attacks on human rights activists, they are complicit. Abuses by police are also rife within the corrections system, as was highlighted by an April 2003 massacre by police of sixty-eight inmates in the prison El Porvenir.

CROSSCUTTING ISSUES: ELITE RULE, CONFLICTS, AND PEACE MAKING

As is apparent from the country histories, several key issues were salient across the subregion. Despite democratization and peacebuilding efforts, these underlying sources of strife have not been completely addressed in any of the nations. In the absence of fully consolidated democracy and fully functional rule of law, the protection and promotion of human rights have been limited. While national human rights institutions are in place, human rights defenders are still subject to attack in some countries. To understand the past and ongoing threats to human rights, it is essential to understand the history of elite domination, military control, and political violence in the region.

Elite rule and civil-military relations.

The history and politics of each nation in the subregion and in the four examined here vary in important ways. However, as outlined above, it is also the case that all experienced to varying degrees control of the state by a small elite, vast economic disparities, and weak or non-existent civilian control over the military with significant penetration by the military into politics, including some instances of direct control over the state. While in the case of Guatemala conflict had been present for some time, in other countries the economic downturn of the 1970s, precipitated in part by debt crises, prompted protests by populations and repression by the security forces. In Guatemala these factors contributed to extended repression, in El Salvador to civil war. In Nicaragua the crisis helped bring the leftist Sandinista regime to power, promoting interventionist responses by the U.S. government in the subregion. Honduras escaped direct internal conflict during the 1980s, though it experienced weak civilian rule, repressive security forces, disappearances, and spill-over from neighboring countries.

Regional conflict and the role of the United States.

The influence of the United States economically and militarily cannot be underestimated. The Soviet Union, whose influence was less extensive than that of the United States, offered material support to the Sandinistas and the FMLN. Soviet involvement helped feed U.S. concern about the threat of Communism in the region. U.S. economic interests continue in the region, and the presence of the United States and U.S. economic interests has tended to exacerbate unstable situations in countries with severe poverty and socioeconomic disparities.

Nicaragua, Honduras, and El Salvador were perhaps the most affected by Cold War rivalries in Central America. U.S. support for the Salvadoran government contributed to the control and repression by the security forces as they battled the FMLN. U.S. policy consistently sought to bring down the leftist Nicaraguan government through the support of the contras and even such activities as mining Nicaraguan harbors. As noted above, Honduras hosted numerous U.S. military installations as well as contra bases. In addition to the Soviet Union, the Sandinistas and Cuba also offered support to the FMLN. It was thus only with the end of the Cold War that these external interests and involvement in the region began to abate, enabling peace negotiations and more extensive democratization to begin. Guatemala, having experienced significant U.S. interference since the 1950s, was less directly involved in these explicitly ideological battles. Its internal conflict was colored by the ethnic divide and the dispossession of the *indios*.

Regional peace processes in the 1980s.

The regional states themselves, as well as the Organization of American States (OAS) more broadly, increasingly affirmed democratic governance through the late 1980s and into the early 1990s as a central principle even as they practiced it rather incompletely at home. A number of regional initiatives, including the Contadora and Esquipulas processes, encouraged resolution of domestic conflicts and fostered more amicable relations among the regional states.

The Contadora process, which arose out of initiatives begun by the U.S. president Jimmy Carter in the late 1970s, only gained momentum in January 1983, when the foreign ministers of four countries of the region met to examine the threats to regional security posed by the internal conflicts. It provided an important multilateral forum that did not include the United States or Cold War concerns. In 1984 the process resulted in a draft Act of Peace for the region, which collapsed under U.S. criticism. While this process largely failed, a key achievement was the creation of a multilateral forum for the discussion of regional problems.

In 1986 Central American presidents meeting in Esquipulas, Guatemala, agreed on the need to address the crises in the region and to create a Central American parliament. In 1987 in Esquipulas the Costa Rican president Oscar Arias presented a peace plan to his fellow Central American presidents that was centered on democracy, and he called upon the three states in civil war to resolve their conflicts. This plan was separate from and parallel to the proposals in Contadora. The parliament was formally created, though in the early twenty-first century it had not yet become a strong force in the region. One concrete result was a regional security treaty completed in December 1996. These efforts contributed to the development of national peace processes in the four countries of this study.

The end of the Cold War.

The end of the Cold War and the changed attitude of the United States toward the subregion clearly enabled the peace processes begun in the 1980s by regional leaders to advance. For the United States the key security concern in the region was no longer defense against Communism but rather defense of democracy. The UN also began to play a more active role. Other key states played important roles, in some instances as "groups of friends" of the secretary-general of the UN. In other instances, they were key donors for peacekeeping and peacebuilding efforts. The United States and other countries exerted more direct pressure on regional states to democratize as a part of resolving their long-running civil wars. For example, the United States and the OAS placed great pressure on the Guatemalan president Jorge Serrano when he attempted a coup by seizing extraconstitutional powers in 1993.

IMPUNITY AND CORRUPTION AS ENDURING PROBLEMS

As Brian Loveman observed, "These 'democracies' were born disabled, unable to enforce the law against those accused of criminal behavior and prevented from exercising fully their constitutional authority" (p. 117). This may be something of an overstatement, but it is the case that impunity and corruption, in governance generally but particularly in the security sector, are enduring problems. Despite efforts at civilianization, purification, and institutional reform of the police and other security forces in El Salvador and Guatemala and more limited reforms in Honduras and Nicaragua, many individuals responsible for human rights abuses remained in these forces in the

early twenty-first century. At the same time there remained, despite training, entrenched habits of excessive use of force and service to elites rather than to the populace at large. The postconflict rise in crime rates facilitated these abuses as populations prioritized diminished crime rates over disciplined police forces. Further, despite oversight bodies, internal discipline continued to be a serious problem. Such weaknesses enabled the involvement of police forces in criminal activities, such as arms trafficking in Guatemala.

Corruption in the security sectors is intimately linked to corruption in politics, including at high levels in some instances. This is certainly a legacy of authoritarian or dictatorial regimes, where corruption and self-serving political leaders were endemic, and many hoped it would diminish in time. However, a study of transitional societies (and others) in Latin America suggests that political corruption does not fade with transitions; political culture is slow to change and difficult to constrain (Whitehead, 2000). The result, then, is fundamental flaws in governance as well as limits to the efficacy of numerous reforms, leading some to conclude that democratization and peacebuilding in the subregion have been incomplete or limited.

POLITICAL CORRUPTION, VIOLENCE, AND HUMAN RIGHTS VIOLATIONS

The rise in violent crime is a common phenomenon in postconflict societies and is not unique to Central American countries. The legacy of conflict is often the habit of resorting to violence to resolve problems, whether personal or political, and is made easier by the accessibility of weapons. Violent crime rose in each of the four countries examined here; it was often undertaken for purely economic purposes and was not linked to specific political ideologies or movements. However, in many instances political agendas can also be discerned, and many apparently "common" crimes were also political ones.

The frequency of politically driven violent incidents is difficult to ascertain due to the dearth of accurate statistics regarding crime, political violence, and corruption. There are of course specific cases documented by governmental and nongovernmental human rights bodies, and the perception is that crime and violence were on the rise in the early twenty-first century. Crime was also underreported in each country, making an accurate assessment of trends yet more difficult. The governments themselves of course concurred that crime was on the rise, and in fact this is the reason the military was used to combat crime in

Honduras. The perception of corruption was widespread according to Transparency International, the leading organization that tracks such trends.

ASSESSMENT

This entry began with the proposition that, while the experience of each of the countries in the subregion examined was in some sense unique, the countries share certain common characteristics and experiences that contributed to political violence and civil war throughout the 1980s. The end of the Cold War and the resolution of the overt political battles provided the opportunity for each of these countries to experience not only negative peace but also positive peace. That is to say, not only were the wars terminated but also sustained peace building efforts held out the promise of addressing the underlying conditions that gave rise to the violence in the first place, whether political, economic, or ideological.

That promise was never truly fulfilled. Peace building, human rights, and governance reform efforts, where they took place, did achieve some measure of institutional reform, the importance of which should not be understated. However, the chronic violence and political corruption in these nations meant that human rights violations and impunity continued to be endemic. Further reforms are necessary to address corruption in the judiciary, the police, and the military. External actors might also engage political participants directly regarding the prevalence of political violence, not only providing technical assistance for governance, but even conditioning assistance on serious efforts to curb abuses and corruption. A failure to do so means that assistance in developing human rights protections and institutions and in reforming old abusive institutions has had only limited effect.

[See also Colombia; Costa Rica; Democracy and Right to Participation; Guatemala; and Organization of American States.]

BIBLIOGRAPHY

Acuerdo de Esquipulas II. August 7, 1987. http://secviccentdocumentosoficiales.blogspot.com/2007/08/ii-cumbre-de-presidentes.html.

Acuerdos de paz: Firmados por el gobierno de la Republica de Guatemala y la Unidad Revolucionaria Nacional Guatemalteca (URNG). Guatemala: Universidad Rafael Landióvar, Instituto de Investigaciones Económicas y Sociales, Misión de Verificación de las Naciones Unidas en Guatemala, 1997.

Amnesty International. Country Reports. http://www.amnesty.org.

Anderson, Thomas P. Politics in Central America: Guatemala, El Salvador, Honduras, and Nicaragua. New York: Praeger, 1988.

Arnson, Cynthia, ed. Comparative Peace Processes in Latin America. Washington, D.C.: Woodrow Wilson Center Press, 1999.

Barahona Riera, Francisco, and Manuel Carballo Quintana, eds. Reconversión militar en Centroamérica. San José, Costa Rica: Fundación Friedrich Ebert, 1995.

Comisionado Nacional de los Derechos Humanos. El difícil transito hacia la democracia. Tegucigalpa, Honduras: Comisionado Nacional de los Derechos Humanos, 1996.

Comisionado Nacional de los Derechos Humanos. Los hechos hablan por sí mismos: Informe preliminar sobre los desaparecidos en Honduras 1980–1993. Tegucigalpa, Honduras: Editorial Guaymuras, 1994.

Commission for Historical Clarification. Guatemala: Memory of Silence. 1999. http://shr.aaas.org/guatemala/ceh/report/english/toc.html.

Declaracion de Esquipulas. May 5, 1986. http://www.sieca.org.gt/Publico/Reuniones_Presidentes/I/declarac.htm.

Domínguez, Jorge I., and Marc Lindenberg, eds. Democratic Transitions in Central America. Gainesville: University Press of Florida, 1997.

Downes, Richard. "The Impact of the End of the Cold War on Inter-American Relations: The Search for Paradigm and Principle." Journal of Interamerican Studies and World Affairs 39, no. 2 (Summer 1997): 197–216.

Farer, Tom, ed. Beyond Sovereignty: Collectively Defending Democracy in the Americas. Baltimore: Johns Hopkins University Press, 1996.

Fuerzas Armadas de El Salvador and ONUSAL. Doctrina militar y relaciónes ejército/sociedad. San Salvador: Fuerzas Armadas de El Salvador and ONUSAL, 1994.

Fuerzas Armadas de El Salvador and ONUSAL. Relaciónes civiles-militares en el nuevo marco internacional. San Salvador: Fuerzas Armadas de El Salvador and ONUSAL, 1994.

Hamilton, Nora, Jeffry A. Frieden, Linda Fuller, and Manuel Pastor Jr., eds. Crisis in Central America: Regional Dynamics and U.S. Policy in the 1980s. Boulder, Colo.: Westview, 1988.

Human Rights Watch. Country Reports. http://www.hrw.org.

Inter-American Court of Human Rights. Velázquez-Rodriguez Case Judgment of July 29, 1988. Inter-American Court. H.R. (Ser. C) No. 4 (1988). http://www1.umn.edu/humanrts/iachr/C/4-ing.html.

International Court of Justice. Case Concerning the Military and Paramilitary Activities in and against Nicaragua (Nicaragua v. United States of America). Judgment of June 27, 1986. http://www.icj-cij.org/docket/files/70/6503.pdf.

Kruijt, Dirk, and Edelberto Torres-Rivas, eds. América Latina: Militares y sociedad. San José, Costa Rica: FLACSO, 1991.

Lentner, Howard H. *State Formation in Central America: The Struggle for Autonomy, Development, and Democracy.* Westport, Conn.: Greenwood, 1993.

Loveman, Brian. "'Protected Democracies' and Military Guardianship: Political Transitions in Latin America, 1978–1993." *Journal of Interamerican Studies and World Affairs* 36, no. 2 (Summer 1994): 105–189.

Millett, Richard L. "The United States and Latin America's Armed Forces: A Troubled Relationship." *Journal of Interamerican Studies and World Affairs* 39, no. 1 (Spring 1997): 121–136.

Montero, Alfred P. "Assessing the Third Wave Democracies." *Journal of Interamerican Studies and World Affairs* 40, no. 2 (Summer 1998): 117–134.

Opazo Bernales, Andrés. *Esquipulas II: Una tarea pendiente.* San José, Costa Rica: Editorial Universitaria Centroamericana, 1990.

Pastor, Robert A. "The Bush Administration and Latin America: The Pragmatic Style and the Regionalist Option." *Journal of Interamerican Studies and World Affairs* 33, no. 3 (Autumn 1991): 1–34.

Peceny, Mark, and William Stanley. "Liberal Social Reconstruction and the Resolution of Civil Wars in Central America." *International Organization* 55, no. 1 (Winter 2001): 149–182.

Rouquié, Alain. *The Military and the State in Latin America.* Translated by Paul E. Sigmund. Berkeley: University of California Press, 1987.

Saldomando, Angel, Carmen Rosa de Leon, Ricardo Ribera, and Carlos Sojo. *Diagnóstico de la investigación para la consolidación de la paz en America Central.* Ottawa, Canada: IDRC, 2000.

Salomón, Leticia. *La violencia en Honduras, 1980–1993.* Tegucigalpa, Honduras: Centro de Documentación de Honduras, 1993.

Samour, Hector. "Las fuerzas armadas Salvadoreñas." *Realidad: Revista de Ciencias Sociales y Humanidades* (September–October 1994): 774–775.

Spence, Jack, David R. Dye, Mike Lanchin, Geoff Thale, and George Vickers. *Chapultepec: Five Years Later.* Cambridge, Mass.: Hemisphere Initiatives, 1997.

Spence, Jack, David R. Dye, Paula Worby, Carmen Rosa de Leon-Escribano, George Vickers, and Mike Lanchin. *Promise and Reality: Implementation of the Guatemalan Peace Accords.* Cambridge, Mass.: Hemisphere Initiatives, 1998.

Sriram, Chandra Lekha. *Confronting Past Human Rights Violations: Justice versus Peace in Times of Transition.* London and New York: Frank Cass, 2004.

Stahler-Sholk, Richard. "El Salvador's Negotiated Transition: From Low-Intensity Conflict to Low-Intensity Democracy." *Journal of Interamerican Studies and World Affairs* 36, no. 4 (Winter 1994): 1–59.

Torres-Rivas, Edelberto, and Gabriel Aguilera Peralta. *Desde el autoritarismo a la paz.* Guatemala: FLACSO, 1998.

United States Department of State. *Country Background Reports and Country Reports on Human Rights Practices.* http://www.state.gov.

Valladares Lanza, Leo, and Susan C. Peacock. *In Search of Hidden Truths: An Interim Report on Declassification by the National Commissioner for Human Rights in Honduras.* Tegucigalpa, Honduras: Comisionado Nacional de los Derechos Humanos en Honduras, 1998.

Vergara, Rafael. *Procesos de negociación comparados en Africa y América Latina.* Guatemala: FLACSO, 1994.

Whitehead, Lawrence. "High-Level Political Corruption in Latin America: A 'Transitional' Phenomenon?" In *Combating Corruption in Latin America,* edited by Joseph S. Tulchin and Ralph H. Espach, pp. 801–817. Washington, D.C.: Woodrow Wilson Center Press, 2000.

CHECHNYA

by Catherine Osgood

Russia's war with separatists in the southern republic of Chechnya from 1994 to 1996, and the second war that reignited in 1999, have been among the bloodiest human rights catastrophes in Europe during the 1990s and in the early twenty-first century. Civilians in Chechnya have been the primary victims of these wars, with hundreds of thousands having been forced to flee their homes since 1994. Many sought refuge and political asylum outside Russia. According to a study by John B. Dunlop published in the *Central Asian Survey* (2000), civilian casualties during the 1994–1996 Russo-Chechen war probably exceeded thirty-five thousand. It appears approximately seventy-five hundred Russian soldiers and four thousand Chechen combatants died during this same period. There are various estimates of casualties since the outbreak of the second Russo-Chechen war, and that figure likely exceeds the number of casualties during the first Chechen war. Accurate statistics on total civilian casualties are difficult to ascertain. Observers' access to the republic has been limited by ongoing violence and by the efforts of authorities to contain the flow of information about human rights abuses. Thousands of civilians in Chechnya have been tortured, raped, detained in so-called filtration camps, and forcibly abducted (or "forcefully disappeared"). Dozens of mass graves have been discovered. Chechnya is on the genocide watch list of the U.S. Holocaust Memorial Museum's Committee on Conscience.

HISTORICAL BACKGROUND

Chechens have lived in the region of Chechnya for at least six thousand years. The Chechen language, part of the Nakh branch of North Caucasian languages, is indigenous to the area and unrelated to any major linguistic group. Chechens are predominantly Sunni Sufis of the Hanafi school, having converted to Islam between the seventeenth and nineteenth centuries. However, during the course of the brutal Russo-Chechen wars beginning

in 1994 and 1999, respectively, there has been a rise in Wahhabism, Islamic fundamentalism, and violent extremism, as well as a breakdown of the social order previously held together by the patriarchal Chechen clan system.

Chechnya is a partly mountainous republic located on the land bridge between the Black Sea and the Caspian Sea connecting access routes between Europe and Asia. The region has been a focal point of the competing interests of regional actors throughout the centuries. A long history of Chechen resistance to outside domination produced a Chechen warrior culture.

Chechens have resisted Russian rule for over four hundred years beginning with the advances of Ivan the Terrible in the 1550s. Serious confrontation erupted between Chechens and Russians during the expansionist project of Peter the Great in the early 1700s. From 1785 to 1791 the Chechen Sheikh Al Mansur led a resistance movement against Catherine the Great's penetration into the North Caucasus. During the Caucasus War of the early 1800s, General Aleksei Yermolov tried to conquer the Chechens by destroying their crops and subjecting them to starvation, raiding settlements and killing scores of villagers, and conducting the first deportations of Chechens from their homes in the lowlands up into the mountains and then to Siberia.

More recent in Chechen cultural memory are Joseph Stalin's 1944 deportations of the entire Chechen population of about half a million people on the premise that they had collaborated with the Nazis during World War II. They were transported in cattle cars to Siberia in the middle of winter along with roughly 200,000 people of other North Caucasian ethnic groups. In some North Caucasus villages, people who were deemed "untransportable" by Soviet authorities were killed on the spot because they were too far from railways or because they were too old or sick to travel. In the most notorious case, Soviet authorities rounded up between 700 and 750 people in the remote Chechen village of Khaibakh and burned them alive in a barn. Following the 1944 deportations, at least 25 percent of the deportees perished within five years from starvation, harsh treatment, and exposure. They were not allowed to return to their homelands until after 1957. In February 2004 members of the European Parliament officially recognized the 1944 deportations of the entire Chechen population as an "act of genocide."

FIRST RUSSO-CHECHEN WAR (1994–1996)

Dzhokar Dudayev, once a major general in the Soviet Air Force, was elected as Chechnya's president in the midst of the Soviet Union's breakup. He proclaimed Chechnya's independence in October 1991. In 1992 Chechnya and Tatarstan were the only two regions that refused to sign the Federation Treaty. The Kremlin negotiated a higher degree of autonomy for Tatarstan, which would remain within the Russian Federation, and Tatarstan later signed the treaty as a result. Chechnya, however, refused to sign the treaty and Dudayev led a de facto independent government. The crisis escalated following attempts by the Russian government to negotiate a compromise with Dudayev, efforts to mobilize Chechen opposition to topple the Dudayev regime, and failed covert efforts to assassinate him. By the fall of 1994, President Boris Yeltsin decided to abandon diplomacy. Within Yeltsin's inner circle pressure mounted to launch a military campaign to capture Grozny and bring down the troublesome Chechen leader. On 26 November 1994 a Russian tank assault on Grozny failed. Yeltsin gave Dudayev an ultimatum to disband his armed formation within two days. The Russian State Duma defense committee chairman Sergei Yushenkov advised Yeltsin that the use of force in Chechnya would result in disaster. He threatened to initiate impeachment proceedings against Yelstin if the Soviet president ordered troops into the republic. Among those who favored military action was Oleg Lobov, secretary of the Security Council, who reportedly asserted that Yeltsin needed a small, victorious war to boost the president's ratings and improve his prospects for reelection. When Dudayev rejected Yeltsin's ultimatum to disband his armed followers, forty thousand Russian troops advanced into Chechnya on 10 December 1994.

Human rights and democracy advocates in Russia sharply criticized the indiscriminate use of force by the military against civilians in Chechnya. Concern also grew that military action in Chechnya would hurt democratic and economic reforms in Russia and possibly lead to a return to authoritarianism. Some asserted that the assault on Chechnya was unconstitutional because according to the Russian constitution adopted in December 1993, armed forces could be used on Russian territory only after a presidential declaration of martial law or a state of emergency, and Yeltsin did not officially declare a state of emergency in Chechnya before authorizing the use of the military. Supporters of Yeltsin's actions cited Article 4 of the Russian constitution, "Russian federal laws are paramount throughout the Russian Federation," which they argued justified the use of force as a constitutional right to respond to the Dudayev regime because it was blocking Russian law in Chechnya.

Elena Bonner, the widow of the acclaimed Russian human rights activist Andrei Sakharov, resigned from President Yeltsin's Human Rights Commission in protest of the military campaign in Chechnya. She urged the U.S. government to contact Yeltsin directly, to ask him to call for a cease-fire and negotiate a political solution with Dudayev. She maintained that Dudayev was willing to compromise on the issue of Chechen independence but wanted international observers present for any talks. Bonner and other supporters of democracy and human rights in Russia warned that the high human cost of a military campaign in Chechnya would divert the course of Russia's political trajectory away from democratization.

Many Western governments feared that a strong, public condemnation of the war or pressure on Yeltsin to enter into negotiations with Chechen separatists would damage their relations with Russia or undermine Yeltsin in the face of his domestic hard-line Communist and nationalist opponents. The Kremlin argued that a successful separatist campaign in Chechnya could spark other separatist movements throughout Russia. The U.S. government shared this concern, particularly because of the fear that Russia's nuclear weapons could end up in the hands of breakaway minority groups. It became U.S. policy to support the territorial integrity of Russia, to deplore the heavy loss of life in Chechnya, to provide humanitarian aid to victims of the conflict, and to urge a political settlement while being cautious to not destabilize the political situation for Yeltsin.

INTERNATIONAL REACTIONS

Top U.S. officials were reluctant to condemn the Russian government's use of force in Grozny so as not to undermine what they hoped would be a new era of increased U.S. cooperation with Russia following the collapse of the Soviet Union and the end of the Cold War. On the day

Russian troops crossed into Chechnya, 11 December 1994, the U.S. deputy secretary of state Strobe Talbott, citing a conversation with the U.S. ambassador to Russia Thomas Pickering, sent a confidential cable with the subject heading "Russian Troops Move into Chechnya" indicating that the Russian government's decision to use force was not unexpected:

> That Moscow decided to move in at this time is not a great surprise. This was clearly one of the options Moscow had been considering as it pursued a dual track policy of building up forces in the region and making an effort to open negotiations with Groznyy on its own terms. Chechen President Dudayev for the past two weeks has said publicly that he thought an "invasion" was imminent. (U.S. State Department cable no. 329213)

The State Department cable set the tone for U.S. policy toward the Russo-Chechen crisis. The U.S. government understood the potential implications of the military operation for Russia's political future and for human rights in Russia, but the United States maintained the position that the crisis was an internal Russian affair:

> This was a very tough decision for Yeltsin and the Russian leadership, with potentially profound implications for Russia's political future. The risks of a military operation in Chechnya, including the possibility of major casualties, long-term partisan warfare, and possible terrorist acts in Moscow, were well known in the Kremlin. At the same time, however, Yeltsin needed to demonstrate that he was in charge, particularly after the embarrassment of a failed covert operation against the breakaway republic late in November.
>
> Moreover, this is an extremely delicate time for Yeltsin, who has been compelled to choose between bad options. We need to be particularly careful in any public remarks we might make on the situation. The key point to make, from our perspective, is that while we recognize that the Chechen crisis remains an internal Russian affair, we hope that further violence can be avoided and that a peaceful resolution can still be found. (U.S. State Department cable no. 329213)

The U.S. government decided to support President Yeltsin with the hope that he would curb human rights abuses by the Russian military and seek a political solution, but the crisis escalated. Thousands of Chechen and Russian civilians were killed when Russian forces began shelling Grozny. The Russian human rights commissioner Sergei Kovalev reported that Russian troops were violating human rights on a massive scale in Chechnya and urged international organizations to pressure the Kremlin to bring an end to the air raids.

As the shelling of Grozny continued, President Bill Clinton stated in a speech in Cleveland, Ohio, on 13 January 1995 that the United States should be "patient" and "unwavering" in its support of Russia. In response, the Russian State Duma defense committee chairman Sergei Yushenkov told the U.S. policy planning director James Steinberg in a meeting on 26 January 1995 that he was "astonished" at the U.S. reaction to the Chechen crisis and at what he perceived to be Western complicity in "crimes against humanity" being committed by the Russian government in Chechnya (U.S. State Department cable no. 02935). Yushenkov argued that although both the Russian government and the Dudayev regime were to blame for the conflict, "The Russian government broke a number of international legal norms, particularly the Geneva Convention, for its use of armed force against civilians and its use of prohibited weapons, including cluster bombs and grad-type rocket launchers" (U.S. State Department cable no. 02935). Yushenkov told Steinberg, "These poorly-planned, poorly-prepared actions have already led to the deaths of some twenty thousand Russian citizens and have left hundreds of thousands homeless; this action clearly qualifies as a crime against humankind" (U.S. State Department cable no. 02935). Yushenkov criticized the United States and Germany for what he said was their "silent agreement" with the Russian government's actions in Chechnya. He pointed out that in Russia "only the fascists and extreme nationalists" supported President Yeltsin's policy in Chechnya. Steinberg noted that Russia had the right under the Helsinki Accords to protect its territorial integrity, but he added that "the U.S. also expressed the view that there are limits to the use of force" (U.S. State Department cable no. 02935). Yushenkov (eight years later, on 17 April 2003, assassinated near his home in Moscow) viewed the Kremlin's military campaign in Chechnya as an attempt to curtail democratization in Russia, and he urged the West to speak "loudly and clearly" to the Kremlin to bring an end to the military campaign.

The indiscriminate use of force against civilians in Chechnya continued unabated. As the death toll rose, Russian public opposition to the war increased, fueled by criticism from much of the country's then independent media. The Russian media's coverage of the brutality of the first Chechen war, particularly that of NTV, which was later targeted and taken over by the state, is credited with creating a "CNN effect" in Russia that brought about popular support for negotiations toward an end to the first war. A few Russian journalists, including RFE/RL's well-known reporter Andrei Babitsky, traveled to Chechnya regularly and faced a number of threats from the authorities.

The Kremlin insisted that human rights abuses were not taking place in Chechnya and largely blocked international coverage of the war. The information blockade about events in Chechnya meant that much of international reporting relied heavily on official Russian government statements. A handful of foreign reporters, among them the French journalists Anne Nivat and Sophie Shihab and the British journalists Thomas de Waal, Carlotta Gall, and Anatol Lieven, managed to enter Chechnya during the first war to report extensively on the situation on the ground as events unfolded and to offer independent viewpoints of the war. In addition, human rights organizations and humanitarian aid organizations such as Human Rights Watch (HRW), Doctors without Borders (Médecins sans frontières), and the International Rescue Committee (IRC) produced detailed reports of widespread human rights abuses and urged the international community to speak out.

Human rights reports by international organizations and media coverage of the plight of Chechen civilians were frequently overshadowed by reports of murders and terrorist acts committed by Chechen extremists that gained wider media attention than the daily horrors of the war itself. It became increasingly difficult for human rights advocates to focus international attention on the humanitarian situation and high civilian death toll, or to advocate negotiations toward a political settlement, when policy makers around the world could point to extremist acts as evidence to support the Russian government's claim that it was fighting terrorists in Chechnya.

The murky details surrounding the April 1995 disappearance of the American aid worker Fred Cuny repulsed many policy makers and human rights advocates in the United States. Cuny, who led the INTERTECT Relief and Reconstruction Corporation, first went to Chechnya in February 1995 and spent time meeting with senior rebel Chechen commanders and Russian generals in an effort to arrange a cease-fire and to enable the evacuation of tens of thousands of civilians from Grozny. The facts concerning Cuny's disappearance during his next trip to Chechnya have never been verified, but some allege that Russian security services convinced a group of Chechens that Cuny was working for the Central Intelligence Agency (CIA) and the Chechens killed him. Others surmise that Russian security services killed him because he was too effective at bringing attention to human rights abuses in Chechnya.

On 14 June 1995, the Chechen warlord Shamil Basayev and a group of over eighty separatist fighters seized a hospital in Budennovsk, taking between fifteen hundred and eighteen hundred hostages and demanding that Russia withdraw its troops from Chechnya and hold direct peace talks with Dudayev. President Yeltsin, attending a Group of Seven (G7) meeting in Halifax, Nova Scotia, at the time, ordered Russian troops to storm the hospital. Basayev's group killed at least seven hostages. Russian security forces and troops attempted to storm the hospital several times using gunfire and grenades, killing over one hundred hostages. Participants at the G7 summit condemned the brutality on both sides of the Russo-Chechen conflict. The Canadian prime minister Jean Chrétien publicly urged Yeltsin to call off the military campaign and to find a political solution. With the help of Sergei Kovalev as mediator, Prime Minister Viktor Chernomyrdin and Basayev negotiated a compromise on 18 June: to release most of the remaining hostages, to provide safe passage for Basayev's group back to Chechnya, and to begin a series of negotiations that would bring an end to the war. Peace talks began under the auspices of the Organization for Security and Cooperation in Europe (OSCE) but broke down quickly when both sides were unwilling to make concessions.

In a repeat of the Buddenovsk crisis, the Chechen warlord Salman Raduyev took approximately three thousand hostages at a hospital in Dagestan on 9 January 1996. Numerous civilians died in the resulting assault by Russian forces. A few days later, on 16 January, Chechen terrorists seized a Turkish ferry. The hostage crises brought on a revamped Russian military assault in Chechnya, with Russian officials vowing to deal a decisive blow to further terrorism.

As the 1996 Russian presidential elections approached, Yeltsin feared that an escalation of the Chechen war would hurt his chances of reelection. In April 1996 Dudayev was assassinated by a Russian missile. A few months later, Aslan Maskhadov, a senior Chechen military leader, and Zemelkhan Yandarbiev, the interim Chechen president who succeeded Dudayev, entered into negotiations under OSCE auspices with General Alexander Lebed. The Khasavyurt Peace Accord was signed on 30 August 1996. The agreement called for the withdrawal of most Russian forces from Chechnya.

However, a final resolution of the republic's status was postponed until 2001. Maskhadov was elected president of the Chechen Republic on 27 January 1997, in an election that OSCE observers judged free and fair. In May 1997 Russia and Chechnya reached an accord recognizing Maskhadov as a legitimately elected leader.

The interim years of Chechnya's de facto independence, between the first and second Russo-Chechen wars, were plagued by instability and low-intensity infighting in Chechnya as various political groups and clans vied for influence. Chechnya was not demilitarized after the signing of the Khasavyurt Accord, and the war-torn republic received very little outside assistance for its reconstruction. Most of the funds earmarked in Moscow for Chechnya's reconstruction were siphoned off by corrupt Kremlin officials and never reached the republic. With high unemployment, a lack of resources for rebuilding, a surplus of weapons, and continued infighting, relations between Chechnya and the Kremlin once again reached a boiling point.

SECOND RUSSO-CHECHEN WAR (1999–)

On 7 August 1999 the Chechen warlord Shamil Basayev, Omar Ibn Al Khattāb, and approximately twelve hundred followers invaded Dagestan with the aim of overthrowing its administration and declaring a joint Islamic state with Chechnya. In September two thousand Chechen rebels launched a second invasion of Dagestan. After a series of apartment bombings in Russia shook the country in September 1999, Russian authorities immediately blamed the attacks on Chechen terrorists. The Chechen president Aslan Maskhadov denied any involvement in the Dagestan raids or apartment bombings. The Kremlin considered the Chechen incursions into Dagestan a direct attack on Russia's territorial integrity, and the international community found it difficult to criticize Russia's right to self-defense. Prime Minister Vladimir Putin became the driving force behind renewed air strikes and another ground campaign in Chechnya to quash the insurgency and to redeem the Kremlin in the face of an embarrassing defeat in the first Russo-Chechen war. Putin gained much popularity for his heavy-handed response to the Chechen rebels and was elected Russian president in 2000.

Some observers, including the former KGB counterintelligence officer Alexander Litvinenko who became a vocal Putin critic, alleged that the Kremlin and Russia's Federal Security Service (FSB) orchestrated the apartment bombings as part of a strategy to legitimize a renewed military campaign in Chechnya and to launch Putin to the presidency. (Litvinenko described the alleged plot in *Blowing Up Russia: Terror from Within*, published in 2002.) Litvinenko died from a lethal dose of the radioactive substance polonium-210 on 23 November 2006. Shortly before his death, Litvinenko accused Putin of being responsible for his murder.

The renewed military campaign in Chechnya was even more brutal than the first. Indiscriminate bombings by the Russian military caused the deaths of scores of civilians. Over 200,000 people fled Chechnya to neighboring Ingushetia. Tens of thousands fled to the South Caucasus and to Europe to seek political asylum. Snipers and Chechen rebels attacked Russian troops almost daily. Russian forces regularly tortured, raped, and killed civilians. The Russian military, security services, and pro-Moscow militia routinely conducted security sweeps or "clean-up operations" known as *zachistki*, in which men and boys of fighting age were rounded up and taken away to filtration camps for torture and interrogation, or they were summarily executed. Many people forcefully disappeared during these *zachistki* were later discovered in mass graves near Russian military bases.

In April 2000, concurrent with the passage of a United Nations (UN) Human Rights Commission resolution on Chechnya supported by the United States, the Parliamentary Assembly of the Council of Europe (CoE) moved to suspend Russia's membership in the council and denied voting rights to the Russian delegates in the chamber in response to human rights abuses in Chechnya. The text of the recommendation to suspend Russia's membership in the council cited "disproportionate, indiscriminate" bombing of the civilian population and "daily violations of human rights, including murders." The CoE called for "substantial, accelerating and demonstrable progress" in ending human rights abuses and taking steps toward a peaceful solution in Chechnya. Less than one year later, despite objections from international human rights organizations that argued Russia had not fulfilled its promises to bring human rights violators to justice, or begun a political process to end the violence in Chechnya, the CoE reinstated Russia's voting rights on 25 January 2001.

Wide popular support existed in Russia at the beginning of the second Chechen war, in large part because of the media's now one-sided reporting. Most of the previously independent media had been taken over by the state and favored the official government position that covered up atrocities and reported the successes of Russian troops against Chechen terrorists. Broad legislation such as the law on extremism and new media laws were enacted to muffle critics of the Kremlin. Independent media outlets and journalists who tried to report on the situation found themselves accused of being terrorist sympathizers and were subjected to threats and harsh treatment by the authorities. In one instance, soldiers held the Russian journalist Anna Politkovskaya of the newspaper *Novaya Gazeta* in a pit, subjecting her to a mock execution and threats of rape because of her efforts to expose human rights abuses.

CHECHNYA AND HUMAN RIGHTS AFTER SEPTEMBER 11

When Al Qaeda terrorists attacked the United States on 11 September 2001, President Vladimir Putin was the first world leader to call President George W. Bush to offer his condolences and solidarity. The Kremlin immediately linked its military campaign in Chechnya to the broader war on global terrorism. Russian officials and security services stepped up the rhetoric that Russia was fighting international terrorism in Chechnya and claimed that Chechen rebels were linked to Osama bin Laden. Although such connections were not proven, the media spin was effective in staving off international criticism of human rights abuses and the harsh crackdown on the Chechen population.

In the absence of a political process to end the second Chechen war, more fighters began turning toward fundamentalist Islam. The conflict transformed from a secular, nationalist separatist movement, as it was widely characterized during the first Chechen war, into a movement with more radical and violent extremist elements. The Kremlin's assertion that it was fighting terrorists in Chechnya soon became a self-fulfilling prophesy.

The cycle of violence continued. In October 2002 a group of Chechen rebels led by Movsar Barayev took over the Dubrovka Theater in Moscow with over 750 hostages. The Putin administration wanted to avoid entering into negotiations with the hostage takers at all costs. The terrorists demanded a Russian troop withdrawal from Chechnya in what appeared to be an amateur, repeat attempt of a Buddenovsk-type crisis to induce negotiations toward a settlement of the conflict. Russian Special Forces used an unidentified sedative gas inside the theater to incapacitate the rebels. In doing so, they subjected all hostages to the highly poisonous gas, which killed more than 120 people and caused lasting respiratory problems for hundreds of others. Russian authorities

declared victory, reporting that all 41 terrorists had been killed.

In an effort to turn over the pacification of Chechnya to an indigenous, pro-Moscow leadership, the Kremlin held a referendum in March 2003 on a draft constitution for Chechnya and organized a presidential election that took place in the republic in October of that same year. Akhmad Kadyrov was installed as the Kremlin-backed Chechen president. The policy of "Chechenization" under Kadyrov's leadership was a strategy designed to distance the Kremlin from the conflict and, in effect, transform it into an internal struggle among Chechens. The number of terrorist acts in Russia, suicide bombings, and revenge killings by Chechen extremists continued to increase. In May 2004 Kadyrov was assassinated by a bomb that had been planted under his seat in a stadium. His son Ramzan subsequently gained popularity and the power of the Kremlin's backing while running a brutal militia (the *Kadyrovtsy*) that responded to separatist violence by cracking down on guerrillas and the civilian population with night raids on homes, forced disappearances, torture, and extrajudicial killings. In March 2007 Ramzan Kadyrov became the Kremlin-backed Chechen president.

On 1 September 2004 a group of terrorists primarily from Ingushetia, Chechnya, and Dagestan seized one thousand hostages at School No. 1 in Beslan, North Ossetia. There is some skepticism about who orchestrated the attack, but the Chechen warlord Shamil Basayev claimed responsibility. The hostage takers shot several people and did not permit the hostages to have food or water. On 3 September then Chechen president Aslan Maskhadov, denying any involvement in the planning of the siege, offered to go to Beslan to negotiate the release of the hostages. The journalist Anna Politkovskaya also offered to help negotiate the release of hostages, but she fell unconscious on the plane from Moscow to Beslan after drinking a cup of tea that she later said had likely been poisoned by Russian security services. Politkovskaya regained consciousness in a clinic in Rostov-on-Don. Contrary to later eyewitness accounts from survivors of the school siege, the Russian official media reported that the rebels in the school did not want to negotiate. Shortly after Maskhadov offered to help negotiate the release of hostages, Russian forces stormed the school. Exactly 332 people, including 186 children, died in the school attack. Ambulances and the fire department were not called to the scene for two hours after a fire broke out in the school gymnasium; eventually, its roof collapsed and 160 people burned to death. Controversy surrounds whether one of the terrorists in the gymnasium ignited the fire that caused the roof to collapse, or if Russian Special Forces ignited the fire with flamethrowers and grenades. Authorities reportedly bribed and intimidated witnesses who expressed views differing from the official version of events, and several independent investigators of the tragedy have been threatened and given harsh treatment in the years since.

In response to the rising threat of terrorism in Russia, in 2002 the State Duma enacted the Federal Law on Counteracting Extremist Activity, which prohibits the advocacy of "extreme" political positions. More significant, it also allows authorities to suspend the activities of civic or religious organizations and political parties if their activities are deemed to be undermining the security or integrity of the Russian Federation, carrying out terrorist activity, or inciting social, racial, nationalistic, or religious animosity. Rights groups and international organizations criticized the law for its vague definition of "extremist activity," which created the possibility of arbitrary enforcement against those who express views challenging government policy, particularly concerning human rights and the North Caucasus. In July 2006 amendments further broadened its definition of extremism, making the law a more effective tool to curtail the rights and freedoms of the media, nongovernmental organizations (NGOs), and individuals.

Hand in hand with the counter-extremism law, in November 2005 the Russian State Duma introduced legislation titled "On Introducing Amendments to Certain Legislative Acts of the Russian Federation," which would require NGOs to reregister and adhere to extensive reporting requirements or face liquidation. The law, which went into effect on 16 April 2006, allows Russian security services to attend any event or meeting convened by any civic or religious organization, thereby allowing intensive monitoring of the organization and pressure from the authorities if they view the subject matter of an activity or meeting as too critical of, or politically sensitive to, the state.

In 2005 Stanislav Dmitrievsky, the managing director of the Russian-Chechen Friendship Society and editor of the newspaper *Pravozaschita* (Human Rights Defense), was accused by the Russian government of "inciting extremism" under the counter-extremism law for publishing two articles written by the Chechen separatist leadership in late 2004. The first article, written by the separatist president Maskhadov, was an appeal to the European Parliament to designate the violence in

Chechnya as "genocide" and urged international support for peace talks. The second article, by Maskhadov's representative in London, Akhmed Zakayev, called on Russian citizens to oppose the war in Chechnya and to not reelect Putin in the 2004 presidential elections. On 3 February 2006 Dmitrievsky was convicted of "inciting ethnic hatred" and sentenced to four years of probation (house arrest) and a two-year suspended sentence. The Russian-Chechen Friendship Society, based in Nizhny Novgorod, was a prominent human rights watchdog organization that sought to bring reconciliation between Chechens and Russians and worked to investigate arbitrary arrests, beatings, rapes, forced disappearances, killings, and other human rights abuses by exposing them to a wide audience in *Pravozaschita*. Citing the counter-extremism law and the NGO law, the Nizhny Novgorod Regional Court decided to shut down the Russian-Chechen Friendship Society on 13 October 2006, in the immediate aftermath of the 7 October slaying of Anna Politkovskaya, the Russian journalist whose murder the organization was investigating. In an interview with *Novaya Gazeta* on 24 October, Dmitrievsky revealed that the Russian-Chechen Friendship Society and Politkovskaya, who had been working on an article about torture committed by the pro-Kremlin Chechen leadership at the time of her murder, were laying the legal groundwork for the creation of an international tribunal on war crimes and crimes against humanity in Chechnya.

The assassination of President Maskhadov in March 2005 came at the height of international discussions about the possibility of peace talks. Maskhadov was widely viewed as a moderate leader who repeatedly called for unconditional peace talks and enjoyed popular support among moderate Chechens as well as many international NGOs seeking to promote a political solution to the war. Maskhadov's assassination diminished the prospects for peace in the North Caucasus. His successor, Abdul-Khalim Sadulayev, survived a little over a year as Chechen president before being shot in a battle between pro-Kremlin Chechen forces and Russian security services. During his term of office, Sadulayev ruled out the possibility of negotiations with the Russian government and called for the unification of rebel forces outside Chechnya to join the fight against Russia. A month after Sadulayev's death, on 10 July 2006, the Chechen extremist Shamil Basayev was killed in an explosion in Ingushetia. Some observers surmised that Basayev's death would lead to the eventual normalization of the situation in the North Caucasus, but fighting spread to Ingushetia where tensions continue to rise. Sadulayev's successor, Doku Umarov, abolished the Chechen separatist presidency in October 2007 and proclaimed himself the emir of a new Caucasus emirate to include other North Caucasus republics. Human rights and democracy defenders have become alarmed by Umarov's extremist statements, statements that demonize Western influences and models of government and express solidarity with Muslim brotherhoods:

> Today in Afghanistan, Iraq, Somalia, Palestine our brothers are fighting. Everyone who attacked Muslims wherever they are, are our enemies, common enemies. Our enemy is not Rusnya [Russia] only, but everyone who wages war against Islam and Muslims. And they are our enemies mainly because they are the enemies of Allah. (Kavkaz Center Web site)

Such rhetoric is an ominous departure from the approach of previous Chechen rebel leaders.

In spite of setbacks to peace and challenges to promoting human rights and justice for victims of atrocities in the Russo-Chechen wars, a few major breakthroughs have occurred. As of June 2008, the European Court of Human Rights had found Russia responsible in thirty-one rulings for serious human rights abuses, including torture, forced disappearances, and extrajudicial executions (http://www. hrw.org/campaigns/russia/russiatrial/). The following are illustrative case examples: In February 2005, October–November 2006, and January 2007 the European Court found Russia guilty of serious human rights abuses and in violation of several articles of the European Convention on Human Rights and Fundamental Freedoms (ECHR). The ruling in February 2005, which found that Russia had indiscriminately targeted civilians, used disproportionate force in military operations, and failed to adequately investigate civilian deaths, was the first international ruling addressing abuses committed by the Russian government during the course of the two Russo-Chechen wars. The European Court ruled on behalf of three Chechen families whose members had been tortured or killed in aerial bombings by Russian forces. In an October 2006 ruling, the European Court found the Russian government guilty of the summary execution of five Chechen civilians in the Estamirov family, including a pregnant woman and a baby, in February 2000. The Court ordered Russia to compensate the Estamirov family with more than $250,000 in damages. Human Rights Watch, Amnesty International, the Russian human rights organization Memorial, and other groups have reported that Russian government forces continue to harass those who have filed applications with the European Court to intimidate them into dropping their cases. At least five applicants to the Court have been killed or forcefully disappeared.

Apart from a few successes in support of human rights in Chechnya, such as the above-mentioned rulings of the European Court as well as the efforts of the CoE in 2000 to suspend Russia's voting rights and to hold the Russian government accountable for its policies, the international community has largely turned a blind eye to human rights abuses in Chechnya. The former U.S. national security adviser Zbigniew Brzezinski, co-chair of the American Committee for Peace in the Caucasus in Washington, D. C., stated that the Chechens have been the third most persecuted people of the last century, with their abuse involving unprecedented cruelty:

> [I]f one considers the fact that in 1944, after 100 years of repression, they were chosen to be eliminated as a nation, which means uprooted from their soil and deported in the midst of a cold winter to an alien territory, in the process of which half of them, almost, died—men, women, and children— it closely approximates what happened to the Jews and the Gypsies, even in terms of statistical proportions. Roughly one-half of the population perished. And since the 1990s, how many more have died? We hear different estimates. But, by and large, I think there is consensus that probably somewhere in the range of a quarter of the total died—not by accident, not by earthquakes, not by climatically induced starvation, but from the hands of others, deliberately. (American Enterprise Institute, *Catastrophe in Chechnya*)

SUMMARY

In the first Russo-Chechen war, the international community decided not to take action beyond cautious criticism of human rights abuses because of pervasive fears that a successful Chechen secession might mean that other ethnic groups with separatist aspirations in Russia would follow suit and that nuclear weapons might end up in their hands. Western governments thus limited themselves to vague, rhetorical support for a "political solution to the conflict and an end to human rights abuses" without pressing specifically for peace talks with moderate Chechen leaders. It was not in the national interests of the United States or other Western governments to appear to support Chechen separatists. The U.S. government decided early on that a more aggressive policy such as economic sanctions, stronger public criticism of human rights abuses, or explicit language to support peace talks would be counterproductive to supporting

President Boris Yeltsin, a policy that they saw as synonymous with promoting democratic and economic reforms in Russia. The general policy was to treat the crisis in Chechnya as "Russia's internal affair." It became clearer over time that it was the silence over Chechnya that was counterproductive to reforms.

Once the United States and other governments had adopted a hands-off policy on Chechnya, it became increasingly difficult to change their position, in part because the Russian government's argument that it was fighting terrorists in Chechnya became a self-fulfilling prophesy as the fighting continued and different factions became more polarized and radicalized. In the post-9/11 climate, the Russian government justified its military campaign in Chechnya by equating it with the global war on terror and met little resistance from the international community. When the war in Iraq began in 2003, the United States found it even more difficult to challenge Putin on the military campaign in Chechnya because the Russian president would retort with criticism of double standards.

Russian forces, the pro-Kremlin Chechen leadership under Ramzan Kadyrov, and Chechen rebel forces continue to commit human rights abuses in Chechnya, and the violence has spread to Ingushetia. In an atmosphere of growing intolerance espoused by both the Russian and Chechen sides of the war, there is little expectation that the human rights situation in the North Caucasus will improve in the near future. Human rights defenders in Russia and critics of the Kremlin are constantly under threat. The apparent contract killing of Anna Politkovskaya on 7 October 2006 and the radioactive poisoning of Alexander Litvinenko in November 2006, irrespective of who may be behind the murders, signaled a dramatic retreat to a dark Stalinist past. The extremist statements of Chechen rebel leader Doku Umarov in late 2007 and early 2008 only indicate that the Russo-Chechen quagmire could worsen. Still, human rights defenders must do what they can to help civilians caught in the middle of the conflict and to seek justice for victims of human rights abuses.

[*See also* Russia; Andrei Sakharov; Demise of Soviet Communism; *and* Joseph Stalin.]

BIBLIOGRAPHY

American Committee for Peace in the Caucasus. *Ingushetia: Trends behind the Recent Violence: Interview with Eliza Musaeva and Tanya Lokshina.* Interview conducted by Iva Savic, October 28, 2007. http://peaceinthecaucasus.org/PDF%20and%20Audio%20files/Eliza%20Musaeva%20and%20Tanya%20Lokshina%20Interview.html

American Enterprise Institute for Public Policy Research. *Catastrophe in Chechnya: Escaping the Quagmire.* Transcript of conference held December 10, 2003.

Amnesty International. *Russia.* http://www.amnesty.org/en/region/europe-and-central-asia/eastern-europe/russia.

Anderson, Scott. *The Man Who Tried to Save the World: The Dangerous Life and Mysterious Disappearance of Fred Cuny.* New York: Doubleday, 1999.

Baiev, Khassan, with Ruth Daniloff and Nicholas Daniloff. *The Oath: A Surgeon under Fire.* New York: Walker & Company, 2003.

Bennigsen, Alexandre, and S. Enders Wimbush. *Mystics and Commissars: Sufism in the Soviet Union.* Berkeley: University of California Press, 1985.

Chechnya Advocacy Network. http://www.chechnyaadvocacy.org/. Web site with links to information about the conflict.

Dunlop, John B. "How Many Soldiers and Civilians Died during the Russo-Chechen War of 1994–1996?" *Central Asian Survey* 19, no. 3/4 (2000): 329–339.

Dunlop, John B. *Russia Confronts Chechnya: Roots of a Separatist Conflict.* Cambridge, U.K.: Cambridge University Press, 1998.

Dunlop, John, B. *The 2002 Dubrovka and 2004 Beslan Hostage Crises: A Critique of Russian Counter-Terrorism.* Stuttgart, Germany: Ibidem-Verlag, 2006.

Evangelista, Matthew. *The Chechen Wars: Will Russia Go the Way of the Soviet Union?* Washington, D.C.: Brookings Institution Press, 2002.

Gall, Carlotta, and Thomas de Waal. *Chechnya: Calamity in the Caucasus.* New York: New York University Press, 1998.

Human Rights Watch. *Justice for Chechnya: The European Court of Human Rights Rules against Russia.* July 2007. http://www.hrw.org/eca/2007/justice_for_chechnya.pdf.

Human Rights Watch. *Russia.* http://hrw.org/doc/?t=europe&c=russia. Web page with links to HRW press releases, briefings, and commentary.

International Center for Not-for-Profit Law. "The Russian NGO Law: Potential Conflicts with International, National, and Foreign Legislation." *International Journal of Not-for-Profit Law* 9, no. 1 (December 2006). http://www.icnl.org/knowledge/ijnl/vol9iss1/art_6.htm.

International Helsinki Federation for Human Rights. *Unofficial Places of Detention in the Chechen Republic.* May 15, 2006. http://www.ihf-hr.org/documents/doc_summary.php?sec_id=58&d_id=4249

Kavkaz Center. *The Official Version of Amir Dokka's Statement of Declaration of the Caucasian Emirate.* November 22, 2007. http://www.kavkazcenter.com/eng/content/2007/11/22/9107.shtml.

Lanskoy, Miriam. "Chechnya's Internal Fragmentation, 1996–1999." *Fletcher Forum of World Affairs* 27, no. 2 (Summer/Fall 2003): 185–205.

Lieven, Anatol. *Chechnya: Tombstone of Russian Power.* New Haven, Conn.: Yale University Press, 1998.

Litvinovich, Marina. *The Truth about Beslan.* Pravda Beslana Web site, August 28, 2006. http://www.pravdabeslana.ru/truth.htm.

McFaul, Michael. "U.S. Foreign Policy and Chechnya: A Joint Project on Domestic Politics and America's Russia Policy." Washington, D.C., Twentieth Century Foundation and Stanley Foundation, March 2003.

McFaul, Michael, and Sanja Tatic. "Russia." In *Countries at the Crossroads: A Survey of Democratic Governance*, edited by Sarah Repucci and Christopher Walker, pp. 465–491. New York: Freedom House, 2005.

Memorial Human Rights Center. *Human Rights Work of Memorial.* http://www.memo.ru/eng/memhrc/index.shtml.

Mendelson, Sarah. "Anatomy of Ambivalence: The International Community and Human Rights Abuse in the North Caucasus." *Problems of Post-Communism*, November/December 2006. An abstract of this article is available at http://www.reliefweb.int/rw/rwb.nsf/db900sid/RMOI-6H63L2?OpenDocument&Click=, where there is also a link to a PDF file of the full text.

Nichol, Jim. "Bringing Peace to Chechnya? Assessments and Implications." Washington, D.C., Congressional Research Services, March 31, 2006. Available through Penny Hill Press (hard copy) and online at http://www.italy.usembassy.gov/pdf/other/RL32272.pdf.

Nichol, Jim. "Renewed Chechnya Conflict: Developments in 1999–2000." Washington, D.C., Congressional Research Services, May 3, 2000. Available through Penny Hill Press.

Nichol, Jim. "Russian Conflict in Chechnya and Implications for the United States." Washington, D.C., Congressional Research Services, January 24, 1995. Available through Penny Hill Press.

Nichols, Johanna. "Who Are the Chechen?" *Linguist List* 6–22, January 13, 1995, ISSN 1068-4875. http://www.hartford-hwp.com/archives/63/077.html.

Orttung, Robert W. "Russia." In *Nations in Transit*, edited by Jeannette Goehring, John Ewing, Eileen G. P. Brown, and Jeremy Druker, pp. 485–505. New York: Freedom House, 2006. http://freedomhouse.org/template.cfm?page=47&nit=406&year=2006.

Piano, Aili, Arch Puddington, and Mark Y. Rosenberg, eds. "Chechnya [Russia]." In *Freedom in the World: The Annual Survey of Political Rights & Civil Liberties*. New York: Freedom House, 2006. http://www.freedomhouse.org/template.cfm?page=22&year=2006&country=7108.

Politkovskaya, Anna. *A Dirty War: A Russian Reporter in Chechnya.* Translated by John Crowfoot. London: Harvill Press, 2001.

Talbott, Strobe. *The Russia Hand: A Memoir of Presidential Diplomacy.* New York: Random House, 2002.

United States Department of State. *Russia: Country Reports on Human Rights Practices (2005).* http://www.state.gov/g/drl/rls/hrrpt/2005/61671.htm.

United States Department of State. "Russian Duma Defense Committee Chairman Denounces U.S. 'Silence' on Chechnya." Cable no. 02935, January 30, 1995.

United States Department of State. "Russian Troops Move into Chechnya." Cable no. 329213, December 11, 1994.

CHILDREN'S CONVENTION
(CONVENTION ON THE RIGHTS OF THE CHILD)

by Samantha Besson and Joanna Bourke-Martignoni

The 1989 United Nations Convention on the Rights of the Child (CRC, sometimes abbreviated as UNCRC) has been widely acclaimed as the first truly comprehensive international human rights instrument. Its inclusion of civil, political, economic, social, and cultural rights within the same text; the fact that it focuses on the "private" sphere of the family alongside the "public" sphere of state activity; as well as the rapidity and extent of its ratification are used to support the assertion that the CRC is a quasi-universal legal instrument in terms of both its thematic and geographic reach.

The United Nations Committee on the Rights of the Child, the specialized UN agencies and procedures with a mandate over children's rights issues, and certain civil society organizations act as the primary monitors of the implementation of the Convention and its two Optional Protocols. Although the process of international monitoring aims to provide a benchmark against which states are expected to monitor and adjust their own performance with respect to the realization of children's rights at the national level, in practice states appear to be more concerned with accountability on the international level. Unlike most of the other core international human rights treaties, the CRC does not allow complaints from individuals alleging violations of their Convention rights to be addressed to the Committee on the Rights of the Child.

This entry will briefly outline the history of children's rights within international law before going on to examine the development of the CRC and the work of the mechanisms established to monitor its implementation.

HISTORY AND DEVELOPMENT

The history of normative instruments for the protection of children's rights at the international level can be traced to the early part of the twentieth century and the work on international conventions prohibiting human trafficking, slavery, and exploitative labor. Following a proposal and intensive lobbying by the nongovernmental coalition Save the Children International Union, in 1924 the League of Nations adopted a Declaration of the Rights of the Child. The Declaration contained five principles, including the obligation to protect children from exploitation and the notion that children should be the first to receive assistance in times of distress.

In 1959 the United Nations General Assembly adopted a slightly more detailed Declaration of the Rights of the Child that enumerated ten principles and exhorted parents, individuals, voluntary organizations, and local and national authorities to strive to observe the principles through the implementation of legislative and other measures.

Despite their stated focus on the rights of children as bearers of human rights, these early instruments took an essentially protective and charitable approach. Throughout the 1970s there was increasing discussion surrounding the need to formulate a binding international convention that would draw together, harmonize, and update existing standards in line with new thinking on the status of children. Although the human rights of children are clearly covered by the existing international human rights instruments, it was widely felt that the rights of children should be encapsulated within a specific convention in order to reflect the relatively recent view of children as subjects of specific rights and to adequately respond to the particular vulnerability of children to abuses of their general and specific human rights. There was, however, some measure of fear that the creation of a new convention dealing exclusively with children's rights would lead to the ongoing marginalization of these issues within the United Nations human rights system. In the end, it was the advocates of a specific child rights convention who were successful in persuading the international community that such a step was necessary in order to ensure the promotion and protection of children's rights.

DRAFTING PROCESS

The original draft of a convention on children's rights was presented to the UN Human Rights Commission by the Polish representative in 1978 as part of the preparation for the International Year of the Child in 1979. The initial text was virtually a copy of the 1959 Declaration with the addition of a monitoring body that was granted only very limited powers. The commission felt that it was necessary to substantially rework the proposal in order to develop an effective international treaty that adequately reflected contemporary ideas about children's rights. A working group consisting of members of the commission was then established to further develop the text into a binding international convention. After many years of negotiation, the working group submitted the final draft of the Convention on the Rights of the Child to the Commission on Human Rights and then to the UN General Assembly in 1989.

An important feature of the drafting process for the CRC was that nongovernmental organizations (NGOs) were closely involved in the development of the text, so that by the time the Convention was actually close to adoption, these organizations had forged strong collaborative relationships not only among themselves but also with government delegations and with specialized agencies such as the United Nations Children's Fund (UNICEF). The involvement of NGOs was largely responsible for the attitude that the implementation of the CRC should occur on the basis of constructive dialogue and have as its hallmarks mutual assistance, support, and cooperation, rather than confrontation. For this reason, the work of the Committee on the Rights of the Child is understood as being advisory in nature as well as performing the function of monitoring the implementation of the Convention. As will be seen below, civil society organizations continue to play a particularly important role in the implementation and monitoring of the CRC.

ADOPTION, RATIFICATIONS, AND ENTRY INTO FORCE

The CRC was adopted by the General Assembly of the United Nations on 20 November 1989, and it entered into force on 2 September 1990. The rapidity with which the instrument gained the twenty ratifications necessary for it to enter into force is unparalleled by the other human rights instruments that have been adopted under the auspices of the UN.

With its 193 ratifications, the CRC is the international human rights instrument with the largest number of parties. Some commentators have observed that the ratification of the Convention has had important follow-on effects, in that many countries that became parties to a multilateral human rights treaty for the first time by virtue of their ratification of the CRC have since gone on to ratify other UN human rights treaties. The rapidity with which some states managed to take the internal legislative and administrative steps needed prior to ratification of the Convention has, however, led to a questioning of the sincerity of the commitment to children's rights in certain ratifying countries as well as to queries about the thoroughness with which the necessary pre-ratification preparatory work was undertaken.

The ratifications by states parties to the CRC have in many cases been qualified by general or specific reservations to its text. The number of reservations to the Convention is partly attributable to the fact that there are more states parties to the CRC than to any other human rights treaty and partly to the subject matter of the Convention, dealing as it does with the "private" sphere of family relations. Reservations, declarations, or statements may be made by states parties in order to exclude or modify the application of one or more provisions of a treaty, thereby limiting the scope of that state's obligations under the instrument. Under Article 51, paragraph 2, of the CRC as well as according to international rules governing the interpretation of treaties, reservations that are "incompatible with the object and purpose" of a treaty shall not be permitted. Several states have made general unilateral statements to the effect that the Convention is to be interpreted in light of religious laws and values or in accordance with their national legislation. Other parties have made extensive reservations to specific articles of the CRC, in particular to Article 1 on the age at which childhood begins and ends, on Article 21 in relation to adoption, and on Article 38 concerning the age limit for participation in armed conflict.

While some states parties have lodged objections against the wide-ranging nature of some of the reservations made to the CRC, the legal effect of these objections is not entirely clear. The Committee on the Rights of the Child, in its General Comment No. 5 (2003) (see below), notes that the aim of "ensuring full and unqualified respect for the human rights of children can be achieved only if States withdraw their reservations." To this end, the committee has successfully persuaded many states parties to remove their reservations to the CRC, in particular regarding the relationship between religious laws and the Convention and concerning Article 21. The overall objective of the dialogue between the states parties and the committee with respect to reservations is the achievement of universal ratification, not only in terms of the number of parties but also with regard to the substantive application of the rights contained in the Convention.

The generality of some of the reservations made to the CRC could be used as an indication that the consensus concerning children's rights is not, in fact, as solid as it first appears. On the other hand, it has been suggested that ratification should be regarded as the first step in a process of increasing compliance and that the impact of reservations upon ratification may be remedied by engaging the states concerned in a dialogue about the ways in which the obstacles to full implementation could be removed.

OPTIONAL PROTOCOLS TO THE CONVENTION

On 25 May 2000 the UN General Assembly adopted two thematic Optional Protocols to the CRC. The Optional Protocol on the Involvement of Children in Armed Conflict and the Optional Protocol on the Sale of Children, Child Prostitution, and Child Pornography both entered into force in 2002.

The protocols create additional reporting obligations for states parties in that they are required to submit initial reports within two years of ratification and periodic reports at intervals of every five years thereafter. The reports are considered by the Committee on the Rights of the Child. Unlike most of the other core UN human rights treaties, there is no provision made within the Optional Protocols to allow for individual petitions alleging violations of these instruments to be brought before the committee.

The Optional Protocols are fairly similar in structure and, interestingly, provide the possibility for states that have signed but not ratified the CRC to become parties. In this way, the United States, which is not a party to the Convention, has ratified both of the Optional Protocols and is therefore required to submit periodic reports on their implementation.

PROVISIONS OF THE CRC RELATING TO IMPLEMENTATION AND MONITORING

Article 4 of the Convention specifies that states have obligations to undertake "all appropriate legislative, administrative and other measures" to ensure its implementation. The committee has interpreted Article 4 as requiring states to carry out a wide range of administrative, legislative, judicial, and other measures to give effect to the CRC; some of these requirements will be discussed in more detail below. Articles 42 and 44 of the Convention specify that states have obligations to raise awareness of the Convention and its provisions among children and adults.

As with other international human rights treaties, the CRC does not formally oblige states to directly incorporate its provisions within their national legal framework. It is clear, however, from the committee's General Comment No. 5 (2003) that it regards the justiciability of Convention rights at the national level and, in particular, the creation of child-sensitive procedures and remedies as essential steps in ensuring the full implementation of the CRC.

The idea that states have positive obligations to adopt domestic measures concerning the acts of private parties is also one that is apparent from the text of the CRC, and it is a notion that has been made explicit in the General Guidelines Regarding the Form and Contents of Periodic Reports (reporting guidelines) that have been drafted by the Committee on the Rights of the Child (see below). For example, the reporting guidelines request that states provide information about the steps that they have taken to prevent and respond to instances of abuse and neglect of children by caregivers. The "indirect horizontal effect" of the CRC, in that it indirectly governs relationships between individuals at the national level as a result of the positive duties it places on the states parties, is one of the features of the Convention that has been widely acclaimed.

With regard to economic, social, and cultural rights, Article 4 of the Convention states that "States Parties shall undertake such measures to the maximum extent of their available resources and, where needed, within the framework of international co-operation." This phrase is similar to the concept of "progressive realization" contained in the International Covenant on Economic, Social, and Cultural Rights. While it would appear on the face of it that resource-poor countries are somehow under a lesser obligation to ensure implementation of economic, social, and cultural rights, the Committee on Economic, Social, and Cultural Rights in its General Comment No. 3 (1990) emphasized that states nevertheless have obligations to "strive to ensure the widest possible enjoyment of the relevant rights under the prevailing circumstances." The

Committee on the Rights of the Child reiterates this point in its General Comment No. 5 (2003) where it provides that "whatever their economic circumstances, States are required to undertake all possible measures towards the realization of the rights of the child, paying special attention to the most disadvantaged groups."

Article 43 of the CRC creates the Committee on the Rights of the Child as the main monitoring mechanism for its implementation. The work of the committee will be discussed in more detail below. Furthermore, the CRC explicitly mentions the role that is to be played by the specialized agencies of the UN, and UNICEF in particular, with regard to fostering the effective implementation of the Convention and ensuring international cooperation for this purpose.

The mechanisms established by the CRC focus on monitoring the overall implementation of the Convention at the national level rather than on individual cases or the violation of specific rights. For this reason, the monitoring process under the CRC is continuous as well as systemic as it aims to evaluate the extent to which the rights contained in the Convention are actually being implemented by states parties.

THE COMMITTEE ON THE RIGHTS OF THE CHILD

The Committee on the Rights of the Child is established under Article 43 of the CRC for the purposes of "examining the progress made by States Parties in achieving the realization of the obligations" undertaken in the Convention. As previously mentioned, the process of reporting by the states parties to the CRC is the primary mechanism through which the national implementation of the Convention's provisions is assessed and monitored. The Committee on the Rights of the Child develops its own rules of procedure and working methods; some of the most salient aspects of these will be outlined in greater detail below. In general, however, the working methods and procedures used by the committee do not differ greatly from those of the other UN human rights treaty bodies.

Article 43 lays out the modalities of functioning of the Committee on the Rights of the Child and provides that its members "shall be elected by States Parties from among their nationals and shall serve in their personal capacity, consideration being given to equitable geographical distribution, as well as to the principal legal systems." The committee members come from a variety of disciplinary backgrounds: lawyers, judges, social workers, psychologists, development economists, doctors, teachers, and children's rights activists. Members also have very different backgrounds and levels of experience in relation to children's rights issues. The process of election, depending as it does upon largely political factors, is open to criticism because considerations of merit may sometimes be secondary to other objectives.

The committee was initially composed of ten individual experts. However, its membership was increased to eighteen in 2003 following recognition that more resources were required to keep pace with the volume of reports being received from the 193 states parties. The committee made a further attempt to deal with the reporting backlog during 2006 when it sat in two chambers, each composed of nine committee members. The delay in reviewing reports is a testament to the fact that the Convention is in some ways a victim of its own success, as the other human rights treaty bodies consider fewer state reports.

Future developments in relation to the proposed reform of the UN treaty body system will almost certainly have a significant impact upon the working methods of the Committee on the Rights of the Child and therefore upon the monitoring and interpretation of the CRC itself. The effects of these systemic changes on the implementation and monitoring of children's rights remain to be seen, however; there is some degree of reticence to these changes among the members of the Committee on the Rights of the Child as well as among a number of civil society organizations, who fear that children's rights may become further marginalized if they are considered together with other human rights issues.

The system of periodic reporting.

Article 44 of the CRC describes the periodic reporting system and provides that states are to submit an initial report on the measures they have adopted to give effect to the rights in the Convention within two years of ratification. States parties are required to report every five years thereafter. The form and content of the periodic reports are governed by the reporting guidelines, which were first issued in 1991 and updated in 1996 and again in 2005. The reporting guidelines provide that reports "must strike a balance in describing the formal legal situation and the situation in practice," and the committee therefore requires information on follow-up, monitoring, resource allocation, statistical data, and challenges to implementation. The reporting guidelines group the substantive Convention rights into clusters: general measures of implementation;

definition of the child; general principles; civil rights and freedoms; family environment and alternative care; basic health and welfare; education, leisure, and cultural activities; and special protection measures.

The concept of "general principles" developed within the reporting guidelines is an idea that is unique to the CRC. The committee has identified Articles 2 (nondiscrimination), 3 (best interests of the child), 6 (right to life, survival, and development), and 12 (respect for the views of the child) as being provisions that are essential to the consideration of each of the rights contained in the Convention. The general principles may be regarded as improving the clarity and focus of state reporting by virtue of the fact that they must be taken into consideration in relation to each of the other rights in the Convention.

On the other hand, there is a risk that deriving general principles that regroup rights contained in different parts of the Convention will lead to "front loading," whereby all of the information that would previously have been considered under the other substantive provisions of the CRC is moved to the beginning of the report. Related to this problem is the concern that by listing certain crosscutting principles, the committee has created a hierarchy of norms within the Convention. Finally, the process through which the general principles were developed and the criteria upon which they are based are not clear, a situation that is problematic given that this decision by the committee has far-reaching effects upon both the structure and content of state reports and the interpretation of the Convention.

The reporting cycle.

The Committee on the Rights of the Child meets in Geneva and normally holds three month-long sessions per year, which are each divided into a three-week plenary session and a one-week pre-sessional working group.

The reporting cycle consists of a review of reports by a working group of the committee, which generally meets in closed session for one week immediately following the previous committee session. The pre-sessional working group decides on a list of issues that is sent to the state as a preliminary indication of the questions that the committee feels should be priorities for discussion at the plenary session. This provides the committee with the opportunity to request additional or updated information in writing from the government, and it enables the state to better prepare itself for the consideration of the report, which generally occurs three to four months after the working group meeting.

One of the major benefits of the working group system is that it permits NGOs to become actively involved in the reporting process. The committee has adopted guidelines to encourage written submissions to the pre-sessional working group from NGOs, and these must be sent to the secretariat of the committee at least two months prior to the pre-sessional meeting. This process allows the committee to compare the information received from civil society organizations with the state report, and based on the written submissions, NGOs are invited to attend the pre-sessional working group. The pre-sessional working group system has, however, been criticized by NGOs that argue that there is only very limited time for discussion during the week-long meeting.

The next phase in the reporting cycle is the consideration of the report in an open, public plenary session, during the course of which members of the state delegation and committee members take the floor. On average, the committee considers nine reports during each three-week session and devotes one day to its public examination of each report as well as two to three additional hours in closed session to discuss its concluding observations for the country. In order to increase the efficiency of the process, the committee has begun appointing two of its members to act as country rapporteurs to lead the discussion on each country report.

Following the dialogue with the state party, the committee meets to discuss its concluding observations, which include both suggestions and recommendations. In general, the concluding observations are structured as follows: introduction, positive aspects, factors and difficulties impeding implementation, principal subjects of concern, suggestions, and recommendations. The observations are made public on the last day of the committee session and are adopted along with the session report. In its reporting guidelines, the committee notes that it is important that states parties make the committee's concluding observations widely available at the national level and that this is in keeping with the spirit of Article 44, paragraph 6, of the CRC.

Follow-up mechanisms.

In general, the formal mechanisms for following up on state reports remain quite limited. It is assumed that the concerns expressed by the committee in its concluding observations will be addressed in a detailed manner by the state party in its subsequent periodic report.

The committee may transmit state reports that contain requests or identify a need for technical advice or assistance on particular issues to relevant agencies and bodies such as UNICEF, the International Labour Organization (ILO), the United Nations Educational, Scientific, and Cultural Organization (UNESCO), the World Health Organization (WHO), the Office of the United Nations High Commissioner for Refugees (UNHCR), and the Office of the High Commissioner for Human Rights (OHCHR). The technical advice could relate to the reporting process itself or could be focused on substantive issues connected to the implementation of Convention rights.

Since 2003 the Treaties and Council branch of the OHCHR has organized several regional and subregional workshops on the implementation of the committee's concluding observations. Also, at the end of 2003 the committee reinstated the practice of making informal visits to states parties with a view to either assisting with the follow-up to its concluding observations or with the preparation of upcoming periodic reports.

General Comments and interpretation of the Convention.

The increasing activism of the Committee on the Rights of the Child is apparent from the number of general comments and thematic recommendations (decisions) that it has adopted in order to assist states and other bodies charged with the implementation of the Convention.

During the first ten years of the committee's existence, no general comments were drafted. Between 2001 and 2003, however, the committee adopted five general comments and since 2003 it has adopted a further five interpretive general comments. These comments cover issues ranging from the aims of education, to the role of independent national human rights institutions in the promotion of children's rights, to HIV/AIDS, adolescent health and development, the treatment of unaccompanied and separated children outside their country of origin, early childhood, corporal punishment, the rights of children with disabilities, and juvenile justice.

General Comment No. 5 (2003), which focuses on general measures of implementation of the Convention, specifies the steps that states parties need to take in order to fulfill their obligations under the CRC. These include a range of judicial, legislative, and administrative measures, such as the removal of reservations to the CRC, ensuring the justiciability of children's rights within national law, the development of comprehensive national action plans on children, conducting child impact assessments and evaluations, improving data collection and analysis, making children visible in budgets, increasing capacity on

children's rights through training, and improving coordination and cooperation on children's rights at the national and international levels.

The legitimacy of the committee's role in adopting authoritative interpretations of the Convention through the use of general comments and recommendations is perhaps less open to question than the process of deriving general principles from the text as described above. Article 45(d) of the CRC itself provides the committee with a broad mandate to make "general recommendations" to states. Nevertheless, the process of adoption of general comments, including the order of priority in which issues are identified as being ripe for interpretation and the use of external consultants and agencies as the lead drafters for particular comments, may give rise to queries surrounding the transparency and legitimacy of the procedure.

Thematic studies and general days of discussion.

Each year since 1992, the Committee on the Rights of the Child has held a general day of discussion on specific Convention provisions or on related issues. These general days of discussion are public meetings, open to delegates from states parties, UN agencies and bodies, NGOs, national human rights institutions, professional bodies, youth groups, researchers, and other interested persons. The discussion leads to recommendations being adopted and, in many cases, these recommendations form the basis for a general comment on a particular issue.

The general days of discussion on children in armed conflict (1992) and on children and violence (2000 and 2001) resulted in recommendations being made to the UN General Assembly under Article 45(c) of the CRC requesting that the UN secretary-general undertake studies on these themes. The UN Study on the Impact of Armed Conflict on Children was adopted by the UN General Assembly in 1996 and the Study on Violence against Children was adopted in 2006. Each of these studies has made important recommendations in relation to the implementation and monitoring of states' obligations under the CRC.

OTHER MONITORING MECHANISMS

As previously mentioned, Article 45(a) of the Convention gives a special role to UN specialized agencies such as UNICEF with respect to encouraging the national implementation of children's rights and in facilitating international cooperation for this purpose. UNICEF in particular has, since the entry into force of the CRC, made great efforts to move its focus from a welfare-based approach toward a rights-based framework anchored in the Convention. Many commentators have noted that while this paradigm shift has influenced the discourse of the organization, it has yet to fully permeate its programming and practical functioning.

The specialized agencies of the UN that work with children's rights issues contribute to the implementation and monitoring of the Convention through the development of programs, studies, and indicators that focus on particular aspects of children's rights in various countries.

Nongovernmental organizations.

The role of NGOs in evaluating and monitoring the implementation of the norms contained in the CRC has already been highlighted. Article 45(a) of the Convention explicitly provides for NGO input to the reporting process and Article 45(b) states that other "competent bodies" may respond to requests for technical advice or assistance on children's rights issues.

The NGO Group for the Convention on the Rights of the Child, which was formed in 1983, played an instrumental part in the drafting of the CRC and continues to act as a liaison between national NGOs and the Committee on the Rights of the Child with respect to monitoring the implementation of the Convention. This group coordinates the submission of alternative NGO reports to the Committee on the Rights of the Child and encourages the work of national coalitions on children's rights issues.

Although the collaborative atmosphere that has developed between civil society organizations, the Committee on the Rights of the Child, and states has many positive aspects, there is a danger that this consensual approach to the CRC and children's rights more generally may lead to a glossing over of important differences in interpretation. It is clear that in other areas, an element of reasonable disagreement with respect to conceptual and legal problems performs an important role in furthering discussion and in finding innovative solutions to underlying differences.

Mainstreaming of children's rights within other parts of the UN human rights system.

Other elements of the UN human rights system also perform significant functions with respect to implementing children's rights. As previously mentioned, the Committee on the Rights of the Child does not have the competence to examine individual petitions from children alleging violations of their rights. Instead, it encourages

children or their representatives to refer to the other UN treaty bodies that do have a mandate to review individual complaints: the Human Rights Committee, the Committee against Torture, the Committee on the Elimination of Racial Discrimination, the Committee on Migrant Workers, and the Committee on the Elimination of Discrimination against Women.

In practice, however, very few individual complaints involving the human rights of children themselves are received by the UN treaty bodies. For example, of the petitions involving children that have been addressed to the Human Rights Committee, the majority concern deportation decisions that would lead to family separation or custody disputes in which one parent requests the right to have access to his or her child or children. Rarely have children themselves made use of the individual communication procedures.

A further implementation and monitoring mechanism for children's rights is the system of special procedures established by the UN Human Rights Council. These procedures, such as the thematic special rapporteurs on the sale of children, child prostitution, and child pornography; on torture; on the right to education; or on extrajudicial, summary, or arbitrary executions, all have urgent action and appeal mechanisms that they can use in favor of individual children or groups of children who are at risk of suffering rights violations. These mechanisms are increasingly taking the situation of children into account in their work and frequently base their interventions upon the relevant provisions of the CRC and its interpretations by the Committee on the Rights of the Child.

Domestic and regional application of the CRC.

In line with the obligations taken on by parties upon ratification, the Convention is being progressively applied by states within their domestic laws. A large number of parties to the CRC have adopted constitutional and legislative provisions that guarantee children's rights, often with direct effect and even imperative weight. While the formal recognition of the rights contained in the CRC is a significant first step toward ensuring the implementation of the Convention in national law, if these provisions are not enforced, monitored, or translated into meaningful policies on children's rights, then they may actually do more harm than good.

In the forty-seven member states of the Council of Europe, children's rights have benefited from the additional protection of the European Convention on

Human Rights, in particular through the binding case law of the European Court of Human Rights. This increased protection can be seen in many areas as a result of the court's dynamic interpretation of the protection of the right to life (Article 2), the right to private and family life as well as the right to identity (Article 8), and the principle of nondiscrimination (Article 14 and Protocol 12), and of the matching positive duties of contracting states.

ASSESSMENT

The CRC has been ratified by 193 states, a fact that gives it the potential to influence the situation of children in virtually every country in the world. As of 2008, however, there was little information available concerning the direct impact of the Convention on the realization of children's rights at the national level—that is, there were few studies on the impact on individual children.

One of the most salient features of the Convention and its current monitoring system is its emphasis on the obligation to establish a strong legislative and policy basis for the promotion and protection of children's rights domestically. The aspect of international accountability, presumably made concrete in the periodic reporting system, is directed toward encouraging states to develop sustainable mechanisms for monitoring and evaluating their own progress in relation to children's rights.

In general, the facilitation of constructive dialogue between states, the Committee on the Rights of the Child, specialized agencies, and civil society has thus far led to significant changes being made to policy, institutions, and legislation at the national level in a large number of states parties. These are important first steps in the process of realizing the rights of children but will need to be backed up with concrete data and continuous monitoring of national efforts if they are to effectively fulfill the Convention's promise.

[See also Civil and Political Rights: International Covenant on Civil and Political Rights; Economic, Social, and Cultural Rights: International Covenant on Economic, Social, and Cultural Rights; International Labour Organization; United Nations Children's Fund (UNICEF); United Nations Educational, Scientific, and Cultural Organization (UNESCO); United Nations General Assembly; United Nations High Commissioner for Human Rights; United Nations High Commissioner for Refugees; United Nations Human Rights Council; and Women: Convention on the Elimination of Discrimination against Women.]

BIBLIOGRAPHY

Alston, Philip, and John Tobin, with Mac Darrow. *Laying the Foundations for Children's Rights.* Innocenti Insight series. Florence, Italy: UNICEF Innocenti Research Center, 2005.

Breen, Claire. "The Role of NGOs in the Formulation of and Compliance with the Optional Protocol to the Convention on the Rights of the Child on Involvement of Children in Armed Conflict." *Human Rights Quarterly* 25 (May 2003): 453–481.

Cantwell, Nigel. "The Convention on the Rights of the Child, Vini, vici . . . et vinci?" In *Understanding Children's Rights*, edited by Eugeen Verhellen and A. Weyts, pp. 395–407. Ghent, Belgium: Ghent University: Children's Rights Centre, 2004.

Child Rights Information Network. The organization's Web site, http://www.crin.org, offers information by country and theme.

Detrick, Sharon, ed. *The United Nations Convention on the Rights of the Child: A Guide to the "Travaux Préparatoires."* Dordrecht, The Netherlands; Boston: Martinus Nijhoff Publishers; Norwell, Mass.: Sold and distributed in the USA and Canada by Kluwer Academic Publishers, 1992.

Fottrell, Deirdre, ed. *Revisiting Children's Rights: 10 Years of the UN Convention on the Rights of the Child.* The Hague; Boston: Kluwer Law International, 2001.

Hammarberg, Thomas. "The UN Convention on the Rights of the Child—and How to Make It Work." *Human Rights Quarterly* 12 (February 1990): 97–105.

Hodgkin, Rachel, and Peter Newell. *Implementation Handbook for the Convention on the Rights of the Child.* New York: UNICEF, 2002.

Lansdown, Gerrison. "The Reporting Process under the Convention on the Rights of the Child." In *The Future of UN Human Rights Treaty Monitoring*, edited by Philip Alston and James Crawford, pp. 113–128. Cambridge, U.K.: Cambridge University Press, 2000.

Office of the United Nations High Commissioner for Human Rights. http://www2.ohchr.org/english/bodies/crc/. Links to comprehensive information about the UN Committee on the Rights of the Child and the UN Convention on the Rights of the Child.

Schabas, William A. "Reservations to the Convention on the Rights of the Child." *Human Rights Quarterly* 18 (May 1996): 472–491.

United Nations General Assembly. *Optional Protocol to the Committee on the Rights of the Child on the Involvement of Children in Armed Conflict and Optional Protocol on the Sale of Children, Child Prostitution, and Child Pornography.* A/RES/54/263, May 25, 2000.

Van Bueren, Geraldine. *The International Law on the Rights of the Child.* Dordrecht, The Netherlands; Boston: Martinus Nijhoff; Norwell, Mass.: Sold and distributed in the United States and Canada by Kluwer Academic Publishers, 1995.

Vandenhole, Wouter. *The Procedures before the UN Human Rights Treaty Bodies. Divergence or Convergence?* Antwerp, Belgium: Intersentia, 2004.

Verhellen, Eugeen. *Convention on the Rights of the Child.* 4th ed. Antwerp, Belgium: Garant, 2006.

CHILE IN THE PINOCHET ERA

by Darren Hawkins

The period of authoritarian rule in Chile (1973 to 1990) and the rise of international concern for human rights are inseparably linked. Prior to 1970 states sometimes proclaimed their allegiance to human rights in international treaties, but rarely did they actually do much to promote or protect human rights in other countries. Indeed, why would they? States do not naturally have strong self-interested reasons to be concerned about how other countries treat their own citizens. State officials may, of course, worry about instability elsewhere leading to high refugee flows into their own countries or about people of their own nationality or ethnicity who live elsewhere, but these limited self-interests are not strong enough to translate into general concern about the well-being of all citizens in other countries. The central problem is that promoting the rights of others can be costly to the state making the effort. States generally do not want to spend their citizens' money or lives ensuring that people in other countries have more rights, especially when they might anger other states in the process, by cutting off aid or trade, for example. Even if it can be said that most people have a moral concern for the well-being of their fellow humans in other countries, states rarely have done anything concrete or specific to help promote the human rights of those living outside their own states.

This pattern changed significantly in the 1970s, when Western states began incorporating human rights concerns into their foreign policies by penalizing human rights violators and by aiding domestic groups in other countries who promoted human rights. Many international organizations also paid more attention to human rights by investigating and publicizing abuses and by shaming abusive governments. International nongovernmental organizations (NGOs) played key roles by collecting and distributing information on abuses and by lobbying others to take more action against abusive governments. Collectively, such international action may be labeled international human rights pressure.

Events in Chile played an important role in triggering these new international efforts, although the extent of Chile's influence is subject to debate. It is somewhat paradoxical that a period of authoritarian rule would contribute to stronger international action in favor of human rights, but it is certainly not unprecedented: Nazi atrocities in Germany in World War II also resulted in international efforts to promote human rights.

Once international pressure occurs, a natural question arises: Does it have any effect? Does it matter to the people suffering repression or to the autocratic leaders? There are good reasons to believe that it will have no effect and good reasons to believe it will have some effect. On the negative side, it seems clear that some countries are willing to suffer immensely from international pressure without ever responding. Such states seem unresponsive, in part, because their leaders use international threats as a rallying point. Although their citizens may not particularly care for their own government, they frequently do not want other countries telling them what to do. States may also be unresponsive because they fear that small reforms will lead to demands for larger reforms, eventually overthrowing the government, as they did in the Soviet Union prior to 1991.

On the affirmative side, repressed individuals can take hope from international pressure and be inspired to redouble their efforts. They can receive money, supplies, and information from international allies. International pressure might also matter to authoritarian rulers, especially if the pressure includes economic or military sanctions. Even without tangible punishments, authoritarian rulers might care about their reputations among other states and worry about future sanctions. Finally, even authoritarian rulers cannot always govern their citizens by sheer force. They must at some point seek at least a minimal level of acceptance from their citizens or else face the potential of widespread noncompliance and rebellion. International action can encourage citizens to openly question their government's rules and spread dissent. It can also raise the fear of widespread domestic dissent among government officials, thereby prompting them to enact reforms designed to placate opponents without undermining their own power too much.

This entry examines these ideas and analyzes the ways in which the situation in Chile may have influenced international human rights actions and how those actions may have then influenced Chile, while drawing careful attention to the limitations of those influences. The extent of the influence is, of course, subject to debate and discussion. Although some argue that the authoritarian government in Chile changed very little over the course of its seventeen years in power, others argue that the changes were larger and more significant. Among those who see significant change, it can be attributed to different factors. For some, change was the product of a struggle for power within the military government. For others, it was the result of international human rights pressure.

A NEW GOVERNMENT IN CHILE

On 11 September 1973 the Chilean military seized power from a democratically elected Chilean government. The military removed President Salvador Allende from office and began a brutal campaign that wound up killing at least three thousand, exiling tens of thousands, torturing tens of thousands, arresting hundreds of thousands, and emotionally or psychologically scarring countless more. For decades prior to the 1973 coup, Chile was a stable democracy. In 1970 the Chilean people freely and fairly elected Allende, a self-proclaimed Marxist. The election of a Marxist at the height of the Cold War triggered deep anxieties and resentment among Chilean conservatives and in the United States. When some of Allende's supporters tried to push him toward Socialism faster than others were willing to go, those anxieties coalesced into political action. Opponents tried to block Allende's progress in the Chilean legislature and through political actions such as strikes. Allende's supporters rallied, and Chilean society quickly became polarized. There were soon long lines for food, paramilitary skirmishes in the streets, and a deadlock in the legislature. The military, with a deep loathing of Marxism and the tacit support of some Chilean political parties and the United States, stepped in and seized power.

In the months before the 1973 coup, Chile became a weak and disintegrating state unable to maintain order. Virtually overnight, the military turned Chile into a predatory state seeking to destroy basic social institutions and then rebuild them in its own image. The new military government was characterized by highly centralized authority, a worldview that emphasized total war on Marxism, and wide-ranging violent repression. In an effort to rid the country of Marxist infiltration, the new military government abolished all social and political institutions in Chile except for a few churches. The government reasoned that because Marxists had infiltrated all social institutions, they should therefore be shut down. The military government also censored the media, suppressed political parties, disbanded Congress, and repressed labor organizations, student groups, and neighborhood organizations. Although many expected a coup, few later claimed they foresaw the degree of violence or the single-minded fury of the military government that would result. Indeed, many thought the military might seize power for a few weeks and then turn over the government to civilian rule again. They were quite mistaken: those few weeks stretched into seventeen years.

A four-man military junta controlled Chile's new government, both its legislative and executive powers. The members of the junta included Augusto Pinochet for the army, José Merino for the navy, Gustavo Leigh for the air force, and César Mendoza as commander of the militarized police. The army was traditionally the most important of these branches, and thus it is perhaps not surprising that Pinochet gained more influence and by December 1974 was named president of Chile. Through this appointment, Pinochet became "first among equals," strong enough to force out later those junta members who openly disagreed with him, as he did with Leigh in 1976. At the same time, he still relied on the support of other branches of the military, whose members sometimes struck more independent lines and forced Pinochet to compromise.

Under Pinochet the military government had a three-fold mission: to eliminate Marxism, to rebuild the economy, and to establish a new political system. The Directorate of National Intelligence (DINA), headed by Colonel Manuel Contreras, was responsible, from 1973 to 1977, for some of the worst human rights violations in its efforts to abolish Marxism from Chile. To reconstruct the economy, the government began rapidly implementing neoliberal economic principles. Those principles focused on reducing the role of government in the economy by cutting the budget, placing fewer taxes on imports, and selling off state-run industries. Instead of immediately focusing on the third task to create a new political system, government officials argued that the military should govern directly for an indefinite period because democracy and constitutional rule could not withstand the assaults of Marxism. Those officials claimed that only the military was capable of excising the "cancer" of Marxism from the Chilean body politic. These three tasks remained central themes until the government lost power in March 1990.

HUMAN RIGHTS ON THE AGENDA

The 1973 coup and subsequent government mission to rid Chile of Marxism led to a human rights travesty that continues to haunt Chileans and others. Torture, kidnapping, intimidation, and murder were important methods utilized to find and eliminate Marxists. In one gruesome account, Pascal Allende, a nephew of the former president, and a wounded colleague sought refuge from DINA officers seeking to kill them. While the fugitives eluded capture in a Catholic parish house, DINA agents open fired on the entrance, killing a maid. DINA operatives later captured and tortured the British doctor who treated Allende and his companion, simply because she provided medical assistance to the government's perceived enemies. Accounts of similar abuses are numerous.

Although a comprehensive accounting of all human rights abuses under the military government has never been undertaken and is probably impossible, in 1990 the new democratic government established the National Commission on Truth and Reconciliation, which in 1991 issued a report on deaths and disappearances in Chile. Using numbers updated by its successor organization, the National Corporation of Reparation and Reconciliation, the commission reported 1,792 deaths attributable to state agents during the most intensive period of repression, from September to December 1973. During this period, security forces made little attempt to conceal their work, making arrests in broad daylight and dumping corpses in public areas. From 1974 to 1977 repression took on a more covert cast as the DINA spread terror by arresting people in the middle of the night, who were then never seen again. The number of fatalities from this period, including disappearances, totals 621. DINA tactics spread fear throughout society and successively dismantled remaining opposition in the Movement of the Revolutionary Left (a radical armed group), the Socialist Party, and the Communist Party. The DINA operated with almost complete autonomy and impunity, although the power of its members created intense friction with the regular armed forces and their intelligence services. To the extent that the DINA was accountable to anyone, it was only to Pinochet, and not to the junta.

In response to the open brutality of the coup and the government mission to exterminate Marxists,

international and domestic human rights groups formed transnational linkages that set precedents for future human rights networks. These groups routinely exchanged vital information and resources that stimulated further international efforts. The resulting networks engaged in strong efforts to monitor the human rights situation, achieve international condemnation, attain international funding for domestic opposition groups and research centers, push international organizations to investigate and publicize the abuses, and lobby powerful Western states to take action.

This international network grew as different groups rallied to support Chileans. International responses to the coup came first from two nongovernmental organizations: Amnesty International and the International Commission of Jurists. Together, these groups contacted the Inter-American Commission on Human Rights (IACHR), a human rights watchdog affiliated with the Organization of American States (OAS). Chilean churches also started human rights organizations that became the core of the transnational network. The churches set up the Committee of Cooperation for Peace (COPACHI), which later became the Vicariate of Solidarity. COPACHI networked with human rights groups in other countries to receive funding and support. One of COPACHI's most critical activities was to investigate alleged human rights abuses and compile detailed reports. COPACHI sent these reports to the International Committee of the Red Cross (ICRC), Amnesty International, Americas Watch, the International Commission of Jurists, the United Nations, the OAS, and others. International actors offered moral support, international visibility, and funding. In addition, journalists writing about the coup and the subsequent violence placed pressure on Western states to respond to the human rights abuses, which added to the pressure on the military government.

These transnational and international responses prompted the junta to put human rights issues at the forefront of its agenda. In its second recorded meeting, the junta discussed how to defend Chile against United Nations accusations initiated by Cuba concerning human rights abuses. Given the number of tasks facing the junta in the days following the coup, this discussion reveals its strong concern for Chile's international image. The UN General Assembly first condemned Chile in December 1974 and, for the first time, criticized an abusive government without linking those abuses to international security issues. Great Britain halted arms sales to Chile in April 1974, and the United States, based on legislation initiated by Senator Edward Kennedy and others, limited economic aid to Chile and ended military aid, but not arms sales.

The international pressure had somewhat contradictory effects on the government. At a superficial level, the government responded to international efforts through an international public relations campaign that included media stories, advertising buys, public speeches, and diplomatic efforts. Inside Chile the government issued new decree laws that pretended to soften the nature of the repression but that, in fact, did not. More problematically, the government may have cracked down harder on internal dissidents.

On the other hand, it seems likely that the pressure posed a threat to the new government's legitimacy, defined as widespread beliefs that an actor's behavior conforms to expectations. In particular, it began to raise questions about whether the government was operating in ways that were perceived to be consistent with Chilean values. Generally speaking, Chileans were proud of their liberal democratic heritage. Chilean political parties were modeled after and had close ties with European political parties. Many Chileans thought of themselves as sharing Western European values of tolerance, respect for basic rights, and social concern for the poor. Although Chilean citizens could do little in the face of such fierce repression to openly question the government, international actors could and did raise questions about the government's behavior and its consistency with the Western, Christian values professed by most Chileans and by the government itself. At a minimum, international pressure kept human rights issues on the government's agenda, despite other pressing economic and political concerns.

THE HUMAN RIGHTS NETWORK GROWS DOMESTICALLY AND ABROAD

Although the military government did its best to root out domestic human rights groups and forced COPACHI to disband, the Catholic Church responded energetically to this challenge. The Church was one of the only social institutions still functioning in Chile and generally supported human rights groups. In 1976 Santiago's archbishop, Cardinal Raúl Silva Henriquez, went a step farther and formed the Vicariate of Solidarity, which became one of Latin America's most widely known and admired human rights organizations. The Vicariate built a transnational network with other religious and human rights groups centered on gathering and publishing information about human rights abuses. The group printed

a bimonthly bulletin, *Solidarity*, in which it recorded and distributed information about disappearances, imprisonments for political views, harassment, torture, and arbitrary arrests to domestic and international organizations and foreign states. To help Chileans domestically, the Vicariate offered medical assistance, food, and legal counsel and presented thousands of writs of habeas corpus in the courts, which rarely acted positively on the requests.

Along with the Vicariate, other groups emerged in Chile to help alleviate human rights abuses. The Social Help Foundation of the Christian Churches and the Service for Peace and Justice aided refugees and exiled families and circulated reports and statistics on human rights abuses. Victims of human rights abuses set up other human rights organizations, including the Association of Families of the Detained-Disappeared, founded in 1974; the Association of Families of Political Prisoners, founded in 1976; and the Association of Families of Executed Political Activists, founded in 1978.

Exiled Chileans formed their own human rights groups in the United States, Europe, and Latin America. These groups created numerous links between human rights groups within Chile and other Western human rights groups. Intergovernmental and nongovernmental organizations stepped up their pressures on the Chilean government based on reports coming out of Chile. In June 1976 the OAS met in Santiago, where the IACHR offered its second report on human rights in Chile, charging the military government with systematic human rights violations. Another report followed in March 1977, showing little human rights improvement. The UN Commission on Human Rights joined international groups by voting to accuse Chile of human rights violations and to call for improvements.

U.S. leaders presented conflicting responses to the human rights abuses in Chile. Publicly, Washington condemned the human rights abuses, but privately the situation was different. In June 1976 then Secretary of State Henry Kissinger publicly announced that Chile's repressive nature was harming relations with the United States, but privately he met with Pinochet to reassure him that his tough language was simply done for show, in an attempt to head off congressional sanctions. Among U.S. politicians concerned with Chilean human rights abuses were Congressman Donald Fraser of Minnesota and Senator Edward Kennedy of Massachusetts. Together, they achieved some success in 1976 when joint House–Senate legislation passed that ended all U.S. military aid and sales to Chile, both public and private, and reduced all government economic aid to $27.5 million per year.

Pressure from the United States added strength to the efforts of the growing transnational network. Sadly, the event that would have the greatest impact on Chilean human rights abuses in 1976 was a car bombing in September, in Washington, D.C. Eventually, U.S. officials discovered that Chilean security officials masterminded the bomb in an attempt to kill Orlando Letelier, a former minister in Allende's government. As a result of the bomb's explosion on U.S. soil, the U.S. government put heavy pressure on the Pinochet government. Arguably, this pressure eventually led to important changes inside Chile.

CHANGING DOMESTIC CONDITIONS

Starting in 1976 the political scene in Chile changed in two ways. First, government officials split into various factions. The chief factions might be labeled rule-oriented actors and force-oriented actors. The rule-oriented faction consisted of a prominent group of legal advisers that proposed a new constitution, rather than ongoing direct military rule, to secure Chile's long-term government stability. These advisers used their positions in government institutions to access and influence top decision makers. Concerned about the government's legitimacy and stability, they sought to create a new constitution that would extend military rule for several years but promise relatively democratic institutions and human rights guarantees in the future. Jaime Guzmán led the rule-oriented actors by arguing for new political institutions that would enable long-term military control over politics. Some refer to these rule-oriented actors as "soft-liners"; however, the term does not accurately capture their proauthoritarian attitudes and their acquiescence to ongoing repression.

The force-oriented faction preferred to postpone new political institutions and a revised constitution for as long as possible. Members of this group believed the military could continue to govern as it had in the past, through repression and the occasional use of "decree laws," and they worried that any new rules would decrease their ability to use force when necessary. At the same time, an important split developed between Pinochet and other junta members that would persist until the end of military rule. Junta members worried about Pinochet's personal centralization of power and consistently sought to limit that power. In part, they worried that political power would undermine the military's cohesion,

professionalism, and commitment to its core mission of defending the country.

Second, economic recovery reduced crisis levels, and security forces finished their mission of dismantling any possible opposition. The economic recovery beginning in 1976 initiated six years of economic growth, in significant contrast to the harsh economic conditions that dated back to 1972. The economy grew at 8 to 9 percent a year, while unemployment levels decreased and real wages began to increase, although not to pre-coup levels. Also at this time, the government completed its task of decimating leftist and extremist groups, using brutal methods. Paradoxically, the government's success in both economic and security issues undermined its claims that ongoing government repression was essential and thus strengthened the arguments of the rule-oriented faction. Fewer domestic difficulties for the government also meant that international pressure would receive more attention.

THE RHETORIC OF HUMAN RIGHTS

Although the point can be contested, the military government demonstrated increasing concern for its legitimacy in response to international pressures in 1975 and 1976. Two years after the military coup, on 11 September 1975, Pinochet first discussed human rights in front of a domestic audience. In 1976, during a speech to mark the government's third anniversary, Pinochet revealed the content of constitutional Acts 2, 3, and 4, major initiatives intended to amend the existing constitution. These rule-oriented actions suggest that the government was concerned with how others perceived it. The amendments themselves were announced but never really implemented, and hence the government's actions remained at the level of rhetoric rather than changed behavior. However, for the government to adopt a rhetoric of human rights marked an important departure from the language it had used soon after seizing power. Act 2 was a general statement of principles and aspirations, Act 3 provided human rights guarantees, and Act 4 specified government power during states of siege and states of emergency, which were constantly in place in Chile. Although the rights promised in Act 3 were strikingly progressive and complete, and would have made any legitimate democracy proud, Act 4 specified different legal states of exception in which human rights could be suspended. In practice, the government invoked the states of emergency to justify ongoing repression and widely ignored the human rights guarantees.

Pinochet, the junta, and key government advisers fiercely debated these acts before announcing them. These debates marked the first partial success for the rule-oriented faction and for junta members contesting Pinochet's power. Merino, the navy commander, repeatedly expressed his concerns about the perceptions of Chile in the international community, while others echoed his points. Merino and some legal advisers were also concerned about the consistency of the junta's new rules with Chile's Constitution of 1925, still technically in effect. It seems likely that both objections were related to concerns about Pinochet's holding too much personal power. Although the constitutional acts constituted rhetoric rather than action, they allowed opponents to accuse the government of hypocrisy and to try to hold it accountable to articulated standards. As will be shown below, this strategy ultimately succeeded in the 1980s.

THE DEMISE OF THE DINA

Although the new constitutional acts constituted a change in language and rhetoric, the government also implemented some small changes in behavior. In 1977 Pinochet announced that the DINA would be replaced by the National Information Center (CNI), which was intended to be (or to appear as) a more traditional intelligence-gathering agency. Debates persist about the extent of real change that occurred. For some, it marked a simple change of name; others see a deeper change as some practices, such as disappearance and torture, seemed to be used with much less frequency. The end of the DINA probably did shift the balance of power in the government between the rule- and force-oriented factions over to those favoring more rules and political institutions. Manuel Contreras, the DINA's leader, had been responsible only to Pinochet for the actions of the security force and was probably one of Pinochet's most influential advisers. Contreras and other force-oriented advisers believed that the rise of the rule-oriented faction was detrimental to Chile because it made the military government too susceptible to foreign influences and placed too many restrictions on the government's behavior. With the DINA disbanded and Contreras relegated to a less visible role, the rule-oriented faction and junta faced fewer competitors within the government.

Why did Pinochet disband the DINA? Several answers are possible. First, the agency had largely accomplished its mission of exterminating Marxists and was expendable. Second, the armed forces and DINA clashed over

intelligence jurisdiction, and those clashes largely annoyed military officials. Third, the United States placed strong pressure on the DINA because its officials were believed to be the architects of the 1976 Letelier car bombing in Washington, D.C. Fourth, rule-oriented officials repeatedly argued that the DINA did more harm than good in an environment in which the government enjoyed security from its enemies but lacked legitimacy. In their view, international pressures would never cease unless the DINA disbanded and new political institutions were created.

ESTABLISHING A NEW CONSTITUTION

In 1977, shortly after the demise of the DINA, the military government in Chile took steps to create long-lasting political institutions. The most significant of these steps led in 1980 to the Political Constitution of the Republic of Chile. As with the end of the DINA, a variety of factors undoubtedly produced the decision to write a new constitution. Some argue that the constitution was the result of continued conflicts between Pinochet and the junta over the length of Pinochet's personal rule. Others focus on the increasing rise of the rule-oriented faction and its plans for long-term stability. It seems likely that international human rights pressures, in part, drove both the junta and its legal advisers. Those pressures aided the pro-constitutional forces in three ways. First, the pressure posed a normative threat, not a security threat or an economic threat. Hence, it made the constitution an appropriate response. Second, and related to the first factor, international pressures posed problems for which legal advisers had expertise: the drafting of legal codes designed to counter those pressures. Third, the pressures created a sense of urgency, pushing the government to act during a period in which organized domestic opposition was meager or nonexistent.

In the late 1970s new human rights groups joined the transnational human rights network, and the network's activities gained new visibility. The largest of these new groups was the Chilean Commission of Human Rights, founded by two Christian Democrats in late 1978. In 1977 the Service for Peace and Justice, a transnational nonviolent human rights group, set up a Chilean chapter, and in 1978 student activists started the National Commission for the Rights of Youth. In 1979 the Vicariate published a definitive and widely disseminated seven-volume report on 613 cases of "disappeared" individuals titled simply *Dónde Estan?* (Where Are They?). This publication helped maintain pressure on the government by raising questions about its legitimacy. In fact, questions about human rights abuses began to appear for the first time in the domestic Chilean media.

The new constitution emerged out of what Pinochet referred to as a "new institutionality," a broad government project dating back to the early days after the coup. The military government and its supporters believed that traditional political institutions in Chile were weak and incapable of resisting Marxism. Officials wanted to create new, stronger institutions that could resist Marxism by making them more elitist and more closely tied to the military. Instead of defining the nature of these institutions and taking positive steps toward creating them, Pinochet's mantra during the first five years of military rule was to establish institutional "goals, not deadlines." As a result, he set up study commissions that proceeded at a leisurely pace toward new political institutions and especially a new constitution. The government established a constitutional commission in late September 1973. It originally had four members, including Enrique Ortúzar and Jaime Guzmán. Ortúzar and Guzmán had personal access to Pinochet and other junta leaders. Guzmán's direct involvement with these leaders over the years established him as a leader within the rule-oriented faction in the military government. The commission set out to articulate a curious blend of traditional liberal democratic values and military-inspired, authoritarian principles. In the commission's second statement, issued on 26 November 1973, it put forth three aims: to maintain Chile as a republican democracy; to decrease the role of political parties and increase that of nonpolitical organized social groups; and to secure the position of the armed forces in protecting internal security. The junta also used the commission to draft problematic legislation, which detracted from its responsibilities in creating a new constitution. Such legislation included the suspension of political parties; the expiration of electoral rolls; the establishment of the constitutional, executive, and legislative powers of the junta; the decentralization of the government; and the formation of government administrative procedures. In the same spirit, the junta created another advisory council on 1 January 1976, the Council of State. The council, which consisted of distinguished political, military, and social figures, including the former Chilean president Jorge Alessandri Rodríguez, became a formal advisory body created to legitimize the government in the face of serious questions about its legitimacy.

Between July and November of 1977, the military government took more steps toward finalizing the new constitution, although Pinochet still resisted firm deadlines and clear definitions of the new political institutions. On Youth Day, 9 July 1977, Pinochet announced plans for a "new institutionality," including, for the first time, a plan for the end of military rule. Pinochet and the junta outlined the plan: by 1980 a Congress would be appointed; by 1985 elections would be held for two-thirds of the legislators, who would then select a president (Pinochet probably hoped for the post himself) to serve a six-year term. Directly following this term, the new constitution would go into effect. The nature of these institutions was mostly undefined. Pinochet apparently disliked liberal democratic solutions of the sort found in most Western democratic states because he believed them to be weak, open to Marxist influence, and subject to the control of political parties that looked out for personal rather than national interests. He preferred allowing very weak political parties (if any at all) and giving a strong governing role to the military. In particular, he was attracted to authoritarian corporatist views of politics, in which various "natural" societal groupings—women, labor, students, and businesses—participate directly in governing rather than funneling their interests through political parties. Rule-oriented advisers, on the other hand, preferred institutions that mimicked classic liberal democratic practices such as direct elections with secret ballots. At the same time, they shared Pinochet's skepticism of political parties and wanted to sharply restrain ideological diversity. Hence, they favored a rather restricted notion of democracy.

As successive drafts of a new constitution moved forward from 1978 through 1980 and increasingly reflected the views of the rule-oriented faction, favoring restricted democracy, the key issue was when such a system would go into effect and how the transition would occur. The rule-oriented civilians drafting the constitution in the Council of State proposed a five-year transition period during which the junta would have limited powers and Pinochet would be bound by all the provisions of the constitution. At the end of the period, military officials would step aside. Pinochet and other relative hard-liners would not accept that formula and worked instead toward a sixteen-year transition. In the end, they compromised somewhat by proposing a new Congress and a plebiscite (referendum) on Pinochet's rule within eight years. If he won, Pinochet could serve an additional eight years. Military officials created the basic rules for this lengthy "transition period" in a set of twenty-nine transitory articles to the proposed constitution. Although those articles finally set a term limit for military rule, the date was ten years away, in March 1990. Furthermore, the new constitution gave relatively few guarantees that the elections anticipated for the late 1980s would be free and fair. The transition articles largely preserved the existing power structure in the military government by giving the presidency to Pinochet but maintaining legislative power in the junta, in which each of the four members had veto power. The articles also enabled the government to continue its repressive policies by authorizing detentions, restrictions on free speech, exile, states of exception, and other measures that limited human rights guarantees. On 11 September 1980, 67 percent (according to official figures) of voters approved the new constitution in an electoral process that lacked many guarantees of a free and fair vote.

ECONOMIC CRISIS, POPULAR PROTEST, AND RENEWED VIOLENCE

A brief period of complacency and triumph followed the adoption of the 1980 constitution but was soon eclipsed by a new period of economic crisis, a rebirth of domestic opposition, and increasing repression. In 1982 the neoliberal economic policies that had brought four years of strong economic growth and capital flows to Chile produced an economic collapse. Chile's economy shrank 14 percent in 1982 and an additional 0.7 percent in 1983. The economic failures produced open and widespread opposition to the government. Mass protests broke out on 11 May 1983 and continued for months afterward. The government responded brutally, killing dozens and jailing tens of thousands. In August 1983 Pinochet appointed the conservative Sergio Jarpa as the new interior minister. His negotiations with opposition leaders promised a return to Chile's traditional democracy, while Pinochet simultaneously used violence to repress street demonstrations. The negotiations soon fell apart as it became clear the government had no intention of handing over power. Between November 1984 and June 1985 the military government reimposed a state of siege on Chile. This increase in repression was exemplified by the shocking murder of three Communist Party members in 1985. The killers slashed their throats in such a severe fashion that their heads were almost entirely severed.

The emergence of mass protests altered the nature and visibility of the transnational human rights network. New groups, such as the Committee of the Rights of the People, formed in late 1980, focused on training other social groups, including labor unions and women's organizations, rather than gathering and sharing information and lobbying international actors. The human rights network continued to operate but became a smaller fish in the bigger pond of mass protests, reemergent political parties, labor unions, and social groups. At first, the domestic opposition called for an immediate transition from military rule, initially seeking that result through street protests and then through negotiations. As it became evident the government would not fall or bargain, the opposition switched tactics and tried to push the government to comply with its own promises to hold a plebiscite on Pinochet's presidency. A lot of effort was put into creating the conditions for a free and fair election. This energetic domestic opposition helped galvanize new international pressure, which also focused on the plebiscite. In the United States the Reagan administration initially supported Pinochet, but by the mid-1980s, it began to see him as a liability, even issuing a signed statement in 1987 detailing necessary conditions for free and fair elections and imposing sanctions in 1988. Along with many European states, the United States funneled substantial money to the domestic opposition, condemned repressive behavior in Chile, and called for a complete return to democracy.

LEGITIMACY AND ELECTIONS IN THE 1980S

The military government's continued quest for legitimacy came to a head in the 1980s, when leaders had to choose between legitimacy, by upholding promises in the 1980 constitution, or illegitimacy, through continued authoritarian rule. Leaders had two options: they could extend authoritarian rule indefinitely by amending the constitution, thereby undermining their legitimacy and risking massive opposition, or they could secure legitimacy for the new constitution by holding a relatively free and fair plebiscite, at the risk of losing power. Government officials generally favored the risks of a plebiscite, in part because of the demands of domestic and international actors. The decision to hold a plebiscite forced leaders to create rules governing the electoral process. The key political questions from 1985 to 1988 concerned when those laws would be enacted and how biased they would be toward the government. Generally, Pinochet and other strong skeptics of democracy preferred delaying those laws as long as possible and writing laws that would favor the government. Others, most notably members of the junta, worried about international and domestic pressures, convinced that the country's reputation and long-term stability required a relatively free and fair plebiscite, planned well in advance.

The result was a stop-and-go legislative process to produce new legislation relating to elections, such as rules governing political parties and voting. During this time, the junta alternately pushed forward and then delayed rules with varying levels of democratic characteristics. One important example was the establishment of an independent electoral tribunal to oversee the plebiscite. Pinochet's advisers prepared the law in 1984, but the junta refused to pass it until Pinochet forwarded other legislation on political parties, voter registration, and the role of the media in the electoral process, which would determine the opposition's chances in the plebiscite. Pinochet refused to do so, and the junta approved the electoral tribunal law in mid-1985 but decided, citing a constitutional technicality, that the tribunal would not operate until after the plebiscite, thereby defeating its entire purpose. A constitutional tribunal set up by the government to assess the constitutionality of key legislation subsequently required the junta to amend the law so that the electoral tribunal would operate prior to the plebiscite. The constitutional tribunal reasoned that a delay in the electoral tribunal's functioning would "expose the very plebiscite to fundamental questions about its legitimacy, with grave damage to the normal development of future institutions."

Other important questions concerned the legal states of emergency that had constantly operated since the 1973 coup and the relative independence of the media. The states of emergency allowed the government special repressive authority. In the face of the 1983 protests, Pinochet wanted to increase the state of emergency to a state of siege. The junta at first opposed this measure but then later approved it, thereby increasing government powers from November 1984 through June 1985 and again from September to December 1986. In both cases, the junta grew insistent that these sieges be lifted so that Chile could appear to be a relatively liberal state. By mid-1988 government legal advisers drafted legislation to guarantee television time to antigovernment campaign ads. Although Chile's television stations were firmly in Pinochet's camp, the government's requiring them to give advertising time to the opposition demonstrates concern for legitimacy.

In the end, the government held a relatively free and fair plebiscite on 5 October 1988, and Pinochet lost by a vote of 55 percent to 43 percent. Before announcing the final results, however, Pinochet apparently made one last attempt to commit fraud by summoning the junta to a late-night meeting while votes were being counted. Junta members resisted whatever pressure he may have exerted and even publicly announced their belief that Pinochet had lost, thereby undercutting any possible plans for fraud. In subsequent months, Chileans elected a new Congress and a new civilian center-left president, Patricio Aylwin Azócar, who took office on 11 March 1990.

This result cost Pinochet his job as president but simultaneously ensured a peaceful transition to democracy and the widespread acceptance of the constitution and other important rules and policies adopted by the junta. Pinochet remained commander in chief of the armed forces and was guaranteed a seat as a senator for life once he stepped down from that post. The military's professionalism, as exemplified by the junta, played a major role in this outcome. Military officers strongly supported Pinochet but also maintained strong respect for the constitution and the rule of law. Military officials serving in government posts publicly professed their loyalty to the constitution over Pinochet and consequently promoted a fair plebiscite. Scholars generally concur that the military's rediscovery of its professional, nonpolitical values, together with the long-standing tradition of civilian rule prior to the coup, aided the transition to democracy.

HUMAN RIGHTS IN CHILE SINCE 1990

With a peaceful transition accomplished, President Aylwin initiated investigations into human rights abuses during the Pinochet era with the formation of the Commission of Truth and Reconciliation. The commission identified 2,279 state-sponsored murders between 11 September 1973 and 11 March 1990. Despite its mandate to investigate only killings, the commission included a section on torture in the report because the testimony it received on the topic was so disturbing. Aylwin worked not only to investigate the murders but also to seek justice. Yet justice seemed elusive after the Chilean Supreme Court upheld a 1978 law granting amnesty to human rights violations occurring prior to that time. Aylwin, disturbed that the justice system would fail to prosecute human rights violators during Chile's critical transition back to democracy, urged prosecutors to continue to investigate regardless of the ruling. The president's stance, which came to be known as the Aylwin Doctrine, allowed prosecutors to gather evidence even if the cases were never tried, an approach the judiciary came to accept.

The Aylwin government also sought to prosecute some of the most highly publicized murders that were not protected under the amnesty law, often because they occurred on foreign soil or after 1978. Among others, officials investigated the murders of a Chilean general and his wife in Argentina; the Letelier murder in Washington, D.C.; the murder of three Communist Party members in 1985; and the attempted murder of a prominent international opponent of the military government, Bernardo Leighton, and his wife in Rome. These investigations attempted to show the Chilean people that the new democratic government sought justice. Despite strides in the judiciary, the real gravity of the human rights violations came into public view through the discoveries of mass graves. Bodies found in Pisagua, in northern Chile, were perhaps among the most shocking discoveries. The dry climate preserved and mummified the victims, who wore terror-stricken expressions. The discovery of other mass graves in different parts of the country sobered the Chilean spirit.

Although it respected the rule of law, which led to the peaceful transition to democracy in 1990, the military did not approve of being investigated for human rights violations. In a defiant response to human rights inquiries, the military on several occasions in the 1990s engaged in a show of force to demonstrate its displeasure at government inquiries. In response, the newly elected government sought compromises with military officials in which both could save face without making substantial progress in the investigations. Although it frequently could not pursue punishment for human rights violations, the government did make strong efforts to give financial as well as moral support to the relatives of human rights victims. Aylwin launched the National Corporation for Reparation and Reconciliation, which by the end of 1992 had given almost 7 billion Chilean pesos to more than forty-five hundred human rights victims. The struggle for truth and justice has continued since then in much the same fashion, with progress balanced by setbacks. In 1997, for example, the Association of Families of the Disappeared pushed the government to set up a DNA bank to help identify missing bodies, thereby offering grieving families some relief. In October of the same year, the military requested that all human rights cases be dropped. Investigations typically produced information, but most court cases resulted in dead ends or endless legal battles.

The most dramatic developments involved the arrests of Contreras, the head of the infamous DINA, and, even more shockingly, Pinochet himself. Contreras was sentenced by a Chilean court to seven years in prison for his role in the Letelier bombing, which was not covered by the amnesty because it occurred on U.S. soil. Pinochet, however, remained commander of the armed forces until March 1998, when he was finally forced by the new constitution to step down. Fortunately for Pinochet, the constitution guaranteed him a permanent seat in the Senate. Unfortunately for him, he traveled in 1998 to Great Britain, where he was detained for 508 days at the request of Spanish prosecutors on charges of human rights violations. The British courts struggled with a variety of legal questions, especially the question of whether Britain or Spain had the jurisdiction to bring charges. The highest British court eventually decided that Britain did have the authority to arrest and extradite Pinochet to Spain, but only on charges of torture occurring after October 1998, the date when Chile, Spain, and Britain all became parties to an international treaty against torture. In the face of enormous political pressure, Britain subsequently found Pinochet unfit to stand trial on grounds of poor physical and mental health and sent him back to Chile. Over the next several years Chilean courts alternatively ruled for and against him in a wide variety of cases while he remained secluded in his Santiago home. Ultimately, Pinochet eluded justice: he died on 10 December 2006.

IMPROVED HUMAN RIGHTS

Paradoxically, strong repression in Chile contributed to strengthening international human rights norms and to the growth of international efforts to protect human rights. The military government led by Pinochet subjected its citizens in Chile to fear, interrogation, kidnapping, torture, and murder. The effects of these abuses live on in the memories of mothers, fathers, wives, husbands, children, and others. Simultaneously, those same abuses triggered the formation of a strong transnational human rights network that served as a model for many other international efforts against domestic repression. That network transmitted key information around the world and helped mobilize international organizations and Western states against Chile. These responses offered hope and protection to the domestic opposition in Chile and threatened the military government's legitimacy. Ultimately, these pressures forced the military government to respond. At first, the government responded superficially, by simply putting the issue on its agenda and changing the way it talked.

As time wore on, the government altered its behavior and created new institutions that ultimately helped force it from office in a peaceful democratic transition. None of these results happened quickly or profoundly enough for human rights activists, but it seems likely that events would have unfolded quite differently if no one had responded at all.

[*See also* Amnesty International; Jimmy Carter; Catholicism; Constitutions and Human Rights; Democracy and Right to Participation; Economic Sanctions; Foreign Policy; Donald Fraser; International Committee of the Red Cross (ICRC); Right to Life; Karl J. Marx; Nongovernmental Organizations: Overview; Organization of American States; Augusto Pinochet; South American Southern Cone: National Security State, 1970s–1980s; Torture: International Law; United Nations Commission on Human Rights; United Nations General Assembly; *and* Universal Jurisdiction.]

BIBLIOGRAPHY

Angell, Alan. "Unions and Workers in Chile during the 1980s." In *The Struggle for Democracy in Chile, 1982–1990*, edited by Paul Drake and Iván Jaksić, pp. 188–210. Lincoln: University of Nebraska Press, 1991.

Arriagada, Genaro. *Pinochet: The Politics of Power.* Translated by Nancy Morris with Vincent Ercolano and Kristen A. Whitney. Boston: Unwin Hyman, 1988.

Barros, Robert. *Constitutionalism and Dictatorship: Pinochet, the Junta, and the 1980 Constitution.* Cambridge, U.K.: Cambridge University Press, 2002.

Branch, Taylor, and Eugene M. Propper. *Labyrinth.* New York: Viking Press, 1982.

Chilean National Commission on Truth and Reconciliation. *Report of the Chilean National Commission on Truth and Reconciliation.* Santiago: 1993.

Chuchryk, Patricia M. "Feminist Anti-Authoritarian Politics: The Role of Women's Organizations in the Chilean Transition to Democracy." In *The Women's Movement in Latin America: Feminism and the Transition to Democracy*, edited by Jane Jaquette, pp. 149–183. Boston: Unwin Hyman, 1989.

Constable, Pamela, and Arturo Valenzuela. *A Nation of Enemies: Chile under Pinochet.* New York: W.W. Norton, 1991.

Dinges, John, and Saul Landau. *Assassination on Embassy Row.* New York: Pantheon Books, 1980.

Drake, Paul W., and Iván Jaksić, eds. *The Struggle for Democracy in Chile, 1982–1990.* Lincoln: University of Nebraska Press, 1991.

Fleet, Michael. *The Rise and Fall of Chilean Christian Democracy.* Princeton, N.J.: Princeton University Press, 1985.

Forsythe, David. "Human Rights, the United States, and the Organization of American States." *Human Rights Quarterly* 13, no. 1 (1991): 66–98.

Fruhling, Hugo. "Stages of Repression and the Legal Strategy for the Defense of Human Rights in Chile: 1973–1980." *Human Rights Quarterly* 5, no. 4 (1983): 510–533.

Garretón, Manuel Antonio. "Popular Mobilization and the Military Regime in Chile: The Complexities of the Invisible Transition." In *Power and Popular Protest: Latin American Social Movements*, edited by Susan Eckstein, pp. 259–277. Berkeley: University of California Press, 1989.

Hawkins, Darren. "Human Rights Norms and Networks in Authoritarian Chile." In *Restructuring World Politics: Transnational Social Movements, Networks, and Norms*, edited by Sanjeev Khagram, James V. Riker, and Kathryn Sikkink, pp. 47–70. Minneapolis: University of Minnesota Press, 2002.

Hawkins, Darren. "State Responses to International Pressures: Human Rights in Authoritarian Chile." *European Journal of International Relations* 3, no. 4 (December 1997): 403–434.

Hawkins, Darren G. *International Human Rights and Authoritarian Rule in Chile.* Lincoln: University of Nebraska Press, 2002.

Kamminga, Menno T. *Inter-State Accountability for Violations of Human Rights.* Philadelphia: University of Pennsylvania Press, 1992.

Loveman, Brian. "Military Dictatorship and Political Opposition in Chile, 1973–1986." *Journal of Interamerican Studies and World Affairs* 28, no. 4 (1986–1987): 1–38.

Loveman, Brian. "Misión Cumplida? Civil Military Relations and the Chilean Political Transition." *Journal of Interamerican Studies and World Affairs* 33, no. 3 (1991): 35–74.

Lowden, Pamela. *Moral Opposition to Authoritarian Rule in Chile, 1973–90.* New York: St. Martin's Press, 1996.

Munck, Gerardo L. "Authoritarianism, Modernization, and Democracy in Chile." *Latin American Research Review* 29, no. 2 (1994): 188–211.

Muñoz, Heraldo. "Chile: The Limits of Success." In *Exporting Democracy*, edited by Abraham Lowenthal, pp. 39–52. Baltimore: Johns Hopkins University Press, 1991.

Muñoz, Heraldo, and Carlos Portales. *Elusive Friendship: A Survey of U.S.-Chilean Relations.* Boulder, Colo.: Lynne Rienner Publishers, 1991.

O'Shaughnessy, Hugh. *Pinochet: The Politics of Torture.* New York: New York University Press, 2000.

Oppenheim, Lois Hecht. *Politics in Chile: Democracy, Authoritarianism, and the Search for Development.* 2d ed. Boulder, Colo.: Westview Press, 1998.

Oxhorn, Philip D. *Organizing Civil Society: The Popular Sectors and the Struggle for Democracy in Chile.* University Park, Pa.: Pennsylvania State University Press, 1995.

Portales, Carlos. "External Factors and the Authoritarian Regime." In *The Struggle for Democracy in Chile, 1982–1990*, edited by Paul Drake and Iván Jaksić, pp. 251–275. Lincoln: University of Nebraska Press, 1991.

Puryear, Jeffrey M. *Building Democracy: Foreign Donors and Chile.* New York: Columbia University–New York University Consortium, 1991.

Remmer, Karen. "Neopatrimonialism: The Politics of Military Rule in Chile, 1973–1987." *Comparative Politics* 21 (January 1989): 149–170.

Schoultz, Lars. *Human Rights and United States Policy toward Latin America.* Princeton, N.J.: Princeton University Press, 1981.

Sigmund, Paul. *The Overthrow of Allende and the Politics of Chile.* Pittsburgh, Pa.: University of Pittsburgh Press, 1977.

Silva, Eduardo. "Chile Past, Present, and Future: The Long Road to National Reconciliation." *Journal of Interamerican Studies and World Affairs* 33, no. 4 (1991): 133–146.

Valenzuela, Arturo. "Chile: Origins, Consolidation, and Breakdown of a Democratic Regime." In *Democracy in Developing Countries: Latin America,* edited by Larry Diamond, Juan J. Linz, and Seymour Martin Lipset, pp. 159–206. Boulder, Colo.: Lynn Rienner Publishers, 1989.

Valenzuela, Arturo. "The Military in Power: The Consolidation of One-Man Rule." In *The Struggle for Democracy in Chile, 1982–1990,* edited by Paul Drake and Iván Jaksić, pp. 21–72. Lincoln: University of Nebraska Press, 1991.

Valenzuela, J. Samuel, and Arturo Valenzuela, eds. *Military Rule in Chile: Dictatorship and Oppositions.* Baltimore: Johns Hopkins University Press, 1986.

Varas, Augusto. "The Crisis of Legitimacy of Military Rule in the 1980s." In *The Struggle for Democracy in Chile, 1982–1990,* edited by Paul Drake and Iván Jaksić, pp. 73–97. Lincoln: University of Nebraska Press, 1991.

Wilson, Richard. "Prosecuting Pinochet: International Crimes in Spanish Domestic Law." *Human Rights Quarterly* 21, no. 4 (1999): 927–979.

CHINA
THE FAMINE OF THE 1960s

by Andrew Wedeman

The failure of the Great Leap Forward in 1959 resulted in what is considered the worst human-made, politically induced famine in modern history. At the time the extent of the famine remained largely hidden from the world. It was not until 1980–1981 that data began to emerge from China indicating the magnitude of the disaster. Based on this information, early studies estimated the death toll at about 16 million. Later analyses raised the estimated toll to 23 million, then 29 million, and up to 43 million. Most analysts now accept an estimate of around 30 million, a figure that would represent roughly 5 percent of China's total population. Estimates of the annual number of deaths put the toll for the first year of the famine (1958–1959) at 4.5 million, rising to 10.9 million in 1959–1960. The number of famine-related deaths declined slightly in 1960–1961 to 9.7 million and then to 4.4 million in the famine's final year. By 1962 the famine had passed. The total demographic toll, however, was even greater. Nationally the birthrate declined by almost half during the famine years, which means between 31 and 33 million fewer births, according to demographers. Children born during the famine years and many other survivors suffered long-term adverse health effects.

Officially the famine was blamed on bad weather, with all but two provinces (Tibet and Xinjiang) reportedly suffering from some combination of drought, flooding, crop disease, and insect infestation. Local government officials and party cadres were also blamed not only for failing to properly implement the policies of the Great Leap Forward but also for responding to the emerging food crisis in a haphazard and derelict manner. After Mao's Zedong death, the party hinted that policy failures at the leadership level might have been a factor. Yet even in the early twenty-first century discussion of the 1958–1961 famine remained a largely taboo historical subject, and its origins remained imperfectly explained in Chinese national discourse.

However, social scientists in the West have convincingly demonstrated that the 1958–1961 famine was a human-made crisis. Weather played a role, they admit, but only in combination with what has been called a policy-induced "perfect storm." Explanations vary in their emphasis. Conventional wisdom ascribes the famine to a combination of inflated production claims that led to excessive government grain procurements, the diversion of labor resources out of the agricultural sector, the failure to complete the fall 1958 harvest, a prevailing atmosphere of political radicalism, the adoption of communal eating, and the government's failure to quickly respond to evidence of mounting food shortages in the countryside. Basically the government neglected to readjust the failing economic policies of the Great Leap Forward and to implement a relief program that might have prevented catastrophic food shortages.

Because the roots of the 1958–1961 famine lie in the Great Leap Forward and its collapse, this article begins by examining its origins and the policies associated with Mao's attempt to radically accelerate China's economic development. It then analyzes the evolution of the famine and concludes with a discussion of the causes of the famine and its consequences.

COLLECTIVIZATION AND THE GREAT LEAP FORWARD

Having ridden a wave of peasant nationalism into power, the Chinese Communist Party embraced a land-to-the-tiller program in 1949–1950. The holdings of landlords were expropriated and redistributed to a new class of small-holding peasant farmers. At first the land-to-the-tiller reforms produced significant gains in agricultural output, with grain production climbing 17 percent in 1950, 8 percent in 1951, and 15 percent in 1952. Thereafter growth rates declined, and total grain production increased less than 2 percent in 1953 and 1954. Frustrated by the "inch forward" in agricultural production and worried that the egalitarian conditions created by the 1949–1950 land reform were giving way to renewed class stratification as some peasant families rose to become "rich peasants" and others once again declined to the level of "poor peasants," the party accelerated agricultural collectivization during the mid-1950s, moving progressively from a program stressing the formation of lower-level mutual-aid teams (in which families pooled labor during the planting and harvesting seasons) to cooperatives in which families invested both their land and their labor in joint production and then to collective farms in which ownership of land and major farm implements (including livestock) were transferred from the individual households to the collective. Families then received payments based on a "work point system."

In the short term collectivization increased agricultural output, with grain production rising over 8 percent in 1955. The following year, however, grain production increased only 5 percent, and in 1957 it grew just over 1 percent. Unhappy with the failure of collectivization to produce the anticipated surge in output and disappointed by the slow pace of industrialization, CCP chairman Mao began to push for the abandonment of the conventional Soviet model with its reliance on collectivization and "squeezing" the agricultural sector. According to Mao, even though China was obviously capital-poor, its abundant supply of labor offered an alternative way of stimulating economic growth. In his view, most agricultural labor was systematically underutilized. Although a vast amount of labor was necessary during the planting season and the harvest, Mao believed farm labor sat mostly idle during the winter months and was underemployed in the period between planting and harvest.

Based on these assumptions, Mao called for a new program using part of China's underutilized rural labor force to construct new irrigation and water conservancy systems that would store water supplies during periods of heavy rain and the spring runoff as well as facilitate the distribution of irrigation water to areas that lacked adequate natural supplies of water. "Surplus" rural laborers would also either be transferred to urban-based industries or employed in new rural industries oriented toward the production of commodities for the farm sector. Mao further suggested that it would be possible to significantly increase the total rural labor force if household chores, such as child care and cooking, were shifted to communal facilities. This would free up female labor for farmwork, which would then allow for further transfers of male labor into construction and industry. Mao thus called for the merger of the collective farms into people's communes. The much larger size of the communes (upwards of ten

thousand families), he claimed, would also allow for much greater specialization of labor and the achievement of new economies of scale. According to Mao, his alternative program would produce a "great leap forward" and would propel the Chinese economy past the advanced industrial economies of western Europe in a few scant years.

Mass mobilization of rural labor for water conservancy projects began in the winter of 1957–1958, followed by the formation of the new communes beginning in the first months of 1958. The initial results appeared to be positive. The Great Leap Forward program was met with considerable enthusiasm and an apparent fervor of activity. "Shock brigades" of nearly 100 million laborers took to the countryside to tame nature and harness China's rivers and lakes by constructing new dams, reservoirs, and canals. Communes began to throw up "backyard steel mills" and other industrial ventures that would turn urban-biased economic orthodoxy on its head. Ten million rural residents were moved into the cities to bolster China's industrial workforce and provide labor for new construction projects. Reports of extraordinary increases in crop yields flowed into the Chinese press, accompanied by pictures of fields bursting with corn, rice, and other grains. Children joined in, clanging pots together in an effort to kill "grain-destroying birds" by forcing them to fly until they dropped dead from exhaustion. A nationwide campaign to exterminate rats produced grisly piles of slaughtered rodents. As of the early fall, it appeared the Great Leap Forward was working. Flush with success, Mao told the party leadership in November that the 1958 grain harvest might double that of 1957.

The winter of 1958–1959, however, brought signs of trouble. Evidence began to surface suggesting that despite provincial claims of record output, grain procurement was falling short of targets, and some cities were facing food shortages. A significant percentage of the iron produced in backyard blast furnaces proved unsuited for industrial purposes. More worrisome was that, even though China had supposedly enjoyed a bumper grain crop, death rates (which had been declining during previous years) began to increase, albeit modestly. However, in China's most populous province of Sichuan, the mortality rate jumped thirteen points from twelve deaths per one thousand in 1957 to twenty-five deaths per one thousand in 1958. Mortality in neighboring Guizhou and Yunnan provinces also went up five points. In Gansu Province the rate increased ten points.

Evidence of more serious problems in the countryside began to appear in the spring of 1959. Touring his ancestral village in Hunan, Minister of Defense Marshal Peng Dehuai discovered that food was in extremely short supply and there was a danger of serious food shortages afflicting the people in the coming months before the new crop reached maturity. Earlier that year, while on a tour of Gansu, he found crops rotting in the field because, he was told, most of the available labor had been assigned to work the backyard steel mills. When he returned to Beijing, Peng was told that soldiers' families had been complaining about severe food shortages. Mao's private secretaries also returned from inspection tours during the spring with tales of starvation and impending economic crisis. During the early summer reports of serious drought in some areas and flooding elsewhere began to trickle in.

When the party leadership met at the mountaintop resort of Lushan in July, Peng submitted a letter outlining what he had seen during his spring travels and arguing that reports of economic breakthroughs in steel and grain production had been wildly exaggerated. Readjustment and retrenchment were necessary; he argued, otherwise, there was a risk of economic crisis. For much of the first three weeks at Lushan, Mao allowed Peng to question the Great Leap Forward, and at the time it appeared that many within the leadership would support his call to halt the program. On 23 July, however, the chairman turned on Peng, charging that his letter was an attempt to blame Mao for the country's problems and was also a treasonous call for an intra-party coup. Mao declared that if the leadership sided with Peng, he would desert the party and raise the flag of rebellion against the CCP. In the face of Mao's outburst, the party leadership immediately abandoned Peng and rallied to Mao. In the days that followed they removed Peng and approved Mao's call for an acceleration of the Great Leap Forward. Economic radicalism therefore continued into the winter of 1959–1960.

By the end of 1959 famine gripped many parts of China. In Sichuan the 1958 famine intensified, sending the morality rate up a further twenty-one points to forty-seven per one thousand, a threefold increase over the 1957 level. Mortality increases were less dramatic elsewhere. Nevertheless mortality rates rose in all but two provinces during 1959. However, both Yunnan and Gansu provinces (where mortality was down compared to 1958) had experienced significant increases the previous year, and in these localities mortality rates remained higher than in the pre–Great Leap Forward period. In all an estimated 11 million people died in 1959 from famine.

In 1960 mortality rates continued to rise in nineteen provinces, with Anhui, Henan, Guangxi, Gansu, and Qinghai reporting double-digit increases. In Anhui, the province hit the hardest, mortality rose nearly fifty-two points from seventeen per thousand to sixty-nine per thousand, almost six times the pre–Great Leap Forward rate. Despite the spread of famine conditions, deaths attributed to the famine reportedly fell slightly, dropping to an estimated 9.6 million.

The following year mortality rates decreased across the country. In Anhui the rate fell from sixty-nine per one thousand to eight per one thousand. Rates in Henan, Gansu, and Qinghai also fell back to pre–Great Leap Forward levels. In Sichuan the mortality rate fell by half but remained a third higher than before the Great Leap Forward policy. In both Liaoning and Shandong, however, mortality rates rose. Decreases in mortality rates did not necessarily signal that the famine was abating. By then many of the weakest members of the population had already died, and in many areas famine deaths had sharply reduced the imbalance between diminished food resources and mouths to feed. The famine thus continued with an estimated 4.4 million deaths attributed to starvation and malnutrition that year.

Birthrates plummeted as food shortages intensified. Nationally births per one thousand population fell from thirty-four in 1957 to twenty-five in 1959, twenty-one in 1960, and eighteen in 1961. As mortality rates increased and birthrates fell, net population growth rates plummeted from a national average net increase of 25 per 1,000 population in 1957 to 19 in 1958, 11 in 1959, and 0.23 in 1960. In 1961 the downward slide ended, and the net rate of population increase rose to six per one thousand. Even then the rate was only a quarter of the 1957 rate. In eight provinces rising mortality and falling birthrates combined to yield net decreases in population. Unofficial estimates of total deaths in five of these provinces are considerably higher.

Official statistics (Table 1) and academic estimates of the death toll tell only part of the story. Anecdotal evidence gathered by Chinese scholars and Western reporters paint a grim picture. Conditions varied across the county. A few areas were largely unaffected or only experienced food shortages. Most areas were hit hard. Some areas were effectively stripped of food, forcing peasants to turn to traditional alternatives, such as wild plants, bark, and grass, all of which were poor nutritional substitutes. Some villages reportedly lost all of their inhabitants to famine. In other villages only a few "hungry ghosts" remained behind. In some areas peasants fled. Some traveled to the cities in hopes of finding food and work.

TABLE 1. Famine-Related Deaths: Provinces Experiencing Net Population Losses.

Province	Peak year	Population peak year (millions)	Low year	Population low year (millions)	Population decrease (millions)	Percentage change	Estimated famine deaths (millions)
Sichuan	1957	70.81	1961	64.59	6.22	−8.78	9.00
Anhui	1959	34.27	1961	29.88	4.39	−12.81	8.00
Shandong	1958	54.22	1960	51.88	2.34	−4.32	7.50
Hunan	1959	36.92	1961	35.08	1.84	−4.98	
Henan	1957	49.79	1961	48.03	1.76	−3.53	7.80
Guizhou	1959	17.44	1961	16.24	1.20	−6.88	
Gansu	1959	12.93	1961	12.11	0.82	−6.34	
Qinghai	1959	2.60	1962	2.05	0.55	−21.15	0.90
Jiangsu	1959	42.90	1961	42.43	0.47	−1.10	
Guangxi	1959	22.05	1961	21.59	0.46	−2.09	
Liaoning	1960	25.59	1961	25.19	0.40	−1.56	
Hubei	1959	31.73	1960	31.52	0.21	−0.66	
Yunnan	1958	19.14	1960	18.95	0.19	−0.99	
Ningxia	1960	2.13	1962	1.99	0.14	−6.57	
Total Loss					20.99		33.20

SOURCE: Guojia Tongji Bu.

Others went to remote areas in search of vacant land and to escape the state and its local cadres. Others became beggars and vagabonds. Still others resorted to banditry. Wives and daughters were sold. Infants and young children were allowed to die from starvation or succumbed to neglect and malnutrition. Many were abandoned. After their parents died or fled, orphans were left to fend for themselves on the streets; few survived. Cannibalism was reported in many localities. Even in less hard-hit localities, malnutrition affected most of the population, first killing those assigned to the most physically demanding tasks, then killing the elderly and young.

The Great Leap Forward and subsequent famine led to an increase in violence in the countryside. Trouble began before the Great Leap Forward and intensified as peasants lost their property. Peasants opposed to collectivization and the communes hid grain and tools, dug up vegetable gardens, cut down fruit trees, and ate their livestock. In many areas local cadres responded by "dragging out" the recalcitrant and subjecting them to public humiliation and beatings. "Rebels" were sent to makeshift jails, where prisoners often starved to death as food supplies dwindled. Laborers assigned to the water conservancy projects and the backyard steel mills were given Herculean tasks and in some cases were subjected to whippings and beatings

if they fell short of quotas. As the procurement season got underway in the fall of 1958, cadres ordered the hard punishment of those who had failed to fulfill their quotas. Peasants who stole food faced the possibility of torture and execution. In some villages the cadres confiscated the peasants' woks and other cooking utensils to dissuade them from stealing food, but this practice also effectively denied them the capability of cooking whatever alternative foods they might scavenge. Roadblocks were thrown up to prevent starving peasants from leaving their homes. Armed guards stopped peasants from boarding trains bound for the cities. In Shanghai and other cities refugees were detained in camps and forcibly repatriated home.

The peasants were not always passive. In some areas they attacked the local cadres, seized food stocks, and sacked granaries. Trains believed to be carrying food were attacked and plundered. In response the cadres called out the militia and turned to the army for help protecting state warehouses and grain depots against peasant attacks. In some areas the deployment of armed soldiers and barbed wire proved insufficient to deter desperate peasants. There were also reports of the military firing on mobs of would-be looters.

Corruption began to spread. Cadres with access to food looked after their own families and relatives. Others demanded bribes and sexual favors in return for food, while others sold scarce supplies on rapidly expanding black markets. As a result, even though many cadres suffered alongside their neighbors and also saw their family members and relatives succumb to hunger and malnutrition, other cadres grew rich from corruption. Cadres sympathetic to the peasants became demoralized, alienated, and in some areas openly insubordinate. At the grassroots level the integrity of the party came under unprecedented stress.

Conditions were somewhat better in the cities. State food policy consistently favored the cities. Supplies extracted from the starving peasantry continued to flow to the cities, where workers, including government officials and party cadres, were eligible for state food rations. As the famine intensified, most urban residents continued to receive grain and other staples. Food, however, soon became scarce, and in many areas rations were cut repeatedly. Endemic hunger and widespread malnutrition caused increased urban mortality even in the absence of mass starvation. According to Mao's personal doctor, even the inner leadership ultimately felt the pinch of hunger as grain supplies dwindled, vegetables became scarce, and meat simply disappeared.

Conditions improved in most areas in 1962, and in a majority of provinces mortality rates returned to their pre-1958 levels. Only Shandong reported a significantly elevated mortality rate that year. Birthrates, on the other hand, jumped to an average of thirty-seven per one thousand, a level not seen since the early days of the People's Republic of China, when the restoration of peace and stability had triggered a baby boom. The combination of declining mortality and rising birthrates restored the rate of net population increase to pre-1957 levels, thus suggesting that the worst of the famine had passed. Persistent food shortages, however, continued into the mid-1960s.

CAUSES OF THE FAMINE

Official claims that the 1958–1961 famine was largely the result of adverse weather conditions and hard evidence that China did in fact suffer from numerous environmental problems during 1959–1961 notwithstanding, it is now generally accepted that the famine was a complex human-made disaster. In brief, the most widely accepted explanation holds that inflated expectations about the ability of the communes to increase agricultural output and pressure to produce record results led grassroots and provincial cadres to inflate reports on the expected size of the 1958 harvest. Based on these exaggerated claims, the state fixed grain procurement quotas at levels that would have left scant reserves for the peasants. Determined to demonstrate their zeal and fearful that failure to deliver would result in punishment, rural cadres filled or even overfilled the state's procurement targets. As a result, many rural localities were left with only a few months worth of food stocks, which was not enough to see them through to the next harvest.

Meanwhile diversion of manpower to the industrial sector, the water conservancy program, and the backyard steel mills created a serious shortage of farm labor. This shortage was not offset by the mobilization of female labor, and as a result, the 1958 fall crop was never fully harvested. In addition the 1959 spring planting was incomplete. Local food supplies were further drained by the establishment of communal mess halls and the advent of the "free supply system," which led to both excessive consumption and increased waste. Food supplies in many areas were thus depleted before the spring crop became available in 1959. Evidence of mounting food shortages were then ignored or covered up, leading to a continuation of the Great Leap Forward and a repeat of the previous year's mistakes in 1959. Once again cadres lied about output, thus causing the state to demand excessive extractions of grain and other foodstuffs. In this context a combination of drought, flooding, and devastating typhoons cut total output and thus exacerbated the human-made problems. Finally, exports of grain, partly to earn hard currency to repay China's Korean War debts to the Soviet Union, diminished domestic grain supplies and left the state without the grain reserves needed to supply a major famine relief effort.

When faced with evidence of widespread hunger, the leadership not only failed to halt grain exports but also failed to import grain in sufficient quantities to offset declining domestic production. The state neither asked for international assistance nor established a system of relief that would have ensured minimal supplies for rural residents, who, unlike urban residents, were not entitled to state-provided rations. The countryside was largely left on its own.

Unwilling to recognize or own up to it errors, including those attributable to Chairman Mao, the party stubbornly clung to the Great Leap Forward policy through 1961. It was only after the country faced mass starvation that the party finally shifted direction and embraced a halfhearted, ad hoc reform program that included cutting back on procurement quotas, shifting labor back into the rural sector, allowing a degree of decollectivization (that included the dismantlement of many of the people's communes), and tolerating the limited restoration of free markets. In many areas the famine was actually brought under control by local initiatives that split up the land and allowed families to return to tending their own crops.

Disagreement exists over the relative importance of these various factors. There is, however, general agreement that it was not a sudden decrease in total food supply that caused the famine. Grain output actually increased in 1958, and despite a 15 percent drop in total grain production the following year, output in 1959 was actually above the levels recorded for the years 1952–1955, which were considered relatively good years for Chinese agriculture. It was not until 1960–1961 in fact that total output fell to crisis levels. Total grain production thus dropped from a peak of 200 million metric tons in 1958, to 170 million metric tons in 1959 and 144 million metric tons in 1960, according to official Chinese statistics issued in the early 1990s. Estimates by American government analysts are slightly lower, but they conform to this basic pattern. In absolute terms therefore declines in total food supply occurred after the start of the famine, not before.

Conventional wisdom places the primary blame for the famine on policy decisions associated with the Great Leap Forward and the effects of grossly exaggerating the harvest's size and the resulting excessive procurement of grain. Diversion of labor into water conservancy and the backyard steel mills hampered efforts to harvest the 1958 crop. More critically the failure to terminate these programs and the decision to continue them into the spring of 1959 caused a devastating decline in production and the rapid spread of famine conditions in 1960. Other factors, including the weather, contributed by further decreasing supplies but only to the extent that they exacerbated the problems created by policy decisions.

If policy decisions were the primary causes of the famine, to what extent were Mao and the CCP leadership to blame? As the chief architecture and proponent of the Great Leap Forward, Mao certainly bears considerable responsibility for the genesis of the crisis. His decision to attack Peng at the July 1959 Lushan conference and force the leadership to continue the Great Leap Forward undoubtedly played a crucial role, causing the localized problems evident in the spring of 1959 to explode into a much more serve famine. Mao was not alone, however.

Other cadres, including provincial leaders in the hard-hit provinces of Henan, Sichuan, and Anhui, pressed the Great Leap Forward with blind zeal and were thus guilty in an even more immediate sense: they should have been more aware of deteriorating conditions than Mao, who largely ignored views that contradicted his own. By the same token local cadres bear a large share of the blame because they were ultimately responsible for the gross inflation of production figures and enforcing the excessive procurement quotas handed down by the central planners.

Ultimately one has to recognize that although individual cadres and officials contributed to the problem, they did so in a political context that made careful deliberation and opposition to radicalism difficult. Throughout the 1950s repeated purges of "rightists" sent the signal that it was better to advance too rashly toward full Communism than to advance too slowly. Once the "wind of exaggeration" began blowing in the spring of 1958, cadres that did not join in the frenzy were flirting with political and occupational suicide. Under such conditions it is perhaps not surprising that many choose to blindly follow the party line even if they harbored doubts about the wisdom of the Great Leap Forward. Fear of Mao, cowardice, and political opportunism thus blocked efforts to abandon the failing policies of the Great Leap Forward and head off the famine while it was still in its early (and perhaps containable) stages. Finally, the absence of effective limits on cadre power played a major role by creating conditions in which many cadres felt they had a mandate to mercilessly squeeze the peasantry economically.

It was not until 1961–1962 that Mao began to comprehend the extent of the famine and became disenchanted (to the point that he allegedly fell into a deep depression) with the "wind of exaggeration." At that point readjustment became possible. However, Mao never renounced the Great Leap Forward. He instead blamed local cadres for excessive zealotry and then quietly stepped aside. With Mao no longer the all-powerful leader, PRC president Liu Shaoqi, Premier Zhou Enlai, and CCP secretary Deng Xiaoping—all of whom supported the Great Leap Forward and failed to stand by Peng when he questioned the Great Leap Forward policies in 1959—began importing food and partially decollectivizing. They shut down the failed backyard steel mills, terminated the failing water conservancy program, and ordered rural workers to return to farming. Mao, in short, was the key to both the genesis of the famine and the eventual decision to address it.

ASSESSMENT

The 1958–1961 Chinese famine was arguably the worst human-made demographic disaster in history. Tens of millions of Chinese died, and hundreds of millions more suffered as a result of the radical economic policies adopted during the Great Leap Forward. The famine stands out because it occurred in peacetime and was not the result of a catastrophic decrease in total food availability. On the contrary, the famine occurred in the context of a period of increasing prosperity brought about by the establishment of the PRC and the consolidation of national power in the hands of the CCP. Perhaps even more ironically, the famine grew out of Mao's distaste for Stalinist development policies that relied on squeezing surplus value out of the peasantry. Mao believed that China could avoid such an antipeasant policy by radically reorganizing its rural sector and thereby dramatically increasing productivity and output. But rather than serve the interests of China's peasantry, Mao's radical policies resulted in economic disaster.

In a sense the famine led to more political chaos. Suspicious that the Liu-Zhou-Deng retrenchment policy would lead to the restoration of class divisions within Chinese society and that counterrevolutionary "revisionism" had perverted members of the CCP (including its innermost elite during the "years of hardship"), Mao initiated a series of political struggles that culminated in the Great Proletarian Cultural Revolution, during which another million people died. Overall, however, the failure of the Great Leap Forward and the resulting famine helped convince some within the party elite that socialized agriculture was an unworkable and perhaps even utopian policy. Agrarian radicalism continued, but in the wake of the famine it was tempered by a new pragmatism that stressed the absolute importance of ensuring stable and adequate food supplies. Never again would the CCP seek to radically restructure the agricultural sector or mobilize rural labor in pursuit of rapid economic change. Moreover the decollectivization policies adopted during the early stages of China's post-1978 economic reform essentially replicated those implemented on a limited basis during the worst days of 1961–1962. In broad terms therefore the reforms that led to the de facto privatization of China's farm sector in the 1980s had their roots in the famine of 1958–1961. As such, the CCP ultimately learned from its catastrophic mistakes. These silver linings should not, however, obscure or somehow justify the suffering and massive abuse of human rights caused by the Great Leap Forward.

[*See also* Right to Food and Adequate Standard of Living *and* Mao Zedong.]

BIBLIOGRAPHY

Aird, John S. "Population Studies and Population Policy in China." *Population and Development Review* 8, no. 2 (1982): 267–297.

Ashton, Basil, Kenneth Hill, Alan Piazza, and Robin Zeitz. "Famine in China, 1958–61." *Population and Development Review* 10, no. 4 (1984): 613–645.

Becker, Jasper. *Hungry Ghosts: China's Secret Famine.* London: John Murray, 1996.

Bernstein, Thomas P. "Stalinism, Famine, and Chinese Peasants: Grain Procurement during the Great Leap Forward." *Theory and Society* 13, no. 3 (1984): 339–377.

Chang, Gene Hsin, and Guanzhou Jame Wen. "Food Availability versus Consumption Efficiency: Cause of the Chinese Famine." *China Economic Review* 9, no. 2 (1998): 157–166.

Domenach, Jean-Luc. *The Origins of the Great Leap Forward: The Case of One Chinese Province.* Boulder, Colo.: Westview, 1995.

Guojia Tongji Bu (State Statistical Bureau). *Quanguo Ge Sheng, Zizhiqu, Zhixia Shi Lishi Tongji Ziliao Huibian [1949–1989] (Compilation of Historical Data for Provinces, Autonomous Regions, and Municipalities [1949–1989]).* Beijing: Zhongguo Tongji Chubanshe (China Statistics Publisher), 1990.

Johnson, D. Gale. "China's Great Famine: Introductory Remarks." *China Economic Review* 9, no. 2 (1998): 103–109.

Kane, Penny. *Famine in China, 1959–61: Demographic and Social Implications.* London: Macmillan, 1988.

Kueh, Y. Y. "A Weather Index for Analyzing Grain Yield Instability in China, 1952–81." *China Quarterly* no. 97 (1984): 68–83.

Kung, James Kai-sing, and Justin Yifu Lin. "The Causes of China's Great Leap Famine, 1959–61." *Economic Development and Cultural Change* 52, no. 1 (2003): 51–73.

Li, Lillian M. *Fighting Famine in North China: State, Market, and Environmental Decline, 1690s–1990s.* Stanford, Calif.: Stanford University Press, 2007.

Lieberthal, Kenneth. "The Great Leap Forward and the Split in the Yan'an Leadership 1958–65." In *The Politics of China 1849–1989*, edited by Roderick MacFarquhar. New York: Cambridge University Press, 1993.

Lin, Justin Yifu. "Collectivization and China's Agricultural Crisis, 1959–1961." *Journal of Political Economy* 98, no. 6 (1990): 1228–1252.

Lin, Justin Yifu, and Dennis Tao Yang. "On the Causes of China's Agricultural Crisis and the Great Leap Famine." *China Economic Review* 9, no. 2 (1998): 125–140.

Li Wei, and Dennis Tao Yang. "The Great Leap Forward: Anatomy of a Central Planning Disaster." *Journal of Political Economy* 113, no. 4 (2005): 840–877.

Li Zhisui. *The Private Life of Chairman Mao: The Memoirs of Mao's Personal Physician.* Translated by Tai Hung-chao, edited by Anne F. Thurston. New York: Random House, 1994.

Peng, Xizhe. "Demographic Consequences of the Great Leap Forward in China's Provinces." *Population and Development Review* 13, no. 4 (1987): 639–670.

Riskin, Carl. "Seven Questions about the Chinese Famine of 1959–61." *China Economic Review* 9, no. 2 (1998): 111–124.

Teiwes, Frederick C., with Warren Sun. *China's Road to Disaster: Mao, Central Politicians, and Provincial Leaders in the Unfolding of the Great Leap Forward 1955–1959.* Armonk, N.Y.: M.E. Sharpe, 1999.

Thaxton, Ralph A., Jr. *Catastrophe and Contention in Rural China: Mao's Great Leap Forward Strategy and the Origins of Righteous Resistance in Da Fo Village.* New York: Cambridge University Press, 2008.

Yang, Dali L. *Calamity and Reform in China: State, Rural Society, and Institutional Change since the Great Leap Famine.* Stanford, Calif.: Stanford University Press, 1996.

Yang, Dali L., and Fubing Su. "The Politics of Famine and Reform in Rural China." *China Economic Review* 9, no. 2 (1998): 141–156.

Yang, Dennis Tao. "China's Agricultural Crisis and Famine of 1959–61: A Survey and Comparison of Soviet Famines." *Comparative Economic Studies* 50, no. 1 (March 2008): 1–29.

CHINA
TIANANMEN MASSACRE

by Ann Kent

The Chinese government's armed suppression of the democracy movement in Tiananmen Square and its surroundings on 3–4 June 1989 was a signal moment in history that became imprinted on the conscience of the world. It marked, in the Soviet leader Mikhail Gorbachev's words, a moment when "military and police violence was used to suppress an attempt by radical groups, particularly students, to step across a boundary in the process of modernization beyond which the [Chinese] Communist Party would have relinquished its monopoly on power" (Gorbachev and Mlynar, p. 193). It was followed by the suppression, if in the main less violent, of related movements around the country. Until then China had been treated as "the human rights exception," not warranting attention from the international community and exempted from international standards, even though it had already ratified most of the relevant international human rights treaties.

The democracy movement's immediate significance for human rights was therefore not that it represented the Chinese people's first meaningful effort to establish human rights and democracy but that its reach, scope, and peaceful character finally persuaded the international community to accept that a significant number of Chinese people aspired to human rights and that the rest of the world had some responsibility to respond to this need. The violent suppression of the movement seven weeks after its inception came as a shock to the Chinese people and to the world at large and only deepened the sense of international responsibility. Thus from 4 June 1989 Tiananmen and human rights provided an almost exclusive prism through which, for a time, the world related to China. Tiananmen also had lasting repercussions for international human rights. Not only did it influence the liberalization of Eastern Europe and the Soviet Union, but it also played a significant and continuing role in shaping the post–Cold War world.

PRECURSORS OF CHINA'S DEMOCRACY MOVEMENT

David Strand has observed that, inasmuch as China has a democratic tradition, it is one harnessing movements rather than institutions. The democracy movement was the culmination of a series of protest movements in China, influenced by Western notions of human rights and democracy, that stretched back into the second half of the nineteenth century. These highlighted the seminal role of intellectuals, students, and workers, acting separately or in loose association, in promoting political and economic progress in their country. In the nineteenth and early twentieth centuries a variety of protests associated with anti-imperialist struggle sometimes harnessed Western religious ideas and concepts of human rights. Of these the most important were the Taiping Rebellion, the Boxer Rebellion, and the May 4 and May 30 movements. By contrast, in the post-1949 period following the establishment of the People's Republic of China, outbreaks of dissent were primarily related to domestic politics but also invoked Western, including socialist, ideas. These included the Hundred Flowers movement, the Cultural Revolution, the Tiananmen incident of 1976, the Democracy Wall movement from 1978 to 1980, and the 1986 democracy demonstrations.

Traditionally, political dissent in China assumed two main forms: peasant rebellions, which were primarily a collective reaction to conditions of extreme economic and social stress and which in some cases resulted in the overthrow of a dynasty, and intellectual dissent or "remonstrance," whereby the literati were in theory obliged to speak out if the ruler departed too radically from Confucian ideals. However, while the actions of the former were often aimed at the overthrow of political elites, those of the latter primarily sought the improvement or reform of those elites. This difference reflected the long-standing alliance between political and intellectual elites exemplified in the Chinese tradition of imperial examinations that produced the country's scholar-officials. Thus the majority of the intelligentsia remained loyal to the court, while a minority of individuals, often working with political factions, influenced the ideas and policies of the incumbent dynasty.

Dissent in the late nineteenth century in China differed from these traditional forms in that it was primarily antiforeign in its goals while harnessing Western ideas for their realization. Thus the Taiping and Boxer Rebellions looked both backward and forward: they contained aspects of the traditional peasant uprising but were also targeted against foreigners and, in the case of Taiping, invoked some of the tenets of Christian religion. However, such uprisings had no direct connections with the intelligentsia, who were engaged in more intellectual and practical responses to the threat from the West.

The original intellectual progenitor of the 1989 democracy movement was thus the May 4 movement of 1919. This was an anti-imperialist movement led by students reflecting popular opposition to the capitulation of a corrupt Chinese government to Western powers at the Paris Peace Conference. Calling for "democracy and science," students attacked the government's preparedness to allow the transfer of German rights in Shandong Province to Japan. Only when workers joined the movement and called for a strike, however, did the Chinese government disavow the terms of the Treaty of Versailles. This movement prepared the way for the erosion of the Confucian system and the gradual influx into China of Western liberal and Marxist ideas.

On the other hand, the May 30 movement had its source in worker unrest. It was sparked by the lockout of striking Chinese workers from a Japanese-owned textile mill. When workers broke into the mill and smashed machinery, one was killed by Japanese guards. This prompted further strikes by workers, supported by student demonstrators shouting antiforeign slogans. When a British police officer called on his constables to fire on the crowd, eleven Chinese demonstrators were killed. Outrage at this atrocity led to a general strike in Shanghai and demonstrations in twenty-eight other Chinese cities. Although arising from different sources, both the May 4 and May 30 movements demonstrated the importance of close association, if not active cooperation, between students and workers. Despite this, even after the success in 1949 of the Communist revolution led by radical intellectuals and peasants, China's intellectuals persisted in their traditional disdain for its worker and peasant classes.

Post-1949 expressions of dissent in China differed from those in the pre-1949 period not only in their domestic focus but in the fact that, for the most part, they were directed and encouraged from above rather than emerging from below. Under the new socialist government established in October 1949, the group itself, whether comprising workers, peasants, or students, was co-opted by the state. Not only was political participation in the form of mass campaigns mobilized from above, but political dissent also had to be initiated and directed by the political leadership. Thus both the Hundred Flowers movement of 1956 and the Cultural Revolution of 1966 were initiated by China's radical leaders, in particular Chairman Mao Zedong, in an effort to both protect and energize the revolution. Following the Hungarian Revolution, which broke out in the wake of de-Stalinization in the Soviet Union, and in an attempt to preempt the spread of unrest to China, Mao launched the Hundred Flowers movement. The initial reluctance of intellectuals to accept their leaders' invitation to "let a hundred flowers bloom; let a hundred schools of thought contend" was ultimately justified when they and their subsequent criticisms became the target of the Anti-Rightist campaign of 1957.

Similarly, the Cultural Revolution was launched by Mao as a mass movement, spearheaded, under his direction, by students and workers, to undermine the entrenched power structures of the Communist Party and the bureaucracy and replace them with new, revolutionary structures as well as to reenergize fading revolutionary ideals by encouraging mass political participation. Apart from eliminating or repressing moderate members of the elite seen to represent a political threat to Mao, such as China's president Liu Shaoqi and the general secretary of the Chinese Communist Party Deng Xiaoping, the judiciary was dismantled, the public security organs were undermined, and summary people's justice was dispensed through revolutionary tribunals. During "struggle meetings" organized by young Red Guards, many leading officials and intellectuals were tortured, killed, or driven to commit suicide.

These revolutionary movements, however, also had significant unintended consequences for human rights and democracy in China. In the case of the Cultural Revolution, the disappearance of the old political, legal, and social structures "crippled the state's institutional infrastructure while training society in the art of covert resistance" (McCormick, p. 57). It not only authorized from above a challenge to authority from below but also for the first time since 1949 encouraged cooperation between revolutionary intellectuals and the worker-peasant classes, producing a linkage of social groups that until then had, for the most part, been kept separate. Following close on the heels of the Cultural Revolution was the incident at the Monument to the People's Heroes in Tiananmen Square on 5 April 1976, which arose during the traditional Qingming festival (of the dead). Beginning as a mass tribute to the moderate premier Zhou Enlai, who had died on 8 January 1976, it developed into a semi-spontaneous gesture of defiance against China's radical leaders when the latter authorized the removal of the wreaths, poems, and posters in Zhou's honor from the square. However, in keeping with past practices, it continued to use traditional forms of respectful dissent.

Two main lessons were derived by thinking Chinese from the Cultural Revolution. The first was the realization that the freedoms of speech, expression, press, and association and the political rights that the Cultural Revolution had temporarily dispensed to one sector of the population while denying them to another could only be universalized if they were institutionalized in a set of legal guarantees and structural forms. The second was that China's elite political leaders, many of whom had been corrupted over time by special privileges, high salaries, and the monopoly of power, could only be made more accountable to the people if a system of "socialist democracy" were adopted. These lessons were incorporated into the charters of the two dissenting movements that overlapped and succeeded the Cultural Revolution, the Li Yizhe movement (1974–1979) and the Democracy Wall movement (1978–1980). Both movements mainly took the form of written critiques in big-character posters and publications in dissident journals. Unlike the Cultural Revolution, they were encouraged by politicians on the right, such as Zhao Ziyang and the newly rehabilitated leader Deng Xiaoping.

The Democracy Wall movement began on 25 November 1978, when political posters were erected on a large wall at Xidan, west of Tiananmen Square in Beijing. The crowds that gathered at the wall over succeeding months discussed such questions as how to put into practice the freedoms of assembly and expression guaranteed by China's constitution, how to establish socialist mass democracy, and how to sweep away obstacles to the policy of the Four Modernizations (in agriculture, industry, science and technology, and military capability) that had been pursued by Deng since the Third Plenum of the Eleventh Central

Committee in December 1978. The leaders of the movement were, for the most part, educated workers with sympathy for ordinary people rather than university students and intellectuals. One of their number, Wei Jingsheng, famously called for a "Fifth Modernization" to accompany Deng's Four Modernizations, that is, democracy, while another, Wang Xizhe, worked to promote the human rights of the "laboring people" of China.

Although the Democracy Wall movement was later suppressed, ironically also by order of Deng, and its leaders arrested, debate continued between reformists and orthodox Marxists on the themes it had raised. Dissent also began to percolate up into the more elite scholarly stratum, including such intellectuals as Yan Jiaqi, Liu Binyan, Su Shaozhi, and Wang Ruowang. Opposing their calls for political reform, in September 1986 the party Central Committee adopted a resolution calling instead for enhanced "spiritual civilization." In response in late November and December, student demonstrations erupted in ten major Chinese cities with calls for civil rights and democracy. The presence of workers in the demonstrations in December ensured that the movement would be short-lived and its leaders punished. Criticized for his indecision in handling the students, the moderate leader and general party secretary Hu Yaobang resigned from his position on 16 January 1987 and was replaced by Zhao.

IMMEDIATE BACKGROUND TO THE 1989 MOVEMENT

China's move in the late 1970s to modernize its economy coincided internationally with the intensification of globalization. Its subsequent human rights crisis arose from the mismatch between the norms of globalization embraced by the government and the different expectations of its citizens. On the one hand, the modernization of communications and the openness associated with the new market system brought a degree of liberalization of the civil rights of freedom of the press, publication, and movement if not of the critical freedoms of speech and association. For the intellectuals of the country, the promise of globalization was precisely its potential for the improvement of such freedoms, and yet they were frustrated by the lack of independent political forums. They pressed the need to open up a social space, independent of party and state, to be inhabited by civil society. Thus in 1987, following on earlier attempts, two leading intellectuals, Chen Ziming and Wang Juntao, set up a nonparty organization, the Beijing Social and Economic Sciences Research Institute, to publish books on controversial political and economic issues and to conduct social surveys of popular opinion. Democracy salons also became a focus of activity at Beijing universities in 1988, as intellectuals met to discuss academic freedom and the meaning of the May 4 movement. In late 1988 a former leading member of the Democracy Wall movement, Ren Wanding, called for the Communist Party to let people decide their future through the ballot box, and by early 1989 intellectuals had banded together to call for the release from prison of another former member, Wei.

By contrast, as numerous opinion polls in the late 1980s showed, the human rights expectations of the ordinary person in the street were geared less to the values of globalization and democracy and more to the distributional norms of socialism, giving rise to the assumption that, despite economic modernization, social justice would continue to be dispensed by an authoritarian and ideologically disciplined government. Such assumptions were fed by, among other things, the continued theoretical status of workers as the leaders of the country and the constitutional guarantees of the right to work and related economic and social rights. Contrary to such expectations and in obedience to the dictates of the new market system, the Chinese government began to dismantle the "iron rice bowl" hitherto guaranteed China's urban workers, thereby initiating a period in which access to housing, health, education, and employment became an expensive privilege rather than an assumed right. Despite their different reform emphases, the common link between students, ordinary citizens, and workers was concern about double-digit inflation and the corruption that had begun to permeate leadership ranks after the onset of economic modernization. A simultaneous sense of rising expectations and popular discontent thus fueled the renewed protests that erupted in April 1989 in response to the death of the disgraced party leader Hu.

The democracy movement that developed from the initial student protests was unprecedented in its reach across all social classes and professions as well as in its spread across the length and breadth of China. It was also unprecedented in its duration and in the amount of international publicity it generated. What became the largest social and political demonstration of peaceful dissent in Chinese history was relayed for seven weeks around the world via television cameras. In view of the extraordinary publicity, foreign to the experience of an authoritarian and secretive government, outside observers who had initially feared the possibility of a government crackdown gradually relaxed as the movement reached its climax in May and began to wind down in early June. The shock of the Tiananmen Massacre was not that it represented the first time that lethal force had been used against protesting Chinese citizens. During demonstrations in Lhasa, Tibet, in 1987 and 1988 and from 5 to 7 March 1989, Chinese security forces had fired directly into the crowds, killing and wounding Tibetans. Martial law had also been declared in Tibet on 7 March 1989, only five weeks before the democracy movement began. The shock was rather that, unlike the attack in Tibet, which was hidden from the outside world, the June attack occurred within the full view of international cameras, even though it was launched at night; that it happened at a point in time when the movement itself seemed to be winding down; and that it killed and wounded thousands of Han Chinese in the center of the capital. Although the government later tried to argue that "no one was killed in Tiananmen Square," this was a purely semantic defense, since most of the people were killed in the surrounding streets opening onto the square.

CHRONOLOGY OF EVENTS

Because Hu was widely admired for his moderate views and lack of personal corruption, his death on 15 April mobilized tens of thousands of citizens to take to the streets in mourning. In an uncanny replay of the scene following the 1976 Tiananmen incident in support of Zhou, on 16 April students laid wreaths for Hu at the Monument to the People's Heroes in Tiananmen Square. They also handed a petition to the National People's Congress calling for a reevaluation of Hu's life and an end to campaigns against "spiritual pollution." On the morning of Hu's memorial service on 22 April, the students were joined in the square by thousands of ordinary Beijing citizens.

Initially, the main demands of the students protesting in the square were for more freedom from the state. As in the past, they concentrated on developing a mass movement rather than the specific political and social institutions that would ensure its success. They called generally for freedom of the press, an end to official corruption, and more democracy. Above all they demanded greater autonomy from the state. Thus they established the Autonomous Students' Association, thereby invoking the right to freedom of association. This was followed by the establishment of the Autonomous Intellectuals' Association and the Beijing Workers' Autonomous Federation (BWAF). Later, particularly after the declaration of martial law on 20 May, the students sharpened their focus and called for greater societal control over the state. Thus they declared the need for free and fair elections to choose leaders, for an independent judiciary, for a legal system meting out equal justice, and for supervision over the government through the press. However, even then they were seeking the reform of the existing political system rather than revolution, there were no reports of calls for the overthrow of the Communist Party or for multiparty elections.

At the height of the movement in Beijing, the demonstrations were attended by students, intellectuals, factory workers, railway employees, entrepreneurs, journalists, employees of a range of state ministries and the Foreign Ministry, employees from the Chinese Academy of Social Sciences, members of the Party Central Committee Cadre School, work units from the PLA and even from the Public Security Bureau, and members of the All China Federation of Trade Unions. Yet true to the basically intellectual and idealistic character of the movement, students assumed the leading role and did not actively seek to enlist workers to their cause until the ebbing of the movement at the end of May. This historical reflex, the students' style of remonstrance, their stress on morality and dependence on political patrons, and their traditional lack of attention to institution building have since been blamed by scholars like Elizabeth J. Perry for the "tragically anticlimactic" outcome of the movement when compared with the changes that occurred in the Soviet Union and Eastern Europe.

Certain critical milestones in the movement stood out: 26 April, when the *People's Daily* editorial attacked the "turmoil" as the work of a "small group of counterrevolutionaries;" 4 May, the seventieth anniversary of the May 4 movement; 13 May, the beginning of mass hunger strikes in Tiananmen Square, following which the democracy movement spread to all major cities in China; 15–18 May, when Soviet president Gorbachev visited China; mid-May, when the BWAF was established; 17 May, when a million people massed in the square, forcing the cancellation of Gorbachev's visit there; 18 May, when Zhao Ziyang, Li Peng, Qiao Shi, and Hu Qili paid a visit to students in the square who had collapsed during a hunger strike and the stormy televised meeting between Li and the hunger strikers on the same day; 19 May, when People's Liberation Army (PLA) troops first tried to reach the square but were turned back by students and

citizens and when Zhao made his last public appearance, pleading with the students to leave the square; 20 May, when martial law was declared in Beijing and the BWAF called a general strike meant to last until the troops were withdrawn; 26 May, when Zhao was stripped of all his posts; 27 May, when students from outside Beijing persuaded the student leaders not to leave the square despite a vote the same day to do so; the night of 29 May, when the Goddess of Democracy made its appearance; the night of 2 June, when troops summoned from outside the capital began to enter Beijing; and the night of 3 June, when the full military assault on the square and surrounding areas began.

To all this activity, Tiananmen Square served as the critical backdrop. Its historical role as the seat of government, its revolutionary significance as the place from which Mao had declared the establishment of the People's Republic, and its importance as a site of historical protest made its occupation by students, workers, and citizens intensely symbolic. In taking over the square, students, workers, and ordinary citizens were undermining the regime's claim to legitimacy. In refusing to leave the square, they were signaling their unwillingness to abandon their hard-won achievements.

During this period intricate political maneuvering was occurring behind the scenes. Books and articles based on firsthand accounts and internal documents published in the *Tiananmen Papers* have revealed the increasingly divisive two-line struggle being waged within the leadership over how to respond to student demands. On the one side was Premier Li, who advocated a hard line and who sought to persuade a wavering Deng, already haunted by the potential of the movement to develop into a full-fledged Polish-style Solidarity alliance between intellectuals and workers, to adopt his strategy. On the other side was General Party Secretary Zhao, who called for dialogue and enhanced political reform. The documents also point to the significant decision-making role taken by retired party elders, who, for instance, assumed the authority to remove Zhao, even though they had no constitutional power to do so.

The military action against the students, workers, and citizens in Tiananmen Square and its environs extended over a week in the full glare of international publicity. Although for the most part on the night of 3 June students were escorted or fled from the square, the first units of the PLA force to enter the square targeted the red and black banner of the BWAF and set fire to its tent headquarters in the northwest corner. The main atrocities occurred in the outer reaches of the square and throughout the city: particularly heavy casualties were sustained at the junction of Xidan and the Boulevard of Heavenly Peace and at Muxidi. Tanks and armored personnel carriers crushed everything in their path, including the citizens, young and old, defying their advance. The Goddess of Democracy met a similar fate. Altogether over two thousand people were killed, thousands were wounded, and many more were arrested. The suppression did not limit itself to Beijing but occurred throughout the country. There, however, protest movements mirroring Beijing's were put down relatively peacefully, particularly in Shanghai. Even in Xi'an and Changsha, local authorities who had used violent methods to suppress protest in late April responded relatively cautiously in June.

Citizens were terrified, but they were also outraged: the abiding image of the onslaught remains the picture of the lone man defying an approaching tank that then maneuvered around him, a picture that reflects not only the courage of unarmed Chinese citizens but also the ambivalence of some officers and soldiers in the Chinese army. Authorities began a hunt for twenty-one chief "counterrevolutionary" suspects and seven leading intellectuals as well as for the leaders of the BWAF. By 13 June the military had issued "shoot to kill" orders against suspects and had sealed the country's borders. Human rights breaches committed at this time included summary executions, torture and ill-treatment of detainees, arbitrary detention or imprisonment, summary trials not conforming to international standards for a fair trial, the arrest of those peacefully exercising their human rights, the negation of the freedoms of association and assembly, the subsequent persistent denial of civil rights in the form of a "general environment of white terror," and a nationwide censorship drive. It was not until 31 October that government authorities announced that the struggle against "counterrevolution" had succeeded and that a "basically closed" Beijing could return to normal. Finally, on 10 January 1990 Premier Li declared the lifting of martial law.

DOMESTIC IMPACT

Apart from breaching innumerable obligations that China had voluntarily assumed when it ratified international human rights treaties in the 1970s and 1980s, the suppression of the democracy movement set back the gradual improvement that had been occurring in China's civil rights and further entrenched the government's tendency to subordinate the values of development and social justice to the imperative of economic growth. It also reinforced the leaders' determination to retain control over the transition process. To this end they invoked long-held popular fears of *shehui luan*, or social disorder.

The suppression thus proved to be a turning point in the relationship between China's leaders and the led. Rather than opting to slow down the modernization and globalization process, thereby allowing Chinese society the chance to adjust more gradually to economic and social change, and rather than expanding popular access to civil and political rights, as the students had demanded, China's leaders chose to accelerate economic reform while reaffirming their Leninist political system. Influenced by the free-market ethos of globalization, they also made a deliberate decision to pursue stability through the "trickle-down effect" of economic growth rather than through more egalitarian redistributive forms of economic and social development. They embarked on a move to downsize and "rationalize" the inefficient state-owned enterprise (SOE) sector and to speed up China's accession to the World Trade Organization. In exchange for the structural instability and human insecurity such a choice entailed, China's leaders struck an implicit social contract with the people to maintain an annual high growth rate of at least 7 to 8 percent in China's gross domestic product (GDP).

In the early twenty-first century the image of Tiananmen represents a beacon for Chinese intellectuals in their efforts to "reverse the verdict" of the 26 April editorial as well as a symbol of the continuing obstacles to political reform in China. In a society where public morality is strongly allied with a sense of political legitimacy, government recognition that the democracy movement was not a counterrevolutionary offense would represent a major step forward in China's political reform, which indeed cannot be effectively advanced without it. Although in November 2005 the disgraced leader Hu was officially rehabilitated, China's leaders continued to insist on the correctness of their verdict on the nature of the movement and their decision to use force to suppress dissent.

The government's market solution to the Tiananmen crisis also had long-term human rights consequences. Its undertaking to maintain a high annual growth rate placed it in a triple bind. The more social instability its international and domestic policies generated, the more its leaders clung to the globalization mantra of economic growth to mask that instability and the more in turn China's economy became tied in with the processes of globalization. Whereas this produced a new class of affluent, middle-class consumers, its negative effects domestically were that, in deference to its new market-driven policies, the government became even more prepared to sacrifice social values that are peripheral to the globalization process. The physical and social well-being of its citizens was imperiled by new policies privatizing the provision of social welfare and tolerating high unemployment in the cause of overall national prosperity. Likewise, the government was free to ignore the civil rights of workers as well as the citizens' need for greater autonomy from the state. Critical to this hiatus was the government's continuing denial of the right of freedom of association, central both to workers' rights and the opening up of civil society. This blind spot permitted, for instance, continued governmental persecution of the Falun Gong, a religious sect charged with attempting to set up a center of power independent of the party and state.

The Tiananmen suppression thus bought the regime time to continue to modernize without further civil disturbance and without having to worry about redistributive policies and inequality. Because of the government's lack of attention to social justice and to the constitutional guarantee of employment, in the 1990s civil disturbance became an increasing problem as the rationalization of industry proceeded. This time, however, the protesters were workers and peasants, and their grievances were articulated more in the name of economic and social rights than of civil rights. From 1994 the intensity of industrial unrest was ratcheted up. By 2002 a veritable explosion of industrial unrest and demonstrations had broken out in the industrial Rust Belt areas of Daqing, Sichuan, Hunan, Hubei, and Lianoning, which was quickly suppressed. The protests, most of them directed against SOEs, were usually over actual and feared job losses, wage or benefit arrears, or allegations of management corruption. Labor disputes, which could be anything from wage conflicts to full strikes, were potent indicators of dissatisfaction. From 1992 to 1999 the number of registered disputes in a year increased fourteen times to over 120,000. Since other cases were not heard and not officially registered, the actual number was probably even higher. In addition, despite a new work-safety law enacted in 2002, in September 2003 alone accidents took the lives of 11,449 workers, an increase of 9 percent over September 2002.

This unprecedented degree of industrial unrest, disputation, and loss of human security reflected the enormous economic and social changes that China's workers were enduring. With the rationalization of industry and the downsizing of SOEs, massive retrenchments had begun. Between 1996 and 2000, according to Human Rights Watch, SOEs laid off 31.4 million workers. Particularly disadvantaged were the forty-to-fifty-year-old bracket of unskilled workers from the Cultural Revolution generation. Competing with them for jobs were 10 million new graduates entering the market each year and rural-to-urban migrants, estimated at 76 million people by 2000. The percentage of women who were laid off was higher than that of men. According to International Labour Organization (ILO) figures, unemployment and underemployment in China also afflicted over 30 percent of the rural population, who had no unemployment benefits. As a result, peasant unrest, particularly over forced resumption of land for developmental purposes, also became an increasing problem.

In the face of such radical socioeconomic change, the government moved to address the growing inequality. From 2002 it worked to adjust its labor policy and improve labor conditions. Whereas before February 2002 only 13 million people received the minimum social insurance, by the end of 2004, according to Chinese government estimates, the numbers of people (in a population base of 1.3 billion) participating in basic pension insurance, unemployment insurance, medical insurance, and industrial injury insurance in urban areas had reached 164 million, 106 million, 124 million, and 68.4 million, respectively. By contrast, in the rural areas, which still hosted the majority of China's population, only 55 million people participated in the social old-age pension system, and only 2.2 million farmers actually received old-age pensions. The minimum wage was increased, and a plan to directly elect union representation in foreign and privately owned factories with less than two hundred employees was instituted, even though these unions were still under the leadership of the official union, the All China Federation of Trade Unions. Increasingly, China cooperated with the ILO branch in Beijing, which worked to alleviate problems of unemployment and the lack of social security. However, the three prongs of China's attempts to remedy the situation—the growth of the nonstate sector, the "reemployment" project, and the program of social insurance—were largely inadequate to the task.

INTERNATIONAL IMPACT

The Tiananmen Massacre forever altered the situation in which China was treated as the "human rights exception." It had the immediate effect of bringing China into the human rights spotlight and constraining its foreign policy. China became the subject of sanctions by international organizations such as the World Bank and the ILO and attracted condemnation and sanctions from individual states. Tiananmen also stymied China's bilateral relations with the United States, Japan, and Taiwan for a considerable period. To offset the effect of bilateral sanctions, China took the initiative to establish "human rights" delegations with Western states, an idea issuing from consultations between Australia and China. Between 1990 and 1991 Australia sent two parliamentary delegations to China to discuss human rights. These were followed by similar delegations from the United States and a host of European states. They were open, accountable missions that produced public reports on their findings. They coexisted with multilateral debate and votes critical of China's human rights in the United Nations (UN) Human Rights Commission. For a time therefore China's human rights were subject not only to multilateral monitoring by international human rights bodies like the Human Rights Commission, the ILO Freedom of Association Committee, the UN Committee against Torture, the UN special rapporteur on torture, the UN Committee on the Elimination of Racial Discrimination, and other treaty bodies but also to unilateral oversight by the United States, the United Kingdom, Australia, Norway, and other European states.

More broadly, the Tiananmen Massacre affected the manner in which the Cold War ended. It became a powerful negative symbol of what could happen if demonstrations in support of human rights and democracy were quelled by force. While the democracy movement influenced the liberalization of Eastern European states, the massacre influenced the way such states democratized. How Tiananmen affected the transition to democracy in Eastern Europe depended very much on the nature of the state involved. In the case of hard-line socialist states, such as Albania and Romania, Tiananmen was used as a positive model to be emulated; in the case of moderate socialist states, such as Hungary and Czechoslovakia, Tiananmen was a negative model to be avoided. By and large, however, Tiananmen influenced political elites in Eastern Europe to ultimately adopt a more conciliatory path to change than had their Chinese counterparts. The most significant example of the Tiananmen effect was the liberalization of the hard-line socialist state of East Germany. As Charles Maier has made clear, Tiananmen Square was still fresh in the minds of both sides in the debate during the critical demonstrations in Leipzig in October 1989, which ultimately determined the fate of the East German regime. Hard-liners like the general party secretary and chairman of the Council of State of the German Democratic Republic, Erich Honecker, who appeared to be heading toward

forcible suppression of the protests, were finally persuaded by those who feared a Tiananmen-style massacre, including many within the Communist Party, including the next leader, Egon Krenz.

Tiananmen also energized the "Asian values" debate that held sway in human rights discourse until the Asian financial crisis in 1997. From 1991, as a way to defend itself from criticism, China encouraged its intellectuals to take on the human rights movement and to debate the "Western" concept of human rights, seen as privileging civil and political rights. In contrast, the Chinese view of human rights emphasized the right to subsistence in particular and economic and social rights more generally. These differences were also highlighted in China's first human rights white paper, published in October 1991. Thus Chinese views both stimulated and fed into a body of theory that was developing more generally in the Asia-Pacific region.

In the early twenty-first century the international emphasis on China's human rights has diminished, and other images of China are invoked by the international community. Because of the success of its socialist market economy since 1992, China's material power and influence, rather than its human rights, have become the main focus of international attention. This outcome has been partly the result of Chinese strategic policy. In contrast to its shift to multilateralism in other areas, from 1997 the government successfully deflected multilateral pressure emanating from, in particular, the UN Human Rights Commission by establishing human rights dialogues with individual states. This shift enabled China to divert the monitoring of its human rights away from multilateral forums under the guise of working to improve its bilateral relations. In other words, having successfully averted bilateral pressures by means of the human rights delegations, China now subverted multilateral pressures by bilateralizing them as human rights dialogues. In contrast to the earlier human rights delegations, these dialogues have been neither transparent nor publicly accountable. As a result of the emasculation of human rights monitoring, the responsibility of the struggle for human rights in China has been effectively returned by the international community to domestic and expatriate Chinese intellectuals and labor activists.

In the longer term, the Tiananmen Square crackdown has continued to exert a contradictory impact on popular demonstrations throughout the world. Thus it arguably provided the model for the suppression of some popular movements like that in the central Asian republic of Uzbekistan in May 2005. There, riots triggered by religious dissent and opposition to President Islam Karimov were quelled when troops opened fire on thousands of protesters in the central square of the city of Andijon, killing as many as two hundred people. However, in general Tiananmen has remained an effective negative example. The horror and adverse publicity generated by China's armed attack on its own people persuaded other governments not to imitate the suppression and, for example, influenced Indonesia's relatively peaceful transition to democracy. In the transition from Suharto's rule in 1998, the symbol of Tiananmen was specifically invoked by Indonesia's political and military leaders as an example to avoid.

Tiananmen also continued to impact China's foreign and international human rights policies in unexpected ways. As a result of the social contract reached between the government and its citizens in the years following the crackdown, any international development that jeopardized China's relentless quest for a higher GDP and economic expansion, whether it was international political instability, the outbreak of war, international recession, or any other unforeseen event, became an anathema to its leaders. The positive result of this has been that China has become preoccupied with the maintenance of international peace and security. The negative aspect has been that, when international crises like SARS and bird flu have occurred, China has been initially more concerned about possible economic repercussions than about its effects on the human right to health of the domestic population and, as a consequence, on that of the rest of the world. Although China is now more sensitized and more responsive to its obligations as a member of the World Health Organization, there is even more of a danger in China than there is elsewhere that local authorities will cover up adverse developments for commercial as well as political reasons.

Internationally, Tiananmen remains a potent symbol of the huge effort, short of humanitarian intervention, that can be mustered when a public human rights emergency arises. By the same token it has highlighted problems of enforcement in the international human rights regime, revealing the difficulty of enforcing obligations from outside unless there is a human rights crisis. Thus later multilateral and bilateral pressures on the Chinese government have proved largely ineffectual, particularly after the UN Human Rights Commission ceased adopting resolutions on China's human rights.

Nevertheless, the Tiananmen Massacre has had a lasting impact on international human rights. For better and worse, it has deeply affected China's domestic and international policies and, for a decade at least, transformed the attitude of the international community toward China and its human rights. More broadly, it has influenced, and continues to influence, the shape of the post–Cold War world. Just as the suppression itself was influenced by Deng's fears of a Polish-style Solidarity movement, so Tiananmen in turn became the ghost at the table determining the manner in which the Cold War ended in Eastern Europe. Many lives in Eastern Europe and later in Asia were spared because of the tragedy of Tiananmen, and some states initially resisting change accepted reform largely because of it. Arguably, citizens continue to be saved in those parts of the world where political and social protests erupt. Although the immediate effects of the trauma may have faded, there is little doubt that in the early twenty-first century, without Tiananmen, both the world and China would be a different places.

[See also China: The Famine of the 1960s; Confucianism; East Asian Values; Foreign Policy; Mao Zedong; and United Nations Commission on Human Rights.]

BIBLIOGRAPHY

Black, George, and Robin Munro. *Black Hands of Beijing: Lives of Defiance in China's Democracy Movement.* New York: John Wiley & Sons, 1993.

Calhoun, Craig J. *Neither Gods nor Emperors: Students and the Struggle for Democracy in China.* Berkeley: University of California Press, 1994.

Cohen, Roberta. "People's Republic of China: The Human Rights Exception." *Human Rights Quarterly* 9, no. 4 (1987): 447–549.

Davis, Deborah, and Ezra F. Vogel, eds. *Chinese Society on the Eve of Tiananmen: The Impact of Reform.* Cambridge, Mass.: Harvard University Press, 1990.

Ding, Yijiang. *Chinese Democracy after Tiananmen.* Vancouver: University of British Columbia Press, 2001.

Dui Hua. "Dialogues at a Crossroads." *Dialogue* 20 (2005): 1–3.

Eckholm, Eric. "Workers' Rights Suffering in China as Manufacturing Goes Capitalist." *New York Times*, August 22, 2001.

Finn, Peter. "Scores of Uzbek Protesters Gunned Down by Troops." *Washington Post*, May 15, 2005.

Gorbachev, Mikhail. *Memoirs.* New York: Doubleday, 1995.

Gorbachev, Mikhail, and Zdenek Mlynar. *Conversations with Gorbachev: On Perestroika, the Prague Spring, and the Crossroads of Socialism.* Translated by George Shriver. New York: Columbia University Press, 2002.

Hicks, George, ed. *The Broken Mirror: China after Tiananmen.* Essex, U.K.: Longman, 1990.

Human Rights Watch. *Paying the Price: Worker Unrest in Northeast China.* New York: Human Rights Watch, 2002.

Information Office of the State Council of the People's Republic of China. *China's Progress in Human Rights in 2004.* Beijing, China: Foreign Language, 2005.

Information Office of the State Council of the People's Republic of China. *Human Rights in China.* Beijing, China: Foreign Language, 1991.

Kent, Ann. *Between Freedom and Subsistence: China and Human Rights.* Hong Kong and New York: Oxford University Press, 1993.

Kent, Ann. *Beyond Compliance: China, International Organizations, and Global Security.* Stanford, Calif.: Stanford University Press, 2007.

Kent, Ann. *China, the United Nations, and Human Rights: The Limits of Compliance.* Philadelphia: University of Pennsylvania Press, 1999.

Kent, Ann. "States Monitoring States: The United States, Australia, and China's Human Rights, 1990–2001." *Human Rights Quarterly* 23, no. 3 (2001): 583–624.

Maier, Charles S. *Dissolution: The Crisis of Communism and the End of East Germany.* Princeton, N.J.: Princeton University Press, 1997.

McCormick, Barrett L. *Political Reform in Post-Mao China: Democracy and Bureaucracy in a Leninist State.* Berkeley: University of California Press, 1990.

Miles, James A. R. *The Legacy of Tiananmen: China in Disarray.* Ann Arbor: University of Michigan Press, 1996.

Perry, Elizabeth J. "Casting a Chinese 'Democracy' Movement: The Roles of Students, Workers, and Entrepreneurs." In *Popular Protest and Political Culture in Modern China: Learning from 1989,* 2d ed., edited by Jeffrey N. Wasserstrom and Elizabeth J. Perry, pp. 74–92. Boulder, Colo.: Westview, 1994.

Pye, Lucien W. "Appealing the Tiananmen Verdict: New Documents from China's Highest Leaders." *Foreign Affairs,* March–April 2001, 148–154.

Schell, Orville. *Discos and Democracy: China in the Throes of Reform.* New York: Pantheon, 1988.

Schell, Orville. *Mandate of Heaven: A New Generation of Entrepreneurs, Dissidents, Bohemians, and Technocrats Lays Claim to China's Future.* New York: Simon & Schuster, 1994.

Solinger, Dorothy J. "Labour Market Reform and the Plight of the Laid-off Proletariat." *China Quarterly* 170 (2002): 304–326.

Solinger, Dorothy J. "WTO Entry: Will China's Workers Benefit from this 'Win-Win' Deal?" *China Rights Forum* 1 (2002): 4–7.

Spence, Jonathan D. *The Search for Modern China.* 2d ed. New York: W.W. Norton, 1999.

Stokes, Gale. *The Walls Came Tumbling Down: The Collapse of Communism in Eastern Europe.* New York and Oxford: Oxford University Press, 1993.

Strand, David. "Protest in Beijing: Civil Society and Public Sphere in China." *Problems of Communism* 39, no. 3 (1990): 1–19.

Unger, Jonathan, ed. *The Pro-Democracy Protests in China: Reports from the Provinces.* Sydney, Australia: Allen and Unwin, 1991.

White, Gordon. *Riding the Tiger: The Politics of Economic Reform in Post-Mao China.* Stanford, Calif.: Stanford University Press, 1993.

Zhang Liang, with Andrew J. Nathan and Perry Link, eds. *The Tiananmen Papers.* New York: Public Affairs, 2001.

CIVIL AND POLITICAL RIGHTS

INTERNATIONAL COVENANT ON CIVIL AND POLITICAL RIGHTS

by David Weissbrodt

Following the adoption of the Universal Declaration of Human Rights in 1948, the UN Commission on Human Rights drafted the International Bill of Human Rights, which contains, in addition to the Universal Declaration of Human Rights, the Covenant on Economic, Social, and Cultural Rights; the Covenant on Civil and Political Rights; and the First Optional Protocol to the Civil and Political Covenant. The three instruments were adopted by the General Assembly in 1966 and entered into force in 1976. The International Bill of Human Rights comprises the most authoritative and comprehensive statement of human rights obligations that governments undertake in joining the UN.

The two covenants distinguish between implementation of civil and political rights on the one hand, and economic, social, and cultural rights on the other. Civil and political rights, such as freedom of expression and the right to be free from torture or arbitrary arrest, are immediately enforceable. Economic, social, and cultural rights are to be implemented "to the maximum of available resources, with a view to achieving progressively the full realization of the rights . . . by all appropriate means, including particularly the adoption of legislative measures." In other words, governments that ratify the covenants must immediately cease torturing their citizens, but they are not immediately required to ensure that all are fed, clothed, and housed.

National self-determination (self-determination for peoples) and decolonization represented a very important part of the UN's agenda when the Covenant on Civil and Political Rights and the Covenant on Economic, Social, and Cultural Rights were being drafted (1946–1966). Hence, the contours of self-determination are set forth prominently in Article 1 of both covenants. This provision is a primary example of a collective human right, as far as the law is concerned. The statement of legal principle found in Article 1, however, has never been followed by a recognized set of rules defining, for example, who is a people entitled to self-determination and what forms self-determination may take, such as statehood or also certain forms of autonomy inside existing states.

Equality and its correlative norm of nondiscrimination are two of the most important precepts of human rights that were codified in the UN Charter as well as the two Human Rights Covenants. The charter's protection against nondiscrimination was elaborated further by the Universal Declaration of Human Rights and the two covenants to protect against discrimination based on race, color, sex, language, religion, political or other opinion, national or social origin, property, birth, or other status.

NON-DEROGABLE RIGHTS IN THE COVENANT ON CIVIL AND POLITICAL RIGHTS

The Covenant on Civil and Political Rights identifies certain rights in Article 4 as non-derogable including the prohibition of discrimination on the grounds of race, color, sex, language, religion, or social origin—that is, those rights that cannot be the subject of suspension during periods of emergency threatening the life of the nation. Article 4 also mentions Articles 6 (the right to life); 7 (prohibition of torture); 8, paragraphs 1 and 2 (prohibition of slavery); 11 (prohibition of imprisonment for inability to fulfill a contractual obligation); 15 (*nullum crimen sine lege* [no crime without law]); 16 (recognition of every person before the law); and 18 (freedom of thought, conscience, and religion) as non-derogable. Furthermore, the Human Rights Committee has interpreted other non-derogable rights, such as the right not to be subjected to arbitrary deprivation of life, as implying that the basic fair-trial provisions of Article 14 cannot be suspended during periods of national emergency.

The Covenant on Civil and Political Rights (1966) protects the right to life in Article 6 as non-derogable by first providing that the right shall be protected by law and that no one shall be arbitrarily deprived of his or her life.

Second, in countries where the death penalty has not been abolished, such a sentence may be imposed only for the most serious crimes in accordance with the law in force at the time of the commission of the crime, and must be carried out pursuant to final judgment by a competent court. Persons sentenced to death have the right to seek pardon or commutation of the sentence. The sentence of death cannot be imposed on persons who were under eighteen years of age at the time of the commission of the crime and on pregnant women.

The Human Rights Committee was established by the Civil and Political Covenant to interpret and apply the covenant's provisions. The committee further defined the obligations under Article 6. For example, the committee in 1982 viewed the right broadly and noted that it includes duties to prevent loss of life in a number of contexts, such as war—especially thermonuclear war, genocide, and other acts of mass violence causing arbitrary loss of life. The right to life also includes positive obligations to reduce infant mortality and increase life expectancy, as well as to prevent arbitrary killings by government security forces and to take effective measures to prevent disappearances of individuals.

The Second Optional Protocol to the International Covenant on Civil and Political Rights, Aiming at Abolition of the Death Penalty (1989), provides for no reservation except for the application of the death penalty for military crimes in time of war. While the Civil and Political Covenant has been ratified by 160 nations, the Second Optional Protocol has 60 states parties.

In Article 7 the Covenant on Civil and Political Rights further provides, as non-derogable, that "no one shall be subjected to torture or to cruel, inhuman or degrading treatment or punishment."

The Civil and Political Covenant also contains a prohibition against slavery and servitude in Article 8. The importance accorded by the covenant to the slavery provision is emphasized by its status as a non-derogable right under Article 4(2). Article 8 contains a provision prohibiting the use of forced or compulsory labor subject to certain limited exceptions.

Article 9 of the Civil and Political Covenant and the other relevant standards assure that a person who is arrested is entitled to be informed at the time of arrest of the reasons for the arrest and promptly informed of any charges. The arrested individual should be brought promptly before a judge or similar officer authorized to exercise judicial power. Civil and Political Covenant

Article 9(3) and other standards strongly discourage detention for arrested persons awaiting trial, but instead recommend guarantees to appear for trial and other non-custodial measures.

Article 9(4) guarantees the right of anyone who is deprived of liberty to take proceedings (such as habeas corpus) before a court to determine the lawfulness of the detention. The Human Rights Committee has expressed the view that detention for forty-eight hours without judicial review is unreasonably long. Article 10 further elaborates on the rights of persons deprived of their liberty by codifying that juveniles should be separated from adults and accused persons should be separated from convicted persons.

Everyone is guaranteed, by Article 12 of the Civil and Political Covenant, the right to freedom of movement and residence within the borders of each state and the right to leave any country, including one's own, and to return to one's country.

The Civil and Political Covenant further elaborates—particularly in its Articles 14 and 15, but also in Articles 9, 2, 6, 7, and 10—upon the fair-trial rights identified in the Universal Declaration. Article 14 of the Civil and Political Covenant recognizes the right to "a fair trial and public hearing by a competent, independent and impartial tribunal established by law." Every person is "equal before the courts and tribunals" under Article 14(1). Article 14 also distinguishes between the sort of fair hearing required for civil cases, on the one hand, and criminal cases, on the other.

Article 17 of the Civil and Political Covenant affirms the right to privacy. The right to privacy under the covenant has been interpreted by the Human Rights Committee to include, for example, the ability of individuals to change their surname, to express concern about intrusions into private telephone communications, and to ensure that effective measures are taken such that personal and body searches are carried out in a manner consistent with the dignity of the person who is being searched.

The Human Rights Committee has authoritatively interpreted Article 18 of the Civil and Political Covenant by noting that the right to freedom of conscience and religion is absolute, but there are significant limitations on the right to manifest one's religion or belief. The Committee has also indicated that Article 18 protects theistic, non-theistic and atheistic beliefs, as well as the right not to profess any religion or belief.

The Covenant on Civil and Political Rights distinguishes in Article 19 between the unqualified right to hold opinions and the far more limited freedom of expression that "carries with it special duties and responsibilities" and is subject to "certain restrictions" in Article 19(3) which must be provided by law and are necessary. The Human Rights Committee in a general comment has noted the important relationship of Article 19 with Article 25 of the covenant (right to participate in public affairs):

> In order to ensure the full enjoyment of rights protected by Article 25, the free communication of information and ideas about public and political issues between citizens, candidates and elected representatives is essential. This implies a free press and other media able to comment on public issues without censorship or restraint and to inform public opinion. It requires the full enjoyment and respect for the rights guaranteed in Articles 19, 21 [peaceful assembly] and 22 [freedom of association] of the covenant, including freedom to engage in political activity individually or through political parties and other organizations, freedom to debate public affairs, to hold peaceful demonstrations and meetings, to criticize and oppose, to publish political material, to campaign for election and to advertise political ideas

The Covenant on Civil and Political Rights codified that "the family is the natural and fundamental group unit of society" in Article 23. The Human Rights Committee has authoritatively interpreted Article 23 in its general comment to mean

> that the concept of the family may differ in some respects from State to State, and even from region to region within a State, and that it is therefore not possible to give the concept a standard definition. However, the Committee emphasizes that, when a group of persons is regarded as a family under the legislation and practice of a State, it must be given the protection referred to in article 23.

The Covenant on Civil and Political Rights addresses the problem of statelessness in Article 24 by providing that "every child has the right to acquire a nationality."

Article 25 of the covenant establishes that "every citizen" shall have the right to participate in public affairs, to vote and hold office, and to have access to public service. The Civil and Political Covenant does not promote a single system of government over others, and its principles can be upheld under different political systems as long as they allow for public participation and for free and fair elections. In its general comment on minority rights, the Human Rights Committee insisted that whatever the political system selected, a government must adopt "measures to ensure the effective participation of members of minority communities in decisions which affect them."

Article 27 of the Civil and Political Covenant provides cultural rights for minorities:

> In those States in which ethnic, religious or linguistic minorities exist, persons belonging to such minorities shall not be denied the right, in community with the other members of their group, to enjoy their own culture, to profess and practise their own religion, or to use their own language.

PROCEDURE

The Human Rights Committee consists of eighteen members from eighteen different nations elected by the states parties to the International Covenant for Civil and Political Rights. Half are elected every two years by the 160 states parties to the covenant. None of the members are government officials. Most of the committee members are academics, judges, or retired ambassadors. They are presently from such countries as Australia, Benin, Colombia, Ecuador, Egypt, India, Ireland, Japan, Mauritius, Peru, Romania, South Africa, Sweden, Switzerland, Tunisia, the United Kingdom, and the United States. Most are experts in relevant aspects of human rights and act in their individual capacity even though they are nominated by their governments. The committee meets three times a year for three weeks each time, alternating their meetings between New York (generally in March) and Geneva (generally in July and October).

The committee has two main functions: (1) to review the compliance reports by states, and (2) to adjudicate individual complaints filed by individuals in countries that have ratified the First Optional Protocol to the International Covenant on Civil and Political Rights. It also produces general comments on issues concerning the implementation of the covenant and elaborating the content of the specific rights delineated in the treaty.

The committee has developed detailed reporting procedures for states parties. The initial report—due within one year after a state becomes a party—usually focuses on the constitution, laws, and structures of the nation as they relate to the fulfillment of the covenant provisions. The committee also expects information about actual practices, including in the first report, but more importantly in subsequent reports.

After a government submits its report, the committee usually decides at which meeting it will review the report. The committee selects a member to serve as a special rapporteur on the country and to lead the questioning of the national representatives when they appear before the committee. The Human Rights Committee and its special rapporteurs have developed a practice of identifying key issues that the national representatives should address when they appear before the committee to present their report. In preparing lists of issues and questions, the committee has developed a practice of consulting with nongovernmental organizations (NGOs)—particularly national NGOs—that can alert the special rapporteur and the committee members to (1) any problems with the compliance of the government with its treaty obligations; (2) the failures of the government to involve civil society in preparing the report; and (3) inaccuracies in the report, which might be the subject of questions when the government representative appears before the committee. In many cases, NGOs prepare their own parallel reports, sometimes referred to as "shadow reports," to answer the official government reports. These shadow reports are often taken into consideration by committee members.

On the day the committee begins to hear the government report in question, government representatives present usually include high-level officials from the capital, as well as diplomats from Geneva or New York. Also in the meeting room are the eighteen members of the committee, a small committee staff of perhaps five or six employees of the Office of the High Commissioner for Human Rights, interpreters, official note-takers, and NGO representatives. With the exception of a few countries for which there is a great deal of NGO interest, the treaty bodies function without much NGO attendance or media attention. Generally speaking, the Human Rights Council and some of the other Charter-based organs receive far more media and NGO participation than the Human Rights Committee and other treaty bodies.

The principal government representative begins the consideration of his or her country report by giving an introductory statement addressing questions raised by the committee's list of issues or addressing the committee about recent developments since the government's report was produced. The committee's special rapporteur raises questions about human rights concerns he or she has identified in the state report or from the information available from NGOs and other sources. The government representatives do not endeavor to answer right away.

Instead, the other members of the committee are each given the opportunity to ask further questions and raise individual concerns. The government representatives are usually given a window of time—for example, an afternoon or an evening—before attempting responses to the questions. There may be follow-up exchanges during which committee members express their views and concerns regarding the government's official responses.

Although the committee does not issue a legally binding judgment on violations by the government, the committee has, since 1992, developed a practice of issuing "concluding observations" on each state report. These country conclusions identify positive developments, note concerns, and offer recommendations. In effect, country conclusions set an agenda for government action until the next reporting deadline, which may be as much as five years later. In their next periodic report, states are asked to address the concluding observations, in particular the concerns and recommendations, and report on progress regarding the protection and enjoyment of rights. For states that are party to the First Optional Protocol, the committee also requests information on remedies provided for any individual cases that have been decided.

The committee occasionally asks for supplementary or more prompt reports when it determines that the initial and periodic reports are incomplete. It has also asked on occasion for emergency reports when it ascertained that events in a particular country indicated that the enjoyment of rights under the covenant had been seriously affected. The committee has established specific guidelines for such reports in order to avoid the tendency that governments have had of being self-congratulatory and not self-critical.

The greatest strength of the periodic reporting process is that it involves a painstaking, professional evaluation of each state party's progress in fulfilling the treaty provisions. The principal limitation is that the treaty bodies and their conclusions rarely receive the publicity they warrant, therefore significantly weakening their impact. Another major limitation is that many governments are late in fulfilling their reporting responsibilities. Several of the treaty bodies have experimented with ways to encourage governments to reply more promptly. For example, a committee might inform the government that if it does not produce its report, the committee will invite the government to appear without having prepared a report and the treaty body will produce country conclusions without the attendance of the government. Such pressures have generally resulted in greater government reporting and cooperation.

In addition to their country conclusions, the Human Rights Committee has developed a practice of preparing general comments to provide governments with authoritative guidance on the meaning of the provisions of the covenant or on other major issues facing the committee. For example, in 1982—before the adoption of the Convention against Torture and Other Cruel, Inhuman, or Degrading Treatment—the Human Rights Committee issued a general comment interpreting covenant Article 7 on the prohibition of torture. The general comment offered an expansive reading of the prohibition of torture to include the prohibition of cruel, inhuman, or degrading treatment or punishment. The committee further noted that it is not sufficient to merely prohibit such treatment or punishment. Instead, governments should make effective

> provisions against detention incommunicado, granting, without prejudice to the investigation, persons such as doctors, lawyers and family members access to the detainees; provisions requiring that detainees should be held in places that are publicly recognized and that their names and places of detention should be entered in a central register available to persons concerned, such as relatives; provisions making confessions or other evidence obtained through torture or other treatment contrary to article 7 inadmissible in court; and measures of training and instruction of law enforcement officials not to apply such treatment.

This general comment was an important step in defining the prohibition of torture set forth by Article 7. It laid the foundation for further development of the interpretation of that right by the drafting of the Convention against Torture, decisions of regional human rights bodies, national legislation, and judicial decisions.

In addition to the state reporting procedure with its country conclusions and the general comments, the Human Rights Committee is authorized under the First Optional Protocol to receive and adjudicate complaints by individuals alleging that their rights have been violated. This complaint mechanism is available to individuals in the 109 nations that have ratified the Optional Protocol. The Human Rights Committee also has the authority—pursuant to Article 41—to consider complaints by one state against another relating to violations of the covenant. As of 2008, however, no state party had invoked this provision.

Before determining that an individual communication is admissible under the Optional Protocol, the Human Rights Committee decides whether certain requirements have been fulfilled. For example, the committee decides whether domestic remedies have been exhausted. This requirement involves verifying whether the individual has previously sought relief from national courts or any other available procedure at the national level. Since 1989 the Human Rights Committee has requested one of its members to serve as the special rapporteur on new communications in determining whether additional information is needed or whether to refer the communication to the state party for its observations on admissibility and the merits of communications. The special rapporteur can also make recommendations regarding admissibility, but the committee as a whole has the ultimate authority to make determinations regarding both admissibility and the merits. Meetings concerning individual complaints are not open to the public. When the committee has determined whether there has been a violation of the covenant, its judgments—which are referred to as "views"—are transmitted to the state party concerned and are eventually published. In all, the Human Rights Committee has handled hundreds of cases and developed an impressive body of human rights jurisprudence.

Although the individual decisions and views of the Human Rights Committee are not enforceable as a matter of law, most governments comply with committee views in individual cases, though sometimes only after the urging of a member of the committee designated as the special rapporteur for the follow-up of views. In their periodic reports, states parties are required to detail compliance with committee views about individual cases. For example, individuals have been released from detention, governments have paid compensation for violations, laws have been improved, and non-citizens have been allowed to remain in the country where they were residing rather than being deported.

The great advantage of these procedures is that they can result in a well-considered judgment on the merits of human rights claims. The disadvantage is that all of these procedures are entirely handled through the exchange of written communications. Without the capacity to hear evidence, receive oral arguments, or visit the country concerned, the Human Rights Committee is unable to handle significant factual disputes.

[*See also* Democracy and Right to Participation; Due Process, Rule of Law, and Habeas Corpus; Limburg Principles on Socioeconomic Rights; Minority Rights: Overview;

Self-Determination; Torture: Convention against Torture; *and* Universal Declaration of Human Rights.]

BIBLIOGRAPHY

Alston, Philip, and James Crawford, eds. *The Future of UN Human Rights Treaty Monitoring.* Cambridge, U.K., and New York: Cambridge University Press, 2000.

Amnesty International. *Combating Torture—A Manual for Action.* 2003. http://www.amnesty.org/en/library/info/ACT40/001/2003/en.

Bassiouni, M. Cherif. "Enslavement as an International Crime." *New York University Journal of International Law and Politics* 23 (1991): 445–517.

Belembaogo, Akila, ed. *The Family in International and Regional Human Rights Instruments.* New York: United Nations, 1999.

Beyani, Chaloka. *Human Rights Standards and the Free Movement of People within the States.* Oxford and New York: Oxford University Press, 2000.

Boyle, Kevin, and Juliet Sheen, eds. *Freedom of Religion and Belief: A World Report.* London and New York: Routledge, 1997.

Clayton, Richard, and Hugh Tomlinson. *Fair Trial Rights.* Oxford: Oxford University Press, 2001.

Coliver, Sandra. *The Article 19 Freedom of Expression Handbook: International and Comparative Law, Standards, and Procedures.* London: Article 19, 1993.

Crawford, J. "The Right to Self-Determination in International Law: Its Development and Future." In *People's Rights,* edited by Philip Alston, pp. 7–67. Oxford and New York: Oxford University Press, 2001.

Fitzpatrick, Joan, ed. *Human Rights Protection for Refugees, Asylum-Seekers, and Internally Displaced Persons: A Guide to International Mechanisms.* Ardsley, N.Y.: Transnational, 2002.

Forsythe, David P. *Human Rights and Peace: International and National Dimensions.* Lincoln: University of Nebraska Press, 1993.

Gross, Oren. "Are Torture Warrants Warranted? Pragmatic Absolutism and Official Disobedience." *Minnesota Law Review* 88 (2004): 1481–1555.

Hannum, Hurst. *Autonomy, Sovereignty, and Self-Determination.* Philadelphia: University of Pennsylvania Press, 1990.

Jones, Thomas David. *Human Rights: Group Defamation, Freedom of Expression, and the Law of Nations.* The Hague and Boston: Martinus Nijhoff, 1998.

Joseph, Sarah, Jenny Schultz, and Melissa Castan. *The International Covenant on Civil and Political Rights: Cases, Materials, and Commentary.* 2d ed. Oxford and New York: Oxford University Press, 2004.

Levinson, Sanford, ed. *Torture: A Collection.* Oxford and New York: Oxford University Press, 2004.

Optional Protocol to the International Covenant on Civil and Political Rights. G.A. res. 2200A (XXI), 21 UN GAOR Supp. (No. 16) at 59, UN Doc. A/6316 (1966), 999 U.N.T.S. 302, entered into force 23 March 1976.

Picolotti, Romina, and Jorge Daniel Taillant, eds. *Linking Human Rights and the Environment.* Tucson: University of Arizona Press, 2003.

Ramcharan, B. G., ed. *The Right to Life in International Law.* Dordrecht and Boston: Martinus Nijhoff, 1985.

Rodley, Nigel S. *The Treatment of Prisoners under International Law,* 2d ed. Oxford: Clarendon Press, 1999.

Second Optional Protocol to the International Covenant on Civil and Political Rights, Aiming at the Abolition of the Death Penalty. G.A. res. 44/128, annex, 44 UN GAOR Supp. (No. 49) at 207, UN Doc. A/44/49 (1989).

Thornberry, Patrick. *International Law and the Rights of Minorities.* Oxford: Clarendon Press, 1991.

Weissbrodt, David S. *The Right to a Fair Trial under the Universal Declaration of Human Rights and the International Covenant on Civil and Political Rights.* Cambridge, Mass.: Martinus Nijhoff, 2001.

Weissbrodt, David, and Rüdiger Wolfrum, eds. *The Right to a Fair Trial.* Berlin and New York: Springer, 1997.

COLLECTIVE/GROUP RIGHTS

by A. Belden Fields

Group, or collective, human rights is one of the more contentious conceptions in the human rights literature. Collective human rights make a lot of sense to people living in societies that have maintained strong group identities and senses of social solidarity. This is especially true in the formerly colonized nations of what we used to refer to as the "third world" and now more often refer to as the South. But group rights, not to mention group *human* rights, are viewed with greater skepticism, and sometimes outright hostility, by thinkers in the West, particularly in the English-speaking world. In the first edition of perhaps the most widely read theoretical human rights textbook in the United States, *Universal Human Rights in Theory and Practice*, Jack Donnelly argued that there could be no such thing as group or collective human rights. He argued that "special difficulties are presented by the group rights of aboriginal peoples" but that "the genuine self-determination of native people is possible within a broader context of internationally recognized *individual* human rights, so long as such peoples are allowed the opportunities to shape, maintain, and influence the evolution of community institutions" (pp. 152–153; italics added). In the second edition Donnelly writes, "Indigenous peoples may present an exception to this general argument against group human rights... But even such rights, I would argue, should be seen as rights of members of indigenous communities" (p. 215). Donnelly seems to remain skeptical of the validity of the idea of group human rights while bowing to the international recognition of such rights, but only in the case of indigenous people protecting their communities from the outside.

After examining some of the major arguments against considering human rights as anything other than rights of individuals, we will elaborate a holistic theory of human rights that requires a specific understanding of group human rights. In this understanding, violations of group human rights are always simultaneously violations of individuals' human rights. However, such violations of group rights cannot simply be seen as the sum of the violations of the rights of those individuals. The group dimension adds something qualitatively different from just a sum of individual human rights violations.

ARGUMENTS AGAINST GROUP HUMAN RIGHTS

While some would look to earlier sources, especially of religious inspiration, others argue that the idea of human rights really began to flourish in the context of the rise of the modern Western nation-state, and of political liberalism and a market economy. In large measure it represented an individualistic reaction against both political absolutism, in which political rights were vested in the king and nobility, and an economy based upon the remnants of feudalism that constrained people to where they were born in the old hierarchical order.

This strong individualism is represented in the writing of political theorists of the epoch, especially in the writings of the English contract theorists Thomas Hobbes and John Locke. While we would not recognize Hobbes, the theorist par excellence of the absolutist state, as a liberal thinker in the way we use the term in the early twenty-first century, he did offer a crucial notion for liberal thinkers that followed him: that the political obligation of any individual is contingent upon the state's recognition of that individual's natural claim to the right to life.

Locke expanded the rights of individuals to liberty (both political and religious) and property as well as life. It was always the individual who was the rights bearer against possible intrusion of either the state or other individuals. It was incumbent upon the state to restrain itself from infringing upon individual rights and to protect individuals within its domain from such infringement by others. In Locke and in Hobbes, the individual was seen as an entity who was free to do anything he desired so long he did not contravene the stated will of the sovereign (Hobbes) or infringe on the rights to life, liberty, or property of others (Locke).

However, this strongly individualistic approach to rights did not go unchallenged in the European Enlightenment. Jean-Jacques Rousseau had a somewhat different view of rights. Rousseau conceived of the citizen as someone who exchanged his natural rights to do what he desired for civil rights that entailed much more obligation to the body politic and much more of a sense of solidarity with other citizens than one finds in the work of Hobbes or Locke. For Rousseau, citizens were not just concerned with protecting themselves from the threat of other people (Hobbes) or pursuing their own property or spiritual interests (Locke); they were by nature able and morally obliged to seek a collective public good that transcends their own individual personal interests. Their rights claims were thus less absolutist than those imagined by Hobbes or Locke in that they had to be consistent with the collectivity's conception (what Rousseau calls the "General Will") of that public good. Rousseau is thus truer to the Aristotelian dictum that man is naturally a political and social animal, but he combines this appreciation for the claims of the community upon its individual members with a necessarily more complex concept of universal rights. Indeed, within Rousseau's own thinking we see the nub of our contemporary arguments over universalism on the one hand as opposed to communitarianism and relativism on the other. Rousseau argued for the universalistic relevance of the values of liberty and equality (for all "men," it should be admitted, and as Mary Wollstonecraft was to rebuke him for in the 1792 publication of her book *A Vindication of the Rights of Woman*). But Rousseau's model in *The Social Contract* is of a small, homogeneous society that determines its own collective will that is specific to that particular society.

Hobbes's thinking is not particularly relevant to today's discussion of human rights, except perhaps to point out that people do view physical security as a primary right and that without some sort of assurance of physical safety and subsistence, as Henry Shue points out in *Basic Rights*, other rights will be seen as less meaningful. But both Locke and Rousseau are very relevant to our thinking about human rights. While both of them are important seminal thinkers, they offer extreme views of rights that are untenable as templates for a modern conception of human rights. Like Hobbes's, Locke's self-interested individualism is excessive. Rousseau, on the other hand, is too totalizing; he lets his conception of the General Will overwhelm individual judgment and conscience to the point that when one's interpretation of

what that will should be is in the minority, one has to admit error.

Somewhere, between the excessively individualist and the overly totalizing positions, we need a conception of human rights that recognizes some collective values that people—constituted within and largely by political communities, cultures, or other social relationships (such as work)—want and need. This obliges us to take seriously the conception and application of group human rights.

A second argument against group or collective human rights is that the seminal founding documents of human rights do not recognize them. As has already been contended, human rights talk began to flourish in the West with the creation of the modern Western state. The two seminal documents in that creation that challenged monarchical governance were the U.S. Declaration of Independence (1776) and the French Declaration of the Rights of Man and of the Citizen (1789). On the surface, these documents can be read as stipulating only individual rights, thus offering historical vindication for the argument that human rights claims from the beginning of the modern Western political era were understood as demanding only individual rights.

But that is merely a surface reading, for the American and French Revolutions, and the above documents that were an attempt to legitimize them, were very much an assertion of collective rights. Those revolutions were claims for recognition as "Americans" (the United States) and as "citizens" (France and the United States). In both cases, going hand in hand with the creation of modern nation-state, they represented claims to recognition of their collective capacities and identities as self-determining citizens.

While there is some opposition to the concept of group rights, especially on the part of Anglo-American theorists and political leaders, there has developed historically a very broad acceptance of them, even in the West, while outside of the West the concept seems not to be problematic. The right to self-determination and the right to development are two rights of special importance to people subjugated by imperialism and colonialism, just as they were crucial rights claims in the French and American Revolutions at the end of the eighteenth century. And, like those earlier documents, they have both individual and collective dimensions. The 1986 UN Declaration on the Right to Development states in Article 1:

1. The right to development is an inalienable human right by virtue of which *every human person and all peoples* are entitled to participate in, contribute to, and enjoy economic,

social, cultural and political development, in which all human rights and fundamental freedoms can be fully realized. [italics added]

2. The human right to development also implies the full realization of *the right of peoples* to self-determination, which includes, subject to the relevant provisions of both International Covenants on Human Rights, the exercise of their inalienable right to full sovereignty over all their natural wealth and resources. [italics added]

The recognition of these rights by the United Nations a good many years after World War II differentiates it from the League of Nations in the interwar period. The League did not oppose colonialism. It simply stripped the losers of the war of their colonies and placed the latter under a mandate system controlled by the victors. The United Nations' position represents a shift in predominant thinking internationally toward a recognition of the collective human rights claims of peoples to determine their own destinies.

In addition to the recognition of the collective rights of self-determination and development, the United Nations Convention on the Prevention and Punishment of the Crime of Genocide, unlike the League of Nations' ignoring of the genocide against the Armenians, asserts the rights of national, ethnic, racial, or religious groups to survive *as groups*. Thus, while the UN convention contains the more obvious prohibition against violence and killing of members of the group, there is also a prohibition against causing mental harm, prevention of birth, or transferring children of the group to another group. In other words, it is not just that individuals within such groups have the right to physically survive but that the collectivity has a right to maintain itself and to defend its collective identity from outsiders who would seek to destroy it—as, for example, the U.S. and Australian governments did with schools that tried to destroy the cultural identities of indigenous peoples. Logic tells us that these were not just rights violations of each individual native or aboriginal person but of the groups themselves. Indeed, Convention 169 (1989) of the United Nations International Labour Organization (ILO), entitled Concerning Indigenous Tribal Peoples in Independent Countries, clearly posits rights for indigenous tribal *groups*. Lest there be any confusion that the ILO convention might be referring to group rights of a different order than "human" rights, it casts the convention in the light of the United Nations' major human rights documents, and it states in Article 3, section 2, that "no form of force

or coercion shall be used in violation of the human rights and fundamental freedoms of the peoples concerned, including the rights contained in this Convention."

But such rights should not be limited to the "exception" of indigenous people as Jack Donnelly argues. For example, any time that hate crimes are committed, genocide being the most grandiose form of these, the entire community as an interactive social entity is harmed and has its collective human rights violated.

A third reason for the rejection of group rights is a very pragmatic one, although influenced by ideology. It is the impulse to keep the list of human rights both short and simple. In *What Are Human Rights?* (1964), Maurice Cranston made the general argument that if human rights are to be taken seriously and actually implemented, they should be severely limited to a certain number of rights around which there is very wide consensus and which could be easily implemented. This led him to advocate limiting human rights to what he regarded as some very basic political rights, such as free speech, habeas corpus, and due process of law. There is wide agreement on these, and the enforcement entails just getting governments to desist from certain unacceptable behaviors against individuals. As Mary Ann Glendon has pointed out in *Rights Talk: The Impoverishment of Political Discourse*, it is also easier for Anglo-Saxon legalists, heavily influenced by the ideology of an individualistic jurisprudence going back to William Blackstone and Jeremy Bentham, to wrap their minds around the idea of individuals, rather than groups, having standing in the courts. However, such pragmatic and ideological considerations should not trump adequate conceptualization. Grappling with complexity often leads to fuller understanding.

Empiricists and quantifiers in the social sciences do indeed simplify for methodological and operational purposes, but this often involves a trade-off in terms of distorting or masking the full meaning of social phenomena and situations. Indeed, in the area of American jurisprudence where there is wide opposition to group rights, all logic is distorted when a clearly collective entity is accorded rights, but only by calling it an individual. That is precisely what is done in the case of the corporation. The convergence of economic interest and political power leads to a recognition of a group right at the same time that many of those who uncritically accept this right deny that other groups or collectivities can have rights.

Although some have argued that the concept of group rights is a fatal blow to individual rights, one need not look at the relationship between these two kinds of rights as a zero-sum game. It is better to say that there can be tensions between the two kinds of rights but that these tensions require negotiation, mediation, or adjudication. These tensions are not best dealt with conceptually through the lens of either extreme individualist or extreme collectivist ideologies, or by political actors using one or the other extreme to advance their own interests.

The tensions would be mitigated if collectivities, especially ethnic groups, were recognized as being dynamic and having diversity within themselves; if the rights of exit of individuals from the groups were recognized, as difficult as the exercise of that right might sometimes be, owing to powerful processes of acculturation and identity formation at early ages; and if group rights were seen as operating simultaneously with individual rights. This latter point does not mean that group rights and individual rights are the same thing, nor does it mean that group rights are the sum of individual rights. This distinction will be discussed more fully in the next section, as will another important argument that some see as the Achilles heel of the concept of group or collective human rights: that group rights cannot be universal, an essential quality of human rights.

COLLECTIVE RIGHTS WITHIN A HOLISTIC THEORY OF HUMAN RIGHTS

The above discussion has made reference to the historical development of human rights in the West. It has argued against an exclusively individualistic interpretation of that historical development. If one were to take a completely consensual approach to the justification of human rights, as Jack Donnelly does, we could just end the discussion here and say that the preceding narrative of the concept as it has appeared in the historical documents proclaiming its validity is enough to justify group or collective human rights. But a deeper theoretical argument is possible and warranted. What follows is a basic exposition of this argument and some of the key concepts leading up to the conclusion. (A more detailed exploration of these concepts may be found in the author's *Rethinking Human Rights for the New Millenium*.) The first two concepts demonstrating the validity of group or collective rights are "potentiality" and "development." Human beings have the potential for development in ways and degrees that are unique among the animal species. They have the potentiality for intellectual development (other species could not write or read this text), creative development (other species do not build their living environment in the elaborate way humans do, nor do they send rockets to

other planets, nor do they create museums or orchestras), and for more expansive affective ties to other human beings—the concept of human rights itself reflects an empathetic concern for the suffering of other people whom we do not even know and who can be thousands of miles away from us. Now these are only potentialities, and it is true that we can act against our better potentialities and be much crueler and more brutal than the brutes. We can stifle the intellectual development of ourselves and other people, for example, forbidding certain groups to learn to read or write or permitting the degeneration of schools that serve certain groups. We can use our creative capacities to make weapons that kill and maim other people or to construct concentration camps and torture centers. We can let our pride, wrath, or greed overcome our capacity for love, friendship, and empathy.

But the positive potentiality is there. The development of human potentialities, both positive and negative, takes place within a web of human relationships that are cultural, social, economic, and political. The development of each individual is a social development. There is no such thing as a totally "self-made" person, no such thing as a completely self-developed and self-sufficient individual. While we have certain individual personality characteristics and talents, the development of our selves depends upon our relations with a wide range of others, including family, friends, teachers, peers, religious or spiritual organizations, workmates, and professional colleagues. The self-determined person is just as fictional as the corporation conceived as an individual; the individual is developed through a process of both co- and self-determination.

Co- and self-determination depends upon people recognizing each other as more than merely natural objects, rather as self-conscious beings, reliant upon each other for their respective development. Humans are not born and sent out in the world to meet each other as already constituted beings who continue to develop themselves purely internally. This way of thinking was repudiated in continental Western philosophy by G. W. F. Hegel and does not have wide currency outside the West.

A fragment of a Zulu aphorism related by Jordan Ngubane in his book *Conflict of Minds* offers a powerful yet succinct way of expressing this idea of co- and self-determination:

My neighbor and I have the same origins
We have the same life-experience and a common destiny;
We are the obverse and reverse sides of one entity;
We are unchanging equals;

We are the faces which see themselves in each other;
We are mutually fulfilling complements;
We are simultaneously legitimate values …
I am sovereign of my life;
My neighbor is sovereign of his life;
Society is a collective sovereignty;
It exists to ensure that my neighbor and I realize the promise
 of being human.

The developmental possibilities of co- and self-determination are materially and culturally conditioned. We would not expect the same sort of intellectual, creative, and even affective development on the part of our cave-dwelling ancestors, or even our contemporary nomads struggling to survive in drought-stricken areas, that we do from people living in wealthy industrialized countries. The flourishing of human rights discourse took place within very specific historical circumstances. In the West, it began among the non-noble upper classes and the bourgeoisie after wealth and property had become more widely diffused than it had been under feudalism. Production and trade in commodities, as well as wage labor, were replacing the more rigid economic relationships of feudalism. The newer political and economic interests were not being sufficiently recognized by the traditional monarchical systems. Revolutionary human rights demands in both France and the United States were responses to these historical systemic transformations because those transformations opened up possibilities for co- and self-determination that were simply not there during the high points of the older systems.

But in both revolutionary instances there were exclusions. Some groups were not recognized as being included under these universal calls for the recognition of human rights. Women, slaves, non-property-owners, Native Americans somehow did not have the proclaimed equal rights. And in subsequent history there were always exclusions despite the universalistic discourse: imperialism, colonialism, slavery, racism, anti-Semitism, discrimination against women, religious persecution, ethnic cleansing, persecution of gays and lesbians, and so on. These exclusions are a form of domination, the exercise of deliberate or structural power over others that frustrates the development of their potentialities. Some of the most important human rights claims are the expression of those who have been excluded, who recognize their own exclusion as a human rights violation and call upon others to recognize it as such.

This approach regards human rights not merely as a set of abstractions handed down by theorists but as a set of social practices acted out in the real world of social interaction, upon which theorists, to be sure, have sometimes had an effect. Looked at in this historical and contextual manner, it becomes clear that we in the West are in no position to simply dismiss the defense of group rights claims coming from more communally oriented societies. Such claims were and continue to be a key ingredient in our own human rights development.

Conceiving of human rights as a social process, a bottom-up approach looks first at the rights claims that victims direct against violators. The table on the next page presents the range of possibilities in terms of human rights perpetrators and the victims of those perpetrators, those who can be considered human rights holders.

It will be noted in the table that if all collective rights violations are simultaneously individual rights violations, it is not the case that all individual rights violations are also group rights violations. Indeed, in all of the categories of victims, there are individual rights violations.

The strongest case for arguing that a widespread human rights violation should only be thought of as a violation of the sum of the individuals' rights—in other words, that group rights are irrelevant—is when the violation is either random or systemwide. If people are systematically denied certain rights by their government, such as due process of law, then we have individual cases in which the totality is the sum of the individual cases. Similarly, if we have random cases of arbitrariness, such as where one never knows if someone charged with a crime is going to get a fair trial, then the rights of some individuals are being violated, but there is no group dimension to such randomness.

But in the other three categories of victims, group or collective human rights are very much involved. The first of these are "ascriptive" groups. These are groups that are identified by the dominant system and its structures as being not only different and distinct but in some senses (morally or intellectually, for example) inferior. Their identity and the kind of social recognition they receive from those more powerful than they are, are fixed. They are usually easily recognizable to others and to themselves. Race, ethnicity, gender, and sexual orientation have been used to mark such people.

When these people are singled out for violent attack, selective criminal prosecution, or discrimination in education, employment, health care, or housing, then there is a violation of the human rights of the group. The case of violent attack is an interesting one. It is there that we find the concept of "hate crime." Some have argued that there should be no such thing as a hate crime, that if a person of a certain group is murdered by someone who demonstrates hatred of the group, it should simply be considered a case of murder like any other. But the nature of the crime, which is often committed against a random (randomness here assumes a very different meaning within a victimized group) member of a race or a gay or lesbian person whom the murderer might not even know personally, is really a statement that the murderer would kill all of those "others" if he possibly could. The victim is merely a stand-in for the entire group. Such attacks are sometimes imaginary, sometimes real, preludes to genocide. The intent, and often the effect, is to terrify and limit the freedom of the hated group and to set an example for other haters of the group to follow. Like its logical and intended culmination, genocide, it is a violation of the rights of the entire collectivity or community of people and their interrelationships. Thus the social meaning of such a crime is vastly different from a murder committed in a context of jealousy, a bank robbery, or a "hit job" by an organized crime mob. It involves a violation of a collective human right, the right of an entire group to live its shared existence without being killed or terrorized.

The non-ascriptive category includes collectivities that are not fixed but are important claimants of human rights. The denial of the rights of people to organize or to speak in the effort to organize politically is a denial of a collective right. John Stuart Mill recognized this when he argued in *On Liberty* (1859) that the denial of someone's right to speak is not just a violation of that person's right to speak but also a denial of others' rights to listen and to use that speech for common civic purposes. If I want to join with others to form a social movement or a political party, and I and the others involved are denied that right, it is not just "my" affair; it is the right of all of us to form a communal endeavor to which we would all contribute time, money, and other resources that we could expend elsewhere if we were only interested in maximizing our own individual interests. A large part of the benefit we receive from such a collective endeavor is the sense of solidarity. The group is thus more than the sum of its parts. The denial of the right to have or sustain such a group also entails the denial of a collective human right.

The same is true of the rights of workers to organize in unions and to bargain collectively (stipulated in Part 3

TABLE 1. Human rights violators and victims: a bottom-up holistic view.

	VICTIMS			
	Individuals	Ascriptive Collectivities and Individuals	Non-ascriptive Collectivities and Individuals	Everyone
VIOLATORS				
States	random and/or systematic denial of right to habeas corpus; denial of due process of law; use of torture to extract confessions	genocide; racially discriminatory laws or enforcement and punishment; criminalization of homosexuality; denial of vote to women; racial, ethnic, or gender discrimination in public education	denial of right to organize politically; denial of right to political expression; denial or worker rights to organize or strike	nuclear tests
Nonstate groups or entitles	terrorism where victims are random	genocide; racist, anti-Semitic, or homophobic violence; racial discrimination in private housing and health care	exploitation and/or denial of workers' right to organize by corporations; child labor	industrial pollution; deforestation; resource depletion
Individuals and families	selling children into prostitution	selling only girls into prostitution; forced female genital cutting and infibulation		

SOURCE: Reproduced by permission from A. Belden Fields, *Rethinking Human Rights for the New Millennium*, New York: Macmillan, 2003, p. 92.

of the International Covenant on Economic, Social, and Cultural Rights and in Convention 98 of the United Nations International Labour Organization). In the United States one of the tactics of employers has been to argue that workers cannot be obliged to pay union dues even when the plant is unionized and unions have achieved benefits for workers in collective bargaining. This is clearly an attempt to weaken unions by breaking the bonds of solidarity and encouraging individual workers to act in their own self-interest, referred to as "free riding." Business in some U.S. states have been successful in pressuring state legislators to pass laws permitting such free riding. They are called "right to work" laws. This is clearly an attempt to negate the significance of the collective rights of workers and an example of the unique ultra-individualism (as well as the power of corporations) in the dominant American ideology. Such extreme individualism also has the effect of destroying the relationship between rights and obligation to anything beyond the individual or family unit.

The final category in the table is the one in which all of us, as humanity, have our rights violated. Examples are nuclear tests, industrial pollution, deforestation, and depletion of scarce resources. Again, this is not just a matter of the sum of the individuals but humanity itself, the preservation of the species, its responsibility to other species and to future generations of both the human and other species. If it is thought that "everyone" or "humanity" is too broad a category to be meaningful in terms of legal or moral rights, it should be remembered that the Nazi war criminals were tried at Nuremberg for "crimes against humanity." What the Nazis did was considered to be an assault upon not only Jews, Gypsies, gays, Communists, and the mentally impaired, but all humanity as an entity that had a right and "legal standing" as a collectivity to have its rights represented by the tribunal.

Now let us return to the argument that group rights cannot be human rights because they cannot be universal. It has already been shown that the right to self-determination is accepted as a human right with universal application. Yet, in practice, it could only apply to a specific group or collectivity that feels the need to exercise that right. Such a group is making a claim that it is a dominated group, that its right to engage in co- and self-determination is being denied by external power. Anyone in the world could theoretically find herself in such a situation if she is part of a collectivity that feels externally dominated. The right exists as a universal principle (right to self-determination; right to co- and self-determination),

but the application will be specific to a particular context in which a collectivity feels deprived of the right.

Similarly, anyone in the world could theoretically find herself subject to wage labor as a way of surviving economically. If people find themselves in this situation and they are egregiously dominated and exploited, as workers in many countries are, one could argue that wherever they are, they could make collective appeals to universal conceptions. This only applies to them so long as they are part of a particular collectivity, workers. But it also applies to them because they are part of the universal category of human beings, not mules or water buffalo. The categories and concepts of particular and universal are not antagonistic here.

Or take the rights of the child or the rights of women. They are obviously not universal in the sense that they apply to everyone. But they are needed and accorded the status of human rights because children and women are human beings and they have often been subjected to specific forms of domination.

Admittedly, not all group rights should be considered human rights. Those that are human rights involve alleviation from extreme forms of domination, cruelty, or threats to physical or cultural existence, as in genocide. There are some group rights that fall short of this but nonetheless raise issues of interest, fairness, and justice. These might be rights claims raised by stockholders, annuitants of retirement programs, or veterans. If the government or private bodies grant these people certain benefits and privileges at a given point in time and then retract them, they might well have legal or moral grounds to argue that they collectively have had their rights violated. But this does not rise to the level of a human rights abuse according to the above criteria.

To argue for group human rights does not mean that it is always easy to evaluate the validity of the rights claims. This is especially the case when there are conflicting rights claims. Perhaps the most serious of these for international politics arises when one or more group claims the right to self-determination in the form of secession, leaving the other group or groups in a state with fewer resources that had been considered common and perhaps less physical security. If such a secessionist rights claim snowballed, it could also result in such large-scale fragmentation of states as to pose a threat to the security of all remaining states. This is the extreme—although sometimes justified under the right of self-determination—end of group human rights claims. Most are for greater physical security or recognition of political, economic, social, or cultural rights. However, the fact that there are conflicts of group rights claims does not differentiate them from individual rights claims. Indeed, there are often conflicts over rights that are usually thought of as individual rights, such as my right to speak but your right not to be unjustly accused or libeled by me, or conflicts over private property rights. Thus, while the conflicts over collective or group rights are by definition on a larger scale and are often more complex than conflicts over individual rights claims (but sometimes no more complex than the rights claims of competing corporations), this is no reason to negate the concept of collective or group human rights.

Groups are not homogeneous or static; if they provide a certain umbrella identity, either imposed by others or adopted by the members or both, there will be variation within the group over ideology and interests, and the group will change over time. To take the case of African Americans in the United States: some are more inclined to separatism as at least a short-term strategy and others to integration; many are very religious but some are secular; among the religious some are Christian while others are Islamic; among the Christians some are Roman Catholic while others are not; some are property owners while others are not. Moreover, the constellation of difference within groups changes over time.

What a group or collectivity with effective political control does not have a right to do is to strip the group members of their individual rights to be different within the group, or to leave the group or its territorial base. These individual rights limit the powerful group's rights to establish or maintain a group identity. It has too often been the case that movements for emancipation from external domination have in the name of solidarity trampled on the rights of individuals in their own movements. This happened in the formation of the United States with the treatment of those who had been loyal to the British; it happened in France during the postrevolutionary Terror; it happened in many of the former colonial areas after World War II. Rather than keeping the three key values of human rights—liberty, equality, and solidarity—in balance, there was an attempt to interpret the latter value in a totalistic manner that negated the other two values.

There will always be some conflicts between group and individual rights claims. The major criterion for dealing with these is the maintenance of a balance between the above key values. This would minimize the harm that group rights claims can do to individuals and that ultra-individualistic rights claims can do to the community. Rousseau did not balance these very well in his theory,

but his attempt to mitigate the very strong individualism of the English contract theorists does offer some insights into how it could be done. Moreover, the holistic (but not totalistic) approach to human rights opens up a more promising possibility for cross-cultural human rights dialogue. It might help get us beyond the well-worn arguments between both Western and non-Western "relativists" who doubt that human rights can be universalistic and almost exclusively Western "individualists" who see the concept of solidarity within and across groups as an anathema to universal human rights.

The concept of solidarity as discussed above should be distinguished from a commitment to what is currently referred to as "identity politics," if that expression is taken to mean a commitment only to the rights or interests of one's own group or collectivity. "Solidarity" within a group is crucial, but it also must expand outward in a concern for the rights of other groups and individuals. The very idea of human rights is that we can, indeed have an obligation to, relate in a solidaristic way to the suffering caused by the rights deprivation of others, even others whom we do not know and are different from us in a multitude of ways. Thus there is no contradiction between a defense of group and collective rights and an attachment to a universalistic conception of human rights. Both are accommodated in this "holistic" approach.

[*See also* Armenians in the Ottoman Empire; Right to Development; Ethnic Cleansing; Genocide; Nuremberg and Tokyo Trials; Self-determination; *and* Right to Work.]

BIBLIOGRAPHY

Barry, Brian. *Culture and Equality: An Egalitarian Critique of Multiculturalism.* Cambridge, U.K.: Polity, 2001.

Cobbah, Joshia A. M. "African Values and the Human Rights Debate: An African Perspective." *Human Rights Quarterly* 9 (1987): 309–331.

Cranston, Maurice. *What Are Human Rights?* New York: Basic Books, 1964.

Donnelly, Jack. *Universal Human Rights in Theory and Practice.* Ithaca, N.Y.: Cornell University Press, 1989 and 2003.

Felice, William F. *Taking Rights Seriously: The Importance of Collective Human Rights.* Albany: State University of New York Press, 1996.

Fields, A. Belden. *Rethinking Human Rights for the New Millennium.* New York: Macmillan, 2003.

Freeman, Michael. "Are There Collective Human Rights?" *Political Studies* 43 (1995): 25–40.

Glendon, Mary Ann. *Rights Talk: The Impoverishment of Political Discourse.* New York: The Free Press, 1991.

Green, Leslie. "Internal Minorities and their Rights." In *The Rights of Minority Cultures*, edited by Will Kymlicka, pp. 257–272. Oxford and New York: Oxford University Press, 1995.

Hartmann, Thom. *Unequal Protection: The Rise of Corporate Dominance and the Theft of Human Rights*. Emmaus, Pa.: Rodale, 2002.

Illumoka, Adetoun O. "African Women's Economic, Social, and Cultural Rights—Toward a Relevant Theory and Practice." In *Human Rights of Women*, edited by Rebecca Cook, pp. 307–325. Philadelphia: University of Pennsylvania Press, 1994.

Jones, Peter. "Human Rights, Group Rights, and Peoples' Rights." *Human Rights Quarterly* 21 (1999): 80–107.

Kukathas, Chandran. "Are There Any Cultural Rights?" In *The Rights of Minority Cultures*, edited by Will Kymlicka, pp. 228–256. Oxford and New York: Oxford University Press, 1995.

Kymlicka, Will. *Multicultural Citizenship: A Theory of Minority Rights*. Oxford: Clarendon Press, 1995.

Kymlicka, Will, ed. *The Rights of Minority Cultures*. Oxford and New York: Oxford University Press, 1995.

McDonald, Michael. "Should Communities Have Rights?" In *Human Rights in Cross-Cultural Perspectives*, edited by Abdullahi Ahmed An-Na'im, pp. 135–151. Philadelphia: University of Pennsylvania Press, 1992.

Ngubane, Jordan. *Conflict of Minds*. New York: Books in Focus, 1979.

Shivji, Issa G. *The Concept of Human Rights in Africa*. London: Codesria, 1989.

Shue, Henry. *Basic Rights: Subsistence, Affluence, and U.S. Foreign Policy*. 2d ed. Princeton, N.J.: Princeton University Press, 1996.

Stavenhagen, Rodolfo. "Universal Human Rights and the Cultures of Indigenous People and Ethnic Groups: The Critical Frontier in the 1990s." In *Human Rights in Perspective*, edited by Asbjorn Eide and Bernt Hagtvet, pp. 135–151. Oxford: Blackwell, 1992.

Taylor, Charles. *Multiculturalism: Examining the Politics of Recognition*. Edited by Amy Gutmann. Princeton, N.J.: Princeton University Press, 1994.

Thompson, Janna. *Taking Responsibility for the Past: Reparation and Historical Injustice*. Cambridge, U.K.: Polity, 2002.

Van Dyke, Vernon. "The Individual, the State, and Ethnic Communities in Political Theory" In *The Rights of Minority Cultures*, edited by Will Kymlicka, pp. 31–56. Oxford and New York: Oxford University Press, 1995.

COLOMBIA

by William Avilés

Beginning in the mid-twentieth century, Colombia became enmeshed in a civil war in which tens of thousands of people's rights, such as those to life, physical integrity, due process, dignity, and liberty, were violated. Between 1985 and 2008 the country's political violence displaced approximately 3 million people, and well over 50,000 Colombians died in political violence. Between 2002 and 2004 eight noncombatants per day were killed for sociopolitical reasons, and on average three thousand Colombians have been kidnapped yearly, giving the country the highest kidnapping rate in the world. The extent and degree of these violations varied during the post–World War II period, but throughout much of this time war and internal strife were a part of the country's social and political makeup.

Human rights in Colombia have been intricately tied to the government's counterinsurgency war, the illegal drug trade, and the inability (or unwillingness) of the country's political and economic elite to address the political, social, and economic inequities that underlie much of this political violence. The actors in the internal conflict in Colombia involved armed guerrilla forces seeking to overthrow the state or establish radical social or economic reform; conservative paramilitary groups working directly for cattle ranchers; large landowners; and narcotics traffickers combating guerrilla assaults while also acquiring greater wealth, land, and control over a multibillion dollar illegal drug industry. In addition, the Colombian armed forces (in particular the army) sometimes worked with paramilitary groups in the perpetuation of human rights violations in their war against the insurgency. Furthermore, the United States' resources and political pressures often contributed to an escalation of Colombia's internal conflict, and U.S. demand for illegal drugs helped finance the survival of violent actors (guerrillas, paramilitary, and narcotics traffickers).

Historically, three important domestic trends underlay the uneven presence of human rights in Colombia despite half a century of uninterrupted electoral democracy. First, state authority was weak or even absent in parts of the country. Second, the dominant political parties and movements employed formal and informal mechanisms to exclude others from the political process. And third, there were inequalities in landownership and economic power. These historical trends long interacted with international factors, such as Colombia's position in the international economy as a provider of primary commodities, that have been conducive to the increasing concentration of land and wealth in fewer hands. This was the case especially with the production and distribution of cocaine, which not only facilitated the concentration of landownership but financed the military operations and activities of central perpetrators of human rights violations. The influence of the United States often backed or legitimized those Colombian governments that pursued policies in line with the strategic interests of the United States or the economic interests of U.S.-based and increasingly transnational capital interests, with uneven consequences for the protection of human rights.

STATE WEAKNESS AND VIOLENCE

After Colombia's independence from Spain (1819), the central government consistently failed to wield and maintain a monopoly over violence. The country's topography long played a role in undermining the integration of a national state, with the Andean Mountain chain splitting the country into three relatively distinct regions that developed for much of its history in relative isolation from the influence of Bogotá, the capital. This regionalization regularly undermined the central government's efforts to squelch or prevent the multiple insurrections and civil wars of the nineteenth century between the Liberal and the Conservative parties. Rival economic elites regularly mobilized the Colombian peasantry. These were ideological wars fought over the role of the church in the nation's politics, free trade, and control over the national government. They had a lasting impact on party identification as tens of thousands of Colombians died, cementing the partisan links in whole communities and families.

The partisan divisions established in the nineteenth century underlay continuing tensions in Colombian politics throughout the first half of the twentieth century. Both parties used their periods in power to undermine and ostracize the other politically through patronage. In addition, the early decades of the twentieth century witnessed increasing social and labor agitation as workers and peasants organized to improve their economic conditions. Continuing partisan and social conflict was the context that preceded the explosion of civil and internal violence referred to as La Violencia. In 1948 the assassination of the populist Liberal leader who was likely the next president, Jorge Eliécer Gaitán, sparked this nationwide civil conflict, which eventually took more than 200,000 lives and resulted in the institutional transformation of the political system. Liberal and Conservative partisans fought over land, governmental power, and political control in communities. The Conservative president Mariano Ospina Pérez (1946–1950) increasingly relied on the army to maintain control, appointing military officials as mayors and governors in regions where the violence became extreme. The police during the Ospina Pérez administration were utilized as a repressive weapon, with party leaders complementing this force through the organization of civilian bands of assassins (*pajaros*) that engaged in selective killings and massacres of Liberal partisans. The *pajaros* were viewed by many as the early precursors of the paramilitary armies that emerged at the end of the century. In response, Liberal bands and guerrilla forces attacked Conservative communities and police and army units. Both sides committed atrocities as a means of terrifying survivors and displacing communities for their party's benefit.

A good deal of the violence in the countryside not only centered on partisan divisions but also involved the seizure of land by force and the extortion and eviction of settlers. Communist militias emerged during this time, often working with Liberals against the Conservative government. The Liberal militia leader Pedro Marín (also known as Manuel Marulanda) later fought with the Communists and helped organize and lead the Revolutionary Armed Forces of Colombia (FARC), the country's largest and longest surviving guerrilla group. By the early 1950s the army was terrorizing the countryside through a "scorched earth" campaign against regions suspected of supporting the Liberal guerrillas, employing bombings, massacres, and arson in its attacks. The continuing social

conflict and violence contributed in part to a military coup in 1953 and the military government of General Gustavo Rojas Pinilla. Rojas Pinilla was removed from power in 1957 by sectors of the military responding in part to a popular mobilization led by traditional party elites.

THE NATIONAL FRONT TO A NEW CONSTITUTION: 1958–1991

Negotiations between party elites ultimately brought the most violent phase of La Violencia to an end in 1958. The resulting National Front agreement ensured that the two parties alternated in power until 1974 (this arrangement continued informally into the 1980s), excluding other parties from political power. Civilian authorities and the armed forces also came to a mutual understanding about their roles. The military was granted autonomy over public order and internal security and conceded policy making and politics to civilian authorities. While contributing to the avoidance of military coups after 1958, this informal arrangement also undermined human rights, because civilian authorities failed to exercise oversight over the armed forces. The two parties monopolized control over the state, and the Colombian army greatly militarized internal order. This in part laid the basis for the emergence of armed challengers to the Colombian state, the two longest-lasting and most important being the National Liberation Army (ELN) in 1964 and the FARC in 1966 (noted above). In response to this insurgent challenge in 1968, the Colombian congress passed Law 48, which allowed the military to legally recruit and utilize members of the civilian population in the collection of information and in the targeting of suspected "subversives."

The militarization of internal order continued the inequalities in the countryside. Rather than implement nationwide agrarian reform, government leaders relied on peasants to colonize new territories and establish new communities with little or no state support in order to reduce the social pressures for reform. Challenges to this system periodically arose in the twentieth century; however, Colombia's landed and political elite effectively co-opted or repressed agrarian reform movements, maintaining a structure of inequality in the countryside that existed in the early twenty-first century. By the early 2000s less than 10 percent of all landowners possessed over 90 percent of the arable land in a country with a 50 percent national poverty rate. This continuing inequality and poverty contributed a rural constituency for the armed actors as well as a workforce for the narcotics trafficking industry.

Colombia enjoyed relative economic and political calm during the 1960s and 1970s. However, the government continued to fight guerrilla armies, containing them but unable to militarily defeat them. Guerrilla armies took advantage of state-neglected and isolated frontier communities to maintain themselves during this period, though they never surpassed a few thousand men before the 1980s. The M-19, an important urban-based guerrilla movement that emerged in 1974, gained notoriety by robbing banks or milk trucks and distributing the loot to poor communities in urban zones. The group's success prompted an escalation in state repression by the Julio César Turbay Ayala administration (1978–1982), which implemented the Security Statute of 1978, subjecting civilians to military courts-martial and implementing other restrictions upon civil liberties. Turbay Ayala governed under a state of siege for much of his presidency. In fact, presidents regularly governed through states of emergency or siege in the decades following La Violencia (approximately 75 percent of the time between the 1960s and the 1980s), which allowed the suspension of constitutional guarantees and greater autonomy for state security forces to repress burgeoning social movements and also strengthening guerrilla insurgencies. Turbay Ayala faced increasing international and domestic pressure to ease his repressive policies, which included mass detentions, accusations of torture, and political assassinations.

Turbay Ayala was followed by the reformist Belisario Betancur (1982–1986), who promoted an agenda of economic redistribution and a negotiated solution with the insurgency. His administration began a trend in Colombia's politics of presidential administrations coming to power with promises to negotiate an end to the internal war only to resort to more repressive and militarized approaches when negotiations broke down. Betancur's redistributive agenda was sidetracked by a Conservative congress. He obtained a truce with M-19 and the FARC in 1984, but his peace process ended with the destruction of the Palace of Justice in 1985 in an effort to retake it from M-19 guerrillas who were holding the country's supreme court hostage. In addition, agrarian and narcotics trafficking elites frustrated with Betancur's peace overtures and their continued harassment by insurgent forces actively organized and financed a new generation of paramilitary groups. One important example was Muerte a Secuestradores (MAS; in English, Death to Kidnappers) which

emerged in 1981 and was financed largely by members of the Medellín cartel in response to escalating guerrilla kidnappings and extortions. MAS set out to kidnap, torture, and kill, with the help of local security officials, all individuals they believed were working with the guerrillas in the Middle Magdalena region of Colombia. Other privately organized groups emerged around the same time and involved local landowners, political leaders, junior officers in the army, and even representatives of the Latin American division of Texaco. By 1983 these paramilitary groups were tied to over two hundred killings, and a 1983 governmental report found that 59 of the 163 members of MAS were active-duty military, though they were not criminally prosecuted for their involvement.

MAS was an early example of Colombia's modern paramilitary groups. These wide-ranging organizations have included death squads organized privately by narcotics traffickers (sicarios) or rural elites and with the assistance of the intelligence agencies; armed militias organized by cattle ranchers, emerald dealers, large landowners and drug traffickers responding to the harassment of guerrilla units (as well as expanding their control over land and resources); and irregular forces formed directly by the state. Financing for such groups has come from domestic interests and multinational corporations such as Chiquita or Coca-Cola. The corporations' subcontractors have financed paramilitary groups to suppress labor unrest and union organizing in their operations.

In the late 1980s and early 1990s Colombian administrations symbolically addressed the issue of human rights but with little substantive policy action. This was partly the result of a vicious war the Medellín cartel launched against the Colombian state in response to the government's increased law enforcement activities against the cartel. Car bombs, assassinations of politicians and police officers, and a wave of kidnappings of political leaders in an effort to intimidate the establishment by drug traffickers raised the general consciousness that human rights needed to be addressed. For example, the Virgilio Barco administration (1986–1990) passed a series of decrees making it illegal for the army to organize paramilitary groups and established a human rights advisory council charged with promoting human rights in the armed forces. This council often concluded that human rights violations were the work of drug traffickers, not the army, despite the fact that human rights organizations regularly reported on the role of the army in perpetuating violations. Paramilitary groups increased their numbers in the last year of the Barco administration, escalating their massacres of peasants, leftists, and trade union activists. Prominent during the late 1980s and early 1990s was the systematic campaign to liquidate the Unión Patriótica (UP). The UP was a political party established by the FARC in 1985, during its peace negotiations with the Betancur administration, in a step toward the FARC's eventual reintegration. Over three thousand of its activists and leaders were assassinated in the first ten years of its founding, which strengthened hard-liners in the FARC unwilling to trust the Colombian state in future peace negotiations. The killing of UP members, trade unionists, and leftist political activists continued into the César Gaviria administration (1990–1994). However, Gaviria's government also facilitated the adoption of a new constitution that stressed human rights and the extension of democracy.

The 1991 constitution guaranteed the rights to life and human dignity, freedom of the press, economic rights, and protections for Colombia's Afro and indigenous minorities. The length of time that a president could call a state of siege was no longer unlimited. In addition, the constitution established the Defensoria del Pueblo, a federal agency with the responsibility to promote human rights ideals and values, to collect information and report on the state of human rights, and to disseminate the principles of human rights law throughout the country.

Finally, the constitution established a Constitutional Court to rule on the constitutionality of specific laws as well as the institution of *tutelas* or writs that citizens can file with a court if they believe that public officials have violated or failed to protect their constitutional rights. Well over 200,000 *tutelas* were filed between 1991 and 2008 as they increasingly were seen as a legitimate tool for the protection of human and constitutional rights for Colombian citizens. While the 1991 constitution is viewed by many as an important democratizing step in Colombia's history, its enactment was followed by a major escalation in political violence and human rights violations.

HUMAN RIGHTS, ESCALATING VIOLENCE, AND PLAN COLOMBIA: 1991–2002

From the mid-1990s through the early 2000s pressure from the United States, the Inter-American Commission on Human Rights of the Organization of American States (OAS), and the United Nations and accumulating evidence of state involvement forced increasing governmental attention to human rights. This included the government's recognition of its role in specific massacres, allowing the United Nations High Commissioner for Human Rights to establish an office in the country, and ratifying the Additional Protocol II to the Geneva Convention on humanitarian law. Protocol II requires that states protect and provide humane treatment to noncombatants and detained individuals within an internal armed conflict. In addition, the administration of Ernesto Samper (1994–1998) publicly acknowledged the government's role in the Trujillo massacres that led to the death of 107 individuals between 1988 and 1990 in or near the town of Trujillo. Samper also provided government funds for relatives of the victims as a partial compensation for their loss.

This progress on an institutional and legal level was undermined by policies that facilitated human rights violations. For example, Samper actively promoted the Convivir, a government-supported program that sanctioned the organization of civilian militias to directly work with the military in gathering intelligence and information. These groups were prohibited by the André Pastrana administration (1998–2002) because of human rights violations, but many later integrated with paramilitary militias (or had been working with them the entire time). Legal impunity continued for members of the military, who often justified their violations of human rights as "acts of service." These should have led to prosecution through the military justice system, but military justice rarely meted out punishment against them. In fact, one consequence of greater international attention and pressure on the Colombian government regarding human rights violations was the expansion in the role and responsibility of paramilitary militias in the repression and elimination of alleged supporters of the guerrilla insurgency.

By the beginning of the 2000s paramilitary groups were the perpetrators of over 70 percent of all politically motivated killings, increasing from a rate of less than 20 percent in the early 1990s. In April 1997 paramilitary units from federal departments united to form the United Self-Defense Forces of Colombia. This created a paramilitary army with the capacity to strike on a national scope. The expanded struggle against guerrillas largely involved terrorizing and killing civilians in communities deemed too supportive of the insurgents. The number of massacres, extrajudicial executions, and internal displacements spiraled upward in the second half of the 1990s and in the early 2000s. The counterinsurgency tactics also helped consolidate the territorial gains of narcotics traffickers while concentrating economic power in fewer hands in the countryside. According to Amnesty International, "Over 60% of the more than 3 million internally displaced people in Colombia have been forced from their homes and lands in areas of mineral, agricultural or other economic importance" ("Trade Unionists under Attack," p. 1).

The Pastrana administration gained some human rights triumphs, but they were of a limited and sometimes contradictory value. A new military criminal code passed in 1999 ostensibly aimed to reduce the military's historic impunity. However, the new code still allowed for the determination on a case-by-case basis whether an alleged crime should be processed by civilian or military courts, no matter the type of crime. Thus a general was sentenced to forty months in jail for allowing over two hundred paramilitary soldiers into the southern town of Mapiripán in July 1997, when forty-nine people were tortured and killed. The Pastrana government also notably attempted to negotiate a peace agreement with the FARC, demilitarizing a major region of the country in exchange for the FARC's involvement in peace talks. These talks did not prevent the FARC from engaging in various human rights violations despite its rhetoric in support of a peaceful resolution of the conflict. Throughout the 1990s and in the early 2000s the FARC pursued a militarized strategy focused on strengthening its resources through taxation of the drug trade and kidnapping civilians for ransom. In addition, the group executed unarmed combatants and intimidated rural communities and governments to ensure its control over specific regions of the country. By 2002 the FARC was at its height militarily but possibly at its lowest in terms of its political legitimacy.

The human rights progress in the Samper and Pastrana administrations were in part a result of pressures from the U.S. government. The Clinton administration rhetorically called upon Colombian administrations to do more to reduce human rights violations, denying visas to military officials linked to human rights violations and signing into law the Leahy Amendment, which ostensibly ensured that U.S. military aid would not be provided to military units that allegedly committed human rights violations. This was an improvement over the positions of the administrations of Ronald Reagan and George H. W. Bush, which placed relatively little emphasis on human rights. Yet in 2000 the Clinton administration greatly expanded

U.S. military aid through the $1.3 billion aid program Plan Colombia. This plan focused primarily on strengthening the coercive sectors of the Colombian state in order to better eradicate coca and opium poppy production, which had expanded. These crops were largely grown in relatively isolated regions, where the FARC and paramilitary groups more or less governed.

The program continued a relationship between the U.S. government and the Colombian military that dated to the 1950s through which the United States. helped train and equip Colombia's first counterinsurgent forces. U.S. military aid in the 1980s and 1990s was regularly justified as part of the U.S. "war on drugs" given that Colombia was the central source of the cocaine that entered the U.S. market. In fact, U.S. drug consumers yearly contributed hundreds of millions of dollars to both guerrilla and paramilitary organizations to help them finance armies and control key production and shipment sites. By 1998 guerrilla and paramilitary groups received approximately $500 million from the drug trade, $300 million from extortion, and over $200 million from kidnappings. The importance of the drug trade continued to be central to paramilitaries and guerrillas in the early twenty-first century.

THE URIBE ADMINISTRATION AND THE "WAR ON TERRORISM": 2002–2008

In the early 2000s the administration of Álvaro Uribe subordinated human rights to an all-out war against the insurgency or "terrorism." This general denial that the state was responsible for human rights abuses was also an open vilification by governmental authorities of human rights groups. The government was elected into office on a hard-line, militarized platform after the failure of Pastrana's peace process. During Uribe's administration the government successfully increased the size and the territorial presence of the security forces through continued U.S. military assistance (approximately $500 to $600 million a year during his administration) and increasing governmental defense spending paid for by special war taxes on Colombia's wealthy. These efforts contributed to a decline in political assassinations, trade union killings, kidnappings, and massacres after a peak in 2001–2002. The government's military offensives against the FARC weakened that group militarily. The FARC declined from its peak of almost twenty thousand members at the end of the 1990s to under ten thousand in 2008. Simultaneously, the government oversaw the demobilization of over thirty thousand paramilitary members, who gave up their arms in exchange for amnesties or light prison sentences. The reduced number of political assassinations and massacres was a reason to celebrate. Whether this represented the consolidation of democratic norms and practices by the Colombian state remained an open question.

The rate of human rights violations in Colombia declined from its peak in 2002 but was at about the rate of that in the mid-1990s, not necessarily a positive time for human rights in the country. In addition, the paramilitary demobilization process has been questioned. Most of the demobilized paramilitary troops were given amnesty for their crimes, and the approximately three thousand mid- to upper-level commanders received sentences of five to eight years. These lighter sentences were granted in part in exchange for information about the crimes these individuals committed during the last two decades of the twentieth century. Critics charged that the majority of testimonies provided little information, and some paramilitary commanders refused to cooperate as required by the demobilization law. Also according to the Organization of American States mission verifying the demobilization process, approximately twenty-two new paramilitary organizations emerged after the "final" demobilization of paramilitary groups in 2006.

Finally, it appeared that the demobilization of paramilitary troops reflected in part the reality that these organizations had established influential networks to local, regional, and national political institutions. In 2008 over sixty congresspeople and governors were under judicial investigation for financing or assisting paramilitary groups in their regions. The vast majority of these politicians were strong political supporters of Uribe. The brother of Uribe's foreign minister was jailed for aiding paramilitary groups, and Uribe's cousin and close political adviser Mario Uribe was accused of conspiring with paramilitary groups. In the spring of 2008 Uribe himself was investigated for his alleged role in planning a 1997 massacre by paramilitary groups that led to the deaths of fifteen individuals, a charge that Uribe vehemently denied. While the investigations themselves illustrated progress in the government's willingness to weaken the impunity long enjoyed by Colombia's political class, they also revealed the extent to which the Colombian state and paramilitary groups worked together to further their respective interests.

Another worrying trend involved the armed forces. The military's expanded role in the internal conflict coupled with the declining role for paramilitary groups were associated with an increase in their direct involvement in human rights violations during Uribe's administration. This included killing unarmed civilians and dressing them up as guerrillas, implying higher rates of guerrilla deaths, so as to secure material benefits and promotions. The internal war persisted, and the FARC continued to engage in human rights violations.

The FARC's activities continued to alienate the general population, even producing massive nationwide anti-FARC protests in February 2008. The public was outraged at the evidence of the suffering of the FARC hostages as well as the length of time (some longer than seven years) that FARC prisoners had been held. The public also condemned the FARC executions of unarmed kidnapping victims when the group feared that the Colombian government might successfully rescue the victims or was unable to arrange a "proper" ransom. In the early twenty-first century the FARC held an estimated seven hundred prisoners, most of them for money and others as political prisoners to exchange for its members in Colombian prisons. Also the FARC recruited minors for its army and threatened or assassinated elected officials who refused to defer to their political demands.

ASSESSMENT

The mass media and U.S. policy makers often present human rights violations in Colombia as reflecting an absent or weak state overwhelmed by internal strife and terrorist actors bent on the state's destruction. The reality, as with many governmental and media frames, is more complicated. The view of a weak state vainly struggling to establish order is only one piece of a larger explanation that involves underlying material and economic inequalities, restrictive politics, the influence of a wealthy narcotics trafficking industry, and the pressures of the United States. These interacted throughout the twentieth century to create incentives for actors to take up arms for political change or to maintain access to legal and illegal resources or to finance state and para-state organizations. The country's governments and political elites have been unable or unwilling to untangle the various elements undergirding the political violence and human rights violations that disproportionately affect the civilian population caught between violent state, para-state, and nonstate actors.

[*See also* Central America in the 1980s *and* Peace and Human Rights.]

BIBLIOGRAPHY

Agence France Press. *Colombian President Says Officials Probing His Role in Massacre.* April 23, 2008. http://www.afp.google.com/article/ALeqM5ixoJlMny-zqGaU2dGxiPlktJhfsQ.

Amnesty International. *Political Violence in Colombia: Myth and Reality.* New York: Amnesty International, 1994.

Amnesty International. *Trade Unionists under Attack in Colombia.* October 2007. http://www.asiapacific.amnesty.org/library/Index/ENGAMR230322007?open&of=ENG-2M3.

Avilés, William. "Paramilitarism and Colombia's Low-Intensity Democracy." *Journal of Latin American Studies* 38, no. 2 (May 2006): 379–408.

Blair Trujillo, Elsa. *Las fuerzas armadas: Una mirada civil.* Santafé de Bogotá, Colombia: CINEP, 1993.

Bushnell, David. *The Making of Modern Colombia: A Nation in Spite of Itself.* Berkeley: University of California Press, 1993.

Center for International Policy. *CINEP: Colombia's Conflict Is Far from Over.* Plan Colombia and Beyond. April 10, 2008. http://www.cipcol.org/?p=580#more-580.

Center for International Policy. *U.S. Aid to Colombia since 1997: Summary Tables.* Center for International Policy's Colombia Program. June 1, 2007. http://www.ciponline.org/colombia/aidtable.htm.

Dávila Ladrón de Guevara, Andrés. *El juego del poder: Historia, armas, y votos.* Santafé de Bogotá, Colombia: Ediciones Uniandes, CEREC, 1998.

Defensoría del Pueblo. *La Defensoría del Pueblo, República de Colombia.* 2007. http://www.defensoria.org.co/red/?_secc=01.

Forero, Juan. "Colombia May Seek Chiquita Extraditions." *Washington Post,* March 21, 2007. http://www.washingtonpost.com/wp-dyn/content/article/2007/03/20/AR2007032001698.html.

Forero, Juan. "Colombian Troops Kill Farmers, Pass Off Bodies as Rebels'." *Washington Post,* March 30, 2008. http://www.washingtonpost.com/wp-dyn/content/article/2008/03/29/AR2008032901118.html.

Forero, Juan. "An Elusive Justice." *Washington Post,* January 25, 2008.

Forero, Juan. "Plot to Kill Colombian Witness Exposed." *Washington Post,* April 26, 2008. http://www.washingtonpost.com/wp-dyn/content/article/2008/04/25/AR2008042503238.html?sub=AR.

Gallón, Gustavo. "Human Rights: A Path to Democracy and Peace in Colombia." In *Peace, Democracy, and Human Rights in Colombia,* edited by Christopher Welna and Gustavo Gallón, pp. 353–411. Notre Dame, Ind.: University of Notre Dame Press, 2007.

Gallón, Gustavo, ed. *Derechos humanos y conflicto armado en Colombia.* Santafé de Bogotá, Colombia: Comisión Andina de Juristas, Seccional Colombia, 1991.

Giraldo, Javier. *Colombia: The Genocidal Democracy.* Monroe, Maine: Common Courage, 1996.

Kirk, Robin. *More Terrible Than Death: Massacres, Drugs, and America's War in Colombia.* New York: Public Affairs, 2003.

Livingstone, Grace. *Inside Colombia: Drugs, Democracy, and War.* New Brunswick, N.J.: Rutgers University Press, 2004.

Maria Bejarano, Ana. "The Constitution of 1991: An Institutional Evaluation Seven Years Later." In *Violence in Colombia, 1990–2000: Waging War and Negotiating Peace,* edited by Charles Bergquist, Ricardo Peñaranda, and Gonzalo Sánchez G., pp. 53–74. Wilmington, Del.: Scholarly Resources, 2001.

Méndez, Juan E. *The "Drug War" in Colombia: The Neglected Tragedy of Political Violence.* New York: Human Rights Watch, 1990.

Palacios, Marco. *Between Legitimacy and Violence: A History of Colombia, 1875–2002.* Durham, N.C.: Duke University Press, 2006.

Rabasa, Angel, and Peter Chalk. *Colombian Labyrinth: The Synergy of Drugs and Insurgency and Its Implications for Regional Stability.* Santa Monica, Calif.: Rand, 2001.

Tate, Winifred. *Counting the Dead: The Culture and Politics of Human Rights Activism in Colombia.* Berkeley: University of California Press, 2007.

United States State Department. *Colombia: Country Reports on Human Rights Practices,* 2007. March 11, 2008. http://www.state.gov/g/drl/rls/hrrpt/2007/100633.htm.

Vivanco, José Miguel, and Maria McFarland Sánchez-Moreno. "Troubled Times." *Progress Magazine,* February 1, 2008. http://www.hrw.org/english/docs/2008/02/01/colomb17975.htm.

Zibechi, Raúl. *Where the Asphalt Ends: Bogota's Periferies.* Americas Program Special Report, Center for International Policy. March 11, 2008. http://www.americas.irc-online.org/am/5057.

COLONIALISM

by Bonny Ibhawoh

A discussion of the legacies of colonialism for human rights can go as far back as the beginning of European overseas empire in the fifteenth century, which included the Iberian conquest and settlement of America. Early European colonialism in the Americas had far-reaching implications for the rights and liberties of the indigenous peoples they encountered in the course of conquest, settlement, and expansion. As their control of the Americas began to wane in the late eighteenth century, European colonial powers, particularly Britain and France, gained new influence and control over territories in Africa and Asia. This marked a new imperial age that spanned much of the nineteenth and early twentieth centuries. It prompted, among other things, the "scramble for Africa," a race by many European countries to acquire territories in Africa for political and economic reasons. The discussion here focuses on this "new" imperialism in Africa, Asia, and the Middle East rather than on earlier Iberian colonialism in the Americas. The discussion here also focuses specifically on the post–World War II notion of universal human rights that emerged within the framework of the United Nations (UN) system and the Universal Declaration of Human Rights (UDHR).

COLONIALISM AND RIGHTS

The link between colonialism and human rights manifests itself on several levels. The first relates to the origins and rationale of European colonialism. Underlying nineteenth- and twentieth-century European colonialism in Africa and Asia were the notions of the "civilizing mission" and "the white man's burden." This was the view, genuinely believed by some and used as a cover for expedient concerns by others, that European colonists had a responsibility as colonizers to spread the benefits of European civilization to colonized peoples. These benefits included the doctrines of Christianity as well as European liberal Enlightenment traditions of freedom, democracy, and the rights of humans. The argument of extending European traditions of rights and liberties to colonized

people in principle, if not in practice, was often used to justify and rationalize European colonialism. In many parts of Africa, the process of European colonial intervention was founded on the need to stop the slave trade and promote legitimate trade. The language of freedom, free trade, liberty, and civilization characterized many of the treaty agreements between the European colonial powers and African chiefs in the early colonial period. European powers saw their role partly in terms of promoting the liberties of colonized people under their influence through active intervention in local politics. They justified their military campaigns against uncooperative communities and the overthrow of indigenous rulers on the grounds of protecting the rights and liberties of European and colonial subjects living in such areas.

The second link between colonialism and human rights has to do with the end of colonialism. Twentieth-century anticolonial nationalist movements in Asia and Africa drew on the same language of rights that had earlier been used to justify colonialism to demand independence and self-determination. The language of universal human rights that gained prominence after World War II was extensively deployed by peoples throughout the colonized world to challenge European imperialism. In India anticolonial nationalists led by Mohandas ("Mahatma") Gandhi took advantage of the new international emphasis on the right to self-determination espoused in the UN Charter to demand independence from British colonial rule. However, although Gandhi and other anticolonial nationalists utilized the language of right to self-determination against European powers, they were not always supportive of the rights discourse on other subjects.

The final link between colonialism and human rights relates to the legacies of colonialism. Although colonialism in many parts of Africa and Asia came to an end in the mid-twentieth century, its legacies continue to dominate discourses about universal human rights. Cultural relativists and pluralists have invoked the history and legacies of colonialism in Africa and Asia to challenge the notion of universal human rights. They challenge and sometimes reject the international human rights body norms developed within the UN as being too Western oriented and not adequately reflective of non-Western-perspectives. They argue that the promotion of a "universal human rights" regime in non-Western societies is evocative of a tradition of European colonialism and cultural dominance. In this regard the universal human rights movement has been compared with earlier Eurocentric colonial projects in Africa and Asia that promoted a homogenizing worldview and cast societies into superior and subordinate positions. The invasion of Iraq by the United States in 2003, partly for articulated reasons of imposing freedom, reinforced this postcolonial skepticism about rights discourse. The following discussion explores these three aspects of the legacies of colonialism for human rights.

RIGHTS, LIBERTIES, AND THE COLONIAL RATIONALE

European colonialism claimed a rights agenda that was inherent in the notions of the "civilizing mission." These rights claims were central to early attempts to justify and rationalize colonial empires. They were also evident in the benevolent paternalism and Christian humanist agendas of some European groups and colonial regimes. Underlying these rights claims were assumptions about the obligations of colonial governments to protect the basic rights and liberties of their subjects. In the case of Britain, colonial authorities sought to extend as far as practicable to the colonies the same standards of law and justice that prevailed in England. Local customs and traditions were allowed to exist alongside the imported English legal system eventually and only to the extent that they did not patently contradict English law. The objective was to create within the empire some legal and judicial standards that represented British ideals of rights and justice. These ideas expressed a broad concern for private rights and individual freedom of action. For France, the emphasis was on extending the republican ideals of the French Revolution—liberty, equality, and fraternity—to its colonial subjects. Colonial discourses on rights and liberty provided a powerful rational for empire, particularly against the background of the antislavery and anti–slave trade movements. But colonial ideals were quite different from colonial practices.

In practice, more pragmatic imperial political and economic imperatives were always considerations in the process of colonial administration. The history of eighteenth- and nineteenth-century European colonialism in Africa and Asia shows clearly that the protection or promotion of the rights of colonial subjects was never really a foremost priority. Yet, even though the rights and liberties of colonial subjects were often violated in the pursuit of overriding political and economic objectives, the rhetoric of rights and liberty remained appealing to colonial officials because it was a powerful device for rationalizing and legitimizing empire.

In addition to extending European legal and libertarian ideas to the colonies, colonial powers also stressed their political and social obligations toward colonized people. Britain, for instance, spelled out its social obligations to its colonial subjects, including "the protection of their liberties in the free enjoyment of their possession" (Boldt, p. 211). It was on the basis of these ideals and obligations that Britain eventually sought to dismantle slavery and other institutions of servitude in Africa as well as the Indian caste system, which limited the freedoms of certain groups within society. Using the imported English legal system, British authorities over time abolished all forms of slave dealings within the territories under their control and prescribed severe penalties for the contravention of antislavery laws. Colonial authorities presented this antislavery posture as evidence of British concern for the basic rights and freedoms of native peoples. They deliberately sought to legitimize colonial rule in terms of Britain's later abolitionist role rather than its record of active slave trading for more than half a century.

The extension of European law to many parts of Africa and Asia in the nineteenth century ushered in new regimes of individual rights whereby previously marginalized groups were able to escape from traditional institutions of servitude and oppression. In India and many parts of Africa, the introduction of new English-style divorce laws provided women opportunities to assert their independence and escape traditional patriarchal control. Colonial authorities put in place laws intended to change local attitudes toward marital relationships. They emphasized the rights of women to have a say in the choice of their husbands and to be able to divorce their husbands under certain conditions. Colonial marriage laws contained provisions that permitted children over the age of twenty-one to marry without their parents' consent. These were intended to check the practices of child betrothal and arranged marriage that were prevalent in many traditional African and Asian societies.

In some cases, colonial laws entirely abrogated indigenous customs regarding marriage, divorce, and custody of children and replaced them with practices that European officials regarded as moral and more in accordance with the principles of natural justice. Whereas many indigenous societies emphasized communal and collective rights, colonial laws tended to emphasis individual rights. Although such colonial reforms did not always go down well with indigenous ruling elites and those interested in maintaining the traditional status quo, they were welcomed by others. Women and other marginalized groups, such as former slaves and persons of lower castes, took advantage of liberal colonial laws and policies to assert their rights and freedoms. They used colonial arguments about women's rights and the need to change "uncivilized" customary practices to escape from restrictive traditions.

But although there was an emphasis on abrogating indigenous institutions and practices that were thought to limit individual rights and freedoms, colonial authorities introduced policies that restricted and violated the rights of colonized people in other ways. Prevailing racial attitudes about the inherent inferiority of colonized peoples and assumptions about their incapability to govern themselves limited the readiness of the European colonists to allow colonial subjects autonomy and self-government. The general pattern among European powers was to implement individual civil rights so long as British power was not reduced.

In this sense, colonialism was inherently a violation of the right of colonized people to self-government. Apart from ruthlessly uprooting the political and social orders in these societies, colonial regimes fell short of their own liberal agendas. Britain, like other European colonial powers, frequently used military force to suppress struggles by colonized people for autonomy and self-government. In 1919 British troops fired indiscriminately on a crowd of unarmed Indian protesters in what became known as the Massacre of Amritsar. British colonial authorities also ruthlessly put down the Mau Mau uprising for land reform and independence in Kenya in the 1950s.

French colonialism followed a similar pattern. The extension of rights to colonized people was an important part of the discourses it deployed to justify colonialism. For much of the colonial period, the French pursued a policy of assimilation that was aimed at incorporating colonized people into French culture as part of the broader agenda of the civilizing mission. Notions of human rights in the context of French republican idealism shaped some colonial policies throughout the French empire from French Africa to French Indochina. At a time of ascendant liberalism in France, republican elites maintained that colonized peoples in Africa and Asia should be freed from the material and moral want that had once oppressed the French nation. As far back as 1792, a revolutionary decree had proclaimed, "All men, without distinction of color, living in the French colonies are French citizens and enjoy all the rights assured in the constitution" (James, p. 115). This represented the aspiration, if not the predominant reality, of French colonialism.

Within French colonial officialdom the prevalent view was that France had an obligation to extend its republican principles of liberty, equality, and fraternity to its overseas territories. However, the dominant approach within French officialdom to colonial administration tended to be authoritarian and repressive. It was assumed that colonized peoples were still to evolve within their own cultures, but they were to do so in a way that respected the universal rights of all individuals. This thinking, which influenced French policy in realms as different as education and labor, convinced committed French Democrats and Republicans that colonialism was actually advancing the cause of human rights and liberty. In line with the French aspiration of extending universal rights to its colonial subjects, the government made elaborate provisions for the representation of its dependent peoples in the central governing institutions in Paris.

Despite this universalist outlook, however, the reality was that French colonialism offered little in the way of democratic institutions or real rights to colonized people. French citizenship and the full range of rights accorded French citizens in France were limited to a few colonized people, and there was virtually no representation of the colonies in Paris. French colonialism in Africa was particularly notorious for its widespread violations of individual rights and liberties. Until the end of World War II, French authorities enforced a brutal system of forced labor in West Africa known as the *indigénat* (indigene) (Thomas, 2005). French colonial policies from education to administration also tended to promote French economic and political interests and assert European values above all else, often undermining the culture and overall welfare of colonized people. Even when reforms were eventually introduced at the end of World War II, racial discrimination and political repression remained prevalent in many French colonies, leading to bitter anticolonial warfare in Indochina and Algeria.

More notorious examples of the excesses of colonialism are the atrocities of the Belgian king Leopold in the

Congo and the Germans in South-West Africa. In the latter case, thousands of Africans, including women and children, were killed by German troops in the Herero uprising in 1904. In the Congo, the Congo Free State was created in the 1880s as a private empire of King Leopold II. This part of Africa was particularly attractive to European powers because of its potential for mining and rubber production, and Leopold sought to maximize production by granting concessions to private companies. These profit-driven concession companies became notorious for the atrocities they committed against the Africans under their control. Colonial and company officials routinely used coercion, torture, arbitrary detention, and mutilation to guarantee the supply of labor in the mines and rubber plantations. These atrocities became so widespread that they prompted a concerted campaign by missionaries and humanitarians to publicize and end the practices. They even drew condemnation from other European colonial powers, leading the Belgian government to take over the colonial administration of the Congo from Leopold in 1908.

But even with King Leopold II in Belgium and the Germans in South-West Africa, the promise of promoting civilization and protecting the liberties of colonized Africans had provided the justification for colonialism. During the mid-nineteenth-century scramble for Africa, Leopold staked his claim to the Congo partly on the grounds of eradicating the residues of the slave trade in the area while promoting Christianity and "civilization." In the end, the atrocities committed under Leopold's rule were as much a violation of the rights of Africans as the inhuman slave trade he sought to suppress.

Although European colonialism promised universal rights, in reality it kept colonized peoples in a state of subjugation. Indeed, the history of European colonialism in Africa and Asia is replete with examples of how colonial policies and actions not only violated the basic rights of colonial subjects but also fell short of the liberal and republican agendas put forward by European colonial powers. English libertarian traditions and French republicanism professed broad concerns for the rights of colonized people, but this did not in fact guarantee human rights conditions in the colonies comparable to those that prevailed in England and France. The purported extension of rights to colonial subjects and the official rhetoric that kept them on colonial agendas seem more a discourse produced to legitimize and rationalize empire than an objective to which European colonial powers were seriously committed.

Despite their limitations, however, colonial discourses on rights and liberties ultimately had a liberating effect. Colonized people were able to appropriate this language of universal rights and use it in their demands for social inclusion and political participation in ways not originally intended by colonial powers. The rhetoric of rights and liberties that underlined colonial propaganda and justifications of empire became an important instrument with which colonized people expressed dissent, challenged colonialism, and articulated nationalist aspirations for self-determination. In this sense, European imperialism forged the tools with which its victims ultimately pried it loose.

NATIONALISM AND DECOLONIZATION

The contemporary human rights movement has been influenced by colonialism. Like colonialism, the human rights movement involves challenges to the practices and sometimes sovereignty of particular regions of the world in the name of universal standards deriving from, and largely enforced by, the West. In the cases of Africa and Asia, such moral discourses were partly shaped by the history of colonialism. Anticolonial nationalist struggles in Africa, in Asia, and elsewhere in the colonized world were among the first mass movements to draw on the universal language of human rights of the post–World War II era. Anticolonial nationalists demanded that the ideals of freedom and self-determination that had been the basis of Allied military campaigns against Nazism in Europe also be extended to them. Thus, although not often recognized as such, anticolonial struggles were not only nationalist movements but also veritable human rights movements. For this reason, it is necessary to reconstruct the histories of twentieth-century anticolonial nationalist movements as human rights histories.

Although the aspiration toward protecting the rights and liberties of colonized people provided a rationale for European colonialism from the very beginning, the world wars made such references to rights even more prevalent as opposition to colonialism gathered momentum. During World War I, President Woodrow Wilson of the United States gave the concepts of decolonization and national self-determination much prominence, although they were not articulated in the language of human rights. In a speech to Congress in 1918, Wilson voiced the objectives of the United States in World War I in what became known as the Fourteen Points. The Fourteen Points, which became the basis for the Treaty of Versailles and the League of Nations, included proposals for securing the independence and self-determination of several European states and societies. Inspired by the Fourteen Points and other wartime developments, people rose throughout the colonized world to rid themselves of imperial domination.

The end of World War I signaled the effective beginning of the great upsurge of anticolonial nationalism, which reached its fruition after 1945. During the Great War, European colonial powers relied extensively on their colonies for contributions of material and labor. In declaring war, European colonial powers such as Britain, France, and Germany were also committing their empires, which included most of Africa and Asia, to the war. The contributions of these colonies to European war efforts were substantial. British colonies in the Indian subcontinent, including present-day India, Pakistan, Bangladesh, and Sri Lanka, provided about 140,000 soldiers and support workers who were engaged in active service during the war. Many of these people served in France, Belgium, and the Middle East. French colonies in Africa contributed an estimated 235,000 soldiers to the war efforts, and French West Africa alone provided ninety-four battalions for the European front.

The contributions of the colonies to European war efforts engendered a sense of entitlement among colonial subjects. Nationalist leaders began to articulate their demands for self-determination and independence not simply as political concessions from colonial powers but as rights—meaning entitlements. In India the period following World War I marked the rise of a vigorous anticolonial nationalist movement. From 1918 the Indian National Congress, under the leadership of Gandhi, launched a series of nonviolent campaigns of civil disobedience, many of which were suppressed by the British colonial government. In Africa former soldiers who had fought in World War I drew on their wartime experiences once they returned home to lead new nationalist movements against colonial domination. They too began to demand independence as a matter of right rather than concession.

WORLD WAR II AND UNIVERSAL HUMAN RIGHTS

Even more than World War I, World War II marked a period of renewed international emphasis on the themes of freedom, democracy, and the fundamental rights of humans. These ideas were of profound importance to colonized people throughout the world and their struggles for independence. Although nationalist claims had been mounting in Asian and African colonies for several years, World War II made self-determination a living principle for the non-European world. During the war, self-determination was proclaimed as a doctrine of universal application and was one of the guiding principles of Allied policy. Allied propaganda presented the war as a fight between the ideals of freedom, democracy, and self-determination and the oppression and tyranny of Nazism and Fascism. However, as the war progressed, it became apparent that the principle of self-determination, which was so forcefully espoused by the Allies, was not intended to reach beyond the confines of Europe or apply to colonized people in the non-Western world. There were also competing claims to self-determination between and within nations as well as conflicts between a national people's right to collective self-determination and individual human rights.

The principle that nations can freely determine their own destinies was accorded international prominence soon after World War I by Wilson. He famously stated at the outbreak of World War I that the central empires had been forced into political bankruptcy because they dominated alien peoples over whom they had no natural right to rule. Wilsonian doctrines of democracy and the right of peoples and nations to govern themselves were also expressed in the Atlantic Charter, a statement on the outcome of a meeting in 1941 between Prime Minister Winston Churchill of Britain and President Franklin Delano Roosevelt of the United States aimed at drawing up a common position on the war. The charter declared, among other things, that both leaders "respect the right of all peoples to choose the form of government under which they will live" and that they wished to "see sovereign rights and self-government restored to those who have been forcibly deprived of them" (Menon, p. 110). The charter was one of the first major documents of global significance to affirm the right to self-determination in both humanistic and universal terms.

The Atlantic Charter became the focus of global discussions and debates about the right to self-determination throughout the colonized world soon after it was issued. Its famous third clause, which affirmed the right of all peoples to choose their own governments, raised the hopes of nationalists everywhere who saw it as an unequivocal recognition of their rights to self-determination and independence. It soon became clear, however, that Churchill did not intend to extend the principle of self-determination espoused in the Atlantic Charter to colonized people in the non-European world.

In a speech before the British House of Commons in 1942, Churchill stated that he and Roosevelt had only European states in mind when they drew up the charter and that the charter was intended as "a guide and not a rule" (Pearce, p. 22). Even more controversial was his widely quoted response to the demands from British colonies that the principle of self-determination affirmed in the charter be extended to them. In rejecting such demands, Churchill stated that he had not become the prime minister of Britain to "preside over the liquidation of the British Empire" (Dukes, p. 89). At about the same time, however, a different message was coming from the other side of the Atlantic. Roosevelt, in keeping with the U.S. anticolonial tradition, maintained that the Atlantic Charter was not intended to apply exclusively to Europe, but to all humanity. Roosevelt's liberal interpretation of the provisions of the charter was more in tune with the expectations of colonized people, who had begun to use it to demand an end to colonial rule.

In British India the Indian National Congress, led by Gandhi and Jawaharlal Nehru, opposed Fascism and Nazism but, drawing on the Atlantic Charter and principles of self-determination espoused by the Allies, also continued its challenge of British colonialism. The Indian National Congress highlighted the contradictions between Allied propaganda that war against Nazi Germany was being fought for the sake of freedom and the denial of these same freedoms to those under British colonial rule. For this reason, the congress refused to support Britain in the war against Germany even though it opposed Nazism and Fascism.

The demands of Indian nationalism went far beyond what Britain was willing to grant. Rather than the full autonomy that Indian nationalists demanded, Britain was willing to grant only some form of limited self-government to the colony. The British argument, which became a standard response of colonial powers to demands for independence, was that the colonies were not completely ready for full autonomy. Britain, like other European colonial powers, stressed what it considered its obligation to maintain political control in the colonies until such time as they were deemed adequately prepared for independence and self-rule. But the Indian National Congress flatly repudiated Britain's right to rule the country and initiated the Quit India movement, which threatened nonviolent mass struggle. The response of the British colonial authorities was to outlaw the congress and imprison its leaders. Similar developments occurred in other Asian colonies, including Burma, the Netherlands Indies, and Indochina, where nationalists rejected tentative imperial reforms and demanded complete independence. These demands for full autonomy were also predicated partly on the idea that the principles of self-determination espoused in the context of wartime Europe also had to be extended to the colonies.

In Africa comparable anticolonial rebellions that broke out against the French in Madagascar and the British in Nigeria and the Gold Coast (Ghana) spurred colonial governments on to reforms and allowed for greater representation of colonized people in governance. The emergence of a new class of Western-educated African elites strengthened the nationalist movements and intensified local opposition to colonial rule. In the Gold Coast a vigorous anticolonial nationalist campaign led by the charismatic Kwame Nkrumah rejected British wartime reforms and demanded complete independence from British rule. Nkrumah's Convention People's Party took as its motto "We prefer self-government with danger to servitude in tranquility." These insistent demands for full independence, along with other global developments, set the stage for the eventual collapse of European imperialism on the continent.

This discourse on self-determination marked a transformation of the Wilsonian notion of self-determination of peoples, a central aspect of international relations since the end of World War I, into a collective human right for national peoples. Anticolonial nationalist movements in the non-Western world tended to emphasize the collective rights of nations and ethnicities rather than individual human rights of a civil, political, economic, social, and cultural nature. Some non-Western nationalist movements, such as that led by Gandhi in India, were prepared to articulate and practice both the collective rights of national peoples and the individual rights of citizens. However, many new governments stressed the collective right of the states and communities while violating individual political, social, and economic rights.

THE UNITED NATIONS AND DECOLONIZATION

The principle of self-determination expressed in the Atlantic Charter formed the basis of the creation of the UN in 1945. The principle found expression in Chapter 11 of the UN Charter, which urges member states with colonies to develop self-government and take due account of the political aspirations of the peoples. This statement reflected the new realities of the postwar order, in which the old imperial order could no longer be justified or sustained—although the British, French, and Dutch tried. Roosevelt, one of the main advocates for the formation of the UN, saw the organization as the ultimate solution to postwar problems, including the agitation for independence by colonized people. In his famous Four Freedoms speech before the U.S. Congress, Roosevelt outlined four fundamental freedoms that he argued humans everywhere in the world ought to enjoy: freedom of speech and expression, freedom of worship, freedom from want, and freedom from fear. Roosevelt sought to extend these principles of universal freedoms to the UN. Thus, unlike the League of Nations, which had essentially been a club of European powers unconcerned with colonial problems, the more broadly based UN was embroiled in them. And the leading power was opposed to continued colonialism as long as Roosevelt lived.

However, the idea that the UN should be actively engaged in colonial problems was not without controversy. In the San Francisco debates over the UN Charter, some colonial powers protested any thought of dismantling the colonial empires or extending the rights of self-determination to colonized peoples. The British delegation objected to dismantling colonies on the grounds that in the early stages of World War II, Britain had been saved from defeat only by the existence of its African colonies, the essential materials that they provided, and the route from the Middle East across Africa that they offered. "If we had been defeated at that time," stated one British delegate, "very likely none of us would be sitting here today" (United Nations, p. 695). Given these conflicting viewpoints among the Allies, the sections of the UN Charter devoted to colonial matters necessarily represented a number of compromises, but in the end the charter endorsed the right of self-determination of peoples. This constituted recognition that old colonial systems could not be sustained within the postwar international order.

The vague human rights provisions of the UN Charter were strengthened by the UDHR, which was adopted by the UN General Assembly in 1948. The adoption of the UDHR marked the international recognition of certain fundamental rights and freedoms as inalienable universal values to which all individuals are entitled simply by virtue of their humanity. At its adoption the UDHR was heralded as "a world milestone in the long struggle for human rights" and "a magna carta for all humanity"

(Krasno, p. 84)—this despite the reality that a third of the world's population was still under colonial domination at the time of its adoption and that most colonized peoples were not represented at the UN and as such had no input in drafting the UDHR. This exclusion of the voices and perspectives of colonized peoples remains one of the strongest limitations of the UDHR's claim to universality. But despite its limitations, the UDHR was significant in the decolonization process because it reinforced the right of self-determination. Like the Atlantic Charter and the UN Charter before it, the UDHR was an international document that could ground the demands of colonized peoples for independence. In direct repudiation of colonialism, Article 21 of the UDHR states that the will of the people shall be the basis of the authority of government and affirms the right of everyone to take part in the government of his or her country. In the drafting of the UDHR, the core negotiating group contained representatives from former colonies, including India, Lebanon, the Philippines, China, and Taiwan, although most African countries, still under colonial rule, were unrepresented.

The UDHR is widely acknowledged as the cornerstone of the contemporary human rights movement. Its adoption by the UN General Assembly marked an important phase in the discourse of rights in the colonized world. Its language of universal rights provided a new framework for articulating long-standing demands for political autonomy in the colonized world. However, it is important not to overstate the impact of the UDHR on the decolonization process in Asia and Africa. Colonized peoples, particularly nationalist leaders, were cautiously optimistic about the impact of the UDHR on their aspirations for independence. This was because some of the key signers of the declaration, including Britain and France, still held onto their colonies in Africa and Asia. The Dutch also tried hard to hold Indonesia and Surinam. One African nationalist leader stated that, although the human rights principles of the declaration were laudable, the imperialist European nations who subscribed to it would find it difficult to implement.

Nevertheless, the UN remained at the forefront of international efforts to assert the right to self-determination of colonized people throughout the postwar period. In 1952 the UN General Assembly decided to include in the Covenant on Human Rights, which became the basis of the two core human rights covenants, an article that affirmed the rights of all peoples to self-determination and the obligation of states having responsibility for non-self-governing people to promote the realization of this right. A subsequent draft article prepared by the Commission on Human Rights stated, "All people and all nations shall have the right to self-determination, namely the right freely to determine their political, economic, social and cultural status" (Raič, p. 229). The commission also recommended a further provision that specified that the demand for colonial self-government be ascertained through a plebiscite held under the auspices of the UN.

Although these initiatives were not always welcomed by European colonial powers reluctant to dismantle their empires, they received overwhelming support from the United States and several Communist nations. At the height of the Cold War, the Soviet Union and the Communist bloc positioned themselves as advocates for colonized people in their struggles against Western European imperialism. The Soviet Union allied with anticolonial Communist and nationalist movements across Africa and Asia in the military and ideological campaign against colonialism. This support was also crucial to the anticolonial initiatives taken by both the UN General Assembly and the UN Security Council. The Soviet support was likely designed more to weaken Western power than genuinely to advance human rights, given Soviet violations of rights at home.

In 1960 the UN General Assembly issued the Declaration on the Granting of Independence to Colonial Countries and Peoples. The declaration reaffirmed the fundamental human rights, the dignity and worth of all humans, and the equal right of peoples of all nations to self-determination. It asserted that all peoples have an inalienable right to complete freedom, the exercise of their sovereignty, and the integrity of their national territory. It also acknowledged that the process of liberation of colonized people was "irresistible and irreversible" (Sohn, p. 319). These principles were subsequently included in the International Covenant on Civil and Political Rights (ICCPR) in 1966, Article 1 of which states, "All peoples have the right of self-determination. By virtue of that right they freely determine their political status and freely pursue their economic, social and cultural development." The same article was included in the International Covenant on Economic, Social, and Cultural Rights (ICESCR), adopted by the UN General Assembly in 1966.

In the UN debates on colonialism and human rights, the presumption was that national self-determination is the starting and indispensable condition for all other rights and freedoms. Individual rights could only be fully achieved when the collective rights of nationhood and self-determination were attained. In the end, the obligations undertaken in the UN Charter, the UDHR, and several other documents created toward self-government and the development of free political institutions had to be accepted by the colonial powers as the new realities of the postwar order.

NATIONALISM AND INDEPENDENCE

After 1945 colonialism was in retreat despite the efforts of various colonial powers to hold onto their colonies. With the UN Charter asserting the interests of colonized peoples and their goal of self-determination, colonialism lost international legitimacy and acceptance. By about the mid-1950s it became clear to European colonial powers that old arguments about the civilizing mission or the gradual reform of colonial rule were no longer acceptable and that nationalist struggles for independence could no longer be held back. Britain was among the first to begin the process of dismantling its colonial empire. Having earlier partitioned its Indian empire into India, Pakistan, and Sri Lanka, Britain bowed to the demands of the Indian National Congress and granted India independence in 1947. The Republic of India was proclaimed soon after, in 1950. However, it was only in 1956, after the Suez crisis, that the United Kingdom pulled back from its global role, which was also about the time that France lost its fight to maintain control of Algeria and Vietnam in 1962 and 1954, respectively. The Dutch also gave up trying to hold principally Indonesia.

The independence of India marked the beginning of the first wave of decolonization processes that swept across Africa and Asia in the 1950s and 1960s. It ushered in the dawn of a new world order that challenged the legitimacy of old colonial empires and asserted the right of self-determination of colonized people. At the UN the emergence of the Asian and African blocs of newly independent nations radically changed the landscape of international politics. Within a span of five years from the end of World War II, India, Pakistan, Ceylon, Burma, the Philippines, Indonesia, Jordan, Syria, and Lebanon had all achieved their independence. By the 1950s another group of former colonial powers gained independence in Asia, Africa, and the Middle East. In Asia, Cambodia, Laos, and a divided Vietnam received independence from France, while Malaysia gained independence from Britain. In Africa, after much international bickering over the fate of the former Italian colonies, Libya became independent and was joined soon afterward by Ethiopia, Somaliland, Morocco, Tunis, and Egypt.

An important event in the postwar decolonization process that had some implications for human rights was the Asian-African Conference of 1955, also known as the Bandung Conference. The conference in Bandung, Indonesia, brought together a group of newly independent Asian and African countries, including Egypt, Indonesia, India, Pakistan, Ethiopia, the Gold Coast (Ghana), Saudi Arabia, and the Sudan, to discuss Afro-Asian cooperation and state their collective opposition to colonialism. Among the primary concerns of the conference were such issues as national sovereignty, racism, nationalism, and struggles against colonialism. In its final communiqué the conference condemned colonial repression in Asia and Africa and in particular the repression of French colonial rule in Algeria, where nationalists had launched a guerrilla war for independence. The conference also adopted the Declaration on Promotion of World Peace and Cooperation, which listed ten principles for handling international relations. Among these were opposition to imperialism and colonialism in all its manifestations and support for the struggle for national independence. The Bandung Conference inspired nationalist movements across Africa and Asia and added to the momentum of global opposition to colonial rule.

Perhaps the most symbolic decolonization process in Africa was in the Gold Coast, where Nkrumah's Convention People's Party led a mass nationalist movement for the independence of the country, which was renamed Ghana, in 1957. The independence of Ghana ushered in the era of decolonization in sub-Saharan Africa. One year after the independence of Ghana, nationalist leaders from across Africa held an All-African People's Conference in Ghana, at which they passed a resolution on imperialism and colonialism. The resolution drew extensively from postwar discourse on universal human rights to demand an end to European colonization of the continent. Among other things, the resolution condemned colonial oppression and subjugation, which denied Africans their fundamental human rights. It also demanded that fundamental human rights and universal adult franchise be extended to every African. In addition, the conference established a human rights committee to examine complaints of human rights abuse across Africa and to work toward redressing them.

The chairman of the conference, Tom Mboya of Kenya, had proposed the conference slogan "Europeans Scram out of Africa" in refutation of the European scramble for Africa

in the nineteenth century that marked the beginning of colonial rule in the continent. Indeed, the 1960s saw the end of European colonial rule in Africa as several countries became independent—Nigeria, Senegal, and Cameroon, in 1960; Uganda, in 1962; and Kenya, in 1963. The notable exceptions were the settler colonies of eastern and southern Africa—Rhodesia, Namibia, and South Africa—where white minority settler governments held onto political power until the 1980s and 1990s.

The process of decolonization in French Asia and Africa was particularly shaped by the outcomes of World War II. Frances's war burden had been intensified by the conflict between the Vichy regime and the Free France of General Charles de Gaulle, which relied heavily on French colonies, particularly those of North Africa. Although de Gaulle was imbued with a strong sense of French nationalism and imperial destiny, he also recognized the need to dismantle the old colonial system. France had fallen victim to Nazi expansionism in Europe and in the drastically changed postwar climate was no longer in a position to hold onto its colonies in Asia and Africa. In West Africa, French colonialism and paternalism inevitably gave way to the idea of a community based on partnership between colonial powers and their former colonies. This new approach was influenced by the postwar universal human rights movement. The constitution of the Fifth Republic acknowledged the "free determination of peoples" and pledged the commitment of France to guide its colonial dependencies toward freedom to govern themselves and toward their own democratic institutions.

COLONIAL LEGACIES AND THE HUMAN RIGHTS MOVEMENT

By the end of the 1960s, most Asian and African countries formerly under colonial rule had become independent. However, the end of colonial rule did not end the discussions about human rights in the context of European colonialism. The legacies of colonialism continued to resonate in discussions about human rights and particularly the international human rights regime that developed under the auspices of the UN. Criticism of the global human rights regime as it relates to the legacies of colonialism centers on two main points. First, there is the argument that the International Bill of Human Rights, and specifically the UDHR, had little or no input from colonized peoples and as such does not wholly reflect non-Western values and aspirations. The point has been repeatedly made that colonized peoples could not fully participate in drafting the international human rights documents. For instance, at the time of the adoption of the UDHR, in 1948, many countries in Africa and Asia were still under colonial rule and were not represented at the UN. They were therefore not party to the drafting of the document, although some of these nations were represented in the drafting process and most of them subsequently endorsed the declaration upon attaining independence. This became one of the grounds on which the universality of the international human rights regime has been challenged. It is also the basis of the arguments for Asian and African values in the conception and promotion of human rights.

References to Asian values in discussions about human rights draw on the history of European colonialism and cultural domination of Asian societies. This is evident in the Bangkok Declaration, a document seen by some Asian countries as a counterdocument to the UDHR. The Bangkok Declaration was drawn up by Asian state representatives to represent the Asian region's position on human rights at the World Conference on Human Rights held in 1993. The declaration states in essence that the notions of human rights enshrined in the UDHR have never been universal and have no roots or sanctions in the traditions of most countries of the world. It also argues that if ideas about "universal human rights" are to be taken seriously, they must be expanded to include other, non-Western notions of human rights. Some scholars have suggested that this position was articulated mainly by authoritarian Asian countries to deflect criticism of their human rights records and that it is generally not shared by democratic Asian countries, such as Japan and South Korea.

European imperialism also continues to feature prominently in early-twenty-first-century debates about the theory and practice of human rights. Proponents of cultural pluralism have repeatedly criticized the human rights movement for being too Western-oriented and reminiscent of the tradition of Western colonialism and paternalism. Some scholars have argued that the human rights movement falls into the historical continuum of the Eurocentric colonial projects in Africa and Asia that disregarded indigenous cultures and imposed a homogenizing Western political and social system on colonized societies. They assert that the human rights corpus put into effect following the atrocities of World War II has its theoretical underpinnings in Western colonial attitudes and that the human rights movement continues to be driven by Eurocentric, totalitarian, or totalizing impulses.

Although these views have been forcefully rebutted by other scholars, they speak to the continued legacies of colonialism for the theory and practice of human rights.

Other scholars have sought to explain the poor human rights record of some countries in Africa and Asia partly in terms of the legacies of colonial rule in these societies. It has been suggested, for instance, that some of the political constraints on the exercise of human rights that manifest in African states can be partly attributed to the colonial experience. Three main features of colonial rule tended to hinder human rights. First, the basic shape of the colonial states themselves was the consequence of European administrative convenience or imperial competition. Second, colonial states installed authoritarian frameworks for local administration, reducing most indigenous rulers to relatively minor cogs in the administrative machinery and leaving until the terminal days of colonialism the creation of a veneer of democratization. Third, colonial states introduced and widely applied European law codes, notably in the urban areas, whereas traditional legal precepts were incompletely codified and relegated to an inferior position in civil law, particularly in the rural areas. These historical realities shape the human rights conditions in many postcolonial societies. It has therefore been suggested that formerly colonized African and Asian countries need to adopt regimes of human rights that not only are founded on basic universal human rights standards but also take into account the distinctive historical legacies of colonialism for human rights in these societies.

[See also Belgian Congo; East Asian Values; Indigenous Peoples; Franklin Delano Roosevelt; Self-Determination; and Universal Declaration of Human Rights.]

BIBLIOGRAPHY

Ansprenger, Franz. *The Dissolution of the Colonial Empires.* London: Routledge, 1989.

Bauer, Joanne. "The Bangkok Declaration Three Years After: Reflections on the State of the Asia-West Dialogue on Human Rights." *Human Rights Dialogue* 1, no. 4 (March 1996): 1–6.

Baumgart, Winfried. *Imperialism: The Idea and Reality of British and French Colonial Expansion, 1880–1914.* Translated by the author with the assistance of Ben V. Mast. New York: Oxford University Press, 1982.

Boahen, A. Adu. *African Perspectives on Colonialism.* Baltimore: Johns Hopkins University Press, 1987.

Boldt, Menno. *The Quest for Justice: Aboriginal Peoples and Aboriginal Rights.* Toronto: University of Toronto Press, 1987.

Boyce, David George. *Decolonisation and the British Empire, 1775–1997*. New York: St. Martin's Press, 1999.

Conklin, Alice L. *A Mission to Civilize: The Republican Idea of Empire in France and West Africa, 1895–1930*. Stanford, Calif.: Stanford University Press, 1997.

Cooper, Frederick, and Ann Laura Stoler, eds. *Tensions of Empire: Colonial Cultures in a Bourgeois World*. Berkeley: University of California Press, 1997.

Dirks, Nicholas B., ed. *Colonialism and Culture*. Ann Arbor: University of Michigan Press, 1992.

Dukes, Paul. *The Superpowers: A Short History*. New York: Routledge, 2000.

Emerson, Rupert. *From Empire to Nation: The Rise of Self-Assertion of Asian and African Peoples*. Cambridge, Mass.: Harvard University Press, 1970.

Ferguson, Niall. *Empire: How Britain Made the Modern World*. London: Allen Lane, 2003.

Ferguson, Niall. *Empire: The Rise and Demise of the British World Order and the Lessons for Global Power*. New York: Basic Books, 2003.

Grierson, Edward. *The Death of the Imperial Dream: The British Commonwealth and Empire, 1775–1969*. Garden City, N.Y.: Doubleday, 1972.

Hack, Karl. *Defence and Decolonisation in Southeast Asia: Britain, Malaya, and Singapore 1941–1968*. Richmond, Surrey, U.K.: Curzon, 2001.

Howard, Rhoda E. *Human Rights in Commonwealth Africa*. Totowa, N.J.: Rowman & Littlefield, 1986.

Ibhawoh, Bonny. *Imperialism and Human Rights: Colonial Discourses of Rights and Liberties in African History*. Albany: State University of New York Press, 2007.

ICCPR. *United Nations International Covenant on Civil and Political Rights* (1966). Entered into force March 23, 1976.

Ita, Eyo. *The Freedom Charter and Richard's Constitution in the Light of the Universal Declaration of Human Rights Signed by the United Nations Assembly*. Calabar, Nigeria: WAPI Press, 1949.

James, C. L. R. *The Black Jacobins; Toussaint L'Ouverture and the San Domingo Revolution*. New York: Vintage Books, 1963.

Khalidi, Rashid. *Resurrecting Empire: Western Footprints and America's Perilous Path in the Middle East*. Boston: Beacon Press, 2004.

Krasno, Jean E. *The United Nations: Confronting the Challenges of a Global Society*. Boulder, Colo.: Lynne Rienner, 2004.

Kuitenbrouwer, Maarten. "Colonialism and Human Rights: Indonesia and the Netherlands in Comparative Perspective." *Netherlands Quarterly of Human Rights* 21, no. 2 (2003): 203–224.

Lorcin, Patricia M. E. *Imperial Identities: Stereotyping, Prejudice, and Race in Colonial Algeria*. London: I.B. Tauris, 1995.

Mamdani, Mahmood. *Citizen and Subject: Contemporary Africa and the Legacy of Late Colonialism*. Princeton, N.J.: Princeton University Press, 1996.

Mann, Kristin, and Richard Roberts, eds. *Law in Colonial Africa*. Portsmouth, N.J.: Heinemann; London: James Currey, 1991.

McLane, John R. *Indian Nationalism and the Early Congress*. Princeton, N.J.: Princeton University Press, 1977.

Menon, Vapal Pangunni. *The Transfer of Power in India*. Princeton, N.J.: Princeton University Press, 1957.

Morsink, Johannes. *The Universal Declaration of Human Rights: Origins, Drafting, and Intent*. Philadelphia: University of Pennsylvania Press, 1999.

Mutua, Makau. *Human Rights: A Political and Cultural Critique*. Philadelphia: University of Pennsylvania Press, 2002.

Pakenham, Thomas. *The Scramble for Africa, 1876–1912*. New York: Random House, 1991.

Pearce, Robert D. *The Turning Point in Africa: British Colonial Policy, 1938–48*. Totowa, N.J.: Cass, 1982.

Raič, David. *Statehood and the Law of Self-Determination*. New York: Kluwer Law International, 2002.

Rudner, David West. *Caste and Capitalism in Colonial India: The Nattukottai Chettiars*. Berkeley: University of California Press, 1994.

Said, Edward W. *Culture and Imperialism*. New York: Vintage Books, 1994.

Shepard, Todd. *The Invention of Decolonization: The Algerian War and the Remaking of France*. Ithaca, N.Y.: Cornell University Press, 2006.

Sisson, Richard, and Stanley Wolpert, eds. *Congress and Indian Nationalism: The Pre-Independence Phase*. Berkeley: University of California Press, 1988.

Sohn, Louis B. *International Organization and Integration: Annotated Basic Documents of International Organizations and Arrangements*. Boston: Martinus Nijhoff, 1986.

Thomas, Martin. *The French Empire between the Wars: Imperialism, Politics and Society*. Manchester, U.K.: Manchester University Press, 2005.

United Nations Conference on International Organization. *United Nations Conference on International Organization, San Francisco, California, April 25 to June 26, 1945: Selected Documents*. Washington, D.C.: U.S. Government Printing Office, 1946.

Welch, Claude E., Jr., and Ronald I. Meltzer, eds. *Human Rights and Development in Africa*. Albany: State University of New York Press, 1984.

COMMONWEALTH OF NATIONS

by Timothy Shaw

The Commonwealth of Nations—its official name is simply the Commonwealth—is an intergovernmental organization made up of Great Britain and its former colonies and associated states. In the early twenty-first century the Commonwealth was made up of fifty-three member states. The original members included Australia, Canada, New Zealand, and South Africa; they were joined by India, Pakistan, and Sri Lanka in the 1940s.

The Commonwealth advances the members' development and human rights. In the early twenty-first century all recognized or accredited Commonwealth states, citizens, companies, and networks were multicultural and multiracial, as well as international or transnational. The interstate Commonwealth Secretariat (ComSec), founded in 1965, is the primary governing agency; the Commonwealth Foundation, formed in 1965, advises on civil society; and the Commonwealth Business Council, established in 1997, promotes multinational corporations.

The Commonwealth, which emerged out of the British Empire as it underwent decolonization after World War II, has always been a rules-based institution, but the values that it has sought to effect have evolved. These were marked by the post-1945 nationalist demands of Britain's colonies that led to global decolonization, the antiapartheid struggles in southern Africa after 1965, and post–Cold War advocacy of democratic governance for development.

This article focuses on the development of human rights in the era of postwar decolonization: from nationalism to the antiapartheid struggle, from basic needs to the United Nations Millennium Development Goals (MDGs), and from economic, social, and strategic insecurity to human as well as national security. How are the values defined, how are they sustained, and what, if any, distinctive contribution has the Commonwealth made?

As both the global Cold War and regional racism in southern Africa formally ended in the late twentieth century, the Commonwealth in 1991 proclaimed a set of principles at its biennial summit in Harare, Zimbabwe. These were expanded and updated at subsequent

Commonwealth Heads of Government Meetings through 2005. The Millbrook Program developed at the New Zealand summit in 1995 established an intergovernmental body, the Commonwealth Ministerial Action Group, to monitor implementation of the principles. The Commonwealth can and does suspend members that violate its human rights principles.

As the Commonwealth came to include a growing number of newly independent members, it moved from relaxed, informal gatherings of heads of governments to the formal intergovernmental ComSec leadership. Simultaneously, it created the Commonwealth Foundation to advance professional associations, civil societies, and nongovernmental organizations (NGOs).

Reflective of a global trend toward the advancement of human rights and democracy, eight of the Commonwealth professional associations in 1987 created the nongovernmental Commonwealth Human Rights Initiative with headquarters in New Delhi, India, and with branches in London for the European Union and in Accra, Ghana, for Africa. As W. David McIntyre noted, "The old Club had become a rules-based international association" (p. 77). In short, symptomatically and perhaps unexpectedly, by the start of the 1990s the old dominions had come to accept both interstate and nonstate approaches to advancing human rights.

Under pressure from the Human Rights Initiative and other human rights groups both in and around the Commonwealth, including professional associations, the ComSec created a Human Rights Unit in the early twenty-first century. Initially in the Constitutional Affairs Division, the unit in 2002 became a freestanding division reporting directly to the secretary-general. In addition to national and regional monitoring and training, including the strengthening of human rights mechanisms, it provides advice for the Ministerial Action Group and Heads of Government Meetings and advances human rights mainstreaming throughout the ComSec.

From the 1960s through the, 1980s the Commonwealth was preoccupied with the resistance to majority rule by racist settler regimes in southern Africa. South Africa left the Commonwealth in 1961 and did not rejoin until 1994. Despite intense controversies, especially surrounding the British prime minister Margaret Thatcher's defiance, the Commonwealth was in the vanguard of the antiapartheid movement. Subsequently, the organization lacked focus even though the Ministerial Action Group suspended members offending the Harare Principles, starting with Nigeria in 1995. In the early twenty-first century the Commonwealth refocused on the advocacy of good governance, first the role of civil society and then that of the private sector.

The Commonwealth's human rights purview expanded from formal to informal democracy, from civil-military relations to division of power, and from constitutionalism to codes of conduct for NGOs and multinational corporations. The source of human rights values expanded to include the work of professional associations—such as the Latimer House Guidelines from the Commonwealth Magistrates' and Judges' Association in 1998 and the Aberdeen Agenda from the Commonwealth Local Government Forum in 2005—NGOs, multinational corporations, and the Human Rights Initiative. Along with global political, social, and economic liberalizations, interstate and nonstate Commonwealth activities have articulated the imperative of human rights in all spheres, not just the formal polity, and at all levels, local to global, especially national.

NATIONALISM AND DECOLONIZATION

The Commonwealth emerged in an unplanned, haphazard way from the British Empire. The "white" dominions essentially achieved self-government between the world wars, so the established, exclusive colonial and imperial conferences gave way to postwar Commonwealth prime ministerial meetings. Initially, these were organized and hosted by the United Kingdom and were held in London. But in the mid-1960s, with the establishment of the ComSec and Rhodesia's Unilateral Declaration of Independence, the new ComSec made arrangements to hold Heads of Government Meetings in any member's capital or other major city. The twentieth anniversary gathering took place in Kampala, Uganda, in November 2007. The meetings attract nonstate organizations that represent civil society, the private sector, and the youth and articulate a range of concerns about human development, human rights, and human security.

Postwar nationalism led to independence in the majority of states, including Caribbean and Pacific islands.

But settler interests in Kenya and central and southern Africa complicated and retarded independence there. Ghana became the first African member in 1957, but South Africa did not participate in the Commonwealth during three decades of increasingly repressive minority rule. This period was marked by controversies and conflicts, initially in Rhodesia, then in South-West Africa, and finally in South Africa itself.

But not all colonies sought independence, notably the island states, and some independent countries retained the British monarchy as the formal head of state and became known as the British Overseas Territories. Among the more affluent overseas territories were Bermuda, the Caymans, Gibraltar, the British Virgin Islands, and the Turks and Caicos, each with a population of more than twenty thousand. These were all parliamentary democracies that endorsed global human rights standards. They received support from both the United Kingdom's Good Government Fund and the European Union to meet global standards in regard to human rights and the status of children and women. In a world of cruise boats, drug running, money laundering, human smuggling, terrorism, and global warming, they were of significant importance. The overseas territories participated in some nonofficial Commonwealth activities, especially at the regional level, and were represented in London through bilateral diplomatic offices and the annual gathering of the United Kingdom Overseas Territories Association.

THE ANTIAPARTHEID STRUGGLE

The Commonwealth was most active and effective following the formal establishment of its ComSec and Foundation in 1965. As the controversial last gasp of racist arrogance, the "unholy trinity" of white settler regimes in southern Africa preoccupied the Commonwealth for more than a quarter of a century. The "wind of change" advocated by Britain's prime minister Harold Macmillan in Cape Town in 1960, the year that Nigeria joined the Commonwealth as an independent state, took three decades to blow away minority rule. Commonwealth member states and civil society networks were central in the series of antiracist struggles, and the first trio of secretary-generals—from Canada, Guyana, and Nigeria—focused on southern Africa.

In addition to promoting independence in Zimbabwe in 1980 and in Namibia in 1990, the Commonwealth created the Eminent Persons' Group in the mid-1980s to facilitate change in South Africa. Although its immediate mission was a failure, the group intensified pressure on the white regime and facilitated changes in the early 1990s. To advance human rights in the region, the Commonwealth established sports sanctions against apartheid regimes in both the Commonwealth Games and the Olympic Games. Zimbabwe was suspended under the Harare Principles in early 2002 and withdrew in December 2003 before the Abuja Heads of Government Meeting could debate its fate. Regrettably, the ability of any agency to moderate the decline of human rights in Zimbabwe was limited, and many exiled Zimbabweans established residences in South Africa and the United Kingdom.

The Commonwealth's concentration on human rights advocacy in southern Africa expanded its membership beyond the countries of the former empire. The formerly Portuguese Mozambique, which had played a crucial role in the independence of Zimbabwe and South Africa and had become more democratic after its own civil war, joined in 1995, twenty years after its independence. That same year Cameroon was admitted even though it was formerly French rather than British. Human rights issues influence the positions of other aspiring states such as Rwanda, East Timor, Somaliland, and Palestine.

GOOD GOVERNANCE: STATE AND NONSTATE

In the postbipolarity and postapartheid era the Commonwealth espoused good governance, building on previous work promoting parliamentary democracy, the rule of law, and civil society. The intergovernmental ComSec was in the vanguard of election monitoring, performing some fifty such missions between 1990 and 2008, while the nongovernmental Foundation advanced the interests of civil society.

The Foundation organized the Commonwealth People's Forums at the Heads of Government Meetings in Durban, South Africa, in 1999 and in Malta in 2005. The meeting in Brisbane, Australia, in late 2001 proceeded even though the intergovernmental summit was postponed because of the events of 9/11. The Foundation celebrated its fortieth anniversary in Malta and animated a unique dialogue on faith and development; it also facilitated forty exhibitions, innumerable performances, side events involving fifty civil society groups, and workshops that discussed economic justice, education, MDGs, networking development, small island states, sustainable development, and human rights. The newly created Civil Society Advisory Committee to the Foundation had a three-hour discussion with Commonwealth foreign ministers.

The Human Rights Initiative prepares a report for each Heads of Government Meeting on a human rights issue. Topics have included policing in 2005, the right to information in 2003, poverty eradication in 2001, and light weapons and human rights in 1999. The series began at Harare in 1991 with the status of human rights in the Commonwealth, advancing the definition and declaration of the Harare Principles.

Both the Human Rights Initiative and the Commonwealth Policy Studies Unit have been concerned with the human rights of indigenous communities throughout the Commonwealth, leading to the creation of the Commonwealth Association of Indigenous Peoples in the late twentieth century. The Commonwealth Parliamentary Association, established in 1911, has more than 15,000 members in 150 branches (federal and state or provincial legislatures) and addresses a broad range of issues beyond voting rights, such as corruption, gender equality, AIDS/ HIV, MDGs, and parliaments in conflict and disaster zones. At the World Trade Organization meeting in Hong Kong in mid-December 2005, the Parliamentary Association, along with the Inter-Parliamentary Union and the European Parliament, monitored progress toward the Doha Round concerning the implications of free trade for development and human rights.

The Commonwealth Business Council was established in 1997, before the United Nation's Global Compact with multinational companies was inaugurated in 2000. Parallel to the Heads of Government Meeting and the Commonwealth People's Forum, the Business Council held a successful conference in Malta in late 2005 that debated such issues as the World Trade Organization Doha Round and corporate governance. In Malta the Business Council also launched a survey on the business environment in the Commonwealth and the first issue of its new magazine *Commonwealth Business*, which included essays on corporate social responsibility and reports on relentless good offices pressures in all members and spheres.

GLOBALIZATION AND CODES OF CONDUCT

Because the Commonwealth was Anglophone, English became the de facto lingua franca of globalization. In the case of the Commonwealth, this role is further facilitated by British-style institutions, regulations, expectations, and media coverage, especially in sectors crucial for business confidence, such as education, government, health, law, and security. Consequently, high-tech sectors, like outsourcing and call centers, are located in Bangalore and other cities of India rather than in, say, Bangkok or Beijing. In turn, Anglo-American rules for services, pension funds, and stock markets mean that Commonwealth multinationals have to approximate global standards for human development and human rights rather than those prevailing in, say, China or Thailand.

The Business Council arranged trisector discussions among states, companies, and civil societies reflective of national and global directions, advancing good corporate citizenship and governance as articulated in the early twenty-first century in the council's Commonwealth Corporate Governance Principles. The rules were facilitated by the tradition of debates and expectations around the Commonwealth. Though myriad international sectoral and other codes of conduct advance corporate social responsibility, Commonwealth companies informed continuing negotiations within the International Organization for Standardization on global guidelines for social responsibility advanced by the Global Reporting Initiative and others. The Business Council was also involved in the fair trade versus free trade debate, including the Ethical Trade Initiative and the Extractive Industries Transparency Initiative, both with profound human rights implications globally. The Commonwealth Telecommunications Organization brought the global North and South together ahead of the World Summit on the Information Society in 2005 in Tunis, and the Business Council advanced global negotiations by bringing a representative set of states and companies to the table.

Commonwealth economies such as the old dominions, distinguished by a high proportion of energy and mining, represent long-established imperial interests as well as information technology reflective of English and Commonwealth educational and professional standards and exchanges. Thus the colonial inheritance of the Commonwealth had some positive implications for economic development and the world-class standards under which it operated. Human rights in the economy cannot be separated from those in the polity and society. The Commonwealth nexus became increasingly mindful of the several interrelated aspects of such rights.

IMPLICATIONS

The continuing role of the inter- and nonstate Commonwealth institutions in advancing human rights is a function of their likely trajectory. Though their demise has been long anticipated, their focus on contemporary issues like development, governance, and small states prolongs their relevance. This is especially so in a context where multilateralism everywhere is under threat from U.S. unilateralism. Nevertheless, the question remains whether the Commonwealth will decline as irrelevant or have a brilliant future in the avant-garde of enlightened globalization.

In part, the answer is a function of the balance between inter- and nonstate nexuses, with the latter holding more promise than the former, especially in the area of human rights. The Commonwealth can punch above its weight if it connects with broader coalitions and networks, such as the Group of Twenty Finance Ministry and Central Bank Governors (G20), which includes Commonwealth members like India and South Africa and nonmembers like China and Brazil. The intrusion of Brazil, Russia, India, and China during the early twenty-first century as the intermediate level between the Organization for Economic Co-operation and Development countries and third world countries (fragile states) may open up new opportunities for the Commonwealth style of low-key diplomacy. Because the Commonwealth includes the "first-level" economies of Australia, Britain, Canada, and New Zealand, the "second-level" economics of Singapore, Malaysia, Brunei, and Bermuda, and the emerging economy of India, it therefore might assume a mediating role with global implications.

The Commonwealth's existence has been overlooked by students of international law and organizations and by analyses of global governance and human rights. Yet its evolution can inform disciplines like political science, international relations, and foreign policy, especially in regard to nonstate actors. The Foundation was ahead of most interstate institutions in its support of the nonstate sector, evolving from an emphasis on professional associations to one on civil society, and subsequent innovations such as the United Nations Global Compact have narrowed the gap.

The Commonwealth also advanced development policies and studies, especially for small island states—the majority of its members—with human rights implications. Almost all Heads of Government Meetings, other ministerial meetings, and Foundation deliberations—especially once majority rule in southern Africa was achieved—concentrated on development. The 2003 report of a Commonwealth group of experts chaired by Manmohan Singh, "Making Democracy Work for Pro-Poor Development," focused on the uneven achievement of Commonwealth states in terms of meeting MDGs. In terms of governance, the Commonwealth has the potential to bring state and nonstate actors together in support of human development and human rights, including with the distinctive Commonwealth Games, the Commonwealth Writers' Prize, and the Commonwealth Lecture.

Finally, notwithstanding criticisms from old nationalist and new antiglobalization movements, given the unique legacy of empire in terms of formal rules of education, government, and law, the Commonwealth possesses an advantage in the definition and implementation of human rights. The Human Rights Initiative and other initiatives in civil society are the focus of the postimperial Commonwealth.

[*See also* Botswana and Lesotho; Democracy Promotion; Right to Development; Economic Sanctions; Human Security; Nigeria; South Africa; Uganda; *and* Zimbabwe.]

BIBLIOGRAPHY

Anyaoku, Emeka. *The Inside Story of the Modern Commonwealth.* London: Evans, 2004.

Biswas, Rajiv. *Breaking with Business as Usual: Perspectives from Civil Society in the Commonwealth on the MDGs.* London: Commonwealth Foundation, 2005.

Green, Richard, ed. *The Commonwealth Yearbook 2005.* Cambridge, U.K.: Nexus for the Commonwealth Secretariat, 2005.

Lee, Donna, ed. "Reflections on the Commonwealth at 40." Themes issue. *Round Table* 94, no. 380 (2005): 291–391.

May, Alex, ed. "Special Issue on Commonwealth Perspectives: Essays in Honour of Peter Lyon." *Round Table* 93, no. 376 (2004): 499–640.

McIntyre, W. David. *A Guide to the Contemporary Commonwealth.* London: Palgrave, 2001.

Randall, Vicky, ed. "Special Issue: The Commonwealth in Comparative Perspective." *Commonwealth and Comparative Politics* 39, no. 3 (2001): 1–164.

Shaw, Timothy M. "Commonwealth." In *Encyclopedia of Globalization*, edited by Roland Robertson and Jan Aart Scholte. New York: Routledge, 2007.

Shaw, Timothy M. *Commonwealth: Inter- and Non-state Contributions to Global Governance.* London: Routledge, 2008.

Shaw, Timothy M. "The Commonwealth(s) and Global Governance." *Global Governance* 10, no. 4 (2004): 499–516.

Shaw, Timothy M. "Four Decades of Commonwealth Secretariat and Foundation: Continuing Contributions to Global Governance?" *Round Table* 94, no. 380 (2005): 359–365.

Srinivasan, Krishnan. *The Rise, Decline, and Future of the British Commonwealth.* New York: Palgrave Macmillan, 2005.

COMMUNITARIANISM AND COMMUNITY

by Brian Orend

Contemporary communitarianism is rooted in two sources: one negative, and one positive. The negative root of communitarianism is its disenchantment with—and subsequent sharp criticism of—aspects of modern human-rights-based societies. These criticisms focus on the conviction that there is a dark side to respecting individual human rights. This dark side deals with the glorification of the self at the expense of social connections to families and churches, neighborhoods and nations. This detachment, communitarians say, has led to isolated and alienated individuals; increased greed; drug, alcohol, and gambling addictions; the growth of secularism and even nihilism; historically high divorce rates; historically low voter turnouts; and the shriveling up of civil society and, indeed, of even basic aspects of etiquette.

The positive root of contemporary communitarianism concerns the substantial and sustaining role that communities play in our development and throughout our lives. This root goes back, in the Western tradition anyway, at least to Aristotle, who declared that humans are naturally social and political animals. Individuals are not self-sufficient; they need to live in communities to survive and thrive. In this view, the romantic—and unreal, abstract—myth of the rugged, rights-bearing individual achieving complete fulfillment in the absence of, or indeed in defiance of, social connection is wrong. We are, rather, social by nature, needful of our communities in an enormous way throughout infancy and childhood, and continuing even throughout adulthood in ways both deep and numerous. Our very selves—which we otherwise wish to protect with rights—have been constituted by our communal memberships, the effects of social institutions upon us, and our shared experiences with family, friends, and colleagues.

We can also distinguish between radical and moderate communitarians; the former believe that the problems attending modern human rights-respecting societies are so severe that substantially different social and political structures are needed. The latter, by contrast, deploy communitarianism more as a corrective device to bring about some desirable—but not radical—transformative reforms in our societies that enhance community living.

This entry will discuss the most important communitarian challenges to recent human rights thought and advocacy. It will then consider how human rights defenders might respond to such challenges. It will lastly search for possible common ground between the two, and highlight future issues to watch for further development.

Before that, though, a quick working definition of human rights is needed. Human rights are basic claims upon people in general, and on social institutions in particular, to those things we all vitally need and that we can reasonably demand. These "things" are what we truly require both to live and to lead minimally good lives in the modern world. There is some dispute about the exact list of things, but many agree it includes five foundational objects: security, subsistence, liberty, equality, and recognition. In any event, two core values are essential aspects to *any* conception of human rights: universality and equality. Universality is the sense that *every human person* has these rights—these elemental entitlements of justice—and equality is the sense that we all have *the same set* of human rights.

COMMUNITARIAN CHALLENGE 1: SELF AND SOCIETY

The first major communitarian challenge, as noted above, is the accusation that human rights disrupt social cohesion, since they express and reward selfish and antisocial attitudes. The image of the rights holder at play here is very much like the character Shylock in Shakespeare's *The Merchant of Venice*—greedy, narrow-minded, self-centered, insensitive to others, insisting on getting his own pound of flesh even though he does not need it and regardless of the damage done to other people. More recently, Mary Ann Glendon has written that our contemporary obsession with "rights talk" in all its forms has had the effect of diminishing both the breadth and depth of the common life we share. With each right we enumerate, we take something out of the realm of public policy and put it into the realm of private entitlement. Not surprisingly, this leads ordinary people to put most of their time and energy into forwarding and asserting their own rights claims, as opposed to tending, in a publicly spirited way, toward the common good. Since claiming personal rights necessarily involves individual assertion, this trend can only undermine people's skills at, and willingness to engage in, the development of such vital virtues as taking on responsibility, negotiating, and being willing to make reasonable compromises so that progress can be made on public policy issues. Our rights culture has produced a sea of Shylocks.

Michael Sandel, William Galston, and Amitai Etzioni have written eloquent testimonials about a collapse in public spiritedness since rights talk came to dominate political life. Over time, they say, rights rupture—they tear apart a shared sense of public life and the common good, finally leaving every man and woman to fend for him- or herself. The individual isolation, "cocooning," and suburban alienation so visible in places like America—described memorably in Robert Putnam's *Bowling Alone*—is cited here by communitarians. What the idea of the rights holder does, they say, is shove to the side the older idea of the good citizen. Instead of the ethics of rights and the politics of individualism, they say we need the ethics of the good citizen, the politics of the common good, and a willingness to compromise our claims out of public spirit and with an eye toward preserving a life rich with community feeling and interconnecting support structure.

The problem is much deeper than mere "selfishness." Communitarians object to the very way in which many human rights advocates view the entire relationship between self and society. We need to distinguish clearly at least two ways of viewing this relation: descriptively versus prescriptively. The descriptive view is of how individuals actually relate to their societies. Communitarians make heavy use of this descriptive sense, stressing the degree of impact that social factors have on how individuals develop, the upbringing they receive, the options open to them, the shaping of the very context of their lives. The self seems fairly small, and socially constituted, from this descriptive perspective. Staunch individualism thus seems, to communitarians, to be a surreal fantasy—a complete abstraction from the clear social facts of our existence. Human rights defenders, by contrast, stress the prescriptive view of the self/society relation, advocating passionately on behalf of personal freedom from the often oppressive hand of such social institutions

as the state. Here the self seems large and vital—it is all that any of us ultimately have—and so it needs separate protections and entitlements against the frequent interferences, and occasional tyrannies, of social institutions.

It is often said that communitarians have an organic conception of society. They view society as more than the sum of individuals who happen to be living in it at a given time. Society is seen almost as a living thing unto itself—hence "organic"—and individuals viewed as parts with roles to play within the whole. Society at its core is an enduring partnership between the past, present, and future—an ongoing, living enterprise—in which we all participate and from which we all benefit. Communitarians thus insist on the need to balance or dilute rights talk with a discourse on social responsibilities.

There is a commitment in communitarianism to the idea of the public good, with a positive role seen for the state and other social institutions, such as schools, in preserving the heritage handed down by previous generations. Conserving a distinctive and long-lasting social way of life is high on the agenda. Communitarians tend as a result to have strong attachments to their own communities and can thus be strongly patriotic, nationalistic, and celebratory of a given way of life. The German philosopher Hegel fortified these instincts with a political theory stressing the value of the nation-state and the role of government in protecting and leading its people's collective way of life.

Reply.

Some of the earliest rights revolutionaries—notably in America and France—were motivated by opposition to communitarian political philosophy. They suggested that what sounded nice in theory turned out in practice to mean the existence of an entrenched elite using talk of "the public good," "protecting a way of life," and "conserving the heritage" to justify its grip on power and the perpetuation of the status quo (which, conveniently, greatly benefited the elite). Against "the dark side" of pro-rights individualism, we might say, we must measure the dark side of radical communitarianism: inequality, lack of diversity and tolerance for different ways of life, rigid hierarchies, dangerous and war-provoking nationalism, and the surrender of individual dreams for the sake of someone else's vision of the public good.

The earliest rights revolutionaries focused on freedom. But what did that freedom consist of? In short, it consisted, ideally, of the freedom to do whatever they wanted, provided that it did not violate someone else's rights, and that anarchy and social chaos did not follow. But, much more concretely and pragmatically at the time, freedom meant liberty from government oppression. These revolutionaries, of the sort who manned the barricades in Boston and Paris in the 1770s and 1780s, were much more suspicious of the power of the state than communitarians were and still are. Where communitarians see the defender of a prized way of life, human rights defenders can see a threatening, potentially oppressive imposer of one group's vision upon all of society. The state does not fulfill our lives, human rights defenders say; it is there to help realize our rights, no more, no less. Government must be carefully watched and limited, lest ambitious authoritarians use its many powers to coerce the rest of the people to fulfill their agenda.

Human rights defenders also tend to be cosmopolitans rather than communitarians, viewing themselves as individual human beings first and foremost—citizens of the world, as it were—and only well down the line as members of a particular nation. In fact, some human rights advocates argue that the celebration of national and cultural difference among communitarians produces an unprincipled moral relativism that violates the universalism demanded by human rights. Human rights provide a universal, global standard of behavior for persons and governments, whereas communitarians irresponsibly allow for governments to violate human rights, provided that such behavior is the "authentic reflection" of their existing national culture. Where is the basis for moral improvement, human rights defenders ask, if all a government is supposed to do is reflect and enforce an existing way of life?

Regarding the fragmentation brought about by rights talk, the human rights defender can reply that it is deeply unclear whether the rise in rights talk has actually caused a collapse in public spiritedness, or rather whether such a collapse was brought about by something else, and that an ethic of rights simply speaks more accurately and honestly to the aspirations of the new age. It could be that, to the extent to which common ground has shrunk, it has been because of major shifts in social structures, and not because of the supposedly corrosive individualism of the rights idea. Some close-knit communities have indeed been ruptured and transformed by emigration and immigration, by technological innovations (especially in communications), and by changes in the economy that stress the value of mobility and the development of a skills set that is saleable worldwide. These social shifts have mixed people of different backgrounds to an unprecedented extent. The differences in beliefs and values have put pressure on political structures to pay less attention to preserving a traditional way of life and more attention to ensuring basic fairness for all. Rights, far from rupturing, actually might fill in a moral gap left behind by the collapse of traditional community values. As the world becomes more globally interconnected, we can actually predict with some confidence a further rise in rights talk. This trend could be for the better, because it shifts public discourse away from controversies regarding whose traditions should prevail toward a more neutral set of concerns regarding equal entitlements for all regardless of background.

This is to say that an emphasis on rights may actually help to smooth over political ruptures, rather than provoking or even creating them. The idea that rights, including human rights, are essentially selfish and antisocial fails to carry with it the stamp of necessity. There are, of course, some people who really do seem to use their rights in a Shylockean, belligerently self-assertive way. But that is more a matter of such people's own psychological shortcomings than it is a legitimate criticism of the very idea of rights. Consider the fact that rights necessarily presuppose a social context. Rights were not invented in order to allow the individual to isolate him- or herself; they were invented to try and ensure elemental fairness among different people living together in society. An emphasis on rights necessarily implies an emphasis on responsibilities, contrary to Etzioni. Why? Because rights can only be made real when other individuals and institutions behave accordingly. Rights are claims *on* others, and on social institutions, to do their part in ensuring that one enjoys one's rights. Rights impose duties, and human rights—claimable by all—impose correlative duties on all. Rights and duties go together, and so, conceptually, it is not true to say that rights are at odds with a social context. Furthermore, the idea of human rights seems as much an affirmation of social solidarity as it does a glorification of the individual person. It is true that human rights are rights individuals have, but *all* individuals get to have them; membership in the human rights club is much more socially inclusive than membership in any other kind of moral or political community. How is this consistent with savage selfishness, or egregious egoism? The institutions demanded by human rights thus actually seem to be an expression of values shared between people, as opposed to those that tear them apart.

Finally, if respect for rights supposedly generates fragmentation and conflict, consider the violation of rights. It does seem true that any moral idea of genuine substance is going to generate some controversy. But what is the alternative? Against the risk that some people will use their rights as an excuse to opt out of social togetherness, we have to weigh the much more serious risk of not enshrining respect for human rights at all. That risk, we know from history, would not only involve actual rights violations but also, through them, the production of division and conflict, resistance, and even violent revolution. The violation of human rights is much more damaging and divisive than the respect for them ever could be.

Common ground.

There is a group of thinkers—including Charles Taylor, Will Kymlicka, Michael Walzer—of moderate, even liberal, communitarians who try to stress common ground between communitarianism and human rights. Walzer, for example, says that if you look close enough, you can see that every society has a moral code that incorporates both "thin" and "thick" elements, with the thin elements nested within the thick, like concentric circles. Walzer claims it is a sociological fact that there is essentially universal endorsement of the thin principles—that is, that these rules are present in every society's moral code. These therefore *universal* rules regulate our conduct with everyone, and they are mainly negative in content— don't murder; don't be aggressive or dominating; don't be cruel or deceptive; don't enslave or torture; and so on. Walzer asserts that the substance of thin morality is essentially the substance of modern human rights theory, minimally conceived. There is genuinely universal commitment to realize everyone's human rights to life and liberty as a matter of moral ideals, and so communitarianism need not equal relativism, much less the rejection of individual human rights. Above and beyond the moral minimum denoted by the thin universalism of human rights, there is and should be, according to Walzer, ample room for moral diversity among cultures and peoples—and such pluralism should be tolerated, even celebrated. This is the "thick," communitarian aspect that gives full flavor and vitality to a moral or national culture. Different cultures can here reasonably disagree on those moral and political choices that do not intrude on the inviolable ground of human rights. The common ground Walzer constructs thus allows sophisticated contemporary communitarians to wholeheartedly endorse human rights, yet also to retain and respect communal differences and the maintenance of distinctive ways of life. It seems, to some extent, that we can have our cake and eat it too when it comes to securing individual rights and satisfying communal life.

Future issues.

Except, of course, when appeals to cultural difference and communal uniqueness are made to try to justify what might seem like human rights violations. Consider how some cultures treat women on the grounds that this is the established product of their ancient society, whereas others view such treatment as violating human rights. These clashes endure today, and definitely figure into issues of future concern. More on this follows in the discussion regarding universalism below.

A second remaining difference between communitarians and human rights defenders concerns cosmopolitanism. Even moderate communitarians like Walzer are clearly more attached to national societies than human rights defenders generally are, and the latter continue to think that the former put too much trust in and emphasis on the state and its role as the protector of its community. Cosmopolitans are clearly more accommodating of moves toward global governance and tend to be very supportive of the growth of international human rights instruments and institutions, in part because these are needed to put further constraints on those who have historically been the biggest human rights violators—unbound and unprincipled national governments.

A third contested issue concerns the concept of group rights. Some communitarians have proposed a strategy of not rejecting, but rather embracing the concept of rights— as it is dominant throughout the world. The strategy is then to advocate for balance between individual rights (such as to life and liberty) and group rights (such as to cultural survival, language education, affirmative action, or national sovereignty). This is an interesting strategic and conceptual move, but it, too, raises enduring critical questions. Some of these are theoretical, as many rights advocates (in the English-speaking world especially) are skeptical of the very idea of group rights. But most of these questions are practical and political: who gets to claim the group right and benefit from it? Who speaks for the group? Above all, what happens when a group right seems to violate an individual right, such as when someone is forced to learn a certain language, or when someone more qualified is passed over in favor of someone less so because of diversity quotas, and so on?

COMMUNITARIAN CHALLENGE 2: UNIVERSAL OR WESTERN ONLY?

Some communitarians, like Abdullahi An-Na'im and Daniel Bell, allege that human rights—in spite of the rhetoric about universality and equality—are in fact pieces of Western democratic ideology that are not automatically applicable to societies with non-Western and undemocratic political structures. An-Na'im, a Muslim of Sudanese origin, supports individual and universal human rights; what he objects to is the establishment of the human rights code without the consent of non-Western societies. When asked, however, what should be removed from or added to the 1948 Universal Declaration of Human Rights, he has no specific suggestions. So he has a general, process-based criticism of current human rights, but not really much of a substantive opposition. Human rights also enshrine a degree of individualism that simply is not shared by some cultures, where social belongingness, family unity, and group success rank higher in concern. The fact that ideas about human rights originated in Western Europe, they say, is not merely an accident; it is an important fact about the world view contained in the human rights idea. This idea bears the indelible stamp of a European, or European-derived, culture, and it is naïve at best, and arrogant at worst, to assume that this culture speaks to everyone, or is applicable to every existing social context regardless of local history. So if a non-Western culture claims, sincerely, that human rights are at odds with its own local customs, then on what grounds can we say that such a culture should nevertheless adopt them, and change its institutions accordingly?

Finally, some left-leaning communitarians like Tony Evans claim that it is no accident that human rights rose to such prominence in the period following World War II, as that period was dominated internationally by the United States, and America has had a bedrock commitment to the idea of natural or human rights dating back to the first days of its own revolutionary origins. Whether by design or sheer dint of its power, America has put human rights front and center. In doing so, it has availed itself of the rhetoric of universal truth and betterment, but, in reality, it is simply doing what all dominant powers in history have always done—remaking the world in its own image, and assuring the world that it looks all the more beautiful as a result.

Reply.

Any effective, pro–human rights response to this accusation of Western bias must start off by acknowledging the mixed record of the history of Western involvement with non-Western cultures; some sensitivity must be shown to this fact. It is also probably true that American hegemony

has been one of the reasons for the sharp rise in the prominence of human rights in the past fifty or so years. These admissions, however, are not devastating to the human rights defender.

The human rights defender could, at this point, raise caution about the so-called genetic fallacy, which refers to a flaw in reasoning, namely, rejecting a theory not on the basis of its own merits but, rather, on the basis of the irrelevant personal characteristics of the person or group who invented it. From the fact that the idea of human rights was first devised in Western European culture, it does not follow that the idea is therefore limited in application only to that part of the world. Isaac Newton, an Englishman, formulated the law of gravity, but the scope of that law stretches well beyond Britain. Furthermore, it does not follow from the fact that the human rights idea originated in Western Europe that Western European culture is therefore an utterly superior cultural form. Good ideas come from all over, and wisdom consists of knowing when to adopt a good idea, as opposed to refusing to do so out of misplaced pride. Just because the good idea of human rights came out of Western European culture does not mean other cultures should resist it, any more than it denotes the sheer supremacy of Western culture. After all, some of the most grievous and appalling human rights violations in all of world history have occurred right in the very heart of Europe.

The human rights defender can also point out that this criticism of universality is often put forward in bad faith (and sophisticated communitarians like Bell actually agree with this). It is surely no coincidence that this criticism is most prominently made by governments in countries with poor human rights records. Such governments—that of China being one of the most prominent—have every self-interested reason to denounce human rights, since the realization of human rights in their countries would challenge their own power, perhaps resulting in institutional transformation. The result is a bogus denunciation of human rights, since it is made not on their merits but on the back of official propaganda that manipulates popular prejudices for the gain of a small cadre of self-serving politicians.

The communitarian claim that significant chunks of humanity do not endorse human rights runs afoul of substantial evidence in favor of cross-cultural consensus on human rights and the desirability of what they are designed to protect. Nearly every country in the world has joined the United Nations, and the charter of that organization commits all its members, among other things, to respect human rights. Most countries have ratified the various international human rights treaties, the most important of which is the International Bill of Rights, composed of the Universal Declaration and the two subsequent International Covenants. And, within their own national constitutions, a great number of non-Western countries enshrine some civil rights. Many non-Western countries, in addition to the above activities, have devised their own articulation of what human rights mean within their own cultural traditions. There are, for example, the African (Banjul) Charter on Human and Peoples' Rights (1981) and the Cairo Declaration on Human Rights in Islam (1990). These international treaties contain substantially the same core ideas as the supposedly "Western" understanding about the need for minimally decent treatment of human beings. Moreover, these states have accepted the 1949 Geneva Conventions that, among other objectives, try to protect the human dignity of both combatants and civilians in armed conflict.

Common ground.

This cross-cultural consensus comes as no surprise, since the human rights idea is so thin, so elemental, and fundamental to most people's understanding of how a person ought to be treated. Most of the world's moral traditions contain the idea that the individual human has worth, and, as Walzer noted, there is recognizable overlap between traditions regarding basic ethical propositions, such as the wrongness of murder and the desirability of promoting human happiness. Furthermore, basic rational judgment is distributed regardless of cultural traditions, and simple self-regarding prudence can go a surprisingly long way toward persuading people about the value of claiming human rights. Human rights protect one's basic needs, after all, and one should respect the rights of others because one wants them to reciprocate. The minimal and baseline nature of human rights protection blunts much of the sharpness of the communitarian's accusations regarding Western arrogance, and associated intolerance of difference. Human rights are not the be-all and end-all of moral and political debate: there is much in ethical life that is not included in them; human rights defenders can grant that to communitarians. There is much room above the minimal threshold for cultural difference, ethical pluralism, and the maintenance and enhancement of unique customs and traditions. Promoting human rights, then, is not the same thing as promoting the Western, or American, way of life.

Charles Taylor has a helpful suggestion here, inspired by John Rawls. He argues that communitarians and human rights defenders can and should focus on the fact that there is a very widespread overlapping consensus between different cultures on human rights—and not go further into debating why each culture wants to respect human rights. If some cultures want to respect human rights because of liberal individualism, whereas others want to do so out of their interpretation of the Qur'an, it makes no practical difference for human rights laws and institutions why each culture agrees. The crucial thing is that they agree.

Future issues.

Some, though, are still skeptical about whether the overlapping consensus is truly universal, given how often human rights are get violated. And others, like Bell, wonder whether agreement that does not reach down to the level of shared values and worldviews can actually be sustained. Still others reiterate the question of what happens when one country or culture uses its cultural difference to justify human rights violations. After all, there might be universal (or near universal) condemnation of actions like murder and torture—but not universal agreement on exactly what those terms mean in every case.

COMMUNITARIAN CHALLENGE 3: FREE-MARKET GLOBALIZATION

A number of contemporary communitarians, like Michael Sandel, Daniel Bell, and Louis Brandeis, view individual human rights as being of a piece with the current spread of free-market globalization—globalization referring to the growing economic interconnectedness between nations, and "free market" referring to capitalism, the mode of economic organization that combines the following three elements: (1) private property ownership of the means of production; (2) free markets as the means of distribution; and (3) money as the means of exchange. People and companies are allowed to own things like money, natural resources, land, and technology. They use these things to produce articles for sale. The selling price is determined by the interaction between supply and demand, and the deal is sealed with money. The motive driving a capitalist economy is personal profit—the desire to increase the amount of what one owns. Versions of capitalism have been the dominant forms of social organization in modern Western civilization since the Industrial Revolution in the 1700s, and they are now spreading worldwide following Communism's general, though not quite universal, collapse after 1989.

Communitarians castigate human rights advocates for being complicit in what they view as the negative consequences of this trend toward free-market globalization—growing inequality between rich and poor, the concentration of wealth in the developed world, centralization of power in corporate head offices and away from local branches, fewer protections and less leverage for working people, and, above all, the increasing homogenization of the world economy at the expense of local communal color and distinctive neighborhoods. Phrases like "McWorld" and "The Monochrome Society" are used in this regard. Bell even claims that globalization undermines families (since many corporations don't have family-friendly policies) and even corrupts democratic processes (since, increasingly, the expense of running for office has rendered politicians dependent on funds donated by corporations and their lobbyists).

We must note here a massive difference between radical and moderate communitarians in this regard. Radicals, inspired by Karl Marx, favor wholesale institutional change away from free-market capitalism and toward more communal and equitable forms of social organization. Moderate communitarians, by contrast, accept the fundamental institutions of capitalism, but wish to see policy reforms instituted so that some of the harsher antisocial consequences of it are mitigated.

Reply.

The reply to these challenges differs widely depending on whether a human rights defender is conversing with a radical or a moderate communitarian. The major problem faced by radical communitarians concerns their inability to put forward a plausible, attractive alternative to a pro-rights free-market democracy. Communism, for example, failed miserably, notwithstanding a few die-hard holdouts like Cuba and North Korea. Moreover, Communist regimes were and are massive human rights violators, with purges, massacres, and daily denials of even the most basic personal freedoms. What are the other options, then? A return to pre-modern religious societies, an impulse we see today in some Islamic societies? But those societies deny freedom of religion, frequently feature very low standards of living, and very often deny women in particular basic freedoms and equality. They were—and are—also highly unequal, especially between the religious elites and the common people.

Another option is the so-called authoritarian social capitalism of East Asian societies like Singapore that try to combine the economic dynamism and growth of capitalism with a profound social emphasis on family and the overall well-being of the nation. But, of course, these regimes deny basic freedoms, especially political participation—to their people. Many also believe that these regimes aren't stable—that the rise in living standards will eventually lead people to demand more say in governance. Plus, there is the issue of whether such modes of organizing society are at all exportable outside the "Confucian cultural sphere" of East Asia. Some of the radical communitarians refer to "economic democracy" as their preferred alternative, but it is so vaguely defined as to not be practical and operational; the version of economic democracy claimed by Tito's Yugoslavia was certainly not known for its commitment to personal freedom or personal satisfaction, and it was eventually abandoned when Communist Yugoslavia collapsed and dissolved in the early 1990s. We all know it is much easier to criticize than to create; it is one thing to note imperfections in liberal democracies, and quite another to construct plausible, attractive alternatives. As Bell notes, the task for contemporary communitarians is to show how to protect and promote valued forms of community—especially the family and nation—without sacrificing too much personal freedom.

Common ground.

Modern welfare-state capitalism attempts to balance concerns for personal freedom with those for socioeconomic equality. All citizens are granted an equal set of personal rights and freedoms, allowing them to choose their own lives for themselves. Free-market business enterprise is allowed, and economic growth and development result. At the same time, a number of laws are enacted to regulate the market and for the benefit of the population—laws against pollution, child labor, and sexual harassment; laws against fraud and anticompetitive collusion; and regulations protecting the health and safety of both workers in their workplaces and consumers in their homes. The government, moreover, uses the tax system to redistribute some income from the richest to the poorest, transferring money from those who have plenty to those who need help generating income and getting access to vital social services like education and basic health care. This moderate, welfare-state capitalism may not be perfect, but it does seem to be a workable, reasonably successful attempt to realize rights while also achieving communitarian values like social peace, concern for the public good, and the maintenance of a real sense of community where envy and resentment are dampened by some sharing of resources.

Future issues.

Realistically, though, some developing nations lack the means to implement strong welfare-state measures to achieve these ends and this between respect for individual rights and a sense of community. The issue of what wealthy nations owe to the developing world in this regard—to make the spread of such regimes possible—is a difficult and enduring one.

Another lingering issue concerns whether, on a global scale, the spread of free-market ideals will challenge local customary practices. With its drive for efficiency, a free-market economy will insist on some standardization and thus "homogeneity" in basic economic structures. In theory, this baseline of economic standardization should be complemented by ever-greater cultural diversity as free markets allow for more and more people to offer their own unique goods and services. Consider the incredible diversity of goods and services, such as kinds of restaurants, now offered compared to only twenty years ago. Yet some fear that the standardization of economic forces can bring with it a standardization in lifestyle that can be stagnant, monotonous, and even oppressive in its own way. Is the entire world destined to end up living the life of the average North American suburbanite? Is that truly such a wonderful and satisfying life, in spite of all the creature comforts?

COMMUNITARIAN CHALLENGE 4: ANTIDEMOCRATIC

This communitarian challenge, inspired by French theorist Jean-Jacques Rousseau, is that human rights are actually antidemocratic. This communitarian challenge comes from democratic socialists, who believe firmly in the rule of the majority as expressed in free and fair elections. They note that human rights can often serve to block the majority from exercising its "general will"—consider, for instance, a property owner refusing to sell his or her land to allow a needed highway to be built. Many of these critics cite the Utilitarian principle, "the greatest happiness for the greatest number," as the very goal of politics. The best political leaders, they say, have public spirit and make those decisions that increase the amount of pleasure and happiness in their communities. A successful statesman is one who leaves his or her people subjectively happier, and objectively better off, than they were before he or she came to power through their vote. But rights often serve as roadblocks on the journey toward maximizing public welfare and happiness. Rights, among other

things, carve out a protected space wherein people are free to do what they wish, regardless of whether the public finds it pleasing, tasteful, productive, or sensible. Indeed, rights are designed, as Ronald Dworkin has said, to serve as trumps, outranking the pursuit of the greatest happiness for the greatest number. Communitarians conclude that individual claims of human rights, trumping public welfare, not only reduce overall social happiness, but they also threaten the balance of good political judgment and ultimately the stability of our shared social existence.

Reply.

This criticism does contain real truth—human rights have antidemocratic aspects to them; they are designed to ensure, for everyone, secure access to the objects of vital human need regardless of what the majority prefers. Human rights were established not only to challenge conservative elitism and to crack open hitherto closed institutions, but also to resist what Alexis de Tocqueville first diagnosed as "the tyranny of the majority." Many of the major human rights disasters of the twentieth century involved the persecution (and worse) of disfavored minority groups. Individuals need protection not only from criminals and dictators but also from a malign majority abusing its democratic control over core social institutions. Respect for rights may thus call for the implementation of some so-called counter-majoritarian measures.

Important examples of these include a codified bill or charter of rights, a judiciary and police system that operate independently from those legislative bodies that enact the democratic will of the majority, and the empowering of the judiciary with the authority to review and perhaps reject legislative measures that violate human rights. Most of these measures are features of the societies in which we live, and they help to ensure that a robust respect for democracy does not degenerate into a nasty mob rule that takes unjustified aim at disfavored individuals or unpopular groups. Judicial review, in particular, continues to serve as a major tool for human rights protection in even the most developed democracies.

It is correct to say that sometimes human rights get in the way of legislative schemes to maximize overall public pleasure and social happiness. But it is wrong to say that this is something for which human rights defenders should apologize or be criticized. That is precisely what human rights are designed to do—provide *everyone*, and not just the greatest number, with secure access to what they vitally need to live a minimally decent life in the modern world. Human rights defenders insist that it is far more important to secure for everyone the social minimum of decent treatment for all than it is to secure the maximization of the majority's happiness.

Common ground.

These reflections and admissions do not add up to the belief that rights are *necessarily* antidemocratic. The relationship is more complex. Surely, the raw historical fact that concern for human rights first fully flourished in democratic societies shows some positive correlation between the two. Furthermore, most human rights advocates argue that some of the most basic human rights—like liberty and security—imply further entitlements to political participation. It is clear that the spirit of democracy and the spirit of human rights still have much in common. Democracy is inspired by the vision of one person, one vote; this vision contains norms of universality and equality, which are central to human rights ideals. Democracy arose, historically, out of anger at severe social exclusion and official oppression; human rights defenders also struggle against such things. Democracy and human rights also share the wisdom of preferring limited government, regularly and concretely accountable to the people. Democracy is, above all, about everyone's right to participate in those institutions that have a major impact on one's life, which indeed shape the structure of our shared social existence. Democracy is ultimately about self-governance. It is about letting people live their own lives. Human rights are likewise expressive of autonomy and personal freedom for self-direction. In both cases, we note that people should be free to govern themselves, so long as they do not abuse such freedom by unjustly harming others. If they do so, they forfeit their rights. We have discovered that, historically, some counter-majoritarian measures are necessary to prevent whole societies from abusing their right of self-governance to harm others in their midst. Thus we at last understand how such apparently antidemocratic measures actually remain faithful to democracy's deepest purpose.

Future issues.

Even if we can see and appreciate this common ground, we can still come up with particular hard cases where there is a clear clash between majority well-being and the interests of individual rights holders. Think of those inventors who refuse to share beneficial information or innovations—like a promising new medicine—without first being assured of making their own fortune. Think of those people who refuse to donate their bodies for medical purposes after they die, in spite of the great good that could be done and the total lack of harm or cost to themselves. Or think of those charged with serious criminal offenses doing everything they can to exercise every last one of their rights without regard to the public interest or to those they have victimized. Such clashes cannot simply be papered over. Difficult decisions have to be made, and they underline the endurance of a real tension—which sometimes is buried, and other times resurfaces—between the will and interests of a community at large and those of an individual rights holder.

COMMUNITARIAN CHALLENGE 5: INTERNAL VALUES CLASH

One last clash, which seems to be a draw yet which is still worth noting, concerns internal clashes of values. Some communitarians criticize human rights advocates for their lack of consensus on the exact full list of which human rights we have, and in particular the clash between "first-generation" human rights to civil and political freedoms and "second-generation" socioeconomic entitlements. Communitarians in particular note the problems that human rights defenders can experience in resolving clashes of rights between people, such as divorce or abortion, or medical triage wherein a doctor has to treat one person and forego another, or war where some people are killed in order to save others. Communitarians like Bell even suggest that such clashes of rights can be resolved by appealing to the social values prevalent in that community. But Bell, to his credit, notes that communitarianism faces its own internal clash of values, such as when the demands of a group of which one is a member clash with the demands of another of which one is also a member. Consider that the demands of the nation-state, such as conscripting an individual to fight in a foreign war, might conflict with the demands of a family that needs that individual to stay home and provide. All ideologies confront hard cases, which reveal tensions and imperfections; here, truly, is where both human rights advocates and communitarians are in the same boat.

[*See also* Collective/Group Rights; Confucianism; Culture and Human Rights; East Asian Values; Globalization; North-South Views on Human Rights; *and* Universality.]

BIBLIOGRAPHY

An-Na'im, Abdullahi Ahmed, ed. *Human Rights in Cross-Cultural Perspectives: A Quest for Consensus.* Philadelphia: University of Pennsylvania Press, 1992.

Avineri, Shlomo, and Avner de-Shalit, eds. *Communitarianism and Individualism*. Oxford and New York: Oxford University Press, 1992.

Bauer, Joanne R., and Daniel Bell, eds. *The East Asian Challenge for Human Rights*. Cambridge, U.K., and New York: Cambridge University Press, 1999.

Bell, Daniel. *Communitarianism and Its Critics*. Oxford: Clarendon Press, 1993.

Bell, Daniel. *East Meets West: Human Rights and Democracy in East Asia*. Princeton, N.J.: Princeton University Press, 2000.

Benhabib, Seyla. *Situating the Self: Gender, Community, and Postmodernism in Contemporary Ethics*. Cambridge, U.K.: Polity Press, 1992.

Campbell, Tom. *The Left and Rights: A Conceptual Analysis of the Idea of Socialist Rights*. London and Boston: Routledge & Kegan Paul, 1983.

Dworkin, Ronald. *Taking Rights Seriously*. Cambridge, Mass.: Harvard University Press, 1977.

Etzioni, Amitai. *The Monochrome Society*. Princeton, N.J.: Princeton University Press, 2001.

Etzioni, Amitai. *The New Golden Rule: Community and Morality in a Democratic Society*. New York: Basic Books, 1996.

Etzioni, Amitai. *The Spirit of Community*. New York: Touchstone, 1994.

Etzioni, Amitai, comp. *Rights and the Common Good: The Communitarian Perspective*. New York: St. Martins Press, 1995.

Etzioni, Amitai, ed. *The Essential Communitarian Reader*. Lanham, Md.: Rowman & Littlefield, 1998.

Etzioni, Amitai, ed. *New Communitarian Thinking: Persons, Virtues, Institutions, and Communities*. Charlottesville: University Press of Virginia, 1995.

Evans, Tony. *US Hegemony and the Project of Universal Human Rights*. Houndmills, U.K.: Macmillan Press; New York: St. Martin's Press, 1996.

Frazer, Elizabeth. *The Problems of Communitarian Politics: Unity and Conflict*. Oxford and New York: Oxford University Press, 1999.

Glendon, Mary Ann. *Rights Talk: The Impoverishment of Political Discourse*. New York: Free Press; Toronto: Collier Macmillan; New York: Maxwell Macmillan, 1991.

Kymlicka, Will. *Liberalism, Community, and Culture*. Oxford: Clarendon Press; New York: Oxford University Press, 1989.

Kymlicka, Will. *Multicultural Citizenship: A Liberal Theory of Minority Rights*. Oxford: Clarendon Press; New York: Oxford University Press, 1995.

Macedo, Stephen. *Liberal Virtues: Citizenship, Virtue, and Community in Liberal Constitutionalism*. Oxford: Clarendon Press; New York: Oxford University Press, 1990.

MacIntyre, Alasdair. *Whose Justice? Which Rationality?* South Bend, Ind.: University of Notre Dame Press, 1988.

Mason, Andrew. *Community, Solidarity and Belonging: Levels of Community and Their Normative Significance*. Cambridge, U.K., and New York: Cambridge University Press, 2000.

Milne, A. J. M. *Human Rights and Human Diversity: An Essay in the Philosophy of Human Rights*. Basingstoke, U.K.: Macmillan, 1986.

Mulhall, Stephen, and Adam Swift. *Liberals and Communitarians*. Oxford and Cambridge, Mass.: Blackwell, 1996.

Orend, Brian. *Human Rights: Concept and Context*. Peterborough, Ontario, and Orchard Park, N.Y.: Broadview Press, 2002.

Pollis, Adamantia, and Peter Schwab, eds. *Human Rights: Cultural and Ideological Perspectives*. New York: Praeger, 1979.

Putnam, Robert D. *Better Together: Restoring the American Community*. New York: Simon & Schuster, 2003.

Putnam, Robert D. *Bowling Alone: The Collapse and Revival of American Community*. New York: Simon & Schuster, 2001.

Rasmussen, David, ed. *Universalism vs. Communitarianism: Contemporary Debates in Ethics*. Cambridge, Mass.: MIT Press, 1990.

Rawls, John. *The Law of Peoples: With the Idea of Public Reason Revisited*. Cambridge, Mass.: Harvard University Press, 1999.

Sandel, Michael J. *Liberalism and the Limits of Justice*. Cambridge, U.K., and New York: Cambridge University Press, 1982.

Tam, Henry Benedict. *Communitarianism: A New Agenda for Politics and Citizenship*. Basingstoke, U.K.: Macmillan, 1998.

Tamir, Yael. *Liberal Nationalism*. Princeton, N.J.: Princeton University Press, 1993.

Taylor, Charles. *Sources of the Self: The Making of the Modern Identity*. Cambridge, Mass.: Harvard University Press, 1989.

Walzer, Michael. *Spheres of Justice: A Defense of Pluralism and Equality*. Oxford: Blackwell, 1983.

Walzer, Michael. *Thick and Thin: Moral Arguments At Home and Abroad*. South Bend, Ind.: University of Notre Dame Press, 1994.

Young, Iris Marion. *Justice and the Politics of Difference*. Princeton, N.J.: Princeton University Press, 1990.

CONFLICT AMONG HUMAN RIGHTS NORMS

by Eva Brems

Human rights claim priority over other interests with which they may enter into conflict. This does not mean, however, that human rights cannot be restricted in the name of other interests. For example, the right to protection of one's private life may enter into conflict with the interest of national security when access to personal data is needed to enable an effective antiterrorism strategy. The fact that privacy is a human right does not imply that a security strategy has to be devised that does not require access to personal data. Yet it means that in designing and implementing this strategy, every restriction of a citizen's privacy right should be justified and proportionate. In other words, when dealing with a conflict between a human right and another interest, the human right carries a priori (that is, reasoning from first principles) more weight. In a legal approach to human rights, tests and criteria are framed in such a way that full respect of the human right is the rule, and its restriction is the exception. In a political or ethical human rights discourse, human rights are regularly used as a conclusive—that is, fundamental and overriding—argument.

EXAMPLES OF CONFLICTING HUMAN RIGHTS

What happens when the other interest that collides with a human right is itself a human right? In such a case both rights will claim priority and any solution that privileges one right over the other risks being seen as arbitrary. This situation is far from theoretical. In fact, conflicts or collisions between human rights abound.

The ticking time bomb: right to life versus prohibition of torture.

The right not to be subjected to torture is one of the rare human rights that is absolute: no exception is possible, according to international law. The right to life, on the other hand, allows for exceptions, in which killing by a state agent may be legitimate. One of the classic theoretical dilemmas involving human rights makes the hypothesis that a terrorist has placed a time bomb in a school. The terrorist is caught, yet refuses to tell in which school the bomb is hidden. Can the terrorist be tortured so as to make him or her provide this information? Is it maybe even mandatory to do so in order to protect the right to life of an unknown number of schoolchildren? Or does the absolute character of the prohibition of torture imply that one evil person's right not to be tortured prevails over the right to life of many innocent others?

Hate speech: freedom of speech versus the right not to be discriminated against.

Another classical example of conflicting human rights involves hate-speech legislation. The right to be protected against discrimination (on grounds of race, gender, sexual orientation, and so on) has come to include, in many legal jurisdictions and documents, a right to be protected against hate speech that is racist, sexist, homophobic, and the like. Under the United Nations Convention on the Elimination of All Forms of Racial Discrimination (1966), it is mandatory for states parties to make racist speech a criminal offense. Hence, most countries have criminalized at least this type of hate speech, thus implicitly giving priority to the prohibition of racist discrimination over the right to free speech in the collision between those two rights. That this is not self-evident is illustrated by the United States, which has adopted the opposite approach, considering many types of hate-speech legislation to be in violation of the right to free speech.

The Danish cartoons: press freedom versus religious rights.

A variation on the same theme is the controversy surrounding the so-called Danish cartoons. In September 2005 the Danish newspaper *Jylland-Posten* published

387

twelve cartoons of the Prophet Muhammad. The paper had ordered these cartoons to challenge the Islamic rule against depiction of the Prophet, as well as to criticize self-censorship in the confrontation with Islam. These cartoons were considered blasphemous by Muslims in Denmark and around the world. Muslim indignation about this incident spread, leading to an economic boycott against Denmark by some Islamic states and to violent popular protests that killed over a hundred people in Nigeria, Libya, Pakistan, and Afghanistan. The controversy also ran high among non-Muslims and within the human rights community. Among the questions being asked were whether the freedom of religion includes a right to be protected against blasphemy, and, if so, whether such a right is outweighed by press freedom.

The paparazzi: press freedom versus the right to protection of one's private life.

Every day the press publishes personal information that the individual(s) concerned would have preferred to keep private. These situations lead to numerous court cases. Sometimes courts uphold press freedom and the right of the public to information to the detriment of the right to protection of private life. In other cases, the privacy right is given priority. Criteria that play a role in such cases include whether a person voluntarily becomes a "public figure" and whether the information that is published relates to that person's public role.

Multiculturalism: religious freedom versus women's rights.

Multicultural societies give rise to a number of human rights challenges, including specific types of conflicting rights issues. In addition to conflicts between human rights of members of different cultural or religious groups, conflicts arise between the individual or collective right to live according to a minority culture or religion on the one hand, and the rights of some members of the minority on the other. Most contentious issues involve women's rights. Does religious freedom include the right of parents to impose religious dress on their daughters? Or should the state protect gender equality by restricting this parental right and prohibiting religious dress, for example, in schools? Does an employer violate religious freedom when he does not hire a Muslim man because he refuses to shake hands with women? And when another employer hires this same man, does he violate the equality rights of his female personnel? Does respect for cultural and religious rights mandate the recognition of religious and customary marriages, regardless of gender inequalities in the personal status rules within the culture or religion concerned? Or does gender equality require states to deny recognition to such marriages?

Affirmative action: nondiscrimination rights of men versus women.

Another situation in which group rights and individual rights collide is affirmative action, especially in its most far-reaching form of gender or ethnic quotas in employment or with respect to political mandates. Quotas and other affirmative action measures are based on the right not to be discriminated against: they aim to correct historical discrimination against a group. Yet in their concrete application, such measures may give priority to a female candidate over a male candidate even though the latter has better qualifications. In that case, the man is rejected only on the basis of his gender, and may therefore invoke the right not to be discriminated against. Hence, there is conflict between the nondiscrimination right of the woman (representative of women as a group) and the nondiscrimination right of an individual man.

Child protection: rights of parents versus rights of children.

Just as the rights of women are bound to collide with the rights of men, the rights of parents are bound to collide with those of children. One typical situation in which this is the case is the placement of children outside their family as a protective measure. This intervention is based on the child's right to protection against abuse or neglect. Yet it restricts or even denies the rights of the parents to a family life with these children. In order to minimize this collision, child-protection measures are typically temporary and aimed at the eventual reunion of the child with his or her parents.

Parliamentary immunity: right of access to court versus freedom of political expression.

Freedom of political expression is valued very highly in a democratic context. Hence, many jurisdictions provide special protection to the freedom of expression of members of parliament through the granting of parliamentary privilege or immunity. This implies in most cases that a member of parliament may not be prosecuted because of an opinion issued in the exercise of his or her function. Thus, when an opinion expressed in parliament constitutes an offense, for example, because it is racist or insulting, parliamentary immunity suggests that the victims are denied the right to bring this case before a judge. In other words, the freedom of expression of the member of parliament conflicts with the victim's human right of access to a court.

Abortion: rights of three parties.

Human rights collisions may involve more than two parties. A typical example is a woman's decision to have an abortion against the wish of her male partner, the coauthor of the fetus. This situation involves at least a conflict between the woman's human right (which might be labeled a right to self-determination, or a privacy right or reproductive right) and the man's human right (right to family life or reproductive right). Inevitably, the discussion arises whether a third rights-bearer should be taken into account, that is, the fetus, which might have a right to life.

Conflicts involving economic and social rights.

Human rights collisions may also occur in the field of economic and social rights, reflecting dilemmas over the allocation of scarce resources. An individual may be denied access to a medical treatment that would significantly improve his or her health, because that person's government prefers to spend the health budget on other types of treatment. People may be homeless because they cannot afford rent and their government refuses to introduce a rent-control policy, privileging owners' right to property over poor people's right to housing. If economic and social rights are to be taken seriously, such conflicts cannot be taken lightly.

WHY HUMAN RIGHTS COLLISIONS ARE SO FREQUENT

Human rights collisions cannot be avoided because of the high number of human beings in the world and the high number of rights they each enjoy. Moreover, human rights are relevant in all spheres of human interaction. There is no indication that the number of rights collisions might diminish in the future; rather, the contrary appears true.

The "list" of human rights keeps growing.

A single authoritative list of all human rights does not exist. Instead, human rights are formulated and interpreted at different levels: the universal, the regional, the national, and the subnational. All of these levels have their own dynamic. New human rights continue to be recognized through the signing of new treaties or protocols, the adoption of constitutional amendments, and the like. For example, the Charter of Fundamental Rights of the European Union includes several "new" rights, such as the right to protection of personal data, the freedom to conduct a business, the rights of the elderly to lead a life of dignity and independence, the right of access to placement services, the right to consumer protection, and the right to good administration. Another way in which human rights lists develop is through interpretation. When fundamental rights can be enforced by courts or other bodies that have the authority to interpret them (for example constitutional courts, the European Court of Human Rights, United Nations treaty bodies), each right becomes increasingly refined through the case law, for example, through the judicial creation of "subrights" not explicitly foreseen by the drafters of the constitution or treaty. For example, Article 8 of the European Convention on Human Rights states the right to protection of one's private life, family life, home, and correspondence. On the basis of this provision, the European Court of Human Rights has recognized the right to protection against severe environmental pollution, the right of members of minority groups to live according to their traditions, the right to individual self-determination, as well as reproductive rights. Another example is the recognition of the human right to water in General Comment No. 15 of the United Nations Committee on Economic, Social, and Cultural Rights, based on the right to health and the right to a decent standard of living. As the list of human rights grows, so does the potential for conflicts between human rights.

Emancipation multiplies the number of rights holders to be taken seriously.

The history of human rights may be read as a history of progressive inclusion through successful emancipation movements. Some of these predate the international recognition of human rights. Documents such as the Magna Carta (1215), which is not a human rights document per se but rather a foundation for constitutionalism (limited government), are the result of a revolt of aristocrats against the king. (The lower classes of England got no personal rights from Magna Carta.) During the French Revolution, the bourgeoisie (middle class) fought the aristocrats. And in the socialist struggle the working classes challenged the power and privilege of the bourgeoisie. After the adoption of the Universal Declaration of Human Rights (1948), several other important campaigns for inclusion have taken place, and continue to take place: decolonization, the emancipation of women, the struggle for the rights of ethnic and other minorities, the movement for the rights of indigenous peoples, the children's rights movement, the movement for racial equality, the struggle for gay rights, and so on. With human rights firmly recognized for all human beings without distinction, at least in legal theory, contemporary campaigns for inclusion deal in the first place with the effective realization of these rights. Exclusion results mostly from the gap between theory and practice. Moreover, campaigns for inclusion go beyond claiming the same rights for everyone. The claim of excluded groups to be fully included in the human rights protection system implies the claim that this system should correspond to their specific needs. Hence, emancipation movements request and obtain additions to the general human rights protection system. In this manner the inclusion of the former colonies has led to the reaffirmation of the right of peoples to self-determination and of the human right to development, though the latter is not included in a treaty. The inclusion of women and children was accompanied by a number of important new United Nations treaties, the Convention on the Elimination of All Forms of Discrimination against Women (1979) and the Convention on the Rights of the Child (1989). More recently, the emancipation movement of persons with disabilities succeeded in obtaining the adoption of the United Nations Convention on the Rights of Persons with Disabilities (2006).

When new rights claims of formerly excluded groups come to the fore, they are bound to conflict with some of the long-established rights of dominant groups. Emancipation comes at a cost. Sometimes women's rights have to be conquered over men's rights. And sometimes the rights of cultural minorities have to be conquered over the rights of the majority. This is the case when emancipation is realized through affirmative action (see above), but also beyond that. Equal rights for women take away men's privileges at home and in the workplace, and participation rights of children reduce parental authority rights. The rights cake does not necessarily grow when it has to be divided into more pieces. Thus, emancipation entails an increase in situations of conflicting human rights.

Human rights obligations apply to a growing range of actors.

Though human rights initially were seen as guarantees in the relation between citizens and the state, their relevance is now broadly if not universally also accepted with respect to nonstate actors: individuals, groups,

organizations, and even corporations. The public authorities have not only the negative obligation to respect fundamental rights (by abstaining from acts that violate them) and the positive obligation to fulfill fundamental rights (by an active policy: legislation, providing means, and so on) but also another type of positive obligation: the obligation to protect fundamental rights. The authorities must offer protection to their citizens against violations of fundamental rights by third persons, including private actors. This leads to an increasing number of human rights claims and therefore a higher incidence of conflicts between human rights claims.

DEALING WITH HUMAN RIGHTS COLLISIONS

Are human rights conflicts a matter for judges or for legislators? To some extent, human rights collisions appear only when human rights are interpreted and applied in a concrete case by judges. Yet frequently human rights collisions manifest themselves at the level of standard setting.

Who decides?

A legislator drafting, for example, privacy legislation or antidiscrimination legislation will be confronted with the matter of conflicting rights. Should the legislator devise a uniform solution for the human rights conflict, or should he or she leave a margin for the courts to deal with the conflict in the most appropriate way in each specific context? Against the legislative approach, it may be argued that bright-line standard solutions to human rights collisions are not appropriate, as they may lead to unfairness in the concrete circumstances of a case. Particular care has to be taken to avoid this, as each solution that gives priority to one right over another involves the sacrifice of a human right. On the other hand, an equally strong argument can be made that the judicial approach results in legal uncertainty, as justice is done only ex post facto, and judges do not provide any clear guidelines in this field. Moreover, judges approach human rights conflicts necessarily from one side only. An individual claims that a particular rule or practice violates a human right. The judge will examine whether or not this is the case. The defendant will claim that the contested rule or practice is intended to protect another human right. Although both human rights are equally fundamental, the right that is invoked by the applicant receives the most attention, because the question to be answered by the judge is whether this right was violated. The other right is implicated only indirectly.

In that respect, legislators are in a better position than judges to deal with conflicting human rights. Legislators can treat both rights equally and are not hindered in their choice of criteria and arguments by a framework that is based on one right only. Ideally, the legislator should have in mind different scenarios that may occur in practice and devise a rule that allows for some nuances and exceptions. Yet at the same time he or she has to be aware that it is not possible to foresee all real-life circumstances and thus leave an opening for judicial overruling. In any case the role of the courts in dealing with human rights collisions cannot be excluded. There will always be cases in which the legislator does not foresee the negative effect of a rule protecting one right on another right. What is more, the choices of the legislator remain subject to national and international human rights law, so that eventually a judge—a domestic judge applying constitutional law or human rights conventions, or an international court such as the European Court of Human Rights—has to decide whether the choice made by the legislator was the right one.

How to decide?

Little research has been undertaken into the criteria and methods used by legislators and courts to solve conflicts between fundamental rights. It appears that legislative approaches are as a rule ad hoc, or limited to the specific conflict that is at issue in a concrete bill. Similarly, most courts—even those that specialize in fundamental rights, such as the European Court of Human Rights—deal with conflicting rights only on an ad hoc basis. Moreover, conflicts between fundamental rights are frequently not recognized as such, resulting in judgments that examine only whether the right invoked by the plaintiff was violated, without even naming the competing right invoked by the defendant.

In general, two approaches are possible: one that is based on reconciling the competing rights and another that resorts to prioritizing the rights. An approach based on reconciling the competing rights will look for a compromise solution that does not subordinate one right to the other. Concessions from both sides are needed to find a solution that optimizes the protection of both human rights. In German constitutional law, this method is called *praktische Konkordanz* (practical coherence). A compromise solution in the parliamentary immunity case mentioned above, for example, might include a narrow

definition of speech that is uttered in the context of the exercise of the parliamentary function, as well as a number of exceptions to the immunity rule in cases in which the harm caused by parliamentary speech is substantial and the benefits to democracy of its utterance are small. A compromise solution in the debate over the recognition of religion-based personal law previously discussed may be found by guaranteeing real individual choice between the religion-based personal law system and the civil law system or by a recognition that is accompanied by state intervention to mitigate the effects of religious personal law that might violate human rights. Yet in a large number of situations, a compromise solution is not possible, and a choice between the conflicting rights has to be made.

Hierarchies of rights at a general level have been proposed by some authors. Yet so far they have failed to carry consensus. Moreover, they appear hard to reconcile with the principle of the indivisibility of human rights, which implies that all human rights have equal value. Prioritization at a general level between pairs of rights seems equally difficult. For example, might one say that the protection of privacy should always prevail over press freedom? or that press freedom should always prevail over privacy?

Hence, prioritization typically has to happen in the specific context of an issue (for example, the issue of paparazzi publishing information about people's private lives) or of a case (for example, the publication of specific information about a specific person's private life). It is not possible to distinguish a clear method of prioritization between competing human rights in legislative or jurisprudential praxis. Yet in general an approach will involve balancing between the competing rights. The balancing exercise ideally appreciates the relative seriousness of the violation of each right that would be caused by full protection of the other right and opts for the least onerous solution from a human rights perspective. Differentiation may be possible if the interfering measure on one side is more serious than on the other (for example, total denial of a right in one scenario versus partial denial of the other right in the other scenario, or restriction of the right of one person versus restriction of the rights of many), or if only one of the scenarios touches upon the core or essence of a human right. In addition, factors related to specific categories of rights may influence their weight in the balancing exercise. In particular, the Convention on the Rights of the Child states that "in all actions concerning children, . . . the best interests of the child shall be a primary consideration" (Article 3, para. 1). This implies that in the balancing between a right of a child and a right of an adult (for example the ticking-time-bomb scenario as described above, or the case of a parent challenging a child-protection measure), additional weight should be attached to the right of the child. This does not mean that the child's right should always get priority, as other factors may lead to even more weight being attached to the adult's right in the particular case. Similarly, the United Nations Committee on Economic, Social, and Cultural Rights has consistently emphasized the need to give priority to the rights of members of vulnerable groups, which include women, children, minority groups, indigenous peoples, refugees, asylum-seekers, internally displaced persons, migrant workers, prisoners, and detainees.

SOME FUNDAMENTAL QUESTIONS

As the examples show, conflicts of human rights occur in widely diverging contexts. They share a bottom-line concern: how to deal with two interests that each merit priority as a matter of principle, yet are mutually incompatible?

Commonalities in rights conflicts.

It may be argued that this common bottom line is less important than the specifics of concrete issues that involve conflicting rights. If this is the case, it may not be particularly relevant to ask the general question "how to deal with conflicting human rights?" Instead, it may be necessary to focus on how to take a correct human rights angle to hate speech, multiculturalism, affirmative action, or blasphemy. One general rule that cannot be avoided, however, is that a solution will not be acceptable from a human rights perspective if it ignores either of the rights in the equation.

A solution may not always be possible.

When dealing with conflicting human rights, the possibility must be taken into account that for some issues a satisfying solution may simply not be possible. It may be impossible to agree on criteria for prioritization or on their interrelationships (for example, is it worse to totally deny the right of one person or to partially restrict the rights of many?). It may be possible that agreed upon criteria do not allow prioritization in a specific case (for example, because the infringement of each right by the realization of the other right would be equally serious). From the perspective of international law, this may be solved by allowing the national authorities a measure of discretion to find the solution they consider most appropriate.

Contingency of the category "conflicting rights."

Finally, the question may be asked whether it is right to assume—as has been done in this entry—that a conflict between two human rights is to be treated in a different manner than a conflict between a human right and a less fundamental interest. This is not self-evident, as the category "human right" itself is variable. Depending on the rights catalog a particular body works with, a certain interest (for example, the interest in a clean environment or the freedom of an entrepreneur to organize his or her business) may or may not be a human right. Moreover, because of the continuous expansion of the list of human rights, an interest that is currently treated as a general interest to be balanced with human rights may at some point obtain human rights status. Does this mean that its relationship with other human rights must necessarily change? For example, in discussions on human rights protection in the context of the fight against terrorism, human rights (for example privacy, religious freedom, the protection against arbitrary detention, the prohibition of discrimination) are pitted against an interest in national security. It has been suggested that there should be a human right to security. If such a right is recognized, should that automatically imply that more infringements of other rights will be allowed in the name of security? In one perspective, recognition of an interest as a human right should have precisely that effect of strengthening its position vis-à-vis other values. Yet, from another perspective, "official" human rights status is secondary to the intrinsic value of the interest concerned. Hence, it may be advisable to look at the respective intrinsic value of conflicting interests regardless of whether any of these interests are recognized as human rights.

[See also Children's Convention (Convention on the Rights of the Child); Crimes against Humanity; Culture and Human Rights; Disability Rights: Overview; Economic, Social, and Cultural Rights: International Covenant on Economic, Social, and Cultural Rights; European Union Charter of Fundamental Rights; Right to Life; Minority Rights: Overview; Terrorism; Rights to Thought,

Speech, and Assembly; Universality; *and* Women: Convention on the Elimination of Discrimination against Women.]

BIBLIOGRAPHY

Alexy, Robert. "Balancing, Constitutional Review, and Representation." *International Journal of Constitutional Law* 3, no. 4 (October 2005): 572–581.

Brems, Eva, ed. *Conflicts between Fundamental Rights*. Antwerp, Belgium: Intersentia, 2008.

Convention on the Rights of the Child. UN Doc. A/44/25. Entered into force September 2, 1990.

De Langhe, Roel. *Botsing van grondrechten voor de rechter.* Nijmegen: Ars Aequi Libri, 1994.

Greer, Steven. "'Balancing' and the European Court of Human Rights: A Contribution to the Habermas-Alexy Debate." *Cambridge Law Journal* 63, no. 2 (2004): 412–434.

Rowan, John. *Conflict of Rights—Moral Theory and Social Policy Implications*. Boulder, Colo.: Westview Press, 2001.

Saint-James, Virginie. *La Conciliation des droits de l'homme et des libertés en droit public Français*. Paris: Presses universitaires de France, 1995.

Zucca, Lorenzo. *Constitutional Dilemmas: Conflicts of Fundamental Legal Rights in Europe and the USA*. New York: Oxford University Press, 2007.

CONFUCIANISM

by Sumner B. Twiss

Confucianism and human rights is a topic much discussed in the past two decades for at least three dominant reasons. First, as the Chinese government increasingly moves beyond its recent Maoist and Marxist past, it is actively exploring its cultural heritage for an appropriate indigenous moral and political tradition to shape its future; according to some, the Confucian tradition may be a viable option if suitably modernized. Second, beyond this governmental project, there are a number of New Confucians, motivated to some degree by cultural nationalism, actively attempting to revitalize and reform the tradition, in part with respect to human rights. Third, external to China and East Asia more generally, especially in the industrialized West, there is some dissatisfaction with aspects of political liberalism (broadly construed), and certain figures are examining alternative communitarian frameworks, the Confucian tradition among them.

These three motivations suggest that many inquiries into Confucianism and human rights are driven by strong normative interests, which must be kept in mind. This entry will examine these inquiries by being especially attentive to their aims, methods, presuppositions, biases, and results. To begin, it is essential to consider benchmark understandings of Confucianism and human rights independently, in their own contexts of usage, before examining how they are brought together in contemporary discussions. It should be noted that, although this entry focuses on Chinese Confucianism, the tradition has also significantly informed other East Asian societies—for example, Japan, Korea, and Vietnam—in various ways, including their systems of governance. Nonetheless, the Chinese context is especially salient for discussions of Confucianism and human rights.

A BRIEF OVERVIEW OF CONFUCIANISM

Confucianism is a millennia-old tradition (since the fourth century BCE) of moral, social, and political thought, with arguably religious dimensions as well, although the latter will not be emphasized here. It represents a mode of living alternatively characterized as the Way of the ancient sages, the Way of the noble person, or the Way of heaven, conceived as a normative standard that prescribes the proper course of human moral development. The norms of this development are predicated on understanding persons as deeply imbedded in and shaped by community, with personal relationships structured around five primary types: father-son, husband-wife, older brother–younger brother, friend-friend, and ruler-subject; the community is conceived as rooted in the family and then extending outward in ever larger concentric circles of familial-like relations up to the state itself (with emperor as patriarch) and even beyond to encompass relations with other sentient beings and nonsentient entities in the cosmos. The five relationships are largely hierarchical, except for friends, and embody distinctive role-responsibilities associated with each pole of the dyad, or bilateral relationship. As structured by their relationships, the people work together for the common good of their communities, construed ideally as a harmonious organic whole, ultimately under the superintendence of the benevolent ruler-patriarch, whose primary role is to coordinate people's interests to achieve a working harmony.

Crucial to the attainment of this harmony is the self-cultivation by all the parties of the dominant virtues of humaneness (benevolence, sympathy, compassion), propriety (respectful deference, civility), righteousness (justice), and practical wisdom (discernment) as expressed especially through the *li*—the rituals of daily life and interaction involving reciprocity in all social relationships and shaping the entire normative social order. The master virtue is *ren* (humaneness) articulated through the *li* and the other virtues, which, if properly developed, result in fully flourishing moral and social persons who constitute fiduciary communities of trust, mutual cooperation, and harmony.

Ideally, self-cultivated persons are well represented by the Confucian sages, Confucius (c. 551–479 BCE) and

Mencius (c. 390–305 BCE), both of whom constantly refer back to ancient sage-kings as role models and their empires as ideal communities, whether or not they actually existed. In this regard, these two classic Confucian sages are in fact preoccupied with the theme of good and humane governance and expend considerable effort in laying out the responsibilities of rulers (and government officials more generally) in providing people with physical security and basic material and cultural needs necessary for the latter's own self-cultivation and for a harmonious community (which was sorely lacking at the time that they taught). Indeed, for thinkers such as Mencius, the very project of moral self-cultivation could take place only after the basic necessities of material livelihood were adequately met.

Against this backdrop, a few additional observations are in order. First, ideal political rule for the classical Confucians was conceived as a benevolent patriarchy involving a successive order of emperor, his ministers (largely a Confucian elite), local magistrates, and the common people. Historically, much of this rule was despotic, and there were no formal mechanisms for bringing abusive rule to account, unless one construes courageous dissent (often severely punished) by some Confucians, political overthrow, or people's rebellion (signaling the ruler's loss of the mandate of heaven) as such mechanisms. A third point is that precisely because the Confucian tradition was greatly influenced by a familial model at varying levels and emphasized the roles of virtues and reciprocal duties, it had little conceptual room for the claiming of rights, much less human rights. A related point is that dispute settlement by legal means, as contrasted with criminal justice, was frowned upon by the tradition in favor of informal mediation. And, implicit in what has been said so far, the tradition was obviously patriarchal, with implications for gender relations in both domestic and public life.

Even though it was clearly patriarchal and hierarchical, classical Confucians did hold the view that all people have the capacity to become flourishing moral persons in the community, if not exemplary sages; this view comes close to maintaining a position of moral equality even within social hierarchy, at least with respect to people's moral potential. Finally, and perhaps most importantly, it is also essential to recognize that, like all traditions, the Confucian one was (and is) open to change and development, in response to both internal social problems and external influences. So, for example, a number of neo-Confucian thinkers (roughly from the tenth century CE onward) began speaking of humane governance in terms analogous to the rule

of law, greater enhancement of local governance, universal education for the citizenry, and even protected open discussion of public policy issues. Indeed, as has been mentioned, currently there is a strong movement of New Confucians now progressively reinterpreting the tradition in robust engagement with the West. The point here is that Confucianism, while conservative, is far from being static and ossified.

HUMAN RIGHTS BENCHMARK

How human rights are conceived is a second crucial benchmark for comprehending and assessing inquiry into Confucianism and human rights. The benchmark for this entry is the current international consensus on human rights—their content, regulative role, and presuppositions. Human rights identify conditions and goods that are minimally necessary for persons and communities to flourish, and although they can be categorized in alternative ways, the most insightful track landmark declarations and conventions: civil-political rights, subsuming norms of personal physical, civil, and legal security as well as those of political empowerment; socioeconomic rights, subsuming goods and services meeting basic personal, social, and economic needs; and collective-developmental rights, subsuming norms of political, economic, and cultural self-determination of peoples as well as special protections for ethnic and religious minorities. These rights are so crucial that the international community regards them as needing to be guaranteed by all states in their respective legal systems and social policies; this is the force or compelling logic of using rights language.

Human rights are intended to guarantee and regulate humane governance of all people by their respective states, avoiding, for example, social pathologies such as totalitarianism, on the one hand, and extreme libertarianism, or minimalist government, on the other. These rights clearly presuppose a social understanding of persons in community, with rights and responsibilities on the part of both citizens and governments to abide by them. Individual human rights of persons are given priority, but collective rights as claims against states (as contrasted with claims against members internal to the community) are important as well. And the international conventions clearly mandate some form of democracy as the proper mode of governance. Within these constraints, the conventions permit a reasonably wide variety of political, legal, economic, and social systems, and they are clearly designed to be reasonably compatible with a diversity of moral and religious traditions. It is important to say that international human rights do not mandate capitalist economies or neoliberal economic policies. While the conventions certainly overlap with Western political institutions, they are not exclusively Western value impositions. While devised and first implemented in the West, they simply stand as a bulwark against, for example, tyranny, starvation, torture, neglect of the poor and marginalized, and discrimination on the basis of race and ethnicity and other markers used for negative discrimination (but may arguably permit positive discrimination such as special provision for the aged).

Human rights are also characterized by the international community, as represented by votes in the United Nations General Assembly, as interdependent and indivisible in the sense that they are interactive and ideally work together for helping to ensure personal and communal flourishing. This is not to deny that some rights might have to be given temporary priority in exigent circumstances and others constrained (and some human rights treaties are written in precisely this way), but none can be emphasized to the exclusion of others, over the long run, without thereby jeopardizing important human interests. It is also not to deny that human rights claims can conflict in particular cases, but it is also expected that such conflicts can in principle be peacefully adjudicated, although there is no mathematical formula for this. The international community also acknowledges that, while practical agreement can be achieved on identifying human rights at the global level, they also need to be more precisely interpreted and justified on regional and local cultural levels in order to significantly influence the development of a human rights ethos in specific social and cultural contexts. This is subject, however, to developing human rights case law in regional jurisdictions and the evolution of international law (e.g., customary international law and *jus cogens* norms).

SPECTRUM OF POSITIONS

In relating Confucianism to human rights, recent inquiries manifest three dominant aims: modernizing or otherwise reforming the tradition so that it will be compatible with human rights; using the tradition to criticize human rights themselves; and attempting to fuse horizons, both East (Confucian) and West (liberalism), into a new post-Enlightenment moral and political vision that is simultaneously communitarian, liberal, and human-rights-oriented. Needless to say, these aims are ideal types that can in fact overlap in particular discussions, but they constitute an analytically useful tool. In pursuing these aims, authors employ various methods, ranging across, for example, philological analysis of key Chinese terms, philosophical analysis of Confucian concept-clusters (e.g., interrelation of the Way, social personhood, rites, communal harmony), and historical analysis of Confucian texts, figures, and political structures and practices over the centuries. Again, these methods can be employed singly or in some combination, but it is nonetheless helpful to keep them in mind.

Inquiries into Confucianism and human rights can be ranged along a spectrum between two extremes. At one end are those who argue that there is an incompatibility or at least deep tension between the tradition and modern human rights. This type of position moves beyond mere complaints that human rights are an anachronism with respect to understanding the tradition. It argues that the Confucian concepts of person, community, the *li* (rituals), and so on constitute a distinctive cluster of concepts that leaves little or no room for the language and conceptuality of any rights whatsoever, much less human rights. This is not, however, a thesis of such radical incompatibility that the tradition cannot be comprehended by outsiders—the latter contention is instantly defeated by obvious translatability—but rather that at a basic level the Confucian concept-cluster cannot be normatively compatible with Western concepts assumed to underpin human rights—for example, radically autonomous, asocial, and egoistic individualism and all that this might entail regarding noncultural selves and communities of estrangement and internal alienation. At the level of deep philosophical presuppositions, therefore, Confucianism is interpreted as being in considerable tension with human rights, although such interpreters often express admiration for the content of human rights and see the Confucian tradition as expressive of some of the latter's values (e.g., socio economic justice concerns). Nonetheless, interpreters within this view vigorously contest the very concept and power of human rights as being compatible with the Confucian tradition and tend to dispute the wisdom of even preferring human rights over the moral and communitarian vision of Confucianism itself (though perhaps modified a bit to take modern gender equality into account). Authors pursuing this approach typically focus on classical Confucian texts (e.g., *The Analects, The Mencius*) and tend to discount later developments in the tradition; in this respect, they are "purists" of a sort and restrict their inquiry to the original definitive works. They also appear to assume an understanding of human rights that diverges considerably from the full international bill of rights, often associating international human rights with more limited philosophical versions of political liberalism and neoliberal economics, especially in the American context. Most U.S. officials do emphasize a strong principle of personal freedom and discount thus far the importance of socioeconomic human rights.

The other extreme of the spectrum of inquiries also focuses on the Confucian classics and argues for broad moral and political analogues to Western liberal understandings of ethics and politics—for example, emphasizing the Confucian virtues, the principle of reciprocity (the Confucian Golden Rule), and the Confucian sages' tolerance of alternative religious and philosophical views, while attempting to link these ethical views to respect for human dignity, human equality, free expression, and freedom of religion. It is even sometimes claimed that the Confucian virtues themselves actually entail human rights, but, beyond simply invoking some sort of correlativity thesis about virtues, duties, and rights, the arguments for this strong claim are somewhat obscure (e.g., some think that duties imply rights and that virtues entail both duties and rights; these are contestable theses). The general thrust of this sort of approach is that classical Confucianism is entirely compatible, indeed continuous, with modern human rights. At the same time, however, authors working within this paradigm discount the complexity and function of human rights, thinking that general parallels between Confucian morality and the content of human rights are sufficient to make the case for their compatibility; for example, the regulative role of human rights and their legal application are completely bypassed. At the same time, they tend to emphasize (like the previous paradigm) classical Confucian texts and fail to deal with not only later developments in the tradition but also the socio-historical record of dynastic abuse of political power.

Between these two extremes, there are various "mixed" positions, four of which merit particular attention. The first presents a historically contextualized argument for the compatibility of many human rights principles with certain aspects of classical Confucianism, but also issues cautionary notes about certain points of tension. The second marshals philosophically sensitive historical arguments for such compatibility when one moves beyond the classics and considers later phases of the tradition. The third involves a self-consciously equal combination of both philosophical and historical considerations aimed at both modernizing the tradition and adjusting, in light of Confucian emphases, certain aspects of Western moral and political views that encompass human rights; the latter

is what was earlier called a fusion of horizons. And the fourth combines philosophical and historical arguments with salient practical considerations to frame a Confucian democratic politics accepting of human rights.

PHILOSOPHICAL APPROACH

The first mixed position is well represented by the work of Joseph Chan. Although he largely focuses on the Confucian classics, Chan brings to them a philosophical perspective informed by the general history of Confucianism and a reasonably sophisticated understanding of human rights close to contemporary human rights norms. He does considerable ground-clearing in arguing on the side of human rights that there are diverse types (though he chooses to concentrate on civil-political empowerments) and that they do not presuppose either an asocial conception of the person or an internally alienated community of self-interested egoists deaf to issues of socioeconomic justice. By the same token, on the side of Confucianism, Chan strongly contests claims that the tradition is solely role-based and duty-oriented by pointing to its more universal elements in the form of the principle of reciprocity and the humane moral and political implications of its central value of *ren* (humaneness). He concedes that historical political appropriations of Confucian thought emphasized hierarchical relationships and duties of obedience to authority, but also argues that the tradition's more universal aspects tempered these—at least in principle. He also concedes the Confucian preference for nonlitigious dispute settlement, but points out that it was in fact possible and permissible to pursue legal redress to protect legitimate interests when informal mechanisms of mediation broke down.

After such ground-clearing, which is more extensive than can be captured here, Chan then takes up the future-oriented question as to whether a Confucian-influenced society in the contemporary world could endorse the content of human rights. He argues that such a society could readily endorse, for example, proscription of torture (as inhumane), freedom of religion and voluntary association, and notions of due process and fair trials (in criminal law). However, it would also constitute a conservative environment that would probably place restrictions, in the interest of encouraging people's proper moral development, on free expression beyond instrumentally necessary public discussion of political and economic policies. That is, insofar as the Confucian tradition tends toward a moral perfectionism—in the form of robust Confucian virtues expressly encouraged by the state—it might well place restrictions on, for example, expressions of racial hatred and the free flow of pornographic materials, since they would be regarded as unwarranted corrupting influences on moral self-cultivation. In his most recent work, Chan elaborates this point by arguing that while Confucianism imbeds important notions of moral and personal autonomy as prerequisite for self-cultivation, it does not provide evidence of having a notion of personal sovereignty, whereby one is entirely free to do or say anything short of physically harming others. This concept of personal sovereignty and its consequences for nearly unbridled free speech, subject only to the constraints of a harm principle, Chan sees as systemic to Western forms of political liberalism. Whether he sees this particular Confucian balancing of free expression and the common good as compatible with human rights is unclear in his discussion, but it should be noted that some Western societies also place restrictions on hate speech (if not pornography) and that arguably, from the perspective of the international human rights community, doing so falls within the society's legitimate interest in maintaining the public order and protecting the rights of all.

Generally speaking, then, Chan argues that a Confucian perspective can support some important human rights within limits, and he construes a Confucian society as being open to ensuring them, but mainly as a "fall-back apparatus," when virtues fail and relationships break down. He further argues that "rights instruments"—presumably referring to legal and political enforcement mechanisms—would, from a Confucian perspective, be considered only a means of last resort; Confucianism definitely prefers nonlegal methods such as education and mediation in order to honor its commitments to fiduciary community and social harmony. Other than this, Chan says little about the exact nature of societal guarantees of human rights—for example, constitutional recognition, an independent judiciary, criminal laws regarding egregious violations, or even mandated universal education—though he certainly does not exclude these instrumentalities. Although this preference for nonlegal mechanisms is surely consistent with modern human rights, nevertheless these need to be backed up by a robust legal system able to not only check egregious human violations but also, and perhaps more importantly, provide citizens with the secure knowledge that they have it as an ultimate recourse.

Chan also argues that a Confucian society, in light of its commitment to family relationships (e.g., filial piety), would likely provide socioeconomic incentives, and perhaps legal remedy, for children to support elderly parents. He does not represent this concern as a distinctive human right, but he clearly thinks that a Confucian society would likely focus attention on its exigency. One might well interpret this claim as expressive generally of a Confucian concern for ensuring through political policy socioeconomic human rights, a concern that Chan mentions with respect to possible social welfare policies in a Confucian society.

HISTORICAL APPROACH

The second "mixed" position is nearly the obverse of the first, with a focus on the changing texts, figures, and political manifestations of the tradition, especially in its postclassical phases, and a somewhat lighter emphasis on employing philosophical argument. This is not to say, however, that this second position lacks a reasonably sophisticated understanding of human rights; quite the reverse, in fact, since its advocates are keenly aware of the political and evolutionary dimensions of human rights. The premier representative of this approach is Theodore de Bary, sinologist and historian of the Confucian traditions in all phases of its development, and, most especially for our purposes, the rich and suggestive neo-Confucian one. De Bary relies on an understanding of human rights that recognizes all aspects of the contemporary international conception as well as various meanings of liberalism—cultural, political, economic, philosophical, educational—informed by the work of Charles Frankl. This preparatory work permits de Bary to identify in later Confucian thought certain "liberal" themes that clearly resonate with human rights—for example, moral autonomy and individual conscience, local political autonomy, public education, and socioeconomic and legal reform.

While all of these themes were present in classical Confucianism, de Bary argues that they crystallized in the thought of neo-Confucians, who, increasingly dissatisfied with the abuses of dynastic political power over the centuries, began searching for systemic remedies. The influences of these proposed reforms must not be overstated, since in historical reality few saw the light of day amidst continuing authoritarian power. Nonetheless, argues de Bary, the reformed proposals manifestly demonstrate that, when considered in its developmental complexity, the Confucian tradition is not only compatible with human rights but also internally open to their application.

The important neo-Confucian reformer cited and studied by de Bary is Huang Zongxi, a seventeenth-century figure who is sometimes called (controversially) "an early champion of native Chinese 'democratic' ideas" (de Bary preface to Huang, p. xii). De Bary makes a convincing case that Huang's political thought was far from being atypical among neo-Confucians. Huang wrote a reasonably systematic political manuscript, *Waiting for the Dawn: A Plan for the Prince*, that laid out what he called "the essentials of a grand system of governance," based on notions that the welfare and the legitimate self-interests of the people were all-important and that the ruler and his ministers were properly understood as servants rather than masters of the community and its people. Huang further argued that the essentials of humane governance require government assurance of adequate subsistence, physical and civil security, universal education, devolution of political authority to local autonomous districts, equality before the criminal law, public input into public policy making, free discussion about public policy issues, and egalitarian or at least equitable land and tax reform.

Clearly, many of these proposals resonate with the content of human rights, though, as might be expected, Huang did not use rights language to make his points, nor indeed did he specify particular means of implementation other than the general political reforms just mentioned, together with the idea of the importance of governance by laws rather than simply relying on governance by men, whose benevolence seemed sorely lacking and corruptible by political power. So, for example, Huang discussed at some length the importance of granting collective political autonomy to local districts for handling social, economic, and administrative matters, the exigency of assigning positions of responsibility to scholar-officials for fixed terms of office and only on the basis of demonstrable merit, and of rotating police responsibilities among households at the community level. A particularly interesting proposal on Huang's part involved conceiving of district schools as mini-parliaments of citizens for free discussion and debate of public welfare issues—that is, viewing schools as political in addition to educational instruments for local decision making and for generating ideas to be forwarded to the central government for its consideration. Another idea involved conceiving of decision making at the highest government level as shared among the emperor, a strong prime minister, and other ministries.

De Bary's claim that Huang's conception of shared humane governance heads in the direction of a constitutional order resembling, for example, the British parliamentary system is not implausible, and Huang's proposals generally were certainly designed to limit the absolute power and abuses of Chinese dynastic rule. Moreover, it is not difficult to discern in Huang's proposed reforms what one might call

"functional analogues" to human rights. Nonetheless, it is hard to dispute Anthony Yu's contention, also working within this approach to Confucianism and human rights, that neo-Confucians (including Huang) failed to provide concrete mechanisms "to curb or bring to justice the transgressive emperor, the patriarch, the judge, the senior ministers, or members of the ruling party." As Yu (2005) puts it in a rhetorically forceful manner, "The logical question that must be asked at every formulation of Confucian social . . . ethics is this: What recourse does a Chinese have when such prescribed norms [fundamental human rights] are not observed or abused, that is, when reciprocity is withheld or rejected?" (p. 123). And he answers that "when government and rulers prove oppressive and tyrannous, the evitable remedy must focus on accountability and change, preferably by peaceful means" (p. 124). The question from this perspective is whether Huang's reforms meet that standard, and the answer is, not quite, since peaceful legal and political recourses are left undeveloped, though Huang opened the door to considering such issues.

VISIONARY APPROACH

The third mixed position is equally well informed by the benchmark conception of human rights, although it works at a level of generality that, like Huang, downplays the issue of societal regulation, beyond speaking of constitutionalism and (especially) democracy. At the same time, though it is clearly historically informed about the Confucian tradition, it tends, like the first position, to use philosophical argumentation but with a different twist: it argues not just for the reform of the tradition but also for a moral and political vision that self-consciously combines aspects of Confucianism with the political traditions of the modern West in what one might call a constructive fusion, incorporating but not limited to human rights. This position is distinguished by its visionary approach to the future and its selective appropriation of central Confucian values to modify Western political ideas. It is perhaps best represented by the work of Tu Wei-ming, who is well known for advocating a "Third Epoch" Confucianism (contemporary New Confucianism) beyond the classical and neo-Confucian periods. Third Epoch Confucianism is a systematic effort to revitalize the tradition following its relative demise in twentieth-century China, including here, for example, the May 4th movement in the early part of that century and the subsequent Maoist period. Unlike other East Asian versions (e.g., by Singapore's political elite) that give an authoritarian "spin" to Confucianism, Tu's Third Epoch Confucianism seeks to build upon and extend the neo-Confucian reforms investigated by de Bary and to reinterpret humanitarian and liberal aspects of Confucianism for the contemporary age. In this respect, Tu's effort is similar in spirit to Abdullahi An-Na'im's attempt to develop a retrospective enlightened interpretation and adaptation of the Islamic tradition with respect to democracy and human rights (i.e., interpreting Islamic law and texts within the frame of contemporary human rights norms).

While emphasizing the core Confucian values of social personhood, fiduciary community, family, and harmonious social order, Tu clearly stands against the "danger of using Confucian values as a cover for authoritarian practices" and calls for a "comparative civilizational discourse on human rights" that is open to being informed by these values ("Epilogue," pp. 299–300). He believes that Confucian values can be used to revise Enlightenment ideas associated with human rights by breaking down, for example, sharp Western distinctions between the private (family) and public (political) realms and between the human and nonhuman spheres. In the former respect, he sees the family as at the root of all politics, especially since it shapes in fundamental ways all future citizens of the nation and world in their understanding of and commitment to fulfill social responsibilities—an insight that he thinks is largely ignored by Western liberal political thinkers. Here Tu may share common cause with feminist critics of liberalism who desire to bring the quality of families into political view. In the latter regard, he is especially emphatic that Confucianism embraces an anthropocosmic vision (i.e., deriving from a sense of union of self and universe) that, from his point of view, properly amends the anthropocentric focus of human rights; this anthropocentric focus has a negative effect on the rights of other sentient beings and the natural environment, which Confucians consider to be valuable and worthy of respect in their own right. Here Tu draws on transcendent or religious dimensions of neo-Confucian visions of being "one body with heaven, earth, and the myriad things" that seek responsible accommodation "between self and community, harmony between the human species and nature, and mutuality between humanity and Heaven" ("Epilogue," p. 302). This is admittedly heady language, but arguably Tu is matching up with an important dynamic within the human rights movement itself that is giving ever-increasing attention to environmental protection and sustainable development (as collective developmental rights) in all parts of the world.

Although he does not really address practical issues of human rights protection and regulation, Tu is unstinting about the need for Confucian reform, especially in its conception of the five primary relationships noted above—here he privileges the equality of friendship and would use it to modify the others (e.g., gender equality in marriage, equality of all under the law)—and the need for a clear commitment to democratic decision making in the realm of politics at all levels. At the same time, he suggests that the Confucian emphasis on social justice, the public good, and the social responsibilities of citizens serves as a counterbalance and warning to an extreme libertarianism that he sees as a growing influence in Western democracies (especially the United States). In sum, Tu argues that a reformed Confucianism along the lines he proposes would be quite compatible with and supportive of, if not indeed even advancing, international human rights. While clearly visionary, Tu's position hardly lacks critical purchase.

POLITICAL APPROACH

The fourth and final mixed position on Confucianism and human rights that has been developed thus far is a blend of the preceding three, involving not only a full comprehension of modern human rights, Confucian history, and philosophical argument but also practical considerations appropriate to the cultural and political contexts of contemporary Confucian-influenced societies. These practical considerations are the distinctive mark of this approach, and its premier representative is Daniel A. Bell, a political theorist who has held appointments at various Chinese universities. Bell interprets the history of Confucian political thought and practice as consistently concerned with checking the excesses of dynastic power while including the functional equivalents of human rights (especially socioeconomic), and he uses the resources of Huang's reform proposals to project a practical Confucian democratic politics: for example, a bicameral legislature with a popularly elected lower house as well as an upper house of representatives selected on the basis of competitive merit pertinent to policy making. The lower house is offered as a corrective to Huang's failure (as a man of his times) to propose mechanisms of popular governance; the upper house is articulated as continuous with Huang's own proposal to institute parliamentary-like mechanisms of policy discussion and deliberation in local communities guided by Confucian scholar-officials—now extended to the national level and modernized. In broad sweep, Bell's proposal appears consistent with the democratic spirit of modern human rights in their political insistence on consensual and democratic governance but tailored to take into account the long-standing Confucian preference for competent officials to play a significant political role.

Beyond this somewhat novel proposal, Bell argues that a Confucian-influenced society would ensure the protection and advancement of significant human rights (e.g., prohibitions of torture, slavery, prolonged arbitrary detention, racial discrimination), although, like Chan, he envisages some—for example, free speech—as likely to be constrained by ideals of the common good and social harmony. Furthermore, he gives higher priority to socioeconomic rights over civil-political rights should temporary conflicts among these arise. Although he would build in constitutional checks against possible human rights abuses—especially for ethnic and religious minorities—Bell says little about the regulative role of an independent judiciary for ensuring the protection and fulfillment of human rights, apparently preferring the Confucian alternative of nonlegal mechanisms of negotiation, mediation, and conciliation. Similar to Chan, Bell regards the legal enforcement of human rights as solely a last resort at best—a proposition in itself unproblematic—but again (as with Chan), it is also important, from a human rights perspective, to provide citizens with the clear protective security of recourse to an independent legal system that is able to protect their legitimate interests.

The strength of Bell's position, then, is its practical political proposal for a human rights ethos sensitive to long-standing Confucian values and practices. Its weakness comes in the form of reticence to discuss more robust legal enforcement of constitutional guarantees of human rights, for when their potential or actual violation is at stake, there appears to be a need for specifying concrete legal mechanisms of interdiction and redress well beyond simply "patient negotiation" and mediation. Many human rights advocates might regard this weakness as Confucianism's main problem, and they are unlikely to be satisfied by Bell's proposal of stiff administrative penalties for extreme abuses by government officials and elected representatives. At the same time, however, they might be heartened by the fact that Bell at least mentions constitutional reform, although this mention does not go far in settling issues about what he calls the "gray areas" of criminal law, family law, and women's rights. The latter two areas in particular are of increasing concern to the

international human rights community, especially in the context of patriarchal social and cultural histories.

ASSESSMENT

Confucianism, then, when viewed historically, philosophically, and politically, can be properly interpreted as compatible with modern human rights with respect to their content, if not legal regulation. This compatibility is perhaps best symbolized by the fact that Chinese Confucian representatives at the United Nations during 1947–1948—for example, P. C. Chang and Wu Teh Yao—clearly influenced the drafting and debate of the Universal Declaration of Human Rights by appealing to classical figures and texts in the tradition. It is also demonstrated in part by certain Confucian-influenced Chinese dissidents throughout the twentieth century who used the tradition to argue for democratic and human rights reforms. Since Confucianism is far from being a static tradition, it appears that it can be amended to provide a minimum of social guarantees for human rights in the form of supportive public policies and political reforms, including constitutionalism and democracy. In this respect, however, there is one caveat: its reformers appear to display resistance to, or at least lack of appreciation of, a strong independent judiciary with the clear power to enforce constitutionally recognized human rights in the face of their potential or actual political abuse. Although these reformers may be aware of the problem, it is far from clear that their proposed informal and administrative mechanisms, in addition to democratic reform, are sufficient to guarantee human rights in Confucian-influenced societies. It is on this point perhaps that the lessons of, for example, contemporary Japan and South Korea may be particularly apt, since with Confucianism still in their background and culture, they are constitutional democracies with independent judicial systems able, at least in principle, to provide checks on and remedies for significant human rights abuses. By the same token, however, if contemporary forms of Confucianism were to be suitably modified to accommodate an independent judiciary, they could contribute significantly to the cause of human rights in the global context: for example, by supporting a more robust appreciation of integrating all types of human rights, by prompting deeper consideration of non legal mechanisms for generating a human rights ethos, and by possibly injecting new human rights ideas into the international discussion (e.g., the rights of the elderly, an anthropocosmic vision emphasizing sustainable human and nonhuman mutuality).

[*See also* Communitarianism and Community; East Asian Values; Philosophy; *and* Vietnam.]

BIBLIOGRAPHY

Ames, Roger. "Rites as Rights: The Confucian Alternative." In *Human Rights and the World's Religions*, edited by Leroy S. Rouner. South Bend, Ind.: University of Notre Dame Press, 1987.

Angle, Stephen C. *Human Rights and Chinese Thought: A Cross-Cultural Inquiry.* Cambridge, U.K.: Cambridge University Press, 2002.

Angle, Stephen C. "Human Rights and Harmony." *Human Rights Quarterly* 30, no. 1 (2008): 76–94.

Angle, Stephen C., and Marina Svensson, eds. *The Chinese Human Rights Reader: Documents and Commentary 1900–2000.* Armonk, N.Y.: M.E. Sharpe, 2001.

Bell, Daniel A. *Beyond Liberal Democracy: Political Thinking for an East Asian Context.* Princeton, N.J.: Princeton University Press, 2006.

Bell, Daniel A. *East Meets West: Human Rights and Democracy in East Asia.* Princeton, N.J.: Princeton University Press, 2000.

Bloom, Irene. "Mencius and Human Rights." In *Confucianism and Human Rights*, edited by Wm. Theodore de Bary and Tu Weiming. New York: Columbia University Press, 1998.

Chan, Joseph. "A Confucian Perspective on Human Rights for Contemporary China." In *The East Asian Challenge for Human Rights*, edited by Joanne R. Bauer and Daniel A. Bell. Cambridge, U.K.: Cambridge University Press, 1999.

Chan, Joseph. "Giving the Priority to the Worst Off: A Confucian Perspective on Social Welfare." In *Confucianism for the Modern World*, edited by Daniel A. Bell and Hahm Chaibong. Cambridge, U.K.: Cambridge University Press, 2003.

Chan, Joseph. "Moral Autonomy, Civil Liberties, and Confucianism." *Philosophy East & West* 52, no. 3 (2002): 281–310.

Cheng, Chung-ying. "Transforming Confucian Virtues into Human Rights." In *Confucianism and Human Rights*, edited by Wm. Theodore de Bary and Tu Weiming. New York: Columbia University Press, 1998.

Confucius. *The Analects*, translated by D. C. Lau. London: Penguin Books, 1979.

De Bary, Wm. Theodore. *Asian Values and Human Rights: A Confucian Communitarian Perspective.* Cambridge, Mass.: Harvard University Press, 1998.

De Bary, Wm. Theodore. *The Liberal Tradition in China.* New York: Columbia University Press, 1983.

De Bary, Wm. Theodore. "Neo-Confucianism and Human Rights." In *Human Rights and the World's Religions*, edited by Leroy S. Rouner. South Bend, Ind.: University of Notre Dame Press, 1987.

Du, Gangjian, and Gang Song. "Relating Human Rights to Chinese Culture: The Four Paths of the Confucian Analects and the Four Principles of a New Theory of Benevolence." In *Human Rights and Chinese Vales: Legal, Philosophical, and Political Perspectives*, edited by Michael C. Davi. Hong Kong: Oxford University Press, 1995.

Huang, Tsung-hsi. *Waiting for the Dawn: A Plan for the Prince: Huang Tsung-his's Ming-I tai-fang lu.* Translated and introduced by William Theodore de Bary. New York: Columbia University Press, 1993.

Ihara, Craig K. "Are Individual Rights Necessary? A Confucian Perspective." In *Confucian Ethics: A Comparative Study of Self, Autonomy, and Community*, edited by Kwong-loi and David B. Wong. Cambridge, U.K.: Cambridge University Press, 2004.

Kelly, F. B. William. *An Independent Judiciary: The Core of the Rule of Law.* Address to Chinese legal professionals. 1995. http://www.icclr.law.ubc.ca/Publications/Reports/An_Independant_Judiciary.pdf.

Mencius. *Mencius.* Translated by D. C. Lau. London: Penguin Books, 1970.

Rosemont, Henry, Jr. "Human Rights: A Bill of Worries." In *Confucianism and Human Rights*, edited by William Theodore de Bary and Tu Weiming. New York: Columbia University Press, 1998.

Rosemont, Henry, Jr. "Whose Democracy? Which Rights? A Confucian Critique of Modern Western Liberalism." In *Confucian Ethics: A Comparative Study of Self, Autonomy, and Community*, edited by Kwong-loi Shun and David B. Wong. Cambridge, U.K.: Cambridge University Press, 2004.

Rosemont, Henry, Jr. "Why Take Rights Seriously? A Confucian Critique." In *Human Rights and the World's Religions*, edited by Leroy S. Rouner. South Bend, Ind.: University of Notre Dame Press, 1987.

Svensson, Marina. *The Chinese Conception of Human Rights: The Debate on Human Rights in China, 1898–1949.* Lund, Sweden: Lund University Department of East Asian Languages, 1996.

Tao, Julia. "The Chinese Moral Ethos and the Concept of Individual Rights." *Journal of Applied Philosophy* 7, no. 2 (1990): 119–127.

Thornton, John L. "Long Time Coming: The Prospects for Democracy in China." *Foreign Affairs* 87, no. 1 (2008): 2–22.

Tu, Wei-ming. *Confucian Thought: Selfhood as Creative Transformation.* Albany: State University of New York Press, 1985.

Tu, Wei-ming. "Epilogue: Human Rights as a Confucian Moral Discourse." In *Confucianism and Human Rights*, edited by William Theodore de Bary and Tu Weiming. New York: Columbia University Press, 1998.

Tu, Wei-ming. "Multiple Modernities: Implications of the Rise of 'Confucian' East Asia." In *Chinese Ethics in a Global Context*, edited by Karl-Heinz Pohl and Anselm W. Muller. Leiden, the Netherlands: Brill, 2002.

Twiss, Sumner B. "Confucian Ethics, Concept-Clusters, and Human Rights." In *Polishing the Chinese Mirror: Essays in Honor of Henry Rosemont, Jr.* New York: Global Scholarly Publications, 2008.

Twiss, Sumner B. "A Constructive Framework for Discussing Confucianism and Human Rights." In *Confucianism and Human Rights*, edited by Willliam Theodore de Bary and Tu Weiming. New York: Columbia University Press, 1998.

Wang, Juntao. "Confucian Democrats in Chinese History." In *Confucianism for the Modern World*, edited by Daniel A. Bell and Hahm Chaibong. Cambridge, U.K.: Cambridge University Press, 2003.

Wong, David B. "Rights and Community in Confucianism." In *Confucian Ethics: A Comparative Study of Self, Autonomy, and Community*, edited by Kwong-loi Shun and David B. Wong. Cambridge, U.K.: Cambridge University Press, 2004.

Yao, Xinzhong. *An Introduction to Confucianism.* Cambridge, U.K.: Cambridge University Press, 2000.

Yasuaki, Onuma. "Toward an Intercivilizational Approach to Human Rights." In *The East Asian Challenge for Human Rights*, edited by Joanne R. Bauer and Daniel A. Bell. Cambridge, U.K.: Cambridge University Press, 1999.

Yu, Anthony C. "Enduring Change: Confucianism and the Prospect of Human Rights Rights." In *Does Human Rights Need God?*, edited by Elizabeth M. Bucar and Barbra Barnett. Grand Rapids, Mich.: William B. Eerdman's Publishing Company, 2005.

Yu, Anthony C. "Which Values? Whose Perspective?" *Review of Asian Values and Human Rights: A Confucian Communitarian Perspective by William Theodore de Bary. Journal of Religion* 80, no. 2 (2000): 299–304.

CONSTITUTIONS AND HUMAN RIGHTS

by Rett R. Ludwikowski

The expansion of constitutionalism is one of the most important phenomena of our time. An analysis of the constitutionalization of rights and fundamental freedoms has become an indispensable component of understanding the major premises of this process. This article examines the process of formation of the modern bills of rights and presents the philosophical background of the doctrines of human rights. It also describes the historically shaped similarities in the regional concepts of human rights protection, which contributed to the internationalization of constitutional guarantees of rights, and the differences that, in the early twenty-first century, still hamper the universalization of the system of the protection of human rights.

ANTECEDENTS OF THE MODERN CONSTITUTIONS AND THE FIRST CHARTERS OF RIGHTS AND FREEDOMS

The term "constitution" has evolved significantly since it came into use. In ancient Greece, it was applied generally to the descriptions of the system of government. In this way, for example, the Solonian reforms gave Athens a new constitution, and Aristotle's *Athenaion Politeia* has been translated as the constitution of the Athenians. In Latin, the word *constitutio* originally meant any highly important legal document. In this meaning it was applied to Justinian's imperial laws, such as *edicta, rescripta, mandata, decreta,* which often have been called *Novellae Constitutiones*.

In the Middle Ages, the word "constitution" was still used most often to describe a collection of laws. In 1164 CE this was clearly the situation when the Constitutions of Clarendon collected "the customs and dignities of the Kingdom of England" in the form of statutes. However, as time passed, the term "constitution" was increasingly associated with charters of fundamental rights and freedoms, including England's Charter of Liberties of 1100, Magna Carta of 1215, Habeas Corpus Act of 1679, and Bill of Rights of 1689. These acts were antecedents of the modern constitutional bills of rights.

Although the idea of human rights was not alien to Chinese, Indian, or Islamic societies, the concept of the rights collected in bills or charters originated in Europe. One of the most striking examples of the gradual process of constitutionalization of rights and freedoms in this region were the numerous liberties and privileges granted to the Polish nobility between the fourteenth and the sixteenth centuries. Some of them were called *konstytucje,* as was the case of the famous constitution *Nihil Novi* of 1505, which guaranteed that "nothing new" would be decided in the Polish-Lithuanian Commonwealth by the kings without the gentry's participation.

The dissemination of the constitutional experience during the nineteenth century encouraged attempts to define the term "constitution" more precisely. The word "constitution" was predominantly used in a twofold way. Following the Aristotelian approach, it was applied to the body of rules and concepts in accordance with which state power is exercised. In this sense, every state would have a constitution. However, a constitution could also refer to a single framework document in which the principles determining the government's form and functions are collected; states may have had organized systems of governance, but they may not have had documents describing how these systems operate.

THE BILL OF RIGHTS AS PREAMBLE TO A CONSTITUTION

The idea of a constitution as a single document, superior to any legislative act and different from mere statutes, was American. Building on this definition, Americans also claimed that a constitution should be more rigid than other laws; a constitution should be passed or amended by special conventions or with requirements higher than those expected for ordinary statutes. The idea of using a bill of rights as a preamble to a constitution was American as well.

Although these ideas matured in America, they had European antecedents. In fact, the transformation of these concepts into an Americanized doctrine was a lengthy process that took almost two centuries. It started in the American colonial period and was concluded with the adoption of the federal Bill of Rights.

The North American colonists came from many parts of Europe, but they brought with them predominantly English political traditions deeply rooted in developing concepts of parliamentary government. The conviction that fundamental rights and freedoms should be delineated in written documents clearly has been a part of this legacy. For Americans, however, the written declarations have not been sufficient; these documents claimed that, in American political circumstances, the list of rights should be supported by special constitutional checks and balances that would guarantee that rights and freedoms would be observed and that the powers, including parliaments, would not act arbitrarily.

After their arrival in America, the colonists claimed that they should retain all the rights of Englishmen. Formally, this position reflected the wordings of the early colonial charters. All of them, beginning with the first Charter of Virginia of 1606, more or less directly borrowed their language from the Magna Carta and declared that all subjects of the British crown would enjoy the same justice and law and would be governed in accordance with principles of a representative government. However, despite all their promising language, the charters were granted but not adopted. As such, they could be revoked or changed, and the privileges and liberties of the colonies could be significantly curbed.

The feeling of insecurity and the growing disappointment in the British treatment of the New World contributed to quickly spreading ideas that the colonies should draft their own lists of rights: these rights would resemble those delineated in the Magna Carta but would be enforceable and less declaratory. The calls for new bills of rights resulted in colonists themselves adopting several acts, such as the 1639 Maryland Act for the Liberties of the People, adopted by the general assembly of this colony; the Massachusetts Body of Liberties, approved in 1641 by the Massachusetts General Court; or the New York Charter of Liberties and Privileges of 1683, enacted by the New York General Assembly. The trend toward writing the colonies' laws became prevalent in the eighteenth century and facilitated the process of drafting the most important documents of the revolutionary era, including the Declaration of Rights of 1774, promulgated by the First Continental Congress; the Declaration on Taking Up Arms, issued in 1775 by the Second Congress; and finally, a year later, the Declaration of Independence.

By the end of the colonial period, the colonists were well prepared to draft their own declarations of rights, and between 1776 and 1783, nine of the newly established states successfully completed this task. However, the process of constitutionalization of the rights and freedoms in these states differed significantly. Two states, Connecticut (until 1818) and Rhode Island (until 1790), decided to retain their colonial charters as their new constitutions; Connecticut supplemented the old act with a short bill of rights. Four states, New Jersey, Georgia, New York, and South Carolina, did not enact separate bills but incorporated rights and liberties in the texts of their constitutions. All other states, starting with Virginia and followed by Pennsylvania, North Carolina, Delaware, Maryland, Vermont, and Massachusetts, prefaced their fundamental laws by separate bills of rights. The 1776 New Hampshire constitution originally did not contain a bill of rights; it was, however, added to the new constitution in 1783. Although the concept of a bill of rights used as a preamble to a constitution was gaining popularity in America, it was not recognized as an indispensable component of the successful constitution-making process. In fact, the implementation of this idea by only some American states affected the U.S. federal constitution's drafting and the process of constitutionalization of the fundamental rights in Europe in the nineteenth century.

BILLS OF RIGHTS IN THE U.S. CONSTITUTION AND IN THE FIRST EUROPEAN CONSTITUTIONS

For the drafters of the earliest written federal and national constitutions—namely, the U.S. Constitution of 1787, the Polish Constitution of 3 May 1791, and the first French Constitution of 3 September 1791—the incorporation of bills of rights into the text of fundamental laws remained an issue of great importance. In fact, in spite of the remarkable interflow of ideas between America and Europe and the important similarities of the first constitutional acts, they did not duplicate each other; and therefore the concepts of the constitutionalization of bills of rights in both continents differed significantly.

The Americans departed from the format that previously had been used by several postcolonial states and adopted the federal constitution without a bill of rights prefixed to it. At the Constitutional Convention, the delegates George Mason and Elbridge Gerry presented a motion to preface the Constitution with a bill of rights. The proposal was, however, opposed by the delegate Roger

Sherman of Connecticut because he felt the state declarations of rights were sufficient and the federal Congress would not violate the rights of the people. These arguments were convincing for the delegates to the convention who, voting as state units, unanimously opposed the motion to elect a committee that would draft a bill of rights.

Although the process of the ratification of the Constitution proved that popular demand for a bill of rights was widespread, the supporters of the original constitutional text claimed that the omission of a bill was not a major defect of the Constitution. James Madison, initially sharing this opinion, became gradually convinced that adding a bill of rights to the Constitution might be a good idea; and Thomas Jefferson, in his letters from France, argued that the lack of a bill of rights might result in the despotism of Congress. A bill would give the judiciary additional opportunity to ensure that fundamental rights would be given appropriate protection. These opinions prevailed, and on 4 May 1789 Madison informed Congress of his intention to present a motion on amending the Constitution by adding a bill of rights. The U.S. Bill of Rights was ratified on 15 December 1791.

The 3 May 1791 Constitution of Poland, the first mature European framework act describing the system of governance of a state, did not have any bill of individual rights; it focused on the protection of group rights—namely, the rights of nobility, burghers, and peasants. Rather than declaring the character of rights as inherent in human nature, the constitution referred to "ancestors as first founders of liberties" and particularly to the kings who—on the basis of the social agreement with the estates—granted "laws, statutes, and privileges."

The French draftsmen of the first constitutional acts looked carefully to the American state constitutions; the constitutions of Virginia, Massachusetts, and Maryland were most widely discussed. The draftsmen were determined to prepare a bill of rights that later would be attached to the constitution. The Marquis de Lafayette prepared the original draft of the 1789 Declaration of the Rights of Man and of the Citizen. It was discussed with the Americans Alexander Hamilton, Benjamin Franklin, and Thomas Paine and reviewed by Jefferson, who sent a copy to Madison for comment. The draft was also presented to the American statesman Gouverneur Morris, who was visiting Paris on private business. Lafayette's draft caused a heated dispute and resulted in the opinion that a declaration of rights should not be published until after the adoption of the first French constitution. Finally, the French Assembly approved a draft that was a compromise between Lafayette's proposal and the drafts of other deputies such as the Comte de Mirabeau; Jean-Joseph Mounier; and Emmanuel-Joseph Sieyès.

On the one hand, the significant interflow of ideas between Europe and America in the eighteenth century seemed to result in remarkable similarities between the French Declaration and the American Bill of Rights. On the other hand, the adoption of the French Declaration almost two and a half years before the ratification of the American Bill of Rights seemed to justify assertions about the French parentage of the American act. In fact, both claims are overstated.

First, the records show that the work on both acts proceeded almost simultaneously; and although the Americans could have been familiar with the early drafts of the French Declaration, they could not have been influenced by its final draft. Madison presented his draft to Congress on 8 June 1789, and Lafayette submitted his to the French Assembly on July 11 of the same year. The third draft of the American amendments was submitted to Congress on 24–25 August, two days before the French Assembly adopted their Declaration on 27 August 1789.

Second, despite the fact that the French drafters of the Declaration were familiar with the American states' bills of rights and the Declaration of Independence, the acts show similarities but do not duplicate each other. Giving just a few examples, it has to be noted that although the French intended to issue a declaration that would have universal appeal, the Americans were more focused on the rights of their own people. The Bill of Rights and the French Declaration emphasized that freedom should be placed ahead of all other rights, while the French act more emphatically stressed the conjunction of equality and liberty and the importance of social equality. The drafters of both acts also differed with regard to religious freedom: Americans emphasized the importance of religious tolerance and the separation of state and church but distanced themselves from the French attitudes that approached, at times, a level of ideological atheism. Despite numerous similarities, the first French and American bills each retained their own specific flavor.

NATURALISTIC LANGUAGE OF THE FIRST BILLS OF RIGHTS

The language of the first American and European constitutional bills of rights was predominantly naturalistic. The French 1789 Declaration of the Rights of Man and of the Citizen proclaimed that the French people, organized in the National Assembly, "have resolved to set forth in a solemn declaration [about] the natural, inalienable, and sacred rights of man." The Declaration clearly stated that these rights are "recognized and proclaimed."

Similarly, the Jeffersonian naturalistic philosophy prevailed in America and was expressed by the most important documents of the American Revolution. "Man [is] a rational animal, endowed by nature with rights and with an innate sense of justice," Jefferson wrote to the American politician and educator William Johnson. Jefferson built this concept into the Declaration of Independence, which proclaimed that it is "self-evident, that all men are created equal, that they are endowed by the Creator with certain unalienable rights, that among these are Life, Liberty and the pursuit of Happiness." The similar naturalistic language, which also prevailed in the American states' bills of rights, is not used verbatim in the U.S. Bill of Rights. The drafters believed that the federal Constitution was a pragmatic act rather than a philosophical manifesto. However, the naturalistic approach to rights had not been abandoned, and it found its expression in the Ninth Amendment, which confirmed that the Constitution enumerated only certain rights while not denying that the people might retain some others.

In contrast to the French and American bills, the language of the second constitution in world history and the first European constitution—the Constitution of Poland of 3 May 1791—was different. Focusing on rights of the main social groups rather than on individual rights, the Polish Constitution did not recognize these rights as "inherent in the human nature." Rather, it referred to "ancestors as first founders of liberties" and particularly to the kings who—on the basis of the social agreement with the estates—granted "laws, statutes, and privileges." In the nineteenth century, the theory of "granted" rights began slowly, but these rights steadily gained an upper hand in Europe.

"RECOGNIZED" RIGHTS AND "GRANTED" RIGHTS

There is one very important difference between the American and European constitutional legacy. The U.S. federal Constitution has survived for more than two centuries, while the European constitutions have changed along with the changing governments. The development of the body of constitutional law in the United States, primarily through the courts' creative interpretation, has been impressive, but the concept of constitutional rights rooted in

the philosophy of natural law has been solidified, to some extent, by the constitutional longevity.

In contrast to the U.S. Constitution, which has survived the test of time, the first European written constitutions did not endure for more than two years. After the partition of Poland, the consolidated front of the Polish Constitution's supporters was not sufficient to keep it alive. The Constitution was never fully implemented, and successive Polish constitutions were simply granted by the foreign emperors who did not "recognize" any natural rights of the Poles; the rights of the Polish society originated in the good will of the rulers. In 1807, in Dresden, after the victorious French campaign against Prussia, accompanied by the Polish anti-Prussian rising, Napoleon simply dictated a new constitution to the Polish administrators of the newly created Duchy of Warsaw. This constitution abolished slavery and confirmed the citizens' equality in law and their freedom of religious worship, but it did not have any elaborate list of rights. It served, however, as a model for a few constitutions granted by Napoleon to the German states of the Union of Rhineland. After the fall of Napoleon, Russia took control of a substantial part of the territory of the Duchy of Warsaw, and in November 1815 the Russian tsar Alexander I gave the newly created Kingdom of Poland a new constitution. Similarly, in the Austrian and Prussian parts of the partitioned Polish territories, the constitutions were granted by the emperors, and the constitutional rights of the Poles were as illusive as the rights of peoples in the other parts of the Austrian and German empires.

The concept of the constitutionalization of rights and freedoms in France was changing as well. The 1789 Declaration of the Rights of Man and of the Citizen listed as a top priority the protection of the natural and inalienable rights of man, such as liberty, property, security, and resistance to oppression. The Declaration, which was added to the Constitution of 1793, still referred to the right to property as a natural law but placed equality before liberty and security, with property taking the last place. The Constitution incorporated more populist components than the prior act of 1791. It granted universal suffrage and introduced the institution of referendum. The Declaration, which supplemented the 1795 Constitution, departed even further from the American concept of mostly "negative freedom" by adding to the rights the List of Duties, which originated from the principle that the people were obliged to do to others what they wished to receive in return. The constitution of 13 December 1799 (Constitution of Year VIII) referred only to the rights of the cities and to few rights of the French citizens. The subsequent Napoleonic constitutions were more pragmatic and dropped the sections on the Rights of Man entirely.

The development of European positivism in the nineteenth century further contributed to the split of the European legal philosophy from the American theory of "recognized" rights. The positivists' inclination to draw all knowledge from purely scientific sources undermined the basic tenets of the naturalistic philosophy of rights. The lists of sacred and inviolable rights did not look sufficiently clear anymore. From the positivistic point of view, the properly adopted constitutional laws protecting rights could not be wrong or illegal; positivistic human rights experts would rather deliberate on "what the law means" than on "what the law should be." The concept of rights that were the grant of power or the result of a social contract became prevalent in Europe. Although the positivistic philosophy made inroads in America as well, it did not push the naturalistic theories into oblivion. The longevity of the U.S. Constitution significantly fossilized the assertions that a man is endowed by nature with rights that belong to human beings simply because they are human.

NEGATIVE AND POSITIVE RIGHTS AND NINETEENTH-CENTURY CONSTITUTIONAL DEVELOPMENTS

In the nineteenth century, the conviction that every respectable country should have a written document of governance containing a bill of rights spread in Europe and Latin America. Borrowing from the experience of the first constitutional states became almost routine. It was especially visible in several Latin American constitutions that clearly were modeled on the U.S. Constitution. Latin American constitutional drafters looked at the Spanish Constitution of 1812 and at the first 1791 French Constitution; they were, however, most strongly influenced by the U.S. presidential system. The Polish Constitution of 1791 spread the idea of constitutionally limited power over Eastern and Central Europe, and Norway's Constitution of 1814 became a model for many Scandinavian countries. Through the nineteenth century, elaborated bills of rights were incorporated in a great number of the modern constitutions, such as the constitutions of Belgium of 1831, Liberia in 1847, the Kingdom of Sardinia in 1848, Denmark in 1849, Prussia in 1850, and Switzerland in 1874, among others.

Although the aspiration to have constitutionally guaranteed fundamental rights gradually became common, some constitutions, namely Latin American acts, listed the rights and freedoms chaotically and blended them with provisions about the administrative structures, division of powers, and revenues of the state. Many of the Latin American bills of rights drawn up in the late twentieth century and early twenty-first century follow this pattern. In contrast, however, the drafters of the European fundamental laws began better organizing their catalogs of rights; and following the models of the French and American states, they started placing these rights as preambles to the constitutional texts.

With all these unquestionable mutual borrowings, several differences warrant attention. In contrast to the American concept of "inherent" rights, the European constitutions declared that rights are constitutionally protected within the boundaries of the laws. The Europeans' inclination to reserve for the parliaments the supreme power did not allow them to impose limitations on the legislature. The constitutional guarantees of rights were supposed to protect people against the arbitrariness of government but not against limitations imposed by legislative bodies. The assumption that rights might be exercised only in the manner expressly provided by law contributed to the development in Europe of human rights–related legislation. In the United States, legislation followed the judge-produced creative interpretation of fundamental rights; in Europe it became the primary source of human rights law.

The first nineteenth-century European constitutions followed the American approach to constitutional rights by providing lists of typical "Thou Shalt Nots." Borrowing also from French constitutionalism, the Europeans began incorporating into their basic laws the provisions on social duties of citizens, including military duties, duties to educate children, and duties to perform some personal services for the state and local communities. The European constitutions also began imposing some positive obligations on the governments—to protect health and environment, to promote development of commerce and trade, and to guarantee affordable housing and basic social benefits for families.

CONSTITUTIONALIZATION OF ECONOMIC AND SOCIAL RIGHTS

Traditionally, Europeans were more eager than Americans to constitutionalize the idea of equality of rights. The U.S.

Constitution, in its original version, did not guarantee universal suffrage, equal rights to women, nor did it prohibit slavery. The European movement to abolish slavery and the slave trade, developed by the Marquis de Condorcet in 1788, resulted in the elimination of slavery in Denmark in 1792. This trend was followed by many European states well before the adoption of the Thirteenth Amendment to the U.S. Constitution in 1865, which abolished slavery. Similarly, before the Nineteenth Amendment, providing for women's suffrage, became the law in 1920, a great number of European states, such as Finland (1906); Norway (1913); Denmark (1915); the Netherlands, Canada, and the Soviet Union (1917); Austria, Germany, Estonia, and Poland (1918); Germany, Luxembourg, and Sweden (1919), enacted legislation guaranteeing a woman's right to vote.

The Americans were not insensitive to the social and economic needs of the common people, but they believed that they did not require constitutional protection: the fulfillment of these goals could be left to private charity or to the initiatives of local communities. During the Great Depression, presidents Herbert Hoover and Franklin D. Roosevelt showed compassion for the suffering of ordinary people. Hoover's unsuccessful attempts to rescue the economy and Roosevelt's New Deal programs were developed to create new jobs and trigger economic development; but these programs never encompassed the mass nationalization actions that became popular in twentieth-century Europe. The New Deal and the later initiatives of the Great Society program of President Lyndon Johnson have never become a symbol of the American economic and social philosophy, and the American courts did not show any intention to interpret the antidiscrimination clauses of the Fourteenth Amendment in a way that would invoke any specific governmental responsibility for the well-being of its citizens.

Traditional European egalitarianism was ahead of its American equivalent in developing the welfare-state doctrine. Rooted in the ideas of the English Fabian Society and the social liberalism of the philosophers Thomas H. Green, Leonard T. Hobhouse, and John Stuart Mill, European welfarism shifted to government the responsibility for individual success—or at least promised individuals equal opportunity in their competition for social benefits.

In the beginning of the twentieth century, the European welfare states began to constitutionalize positive obligations imposed on the governments. This is well illustrated by the 1919 German Weimar Constitution, which guaranteed that the government will enforce the municipal obligations to take care of health, environment, and social welfare and will provide public funds for education. To give another example, the Constitution of Finland of 1919 guaranteed the state's funds for agriculture, commerce, navigation, and fine arts. The Constitution of Yugoslavia of 1921 imposed on the government an obligation to create equal opportunity for citizens in their search for successful professional careers. The state became responsible for national health, general hygienic and social conditions, and for the distribution of free medications to needy citizens. In the interwar period (1918–1939) the assertion that governments have societal obligations and share responsibility for decent standards of life spread all over Europe.

FUNDAMENTAL RIGHTS AND SOCIALIST CONSTITUTIONALISM

The emergence of the Union of Soviet Socialist Republics, after World War I, contributed to the worldwide dissemination of socialist ideology. The socialist legal theory claimed that the socialist system produced a very special type of constitutionalism that, among other features, can be characterized by a new approach to human rights. The socialist doctrine, which attempted to distinguish a socialist "genuine" from a "formal" Western democracy, could be translated into several basic concepts.

First, building on trends popular in nineteenth-century Europe, the socialist jurisprudence claimed that rights were contingent on duties the citizens owed to their countries. Following the provisions of the socialist constitutions, the socialist basic laws became replete with long lists of duties, such as the observance of the Soviet Constitution and the laws, compliance with the standards of socialist conduct, respect for the honor and dignity of the socialist state, labor discipline, and protection of socialist property.

Second, socialist constitutionalism claimed that the enjoyment by citizens of their rights cannot be detrimental to the interest of the society, the state, or other citizens. The assumption that shared interests are superior to individual interests was supposed to contribute to the creation of a "collective mentality"—a precondition for the further evolution of society toward communism. On behalf of the collective interest, all means of production and distribution and all individual values, including rights and duties, were to be subject to public control.

Third, socialist jurisprudence rejected the concept of inherent or natural rights as a purely philosophical category inconsistent with the premises of modern constitutionalism. The rights were "granted" to the people according to the priorities identified by the Communist Party, thus by the vanguard of the people themselves. The priorities could change and the changes could affect the peoples' rights. This rhetoric obviously did not correspond with an idea of permanent or inalienable individual rights.

Fourth, the rights granted by the constitutions were not directly enforceable in the courts. With the exception of a few countries, such as Yugoslavia and Poland, the socialist states did not establish any constitutional courts. The socialist legal doctrine rejected the concept of judicial review, following the assumption that the people's legislative and executive bodies cannot violate peoples' rights. There was no need to evaluate the performance of the people's organs by the people's courts. Socialist jurisprudence reserved the right of review of the laws' constitutionality to the nucleus bodies of the legislative organs, such as the state councils, the standing committees of parliaments, or mixed organs composed of the deputies and constitutional experts. The right to review the legality of the administrative actions had been vested in the procurators who themselves were controlled by the party.

Fifth, to emphasize the superiority of the socialist democracy, the drafters of the socialist constitutions exposed the significance of economic and social rights. Socialist doctrine assumed that economic and social equality is a necessary prerequisite of real political democracy. The social and economic rights, treated by many Western countries as second-generation rights, were usually placed at the top of the socialist constitutional bills of rights. This approach was supposed to symbolize a socialist distributive justice.

MECHANISMS OF JUDICIAL ENFORCEMENT OF CONSTITUTIONAL RIGHTS

The process of forming modern constitutional bills of rights triggered questions about their enforceability. The idea of the rights protected by courts was rejected by the socialist doctrine; and, until the beginning of the twentieth century, it was not well grounded in the European legal doctrine. However, the idea of court-protected rights has been well rooted in the American jurisprudence, where the developing concept of a law-based state implied the existence of mechanisms that individuals could use to claim that their rights are more than pure paper declarations.

The implementation of this idea was contingent on several factors. The document encompassing the bill of rights had to be sufficiently clear. It required the existence of a single framework act, prevailing in conflict over regular legislative acts and sufficiently rigid so the act could not be amended through the regular legislative process. It implied the existence of an organ independent enough to be able to review the acts of the legislative and executive bodies. It was further contingent on the substitution of the principle of supremacy of one organ (legislative or executive) by the concept of well-balanced powers equipped with prerogatives allowing them mutually to observe their activities. On the one hand, the organs hampered each other; but, on the other hand, they were expected to develop models of socially beneficial cooperation. In other words, the establishment of efficient enforcement mechanisms implied the existence of a written constitution implementing the concept of checks and balances; and it reserved to appropriately trained judges the right of review of the constitutionality of the laws adopted by the legislatures and the legality of the executive decisions and actions.

These prerequisites of the constitutional enforcement of rights and freedoms, rooted in the legal system of the United States, were exposed by Chief Justice John Marshall in his 1803 ruling in *Marbury v. Madison*. Following Marshall's precedential ruling on the supremacy of the U.S. Constitution, the Americans adopted a decentralized system of judicial review; it reserved the right of checking on the legislative and executive bodies' acts to all courts, which could declare the law void and null. The American model required the existence of a concrete dispute between the parties involving an issue of constitutionality of the applicable laws. It assumed that the decisions of the higher courts on the constitutionality of statutory laws and validity of other legal enactments would be generalized through the principle of *stare decisis* (adhering to precedent). The concept of a binding precedent, rooted in the philosophy of common law, protected the American model of judicial review from chaos, which could result from colliding decisions of some courts disqualifying the laws that could be applied by the others.

Although some attempts to establish institutions of judicial review were noted in Europe in the mid-nineteenth century, fully developed mechanisms of constitutional enforcement of rights were introduced by the Europeans more than a century after the Americans. In 1847 Greece began experimenting with constitutional review. It vested in that country's supreme court the right to check on the coherence of all legislative acts. In 1867 the Austrians began testing their own model of constitutional review; the Austrian Supreme Constitutional Tribunal and the Supreme Administrative Court were, however, formally established by the constitution of 1 October 1920. In the same year a system of administrative review was developed in Czechoslovakia, and in 1921 Poland also set up the Administrative Tribunal. In the interwar period, similar courts became operational in most of the former states of the Austro-Hungarian Empire.

The so-called Austrian centralized model reserved for a special constitutional tribunal the right of a review of constitutionality of abstract acts submitted by the higher officials of the state (heads of state, governments, groups of deputies). The European tribunals did not exercise the right of "declaratory" review, which implied the pronunciation of a law void *ex tunc*, or since the moment of its enactment. The original Austrian system reserved for the Constitutional Tribunal the initial right to declare the law "voidable" and not "void." The tribunal's decision could be overruled by the vote of a qualified majority of the legislative body. If this result could not be reached, the unconstitutional law became void *ex nunc*, or since the adoption of the tribunal's decision.

The modifications of the classic American and Austrian patterns of review of constitutionality of laws resulted in the emergence of numerous mixed systems. The most popular systems among the countries searching for adoptable models were the German and French concepts of review, blending features of abstract and concrete, decentralized and centralized systems. To emphasize that checking the constitutionality of the laws in Europe was done by special courts or quasijudicial organs and to contrast this model with the American concept of "judicial review," the mixed European models were often referred to as "constitutional review."

The German mixed model attracted the attention of numerous drafters of many currently adapted constitutions. Borrowing from the Austrian traditions, the German Basic Law vests the right of constitutional review of the laws in one Federal Constitutional Tribunal with an impressive jurisdiction. Although the states have their own constitutional courts, reviewing the legality of legislative acts and administrative actions within their jurisdiction, the Federal Constitutional Tribunal is the only institution that can interpret the Basic Law and declare federal statutes as incompatible with the constitutional principles. The tribunal, which became operational in 1951, has the right to review the legality of electoral procedures and

participates in impeachment proceedings. With regard to its main functions, as an institution of constitutional review, it can be reached through five basic channels. First, it reviews abstract issues of constitutionality submitted by the federal government, the state governments, or by one-third of the Bundestag members. Second, it can be activated by the regular courts submitting to the tribunal constitutional questions raised during concrete adversary actions. The courts have to stay the proceedings and obtain the decision of the tribunal on relevant constitutional problems. Third, the tribunal hears disputes dealing with the distribution of competences within the federal administration and between the federal government and the states. Fourth, the tribunal reviews the compatibility of programs and actions of political parties with the democratic principles guaranteed by the Constitution. Fifth, with regard to the enforcement of constitutionally guaranteed rights, the tribunal, since 1969, hears individual complainants on the violation of their rights by public authorities. The decisions of the tribunal are final and binding upon all governmental organs and courts.

The French Constitutional Council, established by the 1958 Constitution of the Fifth Republic, can review the constitutionality of laws only in the relatively short period of time after their adoption by the parliament but before their promulgation. The "preventive" character of the council's review has led to it being recognized as an extension of the legislature, so that the French model was labeled as the "external-political" rather than "judicial" type of review. In fact, the council is a quasijudicial body, composed of nine members appointed by the president of the republic, and the presidents of both chambers of Parliament, equipped with a great deal of autonomy. The council reviews ex officio the organic laws (the main implementing laws listed in the Constitution) and other statutory laws if they are submitted for review by the president of the republic, the prime minister, the presidents of the chambers of Parliament and the group of at least sixty deputies or senators. The council decides about the compatibility of the statutory laws adopted by Parliament with the Constitution, the Preamble, and with the 1789 Declaration of the Rights of Man and of the Citizen, which was reaffirmed by the Constitution of 1958. As France follows a strict concept of the separation of powers, violations of the rights and freedoms by the acts and actions of the government and local administrative bodies are not subject to review of the Constitutional Council but are reviewable by administrative courts, including the supreme administrative judicial organ, the Council of State.

Mixed models of judicial and constitutional review spread in many regions but particularly in the Latin American states and in postsocialist countries. The adoption of any single model of review in Latin America had been particularly difficult. The Latin American states began experimenting with judicial review long before the Europeans established their first constitutional tribunals. They borrowed from the United States' decentralized and concrete model of review; this model, however, did not work smoothly in the countries following civil law traditions. In contrast, the countries of the former Soviet dominance showed reluctance to adopt the U.S. model of review rooted in the concept of common law precedent. They opted for the European centralized and abstract system blended with some features of mixed German or French models. In both regions the attempts to create mixed systems of judicial enforcement of constitutional rights were not overwhelmingly successful and, in many cases, resulted in the excessive politicization of the review process controlled by strong executives or in the judicialization of the constitution by the constitutional courts' excessive eagerness to unnecessarily challenge the great number of adopted laws.

INTERNATIONALIZATION OF HUMAN RIGHTS AND ITS IMPACT ON THE CONSTITUTIONAL BILLS OF RIGHTS AND THE REGIONAL SYSTEMS OF PROTECTION OF RIGHTS

In response to the atrocities committed during World War II, the protection of rights of all people was projected by the postwar international organizations as one of their most important priorities. The more frequent use of the term "human rights" was to signify that besides the protection of citizens' rights by several states, the world needs the protection of the rights of every human being.

The activities sponsored by the United Nations resulted in the adoption of the 1948 Universal Declaration of Human Rights and ratification by a great number of states of the 1966 International Covenant on Civil and Political Rights (ICCPR); the International Covenant on Economic, Social, and Cultural Rights (ICESCR) was also adopted in 1966. These acts, supplemented by the 1966 First Optional Protocol, which authorized the Human Rights Committee to receive communications from victims of human rights violations, and the 1989 Second

Optional Protocol, on the elimination of the death penalty, were, all together, regarded as components of the International Bill of Rights.

Although the term "International Bill of Rights" was first officially applied to the above set of documents by the UN Commission on Human Rights in 1947, the initial compilation of fundamental rights was done in 1942 by a group of jurists from several countries sponsored by the American Law Institute. They prepared the Declaration of Essential Human Rights, which is often regarded as the first International Bill of Rights.

The process of internationalization of human rights affected the national systems of protection of rights, contributed to the development of regional human rights movements, and resulted in a growing consensus that human rights is a global value requiring universal protection. The ratification of the postwar international human rights–related agreements by a great number of states indicated that human rights should be protected by domestic regulations not only as components of customary international law but also as elements of international treaty obligations. Many signatories of the international human rights conventions incorporated into their constitutions the provisions recognizing the supremacy of international agreements over statutory laws. These states began developing human rights legislation confirming their intention to harmonize internal laws with international obligations.

The postwar internationalization of human rights contributed to a growing awareness that the activities of the international organizations had to be supplemented by regional systems of protection of human rights. In Europe, the establishment of such a system was triggered by war crimes, crimes of communist regimes, the incorporation of Eastern Europe into the bloc of Soviet dominance, and the spread of the ideas of European communism in Western Europe. In 1948 The Hague Congress, organized by the International Committee of the Movements for European Unity, initiated the push for a regional human rights declaration. The congress triggered the process of drafting the European Convention of Human Rights (ECHR), which was accomplished in 1949 under the auspices of the Council of Europe. The convention was adopted in 1950 and entered into force in 1953. The European Commission of Human Rights and the European Court of Human Rights became institutions mainly responsible for the implementation of the convention. With time, the original institutional structures protecting the rights were changed. To reduce the backlog of cases waiting for consideration, the signatories of the convention adopted Protocol 11 in 1994. The protocol, ratified in 1997, abolished the European Commission of Human Rights, the organ deciding on admissibility of the actions, and allowed the parties more direct access to the Court of Human Rights.

The process of establishment and integration of the European Communities supplemented the regional European system of protection of human rights by the instruments developed by the community institutions. Although based mostly on the jurisprudence of the European Court of Justice, declarations of the European Commission, Council, and Parliament, and the proclaimed but still unenforceable 2000 European Union Charter of Fundamental Rights, the European Union system of protection of rights enhanced the European system, making it the most efficient regional system in the world.

In comparison with the European system, the Inter-American and African human rights instruments of protection have been less efficient; and no regional human rights system has been established in Asia. The Inter-American system has been based on two overlapping structures: one established by the 1948 charter of the Organization of American States (which entered into force in 1951), the other based on the 1969 American Convention on Human Rights (which entered into force in 1978). The efficiency of this system has been affected by the denial of the United States and Canada to ratify the American Convention on Human Rights. The regional record in human rights protection was also imperiled by ongoing major internal conflicts between Latin American military governments, armed opposition, leftist guerillas, and right-wing paramilitaries. On the one hand, the wide-scale conflicts, touching almost all Latin American countries, created enormous obstacles for regional organizations; on the other hand, the common problems mobilized major social groups, indigenous people, and ethnic minorities and contributed to the internationalization of human rights–related grassroots activities in this region.

In the early twenty-first century, the African regional system is still in the process of development. It was launched by the Organization of African Unity (OAU), established in 1963, and operates in accordance with the 1981 African Charter on Human and Peoples' Rights. In 2001 the activities of the OAU were taken over by its successor, the African Union. In 1998 a new component, the African Court on Human and Peoples' Rights, was added to the system. Although the African court borrows from the experience of European and American regional systems, its efficiency in protecting human rights in Africa requires more than structural development; it is contingent on the evolution of the regional political and legal culture.

RELATIVISM AND UNIVERSALISTIC CONCEPTS OF HUMAN RIGHTS

The process of internationalization of human rights contributed to the growing confidence in the universality of human rights. The numerous postwar proclamations, starting with the 1948 Universal Declaration of Human Rights and followed by the 1968 Proclamation of Teheran or the 1993 Vienna Declaration and Programme of Action, reported on the progress in protection of human rights and the spreading recognition of the interdependence of rights.

At the same time, some reservations as to the successes of universalism have to be noted. Most would agree that human rights is a global value; however, universally adopted standards of enforcement and the hierarchy of rights depend upon the adoption of regional and national implementing legal instruments. The existing obstacles have become visible in the process of ratification of the components of the United Nations–sponsored International Bill of Rights. The United States signed both the ICCPR and the ICESCR, but it ratified only the first. A great number of states signed the covenants with reservations, understandings, and declarations. The significant discrepancies in implementation by national constitutional laws of the basic rights protected by the covenants, such as the right to life, the protection against capital punishment, cruel and degrading treatment or punishment, the right to strike, and the right to equal pay for equal work, are still present. Even the fact that the fundamental international human rights documents, such as the covenants, still cover separately the rights of so-called first and second generation rights—namely, political and civil, and economic and social—speaks for itself.

In addition to this, cultural relativism, most visible in Asia, claimed loudly that the values respected by some people could not be judged in accordance with the standards of others. Relativism in its moderate form recognizes the existence of some fundamental rights but maintains that the standards of the rights' protection may be contingent on some cultural factors. Relativism in its more extreme form emphasizes that the inviolability of rights is not their intrinsic characteristic but is only guaranteed by the peoples' consensus. This trend challenges the universality of rights, claiming that people differ in attempts to list the rights in accordance with some commonly accepted hierarchy. Relativists claim that even the most basic values highly acclaimed in the West, freedom being the most popular, are overexposed and are often alien to the culture of the East. The human rights doctrines of this region stress (more emphatically than in the West) that for the development of human dignity, the value of discipline and spiritual subordination of the individual to divine predestination is more important than personal freedom.

Although the number of states ratifying the most important international human rights–related agreements is growing, in the early twenty-first century problems with uniform implementation of human rights policies still exist. The spreading intention of governments to respect human rights should not be confused with their univocal approval of the same list of rights. The universalization of rights is still a process, not an accomplished fact.

[*See also* African Union: Commission and Court on Human Rights; American Revolution; Association of Southeast Asian Nations (ASEAN); Civil and Political Rights: International Covenant on Civil and Political Rights; Collective/Group Rights; Conflict among Human Rights Norms; Culture and Human Rights; East Asian Values; Economic, Social, and Cultural Rights: International Covenant on Economic, Social, and Cultural Rights; European Convention on Human Rights and Fundamental Freedoms (Council of Europe); European Union; European Union Charter of Fundamental Rights; Global Justice and Human Rights; History of Human Rights; National Courts; Organization of American States; Philosophy; Slavery and the Slave Trade; Universal Declaration of Human Rights; Universality; *and* Universal Jurisdiction.]

BIBLIOGRAPHY

Alston, Philip, ed. *Promoting Human Rights through Bills of Rights: Comparative Perspectives.* Oxford: Oxford University Press, 1999.

Buergenthal, Thomas, Dinah Shelton, and David P. Stewart. *International Human Rights in a Nutshell.* Saint Paul, Minn.: West Group, 2002.

Cappelletti, Mauro, and William Cohen. *Comparative Constitutional Law.* Indianapolis, Ind.: Bobbs-Merrill, 1979.

Donnelly, Jack. *Universal Human Rights in Theory and Practice.* Ithaca, N.Y.: Cornell University Press, 2003.

Edwards, R. Randle, Louis Henkin, and Andrew J. Nathan, eds. *Human Rights in Contemporary China.* New York: Columbia University Press, 1986.

Flanz, Gisbert H., and Rett R. Ludwikowski. *Comparative Human Rights and Fundamental Freedoms.* Dobbs Ferry, N.Y.: Oceana, 2002.

Hilsdon, Anne-Marie, Martha Macintyre, Vera Mackie, and Maila Stevens, eds. *Human Rights and Gender Politics: Asia-Pacific Perspectives.* New York: Routledge, 2000.

Henkin, Louis. *The Age of Rights.* New York: Columbia University Press, 1990.

Henkin, Louis, Gerald L. Neuman, Diane F. Orentlicher, David W. Leebron. *Human Rights.* New York: Foundation Press, 1999.

Humphrey, John P. *Human Rights and the United Nations: A Great Adventure.* Dobbs Ferry, N.Y.: Transnational, 1984.

Hurst, Hannum, ed. *Guide to International Human Rights Practice.* 4th ed. Ardsley, N.Y.: Transnational, 2004.

Ludwikowski, Rett R., and William F. Fox. *The Beginning of the Constitutional Era: A Bicentennial Comparative Analysis of the First Modern Constitutions.* Washington, D.C.: Catholic University of America Press, 1993.

Ludwikowski, Rett R. *Constitution-Making in the Region of Former Soviet Dominance.* Durham, N.C.: Duke University Press, 1996.

Ludwikowski, Rett R. "The French Declaration of the Rights of Man and of the Citizen and the American Constitutional Development." *The American Journal of Comparative Law* 38 (1990): 445–462.

Ludwikowski, Rett R. "Limits of Universalism: Protection of Human Rights in Europe and America in Historical and Comparative Perspective." *Politeja* 2, no. 6 (2006): 7–49.

Merrills, J. G., and A. H. Robertson. *Human Rights in Europe: A Study of the European Convention on Human Rights.* 4th ed. Manchester, U.K.: Manchester University Press, 2001.

Pollis, Adamantia, and Peter Schwab, eds. *Human Rights: New Perspectives, New Realities.* Boulder, Colo.: Lynne Reinner, 2000.

Read, Conyers. *The Constitution Reconsidered.* New York: Columbia University Press, 1938.

Rosenfeld, Michael. "Can Human Rights Bridge the Gap between Fundamental Rights?" *Columbia Human Rights Law Review* 30 (1999): 249–282.

Ruthland, Robert A. *The Birth of the Bill of Rights, 1776–1791.* Boston: Northeastern University Press, 1983.

Schwartz, Bernard. *The Roots of the Bill of Rights.* New York: Chelsea House, 1980.

Smith, Christopher E. *Constitutional Rights: Myth and Realities.* Belmont, Calif.: Wadsworth/Thomson Learning, 2004.

Stone, Geoffrey R., Richard A. Epstein, and Cass R. Sunstein. *The Bill of Rights in the Modern State.* Chicago: University of Chicago Press, 1992.

Subedi, Surya P. "Are the Principles of Human Rights 'Western' Ideas? An Analysis of the Claim of the 'Asian' Concept of

Human Rights from the Perspectives of Hinduism." *California Western International Law Journal* 30 (1999): 45.

Sugiki, Akiko. "Questioning the Universality of Human Rights and Asian Values." *Asia Pacific Research Center*. Kobe, Japan: Kobe Gakuin University, 2004.

Symonides, Janusz, ed. *Human Rights: Concept and Standards.* Aldershot, U.K.: Ashgate, 2000.

Thompson, Kenneth W., and Rett R. Ludwikowski. *Constitutionalism and Human Rights: America, Poland, and France.* Lanham, Md.: University Press of America, 1991.

Weissbrodt, David, Joan Fitzpatrick, and Frank Newman. *International Human Rights.* 3d ed. Cincinnati, Ohio: Anderson, 2001.

Woods, Jeanne M., and Hope Lewis. *Human Rights and the Global Marketplace: Economic, Social, and Cultural Dimensions.* Ardsley, N.Y.: Transnational, 2005.

Wu, Yuan-li, Michael Franz, and John F. Cooper, eds. *Human Rights in the People's Republic of China.* Boulder, Colo.: Westview Press, 1988.

COSTA RICA

by Alison Brysk

Despite periodic shortfalls and growing challenges, Costa Rica has been a steady and surprising model of human rights promotion at home and abroad. How did a small, poor country from a troubled region come to play such a positive role—and what can this teach us about the possibilities for expanding human rights in the world? Costa Rica shows that an internationalist, democratic political culture can inspire policies that safeguard human rights under difficult conditions. At the same time, Costa Rica's unexpected foreign policy activism has been a source of global good citizenship that demonstrates how a dedicated network of small states helps build the international human rights regime.

The parameters permitting the development of democracy were Costa Rica's inconvenient location for colonization, sparse indigenous population, and lack of mineral or plantation wealth, producing light colonial settlement and the development of agricultural production by independent smallholders rather than large labor-exploitative plantations. Costa Rica was spared the classic oligarchy-military-church triumvirate of Latin American dependency and fell at the fringes of U.S. attention during its formative years.

As a result, Costa Rican elites had the latitude and incentive to make a series of progressive policy choices: they established the region's first universal primary education (1869), abolished the death penalty (1882), allowed legitimate political competition (1889), and founded the first international court (1907–1918). Labor rights, universal social services, and basic civil liberties were introduced early in the twentieth century as a conscious strategy to modernize the country. After an electoral dispute in 1948 unexpectedly escalated into a brief but bloody civil war, the horrified Costa Rican elite established a pact declaring José Maria Figueres the founding president of the Second Republic. In 1949 reforms further institutionalized political competition and abolished the military so that it could never again become a tool of political violence. Costa Rica's relatively progressive

political elite thus resulted from a mixture of historical conjuncture and political will and became a self-reinforcing vanguard for human rights promotion.

Throughout the post–World War II period, Costa Rica's political vision was shaped by Latin America's only Social Democratic Party (PLN) that achieved long stretches in government and demonstrated strong influence even in opposition. The social democratic ideal laid the groundwork for a democratic political culture with European linkages, the region's only nonrevolutionary alternative to oligarchy, and a pathway to policy influence for many of the country's intellectuals. Several succeeding Costa Rican presidents, such as the Nobel laureate Oscar Arias Sánchez (president 1986–1990, reelected 2006), imprinted their vision of democracy on the small country at critical junctures. A small circle of democratic diplomats, many of them internationally educated academics, positioned Costa Rica as the "island of peace" in the region, balancing U.S. influence and promoting tourism. An unusually open civil society reinforces and contributes to this "virtuous circle" of positive policy making, including a relatively high level of gender equity and political participation by women. Costa Rica's active and highly respected educational system and media promote a national identity reflected in the nickname for Costa Ricans, *ticos*—peaceful, tolerant, and in an ironic form of cosmopolitan nationalism, "more civilized" than their war-torn neighbors.

As for human rights at home, Costa Rica is regularly certified as having free, fair, and peaceful elections and has a long-standing independent electoral tribunal as well as a more recent ombudsman. Costa Rica's respect for civil liberties scores in the top tier worldwide, government institutions such as police and prisons are generally accountable, and state-sponsored abuses are isolated and usually addressed by government action. On the negative side, chronic gaps in social and economic rights have worsened with globalization, vulnerable groups such as immigrants and indigenous peoples still face some discrimination, and Costa Rica has developed a severe problem with sexual exploitation and trafficking of children—only partially ameliorated by government efforts. From this relatively strong domestic base, Costa Rica has reached out globally to promote human rights as an international identity—far beyond the level of its regional, demographic, or economic peers.

UNITED NATIONS

Costa Rica has played a part in virtually every major human rights initiative and institution—vastly disproportionate to its size, wealth, and power. The country's first ambassador to the United Nations (UN), Fernando Soto Harrison, was vice president of the founding Human Rights Commission. Costa Rica was a founder of the UN Children's Fund and the first country to sign the 1966 International Covenant on Civil and Political Rights as well as the Covenant on Economic and Social Rights. That same year Costa Rica's long-standing diplomatic advocate for human rights, Fernando Volio Jiménez, became president of the UN Human Rights Commission. Costa Rica consistently sought election to this body and held a seat in 1964–1967, 1975–1977, 1980–1988, 1992–1994, and 2001—an unusual span for a single small country. As a measure of human rights activity within these memberships, in 2000 alone Costa Rica cosponsored thirty-four thematic and country-specific human rights resolutions in the General Assembly and voted for seventy, while cosponsoring an additional forty-five measures in the commission itself. During 1988–1990 two Costa Ricans headed the UN Human Rights Sub-Commission for the Prevention of Discrimination and Protection of Minorities.

In addition to good citizenship and support, Costa Rica also helped expand the international human rights regime. The country helped create the UN Office of the High Commissioner for Human Rights (established in 1995), which was based on an initial proposal introduced by Volio Jiménez in 1965 and renewed at periodic intervals for a generation. In 1993 Costa Rica hosted the Latin American regional preparatory conference for the Vienna Human Rights Conference and was later designated vice president of the Latin American regional caucus at the Vienna Conference itself. Costa Rica led the campaign for the 2002 Optional Protocol to the Convention against Torture that mandates periodic inspections of detention facilities, presenting the proposal to the UN Human Rights Commission, lobbying

its hemispheric neighbors, and leading the working group that drafted the instrument throughout most of the 1990s.

During the 1990s Costa Rica also was active on emerging human rights concerns and agenda expansion at the UN. In 1999 Gabriela Rodríguez Pizarro from Costa Rica was appointed special rapporteur for migrants by the Human Rights Commission. Costa Rica played a particularly active role in the UN Durban Conference on Racism and became an active proponent of the International Criminal Court, Mine Ban Treaty, attempts to limit small arms, and campaigns against child soldiers.

THE INTER-AMERICAN SYSTEM

In parallel fashion, Costa Rica helped construct the inter-American system, which is among the strongest regional regimes, and served as an advocate for human rights treaties, institutions, and enforcement within that system. Costa Rica played a key role in establishing both the Organization of American States (OAS) Inter-American Court and the independent Inter-American Institute for Human Rights and hosts both institutions. The Costa Rican president José Joaquín Trejos Fernandez initiated the 1969 San José (Costa Rica) Conference that drafted the hemispheric keystone, the Inter-American Convention on Human Rights. The historic conference was chaired by Costa Rica's foreign minister. Costa Rica was the first country to ratify the convention and the first to accept the jurisdiction of the Inter-American Human Rights Commission as well as the subsequent Inter-American Human Rights Court. Costa Rica was one of the founding members of the (Washington-based) Inter-American Human Rights Commission in 1960, and the Costa Rican Angela Acuña Braun was one of the seven original commissioners. Volio Jiménez also served on the Inter-American Human Rights Commission in between his human rights work at the UN and his domestic posts in Costa Rica.

In his 1978 inaugural address, the Costa Rican president Rodrigo Carazo Odio offered the country as the site for a regional human rights court. The following year Costa Rica's OAS delegation helped draft and lobby for a budget for the new court. Costa Rica secured a special session of the OAS to designate judges and proposed two of the initial seven jurists. Costa Rica was the first state party to submit a case to the court (1981). In 1988–1995 the Costa Rican law professor Sonia Picado became the first female judge on the court and a particularly active presence in inter-American jurisprudence, increasing contentious cases and the enforcement power of the court.

In 1980 Costa Rica signed an agreement with the OAS to host the Inter-American Human Rights Institute for human rights research, education, and promotion. In 1987 Picado became the director of the institute, expanding its mission to include election monitoring and substantial technical assistance to emerging democracies. A new body, Inter-American Center for Electoral Assistance and Promotion (CAPEL), was created for this purpose.

Meanwhile, Costa Rica also advanced numerous human rights initiatives in the wider ambits of the OAS. Costa Rica helped sponsor an Inter-American Declaration on the Rights of Prisoners, the Resolution on the Rights of Migrants, and the 1999 Declaration on the Rights of Indigenous Peoples. In 1994 the Costa Rican OAS official Hermes Navarro del Valle presented the Inter-American Convention on Discrimination against the Disabled, and in 1998 the Costa Rican Jorge Rhenán Segura became president of the working group. By 1999 the Disability Rights Convention had passed, and Costa Rica was the first member state to sign it. The culmination of Costa Rican diplomacy for democratization came in 2001, when Costa Rica hosted the thirty-first meeting of the OAS General Assembly (with the theme of human rights) and used this occasion to help sponsor the Carta Democrática, a regionwide system of reciprocal support for democracy and sanctions for its abrogation.

Costa Rica's advocacy for the interlinked themes of human rights, democratization, and peace bridges the global, hemispheric, and Central American regional levels. During the 1980s Arias convened and brokered the only successful negotiations of the regionwide crisis, resulting in the Esquipulas Accords that resolved civil wars in El Salvador, Nicaragua, and Guatemala. The Costa Rican peace plan provided for mutual disarmament of government and guerrilla forces, withdrawal of external combatants and peacekeeping by the UN, civil society commissions coordinated by the Catholic Church to address underlying conflicts, and human rights accountability to the extent possible in each country. Arias had campaigned on a peace platform against an unpopular U.S.-allied interventionist opponent. He gained support by chronicling the impact of regional conflict on Costa Rica through the loss of investment and a refugee crisis. He predicted a painful loss of U.S. aid but successfully rallied the Costa Rican public to absorb this sacrifice in the name of the national values of peace, democracy, and regional self-determination.

REFUGEES

Within Central America and beyond, Costa Rica's reception of refugees constitutes a litmus test for human rights policy. The generosity and tolerance of all nations are tested by the arrival of vast numbers of needy strangers. Although Costa Rica sits in the middle ranks of developing nations, its resources are limited, so that support of refugees is in some sense a surrogate for foreign aid for struggling neighboring states. Costa Rica has a long-standing tradition of granting political asylum to dissident democratic political figures, even at the cost of annoying neighboring governments. Through the dictatorships of the 1970s and 1980s, the inter-American institutions based in Costa Rica also sheltered some grassroots exiles and human rights workers.

But massive flows of migrants, generated by the Central American wars, posed far deeper challenges. During the 1980s hundreds of thousands of poor Nicaraguans (and some Salvadorans) flooded Costa Rica (whose total population then was around 3 million). A positive sign of civil society support was the establishment of one of Costa Rica's first human rights groups in 1980 on behalf of refugees (Comité Ecuménico Pro Refugiados). At the same time the UN High Commissioner for Refugees (UNHCR) opened a regional office in Costa Rica during the 1980s. Costa Rica provided short-term shelter and humanitarian services for these refugees, although it strongly encouraged voluntary repatriation.

State policy and social attitudes were significantly more ambivalent regarding continuing flows of economic migrants during the 1990s as well as those who chose not to return to their countries of origin. Costa Rica's 2000 census shows 240,000 Nicaraguans, and experts estimate true numbers up to 400,000—which would be around 10 percent of Costa Rica's population. Migrants are eligible for social services and can even safely denounce exploitative labor conditions. But undocumented Central Americans can be deported and are subject to social and employment discrimination. Costa Rica's ombudsman has a special program to track the treatment and access of migrants, and a migration amnesty was declared in 1999–2000 in response to Hurricane Mitch.

Meanwhile, Costa Rica was visited by a new flow of refugees during the late 1990s: Colombians, usually traveling overland on the narrow Isthmus of Panama from

Latin America's bloodiest country to its most peaceful. The UNHCR registered about eight thousand Colombians in Costa Rica of a total refugee population of around fourteen thousand. This gives Costa Rica the highest number of recognized refugees in Latin America. Accordingly, the UNHCR reopened the regional office that had closed during the 1990s. While the Colombians generally have more education and resources than Central American refugees and thus less of a social service impact, their presence created new security problems in Costa Rica through transnational reprisals by Colombian persecutors crossing into Costa Rica.

Costa Rica's response to this population has been conscientious. When over one thousand Colombians arrived in 2000, the Costa Rican Foreign Ministry began meeting with the International Red Cross, and by 2001 Costa Rica had coordinated a Refugee Status Determination Program with the UNHCR. After the UNHCR contributed computer equipment and training to Costa Rica's Migration Department, about half of that year's more than fifty-eight hundred arrivals were granted refugee status. The UNHCR even mounted training programs with Costa Rican border guards to refer rather than apprehend anyone declaring refugee status. Costa Rica's Migration Department automatically issues one-month residency permits to refugee applicants and does not sanction illegal entrants who later apply for refuge. As numbers rose into the thousands, Costa Rica did introduce a visa requirement for Colombians, which may have had a chilling effect on refugees with fewer resources and facing more immediate threats. But for those who made it to Costa Rica, refugee approval rates climbed to almost 70 percent by 2003. Refugee assessment is coordinated with international standards, including UNHCR information on country situations and plausible grounds for claims of persecution (for example, the high incidence of nongovernmental violence in Colombia). Finally, there is an appeals process for refugee applicants, and they are not detained or deported for the duration of this process.

CONTRADICTIONS AND LIMITATIONS

While Costa Rica's policies have been positive on balance, it is important to acknowledge the contradictions and limitations of even this best-case human rights advocacy. Traditional realist considerations periodically persuade policy makers to pursue more conventional strategies of power that ignore human rights in international settings, such as endorsing known human rights violators when they are campaigning for UN positions or acquiescing to internationally condemned U.S. stances. As a peripheral power, Costa Rica sometimes simply lacks the resources to implement at home the international principles the country endorses or cannot participate fully in the international human rights regime. And principled policies in a small state are catalyzed by a limited cadre of dynamic individuals, so that human rights initiatives may be overly dependent on a few charismatic figures and even occasionally entangled in the rivalries such figures inevitably evoke.

Nevertheless, Costa Rica has made a solid contribution to the rights of its own citizens, neighbors, refugees, and global governance that would behoove others to follow. Costa Rica's experience seems to affirm that human rights promotion does not require size, wealth, power, Anglo-American culture, or living in the Northern Hemisphere. Some of the features that provided the opportunity for Costa Rica's human rights policies are fixed: a small scale, dispersed wealth, and generations of democratic institutions. But these resources were mobilized by visionary leaders, dedicated diplomats, and a supportive civil society inspired by a democratic political culture and a positive vision of national identity as a peace promoter and a global good citizen. Political culture and national identity are learned and can be cultivated by media, education, and the international community—slowly and within the parameters set by a nation's history. Costa Rica shows that the political will for human rights promotion can flourish in diverse climates and suggests that global advocates survey more widely for fertile soils to plant principles that can grow into a progressive source of national pride.

[*See also* Central America: The 1980s; Colombia; Civil and Political Rights: International Covenant on Civil and Political Rights; Organization of American States; Refugees; United Nations Children's Fund (UNICEF); United Nations High Commissioner for Refugees; *and* United Nations Sub-Commission on Human Rights.]

BIBLIOGRAPHY

Booth, John A. *Costa Rica: Quest for Democracy.* Boulder, Colo.: Westview, 1998.

Eguizabal, Cristina. "Latin American Foreign Policies and Human Rights." In *Human Rights and Comparative Foreign Policy*, edited by David P. Forsythe. Tokyo and New York: United Nations University Press, 2000.

Hey, Jeanne A. K., and Lynn M. Kuzma. "Anti-U.S. Foreign Policy of Dependent States: Mexican and Costa Rican

Participation in Central American Peace Plans." *Comparative Political Studies* 26 (April 1993): 30–62.

Hurwitz, Jon, Mark Peffley, and Mitchell A. Seligson. "Foreign Policy Belief Systems in Comparative Perspective: The United States and Costa Rica." *International Studies Quarterly* 37, no. 3 (1993): 245–270.

Masís Iverson, Daniel. "Poder político y sociedad." In *Costa Rica contemporánea: Raíces del estado de la nación*, edited by Juan Rafael Quesada Camacho, Daniel Masís Iverson, Manuel Barahona Montero, Tobías Meza Ocampo, Rafael Cuevas Molina, and Jorge Rhenán Segura, pp. 45–96. San José, Costa Rica: Editorial de la Universidad de Costa Rica, 1999.

Pasqualucci, Jo M. "Sonia Picado: First Woman Judge on the Inter-American Court of Human Rights." *Human Rights Quarterly* 17, no. 4 (1995): 794–806.

Quesada Camacho, Juan Rafael. "Evolución a la tica." *In Costa Rica contemporánea: Raíces del estado de la nación*, edited by Juan Rafael Quesada Camacho, Daniel Masís Iverson, Manuel Barahona Montero, Tobías Meza Ocampo, Rafael Cuevas Molina, and Jorge Rhenán Segura, pp. 19–44. San José, Costa Rica: Editorial de la Universidad de Costa Rica, 1999.

Rhenán Segura, Jorge. "Costa Rica y su contexto internacional." *In Costa Rica contemporánea: Raíces del estado de la nación*, edited by Juan Rafael Quesada Camacho, Daniel Masís Iverson, Manuel Barahona Montero, Tobías Meza Ocampo, Rafael Cuevas Molina, and Jorge Rhenán Segura, pp. 311–355. San José, Costa Rica: Editorial de la Universidad de Costa Rica, 1999.

U.S. Department of State, Under Secretary for Democracy and Global Affairs, Bureau of Democracy, Human Rights, and Labor. *Releases: Human Rights: 2003 Country Reports on Human Rights Practices: Costa Rica.* http://www.state.gov/g/drl/rls/hrrpt/2003/27892.htm2003.

Ventura, Manuel. "Costa Rica and the Inter-American Court of Human Rights." *Human Rights Law Journal* 4, no. 3 (1983): 273–281.

Wilson, Bruce M. *Costa Rica: Politics, Economics, and Democracy.* Boulder, Colo.: Lynne Rienner, 1998.

Yashar, Deborah J. *Demanding Democracy: Reform and Reaction in Costa Rica and Guatemala, 1870s–1950s.* Stanford, Calif.: Stanford University Press, 1997.

CRIMES AGAINST HUMANITY

by Jordan J. Paust

Crimes against humanity are among the primary or "core" international crimes recognized by the international community. Human rights are linked to crimes against humanity in the sense that relevant criminal violations by public and private actors necessarily involve violations of human rights as well. As violations of customary international law, crimes against humanity implicate universal jurisdictional competence of states and universal responsibility with respect to both criminal and civil sanctions.

HISTORIC UNDERPINNINGS OF CRIMES AGAINST HUMANITY

In 1945 Justice Robert Jackson's Report to the President on Atrocities and War Crimes, with respect to certain crimes committed during World War II, noted that both "atrocities and persecutions on racial or religious grounds" are crimes against humanity that were already outlawed under general principles of domestic law of civilized states and that "these principles have been assimilated as a part of International Law at least since 1907" (sec. 2, para. 5). Jackson found support for the latter part of his statement in the Frederic de Martens clause in the preamble to the 1907 Hague Convention, No. IV, Respecting the Laws and Customs of War on Land, which affirmed the existence of customary "principles of the law of nations" resulting "from the laws of humanity." The 1868 Declaration of St. Petersburg had also referred to violations of the "laws of humanity" concerning any use of certain types of weaponry during war.

Prior to 1945 there had been other recognitions of crimes against humanity or *crimen contra omnes*. In 1915 the governments of Great Britain, France, and Russia condemned massacres of Armenians by Turks as "crimes against humanity and civilization." In the 1919 Report of the Commission on the Responsibility of the Authors of the War and on Enforcement of Penalties formulated by representatives from several states (the United States, the British Empire, France, Italy, Japan, Belgium, Greece, Poland, Romania, and Serbia) and presented to the Paris Peace Conference, criminal responsibility of persons of any status (including heads of state) was identified in terms such as "offences against . . . the laws of humanity" and "violations," "breach[es] of," and "outrages against . . . the laws of humanity." In 1874 the American author George Curtis labeled slavery a "crime against humanity," and in 1921 a former U.S. secretary of state, Robert Lansing, wrote that the slave trade had become a "crime against humanity" (Bassiouni, p. 66). Related phrases, such as "crimes against mankind," "crimes against the human family," "enemies of the whole human family," and "duties of humanity," had already appeared in late-eighteenth- and early-nineteenth-century opinions of U.S. attorneys general and U.S. federal cases. In *Republica v. De Longchamps* a Pennsylvania court recognized in 1784 that an assault on a foreign consul is a "crime against the whole world"; and U.S. Supreme Court Justice James Wilson recognized in a federal proceeding in 1793 that "duties of humanity" are obligatory "on states as well as individuals." In 1775 the Declaration of the Causes and Necessity of Taking Up Arms expressed American opposition to British political oppression partly on the basis of "principles of humanity." Other U.S. state court cases from the 1850s to the 1930s also identified piracy, the slave trade, rape, and incest as crimes against humanity committed by private perpetrators.

What is interesting with respect to historic recognitions of "laws of humanity" and "crimes against humanity" is that the reach of these precepts was potentially quite broad, perhaps as far-reaching as human rights. They involved several types of conduct and were not limited to state actors, large-scale conduct, or contexts of war.

CUSTOMARY POST–WORLD WAR II DEFINITIONS OF CRIMES AGAINST HUMANITY

During the post–World War II era, several definitions of crimes against humanity under customary international law were formally documented. Each of the customary definitions addressed what are basically two types of crimes against humanity. The first type primarily involves certain inhumane acts committed against "any civilian population" (which is understood to mean against civilians), and the second type involves persecutions on political, racial, or religious grounds. During the subsequent Nuremberg proceedings under Control Council Law No. 10 (a law promulgated by a Control Council of the four states that were occupying powers in areas of Europe after World War II that provided a basis for prosecutions in numerous U.S., British, French, and Soviet military commissions at Nuremberg and elsewhere in occupied sectors in Europe), it was also recognized that genocide is a crime under international law and is "the prime illustration of a crime against humanity." In fact genocide is merely one type of crime against humanity.

Both the Charter of the International Military Tribunal at Nuremberg, in Article 6(c) (1945), and Control Council Law No. 10, in Article 2, section 1(c) (1945), recognized the two general types of crimes against humanity. In each the phrase "against any civilian population" appears only with respect to the first type (addressing various inhumane acts) and does not appear with respect to the second type (addressing prohibited persecutions). Therefore outlawed persecutions on political, racial, or religious grounds could include persecutions of military personnel. The Principles of the Nuremberg Charter and Judgment adopted by the United Nations (UN) General Assembly in 1950 retained this distinction, and both the 1948 Report of the United Nations War Crimes Commission and the Report of the International Law Commission (a body of experts on international law under the auspices of the UN) that formulated the 1950 Principles of the Nuremberg Charter and Judgment recognized that there were basically two types of crimes against humanity addressed during the prosecutions in Europe. With respect to prosecutions in the International Military Tribunal for the Far East, the Tokyo Charter, in Article 5(c) (1946), not only recognized the two general types of crimes against humanity (addressing both certain inhumane acts and certain forms of persecution) but also did not require that either type be committed "against any civilian population." Therefore various inhumane acts and persecutions of those who were not "civilians" could be addressed.

In view of the more limited definitions of crimes against humanity contained in certain instruments constituting modern international criminal tribunals, it is important to compare actual language used in the definitions found in the customary instruments of the post–Word War II international military tribunals (IMTs), Control Council Law No. 10, and the 1950 General Assembly Resolution adopting the Nuremberg Principles. Although they contain some relatively minor differences, there are important uniformities in the customary instruments that stand in contrast to some of the modern instruments.

The following are relevant extracts from the customary instruments. Article 6(c) of the charter of the IMT at Nuremberg reads, "*Crimes against humanity*: namely, murder, extermination, enslavement, deportation, and other inhumane acts committed against any civilian population, before or during the war, or persecutions on political, racial or religious grounds in execution of or in connection with any crime within the jurisdiction of the Tribunal, whether or not in violation of the domestic law of the country where perpetrated." Article 5(c) of the Tokyo Charter reads, "*Crimes against Humanity*; Namely, murder, extermination, enslavement, deportation, and other inhumane acts committed before or during the war, or persecutions on political or racial grounds in execution of or in connection with any crime within the jurisdiction of the Tribunal, whether or not in violation of the domestic law of the country where perpetrated." Article 2, section 1(c) of Control Council Law No. 10 reads, "*Crimes against Humanity*. Atrocities and offenses, including but not limited to murder, extermination, enslavement, deportation, imprisonment, torture, rape, or other inhumane acts committed against any civilian population, or persecutions on political, racial or religious grounds whether or not in violation of the domestic laws of the country where perpetrated." And principle 6(c) of the Nuremberg Principles adopted by the UN General Assembly reads, "Crimes against humanity: Murder, extermination, enslavement, deportation and other inhuman acts done against any civilian population, or persecutions on political, racial or religious grounds, when such acts are done or such persecutions are carried on in execution of or in connection with any crime against peace or any war crime."

MORE RECENT RESTRICTIVE DEFINITIONS

Despite the broad historic reach of crimes against humanity under customary international law and well-documented definitions in the post–World War II era, more recent definitions have restricted jurisdictional coverage and accountability in certain modern international tribunals.

One such definition appears in Article 5 of the 1993 Statute of the International Criminal Tribunal for the Former Yugoslavia (ICTY). Unlike all of the customary definitions noted above, Article 5 of the ICTY statute fuses the two general types of crimes against humanity together as one, listing the second type ("persecutions on political, racial and religious grounds") as merely one form of inhumane conduct and requiring that all categories of crimes against humanity be "directed against any civilian population." Therefore unlawful persecutions of military personnel are not expressly included. Article 5 of the ICTY statute also changes the Nuremberg phrase "committed against" (which in the 1950 Nuremberg Principles is "done against") to "directed against," a phrase that may require a slightly higher threshold of criminal intent than merely "committed" and "done" against. The ICTY article also adds three relevant methods or acts used for commission of crimes against humanity—"imprisonment," "torture," and "rape"—although each is covered by the more general Nuremberg phrase "other inhumane acts" and each expressly appeared in Control Council Law No. 10.

The ICTY definitional orientation was adopted despite the fact that the 1993 Report of the Secretary-General Pursuant to Paragraph 2 of Security Council Resolution 808 using such a focus had noted (in para. 35) that such crimes had been recognized in the Nuremberg Charter and Control Council Law No. 10 and that the law "which has beyond doubt become part of international customary law . . . is embodied in" the Nuremberg Charter and the Genocide Convention (which contains a special definition of genocide that is part of customary international law and has been adopted in all of the modern international criminal tribunal instruments). Presumably the customary definitions contained in the post–World War II instruments will still guide domestic prosecutions, since they are "beyond doubt" those that are accepted under customary international law that any state has competence to adopt and utilize for criminal or civil sanctions.

Moreover with respect to domestic prosecutions that follow the customary instruments, it should not be possible for an accused to escape accountability for criminal persecutions on the ground that they were not "directed against" a "civilian population" as such or in any other way. First, neither the persecution type of crimes against humanity nor genocide under customary international law has such a limiting phrase. Second, as the UN War Crimes Commission indicated in 1948, even when such a phrase is applicable, "single or isolated acts against individuals may be considered to fall outside" the phrase

(United Nations War Crimes Commission, p. 193). Thus it is the commission of an act against ("committed against" or "done against") civilians that is covered and not merely the intentional targeting of civilians as such ("directed against"). Even the slightly higher threshold of criminal intent is met, however, when civilians are targeted. With respect to single acts, it is arguable that commission of one act injuring one victim fits the definition if there is an intent thereby to act against or to target other civilians (such as in the case of a terroristic murder or inhumane act against an instrumental target with the object of producing intense fear or anxiety in a primary target involving other civilians). The same double or terroristic-type targeting may also exist with respect to certain persecutions. Moreover merely using the plural "persecutions" does not answer the question of whether one persecution is sufficient because the definitions also refer to crimes in the plural ("crimes" against humanity, and thus "persecutions" can constitute "crimes").

It should be noted that the 1993 Report of the Secretary-General stated that crimes against humanity are "inhumane" and "very serious." But such labels do not appear in Article 5 of the ICTY statute, nor are they general elements of the offense or limiting criteria for all types of crimes against humanity. Therefore neither the ICTY nor domestic tribunals applying customary definitions need to entertain a defense claim that some relevant acts were not really "inhumane" or "very serious."

THE WIDESPREAD OR SYSTEMATIC LIMITATION

The 1993 Report of the Secretary-General noted that some crimes against humanity were part of a "widespread" or "systematic" attack. But these words had not been considered required elements of the crime that prosecutors must prove, and they do not appear in Article 5 of the ICTY statute. Clearly also the words "serious," "widespread," and "systematic" appear in none of the customary charters or formulations noted above, nor do they exist in the definition of genocide contained in the Genocide Convention and modern international criminal tribunal instruments. Similarly the phrase "widespread or systematic" does not exist in international criminal law instruments that recognize other special forms of crimes against humanity, such as apartheid and the forced disappearance of persons. However, the crime of "apartheid" requires proof of a purpose to "systematically" oppress a "racial group of persons," and although the customary international crime of forced disappearance is not limited by words such as "serious," "widespread," or "systematic," the international community has indicated that "the systematic practice" of such a crime "constitutes a crimes against humanity." Here it should be noted that the customary crime of forced disappearance involves secret detention when there has been a refusal to disclose either the name or the whereabouts of the detained person and the detainee has been deprived of his or her freedom by agents of the state or persons or groups acting with the authorization, support, or acquiescence of the state. A prime example of forced disappearance was U.S. President George W. Bush's admitted "program" of "secret detention" of alleged terrorist and security suspects.

Nevertheless, such phrases sometimes appear in opinions of the ICTY and in connection with particular cases or as occasional rhetorical flourishes. They are at times descriptive of actual events or partly poetic, but such expressions should not be confused with required elements of the general crime under customary international law. It should not be a defense to customary crimes against humanity that an individual's acts were not "systematic" or "widespread." These are not defenses to genocide, slavery, forced disappearance, or more general human rights violations, nor do they appear as elements or defenses in the customary international instruments. The Appeals Chamber of the ICTY recognized in the *Kristić* case that the existence of a plan or policy is not required for crimes against humanity or genocide. However, several ICTY cases have required that relevant conduct be engaged in connection with or be "related to" a widespread or systematic attack on civilians and that the accused know that there is such an attack and that his or her act is part of or "related to" such an overall process.

The 1994 Statute of the International Criminal Tribunal for Rwanda (ICTR) adopted a restrictive approach that limits the jurisdictional reach of the ICTR and the accountability of those prosecuted in the tribunal concerning crimes against humanity. Article 3 of the ICTR statute, like the ICTY statute, fuses the two basic types together (inhumane acts against civilians and persecutions) and also addresses merely those acts that are "part of a widespread or systematic attack against any civilian population." Why this far more limited form of crimes against humanity was utilized has not been explained— perhaps because it is known that international tribunals simply cannot prosecute all crimes against humanity that occur even during a single but sustained outbreak. In any event the ICTR statute limits the types of crimes against

humanity that can be prosecuted before the ICTR. Even then the decision of the ICTR in the *Akayesu* case recognized crimes against humanity involving as few as three, five, and eight direct victims.

More generally nearly all international crimes can occur at one time, at the hands of one public or private perpetrator, and can involve merely a few direct victims. Political persecution, religious persecution, and racial persecution are not less significant than nearly all other international crimes. Yet thresholds of accountability in even newer international criminal tribunals are more limited than those based in customary law reflected in the charters of the IMTs at Nuremberg and Tokyo, Control Council Law No. 10, and the 1950 Nuremberg Principles because they do not cover persecution of all types of persons or inhumane acts and persecutions that are not widespread or systematic.

THE LIMITED JURISDICTION OF THE INTERNATIONAL CRIMINAL COURT

The Rome Statute of the International Criminal Court (ICC) restricts the ability of the ICC to address all forms of crimes against humanity. Article 7(1) of the statute begins the definitional approach to crimes against humanity that are within the jurisdiction of the court with the phrase "for purposes of this Statute," thereby indicating that the definitional approach is limited to the reach of ICC jurisdiction under its statute and is not meant to define crimes against humanity for other purposes. More generally Article 10 and Article 22, paragraph 3 supplement this point. Article 10 reads, "Nothing in this Part shall be interpreted as limiting or prejudicing in any way existing or developing rules of international law for purposes other than this Statute." Article 22, paragraph 3 states that the requirement that a crime be within the jurisdiction of the court at the time it takes place "shall not affect the characterization of any conduct as criminal under international law independently of this Statute."

Nevertheless, Article 7, paragraph 1 severely restricts ICC jurisdiction to crimes against humanity involving certain listed acts that are "committed as part of a widespread or systematic attack directed against any civilian population, with knowledge of the attack." Article 7, paragraph 2(a) further limits jurisdiction before the ICC by defining an "attack" to require "a course of conduct involving the multiple commission of [listed] acts . . . pursuant to or in furtherance of a State or organizational policy to commit such attack." An organizational policy can be that of a private organization, but not all private perpetrator attacks are covered. At least a particular crime need not itself be widespread or systematic to be within the jurisdictional competence of the ICC.

Apartheid is one of the listed acts in Article 7, paragraph 1, but it is defined much more narrowly than in the Apartheid Convention by requiring that it be committed "in the context of an institutionalized regime." Article 2 of the Apartheid Convention is not so limited, and Article 1 recognizes that any form of "apartheid is a crime against humanity." Therefore a comparison with Article 7, paragraph 1 of the ICC statute further demonstrates that the crimes against humanity in the ICC statute are of a more limited sort than those under customary international law. Similarly the customary crime of forced disappearance of persons is one of the listed acts in Article 7, paragraph 1, but it is defined more narrowly than in other instruments by requiring that forced disappearance occur "for a prolonged period of time"—thereby also demonstrating the point that ICC jurisdiction over customary crimes against humanity is limited.

Nonetheless, some of the types of acts that can be part of a crime against humanity under Article 7, paragraph 1 of the ICC statute have been expanded beyond "rape" to include "sexual slavery, enforced prostitution, forced pregnancy, enforced sterilization, or any other form of sexual violence of comparable gravity." Types of "persecution" have also been expanded beyond political, racial, or religious persecution to include that on "national, ethnic, cultural, . . . gender [as defined], or other grounds that are universally recognized as impermissible under international law," which would include human rights law. Yet a clause in the ICC statute severely limits "inhumane" acts that appear in the customary instruments to "inhumane acts of a similar character [to the other acts listed in Article 7, paragraph 1] intentionally causing great suffering, or serious injury to body or to mental or physical health"—thereby demonstrating another instance where the jurisdiction of the ICC does not reach all customary crimes against humanity. This may not be unusual, however, given the fact that the ICC was meant to engage in limited forms of prosecution of limited numbers of individuals, and it is understood that the primary forums for effective prosecution of international crimes remain those within the states of the international community. It should be noted, however, that some writers assert that new customary international law is reflected in the limits set forth in the ICC statute, an argument that would have to rest on the two elements

necessary for the formation of customary law: general patterns of new *opinio juris*, or expectation that something is legally appropriate or required, and general patterns of practice. Some are also concerned that use of the broad definitions under the post–World War II instruments would lead to an overly extensive jurisdiction of states.

SOME SEVERELY LIMITED DOMESTIC CODES AND PRACTICES

Another potentially restrictive definition of crimes against humanity appears in the Canadian Crimes against Humanity and War Crimes Act (sec. 4(3), SC 2000, c. 24). It fuses the two types recognized at Nuremberg into one, requiring that the act or omission be "committed against any civilian population or any identifiable group of persons." Clearly such a requirement does not comply with customary definitions, since not all types must be committed against a civilian population or group of persons. It appears then that accountability since Nuremberg and uniform application of international criminal law are endangered by some forms of imperfect domestic legislation.

The problem is exacerbated by loose rhetoric found in some domestic judicial opinions. While addressing the Canadian law in the 1994 *Regina v. Finta* case, Justice Peter Cory of the Supreme Court of Canada regularly added phrases or descriptions that should not mistakenly be considered as elements of the general crime. Among the phrases used by Cory that are clearly absent from the customary international instruments and that do not reflect elements or limitations under international law are the following: "so grave that they shock the conscience of all right-thinking people"; "cruel and terrible actions which are the essential elements"; "grievous"; "stigma . . . must . . . [be] overwhelming . . . [and have] particularly heavy public opprobrium"; "high degree of moral outrage"; "untold misery"; "immense suffering"; "barbarous cruelty"; "requisite added dimension of cruelty and barbarism"; and the "element of inhumanity must be demonstrated" (*Regina v. Finta*, 1 S.C.R. 701 [1994]). Though critical of some of these phrases, Justice Gerard La Forest stated in dissent that such crimes "obviously involve moral culpability," and the conduct before him "strikes one as morally vile and inexcusable." It is through such limiting efforts that victims of crimes against humanity are betrayed. Unless Canada changes its legislation or such severely limiting interpretations of its law, it will remain unable to fulfill its obligations under customary international law to enact appropriate legislation and to initiate prosecution of those reasonably accused of relevant international crimes if it does not extradite them to another country or render them to an appropriate international criminal tribunal, an obligation captured in part in the phrase *aut dedere aut judicare* (hand over or adjudicate).

The French Cour de Cassation or Constitutional Court was potentially no less misleading in the case of the Nazi officer Klaus Barbie in 1985 when stating that "inhumane acts and persecution committed in a systematic manner in the name of the state practicing a policy of ideological supremacy" constitute crimes against humanity (*Fédération Nationale des Déportes et Internes Résistants et Patriots v. Barbie* [1985] 78 ILR 125). In context the court may not have sought to limit accepted definitions but to highlight the point that the stated acts will fit within the definition of the general crime. Under international law, it is evident that crimes against humanity, including genocide and slavery, simply do not need to be systematic or part of state policy. They can be sporadic or unorganized and engaged in by private perpetrators.

Addressing subsequent trends in France, Leila Nadya Sadat has written that "when articulated by the Court of Cassation in the *Barbie* case, it was unclear what the judges were driving at with this language, which cannot, of course, be found anywhere in Article 6(c) or elsewhere in the IMT Charter or judgment" ("The Interpretation of the Nuremberg Principles," p. 359). In an apt and highly critical summary of developments, including the more recent *Touvier* cases, she added:

> Unfortunately, however, the language of this decision later came to stand for several propositions: first, that the perpetrator must have as his mental intent both an intent to hurt the victim and an intent to attack the group to which the victim belongs (as evidenced by the attack of the victim); second, that only if the perpetrator (i) carried out his crimes on behalf of a State and (ii) that State was one practicing a hegemonic political ideology, could the perpetrator's act or acts be characterized as crimes against humanity. Both propositions are foreign to Article 6(c) and are arguably erroneous. (Sadat, "The Interpretation of the Nuremberg Principles," p. 359)

Such erroneous limitations of accountability, she notes, were extended in 1988, when the court, "in its final word in the *Barbie* case," added a requirement (also erroneous) "that the defendant must intend to further a 'common plan' of a state practicing a hegemonic political ideology" (Sadat, "The Interpretation of the Nuremberg Principles," p. 361). Finally, the French legislature passed a 1992 law containing an improper definition of genocide and its own severely limiting definition of crimes against humanity—ominously deleting "persecution" as such, requiring a common plan and acts organized in carrying it out, and requiring acts "against a civil population group." Despite such severely limiting approaches, actual crimes against humanity in the *Barbie* case involved as few as one, three, seven, eleven, thirty, and forty-four direct victims. Paul Touvier was convicted of being an accomplice to crimes against humanity involving merely the deaths of seven persons.

In contrast, the 1973 Bangladesh International Crimes (Tribunals) Act provided definitions of crimes against humanity and genocide that generally reflected customary international law. In particular the 1973 definition of crimes against humanity retained the two basic types and generally retained the language from the World War II era. The Australian War Crimes Amendment Act of 1988 was preferable to the French legislation. Although it used a limiting phrase, "serious crime," the 1988 act contained two separate categorizations of crime relating to "persecution" and to "intent to destroy, in whole or in part, a national, ethnic, racial or religious group, as such" (sec. 7, para. 3[a]), the latter reflecting part of the definitional orientation regarding genocide. Another section also incorporated crimes against humanity "under international law" as a limit to any claimed defenses by an accused.

The United States has no legislation allowing prosecution of crimes against humanity as such, and this can limit U.S. options with respect to prosecution and extradition. For example, if the United States prefers that a U.S. or foreign national accused be extradited to the United States, the requested state could refuse to extradite because of the lack of dual criminality (that is, because the offense is not a crime under the domestic laws of each state). Similarly the United States could not obtain jurisdiction over a U.S. national who is subject to the jurisdiction of the ICC for an alleged crime against humanity under the principle of complimentarity (which would otherwise ensure a primacy for U.S. prosecution under a U.S. law addressing crimes against humanity). Because Supreme Court cases addressing federal statutes that allow prosecution of piracy and war crimes have recognized the constitutional propriety of incorporating international law "by reference" (that is, by merely referring to relevant international law without defining the crime or identifying its elements), a U.S. statute could simply state:

Crimes against Humanity.

(a) Whoever commits a crime against humanity as defined by customary international law shall be fined not more than $10,000,000, or imprisoned not more than fifty years, or both, unless subsection (b) is applicable.

(b) Whoever commits such an offense in such a way that the death of another human being results therefrom shall be subject to a penalty of life imprisonment.

(c) Whoever commits such an offense shall be liable to pay actual and punitive damages to any victim of such an offense and whoever is alleged to have committed such an offense shall not be entitled to any form of immunity from civil remedies.

Given the number of prior and predictable accused, even with the creation of a new permanent ICC, humankind will remain dependent on national prosecutions for adequate enforcement of international criminal law. From the above it is evident that domestic laws and prosecutorial efforts need to be consistent with the prohibitions of crimes against humanity under customary international law. The same conformity needs to occur with respect to domestic laws that allow victims of crimes against humanity to obtain civil remedies. Some believe that the UN secretary-general should become more directly involved in efforts to end impunity and to assure compliance with customary international standards in domestic laws. Also some suggest that the International Law Commission could recommend the creation of an entity charged with the study of domestic laws for criminal and civil sanctions, one that is also charged with the power to receive reports on domestic legislation and prosecutions from members of the UN and to make suggestions to states. Since fundamental human rights and norms jus cogens are at stake, the UN Human Rights Council could also initiate such a study and implementary effort.

As far back as 1973, a resolution of the UN General Assembly on principles of international cooperation in the detention, arrest, extradition, and punishment of persons guilty of war crimes and crimes against humanity stressed several duties of states to cooperate in bringing those reasonably accused to justice. In particular the resolution expressed the expectation that "wherever they are committed, [such crimes] shall be subject to investigation and the persons . . . [reasonably accused] shall be subject to tracing, arrest, trial and, if found guilty, to punishment" (GA Res. 3074 [XXVIII]). In other resolutions it was affirmed that a refusal "to cooperate in the arrest, extradition, trial and punishment" of such persons is contrary to the UN Charter "and to generally recognized norms of international law" (GA Res. 2840 [XXVI]). More recently the international community affirmed in the preamble to the Rome Statute of the ICC that "effective prosecution" of core crimes, such as crimes against humanity, "must be assured by taking measures at the national level and by enhancing international cooperation," that the community is "determined to put an end to impunity for the perpetrators" of such crimes, and "that it is the duty of every State to exercise its criminal jurisdiction over those responsible for international crimes."

POLITICAL OPPRESSION

One form of crimes against humanity has direct relevance to human rights of individuals to participate in a democratic political process and to the related right of self-determination of peoples. It is the crime against humanity—addressed in the charters of the IMTs at Nuremberg and Tokyo, Control Council Law No. 10, and the Nuremberg Principles—that occurs when individuals are persecuted on the basis of their political opinions. Attacks on "political" groups that are motivated by, or result in, political oppression of such persons can be criminally sanctioned as a crime against humanity. In the early twenty-first century such attacks were also necessarily violations of the precept of self-determination and fundamental human rights of individuals to freedom from discrimination on the basis of political opinion and to participate in a democracy or an authoritative political process that the Universal Declaration of Human Rights recognizes as one based on the "will of the people." As such, attacks on political groups constitute politicide, a violation of the UN Charter (with respect to both self-determination and human rights), and what the International Law Commission has recognized as a crime against self-determination. With respect to opposition to political oppression, it is important to recall that states have a duty under Articles 55(c) and 56 of the UN Charter to take joint and separate action to achieve "universal respect for, and observance of, human rights and fundamental freedoms." Of related interest, in 2005 the UN General Assembly recognized that every state "has the responsibility to protect its populations from genocide, war crimes, ethnic cleansing and crimes against humanity" (A/Res/60/1, 2005, para. 138).

ASSESSMENT

Customary law defines crimes against humanity in a broader manner than the instruments limiting modern international criminal tribunals. This is partly understandable since modern international tribunals do not have the purpose or resources to prosecute all persons who are reasonably accused of having committed crimes against humanity. However, the limiting definitional approaches used in such tribunals should not form the basis for domestic legislation designed to reach crimes against humanity. Certain domestic codes and practices are more narrow than the broad definitions found in customary international law. The international community needs to assure that domestic definitions and prosecutorial efforts reflect and not deny customary international law.

Words that should not appear in any appropriate definition of crimes against humanity or as limits of responsibility include "serious," "widespread," "systematic," "large-scale," "deliberate policy," "grave," "cruel," "terrible," "grievous," "misery," "suffering," "barbarous," "vile," "state policy," "on behalf of a state," "state ideology," "common plan," and "substantial part." Also the two forms of crimes against humanity recognized at Nuremberg should not be fused into one more limited crime regarding inhumane acts against civilians, thereby excluding persecution of military personnel. Additionally the customary international instruments remain as background for interpretation or incorporation by reference with respect to any relevant domestic laws or international statutes that are not expressly limited. Where no relevant domestic law exists or where limiting laws exist, appropriate legislation should be enacted to assure an ability to prosecute all forms of crimes against humanity, thus ending any form of impunity that functions in the absence of adequate legislation and a broader reach within the international criminal tribunals.

[*See also* Criminal Justice: International Criminal Justice; Ethnic Cleansing; Genocide; Holocaust; International Criminal Court; International Criminal Tribunal for Rwanda (ICTR); International Criminal Tribunal for the Former Yugoslavia (ICTY); Nuremberg and Tokyo Trials; Torture: International Law; United Nations Commission on Crime Prevention and Criminal Justice; Universal Declaration of Human Rights; *and* Weapons of Mass Destruction.]

BIBLIOGRAPHY

Bassiouni, M. Cherif. *Crimes against Humanity in International Criminal Law.* 2d ed. The Hague, Netherlands: Kluwer Law International, 1999.

Paust, Jordan J. *Beyond the Law: The Bush Administration's Unlawful Responses in the "War" on Terror.* Cambridge, U.K., and New York: Cambridge University Press, 2007.

Paust, Jordan J., M. Cherif Bassiouni, Michael Scharf, Jimmy Gurule, Leila Sadat, and Bruce Zagaris. *International Criminal Law: Cases and Materials.* 3d ed. Durham, N.C.: Carolina Academic, 2007.

Sadat, Leila Nadya. *The International Criminal Court and the Transformation of International Law: Justice for the New Millennium.* New York: Transnational, 2002.

Sadat, Leila Nadya. "The Interpretation of the Nuremberg Principles by the French Court of Cassation: From Touvier to Barbie and Back Again." *Columbia Journal of Transnational Law* 32, no. 1 (1994): 289–380.

United Nations War Crimes Commission. *History of the United Nations War Crimes Commission.* London: H.M. Stationery Office, 1948.

CRIMINAL JUSTICE

INTERNATIONAL CRIMINAL JUSTICE

by David P. Forsythe

The present entry is a framework essay; it contains only a brief description. Its purpose is to refer the reader to other entries in this encyclopedia dealing with the specific courts, principles, and issues that make up the general subject known as international criminal justice. Since the other entries present appropriate detail, there is no need to repeat those specifics here.

OVERVIEW

International criminal justice refers to the prosecution of individuals for certain crimes as defined initially in international law. Today this refers primarily to genocide, crimes against humanity, war crimes, torture, and possibly crimes against peace (such as waging wars of aggression). [*See* Crimes against Humanity; Genocide; *and* Humanitarian Law (or the laws of war, which may give rise to war crimes).]

Contemporary international and internationalized criminal courts all allow prosecution for genocide, crimes against humanity, and war crimes. They do not provide for jurisdiction over charges of aggression. The partial exception is found in the International Criminal Court, whose Rome Statute, a foundational treaty, allows for jurisdiction over charges of aggression when in the future that concept is precisely negotiated by states. [*See* International Criminal Court.] This is an admission that current statements in international law about aggression or breach of the peace are too vague to provide a proper basis for judicial decisions regarding individual responsibility.

The rest of this entry focuses mainly on international and internationalized criminal courts since 1945, with some attention to the principle of universal jurisdiction as practiced by national legal authorities. [*See* Universal Jurisdiction.] Thus we will analyze in a very general way the contemporary process of holding individuals legally accountable for serious violations of international human rights law and international humanitarian law—the latter being special laws for armed conflict, also called the laws of war.

This entry deals with holding individuals legally accountable for their decisions and actions, which should not be confused with state responsibility under international law. State responsibility for violations of human rights and humanitarian law is dealt with sometimes by the UN Security Council and the International Court of Justice (ICJ, or World Court), by the treaty-monitoring bodies that supervise implementation of the treaties, and by the UN Human Rights Council, which replaced the UN Commission on Human Rights in 2006. [*See* Civil and Political Rights: International Covenant on Civil and Political Rights; Economic, Social, and Cultural Rights: International Covenant on Economic, Social, and Cultural Rights; International Court of Justice; Racial Discrimination Convention; Torture: Convention against Torture; United Nations Human Rights Council; United Nations Security Council; *and* Women: Convention on the Elimination of Discrimination against Women.] For example, in the ICJ, the principal judicial arm of the UN system, states are the petitioners and defendants. That is, regarding binding judgments, the court is only open to states. In the criminal courts discussed here, the cases are brought by international prosecutors, and the defendants are individuals. There are also regional international courts that deal with state responsibility for human rights violations. [*See* African Union: Commission and Court on Human Rights; European Convention on Human Rights and Fundamental Freedoms (Council of Europe); European Social Charter; European Union; *and* Organization of American States.]

BACKGROUND—NUREMBERG AND TOKYO

There were no international criminal trials after World War I; there was discussion in some circles about prosecuting Kaiser Wilhelm II, the emperor of Germany, but the Netherlands granted him asylum. The British talked about possible trials for crimes against humanity of Ottoman officials regarding their treatment of ethnic Armenians in the Ottoman Empire. But eventually the British, seeking the return of POWs held by the Turks, chose not to complicate that return by pursuing legal justice for the Turkish authorities. [*See* Armenians in the Ottoman Empire.]

Revolutionary developments in this domain occurred after World War II, developments that were tainted by questions about due process and victor's justice, but still provided the foundation for later—and more proper—criminal proceedings. German leaders from both government and industry were tried at Nuremberg, and Japanese leaders were tried at Tokyo. [*See* Holocaust; Japanese Atrocities in the 1930s and 1940s; Nanjing Massacre; *and* Nuremberg and Tokyo Trials.]

The United States took a leadership role in the Nuremberg and Tokyo Trials, yet at the same time the United States was striking deals with German and Japanese weapons experts, seeking their cooperation in the coming Cold War in return for exemption from criminal prosecution for possible crimes or complicity in crimes.

This is an example of the difficult choices involved in transitional justice—what is the just decision to make after wars and atrocities? Should one always emphasize criminal prosecution, or is it just to grant amnesties and otherwise avoid the issue of individual criminal liability, considering the larger context? [*See* Transitional Justice *and* Transitions to Democracy and Rule of Law.]

In any event, the United States and the three other major victorious powers in World Word II—the United Kingdom, France, and Russia—proceeded with the Nuremberg Trials despite charges of "victors' justice" and other irregularities. The Tokyo Trials were characterized by more international involvement, but here too there were various irregularities—so much so that several judges issued stinging dissents from the bench.

In addition to the major trials, which resulted in the death penalty for several German and Japanese defendants convicted of either war crimes, crimes against humanity, or aggression, subsequent criminal trials in Germany dealt with many lower-ranking officials. (The Genocide Treaty was only approved in 1948; genocide was not an international crime in 1945.)

THE GAP: 1945–1992

After Nuremberg and Tokyo there were no international criminal courts created for almost five decades. The Cold War in particular prevented easy agreement on how to manage world order in keeping with human rights and the rule of law. The "North-South" conflict, centered on decolonization, was also often brutally contested, all too often with scant regard for individual human rights and independent courts. [*See* North-South Views on Human Rights.]

Many conflicts, including armed conflicts like the Korean War, ended without clear winners and losers, and without the kind of documentary evidence that could lead to conviction in a court of law. Some conflicts that did end decisively did not result in internationally sanctioned criminal proceedings, such as in Hungary in 1956 or Grenada in 1982.

Each of the coalitions in the three-way struggle for power in international relations—East, West, and South—considered the contest too important for effective regulation by international law. Each coalition relied on its own conception of political morality, which often trumped international law. The East saw itself as struggling for human emancipation from capitalist exploitation. [*See* Karl J. Marx.] The West appealed to defense of freedom against Communist tyranny. [*See* Helsinki Accord and CSCE/OSCE *and* Demise of Soviet Communism.] The South gave priority to national liberation from crushing colonialism and neocolonialism. [*See* Algerian War; Belgian Congo; Colonialism; *and* Namibia: Germany's Colonial Wars against the Herero and Nama.]

INTERNATIONAL CRIMINAL COURTS REDISCOVERED

By the end of the Cold War (1989–1991), the decolonization process had been completed with the withdrawal of Portugal from Angola and Mozambique in the 1970s. In the UN Security Council in the early 1990s, the East-West conflict was over, and the North-South conflict, although not over in political terms, was not terribly disruptive in that body—if only because China alone was likely to exercise its veto on behalf of third world causes.

For these and other reasons, the Security Council created two new international criminal courts—for the former Yugoslavia in 1993, and then for Rwanda in 1994. Each was mandated to try major offenders who were responsible for genocide, crimes against humanity, or war crimes. [*See* International Criminal Tribunal for Rwanda (ICTR); International Criminal Tribunal for the Former Yugoslavia (ICTY); *and* United Nations Security Council.]

Initially, there were reasons to be skeptical about the success of these courts; they were created as much out of political face-saving as out of a commitment to human rights and rule of law. To a significant extent, the ICTY was created so that the Western states could show that they were doing something about the atrocities of the Balkan Wars of 1992–1995, while lessening the pressure on these states to commit ground troops to end the carnage. [See Balkan Wars and Humanitarian Intervention: Overview.] Creation of the ICTY showed some initiative, if not decisive and firm action. The ICTR was created after outside parties had failed to intervene decisively to stop the Rwandan genocide. [See Humanitarian Intervention: Policy Making and Rwanda.] Having created the ICTY in Europe, the Security Council would have had a hard time justifying not creating the ICTR in Africa.

Each court functioned for roughly fifteen years, facing various problems and achieving some accomplishments—primarily convicting some individuals for heinous acts, taking some of the leadership of disruptive movements out of circulation, and developing and refining various legal concepts and doctrines. Whether the courts could have a calming impact on their regions by promoting progressive politics and regional peace based on reconciliation is an important question that might take more than one generation to answer. Certain prosecutors had proven dynamic. [See Louise Arbour; Carla Del Ponte; and Richard J. Goldstone.]

If the ICTY and ICTR were created less out of a deep and strategic commitment to a rights-protective world order, and more out of crisis management or the political correctness of the day, then there may be unintended consequences stemming from this approach; decisions based on short-term calculation can have unintended long-term consequences. The United States led in the creation of the ICTY and supported the creation of the ICTR. Shortly thereafter, it was faced with a movement to create a permanent international criminal court, as were China and Russia, and indeed all states. The ICTY and ICTR were ad hoc, created for particular situations, with Security Council–created mandates limited by both time and geography. This was a fairly comfortable process for outside states, which were not subject to the jurisdiction of these courts at the time of creation. (Ironically, when the United States and other NATO states undertook a bombing campaign against Serbia in 1999, ostensibly to stop the forced displacement of ethnic Albanians from the province of Kosovo, NATO member states put themselves under ICTY authority. Since the bombing took place in the territory of the former Yugoslavia, allegations of NATO war crimes properly fell within the jurisdiction of the court.) [See Balkan Wars; Ethnic Cleansing; Humanitarian Intervention: Overview; and North Atlantic Treaty Organization.]

Several like-minded states and a host of nonstate actors, including many human rights nongovernmental organizations, wanted a standing criminal court with no geographical or time limitations. The United States, and perhaps even China and Russia, might have supported such a development as long as it was the UN Security Council (where five states held veto authority) that initiated cases. But in 1998, when states meeting in Rome negotiated a new International Criminal Court (ICC), they refused to defer to U.S. wishes on this point. From that time, the United States not only refused to join the ICC, which began to function in 2002, but actually for a time tried to kill the court through various pressures. China and Russia, along with other important states like India, Indonesia, and Israel, also refused to accept the new court. [See International Criminal Court.]

Nonetheless, though its origins lay in short-term crisis management in 1993, by 2008 the ICC existed and initiated its first case, involving Thomas Lubanga, a militia leader from the Democratic Republic of Congo. [See Democratic Republic of Congo.] The prosecutor had opened several other investigations, including one concerning the very difficult situation in Uganda. [See Luis Moreno-Ocampo and Uganda.] Subsequent ICC investigations produced indictments of individuals in the Central African Republic and also Sudan. More than one hundred states had ratified the Rome Statute creating the court, including all NATO members except Turkey and the United States. And by 2006 even the Bush administration was no longer trying to kill the court and was cooperating with the court as long as the court focused on alleged crimes in places like the Darfur region of Sudan, where Washington assumed no U.S. citizens could be charged with crimes under ICC jurisdiction. [See Darfur.]

INTERNATIONALIZED CRIMINAL COURTS

In addition to international criminal courts, there are internationalized criminal courts. These are courts that were approved by some international process, usually a vote in the UN Security Council, but whose judges and rules of operation are partially national and not fully international. Thus criminal courts in Sierra Leone, Cambodia, East Timor, and Lebanon were made up of both national and expatriate (outside) judges, but operated under international approval. [See Cambodia; Indonesia; and Sierra Leone.] In Kosovo, then a province of Serbia but under international administration, there was a special war crimes chamber that functioned under UN supervision.

UNIVERSAL JURISDICTION

International criminal justice can also be seen as including the principle of universal jurisdiction as exercised by national authorities. Some crimes are considered so heinous, so shocking to the civilized world, that national authorities are authorized to prosecute alleged perpetrators regardless of the place of the crime or the nationality of the defendant. It is very clear in international law that, with regard to human rights, genocide, crimes against humanity, major war crimes, and torture are properly linked to the principle of universal jurisdiction. [See National Courts.] From about 1995, a variety of national courts have exercised universal jurisdiction, with Belgian courts trying Rwandans and German courts trying Serbs, for examples.

The process is well demonstrated by the remarkable Pinochet case. While Augusto Pinochet, the former Chilean head of state, was in the United Kingdom for medical treatment in 1998, he was served with legal papers issued by a Spanish legal official, requesting that the United Kingdom extradite him to Spain to stand trial for the torture of various persons, including Spanish nationals, in Chile. [See Chile in the Pinochet Era.] The relevant British court held that under the UN Convention against Torture, to which the United Kingdom was a party, it was legal for Pinochet to be extradited to Spain. British authorities then decided to return Pinochet to Chile for "humanitarian" reasons in light of his age and health. (Pinochet had strong supporters among British politicians, including former Prime Minister Margaret Thatcher.) Even though Pinochet ultimately did not stand trial in Spain, the British judgment demonstrated Pinochet's individual liability in principle to face charges in various states under the Convention against Torture, as a point of law. This point is probably not lost on other former national leaders who could face similar legal proceedings, and who probably now carefully calculate where they travel. The Pinochet case made clear that having served as a government official, even as head of state, did not provide sovereign immunity against complaints about certain gross violations of human rights (and humanitarian law). Thus, for a former head of state, claims to the protection of state sovereignty did not trump trial for possible responsibility for these gross violations.

ASSESSMENT

Since 1993 the international community, building on the Nuremberg and Tokyo Trials as precedents, has resurrected the idea of international criminal justice. The field of international relations is much changed because of these developments.

International criminal justice has now given rise to many studies about its strengths and weaknesses. There is also the very important question, noted already, of the merits of criminal justice, either national or international, as opposed to other forms of social justice, such as truth commissions, apologies, reparations, lustration (barring former officeholders from public office), and so forth. International criminal justice and transitional justice are now fixtures in many discussions of international relations.

CUBA UNDER CASTRO

by Mayra Gómez

Even long after the end of the Cold War, Cuba under Castro's rule remains a heavily politicized topic. On the one hand, some anti-Castro Cuban exiles and right-wing politicos have condemned Cuba's long-time (and now former) President Fidel Castro as a tyrant, a larger-than-life despot who considered no act of repression too brutal or too vicious to crush his political detractors. At the same time, others further to the left of the political spectrum view Castro as an anti-imperialist visionary and as a defiant leader who championed the rights of the world's poor: a veritable twentieth-century David versus the Goliath of U.S. hegemony. To be sure, Castro still remains at the crossroads of a global political discourse of the twentieth (and now also twenty-first) century, even now some fifty years after he first came to power following the 1959 Cuban Revolution.

The truth about Cuba, however, transcends political sloganeering and simple Cold War dichotomies. This article looks primarily at the issue of the status of human rights in Cuba from 1959 until late in the first decade of the twenty-first century. Indeed, Cuba's human rights record under Castro has been dreary, sometimes encouraging, and often counterintuitive; yet, it should not be reduced to a political caricature. In fact, since the time of the Cuban Revolution, human rights abuses in Cuba have occurred in cyclical waves, with periods of relative calm followed by periods of intensified governmental crackdown on political dissent. This pattern has been recognized for years by leading international human rights groups, such as Amnesty International and Human Rights Watch, but it is nonetheless at odds with the dominant political discourses that assume there has been little change in Cuba's lagging human rights record. As we shall see, the timing and formation of these waves, when viewed in historical perspective, underscore Cuba's changing position within the international system and the varying degrees of internal and external threats experienced by Castro's government.

Prior to the Cuban Revolution, Cuba's human rights record under its President Fulgencio Batista (who ruled Cuba from 1940 to 1945, and then again from 1952 to 1959, having pulled government strings behind the scenes in the interim) was nothing short of dismal. Batista was largely responsible for opening Cuba to large-scale gambling—attracting affluent tourists to Havana's new-fangled casinos—and at the same time turning a blind eye to bourgeoning organized crime. The Batista regime was equally as corrupt as it was brutal, and Cubans suffered daily human rights abuses, including rampant poverty and illiteracy, mock elections, as well as police brutality with little tolerance for political unrest or dissent. Although it is unclear how many political dissidents were abused under the Batista regime, it appears that killings, political imprisonment, and torture were common. Batista himself came to power via his own dramatic coup d'état, suspending elections and suspending Cuba's constitutional guarantees. While the U.S. government was fond of Batista, ordinary Cubans despised him, and civil unrest grew. Students took to the streets in protest, political discord was palpable, and the 26th of July Movement—which would one day culminate in the 1959 Revolution and the ushering in of a new president, Fidel Castro—began to take shape.

The Cuban Revolution of 1959 toppled the Batista regime, ushering in a new era, and solidifying a new political philosophy. To be sure, there have been volumes of books written on the early days of the Revolution, the intricacies of the 26th of July Movement, and its central characters. While the history itself is fascinating, for the purposes of understanding Cuba's human rights record in historical perspective, it is important to note that the days prior to the Cuban Revolution were bleak in terms of human rights. The story of Castro's reign begins with the triumph of the Cuban Revolution, on 1 January 1959.

EARLY YEARS OF THE REVOLUTION: MEETING TRIUMPH AND CRISIS

Set against the backdrop of the Batista regime, the Cuban Revolution triumphed in an atmosphere of euphoria and—like many revolutions—repression. On the positive side, the Cuban Revolution set into motion a range of social and economic reforms that made health care accessible, raised living standards (particularly for the poorest Cubans), and improved literacy rates. As of 2008, Cuba's literacy rate was 99.8 percent, the average life expectancy was seventy-six years (one of the highest averages in the region), and there was 1 doctor for every 170 citizens. In 2000 UN Secretary-General Kofi Annan praised Cuba's efforts: "Cuba's achievements in social development are impressive given the size of its gross domestic product per capita. As the human development index of the United Nations makes clear year after year, Cuba should be the envy of many other nations, ostensibly far richer. [Cuba] demonstrates how much nations can do with the resources they have if they focus on the right priorities: health, education, and literacy." Indeed, the Cuban government was, and continues to be, praised as an example of a developing nation working to secure the economic and social rights of its people. Its record on civil and political rights, however, has been the terrain of much greater international concern and even condemnation.

The period immediately after the Revolution coincides with the first discernible "wave of repression" in Cuba under Castro. This phenomenon is not uncommon, as political science demonstrates that heightened repression is typical of revolutions and postrevolutionary periods. At that time, some of the most severe forms of political repression—indeed, many of the same tactics of Batista's era—were used to forcibly take control of the island and ensure immediate stability. To be sure, the Revolution had many enemies in its early days, both within Cuba and abroad, and early on the newly empowered authorities moved to stamp out anything that could be deemed counterrevolutionary. This often meant rounding up supporters of the previous Batista regime, imprisoning them, and quite often, executing them. Others tagged with the counterrevolutionary label were political dissidents and critics—even initial supporters of the Revolution who later raised questions about its heavy-handed tactics.

Between 1959 and the mid-1960s, rates of political imprisonment in Cuba were higher than at any other period. At the time, the Cuban government estimated it held some fifteen thousand political prisoners. Evidence that would later surface, however, showed that the actual figure was closer to twenty-five thousand political prisoners. Not only was the number of political prisoners inflated during this period, so too was the length of the sentences that political prisoners routinely received.

Many political dissidents received little more than show trials and were sentenced to fifteen to twenty years in a Cuban prison and sometimes more. At times, political prisoners were even resentenced once their original sentence had been served. Human Rights Watch would later say of this period:

> Obviously, many of the regime's drastic measures came in response to national crisis. In the early 1960s, Cuba was clearly a country under siege, and there were a number of active organizations that were attempting to overthrow the government by violent means. Some of these groups received funding and support from the CIA, while others were splinters of Castro's own movement, driven out by the regime's intolerance for dissent, ideological disputes, and, in some cases, personality conflicts. But the categories were confused. Over the next decade, the regime began to imprison more and more non-violent political dissidents and persons considered to be social misfits, applying the labels of terrorist and CIA infiltrator with less and less discrimination. (HRW, 1986, foreword)

In its early days, the Cuban Revolution had to safeguard itself against some rather serious external threats. The stories of CIA-attempted assassinations staged against Castro (for example, the infamous "exploding cigar" plot) and other counterrevolutionary schemes are today seen as legendary blunders. A U.S. Senate Intelligence Committee report would later list eight CIA-instigated plots against Castro's life during this early period, while Castro himself said there were as many as twenty-four. Under Batista, Cuba and the United States had enjoyed an amicable relationship. Following the Revolution, it became increasingly clear to U.S. policy makers that Castro would not cooperate in the same way Batista had. To the chagrin of many powerful American political and business elites, postrevolutionary Cuba nationalized large amounts of property previously owned by American businesses in 1960 and 1961. Cuba expropriated land from U.S. sugar companies, nationalized the telephone service and the oil refineries, and transferred what had been private real estate to the public sector. Although Castro did not originally characterize the Revolution as either socialist or Communist, shortly after Eisenhower refused to meet with Castro in early 1959, Cuba began to align itself both politically and economically with the arch enemy of the United States during the Cold War: the Soviet Union.

Although many are intrigued, if not bemused, by the CIA's plotting and assorted gaffes, the deeper relevance of these events should not be dismissed. In fact, looking closely at the waves of repression in Cuba, it is clear that these kinds of external events were also directly associated with very specific periods of crackdown or human rights abuse. The Bay of Pigs invasion of 1961, funded by the U.S. government and supported by the CIA, provides a good example of this relationship.

Planning for the Bay of Pigs invasion began shortly after Castro came to power. The idea germinated under U.S. President Eisenhower, upon the recommendation of the CIA, and was later executed during the first months of the Kennedy administration. The strategy was to train and arm Cuban exiles to stage a coup d'état against the Cuban state, forcibly overthrowing Castro and ousting the Revolution's leaders once and for all. Even though the CIA invasion failed to meet its objectives, it caused a flare-up in internal political repression. As the government reeled from the externally orchestrated aggression and worked to neutralize the possibility of destabilization from within, Cuban authorities systematically rounded up individuals from within the country suspected of counterrevolutionary activities and charged them, en masse, with political crimes. Because the revolutionary government was either unable or unwilling to distinguish between domestic or foreign-supported enemies of the state and legitimate political dissidents, both were treated with the same degree of tolerance: zero.

The Cuban missile crisis of 1962, the quintessential Cold War showdown between the Soviet Union and the United States, also threatened Cuba's very existence. That same year, the United States put into place what would become one of the longest running embargoes of all time: the U.S. economic blockade against Cuba. Historically, the blockade has been exceptionally severe because of its inclusion of humanitarian and essential goods, such as food and medicine. Partly because of this, the blockade has been politically contentious, and in recent years, has been widely condemned by the international human rights community. Since its inception, the embargo has been meant to weaken the Cuban economy and to foster internal strife within Cuba: getting ordinary Cubans to revolt against a government that cannot meet the needs of its people.

In the face of this adversity, Cuba took steps to maximize internal stability and increased its own internal repression, relying again on arbitrary detention and political imprisonment. It was during this period that Cuba developed its infamous revolutionary tribunals, which operated independently of the judiciary and which were responsible for processing and sentencing all counterrevolutionary crimes.

To some extent, it is difficult to determine the cause-and-effect relationship—did external threats precede internal repression, or was existing repression the justification of external threat? Although it is difficult to unravel the true causality in every instance, it is certainly clear that the two are related and that many times repression in Cuban was, in fact, a response to external threats. This relationship would emerge again in later years.

A speech given by Castro in 1965 provides commentary on the perceived differences between "counterrevolutionary criminals" and "political criminals":

> We always call counterrevolutionary criminals by the name of counterrevolutionary criminals. The counterrevolutionaries try to call themselves political criminals. And I always remember that the definition of "political criminal" which was most accepted as being correct and which seemed to us to be the most correct was that of a great Spanish penologist, who felt that one could speak of political crimes or of political prisoners only in cases of citizens who acted against political laws in a certain instance in an attempt to establish a better social system, a fairer social system, a more progressive social system, a revolutionary social system; but that those who struggled for a conservative social order, for a reactionary social order, for a retrograde social order, for a return to the past could never deserve to be considered political prisoners or political criminals, that is, with the word "political" included.

The definition itself precluded the idea of legitimate opposition to the Revolution, its leadership, and its tactics.

"INSTITUTIONALIZING" THE REVOLUTION AND IMPROVING RELATIONS WITH THE UNITED STATES

Like many Revolutions, despite its tumultuous beginnings, the Cuban Revolution soon began normalizing daily political life on the island. The decade of the 1970s is widely regarded by scholars as one of "institutionalization" of the Revolution. During this time, Cuba's economic situation improved. While the U.S. embargo remained in effect, Cuba enjoyed strong economic ties with the Soviet Union. By 1972 Cuba had become a full member of the Soviet bloc's common market, and began to receive large shipments of Soviet petroleum. By 1974 global sugar prices had hit a historic high. Because Cuban sugarcane was a mainstay crop, the trading profits enabled Cuba to purchase much-needed industrial and consumer goods. Cuba also maintained trade relationships with other countries, particularly within Latin America, and was steadily integrated into the regional economy despite the objections of the United States. As Cuban historian Alfred Padula wrote of the period: "Good times returned to Cuba."

The bilateral relationship between the United States and Cuba also took a turn for the better. The 1970s were a time of decreased tensions between the two, and there were even some signs that the relationship was normalizing. In 1973 Cuba and the United States signed an antihijacking treaty, a small step toward cooperation. In the mid-1970s some within the U.S. State Department were calling for exploratory conversations with Cuba, presumably aimed at improving relations. In 1975 Henry Kissinger declared that there was "no virtue in perpetual antagonism" between the United States and its island neighbor. The election of Jimmy Carter also changed the dynamic significantly. Although diplomatic relations with Cuba were severed shortly after the Revolution, the Carter administration took the bold step of negotiating with Cuba the opening of mutual "interests sections" in Havana and Washington, D.C. Even though the interests sections were not the equivalent of full diplomatic ties, they were an important improvement and demonstrated the potential of a U.S.-Cuba relationship.

During the institutionalization of the Revolution, organs of the group People's Power were created, which were meant to provide citizens with access to the political process, albeit on the terms of the Cuban Communist Party, which itself held its first congress in 1975. In 1976 a new constitution was adopted by the government, guided by the principles of Marxism-Leninism and dedicated to the advancement of the Revolution. At the local level, People's Power organizations supervised elections and held community meetings on matters of importance (People's Power organizations have also been criticized for a more sinister role, namely as part of the state's repressive machinery—identifying suspected dissidents for the authorities). The new criminal code of 1979 also institutionalized many of the criminal methods used to detain and imprison dissidents. These crimes included "enemy propaganda," "disrespect," defamation," "disobedience," "resistance," "contempt," "public disorder," "sedition," and "clandestine printing."

In 1972 Cuba ratified its first international human rights treaty: the International Convention on the Elimination of All Forms of Racial Discrimination. Most notably, however, in terms of human rights abuses, the 1970s were characterized by rapidly declining rates of political imprisonment within Cuba. Political repression loosened its grip, despite the fact that what many viewed as a repressive government infrastructure was being erected at the time. Amnesty International reported that by 1977, some 20,691 former political prisoners had been released by the Cuban government. In an annual report during that period, Amnesty International noted that "the persistence of fear, real or imagined, of counterrevolutionary conspiracies was primarily responsible for the early excesses in the treatment of political prisoners. By the same token, the removal of that fear has been largely responsible for the improvement in conditions." In 1978 the Cuban government admitted to holding some 4,500 political prisoners and stated that it was prepared to negotiate for the release of many of them. By the end of the year, following historic talks with the Cuban exile community, Cuba agreed to release thirty-six hundred political prisoners, at a rate of four hundred per month starting in December 1978.

REASSERTING POLITICAL CONTROL DURING THE MARIEL BOATLIFT

By the end of the 1970s improvements in U.S.-Cuba relations expanded to include permission for family visits, so that Cuban exiles could finally return to Cuba legally to visit relatives, former neighbors, and friends. By the end of the decade, thousands had returned to visit Cuba. The renewed connections inspired many Cubans to also look for a new life abroad, and thus a wave of illegal migration resulted. In April 1980 a small number of Cubans drove a bus through the gates of the Peruvian Embassy in order to request political asylum. Other attempts were made to force entry into the embassies of Venezuela and Ecuador, as well as the Vatican Legation. After one Cuban guard was killed during the chaos that ensued at the Peruvian Embassy, the Cuban government decided to withdraw its guards from the premises. Within a few days, approximately ten thousand Cubans had gathered there to seek asylum and leave the country.

It was this event that was the precursor to the Mariel Boatlift. Following the fiasco at the Peruvian Embassy, Castro announced the temporary lifting of Cuba's "Illegal Exit Law," saying defiantly that everyone who wanted to leave the island could simply leave. Some 125,000 Cubans piled into ramshackle boats and began a mass migration through the treacherous Florida straits to reach the shores of the United States. Those seeking exit were routinely harassed and intimidated. Pro-government mobs would show up at the homes of suspected exiles to hurl insults and sometimes worse.

At the time, the Carter administration had an "open-arms" policy with respect to immigrants from Cuba, granting them refugee status that ensured non-refoulement. However, the Mariel Boatlift, and the realization that Cuba was placing criminals and mentally-ill persons on boats headed to U.S. shores, quickly changed the policy of the U.S. government toward the migrants. The decision of the Carter administration to "get tough" and no longer grant immediate refugee status to Cubans brought the exodus to a halt.

ENTER RONALD REAGAN: COLD WAR TENSIONS REVISITED

To believe former President Reagan and other fervently anti-Castro voices, one would have to agree that Castro's "red menace" threatened not only Cuba but also the entire Western Hemisphere with his draconian and tyrannical ideology. Looking through independent human rights reports from the period, however, reveals a different story. In reality, despite the exaggerated claims of Gestapo-like repression, during the 1980s Cuba maintained a fairly positive and consistent human rights record: there was even a relative decrease in the rate and severity of kinds of human rights abuses seen in previous periods. In 1980 Cuba ratified its second major international human rights treaty, the Convention on the Elimination of All Forms of Discrimination against Women.

During much of the 1980s, the relationship between Cuba and the United States would again resume its Cold War animosity, hardened in part by the conflict in Angola as well as the activities of other leftist and revolutionary movements in Central America. However, in contrast to the early 1960s, there were no crises comparable to the Cuban missile crisis and no equivalent of the Bay of Pigs invasion. While the Reagan administration's condemnation was stern, it was also mostly symbolic (with the exception of course being the embargo, which remained in effect). Cuba's human rights situation did not deteriorate as it had during other periods when its relationship with the United States had been poor. Perhaps the difference lay, in part, in Cuba's strengthened position in the international system by the 1980s, with continuing strong ties to the Soviet bloc as well as to Latin American counterparts. In addition, Cuba's period of political institutionalization strengthened government institutions and ensured greater internal stability.

THE FALL OF THE SOVIET UNION

The fall of the Soviet Union changed everything for the small island nation of Cuba. In the mid 1980s the Soviet Union began implementing a series of significant political and economic changes, under the names of glasnost (supporting transparency in matter of government) and perestroika (ensuring economic restructuring). At the time, Castro was critical of the reforms, although Cuba's relationship with the United States remained close. The eventual breakup of the former Soviet republics and the collapse of the Soviet economy pulled the rug out from under Cuba's own economy. Cuba's GDP plummeted, unemployment rates soared to unprecedented rates, and export crops took a major hit. In the early 1990s, blackouts were common in Havana. Up until the very end, Cuba had been dependent on the Soviet Union for not only economic aid but also access to international trade markets. The crisis forced Cuba to find its own path in a rapidly changing world and a new global economy.

These economic difficulties were compounded to some extent by continued animosity from the United States. In 1992 the Cuban Democracy Act was signed into law by President George H. W. Bush. That legislation called upon the president to encourage the governments of countries that conduct trade with Cuba to restrict their trade and credit relations. At the signing ceremony in Miami, President Bush noted: "People are choosing liberty all over the world by their votes. The Cuban people deserve no less. That's why this Cuban Democracy Act strengthens our embargo. It will speed the inevitable demise of the Cuban Castro dictatorship. The legislation that I sign today reflects our determination, mine and yours, that the Cuban government will not benefit from U.S. trade or aid until the Cuban people are free. And it reflects another belief: I'm not going to let others prop up Castro with aid or some sweetheart trade deal." A few years later, in 1996, President Clinton signed into law the Helms-Burton Act (named for its chief champions, Republican Senator Jesse Helms and Republican Representative Dan Burton), otherwise known as the Cuban Liberty and Democratic Solidarity Act. The stated purpose of the forty-two-page act was "to seek international sanctions against the Castro government in Cuba, to plan for support of a transition government leading to a democratically elected government in Cuba, and for other purposes." The Helms-Burton Act, which makes it impossible for a U.S. president to end or limit the embargo until the current government falls or "transitions," has been widely criticized as counterproductive by European and other governments.

The economic instability caused by the collapse of the Soviet Union once again plunged Cuba's human rights situation into a downward spiral. Early on in the crisis, Amnesty International noticed that human rights abuses in Cuba were undergoing a change and reported that "whereas in the past [prisoners of conscience] would probably have been charged with state security offenses, such as enemy propaganda, a new pattern seems to be emerging whereby they are being charged with public order offenses." Dissidents were increasingly being charged with new kinds of crimes, and long-term political imprisonment—formerly the main concern of international human rights monitors— took a back seat to short-term detention and repeated harassment. "Rapid response brigades" or "acts of repudiation" subjected political dissidents to intimidation, vandalism, assault, and harassment, sometimes goading them to leave the country. Often, these rapid response brigades would gather outside of the house or the workplace of a perceived counterrevolutionary. Although they were to have the appearance of a spontaneous community protest, these were in fact state-sponsored events, and the police did not intervene to protect those being targeted.

These hardships caused many Cubans to riot against the government for the first time. These riots, similar to the scene at the Peruvian Embassy years before, again resulted in the temporary lifting of Cuba's Illegal Exit Law. In the mid-1990s tens of thousands of Cubans would attempt to leave the country by raft. Most of them were regarded as economic migrants, as opposed to the politically motivated exiles of decades prior, although in reality there was some mixing of the two categories. Most of them were later returned to Cuba after having been intercepted by the U.S. Coast Guard off the coast of Florida.

It was not until several years after the collapse of the Soviet Union that Cuba would begin to regain some of its former stability. Some important human rights accomplishments were made, however. Cuba ratified the Convention on the Rights of the Child in 1991 and the Convention against Torture and Other Cruel, Inhuman, or Degrading Treatment or Punishment in 1995. In the mid-1990s Cuba reopened itself to foreign investment, and the use of U.S. dollars within its domestic economy was legalized. Both of these developments served to stabilize the economy, although the introduction of the U.S. dollar was also widely criticized as creating a two-tiered economy in Cuba as well as a new black market.

In the early 1990s human rights organizations had heavily criticized the repressive tactics of Cuba's rapid response brigades. But by the mid-to late 1990s, human rights organizations reported that the acts of repudiation were much less frequent and that the rapid response brigades were much less active. After the visit of Pope John Paul II in January 1998, the Cuban government took another positive step toward improving its human rights practices, announcing its decision to free 300 political prisoners it still held; 112 were released later. However, Cuba would continue to repress political opposition when it seemed necessary. During the Ibero-American Summit, held in Havana in late 1999, Cuban authorities reportedly detained some 260 dissidents, including human rights advocates, political opponents, and journalists. One month after the detentions, all were released without charges save for eleven people, all of whom were reportedly peaceful opponents of the government.

The arrival of six-year-old Elian Gonzalez in the United States in 1999 once again tested U.S.-Cuba relations and shone a spotlight on the Cuban exile community in Miami. Elian had arrived in the United States after fleeing Cuba with his mother and twelve other Cubans. The boat that had carried them sank in the dangerous waters on the way to Florida, drowning Elian's mother. Young Elian survived by clinging to a small inner tube with two other survivors. Unbeknownst to the boy, he would become the center of a decades-old political rivalry. Hard-line anti-Castro members of the Cuban-American community in Miami went against the tide of international opinion, insisting that Elian remain with his great uncle in the United States, rather than return home to Cuba to live with his father. When the U.S. federal government mandated the return of the boy, the child's relatives in Miami refused to comply. Eventually, Elian was taken by force and was reunited with his father.

At the time the fervent position of some in the Cuban-American community caused the exiles to lose face internationally and to lose some of their political clout domestically. Declining public perception of the Cuban-American community, combined with U.S. business interests accessing Cuba's consumer markets, created some political space in the United States for punching a small but significant hole in the decades-old embargo. A law passed by the U.S. Congress in 2000, signed into law by President Clinton, authorized cash-only purchases of U.S. food and agricultural products as well as medicines for humanitarian purposes. The first purchases were made in

November 2001, and today the United States is one of Cuba's main food suppliers, selling chickens, eggs, rice, beans, corn, and wheat to its island neighbor. Although the relationship is limited, the Cuban market had captured the attention of the U.S. business community; and in the future it is likely that the embargo will continue to wither away. The UN General Assembly has for years called for an end to the U.S. embargo against Cuba, and it continues to call for a complete lifting of the blockade.

A NEW DAY?

In May 2002 former President Jimmy Carter visited Cuba. In Havana, he called for an end to the embargo, saying, "Our two nations have been trapped in a destructive state of belligerence for forty-two years, and it is time for us to change our relationship." Only time will tell how the relationship evolves. And although in 2004 the administration of George W. further restricted travel limitations to and from Cuba (including weight restrictions on registered luggage, family visits reduced to one every three years, and fewer educational and sporting exchanges allowed), these restrictions were relaxed in 2009 under the Obama administration.

The Cuban government has extended invitations for visits to some of the Special Mechanisms on the UN Human Rights Council (formerly the UN Commission on Human Rights) but has also denied others. The personal representative of the UN high Commissioner for human rights on the situation of human rights in Cuba, Christine Chanet (whose mandate recently ended), noted in a 2007 report that although the Cuban government does not recognize her mandate, "Positive aspects must once again be noted in the sphere of economic, social and cultural rights, especially in the areas of education and health, where the Cuban authorities are making major efforts, in particular as regards funding."

At the same time, however, the personal representative recalled the "wave of repression" that was unleashed in March–April 2003 in Cuba, the pretext being the active role played by the United States Interests Section in Havana vis-à-vis the political opposition. Nearly eighty members of civil society were arrested. They were tried and sentenced to prison terms ranging from six to twenty-eight years, either under Article 91 of the Criminal Code, or on the basis of Article 91 combined with the provisions of Act No. 88 on acts "contrary to the independence and integrity of the State." According to the most recent

(2008) Annual Report of Amnesty International, Cuba continues to detain some sixty-two "prisoners of conscience." Still, on International Human Rights Day in 2007, Cuba's Foreign Minister Felipe Pérez Roque announced during a press conference the government's intentions to ratify two of the most important international human rights treaties: the International Covenant on Economic, Social, and Cultural Rights and the International Covenant on Civil and Political Rights. While Cuba has yet to carry this out, on 28 February 2008 Cuba became a signatory to both covenants, and on 2 February 2009 Cuba ratified the International Convention for the Protection of All Persons from Enforced Disappearance.

ASSESSMENT

Cuba's future is a subject of much speculation. After a year in which Fidel Castro looked visibly frail and aging, and in which media conjecture about a post-Castro Cuba ran rampant, the personal representative cautioned, "The tension between Cuba and the United States of America has created a climate which is far from conducive to the development of freedom of expression and freedom of assembly. United States laws and the funding provided for 'building democracy in Cuba' make members of the political opposition on the island appear to be sympathetic to foreign influences and provide the Cuban authorities with an opportunity to tighten repression against them." So for the foreseeable future, it seems that Cuba and the United States will remain joined by the bonds of history. In November 2008, for the sixteenth consecutive year, the UN General Assembly passed a resolution calling on the U.S. government to end its embargo on Cuba. However, at least for the time being, it appears that the embargo will remain in effect under the Obama administration. However, after almost fifty years, support for the embargo within the United States is waning. Even some younger Cuban Americans, who do not always share the political views of their exiled parents, are beginning to question the hard-line approach. In the last presidential election, a majority of these young Cuban Americans voted for Obama.

The era of Castro has come to a close. In 2006 a visibly elderly and frail Fidel Castro transferred his presidential responsibilities to the first vice-president of Cuba, his brother Raul Castro. In 2008 Fidel Castro stepped down from the office permanently, and Cuba's National Assembly elected Raul Castro as the next president of Cuba.

[*See also* José Ayala Lasso; Democracy Promotion; Film; Jacobo Timerman; *and* Organization of American States.]

BIBLIOGRAPHY

Americas Watch. *The Treatment of Political Prisoners in Cuba and the American Response.* New York: Americas Watch, 1983.

Amnesty International. *Amnesty International Annual Report.* London: Amnesty International, 1975–76.

Amnesty International. *Amnesty International Annual Report.* London: Amnesty International, 1979.

Amnesty International. *Cuba: Silencing the Voices of Dissent.* London: Amnesty International, 1992.

Amnesty International News Release. *Cuba: Amnesty International Fears Further Escalation of Repression of Dissidents inside Cuba.* London, Amnesty International, March 1, 1996.

Baloyra, E. A., and J. A. Morris, eds. *Conflict and Change in Cuba.* Albuquerque: University of New Mexico Press, 1993.

Bengelsdorf, C. *The Problem of Democracy in Cuba: Between Vision and Reality.* New York: Oxford University Press, 1994.

Center for International Policy. "Toward Détente with Cuba: Issues and Obstacles," *International Policy Report* 3, no. 3 (1977).

Chanet, C. "Report of the Personal Representative of the United Nations High Commissioner for Human Rights on the Situation of Human Rights in Cuba, Ms. Christine Chanet." UN Doc. A/HRC/4/12 (2007).

Del Aguila, J. M. *Cuba: Dilemmas of a Revolution.* Boulder, Colo.: Westview Press, 1993.

Farber, Samuel. *The Origins of the Cuban Revolution Reconsidered (Envisioning Cuba).* Chapel Hill: University of North Carolina Press, 2006.

Human Rights Watch/Americas. *Twenty Years and Forty Days: Life in a Cuban Prison.* New York: Human Rights Watch, 1986.

Human Rights Watch/Americas. *Tightening the Grip: Human Rights Abuses in Cuba, August 1991–February 1992.* New York: Human Rights Watch, 1992.

Padula, A. "Cuban Socialism: 30 Years of Controversy." In *Conflict and Change in Cuba,* edited by E. A. Baloyra, and J. A. Morris, Albuquerque: University of New Mexico Press, 1993.

Pérez, L. *Cuba and the United States: Ties of Singular Intimacy.* Athens: University of Georgia Press, 1990.

Perez-Stable, M. *The Cuban Revolution: Origins, Course and Legacy.* New York: Oxford University Press, 1998.

CULTURE AND HUMAN RIGHTS

by Yvonne M. Donders

Yanomami Indians in Brazil fighting for protection of their traditional lifestyle; Indians of the Awas Tingni community in Nicaragua claiming the demarcation of their land; Aborigines in Australia trying to overcome a history of inhumane treatment; Kurds in Turkey seeking political recognition and language rights; Muslims and Sikhs protesting a 2004 French law banning the wearing of conspicuous religious symbols in schools; Sami in Scandinavia trying to protect their reindeer-herding activities; Roma in several parts of Europe battling racism and discrimination—these are all examples of communities and individuals striving for the preservation and protection of their cultures.

People attach great importance to culture, because it shapes thinking and behavior, is a dynamic source of creativity, and provides a sense of belonging. In other words, culture is an important part of human dignity. With globalization, the increased flow of people and communications has fostered multicultural societies and even the sense of a universal culture. At the same time, individuals and communities fear erosion or loss of their traditional cultures, leading to a growing reaffirmation of local specificities. As a result, there is an increasing demand for the protection of culture as a human right.

All of the core United Nations human rights treaties pertain to cultural rights (in order of adoption): the International Convention on the Elimination of All Forms of Racial Discrimination (ICERD, 1965); the International Covenant on Civil and Political Rights (ICCPR, 1966); the International Covenant on Economic, Social, and Cultural Rights (ICESCR, 1966); the Convention on the Elimination of All Forms of Discrimination against Women (CEDAW, 1979); the Convention against Torture and Other Cruel, Inhuman, or Degrading Treatment or Punishment (CAT, 1984); the Convention on the Rights of the Child (CRC, 1989); the International Convention on the Protection of the Rights of All Migrant Workers and Members of Their Families (ICRMW, 1990); the Convention on the Rights of Persons with Disabilities (CRPD, 2008); and the International Convention for the Protection of All Persons from Enforced Disappearance (which had not yet entered into force as of early 2009).

CULTURAL RIGHTS IN THE HUMAN RIGHTS DISCOURSE

Cultural rights have always been part of the human rights discourse, being one of the so-called categories of human rights, along with civil, economic, political, and social rights. However, cultural rights have historically received less attention than these other rights, and consequently are conceptually and legally less developed. The place of cultural rights in the human rights discourse has also been problematic. Debate has centered on whether the promotion and protection of cultural rights are consistent with the idea of the universality of human rights, and whether cultural rights, by emphasizing differences, are inherently in contradiction with the human rights principles of equality and nondiscrimination. Moreover, no clear consensus exists about which rights fall within the category of cultural rights. Must such rights explicitly refer to culture or do they include all human rights that have a cultural implication? This lack of clarity has further obscured the implementation of cultural rights.

Universality versus cultural relativism.

One long-standing debate concerns the competing theories of universality and cultural relativism. Universality asserts that every person has certain rights by virtue of being human. These rights are meant to protect human dignity; they are therefore inalienable and are understood to belong to all persons. While the universal enjoyment of human rights is generally not a matter of dispute, the universal character or content of these rights is rebutted by the theory of cultural relativism. Cultural relativism claims that there are no universal human values or rights, and that the variety of cultures in the world implies that human rights can, and may, be interpreted differently.

The question arises as to whether the promotion and protection of cultural rights, which lead to an increased emphasis on and valuing of cultural specificities, are a form of cultural relativism. Some have argued that the promotion and protection of cultural rights are themselves inconsistent with the notion of the universality of human rights. Others have maintained that the fact that cultural rights draw special attention to the customs and behaviors of particular communities does not stand in the way of the universality of human rights norms. The universality of human rights implies that human rights are enjoyed by all persons on the basis of their human dignity. At the same time, the *implementation* of these rights may allow for cultural relativism. This is what the scholar Jack Donnelly has called "relative universality." In this view, variation in practices by countries or cultures can be consistent with the principal of universality. For example, while the right to political participation is a universal norm, the implementation of this right may, or perhaps should, be adjusted to regional or local necessities.

Similarly, cultural rights could be universally applicable to all communities and individuals regardless of their language, traditions, geographic place, and so on, on the ground that culture is an important element of human dignity. Thus cultural rights could be understood to have a universal character.

Equality and nondiscrimination.

Cultural rights have also been seen as clashing with the fundamental human rights principles of equality and nondiscrimination. Cultural rights seem to be based on the fact that individuals and communities want to be recognized as different in some respects from the larger society, and to be treated differently. It has thus been asserted that cultural rights have a specifying and differentiating effect instead of achieving equality, as human rights are intended to do.

A counterargument is that equality and nondiscrimination, as key principles of human rights, entail the recognition of diversity and the right to be different. Having equal rights is not the same thing as being treated equally. Indeed, equality and nondiscrimination imply not only that equal situations be treated equally but that unequal situations be treated unequally. At the international level, the UN's Human Rights Committee, which monitors implementation of the ICCPR, recognized in 1989 that "the enjoyment of rights and freedoms on an equal footing . . . does not mean identical treatment in every instance" (General Comment No. 18, "Non-Discrimination," para. 8). Not all difference in treatment constitutes discrimination, as long as the criteria for such difference are reasonable and objective

and serve a legitimate aim. Legal doctrine generally distinguishes between "differentiation," "distinction," and "discrimination." Differentiation is lawful difference in treatment; distinction is a neutral category used when it has not yet been determined whether difference in treatment is lawful or not; and discrimination is difference in treatment that is arbitrary and unlawful. Consequently, only treatment that results in discrimination is prohibited.

It has been established in international law that "affirmative" or "positive" action is not in contradiction with nondiscrimination. Affirmative action is sometimes also referred to as "positive discrimination," but some have argued that this is a contradiction in terms: either the distinction is justified and legitimate and thus cannot be called discrimination, or it is not justified and thus cannot be called positive. Affirmative action to remedy historical injustices and social discrimination, or to create diversity and proportional group representation in order to obtain effective equality, has been acknowledged as lawful under several international human rights instruments. The ICERD, for instance, states the following in Article 1, paragraph 4:

> Special measures taken for the sole purpose of securing adequate advancement of certain racial or ethnic groups or individuals requiring such protection as may be necessary in order to ensure such groups or individuals equal enjoyment or exercise of human rights and fundamental freedoms shall not be deemed racial discrimination, provided, however, that such measures do not, as a consequence, lead to the maintenance of separate rights for different racial groups and that they shall not be continued after the objectives for which they were taken have been achieved.

The Human Rights Committee has further stated that the principle of equality under Article 26 of the ICCPR may sometimes require states to take affirmative action to diminish or eliminate conditions that cause or help to perpetuate discrimination prohibited by the covenant (General Comment No. 18, "Non-Discrimination," para. 10). Affirmative action may also be relevant in relation to cultural rights. For example, in 1999 the Committee on Economic, Social, and Cultural Rights, which monitors implementation of the ICESCR, determined that temporary special measures intended to bring about de facto equality between men and women and/or for disadvantaged groups in regard to education is not a violation of the right to nondiscrimination. Such special measures could also include separate educational systems or institutions, as long as these do not lead to completely separate standards for different groups

(General Comment No. 13, "The Right to Education," paras. 32–33).

In other words, it can only be determined on a case-by-case basis whether the actual implementation of cultural rights constitutes a lawful or justified distinction or whether it is discrimination. Although cultural rights seem to differentiate, they could be based on the principle of equality insofar as they are to be enjoyed by all communities and individuals alike and are intended to obtain effective equality. With regard to their implementation, there may be differences in treatment and necessary means without this being in contradiction with the principle of equality.

NATURE AND SCOPE OF CULTURAL RIGHTS

The preambles to both the ICCPR and the ICESCR state that all human rights—civil, political, economic, social, and cultural—are interrelated, indivisible, interdependent, and equally important. Nonetheless, the different categories of human rights have not developed at an equal pace. The development of cultural rights has been inhibited by the vagueness of the term "culture," which raises doubts as to which rights are cultural rights and leaves their normative content unclear.

Which rights are cultural rights?

Although cultural rights are mentioned in the name of the ICESCR, the text of the covenant does not specify which of its provisions are cultural rights. Since there is no definition of "cultural rights" in any of the international human rights instruments, there is no agreement on which rights should be labeled cultural. Which rights are included depends on the underlying concept of culture that is used. (For a discussion of the multitude of ways in which "culture" is defined and understood, see Kroeber and Kluckhohn.)

"Culture" is a broad term that can refer to different things. One can think of the human culture in general, the culture of a specific community or period, or the culture of individuals in the context of their civilization. Over the years, the concept of culture has developed from a singular, normative notion conveying an elitist idea of civilization and necessary progress, to a plural, value-free notion that is used to describe differences among individuals and communities. The modern notion of culture is not easy, perhaps even impossible, to define. Without providing an overall definition, though, we can describe several characteristics of culture. An important feature of culture is that it is dynamic and does not have precise boundaries. It is a complex system of beliefs and practices that can change and develop. Consequently, culture is not inactive or static, but dynamic; it is not only a *product*, such as arts and literature, but also a *process*. Culture has both an objective and a subjective dimension. The objective dimension is reflected in visible characteristics such as language, religion, or customs, while the subjective dimension is reflected in shared attitudes, ways of thinking, feeling, and acting. Also, culture has both an individual and a collective dimension. Cultures are developed and shaped by communities, which individuals identify with, building their personal cultural identities. Culture is developed and passed on by cultural institutions such as educational and media organizations, as well as historical archives, museums, and theaters.

How can such a broad notion be translated into human rights norms? The complexity of the concept of culture is visible in the development of thinking about cultural rights. One could say that the broader the concept of culture, the broader the scope of cultural rights. If culture is considered from a narrow perspective as corresponding to cultural products such as arts, literature, and material and immaterial cultural heritage, then cultural rights could include the protection of such cultural heritage, as well as the right to have access to cultural products and heritage in museums, theaters, and libraries. If culture is considered in broader terms, from the perspective of the process of artistic and scientific creation, cultural rights would include, for example, the rights to freedom of expression, artistic and intellectual freedom, and rights related to the protection of producers of cultural products, including copyright. And finally, if culture is considered as a way of life, the sum of material and spiritual activities and products of a community, then cultural rights comprise all kinds of rights pertaining to the maintenance and development of cultures, such as the right of self-determination, including cultural development, the rights to freedom of thought, religion, and association, and the right to education. In this broad sense, cultural rights are sometimes seen as equivalent to *the right to culture*, in the sense of the right to preserve, develop, and have access to a culture. Others prefer to make a distinction between cultural rights as a category of human rights that relate to culture, and separate cultural rights, such as the right to culture, that fall within this category.

Drawing from the international human rights instruments that address cultural rights, a general distinction can be made between cultural rights in the narrow sense and cultural rights in the broad sense. The group of narrow cultural rights contains those provisions that explicitly refer to culture, such as the right to participate in cultural life [ICESCR, Article 15, para. 1(a); CEDAW, Article 13(c); CRC, Article 31; and ICRMW, Article 43], or the right to equal participation in cultural activities (ICERD, Article 5). Other cultural rights in the narrow sense include minorities' rights to enjoy culture (ICCPR, Article 27), the right to education for children with due respect for their cultural identity (CRC, Article 29), and the rights of migrant workers to respect for their cultural identity and to maintain cultural links with their country of origin (ICRMW, Article 31). The group of broad cultural rights might also include other civil, economic, political, or social rights that have a link with culture. It might be defensible to say that all human rights have a link with culture, but the rights specifically meant here are the rights to self-determination (ICCPR and ICESCR, Article 1), to freedom of thought and religion (ICCPR, Article 18; ICRMW, Article 12), to freedom of expression (ICCPR, Article 19; ICRMW, Article 13), to freedom of association (ICCPR, Article 22; ICRMW, Article 40), and to education (ICESCR, Articles 13 and 14; CEDAW, Article 10; ICRMW, Article 30).

Apart from the general human rights instruments, cultural rights can be found in human rights instruments designed for minorities and indigenous peoples. Since the culture of these communities is often in jeopardy, the protection of their cultural rights has here a prominent place. The UN Declaration on the Rights of Persons Belonging to National or Ethnic, Religious, and Linguistic Minorities (1992) enumerates several cultural rights, such as rights to enjoy one's culture, to use one's language, and to practice one's religion (Article 2), as well as educational rights (Article 4). States also have the duty to protect the cultural, religious, ethnic, and linguistic identity of minorities (Article 1). The UN Declaration on the Rights of Indigenous Peoples (2007) also lists several cultural rights, such as the right not to be subject to the destruction of one's culture and the right not to be deprived of one's cultural values (Article 8), and the right to practice and revitalize cultural traditions and customs, including manifestations of culture (Articles 11 and 12). It should be noted that these declarations, unlike the core human rights treaties, are not legally binding. They reflect principles that have a moral and political force and should therefore be respected by states.

The regional human rights instruments in Europe, Africa, and the Americas also address cultural rights. The European Convention on Human Rights and Fundamental Freedoms (ECHR, 1951) and the European Social Charter (1961, revised 1996), adopted by the member states of the Council of Europe, do not contain cultural rights in the narrow sense. They do, however, incorporate cultural rights in the broad sense, such as nondiscrimination and the right to freedom of religion and association. The right to education is included in the First Protocol to the ECHR. Cultural rights in the narrow and in the broad sense are present in several European instruments on minorities, including the European Charter for Regional or Minority Languages, adopted in 1992, and the Framework Convention for the Protection of National Minorities, adopted in 1995. An attempt to draft an additional protocol to the ECHR on cultural rights failed. Provisions discussed among experts and states included, for instance, a right to cultural identity, the right to choose to belong to a group, the protection of cultural heritage, the right to participate in cultural activities, the right to set up cultural and educational institutions, the right to use the language of one's choice, and the right to a name. In the end, however, the member states of the Council of Europe hesitated to adopt legally binding provisions on culture, because they found their potential consequences and implications too uncertain. They also argued that most of the proposed rights would in practice not add much to the provisions already in the ECHR. In January 1996 a decision was made to suspend work on this protocol, and as of 2008 no new attempt to adopt an instrument on cultural rights had been undertaken at the European level.

The American Declaration on Human Rights (1948), adopted by the member states of the Organization of American States, contains cultural rights in the broad and in the narrow sense, including the right to take part in the cultural life of the community (Article 8). The American Convention on Human Rights (1969) contains, inter alia, the rights to equal protection, to property, and to freedom of religion, movement, and residence. In 1988 the signatories to this convention signed the Protocol of San Salvador, which focuses on economic, social, and cultural rights and contains provisions similar to those of the ICESCR, including the right to education and the right to take part in the cultural life of the community (Article 14).

The states represented in the African Union adopted the African Charter on Human and Peoples' Rights (1981), which incorporates all categories of human rights—civil, cultural, economic, political, and social—in a single instrument. The charter includes cultural rights in the broad sense, such as freedom of religion and association and the right to education. It also contains cultural rights in the narrow sense, such as the right to take part in the cultural life of the community (Article 17) and the right of peoples to their own cultural development (Article 22).

Cultural dimension of human rights.

Although some human rights, at first glance, may not have a direct link with culture, most have important cultural implications. Several international judicial bodies, including the European Court of Human Rights and the Inter-American Court of Human Rights, have acknowledged the cultural dimension of human rights provisions.

The European Court has, for example, decided that the right to freedom of association (ECHR, Article 11) extends to cultural organizations, in cases such as *Sidiropoulos and others v. Greece* (1998), *Stankov and the United Macedonian Organisation Ilinden v. Bulgaria* (2001), and *Gorzelik and others v. Poland* (2001). The European Court further addressed the cultural dimension of the right to private life (ECHR, Article 8) when it recognized that living in caravans is part of the traditional lifestyle of gypsies (the term used by the Court for Roma) to be protected under this right. This was determined, for example, in the cases of *Buckley v. the United Kingdom* (1996) and *Chapman v. the United Kingdom* (2001).

The Inter-American Commission on Human Rights has issued several judgments on indigenous peoples and the protection of their cultures under the right to life and the right to health. An interesting case in this respect is that of *Yanomami Community v. Brazil* (1985). The Inter-American Court of Human Rights has acknowledged the specific interpretation of the right to property with respect to the culture of indigenous peoples. The landmark case in this regard is *Mayagna (Sumo) Indigenous Community of Awas Tingni v. Nicaragua* (2001).

The UN's Committee on Economic, Social, and Cultural Rights, in monitoring the ICESCR, has acknowledged the cultural elements of, for instance, the rights to food, health, and housing. It has determined that the right to adequate housing implies, among other things, that the construction of houses, building materials, and building policies "must appropriately enable the expression of cultural identity and diversity of housing" (General Comment No. 4, "The Right to Adequate Housing," 1991, para. 8[g]). With regard to the right to adequate food, the committee has stated that the guarantees provided should be culturally appropriate and acceptable (General Comment No. 12, "The Right to Adequate Food," 1999, paras. 7, 8, and 11). With regard to the right to health, the

committee has determined that "all health facilities, goods and services must be . . . culturally appropriate, *i.e.*, respectful of the culture of individuals, minorities, peoples and communities" [General Comment No. 14, "The Right to the Highest Attainable Standard of Health," 2000, para. 12(c)].

Cultural rights as individual or collective rights.

Cultural rights can be considered as individual rights, as group rights (rights of individuals as part of a community), or as collective rights (rights of communities as a whole). While most provisions in international human rights instruments define cultural rights as individual rights, their enjoyment is firmly associated with the larger community. The individual right to participate in cultural life, for example, can only be enjoyed by members of a cultural community. In other words, cultural rights have an individual and a collective dimension.

Almost all provisions in international human rights instruments have been defined in individual terms. Only the right of self-determination is included in the ICESCR and the ICCPR (common Article 1) as a right of "all peoples." Another exception is seen in the African Charter on Human and Peoples' Rights, which includes several collective cultural rights of peoples, as mentioned above.

Generally speaking, however, the state approach toward cultural rights has focused mainly on the individual. States remain cautious about empowering communities as a whole with cultural rights for fear that such a collective approach might endanger the stability of the society. Despite this concern, the collective dimension of cultural rights has not been entirely disregarded, as is illustrated by the development of rights of minorities and indigenous peoples. Such claims for collective rights, especially in relation to culture, have been met. For instance, the UN Declaration on the Rights of Persons Belonging to National or Ethnic, Religious, and Linguistic Minorities refers to minorities as such on several occasions. However, these provisions are formulated as duties on the part of states and not as rights for the communities involved. States, for example, have the duty to protect the cultural, religious, ethnic, and linguistic identity of minorities (Article 1). This means that minorities are not the subjects, but the beneficiaries, of these provisions. The UN Declaration on the Rights of Indigenous Peoples goes further in its collective approach. This declaration enumerates several collective rights for indigenous peoples, including cultural rights in both the narrow and broad sense.

STATE OBLIGATIONS CORRESPONDING TO CULTURAL RIGHTS

Rights imply a claim by the holder against an addressee, who is expected to do something or to refrain from doing something with respect to the holder. In the case of human and cultural rights alike, the chief addressee is the state. What is the nature of state obligations with regard to cultural rights?

Negative and positive obligations.

Generally, state obligations can be divided into negative and positive. Negative obligations require the state to refrain from some action, whereas positive obligations require state action. Although in the past a firm but not absolute distinction was made between rights that demand state abstention, or negative obligations, and rights that require state action, or positive obligations, there is now general consensus that all categories of rights may be subject to positive as well as to negative state obligations. After all, states must sometimes take positive measures to protect civil and political rights. They must, for example, be proactive in scheduling and organizing elections, as well as in creating and maintaining court systems. Also, economic and social rights may sometimes require states not to act, for example, with respect to educational and scientific freedoms.

Accordingly, cultural rights may involve positive as well as negative obligations. But while there is general agreement that states have negative obligations in relation to cultural rights, positive obligations associated with these rights have been the subject of dispute. For example, if a state has a negative obligation to respect the use of individuals' language of choice in the home, does it then have a positive obligation to provide language facilities so that these individuals can use their language of choice when dealing with public authorities? If the United States, for example, allows the use of Spanish in various cultural festivals, can it then require all citizens to use English in court proceedings and on election ballots? Another example concerns the right to education. The state may be obligated to respect a cultural community, small or large, that wishes to organize the teaching of its own values. But is the state also obliged to financially support the development of educational facilities for all minority communities, no matter their size and number?

"Progressive realization" of economic, social, and cultural rights.

Cultural rights that are part of the ICESCR fall under the supervisory regime of that treaty. The key provision in the ICESCR with regard to state obligations is Article 2, paragraph 1, which specifies that states should take steps to the maximum of their available resources, "with a view to achieving progressively the full realization of the rights recognized in the present Covenant by all appropriate means, including particularly the adoption of legislative measures." The debate on the meaning of "progressive realization" is ongoing. An important interpretation of Article 2, paragraph 1, of the ICESCR is General Comment No. 3 concerning the nature of state obligations, adopted by the Committee on Economic, Social, and Cultural Rights in 1990. In this document, the committee stated that the obligation to take steps or measures as laid down in Article 2, paragraph 1, has an immediate character. States should start the implementation immediately and move as fast as possible toward the goal of total realization. Furthermore, taking the appropriate measures implies not only legislative measures, but also administrative, financial, educational, social, and other measures. States are free to determine which measures they consider best to implement the material provisions of the ICESCR, whereby the committee determines whether the state has taken the appropriate steps.

Article 2, paragraph 2, of the ICESCR contains a provision that obliges states to take measures to immediately ban de jure discrimination in the enjoyment of the rights in the covenant. The idea of progressive realization is not applicable here, since the term "to ensure" is used. The principle of nondiscrimination may also have implications for the implementation of cultural rights. If, for example, the state finances a cultural institution for one community, it should also take financial measures for the benefit of other communities.

The ICESCR's progressive realization principle applies only to cultural rights in the ICESCR. The ICCPR and other relevant human rights instruments demand that immediate steps be taken by states, irrespective of the availability of resources. Article 2 of the ICCPR requires states to undertake to respect and ensure the rights of the ICCPR. The understanding in the treaty is that cultural rights, such as freedom of religion, expression, and association, should be guaranteed immediately and without discrimination.

Tripartite typology: obligations to respect, protect, and fulfill.

Three types of state obligations can, in principle, result from all human rights, whether civil, political, economic, social, or cultural in nature: the obligation to *respect*, the obligation to *protect,* and the obligation to *fulfill.* This so-called tripartite typology, developed by scholars, was articulated at the international level in 1987 by Asbjørn Eide, then the UN's special rapporteur on the right to food. The obligation to respect means that states should refrain from "anything that violates the integrity of the individual or infringes on his or her freedom, including the freedom to use the material resources available to that individual in the way he or she finds best to satisfy the basic needs." The obligation to protect means that the state should take the necessary measures "to prevent other individuals or groups from violating the integrity, freedom of action, or other human rights of the individual—including the prevention of infringement of the enjoyment of his material resources." The obligation to fulfill means that the state should take measures "to ensure for each person within its jurisdiction opportunities to obtain satisfaction of those needs, recognized in the human rights instruments, which cannot be secured by personal efforts" (*Final Report of the Special Rapporteur on the Right to Food,* paras. 67–69).

The tripartite typology has gained international recognition and is widely used by academics. The Committee on Economic, Social, and Cultural Rights has used it in its general comments on, for example, the rights to food, education, health, and water, to determine the corresponding state obligations of these rights. The typology is designed to clarify the different levels of obligations of states in relation to specific rights. It is therefore not helpful for the clarification of cultural rights as an entire category, but could be used to determine certain state obligations of specific cultural rights.

For example, when applied to the right to take part in cultural life, the three levels of obligations imply a variety of measures to be taken. States should first *respect* the freedom of the individual to choose, develop, assert, and change a preferred cultural orientation, as well as the freedom to collect and distribute cultural information. Second, states should *protect* the individual's right to take part in cultural life against third parties who, by the assertion of their culture or engagement in cultural activities, disrupt the enjoyment of this right. Finally, states have an obligation to *fulfill* that is met by taking active steps to achieve widespread cultural participation and accessibility. Concrete measures may, for example, include improving access to cultural life through cultural funds or the establishment of an institutional infrastructure to promote popular participation in cultural life. The obligation to fulfill also entails, for example, state

protection of cultural heritage for generations to come, including the protection of monuments, sites, cultural property, and museums. More specific measures could be exemptions from laws that penalize cultural practices, for example, special hunting and usufruct laws; the funding of ethnic associations or multilingual ballots or special voting measures; or the protection of symbolic claims, such as religious holidays. Since the right to take part in cultural life includes not only access to culture but active participation in the decision-making process on cultural matters, the state should also ensure that individuals are free to take part in the general political process. States should, for example, ensure representation of different communities in relevant decision-making bodies, or at least consult them or have them participate in matters of their concern, such as cultural development.

LIMITS ON THE ENJOYMENT OF CULTURAL RIGHTS

It has been argued that the promotion and protection of cultural rights can lead to support for questionable cultural activities such as the discriminatory treatment of women, examples of which are forced marriages, bride price, female genital mutilation, widow cleansing (a traditional practice in which a widow is forced to have sexual relations in order to be "cleansed" of her husband's evil spirit and/or to secure property within the family), and unequal treatment with regard to land ownership or inheritance. Cultural rights, as is true of other human rights, cannot be enjoyed without limit. The general framework of such limitations is outlined in Article 29, paragraph 2, of the Universal Declaration of Human Rights, in which it is stated that "in the exercise of his rights and freedoms, everyone shall be subject to only such limitations as are determined by law solely for the purpose of securing due recognition and respect for the rights and freedoms of others and of meeting the just requirements of morality, public order and the general welfare in a democratic society."

From this text it can be derived that the enjoyment of cultural rights may be limited by law. Article 4 of the ICESCR, for example, gives states the possibility of limiting the enjoyment of the rights in the covenant, but only on the condition that these limitations are "determined by law only in so far as this may be compatible with the nature of these rights and solely for the purpose of promoting the general welfare in a democratic society." This limitation clause is not meant to provide states with a simple excuse not to implement the provisions of the ICESCR.

Limitations may not be in contradiction with the nature of the rights in the covenant; otherwise, the provisions would no longer have any value and substance.

Second, as outlined in Article 29, paragraph 2, of the UDHR, the enjoyment of human rights by one person may not unjustifiably limit or violate the enjoyment of human rights by others. In other words, the enjoyment of cultural rights can be limited by the enjoyment of human rights by others. In fact, many human rights are inherently capable of clashing in certain situations. For example, the 2005 publication in a Danish newspaper of cartoons depicting the Prophet Muhammad, which led to widespread protests and rioting by Muslims, demonstrated tension between freedom of religion and freedom of expression. As there is no hierarchy with respect to the different human rights, there are no general rules as to which right should prevail over another. Instead, particular situations must be carefully evaluated to determine which right prevails.

The question remains how to deal with cultural *activities* or *practices*—which are not the same as cultural *rights*—that are in conflict with or limit the enjoyment of human rights. Such practices, it is argued, should not be protected by cultural rights. It is hard to make general statements about the acceptability of cultural practices and their relation to human rights, since these practices are diverse and their possible conflict with human rights could best be treated on a case-by-case basis. However, some have argued that cultural practices that are clearly in conflict with international human rights norms cannot be justified on the basis of protection granted by "cultural rights." As Article 29, paragraph 3, of the UDHR outlines, "These rights and freedoms may in no case be exercised contrary to the purpose and principles of the United Nations." An appropriate criterion could therefore be that cultural practices should not be in conflict with the value of human dignity and internationally accepted human rights norms. However, it remains difficult to assess to what extent certain cultural practices are in conflict with these values and norms.

It has been argued that cultural practices considered inconsistent with human rights are most successfully challenged from within the cultural community itself, rather than change being imposed from outside. Human rights instruments, however, affirm the responsibility of states to find ways to promote such change. CEDAW, for instance, states in Article 5 that "States Parties shall take all appropriate measures: (a) To modify the social and cultural patterns of conduct of men and women, with a view to achieving the elimination of prejudices and customary and all other practices which are based on the idea of the inferiority or the superiority of either of the sexes or on stereotyped roles for men and women." The Protocol to the African Charter on Human and Peoples' Rights on the Rights of Women in Africa, adopted in 2003, includes a similar provision in Article 2, paragraph 2: "States Parties shall commit themselves to modify the social and cultural patterns of conduct of women and men . . . with a view to achieving the elimination of harmful cultural and traditional practices and all other practices which are based on the idea of the inferiority or the superiority of either of the sexes."

CONTINUING DEVELOPMENT OF CULTURAL RIGHTS

Attention to cultural rights increased in the late twentieth century as scholars and policy makers addressed cultural diversity and the problematic issues arising from multicultural societies. Developments have taken place in the form of the adoption of international standards and elaboration of the normative content of cultural rights. In the opening decade of the twenty-first century the member states of the United Nations Educational, Scientific, and Cultural Organization (UNESCO) adopted two instruments on cultural diversity: the Universal Declaration on Cultural Diversity (2001) and the Convention on the Protection and Promotion of the Diversity of Cultural Expressions (2005). While both instruments emphasize the importance of cultural rights, neither contains substantive cultural-rights provisions.

Article 5 of the Universal Declaration on Cultural Diversity, which describes cultural rights as "an enabling environment for cultural diversity," states the following:

Cultural rights are an integral part of human rights, which are universal, indivisible and interdependent. The flourishing of creative diversity requires the full implementation of cultural rights as defined in Article 27 of the Universal Declaration of Human Rights and in Articles 13 and 15 of the International Covenant on Economic, Social and Cultural Rights. All persons have therefore the right to express themselves and to create and disseminate their work in the language of their choice, and particularly in their mother tongue; all persons are entitled to quality education and training that fully respect their cultural identity; and all persons have the right to participate in the cultural life of their choice and conduct their own cultural practices, subject to respect for human rights and fundamental freedoms.

This provision confirms the importance of cultural rights and enumerates several of them, including the right to participate in cultural life, the right to freedom of expression, and the right to education. No specific reference is made to the right to freedom of religion, because the member states could not agree on its inclusion in the Declaration. As a result, an important aspect of cultural diversity and cultural rights is not referred to in this document. Article 5 further deals with the limits to the enjoyment of cultural rights, namely that the conduct of cultural practices must be respectful of human rights. The Declaration on Cultural Diversity is not a legally binding instrument and mainly contains principles to be respected by the member states of UNESCO. After its adoption, the member states discussed drafting a binding instrument on cultural diversity. One option considered was to adopt a new instrument on cultural rights. Instead, the UNESCO member states adopted the Convention on the Protection and Promotion of the Diversity of Cultural Expressions.

According to Article 2, paragraph 1, of this convention:

> Cultural diversity can be protected and promoted only if human rights and fundamental freedoms, such as freedom of expression, information and communication, as well as the ability of individuals to choose cultural expressions, are guaranteed. No one may invoke the provisions of this Convention in order to infringe human rights and fundamental freedoms as enshrined in the Universal Declaration of Human Rights or guaranteed by international law or to limit the scope thereof.

Here also, several cultural rights are enumerated and the possible limitation of these rights is included.

Although the convention does not contain substantive cultural rights of individuals or communities, several provisions speak of measures that *may* be taken by states to protect cultural diversity. These measures are similar to state measures following from human rights treaties for the implementation of cultural rights. For example, according to the convention, states may take measures that "provide opportunities for . . . the creation, production, dissemination, distribution and enjoyment of such domestic cultural activities, goods and services, including provisions relating to the language used for such activities, goods and services" (Article 6, para. b). This provision furthermore speaks of measures to establish and support public institutions, to support artists and others involved in the creation of cultural expression, as well as measures to enhance the diversity of the media (Article 6, paras. f–h). Such measures could also include public financial assistance (Article 6, para. d). The convention also holds that states should encourage individuals and groups to create, produce, disseminate, distribute, and have access to their own cultural expressions, "paying due attention to the special circumstances and needs of women as well as various social groups, including persons belonging to minorities and indigenous peoples" (Article 7, para. a).

In the 1990s a group of academics from around the world began working on the elaboration and clarification of cultural rights. Their deliberations resulted in the Fribourg Declaration on Cultural Rights, which was presented to international intergovernmental and nongovernmental organizations in May 2007. The aim of the declaration was not to adopt a new set of rights, but to group cultural-rights provisions from existing international human rights instruments in order to enhance their visibility and coherence and to advance their realization. The declaration has been widely supported by scholars and institutions, as well as by members of the various treaty bodies of the UN. As it is an academic document, it does not have legally binding force on states. It could, however, serve as a reference document for the further development and advancement of cultural rights.

[*See also* Globalization; Indigenous Peoples; Kurdish Nationalism and Rights; Minority Rights: Overview; Religious Freedom; *and* Roma in Europe.]

BIBLIOGRAPHY

Alston, Philip, and Gerard Quinn. "The Nature and Scope of States Parties' Obligations under the International Covenant on Economic, Social, and Cultural Rights." *Human Rights Quarterly* 9, no. 2 (1987): 156–229.

Bossuyt, Marc. *Prevention of Discrimination: The Concept and Practice of Affirmative Action.* UN Doc. E/CN.4/Sub. 2/2002/21, June 17, 2002.

Donders, Yvonne M. "The Legal Framework of the Right to Take Part in Cultural Life." In *Human Rights in Education, Science, and Culture: Legal Developments and Challenges*, edited by Yvonne Donders and Vladimir Volodin, pp. 231–272. Paris: UNESCO/Ashgate, December 2007.

Donders, Yvonne M. *Towards a Right to Cultural Identity?* School of Human Rights Research Series, no 15. Antwerp, Belgium: Intersentia, 2002.

Donnelly, Jack. "The Relative Universality of Human Rights." *Human Rights Quarterly* 29, no. 2 (2007): 281–306.

Donnelly, Jack. *Universal Human Rights in Theory and Practice.* 2d ed. Ithaca, N.Y.: Cornell University Press, 2003.

Eide, Asbjørn. "Cultural Rights as Individual Human Rights." In *Economic, Social, and Cultural Rights: A Textbook*, edited by Asbjørn Eide, Catarina Krause, and Allan Rosas, pp. 289–302. 2d rev. ed. Dordrecht, the Netherlands: Martinus Nijhoff, 2001.

Eide, Asbjørn. *Final Report of the Special Rapporteur on the Right to Food*. UN Doc. E/CN.4/Sub.2/1987/23, 1987.

Fribourg Declaration on Cultural Rights. http://www.unifr.ch/iiedh/droits-culturels/odc-pres.htm.

Hansen, Stephen A. "The Right to Take Part in Cultural Life: Toward Defining Minimum Core Obligations Related to Article 15(1)(A) of the International Covenant on Economic, Social and Cultural Rights." In *Core Obligations: Building a Framework for Economic, Social, and Cultural Rights*, edited by Audrey Chapman and Sage Russell, pp. 279–304. Antwerp, Belgium: Intersentia, 2002.

Kroeber, A. L., and Clyde Kluckhohn. *Culture: A Critical Review of Concepts and Definitions*. Cambridge, Mass.: The Museum, 1952.

Kymlicka, Will. *Multicultural Citizenship: A Liberal Theory of Minority Rights*. Oxford: Clarendon; New York: Oxford University Press, 1995.

"Limburg Principles on the Implementation of the International Covenant on Economic, Social and Cultural Rights." UN Doc. E/CN.4/1987/17, 1987. Also in *Human Rights Quarterly* 9 (1987): 122–135.

Marks, Stephen. "Defining Cultural Rights." In *Human Rights and Criminal Justice for the Downtrodden: Essays in Honour of Asbjørn Eide*, edited by Morten Bergsmo, pp. 293–324. Leiden, the Netherlands: Martinus. Nijhoff, 2003.

Meyer-Bisch, Patrice, ed. *Les droits culturels: Une catégorie sous-développée de droits de l'homme; Actes du VIIIe Colloque Interdisciplinaire sur les Droits de l'Homme*. Fribourg, Switzerland: Editions Universitaires, 1993.

Niec, Halina. *Cultural Rights and Wrongs*. Paris: UNESCO; Leicester, U.K.: Institute of Art and Law, 1998.

O'Keefe, Roger. "The 'Right to Take Part in Cultural Life' under Article 15 of the ICESCR." *International and Comparative Law Quarterly* 47, nos. 3/4 (1998): 904–923.

Parekh, Bhikhu. *Rethinking Multiculturalism: Cultural Diversity and Political Theory*. Basingstoke, U.K.: Macmillan, 2000.

Prott, L.V. "Cultural Rights as Peoples' Rights in International Law." In *The Rights of Peoples*, edited by James Crawford, pp. 161–175. Oxford: Clarendon; New York: Oxford University Press, 1988.

Steiner, Henry J., Philip Alston, and Ryan Goodman. *International Human Rights in Context: Law, Politics, Morals; Texts and Materials*. 3d ed. Part C, pp. 517–668. Oxford: Oxford University Press, 2008.

Symonides, Janusz. "Cultural Rights." In *Human Rights: Concept and Standards*, edited by Janusz Symonides, pp. 175–227. Paris: UNESCO, 2000.

Türk, Danilo. *The Realisation of Economic, Social, and Cultural Rights*. Final Report, UN Doc. E/CN.4/Sub.2/1992/16, July 3, 1992.

Van Boven, Theo C., Cees Flinterman, and Ingrid Westendorp, eds. *The Maastricht Guidelines on Economic, Social, and Cultural Rights*. SIM Special Report No. 20, pp. 1–12. Utrecht, the Netherlands: SIM, 1998.

CUSTOMARY INTERNATIONAL LAW

by Connie de la Vega

I n order to be considered customary international law, a provision or prohibition must be (1) state practice—evidenced by long-term, widespread compliance by many states; and (2) *opinio juris*—states' belief that compliance with a standard is not merely desired, but required by international law. It is important to distinguish customary international law, which is law applying to states, from customary law, which applies to the indigenous practices in many nations, including many African countries. States are bound by customary international law norms unless they have persistently objected to them.

DEFINITION AND CREATION OF CUSTOMARY INTERNATIONAL LAW

A general practice that is accepted by law as nations can become international custom and thus a source of international law. Article 38(1) of the Statute of the International Court of Justice (ICJ), which was adopted as part of the Charter of the United Nations on 26 June 1945 and came into force on 24 October 1945, recognizes international custom as a source of law in resolving disputes between states: "The Court, whose function is to decide in accordance with international law such disputes as are submitted to it, shall apply: . . . b. international custom, as evidence of a general practice accepted as law; c. the general principles of law recognized by civilized nations." Article 38(1) is accepted as a definitive statement of the sources of international law. Thus, in international relations there is a complicated process that creates international law.

Both practice and adopted laws and principles constitute the sources of international law and are applied by international bodies as well as national courts. As the U.S. Supreme Court held in 1900 in *The Paquete Habana*, customary international law is "part of our law, and must be ascertained and administered by the courts of justice of appropriate jurisdiction," which could be ascertained by the works of jurists and commentators when there was no controlling treaty or other law (175 U.S. 677).

General principles of law recognized by states now refer to states' acceptance of principles in international agreements as well as their own laws, though works of jurists and commentators are still useful for identifying international customary law. Acceptance of principles includes government policy statements and opinions by legal officers as part of the increasing practice of negotiating and approving international instruments. Legal briefs endorsed by states, as well as national judicial opinions, would also be relevant to the identification of customary norms. The widespread negotiation, promulgation, and acceptance of human rights treaties, declarations, resolutions, and other instruments have been recognized as indicative of state practice as well as of the *opinio juris* requirement.

One commentator, the jurist Ved Nanda, has noted that one way to establish *opinio juris* is to "distinguish between those habitual practices that are regarded as binding legal obligations [and] those that result simply from courtesy or diplomatic protocol, or from domestic policy considerations, and from which departure can ensue without breach of international law" (Nanda, p. 1333). In the realm of human rights, the human rights treaties themselves may be deemed to enunciate the intentions of the parties and thus their provisions are clear evidence that the countries are acting pursuant to them. Some commentators have raised the question about the role that state practice plays in determining whether an international customary norm exists and whether that analysis is appropriate in the human rights arena. Nonetheless, customary international law and general principles of law are relevant and useful concepts to apply to human rights discourse. A recent example may be found in the 2005 U.S. Supreme Court case holding the death penalty for juveniles unconstitutional. One of the grounds for that ruling included reference to treaties, resolutions by UN bodies, and the practice of other nations.

Commentators have noted that only widespread, rather than unanimous, acquiescence is needed. The Restatement of the Foreign Relations Law of the United States has noted that "there is no precise formula to indicate how widespread a practice must be, but it should reflect wide acceptance among the states particularly involved in the relevant activity." Often there is disagreement on when a practice, or rule, has ripened into a customary international norm, but consensus has been reached on some human rights. Human rights that have been recognized as customary international law include a number of prohibitions: genocide; slavery or slave trade; murder or the causing of the disappearance of individuals; torture or other cruel, inhuman, or degrading treatment or punishment; prolonged arbitrary detention; systematic racial discrimination; the application of the death penalty and life without parole sentences for offenders under eighteen years of age; and consistent patterns of gross violations of internationally recognized human rights. As the UN human rights bodies, including the Commission on Human Rights and its replacement body, the Human Rights Council, have expanded their consideration of rights to those in the economic, social, and cultural arenas, recognition of customary legal standards may be expanded to certain aspects of those rights, which include the right to food, health, and education.

THE PERSISTENT OBJECTOR DOCTRINE

A customary international norm binds all governments, including those that have not recognized it, as long as they have not expressly and persistently objected to the norm from the inception of its development. In this context, it is important to note that customary international norms are different from *jus cogens*, or "higher law" norms. With respect to the latter, states are bound whether or not they have persistently objected to *jus cogens* norms.

The persistent objector doctrine arose as a corollary to the fundamental principle of state sovereignty. In order to qualify as a persistent objector, the state must object when the norm is in its formative stages, throughout its development, and at every relevant opportunity. The objections by the state must be clear, consistent, and affirmative—silence does not qualify as an adequate objection. This is why many governments take to the floor at the United Nations and other forums to explain their position on a matter with legal implications. They do not wish their silence to be taken as agreement with the possible emergence of a rule of customary international law to which they object.

The ICJ has applied the doctrine of persistent objection in only two cases. In a case between Peru and Colombia (I.C.J. 266, 1950), Peru raised the doctrine against provisions of a treaty that had risen to the level of a customary international norm. Peru was found to be a persistent objector, not only because it failed to sign the treaty in question, but also because it had specifically repudiated the asylum provisions in question. In a dispute involving custom limiting the extent of territorial waters, the ICJ ruled that Norway had continuously opposed any attempt to apply the rule to its coastline and thus was a persistent objector to the development of the norm. The ICJ has not clarified the form the objection should take, how consistent it must be, or to what kinds of customary international law it applies.

THE ICRC STUDY ON CUSTOMARY INTERNATIONAL HUMANITARIAN LAW

The International Committee of the Red Cross (ICRC) conducted a ten-year study that raised interesting issues regarding the formulation of customary international law. The study was completed in 2005 and attempted to identify the rules of customary international law on armed conflict or humanitarian law. Previously, many actors made various claims about customary international law in this subject area, but there remained much ambiguity. The study is instructive on the various issues that come up during the attempted identification of such norms as well as the role that governments may play in the process, since it involved extensive and broad-based research to identify the existence of norms of customary law in that area.

After the publication of the report, legal advisers from the U.S. government objected to various aspects of the methodology used by the ICRC to identify the customary international humanitarian law. With respect to state practice, their objections focused on five topics: (1) the state practice cited is insufficiently dense to meet the "extensive and virtually uniform" standard required to demonstrate the existence of a customary norm; (2) the type of state practice included placed too much emphasis on written materials rather than actual operational practice; (3) the study gave too much emphasis to statements by nongovernmental organizations and the ICRC itself, when those statements do not necessarily reflect norms accepted by states; (4) negative practice by states was given inadequate weight; and (5) the study failed to pay enough attention to the concept of specially affected states—those states that have a history of participation in armed conflict should be given greater weight. The United States in effect argued that with respect to those who are war prone, their objections, instead of being grounds for establishing that they were persistent objectors, might be grounds for arguing against the creation of a norm. With respect to the second point, the government lawyers objected to the use of nonbinding General Assembly resolutions since states often agree to such resolutions in order not to break consensus and not because they believe that those provisions reflect customary international law.

The U.S. attorneys also argued that the study merged the practice and *opinio juris* requirements into a single test. While they agree that the same action might be evidence of both state practice and *opinio juris*, they disagreed that the latter can simply be inferred from practice. In other words, the United States was asking for a rigorous standard for *opinio juris*, namely that states needed to indicate clearly their belief that their practice was required by international law. It was the U.S. position that more positive evidence beyond mere treaty obligations is needed to establish that states consider themselves legally obligated to follow a particular course of action.

Regarding sources of law, the U.S. attorneys disagreed that treaties necessarily are evidence of customary international law since states do not necessarily consider them as such when they ratify the treaties. In addition, they especially were concerned with the use of military manuals to establish *opinio juris* without distinguishing between those that were prepared solely for training and those that were approved as official government statements.

The attorney for the ICRC responded as follows to these objections. First, with respect to the density of practice requirement, there is no mathematical requirement for how extensive the practice must be since it will depend on the subject matter. Some practices will generate a great deal of discussion, while others do not, but nonetheless the two types of practices may be considered custom. Two examples were given to exemplify this point. Complex factors affecting the rule on not attacking civilians, compared to permissible attacks on combatants, arise regularly in connection with armed conflicts and are addressed in nearly all military manuals, international forums, and judicial proceedings on war crimes. On the other hand, practice regarding the protection of the white truce flag is rarely discussed. However, both the prohibition on attacking civilians (and civilian objects) and respecting the white flag may be considered customary norms. This is the case even though there are few cases on the use of the white flag because it is always respected, thus confirming the validity of the customary international norm.

To quantify the density of a practice, it is also necessary to determine the correct value of each practice. Thus, a military manual may represent numerous precedents as it is used to train many personnel who will presumably act in accordance with the rules in the manual. It is also necessary to take the nature of the rule into account as prohibitive and permissive norms may be manifested in different ways. Prohibitive rules may be supported by affirmative statements as well as abstention from conduct, which is difficult to quantify even though a particular norm might be followed every day. Permissive rules may be supported by acts or the absence of objections, but not by a dense enough practice that would be necessary for other norms. An example of such a customary rule is the principle of universal jurisdiction, which may not be practiced extensively because of other factors such as the availability of international procedures.

The ICRC lawyer also noted that a study on customary international law has to look at the combination of what states say and what they do. Thus, for example, while attacks against civilians, pillage, and sexual violence are prohibited, violations are reported regularly. Support in this case that these are violations comes from affirmative acts, such as military manuals, national legislation, national and international case law, resolutions of international organizations, and official statements. The study considered not only resolutions of the United Nations and the regional bodies, but also the voting record of each country at those bodies. And the resolutions were only part of the larger record for each norm.

Since the ICRC had been mandated to prepare the study, it deemed that its own official statements were relevant to support the customary nature of a rule. Nongovernmental statements were not given any weight in the determination of what was customary but were included as a residual category of materials that were relevant to the norms.

The study also did not assume that a norm was customary simply because it was contained in a widely ratified treaty. The distinction between contracting and noncontracting parties was taken into account and lists of those countries were compiled. The study did note that some states had more experience and participation in some areas but did not consider that the doctrine of "specially affected" as identified by the ICJ with respect to the law of the sea necessarily applied to humanitarian law, since all states have the potential of becoming involved in armed conflict and thus being "specially affected."

While the commentaries in the study did not set out a separate analysis of practice and *opinio juris*, scrutiny did take place for each norm to determine whether the practice evidenced a rule of law and not merely a policy.

And the study did not simply infer *opinio juris*, but the conclusion that it existed was the result of the consideration of all the relevant practice.

One interesting point made by the ICRC attorney is that the portrayal of customary international norms will usually be a great deal simpler than the rules found in treaties. This makes sense as often the negotiation of treaties can result in a great deal of detail that is not possible in describing a customary norm. Nonetheless, customary humanitarian law has filled important gaps in treaty law applicable to noninternational armed conflicts. And because customary international law is an evolving process, the study cannot be seen as the final word on the humanitarian norms.

In this particular example, it might be noted that the ICRC is the "guardian" of international humanitarian law and that a private humanitarian actor might be presumed to look favorably on the expansion of that law via customary international law. On the other hand, since the United States often finds itself engaged in armed conflicts, as was true of former powers such as France and the United Kingdom, it might be presumed to look with favor to a smaller body of rules making international humanitarian law, including custom, which would provide it more leeway in the use of military force. It is likely that the identity and roles of these two actors—the United States and the ICRC—affect the positions they take on the clarification of customary international law in the domain of international humanitarian law.

ASSESSMENT

Customary international law is a source of law for governing conduct between states as well as for establishing and protecting human rights. Indeed, many human rights norms, such as the prohibition of slavery, developed first as customary international law. As the ICRC study indicates, there are numerous sources for establishing both the practice and *opinio juris* aspects of a customary international norm, and the interrelationship between the two is complex and varied. While governments may commit acts that violate those norms, it is not necessarily the case that they disagree with the existence of the norm. Such is the case with torture, which is universally denounced by states, but continues in practice nonetheless. Even with all the difficulties involved in identifying the emergence of customary international law, courts still turn to it in specific conflicts, and states do accept in general that it is a valid type of law.

[*See also* Children's Convention (Convention on the Rights of the Child); Conflict among Human Rights Norms; Culture and Human Rights; Genocide; Global Justice and Human Rights; History of Human Rights; Humanitarian Law; International Committee of the Red Cross (ICRC); International Court of Justice; Jus Cogens; Racial Discrimination: Origins and Patterns; Slavery and the Slave Trade; *and* Torture: International Law.]

BIBLIOGRAPHY

Asylum Case (Colombia v. Peru). I.C.J. 266, June 13, 1950.

Bellinger, John B., III, and William J. Haynes II. "A U.S. Government Response to the International Committee of the Red Cross Study *Customary International Humanitarian Law.*" *International Review of the Red Cross* 866 (June 2007): 443–471.

Brownlie, Ian. *Principles of Public International Law*. 4th ed. Oxford: Clarendon Press; New York: Oxford University Press, 1990.

Charney, Jonathan I. "Universal International Law." *American Journal of International Law* 87, no. 4 (October 1993): 529–551.

de la Vega, Connie, and Jennifer Jean Brown. "Can a United States Treaty Reservation Provide a Sanctuary for the Juvenile Death Penalty?" *University of San Francisco Law Review* 32, no. 4 (1998).

Fisheries Case (United Kingdom v. Norway). I.C.J. 116, December 18, 1950.

Fitzpatrick, Joan. "The Relevance of Customary International Norms to the Death Penalty in the United States." *Georgia Journal of International and Comparative Law* 25 (1996): 179–180.

Henckaerts, Jean-Marie. "Customary International Humanitarian Law: A Response to U.S. Comments." *International Review of the Red Cross* 866 (June 2007): 473–488.

Hunter, David, James Salzman, and Durwood Zaelke. *International Environmental Law and Policy*. 3d ed. New York: Foundation Press; St. Paul, Minn.: Thomson/West, 2007.

Loschin, Lynn. "The Persistent Objector and Customary Human Rights Law: A Proposed Analytical Framework." *University of California at Davis Journal of International Law and Policy* 147 (1996): 150–151.

Military and Paramilitary Activities in and against Nicaragua (Nicaragua v. United States). I.C.J. 14 (Judgment of June 27, 1986).

Nanda, Ved P. "The United States Reservation to the Ban on the Death Penalty for Juvenile Offenders: An Appraisal under the International Covenant on Civil and Political Rights." *DePaul Law Review* 42 (1993): 1311–1333.

North Sea Continental Shelf Cases (Federal Republic of Germany v. Denmark; Federal Republic of Germany v. Netherlands). I.C.J. Rept. 3 (1969).

The Paquete Habana. 175 U.S. 677 (1900).

Restatement (Third) of the Foreign Relations Law of the United States. Section 102 (1987).

Roper v. Simmons. 543 U.S. 551 (2005).

Simma, Bruno, and Philip Alston. "The Sources of Human Rights Law: Custom, *Jus Cogens*, and General Principles." *Australian Yearbook of International Law* 12 (1992): 82–108.

Weissbrodt, David. "Execution of Juvenile Offenders by the United States Violates International Human Rights Law. *American University Journal of International Law and Policy* 339 (1988): 367–369.

Weissbrodt, David, Joan Fitzpatrick, and Frank Newman. *International Human Rights: Law, Policy, and Process.* 4th ed. Cincinnati, Ohio: Anderson, 2008.

CYPRUS FROM 1964

by James Ker-Lindsay

Situated at the farthest eastern end of the Mediterranean Sea, the small island of Cyprus has played a disproportionately large role in the development of human rights in the modern era. Over the course of forty years the conflict between the island's Greek and Turkish communities touched on a range of substantive human rights issues, including questions relating to self-determination, minority rights, the treatment of internally displaced persons, and the introduction of settlers into areas deemed to be under occupation. However, it is perhaps with regard to the question of property rights that the island has become best known.

During the 1974 Turkish military invasion of the island, many thousands of Greek Cypriots were forced to flee their homes. Twenty years later and following numerous attempts to reunite the island, the European Court of Human Rights (ECrtHR) ruled that Turkey was in military occupation of the northern third of the island and ordered the Turkish government to pay compensation to Titina Loizidou for the ongoing loss of use of her property. This landmark judgment effectively cemented the principle that the invasion and occupation of territory cannot be legitimized with the passage of time. The land remained the property of its original owners, and states were liable to pay ongoing compensation to the owners for the loss of use of that property. However, the ruling also opened up important new questions. Most notably it raises questions about the degree to which a political settlement underpinned by a regime of compensation for property lost, rather than full restitution as laid down by the ECrtHR, can be held to be in conformity with the new principles laid down by the court.

ORIGINS AND COLLAPSE OF THE CYPRIOT REPUBLIC, 1960–1974

In 1960, following a four-year armed campaign to end eighty-two years of British colonial rule, Cyprus became an independent state. Under the constitution a complex power-sharing agreement was established between the majority Greek Cypriot community, which represented 78 percent of the population, and the minority Turkish Cypriot community, which made up 18 percent of the population. (The remaining 4 percent included the Maronite, Latin, and Armenian religious communities. Although each of these groups was entitled to a member in the House of Representatives, that representative could only vote on issues directly affecting his or her community. For the purposes of voting and political participation, each community opted to be considered a part of the wider Greek Cypriot community.) For the most part power was shared between the Greek and Turkish Cypriot communities on a ratio of 70 to 30. However, in the armed forces, the ratio was 60 to 40. At the same time both communities were given autonomy in a number of policy areas, such as education and religion.

The center of power in the state was the Council of Ministers, made up of seven Greek Cypriots and three Turkish Cypriots. Of the ten positions available, Turkish Cypriots were constitutionally required to hold one of the three key ministries: finance, defense, or foreign affairs. At the top of the state hierarchy were the Greek Cypriot president and the Turkish Cypriot vice president. Both held considerable veto power over legislation. Nevertheless and unusually, the ultimate responsibility for ensuring that the island's territorial integrity, sovereignty, and independence were protected was given to Greece and Turkey, the two "motherlands," who also retained a military presence on the island, and the United Kingdom, which also retained 99 square miles (255 square kilometers) as sovereign territory for military purposes. Collectively Greece, Turkey, and Great Britain became known as the guarantor powers. This system led to accusations that, although Cyprus was notionally independent, in reality the sovereignty of the new state was severely limited.

The creation of the Republic of Cyprus was not greeted by any wide-scale enthusiasm on the island. Indeed for Greek Cypriots the republic was a disappointment. The four-year struggle to end British colonial rule had not been fought to create an independent state. Instead, it had been waged to bring about the island's political union with Greece (enosis). This had been a long-standing dream of Greek Cypriots since the nineteenth century, and a referendum organized by the Orthodox Church of Cyprus in the early 1950s indicated that 96 percent of Greek Cypriots supported the idea of enosis. Moreover, while frustration about independence existed, there was also popular resentment against the constitutional structure of the new state that had given Turkish Cypriots, who represented less than one-fifth of the population, almost equal say over the governance of the country. In contrast, Turkish Cypriots viewed the Republic of Cyprus with a degree of ambivalence. Although the decision to create an independent state meant that the island had not united with Greece, which was undoubtedly a positive factor in the eyes of Turkish Cypriots, it nevertheless represented a compromise. Just as Greek Cypriots had wanted the entire island united with Greece, Turkish Cypriots sought a settlement that would have partitioned the island between Greece and Turkey, a policy known as *taksim* (Turkish for "division"). However, given the eventual outcome, the group's strong position in the government of the republic was a welcome result for most Turkish Cypriots.

Despite initial hopes that the power-sharing system put in place would eventually lead to a viable and functioning state, just two years after independence major differences began to emerge between the Greek and Turkish Cypriot communities. The first main issue to arise centered on the provision for the establishment of separate municipalities in Cyprus's main towns and cities. The Greek Cypriots, led by Archbishop Makarios, the first president of Cyprus, argued that the system was simply unworkable and that unified municipalities needed to be established. The Turkish Cypriots, led by Fazil Kuchuk, the vice president, argued that any changes could not be considered until the separate municipalities had been established as envisaged in the constitution. Thereafter a number of other points of difference began to emerge. These included questions relating to taxation and the degree to which the two communities should be integrated within existing security forces. By late 1963 Makarios had decided that major constitutional changes were required to ensure what he viewed as the smooth running of the state. In November of that year he proposed thirteen amendments to the constitution. These changes included eliminating the rights of the president and the vice president to veto legislation, creating unified municipalities, unifying the justice system, and a proposal to reduce the participation

of Turkish Cypriots in the civil service in accordance with their proportion in the wider population. Turkey immediately rejected the proposals, viewing them as an effort to undermine the Turkish Cypriot position within the state hierarchy, and in the weeks that followed there was a noticeable rise in tensions between the two communities.

On 21 December 1963 fighting broke out in Nicosia, the island's capital. In the days that followed the clashes spread to several other towns. Soon thereafter Turkish Cypriots effectively ceased to play a part in the government of Cyprus. At the same time large numbers of Turkish Cypriots began to gather together in various parts of the island. In the early twenty-first century the two communities continued to dispute what actually transpired during this time period. The Greek Cypriot interpretation of events is that Turkish Cypriot leadership, in pursuit of a policy to partition the island, ordered Turkish Cypriots to abandon their posts in the civil service and move into enclaves under Turkish Cypriot administration. There they would exist under the protection of Turkish Cypriot militias and the Turkish army units legally stationed on the island under the 1960 constitution. Conversely, Turkish Cypriots argue that they were prevented from participating in the government by Greek Cypriots and were forced to congregate in enclaves for self-defense. Whatever the truth of the matter, and the historical record shows that there are elements of truth in both accounts, the events of that period effectively marked the end of Turkish Cypriot participation in the government of Cyprus. To Turkish Cypriots, this marked the point when they were deprived of their rights as citizens of the Republic of Cyprus and forced to abandon their co-equal role in the state.

Over the course of the following weeks and months Greek Cypriots secured their position as the legitimate authority in Cyprus. This was ultimately confirmed on 4 March 1964, when the United Nations (UN) Security Council passed Resolution 186, which tacitly acknowledged that the government of Cyprus was now a Greek Cypriot–controlled entity. Importantly the resolution also established a peacekeeping force in Cyprus (the UN Peacekeeping Force in Cyprus or UNFICYP) and recommended the appointment of a mediator to try to reach a political solution between the two communities. In 1965 Galo Plaza Lasso, the UN mediator, presented his report. Controversially he suggested that Greek Cypriots put aside their pursuit of union with Greece. As for Turkish Cypriots, he recommended that they be offered greater political autonomy but rejected calls to create a federal system on the island. Turkey and Turkish Cypriots promptly dismissed the report, arguing that the mediator had no right to make formal proposals to the two sides. They therefore called on Plaza to resign. Greek Cypriots, although disagreeing with Plaza's rejection of enosis, argued that they would not accept a replacement mediator. Under these circumstances the UN secretary-general had no choice but to abandon the mediation effort. Instead, he established a Mission of Good Offices, which sought to take a less interventionist role. Going forward, any settlement would have to be reached on the basis of direct negotiations between the leaders of the two communities.

Meanwhile Greek Cypriots had introduced emergency legislation to manage the running of the state in the absence of Turkish Cypriots. These measures included a decision to abandon separate communal chambers and increase the size of the House of Representatives. Similarly the positions in the government that had been held previously by Turkish Cypriots were filled by Greek Cypriots. All these measures effectively ended the partnership state that had been established in 1960. By this point Greek Cypriots were in full control of the Republic of Cyprus, and Turkish Cypriots had become increasingly isolated in the enclaves scattered around the island. Again although Greek Cypriots argue that this isolation was self-imposed, Turkish Cypriots insist that they had no choice but to congregate in safe areas in order to avoid attacks by Greek Cypriot forces. Whatever the merits of the two arguments, life in the enclaves was extremely difficult, with access to food and medicine often limited. This led to a marked deterioration in the quality of life of Turkish Cypriots.

In 1967, following another major bout of fighting between the two communities, Turkey mobilized its armed forces and prepared for an invasion. A crisis was averted when the Greek government agreed to remove a substantial number of its forces from the island and Greek Cypriots agreed to lift the restrictions placed on Turkish Cypriot enclaves. As a result, Turkey ensured that regular supplies were able to reach Turkish Cypriot areas. This led to a dramatic improvement in the position of Turkish Cypriots, and shortly afterward Turkish Cypriots announced the formation of their own autonomous administration. Although this move was condemned by Greek Cypriots, a new round of negotiations began between the two communities in 1968. These lasted for the next six years and mainly focused on the question of granting Turkish Cypriots greater autonomy. However, this concept was again rejected by Makarios, who still hoped to put in place constitutional changes that would recognize Greek Cypriot majority rule and grant Turkish Cypriots minority rights rather than the coequal standing they were granted under the 1960 agreements.

DIVISION OF THE ISLAND

In 1974 the situation in Cyprus changed dramatically. Following several years of tensions between Athens and Nicosia, on 15 July the Greek military government staged a coup against President Makarios. In his place they installed a violent supporter of enosis known for his anti-Turkish views. Fearing that this was a prelude to a formal move to unite Cyprus with Greece, the Turkish government asked Great Britain to stage a joint intervention. London refused. Ankara therefore decided to take unilateral action. On 20 July 1974 Turkey invaded Cyprus. Within three days the military administration in Athens had collapsed, leading to a restoration of democracy in Greece. Shortly afterward a cease-fire was reached, and peace talks were convened in Geneva, Switzerland, that included the three guarantor powers: Britain, Greece, and Turkey. However, these talks broke up after several days. Thereafter a second round of negotiations was convened, this time involving the Greek and Turkish Cypriot communities. At this stage Ankara demanded that Greek Cypriots accept the creation of a federation on the island. A request by Greek Cypriots to consider the proposal was refused.

On 14 August Turkey ordered a second phase of the invasion. In the days that followed, Turkish forces fanned out east and west from their positions. By the time the next cease-fire was established, Turkey controlled 36 percent of the island's territory. The consequences of this were profound. In addition to the thousands killed and wounded, 160,000 Greek Cypriots were forced to flee their homes, becoming internally displaced persons (although in Greek Cypriot parlance they are more generally referred to as refugees). In the eyes of Greek Cypriots, the Turkish military operation amounted to little more than ethnic cleansing. Its aim was to not return the situation on the island to the status quo ante. Instead, the Turkish action aimed solely at driving out Greek Cypriots from their ancestral land in order to create an ethnically homogenous Turkish Cypriot zone. For Turkish Cypriots, the Turkish army was viewed as a liberator. After ten years of living in relative isolation, the Turkish Cypriots considered the invasion an opportunity to cement their autonomy with a territory of their own.

The invasion placed an enormous strain on the UN, which took responsibility for managing the humanitarian aspects of the crisis, and on the government of Cyprus, which also had to contend with the fact that the invasion had resulted in the loss of many of the most economically important areas of the island, such as the citrus-growing areas around Morphou and the major port at the eastern city of Famagusta. At the same time the division also resulted in major changes for Turkish Cypriots, many thousands of whom made their way to the areas under Turkish control. Meanwhile many others began to congregate in the British military bases on the south coast of the island, waiting for a chance to move north. To facilitate this, several agreements were put in place during the autumn that allowed these Turkish Cypriots to be transported via Turkey to northern Cyprus. In addition, a number of other steps were taken to manage the humanitarian dimensions of the island's division. For example, the UN established a Committee for Missing Persons (UNCMP) to investigate the whereabouts of over sixteen hundred Greek Cypriots and eight hundred Turkish Cypriots whose fates were unknown. This remained an ongoing process in 2008. And while the remains of a number of missing persons have been identified, the process has been frequently hampered by political ill will between the two communities. As a result, many other cases were still open and the work of the committee continued in the early twenty-first century.

INITIAL ATTEMPTS AT REUNIFICATION

The division of the island fundamentally altered the parameters of a political settlement. Whereas previous discussions had centered on giving Turkish Cypriots some degree of autonomy within the context of a unitary state, in the aftermath of the invasion the search for a solution now became focused on a federal settlement. This change was officially confirmed in 1977, when both sides signed the first of two high-level agreements confirming that any future solution would be based on the creation of a federation made up of two zones, the principle of bizonality, and the incorporation of two communities, the principle of bicommunality. This was reconfirmed in a second high-level agreement signed in 1979. Although this may have seemed like a relatively straightforward formula, in reality the two communities held widely differing views as to what it meant. The Turkish Cypriots assumed that the notion of bizonality and bicommunality were intrinsically linked and that any settlement would see the

establishment of an exclusively Turkish Cypriot federal state alongside an exclusively Greek Cypriot federal state. These two would then join to form the federal republic. For Greek Cypriots, the notions of bizonality and bicommunality were not directly linked to one another. Although it was accepted in principle that one state would be predominantly Turkish Cypriot and the other predominantly Greek Cypriot, neither state would be wholly made up of one community or the other. This issue was further complicated by the arrival of significant numbers of mainland Turkish settlers on the island, changing the demographic structure of the Turkish Cypriot community. However, the exact numbers were contested. Most Turkish Cypriot authorities adopted a lower-end estimate, putting the number at around forty thousand. By contrast, Greek Cypriots insisted that the number exceeded 100,000, in which case the settlers outnumbered Turkish Cypriots and therefore represented over 50 percent of the population on the northern part of the island.

On 15 November 1983 efforts to reunify the island suffered another severe setback when Turkish Cypriots unilaterally declared independence and founded the Turkish Republic of Northern Cyprus (TRNC). Although the new state was immediately recognized by Turkey, the move was declared illegal by the UN Security Council, which passed two resolutions (541 and 550) calling on the international community to refrain from recognizing the new state or otherwise supporting the TRNC. Despite this apparent setback, the UN continued its efforts to reach a settlement in Cyprus. In 1984 a new round of talks commenced. This time the talks foundered after the Greek Cypriot leadership rejected a blueprint presented by the UN. Afterward Rauf Denktash, the Turkish Cypriot leader, made it clear that he would not be willing to accept such a deal again. As a result, his position became increasingly intransigent, and by the late 1980s it was clear to most international observers that no settlement was likely as long as Denktash remained the Turkish Cypriot leader.

HUMAN RIGHTS CASES AGAINST TURKEY

In the late 1980s the pressure on the Turkish government to reach a settlement began to increase. In 1989 Loizidou, a Greek Cypriot refugee from the northern coastal town of Kyrenia, was arrested and held for several hours by Turkish forces while participating in a rally that aimed to cross the Green Line, the de facto boundary dividing the parts of the island controlled by Greek Cypriots and

Turkish Cypriots. In the aftermath of her detention, she filed a case against Turkey at the ECrtHR. Her attorneys' argument was that, because of the Turkish military occupation of the northern part of the island, Loizidou had lost control over her property. This represented a clear contravention of Article 8 of the European Convention on Human Rights, which protected the individual's right "to respect for his private and family life, his home and his correspondence." In response the Turkish government asserted that under international law it could not be held liable for the actions of the Turkish Republic of Northern Cyprus, which, it argued, was an independent state. Moreover, according to laws passed by the TRNC, Loizidou was no longer the owner of the property in question. On 19 December 1996 the court issued its first ruling. In a landmark decision it proclaimed that, for the purposes of Article 8 as well as Article 1 of Protocol 1 of the convention, Loizidou remained the legal owner of the land. Any attempt by the TRNC to deprive her of her property was therefore unrecognized. Second, the court held that the Turkish government, through the presence of large numbers of its troops on the island, was ultimately responsible for the actions of the TRNC, which was deemed to be a subordinate administration.

Two years later the court issued a subsequent judgment awarding Loizidou CY£300,000 (Cyprus pounds) in pecuniary damages for the loss of use of her property, CY £20,000 in nonpecuniary damages, and costs. The annual interest rate for default was set at 8 percent. The ruling represented a watershed moment as Turkey had been declared to be an occupying power. However, the Turkish government rejected the court's decision as politically motivated and announced that it would not comply with the ruling. Moreover the Turkish government argued that any effort to comply with the ruling would potentially disrupt efforts to find a political solution to the Cyprus problem. The decision to ignore the court's ruling, however, had direct implications for Turkey's continued participation in the Council of Europe (CoE). This in turn also raised questions about Turkey's hopes for eventual membership in the European Union (EU), as compliance with ECrtHR rulings was a basic requirement for membership.

Simultaneously Turkey came under increasing pressure from other quarters. On 8 September 1992 another case was brought against Turkey at the European Commission of Human Rights. This time it was lodged by a Turkish Cypriot, Djavit An, who argued that he had been deprived of his right to peaceful assembly as a result of the decision by Turkey and Turkish Cypriot authorities to prevent him from attending bicommunal events across the Green Line. He argued that this was a violation of his rights under Article 25 of the Convention for the Protection of Human Rights and Fundamental Freedoms. The case was eventually put before the ECrtHR on 1 November 1999; the court issued its ruling on 20 February 2003. Once again it confirmed Turkey's responsibility for human rights violations in northern Cyprus, fining the Turkish government 15,000 euros for having deprived An of his rights and an additional 4,715 euros for legal costs and expenses.

Another important issue centered on the way Turkey appeared to be encouraging a number of its citizens to relocate to Cyprus. Greek Cypriots argued that this settlement process was in direct contravention of international law. Specifically it represented a violation of article 49(6) of the 1949 Convention (IV) Relative to the Protection of Civilian Persons in Time of War (otherwise known as the Fourth Geneva Convention), specifically relating to the deportation and transfer of persons into occupied territory. Article 85 of Protocol I of the convention stipulates that a grave breach of the protocol would take place with the willful "transfer by the Occupying Power of parts of its own civilian population into the territory it occupies." As a result, Greek Cypriot politicians argued that Turkey's actions regarding the settlers represented a war crime and made it clear that any settlement of the Cyprus issue must necessarily be tied to steps to ensure that all new settlers returned to Turkey. This, however, raised a number of serious questions. Quite apart from the fact that many settlers had since married Turkish Cypriots and therefore would be entitled to stay on the island in the event of reunification, many others argued that the settlers could not be forced from the island. In many cases, they had given up all their ties to a village in mainland Turkey. And in other instances, when families had tried to return home, they had been ostracized by their former communities. For the children of the settlers, Cyprus was home. It therefore became clear that the issue was not nearly as cut-and-dried as made out by Greek Cypriots. Most observers recognized that any solution would have to balance the overall legality of the settlement program against the human rights of the settlers.

OPENING OF THE GREEN LINE

By the late 1990s the efforts to reunite the island of Cyprus were undergoing a profound transformation.

The EU's decision to open membership talks with Cyprus, coupled with increasing pressure on the Turkish government from the ECrtHR, posed a direct threat to Turkey's own EU membership aspirations. Therefore in November 2001 a new peace initiative was launched at the behest of the Turkish Cypriot leadership. However, initial optimism that the two sides would be able to reach a settlement by the following June, as had been suggested by both parties, quickly dissipated. Within weeks of the start of talks, they were deadlocked. In November 2002, acting with the support of the UN Security Council, Secretary-General Kofi Annan unveiled a blueprint for the settlement of the problem. This quickly became known as the Annan Plan. As had been agreed to in the 1977 and 1979 high-level agreements, the plan foresaw the creation of a bizonal, bicommunal federation in Cyprus. However, the Turkish Cypriot leader refused to accept such an agreement, and in March 2003 the UN secretary-general was forced to abandon his initiative. Fearing the consequences that this might have for Turkey and in order to stave off growing resentment among Turkish Cypriots, the Turkish Cypriot leadership ordered that all restrictions on crossing the Green Line be lifted. After thirty years Greek Cypriots would be allowed to cross the line freely. The effects of the decision were profound. In the days and weeks that followed the decision, tens of thousands of Greek Cypriots queued daily to visit their former villages and homes. Although Greek Cypriots could now cross the Green Line at will, Turkish Cypriot authorities nevertheless made it clear that there would be no restitution of the properties originally belonging to them. People could visit their homes, but they could not reclaim them and subsequently return to live there. In this regard the opening of the line did nothing to address the issues raised in the Loizidou case.

The opening of the Green Line also meant that many thousands of Turkish Cypriots now had their first opportunity in decades to cross freely to the southern part of the island. However, unlike the Turkish Cypriot authorities that had expropriated Greek Cypriot properties, the Cypriot government had made no similar claim against Turkish Cypriot land. Instead, Turkish Cypriot properties owned by Turkish Cypriots who had left the areas under the control of the government of Cyprus had been placed under a form of trusteeship. Although the title still belonged to the Turkish Cypriot owner, many of these properties had been rented out to Greek Cypriot refugees. Once the line was opened, many Turkish Cypriots began to reclaim their land. This placed the Cypriot government in a difficult position. If it refused to return the property, it would be liable to face highly embarrassing action before the ECrtHR. However, any move to give back the land and evict the Greek Cypriot tenants would be costly in political terms. Refugee groups would argue that they were being displaced for a second time and that, although Greek Cypriots were prepared to return Turkish Cypriot land, Turkey and the Turkish Cypriots were still refusing to hand back Greek Cypriot properties.

For this reason the government attempted to limit the number of cases by introducing a requirement that any Turkish Cypriot wishing to reclaim land must be a resident in the areas controlled by the government of Cyprus for at least six months. This deterred the great majority of Turkish Cypriots, but cases soon emerged in which this condition had been met and a claim was filed for the return of property. At first the government tried to delay action for as long as possible, but eventually it was taken to court by Mustafa Arif, a Turkish Cypriot with property in the south of the island. In September 2004 the Supreme Court ruled that property belonging to Arif should be returned. Thereafter a subsequent court ruling found that Arif met the necessary conditions for his property to be returned. The court, however, did order that the implementation of the ruling be delayed pending an appeal by the government and by the inhabitants of the property. In February 2006 the government, recognizing the legal consequences of a defeat in court, which would open the way for many other properties to be returned to their original owners, decided not to challenge the case and found alternative accommodations for the Greek Cypriots living on Arif's property. The Cypriot government argued that Arif's claim was an "isolated case" and could not be regarded as a precedent. Naturally this raised questions about the degree to which Greek Cypriots were adopting a double standard with regard to property issues.

In the autumn of 2003 Turkey eventually decided to comply with the ECrtHR ruling in the Loizidou case. After five years of fighting the decision, Turkey's decision to satisfy the court's judgment was driven by several factors. Most importantly it was a direct result of the growing pressure that was being brought to bear on Turkey by the EU. At the European Council in Thessalonica in June of that same year, members of the EU had reiterated the importance of full compliance with the rulings of the ECrtHR and made it clear that such compliance was a prerequisite for membership in the EU. In view of the Turkish government's wish to proceed with a petition for membership, which was linked with a hope to start formal membership talks later that year, Ankara at long last decided to settle the case and pay the ECrtHR-mandated fines. The decision was in part shaped by a political decision made by the CoE several days earlier to delay implementation of the judgment calling for the property to be returned to Loizidou until the end of 2005. Although this decision was vigorously opposed by the Republic of Cyprus, which found support from Greece and Russia, the other states present agreed to the delay. On 7 December 2003 Turkey paid Loizidou the sum of 1.2 million euros. To Greek Cypriots, the decision was hailed as proof that the TRNC was nothing more than a subordinate administration of Turkey and that the Turkish government was ultimately responsible for any human rights abuses that had taken place in northern Cyprus. In contrast, the Turkish government maintained that its basic position remained intact. It had simply decided to comply with the "unjust and erroneous" ruling in order to fulfill its common responsibility and preserve the credibility of the court.

THE ANNAN PLAN AND EU ACCESSION

Following Turkish Cypriot parliamentary elections in December 2003, which brought to power an administration committed to reunification, talks resumed between the two sides in February 2004. With just three months until the island was scheduled to join the EU, the secretary-general made it clear that the talks would be held according to a strict timetable. Following an initial round of negotiations between both sides in Cyprus, a second phase of discussions occurred in Switzerland involving both Greece and Turkey. When this failed to produce a conclusive set of proposals, Annan himself stepped in to move forward a draft agreement. It was widely praised by the international community, which saw the document as essentially fair. Despite complaints from many Greek Cypriots that the plan was contrary to the principles of the EU, the European Commission, which had been involved in drafting the agreement, gave its approval. Similarly both the Turkish government and the Turkish Cypriot administration supported the agreement. However, the plan was quickly rejected by the Greek Cypriot leadership. In an emotional speech delivered to Greek Cypriots on 7 April 2004, Tassos Papadopoulos, the president of Cyprus, called on the people to reject the agreement. Specifically he argued that it did little to reunite the island but instead would cement the division and in doing so would legitimize many of the most

unacceptable aspects of the division, such as the presence of a large number of Turkish settlers on the island. Finally, many Greek Cypriots believed that the plan was being rushed through in an attempt to secure a settlement in advance of the island's membership in the EU. This raised suspicion that the agreement contained a number of clauses contrary to EU *acquis communautaire* (body of laws). The argument was therefore put forward that once the island joined the EU, the plan would no longer be acceptable. However, little existed to support this view. The European Commission had already made it clear that the plan was in accordance with the acquis. Moreover the exceptions (derogations) that had been requested were, with one exception, temporary and therefore in perfect accord with the standard principles of the EU.

To be sure, there were many elements of the plan that were justifiably open to criticism. For example, many pointed to the question of security and the mechanisms for ensuring that the plan would be implemented according to the agreed timetable. As Papadopoulos pointed out, Greek Cypriots would be expected to meet their end of the bargain, participating in a joint government with Turkish Cypriots almost immediately, whereas Turkish Cypriots would have several years to surrender property and ensure that large numbers of Turkish troops left the island. Many also resented the fact that the plan failed to ensure that all Greek Cypriots would receive back the property they had lost. Although those who had lost property in Morphou and Famagusta would experience the return of all their property, many others, especially those living near Kyrenia and in the Karpas Peninsula, would be entitled to recover only a third of their property, receiving compensation and bonds for the rest of their lost land. At the same time many asserted that the proposals to allow over forty thousand Turkish settlers who had arrived on the island since 1974 to stay in Cyprus amounted to an unacceptable illegal policy put in place by Turkey. It was against this backdrop that on 24 April 76 percent of Greek Cypriots voted against the UN plan, as compared with 65 percent of Turkish Cypriots voting in favor of it. The plan therefore failed to come into force and a week later, on 1 May 2004, Cyprus joined the EU as a divided state.

Despite initial hopes that a new process would start soon after accession, in the first four years that followed there was little movement on the Cyprus issue. Whereas in July 2006 the two sides reached an agreement paving the way for a consultation process, this failed to produce any significant results. Instead, it was not until early 2008 that momentum began to develop for a new peace process following the election by the Greek Cypriots of Dimitris Christofias, a known moderate, as president. Within weeks the leaders of the two communities agreed to the start of technical discussions between a number of expert committees. These covered a range of key topics, including governance, security, and property. In September 2008 high-level negotiations began between the two sides.

ASSESSMENT

After 1960 Cyprus raised questions relating to a number of human rights. Most notably these issues relate to the conflict between the Greek and Turkish communities on the island. This led to significant human rights abuses by both sides. However, as is the case with most conflicts, in Cyprus the finger of responsibility for human rights violations and abuses cannot be pointed solely at one side or another. Neither is it simply a matter of blaming the external parties that played a part in events on the island. Similarly neither community can claim to be the sole victim of the situation. A degree of blame must be apportioned to all sides for human rights abuses on the island over the course of forty years. In the early 1960s Greek Cypriot extremists had been clearly determined to limit the role of Turkish Cypriots in the central administration of the state. At best this plan aimed to see them reduced to a minority with minority rights rather than a politically equal community. At worst it would have seen large numbers of Turkish Cypriots murdered or driven from the island. In a similar vein, throughout the 1960s the Cypriot government, which was by that point controlled by Greek Cypriots, impeded the delivery of food and medical supplies to Turkish Cypriot enclaves. However, it must also be recognized that Greek Cypriots were victims of what can be regarded as ethnic cleansing in 1974. The aim of the Turkish armed forces and Turkish Cypriot leadership was to create an area in Cyprus that would be almost exclusively, if not wholly, Turkish in identity. In doing so, Turkish Cypriots, the victims of human rights abuses during the period from 1964 to 1974, became accomplices in human rights violations committed against the Greek Cypriot community during and after the Turkish invasion.

The failure to reach a settlement in the years that followed the division of the island eventually paved the way for a number of human rights violations cases to be brought against the Republic of Turkey. These cases fundamentally reshaped the parameters of the problem in legal, if not political, terms. Without a doubt, the most significant development in terms of human rights to have emerged from the Cyprus issue is the Loizidou case. Quite apart from the consequences it has had on Turkey's standing in international circles and the effect it will have on the country's prospects for EU accession, it has also led to what Achilleas Demetriades, the attorney for Loizidou, referred to as the "economic quantification" of human rights abuses. No longer do wide-scale human rights abuses perpetrated by governments simply carry a political penalty on the international stage. They also risk clearly discernible economic costs. This marks an important development, at least as seen by Greek Cypriots, in the future evolution of human rights. Ironically and importantly the consequences of this decision also have an affect on Greek Cypriots. Following the events of 1974, many Turkish Cypriots decided to move to the areas under Turkish control and abandon their properties. These were then placed under the administration of the guardian of Turkish Cypriot properties.

However, after the Green Line opened in 2003, many Turkish Cypriots sought to reclaim their own properties only to find that path obstructed. This led to the possibility of cases being brought to the ECrtHR by Turkish Cypriots. Needless to say, this would be highly embarrassing as well as politically damaging to Greek Cypriots. Nonetheless, handing back properties to Turkish Cypriots, which in many cases might require evicting Greek Cypriot refugees, would be politically costly for Greek Cypriot leaders as long as Greek Cypriot land and property in Turkish Cypriot–controlled northern Cyprus remain inaccessible. Greek Cypriots would also find it unacceptable that they ultimately become liable for the taxes on property that Turkish Cypriots decided to abandon.

To many, if not most, outside observers, one of the major problems preventing a settlement in Cyprus is that the term "human rights" has been misinterpreted, either deliberately or in error, by the two communities. It is clear that the notion of human rights means one thing to a Greek Cypriot and something entirely different to a Turkish Cypriot. In the minds of Greek Cypriots, the Cyprus issue has been a question of invasion and occupation by Turkey. Few Greek Cypriots have recognized that the roots of the problem lie in the period before 1974, when Turkish Cypriots were forced to live in enclaves and deprived of their constitutional rights to participate in the central government. Instead, for Greek Cypriots the language of the problem has focused on the need to reclaim property lost during the invasion and to ensure the return of all refugees to their former homes. For Greek Cypriots, the term "human rights" is shorthand for property rights involving the individual. Conversely, Turkish Cypriots have tended to ignore the major humanitarian consequences of 1974 for Greek Cypriots. Most do not view the Turkish army as an occupation force that has deprived Greek Cypriots of their homes and property. Rather, they see the army as guaranteeing the safety and security of the Turkish Cypriot community. Furthermore, any attempt to reach a settlement must ensure the political equality of the Turkish Cypriot community in the governance of a future Cypriot state. In contrast, "human rights" for Turkish Cypriots has come to mean communal political rights.

Any attempt to broker an agreement based solely on one reading of this term would prove impossible. Full respect for the right of Greek Cypriots to return to their homes would render meaningless any bizonal, bicommunal federal agreement. By allowing all Greek Cypriot refugees to return to their pre-1974 homes, the Turkish Cypriot component state would become inhabited by a Greek Cypriot majority. However, any effort to severely limit or completely deny the right of Greek Cypriot refugees to return to their homes would lead to considerable resentment among them. To this extent, the notion of a bicommunal and bizonal federation must naturally ensure a degree of exclusivity to each of the two states if the concept is to have meaning and validity. This does not mean, however, that two ethnically exclusive states have to be formed. There must be a balance between both, and a full and unfettered application of "human rights" as seen by one or the other community cannot take place. Instead, a politically negotiated settlement must be reached that straddles the two competing interpretations of human rights—one predominantly based on communal civil and political rights, and the other largely conceptualized in terms of the individual's right to own property—which necessarily has wider political ramifications.

[*See also* Ethnic Cleansing; European Union; Foreign Policy; Internally Displaced Persons; Self-Determination; *and* United Nations High Commissioner for Refugees.]

BIBLIOGRAPHY

Brewin, Christopher. *The European Union and Cyprus.* Huntingdon, U.K.: Eothen, 2000.

Chrysostomides, Kypros. *The Republic of Cyprus: A Study in International Law.* Cambridge, Mass.: Kluwer Law International, 2000.

Diez, Thomas, ed. *The European Union and the Cyprus Conflict: Modern Conflict, Postmodern Union.* Manchester, U.K.: Manchester University Press, 2002.

Dodd, Clement, ed. *Cyprus: The Need for New Perspectives.* Huntingdon, U.K.: Eothen, 1999.

Joseph, Joseph S. *Cyprus: Ethnic Conflict and International Concern.* 2d ed. Houndmills, Basingstoke, U.K.: Palgrave Macmillan, 1997.

Kyle, Keith. *Cyprus: In Search of Peace.* London: Minority Rights Group, 1997.

Necatigil, Zaim M. *The Cyprus Question and the Turkish Position in International Law.* Oxford: Oxford University Press, 1989.

Richmond, Oliver, and James Ker-Lindsay, eds. *The Work of the UN in Cyprus: Promoting Peace and Development.* Houndmills, Basingstoke, U.K.: Palgrave Macmillan, 2001.

ROMÉO DALLAIRE

by Howard B. Tolley Jr.

As commander of the United Nations Assistance Mission for Rwanda (UNAMIR), Lieutenant General Roméo Dallaire made heroic but unsuccessful efforts to protect the Tutsi from genocide in 1994. On his first assignment with command responsibility in a combat zone, Dallaire confronted génocidaires (perpetrators of genocide), protected their victims, and sounded constant alarms ignored by others.

Overwhelmed by a sense of personal responsibility for the genocide, Dallaire suffered post-traumatic stress disorder and repeatedly attempted suicide. Since his recovery and his retirement from the military in 2000, Dallaire has in effect waged a "Never Forget Rwanda" campaign in order to make real the promise of "Never Again."

THE PRE-RWANDA YEARS: 1946–1993

Dallaire's father, a French-Canadian noncommissioned officer, fought with Allied forces that liberated Belgium and the Netherlands from the Nazis. He married a Dutch nurse, who gave birth to their first child, Roméo, on 25 June 1946. Six months later, Dallaire's mother brought him to settle in Montreal, Quebec. He attended Catholic schools but also made friends in a scout group sponsored by a Presbyterian church. In street fights, he alternately aligned with rival French- and English-speaking gangs.

In his teens, Dallaire decided to pursue a military career and made considerable effort to improve a weak academic record for admission as a cadet to Collège Militaire Royal de Saint-Jean in Montreal. When completing university at the Royal Military College in Kingston, Ontario, he encountered prejudice against French-speaking students, who were regarded as potential separatists. He demonstrated a loyal commitment to federalism when his artillery unit guarded the National Assembly against terrorist secessionists in 1970. A possible beneficiary of affirmative action for French Canadians, he rose in rank on a fast track. Dallaire attended staff colleges in the United States and the United Kingdom. He commanded an artillery regiment and a mechanized brigade

and participated in NATO live-fire exercises in Germany. Upon returning home, Dallaire married, and he fathered three children. He became the commandant of Collège Militaire Royal de Saint-Jean with the arrival of a post–Cold War new world order in 1990.

At the height of the U.S.-Soviet rivalry, Canada's Lester Pearson had promoted UN peacekeeping to create a neutral buffer force monitoring a cease-fire between states at war. Dallaire trained Canadian peacekeepers for a different type of UN mission within states torn by civil war— Bosnia and Cambodia. Crimes against humanity in failed states increasingly forced the UN to take sides by making rather than keeping the peace. When called to command a force in Rwanda, Lieutenant General Dallaire's Catholic, francophone, minority, and family background made it feel to him like a career dream come true.

UN FORCE COMMANDER: HEROIC FAILURE

After years of civil war and ethnic massacres, in August 1993 Rwanda's Hutu strongman, Major General Juvénal Habyarimana, reluctantly agreed to the Arusha Accords with Hutu opposition parties and the Tutsi-dominated Rwandan Patriotic Front (RPF). The agreement provided for a weapons-free zone in the capital, Kigali; integration of RPF units in Rwanda's military; repatriation of Tutsi refugees; and power sharing among six rival parties in a new transitional government. Dallaire's initial deployment to the region was as commander of a UN observer force in Uganda monitoring a ban on arms transfers by Tutsi exiles across the Rwandan border.

The August accords called for a UN deployment within a month. The UN Security Council did not approve it until October, and the troops arrived between November and February. The day before Dallaire arrived in October, Tutsi soldiers killed the elected Hutu president in Burundi, Rwanda's neighbor to the south. Over a hundred thousand terrified refugees fled to Rwanda, fueling Hutu antagonism toward the RPF.

Dallaire's recommendation for 5,500 troops was scaled back to 2,500. Although the Arusha parties requested a force to protect the civilian population, the Security Council restricted UNAMIR to a neutral, monitoring role with a minimal budget. Dallaire independently drafted robust rules of engagement authorizing use of lethal force to prevent crimes against humanity. His superiors never questioned the rules, and Dallaire hoped they would support effective military action if needed. An unresponsive UN bureaucracy frustrated his efforts to obtain basic telephone service, office furniture, supplies, and equipment.

Twenty-three governments contributed a diverse assortment of troop units and selected officers, but most arrived from developing states without the required equipment and logistical support. Rwanda's former colonial ruler, Belgium, contributed four hundred well-trained and adequately equipped troops. Nine hundred ill-prepared Bangladeshi troops posed repeated problems. Canada supplied only one additional officer, Major Brent Beardsley, who became the force commander's military assistant and trusted confidant. Old transport vehicles and armored personnel carriers arrived in need of extensive repairs. UNAMIR set up a Kigali headquarters in the Amohoro Hotel adjoining a large athletic stadium. As violence escalated and the ruling party failed to implement the accords, ragtag units of unarmed UN observers and lightly armed peacekeepers were deployed beyond Kigali in a northern demilitarized zone and scattered sites throughout the country.

There was no unity in the UN chain of command. Numerous civilian superiors pursued different political agendas. Dallaire's military subordinates also reported to contributing governments that countermanded his orders.

Cameroonian Jacques-Roger Booh-Booh served as the secretary-general's special representative for facilitating the political transition and head of mission in Kigali. The RPF viewed the Franco-African Booh-Booh as sympathetic to the Hutu government and its French patrons. Hutu extremists considered Dallaire pro-Tutsi and, when facing defeat, broadcast calls for assassinating the commander with the mustache. When Dallaire sought reinforcements, Booh-Booh favored withdrawal.

The force commander reported continuously by cable to a triumvirate in the UN Department of Peacekeeping Operations (DPKO), headed by Undersecretary-General for Peacekeeping Operations Kofi Annan, that included his fellow Canadian and friend General Maurice Baril. In January, Dallaire requested protection for an informant who warned of plans to massacre Tutsi in Kigali as well as Belgian peacekeepers. He announced plans to seize a weapons cache and closed with an enthusiastic call to arms: "Where there's a will, there's a way. Let's go!"

At UN headquarters there was no will to take sides or use force unless peacekeepers were attacked. The DPKO denied permission to seize the weapons and directed Dallaire to inform Habyarimana and the U.S., French, and Belgian missions of the threat. Rather than empower Dallaire with a deterrent force, the major powers insisted that UN officials threaten to withdraw UNAMIR as a way to press Habyarimana to implement the Arusha Accords.

As political assassinations and killings spread, Dallaire warned of massacres that would be fueled by Hutu hate radio foretelling mass slaughter. DPKO failed to share his dire warnings with the Security Council. Dallaire worried that Rwanda's representative on the Security Council functioned as an informant for the Hutu extremists. Secretary-General Boutros Boutros-Ghali never sought information directly from Dallaire until five days after Hutu power extremists launched both a coup d'état and their well-planned final solution to the "Tutsi threat."

It is still unknown who killed President Habyarimana by shooting down his plane on 6 April 2004. Hutu extremists immediately blamed the RPF and Belgium. Within twenty-four hours they had assassinated moderate Hutu leaders, murdered ten Belgian peacekeepers, and begun exterminating Tutsi. Before their execution, Dallaire learned that the Belgians were being held in a well-fortified army camp. He concluded that UNAMIR had insufficient troops to mount a successful rescue mission. After recovery of the mutilated corpses, the Belgian government decided to remove its remaining peacekeepers.

Dallaire believed that a decisive show of force with effective UN support could defeat the Hutu extremists and restore order. He also felt a moral duty to protect targets on the death lists in Kigali. UNAMIR secured a stadium, hotels, schools, and churches. He desperately sought to save the Arusha Accords by promoting RPF collaboration with moderate Hutu in the military but failed to prevent resumption of the civil war.

The Department of Peacekeeping Operations insisted on strict neutrality and recognized the new extremist regime as an acceptable successor to the government that consented to the Arusha Accords. UN headquarters directed the Kigali mission to seek a cease-fire and offered no support for the protection of Rwandans. Instead, DPKO called on Dallaire to secure the airport and assist French and Belgian paratroopers just hours before they arrived to evacuate expatriates on 9 April. The United States placed marines on call in neighboring Burundi to support an overland convoy of departing U.S. nationals. A Belgian unit redeployed from a school to the airport, thus abandoning to slaughter over two thousand people who had sought UNAMIR protection. A contingent commander, from Bangladesh, citing orders from home, rejected UNAMIR assignments that endangered his men. France evacuated Hutu allies and used UNAMIR vehicles.

None of the intervening powers offered assistance to UNAMIR's protection efforts, and they refused to evacuate any endangered Rwandans in their employ. An infuriated Dallaire concluded that for the Western powers some people were more human than others. NATO allies that had committed sixty thousand troops to prevent ethnic cleansing in the former Yugoslavia put fewer than two thousand boots on the ground in Rwanda and restricted them to a three-day evacuation of their own white nationals completed by 12 April. The departure of the Belgian contingent days later further embittered a commander whose father had fought to liberate the Low Countries from the Nazis fifty years earlier.

Although he still wanted the Security Council to approve an increased force of five thousand, Dallaire was offered the option of either total withdrawal or reduction to a skeleton force. Despite considerable resistance from the United States, he was allowed to continue with 270 troops and directed to work for a cease-fire. A committed Ghanaian deputy arranged for several hundred of his capable men to remain, leaving UNAMIR with about five hundred troops by 25 April.

UNDER THE GUN

In the one hundred days after 6 April 1994, an estimated eight hundred thousand people were killed in what Dallaire learned to call genocide. He bravely risked his life on repeated missions to negotiate with the combatants, to rescue victims, and to protect humanitarian relief workers. UNAMIR forces lived in squalor—short on rations, water, and fuel. They struggled to protect and feed over twenty thousand refugees at sites in Kigali, including medical facilities staffed by the International Committee of the Red Cross and Doctors without Borders (Médicins sans frontières). With rival armies controlling sectors of Kigali, Dallaire facilitated short truces that enabled threatened noncombatants to move safely across enemy lines.

Lamenting the lack of a broadcast capability to counter radio broadcasts directing génocidaires to Tutsi targets, he failed to persuade the UN to take out the extremist station or block its transmissions. In order to shame the international community into action, Dallaire shielded visiting journalists courageous enough to confront the mounting piles of bodies on the streets and bloated corpses on the rivers. He failed to persuade RPF commander Paul Kagame to alter his narrow antigovernment military strategy and do more to halt the genocidal "self-defense" by Hutu extremists.

By late May, the DPKO and the Security Council were forced to acknowledge a humanitarian disaster involving several hundred thousand deaths. The United States objected to including the term "genocide" in the authorizing resolution but voted for UNAMIR II with five thousand troops mandated to halt the slaughter. Well before the promised manpower and personnel arrived two months later, France with Security Council approval had created a humanitarian protection zone in southwestern Rwanda and the RPF had won the war. Upstaged by the Security Council's approval of the French "Operation Turquoise" and diverted by the RPF's threat to attack French troops harboring Hutu extremists, Dallaire was powerless to prevent an exodus of the extremist government and nearly 2 million Hutu refugees, mostly into Zaire. Dallaire wanted UNAMIR II troops to replace the French at the earliest possible time, and he prepared a Homeward Bound plan to avert destabilization of Zaire. Trauma prevented him from soldiering on. After several incidents of erratic behavior, a new force commander assumed responsibility for helping postgenocide Rwanda.

CASUALTY AND SCAPEGOAT

Before departing Rwanda, Dallaire had become suicidal, recklessly exposing himself to unnecessary risk. The daily sights, smells, and sounds of indescribable atrocities created an unbearable sense of failure. Compulsive work at new command posts in Canada delayed treatment of his post-traumatic stress disorder (PTSD) for several years. A six-month medical leave led to extensive medication and therapy. He collaborated in a training video on PTSD and helped his therapist write a book detailing the mental health wounds of peacekeepers in Rwanda. In public lectures and interviews, Dallaire continued to reproach himself with graphic descriptions of the bloodied, dismembered victims he had failed to save. Six years after his return from Rwanda, and several years after beginning therapy, police found him unconscious from a toxic mix of drugs and alcohol on a park bench.

Survivors and buck passers have pursued Dallaire on several fronts. Family members of murdered Hutu leaders he had promised to protect and relatives of those slaughtered at the school abandoned by the Belgians initiated civil litigation. Unable to place Dallaire in the dock, the Belgian military attempted to court-martial their own top officer in Rwanda. In their view, UNAMIR commanders violated their cardinal obligation to rescue fallen comrades. Secretary-General Kofi Annan would not allow Dallaire to testify for the defense—he could only answer questions in writing. Just as Security Council members had become gun-shy based on the fatalities suffered in Mogadishu, Dallaire also learned from that futile rescue effort. He insisted that an attack on the army camp would not have saved the Belgians but would have resulted in significant UNAMIR casualties and jeopardized the larger mission. His deputy was acquitted.

The Belgian and French parliaments both completed investigations that, while faulting Dallaire, also spread the blame far beyond the force commander. Detractors in Canada lamented that Dallaire's inexperience, political naïveté, and gung ho approach made him less fit for the Rwanda assignment than veteran officers from other peacekeeping missions. Two studies (one by Scott R. Feil, the other by Alan J. Kuperman) examining whether the intervention recommended by Dallaire would have averted genocide reached conflicting results. The most thorough official investigations completed by the UN and OAU assigned primary responsibility for the Rwanda debacle to others while commending Dallaire's efforts.

WITNESS FOR THE PROSECUTION AND HONORED WARRIOR

Prosecutors and defendants at the International Criminal Tribunal for Rwanda have solicited Dallaire's testimony in three cases. Dallaire welcomed the opportunity to hold evildoers accountable, especially the génocidaire in chief, Thèoneste Bagosora, who had threatened to kill him.

Dallaire's best-selling memoir *Shake Hands with the Devil: The Failure of Humanity in Rwanda* (2004) indicts UN Secretariat officials and the world's major powers in the court of public opinion. While acknowledging his own defects and attributing primary responsibility to the Rwandans, his detailed bill of particulars exposes incompetence, hypocrisy, racism, political machinations, and a critical lack of will. Yet, Secretariat DPKO leaders who opposed more muscular UN involvement in Rwanda presented themselves as trying to save UN peacekeeping from another disaster after the withdrawal from Somalia in 1993.

Canadian filmmakers promoted Dallaire's views in *The Last Just Man* (2001). *Shake Hands with the Devil* became the subject of a 2004 Emmy award–winning documentary and a 2007 feature film. Appointed as a Liberal member of Canada's Senate in 2005, Dallaire has campaigned for humanitarian intervention against genocide in Darfur and sought to end the use of child soldiers.

Over a dozen U.S. and Canadian universities have recognized Dallaire with honorary doctorates. Harvard's Kennedy School of Government granted him a fellowship at the Carr Center for Human Rights Policy, and he has lectured widely at other universities. His military honors include the Canadian Meritorious Service Cross, Officer of the Order of Canada, and Grand Officer of the National Order of Québec. The United States conferred the Legion of Merit in noting his assistance in the evacuation of U.S. nationals. Dallaire's human rights awards include one for genocide prevention from the Aegis Trust (United Kingdom) and the Pearson Peace Medal for his contribution to multilateralism. Based on the tough choices Dallaire confronted, an educational software firm developed *Pax Warrior* for students to role-play the UN force commander under siege.

Dallaire transferred the soldier's traditional allegiance to "God and country" into a commitment to humanity and the UN. The humanitarian idealism that became a nightmare for him offers a profile in moral courage for others.

[*See also* Genocide *and* International Criminal Tribunal for Rwanda (ICTR).]

BIBLIOGRAPHY

PUBLISHED WORKS

Adelman, Howard, and Astri Suhrke. *The Path of a Genocide: The Rwanda Crisis from Uganda to Zaire.* New Brunswick, N.J.: Transaction Publishers, 1999.

Anyidoho, Henry K. *Guns over Kigali: The Rwandese Civil War—1994: A Personal Account.* Accra, Ghana: Woeli Publishing Services, 1997.

Barnett, Michael N. *Eyewitness to a Genocide: The United Nations and Rwanda.* Ithaca, N.Y.: Cornell University Press, 2002.

Castonguay, Jacques. *Les Casques Bleus au Rwanda.* Paris: Harmattan, 1998.

Dallaire, Roméo. "The End of Innocence: Rwanda 1994." In *Hard Choices: Moral Dilemmas in Humanitarian Intervention,* edited by Jonathan Moore, pp. 71–86. Lanham, Md.: Rowman & Littlefield, 1998.

Dallaire, Roméo. "The Media Dichotomy." In *The Media and the Rwanda Genocide*, edited by Allan Thompson, pp. 12–19. London: Fountain Publishers, 2007.

Dallaire, Roméo, and Brent Beardsley. *Shake Hands with the Devil: The Failure of Humanity in Rwanda*. New York: Carroll & Graf, 2004.

Des Forges, Alison L., Human Rights Watch, and Fédération Internationale des Droits de l'Homme. *"Leave None to Tell the Story": Genocide in Rwanda*. New York: Human Rights Watch and International Federation of Human Rights, 1999.

Feil, Scott R., Carnegie Commission on Preventing Deadly Conflict, and Carnegie Corporation of New York. *Preventing Genocide: How the Early Use of Force Might Have Succeeded in Rwanda*. Washington, D.C.: Carnegie Commission on Preventing Deadly Conflict, 1998.

Kuperman, Alan J. *The Limits of Humanitarian Intervention: Genocide in Rwanda*. Washington, D.C.: Brookings Institution Press, 2001.

Mamdani, Mahmood. *When Victims Become Killers: Colonialism, Nativism, and the Genocide in Rwanda*. Princeton, N.J.: Princeton University Press, 2001.

Melvern, Linda. *A People Betrayed: The Role of the West in Rwanda's Genocide*. London: Zed Books, 2000.

Off, Carol. *The Lion, the Fox, and the Eagle: A Story of Generals and Justice in Yugoslavia and Rwanda*. Toronto: Random House Canada, 2000.

Organization of African Unity, International Panel of Eminent Personalities to Investigate the 1994 Genocide in Rwanda and the Surrounding Events. *Rwanda: The Preventable Genocide*. Addis Ababa, Ethiopia: Ipep/Oau, 2000.

Power, Samantha. *A Problem from Hell: America and the Age of Genocide*. New York: Basic Books, 2002.

United Nations Security Council. Report of the Independent Inquiry into the Actions of the United Nations during the 1994 Genocide in Rwanda, December 15, 1999. http://www.ess.uwe.ac.uk/documents/RwandaReport1.htm

United Nations. *The United Nations and Rwanda, 1993–1996*. Vol. 10. New York: Dept. of Public Information, United Nations, 1996.

FILMS

Barker, Greg, writer and codirector. *Ghosts of Rwanda*. 2004. Produced for the PBS series *Frontline*.

George, Terry, writer and director. *Hotel Rwanda*. 2007. Feature film.

Raymont, Peter, director. *Shake Hands with the Devil: The Journey of Roméo Dallaire*. 2004. Documentary.

Robinson, Mike, and Ben Loeterman, writers and producers. *The Triumph of Evil*. Boston: WGBH Educational Foundation; distributed by PBS Video, 1999.

Silver, Steven, director. *The Last Just Man*. 2002. Documentary.

Spottiswoode, Roger, director. *Shake Hands with the Devil*. 2007. Feature film.

Witness the Evil. 1998. Canadian military training video about PTSD.

DARFUR

by Linda S. Bishai

Before 2004, it is safe to say, most Westerners had never heard of Darfur in the western part of Sudan, and many had only vague recollections of Sudan as a country that had once hosted the terrorist Osama bin Laden, who planned the attacks on New York and Washington, D.C., on 11 September 2001. As the humanitarian disaster took shape in Darfur, however, the whole world came to associate that area with the term "genocide." The term was inserted into American public discourse on 9 September 2004 by then Secretary of State Colin Powell in testimony before the Senate Foreign Relations Committee. This was a presidential election year for the United States, and there had been pressure on the White House to use the term after Congress passed a resolution finding that the situation in Darfur merited the use of the term "genocide." Secretary Powell did state that genocide had been committed in Darfur, but he was also quick to say that this determination did not require any new action by the U.S. government because it was already doing everything it could to deal with the problem. Although the U.S. government disclaimed any imperative stemming from its use of the word "genocide", the label prompted a tidal wave of popular activism in North America and Europe and forced politicians to take positions on what had previously been a fairly obscure conflict.

This analysis of Darfur and its relation to genocide is divided into four sections. The first focuses on the historical roots of the conflict in Darfur as well as the Sudanese civil war between the north and the south. The second provides an overview of the responses of key actors to the conflict. One of the complicating factors about Sudan is how many outside parties—state and nonstate—have become involved. The third section summarizes the international response to the crisis in Darfur, from diplomatic rebukes to critical support for the regional response by African Union troops followed by UN forces on the ground. The fourth and final section examines important questions for human rights raised by the situation in Darfur, including the rise of global political activism, the

distinction between political and humanitarian crises, and the need for political approaches to address long-term solutions.

THE HISTORY OF THE DARFUR REBELLION

The rebellion and violence in Darfur are rooted in complex layers of identity, neglect, and competition for diminishing resources. Ignoring its long history as an independent Islamic sultanate, the British annexed Darfur to the rest of Sudan in 1916, fearing that it would enter World War I in aid of the Ottoman Turks. Once within Sudan's borders, Darfur, like much of the country, became peripheral to Khartoum in the political as well as geographical sense. After gaining independence from Britain in 1956, Sudanese rulers—both elected and military dictators—continued to disregard Darfur, only occasionally feigning interest in it as a bargaining chip to gain arms and funds from Libyan leader Muammar al-Qaddafi. Qaddafi's interest was to use Darfur as a base for incursions into Chad and also as a bridgehead in his vision for militant pan-Arabism in the region. To this end, Qaddafi lent his support to the creation of the Tajammu al-Arabi (the Arab Gathering), founded in Darfur in 1986 for the express purpose of securing the "Arab" nature of Darfur. The Arab identity issue has become a significant motivating factor in determining alliances and patterns of violence in Sudan's continuing series of conflicts, including Darfur.

During the long-running civil war with the south, the Sudanese government made heavy use of troops from southern Darfur—the Arabized Murahaleen—who saw the war as an Islamic jihad to dominate and Arabize the non-Arab south. The Murahaleen were recruited to deal with the bases of the Sudan People's Liberation Army (SPLA) in Bahr el Ghazal, the portion of the south bordering on Darfur, but their pan-Arabist zeal and history of feuding with the southern Dinka tribe resulted in brutal attacks mostly on civilians. The Murahaleen were allowed to pillage, rape, and enslave the villages they attacked in the name of putting down the rebellion. The government allowed them the use of its railways to transport spoils back to southern Darfur and counted itself lucky that its war with the south could be fought without seriously taxing the privileged northern population.

Although happy to make use of Darfur's militant Arabist volunteers, the government of Sudan did not wish to be troubled with investing in Darfur's much-needed infrastructure and public services. Education has been a particular problem for Sudan's peripheral provinces, and Darfur—with a soaring illiteracy rate—had very few schools relative to its population. In addition, the northern elites promulgated a curriculum that emphasized the lack of civilization of the peripheral provinces, so that Darfurian children, though all Muslim, were raised to feel socially and culturally inferior to the riverine Arabs living in the Khartoum area. Darfur's lack of political power was keenly felt after two years of drought in the early 1980s resulted in terrible famine in Darfur. The Khartoum government refused to acknowledge the crisis and did not provide the resources necessary to deal with the devastating effects. An estimated ninety-five thousand people died from the famine and the neglect of the government.

The famine also wreaked havoc with the historic and delicately balanced relationship between tribal identities, livelihood groups, and the dated land tenure system. During Darfur's sultanate period, the Sultan granted land rights called *hawakir* (singular *hakura*) to religious leaders and administrators. They in turn could collect taxes from those who cultivated or used the land. This system coexisted with a more fluid geography of tribal *dar*, or homelands, that shifted according to a tribe's needs and relative influence. British colonial rules favored land cultivators over cattle herders, and successive policies by postindependence governments failed to clarify the issue of competing rights and access to land in Darfur. So when encroaching desert to the north combined with the shocking effects of famine, Darfurians found that their traditional mechanisms, including customary right of passage for herders during seasonal migrations, were challenged to the breaking point. With the food supply critical, both farmers and herders tried to expand their access to land for cultivation. Rights of access began to be fenced off so that additional lands could be used for food. The complex identity politics of the pro-Arab regimes in Khartoum that recruited and rewarded the Tajammu al-Arabi and Murahaleen and promoted the concept of holy war

against the south did not soothe these conflicts over land and food access. Given that many (though not all) self-identified Arab tribes were herders of cattle and many (though not all) self-identified African tribes were cultivators of land, it is not surprising that resentment among these groups developed and remained ripe for exploitation in 2003, just when Khartoum needed cheap and effective counterinsurgency tactics against Darfur's rising rebel groups.

Aside from administrative neglect by the central government, Darfur also suffered by its proximity to Chad. Libyan leader Colonel Qaddafi regarded Darfur as his natural playground and staging area for a rebellion against the Chadian president, Hissen Habré. Throughout the 1980s, in exchange for funneling resources (both financial and military) to the Sudanese government, Qaddafi was allowed to fuel a Chadian civil war from his bases in Darfur, including the arming of pro-Arab militias in Darfur. The Chadian war spilled over the border into Darfur in 1989, and Chadian forces occupied three Darfurian cities. When Qaddafi's choice, new Chadian President Idriss Déby, was finally installed, Qaddafi's interest in Darfur subsided. But the region remained war-torn and in the throes of another famine. Again, the government in Khartoum denied the serious nature of the famine and uncounted numbers suffered its effects.

By now, many of Darfur's tribal groups had formed militias and begun to spar over resources and influence. The politicization of Arab identity by the Khartoum government and by Qaddafi began to polarize Darfur's many tribes into two essential identity groups—Arab and African—and throughout the 1990s and early 2000s, Arab and African groups engaged in continuous but sporadic fighting. But despite the tribal tensions over ethnic favoritism and scarce resources, it was development and economic policies that motivated a group of militant Darfurians to agitate for political change in 2000 with the publication of *The Black Book*. Published privately and anonymously, *The Black Book* provided detailed illustrations of Khartoum's neglect of the peripheral provinces and Darfur in particular. Meant to shame and condemn, the publication did not reveal anything unknown to Khartoum's elite, but the effrontery of its writing and distribution was a new and threatening indicator of the trouble brewing in the west.

Ironically, it was the increasingly successful results of the north-south peace negotiations that triggered the start of the sustained armed violent conflict in Darfur. The clearer it became that the south would gain not only autonomy but also shared wealth and power from the central government, the more intolerable was Darfur's deprivation. In 2002 armed rebel groups formed in Darfur and began to conduct a series of attacks on government facilities in Darfur, including police stations, convoys, and military outposts. Two groups drawn largely from African tribes emerged in 2003 as forces to be reckoned with. The Sudan Liberation Movement/Army (SLA/M) and the Justice and Equality Movement (JEM) were allies in purpose if not in structure and operations. The SLA originated as a secessionist movement but scaled back to a secularist political agenda and autonomy from Khartoum. The JEM formed as a result of disagreements among the Islamists in Khartoum and continues to advocate an Islamist national policy. Both groups were determined to exert pressure on the government through military force, at a minimum gaining enough power to negotiate for their interests at the center but also with the ultimate goal of transforming the government itself. Unfortunately, the armed rebel movements were not able to protect the civilian population from the inevitable retaliation by Khartoum. In April 2003, after several small raids had provoked the government's attention, the SLA and JEM coordinated a large attack on an army garrison in the Darfurian capital city of El Fashir, destroying military planes and helicopters and reportedly killing more than seventy men.

The unprecedented success of the raid on El Fashir plus a series of subsequent successful attacks proved intolerable to the Sudanese government, but its army was overtaxed from dealing with the war in the south and an insurrection in the east. There may also have been fears that the significant numbers of Darfurians in the national army would make it unreliable in countering the rebels. Needing a change of tactics, the Sudanese government began to coordinate its air power with the armed Arab militias it had relied on in the past to quell Darfurian rebellions. The Janjaweed had originally been piratelike raiders preying on Arab and African alike, but over time they had become increasingly associated with the pro-Arab Islamists and so presented a convenient paramilitary tool for the government as it sought new ways of dealing with the strength of the Darfurian rebellion. The government began to coordinate closely its counterattack with the Janjaweed, and the targets were villages in regions where the SLA and JEM drew their support. With improved arms and military intelligence, the Janjaweed struck with devastating effect. By the spring of 2004 thousands had been killed and hundreds of thousands were displaced.

As refugees streamed into Chad, international aid workers and observers responded. UN personnel soon noticed the targeted nature of the killing and destruction—African tribes such as Fur, Zaghawa, and Masalit saw their villages destroyed while neighboring Arab villages were left unscathed—and released the information.

Reports of the human rights violations in Darfur spread rapidly across the world and by the time the U.S. government labeled the killings genocide, most people with access to a television would have heard of Darfur. Interviews with survivors revealed a striking pattern of brutality that echoed the tactics used by the Sudanese government in its war in the south (Amnesty International; Power). Large cargo planes would fly over a village and drop crude canister bombs packed with projectiles and explosives. Helicopter gunships would then fly over the villages, firing on anything that moved. As homes burned and inhabitants tried to flee, people were rounded up and shot by the Janjaweed, armed men on horseback or in pickup trucks. Small children and infants were tossed into fires, men and youth were massacred and often mutilated, and women and girls were held and raped if not killed. The raiders then helped themselves to whatever belongings and wealth they could find. Those who managed to survive the destruction of their village had nothing left if they returned. Survivors often told stories of being called *abd* (slave) and being told that the land belonged to the Arabs and that the government did not want them there. Even residents at internally displaced person (IDP) and refugee camps were unsafe, as they were frequently attacked if they left the camp to collect firewood or to forage for food. Water was scarce and sanitation a serious problem. Disease spread rapidly and government authorities often snubbed IDPs attempting to find relief in Darfur's cities.

The Janjaweed attacks were so successful and numerous that the scale of the disaster grew rapidly and lent credibility to comparisons with the Rwandan genocide, which was being remembered during its tenth anniversary in 2004. In March of that year, the UN human rights coordinator for Sudan, Mukesh Kapila, labeled Darfur "the world's greatest humanitarian crisis." UN Secretary-General Kofi Annan conceded that the risk of genocide was real even while the UN Commission of Inquiry reported that although mass violations of human rights and crimes against humanity were taking place, "genocidal intent" was missing in Darfur. Meanwhile, the government of Sudan delayed humanitarian workers attempting to reach Darfur with frustrating bureaucratic permission processes and the pretense of providing clear access.

The storm of coverage and concern over Darfur could not have come at a worse time for the government of Sudan, engaged as it was in wrapping up the delicate negotiations of the Naivasha Agreement that would end the civil war with the south and create a transitional government. Maintaining control over the north while finalizing negotiations with the south was one priority; shutting down the efforts of Darfur and the east to gain leverage for a similar power and wealth-sharing agreement was another.

KEY ACTORS

Despite impatient recriminations by human rights activists that nothing has been done and no one is noticing, the coverage of Darfur as a tragedy for which global responsibility must be taken has been relentless and widespread. This has provoked unprecedented and broad, if somewhat unfocused, initiatives from many sectors of the international community, both public and private. Private-sector responses in the United States and Europe have included organized marches—notably a global march in forty countries on 17 September 2006, celebrity speeches and public appearances, art exhibitions, print articles, television news stories, Web logs, fund-raising campaigns by school children, campus divestment activism, a green rubber wristband "not on my watch" campaign, and even a Darfur scorecard Web site that rates members of the U.S. Congress according to their level of commitment to the Darfur issue. Darfur has become a household name, surfacing in media that normally would never cover foreign human rights abuses. Even comic strips (*Get Fuzzy*), fashion magazines (*Vogue Hommes*), and video games (*Darfur Is Dying*) have addressed the crisis.

The United States.

The sustained interest on the part of the general public has kept Darfur much closer to the top of the agenda among Western leaders and the United Nations than almost every other issue on the African continent. The United States has devoted significant personnel and resources to Sudan in general and Darfur in particular. Former U.S. President Bush George W. made Darfur a strong personal priority and has continued to address it as a case of genocide and a compelling moral issue. To that end, a series of diplomats were assigned to focus on Sudan and on Darfur. Robert Zoellick, then deputy secretary of

state, played an active role in the series of Darfur peace talks that took place at Abuja, Nigeria, from 2004 to 2006. Mediators pressed hard to achieve a signed document, even without acceptance by most of the splintering Darfurian rebel groups. Bush then designated a special envoy to Sudan, a sign of special presidential attention to the issue. Andrew Natsios, former head of the U.S. Agency for International Development, was appointed in 2006, and former ambassador Richard Williamson assumed the position in late 2007. The Bush administration called for international targeted sanctions in addition to previously existing general sanctions on the Sudanese regime and also supported efforts in the UN Security Council to bolster the presence of the United Nations in Sudan. The U.S. Congress—uncharacteristically united on this issue—has been remarkably active on Darfur. Since 2004 Congress has passed numerous resolutions in both the House and the Senate, and has legislated on a bipartisan basis to enact sanctions against the government of Sudan, provide significant funding for humanitarian aid, and provide funds first for the African Union (AU) forces and subsequently for the AU/UN hybrid force in Darfur.

The European Union.

The European Union (EU) has also been active on the Darfur issue, most notably in its support for the AU force in Darfur and the increasingly critical EU force in Chad. The United States and the EU resisted calls by activists to involve NATO extensively in Darfur, but NATO has been involved in technical support—advising and training the AU troops. The EU itself has also provided significant funding and technical expertise, including European officers embedded with African forces on the ground in Darfur. These efforts yielded mixed results, hampered by the severe challenges of commitment, recruitment, training, supplying, and deploying of troops by the newly formed AU organization. The EU also provided more than 500 million euros in humanitarian aid and maintains a significant presence both officially and through many private organizations on the ground in Khartoum. European states have joined the United States in calling for the Sudanese government to act responsibly and in exerting pressure at the Security Council.

Regarding sanctions, the EU has maintained a less confrontational approach than the United States. A long-standing arms embargo on Sudan remains in effect, though this is nearly meaningless in the context of a huge free-flowing arms market throughout the African continent. The EU dutifully implemented the sanctions specified by Security Council resolutions, targeting those who directly participate in the conflict. The EU has been slow, however, to enact trade or targeted sanctions in Sudan, and many EU companies actively continue to develop business relationships in the country. This has led to accusations by activists that the EU is not doing enough to pressure the Sudanese government on Darfur. The European response has been to cast doubt on the effectiveness of government sanctions in this case. Recent campaigns for divestment in Sudan and in particular its oil sector have, however, begun to be effective, with several notable European companies, such as Rolls-Royce, cutting their business ties with Sudan.

Finally, the EU has committed to providing peacekeeping and humanitarian troops to a force (EUFOR) to be deployed in Chad and the Central African Republic (CAR). The UN Security Council approved the creation of EUFOR in September 2007 to support the extensive humanitarian staff and facilities fielded by the UN to handle refugees from Darfur and Chadian IDPs located mostly in eastern Chad. The force is mandated to protect the refugee/IDP populations, to aid the administration of humanitarian assistance, and to protect UN personnel and property, which continue to be subjected to significant kidnapping and theft. Although technically a joint European force, EUFOR-Chad relies largely on France, a former colonial power in Chad, as its main contributor. Continued French presence in Chad has drawn skepticism that EUFOR can remain neutral in the highly politicized atmosphere of eastern Chad with its cross-border rebel groups and proxy wars between Chadian President Idriss Déby and Sudanese President Omar Beshir. Perhaps fearing EUFOR intervention on Déby's behalf, Sudanese-backed Chadian rebels stormed the capital, N'Djamena, in January 2008 before the European troops' arrival in the city. The attempted coup failed, and EUFOR began deployment in early 2008.

The United Nations.

The UN has long been involved in Sudan, notably through humanitarian efforts with Operation Lifeline Sudan during the north-south civil war. Additionally, it had been a significant actor in brokering and monitoring the Comprehensive Peace Agreement (CPA), ending the civil war between the north and the south of Sudan. In fact, the UN already had a mission in Sudan (UNMIS) with more than ten thousand personnel (mostly military) charged with supporting and monitoring the implementation of the CPA. UNMIS also coordinates numerous other UN agencies and programs actively operating in Sudan, including the UN High Commission for Refugees (UNHCR), the UN Children's Education Fund (UNICEF), the UN Development Programme (UNDP), and the World Food Programme (WFP). After several years of delicate parsing of resolutions in the Security Council in the face of opposition from the government of Sudan, the UN has finally begun to deploy a hybrid peacekeeping mission in Darfur, the UN African Union Mission in Darfur (UNAMID). UNAMID both encompasses and relieves the strained and weary troops of the African Union Mission (AMIS). UNAMID was not expected to reach its full troop strength of 26,000 until the autumn of 2008.

The UN has signaled Sudan as a priority by maintaining a series of high-level envoys in the country, most notably the special representative of the secretary-general for Sudan Jan Pronk, who served from 2004 to 2006. Pronk made international headlines when his statements about casualties and low morale among the Sudanese army forces in Darfur caused the Sudanese government to declare him persona non grata and led the secretary-general to recall him for consultations immediately. He was not replaced until 2007, when the secretary-general appointed Ashraf Qazi, who had previously served in a similar post in Iraq. In another significant move, the UN appointed globally prominent Jan Eliasson, former foreign minister of Sweden and former president of the UN General Assembly, to be the UN special envoy for Darfur. Eliasson and his AU counterpart, Salim Salim, have attempted to broker a continuing series of negotiations between the Sudanese government and the disparate representatives of Darfurian rebel groups.

In addition to its diplomatic and military presence, the UN has been supporting and coordinating massive humanitarian missions in both Darfur and Chad, as violence and people have spilled back and forth across the border. These missions have calculated the casualty numbers at around 200,000 people killed and nearly 2 million displaced, although some humanitarian groups have used the figure of 400,000 dead. Because access is so restricted and security is so compromised, the casualty numbers for Darfur continue to be a hotly contested matter. Sudan's president said in November 2006 that the number was no more than 9,000 killed, and that casualty numbers have been greatly exaggerated by the West in order to justify intervention. In September 2004, after Secretary Powell's testimony to Congress mentioned genocide, the UN Security Council authorized an International Commission of Inquiry on Darfur "to investigate reports of violations of international humanitarian law and human rights law...[and] to determine also whether or not acts of genocide have occurred."

In the spring of 2005 the Security Council—in the first such move since the creation of the court—referred the situation to the International Criminal Court (ICC) for investigation (Security Council Resolution 1593). With no access to Darfur, the ICC prosecutor proceeded by interviewing hundreds of refugees and Sudanese migrants outside the country. In February 2007 the ICC issued two indictments on counts of war crimes and crimes against humanity. The named indictees were Ahmed Haroun, a former state minister at the ministry of interior and current minister of humanitarian affairs, and Ali Kushayb, a top leader of the Janjaweed militia. Khartoum's response was to condemn the indictments, deny the charges, and refuse cooperation with the court. Though they did arrest Ali Kushayb, stating that he would be tried by Sudan in a special court designed for that purpose, Kushayb was later released for lack of evidence. Afterward, the government remained inactive on creating judicial processes in Sudan for crimes against humanity or war crimes. Later that same year, the government—in an audacious move that stunned human rights activists—appointed Haroun to co-chair a governmental committee charged with investigating human rights abuses.

The African Union.

In 2002 the Organization of African Unity (OAU) gave way to a new institution—the African Union (AU)—intended to reflect greater cooperation and more robust mechanisms for responsibility and accountability in state actions. The AU's new mandate allows for collective intervention when a member state commits war crimes, genocide, or crimes against humanity. This significant step reflects the recognition by African leaders that they should handle African conflicts among themselves rather than depend upon the political whims of the international community. Nonetheless, the AU still relies on international monetary and technical support to enable its collective actions.

Western politicians encouraged AU involvement in Darfur as a positive and hopeful sign, though regional experts expressed concern that the organization was not robust enough to handle a situation as complex and a government as recalcitrant as Sudan's. The AU involved itself slowly, first by encouraging all parties to commit to a cease-fire in 2004. It then formed a cease-fire commission and sent a handful of troops to monitor the situation in Darfur. The AU then increased the number of observers and deployed three hundred soldiers for their protection. As the complexity and danger of the situation became apparent, the AU committed to further troops, eventually reaching seven thousand by 2006. The observer mission, AMIS, challenged the new organization to live up to its motto of African solutions to African problems. AU officials, however, insisted on limiting the AMIS's mission to observation and monitoring, refusing even to consider a peacekeeping mandate. Initially, there was some improvement and some hope that the presence of African troops in Darfur would deter the attacks. The challenge of operating with so few troops over such a large territory and in an extremely underdeveloped environment meant that the high expectations for AMIS were inevitably let down.

China.

China's extensive business and trade relations with Sudan have complicated efforts by the United States and Europe at the UN Security Council, watering down the resolutions on sanctions and providing some insulation for the Beshir government. China began investing in Sudan in the mid-1990s, when the country's pariah status limited its options for foreign investment. The Sudanese government spent most of its early profits from Chinese oil investments to buy Chinese-made weapons for use in its war with the south, still raging at that time. China has been the primary supplier of arms to the Sudanese government. In addition to a 40 percent ownership in Sudan's main oil consortiums, China purchases nearly 70 percent of Sudan's exports, most of which is oil. This mutually agreeable relationship has helped Sudan to weather global condemnation on the issue of Darfur, and China shows no inclination to pay more than modest lip service to the idea that the Sudanese government should demonstrate responsible leadership.

In early 2007 China provided Sudan with a $13 million loan interest-free, apparently to facilitate the building of a new presidential palace. China's unwillingness to pressure Sudan on Darfur led antigenocide activists to start a global campaign to taint the 2008 Olympic Games in Beijing as the "Genocide Olympics." They also organized large protests around the route of the Olympic torch as it traveled to Beijing. Famed Hollywood director Steven Spielberg withdrew from his position as artistic adviser for the games, and several Western heads of state pledged a boycott of the games' opening ceremonies. After demonstrations by Tibetan monks, Chinese control of Tibet became intertwined with the cause of Darfur for Olympic protesters. These tactics embarrassed China, but the response was a greater attempt to control the Olympic process and to depict protesters as criminals rather than to respond to global concerns on Darfur or Tibet. The Chinese government insisted that its role in Darfur has been constructive and that Chinese policy has simply been misunderstood.

Nongovernmental organizations.

Perhaps the most unique aspect of the current Sudanese crisis in Darfur is the extent to which nongovernmental organizations (NGOs)—both national and international—have become influential in the political process. Large established groups such as Amnesty International, Human Rights Watch, Doctors without Borders, and the International Crisis Group have been active globally despite lack of coverage of many conflicts in the developing world. The Darfur crisis saw a new order of magnitude of involvement that extended well past the traditional global NGOs. Much of this involvement has focused on the obligation that a defined genocide requires of the global community. The United States Holocaust Memorial Museum led the charge early on by declaring a genocide emergency in Darfur in 2004, sponsoring exhibitions and talks on the situation, and promoting activism in the form of political pressure. *New York Times* columnist Nicholas Kristof began to publish a series of searing articles on Darfur, describing what he saw as a moral disaster being ignored. Kristof also published photographs of the devastation, deaths, and victimized people that became more difficult to ignore than print media. A growth spurt in activist organizations followed, and Darfur soon became a cause célèbre among young people drawn by the call to make an impact on what seemed like a clear violation of human rights with a clear solution.

The most prominent of these groups was the Save Darfur Coalition, founded in 2004. Save Darfur is an organization of smaller disparate groups, many of them religious, concerned with bringing attention and focus to the issue of Darfur. Save Darfur became extremely effective at both fund-raising and awareness-raising. The coalition sponsored rallies, garnered celebrity spokespersons, started the green bracelet movement, and produced compelling ads in print and television calling for the U.S. government to take action in Darfur and calling on businesses to divest their interests in Sudan. By 2007 the coalition had attained such visibility that its methods and aims also came under intense scrutiny.

The global grass roots campaign had succeeded in pressuring politicians in the United States and Europe to show concern for Darfur, even as Iraq and Afghanistan were drawing resources and attention. But the American public, and some politicians, interpreted the call to action as a call for military intervention—a course most experts condemned as ill-conceived and detrimental considering the complexity of the situation. Later, Save Darfur refined this message to one of calling for sustained political pressure on the Sudanese and Chinese governments. Humanitarian groups also criticized Save Darfur for raising millions of dollars and refraining from spending any of it directly on aid in Darfur, though the organization has never claimed to be anything other than activist. Save Darfur has undeniably changed the rules of international activism, focusing on political action and involvement rather than the more traditional fund-raising for humanitarian aid. It remains to be seen whether Save Darfur and similar organizations can sustain their activities over time in a situation that looks increasingly like an intractable conflict.

In the face of all this activity, Darfur remains an issue of compelling but indefinite urgency. How did it start and why has it been allowed to continue?

SUMMARY OF INTERNATIONAL DEVELOPMENTS

Throughout 2004 the primary response of the United States, Europe, and the UN was verbal outrage and humanitarian aid. Much of the attention remained focused on keeping the north-south Comprehensive Peace Agreement (CPA) on track. External pressure continued to be necessary to solidify and guarantee the arrangement, and Darfur presented an unwanted and worrying distraction. Iraq and Afghanistan absorbed most of the military and foreign policy concerns of the United States and to some extent Europe, and they were wary of engaging beyond the potential victory of brokering the CPA. The government of Sudan had also made it clear that it would not welcome external assistance on Darfur and that it would resist any efforts made by the UN as violations of its sovereignty. Given the lack of political will, the Security Council made little effort to mandate any kind of force for Darfur early on, leaving the stage empty for the appearance of the newly formed African Union organization (AU), which authorized a cease-fire monitoring mission.

The AU mission was beset by troubles from the beginning. To begin with, the cease-fire AMIS was supposed to monitor did not really exist. Massacres, rapes, and large movements of population continued in the presence of the monitoring troops. Since their mandate did not include civilian protection or police enforcement, AMIS forces stood by and recorded, but did not stop, attacks on civilians and the destruction of villages. Darfurians had assumed that AMIS troops were intervening for their protection. When attacks continued in the presence of the troops, the civilian population lost confidence and the rebels even began to harass the troops, pursuing their vehicles and supplies as valuable wartime booty. Worse, the Sudanese government began to fly its own gunships, painted white to resemble observer craft from UNMIS, further confusing the population about the purpose behind the presence of international troops and observers.

The limited response by AMIS reflects the significant problems of a limited mandate and one that was based on the consent of the Khartoum government. Although the AU Peace and Security Council has the authority to make binding decisions that could have required the Sudanese government to cooperate more openly with AMIS, it refrained from any form of coercion and elected to rely on consent. AMIS's mandate to monitor and report activities and protect humanitarian operations under imminent threat rested on the crucial—but unfortunately wrong—assumption that the Sudanese government would be providing protection for the civilian population.

Despite the great challenges Darfur presented, AMIS troops did sometimes make a positive difference. Their presence did have a deterrent effect at first on government troops operating in areas near vulnerable populations. AMIS troops also undertook outreach to local community leaders and held regular meetings to hear about their concerns. This kind of trust-building process is important to keep local mechanisms functioning in the face of complete social disruption. The troops often patrolled in places where an attack was expected, hoping to deter violence and protect civilians without violating their mandate. Though limited in number, many of the AMIS troops were committed to their mission, with officers trained by special programs of the U.S., British, and French militaries. Rwandan troops made up a significant proportion, and their unique national experience with genocide gave them particular motivation to make a difference in Darfur. Nonetheless, after two years in Darfur without an end in sight, with the killing continuing and with funding sources drying up, the AU troops began to flag. The AU, already the lead intermediary in talks between the government and rebel groups, began to join

with the United States, the EU, and the UN to exert tremendous pressure for a negotiated agreement.

A series of talks were held in Abuja, Nigeria, with the AU as primary mediator. Challenges such as very low trust among the parties, superior negotiating skill of the Sudanese government, and rivalries within the SLM/A complicated the progress of the talks. The SLM/A eventually split into two primary factions, one led by Abdel Wahid Mohamed el-Nur (sometimes spelled el-Nour), a Fur, and the other led by Minni Minnawi, a Zaghawa. The two leaders disagreed on the approach to be taken in the negotiations, but rather than resolve this split, the international mediators pressed anxiously for signatures by a final deadline. In the end only one of the major rebel groups, the Minni Minnawi faction of the SLM/A, signed the Darfur Peace Agreement (DPA) in May 2006 with the government of Sudan. Though the negotiators and signatories celebrated the DPA at the time, it has become clear that the failure of the other groups to sign was a profound limitation on the impact of the agreement. Attempts to encourage the nonsignatories to participate later in the terms of the agreement yielded little movement, and the rebel movements continued to splinter into multiple factions.

Although the DPA included significant concessions by the government of Sudan, it did not do enough to assure the nonsignatories that their concerns would be addressed. Partially, this may be due to the difficulty of the trust issues and resistance to the rushed timetable of the negotiations. Also, the DPA, while it mirrored many of the features of the Naivasha Agreement, did not allow for participation in the government of national unity in the way that the CPA grants the southern SPLM/A. The CPA clearly inspired Darfurian negotiators with hopes of a similar power and wealth-sharing arrangement, but the CPA itself—as a closed agreement that both north and south refused to reconsider—actually limited the options available for Darfur. Some provisions of the DPA were implemented—for example, Minni Minnawi was appointed senior assistant to the president and chair of the Transitional Darfur Regional Authority that oversees the terms of the DPA. Other provisions such as development funds and victims compensation require further agreement before they can be implemented.

As the international mediators came to acknowledge that the DPA would not bring peace to Darfur, they pushed harder for a UN-led peacekeeping mission, larger and more robust than AMIS. After repeated efforts to dodge the issue, claiming Darfur was a tribal conflict being adequately handled by the state, the Sudanese government finally agreed to a hybrid AU/UN force in which most of the soldiers were African. The Security Council formally approved the UN Mission in Darfur (UNAMID) on 31 July 2007 with an African joint AU/UN special representative and an African hybrid force commander. The three-phase deployment began in December 2007 despite hedging by the Sudanese government on troop composition and equipment. UNAMID's mandate is far more robust than that of AMIS, prioritizing the protection of the civilian population and humanitarian aid. The first troops to join the force were the ones already present in AMIS. At full strength, UNAMID will be the largest of the UN-sponsored peacekeeping missions, but it faces significant challenges deploying in what remains an active conflict zone.

IMPORTANT QUESTIONS FOR HUMAN RIGHTS

The question of whether the pattern of government-supported Janjaweed attacks constitutes genocide has already been much debated. The UN Convention on the Prevention and Punishment of the Crime of Genocide (1948) describes genocide as acts "committed with intent to destroy, in whole or in part, a national, ethnical, racial or religious group." There is evidence to support either conclusion in the case of Darfur. Much hinges on the emphasis given to the issue of intent to destroy a group in its entirety, or in substantial part. Most commentators can agree that the events have been horrific and shocking and that they trigger liability for crimes against humanity on an international scale.

Yet the debate about the genocide label has not faded. Activists often point to the political obligations of states under the Convention against Genocide, arguing that this makes it more important to call such activities genocide when they see them. It is certainly questionable whether the Save Darfur Coalition could have raised the millions of dollars that it did had it not been able to make use of the emotional weight that the term "genocide" carries.

The word itself is potent with emotional and political meaning, and yet Darfur has been allowed to linger under the noses of the very international community that says "genocide" should be impossible. Millions of people marched in 2006 to save Darfur and yet it has not been saved. Perhaps the word genocide is too blunt an instrument to capture the complexity of Sudan. Any decent understanding of Darfur must account for a quarter

century of history and complex patterns of identity formation. For those wishing only to stop the violence in the short term rather than attempt sustainable peace, Darfur presents a human rights dilemma. The use of the term "genocide" failed to spark the kind of immediate powerful response for Darfur envisioned by human rights activists. It also arrived simultaneously with a globally unpopular intervention in Iraq, restraining the primary suppliers of international humanitarian force and playing into the hands of an Islamist government all too eager to spin the example of Iraq to its advantage. Continuing complexities in Kosovo also reminded policy makers that it was easier to launch an intervention than to pacify a situation on the basis of consensus afterward.

What then of the term "genocide"? Has its use in the case of Darfur actually weakened its descriptive or peremptory value? It is worth questioning whether the legal distinction between crimes against humanity and genocide remains in effect. For instance, when does a pattern of violence by a state become so shocking that it must trigger external responsibility for the sake of some concept of human decency (whether it is called genocide or not)? Whether crimes against humanity or genocide, Sudanese actions in Darfur raise the question of "the responsibility to protect": what responsibility do external actors bear toward those they would protect in terms of disrupting local patterns of governance, political power, and culture? In the case of Darfur, the first instinct of the international actors was to keep the focus on the hard-won north-south agreement and leave Darfur to the African Union as the relevant regional actor. The efforts of the AU in Darfur have been valiant if problematic. The organization is young and struggling for funds, personnel, and equipment—Darfur presented too large a challenge too soon. Does the imperative of saving lives outweigh the value of encouraging regional solutions to a humanitarian crisis? If saving lives in large numbers generates its own imperative, then perhaps resources are better committed to preventable public-health impacts such as malaria and tuberculosis. Yet deaths from malaria, though perhaps a violation of a right to health care, do not result from shocking crimes and are therefore less noted in the global media and trigger no direct obligation under international law.

Darfur also showcases for the first time the power of the new grassroots activism that may well have major effects on the interpretation and implementation of human rights. Networks can spring up nearly instantaneously to generate events and organizational structures around a common motivating theme such as stopping genocide. Often these structures are driven by young people who have mastered the connectivity of the Internet and use it to further their commitment to the moral issues they feel are overlooked by domestic politics. This kind of organization has become a political force in democratic societies where the interests of a motivated electorate matter. In the case of Darfur and the stop genocide movement, there is perhaps a new order of magnitude for interest in human rights and the will to be politically active about it. A main concern may be that such movements gain their power from the force of simple compelling messages, and as in the case of Darfur, they do not necessarily convey the complex array of issues, actors, and potential complications that require untangling before a helpful response can be formulated.

An example of this dynamic occurred in the 2007 call for an enforced no-fly zone over Darfur. This seemed like a good idea since Sudan routinely violated the Security Council resolution banning government military flights in the region. This viewpoint was promulgated by several prominent activists and even by members of the U.S. Congress gearing up for presidential campaigns. However, once the issue reached the ears of the humanitarian aid workers on the ground in Darfur, they put up fierce resistance. Bringing foreign jets into Sudanese airspace, they argued, would prompt immediate retaliation by the Sudanese government, most likely by blocking roads and convoys of aid and by simply denying visas for aid workers to enter the country. Humanitarian work, they asserted, would certainly suffer. Once this response had a chance to spread, the calls for the use of air power diminished. For human rights activists, the awesome power to unleash rapid popular response had been demonstrated, but judicious use of this power remained a challenge.

The case of Sudan reveals a critical distinction that should be recognized in considerations of human rights. This is the distinction between a political and a humanitarian crisis. They are easily blurred as they so often occur together, yet the violation of human rights must be situated within its political context in order to be addressed responsibly. Sudan provides an exceptionally complex geography of serial civil wars, tribal identity, race, ideology, oil, and livelihoods, to name a few key issues. The continued resistance of the central government to international involvement or political reform has masked an internal political crisis in which the government has been struggling against numerous armed rebellions and the collapse of its ruling ideology. The repeated and extreme violations of human rights—and possibly genocide—have

not occurred in a vacuum. It is imperative that the responses to these violations not occur in a vacuum either. Sudan starkly illustrates that an effective response to human rights violations requires sustained attention to politics and careful cultivation of trust among the international and domestic actors.

> The key lesson I have learned in nearly forty years of humanitarian work . . . is that in between theory and practice is a very important field called politics. Like any other field, aid work is intertwined with politics. We must always be conscious of this.
> —Dr. Bernard Kouchner, cofounder, Doctors without Borders (*Médecins sans frontières*), 2 March, 2004.

[*See also* African Union: Banjul Charter; African Union: Commission and Court on Human Rights; Amnesty International; Crimes against Humanity; Doctors without Borders; Ethnic Cleansing; Foreign Policy; Genocide; Human Rights Watch; Humanitarian Law; Internally Displaced Persons; International Criminal Court; International; Jus Cogens; Refugees; Rwanda; United Nations High Commissioner for Refugees; *and* United Nations Security Council.]

BIBLIOGRAPHY

African Union. *Report of the Chairperson of the Commission on the Situation in Darfur, the Sudan.* Addis Ababa, Ethiopia, October 2004. http://www.africa-union.org/News_Events/Communiqués/Report%20-%20Darfur%2020%20oct%202004.pdf.

African Union. *Report of the Chairperson of the Commission on the Status of the Implementation of the Peace and Security Council Decision of 10 March 2006 on the Situation in Darfur and the Conclusion of the Abuja Peace Talks.* Addis Ababa, Ethiopia, May 15, 2006.

Amnesty International. *Darfur: Too Many People Killed for No Reason.* London: Amnesty International, February 2004.

Anonymous. *al-Kitab al-Aswad* (The Black Book). 2000. A partial English translation is available at http://www.sudanjem.com/sudan-alt/english/books/books.htm.

Daly, M. W. *Darfur's Sorrow: A History of Destruction and Genocide.* Cambridge, U.K.: Cambridge University Press, 2007.

De Waal, Alex. "Counter-insurgency on the Cheap." *London Review of Books* 26, no. 15 (August 2004). http://www.lrb.co.uk/v26/n15/waal01_.html.

De Waal, Alex. *Famine That Kills: Darfur (Sudan), 1984–1985.* Oxford: Clarendon Press, 1989.

De Waal, Alex, ed. *War in Darfur and the Search for Peace.* Cambridge, Mass.: Harvard University Press, 2007.

The Elders. *The Elders Report on the Mission to Sudan,* December 12, 2005. http://www.theelders.org.

Flint, Julie, and Alex de Waal. *Darfur: A Short History of a Long War.* London: Zed Books, 2005.

Human Rights Watch. *Darfur in Flames: Atrocities in Western Sudan.* Washington, D.C.: Human Rights Watch, 2004 http://www.hrw.org/reports/2004/sudan0404/sudan0404.pdf.

International Commission of Inquiry on Darfur. *Report of the International Commission of Inquiry on Darfur to the United Nations Secretary General.* Pursuant to Security Council Resolution 1564 of 18 September 2004, Geneva, Switzerland. 25, January 2005. http://www.un.org/News/dh/sudan/com_inq_darfur.pdf).

International Crisis Group. *The AU's Mission in Darfur: Bridging the Gaps.* Africa Briefing 28, Nairobi, Kenya, and Brussels, Belgium, July 6, 2005.

Kristof, Nicholas. "The Secret Genocide Archive." *The New York Times,* February 23, 2005.

Lesch, Ann Moseley. *The Sudan: Contested National Identities.* Bloomington: Indiana University Press, 1998.

Million Voices for Darfur. January 22, 2006. http://www.save-darfur.org/pages/previous_ initiatives.

Nathan, Laurie. "No Ownership, No Peace: The Darfur Peace Agreement." In *Crisis States Working Papers Series 5.* London: London School of Economics Crisis States Research Centre, September 2006.

O'Neill, William G., and Violette Cassis. *Protecting Two Million Internally Displaced: The Successes and Shortcomings of the African Union in Darfur.* Washington, D.C.: The Brookings Institution–University of Bern Project on Internal Displacement, November 2005.

Power, Samantha. "Dying in Darfur." *The New Yorker,* August 30, 2004.

Prunier, Gérard. *Darfur: The Ambiguous Genocide.* Ithaca, N.Y.: Cornell University Press, 2005.

Rubin, Elizabeth. "If Not Peace, Then Justice." *The New York Times,* April 2, 2006.

Strauss, Scott. "Darfur and the Genocide Debate." *Foreign Affairs* 84, no. 1 (January/February 2005): 123–133.

CARLA DEL PONTE

by Heikelina Verrijn Stuart

More than anyone else, Carla Del Ponte has been the face of the International Criminal Tribunal for the Former Yugoslavia, so much so that her departure from the tribunal in The Hague in December 2007 took place in an atmosphere of finality, as if it also meant the closure of the tribunal.

Del Ponte was chief prosecutor from 1999 to 2003 at the United Nations International Criminal Tribunal for Rwanda (ICTR) and from 1999 to 2007 at the United Nations International Criminal Tribunal for the Former Yugoslavia (ICTY). She was the first prosecutor at the ad hoc tribunals with experience as a crime fighter. Her time in office will always be associated with the high point of the tribunal for the former Yugoslavia, the moment Slobodan Milošević, the former president of the Federal Republic of Yugoslavia and later of Serbia, was arrested, and with its low point, when he died in his prison cell in the UN detention unit in Scheveningen, after lengthy proceedings and without a conviction on any charges. When Del Ponte left The Hague, the two most wanted suspects for genocide and crimes against humanity were still at large. The general feeling at the time was that if this tough prosecutor had not succeeded in getting the former Bosnian Serb president Radovan Karadžić and the former Bosnian Serb general Ratko Mladić arrested, nobody would. Half a year later, in July 2008, Karadžić was transferred to the tribunal by the Serb authorities in Belgrade. Del Ponte had for eight years maintained that both Karadžić and Mladić were within reach of the authorities of Serbia or of the Bosnian Serb entity Republica Srpska and could be arrested if only there was the political will in Serbia.

In Del Ponte's book *Madame Prosecutor,* she notes, "A sense of failure loomed larger as the end of my mandate, December 2007, approached." However, in Del Ponte's eight years at The Hague, ninety-one suspects were taken into custody, sixty-three indictments were served, and forty-four trials were conducted. The UN detention unit housed prime ministers, ministers, and generals from all sides of the conflict.

LIFE AND WORK BEFORE THE TRIBUNALS

Del Ponte was born on 9 February 1947 in Bignasco, a village of about two hundred inhabitants high in the Swiss Alps behind Locarno. She completed her studies for the baccalaureate examination in the German-speaking region of Switzerland and chose to go to the university in Berne to study medicine, mainly out of spite against her father, who wanted her to become a proper housewife. A year later she switched to law in Geneva, where she got her degree in 1972.

After a time as a defense attorney, in the 1980s Del Ponte became *juge d'instruction*, an examining judge, who conducts investigations and passes on the results in a file to a prosecutor who presents the case in court. She specialized in financial corruption, fighting the consequences of the Swiss banking system, which makes it possible to keep personal identity and the source and destination of money secret in order to evade taxes and to cover trails leading back to criminal activity. Her high-profile cases included the Sicilian-based "Pizza Connection," which distributed an estimated 1.6 billion dollars in heroin and other illicit drugs through a network of pizzerias in the United States, and an investigation of Roberto Calvi, who had been chairman of Italy's second-largest bank, which had links with the Vatican and the Sicilian Mafia.

Del Ponte became a public prosecutor in 1988. Her work with the Italian judge Giovanni Falcone, who was killed by the Sicilian Mafia in 1992, resulted in arrests of Mafia bankers and the freezing of illegal assets and made it necessary for her to be accompanied by security guards from then on. In 1994 Del Ponte became Switzerland's federal attorney general. The criminalization of money laundering in Swiss law laid the basis for investigations into political leaders like Boris Yeltsin, then president of Russia, and Benazir Bhutto, Pakistan's former prime minister.

THE HAGUE

In 1998, the year the International Criminal Court (ICC) was established, Del Ponte dreamed of becoming the chief prosecutor of this new court. She became chief prosecutor of the Yugoslavia and Rwanda tribunals instead. These two UN tribunals, one established by the Security Council of the United Nations in 1993 during the war in the Balkans and the other in 1994 after the genocide in Rwanda, shared a chief prosecutor. The Security Council officially appointed Del Ponte to the post on 11 August 1999.

In her book Del Ponte describes continuous clashes between politics and justice in the course of her work. How ugly these clashes could become has also been described by Del Ponte's spokesperson Florence Hartman in her book *Paix et châtiment* (Peace and Punishment, 2007) and were depicted in the film *Carla's List* (2006), made by Marcel Schüpbach, who accompanied the chief prosecutor on her many journeys. In her earlier fights against money laundering and against the Mafia, she had walked into what she called a *muro di gomma* (a wall of rubber); during her years as chief prosecutor of the two tribunals, she would walk into the same rubber wall wherever she went, in Belgrade and Zagreb, at NATO and European Union headquarters in Brussels, at the United Nations in New York, and at U.S. government offices in Washington, D.C. Her description of her encounters with George Tenet, then director of the Central Intelligence Agency, is particularly revealing. During her first visit as chief prosecutor to Washington, D.C., in late September 2000, she turned to "one of the world's most-powerful men to ask for his help" in finding Karadžić. "He assured me that the CIA was active in the manhunt but that apprehending someone like Karadžić, who never speaks over the telephone or signs a document, is a daunting task. . . . Then he said, 'Karadžić is my Number One priority.'" However, her second meeting with Tenet, in the spring of 2001, was a different matter. Del Ponte remarks in her book, "Perhaps it was a mistake to figure that Tenet, the superpower's top spy, the man of the Mediterranean with a blunt, direct style, would not interpret candor as disrespect: 'George, I saw you in September. You told me then that Karadžić was a top priority of the CIA. But here we are six months later, and, given the results, I find it hard to believe you.'" According to Del Ponte, Tenet had replied "Look, Madame, I don't give a shit what you think."

More than a lawyer, Del Ponte was a crime fighter, albeit one without a police force. Her aim was finding, arresting, and prosecuting the suspects on her list. But she was completely dependent on states for obtaining evidence, finding and arresting suspects, and protecting victims and witnesses, and this brought her toe to toe with politicians all over the world, pressuring them to do what they were obligated to do as UN members to cooperate with the UN war crimes tribunals. However, she met animosity wherever she went, often hidden behind diplomatic words and warm promises. And in the countries where she wanted to be the champion of the victims, she was met with mistrust. In Serbia she was the one who "only" prosecuted Serbs. In Croatia she was thought to have an anti-Croat bias, targeting their war heroes, like the former general Ante Gotovina, who had recaptured the border area of Krajina between Croatia and Serbia, which had been taken by the Serbs in 1991. In Republica Srpska she was simply considered an enemy, chasing their heroes Karadžić and Mladić. In Kosovo the ruling Kosovar Albanians, who were in power thanks to the intervention of the North Atlantic Treaty Organization (NATO) in 1999, loathed her for indicting their prime minister, Ramush Haradinaj. In Bosnia she was respected, but many victims groups believed she was not doing enough.

Del Ponte's confrontations with political leaders and her threatening them with sanctions outside her own power brought on reproaches of acting as a politician herself. At one stage, even Kofi Annan, the UN secretary-general, told her to stay away from politics. In response to her ongoing pressure on Serbia's president Vojislav Kostunica, who was not supportive of the attempts by his prime minister Zoran Djindjic to transfer Milošević to The Hague, Annan wrote: "I note from recent reports in the press that you would appear now to have broadened the scope of your remarks and to have entered into the discussion of more general political issues, such as the granting and withholding by States and international organizations of economic assistance to the Federal Republic of Yugoslavia. . . . In view of the very sensitive situation prevailing within the Federal Republic of Yugoslavia and the delicate position in which Mr. Kostunica finds himself . . . I would accordingly encourage you in the future to confine your interventions to matters that are more directly within the sphere of your lawful concern" (letter from Annan to Del Ponte, 6 March 2001).

At last she found someone she could work with in Belgrade. Zoran Djindjic had become prime minister in January 2001 after the fall of the Milošević regime. He would ultimately succeed in transferring the former president of Serbia and Yugoslavia to the ICTY. Milošević was arrested on 1 April 2001 and arrived in The Hague on 29 June 2001. In many respects Djindjic reminded Del

Ponte of Falcone, and like the other man Del Ponte had respected and admired, Djindjic was killed. On 12 March 2003 he was shot outside the main government building in Belgrade. Milošević was charged with sixty-six counts of genocide, crimes against humanity, and war crimes, committed in conflicts in Bosnia, Croatia, and Kosovo. In her opening statement at the Milošević trial, the chief prosecutor stressed that nobody was above the law.

The prosecution of a former president of a European state was a landmark in international law and international politics. Milošević conducted his own defense, using the trial as another forum for his political convictions. He famously declared, in English, "I consider this tribunal false tribunal, and indictments false indictments." Milošević's self-representation in court and the deterioration of his health led to fewer trial days, with only half days spent in court and many suspensions. When he died in his cell on 11 March 2004, the overall trial had been ongoing for four calendar years, although in actual working days this amounted to ninety days, thirty per war, according to the arithmetic of the prosecutor Geoffrey Nice at a roundtable at the Centre for Holocaust and Genocide Studies in Amsterdam on 5 November 2007.

The outside world reacted to the death of Milošević as if the ICTY had imploded. However, more suspects were on trial than ever. Only high-ranking persons were tried; others were referred to the local war crimes chambers in Zagreb, Sarajevo, and Belgrade. The judges started playing a more active role in limiting indictments and numbers of witnesses. Major trials started, among them the prosecution of Radislav Krstić and others for the massacre of seven to eight thousand Muslim men in Srebrenica in 1995; the case against three high-ranking Serbian military officials for a massacre of mostly Croats in Vukovar; the trial of the former Serbian president Milan Milutinović and others for incidents in the war in Kosovo; the case against Vojislav Šešelj, the ultranationalist leader of the Serbian Radical Party; the case against the former Bosnian Serb leader Momčilo Krajisnik; and the case against the Bosnian general Rasim Delić, who had allegedly made use of mujahideen fighters during the war. By Del Ponte's own count, more than thirty-five hundred Balkan stories have been told by victims in the courtrooms of the ICTY.

In 2000 the judges and prosecutors started mapping out a completion strategy for the ICTY. On 28 August 2003 the Security Council laid down the completion strategy in Resolution 1503: all investigations should be wrapped up in 2004, first-instance trials should be finished in 2008,

and appeal trials in 2010. Del Ponte issued the last indictments in the beginning of 2005.

Increasingly, Del Ponte would find ways to hold persons of all ethnic groups involved in the wars in the former Yugoslavia responsible. Her deputy prosecutor David Tolbert said in an interview that the policy to prosecute all sides was systematically applied under Del Ponte. By focusing on dividing resources and lawyers equally over investigations, Del Ponte gave difficult prosecutions a chance. One of her most daring prosecutions was the one against Kosovo's prime minister Ramush Haradinaj, a protégé of the international organizations in Kosovo, who wanted him to broker peace with Serbia. As one of the leaders of the Kosovo Liberation Army, he had used unlawful methods, according to the indictment. It became a prosecution against all odds, with witnesses withdrawing their statements after they had received threats and other witnesses refusing to appear. Here, justice against a victor fell flat. The defense was so certain of an acquittal that it did not present a case. On 3 April 2008 Haradinaj was acquitted for lack of evidence. The then ongoing trial of the Croat general Ante Gotovina, one of the leaders of Operation Storm in 1995, was made difficult because it was a trial against a person who has been considered a hero in his country and belonged to the local victors and it thus clashed with the reality of power politics.

RWANDA

The UN tribunal for Rwanda is housed not in Rwanda itself but in Arusha in neighboring Tanzania, a long way from Kigali, the capital of Rwanda. The result, much to Del Ponte's annoyance, was that victims and witnesses had to make a long journey and that the media, who were mainly stationed in Nairobi in Kenya, a five-hour drive to Arusha, only sparingly covered the trials. Del Ponte chose to live in Kigali, a better hub to the rest of the world.

On Del Ponte's first visit to Arusha, on 23 November 1999, she found forty-eight indictments already issued and twenty-nine suspects in detention. Jean Kambanda, the prime minister of the extremist Hutu government, had already pleaded guilty to genocide. Louise Arbour, Del Ponte's predecessor as chief prosecutor, had formulated a strategy to combine cases thematically. Thus, trials were organized against the highest military leaders of the Hutu, against the political leaders during the genocide, and against people connected to the media who had played a pivotal role as propagandists in the genocide.

During her second visit, Del Ponte went into the countryside of Rwanda and had her first confrontation with the horrendous outcome of the genocide. She saw massive amounts of bodies and human bones and spoke with many victims. In her book she notes that she realized how limited her role was: "I suffer through conversations with victims and survivors. What can you do to improve their lives or ease the burden? Nothing significant, nothing lasting."

As Arbour had already realized, the prosecution of others besides the Hutu génocidaires proved impossible. In this respect, the difference with the work at the ICTY was huge. Del Ponte's successor at the ICTR, Hassan Jallow, pointed out the difference: "The ICTY is essentially a war crimes court. The ICTR is essentially a genocide court. There are no two parties to a genocide. There was a parallel military conflict, but genocide was an overwhelming huge crime basis. This is why we have concentrated on that." The ICTR was the tribunal of the victims, of the beaten who had ended up being in power. Thierry Cruvellier, the only journalist who closely followed the trials at the Rwanda tribunal, therefore called his book *Le tribunal de vaincus*, in which he shows how the tribunal never had a chance to fulfill its mandate to investigate and prosecute perpetrators of all sides. The victims would not let that happen, and the international world felt so guilty that politicians would not support Arbour and Del Ponte in their efforts.

The genocide in Rwanda had taken the lives of 500,000 to 800,000 Tutsi and moderate Hutu. The Tutsi Rwandan Patriotic Front (RPF) won the subsequent war, and Paul Kagame was elected president of Rwanda in 2000. Del Ponte, like Arbour before her, realized that the RPF troops had also committed serious war crimes. The central point of conflict between Kagame and Del Ponte was the assessment of the missile attack in April 1994 that killed Juvénal Habyarimana, the Hutu president at the time, who had brokered a power-sharing agreement between Hutu and Tutsi. Del Ponte's special investigation into the role of the RPF, especially into the possibility that they had instigated the missile attack on Habyarimana's plane, resulted in an increasingly bad relationship with the Tutsi government. Del Ponte has continued to maintain that this tension led to her dismissal as chief prosecutor of the ICTR in 2003. The alleged political interference by the United Kingdom and to a lesser extent the United States to get her fired was, by this account, rooted in their support for the Rwandan Tutsi government. After Del Ponte left Arusha, the investigation of the RPF was never officially closed, but Jallow let it die a silent death.

The official reason given by the UN for dismissing Del Ponte was that a single chief prosecutor was not enough for an efficient completion strategy for the two tribunals. At her first big press conference in 2000, after a hundred days in office, Del Ponte had announced that she was planning to divide her time equally between the two tribunals, but in Rwanda she remained largely an outsider. The Rwandan government prosecutor Gerald Gahima, talking disparagingly to BBC News on 29 July 2003 about a "part-time prosecutor based on another continent," said, "We need someone who devotes adequate time to the affairs of the tribunal. Rwanda does not deserve second-rate justice."

However, the ICTR had its large, complicated, and more or less successful cases, and Del Ponte played a role in some of them. On 2 April 2002, six years after his detention, Théoneste Bagosora, the former head of the Ministry of Defense and the alleged architect of the genocide, went on trial with three others. In her opening statement, Del Ponte spoke of "crimes committed in Rwanda whose gravity shocked the human conscience. They plunge all of humanity into mourning" because they "affect that which is the most sacred." The trial of Bagosora, who had said in 1992 that he was coming to Kigali "to prepare the apocalypse," lasted until June 2007, with a judgment issued in February 2009.

When Del Ponte arrived at the ICTR for the first time, among the forty-eight indicted persons was Jean-Bosco Barayagwiza, who had allegedly been a strong, hands-on supporter of the genocide. He had narrowly escaped prosecution. He had been detained in Cameroon and after his transfer to Arusha had been held for three months without having been brought before a judge. For this reason the ICTR Appeal Chamber dismissed his charges. But Del Ponte managed to get this decision reviewed, and Barayagwiza stood trial with others in the so-called media trial. He had allegedly played a crucial role in the planning and execution of the massacres and had been a member of the steering committee of Radio Télévision Libre des Milles Collines and, as such, was responsible for the genocidal propaganda. He was sentenced to twenty-seven years in prison, and his appeal is pending.

CRITICISM

Del Ponte clashed not only with politicians but also with people in her offices. The outspoken chief prosecutor had to deal with equally outspoken members of her team, most of whom would criticize her only off the record, but some of whom made their grievances public. The Milošević prosecutor Nice was one of her most ferocious critics. He blamed Del Ponte for being a bad manager, a bad lawyer, a politician, and for making huge errors of judgment. He blamed her for being interested in cases only when they would generate huge publicity. In an interview with Dutch NOVA TV, broadcast on 29 December 2007, he said, "The problem with the Milošević trial was that it provided such a potential for publicity that she wanted to get involved in it, more than she wanted to get involved in other trials." But in court, Nice was in charge. "She was never knowledgeable enough about the facts of the case or necessarily of the law to make close liaison on matters of detail appropriate." Del Ponte replied to media questions about Nice's criticisms of her by suggesting that he was not a team player and could not accept the leadership of a woman. Nice retorted that he admired and worked harmoniously with the woman who had appointed him, Arbour.

Asked during her last press conference what kind of leader of the organization she was, Del Ponte said, "My leadership is to take all responsibility for what happens in my office because I am the chief prosecutor. And to discuss fully with my collaborators before taking a decision." But in her book she expresses some regrets: "I should have acted more quickly to reassign or dismiss some incompetent attorneys. I should have found the time to become more of a presence on the hallways of the Office of the Prosecutor; I underestimated the value this would have had for morale."

Other criticisms came also from outside her office. Her agreement with the Serbian government that the crucial documents of the Supreme Defense Council should not be made public after they had been transferred to the ICTY as evidence has been hotly discussed. The fact that she did not indict NATO authorities for bombing civilian targets in Belgrade in 1999 has been a subject of debate, not only in Serbia but also among international lawyers. And the fact that she had let Biljana Plavšić, the former president of the Republika Srpska, get away with a less-than-genuine plea agreement and a refusal to give evidence against Milošević and other important suspects was, with hindsight, widely seen as an error of judgment.

Del Ponte only takes the blame for the last incident, acknowledging that she realized too late that she had been played by the "iron lady" from Republika Srpska. Plavšić later said in an interview with Banja Luka Alternative TV in 2005 that she had not spoken the truth in her plea statement in court and had only pleaded guilty because she had no choice, for lack of witnesses who wanted to testify on her behalf.

In her book Del Ponte lays the blame for the failure to bring the NATO indictment with the people in power in Brussels and Washington, who refused to support her investigations with evidence. And regarding the secrecy about the Serbian documents, which served only the Serb government, who was party in a procedure with Bosnia before the International Court of Justice (ICJ) on the basis of the Genocide Convention, she points to the judges of the ICTY and the ICJ, who accepted that the documents should remain under seal.

AFTER THE HAGUE

Switzerland appointed Del Ponte ambassador to Argentina in 2008. When her book was published the same year, Swiss officials told her not to speak in public about the contents. Her criticism of political authorities and of the constant dominance of politics over justice was considered incompatible with her new diplomatic role in Buenos Aires. Thus, the book had to find its way to the public without press coverage or interviews.

At the ICTY Del Ponte was succeeded by Serge Brammertz from Belgium, who had been federal prosecutor in his home country, became deputy prosecutor at the ICC in 2003, and was head of the International Investigation Commission into the murder of the former prime minister of Lebanon, Rafiq Hariri, in 2006.

[*See also* Balkan Wars; Criminal Justice: International Criminal Justice; Genocide; International Criminal Tribunal for Rwanda (ICTR); International Criminal Tribunal for the Former Yugoslavia (ICTY); Slobodan Milošević; *and* Rwanda.]

BILIOGRAPHY

Côté, Luc. "Reflections on the Exercise of Prosecutorial Discretion in International Criminal Law." *Journal of International Criminal Justice* 3 (2005): 162–186.

Cruvellier, Thierry. *Le tribunal des vaincus: Un Nuremberg pour le Rwanda?* Paris: Calman-Lévy, 2006.

Cruvellier, Thierry. "The Troubled Mandate of the ICTR." *International Justice Tribune*, November 19, 2007.

Del Ponte, Carla. "Investigation and Prosecution of Large-Scale Crimes at the International Level: The Experience of the ICTY." *Journal of International Criminal Justice* 4 (2006): 539–558.

Del Ponte, Carla, in collaboration with Chuck Sudetic. *Madame Prosecutor: Confrontations with Humanity's Worst Criminals and the Culture of Impunity.* New York: Other Press, 2009.

Originally published as *La Caccia: Io e i criminali di guerra*, Rome: Giongacomo Feltrinelli Editore, 2008.

Gattini, Andrea. "Evidentiary Issues in the ICJ's Genocide Judgement." *Journal of International Criminal Justice* 5 (2007): 889–904.

Hartmann, Florence. *Paix et châtiment*. Paris: Flammarion, 2007.

Nice, Geoffrey. "Hidden from Public View." *International Herald Tribune*, April 16, 2007.

Reydams, Luc. "The ICTR Ten Years On: Back to the Nuremberg Paradigm?" *Journal of International Criminal Justice* 3 (2005): 977–988.

Simons, Marlise. "Genocide Court Ruled for Serbia without Seeing Full War Archive." *New York Times*, April 9, 2007.

Verrijn Stuart, Heikelina. "International Criminal Tribunal for the Former Yugoslavia: Justice against All." *International Justice Tribune*, December 3, 2007.

DEMOCRACY AND RIGHT TO PARTICIPATION

by Peter R. Baehr

This entry deals with the human right of public participation and its relationship to democracy. It discusses the principle of popular sovereignty, restrictions on majority rule, the major international human rights instruments, and political participation in practice. The right to political participation is generally considered an essential part of some manner of a democratic system of government. One of the principles adopted by the World Conference on Human Rights in Vienna in 1993 states that democracy, development, and human rights are "interdependent and mutually reinforcing." Democracy was considered to be based on the freely expressed will of the people to determine their own political, economic, social, and cultural systems and their full participation in all aspects of their lives.

Although no standard definition of the terms "democracy" and "democratic" is universally accepted, the commonly held view is that a democratic system of government is based (or at least claims to be based) on the will of the majority of the people. The political scientist Robert A. Dahl considers the continuing responsiveness of the government to the preferences of its citizens a key characteristic of a democracy. Sovereignty rests with the people ("popular sovereignty"). The precise form such a democratic system of government takes may differ widely. One may distinguish, for instance, majoritarian, consensual, limited, aspiring, executive, federal, confederal, unitary, and others.

Even systems that are clearly totalitarian or authoritarian usually pay at least lip service to the democratic ideals: the notion of democracy has such a broad appeal that authoritarian regimes prefer to call themselves democracies of some kind or another. As Fareed Zakaria has noted, "Democratically elected regimes, often ones that have been reelected or reaffirmed through referenda, are routinely ignoring constitutional limits on their power and depriving their citizens of basic rights and freedoms" (p. 22)Such regimes he calls "illiberal democracies" that

do not meet minimum standards of what a democracy is supposed to be. Thus, next to the parliamentary and presidential democracies as practiced in most Western states (usually called "liberal democracies"), the Communist states of Eastern Europe called themselves "people's democracies," while the Soviet Union itself, though a one-party state under the leadership of the Communist Party, based its decisions on a system of "democratic centralism." At the time, Indonesia's president, Sukarno, ruled his country by a system that he called "guided democracy." Also, in the early twenty-first century, democracy in some non-Western states may amount to no more than informal consultations or legally approved ways to express grievances. Such rights are granted to all members of the adult population. The North African state of Libya, headed by the long-time ruler Muammar al-Qaddafi, offers "direct democracy," which includes the holding throughout the country of people's congresses at which citizens debate issues facing their government and ostensibly make decisions.

There are limits, however, to what can be called a democratic system. Political systems that systematically exclude certain adult groups from public participation, for example, on the basis of gender (in the past in certain cantons in Switzerland and in the early twenty-first century in some Arab states) or color of skin (during apartheid in South Africa), cannot be considered democratic. Although the classical Athenian city-state is often called "the cradle of democracy" as the concept was coined there and then, it limited public participation to male, native, freeborn citizens and therefore cannot be considered a "democracy" in any modern sense of the word.

Democracy is also referred to as government by, or on behalf of, the majority of the population. This, however, is not sufficient. Democracy also entails respect for the rights of the minority (or minorities), including fair and transparent procedures to offer those groups the possibility to gain a majority status or at least the protection of their rights and interests. In other words, they should be granted full freedom of expression, the right to assembly and organization, and the right to take part in the electoral process. It is especially in order to safeguard these rights of the minority that a full-fledged democratic form of government includes a number of fundamental human rights that cannot (or cannot easily) be disregarded. The more strongly civil and political rights are enforced in a society, the more democratic it becomes. For that reason, these human rights are usually contained in the constitution of a state, which cannot be easily amended.

The right to political participation can be put into practice in various ways, including by the right to take part in the conduct of public affairs or by the more specific right to take part in elections but also, in some states, by the right of petition, the holding of referenda or plebiscites, and other ways of consulting the will of the people. If the condition of holding periodic popular consultations in a fair and equal manner is met and if there are satisfactory ways to protect the rights of political and other minorities, such a system of popular participation can be called a democracy. A good definition was given in 1942 by the Austrian writer Joseph Schumpeter. He defined the democratic method as "that institutional arrangement for arriving at political decisions in which individuals acquire the power to decide by means of a competitive struggle for the people's vote" (p. 269). Many criticisms have been expressed of that form of government, for example, that it perpetuates elite domination or that it leads to ill-judged citizen choices. But as Winston Churchill, the British prime minister, once said, "Democracy is the worst form of government, except for all those other forms that have been tried from time to time" (*Official Report, House of Commons*, pp. 206–207).

THE PRINCIPLE OF POPULAR SOVEREIGNTY

Democracy and political participation are founded on the principle of popular sovereignty, the idea that the people should be able to determine their own system of government and that it should at least control the general lines of policy making. This idea was first formulated by the British philosopher John Locke and the French philosopher and political thinker Jean-Jacques Rousseau. It formed the basis of France's Declaration of the Rights of Man and of the Citizen (1789), which states that "the principle of sovereignty resides essentially in the nation"

and of other similar documents. A number of questions remained unresolved, however— among them, who does belong to the "people" or "the nation" and how and by whom was the will of the nation to be expressed. Rousseau argued that there existed a "general will" that represented the rational interests of the entire nation. This general will was seen as being different from (and more than) the accumulated wishes of the individuals that made up the nation ("the will of all"). The only acceptable way to determine that general will was, in Rousseau's view, a system of direct democracy, "where the people find it easy to meet and in which every citizen can easily get to know all of the others"—following the model of the classical Greek city-state—and reach decisions on policy matters. He rejected the idea of government by representation, which, he felt, could never fully express the general will. Once that general will was established, everybody was supposed to follow its directives. In Rousseau's famous words, whoever refused to follow the general will "will be forced to be free."

Although one may question the idea of popular sovereignty and its implications, its importance lay in its direct opposition to then current theories of divine sovereignty, the sovereignty of God, in whose name or by whose grace emperors, kings, and other worldly leaders reigned. This concept could already be found in the U.S. Declaration of Independence (1776), which proclaimed "that . . . governments are instituted among men deriving their just powers *from the consent of the governed*" (italics added).

The subjection of individual preferences to the "general will" of the full community does not tally with modern views of democracy, which protect the individual by guaranteeing his or her fundamental human rights. The protection of the individual and the protection of minorities are constraints to the absolute power of popular sovereignty as seen by Rousseau. There remains an ingrained fear in the early twenty-first century that certain individuals or groups, claiming to represent "the general will," may take or use political power to form a civilian or military dictatorship—something radically different from the ideal of direct democracy with full participation by all the people that Rousseau had in mind.

RESTRICTIONS ON MAJORITY RULE

Majority rule does not necessarily imply respect for human rights. If the majority—or those claiming to represent that majority—were left to their own devices, this might have negative consequences for those not belonging to that majority. The American human rights expert Jack Donnelly put this problem very aptly: "The people often want to treat some in their midst with extreme cruelty" (p. 610). Nazi leaders in Germany often referred to the "gesundes Volksempfinden" (healthy sentiments of the people), which supposedly legitimized Hilter's actions against the Jews and other "Untermenschen" (inferior people) (Rosenberg).

To protect the rights of the political minority, other minorities, or individuals, it is necessary to reign in the absolute power of the majority. Such reigning in is usually done in the constitution of a state, which means that in a (liberal) democracy, majority rule is accompanied by "constitutionalism." Constitutionalism provides the legal and political framework for safeguarding the dignity and human rights of all citizens, both members of the majority and minorities. For example, the first ten amendments to the Constitution of the United States, often called the Bill of Rights, are meant to help safeguard the rights of all Americans. The advantage of having these rights incorporated in a state's constitution is that amending it usually requires special procedures, for example, in the United States a two-thirds majority in both houses of Congress plus ratification by three-quarters of the states.

The death penalty further underscores the importance of making it difficult to change basic rights. In all states of Europe, this form of punishment has been outlawed as an unacceptable infringement of the right to life. However, in the early twenty-first century in most European states there is a sizable minority of some 40 percent in favor of reintroducing the death penalty. In cases where some horrendous or abominable crimes were committed, that figure may well rise to more than 50 percent. Nevertheless, as the prohibition of the death penalty is usually incorporated in states' constitutions, it will not be easy to reintroduce the death penalty unless the required qualified majority for such a change to the constitution is attained.

The most extensive protection of individual rights is contained in the constitution of the southern African republic of Namibia, which includes in Chapter 3 some twenty articles dealing with fundamental rights and freedoms. Under Article 131, Chapter 3 can never, under any circumstances, be changed: "No repeal or amendment of any of the provisions of Chapter 3 hereof, in so far as such repeal or amendment diminishes or detracts from the fundamental rights and freedoms contained and defined in that Chapter, shall be possible under the Constitution, and no such purported repeal or amendment shall be valid or have any force or effect." In other words,

a revolution or some other extralegal changeover would be required to change this part of the Namibian constitution. One may well wonder whether such 100 percent protection, which may lead to inflexibility, is what a society needs. In all other states some kind of qualified majority is preferred.

Majority rule does not necessarily mean rule by an absolute majority of all those entitled to vote. In some countries, such as Belgium, voting is compulsory, which means that between 80 and 90 percent of voters turn up at the polls. In most countries, however, people are free to go to the polls or not. In the United States, for example, no more than about 40 percent of eligible voters take part in the presidential elections. Its electoral system is based on the states. This may mean that the president is elected not only by a minority of those entitled to vote but also by a minority of those who do vote. For example, in 2000 George W. Bush was elected into office as president by fewer popular votes than his opponent, Al Gore, because Bush commanded a majority of the votes in the Electoral College, which elects the president. The Electoral College was created by the Founding Fathers of the American Constitution, who were wary of popular passions at the time and therefore put this limitation on the direct impact of the popular vote. In addition, they devised a system of "checks and balances" that limits presidential power. With regard to human rights, one can argue that some of these checks and balances, such as freedom of expression, freedom of assembly, and freedom of association, may help support majority rule, whereas others, such as the protection of minorities and freedom of religion, restrict such rule.

THE MAJOR INTERNATIONAL HUMAN RIGHTS INSTRUMENTS

The right of participation is mentioned in a number of international treaties and other documents. The first of these was the Universal Declaration of Human Rights, adopted by the General Assembly of the United Nations (UN) in 1948. Article 21 of the declaration states, "Everyone has the right to take part in the government of his country, directly or through freely chose representatives."

Johannes Morsink, the author of a major textbook on the Universal Declaration of Human Rights, has made the point that, although World War II was fought for saving democracy, the term "democracy" as such does not appear in the declaration, and the word "democratic" is mentioned only once (in Article 29, para. 2). His explanation for the absence of those terms is that the drafters "got caught in the rhetoric of the Cold War" (p. 61). Others, too, have observed that the Soviet Union especially saw the declaration mainly as a tool in the Cold War struggle.

The Universal Declaration of Human Rights was followed by the legally binding International Covenant on Civil and Political Rights (ICCPR), whose Article 25 reads, "Every citizen shall have the right and the opportunity . . . to take part in the conduct of public affairs, directly or through freely chosen representatives."

The wording of this article was deliberately left somewhat vague to accommodate the various existing political systems. A state does not have to follow the Western democratic model in order to satisfy the requirements of this article. In fact, at the beginning of 2006, no less than 154 states had become party to the ICCPR. However, some of these do not meet the requirements to be called democracies. The article only requires governments to be in some way accountable to their citizens and does not allow for an absolutist reign; it is thus based on the principle of popular sovereignty. How that sovereignty is exercised is left open, however. As Sarah Joseph, Jenny Schultz, and Melissa Castan point out in their major commentary on the ICCPR, "Numerous political systems seem compatible with article 25 (a), including Westminster systems, 'presidential' systems, bicameral systems, unicameral systems, unitary systems, and federal systems" (p. 654).

Another relevant article is the common Article 1 of the ICCPR and the International Covenant on Economic, Social, and Cultural Rights (ICESCR), which provides for the right of self-determination of all peoples. The second sentence of that article refers to the right of internal self-determination: "By virtue of that right they freely determine their political status." The recognition of this right of internal self-determination implies that it must be possible to hold governments accountable. Internal self-determination is different from external self-determination, which was mainly used by colonized people in the third world trying to free themselves from (Western) colonial rule. Most governments, for obvious reasons, refuse to accept, with respect to the latter, that such self-determination could lead to secession and the formation of another state.

The right of participation is explicitly limited to the citizens of a country. In a general comment, the UN Human Rights Committee indicated in 1995 that at the municipal level, the right of political participation can also be conferred on noncitizens, but the state must indicate whether any groups, such as permanent residents, enjoy these rights on a limited basis, for example, by having the right to vote in local elections or to hold particular public service positions.

The right of political participation of women is explicitly mentioned in the Convention on the Elimination of All Forms of Discrimination against Women, adopted in 1979. The preamble to that convention stresses that discrimination against women is an obstacle to the participation of women, on equal terms with men, in the political, social, economic, and cultural lives of their countries; that it hampers the growth of the prosperity of society and the family; and that it makes more difficult the full development of the potential of women in the service of their countries and of humanity.

Article 7 ensures to women the rights:

b) To participate in the formulation of government policy and the implementation thereof and to hold public office and perform all public functions at all levels of government;

c) To participate in non-governmental organizations and associations concerned with the public and political life of the country.

One of the ideas behind this convention is that such participation will help ensure that greater attention is paid to the specific demands of women, thus helping eliminate discrimination against women in society. The Committee on the Elimination of Discrimination against Women recommended in 1997 that the article should be applicable not only to the subjects explicitly mentioned but also to the governing boards of public bodies, political parties, labor unions, professional organizations, and institutions working in the field of economic policy making.

According to the treaty, states, not private bodies, are responsible for implementing the obligations against the treaty. However, under Article 2, paragraph e, states must "take all appropriate measures to eliminate discrimination against women by any person, organization or enterprise." This means that, for example, with regard to political parties and labor unions, states must ensure that these bodies do not discriminate against women, although they themselves are not directly bound by the treaty. In the case of the Netherlands, this has led to measures against one orthodox-fundamentalist Christian political party, the Staatkundig Gereformeerde Partij (SGP), which, until 2006, did not admit women to its membership. The Committee on the Elimination of Discrimination against Women noted in 2001, "with concern that, in the Netherlands, there is a political party represented in the Parliament that excludes women from membership, which is a violation of article 7 of the Convention." The committee recommended that "the State party take urgent measures to address this situation, including the adoption of legislation that brings the membership of political parties into conformity with its obligations under article 7 (para. 219–220)." Such legislation had not been adopted two years later, but a court ruled that the financial governmental subvention to the SGP that is available to all parties represented in parliament must be withdrawn. Although progress has been made, the world average of women in parliament, according to the Inter-Parliamentary Union, was no more than 15.7 percent in 2005.

Children are not accorded the right to political participation as such. In all societies there is a minimum age limit (usually eighteen years) to the right to vote. This does not mean, however, that children are entirely without political rights. Under the Convention on the Rights of the Child, which was adopted in 1989 and had been ratified by 191 states as of the early twenty-first century, children are given the right to active participation in social life. This includes the right to be heard in any judicial and administrative proceedings; the right to freedom of expression; the right to freedom of thought, conscience, and religion; the right to freedom of association and peaceful assembly; and the right to privacy. States should also ensure that children enjoy basic economic rights, such as access to education, health institutions, social security, and so forth. These rights have been summarized as protection, participation, and provision, the "three P's" of children's rights.

The International Convention on the Elimination of All Forms of Racial Discrimination, adopted in 1965, includes "political rights, in particular the rights to participate in elections . . . on the basis of universal and equal suffrage, to take part in the Government as well as in the conduct of public affairs at any level and to have equal access to public service" (Article 5, para. c). The system of apartheid in South Africa gave a legal basis to racial discrimination, which limited the participation of nonwhites in the political life of the country. Following the elimination of apartheid, no system in the world legally permits racial discrimination and thereby limits the political participation of persons of a particular racial background.

The World Conference against Racism, Racial Discrimination, Xenophobia, and Related Intolerance, held in Durban, South Africa, in 2001, recognized in its final declaration "that the equal participation of all individuals and peoples in the formation of just, equitable, democratic and inclusive societies can contribute to a world free from racism, racial discrimination, xenophobia and related intolerance" (p. 7). The convention's program of action recognized that participatory governance responsive to the needs and aspirations of the people is essential for the effective prevention and elimination of racism, racial discrimination, xenophobia, and related intolerance.

The above documents are global in their aims and scope. Similar documents exist at the regional level. Thus, for example, the American and African human rights treaties contain references to the right of political participation. The Council of Europe Convention for the Protection of Human Rights and Fundamental Freedoms (1950) limits itself to a provision for holding "free elections at reasonable intervals by secret ballot" (Protocol 1, Article 3). In the preamble to the convention, reference is made to those fundamental freedoms that are the foundation of justice and peace in the world and are best maintained by "an effective political democracy"; at various places in the convention, reference is made to "a democratic society."

The American Declaration on the Rights and Duties of Man (1948) provides (in its Article 20) for the right of all persons having legal capacity to participate in the governments of their countries and to take part in popular elections. The legally binding American Convention on Human Rights, adopted in 1978, contains a chapter on the right to participate in government. Its Article 23 reads:

Every citizen shall enjoy the following rights and opportunities:

1. to take part in the conduct of public affairs, directly or through freely chosen representatives;
2. to vote and to be elected at genuine periodic elections, which shall be by universal and equal suffrage and by secret ballot that guarantees the free expression of the will of the voters; and
3. to have access, under general conditions of equality, to the public service of his country.

As in the case of the ICCPR, this right is explicitly limited to citizens. By implication, one must conclude that noncitizens do not have these rights. The said provision is nonderogable (that is, it cannot be suspended or abolished) "in time of war, public danger, or other emergency" (Article 27, para. 1). Article 29 provides that "no provision in the convention shall be interpreted as . . . precluding other rights or guarantees that are inherent in the human personality or derived from representative democracy as a form of government" (Article 29, para. c).

In 1991 the General Assembly of the Organization of American States (OAS) adopted what has become known as the "Santiago Doctrine." The doctrine created a mechanism to respond to an irregular interruption of the democratic political institutional process in any member state of the organization. Democracy thereby became an international (regional), not merely a domestic, matter. When the U.S. government in 2005 tried to endorse a coup d'état in Venezuela against the democratically elected Hugo Chávez government, the members of the OAS supported the Venezuelan government in the name of democracy.

Article 13 of the African Charter on Human and Peoples' Rights (1981) reads:

1. Every citizen shall have the right to freely participate in the government of his country, either directly or through freely chosen representatives in accordance with the provisions of the law.
2. Every citizen shall have the right of equal access to the public service of his country.
3. Every individual shall have the right of access to public property and services in strict equality of all persons before the law.

Note the restriction of the first two paragraphs to citizens, whereas the rights listed in the third paragraph apply to all individuals.

In 1990 the African Charter for Popular Participation in Development and Transformation (Arusha Charter) was adopted at a conference attended by representatives of African governments as well as nongovernmental organizations (NGOs). According to the charter, popular participation is in essence "the empowerment of the people to effectively involve themselves in creating the structures and in designing policies and programmes that serve the interests of all as to effectively contribute to the development process and share equitably in its benefits." The attainment of equal rights by women in the social, economic, and political spheres must become "a central feature of a democratic and participatory pattern of development." The charter consists of a number of recommendations to governments, "the people and their organizations," the international community, NGOs, the communication media, women's organizations, labor unions, and youth and student organizations, ending in a plea for monitoring popular participation. The charter was transmitted to the Assembly of Heads of State and Government of the Organization of African Unity, which, however, had not taken any measure to give effect to this right of popular participation as of the early twenty-first century.

POLITICAL PARTICIPATION IN PRACTICE

Elections are the most common way political participation is exercised in practice. This practice is explicitly stipulated as a human right in the ICCPR: "To vote and to be elected at genuine periodic elections which shall be by universal and equal suffrage and shall be held by secret ballot, guaranteeing the free expression of the will of the electors" (Article 25, para. b).

The only acceptable restriction is a minimum age requirement, usually eighteen years. Just about all political systems use some form of elections to select their political leaders. These elections may be free and fair or manipulated and unfair in various degrees. In the Communist states of Eastern Europe, elections that resulted in majorities of more than 90 percent for the ruling elite were no exception. In the early twenty-first century as well, not all elections in all countries could be considered equally fair and free. In some countries, voters may have to choose by throwing their ballots, depending on whether they vote for or against the government, in clearly indicated boxes, often under the critical eyes of security officers. Apparently, although all regimes need some kind of legitimization through "elections," the result may have little resemblance to the "clearly expressed preference of the voters." It is estimated that genuine competitive contests take place in only one-third of the states. To demonstrate and check whether political systems do indeed offer a fair and free choice to the voters, neutral, often foreign, observers are invited to monitor the conduct of the elections.

Elections are usually contested by political parties that present lists of candidates for office. In many countries these parties are ideologically inspired. Different political traditions exist. Some countries, such as the United States, have a two-party system; most western European states have multiparty systems. In two-party systems the party that gains a majority forms a government, whereas in multiparty systems, negotiations among the parties after the election result in a government coalition. Elections may be organized on a district or constituency basis ("winner takes all"), as in the United States and the United Kingdom; by proportional representation, as in the Netherlands and most of the Scandinavian countries; or in a mixed system, as in Germany. A district system can lead to malapportionment, by redrawing the boundaries of districts to favor certain parties (called gerrymandering in the United States).

To be free, elections must also include a fair procedure for selecting the candidates. Some countries, such as the United States, hold primaries, which can also be more or less fair. Holding an election campaign can be extremely expensive, which only a few people can afford. In the United States, spending for election campaigns is subject to more or less effective regulations and rules that aim at guaranteeing a fair process. A contested election means that the voters have some kind of choice, but it is usually the political elite that decides between whom that choice will be made.

Political participation can also include referenda, or popular initiatives on a particular question or issue. These are implicitly mentioned in the ICCPR: "to take part in the conduct of public affairs, directly or through freely chosen representatives" (Article 25, para. a). Such referenda may be legally decisive or merely consultative, but the popular initiatives may also have the political force of legislative mandates. Many countries have a regular practice of referenda; in a country like Switzerland, voters are frequently asked to express their views at the national or local level.

A special case is constituted by the referenda on various aspects of European integration and, in 2005, in a number of member states of the European Union, on a draft constitutional document. Although this last document was only subject to parliamentary approval in some countries, referenda were held or planned in the Czech Republic, Denmark, France, Ireland, Luxembourg, the Netherlands, Poland, Portugal, Spain, and the United Kingdom. Although the document was accepted in Spain and Luxembourg, the voters in France and the Netherlands rejected it by sizable majorities (55 percent in France and 62 percent in the Netherlands). After that, the planned referenda in the other states were postponed. Subsequently, the document was considered politically dead, raising the issue of whether it is justified or acceptable that a majority of the voters in two countries can thwart the preferences of the voters (or their parliamentary representatives) in a great number of other countries.

A plebiscite is a referendum to give expression to the right of external self-determination. It gives the voters the opportunity to decide on the future makeup of the state: independence, joining another state, and so forth. Well-known examples are the series of plebiscites held in Europe after World War I to decide on the political futures of the respective countries or areas. The plebiscite in Upper Silesia in 1921 resulted in an overwhelming vote in favor of joining Germany rather than Poland. The vote on the future of the Saar Province in 1935 led to reunion with Germany rather than with France. After World War II such plebiscites were held in British Togoland, where the majority voted in favor of joining Ghana in 1955, and in North Cameroon, which joined Cameroon in 1961. West Samoa chose independence in 1961. Subsequently, plebiscites came into disuse. Preparations began in 1995, under the guidance of a UN mission, for a plebiscite to allow the inhabitants of the former Spanish colony of Western Sahara to choose between independence and joining Morocco. Although special representatives of the UN secretary-general have tried repeatedly to organize the event, it has repeatedly been "rescheduled," mainly owing to procrastination on the part of the Moroccan government.

Political participation can also take the form of submitting a petition. This is an age-old right consisting of a formal request by a group of citizens to a person in authority for a specific decision, a grant or benefit, or redress of a grievance. Petitioning is mentioned in most national constitutions. It was debated at length whether or not to include a right to petition to the UN in the Universal Declaration of Human Rights, but in the end the matter was postponed indefinitely. Such a right does exist, however, at the European level, for which the European Parliament established a Petitions Committee. This committee receives some fifteen hundred requests per year to right a wrong or to correct what is considered an injustice. The committee may intervene if the issue is a truly European one or if a member state of the European Union or a European Union institution is alleged to have infringed on a citizen's right under European Union law. This process may help bridge the growing gap between citizens and what is seen by many as the ever-increasing bureaucracy in Brussels. The European ombudsman created in 2002 fulfills a similar function.

The right to resist oppression can be seen as an ultimate form of political participation. This right was first systematically analyzed in the *Vindiciae contra Tyrannos*, published in 1579. Two years later, when the Netherlands repudiated its allegiance to King Philip II of Spain, the

States-General adopted an Act of Abjuration that read in part, "And that God did not create the subjects for the benefit of the Prince, to do his bidding in all things whatever godly or ungodly, right or wrong, and to serve him as slaves, but the Prince for the benefit of the subjects, without which he is no Prince."

A first draft of the Universal Declaration of Human Rights contained an explicit provision on the right to resist oppression and tyranny, but the delegation of the Soviet Union was not in favor of such a provision "for it might provide the possibility for fascist elements to overthrow the Government" (Morsink, p. 309). At a later point, the U.S. delegation was not in favor either, as the leader of the delegation, Eleanor Roosevelt, declared that the "recognition . . . of the right to resist acts of tyranny and oppression would be tantamount to encouraging sedition" (Morsink, p. 310). What remained was merely an indirect reference in the preamble of the declaration: "Whereas it is essential, if man is not to be compelled to have recourse, as a last resort, to rebellion against tyranny and oppression, that human rights should be protected by the rule of law." It is not explicitly mentioned in any of the legally binding instruments.

ASSESSMENT

Various rationales are given for having a human right to democracy and political participation. It can be seen as a good thing for individuals, good for a nation's stability and welfare, or even good for the maintenance of international peace and security under certain conditions.

Everybody seems to be in favor of democracy; yet, there is little agreement worldwide on what the concept is exactly meant to include. It provides some vague ideas that "the people" are supposed to govern themselves and that there should therefore be some broad measure of popular participation in public life and its government. However, it is also clear that not all people are always eager to engage in such participation, while there are always some who do. The latter group may be motivated by personal ambition or greed or by a genuine concern for the welfare of their fellow citizens. Only small societies can afford to practice the kind of direct democracy in which everyone gathers under an oak (or some other kind of tree) to discuss government business in the manner that Rousseau and his fellow thinkers envisioned. But even in those cases, it is unlikely that all the people will take part in the public debate in an equal manner; people tend to be different in their inclinations and talents. In the

much larger political societies, called "states," that make up the early-twenty-first-century international political system, these limitations to political participation are even more clearly present. This makes the right of popular or political participation a far-off, somewhat academic ideal that can at best be only partly achieved.

The principle of popular sovereignty is accepted in most societies and given the practical form of elections. Elections for public office are held in just about all states at both the national and the local levels. Although there are many different electoral systems, none seems to be fully satisfactory in the sense of assuring 100 percent political participation (or rather, those systems that claim to produce such nearly total participation are based on fraud or manipulation). The best results that can be achieved occur within systems that offer a maximum of transparency of procedure combined with a full measure of secrecy in the voting process itself. The high financial cost of conducting a campaign that reaches the voters makes candidacy in many societies almost impossible for those with a middle income or less. This also means that wealthy people or those supported by such wealthy persons hold a tremendous advantage.

If the minority (or minorities) in a society is to be given the chance to achieve majority status, then the current majority rule must be constrained by a system of human rights protection. In most societies it is the constitution (written or unwritten) that offers such protection. A constitution cannot solve all problems, however; basic constitutionally guaranteed human rights may clash. Clashes have occurred, for instance, between the right of freedom of expression and that of religion or nondiscrimination. The legal way out of such conflicts is offered by a political willingness to seek compromises combined with an independent court system. But in some situations that solution is not acceptable for all, and conflicts or even outbreaks of violence, including the killing or wounding of opponents or burning of embassies, may occur. This, too, can also be considered a manner of "public participation," but not in an acceptable way. Violence usually means that the weaker individuals or groups will be on the losing side. No society can afford to have such violent participation on a permanent basis.

Political participation is reserved for citizens. Noncitizens, including immigrants and refugees, tend to be discriminated against in this respect. Societies must find ways to accommodate the interests of noncitizens and to offer them an opportunity for acquiring citizenship. Problems tend to be aggravated if the number of noncitizens increases, which can lead to forms of xenophobia on the part of the original population (which may include those who only recently acquired citizenship and want to protect their newly acquired status). Most societies are reluctant to grant voting rights at the national level to noncitizens. However, at the local level there seems to be less reluctance.

The political party was once the major mechanism for organizing candidates for office, but the popularity of parties is decreasing in many countries. This may create problems in organizing participation in the electoral process in the long run. It does not necessarily mean that people are becoming less interested in public issues; people may express their views through NGOs that do not take part in the electoral process but that try to influence the political decision-making process. NGOs have been accused of not making clear on whose part or on whose authority they express their views. The same is often also true of political parties, whose leadership is not necessarily always responsive or accountable to the membership.

Initiatives, referenda, and plebiscites are means of consulting the views of the voters on certain specific issues in between and beyond regular elections. How many of those entitled to vote turn up depends on the nature of the issue and the frequency of these popular consultations. Many systems provide for a minimum turnout for the result of the referendum to be decisive. As an additional means next to parliamentary decision making, such popular consultations should be considered useful if not organized in excess.

The right of petition is an old but relatively modest manner in which to request certain measures from the government. More radical is the right to resist as an ultimate form of political participation if a government makes a majority-backed decision that is fully unacceptable to the minority, for example, abridging the fundamental rights of that minority. Then the right to participation may take the form of nonviolent resistance.

Finally, the outside world may interfere by peaceful or military means in the political process. Such interference should be proportionate, limited, and geared to achieving no more than the purpose of improving the human rights situation as envisioned. Such means may turn out to be counterproductive. Misuse of the term "humanitarian intervention" for what are essentially purely foreign policy aims should be avoided.

[See also African Union: Banjul Charter; Amnesty International; Children's Convention (Convention on the Rights of the Child); Civil and Political Rights: International Covenant on Civil and Political Rights; Economic, Social, and Cultural Rights: International Covenant on Economic, Social, and Cultural Rights; European Convention on Human Rights and Fundamental Freedoms (Council of Europe); European Union; Foreign Policy; Humanitarian Intervention: Overview; Minority Rights: Overview; Organization of American States; Self-Determination; South Africa; United Nations Commission on Human Rights; United Nations Security Council; Universal Declaration of Human Rights; Women: Convention on the Elimination of Discrimination against Women; and Women: Women's Rights.]

BIBLIOGRAPHY

Act of Abjuration. In *Human Rights and Foreign Policy*. Memorandum presented to the Lower House of the States General of the Kingdom of the Netherlands on May 3, 1979 by the Minister for Foreign Affairs and the Minister for Development Co-operation, Ministry of Foreign Affairs of the Kingdom of the Netherlands, 1581.

African [Banjul] Charter on Human and Peoples' Rights. University of Minnesota Human Rights Library.

American Convention on Human Rights. Human Rights and Constitutional Rights, Columbia Law School. http://www.hrcr.org/docs/American_Convention/oashr5.html.

Arat, Zehra F. *Democracy and Human Rights in Developing Countries*. Boulder, Colo., and London: Lynne Rienner, 1991.

Constitution of the Republic of Namibia. Windhoek: Ministry of Information and Broadcasting, 1991.

Convention for the Protection of Human Rights and Fundamental Freedoms, as amended by Protocol 11. Signed at Rome on November 4, 1950.

Dahl, Robert A. *Polyarchy: Participation and Opposition*. New Haven, Conn., and London: Yale University Press, 1971.

Donnelly, Jack. "Human Rights, Democracy, and Development." *Human Rights Quarterly* 21, no. 3 (1999): 608–632.

French Declaration of the Rights of Man and of the Citizen. In *The Human Rights Reader*, edited by Walter Laqueur and Barry Rubin. 2d ed. New York: New American Library, 1989.

Held, David, ed. *Prospects for Democracy: North, South, East, West*. Cambridge, U.K.: Polity, 1993.

Joseph, Sarah, Jenny Schultz, and Melissa Castan. *The International Covenant on Civil and Political Rights: Cases, Materials, and Commentary*. 2d ed. Oxford: Oxford University Press, 2004.

Klütz, Alfred. "Volksschädlinge am Pranger" [Those Who Damage the People to the Pillory]. *Faks.chronica* 13 (1940): 769ff.

Koh, Harold Hongju, and Ronald C. Slye, eds. *Deliberative Democracy and Human Rights*. New Haven, Conn., and London: Yale University Press, 1999.

Kufuor, Kofi Oteng. "The African Charter for Popular Participation in Development and Transformation." *Netherlands Quarterly of Human Rights* 18, no. 1 (2000): 7–22.

Langlois, Anthony J. "Human Rights without Democracy? A Critique of the Separationist Thesis." *Human Rights Quarterly* 25, no. 4 (2003): 990–1019.

Laqueur, Walter, and Barry Rubin, eds. *The Human Rights Reader*. 2d ed. New York: New American Library, 1989.

Morsink, Johannes. *The Universal Declaration of Human Rights: Origins, Drafting, and Intent*. Philadelphia: University of Pennsylvania Press, 1999.

Nowak, Manfred. *U.N. Covenant on Civil and Political Rights: CCPR Commentary*. 2d ed. Kehl, Germany: N.P. Engel, 2005.

Official Report, House of Commons. Vol. 444. Speech of Winston Churchill before the House of Commons, November 11, 1947.

Powell, G. Bingham. "Liberal Democracies." In *Encyclopedia of Government and Politics*, 2d ed., edited by Mary Hawkesworth and Maurice Kogan, pp. 205–222. London and New York: Routledge, 2004.

Report of the Committee on the Elimination of Discrimination against Women. Twenty-fifth session, UN Doc. A/56/38, July 2–20, 2001.

Report of the World Conference against Racism, Racial Discrimination, Xenophobia, and Related Intolerance. A/CONF.189/12, August 31, September 8, 2001.

Rosas, Allan. "Democracy and Human Rights." In *Human Rights in a Changing East-West Perspective*, edited by Allan Rosas and Jan Helgesen, pp. 17–57. London and New York: Pinter, 1990.

Rosenberg, Alfred. *Der Mythus des Zwanzigsten Jahrhunderts*. München, Germany: Hoheneichter Verlag, 1930.

Rousseau, Jean-Jacques. *The Social Contract* (1762). Chicago: Henry Regnery, 1948.

Schumpeter, Joseph A. *Capitalism, Socialism, and Democracy*. 2d ed. New York: Harper, 1947.

Steiner, Henry J. "Political Participation as a Human Right." *Harvard Yearbook of International Law* 1 (1988): 77–134. Reprinted in *International Human Rights in Context*, edited by Henry J. Steiner and Philip Alston, pp. 890–899. Oxford: Oxford University Press, 2000.

United Nations. *Convention on the Elimination of All Forms of Discrimination against Women*. Division for the Advancement of Women. http://www.un.org/womenwatch/daw/ cedaw/text/econvention.htm#article7.

United Nations. *International Convention on the Elimination of All Forms of Racial Discrimination*. Office of the High Commissioner for Human Rights. http://www.unhchr.ch/html/menu3/b/d_icerd.htm.

United Nations. *International Covenant on Civil and Political Rights*. Office of the High Commissioner for Human Rights. http://www.unhchr.ch/html/menu3/b/a_ccpr.htm.

United Nations. *International Covenant on Economic, Social, and Cultural Rights*. Office of the High Commissioner for Human Rights. http://www.unhchr.ch/html/menu3/b/a_cescr.htm.

United Nations. *Universal Declaration of Human Rights*. Office of the High Commissioner for Human Rights. http://www.unhchr.ch/udhr/lang/eng.htm.

United States Declaration of Independence. In *The Human Rights Reader*, 2d ed., edited by Walter Laqueur and Barry Rubin, p. 107. New York: New American Library, 1989.

Vienna Declaration and Programme of Action. UN Doc. A/CONF.157/23, July 12, 1993, adopted by the World Conference on Human Rights, June 25, 1993.

Zakaria, Fareed. "The Rise of Illiberal Democracy." *Foreign Affairs* 76, no. 6 (1997): 22–43.